# On Work

For Kate, John and Nick,
with the hope that they may
continue to enjoy their work

# ON WORK

## Historical, Comparative and Theoretical Approaches

*Edited by*

R. E. PAHL

Basil Blackwell

First published 1988
Reprinted 1989

Basil Blackwell Ltd
108 Cowley Road, Oxford OX4 1JF, UK

Basil Blackwell Inc.
432 Park Avenue South, Suite 1503
New York, NY 10016, USA



*British Library Cataloguing in Publication Data*
On work: historical, comparative and
theoretical approaches
1. Work – Social aspects
I. Pahl, R.E.
306′.36 HD6955
ISBN 0–631–15761–1
ISBN 0–631–15762–X Pbk

*Library of Congress Cataloging in Publication Data*
On work: historical, comparative and theoretical
approaches/edited by R.E. Pahl.
p. cm.
Includes index.
ISBN 0–631–15761–1
ISBN 0–631–15762–X (pbk.)
1. Work. 2. Sexual division of labor.
3. Women – Employment.
4. Labour supply – Effect of technological
innovations on. I. Pahl, R.E. (Raymond)
Edward), 1935–
HD4904.05 1988 87–25357
331—dc19 CIP

Typeset in 10 on 11pt Plantin
by Times Graphics, Singapore
Printed in Great Britain by Billing & Sons Ltd, Worcester

# Contents

# Acknowledgements

The editor and publishers are grateful to the following for permission to reproduce previously published material:

Academic Press, Inc. (London) Ltd for 'Labour Market Segmentation and Workers' Careers' by G. Solinas, *Cambridge Journal of Economics*, 1982.

The American Sociological Association for 'Rethinking Internal Labour Markets: New Insights from a Comparative Perspective' by David Stark, *American Sociological Review*, vol. 51, 1986, pp. 492–504.

Associated Book Publishers (UK) Ltd for 'Work Employment and Unemployment in the Development of Industrial Society' by Krishan Kumar, *Sociological Review*, vol. 22 (2) pp. 185–233, May 1984, Routledge and Kegan Paul plc; and 'The Subcontracting of Cleaning Work in Israel' by Deborah Bernstein, *Sociological Review*, vol. 34 (2) pp. 396–422, 1986, Routledge and Kegan Paul plc.

Cambridge University Press for 'Women's Work: Mechanisation and the Early Phases of Industrialisation in England' by Maxine Berg from *The Historical Meanings of Work*, ed. Patrick Joyce, 1987.

Campus Verlag for 'Labour Market and Second Economy in Hungary' by P. Galasi and G. Sziracski from *Worker Behaviour in the Labour Market* by G. Kertesi and G. Sziracski, 1985.

Frank Cass & Co. Ltd. for 'Conceptualizing the Labour Force: The Underestimation of Women's Economic Activities' by Lourdes Beneria, *Journal of Development Studies*, (17) pp. 10–28, 1981.

Century Hutchinson Ltd for 'Ways of Getting a Living in 18th Century England' from *Life and Labour in England 1700–1800* by R. W. Malcolmson, Hutchinson, 1981; and 'Taylorism, Responsible Autonomy and Management Strategy' by Stephen Wood and John Kelly from *The Degradation of Work*, ed. Stephen Wood, Hutchinson, 1982.

Croom Helm Ltd for 'Domestic Labour and the Household' by Maureen M. Mackintosh from *Fit Work for Women*, ed. S. Burman, 1979.

Jonathan I. Gershuny for 'Technology, Social Innovation and the Informal Economy'.

Judith Mara Gutman for 'Work Culture and Society in Industrialising America 1815–1919' by Herbert Gutman, *American Historical Review*, 1973.

Gower Publishing Company Ltd. for 'Managerial Strategies, New Technology and the Labour Process' by John Child from *Job Redesign,* eds. David Knight et al., 1985.

Dag Hammarskjold Foundation for 'Women as Food Producers and Suppliers in the Twentieth Century' by Shimwaayi Muntemba, *Development Dialogue*, 1–2, 1982, pp. 29–50.

The Controller of Her Majesty's Stationery Office for 'Homeworking in Britain: Key Findings from the National Survey of Home-Based Workers' by Catherine Hakim, *Employment Gazette*, February 1987; and 'Who Cares? A Review of Empirical Evidence from Britain' from *With Due Care and Attention* by Gillian Parker, Family Policy Studies Centre, Occasional Paper no. 2, Jan. 1985 funded by the DHSS.

Jane Humphries for 'Protective Legislation, the Capitalist State and Working Class Men', *Feminist Review*, Spring 1981.

Macmillan Publishers Ltd and Sheridan House, New York for 'The Greening of Women's Labour' by Ruth Pearson from *The Changing Experience of Work*, eds Kate Purcell et al., 1986.

Martin Meissner, Elizabeth W. Humphreys, Scott M. Meis and William J. Scheu for 'No Exit for Wives: Sexual Division of Labour and the Cumulation of Household Demands', *Canadian Review of Sociology and Anthropology*, 12, 1975 pp. 424–39.

Christopher Middleton for 'The Familiar Fate of the *Famulae*: Gender as a Principle of Stratification in the Historical Division of Labour'.

Enzo Mingione for 'Informal Activities and Low Income Life Styles in Urban Mezzogiorno'.

Fergus Murray for 'The Decentralisation of Production and the Decline of the Mass Collective Worker', *Capital and Class*, no. 19, Spring 1983.

Plenum Publishing Corporation for 'Making Work: The Perspective from Social Science' from *Making Work* by William Ronco and Lisa Peattie, 1983.

Nanneke Redclift for 'Gender, Accumulation and the Labour Process' from *Beyond Employment* by Nanneke Redclift and Enzo Mingione, Basil Blackwell Ltd, 1985.

Sage Publications, Inc. for 'Office Automation and Women's Work: The Technological Transformation of the Insurance Industry' by Barbara Baran from *High Technology, Space and Society*, ed. M. Castells, 1985.

Sean Sayers for 'The Need to Work: The Perspective from Philosophy', *Radical Philosophy*, 46, Summer 1987, pp. 17–26.

Endre Sik for 'Reciprocal Exchange of Labour and Social Stratification: a Hungarian Case Study'.

Socialist Review for 'Piece Rates, Hungarian Style' by Michael Burawoy, *Socialist Review*, no. 79, (Jan./Feb.) 1985.

Springer Verlag GmbH & Co. for 'Household Composition, Social Networks and Household Production in Germany' by Wolfgang Glatzer and Regina Berger from *The Economics of the Shadow Economy*, eds Wolf Gaertner and Alois Wenig. pp. 330–51, 1985. Copyright © 1985 Springer Verlag.

University of Chicago Press for 'Thirty Years of Making Out' from *Manufacturing Consent* by Michael Burawoy, 1979; 'Accumulation, Reproduction and Women's Role in Economic Development: Boserup Revisited' by Lourdes Benería and Gita Sen, *Signs*, vol. 7, no. 2, pp. 279–98, 1981; and 'The Comparative Advantages of Women's Disadvantages: Women's Workers in the Strawberry Export Agribusiness in Mexico' by Lourdes Arizpe and Josephina Aranda, *Signs*, vol. 7, no. 2, pp. 453–73, 1981.

The editor and publishers are also grateful to Paul Goodrick for translating 'Informal Activities and Low Income Life Styles in Urban Mezzogiorno' by Enzo Mingione and to Katalin Pickvance for translating 'Reciprocal Exchange of Labour and Social Stratification: a Hungarian Case Study' by Endre Sik.

# Preface

This book grew out of a plan to provide a short, relevant and accessible book on the current confusions and debates about work. However, the world of work is in the process of such diverse and challenging developments that it seemed necessary first to bring together some of the most significant contributions written in the last decade. The introductory essays to each part, taken with the epilogue, amount to an extended discussion of my own perspective on work.

The reading and preparation that was involved in compiling a book of this nature has been necessarily time consuming. I am very grateful to Robin Guthrie and the trustees of the Joseph Rowntree Memorial Trust who have supported my work, of which this book is a part, over the past two years. It follows from the Trust's active involvement in a number of projects focused on the theme of 'work and society', and I hope that this book will help to keep the debates alive.

This book is intentionally comparative along a number of dimensions. I have long found Hungary and Italy two of the world's most interesting societies and a significant part of this book is devoted to specific developments in the world of work in these countries. It is a pleasure to acknowledge the warm and friendly welcome I have received on my various visits. Comparative sociological analysis may have many intellectual challenges but it also brings many rewards of convivial gatherings and lasting friendships.

I have received much help from many people at the University of Kent at Canterbury. Anna Ireland of the University Library was unfailingly helpful in finding elusive articles and in checking sources. Nanneke Redclift provided critical help and advice on part III and Krishan Kumar was a constant source of inspiration and tolerant scepticism. The undergraduates on whom I tried out some of the ideas in the introductions provided more help than they probably realized at the time. I should also like to thank Harriet Barry, Brian Goodale and Kate Chapman of Basil Blackwell, who had a particularly awkward job in steering this book through the press. Finally, it is a pleasure to acknowledge the ever-cheerful efficiency with which Sue Macdonald of Darwin College coped with typing the manuscript, often under considerable pressure from other responsibilities.

R. E. P.
Canterbury

# Introduction: Work in Context

Work is becoming the key personal, social and political issue of the remaining years of the twentieth century: confusion and ambiguities about its meaning, nature and purpose in our lives are widespread. Those who reflect and comment on such issues may sometimes be guilty of preferring wishful to critical thinking; others stolidly maintain their loyalties to established debates. Thus, in the former case, authors discuss work as having a very different or perhaps an altogether uncertain future, whereas, in the latter case, authors engage in debates about the labour process, deskilling, segmented labour markets and suchlike as if nothing fundamentally has changed.

There seems to be a basic uncertainty about whether we are truly at a turning point in the relationship between work and society or whether, if we distance ourselves a little from contemporary events, the world is as much dominated by the need to work as it has ever been. This book brings together material to show something of the contours of a restructured world of work. Debates and arguments using different languages and adopting different assumptions, while valuable in themselves, may have the effect of combining collectively to numb people's minds so that it is harder for them to get an overview of what the issues now are and how they relate to each other. In this and the introductory essays to each part readers will be encouraged to keep these main issues in focus.

First, and perhaps most importantly, it is clear that not all work is remunerated. Someone arriving from another planet might be surprised and puzzled by the way we distinguish between work and employment and the differential rewards that are paid to employees based on the kind of work they do and the kind of person they are. Interesting, creative and varied employment is highly rewarded; dull, repetitive and routine work is poorly rewarded. Men receive more money than women, and this is related to social attitudes and conventions more than the actual amount or quality of work that the individual or the gender category does. This issue of remunerated work or employment involves an understanding of *where* the jobs are, that is the geographical division of labour; *who* does the job, in the social division of labour and the sexual division of labour in particular; *what* sort of jobs they are, that is the technical division of labour; and *how many* jobs there are and how the demand for employment by those seeking remuneration matches the demand by employers for employees.

Secondly, there is all the work outside employment. Such work may be exhausting or exhilarating; it may be done under conditions of oppressive exploitation or it may be voluntary work hard to distinguish from play. Some of the most demanding work outside employment, such as child care, can also be remunerated when done for others; so clearly it is not the nature of the task that matters most in determining whether or not it is to be financially rewarded and whether it is to count as 'work', but rather the social relations in which the task is embedded. Again, in the production of goods and services it is not always financial considerations that determine whether we have, for example, home-made or bought jam. Technological developments allow us to produce more and different goods and services in the home, but it does not necessarily follow that we have the money, time or inclination to do so. There are many questions relating to unpaid work and how this relates to employment. Work outside employment can only increase relative to paid employment if, overall, people have sufficient time and financial resources. The lifestyle of the gentleman is possible only if it is based on unearned income based on profits or rents. The divisions of labour in work outside employment cannot be divorced from the divisions based on remunerated work. Those quasi-utopians who see work outside employment as an alternative to remunerated work must consider the financial implications of what they advocate.

Divisions of labour are changing, then, at a global, national and individual level and such change produces new perceptions of and attitudes to work. Young people not fully committed to the world of employment, older people who have been unemployed for over a year, and those who have few wants or sufficient wealth are among the categories who can question the notion that their occupational identity should be central, or that the endless pursuit of financial rewards is the best or only way to spend their lives. Such considerations raise questions about the so-called work ethic that arguably once ensured that most men were kept out of mischief by being busily employed. People can engage in employment because they have to, because they feel obliged to or because they want to: they work for money, they work out of a sense of duty or they do it for fun or for self-expression. Some people, it is true, have to work to avoid starvation, but in the developed world (the OECD countries) they are happily a small minority. But if even employers are becoming less enthusiastic about all their workforce being equally committed to a lifelong career, then a degree of instrumentality may be encouraged, even amongst those previously committed to such careers and loyal service to the company. Employers may prefer a rapid turnover of intensely committed workers, rather than a lifetime's service from people who approach their job in a more leisurely way. Yet whether one adopts a crudely instrumental approach to paid employment or whether one has a more expressive orientation, the problem still remains in the affluent capitalist nations as to *how much* money or other forms of reward is necessary or desirable. The manager who prefers to stay amongst friends rather than accept promotion elsewhere, the teenager who rejects a boring and monotonous job, the self-employed carpenter who turns down work because he wants to go fishing, the professor who rejects the offer of being chairman of his professional association because it would take time away from his gardening (or even his research), will all discuss their decisions with their friends and will receive at least as much sympathy and support as criticism. Increasingly, people are facing personal decisions about degrees of involvement in employment or self-employment. By having varied experiences in and out of the labour market they perceive more clearly the advantages and disadvantages of each sphere. Now, increasingly perhaps, such choices and alternatives are being more widely shared and understood.

The idea that attitudes towards work and employment may be changing is obviously dependent upon knowledge of some previous time and set of circumstances that may serve as a base from which to measure such changes. Clearly, the search for some golden age, where the divisions of labour were in some kind of celestial harmony, is a fruitless exercise. Yet, curiously, few of the great thinkers who have turned their minds to the problems of work have managed to avoid an explicit or tacit retrospective utopia, whether it be the Garden of Eden of Judaic myth, the self-employed craftsman of Karl Marx or William Morris, or the Beveridge-style welfare state - based on the full employment of male heads of households - that was the goal of social democratic politicians after the Second World War. However, the idea that medieval craftsmen or the affluent automobile workers of Detroit or Wolfsburg in the 1960s were the archetypal inhabitants of a golden age has only to be stated to be rejected.

Evidently work inside and outside employment is affected by technology, employers' practices, global economic development, feminist, socialist and managerialist ideologies and much else besides. Whether, proportionately, more people in the advanced industrial nations are now deliberating the trade-offs between different types of activity than ever before is hard to determine. What does seem clear is that more people are becoming self-consciously aware of the processes of which they form a part.

The individual both moulds and is moulded by his or her work; the state is judged by the way work is organized and distributed; the employer creates types of task and levels of reward. The politics of work is a personal matter as much as an issue of contemporary debate in society at large.

In this book five major themes form the basis of each main part. In part I the emphasis is the emergence of the male breadwinner, the collective mass worker and the concepts of 'unemployment' and 'the unemployed'. The pre-industrial world of household production and household strategies with its distinctive work rhythms and practices was undermined by the forces of industrial capital expansion and accumulation. In the late eighteenth and nineteeth centuries women lost much of their productive economic role and function associated with the rise of the male breadwinner: traditional ways of working collapsed under the constraints of employment and unemployment. In part II the dominance of the male breadwinner and the collective mass worker are shown to be receding in their turn, displaced by new divisions in internal and external labour markets and new strategies of employers, workers and households. In part III the emphasis shifts to the world's work that is done by women and the new conceptual and theoretical developments that have developed out of feminist thinking since the early 1970s. Part IV explores the forms of work outside employment that have come to be of more central interest in recent years. Distinctive forms of work can be described only in certain contexts: the reciprocal exchange of labour described by Sik for Hungary is unlikely to be found to the same degree in Paris, London and Frankfurt. However, women typically pool their resources in caring for, carrying and collecting children: this is a traditional form of work with deep roots. The balance or mix of all forms of work is changing, as various papers in this part illustrate in detail. In part V there is documentation of the processes and patterns of a disaggregrated capitalism that has now spread throughout the globe, creating strains and contradictions that parallel in certain respects the situation historians described for Britain in the late eighteenth century. Finally, in part VI, the question 'Why work?' is posed both philosophically and in more traditional social science terms. The book concludes with a sceptical note about the future-of-work industry.

This book is organized on the assumption that we are living through a period of change that is qualitatively and quantitatively different from that typical of most of the twentieth century. In a sense, the years between the late eighteenth century and the mid twentieth century can be seen as the period of the slow but remorseless emergence of the age of the male breadwinner and the collective mass worker in Western industrial societies. The economic crises of the 1970s and 1980s have provided the critical turning point to a new phase of disaggregated capitalism. Charting these emerging forms of work and new divisions of labour is the task for social scientists in the 1990s. Some signs of this future pattern can be quite clearly seen, such as the universal and irreversible increase in married women's employment; others are still unclear. However, it is better to aim at some comprehension of the contemporary world of work, even if our understanding must necessarily be limited and, perhaps, partially inaccurate, than to rely on apparent clarity and a more comprehensive understanding of a world that is rapidly passing. This is intended to be an unconventional approach to the study of work. I hope that it will also come to be seen to illuminate more accurately the processes of which its readers now, or will shortly, form a part. The year 2000 is now, in 1987, closer than 1973, the year of the dramatic rise of oil prices which symbolized the end of the years of relative economic stability. The contributions to this book provide a particular perspective of work in its historical and comparative context midway through the last quarter of the twentieth century. Readers in the year 2000 will be able to judge the accuracy of that perspective.

# Part I

# Ways of Working in Former Times

# Editor's Introduction: Historical Aspects of Work, Employment, Unemployment and the Sexual Division of Labour

## ATTITUDES TO WORK

In our present confusions about the meaning of work, it is possible that the past may provide some help in understanding the future. Clearly, it is not easy to discover what ordinary people felt about their experience of work and how they divided up the various work tasks that had to be done between the various members of the household. If we start from the assumption that people did not much enjoy their struggles with nature we are surely nearer the truth than the alternative stereotype of the happy, dancing peasant lurching about in a Bruegelesque way, full of too much strong ale. Labour services were resented: the Anglo-Saxon ploughman complained of the burden of his lot and the manorial overseer carried a stick. The claims of the peasants' revolts at the end of the fourteenth century appeared to be less about the quality of the work and more about excessive demands for labour and burdensome taxes. The complaint that Langland makes in *Piers Plowman* about the idle peasants not showing sufficient enthusiasm for work smacks of contemporary harangues against the workshy. Even St Benedict in setting out his *Rules for Monasteries* did not seem to expect the monks to be enthusiastic about their work and had to encourage them not to complain when they were obliged to get in the harvest.

Of course, it is not unreasonable to expect the ploughman and his wife to be feeling pretty miserable struggling through the mud behind the oxen, but it is often assumed that the craft workers were happy, taking intrinsic satisfaction from their work. In Frederick Antal's classic study of *Florentine Painting and its Social*

*Background*[1] there is much to demystify such a notion. Thus, we are told that Giotto was a sharp businessman who operated as a professional money-lender and increased by usury what he earned by his art. St Francis objected to art as much as to wealth for he perceived art to be connected with wealth. Yet not all artists in fourteenth-century Florence became affluent; they were too bound by contracts to their patrons. It is hard for us to remember now, when contemplating the masterpieces of the Renaissance, that these were mostly completed by jobbing craftsmen – there was no distinction between arts and crafts in the fourteenth century – organized in workshops where painters and their apprentices and journeymen carried out their commissions. The most striking thing was the extraordinary versatility of the medieval workshop. It was normal practice for a craftsman to be equally skilled as painter, sculptor and even architect and to be knowledgeable about a whole range of technical processes. These workshops carried out the jobs they were given and a patron had to pay more to be sure to get a named contractor to do the fresco or whatever. This was often quite difficult to achieve and Giotto ended up entirely as an entrepreneur, subcontracting all his work to pupils. Patrons would attempt to draw up detailed contracts with penalty clauses, the size and number of figures to be portrayed, the quality of the pigments to be used and so on. These contracts, Antal claims, deprived the artists of all rights with no means of redress. They were entirely subordinate and as dependent as workers in all other branches of production. Fees were generally low and, in the case of monastic commissions, payment was even made in kind. Antal emphasizes that Giotto was truly exceptional: most artists spent long periods unemployed, few could even manage to acquire a house, and the great majority lived with their families in a state of permanent financial stringency.

It is very unlikely that the craftsmen in the Florentine workshops of the fourteenth century were that much more contented than the English agricultural workers. Increasingly they were tied to reproducing standard altar pieces for stock: routine pictures were mass produced for foreign markets and more remote parts of Italy. Even in the early fifteenth century, artists continued to be economically exploited, although a rising upper middle class was then holding artists, scholars and educated people in more esteem. For the first time men from middle-class backgrounds were becoming artists from talent and conviction; Masaccio was the son of a provincial lawyer and Brunelleschi came from a wealthy family. However, this may not have advantaged ordinary craftsmen. Brunelleschi helped to crush a strike of builders working in the cathedral and cut their wages.

Most of what one reads about those most likely to have an intrinsic commitment to their work suggests that pre-industrial attitudes were not much different from those found today. However, there may have been more free time: in France 111 saints' days and festivals existed under the *ancien régime*. It is unlikely that the majority of the people could escape from their own everyday tasks of child and animal care and the gathering and production of fruit and vegetables, but contemporary working people are unlikely to have more 'free' time. However, historians find it impossible to evaluate the quality of working life for ordinary people in pre-industrial times. All that can be done is to hold a very sceptical

1. F. Antal, *Florentine Painting and its Social Background*, Kegan Paul, 1947.

stance against those who romanticize the past: there was no pre-industrial golden age of satisfying work.

In England many people's images of the past are coloured by the myths of Merrie England portrayed by a literary elite. Most anthologies of English poetry present a very partial and glamorized view of country life. Only very recently has there been any scholarly interest in the writings of ordinary working men and women. The plebeian poets of the early eighteenth century provide what seems a more accurate protrayal of working life. Stephen Duck, for example, writing in about 1720, describes agricultural work in a way not dissimilar to that provided by contemporary sociologists such as Ely Chinoy or Huw Beynon,[2] who write about the work experiences of automobile workers.

When sooty peas we thresh, you scarce can know
Our native Colour, as from Work we go:
The Sweat, the Dust, and suffocating smoke
Make us so much like Ethiopians look
We scare our wives, when Ev'ning brings us home;
And frighted Infants think the Bugbear come.
Week after week, we this dull Task pursue,
Unless when winn'wing days produce a new;
A new, indeed, but frequently a worse:
The Threshal yields but to the Master's Curse.

Let those who feast at ease on dainty fare
Pity the reapers, who their feast prepare:
For toils scarce ever ceasing press us now;
Rest never does, but on the Sabbath, show:
And barely that our Masters will allow.
Think what a painful life we daily lead;
Each morning early rise, go late to bed;
Nor, when asleep, are we secure from Pain;
We then perform our labours o'er again:
Our mimic fancy ever restless seems;
And what we act awake, she acts in dreams.
Hard Fate! on Labour ev'n in Sleep don't cease:

However, Stephen Duck's complaints about the burdens of male manual work were marred by sexist comments about 'prattling Females, arm'd with Rake and Prong' that sparked off a feminist response 250 years ago as sharp as any today. Mary Collier (1690–176?), tuned to the feminist thinking of the late seventeeth century, castigated Duck for ignoring the triple burden of working women – wage labour, housework and the rearing of children:

When Ev'ning does approach, we homeward hie
And our domestick Toils incessantly ply:
Against your coming Home prepare to get
Our Work all done, Our House in order set:
Bacon and Dumpling in the pot we boil,

2. E. Chinoy, *Automobile Workers and the American Dream*, Doubleday, New York, 1955; H. Beynon, *Working for Ford*, revised Penguin edition, Harmondsworth, 1984.

Our Beds we make, our Swine we feed the while;
Then wait at Door to see you coming Home,
And set the Table out against you come;

Our Children put to Bed, with greatest Care
We all Things for your coming home prepare:
You sup, and go to Bed without Delay,
And rest yourselves till the ensuing Day;
While we, alas! but little Sleep can have,
Because our froward Children cry and rave.

Mary Collier is surely right to reprove Stephen Duck, and she reflects the important truths that all forms of work were equally necessary and important and that the essential unit for getting all forms of work done was the household. The analytical distinction that can arguably be made between work for production and work for reproduction could also have been made in the past, but was not very important. Individuals were largely obliged to be members of households; they had to get a livelihood, had to get by, and would have seen little need to philosophize about whether or not the roof should be repaired or the cow milked. In practice, households in pre-industrial England, as elsewhere, had to be based on an economic partnership between men and women and other household members. A *household work strategy* developed, which made the best use of resources for getting by under given social and economic conditions. This emphasis on the household rather than the individual as the basic economic unit is a more fruitful way to approach the work of production, reproduction and consumption. This focus makes no *a priori* assumptions about either internal conflict or consensus within the household and none about the necessity for identifying putative household heads. Households are simply units for getting various kinds of work done. They were not, of course, isolated units: households were bound to each other in many complex ways and the boundaries between them were often very fluid, as members moved back and forth at different stages of the life cycle. Certainly, in the past the Church and more recently the state have imposed gender ideologies and hierarchies within the household – the former as a reflection of the development of hierarchy and organization within the Church, and the latter as a convenient way of gathering taxes. Even in Britain today, it is the Inland Revenue and the Office of Population Censuses and Surveys (OPCS) that are still most concerned about defining the 'head of household'.

## DIVISIONS OF LABOUR

Evidently, household work strategies were heavily determined by social and material conditions in pre-industrial times. While, in theory, literate commentators might attempt to define what was women's work and what was men's, in practice there was likely to be substantial variation. As M. Segalen laconically remarks, referring to peasant families in France, 'the household had to produce in order to live, and often lived in order to produce, production guaranteeing the perpetuation of the human grouping.'[3] She goes on to observe that there has been

3. M. Segalen, *Love and Power in the Peasant Family*, Basil Blackwell, 1983.

no systematic historical analysis of the distribution of tasks carried out by members of the household. She doubts whether the concept of 'domestic life', separate from the life of production, is meaningful in terms of the peasant household, where what has to be done is determined more by cycles of work connected with the seasons and the reproductive cycle. Reporting on accounts by French folklorists, Segalen shows how tasks are intermeshed on the farm:

> There is no distinction in kind drawn between cultivation and cooking. Preparing a meal or giving the pigs their swill, all come under the household; men, women and children, servants and animals are all equal beneficiaries of this work. Thus, work in the kitchen should no more be considered part of a strictly defined category of housework than tilling the soil should be excluded from the category of 'production' in so far as it is an activity of preparing the soil.

Tasks are divided, but they are also complementary: certain tasks connected with the hearth, home and garden were evidently largely reserved for women, although very often what is conventionally called 'housework' would more likely be done by servants or young girls. Certainly, in the order of priorities, housework came below working in the fields and caring for the children and animals. Much time would have to be spent in the garden digging, sowing, hoeing and harvesting. Yet Segalen notes that even the most gender-linked tasks are taken over by the other partner in certain regimes. In the case of bread-making – traditionally a female task – by breaking down the task into its constituent elements, she suggests that it is not always so clear who in practice does the task, since both men and women may share different aspects of the work. In one area women make the dough but men knead it; elsewhere men handle the process of heating up the oven or perhaps the whole baking process. This interchangeability of apparent gender–task linkages makes Segalen wonder whether the term 'domestic' has any precise meaning: 'Certain activities were carried out by either men or women, depending on the region. Everything to do with livestock was dealt with in this way. While sheep were rather regarded as being the men's province . . . cows could be the responsibility of either one or the other.' Evidently, according to Segalen, any attempt to document precisely the gender-linked division of tasks in French peasant households as a basis for generalization is hardly a realistic enterprise. There would be a division of labour in any one household, to be sure, but the variations appear endless: 'The amount of feminine contribution to the work on the land depended on the composition of the household and the particular stage of its evolution, on its economic level, on the time of year, and finally perhaps on cultural models which are the most difficult of all to come to grips with.' That generalization must be hard to refute: it is quite clear that women played an essential role in production and their labour was essential to the economic survival of the household unit.

## WORK AND EMPLOYMENT

Employment is simply one form of work. In the past work was synonymous with toil: an agricultural worker might do some digging or ploughing as part of the collective household labour needed for that household to achieve a modest livelihood; other digging or ploughing could be done as wage labourer. The distinction between remunerated or non-remunerated labour did not prevent either being equally unpleasant on a cold, wet day. It may be that a given worker might bring different orientations to the task so that there could be more or less resentment and awareness of oppression, depending on whether the work was for the household or for the abbots of the local monastery. Perhaps wage labour was perceived as more constraining in the sixteenth century, as work in the domestic dwelling is perceived as more constraining by some women today.

Clearly, it is necessary to make precise analytical distinctions between social orientations, social, economic and physical constraints and the nature and content of the rewards for labour. The precise mix between orientations, constraints and rewards is likely to vary both historically and geographically and also by class, age, sex and life-cycle stage. Simply naming the activity that one gets paid for as work will not adequately serve as a definition.

The notion that one should obtain most, if not all, of one's material wants as a consumer by spending the money gained through employment emerged for the first time in the nineteenth century. Whilst there has, indeed, been a market for labour for at least 800 years in England so that most households probably had some source of income, however erratic and irregular that might be, income generation was not an essential basis for livelihood. Malcolmson remarks that, even as late as the eighteenth century, 'in most households an adequate subsistence depended on a complex of various forms of task work and wage labour: regular, full-time employment at a single job was not the norm' (see chapter 2). Indeed, from as early as the seventeenth century, there was substantial resistance to the spread of wage labour. To give all of one's labour power in return for a wage was seen as a grievous loss of independence, security and liberty. 'It takes centuries,' observed Marx, 'ere the "free" labourer, thanks to the development of capitalist production, agrees, i.e. is compelled by social conditions, to sell the whole of his active life, his very capacity for work, for the price of the necessaries of life, his birthright for mess of pottage.'

In pre-industrial times, then, most of an individual's work was done in and for the household. The viability of the household was the crucial priority in life and the work of all members of the household had to be coordinated to achieve that end. Different members had different tasks and these became conventionally established, as we have seen. There was no *a priori* assumption that wage labour was a superior form of work or that men were the natural wage earners. Very often women were the main money earners, either by selling produce at markets or by producing textile goods in their homes in the proto-industrial era of the eighteenth or early nineteenth centuries.

## THE RISE AND FALL OF THE MALE BREADWINNER

For an untypical period of 100 years or so, households were dependent on a male chief earner, who was, in theory, paid a family wage to support his wife, children and possibly elderly dependants as well. How this curious shift to a single male breadwinner supporting his household of dependants took place is a complex matter to resolve and has given rise to considerable debate in recent years (see chapter 4). On the one hand some stress the advantages to capitalism as a system in having its workers cheaply and effectively 'reproduced'. Clearly, if workers are well fed and cared for and are kept in good health they will operate more efficiently. 'Providing for' a wife and children is likely to be a stabilizing factor on incipient rebels and is also likely to encourage commitment to employment and a willingness to work hard and long. Furthermore, if workers are individually cared for in individual homes their propensity to acquire and to consume goods and services may be enhanced. They may, further, be encouraged to pursue the advancement of their social status through styles of consumption, rather than the advancement of their collective position in relation to the means of production through collective class action. Hence, it is argued, there is sense in enhancing the wages of male manual workers at the expense of female workers and also in 'protecting' women and children from engaging in certain forms of dirty, difficult or dangerous work.

Such a view has been criticized for being cynical and for having an inflated and unrealistic view of the general wiliness and machiavellian nature of mid-nineteenth-century capitalists. An alternative approach stresses the humanitarian concern of individual employers, whose own wives were safely cocooned in bourgeois domesticity and who, not unreasonably perhaps, imagined that such a goal was equally appropriate for their workers. Such people may have come to understand something of the impact of the harsh conditions of employment on disease and mortality rates, particularly for women and children. At the same time the shift to heavy manufacturing in what are now called the 'smoke-stack' industries generated what was taken to be more appropriately male employment. As the captains of industry began to equip their factories with new and expensive machinery they extrapolated their own views about who should do what work on to their workforce. This argument is, therefore, based on a combination of sentimental charity and bourgeois morality, coupled with the development of technology in parts of primary and manufacturing industry.

Such a position, in its turn, was attacked by those who claimed that there was an unholy alliance between male employers and male workers. The former did not wish to encourage an alternative value system allowing women more economic equality: that might open the way to social and political equality, which could endanger their own privileged position. Their workers, on the other hand, feared the competition of effective, efficient and potentially lower-paid workers: reducing the role of married women employees might enhance their own labour market position and have the further advantage of providing a cosy, caring home to which they could retreat for comfort and material sustenance and support. This argument has been adduced by those writing from a feminist perspective, who have adopted what might be called a 'patriarchy first' position. A collusion between men, whether bourgeois or proletarian, may be expected in a tacit conspiracy to encourage and to enhance the subordination of women.

However, there is a fourth position, also put forward by those who openly assert that they write from a feminist perspective, that refutes the 'patriarchy first' perspective. Jane Humphries in chapter 4 claims that in the case of the 1842 Mines Regulation Act men were not acting primarily out of gender-based self-interest. Coal miners needed the extra income provided by their wives and children and family teams were a convenient and efficient means of getting the work done, given the technology of the time. The prevention of the employment of women and children would result in the male coal miners doing more work, without a commensurate increase in wages. The workers were thus likely to become collectively poorer. Secondly, it was not clear that there was much demand amongst miners for a cosy home in which they could dominate in private when the tradition was for collective and communal social life based on the pub or the chapel. It is not clear what the precise advantages for the miner would be in having his wife left to scrub the step without any wage for her labours. More plausibly, the men may have been genuinely concerned for the health of their wives and children and were thus prepared to work harder and, later, to organize collectively in order to be paid wages sufficient to support their dependants.

Evidently, the shift to the model of a male breadwinner was a long and complex process and in many places and industries it was never fully achieved. Nevertheless, the system of social security outlined by Sir William Beveridge in his report, first published in 1942 and a best seller in both Britain and America, was based on a fundamental assumption of a wage earner and his dependent family. Women were acknowledged by him to be doing 'vital unpaid service' in the home, caring for children and the elderly. As the economist Gertrude Williams wrote in 1945:

> One of the happiest innovations proposed in the Beveridge Report is the emergence of the housewife as a separate and honoured category of the population. In wartime no one disputed the complete partnership of women in communal life and there is unstinted appreciation of her contribution to war industry. But rearing babies through happy, healthy childhood to independent maturity is even more important than wiring aeroplanes, and is a very much more absorbing and exacting task.[4]

After the Second World War the domination of the male wage earner ensured that the confusion arising from the elision of work with employment continued for a further two or three decades. Thus in 1958, in a widely used American textbook *The World of Work* by Robert Dubin,[5] work was defined as 'continuous employment in the production of goods and services, for remuneration'. Professor Dubin asserted that 'from the standpoint of the life history of the individual, the significant work he performs is done continuously by him.' Dubin then goes on to claim that 'in a sociological sense, only those expenditures of human energy producing goods or services are defined as work.' However, that definition does not include housework, solely because, even though the housewife certainly produces goods and services, she does not get paid and hence 'falls outside the subject matter of our field'.

Some thirty years later, such an explicit focus on men's remunerated employment appears archaic. Throughout history most work has been done by women and most has not been remunerated (see part III). Now, in the last years of the twentieth century, the participation rates of women in formal employment have never been higher and the growth of redundancy, unemployment and early retirement amongst men has led to a return to patterns of unremunerated work amongst men. They may no longer cut turf or timber for their fires or rear hogs in

4. G. Williams, *Women and Work*, Nicholson and Watson, London, 1945.
5. Robert Dubin, *The World of Work*, Prentice-Hall, Englewood Cliffs, 1958.

scrub woodland but they may install their own storm windows or build on a patio with their own tools, with their own labour and in their own time. Most would see such work for themselves, or self-provisioning, as highly productive. These issues are explored in part IV, and especially in chapter 26.

If most people who equate work with employment are trapped in the concepts and ideology of a period now passed, how should the notion of work be appropriately conceptualized in order to illuminate current reality? What is it that analytically distinguishes work from 'all purposeful activity', and what is the special position of paid employment in the overall spectrum of work? How is unpaid domestic work and all the other forms of unpaid or informal work to be brought into a common analytical schema?

Undoubtedly there is much contemporary confusion about the nature of work but, happily, one consequence of this is that old stereotypes, based on the male manual worker, do not now require to be dispelled with the same urgency. Nevertheless, whilst the old stereotypes may be crumbling, old concepts still have an unexpected currency, largely perhaps because the social institutions of the age of male employment, such as trade unions and the social security system based on the male breadwinner, have not been superseded. Conceptual classification does not necessarily produce new and appropriate institutions: it is certainly hard to make new curtains without first locating and measuring the windows and the need for conceptual clarification may be greater than is commonly realized, as the contributors to part III demonstrate.

## THE FUTURE OF WORK IS IN THE PAST?

It is sometimes said that the future of work is in the past. The implication is that there are aspects of the way work was organized in former times that may provide a guide to a world that perhaps now is relearning that employment is only one form of work.

The ways in which knowledge of the past helps in both understanding the present and in creating a future are by no means self-evident. Middleton's elegant and well-crafted essay which begins part I is a theoretically sophisticated attempt to disentangle confusions in contemporary labour market analysis by describing patterns of segregation and sex-linked wage differentials in early modern England. He admits that he presents highly selective evidence and that 'wage work was very much a subsidiary form of labour in feudal England.' Nevertheless he presents a convincing case that 'segregation and inequality in the organization of labour have persisted with remarkable tenacity through profound changes in the wider social order of class and gender relations.'

Certainly not all historians would be comfortable with Middleton's use of the very early evidence, although his analysis of wage levels after the seventeenth century is widely accepted. Similarly, many feminists may not be so ready to accept Middleton's logical demolition of the concept of patriarchy. Snell, on whom Middleton heavily relies, has been critical of 'historiographical assumptions of long-held and extreme sexually exploitative attitudes in the past. Such assumptions usually ignore social detail and specificity (often being based on upper-class literary evidence), and presume little discontinuity from preceding centuries

of the mid-nineteenth-century status of women.'[6] Middleton certainly cannot be accused of doing this and there is no dispute between his and Snell's interpretation of agricultural wages. However, Snell's other work on female apprenticeships provides some surprising conclusions, indicating, as it does, that up until the late eighteenth century women were apprenticed to a variety of trades. R. A. Leeson has also described how

> Fourteenth-century masons were urged to be together as 'systerers and bretheren'; the London carpenters had 'brothers and sisters'; men and women paid 'quarterage' to the blacksmiths; and the coopers' rules included 'sisters' until the sixteenth century. Women were found in a number of trades from brewer to leadbeater. They staged whole scenes in the pageants which marked the annual gild celebrations. Women were more often mistresses, taking over the workshop from their husbands; they were more rarely apprentices, though there was no widespread direct bar to their admission to the trades until the sixteenth century. The Lincoln fullers' rules, though, suggest that the travelling stranger was likely to be a man. Only rarely in the exclusive town crafts does one come across the travelling journey-woman. That is not to say she did not take the road, but she has left a much fainter trace.[7]

Similarly M. D. George gives many examples of girls in eighteenth-century London being apprenticed to trades and she concludes: 'When we reach the level of the "labouring poor" it can almost be said that there is no work too heavy or disagreeable to be done by women.'[8] According to Alice Clark, the decline of women's position in crafts and trade took place in the seventeenth century with the spread of 'capitalistic organization' when

> the numbers of women who could find no outlet for their productive activity in partnership with their husbands were increasing and their opportunities for establishing an independent industry did not keep pace; on the contrary, such industry became ever more difficult. . . . the wife of the prosperous capitalist tended to become idle, the wife of the skilled journeyman lost her economic independence and became his unpaid domestic servant. . . . The masters no longer depended upon the assistance of their wives, while the journeyman's position became very similar to that of the modern artisan; he was employed on the premises of his master. . . . his wife and daughters . . . remained at home. . . . The alternatives before the women of this class were either to withdraw altogether from productive activity, and so become entirely dependent upon their husband's goodwill, or else to enter the labour market independently . . . in competition not only with other women, but with men. . . . At this time the idea that men 'keep' their wives begins to prevail.[9]

Snell's analysis of parish apprenticeships over three centuries up to 1834 demonstrates that 34 per cent of all apprenticeships were for girls: 'The eighteenth-century figures suggest relatively extensive female participation in the trades.'[10] It seems clear that women's position in work outside the home went

6. K. D. M. Snell, *Annals of the Labouring Poor: social change and agrarian England 1660–1900*, Cambridge University Press, 1985, p. 271.
7. R. A. Leeson, *Travelling Brothers*, Paladin Books, St Albans, 1980, p. 27.
8. M. D. George, *London Life in the Eighteenth Century*, Penguin, 1965, p. 172.
9. Alice Clark, *Working Life of Women in the Seventeenth Century* (1919), quoted in Snell, *Annals of the Labouring Poor*, p. 276.
10. Snell, *Annals of the Labouring Poor*, p. 278.

through a particularly bad period from the mid eighteenth to the mid twentieth century. It is fallacious to assume that the capitalist system is somehow committed to developing and expanding consistently by exploiting women more than men. Capitalism works infinitely more subtly and with far more complexity than many simple models suggest. Certainly it appeared that women were more useful in their domestic roles in an earlier phase of capitalism. However, there is no absolute logic about this and the signs are that women are now becoming more central as employees in the labour market. In Britain a half of all women between sixteen and sixty and three-quarters of all men between sixteen and sixty-five are economically active. The female activity rate is consistently rising as the male activity rate consistently falls. This is not, of course, to say that women are now being 'liberated' from the home by capitalism: rather a certain phase in the sexual division of labour is coming to an end.

Snell admits that 'one so frequently encounters the historiographical assumption that the acute sexual division of labour which had developed by 1850 existed long before then, in all classes',[11] and he goes on to cite evidence about the prevalence of women apprenticed to blacksmiths and farriers. The Select Committee on the Employment of Women and Children in Agriculture reported in 1843 that 'the physical condition of the girls is better than that of the boys . . . they bear the heat of the forge better, and often become strong by the work.' Such activity rendered the girls, as the report put it, 'perfectly independent. They often enter the beer shops, call for their pints, and smoke their pipes like men.' The report found 'little difference in their circumstances from those of men'. Similarly, E. P. Thompson, writing about the active role of women in popular unrest in the eighteenth-century, remarked ironically: 'These women appear . . . to have been unaware that they should have waited for some two hundred years for their liberation.'[12]

Clearly the economic position of women declined, but it would be wrong and dangerous to look to the eighteenth century as another golden age for women. They were certainly not involved in trades to the same extent as men, and nor were they as economically independent. The decline of female apprenticeship may be associated with the fall of female marriage rates and demographically linked labour shortages. More important, perhaps, was the growth of male unemployment after the Napoleonic wars. When an eighth of the male workforce was in the forces, it is perhaps not surprising that there should be quite dramatic fluctuations in the sexual divisions of labour. Associated with these factors was the increasing capitalization of the trades and its relation to the decline of artisan family economies. The more industries became more highly organized, the more women's employment was attacked as competing with that of men.

Middleton's chapter illustrates extremely well the nature of the issues and the difficulties in coming to firm and final judgements. Snell's work on the apprenticeship of women is equally stimulating and controversial. It is clear that there is need for considerable caution in making generalizations about men's work and women's work in former times. Until recently the historical studies available to sociologists interested in the history of work have been very limited.

11. Ibid., p. 296.
12. All cited in ibid., pp. 297–8.

However, there are now welcome signs of change and we may expect very substantial contributions by historians in this field during the next decade. Middleton's attempt to use historical sources to illuminate contemporary debates is echoed also by Snell. Contemporary questions about the sexual divisions of labour require detailed and complex historical research if we are to understand them more completely. All the chapters in part I are concerned, in their distinctive ways, to challenge over-simple 'golden-ageism'.

Lest I be accused of ethnocentrism I should, of course, acknowledge that part I is intentionally devoted to the history of work in what are now Western industrial societies. There may still, however, be something to learn that is relevant to more agriculturally based societies today. Malcolmson quotes Joan Thirsk, the economic historian, who claimed that an economy of dual occupations 'was the best insurance that men with almost no savings and certainly no capital resources could have devised. If misfortune attended one activity, there was always the other to fall back on.' It is unclear why she limits her claim to men, since women also engaged in a variety of forms of work and most people, whether men or women, gained their livelihood from more than one occupational source, as Malcolmson illustrates for eighteenth-century England.

Berg's focus on women's work in the early phases of industrialization in England makes it clear that existing attempts at generalization, whether by feminists or traditional social historians, are often based more on speculation than on hard evidence. Her detailed account of women's work in textiles and the metal trades demonstrates the difficulty of making generalizations in the face of empirical diversity. She dispels 'simple assumptions' about fundamental transformations in women's employment and skills brought about by the concentration of employment in mills and factories. In the light of the complexity of the empirical data she adduces, she argues that 'The household economy as it has been understood is a myth' based on an ahistorical and a static conception of the past, leading to 'uninteresting unidirectional accounts of women's subordination'. She points to parallels between her research on women's work in the late eighteenth and early nineteenth centuries and Pearson's work on the contemporary world (see chapter 20).

Clearly Keith Snell's research, to which I have already referred, has had a considerable impact on the historiography of early industrial England. As Berg concludes:

> The idea of a transition in the eighteenth century from a community-based workforce where women may have played a prominent role to the more individualist, market-oriented and, by association, more male workforce needs to be unravelled, and tested against the complex character of the contact between market and custom, individual and community which developed in the early industrial period.

This call for caution is important, since it makes most of the conventional accounts of the impact on women of the changing patterns of work in the period she reviews open to considerable doubt. It is useful to remember that were it not for the way feminists have drawn attention to the oppressive implications of the changing divisions of labour for women, there would not have been the same impetus for historians to reappraise conventional views. However, it is of course also true that more recent 'conventional views' have been informed by certain feminist speculations that Berg disputes.

Berg concludes by emphasizing the role of women in consumption which was 'the activity that bound community and capitalism together'. The logic of this perspective is that women were important in *facilitating* the crucial transformations in work patterns of that period. Perceiving women as a docile element being acted upon by the forces of history may have helped to create fallacies that may be hard to dispel.

The nineteenth century was the crucial period of transition, with the emergence of the male chief earner supporting 'his' dependent family; with the socialization of workers, with pre-industrial customary forms of behaviour, into the time disciplines of industrial capitalism; and with the emergence of a new social category – the unemployed. The remaining three contributions to part I deal with each of these issues in turn.

Humphries's work has already been referred to at some length above. She explores the complexities and contradictions surrounding a contentious and crucial piece of legislation that had wide-ranging consequences for the sexual divisions of labour. She makes it clear how 'paradoxically, coal mining men sought to abolish a system which seems to have operated in their favour, and to replace it with a system which was highly likely to force them into longer hours and harder work.' In order to understand this paradox, Humphries has to explore the circumstances of working-class family life in the context of working-class communities. Unlike those who wish to stereotype both men and women Humphries argues that 'the collier way of living was not only a way of surviving, but a way of relating, valuing and loving.' It is a tragedy of the contemporary world that such a statement still needs repeating with no less emphasis.

Gutman's historical survey of changing orientations to work in nineteenth-century America shows how the new industrial workers were only gradually socialized into a commitment to employment. The assumption that there was some kind of primordial 'Protestant' work ethic in the United States is hard to sustain, despite some valiant attempts to the contrary.[13] Gutman acknowledges the pioneering work of E. P. Thompson in this area and confirms that all elements of the American working class made the transition to industrial society uneasily, involving as it did, in Thompson's words, 'new disciplines, new incentives, and a new human nature upon which these incentives could bite effectively'. What the American and British worker fought *against* so vigorously in the nineteenth century they now, paradoxically, fight *for* equally vigorously. Employment has shifted from being a burden to be resisted to a necessity that cannot be forgone. The traditional work habits were reshaped by a variety of forces including new forms of consumption and piecework. Gutman quotes the Connecticut Bureau of Labour Statistics reporting in 1885 that piecework was 'a moral force which corresponds to machinery as a physical force.' We return to the dominations of forms of payment and production-line technology in part II.

The final transformation, discussed by Kumar, is the changing attitude to the 'unemployed', who emerged for the first time as a distinct social category at the

13. For a substantially different view, largely based on middle-class diaries, biographies and novels, see Daniel T. Rodgers, *The Work Ethic in Industrial America*, University of Chicago Press, 1978.

end of the nineteenth century. To understand the conditions of those without employment and the means of subsistence Kumar focuses on the English poor relief system in the seventeenth and eighteenth centuries. The existence of a national system under the old Poor Law from 1601 to 1834 provides a unique source of information for exploring the condition of the labouring poor.[14] No other European country possessed such a system. As the total of those unemployed in the OECD countries (that is the main capitalist industrial societies) in 1986 reached 31 million, it is valuable to consider how similar problems were handled in previous times. In particular, Kumar draws on the work of historians such as Malcolmson and others to emphasize the irregularity of wage labour – in that 'concealed unemployment' was endemic – and the need for different work 'mixes'. He makes the link between the arguments and information of chapters 2, 3 and 5 and the emerging idea of unemployment as a distinct condition. In the same way that employment came to dominate as the only work that 'counted', since survival depended overwhelmingly on having a source of income, so its reciprocal, unemployment, became synonymous with poverty. This emergence of a polarity between employment and unemployment is in marked contrast to the continuum of mixes of different forms of work typical of earlier times. It may be that in the last years of the twentieth century we are witnessing a return to a world where the continuum is more apposite than a polar or dualistic concept. However, those who can do without money to provide goods and services are in a very small minority as ordinary people's alternative means of subsistence have been gradually eroded over the last 200 years.

14. For two recent outstanding yet contrasting discussions of these issues see Gertrude Himmelfarb, *The Idea of Poverty: England in the early industrial age*, Knopf, New York, 1984; Random House, Toronto, 1984; Faber and Faber, London, 1984; and Snell, *Annals of the Labouring Poor*.

# 1

# The Familiar Fate of the *Famulae*: Gender Divisions in the History of Wage Labour

CHRIS MIDDLETON

The past is a foreign country: they do things differently there.
L. P. Hartley, *The Go-Between*

Both the sexual division of labour and male domination are so long standing.
H. Hartmann, 'Capitalism, patriarchy, and job segregation by sex'

Wage labour is not an invention of the capitalist economy. As far back as the thirteenth century large feudal estates would meet part of their labour need by employing staffs of stipendiary wage workers. But these workers, known as *famuli*(m)/*famulae*(f), were not in any sense proletarians. They were a form of bonded labour, and their services did not appear for sale on any labour market.

Among the lists of *famuli*[1] which survive from the thirteenth century are a set for eighteen manors on estates belonging to the Earls of Cornwall, the Abbots of Crowland and the Bishop of Winchester (Postan, 1954, appendix II). They are an important source of information for anyone interested in the sexual division of labour under feudalism. Although this was a society in which wage labour had little status and most *famuli* would probably have been recruited from the poorer families in the community (Britton, 1977, p. 92), the records list a considerable number of labourers who were recruited for their special skills. Nearly all the specialists so listed were engaged in activities conventionally defined as 'men's

This is a revised version of a paper presented to the Economic and Social Research Council symposium on segregation in employment held at the University of Lancaster, July 1985. I should like to thank Sheila Miles for her loving support and many helpful contributions to the essay.

1. I have used the generic masculine case (a) where I am referring to original documentation and (b) where it would be misleading to imply both sexes because very few women were involved.

work' (ploughmen, shepherds, herdmen, millers etc.), whereas openings for skilled women (predominantly in the dairy and, perhaps, the garden) were comparatively few.[2] The great majority of female workers were recorded as 'servants'. Thus (even though a servant was not necessarily a domestic drudge and some may even have been employed in predominantly agricultural tasks) there is evidence here of a pattern of job segregation by sex which has a remarkably familiar ring:

1 Recruitment to most positions appears to have been governed by a person's sex.
2 There were far fewer opportunities for women and girls in this relatively secure (though hardly prestigious) form of paid employment.
3 The *range* of specialist work open to them was much narrower.
4 Most women were recruited to service positions of an unspecified nature (for example, 'one woman-servant') whereas adult males were widely employed in specialist capacities.
5 There was a marked tendency for women to be employed in domestic services.

The aim of this chapter is to consider the relevance of evidence of this kind (more examples are presented below) to debates about the role of gender divisions in the segmented labour markets of contemporary capitalism. If patterns of gender segregation and inequality are observed to persist from one mode of production to another it must make us wonder (at the very least) about the validity of accounts which try to explain their origins and functioning by reference to processes that are *specific* to capitalist or market economies. In questioning such theories, however, I do not want to fall into the opposite trap of positing some autonomous and everlasting realm of patriarchal oppression. The argument that follows, therefore, falls into three parts.

Firstly, I consider how questions of gender segregation and inequality have been analysed within 'class-derivationist' theories of labour market segmentation and suggest that, contrary to a belief implicit in much feminist criticism, such theories have not treated gender divisions as a by-product of class relations. I argue that 'class-derivationist' and 'feminist'[3] accounts of gender segregation in the labour market share more common ground than is generally supposed, since both have tended to regard the conditions governing women's entry into the labour market as the decisive variable for explaining divisions within it.

Secondly, a range of historical evidence is advanced to suggest that the terms of women's entry into the labour market may not, in fact, be the critical issue. There are strong indications that the patriarchal organization of wage work in pre-industrial England (which often resembled that informing the labour market under industrial capitalism) was compatible with significant variations both in the character of the labour supply and in the conditions under which labour 'offered'

2. References to 'skilled work' in this chapter rest on what appear to be the contemporary definitions of 'skill' or specialist work.
3. 'Feminist' as used here refers only to theorists who perceive gender hierarchies as constructed independently of class formations.

its services. I should perhaps stress at this point that the evidence presented here is highly selective in character, concentrating on some major *continuities* in occupational segregation and inequality rather than on any variations in the sexual division of labour.[4] This approach has been adopted with a particular end in view. Most studies of gender stratification in capitalist labour markets claim either that segmentation itself is a function of capitalist development or that the source of gender divisions within the labour market can be traced to a kind of family-household system specifically associated with capitalist social formations. The historical evidence deployed below is intended to throw doubt on both of these interpretations.

Thirdly, evidence that shows how patterns of gender segregation and inequality in the organization of labour have outlived transformations in the mode of production would seem at first sight to point towards the existence of a system of 'patriarchy' that is independent of class relations. But in the final section of this chapter I suggest that such arguments actually involve an unacceptably tendentious use of historical evidence. Moreover, the unrepresentative character of the particular evidence presented here (i.e. the disregarding of examples of labour organization where segregation and inequality were less entrenched or took unfamiliar forms) takes on a new significance in this context. Such variations cannot be overlooked in any general history of the sexual division of wage labour, or in any attempt to construct a pan-historical theory of patriarchy (for discussion of such alternatives see Medick, 1976; Kriedte, Medick and Schlumbohm, 1981; Middleton, 1985).

## THE PLACE OF GENDER IN THEORIES OF OCCUPATIONAL SEGREGATION

Theories of labour market segmentation have generally been developed in isolation from feminist accounts of the sexual division of labour, and the appropriate relation between them has therefore become a matter for controversy. Some writers foresee no great difficulty in combining their respective insights, viewing these as complementary, but many feminists are less sanguine about the prospects for a successful coupling. The latter have argued that 'orthodox', class-derived theories of labour market segmentation are irretrievably flawed by their treatment of patriarchy as an element to be incorporated into a predetermined structure of labour market relations, while ignoring the way gender divisions are instrumental in the initial shaping of that framework.

Although it is becoming widely accepted that there can be no single, universally applicable explanation for labour market segmentation, a limited number of alternative interpretations have been identified. In particular, a dichotomous distinction has often been drawn between those theories which argue that the labour market became segmented for reasons unrelated to gender (notably the imperatives of capital accumulation and/or conflicts between capital

4. The focus on wage work is a function of this stress on continuity. Wage work was very much a subsidiary form of labour in feudal England, though it steadily increased in importance during the centuries covered here.

and labour) and those which claim that gender divisions were themselves responsible for determining the shape of the labour market in important respects.

Class-based interpretations of occupational segregation can be subdivided into theories which focus on capitalist initiatives, and theories which emphasize strategies evolved by workers in the course of their struggle to improve the terms on which they sell their labour power. These approaches have been criticized by feminists for seeing gender divisions within the labour process as, respectively, a 'by-product of the dynamics of capital accumulation and capital restructuring' (Beechey, 1983, p. 41) or a 'by-product of struggles between capital and labour' (Walby, 1983, p. 158). I am not convinced, however, that this properly represents the views of theorists within the class-derivation tradition. Although these theories may lack an adequate conception of patriarchal forces, it is not true that they have seen the imperatives of capital accumulation or class struggle as major determinants of *gendered* segregation in the occupational sector. It is the segmentation of the labour market, not gender divisions as such, which they see as deriving from the capitalist process. Thus, rather than the usual twofold classification outlined in the previous paragraph, it would be more accurate to distinguish three possible positions:

1 Gender divisions in the labour market are a by-product of processes of capital accumulation and/or class struggle.
2 Segmented labour markets are created by processes of capital accumulation and/or class struggle. Gender divisions become superimposed on the market for reasons which lie *beyond the scope of the model.*
3 Gender divisions are not derivative of capital accumulation and/or class struggle. They are independently responsible for structuring labour markets according to 'patriarchal' principles (although that term may not always be used).

In brief, class-derivation theories are usually accused of adopting position 1, whereas I shall argue that position 2 is much more typical of their approach.

Class-derivation theories of labour market segmentation show little uniformity in their treatment of gender and its links to processes of occupational segregation. In some accounts these matters assume considerable prominence, in others they appear to be quite peripheral. Yet, despite these divergences, all the studies we examine here are consistent in arguing that gender becomes a relevant factor in the labour market because of conditions which are *external* to the market. These concern either the differential characteristics of men and women workers (real or perceived) or the circumstances governing each sex's availability for wage work – neither of which is seen as determined wholly by capital accumulation or class struggle.

Theories that focus on employer initiatives include the two 'mainstream' theories of labour market segmentation, i.e. dual labour market theory (Doeringer and Piore, 1971; Barron and Norris, 1976) and radical theories (Reich, Gordon and Edwards, 1973; Gordon, Edwards and Reich, 1982). Braverman's deskilling thesis (1974) and many accounts of the industrial reserve army would also fall under this heading. Their disagreements and differences of emphasis, in both describing and explaining the development of labour market processes, are well known, but for all that there is an essential congruity in their treatment of gender division. All these approaches explain developments in the structure of the labour market in terms of 'demand-side' economics. Gender differences, on the contrary, are identified as an attribute (real or perceived) of the supply of labour. Gender divisions are therefore seen as having been constructed by social relationships outside the province of labour market theory. Edwards provides what is perhaps the clearest acknowledgement of this perspective. He states that on the one hand 'the fundamental differences [between labour market segments] are not so much among the workers as among the jobs that workers hold. . . . if we are to understand the historical forces that established and maintain the divisions, we must look to the job structure.' On the other hand, however, 'for both blacks and women, the separate dialectics of race and sex condition their participation in the capitalist economy. . . . the dynamics of racial and sexual divisions require *separate analysis*' (Edwards, 1979, pp. 166, 197, 195, my emphasis). In this interpretation, then, distinctions of gender are superimposed on a predetermined framework of labour market divisions.

Theories which concentrate on capitalist initiatives have been criticized for exaggerating the employers' capacity to manipulate the labour market and, correlatively, for underestimating the degree to which gender segregation in the labour market is attributable to the effects of working-class action. Sex discrimination, in this latter view, has been used by workers as an instrument of class struggle. Rubery, for instance, develops Braverman's arguments on deskilling. All workers, she suggests, are threatened by the deskilling process and 'this threat may induce defensive actions on the part of the workers to stratify the labour force, control entry to occupations and maintain skill status long after these skill divisions have become irrelevant' (Rubery, 1980, p. 257). Segmentation arises because the existing labour force organizes and protects itself against competition from new influxes of workers (comprising, in the recent history of capitalism, female and immigrant labour). In a similar vein Humphries has argued that nineteenth-century workers resisted the cheapening of labour power by attempting to limit the number of married women entering the labour market (Humphries, 1977). This would not result in gender segregation *within* the labour market, of course, but it might help to explain women's poorer market capacity and thus their consignment to secondary sector occupations. Gender discrimination in the labour market is once again explained in terms of the determinants of labour supply.

How do these various theories account for the allocation of men and women to separate labour markets? On one interpretation women's recruitment into the secondary sector can be viewed essentially as historically contingent (though not necessarily accidental if one takes into account the wider sexual division of labour). Edwards, for instance, argues that 'women entered the labor-force during the regime of monopoly capitalism. In contrast to nineteenth-century immigrants . . . later groups entered when developmental forces were pushing towards a segmented, rather than a homogeneous workforce (Edwards, 1979, p. 194). Presumably, then, we are to understand that if women had entered the labour market in the nineteenth century they would have joined a workforce which was becoming progressively more homogeneous, and their relegation to the secondary labour market would have been less assured.

A similar sense of historical contingency informs Rubery's position. It is women's status as a recently generated supply of wage labour which leads to a restructuring of the labour force and also determines their own fate within it. Their status as newcomers derives from a 'release' of female labour from domestic production – which is due in turn, one may assume, to its previous elimination from the waged sector (see Humphries, 1977). Rubery also alludes to women's particular 'supply' characteristics as a reserve army of labour.

However, the main thrust of radical theory focuses on monopoly capitalism's 'divide and rule' strategies to forestall working-class opposition, and women's consignment to the secondary labour market is interpreted in this light. Edwards suggests that pre-existing divisions of race and sex are manipulated in order to foment working-class disunity but (in contrast to the formation of the bifurcated primary market) discrimination has not been forced upon employers. Rather, the lack of any effective bargaining strength among blacks and women made discrimination possible (Edwards, 1979, p. 195). From this perspective, then, there was nothing fortuitous about the segregation of men and women in the labour market. The explanation consists of two elements: gender discrimination was the result of deliberate policy on the part of employers, but their success is conditional on *extraneous* factors which have been responsible for differentiating the market capacities of men and women.

Barron and Norris (1976) spell out for us some of these characteristic differences. In their view the maintenance of a secondary labour market depends on the availability of a supply of workers who are prepared to tolerate the low pay, insecurity and other disadvantages associated with jobs in that sector. In Britain, at least, women form the largest single category of such workers. In discussing women in the secondary sector they are more careful than most to distinguish between actual characteristics and stereotypical representations, and so avoid the trap of simply assuming that workers in the secondary labour market lack stable work habits (Piore, Edwards) or that women provide a cheap and unskilled workforce (Braverman, Rubery). Yet, even in Barron and Norris's account, the characteristics of women workers (real or ascribed) cannot be deduced from the operations of the labour market. As with all the other accounts we have reviewed, they enter the analysis as an exogenous 'given'.

It seems to be generally assumed that the source of women's weak bargaining position and/or low level of motivation in the labour market can be located in the family-household system and women's continuing responsibility for the domestic welfare of its members. However, few analyses of labour market segmentation have actually investigated this wider sexual division of labour in detail. It is perhaps to be expected that theories emphasizing the employers' responsibility for segmentation will treat conditions governing the supply of labour as peripheral. But even studies which concentrate on workers' strategies (and thus do make 'supply-side' economics a central feature of their analysis) are content to refer somewhat casually to 'traditional' family forms and 'traditional' patterns of job segregation (Humphries, 1977; Rubery and Tarling, 1982).

An exception to this is a recent article by Brenner and Ramas (1984). The authors examine the background to the kind of worker-instituted segregation discussed by Humphries and Rubery, agreeing with Humphries that the exclusionary tactics of nineteenth-century trade unions were contingent strategies evolved in the course of the class struggle, rather than a sign of rampant sexism. The exclusivist policies were determined by the competitive nature of the labour market. They acquired a gendered dimension because women had *already* been marginalized in the wage sector and entered the labour market at a disadvantage. The process of marginalization (withdrawal from full-time wage-work) had occurred long before the mid nineteenth century and was explicable in terms of the particular social exigencies of biological reproduction prevalent at the time.

According to Brenner and Ramas, there was no realistic economic alternative to a division of labour in which one person undertook full-time wage work while the other became a 'full-time' domestic labourer. It was then more or less inevitable that mothers should be assigned to the home because of their biological role in reproduction and the nursing of infants. Thus, although the operation of the labour market was indeed 'sex-blind', it could still account for sex segregation because women now entered the labour market at a disadvantage arising from their domestic responsibilities. This was best considered in strictly material terms. Women's skills were undervalued not for any reasons of ideology, but because women were less able to organize. Their bargaining position was materially weak (Brenner and Ramas, 1984).

To sum up the argument so far: most class-derivation theorists do not claim to explain gender as a principle of stratification in the labour process, though they do suggest ways in which employers or male workers may reinforce existing gender divisions while pursuing class objectives. On the contrary, they have taken as *given* various attributes (real or ascribed) of women as a supply of labour: low or unrecognized skills, a readiness to accept low pay, low bargaining strength, alternative domestic commitments, etc. These characteristics presuppose a sexual division of labour, discriminatory practices or ideologies operating beyond the boundaries of the labour market. Yet this is exactly the area that many feminist critics have been keen to explore and which many have privileged within their own analytical approaches. One thinks perhaps of Delphy's domestic mode of production; of Barrett's discussion of familial ideology; and of Beechey's earlier emphasis, since qualified, on the special characteristics of married women workers. On this reading, class-derivation theories of labour market segmentation and feminist analyses of the sexual division of labour do not seem to be incompatible.

But while a theoretical *rapprochement*, centring on the question of the circumstances that govern women's entry into the labour market, seems feasible, one may query whether this is really the critical issue. It is at this point that a broader historical canvas may prove illuminating. How satisfactory could we regard the current state of theory if it could be shown that comparable patterns of gendered segregation and inequality were prevalent in non-capitalist modes of production, where there was often no market in labour and/or where family-household structures were markedly different from those associated with industrial capitalism? It is to this evidence that we now turn.

## WAGE LABOUR IN FEUDAL ENGLAND

Let us return first to the case of the medieval *famuli*. It should perhaps be emphasized that most of the farm workers recruited for their special skills would not be 'specialists' in the modern sense of the word. Many specialist farming skills had a seasonal application only and versatility was essential. Moreover, the *famulus*, though common enough in some areas, was not the typical labouring figure in the rural landscape, as demesne farming in most regions relied heavily on the obligatory, part-time, unwaged labour of the bonded tenantry. Yet it would be unwise to belittle the significance of these estate records, for they testify to the fact that the rudimentary elements of occupational specialization (and perhaps of occupational identity too) were present in one of the few sectors of the rural economy where such a development could be sustained – that is where the unit of labour was sufficiently large and the technical division of labour sufficiently advanced to allow for the frequent and regular use of specialist skills. The records show clearly that these embryonic occupational identities were largely confined to men.

No such configuration was possible on the peasant holding, where the limits of size dictated a flexible response; yet even here one finds that many activities were designated as either 'men's work' or 'women's work'. Ploughing and mowing (with the heavy scythe) were almost invariably done by men, while other predominantly male tasks included reaping, threshing, hedging, ditching, and the gelding and spaying of livestock. 'Women's work' in the fields included planting, weeding, and gathering straw, stubble and chaff; winnowing was usually done by women, and they often undertook the washing and shearing of sheep. Closer to home, they took care of the poultry, the dairy and the garden. But flexibility was important and few of the above tasks appear to have been sexually exclusive. No doubt, the extent and nature of men and women's participation was affected by technological developments and changing conditions of labour supply, but there is evidence of women performing *all* the above tasks at some time or another (though it must be said that the evidence on their involvement in mowing and ploughing is somewhat tenuous) (Hilton, 1947, pp. 145–7; Roberts, 1979; Power, 1975, pp. 71ff; Casey, 1976, pp. 227–31).

The important question, of course, is whether these tendencies towards segregation by sex became more pronounced when circumstances allowed or favoured occupational specialization; and, if this did happen, one then needs to ask whether and in what ways these divisions took on a hierarchical form. With this in mind let us continue our examination of rural wage labour in the medieval economy.

Apart from the *famuli* two other kinds of wage labour were employed as adjuncts to the system of rental exploitation: a stratum of skilled artisans; and day labourers. The occupational experiences of the former could very enormously. Smiths, for example, might be more or less full-time craftsmen plying their trade from a single village, whereas thatchers and common carpenters would normally provide their specialist services on a seasonal or part-time basis, engaging in farm work for the rest of their time. Yet other craftsmen, especially masons, the more specialist carpenters and others engaged in the building trade, tended to form a migratory but highly paid labour force. Women are sometimes recorded as being paid for assisting in these trades (thatching, in particular), but otherwise all the craft workers were men.

At the other end of the wage-labouring scale was feudalism's version of the reserve army of labour drawn from a class of landless labourers, cottars, and younger or unmarried siblings whose inheritance had excluded them from the family holding. The rise in population and the pressure this placed on the land made them especially numerous in the century before the Black Death of 1348. Most eked out a subsistence living from a combination of grazing and gathering rights, and supplemented their income from day wage labour. These, the poorest labourers of all, undoubtedly included a large proportion of women in their ranks, and it is unlikely that the sexual segregation of labour was as strict among them as it was among the other groups of workers we have discussed so far. Yet even here there were distinct patterns of recruitment for men and for women. Women and children could usually find work only on a seasonal basis even though their earnings must have been vital to families living so close to the breadline (Rogers, 1866, vol. I, pp. 289ff; 1894, pp. 169–70). Where regular, paid day labour was available it seems to have been largely a male prerogative, and we can only guess at the plight of any 'independent' female cottars and labourers living alone, of whom, according to both Russell and Hilton, there may have been considerable numbers (Russell, 1948, pp. 61–9; Hilton, 1975, pp. 27–36).

Information on wages in medieval England is far too sketchy for any detailed comparison of male and female rates to be possible. The best series of data available to us is an extensive but frustratingly patchy listing of payments for the years 1259–1400 compiled by Thorold Rogers more than a century ago (Rogers, 1866). The evidence is difficult to interpret because, as well as being sparse, it is spread thinly over many decades and many regions. Interpretation is made even more difficult by the fact that payments were often by the piece rather than for a specified period, were often made wholly or partly in kind, and might cover the work of more than one labourer. For the following brief discussion I have excluded all data which cannot be expressed unequivocally as a day rate for an individual agricultural labourer. The figures refer to 'the going rate' on a particular estate in any given year.

One fact does stand out sharply from Rogers's listings: wages for women were lower than wages for men. But even this bald statement, though undoubtedly true, is really based on an inference. What the figures actually show is that wages for work normally performed by women were, on average, significantly below those paid for 'men's work'. The sex of the labourer actually employed to perform the work was rarely made explicit. In the eighty years prior to the Black Death (1268–1347) the median day rate for men's work was 2.5d ($N = 25$; range 1–4d) while that for women's work was only 1d ($N = 17$; range 0.75–1.5d). Rates rose sharply thereafter for the rest of the century (1349–94) to medians of 3d for men's work ($N = 13$; range 2–8d) and to 2d for women's work ($N = 5$; range 1–2d) (adapted from Rogers, 1866, vol. II, pp. 576–83). Other figures in the listings resist even the simplest computation, but do bear out the general impression of inequality between male and female earnings.

It is hard to tell whether differences in wage rates were solely a function of the sexual division of labour, or whether women also received less for performing identical work. Some sources suggest that men and women were paid equally for the same work. Rogers certainly believed this to be the case for harvesters in the thirteenth century, and Hilton came across an example of women reapers being employed at the same rates as men in Gloucestershire, though since this was in the 1380s it may conceivably have been attributable to labour shortage (Rogers,

1866, vol. I, p. 281; 1894, p. 170; Hilton, 1975, pp. 102–3). Against this, we have the anonymous author of a late-thirteenth-century farming guide, entitled *Hosebondrie*, advising estate managers to employ women for certain tasks because they would accept 'much less money than a man would take' (Oschinsky, 1971, p. 427; cited in Bennett, n.d.). It is possible, of course, that men and women received the same rate when payment was by the piece. If that were the case one would really need to know whether men and women could complete the task in the same time span, or whether, as has been suggested, men had a higher productivity in certain circumstances (Roberts, 1979, p. 9).

In conclusion, we can say that women are rarely documented in medieval records as performing agricultural work of a skilled or prestigious nature, and they appear to have received considerably less pay than men.

## THE EXPANSION OF WAGE LABOUR: FARM SERVANTS AND DAY LABOURERS

I want now to describe a number of developments in the organization of wage labour which were associated with the rise of agrarian capitalism. In England, feudal relations never properly recovered from the havoc wrought by famine and plague over the course of the fourteenth century. From the peasants' point of view the repeated catastrophes had all the makings of some singularly perverse miracle. The hunger for land was transformed 'overnight' into a chronic labour shortage. Land became plentiful, strengthening the cultivator's hand in his struggle against the landlord and raising the standard of living. The proportion of small holding families supplementing their income through wage work was drastically reduced. All strata of peasants prospered but, above all, the fifteenth century became the age of the yeoman farmer, i.e. the age of the middling peasant relying heavily on family labour.

However, signs that the commercialization of agriculture was spreading were already visible by the Tudor era (early sixteenth century) (Tawney, 1912). The yeoman class began a classic process of fragmentation; some families rose to become prosperous capitalist farmers, while others, unable to consolidate their fortunes in this way, were increasingly forced to resort to wage labour. Meanwhile, many of the great landed estates, no longer able to function on the basis of obligatory labour, were converted into capitalist enterprises, with one eye on market opportunities and the other on the price and productivity of labour. The development of agrarian capitalism was thus associated with, and arguably responsible for, a vast increase in the proportion of the rural population who were dependent on wage labour.

Despite the disappearance of bonded labour the crucial separation of the wage-labouring population into 'living-in' servants and day labourers persisted. Indeed, this division became a key organizing principle of agricultural labour in a way that had never been true of the medieval economy. By the sixteenth century farm service involved a far higher proportion of the labouring population, and it had also acquired new functions and meanings. The farm servants who lived in, 'servants in husbandry', were predominantly young and single, and entered their master's household as youthful dependants.[5] They were hired annually, but it would be wrong to see them as youthful proletarians with long-term contracts. They became hired members of a working family. As in earlier times these servants were agricultural workers rather than domestic menials, but since they were obliged to perform whatever duties their master required, many, especially women and girls, would have been kept busy round the house as well as in the fields. Their time was at their master's disposal for the duration of the contract.

Farm service had become the main institutional source of continually available labour in a social structure where coresident families were generally small.[6] It flourished because of the importance of the small farmer, offering him (and only occasionally her) a flexible solution to any cyclical imbalance between labour needs and resources which might arise from the family's developmental cycle. One historian succinctly expressed it thus: 'Service in husbandry solved the cyclical problem by eliminating it. The family was simply redefined' (Kussmaul, 1981, p. 24). Service was also an important means of social control, ensuring that adolescents were attached to a man of property until such time as they married (which, for much of the period, could be expected to happen sometime in their mid-twenties) (Stone, 1977, p. 22). From the servants' point of view their term of employment offered a training in farm work and domestic production, and effectively acted as a forced method of saving before marriage. But the arrangement was not one of their own choosing (Hajnal, 1965, p. 132).

The position of day labourers was quite different. Typically, they were married adults, living independently of their employer and hired only when he needed them; thus their experience of work was likely to be seasonal, intermittent, and dependent on the vagaries of the weather and their own state of health. The division between service and day labour had become, for the majority of agricultural workers, a matter of successive stages in their personal biography: a position characterized by relatively secure employment but semi-servile status was exchanged, on marriage, for an uncertain and often poverty-stricken independence. Moreover, even though families at every level of society sent their children into service, there can be very few doubts about the stigma that attached to it, for women quite as much as men. Little Moll Flanders's aversion to going into service was a fiction based solidly in social fact. It is confirmed by the observation that so many of the rural poor preferred a precarious independence to the protection of service: there were very few older servants.[7]

There appears to have been a relatively strong association of women with household service. The ratio of servants to day labourers was significantly higher among women than for men (Kussmaul, 1981). While unmarried persons of both sexes were supposed to enter service so that they should be brought under a master's authority, the number of males remaining unplaced far exceeded that of

5. The labels 'servant' and 'labourer' were not applied with quite such discrimination as the discussion here might imply. But the institutional distinction was drawn sharply enough.

6. The new consensus, especially strong among historians, describes the family in early modern England as 'nuclear'. This is quite misleading as the only significant continuity with the modern nuclear family form is in the *size* of the coresident unit. The description ignores all other aspects of familial institutions, including even the coresident unit's internal structure.

7. Roberts (1985) provides references to girls who, like Moll Flanders, were reluctant to go into service.

females (Emmison, 1976, pp. 147–64),[8] and there is some evidence that it was the young unmarried woman who was most vigorously forced into service (Scott, 1973, p. 41). It appears, in consequence, that the total number of women servants may have been higher than that of men: Gregory King estimated that there were 300,000 female servants in 1695 compared with 260,000 male (King, 1810, p. 39).[9] Thus the protection which service offered against the uncertainties and irregularity of the labour market may have been extended to rather more women than men, but it did so only by reaffirming their subservient status. Girls in service were not only expected to acquire the skills they would need as a farm labourer's wife, but also the virtues of a submissive demeanour. (The particular tasks she would be asked to perform – and especially the balance between indoor and outdoor work – would vary according to the size of household she had entered and the kind of farming it practised; Scott, 1973, pp. 43–4.)

While the experience of independent labourers as a whole was one of chronic underemployment, women appear to have fared even worse than men. On average they worked fewer days in the year, and it was rare indeed for them to find regular employment outside their own homes. Where they did manage to do so, as on the Lancashire estate of Swarthmoor Hall for example, it was usually by combining agricultural work with menial household tasks such as washing and scrubbing, or with cooking for the field labourers (Scott, 1973, pp. 128–30).

This does not mean that they were unable to bring any earnings into the household. In most parts of the country the economic viability of labouring households depended on a mix of self-sufficient husbandry, wage labour, and petty-commodity production. Although women could rarely earn as much as men through wage labour, their contribution in the two other respects was substantial and their involvement in rural industry connected them to the market. Indeed there was often little visible difference between commodity production for the merchant capitalist and wage work under 'proto-capitalism' (Middleton, 1985). The importance of regional variation must again be noted here, for women undoubtedly had more opportunity to make a financial contribution to the household wherever rural industry took a firm hold. This happened mostly in the

8. Records of the Lexden Hundred petty sessions, 1568–9, give the following totals (calculated from Emmison, 1976, p. 152):

| | *Males* | *Females* |
|---|---|---|
| Masterless | 229 | 66 |
| Orders (to find or serve masters) | 57 | 8 |
| | 286 | 74 |
| (Women as proportion of total = 20.6%) | | |
| Hirings | 83 | 22 |
| (Women as proportion of total = 21.0%) | | |

The lower number of females in these records is intriguing, given all the other pointers to the large number of female servants, but could conceivably reflect more informal channels whereby girls were put into service.

9. Even if, as Stone suggests, service was an important institution for controlling unruly male youth, it was possibly still more important for its control over young women.

smallholding and pastoral regions of the north and west, rather than the arable counties which we examine in more detail later.

Between the sixteenth and eighteenth centuries the preponderance of the large capitalist farm in the agrarian economy advanced inexorably through discontinuous but cumulative processes of dispossession and amalgamation, expanding especially in the southern and eastern counties of arable (and also lowland sheep) farming. Farming methods and technology became subject to the competitive 'disciplines' of the market (though, as we shall see, acceptance of those disciplines may have been limited by the persistent influence of patriarchal ideology and conventions). In comparison with the smaller farms these large estates employed proportionately fewer farm servants but relied heavily on day labour.[10] In some areas they were undoubtedly the principal source of *regular* work for independent labourers. It was here that the trend towards occupational specialization was most marked, and the number of skilled labourers employed on the largest estates was often quite remarkable. (One should still remember, though, that regular full-time work in a single job was not yet the norm, and the concept of occupational categories 'as applied to particular individuals and social groups . . . should be treated with caution'; Malcolmson, 1981, p. 23.)

It seems that few of the opportunities arising on these estates were open to women. For them, skilled agricultural work continued to be restricted to the dairy and market garden. In fact, the pattern of occupational specialization on the large capitalist farms seems to have resembled, but in a more entrenched form, the model of gendered segregation that we observed among the medieval *famuli* (Everitt, 1967, pp. 430ff ). However, the work experience of women could not remain unaffected while prospects for men were improving. Changing technology and divisions of labour often meant a deteriorating situation for women within the labour process. As agriculture grew more specialized and the distribution of tasks became less fluid, the work of ordinary labourers tended to become even less varied and rewarding than it had been before.

## HARVEST LABOUR: A CASE STUDY OF DAY LABOUR

A clear illustration of the kind of effects which advancing technology and specialization could have is provided by the history of harvesting. The harvest was always the season of greatest demand for day or weekly labour, whether it be met by the obligatory 'boonworks' exacted from the feudal peasantry or, in later centuries, by the hiring of wage workers. It called for the involvement of all members of the community – men and women, old and young alike – and at no other time of the year could so many women be found working outside their households. It was also the season when wages tended to be most buoyant for, in so far as any agrarian labour market could be so described, the harvest was a sellers' market.[11]

The focal work of the harvest, and the best paid, was the actual cutting of the

10. The greater reliance on day labour on the large estates may have been a function of their close connection with arable farming – which is more seasonal in its demands for labour.

11. For an indication of the way this sellers' market could be exploited, see Malcolmson (1981, p. 36).

crop. This could be done either by reaping with a sickle or by mowing, two-handed, with the heavier and more productive corn scythe. Male harvesters predominated in this part of the work, but at the beginning of our period they certainly held no monoply. The records contain numerous references to female reapers and even a few to female mowers.[12] As one might expect, there is some evidence of more women being conscripted into laborious harvest work during the second half of the fourteenth century (i.e. the period of greatest labour shortage), but the gradual replacement of sickle by scythe had a deleterious effect on women's involvement in the harvest (Roberts, 1979). Wherever the new corn-cutting technology was introduced, which happened with gathering momentum from the later Middle Ages, women ceased to be employed as shearers. In the opinion of Michael Roberts, and also in that of many contemporary writers, the critical factor in this was the additional size and weight of the scythe which 'emphasized the strength and stature required of the mower, effectively confining its use to the strongest men' (Roberts, 1979, p. 8).

Roberts has stressed the gradual rather than catastrophic nature of the changeover to the scythe. Scythes could cut greater quantities of corn with less labour, but resulted in more of the crop being lost or damaged. For a long period, therefore, they were used only to mow the cheaper quality grains, leaving wheat and rye to be cut by sickle. Another factor inhibiting their introduction was the availability of a large labour force in the corn-growing counties fed by a seasonal migration to the south and east, which reduced the pressure for high individual productivity. But a third consideration, paradoxically, were the temporary *shortages* of male labour (especially in times of war and civil war) since these emphasized the farmers' continuing reliance on female labour. Thus female reapers were not displaced 'in one fell swoop'. But the vulnerability of their position as shearers was nevertheless becoming ever more apparent as capitalist principles of economy gained ascendancy.

The adoption of the corn scythe did not eliminate women from the harvest entirely. Although a mower could cut larger quantities of corn more quickly than a reaper, he 'left the corn he had cut in more disarray and, as a result, more subsidiary workers were needed to gather the produce of a mower than were necessary for each individual reaper' (Roberts, 1979, p. 13). Thus the introduction of the new technology had complex implications for the pattern of women's work in the harvest fields. Women were displaced from the highly paid work of shearing but, for a long period, the total number of days worked by them (mainly as poorly paid rakers and followers) may actually have risen. Is this a classic case of deskilling following the introduction of new technology?

Research by Snell (1985), using data on seasonal unemployment in the grain-growing counties, has demonstrated that the move towards male domination of the harvest accelerated during the course of the eighteenth century. The trend was especially noticeable towards the end of the century, which also happened to be a period of intensive specialization in cereal farming. Through an imaginative use of rural settlement examinations, Snell discovered that the seasonal distribution of agricultural unemployment (as measured by applications for poor relief in the rural parishes) followed similar patterns for both sexes until about 1760.

12. Roberts (1979, p. 6, n. 24) has queried the reliability of some of these references.

After that the distribution curves diverged sharply. The male curve preserved its characteristic indications of employment security during the summer months for the whole period of analysis (1690–1860). Indeed, the steepness of the curve was accentuated after 1793, indicating an even greater concentration of male employment in the harvest season from around the turn of the nineteenth century. By way of contrast, the seasonal distribution of female unemployment displayed a similar pattern to that of men during the first half of the eighteenth century, but then shifted towards one with a rising curve of unemployment lasting right through the harvest months. In many parishes, it seems, women wage workers had not merely become marginal to the harvest effort but had been eliminated from it – apart from the very short-term work of gleaning.

Women's exclusion from harvest labour in the arable counties did not mean they were completely lost to agricultural work, though their participation rates almost certainly declined. Frequency indicators taken from the 1834 report of the Poor Law Commission suggest that their activity had come to be concentrated on the spring work of weeding corn, on hay-making and stone picking, and on gleaning as mentioned. Their involvement in other kinds of field work (which included reaping, wheat planting, and root crop production) received far fewer mentions (Snell, 1985, pp. 55–6). This confirms the impression of their seasonal unemployment curves which show that the lowest rates of female unemployment were now in the spring which, as Snell emphasized, was 'a period of the year characterised in the east by relatively slight labour costs and by a low demand for labour' (Snell, 1985, p. 22). Or, to put it from the women's perspective, they had less work and less money.

We have shown how, over the course of several centuries, the sexual division of harvest labour was transformed; and we have identified two distinct movements within the overall process of change. First, we noted how the segregation of the sexes was intensified by the introduction of the corn scythe and how this led to a channelling of female harvesters into subsidiary activities. Roberts's explanation for this, once the decision to adopt the corn scythe has been taken, is predicated on a physiological-cum-technological determinism: women do not have the physical capacity to mow. Whatever we may think of his suggestion, the ramifications of this process – how technological innovation led to a stricter sexual *hierarchy* of harvest labour – still need to be analysed sociologically.

The second movement entailed the exclusion of women from the harvest fields. This came at the end of the period discussed by Roberts, was relatively abrupt, and was confined for the most part to the corn-growing counties. Snell's analysis, while not denying the relevance of technological innovation, gives more weight to socio-economic forces. A series of linked developments had exacerbated seasonal fluctuations in the demand for labour and simultaneously undermined the labourers' capacity to withstand periods of unemployment. The alteration in the pattern of demand was primarily a consequence of the shift to specialized crop farming: first because cereal production is sporadic in its demands for labour, and secondly because it curtailed the availability of alternative employment. (Dairy farming, which had once provided work in the spring, was now much reduced.) Meanwhile, the labouring population had been turned into proletarians. Through the loss of smallholdings, the erosion of common rights, and the decline in many districts of rural industry, agricultural workers had become entirely dependent on wage income. Seasonal unemployment simply pushed them on to the parish. In effect, an economy of underemployed labour had been transformed into one of structural unemployment. If women had continued with their agricultural involvement under these circumstances, male vulnerability to seasonal unemployment would have been even greater. Accordingly, Snell thinks it likely that pressure arose from within the labour force itself to exclude female competition (Snell, 1985, pp. 57–66).

## WAGE DISCRIMINATION: SERVANTS AND LABOURERS

Any estimate of the degree of gender inequality among agricultural wage workers has to allow for the relatively high proportion of girls and women in service, and then come to terms with the futility of attempting any quantitative comparison between servants' and day labourers' incomes. Farm servants were in the singular position of being half family members, half hired helps. The provision of food and board for them was part of an obligatory relationship as well as a material necessity. This is not to deny that farmers were conscious of costs, and in fact some contemporary writers did try to assess the relative advantages of employing servants and day labourers. Timothy Nourse, discoursing on the needs of the family economy, suggested that: 'Domesticks [i.e. servants] may be a greater Charge, because we are obliged to pay and provide for them even when they do us no service . . . [while] Day-Labourers ly more easilie upon us, as being paid no longer than they work' (Nourse, 1700; cited in Kussmaul, 1981, p. 101). He concluded, nevertheless, that the advantage of having workers available whenever needed outweighed the higher outlay in wages. But this tells us little about the relative material situations of servants and labourers. If servants were a greater drain on their master's purses, this does not mean that they enjoyed a higher standard of living overall, for their time belonged to their employers and so, unlike day labourers, they could not supplement their wage incomes from other sources.

Evidence on wages in pre-industrial England after the mid fourteenth century comes in two forms: direct evidence of wages paid from account books (which is fairly reliable, but scarce); and the indirect evidence of legally assessed maximum wage rates. The history of wage regulation began in the immediate aftermath of the Black Death, when the Statute of Labourers (1350–1) was enacted in an effort to hold wages down to their pre-plague levels. As we have seen, this early legislation enjoyed very limited success. Rates continued to be determined centrally by Parliament, however, until 1562–3 when the Statute of Artificers devolved responsibility for setting maximum wages to county level via justices of the peace acting in quarter sessions. Thereafter, wage assessments showed wide variations from one county to another. However, the few surviving accounts of actual wages paid do suggest that payments in excess of the prescribed rates became a comparatively rare occurrence (Clark, 1919, chapter 3; Kussmaul, 1981, pp. 35–9). Does this mean that the legislation was successful in forcing wages down? It is possible that some such regulatory effect may have been realized, but an alternative and more likely inference is that, occasional 'economic panics' apart, the flexibility introduced by the policy of fixing wages at county level enabled the JPs' proclamations to reflect local conditions and practice.

Historians are broadly agreed in their assessment of farm servants' living standards. They were very well fed, reasonably well housed according to the standards of the day, and abysmally low paid. Gender inequality among servants hinged on the last of these, and the evidence is unambiguous. Kussmaul (1981) has summarized it simply: 'Women systematically received only a fraction of men's wages.' This statement certainly conveys the essence of the position, while not being strictly true in the letter in so far as it is virtually impossible to discern any 'system' in the wide regional and temporal variations in the fraction's size.

Kussmaul herself has calculated the ratios (expressed below in percentages) of highest female to highest male wages, and of lowest adult female to lowest adult male wages, for a random sample of thirty quarter sessions assessments in various English counties over the period 1564–1724. She found a median of 57 per cent and a mean of 61 per cent. The range was from 30 per cent to 83 per cent (Kussmaul, 1981, appendix 2). Figures presented by Roberts over a roughly similar period, but covering only ten assessments in four counties (Kent, Essex, Staffordshire and Wiltshire), produce a median of 57 per cent and a mean of 52 per cent (Roberts, 1979, p. 19). Two later sets of figures for Lincolnshire at the end of the eighteenth century show even higher average discrepancies. The mean annual female wage at the Spalding hiring fairs (1768–85) was only 44 per cent of the male wage, while an account book from Tetney gives a median of 49.5 per cent for the years 1780–1803 (Kussmaul, 1981, pp. 37, 182). One would not be justified in concluding that the Lincolnshire figures indicate a widening gap, however, because there is strong evidence of wide regional variation in the proportions of male to female servants' wages. Indeed, the assessments presented by Roberts, which were selected precisely in order to let valid comparisons be made over time, show a truly remarkable constancy in the extent of inequality in each county for periods of 106, 39, 81 and 82 years respectively (see figures for servants' wages in figure 1.1).

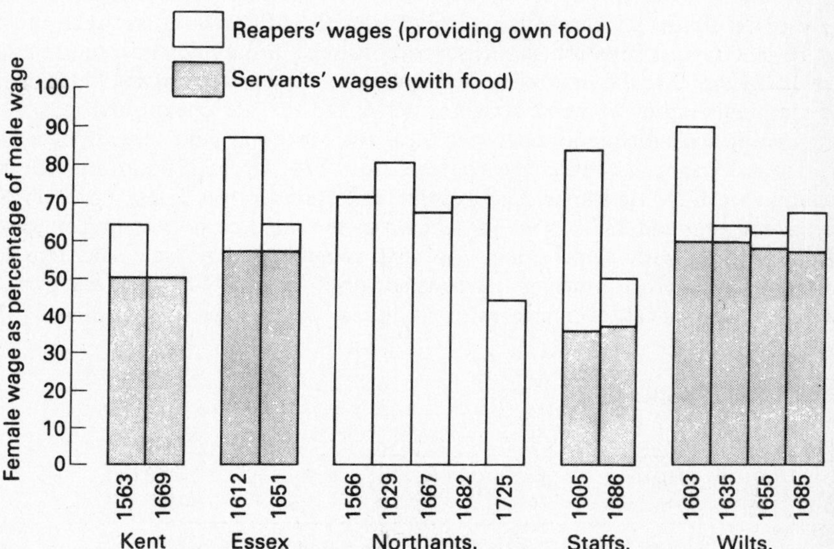


FIGURE 1.1 Ratio of female to male assessed wages, 1563–1725
*Source:* Adapted from M. Roberts (1979), p. 19

Two final points on servants' wages can be made with some degree of certainty. The first is that the range of variation in men's wages is far greater than that for women's wages. Thus, for example, the list of annual wages for Spalding, 1786–7, shows a range for all females of only £1–4 ($N = 78$), with all but four of the women receiving between £2 and £4. The equivalent range for males is £2–11 ($N = 67$), with a much more even distribution of men between the different wage levels. The other, and no doubt related point, is that whereas young boys could expect to receive substantial wage rises as they grew older, girls' and womens' wages showed very little increase with age.

Day rates for independent labourers were higher than those for farm servants, but show a similar pattern of gender inequality. In the following discussion we shall again concentrate on harvest evidence.

One of the fullest estate records giving details of rates for male and female day labour are those kept by the Yorkshire farmer, Henry Best. The figures in table 1.1 have been computed from his harvest accounts for 1641. Thus on Best's farm the median wage for female harvesters was 75 per cent of that of male harvesters; the mean was 72 per cent. This indicates a somewhat narrower differential between male and female day rates than existed for servants. It would obviously be useful to know whether this is merely evidence of a regional variation, or whether it reflects a systematic variation between the different kinds of labour. Fortunately, we are able to make some direct, same-year comparisons of gender differentials for harvest reapers and servants for four of the counties referred to in figure 1.1. In every case but one the differential for male and female reapers is less than the differential for servants. (The exception is for Kent, 1669, where female wages were assessed as exactly half those for males both for reapers and for servants. No figures on assessed wages for servants are available for Northamptonshire.) This does suggest then that sex discrimination in wage levels was significantly greater among servants than it was among day labourers.

However, figure 1.1 also tells a story of widening differentials between male and female harvest labourers across several counties in the midlands, south, and east. It appears that the increasing segregation of work in the harvest fields, and the marginalizing of women's activities there, had the not unexpected result of heightening wage inequalities between the sexes. More complete series of data for agricultural wages in general are available from 1741 (from 1706 in the case of Buckinghamshire, Berkshire, Oxfordshire and Hampshire). These cover 1924 hirings for men and 837 hirings for women in the main corn-growing counties. They indicate, with some minor regional variations, that male and female differentials remained more or less constant until about 1760, when male rates began to surge ahead of female rates. Male real wages stayed above their 1741

TABLE 1.1

| | *N* | *Median* | *Mean* | *Range* |
|---|---|---|---|---|
| Males | 88 | 8d | 7.8d | 5–10d |
| Females | 76 | 6d | 5.6d | 4–6d |

*Source:* Robinson, 1857. Adapted from account lists in Roberts, 1979, appendix B.

level until about 1790 when they failed to keep pace with the rapid price inflation. But female real wages declined steadily from 1760 and by the first decade of the nineteenth century were about half their 1741 base rate. Thereafter they began, once again, to start closing the gap on male wages. These trends show very clearly the income effects of women's virtually total exclusion from harvest labour in the last third of the eighteenth century and their removal to the low-paid, low-demand spring season (Snell, 1985, pp. 29–34).

## GENDER AS A PRINCIPLE OF STRATIFICATION IN THE HISTORICAL ORGANIZATION OF LABOUR

The most striking point to emerge from all this evidence must surely concern the sheer longevity of some highly familiar features of gender stratification. Segregation and inequality in the organization of labour have persisted with remarkable tenacity through profound changes in the wider social order of class and gender relations. Let us now recapitulate the main findings and assess their implications for theories of occupational segregation.

1 Gender has consistently served as a principle of stratification in the organization of labour. This has been so even where no labour market existed. The clearest example encountered here has been the organization of *famuli* labour on the feudal demesnes, but we also observed that medieval peasant farming involved gender segregation even though the labour process on a smallholding could hardly tolerate an inflexible approach. For a later period, there is evidence of a well-developed gender hierarchy operating within the servant class, though here too it seems highly unlikely that the servant hiring fairs functioned as impersonal labour markets (Kussmaul, 1981). In all these contexts it seems inappropriate to talk of factors governing the terms of women's 'entry' into the labour process. Similarly, the notion of 'bargaining strength', especially in relation to worker organization, is hardly applicable to situations of this kind.

2 Until the late eighteenth century (in the arable south-eastern counties) the economy was characterized by chronic underemployment. Thus, even where labour markets were in the process of emerging (though often still highly personalized) it is doubtful whether the 'availability', 'commitment' or 'dispensability' of different groups of workers loomed as a major factor in determining their variable conditions of employment.

3 Male workers have also been stratified by skill, status and income despite the lack of a labour market. Indeed, the extent of differentiation among male workers appears to have been consistently greater than that among female workers. The experiences of men as a group have been more diverse than those of women, both with regard to the variety of jobs available to them, and to the range of incomes they have been able to secure. (This does mean, of course, that not all men shared in the 'prerogatives of patriarchy' to the same extent.)

4 Stability and security of employment in early modern England were not associated with skill, high overall wages, or status. Many skills could only be utilized on a seasonal basis and most farmers relied on day labour for work requiring these skills. Many skilled labourers, therefore, belonged to a seasonal reserve army of labour. Farming households employed servants on annual contracts to meet their needs for routine agricultural labour.

5 Women have long been associated with the household and domestic tasks, but there is no evidence that women's disadvantaged position in the occupational structure was a consequence of their responsibility for or commitment to their families. In pre-industrial England their connection with the household was intensified by marriage (Middleton, 1979), but certainly not dependent on it: single women regularly performed domestic services in the households of strangers. Women in service were almost invariably unmarried and childless, but gender still provided a template for occupational segregation in this sphere. Indeed, it is fairly certain that wage differentials between men and women servants were even wider than those for other contemporary groups of wage workers.

6 There is very little evidence of segregation in the countryside arising as a result of male workers closing ranks against unskilled and low-paid female competition. (The towns and professions were another matter entirely.) The one exceptional case we came across was that of the highly proletarianized harvest labourers discussed by Snell. But this example is interesting for its reversal of the more recent process of male working-class defensive action described in the combined writings of Humphries and Rubery. According to their analysis the channelling of women into secondary sector jobs in the early twentieth century followed on from, and was largely a consequence of, their earlier expulsion from the labour market. For female harvest labourers the sequence was reversed: they suffered exclusion only *after* a long and secular process of increasing segregation. The sense of historical contingency which we remarked in Rubery's position is rather undermined by this observation; it appears that sex discrimination could be directed quite as much against established women workers as against outsiders and newcomers.

Studies of economic life in pre-industrial England show that gender was a basic principle of occupational division and inequality from as far back as the thirteenth century. In most cases the organization of labour was inseparable from questions of political authority and marital status. Gender, most emphatically, was *not* a distinction to be grafted on to a pre-existing framework of segregation because of the particular attributes of women workers or the circumstances under which they sold their labour. It is not surprising perhaps to find that theoretical models devised to account for occupational segregation in capitalist economies do not fit easily when wrested out of context and applied to other historical formations. But a retreat into historical relativity is no solution either. The utter durability of gender as a basic principle in the organization of wage labour, despite profound changes in the mode of production, must cast doubt on the validity of models that attribute its occurrence under industrial capitalism to class dynamics or family-household systems that are specific to that mode.

## INTERPRETING HISTORICAL DATA ON THE CONTROL OF WOMEN'S LABOUR

The evidence we have considered shows that patriarchal forms may have a remarkable capacity for survival. In the sphere of wage labour at least, the quotation from Hartmann (1976) with which we opened this article seems fully justified: 'the sexual division of labour and male domination are . . . long standing' indeed. Such findings will no doubt be received as meat and drink by those who believe in the existence of an autonomous system of patriarchy and wish to assert its independence of the mode of production and class structure. Patriarchy, according to this view, is established as an order of reality that remains largely unaffected by major shifts in other elements of the social structure. The data on long-term trends in the organization of wage labour are so vulnerable to this kind of misinterpretation that they cannot be left to speak for themselves. I will therefore conclude by indicating why this view is unacceptable.

The idea of patriarchy is rooted in an apprehension of male dominance as virtually ubiquitous. Certain writers, of course, have happily embraced the ahistorical implications of this perception. Conservatively inclined sociobiologists and evolutionary ethnologists contend that patriarchy is both universal and inevitable, and their claims have been echoed, though rather less happily, by their counterparts within radical feminism who identify women as an invariably oppressed sex.[13] Such arguments are unlikely to convince the historically minded, and their logical inconsistencies have been too thoroughly exposed elsewhere to require further comment here (see for example critiques by Sayers, 1982; Rose, Lewontin and Kamin, 1984).

A more serious challenge is posed by theories of patriarchy that are sensitive to historical issues. The major contributions here have come from within the Marxist-feminist tradition, where we find a resistance to universalistic conceptions coupled with uncertainty and division as to the concept's utility (e.g. Beechey, 1979; Rowbotham, 1982; Alexander and Taylor, 1982). Should the concept be repudiated as inherently ahistorical, or can it be developed as a means to explore the relationship between gender oppression and modes of production? Writers like Hartmann (1979) and Cockburn (1983) have argued strongly that patriarchy is an important and necessary concept for historically conceived feminist research. They have vigorously defended the formulation of distinct feminist categories and theories on the grounds that previous attempts to *integrate* feminism and Marxism have led either to the marginalization of feminist concerns or else to their incorporation within the conceptual framework of the more established tradition. While I can only concur with their overall assessment of past work in this area, the solution they propose is not, in my view, a particularly satisfactory one and is, moreover, logically flawed. It remains to show the nature of this disagreement.

Marxist feminists who favour the concept of patriarchy are engaged in two distinct though closely related projects. The first is to 'historicize' the concept in order to give it *explanatory* power in historical and comparative research. 'Patriarchy' would then possess a theoretical status within feminist theory similar

13. It should be recorded that not all radical feminists adopt this position.

to that enjoyed by the concept of 'class' within Marxism. The second objective, which is implied by the first, is to establish the existence of patriarchy as an *independent* order of inequality and control. This is seen as the only way to avoid the kind of reductionist theorizing that analyses 'the sexual subordination of women . . . as a by-product of class processes' (Cockburn, 1983, p. 6).

Since there is no one Marxist-feminist concept of patriarchy we will have to limit the scope of our discussion in considering these points. Thus the following comments refer only to historical and materialist treatments of patriarchal labour relations. Theories of patriarchy conceived as ideology or as governing the social relations of reproduction, for example, are not touched upon.

There have actually been rather few attempts to trace the pattern of job segregation and control by sex through the course of a transition from one mode of production to another. Hartmann's has been one of the most influential. She argues that, 'before capitalism, a patriarchal system was established in which men controlled the labour of women and children in the family, and that in so doing men learned the techniques of hierarchical organisation and control. . . . the problem for men became one of maintaining their control over the labour power of women' (Hartmann, 1976, p. 138). This seems fairly representative of Marxist-feminist approaches to patriarchy on three counts: in its sense of the patriarchal order as a system functioning on its own account; in its awareness of the historical specificity of patriarchal forms; and finally in its stress on men acting collectively *as men* (rather than as capitalists, peasants, trade unionists etc.) in order to maintain their privileges and control.

Let us deal first with the explanatory potential of this perspective. One problem seems to be that the concept is required to meet two contradictory objectives. As we saw, the term 'patriarchy' first found favour because of a need for a language that would reflect the sheer prevalence of male-dominated institutions across a wide range of social structures and modes of production. It is an idea rooted in a sense of continuity and sameness, and one sustained by the kinds of evidence described in this chapter. But Marxist-feminists are alert to cross-cultural variations and historical diversity. They acknowledge that the different manifestations of patriarchy cannot be dismissed as unimportant. Faced with this perplexing dilemma the historical project of Marxist-feminist research has been to create a theory which would reflect this continuity in sexual oppression, yet could account for the changes too. It has often been defined as one of tracing and explaining the changing *forms* of patriarchy (e.g. Mackintosh, 1977; McDonough and Harrison, 1978, p. 26; Beechey, 1979). But this solution unintentionally places strict limits on the significance of history and, ironically, of patriarchy too. If it is only the form of patriarchy that undergoes change, the patriarchal *essence* must presumably remain constant – immune as it were from historical influence. In that event the concept of patriarchy must lose the explanatory power it is meant to possess. Things have to happen *to* patriarchy to precipitate the observed changes; it ceases to be a motor of history itself.

The theory also lacks any means of showing *why* men should control women's labour or seek to organize purely on the basis of their sex in order to maintain it. Some might think that the question itself is curiously redundant: does not the power that men exert over women make their commitment to patriarchy self-evident? After all, the argument runs, we do not feel it is necessary to ask why capitalists seek to maintain control over their workers.[14] This defence of the concept certainly has some resonance, but on closer examination it proves to be tautologous, and the comparison with class cannot be sustained. Logically speaking, we cannot explain men's control over women's labour by pointing to the power that it gives them, for this is but to confuse an explanation with the explicandum. The tautology could only be resolved by contending that men are stained by 'original sin' (i.e. an untutored desire to dominate women), but that would be a return to the realm of a discredited biological determinism.[15] 'Patriarchy' is a mental construct that categorizes a set of related phenomena, organizing and expressing them in a particular informative way. This is not to gainsay the existence of patriarchal relations, since the phenomena referred to are real enough; but if patriarchy's existence has been deduced from evidence showing women's oppression by men then logically the concept cannot be used to *explain* that evidence.

The comparison of patriarchy with Marxist theories of class structure is also inappropriate. Hartmann herself has acknowledged the essential difference between them while failing, in my view, to recognize its full implications. In the sense that they do not specify the biological characteristics of the particular individuals who comprise them, Marxist categories of class are 'empty places'. A class is *defined* by its social relationship to another class, and it is the quality of that relationship which provides the category with its internal conceptual unity. Moreover, these categories do not exist *sui generis*, but are theoretically contingent. They have been devised as part of an explanatory model intended to account for various observable processes such as industrialization, capital concentration, the restructuring of the labour process and over-production – and their utility depends on their capacity to perform that task. Even to refer to such Marxist categories as serf and landlord, capitalist and proletarian is to presuppose a specific kind of social relationship between them, contained within a theoretical framework which gives the terms their meaning and explanatory power. None of these things holds true for the distinction between men and women. The categories of gender are defined, in the first instance, according to biological criteria, while the nature of the social relationship between them has to be empirically demonstrated, and only then explained. A concept such as patriarchy which is intended to portray that relationship should be seen as a descriptive rather than an explanatory term. Certainly, it cannot be both.

Even if it is accepted that the concept of patriarchy has no explanatory value it would still be possible to interpret our findings as evidence for an institutional order of patriarchy that was independent of the mode of production. There can be no brooking the central empirical point that Hartmann makes: women's labour

14. The point was made forcefully at the ESRC symposium where this essay was first presented. Some women greeted the suggestion that there was any need to ask why men should seek to control women's labour with some mirth. In their eyes the question seemed utterly superfluous.

15. Briefly, the hidden circular structure of reasoning is as follows:
(a) Men have power which they enjoy and derive benefit from.
(b) Why do men have power?
(c) Because men have organized to obtain and retain power.
(d) Why have men so organized, and why have they succeeded?
(e) Because men have power which they enjoy and derive benefit from.

was under male control. Her deductions, however, are not substantiated and actually fly in the face of the evidence. First of all there is the dubious implication (more explicitly argued in Hartmann, 1979, pp. 11–12) that *all* men shared in the control of women's labour. The history of pre-capitalist English labour would not support this contention. Here was a society, especially during the era of high feudalism, where a very substantial minority of the population never married at all and, whatever other differences may have obtained between single women and single men, there is no evidence to suggest that the latter held any authority over women's productive or sexual labour. Moreover, a man's marital status or prospects were intimately bound up with the system of landholding: those who held no land or had no other means of livelihood would not normally expect to marry. A man's access to the control of female labour was conditional on his position in the class structure. There can be no way of understanding the patriarchal organization of labour except in relation to the matrix of feudal property relations, so it would be incongruous to elaborate a separate theory of patriarchy or sex/gender systems.[16] Hartmann's insistence on conceptualizing men as a cohesive and homogeneous group leads her to gloss over these differences, and she ends up by describing men as sharing objectives and problems that have no basis in real life.

Even when due allowance has been made for the selective presentation of evidence in this chapter, the impression of continuity in the patriarchal organization of wage labour remains very strong. It is all the more important, therefore, that we retain a proper empathy for cultures that are remote from us. The past really is a foreign country, and we cannot assume that familiar signs are indicative of a familiar reality. As Philip Abrams has written: 'Doing justice to the reality of history is not a matter of noting the way in which the past provides a background to the present; it is a matter of treating what people do in the present as a struggle to create a future *out* of the past' (Abrams, 1982, p. 8). Continuities there certainly are, and they need to be explained. But the past contains no simple messages for us, and historical regularities are no more amenable to explanation through universalizing concepts than are the vagaries of historical change. It may prove necessary to construct different explanations for apparently similar findings depending on their social context. Gender segregation and inequality may be grounded in different structural relationships at different times; they may have different rationales and mean different things to their participants. Thus, for example, it is my suspicion that the patriarchal control of women's labour in feudal England was not a self-sustaining phenomenon, but had its roots at all levels of society in preoccupation with questions of fertility. A property-based concern with the frequency, circumstances and timing of procreative activity provided the rationale for close economic and personal control over all kinds of female activity (see Middleton, 1981). If that interpretation is correct the causes of segregation

16. Cockburn prefers the notion of sex/gender systems (developed by Gayle Rubin, 1975) to that of patriarchy as it escapes the inbuilt assumption that men are always dominant. She is, however, happy to use the term 'patriarchy' when referring to male-dominated sex/gender systems and she observes that they are very long lived. Most of the points made here in respect to patriarchal theory apply equally well to theories of the sex/gender system since this system is regarded as being separate from the class structure (Cockburn, 1983, p. 8).

and inequality in the feudal era were very different from the causes of similar phenomena in the capitalist labour market. In effect, what I am proposing reverses the conventional formulation of Marxist-feminism's project as the examination of changing forms of patriarchy. It suggests that even when patriarchal forms persist more or less unchanged, we cannot assume that the underlying structure determining women's oppression has remained constant. This is not to deny the feminist claim that men act together as men, but it is to suggest that they rarely, if ever, act together *just* as men, purely on the basis of their sex. The position I am advocating is not a reductionist one. It does not analyse patriarchal relations as a by-product of class processes, any more than it would allow class relations to be analysed without reference to gendered structuring. Peasant men in feudal England did not seek control of women's labour because they were peasants, but neither did they do so because they were men. They did so because they were male peasants striving to carve out their futures according to male peasant values under constraints imposed by a particular mode of production and reproduction. Patriarchy and class are neither 'relatively autonomous' nor reducible one to another. They comprise an integrated structure of relationships.

## REFERENCES

Abrams, P. (1982) *Historical Sociology*, Bath, Open Books.

Alexander, S. and Taylor, B. (1982) 'In defence of "patriarchy" ', in M. Evans (ed.) *The Woman Question*, Fontana. (See also Rowbotham, 1982.)

Barron, R. D. and Norris, G. M. (1976) 'Sexual divisions and the dual labour market', in D. L. Barker and S. Allen (eds) *Dependence and Exploitation in Work and Marriage*, Longman.

Beechey, V. (1979) 'On patriarchy', *Feminist Review*, 3.

Beechey, V. (1983) 'What's so special about women's employment?', *Feminist Review*, 15.

Bennett, J. (n.d.) 'Medieval peasant marriage: an examination of marriage licence fines in the Liber Gersumarum', unpublished paper.

Braverman, H. (1974) *Labor and Monopoly Capital: the degradation of work in the twentieth century*, New York, Monthly Review Press.

Brenner, J. and Ramas, M. (1984) ' Rethinking women's oppression', *New Left Review* , March–April, pp. 33–71.

Britton, E. (1977) *The Community of the Vill: a study of the history of the family and village life in fourteenth-century England*, Toronto, MacMillan.

Casey, K. (1976) 'The Cheshire cat: reconstructing the experiences of medieval women', in B. Carroll (ed.), *Liberating Women's History*, London, University of Illinois Press.

Clark, A. (1919) *Working Life of Women in the Seventeenth Century*, Frank Cass (reprinted 1982, Routledge and Kegan Paul).

Cockburn, C. (1983) *Brothers*, London, Pluto Press.

Doeringer, P. B. and Piore, M. J. (1971) *Internal Labour Markets and Manpower Analysis*, Lexington, Mass., Lexington Books.

Edwards, R. (1979) *Contested Terrain*, London, Heinemann.

Emmison, F. G. (1976) *Elizabethan Life: home, work and land*, Chelmsford.

Everitt, A. (1967) 'Farm labourers', in J.Thirsk (ed.), *The Agrarian History of England and Wales. Vol. IV: 1500–1640*, Cambridge, Cambridge University Press.

Gordon, D. M., Edwards, R. and Reich, M. (1982) *Segmented Work, Divided Workers*, Cambridge, Cambridge University Press.

Hajnal, J. (1965) 'European marriage patterns in perspective', in D. V. Glass and D. E. C. Eversley (eds), *Population in History*, London, Arnold.

Hartmann, H. (1976) 'Capitalism, patriarchy and job segregation by sex', in M. Blaxall and B. Reagan (eds), *Women and the Workplace*, London, University of Chicago Press.

Hartmann, H. (1979) 'The unhappy marriage of Marxism and feminism: towards a more progressive union', *Capital and Class*, 8.

Hilton, R. H. (1947) *The Economic Development of some Leicestershire Estates in the 14th and 15th Centuries*, London.

Hilton, R. H (1975) *English Peasantry in the Later Middle Ages*, Oxford, Clarendon.

Humphries, J. (1977) 'Class struggle and the persistence of the working class family', *Cambridge Journal of Economics*, 1 (September), pp. 242–58.

King, G. (1810) *Natural and Political Observations*, London.

Kriedte, P., Medick, H. and Schlumbohm, J. (1981) *Industrialisation before Industrialisation*, Cambridge, Cambridge University Press.

Kussmaul, A. (1981) *Servants in Husbandry in Early Modern England*, Cambridge, Cambridge University Press.

McDonough, R. and Harrison, R. (1978) 'Patriarchy and relations of production', in A. Kuhn and A. M. Wolpe (eds), *Feminism and Materialism*, London, Routledge and Kegan Paul.

Mackintosh, M. (1977) 'Reproduction and patriarchy', *Capital and Class*, 2, pp. 119–27.

Malcolmson, R. W. (1981) *Life and Labour in England 1700–1780*, London, Hutchinson.

Medick, H. (1976) 'The proto-industrial family: the structural function of the household and family during the transformation from peasant society to industrial capitalism', *Social History*, 3, pp. 291–316.

Middleton, C. (1979) 'The sexual division of labour in feudal England', *New Left Review*, 113–14, Jan–April, pp. 147–68.

Middleton, C. (1981) 'Peasants, patriarchy and the feudal mode of production in England: a Marxist appraisal' parts 1 and 2, *Sociological Review*, 29(1), new series, pp. 105–54.

Middleton, C. (1985) 'Women's labour and the transition to pre-industrial capitalism', in L. Charles and L. Duffin (eds), *Women's Work in Pre-Industrial England*, London, Croom Helm.

Nourse, T. (1700) *Campania Foelix*.

Oschinsky, D. (1971) *Walter of Henley and Other Treatises on Estate Management and Accounting*, Oxford.

Postan, M. M. (1954) 'The *famulus*: the estate labourer in the twelfth and thirteenth centuries', *The Economic History Review*, supplement no. 2, London.

Power, E. (1975) *Medieval Women* (ed. M. Postan), Cambridge, Cambridge University Press.

Reich, M., Gordon, D. M. and Edwards, R. C. (1973) 'A theory of labour market segmentation', *American Economic Review*, 63(2), pp. 359–65.

Roberts, M. (1979) 'Sickles and scythes', *History Workshop Journal*, no. 7, spring.

Roberts, M. (1985) 'Words they are women, and deeds they are men: images of work and gender in early modern England', in L. Charles and L. Duffin (eds), *Women's Work in Pre-Industrial England*, London, Croom Helm.

Robinson, C. B. (ed.) (1857) *Rural Economy in Yorkshire in 1641*, Durham.

Rogers, J. E. T. (1866) *A History of Agriculture and Prices 1259–1400*, vols I and II, Oxford, Clarendon.

Rogers, J. E. T. (1894) *Six Centuries of Work and Wages*, London, Swan Sonnenschein.

Rose, S., Lewontin, R. and Kamin, L. (1984) *Not in our Genes: biology, ideology and human nature*, Harmondsworth, Penguin.

Rowbotham, S. (1982) 'The trouble with "patriarchy" ', in M. Evans (ed.), *The Woman Question*, Fontana. (See also Alexander and Taylor, 1982.)

Rubery, J. (1980) 'Structured labour markets, worker organisation and low pay', in A. H. Amsden (ed.), *The Economics of Women and Work*, pp. 242–70.

Rubery, J. and Tarling, R. (1982) 'Women in the recession', *Socialist Economic Review 1982*, Merlin Press.

Rubin, G. (1975) 'The traffic in women: notes on the political economy of sex' in R. Reiter (ed.), *Towards an Anthropology of Women*, New York, Monthly Review Press.

Russell, J. C. (1948) *British Medieval Population*, Albuquerque.

Sayers, J. (1982) *Biological Politics: feminist and anti-feminist perspectives*, Tavistock.

Scott, R. J. (1973) 'Women in the Stuart Economy', London University, unpublished M. Phil. thesis.

Snell, K. D. M. (1985) *Annals of the Labouring Poor: social change and agrarian England , 1660–1900*, Cambridge, Cambridge University Press.

Stone, L. (1977) *The Family, Sex and Marriage in England 1500–1800*, London, Weidenfeld and Nicolson.

Tawney, R. H. (1912) *The Agrarian Problem in the Sixteenth Century*.

Walby, S. (1983) 'Patriarchal structures: the case of unemployment', in E. Gamarnikow et al. (eds), *Gender, Class, and Work*, London, Heinemann.

# 2

# Ways of Getting a Living in Eighteenth-Century England

R. W. MALCOLMSON

Our concern here is to explain how, in the eighteenth century, people with little or no private property provided for their own subsistence. How did labouring men and women support themselves? And what were the principal determinants of their standard of living? It is clear that their sustenance came from many different sources and was produced in many different ways. Most men no longer lived as peasants, and the predominance of industrial employment lay in the future. But it is misleading to speak of this society as 'pre-industrial', for manufacturing was widespread and of vital importance. Yet at least three-quarters of the English people in 1700 still got a major portion of their living directly from some form of agricultural work. In order to appreciate the character of labour in this period it is best, I think, if we recognize the need to distinguish and describe both the actual tasks that people performed and the circumstances that conditioned the performance of these tasks. In most households an adequate subsistence depended on a complex of various forms of task-work and wage-labour: regular, full-time employment at a single job was not the norm. Occupational categories, then, as applied to particular individuals and social groups - farm labourer, weaver, housewife - should be treated with caution, for they tend to obscure the complexities and intricacies of the real world of labour as it was experienced by individuals and families. It is better to speak of the work itself - farm labour, weaving, housewifery - and to try to understand how such work contributed to a family's living. Moreover, labour of any kind was rooted in a particular local economy and derived much of its character from the specific opportunities and limitations of the local environment; and in the eighteenth century there was an immense diversity of local economies. The means of subsistence, then, varied markedly from

This essay was first published as chapter 2 in R.W. Malcolmson, *Life and Labour in England 1700–1800*, Hutchinson, 1981. It has been slightly shortened for this volume.

place to place, and from family to family. But a recognition of diversity does not mean that useful generalizations are impossible. For underlying this diversity there were common patterns of living and widely shared social and economic objectives. What, then, were the principal conditions which constrained, or supported or enhanced the material circumstances of life? Which social and economic determinants were of central importance to the everyday subsistence of the labouring people?

## THE COUNTRYSIDE AND COMMON RIGHTS

The productive enterprises in eighteenth-century England, the social units in which work was done, were mostly small in scale. Large units of production were exceptional. Factories were almost non-existent until the end of the century, and most coal pits, outside of the Tyneside region, were still modest undertakings, worked by a handful of men; only a very few enterprises, such as the naval shipyards and Crowley's iron works, could be regarded as undeniably concentrated units of production. Most work was done on a family farm, in a workshop, in the streets of a town, or in a household. In fact, the household was the central unit of production in the eighteenth century. A large proportion of manual labour, whether in agriculture, industry or service – probably the majority of such work – was directly implicated in the productive activities of the family household. The household was not merely a unit of consumption in which its members spent money that was earned elsewhere: an individual's actual work was normally done, not outside the household, but as part of the household's own productive economy. For most labouring people, then, the viability of the household economy was the crucial priority in life. An appreciation of the components of this economy is an essential prerequisite for our historical understanding.

In the first half of the eighteenth century, when about three-quarters of the English population lived in villages, hamlets, and scattered farmsteads and cottages, the viability of a working man's household economy depended heavily on the degree to which his family could gain some sort of (often partial) living from the land. The agrarian economy was of central importance to almost all of these families, but the specific character of this importance, and the particular benefits derived from the land, varied greatly from household to household and from parish to parish. Men with small farms – farms of perhaps ten, fifteen or twenty-five acres – enjoyed a modest degree of independence and prosperity. Some of them held freeholds; others enjoyed long leases, often by copyhold. They were usually known as husbandmen or, in later years, as smallholders. However, by the early eighteenth century the bulk of the rural working people held less land than this, and often no land at all, aside from a cottage garden. These people, the hundreds of thousands of cottagers, country labourers, and smallholders with one or two acres, usually owned no land and cannot be considered as members of the landholding class, if we understand this class to comprise men with, at the least, enough land, securely occupied, for a more-or-less self-sufficient farm. But even if most country people held no land in this sense, it does not necessarily follow that they were unable to get a major portion of their living from the land. In fact, the central concern of many of these families was, first, with rights of access to the use of land, and second, with the availability of employment on nearby farms. By means of the former they produced some of their own provisions and thus achieved a degree of domestic self-sufficiency; by means of the latter they obtained wages that allowed them to buy other necessities in the marketplace, pay the rent for their cottages, and purchase recreational pleasures. In this way an economy of self-reliance and an economy of wage-dependence could be linked together.

This economy of self-reliance was heavily dependent on the existence of common rights. It is important to appreciate that the notion of the absolute private ownership of land and its resources was not yet fully triumphant. Indeed, in many parts of the country – especially in regions where there were forests, or heaths and 'wastes', or simply unenclosed fields – no one landowner enjoyed exclusive rights to the use of particular tracts of land. In these areas numerous other individuals, most of them local men with little or no private property, claimed the right to make use of the land for certain customary purposes: purposes that were directly related to their own livelihoods. The rights these people claimed were usually supported by appeals to custom, by ideas of usage from time immemorial. 'Custome', as one writer put it around 1700, 'is a law or right, not written, which being established by long use and the consent of our ancestors, hath been and is dayly practised.'[1] Custom, in this context, was not simply the equivalent of 'tradition': custom had the power of law and could be enforced in the manorial courts. As the Webbs once remarked, these manorial customs, which were very widespread, 'were legally binding on both the Lord and his tenants'.[2] (A later eighteenth-century observer, sensing the tension between the older claims of custom and the newer claims of private property, whose 'real' rights the law was coming to favour, said of the poor around 1780 that 'though perhaps they have no real right to the commons, yet prescription and long usage seem to give them an apparent claim'.)[3] The conception of land appropriate to this discussion is one, not of landownership, but of land being used: used for different purposes by different people, none of whom was acknowledged to have absolute possession. A lord (or lords) would have rights to use such land – rights which, though they might be more extensive than those of other users, were never exclusive; and the poorer members of the community – or at least some of them, the 'commoners' – also had rights of access to the land for purposes that were sanctioned by customary practice. The land was there: nobody possessed it completely, many people enjoyed its material benefits in different ways and to varying degrees. To the commoners land existed to be used by those who needed it, not owned as private property.

What were the concrete advantages of these common rights to men of modest means? Most of the benefits of commons stemmed from two kinds of rights: grazing rights for livestock, and rights to gather, for household use, certain natural resources of the land. Grazing rights were particularly important for they

1. Richard Gough, *Antiquities and Memoirs of the Parish of Myddle, County of Salop* (Fontwell, Sussex: Centaur Press 1968), p. 34; Gough composed his work at the very beginning of the eighteenth century.
2. Sidney Webb and Beatrice Webb, *The Manor and the Borough* (London 1908), pp. 15–16 (cf. pp. 4, 9, 18–19, 64, 75–9 and 116).
3. T. R. Nash, *Collections for the History of Worcestershire* (2 vols, London 1781–2), vol. 1, p. xii.

allowed men with only tiny holdings, holdings too small for grazing, or with no holdings at all, to maintain a small number of livestock on the common lands and thus enjoy those direct and tangible rewards which stock-keeping generally involved. Although such commoners might be able to grow no grain of their own, their modes of sustenance were deeply implicated in some form of pastoral economy. Even very poor men could benefit from these common rights. As one writer put it in 1726:

> there are in most Counties a Sort of Cottagers, that have Custom and Right of Commoning, tho' they Rent nothing but their Houses: And if it were a meer Hovel built upon the Waste, who would hinder a poor Man from keeping an Ewe and Lamb, or if he compass one, a little Heifer? For these can run upon a Green, or among the Lanes and Highways, till the Crop be ended; and then away with them into the common Fields, for the coming Season, as freely and unmolested as he that rents 100 l. per Annum, and by this Advantage in some Places divers poor Families are in good Part sustained.[4]

Access to common land for grazing allowed commoners to keep a cow or two, or some sheep or pigs – a labouring man who kept sheep could rent them to a farmer because of the value of their dung[5] – perhaps a few geese, or a horse which could be employed in the carrying trade. The specific nature and limitations of the rights enjoyed varied from place to place: stinting regulations were often enforced, pigs might be prohibited from feeding on parts of the common, grazing on certain unenclosed (but cultivated) fields would only be permitted during the months between the end of the harvest and the winter sowing. But whatever particular restrictions may have existed – and many of them were designed to protect the commons from exhaustion – substantial and widely enjoyed benefits always remained. In areas of wide expanse – the fens of East Anglia, Dartmoor and other moorland districts, the open field countryside of central England, forests throughout the country – cottagers and smallholders sustained a viable, if often tenuous, economy because of their ability to keep stock; and in many individual parishes in regions of intensive arable husbandry villagers enjoyed similar advantages from a local marsh, waste or other uncultivated piece of land, or from rights of access to unenclosed fields at times when no crops were growing.

Common rights were certainly important in rural England, and their value and extent have too often been undervalued and depreciated by certain economic historians, especially by those whose enthusiasm for commercial farming sometimes runs away with them. But the fact still is that the actual economic value of commons varied greatly from place to place, sometimes to the point of irrelevance; and that wage-payment, in contrast, existed virtually everywhere and was probably the single most important means of support for the majority of labouring families in the early eighteenth century. Already in many parishes people relied almost completely on wages; and even in regions where common rights helped to sustain a partly self-sufficient household economy, the income

4. *Northampton Mercury*, 17 October 1726.
5. The Swedish visitor Pehr Kalm described the economy of these 'sheepmen' in *Kalm's Account of His Visit to England on His Way to America in 1748*, trans. Joseph Lucas (London 1892), pp. 301–3.

available from wage-labour was normally an important component of the family's subsistence. Let us turn, then, to consider the sources from which these wages were obtained.

## WAGES IN AGRICULTURE

In rural England the single most important source of wage-payment was farm labour. Since hardly any farming families were able to provide on their own all the labour needed on their farms at all times of the year, they were obliged to hire labourers to assist them with the tasks of the farming year – indeed, on the larger farms, labourers did almost all of the manual work. Arable and mixed farming, like most other forms of productive enterprise, was still very labour-intensive, and farmers depended heavily on their workmen to perform the large number of jobs that had to be done by hand. There were two main ways in which these workers were hired. Some of them, the 'servants in husbandry', were hired by the year and lived with their masters, where they received room and board in addition to an annual wage; they were regular, full-time agricultural labourers, continually under the authority of their employers to do whatever work was demanded of them. These farm servants were almost always unmarried, and most of them were less than 25 years old. They worked and lived in other people's households, not in their own or those of their parents. Other workers, in contrast, were hired not as live-in servants but as wage-labourers who were paid by the day or the task as their services were needed to supplement the labour that was available from the farmer's own household. These men and sometimes women, who lived in their own (usually rented) cottages, were employed at the farmer's convenience, normally intermittently rather than regularly, to perform specific tasks according to seasonal demands.

The farming jobs for which labourers might be hired would vary, of course, from place to place, depending on the nature of the soils and the types of farming which were practised. In arable regions the seasons of ploughing and sowing, in autumn and spring, provided considerable opportunities for the employment of day-labourers. And at other seasons of the year workers would be hired, usually for short periods of time, for clearly defined purposes: threshing in the winter months; repairing hedges, building fences, digging and scouring ditches; felling trees, barking, chopping wood and faggoting in more wooded areas; mowing clover or grass, spreading manure, picking turnips, pulling woad; and in fielden parishes workers would be hired for such tasks as weeding, hoeing, harrowing and marling. In upland and sheep-corn districts men would be employed to help with the washing and shearing of sheep.

The season of easily the greatest demand for hired labour was the summer, the season of harvest. For each crop, as it ripened, there was just the right moment for harvesting, and when that moment arrived farmers wanted to get the job done as quickly as possible, while crop conditions were at their best and (they hoped) the weather stayed dry. Speed was of the essence, for delays could cause losses, and there was a great deal of work to accomplish in a short period of time. 'Esteem fair weather as precious, and mispend it not', recommended one authority, reflecting the conventional wisdom. During the wheat harvest, said Arthur Young of the farmer, 'Bad weather now greatly injures his profit: he must have many hands at work, to make the best use of fine seasons.'[6] A successful harvest, then, was only possible with the assistance of a large body of labourers hired especially for the occasion. So great was the demand for labour during the four or five weeks of the corn harvest that industrial workers often abandoned their ordinary labours in order to work as reapers, harvest gangs of skilled men were formed to negotiate favourable terms with farmers, and groups of Irishmen were commonly found migrating from farm to farm, some of whom may even have been grudgingly welcomed by farmers who desperately needed a few more hands. The overriding importance of getting in the crop ensured that August was a month of full employment. Similarly, though less intensively, haymaking, usually in July, afforded considerable short-term employment in many parishes; and in parts of Kent and Surrey hop-picking imposed at least as heavy demands upon the supply of labour as those experienced in corn-growing areas. Around 1790 William Marshall reported that 'whole families, indeed, the whole country, may be said to live in the fields during the busy season of hopping'. Even the daughters of tradesmen and other men of property, he claimed, 'are seen busy at the hop bins', and Maidstone 'is nearly deserted, in the height of the season. . . . Beside the people of the neighbourhood, numbers flock from the populous towns of Kent; and many from the metropolis; also from Wales; hop picking being the last of the summer works of these itinerants.'[7]

Wages from employment at farm labour, then, would have been an important component of the household economy of almost all country people, and even, because of harvest wages, of some town dwellers. Wage levels in the mid eighteenth century varied from region to region, but most of them probably fell within a normal range of 10d to 1s 3d per day; many employers gave their men allowances of beer (or cider in the west country) in addition to money wages. Summer day-wages were often slightly higher than those in winter, partly because of the longer working day. The greatest rewards for labour were always received for harvesting: harvest wages were normally at least 50 per cent higher than those offered at other seasons, and farmers at this time of the year, recognizing the need to maintain good morale among their workers, were particularly inclined to be liberal with their provisions of food and drink – these, indeed, were perquisites which the labourers expected as a matter of customary right. When women were employed in the fields – and they sometimes were, especially at harvest, but also for such casual jobs as weeding and raking – they were usually allowed about half the wages given to men.

There were undoubtedly a few men who were employed more or less continuously at farm labour throughout the year: on the completion of one task they were hired again for different work, and by successfully linking together a series of seasonal jobs they were able to attain virtually full-time employment. But this was not the normal pattern of employment. Men who were hired as farm

6. Cardanus Riders, *Riders British Merlin* (London 1683), under 'Observations on August'; and Arthur Young, *Farmer's Kalendar*, p. 231. See also William Ellis, *The Modern Husbandman*, (8 vols, London 1750), vol. 5, pt 1, p. 2.

7. William Marshall, *The Rural Economy of the Southern Counties* (2 vols, London 1798), vol. 1, pp. 258 and 242; see also Peter Mathias, *The Brewing Industry in England 1700–1830* (Cambridge: Cambridge University Press 1959), pp. 491–3.

labourers for, say 250 to 300 days of the year (a full working week comprised six days of labour), were considerably less numerous than those who were hired for less than 250 days, many of them for very much less. Winter, for instance, was a slack season; the demand for farm labour was low, and consequently many country people who had fairly regular employment between about March and November were unable to find enough work during the winter months.[8] Others still were only hired for the peak seasons of labour, in the spring and summer. Moreover, in pastoral regions there was a less active demand for hired labour throughout the entire year. Pastoral farming was not as labour-intensive as arable husbandry; sheep, in particular, required the services of only a small body of workmen. Consequently, in places where much of the soil was too poor for commercial cultivation - in upland regions especially - or where arable land had been converted to grass, families that did not occupy (even small) farms of their own, or had no access to common lands, would have been hard pressed to support themselves by relying largely on wages from farm labour. In both lowland and upland districts the irregularity of agricultural work might have been tolerable for families that enjoyed common rights, for then the weight of wages in the equilibrium of the household economy would have been rather more modest: they would have been supplements to the partly self-sufficient modes of petty agrarian production which, as we have seen, were sustainable when commons existed. But in many parishes there were no commons at all. The result, then, was that agricultural underemployment, especially during the winter months, was a widespread and basic reality of life. Wages from farm labour were important to the great majority of rural households - indeed, they were probably vital, for harvest wages alone were a tonic for most plebeian families in arable regions; however, though necessary to a family's basic comfort and subsistence, they were often insufficient by themselves. Further support had to be sought through other, non-agricultural forms of employment.

These considerations help to explain why, by the early eighteenth century, many rural households had come to be engaged in some form of industrial by-employment. Agricultural underemployment forced people to look for additional ways of getting wages: ways that would supplement the livelihood they gained from agriculture, and that could be carried on in their own cottages. At the same time merchant-manufacturers in a variety of industries - such capitalists as clothiers, lace merchants, stocking masters, iron masters, and button dealers - were searching for abundant supplies of cheap labour, and they saw in the material circumstances of the countryside the possibility of profit to themselves: profit that could be obtained without fear of having to take account of the regulatory constraints of the trade guilds, virtually all of which were city-based. There was a certain basic compatibility, then, between the aspirations of these merchant-industrialists and those of the country people. The former wanted labourers to do the actual manufacturing - the 'working up' of the unfinished goods at the various stages of production - that their numerous trades required; and the latter wanted to be able to earn extra income by means of some

8. See, for instance, the explicit reference to this seasonality of employment in Westmorland in T. S. Willan, *An Eighteenth-Century Shopkeeper: Abraham Dent of Kirkby Stephen* (Manchester: Manchester University Press 1970), p. 64.

employment that could be conveniently grafted onto the traditional modes of subsistence associated with the rural cottage economy. These were the roots of the domestic or putting-out system of industry, a system in which cottage manufacturing was engaged in by those families that were not fully and intensively employed on the land.

## RURAL INDUSTRY

During the reigns of the later Stuarts the meshing of agricultural and industrial employments was so pronounced in certain upland and pastoral regions that some historians have spoken of the existence of an economy of dual occupations: a household economy in which there was such an integral relationship between farming (normally stock-keeping) and some kind of cottage industry that it may be misleading to speak of 'by-employments' at all, for it is often the case that one means of livelihood cannot be clearly identified as predominant and the other as subsidiary. In rural south Lancashire, for instance, families frequently combined small-scale farming with textile work, especially weaving. Many men who were occupied as weavers also grew oats and potatoes or were otherwise employed in husbandry. When Richard Pococke was travelling in the Burnley area in 1751 he was told by a local youth, who was asked about his mode of living, 'that his father paid six pounds a year [for his holding], kept a horse, three cows, and forty sheep; that his father and he wove woollen both for their clothing and to sell'.[9] In the Rossendale region of south Lancashire, where there were no large landed proprietors, smallholdings were very common: families subsisted by grazing stock on the pasture and waste lands (little land was given over to tillage) and by making cloth; and the term 'yeoman', it is said, often indicated a 'landholder who divided his time between farming and weaving.'[10] A similar situation existed in many parts of the West Riding of Yorkshire, where families with modest landholdings were actively engaged in the woollen industry, many of whom worked independently of any large clothier. Here, according to Herbert Heaton, the 'alliance of land and loom was a great benefit to the clothing population, especially to the weavers, who often were compelled to lay aside the shuttle because of scarcity of yarn, but who were able to fill up this time by working in their garden, or by performing some necessary piece of work on the land attached to their house'.[11] Similarly, in south Yorkshire and the west Midlands during the late seventeenth and early eighteenth centuries many of the metalworkers - nailers, cutlers, scissorsmiths, scythesmiths - were also part-time farmers, some with only a few head of livestock, others with a much more substantial involvement in farming. By combining two occupations they were better able to cope with seasonal unemployment and other sorts of economic fluctuation, for a slump in one line of

9. A. P. Wadsworth and J. de L. Mann, *The Cotton Trade and Industrial Lancashire 1600–1780* (Manchester 1931), pp. 314–23 and 337–8; and J. J. Cartwright (ed.), *The Travels Through England of Dr. Richard Pococke* (2 vols, Camden Society, n.s., vols 42 and 44, 1888–9), vol. 1, pp. 203–4.

10. G. H. Tupling, *The Economic History of Rossendale* (Manchester 1927), ch. 6, especially p. 168.

11. Herbert Heaton, *The Yorkshire Woollen and Worsted Industries from the Earliest Times up to the Industrial Revolution*, 2nd edn (Oxford: Clarendon Press 1965), pp. 290–4.

work did not necessarily spell complete disaster, and thus they were less likely to succumb to a condition of impoverishment, misery, and dependence. An economy of dual occupations, as Joan Thirsk has argued, 'was the best insurance that men with almost no savings and certainly no capital resources could have devised. If misfortune attended one activity, there was always the other to fall back on'.[12]

Even in places where dual occupations cannot be regarded as the norm, a significant minority of households often derived substantial benefits from both agriculture and some form of trade. Professor Hoskins found that in Wigston Magna, Leicestershire, 'there were at least a dozen tailors . . . in the late seventeenth century and nearly as many shoemakers. Almost without exception, they combined their trade with the cultivation of some land.'[13] Around the same time in Middle Clayton, north Buckinghamshire, a parish completely owned by the Verney family, small-scale farming households were also engaged at various times in such diverse trades as building, blacksmithing, tailoring, innkeeping, carrying and carting, and making potash (a local speciality); one farmer took up weaving, another glove-making.[14] Around 1770 the woollen industry was well established in West Haddon, Northamptonshire, and at least one-fifth of these weavers and wool-combers also had small holdings of land.[15] Dual occupations were even found in some small country towns: until the middle of the eighteenth century the woollen weavers in Banbury, Oxfordshire, 'were mostly part-time workers, combining weaving with agricultural work.'[16] In the area of Frampton Cotterell, Gloucestershire, north-east of Bristol, a district that was full of rural industry, many men who were identified in contemporary documents as tailors, masons, weavers and other clothworkers, tanners, cordwainers, feltmakers and coal-miners can be shown from the probate inventories 'to have retained a substantial involvement in agriculture, in many cases equal in extent to that of yeomen and husbandmen . . . , in some cases so much so that, were it not for indisputable written attribution of their primarily non-agrarian occupation, one would have assumed they were either yeomen or husbandmen.'[17]

12. Joan Thirsk, 'Horn and thorn in Staffordshire: the economy of a pastoral county', *North Staffordshire Journal of Field Studies*, vol. 9 (1969), p. 11. For evidence on the dual occupations of the metalworkers see Marie B. Rowlands, *Masters and Men in the West Midland Metalware Trades before the Industrial Revolution* (Manchester: Manchester University Press 1975), pp. 41–3; and three works by David G. Hey: *The Village of Ecclesfield* (Huddersfield: Advertiser Press 1968), p. 57; 'A dual economy in south Yorkshire', *Agricultural History Review*, vol. 17 (1969), pp. 108–9; and *The Rural Metalworkers of the Sheffield Region: A Study of Rural Industry Before the Industrial Revolution*, Leicester University Department of English Local History Occasional Papers, 2nd series, no. 5 (Leicester University Press 1972), pts 1–3. Some general observations on dual occupations are offered by Joan Thirsk in 'Seventeenth-century agriculture and social change', in Thirsk (ed.), *Land, Church, and People: Essays Presented to Professor H. P. R. Finberg* (Reading: British Agricultural History Society 1970), pp. 171–2, and 'Roots of industrial England', in A. R. H. Baker and J. B. Harley (eds), *Man Made the Land: Essays in English Historical Geography* (Newton Abbot, Devon: David & Charles 1973), pp. 106–8.

13. W. G. Hoskins, *The Midland Peasant* (London: Macmillan 1957), p. 204.

14. J. P. F. Broad, 'Sir Ralph Verney and his estates, 1630-1696' (unpubl. D. Phil. thesis, Oxford University, 1973), pp. 191–4.

15. J. M. Neeson, 'Common right and enclosure in Northamptonshire' (unpublished Ph.D. thesis, University of Warwick 1977), pp. 237–8.

16. *Victoria County History, Oxford*, vol. 10 (1972), p. 64.

17. John S. Moore (ed.), *The Goods and Chattels of Our Forefathers* (Chichester: Phillimore 1976), pp. 26–7.

Occupational designations, then, can be seriously misleading, for in their apparent straightforwardness they often conceal much of the complexity of the household economies from which people supported themselves. A man was not always simply a farmer, or a weaver or a metal worker, or – the most difficult of all to interpret – a labourer, any more than most married women today could be usefully represented as 'simply' housewives. We want to learn about the actual activities in which people were involved. And people's livelihoods, even when they particularly depended on a single kind of employment, were usually derived from more than one occupational source. In the clay ahd heath regions of Dorset small farmers might be occupied in such by-employments as making ropes or nets, tanning, glove-making, and (on the Isles of Portland and Purbeck) the quarrying of stone.[18] Rural industry was common in the Arden district of Warwickshire by the early eighteenth century: some households were actively engaged in both farming and a craft, though others gained the bulk of their livelihood from some form of manufacturing (metalworking, weaving, wood working).[19] Smallholders, commoners and cottagers in forest areas frequently found employment in carpentry, joining, sawing and coopering, as well as in such woodworking crafts as the making of rakes or ladders or hurdles.[20] In Kent fishermen 'might also be partly agricultural workers: thus in Thanet the mackerel season began in May when the barley sowing had ended, and the herring fishing took place between the end of the August harvesting and the wheat sowing in November'.[21] Such dovetailing of seasonal occupations was found as well among the miners in Cornwall, who often worked in the pilchard fishery during the peak autumn season,[22] and it was evidenced more generally in the priority that many industrial workers gave to harvest employment during the late summer, a season when the best wages were to be found in agriculture. Even a contrary piece of evidence reinforces our sense of these occupational interconnections: in July 1767, after a visit to Witney in Oxfordshire, famed for its making of blankets, Arthur Young reported that 'none of the manufacturers ever work for the farmers', but he regarded this as a 'remarkable circumstance'.[23] The iron industry probably

18. J. H. Bettey and D. S. Wilde, 'The probate inventories of Dorset farmers 1573–1670', *Local Historian*, vol. 12, no. 5 (February 1977), pp. 231–2.
19. J. M. Martin, 'The parliamentary enclosure movement and rural society in Warwickshire', *Agricultural History Review*, vol. 15 (1967), pp. 23–4.
20. Numerous accounts of forests allude to the woodworking industries that were conducted in their vicinity. See, for instance , J. E. Linnell, *Old Oak: The Story of a Forest Village* (London 1932), pp. 3–4, on Whittlewood Forest in southern Northamptonshire. In King's Cliffe, Northamptonshire, a small market town on the edge of Rockingham Forest, twenty-six of the able-bodied men who were liable for the militia in the 1760s were listed as wood turners (Pettit, *Forests of Northamptonshire*, pp. 160–1; see also p. 182). It may be noteworthy that the large and prominent Boughton Green Fair, which was held in central Northamptonshire, about midway between Rockingham Forest to the north and Whittlewood and Salcey Forests to the south, was said to be noted for (among other things) the sale of 'timber, poles, ladders, cooper's ware, and tunnery': John Ogilby and William Morgan, *The Traveller's Pocket-Book*, 19th edn (London 1778), p. 186. See also Alan Everitt, 'Urban growth, 1570–1770', *Local Historian*, vol. 8, no. 4 (1968), p. 120.
21. C. W. Chalklin, *Seventeenth-century Kent* (London: Longman 1965), p. 45; see also p. 150.
22. John G. Rule, 'The labouring miner in Cornwall *c.*1740–1870: a study in social history' (unpubl. Ph.D thesis, University of Warwick, 1971), pp. 76 and 96.
23. Arthur Young, *A Six Weeks Tour, Through the Southern Counties of England and Wales*, 2nd edn (London 1769), p. 132.

offered less opportunity for ancillary employments than many other sectors of production – much of its labour was not organized under the putting-out system, for forges and furnaces required specialized work-places – but even here, according to T. S. Ashton, 'many labourers . . . held small plots of land which they cultivated in their spare time and which saved them from idleness when shortage of water, or other cause, brought the ironworks to a temporary stand.'[24]

## SELF-SUFFICIENCY IN EIGHTEENTH-CENTURY ENGLAND

A labouring family around 1700 normally got its support, not from just one or two sources, but from a variety of activities. Its productive economy, one might say, was extensive rather than intensive. People tried to knit together a viable sustenance from a wide range of employments. We have already mentioned the value of common rights and the uses to which common lands were put. Even in places where few commons existed, many people had small cottage gardens where they could grow potatoes, cabbages, peas and beans; cottagers very commonly kept a pig or two, which could be fattened on almost anything; some had chickens or geese, a few kept bees. ('As the poorest family can often maintain a cat or a dog, without any expence', wrote Adam Smith, 'so the poorest occupiers of land can commonly maintain a few poultry, or a sow and a few pigs, at very little. The little offals of their own table, their whey, skimmed milk and butter-milk, supply those animals with a part of their food, and they find the rest in the neighbouring fields without doing any sensible damage to any body.')[25] Some of this produce they sold in the market, much of it they consumed directly. For most of them farm labour was an important source of income; and increasingly country people were taking up ancillary employments – spinning, weaving, knitting, glove-making, metalworking, and the like – to supplement the livelihood they gained from agricultural wages, a smallholding, or common rights. The returns from gleaning would provide some of the following year's bread, perquisites might be forthcoming from farmers and landlords (fuel allowances, cheap wheat, holiday treats and gratuities), a part of the wages from children in service would be returned to their parents, from a small plot of hemp or flax yarn could be spun (in 1776 Arthur Young noticed many hemp gardens between Wolverhampton and Shrewsbury),[26] and there were few deterrents against the casual 'poaching' of small game prior to the age of large game preserves and assiduous gamekeepers. It was standard practice for families to get their earnings from a variety of seasonal employments. In Selborne, Hampshire, for example, it was said by Gilbert White that 'besides the employment in husbandry the men work in hop gardens, of which we have many; and fell and bark timber. In the spring and summer the women weed the corn; and enjoy a second harvest in September by hop-picking.'

24. T. S. Ashton, *Iron and Steel in the Industrial Revolution* (Manchester 1924), p. 197. Similarly, Cornish miners commonly had small plots of land – perhaps a couple of acres – attached to their cottages: Rule, 'Labouring miner' (Ph.D.), pp. 95–100.

25. Adam Smith, *The Wealth of Nations* (New York: Modern Library 1937), p. 226.

26. Arthur Young, *Tours in England and Wales (Selected from the Annals of Agriculture)*, London School of Economics and Political Science Series of Reprints of Scarce Tracts in Economic and Political Science, no. 14 (London 1932), pp. 144 and 162.

They also did some spinning during the winter months.[27] A family's living, then, was usually obtained from a number of part-time and seasonal activities, and the more they could sustain this diverse economy, the better their security would be.

We can see from many sources that plebeian households tried to attain at least a moderate degree of domestic self-sufficiency. The more they could produce directly for their own consumption, the less they would have to buy from the marketplace; and if their dependence on market purchases could be minimized, they would be less dependent for their livelihood and conveniences on the wages provided by employers. Providing for one's own needs by one's own efforts, without the mediation of wage-employment, made for greater self-reliance and independence, and these were goals that most people respected. They were also goals that many families were still able to satisfy, at least in part: getting a living outside the economic arena of contractual wage-payments was feasible and widely practised. Keeping a pig and some poultry, digging peat or collecting brushwood for fuel, having a plot of hay to provide fodder for a cow, growing potatoes or other vegetables in a cottage garden, collecting nuts or berries, making at least some of one's own clothing (shoes were always excepted, and thus the shoemaker was one of the most ubiquitous of craftsmen): these were some of the ways in which families would supply their own needs. It was said that in the Chichester area in the early eighteenth century 'spinning of household linen was in use in most families; also making their own bread, and likewise their own physic'.[28] In many places people made their own rushlights, by dipping rushes in animal fat, and were thus able to avoid buying candles. Gilbert White offered a detailed account of this – as he called it – 'very simple piece of domestic economy'. He was assured by an 'experienced old housekeeper . . . that one pound and a half of rushes completely supplies his family the year round, since working people burn no candle in the long days, because they rise and go to bed by daylight.' (In some places rushes were also used for plaiting mats or chair-bottoms.) This was the sort of economy that valued thrift and condemned waste: all resources were to be used for some purpose.

Whatever the changing pressures that impinged upon, or even transformed, people's lives, the efficiency of the family economy continued to be the compelling priority in plebeian life. And this family economy was not normally centred around a single breadwinner: rather, it was assumed that the family's sustenance would depend on the productive contributions of all its members, each of whom helped to sustain the whole. A wife was always a working woman – indeed, marriage itself was, in part, an economic partnership – and children were usually put to work at an early age. Contemporary sources are full of references to the gainful employment of women and children. We have already noticed that women were actively engaged in a wide range of domestic industries – spinning, carding, knitting, lace-making, silk-winding, glove-making, the making of shirt buttons, the repairing of fishing nets; and in many of these trades children – especially girls – were expected, from an early age (perhaps at around six or

27. Gilbert White, *The National History of Selborne* (London: Dent Everyman 1949), pp. 15–16; first published 1788.

28. Francis W. Steer (ed.), *The Memoirs of James Spershott*, Chichester Papers, no. 30 (Chichester 1962), p. 15.

seven), to help their mothers by performing such simple but necessary tasks as quilling, covering wire for the making of buttons or winding thread on bobbins. As they grew older these children would be taught the requisite skills of a particular handicraft, usually getting small earnings as they learned, earnings that were regarded as contributions to the family economy. William Hutton, whose father was a wool-comber, was born in Derby in 1723, and he recalled in his memoirs that in 1729 there was talk about sending him to work. 'Consultations were held about fixing me in some employment for the benefit of the family. Winding quills for the weaver was mentioned, but died away. Stripping tobacco for the grocer, in which I was to earn fourpence a week, was a second; but it was at last concluded that I was too young for any employment.' The next year, however, at the age of seven, he was sent to work in Lombe's silk factory in Derby.[29] In lead, tin and copper mining districts women and children were commonly employed at such jobs as breaking, sorting and washing the ore and pushing wagons and barrows; and young boys were normally hired to control the ventilation trap-doors in coal mines. Women were often employed in nail-making shops, and in London the wives of labouring men contributed to their families' sustenance by sewing and stitching, hawking goods in the streets or taking in laundry. In 1782 two-thirds of the housewives in Cardington, Bedfordshire, were engaged in a cottage handicraft, usually either lace-making or spinning, and many girls were similiarly employed.[30] Female and child labour was not, for the most part, a matter of free choice: it was a matter of necessity. Few families could subsist for long from the earnings of only the head of the household. The smooth functioning of the family economy, then – an intimate economy of closely knit interdependence – was a fundamental preoccupation of almost all labouring people. And for most of them the family was also a central unit of social experience and personal relations: the small stage on which the everyday transactions of life were acted out.

29. Llewellyn Jewitt (ed.), *The Life of William Hutton* (London 1872), pp. 105–6.

30. N. L. Tranter. 'Demographic change in Bedfordshire 1670–1800' (unpubl. Ph.D thesis, Nottingham University, 1966), pp. 293–7.

# 3

# Women's Work, Mechanization and the Early Phases of Industrialization in England

MAXINE BERG

## THE PREVAILING ASSUMPTION

The fundamental transformation of the meaning of work in the day to day lives of individuals and families is usually believed to have come with the reorganization of production which separated the household from the workplace at some point during industrialization. The separation in space between household and workplace became the foundation for the separation in conception between market activities and communities. Families were divided from the trades, consumption from production, women's activities from men's, and ultimately the ethos of mutuality and moral imperative from the ethos of the individual and market imperatives. The division between home and work is also associated with wider divisions between the 'private' and the 'public' spheres; the division has accounted for a sexual division of labour going far beyond original divisions rooted in biological reproduction and family life. It is a division which is fundamentally historical, and it carries with it the assumption of some past historical time when home and work were one and the same.

The historical meanings of work were in some way changed with the movement of work away from the home: it is therefore important to go back to those early stages of industrial capitalism when most production was carried out in the

I am grateful to Patrick Joyce for suggestions on the revision of this paper, and to Ludmilla Jordanova for her criticism of an early version. The 1985 Warwick Workshops on Proto-industrial Communities provided stimulating discussions of eighteenth-century industrial work. Claudia Goldin's 'The economic status of women in the early Republic: some quantitative evidence', *Journal of Interdisciplinary History*, 16: 3 (1986), which was published after this essay went to press, raises some similar points to mine for the case of early industrial Philadelphia. This essay was first published in Patrick Joyce, ed., *The Historical Meanings of Work* (Cambridge University Press, 1987).

home, but the first phases of mechanization and factory production were presenting new challenges. This chapter will thus focus on production conditions – workplace organization, techniques of production and their community context – in eighteenth-century industry, especially in those industries which underwent significant expansion and transformation in the eighteenth century – textiles and metals.

Assumptions about the changes in the meaning of work no longer carried on within the home and family setting have been particularly important in recent writing on gender divisions in the workforce. Most research on women's current subordination in the workforce rests on the assumption of a fundamental historical transition in women's workforce participation and status in the eighteenth or early nineteenth century, coterminous with the rise of industrial capitalism. This assumption pervades much Marxist–feminist analysis of women's work; it is at the core of debates on patriarchy and capitalist production.[1] The search for an historical basis of subordination remains fundamental and has taken the form of seeking a transition in production relations, in trade union and class relations, in the role of the state and in ideology.[2]

The analysis of a historical transition in women's employment is a part of larger debates on the transition from feudalism to capitalism, and the transition in the labour process from handicraft and domestic manufacture to modern industry, the factory system and industrial capitalism. The enormously complex and many-sided processes of change which mark the transformation from a pre-industrial to an industrial world have been studied by generations of historians trying to unravel the content and timing of fundamental changes stretching from the late seventeenth to the early twentieth centuries. Where, once, we spoke with some certainty of an Industrial Revolution, concentrated within a relatively short fifty-year period, our conception of industrialization is now of a longer, more complex process. With this shift of focus, older certainties about the fundamentals of the transition to capitalism have been questioned, so that we can no longer say just when capitalist social relations overcame feudal traditions, or indeed what constituted the fundamental cause of transformation.[3]

Hence the search for the historical basis of the inequities faced by women in the workplace has become one fraught with dead ends, wrong turnings and an ever-receding destination. One result of this is an appeal to ever more elastic terminology which becomes invested with explanatory value. Key concepts appealed to by Marxist feminists and other historians alike are the 'family-wage

1. Heidi Hartmann, 'The unhappy marriage of Marxism and Feminism: towards a more progressive union', Lydia Sargent, ed., *Women and Revolution* (Boston, South End Press, 1981); Sheila Rowbothom, 'The trouble with patriarchy', *New Statesman* (21–8 December 1979); Sally Alexander and Barbara Taylor, 'In defence of patriarchy', in R. Samuel, ed., *People's History and Socialist Theory* (London, Routledge, 1981).

2. Michele Barrett, *Women's Oppression Today* (London, Verso Books, 1980); Jane Humphries, 'Class struggle and the persistence of the working class family', *Cambridge Journal of Economics*, 1:3 (1977); Sally Alexander, 'Women, class and sexual difference', *History Workshop Journal*, 17 (Spring 1984); Catherine Hall, 'The early formation of Victorian domestic ideology', in S. Burman, ed., *Fit Work for Women* (London, Croom Helm, 1979).

3. See T. H. Aston and C. H. E. Philpin, eds., *The Brenner Debate* (Cambridge University Press, 1985).

economy', or simply 'family economy' and the 'family-household system'.[4] In fact these terms cover a variety of meanings. The 'family-wage economy' was a unit made up of family members who worked for wages in the family interest. It succeeded the old 'family economy' of the household mode of production[5] yet the hold of the family economy on behaviour, mentalities and social structures continued as long as all family members had some economic function.[6] Marxist feminists argue that this 'family economy' was overtaken by the 'family-household system', a combination of a household structure based on the dependence of members on the paid labour of husbands or fathers and the unpaid labour of the wife/mother in domestic tasks, and the ideology of the family, 'the private sphere beyond the public realm of commerce and industry'. Developments in the mid nineteenth century forced women into the domestic sphere and created the basis for a sexually segregated labour market.[7]

Whatever the stages of the transitions from family economy to family wage economies and on to the family household system, there lies at the heart of these debates the still more fundamental separation of home and workplace. The belief that the historical separation of the workplace from the home and personal life with the development of capitalism was accountable for women's particular oppression was and still is much debated in Marxist-feminist literature.[8] But accounting for the socially constructed gender differences which lie deeply embedded in the sexual division of labour has taken feminists far beyond the economy, production relations or Marxist economic categories into broader spheres of ideology and social constructs. They have subsequently called for the study of links between the organization of production and gender divisions.[9] Nevertheless the history of waged and unwaged work has remained a vital component of the analysis of these connections. And the assumption of an earlier historical epoch where work and home life were integrated underpins the general focus of much contemporary research on women's subordination.

Throughout the current debate there exists consensus about the model of a pre-capitalist system of production based on the family work unit, which allowed women to combine their productive work with children and housework. The transition to an industrial capitalism which separated production from the home to the workshop or factory is then said to account for the declining opportunities for women. The timing of this transition in England has been variously placed at points ranging from the early eighteenth century to the mid nineteenth century,[10]

4. Michele Barrett and Mary McIntosh, *The Anti-Social Family* (London, Verso Books), p. 79; David Levine, 'Industrialisation and the proletarian family in England', *Past and Present*, 107 (May 1985); Louise Tilly and Joan Scott, *Women, Work and Family* (New York, Holt, Reinhart and Winston, 1978); Joanna Brenner and Maria Ramos, 'Rethinking women's oppression', *New Left Review*, 144 (March–April 1984).
5. See Tilly and Scott, *Women, Work and Family*, ch. 6.
6. See David Levine, 'Industrialisation and the proletarian family.'
7. See Barrett, *Women's Oppression Today*, and Brenner and Ramos, 'Rethinking women's oppression'.
8. The early discussion centred on Eli Zaretsky, *Capitalism, The Family and Personal Life* (New York, Harper and Row, 1976). Also see Hartmann, 'The unhappy marriage'.
9. Maureen Mackintosh, 'Gender and economics: the sexual division of labour and the subordination of women' in K. Young, C.Wolkowitz and R. McCullagh, *Of Marriage and the Market* (London, CSE Books, 1981).
10. I. Pinchbeck, *Women Workers and the Industrial Revolution* (1930 and London, Virago, 1981) and E. Richards, 'Women in the British economy', *History*, 53 (1974).

and the focus lies on differences in working conditions under the 'domestic system' and those under the factory system.

The key historical questions about this transition were set in the 1920s and 1930s by Lillian Knowles, Alice Clark, Dorothy George and Ivy Pinchbeck. Alice Clark asked how economic development in the seventeenth and eighteenth centuries had affected the productivity and status of women, and argued that their jobs were narrowed and their position degraded with the 'triumph of capitalistic organisation' and the decline of the household economy. Yet Lillian Knowles, Ivy Pinchbeck and Dorothy George all found a vital and positive transition in the rise of the factory system which took women out of the home to work, and they took pains to debunk the idea of historical golden ages in the conditions of domestic manufacture.[11]

The crucial questions debated by these historians were, first, what conditions prevailed for women under domestic manufacture? And, second, did the displacement of work away from the home to workshop or factory enhance or reduce their condition? Dorothy George blamed domestic manufacture for keeping wages low and for being largely dependent on the excessive labour of women and children.[12] Ivy Pinchbeck argued that the family industrial unit established a tradition of low wages which subsequently affected women's wage levels when they did enter the factory.[13] But Alice Clark argued that women in the seventeenth century had occupied an assured position whenever the 'system of family industry prevailed', and that the greater equality in their economic positions depended upon whether enterprises were carried on at home or elsewhere.[14]

This issue of women's work in domestic manufacture has never been resolved. It has remained crucial to assumptions underlying feminist debates, but in spite of raising the historical problem in the twenties and thirties, the work of these historians has not been followed up. Research on women's work, especially industrial work in the eighteenth century and early nineteenth century, remains very limited. Apart from what can be gleaned from a few general surveys, some substantial research on women in agriculture, and Keith Snell's very recent research on women's apprenticeship in the south of England, we know very little of women's working lives in this crucial historical period.[15] As Olwen Hufton has recently revealed in her survey on women's history,

11. For a disscussion of these positions see Joan Thirsk, 'Forward', in Mary Prior, ed., *Women in English Society* (London, Methuen, 1985) and M. Berg, 'Introduction', *The Age of Manufactures, 1700–1820* (London, Fontana, 1985).

12. Dorothy George, *England in Transition* (Harmondsworth, Penguin, 1931), p. 99.

13. Pinchbeck, *Women Workers*, p. 126.

14. Alice Clark, *Working Life of Women in the Seventeenth Century* (1919 and London, Virago, 1982).

15. See N. McKendrick, 'Home demand and economic growth: a new view of women and children in the industrial revolution', in N. McKendrick, ed., *Historical Perspectives* (Cambridge University Press, 1974); Richards, 'Women in the British economy'; R. Masch, 'Women in an age of transition 1485–1714', in B. Kanner, ed., *Women in England from Anglo Saxon Times to the Present: Interpretive Bibliographical Essays* (Hampden Conn., Anchor Books, 1979); M. Roberts, 'Sickles and scythes: women's work and men's work at harvest time', *History Workshop Journal*, 7 (1979); K. Snell, 'Agricultural seasonal unemployment, the standard of living, and women's work in the south and the east 1690–1860', *Economic History Review*, 2nd series, 34 (1981); K. Snell, *Annals of the Labouring Poor* (Cambridge University Press, 1985) ch. 6. Also see Mary Prior, 'Women and the urban economy: Oxford 1500–1800', in Prior, *Women in English Society*.

> We are thus carried into the realm of women and work and are confronted with a curious paradox. We all know that women in pre-industrial society worked . . . Sense tells us that in the proto-industrial phase their role was crucial. They were the more numerous sector of the cheap labour force. Yet we have very little detailed modern research bearing on the nature and importance of their labour.[16]

Feminists are prepared to pronounce with confidence on the great transition from the household manufacture or domestic industry to the factory system, but as yet we know little of what this 'transition' really involved for women.

## PROTO-INDUSTRIALIZATION AND FAMILY LABOUR

If feminism has not in this country generated an economic history of women since the early classics, current trends in economic and social history have nevertheless made one possible. The recent debate over proto-industrialization, whatever one's reservations over the concept, has revived interest in the eighteenth century, and has shifted the formerly agrarian focus of research on to the industrial activities of the countryside. The demographic orientation of the historians of proto-industrialization did lead them to raise important questions about the family economy in the phase of transitional industrial expansion before full industrialization. But it blinkered them in other respects, for few of these historians, at least until recently, have written about the place of women in proto-industrialization in terms other than those of breeding and child rearing.[17] Some of the original contributions to the debate did, however, point out women's special role in the labour force. Hans Medick and David Levine argued that the new domestic industries thrived on cheap, infinitely expandable supplies of labour.[18] These industries increased the intensity of labour, and the productive effort of women and children contributed indispensably to the family subsistence wage. But this decisive marginal work effort in the family went underpaid. A large proportion of the labour time of these women and children went to merchant capitalists in the form of extra profit. Medick and Levine also credited proto-industrialization with bringing about a transformation of the division of labour between the sexes, giving women a greater and more equal position in the labour force than hitherto. But this argument consigns to women a rather minor role in agriculture and indeed in the urban trades before proto-industrialization. Other historians have, however, marshalled substantial evidence of just the reverse.[19]

Before we can pronounce on the implications of the separation of work from home, we must examine the conditions of domestic manufacture, and especially

16. Olwen Hufton, 'Survey articles, women in history I. Early modern Europe', *Past and Present*, 101 (1983) 132.

17. For a survey of this debate see ch. 3 in Berg, *Age of Manufactures*, and Leslie Clarkson, 'Proto-industrialisation: the first phase of industrialisation?'

18. See David Levine, 'The demographic implications of rural industrialisation: a family reconstitution study of Shepsted, Leicestershire, 1600–1851'; Hans Medick, 'The proto-industrial family economy'. Both reprinted in P. Thane and A. Sutcliffe, eds, *Essays in Social History*, vol. II (Oxford University Press, 1986).

19. Snell, *Annals*, ch. 1, and R. Du Plessis and M. C. Howell, 'Reconsidering the early modern urban economy: the cases of Leiden and Lille', *Past and Present*, 99 (1982).

the place of women within this. The employment of women in the dispersed handicraft production of the seventeenth and eighteenth centuries may not have been novel, but the rapid expansion of these industries and their reliance on low-paid labour entailed higher proportions of female and child labour. Yet this reliance on women's labour and, more significantly, children's labour is now little remarked upon in reference to handicraft and even early factory industry. It was once singled out as the keynote of the system. Dorothy George devoted a chapter of her *England in Transition* to child labour, and argued strongly that the custom of child labour at an early age was deeply rooted in the domestic system, and was only seriously challenged with the coming of the factory system. 'What was new and revolutionary', she argued, 'was that for the first time toiling children were regarded as an outrage, not something to be admired . . . it was the sense of something monstrous in the factory system which directed attention to the yet more monstrous exploitation of the labour of young children.[20] Historians are only now returning to consider the place of this child labour. David Levine has argued recently that handicraft manufacture coincided with high fertility and high proportions of children in the population. The labour of children was an elastic resource, with children aged five to fourteen comprising one-sixth to one quarter of the total population. With the decline in the handicraft trades came a decline in the demand for female and child labour. The result was a sharp reversal in the rates of population increase; the age of first marriage for women rose. With the relocation of the workplace away from the family by the mid nineteenth century the family's material base was changed from a locus of production to one of reproduction and consumption. Women become identified with the domestic sphere, while sexuality and especially masculinity was related to work. Working class boys learned to labour 'as an expression of their masculinity'. Levine argued that it was the flow of wealth within the family that determined fertility, it was not until as late as the 1920s that wealth flowed from parents to children instead of the reverse, and that the imperatives of the family economy started to recede.[21]

## THE FEMALE WORKFORCE AND INDUSTRIAL EMPLOYMENT IN EIGHTEENTH-CENTURY INDUSTRY

This chapter will now examine the case for a transition in the role of women in the industrial workforce in the eighteenth century. It will look at changes which took place within an industrial production still largely dominated by households and small workshops. The chapter will focus on those early changes in technology which defined the Industrial Revolution, and their implications for women's employment and skills, and compare the experiences of women workers in the textiles industries and metal trades. This mechanization has come to be seen as synonymous with the demise of home based handicraft production. I will also raise the problem of community and work networks for women, but as evidence on this area is so very limited, I can do no more than to ask some questions. I will

20. George, *England in Transition*, pp. 132–3. Compare R. Gray, 'The languages of factory reform in Britain, 1830–1860', in Patrick Joyce, ed., *The Historical Meanings of Work*.
21. Levine, 'Industrialisation and the proletarian family', p. 197.

TABLE 3.1 Occupations in eighteenth-century England

| | | | |
|---|---|---|---|
| | *Commerce and Industry* | | |
| King | | Lindert | |
| Merchants & traders by sea (greater) | 2,000 | All commerce | 135,333 |
| Merchants & traders by sea (lesser) | 8,000 | Manufacturing trades | 179,774 |
| Shopkeepers & tradesmen | 40,000 | Mining | 15,082 |
| Artizans & handycrafts | 60,000 | Building trades | 77,232 |
| | 110,000 | | 407,421 (excluding labourers) |
| | *Agriculture* | | |
| King | | Lindert | |
| Freeholders (greater) | 40,000 | All agriculture | 241,373 (excluding labourers) |
| Freeholders (lesser) | 140,000 | | |
| Farmers | 150,000 | | |
| | 330,000 | | |

draw on a survey of present knowledge informed by economic analysis of labour markets, and I will pose questions of whether changes in work processes increased or reduced opportunities for women. My major work on only two of the most advanced sectors shows a diversity of experience that makes generalization very difficult.

Quantitative evidence about women in industrial occupations in the eighteenth century is non-existent. Conjecture is combined with broad estimates to convey an idea of a high proportion, but beyond this, there is little we can say with certainty. Occupational structure for the eighteenth century can be gleaned from contemporary estimates and recent revisions of these (see table 3.1). Peter Lindert's new social tables are now fairly widely used in preference to the estimates of Gregory King (1688), Joseph Massie (1759) and Patrick Colquhoun (1811). His tables convey a sense of an occupational structure much more industrial than previously assumed. His estimates also show that though occupational structure was relatively stable before 1755, agriculture and manufacturing increased faster than average and, in the last half of the eighteenth century, manufacturing employment increased substantially, dominated by textiles. By his estimate, employment in textiles more than tripled in the second half of the eighteenth century.[22]

There is, however, no certainty in these estimates; they come with high margins of error.[23] The tables are, furthermore, subject to the other serious

22. Peter Lindert, 'English occupations 1670–1811', *Journal of Economic History*, 40:4 (December 1980) 702–5, and 'Revising England's social tables, 1688–1812', *Explorations in Economic History*, 19 (1982).

23. Lindert, 'English occupations', p. 701; E. A. Wrigley, 'Urban growth and agricultural change: England and the Continent in the early modern period', *Journal of Interdisciplinary History*, 15:4 (Spring 1985) 698 n. 11. Lindert reckons that for his finer occupational groupings (fewer than 40,000) the true numbers could be one-third to three times his estimates. Estimates for shoemakers, carpenters etc. were 'little more than guesses'. And for categories with over 100,000 persons (agriculture, commerce, manufacturing etc.) the true value could be three-fifths to five-thirds the estimates. Lindert's tables have also been seriously doubted by Wrigley, who finds numbers in agriculture seriously underestimated.

reservation expressed by David Levine, that Lindert's analysis focuses on the occupations of men (they are based on male burial records) not those of women, youth and children, and also fails to account for the multiplicity of different activities by industrial and non-industrial workers.[24] Levine, nevertheless, chooses to use the tables as a base line indicator of economic activity. We may have doubts over the aggregate estimates, but they do give us a picture of a substantially industrial occupational structure in the eighteenth century. Though there are no figures, it is almost certainly the case, as Levine points out, that there was a substantial female and youthful industrial population.[25]

Conjectures on the employment structures of individual textile industries confirm this impression. Adrian Randall has calculated that in the West Country woollen industry in the period 1781–96, women accounted for higher proportionate numbers of workers than men, and children higher numbers than men.[26] As most of the women involved were spinners, there is no reason to think the ratio would be different for the industry in other parts of the country, at least before the spread of the spinning jenny. Spinning also provided the greatest employment in the linen industry, and this was again the employment of women.[27] Adam Smith calculated that in addition to flax growers and dressers, three or four spinners were necessary to keep one weaver in constant employment.[28] Women also predominated in the silk manufacture; Natalie Rothstein has estimated that in 1765 the proportion of women and children to men in the London silk trade was 1400 to 100. Out of approximately 4000 employed in Spitalfields, most were women and children.[29] When silk throwing started to move out of London to the home countries it was to tap an even larger female labour market in farming communities.[30] Lacemaking in the eighteenth century was almost exclusively a female trade.[31] Hand knitting occupied the hands of women, children and old men over many areas such as the dales of the West Riding even after the widespread use of framework knitting.[32] Framework knitting, though carried out

24. Levine, 'Industrialisation.'
25. Ibid.
26. Adrian Randall, 'The West Country woollen industry during the Industrial Revolution' (unpublished Ph.D. thesis, University of Birmingham, 1979), vol. II, p. 249. Numbers needed to produce twelve broadcloths:

| | *1781–96* |
|---|---|
| Men | 167 |
| Women | 186 |
| Children | 306 |
| | 659 |

27. See A. J. Durie, 'The Scottish linen industry 1707–1775, with particular reference to the early history of the British linen company' (unpublished Ph.D., University of Edinburgh, 1973), p. 159; Brenda Collins, 'Proto-industrialisation and pre-famine emigration', *Social History*, 7:2 (1982) 132–4.
28. Adam Smith, *The Wealth of Nations* (1776 and Oxford University Press, 1976), vol. IV, vii, p. 644.
29. N. K. Rothstein, 'The silk industry in London, 1702–1766' (unpublished MA thesis, University of London, 1961), ch. 2.
30. See J. Lown, 'Gender and class during industrialisation: a study of the Halstead silk industry in Essex 1825–1900' (unpublished Ph.D. thesis, University of Essex, 1984), ch. 2.
31. G. F. R. Spencely, 'The English pillow lace industry 1845–80: a rural industry in competition with machinery', *Business History*, 70 (1970).
32. J. D. Chambers, 'The rural domestic industries during the period of transition to the factory system', *Second International Congress of Economic History*, Aix-en-Provence, 2 (1962).

TABLE 3.2 Estimates of economic growth: value added in British industry (£m, current)

| | *1770* | *%* | *1801* | *%* | *1831* | *%* |
|---|---|---|---|---|---|---|
| Cotton | 0.6 | 2.6 | 9.2 | 17.0 | 25.3 | 22.4 |
| Wool | 7.0 | 30.6 | 10.1 | 18.7 | 15.9 | 14.1 |
| Linen | 1.9 | 8.3 | 2.6 | 4.8 | 5.0 | 4.4 |
| Silk | 1.0 | 4.4 | 2.0 | 3.7 | 5.8 | 5.1 |
| Building | 2.4 | 10.5 | 9.3 | 17.2 | 26.5 | 23.5 |
| Iron | 1.5 | 6.6 | 4.0 | 7.4 | 7.6 | 6.7 |
| Copper | 0.2 | 0.9 | 0.9 | 1.7 | 0.8 | 0.7 |
| Beer | 1.3 | 5.7 | 2.5 | 4.6 | 5.2 | 4.6 |
| Leather | 5.1 | 22.3 | 8.4 | 15.5 | 9.8 | 8.7 |
| Soap | 0.3 | 1.3 | 0.8 | 1.5 | 1.2 | 1.1 |
| Candles | 0.5 | 2.2 | 1.0 | 1.8 | 1.2 | 1.1 |
| Coal | 0.9 | 4.4 | 2.7 | 5.0 | 7.9 | 7.0 |
| Paper | 0.1 | 0.4 | 0.6 | 1.1 | 0.8 | 0.7 |
| Total | 22.8 | | 54.1 | | 113.0 | |

*Source:* N. F. R. Crafts, *British Economic Growth during the Industrial Revolution* (Oxford, 1985), p. 22.

early in the eighteenth century by men, relied heavily on the ancillary labour of women and children. Increasingly over the eighteenth century, once apprenticeship regulations were bypassed, women and children also worked the frames.

> The knitter's wife was also one of his greatest industrial assets. When he worked on fancies and completed the whole article, she seamed and finished it. After he became a specialist at a single process on the frame, she supervised and assisted the younger children in winding the yarn and keeping the shuttles filled . . . Occasionally women worked on the frame, but usually as an emergency measure, although after the 'long depression' many women kept their husband's frame busy far into the night in order to eke out the husband's income.[33]

The early factory cotton industry was also dominated by women's and children's labour. Most of the mills surveyed in 1816 were small scale and employed significantly more women than men, and roughly equal numbers of adults and children. The few large-scale mills at the time employed roughly equal proportions of men and women; adults and children.[34] The textile industries formed the largest manufacturing sector in eighteenth-century England. On the evidence of these individual sectors, women dominated all its major manufactures. The other major eighteenth-century manufacturing industries were the leather trades and the metal-working industries. Women were employed in limited sections of the leather industries. They were widely employed in certain sectors of the metal trades, particularly in nailmaking, but also in a wide range of hardware trades. Employment data for eighteenth-century industries is not available, but some indication of the relative significance of the various

33. E.G. Nelson, 'The English framework-knitting industry', *Journal of Economics and Business History*, 2:3 (1930).
34. See Select Committee on the Employment of Children in Factories, PP 1816, (397) iii, pp. 211–19, 374, 378. Also see F. Collier, 'An early factory community', *Economic History Review*, 2 (1930).

eighteenth-century industries can be gleaned from estimates of the contribution of individual industries to increases in the national product (see table 3.2 above).

Though male occupations such as leathermaking, building, and coal were very important, the textile industries were clearly dominant, and mixed trades such as iron and brewing were also significant.

Another indication of the high potential figures for female employment can be recovered from the listings which survive of inhabitants for the two parishes of Cardington, Bedfordshire and Corfe Castle, Dorset.[35] Such detailed listings are rare, but these two examples form a source. They reveal high participation rates in both places in the eighteenth century, but experience in the nineteenth century diverged sharply. In the 1790s employment opportunities for women in spinning and knitting in Corfe Castle were respectable, but by 1851 had virtually disappeared with the contraction of cottage industry. In Cardington female employment in lacemaking was high and remained so through 1851. Indeed, activity rates for married women aged twenty to thirty-nine in Cardington in 1752 was a remarkable 82 per cent. In our own time a high rate for married women was 58 per cent, the figure for 1971, but this was for the narrower category of the age group forty-five to fifty-four, those without young children at home.[36]

The contraction of such opportunities with industrialization would certainly confirm the argument of Eric Richards that the nineteenth century brought a great decline in women's industrial employment caused by a contraction in rural industry. Other research has shown a great decline not just in women's work, but in male employment and in village trades as a whole, a decline closely linked with the enclosure of the commons.[37]

A contraction of women's employment opportunities was reflected not only in this contraction of domestic industries, but also in a striking decline in the range of trades to which women were apprenticed in the eighteenth century. Keith Snell has drawn a rather remarkable picture of widespread female apprenticeship in the southern and eastern counties of England in the early half of the century. Thirty-four per cent of the apprenticeships he examined were for girls and these were appointed to as many as fifty-one trades, more than in the case of men. Many were apprenticed to the same trades as their fathers, and their premiums were comparable to those of boys. Girls apprenticed by the parish were furthermore to be found in the widest range of occupations. By the nineteenth century the number of female apprentices had fallen, women were apprenticed to less than half the trades that men were, and these were largely restricted to the household and clothing manufactures.[38]

This picture of widespread female employment across the trades in the pre-industrial and early industrial period fits with other pictures of the pre-industrial crafts in Europe.[39] The reasons suggested for the great contraction after this are,

35. Osamu Saito, 'Who worked when: life time profiles of labour force participation in Cardington and Corfe Castle in the late 18th and mid 19th century', *Local Population Studies* (Spring 1979).

36. Ibid. pp. 15–16.

37. J. M. Martin, 'Village traders and the emergence of a proletariat in south Warwickshire 1750–1851', *Agricultural History Review* (1985).

38. Snell, *Annals*, ch. 6, p. 331.

39. Du Plessis and Howell, 'Reconsidering the early modern urban economy'; N. Zemon Davis, 'Women in the crafts in sixteenth century Lyons', *Feminist Studies*, 8 (1982).

however, difficult to reconcile. Alice Clark in 1919 accounted for it by the movement of manufacture and business out of the home. Keith Snell produces similar reasons. He argues that demographic conditions in the late seventeenth century to the eighteenth century favoured female employment. Low population pressure was combined with a high age of marriage and more single women. Between the late seventeenth century and the 1780s the age of first marriage for women fell from twenty-seven to twenty-four, and the proportion of women never marrying fell from 15 per cent to 7 per cent. But these demographic trends coincided with both the growing capitalization of the trades which took work out of the framework of the family economy, and with a glutting of the trades in the early nineteenth century. Substantial male unemployment meant the barring of female labour from many trades.

This perspective is also endorsed by research in the organization of the trades. Where women earlier in the eighteenth century had belonged to many of the trade organizations, by its end they were increasingly excluded. In 1769 the Spitalfields silk weavers excluded women from higher-paid work, and in 1779 journeymen bookbinders excluded women from their union. The Stockport Hatmakers' society in 1808 declared strikes against women in the trade, and the Cotton Spinners' Union in 1829 excluded women. The handloom weavers refused to admit women to their unions, and in 1834 the London tailors struck work to drive women from the trade.[40]

There is, however, a substantial amount of evidence to indicate a rather more complex pre-industrial and proto-industrial experience than is allowed for in these analyses of the crucial transition in women's employment opportunities. First the pre-industrial experience was highly variable between industries and parts of the country. The women of fourteenth- and fifteenth-century Leiden may have occupied the trades in considerable numbers and status, but this was not necessarily the position in England. The experience of fourteenth-century Shrewsbury and sixteenth- and seventeenth-century Salisbury showed a clear sexual division of labour with women predominantly found in occupations associated with domestic labour, or in the 'casual menial end of the market, an area which may not have involved large numbers at any one time, but which must have given employment to a significant number of women at some stage during their life cycle'.[41] Though women may have worked across a wide range of trades, their roles were restricted; they rarely entered fully into the 'mysteries' of the craft, and capital, including tools and workshops, was bequeathed where possible to sons.[42] Women went on to only limited opportunities in eighteenth-century Oxford. They played only a small role as market traders even in the casual sectors, and this became even more circumscribed with gradual market deregulation, when many dealings moved to the male social world of the inn or public house.[43] There were expanding opportunities for women in the new ready-made clothing

40. Barbara Taylor, *Eve and the New Jerusalem* (London, Virago, 1983).

41. See Diana Hutton, 'Women in fourteenth century Shrewsbury', in Lindsey Charles and Lorna Duffin, *Women and Work in Pre-Industrial England* (London, Croom Helm, 1985); Sue Wright, 'Charmaids, housewyfes and hucksters: the employment of women in Tudor and Stuart Salisbury,' in Charles and Duffin, *Women and Work*, p. 116.

42. Michael Roberts, 'Images of work and gender', in Charles and Duffin, *Women and Work*, p. 140.

43. Wendy Thwaites, 'Women in the market place: Oxfordshire 1690–1800', *Midland History*, 9.

trades of mantua-making and millinery, but these trades were unregulated, and destined by the early nineteenth century to suffer flooded labour markets and sweating.[44]

If these cases would confirm a long-standing restricted and subordinate position for women workers, pre-dating any transition to industrial capitalism, the important position of the silk women of London provides the necessary exception. Women made up virtually the whole labour force of the silk industry in London at least until the end of the fifteenth century, and they carried out all procedures in the manufacture of narrow silks, ribbons, corses, and lace.[45] Broad silk weaving was introduced in Norwich from the sixteenth century, but its great expansion came with the Huguenots in 1685–7, when 100,000 arrived in the country and transformed the Spitalfields trade. The broad silk weavers from France brought a new division of labour where weaving was done by men, and winding, quilling and warping by women and children. Narrow silk weaving suffered a great decline in status, and the women occupied in the ancillary processes of broad silk weaving were low-paid workers whose job was also considered a suitable activity for workhouses and parish apprentice girls. This said, it was also true, however, that the silk women, though once exercising a monopoly over a luxury trade, had never held a guild status. In London itself they thus lacked the formal craft status and power of men in other trades; they also lacked the status given by the guilds in other major European towns engaged in silk manufacture.[46]

The decline of apprenticeship also forms a problematic divide, for though women were apprenticed, and took apprentices themselves, the meaning attached to this cannot be assumed to be the same as that for men. Recent research by Deborah Lantz on eighteenth-century Essex and Staffordshire reveals that quite high proportions of girls were apprenticed; one-tenth to one-third of apprentices were girls, depending on the type of indenture. But the skill content and the training component of many of the trades to which they were apprenticed were modest, and for girls in particular a training in values and behaviour was as much a part of the purpose of apprenticeship as any industrial training.[47] There were orthodox indenture procedures and apprenticeship patterns in the London silk trade, but these did not lead to the foundation of a guild. Apprenticeship for girls was about maintenance and general training before marriage, while boys underwent systematic industrial training and entered a guild.[48]

Women did themselves take apprentices but in small numbers. Very small numbers were recorded for Wiltshire and Warwickshire in the seventeenth and eighteenth centuries; apprenticeship, moreover, was predominantly recorded in the name of a couple, or of a husband alone.[49] In Oxford the number of

44. Mary Prior, 'Women and the urban economy: Oxford 1500–1800', in Prior, *Women in English Society*.

45. See K. E. Lacey, 'Women and work in fourteenth and fifteenth century London', in Charles and Duffin, *Women and Work*, pp. 55–7.

46. Lown, 'Gender and class', pp. 92–118.

47. Deborah Lantz, 'The role of apprenticeship in the education of eighteenth century women', unpublished paper in Warwick Working Papers in Social History – Workshops on Proto-industrial Communities, 1986.

48. Lown, 'Gender and class', p. 100.

49. Roberts, 'Images', p. 143.

widows taking apprentices varied from 0.2 per cent to as high as 8.5 per cent of the total apprenticeships taken out over the whole period 1601 to 1800.[50]

The argument for a reduction in female employment and job status with the contraction of domestic industry is problematic when placed against the substantial evidence of very limited opportunities in the pre-existing period. Pinning one's hopes for explanation to the vicissitudes of female apprenticeship is no more rewarding. Domestic industry, furthermore, poses its own special problems. On the one hand, the growth of the new consumer industries, the proto-industrial manufacturers, was at the cost of guild-regulated urban trades. Women, as well as men, in traditional industries lost out in the regional and industrial restructuring of eighteenth-century industry, but the new putting-out industries were also predominantly employers of women. They did not, on the whole, require formal apprenticeships, so that entry for women was easier. But equally, the whole point of the relocation of industry from town to country was the search for cheap labour, and merchants found an infinitely expandable pool in the large numbers of spinsters as well as the wives and daughters of agricultural labourers, miners, cottagers and squatters in rural areas, and in the still small but rapidly expanding unincorporated towns or suburbs. Women proliferated in these industries to be sure, but because they were cheap labour. Women endured the time discipline imposed on such domestic industries by market dates, raw material delivery times and putting-out networks – a discipline greatly amplified by the intensification of labour through the driving down of piece rates.

The close relationship between this domestic manufacture and the family economy is accepted *prima facie* as the reason for high participation rates of women. Industry carried out at home supposedly allowed a flexible integration of productive and domestic labour; indeed feminists have recently argued that pre-capitalist manufacture, because it was centred on the home, was more compatible with child-bearing and rearing and in particular breast-feeding.[51] But this is speculation; the extent of any such compatibility depended on work, status, industry and the economic cycle.[52] The experience of a late eighteenth-century female nail-worker was not the same as that of a pottery worker or buttonmaker; the vagaries of international markets brought bouts of highly intensive labour followed by phases of unemployment. Though women were the most important part of the proto-industrial workforce, the intensity of labour from a woman with young children even if she was working at home was not likely to be high. It was the numbers of these women available for some work at less than subsistence wages, the numbers of their children who made some contribution to work, and especially the numbers of youths, who yielded both high labour intensity and high productivity, which made household manufacture so lucrative to merchants. It was the life cycle of the labour force as well as its supply that was crucial. The expansion of the unregulated domestic industries may have enhanced women's employment opportunities, but there is little evidence that they enhanced their job status or wages. The highest paid female workers of the eighteenth century were girls and young women who worked away from home in workshops in the

50. Prior, 'Women in the urban economy', p. 109.
51. Brenner and Ramos, 'Rethinking women's oppression', p. 52.
52. Christoper Middleton, 'Women's labour and the transition to pre-industrial capitalism', in Charles and Duffin, *Women and Work*, pp. 198–200.

hand weaving, calico printing and pottery trades, metal and hardware workshops and small jenny factories.[53]

## WOMEN AND MECHANIZATION

One important case made for a general exclusion of women from productive work in the eighteenth century, and their concentration in positions of low pay and low skill, has been the differential effect of mechanization in the eighteenth century upon women. Several historians have drawn attention to the existence of an eighteenth-century 'machinery question', a machinery question before the introduction of the big power technologies and large-scale factories of the nineteenth century. Clapham argued long ago that spinning machinery, knitting and lockworking implements had left women's hands idle and family earnings curtailed in an age of hunger and high prices.[54] Eric Jones argued more recently that mechanization drove many of the handicraft districts into industrial oblivion, cutting deeply into the base of 'mother and daughter power' in the south and the east.[55] Adrian Randall has stressed that in the woollen industry, it was the first wave of mechanization in the eighteenth century which had the most sweeping changes for workers, especially women.[56] But this decline in employment for women was by no means final. To argue so would be to ignore the extent to which industrialization also involved the use of more, cheaper labour more intensively. Cheap women's labour, particularly in woollen and linen manufacture, was driven by mechanization to even lower wage levels, and became a source for new rural industries in lace, straw plait manufacture, glovemaking and shirt button making, boot and shoemaking, nailmaking and in the new urban sweated trades, especially in tailoring which flourished from the 1830s.

But the impact of technological change on women's employment cannot be assessed in the aggregate. It cannot be proved at the aggregate level that technological change creates either more or less employment. The issue needs to be examined at the level of the individual industries and individual innovations. Two fruitful industries of investigation and comparison in the eighteenth century are the textile industries and the metal trades. Both industries experienced substantial change in technology in the eighteenth century and we can examine in some detail the impact of technology on the division of labour and on women's productivity and employment.

### *Textiles*

Hand spinning was the archetype of women's employment in the eighteenth century. The women who practised the trade right across the country were

53. See Berg, *Age of Manufactures*, p. 173.

54. J. H. Clapham, *An Economic History of Modern Britain*, 3 vols (Cambridge University Press, 1938), vol. I, p. 183.

55. E. L. Jones, 'Constraints on economic growth in southern England 1650–1850', *Proceedings of the Third International Congress of Economic History* (Munich, 1965).

56. A.Randall, 'Worker resistance to machinery – the case of the English woollen industry', in Warwick Working Papers in Social History – Workshops on Proto-industrial Communities, 1986.

invariably among the lowest paid of workers. Eden in the 1790s found the earnings of the female domestic spinners of Essex, Norfolk, Oxfordshire, Leicestershire and Yorkshire ranged from 1s 6d to 3s a week, while the women who worked in three Yorkshire factories at the time earned 4s to 5s a week. Julia Mann described the hand spinners as 'an unorganised mass of sweated labour'.[57]

In the linen industry in Scotland in 1751 it was argued that a good spinner producing 1½ spindles a week in twelve-hour days 'can gain between 15 and 16d a week, but the price of corn at 3d a sack leaves a woman 1d a week for clothing, firing house rents, etc. Therefore she must starve.'[58] In spite of the low wages of spinners, constraints were felt in the supply of yarn, and three machines were invented which revolutionized spinning: Arkwright's water frame (1769), Hargreaves' jenny (1770) and Crompton's mule which came into use in the 1780s. All of these machines were used first in the cotton industry, but the jenny was soon introduced to the much larger woollen industry. The jenny was introduced among a range of new techniques in the woollen industry: scribbling and carding machinery, spinning machinery, the flying shuttle and the gig mill. All were introduced within a ten-year period to an industry which had previously known only one powered technique, its fulling mills. The jenny had an immediate, but differential impact on women workers. Randall explains that from 1781–96 to 1805 the number of women per cloth fell to 18 per cent of its former total; their job losses being due directly to the jenny and the slubbing billy.[59] The worst hit areas were agricultural and rural parishes. Eden described such an area where 'hand spinning has fallen into disuse . . . and the poor from the great reduction in the price scarcely have the heart to earn the little that can be made.'

Resistance to the machine was proverbial and widespread. Jennies were destroyed across Lancashire in 1769, and there were famous riots around Blackburn in 1779, which Wadsworth and Mann described as a state of 'guerilla warfare'. Resistance in the West Country was widespread, and it was not until the early 1790s that the machine spread in any numbers in Wiltshire and Gloucestershire. A magistrate in Somerset in 1790 described how he was called in by two manufacturers to protect their property:

> from the Depredations of a lawless Banditi of colliers and their wives, for the wives had lost their work to spinning engines . . . they advanced at first with much Insolence, avowing their intention of cutting to pieces the Machinery introduced in the woollen manufacture; which they suppose, if generally adopted, will lessen the demand for manual labour. The women became clamorous. The men were open to conviction and after some Expostulation were induced to desist from their purpose and return peaceably home.[60]

But the impact of the jenny on women's employment was not clear-cut. It was a great deal more damaging in agricultural areas than in textile centres.[61] The early

57. Frederick Eden, *The State of the Poor*, 5 vols (1797 and London, printed by J. Davis for B. and H. White, 1966), II, p. 385, III, pp. 739, 814, 876; Chambers, 'Rural domestic industries', p. 438.
58. Cited in Durie, 'Scottish linen industry', p. 159.
59. Randall, 'Labour and the Industrial Revolution', vol. II, p. 253.
60. Cited in J. L. and B. Hammond, *The Skilled Labourer 1760–1832* (1919 and New York, Longman, Green and Co., 1970), p. 149.
61. Randall, 'Labour and the Industrial Revolution', p. 253.

jenny of twelve to twenty spindles was operated by women in the home. It was part of the domestic system, the machine of the poor. When it came to the Holmfirth district of Yorkshire in 1776 it was 'hailed as a prodigy'. 'Every weaver learned to spin on the jenny, every clothier (or manufacturer) had more work in his house, and also kept a number of women spinning yarn for him in their cottages.'[62] In the context of fairly competitive yarn prices and little industrial concentration in the early Lancashire cotton industry, the machine benefited those who owned and operated the machines themselves. It was the cottage producers and those who ran small centralized workshops who reaped the first gains in efficiency from the jenny, and they did so until merchants and factors saw the gains to be had through setting up their own jenny factories.[63] Some women, mainly those in clothworking families, clearly gained from the jenny. It increased their productivity in proportion to the number of spindles, and wages initially increased.

But as William Reddy has argued, the very design of the machine lent itself to large-scale production, and large jennies usually of sixty to eighty spindles were soon combined with machine carding and installed in the so-called jenny factories. These jennies were still operated by women, but in going to the factories they had lost the entrepreneurial control of their own labour as well as early windfall gains to a male manufacturer. The women's wages fell; those who had been earning 8s to 9s a week on jennies of 24 spindles could now earn only from 4s to 6s. The early jennies were part of the domestic system, the machines of the poor; the larger ones were in the hands of merchant manufacturers. As a contemporary petition proclaimed: 'That the Jenneys are in the Hands of the Poor, and the Patent Machines are in the Hands of the Rich; and that the work is better manufactured by small Jenneys than by large ones.'[64]

Most of the jennies introduced into the woollen industry, especially in the south west, made their entry in times of booming trade in the early 1790s. But levels of resistance depended on more than the trade cycle; they depended on a gestation period for fostering popular resentment, and on levels of community and trade organizations in a district.[65]

The jenny had quite devastating effects on women's employment in some areas; but for some textile families at least, the early jenny was a veritable 'women's technology'. Another major spinning technology, the water frame, relied from the outset on the labour of children and especially girls and young women. The spinning mule, however, which was to become the most efficient technique, rapidly became an enclave of male labour. This machine, too, started as a hand technology, used in small workshops within the framework of the domestic system. Before power was applied it required substantial physical strength, and male labour was employed. But the technique was not competitive with the jenny or water frames, run by low-wage female labour. After power was applied the machine still required substantial stamina and the continued attendance of a skilled operative; more significantly, substantial amounts of capital were required to buy or build the machine, and engineering skills were required to maintain and

62. C. Aspin and S. Chapman, *James Hargreaves and the Spinning Jenny* (Preston, Helmshore Local History Society, 1964), p. 57.

63. William Reddy, *The Rise of Market Culture* (Cambridge University Press, 1985), ch. 2.

64. Pinchbeck, *Women Workers*, pp. 150–1.

65. Randall, 'West Country woollen industry', vol. I.

repair it. In spite of these obstacles, women could and did learn the skills and were quite widely used on the smaller mules even into the 1830s.[66] It was the Mule Spinners' Union, not the machine, which excluded women workers. It consistently struck over women workers from 1810, and in 1829 explicitly forbade women joining the union.

Silk throwing was carried out almost entirely by women before the introduction of throwing mills. Most worked in their own homes with simple throwing equipment made of wood. Though throwing mills existed from the first quarter of the eighteenth century, they began to replace home production significantly only from the later part of the century. Some throwers, mostly men with high earnings gained in putting work out, turned to building throwing mills employing over 100 workers, in rural areas close to the East End of London. The new machinery and skills also drew on women's and girls' labour, but now from the declining textile regions of Essex where high female unemployment and large numbers of workhouses provided a pool of cheap labour.[67]

The new spinning machinery undoubtedly destroyed a large source of casual female employment. But some women found more or less lucrative employment in the rationalized structures and mechanized processes introduced from the later eighteenth century.

Was women's experience in the weaving and finishing processes any different? Contrary to popular belief, hand weaving was not a skilled male pursuit, transposed to unskilled women workers only with the advent of the power loom and factory. It was widely practised by women, particularly in the silk industry, but also to a considerable extent in wool, linen and cotton. The techniques which threatened this employment were the Dutch engine or double engine loom, the Jacquard, the flying shuttle and the power loom.

In the silk industry, three quarters of the single hand weavers in Staffordshire and Warwickshire were women. Men played only a small part in the industry in Macclesfield, and it was there, in 1719, that women, boys and girls were the most violent assailants of ladies wearing calico gowns.[68] In Spitalfields, regulations against women weavers, other than widows or daughters supporting old parents, existed from early in the eighteenth century, but these lapsed or were revived according to the demand for labour. Women used both single and double engine looms in the 1760s, to such an extent that this was a cause of the great hostility of male weavers in 1769. And women were again widely employed in weaving in the Napoleonic Wars.[69]

Across the silk, woollen and cotton industries spread the introduction of new weaving technologies, particularly the broad loom, the Jacquard loom, the double engine loom and the Dutch loom. Judy Lown has shown that in Spitalfields women were mainly employed in plain or narrow silk weaving, while men worked

66. W. Scott-Taggart, 'Crompton's invention and subsequent development of the mule', *Journal of the Textile Institute*, 18 (1927) 28; H. Catling, 'The development of the spinning mule', *Textile History*, 9 (1978) 43; E. Baines, *A History of the Cotton Manufacture in Great Britain* (1835 and London, H. Fisher, R. Fisher and P. Jackson, 1966).

67. Lown, 'Gender and class', pp. 123, 144–59.

68. G. B. Hertz, 'The English silk industry in the 18th century', *English Historical Review*, 24 (1909).

69. Dorothy George, *London Life in the Eighteenth Century* (London, K. Paul, Trench, Trubner, 1925), pp. 184–6.

the broad looms brought over from the continent for larger silk pieces, then on the Jacquard from the early nineteenth century for fancy work. Both the techniques and their products were regarded as more highly skilled, and women became associated with subsidiary roles in silk weaving and ribbon weaving.[70] But nevertheless, by the early nineteenth century, women were doing broad silk weaving from Macclesfield to Spitalfields.[71] Broad loom and Jacquard loom weaving, however, also brought new categories of employment. The drawboys and drawgirls were employed in fancy weaving to 'read' a pattern on to the cards, but this was considered menial labour. At the first opportunity (such as the edict in France in 1786, permitting women to weave) the drawgirls abandoned their arduous and undervalued employment and took to the loom. The effect of the shortage of ancillary labour was to hasten the development of the Jacquard system of automatic design control.[72]

The introduction of the double engine loom in Macclesfield in the 1730s was greeted with rioting by female button workers. The Dutch engine loom was the occasion for separating the Coventry ribbon-weaving industry into a skilled male section using the new looms, and an unskilled female section using single hand looms. But this exclusion operated only until shortly after 1815 when the hold of larger manufacturers was challenged by small capitalists employing cheap labour, notably women, on the machines.[73] Women weavers were common in the Yorkshire and the West Country woollen industry, though crisis years provided occasions for attempts to exclude them from the use of the more efficient double looms, if not from the trade itself. Over the course of the eighteenth century the double loom was increasingly worked by women, youths and apprentices in the West Country. In the later 1790s women became weavers in large numbers, but by the early nineteenth century men displaced from scribbling and finishing processes turned in high proportions to the loom. Where, before mechanization, 57 per cent of the male workforce went into weaving, by 1828 this was as high as 84 per cent.[74] But women were also a substantial part of the weaving workforce among the illegal weavers put to the flying shuttle or spring loom in the early loom shops. Several clothiers from Yorkshire and the West Country also reported to the 1806 Woollen Committee that women and girls were employed weaving, and wives and daughters as well as men used the loom in cottage industry.[75]

The experiences of the linen and cotton industries were no different. When linen spinning passed out of the hands of female domestic spinners, these turned increasingly to hand weaving, and one-third of all the weavers in the south Scotland linen industry by the beginning of the nineteenth century were women and children. In the early cotton industry the divisions were to manifest

70. Lown, 'Gender and class', pp. 109–18
71. Select Committee on Apprentices, PP 1812–13.
72. Daryl Hafter, 'The programmed brocade loom and the decline of the drawgirl', in M. M. Trescott, ed., *Dynamos and Virgos Revisited: Women and Technological Change in History* (Metuchen, NJ, Scarecrow Press, 1979), p. 56.
73. S. Timmins, ed., *The Resources . . . of Birmingham and the Midland Hardware District* (London, R. Hardwicke, 1866), pp. 179–89.
74. Randall, 'West Country woollen industry', vol. II, pp. 263, 306.
75. Select Committee on the Woollen Manufacture, PP 1806, testimonies of John Platt, W. Howard, Stephen Smith.

themselves both in machinery, and in geography. Women were employed in the less skilled country branches of the trade using the ordinary hand loom, not in the urban smallware trade where master weavers used the Dutch loom in large workshops.[76] Women, children, Irish migrants and the aged were concentrated in the coarser, less skilled, branches of cotton weaving, and it was their jobs which were threatened by the new power looms, looms which paradoxically also drew on the labour of young women. Male craft workers weaving fine or figured cloth had nothing to fear from the machine until well into the second third of the nineteenth century.[77] The power loom, like the spinning jenny before it, did not set unskilled women against male craft workers. It set women against women, especially young women working in the shops or mills against older married women working at home.

Finishing processes in the cloth manufacture were frequently skilled male crafts, though girls and young women were widely employed as assistants, particularly in bleaching and calico printing. Boys apprenticed to the woollen manufacture were taught the highly skilled parts of the trade - dyeing, putting cloth into the fulling mill, and sorting wool, only in the last two years of their apprenticeship. Girls and women performed most other processes in the manufacture, but rarely these.[78] New techniques introduced into finishing processes clearly affected male employment. The two techniques that fuelled the classic Luddite attacks, the gig mill and shearing frame, displaced six out of seven and three out of four men respectively.[79] But it was calico printing techniques which demonstrated the most remarkable gender typing of technological development. In this case more mechanized processes were bypassed and labour intensive technologies specifically developed along with an advanced division of labour in order to tap a female labour force. Four such technical innovations were developed over the second third of the eighteenth century. The first was 'picotage' or the patterning of printing blocks with pins or studs tapped into the blocks. This was delicate work, for one large block contained 63,000 pins, but it was a job done by women who earned 12–14s a week after their apprenticeship. Another labour-intensive process introduced at the time was 'pencilling' or the hand-painting of patterns directly on to the cloth. This was performed by women who worked in long terraces of cottage-like workshops under the superintendence of 'mistresses'.

> In the shop each woman had her piece suspended before her with a supply of hair pencils of different degrees of fineness according to the size of the object . . . to be touched, and containing colour . . . according to the pattern required . . . a good workwoman might earn £2.00 a week, though it was likely most earned a lot less.

The style of patterns changed little from year to year. This laborious work was

76. A. P. Wadsworth and J. De L. Mann, *The Cotton Trade and Industrial Lancashire, 1600–1780* (Manchester University Press, 1931), pp. 285, 325, 323, 336.
77. N. Murray, 'A social history of the Scottish handloom weavers 1790–1850' (unpublished D.Phil. thesis, University of Strathclyde, 1976), pp. 55–62; M. Berg, 'The introduction and diffusion of the power loom' (unpublished MA dissertation, University of Sussex, 1972).
78. See testimonies of wide range of clothiers in Select Committee on Woollen Manufacture.
79. Randall, 'West Country woollen industry'.

done by women, and so was regarded as an unskilled process which bypassed the employment of the highly paid craftsmen who engraved and used wooden printing blocks and, after 1760, copper plates. Copper-plate printing, introduced in 1760, followed by roller-printing in 1785, constituted the real technical improvements of the industry, but they required the use of highly organized and highly paid 'gentlemen journeymen', so that such manufacturers as Peel bypassed these and instead organized 'protofactories' using elementary labour-intensive techniques and extensive division of labour, along with special training and disciplining of workers. The scarcity, together with the very high status, of skilled calico printers was the main stimulus behind the attempts by entrepreneurs to look for alternative methods of production on which they could employ low-paid women and girls.[80]

## *The Metal Trades*

The industrial revolution is usually conceived of in terms of power-driven technologies and large-scale factories in the textile industries, and a transposition of work from male craftsmen to a female factory proletariat. However, as I have shown in the case of textile workers, many of the techniques introduced were developed initially on a small scale within the framework of the domestic system, and women had dominated the industry long before the appearance of power-driven machinery. The development of the metal trades was another important aspect of eighteenth- and early-nineteenth-century industrialization. On the one hand, there were the classic puddling and blast-furnace technologies of iron processing; on the other, a range of new technologies in the working of metals, new technologies which, in the nineteenth century, would be associated with the engineering industry. In the eighteenth century the metal trades were much more diffuse and less specialized, producing goods ranging from swords, cutlery and agricultural implements to hardware goods, guns, tools, machinery and 'toys'.

Metals or small hardware goods and ornamental ware have usually been assumed to be the preserve of the male craftsman; on the face of it, not an unreasonable assumption given the historic association of the engineering industry with male workers, other than in wartime. Even in 1980, the engineering industry, while providing 13 per cent of total employment in Britain, afforded only 7 per cent of women's employment.[81] The male preponderance in metal-related industries perhaps goes back to the religious and mythical association of the armourer and the warrior – Hephaestus and Achilles. The forge historically conjured up images of strength, power and domination, and the very term engineering originally applied only to those in the military profession. Carlo Cipolla has pointed out how, in the fourteenth century, the workmen who made the bells which tolled out the rhythms of peaceful village and town life also made the cannon that continually blasted apart the peace tolled by the bells.

80. S. D. Chapman and S. Chassagne, *European Textile Printers in the Eighteenth Century: a Study of Peel and Oberkampf* (London, Heinemann Educational, Pasold Fund, 1981), p. 95–96, 194.

81. Cynthia Cockburn, 'Caught in the wheels: the high cost of being a female cog in the male machinery of engineering', in D. Mackenzie and J. Wajeman, *The Social Shaping of Technology* (Milton Keynes, Open University Publications, 1985), p. 55.

Seventeenth- and eighteenth-century developments in gun manufacture and in the great arsenals were technically interrelated with the early hardware and engineering trades. Sophistication in the technology of producing guns also entailed new forms of fighting. As Cipolla has argued, the whole art of gunnery produced a new type of warrior – cold-blooded and technically inclined – who in the middle of the fight had to stop and carry out a series of measurements and calculations; he was no longer the hot-blooded warrior of the old days.[82]

But women also worked in significant numbers across the metal trades – in large numbers in some, not at all in others. Technical change in the eighteenth century in these trades in contrast to textiles was almost entirely associated with the workshop and domestic manufacture. What did this high-productivity household and workshop manufacture mean for the women who worked in these trades?

First, innovation did not displace the household workshop. The earliest working equipment of the metal trades were anvil, hammer, file and grindstone. If we look specifically at the metal trades of Birmingham, major eighteenth-century innovations were the stamp, press and draw-bench, and the lathe. These tools, along with the division of labour, certainly did combine to save time and effort. Shelbourne cited mixed metals and stamping machinery used with the division of labour to produce cheap buttons. And there were besides 'an infinity of smaller improvements which each workman has and keeps secret from the rest'. In Britain's Soho works, it was not just the skilled artisans who contributed to success but 'the number of ingenious mechanical contrivances they avail themselves of, by means of Water Mills, which much facilitates their work and saves a great portion of time and labour'. In Birmingham, machinery was, however, in the main hand operated, only supplemented in some cases by horse and water power. Steam power, though the most famous product of the town, was hardly ever used there before 1800, and by 1815 there were still only forty engines in the town.[83]

Evidence that the Birmingham toy trades made use of apprentices, non-apprenticed and women's and children's labour from the start in many of the processes makes it difficult to assess the impact of new technology on skills and the status and structure of the labour force. Apprenticeship and the sexual division of labour were not necessarily any index of changes in the labour process. Certainly the new technology did affect the division of labour in the trades. Contemporaries argued simultaneously that the techniques used in Birmingham did not reduce the skill or labour required in production processes, and that the new machinery allowed extensive use of child labour. Taylor and Garbett, for instance, reported that Birmingham machines reduced the manual labour and enabled boys to do men's work. Shelbourne cited a division of labour that made work so simple that 'five times in six, children of 6 or 8 years old do it as well as men.'[84] And Dean Tucker described the close connection between machinery and child labour in Birmingham: 'When a Man stamps on the metal Button by means of an Engine, a

82. This point about the association of technology with war was made by Cynthia Cockburn. Also see Carlo Cipolla, *Guns, Sails and Empires* (London, Collins, 1965), for a development of the argument.
83. E. Hopkins, 'Working hours and conditions during the Industrial Revolution: a reappraisal', *Economic History Review*, 35 (1982).
84. Edward Fitzmaurice, *Life of William Earl of Shelbourne*, vol. I, 1737–1766 (London, Macmillan and Co., 1875), p. 404.

Child stands by him to place the Button in readiness to receive the Stamp, and to remove it when received and then to place another.'[85] But equally, the differentiation of existing trades and the proliferation of a number of new trades reflected changes in product as well as in processes. It is particularly difficult to gain any clear idea of the sexual division of labour in trades which displayed such varied industrial structures. It is said, however, that the adoption of machines for stamping and piercing extended the range of female employment, especially for young girls.[86] And it was recognized that women's work was widespread in the japanning and the stamping and piercing trades. Girls were specifically requested in advertisements for button-piercers, annealers, and stoving and polishing work in the japanning trades. Another advertisement for button-burnishers in 1788 also sought 'a woman that has been used to looking over and carding plain, plated and gilted buttons, also a few women that have been used to grind steels, either at foot lathes or mill'.

The delicacy of the work in buttonmaking and piercing, as well as in the hand-painting of designs, was regarded as the special province of women and girls with their smaller hands and the deftness and concentration already acquired at household needlework. The lacquering and japanning trades required stove management and even in the nineteenth century it was women who worked in the trade. The small lacquering rooms in the brass trades, only twelve by fifteen feet and eleven feet high, characteristically contained a couple of iron plate stoves and five to six women workers.[87]

In the Black-Country trades there was no lighter alternative work open to women, and they worked beside the men in heavy industry – on the pit-bank, in the nail manufacture, and in the manufacture of chains, saddlery, harness and hollow ware. But in many of these trades, and in particular in nailmaking, they had long been degraded workers. The most noted women workers of the West Midlands trades were the nailers. Their subservience in this degraded and poverty-stricken trade reflected the wider subservience of their sex. William Hutton, on his travels in 1741, provided an exemplary male image of this workforce.

> In some of these shops I observed one, or more females, stript of their upper garment, and not overcharged with their lower, wielding the hammer with all the grace of the sex. The beauties of their face were rather eclipsed by the smut of the anvil; or in poetical phrase, the tincture of the forge had taken possession of those lips, which might have been taken by the kiss. Struck with the novelty, I enquired, 'whether the ladies of this country shod horses?' but was answered, with a smile, 'they are nailers'. A fire without head, a nailer of a fair complexion, or one who despises the tankard, are equally rare among them.[88]

Yet certain women did have a knowledge of a wide range of trades. Many

85. Cited in Roy Porter, *English Society in the Eighteenth Century* (Harmondsworth, Penguin, 1982), pp. 213–14.

86. D. C. Eversley, 'Industry and trade, 1500–1800', *Victoria History of the Counties of England: Warwickshire*, vol. VII (London, Constable and Co., 1965), pp. 110–11.

87. See Berg, *Age of Manufactures*, ch. 13.

88. W. Hutton, *A History of Birmingham to the End of the Year 1780* (Birmingham, Pearson and Rolleson, 1781).

women carried on with their husbands' businesses after their death, and though they may have employed some journeymen they would themselves have had to have a great deal of practical experience and knowledge to make a success of running what were in the main small artisan businesses. These women ran the businesses not only where one might have expected women's work – as in toy, button and bucklemaking, and japanning. But widows and daughters also appeared in strength in the iron business, in plumbing and glazing, in the brass founding and pewtering trades, and among the hammer, anvil and edgetool making trades (see appendix 3.1). A survey of *Aris's Gazette* from 1752 to 1790 indicates that women were taking over husbands' businesses or dealing with various problems which arose in the trades over a wide range of processes. Notices appeared over this whole period from nine female ironmongers, eight plumbers and glaziers, seven buttonmakers and seven bucklemakers, six watchmakers, five brass manufacturers and braziers, five toolmakers, and five chain and toymakers. There were notices from three women running ironworks, three female plateworkers, two nailworkers, two women running coalworks, as well as individual locksmiths, japanners, wireworkers, and file cutters[89] (see appendix 3.2).

Women occupied an important place in the eighteenth-century Birmingham toy trades, as workers and employers. And though the evidence available does not indicate the extent to which there was a 'sexual division of labour' between individual trades and processes, it does indicate an economic and social subservience to men, for their wages were much lower, and they appear as tradeswomen and owners of business in their own right in effect only where they were continuing the business of a deceased husband or father. But we cannot deny the knowledge and expertise possessed by such women in these trades, for their businesses were mainly small-scale or at most medium-scale enterprises. And success for women as much as for men in these Birmingham trades was dependent on skill and on knowledge.

In the nineteenth century women were still employed over a wide range of processes in the Birmingham trades, but these were by and large concentrated in the newer, lighter or more unskilled branches. Women did the lacquering in the brass shops, japanning in the tin plateware manufacture, and barrel boring in the gun trade. In the button trade there was a division between the old and more skilled branches such as the metal and pearl button section which employed men, and the new covered and linen button section, which employed women. Men made high-class jewellery, and women and girls were left to the cheap end of the trade in gilt articles and chains. In stamping and piercing the tools were fitted into the press by male toolworkers who also attended to the condition of the tools in cutting the larger stamped work. But women worked even with the large presses, though girls were left to cut out smaller examples of the work. When women were employed in piercing and cutting-out work, they received only 8–12s a week and girls got 6–8s; while the toolmaker who superintended the work claimed 30–40s.

Surveys of education in Birmingham carried out in the mid nineteenth century found that while half the working girls surveyed were in button manufacture and in service, the button trade was strictly subdivided by gender and age. In pearl button manufacture, for example, men cut the pearl from shell then turned it on a

89. Berg, *Age of Manufactures*, p. 313.

lathe, women drilled holes and polished, boys filled edges and girls carded. In the metal button trade, little button girls from the age of nine were employed as 'putters-in', feeding the press with raw materials. They were paid at 1s to 2s 6d a week, while women got 7s to 10s. Women's and children's wages in the trade fell during the nineteenth century as mechanization cheapened piecework.[90]

It seems, on the basis of close study of the textile and the metal manufacturers, that there is no straightforward case to be made for a great transition in women's role in the workplace in response to mechanization. In the nineteenth century, as before in the eighteenth, women worked at a broad range of processes. In textiles attempts were made from early in the eighteenth century to exclude them from using more advanced techniques, and large numbers of women were indeed left behind by the revolution in technology to continue their traditional reliance on hand processes used at home. But the attempts at exclusion were rarely successful, for the market and profitability ultimately set the terms of industrial structure; while large numbers of women ultimately lost out on domestic employment in textiles, others were drawn in to use the new machines in workshops and factories, usually at lower wages than their male counterparts.

The metal industries tell a different but related tale of widespread women's employment in both centuries. The new techniques only reinforced gender divisions there in the trades from early in the eighteenth century. The celebrated female nailworkers were sweated women workers by the mid eighteenth century, long before any mechanization. But women's wages, working conditions and job status relative to those in the rest of the country did decline in the nineteenth century, not so much in response to mechanization, however, as to a dramatic change in the fortunes of the Birmingham traders, from new growth sector to relatively declining industry. Cost-cutting rationalization, not the windfall gains of a new industry, governed job opportunities for women as well as men.

## THE ORGANIZATION OF PRODUCTION AND WOMEN'S COMMUNITY NETWORKS

The difficulty of assigning a clear-cut transition in women's roles to the introduction of machinery also arises in examining the relationship between the organization of production and women's trade organization. It is difficult to uncover very much about the role of women in eighteenth-century trade societies. We occasionally uncover some evidence of female membership, but little else. And this evidence tells us nothing of the greater part of women's employment in those trades with no formal organization or in the rural domestic industries. Traditional assumptions of low levels of worker organization among dispersed rural labourers have been discounted by recent research, which has demonstrated the high levels of organization among country workers, not only in industrial disputes but in food and enclosure riots. Research has shown bonds formed among agricultural, urban industrial and rural industrial workers. Protests against enclosure were frequently led by workers from the towns, or

90. C. Heward, 'Home, school and work: changes in growing up in the Birmingham jewellery quarter, 1815–1881' (unpublished MA thesis, University of Warwick, 1982).

industrial workers squatting on the commons. Opposition to enclosure was strongest where open fields and rural industry coincided, and the decline of food rioting in areas of southern England has been attributed to the decline of the industrial communities themselves.

Women were an important section of these rural communities, and frequently played a leading part in local custom and protest; there is evidence that they led food riots, organized gleaning, mobbed poor-law officials and played an important part in instances of rough music or charivari and seasonal rites. There is little evidence indeed to tell us of their role in the details of organizing production, though sense tells us that in largely female workforces, networks formed among women must have been vital in the training and recruitment of the labour force. Certainly in woollen and worsted spinning, women acted as intermediaries, 'putting out yarn' to their neighbours.[91]

I have tried to demonstrate so far that the idea of a fundamental transformation in women's employment and skills with the separation of work and home rests on simple assumptions about pre-industrial and early industrial household production. Sexual divisions and hierarchy already present in many early eighteenth century household industries were sometimes reinforced even within the household by mechanization. Or they could be reassembled in new ways by both mechanization and outside workshop or factory production which in the process brought some, at least short-term, opportunities to some women. The implications of eighteenth-century mechanization and reorganization of production within and outside the home really cannot be assessed outside its context in growing and declining sectors, and competitive or monopolistic structures. The household economy as it has been understood is a myth. But dissected as a changing part of a dynamic process of industrial and capitalist growth or decline it can help to reveal undiscovered directions and possibilities.

A historical assumptions of static structures and even a static past have entailed rather uninteresting unidirectional accounts of women's subordination. They have also reinforced the faithful rendering of the creed of community. Much has been written about the close community networks, the corporate identity, the plebeian culture and the moral economy of pre-industrial England, but the connection between the world of the local community and the world of work has been less frequently explored.[92] Kinship and community have been equated with notions of mutuality, but this has been assumed, not investigated. By extension, it has also been assumed that the cohesiveness of the local community and with this the social and organizational role of women was broken by the advance of capitalist competition and the market. Where once home and local community formed the location and framework of labour, its harmony and corporate identity were said to dissolve under the impact of population growth and migration, as well as the movement of production outside the home. But this assumption of close ties among workers, and especially among women, needs to be examined anew; it is only one side of the story. For equally there were many divisions, and

91. These arguments are developed in pp. 164–7 of my book, *Age of Manufactures*.

92. An exemplary study is G. M. Sider, 'Christmas mumming and the New Year in Outport Newfoundland', *Past and Present*, 71 (1976) 102–25.

these divisions may well have been even greater before the late eighteenth century than they were to be after.

There are many strong arguments for the importance of community. Neighbourhood and community ties structured the work unit of the rural handicraft industries. The rural workforce was certainly not an unorganized one, in contrast to the urban, and in addition, as Chambers argued over twenty years ago, 'the values of the domestic worker were also the values of the society in which he lived'. It was the local communities which hid the Luddites and which in the East and West Midlands supported the resistance of their framework knitters and silk weavers to the advance of machinery.

Some of these community ties were based in agrarian relations, and several historians, including Keith Snell, J. M. Neeson, J. M. Martin and Pat Hudson, have recently argued for the close interdependence between common right and the structures and extent of domestic industry. They have also demonstrated how closely connected was the decline of rural manufacturing with enclosure. The destruction of one of the major institutions of community – common right – seemed to break the resilience of the handicraft sector. But as Keith Snell so cogently argues in his *Annals of the Labouring Poor*, other institutions came into play – notably the settlement provisions of the Old Poor Law. Outdated legal provisions on settlement rarely relevant at the time they were introduced in the seventeenth century, came into play in the later eighteenth century. They transformed a relatively mobile rural population in the early eighteenth century into the 'stay-at-home' agricultural labourer of the nineteenth century. The enforcement of these settlement laws ended the earlier ease in gaining settlements, forcing high proportions of the rural workforce to take their fathers' settlements. Snell argues that in the case of the artisan and proto-industrial trades, this perpetuated families practising certain trades in the same place over the generations. They developed familiarity with parochial issues stretching back in to their family history, 'creating a community and political consciousness which could never have existed to the same degree when up to sixty percent of village populations might disappear every twelve years through migration and low life expectancy'.[93]

The juxtaposition of community mentality versus individual action and of moral economy against the market is difficult to pursue in any clear-cut manner in discussion of changing industrial work structures in the eighteenth century. There is certainly a new and strong tradition of research rekindling the debate on the moral economy, and now exploring this in industrial contexts. William Reddy has contrasted the 'language of the crowd' with the 'language of market culture', demonstrating the existence of a community of shared values and expectations, beliefs and attitudes among eighteenth- and early nineteenth-century textile workers. But gradually this language of the crowd began to recede. Market language, categories and culture became the public code, limiting industrial action and political behaviour to a narrow range of monetary calculations.[94] Applying this model plus Thompson's concept of the 'moral economy of the poor'

93. Snell, *Annals*, ch. 7.

94. Reddy, *Rise of Market Culture*. Also see Reddy, 'The textile trade and the language of the crowd at Rouen 1752–1851', *Past and Present*, 74 (1977), 62–89.

to the West Country, Randall has also argued for the common basis of strikes and food riots in a strong community consensus. Trade consciousness was thus synonymous with community consciousness.[95] But the explanatory value of this sharp dichotomy between the area of moral imperatives and the market breaks down in areas undergoing industrial change. The dichotomy raises the thorny question of the definition of community.

There were divisions between artisans with a long and stable stake in the community or in the trade society, and casual outworkers in temporary residence. There were divisions created by the differential impact of international price fluctuations on neighbouring communities producing slightly different products. There were divisions inherent in the division of labour itself, especially the division between men and women workers. There was, in addition, no reason, as has been argued so cogently by Olivia Harris, why the existence of kin or community should imply a behaviour code based on mutuality, morality or custom.

> Both the language of kinship and the way co-residence is represented, contain underlying assumptions about the exclusion of economic relations based on direct exchange and precise calculation, and the presence of other relations of generosity without calculation. This ideology . . . should not, however, be confused with what relations actually obtain between kin and non kin . . . The degree to which people exhibit such behaviour to each other is a matter for investigation rather than assumption.[96]

Community was not, furthermore, something simply associated with a pre-industrial past, something bound up with custom and common right and outside of interaction with the market. Nor was it external and unchanging in the way that community is often invoked against the market and industrialization. Community and the custom to which it is related is, rather, a living product – it is not egalitarian, nor is it free of relations of power and subordination. Divisions of interest within any one community may be marked, yet the 'interests of the community' be defined in terms of the group which at that moment wielded some authority.[97] Community was frequently invoked, for instance, when the livelihoods of skilled and craft workers were at stake; rarely when those of squatters, casual labourers and women were threatened. These people were regarded as mobile, anonymous, 'without community'. The creation of new products, the use of new techniques and access to a whole range of markets could form the basis for different types of community – such as existed in eighteenth-century Birmingham and its hinterland. Here, close family connections between town and

95. See debate between D. E. Williams 'Morals, markets and the English crowd in 1766', *Past and Present*, 104 (1984) and A. Charlesworth and A. J. Randall, 'Morals, markets and the English crowd – a comment', *Past and Present* (forthcoming). Also see A. J. Randall 'The industrial moral economy of the Gloucestershire weavers in the eighteenth century', in John Rule, ed., *Labour and Trade Unionism in Eighteenth Century England* (London, Longman, forthcoming).

96. Olivia Harris, 'Households and their boundaries', *History Workshop Journal*, 13 (Spring 1982), 146–9.

97. These points were raised by David Washbrook in his talk, 'Markets and custom in 18th century South India', in a session on 'Market custom and moral economy', Warwick Workshop on Proto-industrial Communities III, Custom Culture and Community, July 1985.

country, and rural traditions of partible inheritance appear to have allowed the easy transmission of skills and capital. Industrial concentration and monopolization of the market cut off the possibility of such flexible community structures in the West Country, and the textile community there became one entrenched in its own traditions, traditions which were, however, the artifact of fairly recent processes of monopoly and proletarianisation.

The imposition of a strict dichotomy between the community and the market is particularly difficult when applied to women workers. Women have been traditionally identified with the idiom of the mutuality of the family and the community. They are assumed to accept this code of behaviour, and the priority they give to family and home places them at a disadvantage in the labour market. They behave, in other words, like Chayanovian peasants, placing family before profitability, when male workers have 'learned the rules of the game' in operating the labour market to their best advantage. But just as Chayanov's peasant has been dissected and found to be mythical,[98] so must the sceptic question our traditional attitudes to identities and communities among women.[99] Bonds among women and female networks were closely tuned to the family lifecycle. The large youthful labour force of early industrial England made up predominantly of girls and young women cannot be assumed to have found its sole priorities and connections within the 'family economy' of married women and mothers. The changing historical divisions and networks created among working women with the impact of both the new industrial work opportunities and the industrial decline that characterized the eighteenth century need to be examined before historians can pronounce on women's identity with the values of the community.

Another arena where the dichotomy between custom and commerce breaks down is in the area of consumption. Women were central to informal popular protests on issues concerning consumption, in the food riots and in later protests over the adulteration of food. They carried over these traditions of protest in their role in enforcing moral codes of behaviour and sexual relations within their communities.[100] But they also organized consumption in a manner which brought the community and the market together.

Economics was at the basis of mutuality just as much as of the market. In eighteenth-century England the community consumption which Hans Medick had attached to E. P. Thompson's 'plebeian culture' was economic both in its manifestation and in its motivation. Time and especially money spent by the poor on cultural ritual, gifts, feasts and luxury consumer display were a form of 'social

98. See M. Harrison, 'Chayanov and the economics of the Russian peasantry', *Journal of Peasant Studies*, 2 (July 1975).

99. For analysis and research in this mould see J. Baker Miller, 'Ties to others', in M. Evans, ed., *The Woman Question* (London, Fontana, 1982); M. P. Ryans, 'The power of women's network', in J. L. Newton et al., *Sex and Class in Women's History* (London, Routledge, 1983); E. Ross, 'Survival networks: women's neighbourhood and sharing in London before World War I', *History Workshop Journal*, 15 (Spring 1983) ; R. Whipp and M. Grieco, 'Family and the workplace', *Warwick Economic Papers*, 239 (1983).

100. See Sian Moore, 'Women's politics within the industrial community: Bradford, West Yorkshire, 1780–1845', Warwick Working Papers in Social History – Workshops on Proto-industrial Communities, 1986.

exchange', a means of strengthening bonds of neighbourhood and friendship.[101]

Anthropologists such as Mary Douglas have also treated consumer goods as an information system or means of communication, 'A household's expenditures on other people gives an idea of whether it is isolated or well involved.' Consumption, and particularly luxury consumption, convey the fine gradations of social class, age and hierarchy as well as cementing particular kinds of degrees of social relationship. Goods are 'the medium, less objects of desire than threads of a veil that disguises the social relations under it'.[102]

It can be argued that this consumer culture was very important to the community networks formed among women in the eighteenth century. The household production unit was also a unit of consumption. The consumer needs of the household had to be maintained and organized. To what extent was it women who organized household consumption, and indulged in private and social luxury consumption? We know this was the case in early twentieth-century Europe. In London, wives' skills and tastes could do as much as husband's wages to determine how comfortably their families lived. Among the Amsterdam seamstresses the first task of a married woman was housekeeping. She saved on the family budget by sewing clothes for her family, and tidiness became ' the most valued quality in housekeeping'.[103]

In eighteenth-century England too, there is at least indirect evidence to show that women organized a large proportion of household consumption. It is evident that many of the new consumer industries reproduced goods which women already made for household consumption. Women's hands were busied producing yarn, stockings and clothing for their families. They also took pride in their labour-intensive efforts to bypass the market and so to clothe their families better and with a smaller outlay of precious cash earnings.

In both England and Scotland most linen was made by private families for their own use. Though needlework and cooking had existed throughout the early modern period as the essential elements of housewifery performed by women, the demands made by these on women's time became more intensive and a higher degree of skill was called for as new lighter materials in grades of cotton and linen, and new furnishings and cooking implements, were introduced over the course of the eighteenth century. The amount and the variety of household consumption increased, and women's household tasks increased alongside. A woman's labour-power was an important asset, but her consuming power for the household was also an asset of rising significance in the eighteenth century. It is no mere coincidence that many of the new domestic manufactures of the seventeenth and eighteenth centuries were also consumer industries catering to a mass market, and that their labour force was made up predominantly of women.[104]

It has been argued that the so-called 'home market' of the eighteenth century

101. Hans Medick, 'Plebeian culture in the transition to capitalism', in R. Samuel and G. Stedman Jones, *Culture, Ideology and Politics* (London, Routledge, 1982), p. 92.

102. M. Douglas and B. Isherwood, *The World of Goods: Towards an Anthropology of Consumption* (1978 and Harmondsworth, Penguin, 1980), pp. II, 202.

103. Ross, 'Survival networks', pp. II, 14.

104. Joan Thirsk, *Economic Policy and Projects: The Development of Consumer Society in Early Modern England* (Oxford University Press, 1978), pp. 22–23.

was largely a women's market. The consumer industries of the early Industrial Revolution were 'those in which women took the decision to consume: the cotton, woollen, linen and silk industries, the pottery industry, the cutlery industry, the Birmingham small trades.'[105] But discussions of consumption in the eighteenth century are thus far almost wholly tied to the evidence of inventories, and these have been left largely by those from established craftsmen or tradesmen backgrounds and middle incomes or higher. Such evidence cannot give us clues to labourers' consumption or the mass markets of the poor. What we have to say about the growth of consumption and the market consumer culture is thus tied to a relatively limited social group. It is also the case that, though social status and not just basic needs was behind much of this consumption, the character and composition of a range of consumer goods varied enormously between social groups.[106] The relationship of women to this consumer market would similarly take on this complexity of interaction with production and consumption. Among some social groups labour-intensive and costly home-production of commodities was valued more than the option to purchase those goods in the market. Both, however, were manifestations of consumption. Consumption reveals the great range of connections between the home and the market which the rise of market culture helped to create, rather than to destroy.

We can ask moreover to what extent women's organization of this household consumption actually created a consumer culture centred on the marketplace. Household management was also dependent on a knowledge of the price, a knowledge acquired through long-term participation in the market, and through the information acquired in the networks formed among consumers, particularly women. It was this process of haggling and bargaining in the markets, according to 'that sort of rough equality which though not exact, is sufficient for carrying on the business of common life' which Adam Smith argued actually determined the extent to which the value of commodities accorded with their price.[107]

The consumer culture did not contradict the household economies and production of early industrial artisans. It was but one part of household management. Similarly these proto-industrial workers and consumers were not obviously aware of any special distinction between the market and the moral economy. Many of the seasonal activities, rituals and customs were important sources of income in themselves, making it worthwhile leaving off waged work for one or more days at a time. Where waged work and household management intertwined, other time and money economies took their own priorities, and they frequently concerned female members of the workforce.

Community relations and networks were integrated into the priorities of workplace relations not just, as in earlier periods, because the household was both the unit of production and the unit of residence. In the early industrial economy of the eighteenth century, consumption was the activity which bound community and capitalism together. The new industries produced consumer goods; they transformed goods formerly produced (largely by women) within the household

105. N. McKendrick, 'Home demand, and economic growth', p. 197.

106. L. Weatherill, 'Consumer behaviour, the ownership of goods and early industrialisation', paper to Warwick Workshop on Proto-industrial Communities, Custom, Culture and Community, 1985, to be published in *Continuity and Change* (1986).

107. Adam Smith, *Wealth of Nations*, vol. I, p. 49.

to meet basic needs into commodities to be sold on a world market. The new industries also tapped a women's labour force, a labour force which brought valuable skills and social networks. It was also a cheap labour force, bound as it was within the household. But the communities into which this capitalist production penetrated themselves became consumer and market communities. Social status and participation, custom and community continued to hold sway and to impinge upon work, but they did so in new ways, in ways expressed increasingly through consumption, by the individual, by the household and by the whole community.

The impact of custom and community on the workplace was not, however, a casualty of industrialization; rather it took on other forms. Before we can understand the change which did come with the later phases of industrialization we must understand the content and dynamics of custom as well as the household itself. Appeals by historians to pre-industrial social values, non-market behaviour, family subsistence economy and backward-sloping labour-supply curves are all inadequate. Certainly the behaviour and characteristics subsumed under these terms affected the rhythms of work, the division of labour, and the use and reception of new technology. But they were neither timeless nor homogeneous and as yet we know very little indeed about them. One important aspect of these characteristics during the early phases of industralization was the special integration of waged work, household subsistence and consumption, and community networks. It was women who filled the interstices of all these centres of activity. And it was the mixed character of women's household, waged and community work, whose purpose above all others was to ensure the subsistence of their families, which made women workers so vulnerable to exploitation, and their labour such a lucrative source of profit to capitalists.

The idea of a transition in the eighteenth century from a community-based workforce where women may have played a prominent role to the more individualist, market-orientated, and, by association, more male labour force needs to be unravelled, and tested against the complex character of the contact between market and custom, individual and community which developed in the early industrial period. Clear-cut divisions are difficult to identify, and were they to emerge, may well have been caused by rather than eliminated by the processes of industrialization.

## CONCLUSION

The identification of a great transition in women's working lives with the advent of industrialization seems on present evidence to be an impossible task. But perhaps it is after all a chimera of simplistic linear notions of Marxist historiography. Circular and cyclical ideas must be at least as germane to our understanding of industrialization; the existence of a complex array of paths of development calls for a less deterministic history. This is particularly important in the study of women's work, where the parallels between women in eighteenth-century domestic industry, in the sweated homework of the nineteenth century, and in the new subcontracting proliferating today in metropolitan and Third

World countries are more significant than many historians and social scientists are prepared to admit.[108]

## APPENDIX 3.1 WOMEN IN THE BIRMINGHAM TRADES

### *Widows Announcing Intention of Carrying on Businesses of Deceased Husbands*

| | |
|---|---|
| Adams, Mrs (1777) | Iron works |
| Aston, Alice (1772) | Plumber and glazier |
| Bailey, Barbara (1776) | Jackmaker and whitesmith |
| Baker, Mary (1767) | Plateworker |
| Baldwin, Mrs (1778) | Watchmaker |
| Barnes, Ann (1791) | Ironmonger |
| Beddow, Elizabeth (1793) | Locksmith |
| Bell, Elizabeth (1767) | Glass pincher and buttonmaker |
| Bentley, Hannah (1774) | Blacksmith |
| Bradnock, Mary (1797) | Gilder, silverer and stamper |
| Bransby, Mary (1775) | Plumber and glazier |
| Chandler, Sarah (1774) | Buttonmaker |
| Dawson, Mary (1783) | Plumber and glazier |
| Deakin, Jane (1773) | Whitesmith and ironmonger |
| Fletcher, Sarah (1786) | Steel watch, toy and chainmaker |
| Garrison, Elizabeth (1784) | Brazier, pewterer and fine plate worker (father's business) |
| Gill, Anne (1756) | File cutter |
| Grove, Ann (1791) | Plumber and glazier |
| Hill, Sandra (1796) | Manufacturer of anvils, bisk irons, vices, hammers, all kinds of tinman and braziers' tools, press screw, mill pillers |
| Hoffmeyer, Elizabeth (1779) | Clockmaking |
| Hopkins, Mary (1763) | Ironmonger |
| Hughes, Mary (1793) | Nailor |
| Lane, Elizabeth (1767) | Licensed to sell plate |
| Lane, Sarah (1783) | Edge Tool maker and hammermaker |
| Lard, Lydia (1795) | Toymaker |
| Mercer, Elizabeth (1772) | Brazier and tin plate worker |
| Moore, Felicia (1795) | Sadler's ironmonger |
| Osbourne, Ann (1779) | Japanned clock dial manufacturer |
| Pagett, Mary (1767) | Wire drawer |
| Parker, Mary (1788) | Plater |
| Parkes, Sarah (1777) | Clock and watchmaker |
| Parratt, Ann (1765) | Ironmonger |

108. See Ruth Pearson, ch. 20 below, and her 'Homework, outwork, subcontracting: women's work in historical and international perspective', University of East Anglia Working Paper, 1986.

| | |
|---|---|
| Richardson, Mary (1773) | Tinman and coffin platemaker |
| Sly, Susannah (1786) | Plate |
| Russell, Mary (1767) | Bucklemaker |
| Whittaker, Martha (1797) | Wire worker and flour machine maker |
| Tuft, Margaret (1789) | Toy and watchchain maker |

*Source: Aris's Gazette*, advertisements of trade announcements, 1750–96.

## APPENDIX 3.2 WOMEN IN THE BIRMINGHAM TRADES

*Tradeswomen Mentioned in Connection with Miscellaneous Problems of Business*

| | |
|---|---|
| Allen, Ann (1796) | Gilt toymaker |
| Baker, Mary (1767) | Licensed to sell plate |
| Baldwin, Mrs (1778) | Watchmaker |
| Barber, Elizabeth (1791) | Bucklemaker |
| Barnseley, Mary (1789) | Hammermaker |
| Bennitt, Eleanor (1794) | Nail trade |
| Bodington, Hannah (1765) | Milliner and bucklemaker |
| Bramwell, Ann | Nailer |
| Browne, Jane (1763) | Coal works |
| Clare, Sarah (1791) | Brass founder and silverer |
| Cooke, Mrs (1756) | Buckle rings and chapemaker |
| Cross, Mrs (1778) | Gun polisher |
| Darby, Rebecca (1797) | Ironworks |
| Davies, Mrs (1794) | Journeyman plumber, glazier and painter |
| Dudley, Mrs (1765) | Coalworks |
| Dumold, Mrs (1790) | Plumber and glazier |
| Evans, Ann (1767) | Owner of china warehouse |
| Fowke, Ann (1749) | Enginemaker |
| Godfree, Hannah (1775) | Buttonmaker |
| Goodchild, Mrs (1752) | Ironmonger |
| Greaves, Hannah (1790) | Plumbers and glaziers |
| Green, Mrs (1784) | Plumber and glazier |
| Hadley, Sarah (1745) | Anvil maker |
| Hartwell, Mrs (1793) | Watch manufacturer |
| Hopkins, Mary (1763) | Ironmonger |
| Latham, Jane (1762) | Bucklemaker |
| Orton, Elizabeth (1769) | Ironmonger |
| Parkes, Elizabeth (1789) | Ironmongers and cutlers |
| Piddock, Ann (1784) | Platers and bucklemakers |
| Reece, Mary (1769) | Ironmonger |
| Reynolds, Martha (1754) | Brazier |
| Rooker, Mary (1763) | Brass founder |
| Saul, Mary (1789) | Buttonmakers |
| Seagen, Ann (1784) | Plumber and glazier |

| | |
|---|---|
| Room, Mary (1792) | Japanner |
| Rowley, Mrs (1789) | Spoon maker |
| Salt, Ann (1797) | Hardware dealer |
| Stevens, Mary (1777) | Toymaker |

*Women in the Button Trade*

Wanted advertisements for women and girls:
- Button piercing (1773 and 1775)
- Filling and dipping buttons and annealing shells (1772)
- Carding plain, plated and gilt buttons (1788)
- Grinding steels at foot lathe or mill (1788)

*Source:* As appendix 3.1

# 4

# Protective Legislation, the Capitalist State and Working-Class Men: the Case of the 1842 Mines Regulation Act

JANE HUMPHRIES

In the nineteenth century, working people fought for and frequently obtained legislation which protected them from dangers confronted in the workplace, and which prevented increases in absolute surplus value appropriation by the prolongation of the working day. Much of the legislation enacted had a selective impact on the activities and hours of work of women and children. While there has been little reaction to the differential treatment of child labour, interest in the subordination of women has called attention to legislation which dealt specifically with women's labour. One early attempt by the British state to regulate female and child labour, the Act of 1842 governing underground work in coal mines, provides evidence to locate such intervention in the complex contradictory tendencies of early capitalist society.

The chapter begins with an examination of interpretations of sex-specific protective legislation commonly encountered in the Marxist and feminist literatures. These interpretations are then challenged by a study of the 1842 Mines Regulation Act. The chapter ends with a sketch of an alternative explanation of state intervention. It is hoped that particular case studies will

This essay was first published in *Feminist Review*, no. 7, spring 1981. The author would like to thank those colleagues at the universities of Massachusetts and Cambridge who found time to comment on earlier drafts of this essay. Seminars at these institutions, and at Birkbeck College, provided forums for interesting and relevant discussion. The essay also gained from its presentation as part of the Union for Radical Political Economics Program at the American Economic Association Meetings in Atlanta, Georgia, December 1979. Catherine Hall, Michèle Barrett and Sue Himmelweit of *Feminist Review* have been most helpful and most patient. Special thanks are due to Catherine Best.

clarify the current debates around the welfare state in general and sex-specific legislation in particular.

## ALTERNATIVE PERSPECTIVES ON SEX-SPECIFIC LABOUR LEGISLATION

Recent theorization of the capitalist state has emphasized the logical derivation of the form of the state from the functions that it must fulfil within competitive capitalism in order to secure the reproduction of capital *as a whole* (Holloway and Picciotto, 1978). Thus the state, derived as 'ideal collective capital', must be concerned with counteracting the deficiencies of private capital and with organizing individual capitals into a viable body (Altvater, 1978; Blanke, Jurgens and Kastendiek, 1978). For example, Muller and Neususs (1978), in an article based on Marx's treatment of the Factory Acts in *Capital*, deduced the necessity of the state as a particular form 'alongside and outside bourgeois society' from the self destructive character of capitalist society, particularly capital's 'unrestrained passion, its werewolf hunger for surplus labour' (Marx, 1967: 252). A related tendency de-emphasizes the extent to which protective legislation was the result of long and bitter struggle between the classes, and instead interprets it in terms of the long-run functional prerequisites of capitalism. Marx emphasized that as labour is the source of surplus value, its availability constitutes a condition of existence of the capitalist mode of production (Marx, 1967: 239). Moreover, the development of capitalism implies changing needs in terms of the quantity and quality of labour. It is not just that the capitalist 'profits, not only by what he receives from, but by what he gives to, the labourer', but that he also benefits from the welfare provisions of the capitalist state in so far as they secure the reproduction of labour power and/or appropriate changes in the quantity and quality of labour available.

Predictably there exists a similar 'capital logic' view of the protection afforded women workers as they stand right at the heart of this contradiction between capital's immediate interests in the exploitation of labour and longer run collective interest in its renewal over time. On the one hand the logical development of the capitalist mode of production implies an increased demand for female and child labour (Marx, 1967: 394), which does appear to have been characteristic of early nineteenth century Britain. On the other hand, this 'progressive' tendency in capitalism puts particular pressure on the reproduction of labour power because of women's traditional responsibilities in this sphere and the difficulties involved in combining waged work with these duties. McIntosh describes the outcome of this tension:

> In the nineteenth century it was a matter of great concern to the bourgeoisie that industry was working its labourers so hard and paying them so little that it exhausted them before the next generation was produced. No individual firm would benefit from stopping this; but the state under pressure from the 'Ten Hours' movement, as well as from elements of the bourgeoisie, was able to restrict hours of work, especially of women and children, and to insist on somewhat improved conditions. (McIntosh, 1978: 262)

Thus, according to this capital logic interpretation, the need to ensure the reproduction of labour power (to the extent that it cannot be so secured via the market) led the state as the ideal collectivity of capitals to concede limitations on hours of work (Marvel, 1977; Muller and Neususs, 1978); the growth of public education; and so on. Precisely the same concerns imply the promotion and retention of a particular form of the family (Wilson, 1977) and specifically a constraint on the employment of large numbers of women and children, and a preference for the redeployment of both in other activities designed to safeguard the quality of future workers. Children were channelled into public schools and vocational training, and out of too early and arduous employment which could only cripple their minds and bodies. Women were directed to use-value production in the home where they could also play an important role in the socialization of their children and the recuperative relaxation of their family's wage earners, with obvious implications for their social subordination.[1]

Dissatisfied with neo-Marxist analyses, some feminists have developed an approach which they consider more useful in the analysis of women's subordination. According to this 'patriarchy first' approach (the term to be understood as a label, a crude mnemonic rather than a satisfactory summary of a complex position),[2] limitations on women's participation in social production, their concentration in certain industries for only certain years in their life cycles, and more generally, the removal of their labour to the private sphere, were in the interests not only of capital, but also of *male workers*. Specifically, working men are viewed as fearful that women would infiltrate industry, usurp men's jobs (because employers would prefer the cheaper, more docile female labour), and lower the rate of pay for all. Not only would this be a disaster in terms of men's position within commodity production, but it would also liberate women from dependence on men and smash the traditional hierarchical division of labour within the home.

These material tensions have been widely employed to explain the ambivalence of male-dominated labour organizations to women workers, and working men's support for legislation which either excluded women from certain trades or required differential conditions for women workers, and therefore penalized their employment. Of course even among authors sharing this general perspective, there are differences in emphasis and detail, and the general orientation has not gone unchallenged. Different positions are briefly illustrated from the literature and the points of contention summarized below.

1. Of course, as with all tendencies linked to the accumulation process, these developments were uneven over time and space, affected by both cyclical and secular trends within particular economies, and by conditions (technology, market structure, location, etc.) within specific industries.

2. The term 'patriarchy first' was suggested by Heidi Hartmann's and Ann Markusen's description of the position which emphasizes class relations in the analysis of patriarchy, and which they see as the antagonist of their own direct focus on the relations between women and men, as *class first* (Hartmann and Markusen, 1980). Although the present author is not particularly enthusiastic about the categorization of different theoretical positions in terms of an alleged 'primary focus', and even less enthusiastic about Hartmann and Markusen's forcing of their own previous work into the procrustian bed of their dubious theoretical boxes, these labels do capture something of the ongoing debate among feminists. (Although Hartmann and Markusen would undoubtedly deny me that title.) For other, more scrupulous criticism of the author's previous work which bring out the points of contention, see Sen (1980) and Barrett and McIntosh (1980).

In a recent (1979) forthright statement of the 'patriarchy first' position, Heidi Hartmann criticized Marxists for their underestimation of pre-existing patriarchal structures which she sees as counteracting the tendency for women and children to be drawn into the labour force. Working men were united against universal proletarianization not only because they feared intensified competition in the labour market, but, more importantly for Hartmann, because wage-earning wives and children threatened male authority and derived privilege within the home:

> The industrial revolution was drawing all people into the labour force, including women and children; . . . that women and children could earn wages separately from men both undermined authority relations . . . and kept wages low for everyone. . . . Working men . . . recognized the disadvantages of female wage-labour. Not only were women 'cheap competition' but working women were their very wives, who could not 'serve two masters well'. . . . While the problem of cheap competition could have been solved by organizing the wage-earning women and youths, the problem of disrupted family life could not be. Men reserved union protection for men and argued for protective labour laws for women and children. . . . In the absence of patriarchy a unified working class might have confronted capitalism, but patriarchal social relations divided the working class, allowing one part (men) to be bought off at the expense of the other (women). (Hartmann, 1979: 15–16)

Capital's interest in the reproduction of labour power appears as important only because it facilitates an unholy 'partnership' between working men and capitalists.

Barbara Taylor's study of conflict between men and women workers in the London tailoring trades in the nineteenth century (1979) reversed Hartmann's emphases. While fully aware that male hostility to women workers, and women's unions, was partially prompted by the perceived threat to male dominance within the home, she gives prominence to competition within the labour force and her analysis suggests that such fears were not without their material base. Moreover her work carries an important political implication that stands in opposition to that emerging from Hartmann's analysis. There is no coincidence of interest between masters and men in the exclusion of women from tailoring. The masters appear as concretely involved with the maintenance of cheap female labour, with the use of women workers as scabs, and with the exacerbation of conflict between men and women in the trade. The employment of women in the slop trade was essential to the capitalists' struggle to control the labour process and the supply of commodities and to deskill and reduce wages; in short to secure the real subsumption of labour to capital in a trade with strong artisan tradition. Capital's success is illustrated by Mayhew's description of the state of the occupation by mid-century (Thompson and Yeo, 1973).

In general, feminist authors have castigated male trade unionists for not responding by organizing their sisters, and bemoaned the long term implications of male apathy both for the reinforcement of patriarchal structures and for the atomization of the working class. But female trade unionists, particularly in the nineteenth century, were anxious that the danger to the labour movement of female competition, and the very real problems involved in organizing women workers, not be underestimated. Moreover, the women historians of the factory reform movement recorded their rejection (occasionally echoed by women trade unionists today) of the interpretation of protective legislation as a plot to disable women workers (Hutchins and Harrison, 1903).

More recently it has been argued that working people's actions and attitudes cannot be understood independently of the contradictions and conditions of capitalist production relations (Rubery, 1978; Humphries, 1977a and 1977b). In Humphries (1977a and 1977b), the working-class family is described, not as an instrument of social control, or as an arena for male exploitation of female labour power, but as an institution which sometimes united working men and women around common interests and promoted social obligation, and hence provided a space for the development of class consciousness. Similarly the payment of male wages sufficient to maintain a wife and children, which Hartmann sees as the material basis for working men's exploitation of their wives and daughters – as the thirty pieces of silver with which bourgeois men 'bought off' their proletarian counterparts – could, alternatively, be seen as the (imperfectly realized) historically specific goal of working-class men and women struggling in a hostile environment for a better life.

Not surprisingly, given the disagreements among authors, several questions emerge from this brief survey:

1 How important was capital's concern for the reproduction of the working class in the emergence of state regulation of female labour?
2 Did working men support sex-specific protective legislation and was their support important? While convincing answers require detailed empirical work, it must be realized that, whatever the interests of collective capital and the male working class as a whole, *individual* working men like *individual* capitalists had a strong material interest in continued female employment in so far as the latter benefited from employing cheap and (perhaps) docile female workers, and the former from the higher family income secured by working wives and daughters. The potentially conflicting interests of individual capitalists and the capitalist class, and of individual working men and the male working class, require attention. Although the former has been the subject of theoretical scrutiny – indeed the functionalist derivations of the capital logic school are premised precisely on such tensions – their historical development and implications have been neglected.[3] The contradiction between the material well-being of individual working men and the progress of the male working class has received little or no explicit attention despite its rather obvious importance in the 'patriarchy first' argument.
3 Questions 1 and 2 suggest that another question centres on the potential existence of a coincidence of interest and therefore political alliance between the capitalist class and working-class men. Although such a 'partnership' has been presented as a historical reality (Hartmann, 1979), its theorization and empirical investigation remain vague.
4 The motivations of working-class men also appear problematic. What were the interests of male workers? What benefits and privileges did they seek to

3. An exception here is Howard Marvel's (1977) excellent analysis of early English factory legislation.

establish and maintain? The political implications are very different if the emphasis is on the preservation of trans-historical patriarchal structures as opposed to a sexual antagonism within the labour force derived from a historically specific phase in capitalist development.

5 Authors also disagree about the possibilities open to the working class, reflecting different visions of the problems involved in organizing women workers and the realities of nineteenth century worklife. Without pretence to a resolution of all these differences, this essay provides an interpretation of sex-specific protective labour legislation as it relates to this literature, and in the context of one particular historical case: the exclusion of women from underground work in coal mines in Britain in 1842.

## THE INDUSTRIAL REVOLUTION, THE COAL INDUSTRY AND THE 1842 COMMISSION: THE CONTEXT OF THE CASE STUDY

In two centuries, coal mining developed from an ancient but small-scale industry into a central pillar of British industrialization. The industry's expansion began as early as the sixteenth century, but, paralleling other deep-seated structural changes, gathered momentum in the 1700s (Nef, 1966). Coal mining was not only a growing industry, it was also of particular strategic importance in the process of industrialization, so much so that one historian of the industrial revolution has claimed its most important achievement was that it 'converted the British economy from a wood and water basis to a coal and iron basis' (Deane; 1967: 129). There is also evidence that developments within coal mining reflect, in microcosm, changes characteristic of emergent capitalism (Nef, 1966).

In 1840 the government, as part of the frequent social investigations authorized by the anxious rulers of a rapidly changing society, ordered an inquiry into the conditions and extent of child labour in coal and ironstone mines. Four distinguished and experienced commissioners were appointed to direct a score of subcommissioners who were engaged to visit mining districts to investigate work conditions, to document the relative importance of child labour, and so forth[4]

The 1842 Commission produced a mass of information about the coal industry, including the existence in several regions of female underground labour. As a result, Parliament enacted legislation prohibiting women from working underground. This was the first and one of the most extensively documented pieces of discriminatory labour legislation.

As workers themselves were interviewed as well as proprietors, agents, coroners, doctors and other representatives of the ruling class, there is considerable evidence of working-class opinion of differences between workers and supervisors or managers. In addition these documents may afford some insight into the motivation of the ruling class both by demonstrating the concerns of the owners and agents and by exposing any tensions which existed between these representatives of industrial management and the representatives of the ruling

4. The commissioners were the economist Thomas Tooke and the physician Southwood Smith, both of whom had been commissioners in the investigation into factory conditions of 1833, and two factory inspectors, Leonard Horner and J.R. Saunders.

class in political power in Parliament. But of greater immediate concern are the questions raised by the 'patriarchy first' school: (1) What were working men's opinions of women working underground? (2) Did they support the exclusion of women because they were afraid for their jobs and concerned that the presence of women in the industry would lead to a reduction in wages? (3) Did they also dislike their wives and daughters working in the mines because it threatened their patriarchal power, and/or prevented the women from producing home comforts which men with non-working wives enjoyed?

As a first step toward answering these questions, the following section provides an overview of the importance of female workers in coal mining in the early nineteenth century. Note that women were not employed underground in all districts, and that their relative importance in the subterranean labour force varied from region to region. Thus the elimination of women from underground work did not require state intervention in all coal fields. A deeper understanding of this diversity would require closer attention to variation in the historical process of the formation of a collier class in the different districts.

The next section discusses the coal mining labour process in the 1840s with particular emphasis on the sexual division of labour and the exercise of supervision and control underground, both of which are described in the third section as related to a system of *family* labour. The picture of the industry which emerges suggests that in general male workers were not afraid that women would steal their jobs, or that competition from female labour would undercut wages.

The fourth section examines the hypothesis that the colliers' defence of patriarchal privilege within the home prompted their opposition to wives and daughters working underground. In the fifth section we look in more detail at the apparent interests of capital and how these concerns may have interacted with those of working-class men. Finally we evaluate the 'patriarchy first' argument in the light of the evidence provided in the 1842 Report.[5]

## 'NOT A RELIC OF FEUDAL "BARBARISM" ': THE EXTENT AND HISTORY OF FEMALE UNDERGROUND WORK IN COAL MINES

The 1842 Commission was formally charged to inquire into the employment in mines and collieries of children who were not covered by existing legislation regulating juvenile employment. The letter of instruction does not specifically mention female labour, its inclusion being an afterthought dating from 1841. References to women's and girls' employment are common in the subcommissioner's reports, and one whole section in the summary volume, *Sex: Employment of Girls and Women in Coal Mines*, attempts a digest of this material.

Despite alleged surprise at the extent of this phenomenon, women's and girls' employment underground was not unusual. Although only characteristic of some colliery districts of England, particularly Yorkshire, Cumberland and Lancashire, in the east of Scotland 'their [women's] employment is general' and in south

5. The following sections draw heavily on the 1842 Report, but detailed page references have been omitted in the interests of readability. These are available from the author at Newnham College, Cambridge University.

Wales 'not uncommon' (Parliamentary Papers XV, 1842: 24; see also Ashton and Sykes, 1929). Even within a coalfield, women were employed in some districts but not in others (Hammond and Hammond, 1978: 18). There was also variation in the incidence of recourse to female labour among those regions where women were employed. Thus, whereas the commissioners estimated that twenty-two adult women were employed per 1000 adult men in Yorkshire, in east Scotland as many as 338 women were employed per 1000 men.[6]

Regional variation in recourse to female labour was a product of the historically specific and regionally diverse ways in which a collier proletariat had been constituted. Women had not always worked underground, so their presence there in 1842 was, as Nef insists, 'not a relic of feudal "barbarism"' (Nef, 1966: 167). Female underground employment was a relatively modern phenomenon produced by those same forces which led to the specialization and wage dependence of men, for these forces could not but affect the women of the communities that were to become pit villages. Women were, however, generally proletarianized later and less consistently, which led by 1842 to significant regional variation in recourse to female labour. Whether or not women became underground workers depended upon a variety of local and regional circumstances including: the relative importance of landowner/proprietors, their political power, the degree of labour scarcity, the availability of other employment including access to land, and the resistance of the working class to the imposition of capitalist relations of production.[7]

## 'CHRISTIANS ARE HANDIER THAN PONIES': WOMEN AND CHILDREN IN THE COALMINING LABOUR PROCESS

By 1800 two principal methods of working coal had developed: (1) The bord and pillar system which was general in the north of England, in south Wales, and in Scotland; (2) the longwall system which was used primarily in the midlands but which spread to other regions during the course of the nineteenth century (P. P. XVI, 1842: 325ff; Ashton and Sykes, 1929). Each labour process was associated with a particular hiring or recruiting practice, which in the bord and pillar system was based on the hewer and in the longwall system on a 'butty' or chartermaster.

6. Instructed to gather quantitative evidence on the extent of juvenile employment, the commissioners surveyed the employers by issuing a questionnaire which requested a classification of workforces by age and sex. The returns were the statements of employers themselves and could therefore have been subject to falsification in the (perceived) interest of the employing class. Undoubtedly some distortion occurred, as it is clear that in other aspects of the inquiry the employers' responses invariably diverged from those of lower-level management, and, in turn, the views of the agents and managers were always different from those of the colliers themselves (see P. P. XV, 1842: 108 and 110). Whether inaccuracies on the part of the coal owners are ascribed to ignorance or wilful deception, the implications for these data are obvious. They are likely to *underestimate* the employment of women and children relative to men. Underestimation was also probable in that returns came disproportionately from 'the highest class of employer', that is from that fraction of capital thought to be less dependent on female and child labour (P. P. XV, 1842: 38).

7. A more detailed description of regional differences in the mode of creation of a collier proletariat and the implications for women members of the coalmining communities is included in the author's 'The creation of a proletariat: the case of the coalminers'.

The two systems can be interpreted as responses to different geological and geographical conditions, to the context of labour scarcity and to the problems involved in the creation and retention of a collier workforce.[8] The bord and pillar system is the focus of attention here as it predominated in the major coalfields and was invariably the method used where women were employed underground.[9]

The bord and pillar system involved driving headways along the grain of the coal from which the bords or stalls of the hewers (known as 'getters') were cut into the coal face. The tendency to 'rob' the pillars, which were left standing to support the roof, was soon integrated into the labour process, though it remained a highly skilled and very dangerous operation. The difficulty of the getter's work was exacerbated by the cramped space within which he operated.

In addition to the hewers, large numbers of ancillary workers were required to transport the coal underground, to repair the railways, to open and close air doors, and so on. In the bord and pillar system, the collier himself was responsible for the recruitment, reward and supervision of the labour assisting in the transport of the coal, but the mine owner or his agent hired those workers responsible for the upkeep of the pit.

The variation in the relative importance of women workers was not paralleled by heterogeneity in the task undertaken. *Everywhere they were employed women did the same work.* They were primarily transport workers, that is they moved the coal from the face to the horses, if horses were used, otherwise to the bottom of the shaft. In some pits their responsibilities extended to filling the corves in which the coal was moved, 'riddling' (sieving out the dust), and even occasionally moving coal through workings of different levels on their backs, called 'bearing'. Specific geological conditions combined with local custom to provide variation in the methods of hauling the coal. Where rails could be laid, wheeled corves were used which were pushed along from behind by workers called 'putters' or 'hurriers', or pulled by workers harnessed to the front, appropriately called 'drawers'. More usually however, 'drawers' were workers labouring in pits where the seams were judged too thin to justify the expense of laying rails and where the carts had to be dragged along the pit bottom. In this case they were usually shod with iron and the worker would be harnessed to this sled by a belt and chain.

In many mines, geological conditions, lack of capital, cheapness of labour, and apathy on the part of the owners, combined to cause reliance on human labour to move the coal even to the surface. For example, in the thin seam pits the expense of raising the gates meant that horses were judged 'not so handy as Christians' (P. P. XVI, 1842: 228).

Women shared these jobs with children. In the thin seam coal pits, where access to the coal face involved passage through very low doors, children were preferred for their smaller size. To a lesser extent women were employed as maintenance workers. Again they competed for these jobs with children. One such task – the opening and closing of doors designed to circulate air through the pit – required

8. This point is expanded in the paper described in footnote 7.

9. However the extension of the longwall system into other districts cannot be simplistically linked to the desuetude of women's labour underground. The Northumberland-Durham region where women had ceased to be employed by the late 1700s, for example, has exhibited successful resistance to the longwall system down to the present day (Douglas, 1977).

little physical strength or mental cognition, and was therefore entrusted to very young children who could be hired cheaply. Unfortunately the responsibility of the work was out of all proportion to its other demands. Inattention could destroy whatever ventilation existed and have tragic consequences, as the commissioners discovered (for example, P. P. XVI, 1842: 564–5).

Was this sexual division of labour universal? Did women ever escape their customary roles and actually get coal? The sources suggest that women coal getters, although not unknown, were very rare (Hammond and Hammond, 1978: 24; P. P. XV, 1842: 24). The voluminous evidence produced by the subcommissioners contains few references to women getting coal. The rare female coal getters were usually esteemed by their comrades. John Wright, remembering his parents, noted that his mother 'used to get coals' and underlined the respect thereby due with: 'there are very few women ever become coalgetters' (P. P. XVII, 1842: 207). Edwin Ellis, a surgeon at Silkstone, a colliery where women workers were particularly important, has an even more dramatic comment: 'The work these women do will be generally hurrying; but sometimes a women 'gets' and one I have known to do so, she earned more than her husband, and I have known her to get in an advanced state of pregnancy' (P. P. XVI, 1842: 248). When women do appear as coal getters, surrounding evidence usually suggests extenuating circumstances. Rebecca Hough, at work in Silkstone colliery, is described as 'getting', but Rebecca describes herself as a 'regular hurrier' and explains that her current activity is but helping the getter which she 'often does three or four times a week'. Mr Cawthorne, the underground steward, puts this incident further in perspective: 'The girl you saw in the bank-face getting has not too much hard work. Her master does not come regular at all' (P. P. XVI, 1842: 257). In other words Rebecca was getting (and not very successfully) because the hewer with whom she worked had taken an unofficial holiday.

Fifty-year-old Elizabeth Boxter described the context of her hewing thus:

> I hew the coal, have done so since my husband failed in his breath; he has been off work twelve years. I have a son, daughter, and niece working with me below, and we have sore work to get maintenance; have had nine children, seven are in life, the youngest is ten, and has wrought below two years and more (P. P. XVI, 1842: 475).

Here incapacitation of the husband-father and dependence of several children forced Mrs Boxter to take over her husband's job, a move which must have required the sanction of the mine owner or agent. Significantly this was in a small colliery where the management seems to have been haphazard. Note too that Mrs Boxter leaves at midday, having gone down at 4.00 a.m., 'to do work at home as father is bedridden' (P. P. XVI, 1842: 475).

Not only was hewing a *male* job, it was reserved for *adult* males. Although lads might assist the hewer and gradually be taught technique, in the northern regions they rarely aspired to getter status until they were eighteen or even twenty-one years old: witness the number of seventeen- and eighteen-year-old hurriers reported. In Scotland too, although seventeen- and even sixteen-year-old hewers are recorded, progress towards getter status was constrained by age-linked milestones which were institutionalized by regarding boys of various ages as quarter, half and three-quarters men. The use of the pick was limited to three-quarters men.

Within the graduations of the collier workforce, girls were apparently considered female *children* rather than young *women*. No distinctions existed between the labour of boys and that of girls. Although it is difficult to locate coalfields or mines where girls were employed and women were not, the former do seem more common than the latter in many areas. Indeed there is evidence that girls left the pits at the age when their male counterparts became hewers. Moreover when discussing the propriety of employing females underground, both workers and management distinguished between grown women and girls. Thus a resident of Silkstone testified: Till they [girls] are twelve or fourteen years old they may work very well, but after that it's an abomination, (P. P. XVI, 1842: 248, and see also 28–9).

To summarize: the coalmining workforce was divided into non-competing groups distinguished by age and sex. Hewing was monopolized by adult males; women and children performed the numerous support tasks. Discrimination seems to have existed, at least in the minds of employers, between (scandalous) adult female labour and (acceptable) child female labour. Girls' habit of leaving the work when they were seventeen or eighteen years old suggests that the working class, too, distinguished girls' from women's labour, and while tolerating the former, resisted the latter. Several questions are apparent: first, how did such a clear division of labour develop in coalmining, and how was it sustained, especially in the context of relative labour scarcity? Second, given that the coalmining labour process is notoriously difficult to oversee (Douglas, 1977), how were these workers supervised and controlled? The answers to these questions require an understanding of underground labour as *family* labour.

## 'I EXERCISE NO CONTROL . . . I MERELY PAY THE MEN': FAMILY LABOUR IN THE COALMINES

Economic historians, particularly of the textile industry, have documented the existence of family-based employment in the early factory system. Here the employer hired only the principal workers, leaving to them the task of recruiting their helpers (Smelser, 1959; Anderson, 1971; Lazonick, 1979; Humphries, 1977a and 1977b). In the early spinning factories the employer would hire the spinners and they in turn would hire the piecers and other assistants. The employer would then pay the spinner according to the yarn produced, and the spinner, in turn, would meet the explicit or implicit contract made with the assistants or their parents. If the helpers were other co-residing family members, the money would simply be used to secure the family subsistence, the children receiving a few coppers on their own account.

In coalmining, in those districts where women worked, management hired only the principal operatives. As in the spinning factories, and for similar reasons, recruitment and supervision were left to the workers themselves. Many centuries before spinners, coalminers had turned to their own families for help. Mine owners and managers, like millowners of a later date, faced frequent and chronic labour shortages. It was impossible to find appropriate quantities of male labour in the isolated colliery communities and the distinct habits and customs of the collier people were not agreeable to migrants from other areas. The coalminers' own kin were the obvious solution. Even today, coalmining is difficult to supervise (Douglas, 1977). In nineteenth century conditions the performance of not only the individual hewers, dispersed at work over considerable distances, but also the helpers, constantly moving along narrow underground passages, simply could not be monitored. Production was maintained by fixing a piece rate that would allow the miners to get their customary subsistence *if* they worked hard and *drove their assistants to similar heroic efforts*. Familial authority relations assisted in the latter. Thus the decentralized system lifted a difficult, if not impossible, task from the shoulders of the mine owners. Other practices of mine owners were consistent with this preference for a system which reduced their involvement. Management was frequently entrusted to an agent whose objective was to maximize output, and who had little incentive to become embroiled in the toil and trouble of recruiting.

Lack of interest in the enterprises which produced their wealth undoubtedly was related to the social origins of many coal proprietors who were often large landowners, men with other sources of wealth and power, and access to other arenas within which to display that wealth and power. They had other dominions than their own workers. Although this studied aloofness was known to evaporate when confronted by threats to their vested interests (Hammond and Hammond, 1978; see also Mee, 1976; Ashton and Sykes, 1929), it served them well in the context of a government inquiry which revealed reprehensible conditions and scandalous practices. The coal owners took shelter behind the decentralized system which had developed to serve their interests. Masters proclaimed their inability to improve working conditions, to prevent brutal treatment of juvenile workers, and to cease to employ women and children. The system of family labour had taken such matters out of their control. Power lay in the hands of the colliers themselves: 'the masters did not interfere' (P. P. XVII, 1842: 164). John Barber, a Yorkshire coal owner insisted that he did not employ the children: 'Each collier employs whoever he likes . . . I exercise no control over them. I merely pay the men for the coal which they bring to the bank' (P. P. XVII, 1842: 236, see also XVI, 1842: 243). The apogee of genteel disinterest is reached in the testimony of the proprietor of Oaks Colliery, Ardsley, who, claiming ignorance of whether or not girls were employed in his pit, explained his presence there by his disposition to ride over 'as an amusement' (P. P. XVI, 1842: 254).

As in the factories, family labour in the mines had advantages for the workers. It increased discipline and therefore relieved the hewer of the need constantly to supervise the ancillary labour process. The need to *control* helpers explains the recourse to girls' labour, not necessarily because they were more docile, but because miners preferred to employ *daughters* over whom they had parental authority, rather than boys from another family. Thus John Brammal argued: 'I think the reason why girls are employed is because the colliers like to have the children more under their command and bring their own girls in preference to employing other people's boys' (P. P. XVI, 1842: 237). James Ibbetson, a twenty-year-old hewer who did not think female employment 'proper', nevertheless employed his two sisters to hurry for him. He acknowledged that he could get boys but 'my sisters are more to be depended on' (P. P. XVI, 1842: 291). Not only did family labour mean more control and dependability, often it was the *only* source of labour. Other helpers were simply not available. Such circumstances condemned Sarah Ambler to work she disliked and forced Mary Smith to give up a preferred job in service (P. P. XVI, 1842: 124 and 447). There is evidence enough of adult labour's recourse to verbal abuse and physical violence even against their own relatives, but many witnesses believed that familial affection softened the harshness of the underground regimen. Certainly drawers who worked for people to whom they were not related seem more frequently ill-used, and the workhouse orphans the most vulnerable of all. Significantly in many pits, parents alone could mete out punishment, and children would appeal to their parents for redress if they were chastised by some unrelated individual. Occasionally there would be appeals to management, who in theory opposed physical force, but in practice exercised a far from benign neglect. Sometimes parents would be afraid to complain, but there were instances of parents taking offenders before a magistrate for retribution. There are as many examples of parental affection and protection as there are of child abuse.

The dangers of underground work provided yet another motive for employing family members as they might render assistance when others would not. The Commission did reveal several such acts of bravery, witness Elizabeth Dickinson's rescue of her father from 'bad air' and Margaret Watson's attempt to save her brother from choke damp (P. P. XVI, 1842: 456 and 458).

It is also difficult in the coalmining labour process clearly to demarcate the production of an individual hewer and ensure that he is not cheated either by other workers or by management. Family labour promoted honesty between members of the mini-production team then as today (Samuel, 1977: 56ff). In nineteenth century conditions it secured for the hewer a guardian of his interests at the shaft or the horsegate, where the coal was weighed and recorded; his wife or child would be there to correct mistakes, intentional or otherwise, by the weightman.[10]

But for the miners, like the textile workers, the overwhelming incentive to employ family labour was that the wage did not then have to be shared with outsiders. Indeed some observers argued that this motivated not only the proletarianization of the wife and children but their acquisition in the first place. The employment of women in the mines was held to induce early marriage and large families. 'Where women are encouraged to work below they get husbands very early, and have large families' (P. P. XVI, 1842: 442; see also 459). Single hewers had to pay wages to their assistants which were a substantial drain on their earnings. William Muckle, a seventy-year-old hewer, looking back over his fifty-seven years below ground, noted that colliers were 'obliged to get a woman early, as at that time all the profits of a collier's wages were taken to pay the bearers' (P. P. XVI, 1842: 452). Marriage was an economic necessity, and Janet Selkirk was being realistic rather than cynical when she observed that 'Men only marry us early because we are of advantage to them' (P. P. XVI, 1842: 457). 'Not only did women's employment promote early marriage, it also allegedly affected the choice of a partner. Strength was the usual criterion, rather than 'aptitude for domestic duties' or 'liking' (P. P. XVI, 1842: 442). In short, not only did the sexual division of labour underground protect working-class men from competition from women of the same class, but also in conjunction with the decentralized system of hiring and recruitment it provided a *positive inducement* to employ women

10. It was not until 1860 that the checkweightman system was established whereby the checkweightman functioned as the miners' representative in the monitoring of production (Douglas, 1977: 244).

and children. By enlisting the help of their wives and daughters, men avoided the cost of hiring non-family labour and thereby maximized family income. The last phrase needs clarification.

There were witnesses who alleged that parents did have options, that greed, bad management and alcoholism were responsible for the proletarianization of children, and who told anecdotes to substantiate their claim. But overwhelmingly the evidence suggests that the contribution of the women and children was not mere gilt on the gingerbread but *essential* to the family's wellbeing. Many representatives of management, and the subcommissioners themselves, were so persuaded.

Generally the workers themselves argued that given the concrete conditions of their lives, that is, the diet needed to maintain physical efficiency in the face of gruelling labour, the likelihood of incapacity and associated unemployment, family size and the burden of dependent children, and the attitude of the post-1843 Poor Law administration, and *given the level of hewers' wages*, other family members had to work. But simultaneously there were those who argued that it was just such a family labour system that kept men's wages where they were. For despite the lack of direct competition between grown men and women, there are occasional references to female employment lowering male wages (see, for example, P. P. XVI, 1842: 250, 284 and 285).

This argument was developed not in terms of competition between men and women but in terms of the natural price of labour and its relationship to the reproduction cost of the family as a whole. With women and children working the male wage need provide only a part of the family's subsistence, this part representing their 'natural price', but with women and children out of the labour force, the shortfall between the current level of *male* wages and the income historically needed to sustain the collier *family* had to be covered. Thus while it was widely argued that the earnings of women and children were essential to secure the historic subsistence, both colliers and management did not contemplate the withdrawal of women and children in isolation, but anticipated ramifications in the labour market either on the wages of men, the hewer's wage becoming in fact 'a family wage', or by the government providing alternative 'more suitable' employment for wives and children or income subsidies towards their maintenance.

The conclusions from this section are:

1 The hewers neither individually nor collectively feared competition from female labour.
2 Many hewers had an interest in the retention of female and child labour underground as the employment of their own wives and children increased their family's income.
3 It was not clear that the regulation of female and child labour would be accompanied by other changes which would compensate families for earnings thereby lost. Offsetting financial gains might be forthcoming from the actions of government providing alternative employment opportunities, or income transfers, or from an increase in hewers' wages which would allow the husband/father to maintain his immediate kin.

In the *laissez-faire* context of early nineteenth century Britain, the first or second possibility was distinctly improbable. Demands that the authorities intervene in either way were probably not expected to bear fruit, but were part of the rhetoric of class struggle. A rise in hewers' wages was more likely. Mr Symons thought that the market mechanism would ensure that after protective legislation hewers' wages would increase, with the consumers footing the bill by paying higher prices for their coal (P. P. XVI, 1842: 169). However, the burden of supporting a family on an individual wage was likely to involve an increase in the length of the hewer's working week, to require greater effort and more constant application – the kind of grinding regularity which wore men out. Certainly these had been the results in areas where women's labour underground had been prohibited.

What is remarkable, under these circumstances, is that male colliers almost universally wanted state intervention to regulate the labour of women and children, and the overwhelming majority of hewers believed that women should be prohibited from working below ground. This is true even of those husbands, fathers and brothers whose economic interests were directly served by their wives, children and sisters working. (For example, see P. P. XVI, 1842: 291 and 452.) Paradoxically, coalmining men sought to abolish a system which seems to have operated in their favour, and to replace it by a system which was highly likely to force them into longer hours and harder work. In search of an explanation it is necessary to follow the pitman out of the coal mine and into his home.

## 'RESPECTABLE WOMEN, AND FOR OUGHT I KNOW USEFUL WIVES': PITWOMEN'S COMPETENCE IN THE HOME

It has long been suggested that the proletarianization of wives and children strained traditional family relationships. Wage labour distracted women and children from their domestic duties and conjugal and filial responsibilities. Women's housekeeping talents decayed, and the inter-generational transfer of such skills collapsed, as mothers had no time to teach and daughters no time to learn. Wage labour bred a spirit of independence that was incompatible with patriarchal subordination. Precisely these implications of mass proletarianization of women and children led not only Marx and Engels, but other social commentators of the nineteenth century to conclude that the working-class family was in decay (Engels, 1972: 145ff; Marx, 1967: 388–403; Humphries, 1977a and 1977b). Radical feminists deduce the opposition of working men to the waged work of wives from the same data. The wife who stayed home and busied herself with domestic tasks was more dependent and more manageable, and although her earnings had to be forgone, her labour was the source of use-value production over which the husband had monopoly rights. In short, working men's opposition to the proletarianization of their wives and children is seen as rooted in a desire to maintain their patriarchal privileges within the home.

Patriarchal privileges consist of domestic comforts and personal services produced primarily by wives, but also by children, which improve the husband-father's quality of life. The latter's familial authority constitutes a condition of existence of his access to, and right to exclude others from, such use-value production.

The questions here are: in those regions where women and children were employed, were the patriarchal privileges of the male colliers threatened, and does this explain their advocacy of protective legislation? Discussion of these issues involves an assessment of the evidence on the domestic capability of collier women, followed by an analysis of the importance of 'domestic comfort' within the collier lifestyle. The threat to partriarchal control is then shown to be mitigated by the system of family labour within which the hewer generally retained control of both his family's labour and earnings.

Intra-family relations are, in general, more difficult to reconstruct than are the social relations of the workplace. The evidence on the labour process provided by the 1842 Commission is concrete and detailed. There are descriptions of tasks, conditions and authority relations; there are tables which provide a quantitative dimension to personal testimony; and, there are even pictures that help to visualize the world underground. The subcommissioners devoted much less time to the homelife of the colliers. They visited pitmen's homes and asked relevant questions, but while they observed the labour process, it was not possible to get a similar grasp on the dynamic of intimate family relations. Much of the evidence consisted of observation and opinion from upper-class witnesses, and was therefore filtered through the alembic of their preconception and prejudice. The subcommissioners had never been coalminers and had few prior opinions about work underground. But they did have families, and important preconceptions about family life. The working-class family, a historically specific product of concrete economic conditions, was assessed with regard to standards that were themselves the products of wholly different material circumstance and historical experience. It is not the intention here to reconstruct collier family life but only to isolate several factors of immediate interest.

There is testimony that pitmen's wives were derelict in their domestic duties, and that this reduced the comfort of their cottages. But such evidence was seldom presented at first hand. True, the subcommissioners visited comfortless and filthy cottages, but frequently these conditions reflected poverty and bad housing rather than incompetent housewives. Evidence on the latter is invariably hearsay and although miners themselves, in response to specific questions, did complain about the domestic incompetence of collier women, most criticism came from bourgeois witnesses.

The subcommissioner most concerned with the impact of female proletarianization on homelife was W. R. Wood. His strong conclusion is quoted in the summary:

> the employment of female Children . . . has the effect of preventing them from acquiring the most ordinary and necessary knowledge of domestic management and family economy, that the young females in general . . . are nearly ignorant of the arts of baking and cooking, and, generally speaking, entirely so of the use of the needle; that when they come to marry, the wife possesses not the knowledge to enable her to give to her husband the common comforts of a home. (P. P. XV, 1842: 33)

The authority assumed by Wood's opinion is surprising given its narrow basis in the evidence of only four witnesses: Henry Leah and Charles Hardy, both coal proprietors, the Reverend Joshua Fawcett, vicar of Low Moor, and Mr Muir, a surgeon at Bradford. Of Wood's ninety-eight other witnesses, only Christopher Hird Dawson, another proprietor, said anything to support this judgement, and the majority of collier men, women and children, said much which directly *disputed* it. All three adolescent girls interviewed at Low Moor claimed some domestic skills. John Laycock, whose first wife had drawn coals, but whose second wife had never worked for wages, provided further contradictory testimony. Although clearly invited by Mr Wood to distinguish the two according to their domestic talents, the collier declined, insisting that his first wife had been a good homemaker despite her underground employment.

Returning to the bourgeois testimony, Mr Hardy's treatment of the lack of domesticity was cursory, and Mr Muir's non-existent, he being more concerned to ascribe the low standard of living of the miners to the impact of beer houses. These witnesses all conflated the issue of domestic competence with that of female 'morals' and were, in general, more interested in the latter topic (for example, see P. P. XVI, 1842: 246–7). This is true for the Commission as a whole, with important implications as developed below.

In the sample as a whole the evidence is by no means unanimous in condemnation of the collier housewives. Struggling with the nineteenth century equivalent of today's 'double shift', Betty Harris fitted her domestic duties around her wage labour. Despite a 'very bad mother', Esther Craven could hem and sew and mend her own stockings. Mrs Boxter, after an early start, left the pit at noon to perform her household tasks (see above). Collier George Hirst's considered judgement challenged that of many of his 'betters': 'I have seen many who have made respectable women, and for ought I know useful wives' (P. P. XVI, 1842: 297).

Thus the Commission's conclusion that poor living conditions resulted from incompetent housekeeping, itself a product of the distraction of waged labour, is not entirely supported by the evidence, which instead depicts numerous qualified women struggling to perform their perceived duties. In addition the evidence that girls frequently left the pit when they reached their late teens (see above) suggests that, family circumstances permitting, daughters were withdrawn from wage labour to be instructed in homemaking in preparation for marriage.

Nor can regional differences in the degree of home comfort be ascribed simply to geographical variation in recourse to female labour. True, in east Scotland where women habitually worked, the cottage interiors were frightful, whereas Mr Mitchell described comfortable and well-appointed homes in the Wear and Tyne Valley. But standards were not uniform within these two areas. Mitchell reported that even in the north-east where women had not worked underground for six decades, there were wives who were 'neither so attentive to themselves, their children, or their houses, as the husbands have a right to expect' (P. P. XVI, 1842: 136). In contrast, even in east Scotland some women managed to impress Mr Franks. Moreover in south Yorkshire, where it was customary for women to work, descriptions of interiors convey a sense of comfort and care, as compared with west Scotland, where even though women generally remained at home, the houses had little 'decency, cleanliness, or comfort' (P. P. XVI, 1842: 313).[11] Perhaps a more convincing explanation of the degree of domestic comfort was income level, the horrors of Scotland and the relative cheer of northern England simply reflecting income differentials across coal fields.

11. Classic studies also suggest that there is little evidence that the quality of housekeeping varied between working and non-working wives; see Cadbury, Matheson and Shann (1907).

Yet other evidence suggests that use-value production in the home was unlikely to be as important to the colliers' lifestyle as it was to the coal owners, clergymen, doctors and lawyers who lived alongside them. The coalminers' incomes were clearly lower, and their style of life more humble. Their diet, while substantial compared to that of comrades in other trades, was extremely simple. Even without running water, electricity, etc., the preparation of their meals could not have been too demanding, at least in terms of skills. Although there is conflicting evidence in the 1842 Report on coalminers' clothing, it seems unlikely that they were as concerned about personal appearance as the bourgeoisie, although in some districts both sexes took pleasure in dressing well after work.

Cultural differences around attitudes to property are also discernible. Colliers were not renowned for their thriftiness, even if their incomes had allowed it. They did not acquire money or property, and frequently ended their lives in destitution (Razzell and Wainwright, 1973: 232). But there were other reasons for not investing in household effects. One women tried to explain the paucity of her furniture to Mr Franks by relating how 'troublesome' it was when 'flitting', an explanation which clearly left the subcommissioner aghast! He had never had to pile his family's possessions on a handcart and relocate where there was work; or scramble across town in the middle of the night, a 'moonlight flit', to avoid debts or overdue rents. Thus the spartan existence of the collier folk may not have meant domestic discomfort, but rather a way of life in which leisure hours were unlikely to be spent around the domestic hearth. Other evidence supports this view.

Not surprisingly after long hours of oppressive confinement, many of the pitfolks' leisure activities took place out of doors. Colliers were often keen gardeners. The potato patch stretched the wage in an important way. But man does not live by bread alone and pitmen were also fond of flowers, often emerging triumphant over better-heeled competition in local horticultural exhibitions. Both children and adult sports enthusiasts played their games of 'crackers', 'nor and spell' and 'bumball' and enjoyed dogfighting, cockfighting, racing whippets, prizefighting, etc. Other community-focused institutions were the chapel and the alehouse, the latter enjoying far more popularity.

Women also had their own specific community-based institutions. Back-to-back housing enforced familiarity among neighbours and community ovens meant that baking was done in concert if not in common. Women also socialized while their families were at work, much to the indignation of at least one rent collector!

Much is made in the Report of the 'separateness' of the pit people, of their ostracism by workers in other trades. The other side of this coin was the closeness of relationships *within* the mining community, a solidarity cemented by endogamy as well as the necessity of comradeship in a labour process where individual safety depended on collective responsibility. Endogamy, in turn, was related to the distinct customs and culture of the colliers. James Hogg described the impact of such practice on the village of East Houses: 'The population was some 800 or thereabouts and I believe there were only three of four families who were not relations in blood' (P. P. XVI, 1842: 443). In such circumstances of intermarriage and interdependence, the individual home paled into insignificance beside the community focus and village activity.

It is telling that the colliers' objections were not to their wives and children working for wages, but to the specific work available in coalmining regions. Presumably millwork or agricultural labour distracted women from their domestic duties just as much as coalmining did; indeed if the hours of work in the factory or on the land exceeded the length of the hurriers' working day, a greater dislocation in domestic arrangements would have resulted. If working men's support for protective legislation was motivated by a desire to secure use-value production in the home, the hewers would have been indifferent to the nature of the work available, and equally opposed to all forms of paid employment for their wives and daughters. Nor can it be argued that the hewers were reacting to threats to their familial authority posed by the economic independence of wage-earning wives and children. Remember that the hewers controlled, organized and disciplined family workers within the coalmining labour process. Proletarianization did not liberate women and children from familial authority relations; rather such relationships acquired new meaning and significance within the capitalist enterprise.

More important still, the *financial* independence of the ancillary workers was largely illusory. The hewers generally received the earnings of their mini-production teams. Wages were paid to individual hurriers only in unusual circumstances. If no family members were available, the hewer would try to obtain a parish apprentice who would be bound to work in return for room and board. Only in the last resort would a hewer hire a helper with whom he had to share his wages, and even then the hurrier's share of the earnings would rarely be received by the boy or girl concerned; almost invariably the financial transactions were between the hewer and his helper's parents. Thus even if ancillary workers were not in immediate family employment, they were rarely in command of their own earnings.

Even if subsidiary workers had received their own wages, financial independence would still have eluded them. One crucial function of the working-class family, here as elsewhere, was that it provided a framework for both work and income sharing which was essential to the workers' reproduction (Humphries, 1977a and 1977b). Together a group of people could reproduce themselves within the collectivity, but individuals alone and unassisted faced impossible conditions. Thus Thomas Moorehead, a pauper apprentice, found that despite the ill-treatment of his former master, running away exacerbated his problems. Only after his inclusion in another collier's household did he secure a situation which ensured his survival.

Within the family, equity in distribution almost certainly did not prevail. Undoubtedly there were cases where the father received a disproportionate share of resources, sometimes squandering these to the misery of his family (for example, see P. P. XVII, 1842: 246). Collier mothers, as mothers elsewhere, would sacrifice for their children's wellbeing. But there is also evidence of compassionate and sharing fathers and dissolute and heartless mothers.

Inequality in the allocation of food did not necessarily represent selfishness or greed, but was a rational strategy if heavy physical work was undertaken by some family members but not others. The proletarianization of women probably meant that their diets improved, both because family incomes increased and because relative shares shifted in their favour. As individuals, women and child workers may not have secured all the benefits of their *incremental* earnings, some being redistributed to other family members, but the crucial point is that their wages could not have secured their reproduction in the customary style within some income pooling arrangement. The hewer had a similar interest in the family. His wages were higher than those of the transport workers, but not sufficiently higher to finance customary subsistence if he also had to pay subsidiary workers and for room and board.

Several comments are in order here. First, it should not be assumed that the payment of wages to the male hewer both reflected and reproduced patriarchal control. The control was *parental* not patriarchal. The purse strings were not invariably held by the father, much to the dismay of those bourgeois witnesses whose experience involved a more rigid sexual division of labour. When women were widowed, authority over family wages was theirs alone, and they drew their children's pay even if they themselves did not work at the pit.

Second, although proletarianization does not automatically liberate women and children, it must be acknowledged that it does shift the limits of patriarchal and parental authority. If pushed too far by inequities, children would try to secure some other arrangement. In the circumstances this did not involve opting for an independent life, but simply throwing in their lot with another collectivity. It was a change in *subjects* that was sought, not a change in *structures*.

Finally it is necessary to guard against too instrumentalist an interpretation of the arrangements described above. It is misleading to separate the material foundations of family life from its emotional existence, to put 'affect' or feeling here, and 'economics' or interest there. Precisely such false separation makes the social scientist of the family susceptible to the colonizing prejudice of the bourgeois observers of the nineteenth century working class, and to infection by their interpretation of working people as 'economic' in the meanest and most calculating way. The collier way of living was not only a way of surviving, but a way of relating, valuing and loving.

## COLLECTIVE CAPITAL, COMPETITIVE CAPITAL AND RULING-CLASS SEXUALITY: THE INTERESTS OF THE RULING CLASS

Turning to the interests of the ruling class, existing explanations of protective legislation emphasize that the prodigal and careless attitudes of employers to the consumption of *labourers* as well as labour power, worked against their interests *as a class* which required an increasing supply of high quality workers. It can readily be shown that the pursuit of immediate gain in the coal industry involved a reckless disregard for the lives and health of the colliers, who were frequently killed and maimed in preventable accidents, and rapidly worn out by long hours of heavy work in appalling conditions.

All the subcommissioners emphasized the dangers of coalmining. Dreadful examples of violent death and disablement capture the imagination, and there is ample evidence of the slow, debilitating and ultimately fatal diseases that were the miners' lot. The *Morning Chronicle* described the hewer as 'past his prime at forty'

(Razzell and Wainwright, 1973: 232), and the commissioners agreed. Arthritis, asthma and pneumoconiosis took a horrific toll: 'Most of the men begin to complain at thirty to thirty-five years of age and drop off before they get to the length of forty' (P. P. XVI, 1842: 450). Women did not seem to suffer so chronically from lung complaints, but were crushed by the hard labour and became 'old women at thirty' (P. P. XVI, 1842: 467). Nor was this terrible toll in terms of human lives the inevitable consequence of the early development of a dangerous industry. Many of the accidents and much of the disease were products of the avarice of the coal owners, of their miserly search for every last penny of profit and every last possible economy in costs even if this meant increased risks for their workers.

With respect to child labour: even if a child escaped violent death or severe injury, early employment in coal mines produced crippled gait and stunted growth. Both parents and children complained that excessive hours produced sheer exhaustion and many colliers made connections between weakness as adults and overwork as a child. There is little wonder that colliers appeared 'rather decrepit' (P. P. XVII, 1842: 811).

Although many employers and managers ignored the evidence that was provided for them, insisted on the constitutional soundness of mining children and denied any long run adverse effects, others were more humane or sagacious. There was recognition that too-early employment inhibited children's physical development, and prevented their exposure to the social control of a Victorian education. George Shaw was not alone in believing that the interests of capitalists and workers coincided on the issue of limitations on child labour:

> If a law was passed preventing the labour of children in pits till they were eleven years old, I think it would be better for the master, because the lads at that age would be more able to work, and would become better men and more valuable to their employers. (P. P. XVI, 1842: 239–240; see also 474)

Recognition of these interests was not universal. Other employers fought the Bill tooth and nail, poured resources into an anti-protection campaign and evaded the law in its operation. Lords Londonderry, Durham, Granville and Melbourne used their huge political power in the House of Lords to nullify certain clauses in the law and reduce the classes of labour to be protected (Challinor and Ripley, 1968).

Employers' collective interest in the reproduction of the collier proletariat predicates concern with the impact of underground work on women's effectiveness in reproduction, that is, with their ability to bear and rear strong, healthy babies. Many women miners testified to the subjugation of motherhood to waged work. They continued to work while pregnant, even to the hour of confinement, so that on occasion babies were actually born in the pit or by the pit bank. Nor were women allowed much respite after delivery, but were usually back underground within a few days. Women's health fell victim to these incompatible demands. They miscarried frequently, and babies were often stillborn. Isobel Wilson miscarried five times while coalbearing, and Isobel Hogg's daughter was 'not expected to recover' from a miscarriage produced by working when pregnant.

Nor did a woman's continued employment after her baby's birth bode well for his/her survival. While the relative incidence of infant mortality in the colliery districts where women worked remains to be examined, there are good reasons to believe that a mother's absence reduced a baby's chances of survival (P. P. XV, 1842, 163). Although the contemporary emphasis on vicious childminders, heartlessly administering their opium derivatives, may be largely the product of middle-class imagination, without sterilization and nutritionally appropriate bottle feeds, inability to breast feed was a real disadvantage (Dyhouse, 1978).

It would have been appropriate for the authors of the 1842 Report to have emphasized the incompatibilities of maternity and underground work, and of a robust male population and overwork during childhood. Despite the voluminous testimony on the former theme, it is not stressed in the subcommissioners' precis, or in the commissioners' summary. The sections devoted to women in the latter volume are instead engrossed with the moral and sexual implications of women's work underground. Before turning to an explanation of this preoccupation, two other arguments must be introduced. First, in addition to the rather amorphous interest in improving the labour force, the employers also shared an interest in the regularity and punctuality of the coalminers. Absenteeism has been the emblem of the miners' independence down to the present day (Douglas, 1977). The image obtained from the 1842 Report is of undisciplined and independent workers, who would come and go as they pleased, and celebrate St Monday at the beginning of the week, even if the remorseless pressure of the piece-rate meant working up a storm by Friday. The coal owners found such behaviour disconcerting, and, as mines became increasingly capitalized, costly. It became financially imperative to get the hewers to descend and ascend at particular hours and to work regularly. Representatives of management felt that a prohibition on female and child labour, by making colliers responsible for the whole of *family* maintenance, would force them to change their irresponsible habits. Thus John Thompson, mining oversman, argued that if colliers became more steady in their work 'they would not need the assistance of such quantities of infant labour' (P. P. XVI, 1842: 468).

Evidence from pits where women had been excluded suggested that such a policy did have a steadying impact on male labour. Thomas Bishop ascribed the regularity and discipline of Sir William Baillie's colliers to 'self dependence, as females are entirely prohibited from working below ground' (P. P. XVI, 1842: 474). Mr James Wright recounted the effects of excluding women from R. B. Woodlaw Ramsey's and the Duke of Buccleugh's mines. In the former case, although 'some families left . . . being desirous to avail themselves of the labour of their female children . . . the colliers are much more regular in their labour than heretofore' (P. P. XVI, 1842: 441). John Wright, the current manager of Woodlaw Ramsey's pits, reported the effects of the prohibition of female labour as later marriage, allegedly for different reasons, and more working days per fortnight (P. P. XVI, 1842: 451).

Although routinization benefited the colliery owners, it was precisely such grinding regularity which threatened the hewer's health. Absenteeism was justified by the need for respite, and even some managers agreed that more constant male labour was impossible in existing conditions. Thus James Wright held that greater reliance on men would necessitate improvements in ventilation, roadways and drainage, so 'as to enable men who now work only three or four days a week to discover their own interests in regularly employing themselves' (P. P. XVI, 1842: 441–2). How soon these adjustments were forthcoming remains a matter for speculation. In the interim, the hewer found himself working more regular and longer hours to earn the family wage. The effects on his health and welfare must have been negative.

A case which rests only on the long-run collective interests of a group of politically and ideologically non-homogeneous employers, especially when the mechanism whereby such half-perception was translated into state activity remains unexplained, is not wholly convincing. However, divisions among the coal proprietors were not solely determined by a correct or incorrect diagnosis of class interest. Some employers had a vested interest in, and therefore supported, state intervention because it was perceived as bestowing on them a competitive advantage relative to other employers, who by the same token, adamantly opposed an intervention which they viewed as disadvantaging their business ventures.

Several such divisions are immediately obvious. For example, employers in regions where female workers were not used had a vested interest in legislation which prohibited such employment elsewhere, requiring other employers to recruit and train substitute male workers, or to shift to a more capital-intensive technology, both of which would cause dislocations in production and place them at a competitive disadvantage. This interest is reflected in the frequently encountered statement from owners/managers of enterprises where females were employed, that they wished other employers would be forced to discontinue such practices.

*Ceteris paribus*, the more capitalized the enterprise, the less the reliance on female and child labour, and the more likely the owners would be to identify state intervention as in their particular interests. This fraction of capital was also the most interested in a labour policy which would ensure discipline, punctuality and regularity (see above), and has been identified as the most likely to support state intervention in other industries (Marvel, 1977).

Employers also differed according to the size of the seam being worked. In the thin seam coal pits, the cramped subterranean working spaces necessitated extensive use of child labour, not only as transport workers, but even to hew the coal. Not surprisingly, we find masters and managers of thin seam pits adamantly opposed to any regulation of child labour, which they argued would make it impossible to work their particular bed. Several managers argued that unless children came very young, they would never acquire the gait and stance of the coal miner, quaint euphemisms for the deformation that resulted from too early employment. Less pessimism was displayed by Mr Ellison of Birkenshaw, who believed that the gates could be made sufficiently high to admit mules. But, though 'acquainted with coal mines all his life', Ellison was not a coal owner; his profits were not at stake. It seems safe to predict that, in general, the proprietors of thin seam pits opposed regulation as inimical to their interests.

Whatever the particular interests of the employers, whether they were converted to the cause of state intervention by their long-run class-based interests, or by some individual competitive advantage, it was obvious that they could not hope to act individually and secure their ends. New rules of behaviour had to be imposed simultaneously on all operators. Individual employers, even if they believed that certain changes were desirable, could not introduce them alone without penalizing their competitive position in the industry. True, certain employers had ceased to use female labour in advance of the law, but this was only possible in isolated locations where they employed a substantial proportion of the local working class. Even here they ran the risk of colliers seeking other positions where they could take advantage of the labour of their family's women and girls, a chance which smaller scale employers in more populated areas could not take. The general conviction was that individual employers could not secure change; a *prima facie* case for state intervention existed.

The Victorians' golden rule that it was better to be preoccupied than occupied with sex (Pearsall, 1971: 15) is demonstrated in the 1842 Report, which reveals the commissioners, subcommissioners and bourgeois witnesses as obsessed with the *morals* of collier women. 'Morals' meant sexual behaviour. Drunkenness, immodesty and profanity were also relevant but only because they were viewed as symptomatic of promiscuity. Consideration of female morals intruded into all areas of investigation. The study of the impact of proletarianization on homelife and the standard of domestic comfort, as already suggested (see above), was diverted into a cant-filled discussion of morality, which emerged as the primary concern of bourgeois witnesses.

The investigation of women's work underground was similarly diverted. Mr John Thorneley's testimony was typical. There was no discussion of the nature of women's work or the extent of their physical suffering. Thorneley immediately embarked on a diatribe against the sensual and animalistic colliers:

> The system of having females to work in coal pits . . . I consider to be the most awfully demoralizing practice. The youths of both sexes work often in a half-naked state and their persons are excited before they arrive at puberty. Sexual intercourse decidedly frequently occurs in consequence . . .women brought up in this way lay aside all modesty, and scarcely know what it is but by name. (P. P. XVI, 1842: 246)

The subcommissioners themselves were not above this salacious prepossession. Mr Symons, for example, rather than appreciating the physical effort involved in dragging unwheeled corves along underground passages, and the indignity of the belt and chain, was instead obsessed with the location of this harness on the female anatomy. He noted more than once that the chain passed between the legs of the women and girls and proceeded to describe the implications of potential wear on the drawer's clothing: 'The chain passing high up between the legs of two of these girls, had worn holes in their trousers, and any sight more disgustingly indecent or revolting can scarcely be imagined than these girls at work' (P. P. XVI, 1842: 181). In his interrogations he devoted much time and effort to ascertaining the likelihood of the chains wearing holes in girls' trousers. Girls working without shirts had a similar effect on Symons. Significantly his image of this scene of exploitation was the scene of sexual sales – the brothel!

Edward Newman, a solicitor who lived alongside the Silkstone colliers, provided the most patently prurient testimony:

> At Silkstone there are a great many girls who work within the pits and I have seen them washing themselves naked much below the waist as I passed their doors, and whilst they are doing this they will be talking and chatting with any man who happens to be there . . . the moral effect of the system must be very bad. (P. P. XVI, 1842: 250)

That Newman was not just an observant co-resident but a peeping tom, who consciously or unconsciously regarded collier girls as sex objects, was revealed by his subsequent admiration of their after-work finery including their ear-rings which he reported were fully two inches long!

Of course comments on female promiscuity are not limited to the bourgeois witnesses. Working colliers too expressed anxiety over the morals of women and girls. But working-class comments were integrated with expressions of concern for the physical welfare of women, and for the effects of their labour on the family wage and therefore on working-class welfare; and often morals were unmentioned. Sometimes expressions of concern over morality are tagged awkwardly onto the end of a deposition, as if the witness was prompted by the subcommissioner (see witnesses 146, P. P. XVI, 1842: 286–7).

Moreover working people frequently defended the morals of pit women, and took the subcommissioners to task for suggesting impropriety. Benjamin Mellor did not object to his daughters working below, and expressed the opinion that there was less immorality in pits than in service to the ruling class! Mr Mellor's postscript also gives some insight into sexual relations between pitmen and women: 'If a man was to offer any insult to a girl in a pit she would take her fist and give him a blow in his face' (P. P. XVI, 1842: 248). Mrs Fern, clearly being questioned about subterranean morality, produced a truism worthy of the bourgeois commentators themselves: 'There are good and bad in pits as well as above ground' (P. P. XVI, 1842: 263).

In reality naked exploitation was a greater evil than naked bodies. Why then did the latter get so much more vivid press? Why were these social investigators so obsessed with the sexual mores of working women? One possible explanation lies in ruling-class concern for social stability, particularly for the survival of the family as an institution which secured the privatized daily and intergenerational reproduction of the working class. But however threatening sexually 'liberated' women were to the bourgeois world-view, they do not appear to have disrupted family formation and stability, or traditional modes of child-rearing, as the subcommissioners recognized. True, the colliers had their own esoteric ordering of betrothal, nuptials, conception and childbirth, but it was one rooted in ancient peasant tradition, and not at all incompatible with the material reality of the miners' lives. It might have been five weeks *after* Ann Smith had borne Peter Fairdrie's brother's child that they married, and the *day* after she was married that Betty Wardle delivered her child in the pit, but the ultimate results of these (to the bourgeois mind shockingly disordered) sequences did not contradict the working class's acceptance of responsibility for its own maintenance and intergenerational reproduction.

Subcommissioner Symons was partly correct when he reported that colliers generally married 'the girls they seduce' (P. P. XVI, 1842: 197). But he was wrong to describe the process of collier courtship as 'seduction'. A model which equated sex before marriage with male enticement of female to wrongdoing belonged to his own class, not to to that of the miners. Among the latter, pre-marital sex was differently understood and executed. 'Bastardy' was a 'misfortune' and not a 'crime'. 'Ante-nuptial marriage', cohabitation and pre-marital pregnancy constituted a different mode of family formation, but it was one that worked, both for the mines and for capital. The collier class survived despite the ravages of capital upon it.

An alternative explanation of the prepossession of ruling-class men with the sexuality of the objects of their scientific scrutiny focuses on the sexual ideology prevalent within the ruling class. The construction of bourgeois sexuality has been linked to the material interests of elite families in the concentration and inheritance of property (Cott, 1978: Stone, 1977; Cominos, 1972; Thomas, 1959). Perhaps not surprisingly, the classical Marxist explanation for the oppression of women advanced by Engels in *The Origin of the Family, Private Property and the State* seemed most appropriate to his own Victorian peers. For men whose identity and meaning were determined by the property they owned, the purity of women before marriage, and their fidelity during marriage, were essential to guarantee certainty about inheritance. Female impurity and infidelity menaced the integrity of the bloodline and threatened to bestow the fruits of accumulation and exploitation on a usurper. 'We hang a thief for stealing sheep,' remarked Dr Johnson, 'but the unchastity of a woman transfers sheep and farm and all from the right owner.' Hence the development of monogamy; but unchastity and infidelity by men caused no such legal problems around legitimate inheritance and so the double-standard characterized sexuality both before and after marriage.

The Victorian age, the age of property *par excellence*, predictably saw such sexual oppression reach its apogee. The institutions which controlled women's sexuality, monogamy, marriage and divorce laws, the medical profession, etiquette, etc., were buttressed by, and produced and reproduced, a female sex role stereotype in which chastity and modesty were the quintessential female virtues. In this context, control and domination of women in order to safeguard property rights developed into notions of women *themselves* as men's property. The ruling-class ideal woman became not just pure but passionless as a reification in nature of the double-standard (Thomas, 1959).

Among the propertyless proletariat there was no foundation for either the institutions of such repression or related ideology. Thus the value attached to chastity was directly related to the degree of social hierarchy and property ownership. The male dominance and female subordination which characterized the working class had different foundations, different forms and different ideological implications.

The ruling-class world-view clearly distinguished working women from bourgeois women. In Victorian Britain generally, the working classes were separated and isolated from contact with their 'betters'. They lived in different districts, no longer mingled at their place of work, and spent their leisure hours in different amusements. Ideologically the working class was depicted as 'another race', 'a barbarous people', *different* from their masters and rulers. But simultaneously the double-standard demanded working women as the outlet for ruling-class male sexuality, and this required a contact and familiarity which violated the organization and image of inter-class relations generated elsewhere in the society.[12] Hypocrisy and denial smoothed things over on the surface, but the

12. Thus Sigsworth and Wyke see prostitution as 'a physical expression of the class structure of Victorian society'. While all the available evidence points to a supply of prostitutes drawn from the working classes, the demand upon which contemporary opinion concentrated came from the wealthier classes of society: 'Prostitution not only satisfied the sexual appetites of the middle-class male, it also performed the important social function within the context of the Victorian family of preserving the virgins of the wealthier classes and shielding their married women from the grosser passions of their husbands' (Sigsworth and Wyke, 1972: 87).

pretence by the male bourgeois that he was more 'moral' than the reality, a pretence carried even into self-deception, compromised his integrity. Guilt and unease simmered below the surface (Pearsall, 1971).

Superimposed on this contradiction was the incompatibility between the exploitation of female workers with their very *womanhood* as conceived by the male bourgeoisie. Working women could not but be thought of in relation to the male bourgeois's own sister, wife and mother. These contradictions were painfully manifest in the conflicting images and ideals of the Victorians and firmly rooted in the material organization of production and human reproduction in a viciously exploitative, patriarchal and class society. They explain the obsession of the bourgeois social commentators, their personal anxiety and the scandal occasioned by the publication of their findings.

## CONCLUSION

The 1842 Mines Regulation Act inaugurated sex-specific protective legislation. For the first time the authorities limited the exploitation of a class of workers on the basis of gender, a distinction which has characterized protective labour legislation ever since. The introduction of this legislation was prompted by the publication of the report of the Royal Commission on the Employment of Children in Mines which has helped to reconstruct the nature of the coalmining family's existence. In turn, this historical evidence suggests that widely accepted explanations of sex-specific protective legislation are not applicable in this particular case.

Theoretical problems with the 'patriarchy first' position aside, in the coalmining context it cannot be argued that the male hewer was afraid that female competition would create unemployment, reduce male wages and lower the standard of living for all. The other strand of the 'patriarchy first' argument, which derives working men's support for protective legislation from their desire to secure and retain privileged access to privatized domestic production, is inconsistent with the reality of collier life. More generally this position is historically underinformed.[13] It has more to say about the material bases of tension between middle-class men and women in monopoly capitalism than it does about the long-dead subjects of this study. In turn, neo-Marxist analyses of the state provide some insights into the ruling-class motivation, but a completely satisfying explanation remains to be developed.

The conclusions then seem largely negative. Existing theorizations have proven inadequate to the understanding of an important historical example. It could be that the 1842 Act is an exception; but in history exceptions seldom prove rules. It is likely that further historical research will uncover other inconsistent cases, and will eventually force theoretical revision. But not all the conclusions are negative. One alternative explanation of the attention of bourgeois society to

13. There has been little empirical work on the relative appropriation of labour time from individual family members and its relation to their relative shares in family income. The 'patriarchy first' school obtains some support from Laura Oren's essay in *Clio's Consciousness Raised: New Perspectives on the History of Women*, edited by Mary S. Hartman and Lois Banner (1974). Alone this evidence is not sufficient to sustain their argument in the face of conflicting evidence such as that cited here. Clearly this is an issue which requires more research.

the plight of collier women was briefly introduced. This argument built on the contradiction between the dramatic revelation of massive exploitation of women *workers* and the sex role standards which prevailed within the ruling class, and which were themselves conditions of existence of the *sexual* oppression of women within that class.

An explanation of this kind however raises more questions than it answers. Further work is required to describe the sex role standards prevalent within a particular class, their material base, and the nature of any inter-class contradictions identified. Particularly important would be the demonstration of cultural imperialism, the permeation of ruling-class sensibilities and values (and therefore behaviours) into working-class sexuality. The convergence of the ideological accoutrements of patriarchy within classes must be dealt with in the broader context of questions about the nature and meaning of ideology in general. Particularly it must be asked whether a separate working-class culture, implying distinct values, norms and behaviours, could survive in Victorian class society. If it did survive, as suggested here, in nineteenth century pit villages, what were its conditions of existence and how were they secured? How did its pattern of development relate to the massive social change of this time?

In addition to these specific suggestions for future research, the current study has one more general implication. Feminists and Marxists alike would be well advised to pay more attention to the organization of human reproduction, conceived as a material practice, and therefore co-equal in status in the analysis to the organization of production. Analyses conducted with a more sympathetic and careful eye in this direction may not only elucidate particularly opaque actions by the capitalist state, but may with advantage impact back upon the ongoing endeavour to construct a Marxist-feminist theory. At least this author thinks so!

## REFERENCES


Altvater, E. (1978) 'Some Problems of State Interventionism' in Holloway and Picciotto (1978).

Anderson, M. (1971) *Family Structure in Nineteenth Century Lancashire* Cambridge: Cambridge University Press.

Ashton, T. S. and Sykes, J. (1929) *The Coal Industry of the Eighteenth Century* Manchester: Manchester University Press.

Barrett, M. and McIntosh, M. (1980) 'The "Family Wage": Some Problems for Socialists and Feminists' *Capital and Class* no. 11.

Blanke, B., Jurgens, V. and Kastendiek, H. (1978) 'On the Current Marxist Discussion on the Analysis of Form and Function of the Bourgeois State' in Holloway and Picciotto (1978).

Cadbury, E., Matheson, M. C. and Shann, G. (1907) *Women's Work and Wages: A Phase of Life in an Industrial City* Chicago: University of Chicago Press.

Challinor, R. and Ripley, R. (1968) *The Miners' Association: A Trade Union in the Age of the Chartists* London: Lawrence and Wishart.

Cominos, P. T. (1972) 'Innocent Femina Sensualis in Unconscious Conflict' in Vicinus (1972).

Cott, N. F. (1978) 'Passionlessness: An Interpretation of Victorian Sexual Ideology, 1790–1875' *Signs: Journal of Women in Culture and Society* Winter.

Deane, P. (1967) *The First Industrial Revolution* Cambridge: Cambridge University Press.

Douglas, D. (1977) 'The Durham Pitman' in Samuel (1977).

Dyhouse, C. (1978) 'Working Class Mothers and Infant Mortality in England, 1895–1914' *Journal of Social History* Winter.

Engels, F. (1972) *The Origin of the Family, Private Property and the State* New York: International Publishers.

Hammond, J. L. and Hammond, B. (1978) *The Town Labourer* London: Longmans.

Hartmann, H. I. (1979) 'The Unhappy Marriage of Marxism and Feminism: Towards a More Progressive Union' *Capital and Class* no. 8.

Hartmann, H. I. and Markusen, A. R. (1980) 'Contemporary Marxist Theory and Practice: A Feminist Critique' *Review of Radical Political Economics* Summer.

Hartmann, M. J. and Banner, L. (1974) editors, *Clio's Consciousness Raised: New Perspectives on The History of Women* New York: Harper.

Holloway, J. and Picciotto, S. (1978) *State and Capital: A Marxist Debate* London: Edward Arnold.

Humphries, J. (1977a) 'Class Struggle and the Persistence of the Working-Class Family' *Cambridge Journal of Economics* September.

Humphries, J. (1977b) 'The Working Class Family, Women's Liberation and Class Struggle: The Case of Nineteenth Century British History' *Review of Radical Political Economics* Autumn.

Hutchins, B. L. and Harrison, A. (1903) *A History of Factory Legislation* London: P. S. King and Son.

Kuhn, A. and Wolpe, A. M. (1978) editors, *Feminism and Materialism* London: Routledge and Kegan Paul.

Lazonick, W. (1979) 'Industrial Relations and Technical Change: The Case of the Self-Acting Mule' *Cambridge Journal of Economics* September.

McIntosh, M. (1978) 'The State and the Oppression of Women', in Kuhn and Wolpe (1978).

Marvel, H. (1977) 'Factory Regulation: A Reinterpretation of Early English Experience' *Journal of Law and Economics* October.

Marx, K. (1967) *Capital*, vol. I, New York: Charles Scribeners' Sons.

Mee, G. (1976) 'Employer–Employee Relationships in the Industrial Revolution: The Fitzwilliam Collieries' in Pollard and Holmes, 1976.

Muller, W. and Neususs, C. (1978) 'The Welfare-State Illusion' and the 'Contradiction Between Wage Labour and Capital' in Holloway and Picciotto (1978).

Nef, J. U. (1966) *The Rise of the British Coal Industry* Hamden, Connecticut: Archon Books.

Parliamentary Papers (1842) vols XV, XVI and XVII, *Children's Employment Commission* (also reprinted (1968) Shannon: Irish University Press).

Pearsall, R. (1971) *The Worm in the Bud: The World of Victorian Sexuality* Harmondsworth, Middlesex: Penguin.

Pollard, S. and Holmes, C. (1976) editors, *Essays in the Economic and Social History of South Yorkshire* Doncaster: South Yorkshire County Council.

Razzell, P. E. and Wainwright, R. W. (1973) editors, *The Victorian Working Class, Selections from Letters to the Morning Chronicle* London: Frank Cass.

Rubery, J. (1978) 'Structured Labour Markets, Worker Organization and Low Pay' *Cambridge Journal of Economics* March.

Samuel, R. (1977) editor, *Miners, Quarrymen and Saltworkers* History Workshop Series, London: Routledge and Kegan Paul.

Sen, G. (1980) 'The Sexual Division of Labour and the Working-class Family: Towards a Conceptual Synthesis of Class Relations and the Subordination of Women' *Review of Radical Political Economics* Summer.

Sigsworth, E. M. and Wyke, T. J. (1972) 'A Study of Victorian Prostitution and Venereal Disease ' in Vicinus (1972).

Smelser, N. J. (1959) *Social Change in the Industrial Revolution: An Application of Theory to the British Cotton Industry* Chicago: University of Chicago Press.

Stone, L. (1977) *The Family, Sex and Marriage in England – 1500–1800* London: Harper and Row.

Taylor, B. (1979) ' "The Men Are As Bad As Their Masters" . . . Socialism, Feminism and Sexual Antagonism in the London Tailoring Trade in the Early 1830s' *Feminist Studies* Spring.

Thomas, K. (1959) 'The Double Standard' *Journal of the History of Ideas* April.

Thompson, E. P. and Yeo, E. (1973) *The Unknown Mayhew* Harmondsworth, Middlesex: Penguin.

Vicinus, M. (1972) editor, *Suffer and Be Still* Bloomington: University of Indiana Press.

Wilson, E. (1977) *Women and the Welfare State* London: Tavistock.

# 5

# Work, Culture and Society in Industrializing America, 1815–1919

HERBERT G. GUTMAN

The work ethic remains a central theme in the American experience, and to study this subject afresh means to re-examine much that has been assumed as given in the writing of American working-class and social history. Such study, moreover, casts new light on yet other aspects of the larger American experience that are usually not associated with the study of ordinary working men and women. Until quite recently, few historians questioned as fact the ease with which most past Americans affirmed the 'Protestant' work ethic.[1] Persons much more prestigious and influential than mere historians have regularly praised the powerful historical presence of such an ethic in the national culture. A single example suffices. In celebrating Labor Day in 1971, the nation's president saluted 'the dignity of work, the value of achievement, [and] the morality of self-reliance. None of these,' he affirmed, 'is going out of style.' And yet he worried somewhat. 'Let us also recognize,' he admitted, 'that the work ethic in America is undergoing some changes.'[2] The tone of his concern strongly suggested that it had never changed

This essay was first published in *American Historical Review*, June 1973, and was reprinted by Basil Blackwell, Oxford, 1977. It has been shortened for this collection. Earlier versions were delivered at the Anglo-American Colloquium in Labour History sponsored by the Society for the Study of Labour History in London, June 1968; and at the meeting of the Organization of American Historians in Philadelphia, April 1969. Several friends and colleagues made incisive and constructive criticisms of these drafts, and I am in their debt: Eric Foner, Gregory S. Kealey, Christopher Lasch, Val Lorwin, Stephan Thernstrom, Alfred F. Young, and especially Neil Harris and Joan Wallach Scott. So, too, it has profited much from comments by graduate seminar students at the University of Rochester. My great debt to E. P. Thompson should be clear to those who even merely skim these pages.

1. See especially the splendid essays by Edmund S. Morgan, 'The Labor Problem at Jamestown, 1607–18', *AHR*, 76 (1971): 595–611, and C. Vann Woodward, 'The Southern Ethic in a Puritan World', in his *American Counterpoint, Slavery and Racism in the North-South Dialogue* (Boston, 1971), 13–46.
2. Quoted in the *New York Times*, Apr. 2, 1972.

before and even that men like Henry Ford and F. O. Taylor had been among the signers of the Mayflower Compact or, better still, the Declaration of Independence.

It was never that simple. At all times in American history – when the country was still a preindustrial society, while it industrialized, and after it had become the world's leading industrial nation – quite diverse Americans, some of them more prominent and powerful than others, made it clear in their thought and behaviour that the Protestant work ethic was not deeply engrained in the nation's social fabric. Some merely noticed its absence, others advocated its imposition, and still others represented an entirely different work ethic. During the War of Independence a British manufacturer admitted that the disloyal colonists had among them many 'good workmen from the several countries of Europe' but insisted that the colonists needed much more to develop successful manufactures. 'It is not enough that a few, or even a great number of people, understand manufactures,' he said; 'the spirit of manufacturing must become the general spirit of the nation, and be incorporated, as it were, into their very essence. . . . It requires a long time before the personal, and a still longer time, before the national, habits are formed.' This Englishman had a point. Even in the land of Benjamin Franklin, Andrew Carnegie, and Henry Ford, nonindustrial cultures and work habits regularly thrived and were nourished by new workers alien to the 'Protestant' work ethic. It was John Adams, not Max Weber, who claimed that 'manufactures cannot live, much less thrive, without honor, fidelity, punctuality, and private faith, a sacred respect for property, and the moral obligations of promises and contracts.' Only a 'decisive, as well as an intelligent and honest, government', Adams believed, could develop such 'virtues' and 'habits'. Others among the Founding Fathers worried about the absence of such virtues within the labouring classes. When Alexander Hamilton proposed his grand scheme to industrialize the young republic, an intimate commented, 'Unless God should send us saints for workmen and angels to conduct them, there is the greatest reason to fear for the success of the plan.' Benjamin Franklin shared such fears. He condemned poor relief in 1768 and lamented the absence among contemporaries of regular work habits. 'Saint *Monday*,' he said, 'is as duly kept by our working people as *Sunday;* the only difference is that instead of employing their time cheaply at church they are wasting it expensively at the ale house.' Franklin believed that if poorhouses shut down 'Saint Monday and Saint Tuesday' would 'soon cease to be holidays'.[3]

Between 1815 and 1843 the United States remained a predominantly preindustrial society and most workers drawn to its few factories were the products of rural and village preindustrial culture. Preindustrial American society was not premodern in the same way that European peasant societies were, but it was, nevertheless, premodern. In the half century after 1843 industrial development radically transformed the earlier American social structure, and during this Middle Period (an era not framed around the coming and the aftermath of the

3. 'A Manufacturer', London *Chronicle*, Mar. 17, 1778, quoted in *Pennsylvania Magazine of History and Biography*, 7 (1883): 198–9. John Adams to Tench Coxe, May 1792, quoted in *National Magazine*, 2 (1800): 253–4, in Joseph Davis, *Essays in the Earlier History of the American Corporation* (New York, 1917) 1: 500; Thomas Marshall? to Alexander Hamilton, Sept./Oct. 1971, in Harold C. Syrett, ed., *The Papers of Alexander Hamilton*, 9 (New York, 1965): 250–2; Benjamin Franklin, *Writings, 1767–1772*, ed. A. H. Smith (New York, 1907), 5: 122–7, 534–9.

Civil War) a profound tension existed between the older American preindustrial social structure and the modernizing institutions that accompanied the development of industrial capitalism. After 1893 the United States ranked as a mature industrial society. In each of these distinctive stages of change in American society, a recurrent tension also existed between native and immigrant men and women fresh to the factory and the demands imposed upon them by the regularities and disciplines of factory labour. That state of tension was regularly revitalized by the migration of diverse premodern native and foreign peoples into an industrializing or a fully industrialized society. The British economic historian Sidney Pollard has described well this process whereby 'a society of peasants, craftsmen, and versatile labourers became a society of modern industrial workers.' 'There was more to overcome,' Pollard writes of industrializing England,

> than the change of employment or the new rhythm of work: there was a whole new culture to be absorbed and an old one to be traduced and spurned, there were new surroundings, often in a different part of the country, new relations with employers, and new uncertainties of livelihood, new friends and neighbours, new marriage patterns and behaviour patterns of children within the family and without.[4]

That same process occurred in the United States. Just as in all modernizing countries, the United States faced the difficult task of industrializing whole cultures, but in this country the process was regularly repeated, each stage of American economic growth and development involving different first-generation factory workers. The social transformation Pollard described occurred in England between 1770 and 1850, and in those decades premodern British cultures and the modernizing institutions associated primarily with factory and machine labour collided and interacted. A painful transition occurred, dominated the ethos of an entire era, and then faded in relative importance. After 1850 and until quite recently, the British working class reproduced itself and retained a relative national homogeneity. New tensions emerged but not those of a society continually busy in (and worried about) industrializing persons born out of that society and often alien in birth and colour and in work habits, customary values, and behaviour. 'Traditional social habits and customs,' J. F. C. Harrison reminds us, 'seldom fitted into the patterns of industrial life, and they had . . . to be discredited as hindrances to progress.' That happened regularly in the United States after 1815 as the nation absorbed and worked to transform new groups of preindustrial peoples, native whites among them. The result, however, was neither a static tension nor the mere recurrence of similar cycles, because American society itself changed as did the composition of its labouring population. But the source of the tension remained the same, and conflict often resulted. It was neither the conflict emphasized by the older Progressive historians (agrarianism versus capitalism, or sectional disagreement) nor that

4. Sidney Pollard, 'The Adaptation of the Labour Force', in *The Genesis of Modern Management. A Study of the Industrial Revolution in Great Britain* (Cambridge, Mass: Harvard University Press, 1965), 160–208. Striking evidence of the preindustrial character of most American manufacturing enterprises before 1840 is found in Allen Pred, 'Manufacturing in the American Mercantile City, 1800–1840', *Annals of the American Association of Geographers*, 56 (1966): 307–25. See also Richard D. Brown, 'Modernization and Modern Personality in Early America, 1600–1865: A Sketch of a Synthesis', *Journal of Interdisciplinary History*, 2 (1972): 201–28.

emphasized by recent critics of that early twentieth-century synthesis (conflict between competing elites). It resulted instead from the fact that the American working class was continually altered in its composition by infusions, from within and without the nation, of peasants, farmers, skilled artisans, and casual day labourers who brought into industrial society ways of work and other habits and values not associated with industrial necessities and the industrial ethos. Some shed these older ways to conform to new imperatives. Others fell victim or fled, moving from place to place. Some sought to extend and adapt older patterns of work and life to a new society. Others challenged the social system through varieties of collective associations. But for all – at different historical moments – the transition to industrial society, as E. P. Thompson has written, 'entailed a severe restructuring of working habits – new disciplines, new incentives, and a new human nature upon which these incentives could bite effectively'.[5]

Men and women who sell their labour to an employer bring more to a new or changing work situation than their physical presence. What they bring to a factory depends, in good part, on their culture of origin, and how they behave is shaped by the interaction between that culture and the particular society into which they enter. Because so little is yet known about preindustrial American culture and subcultures, some caution is necessary in moving from the level of generalization to historical actuality. What follows compares and contrasts working people new to industrial society but living in quite different time periods. First, the expectations and work habits of first-generation predominantly native American factory workers before 1843 are compared with first-generation immigrant factory workers between 1893 and 1920. Similarities in the work habits and expectations of men and women who experienced quite different premodern cultures are indicated. Second, the work habits and culture of artisans in the industrializing decades (1843–93) are examined to indicate the persistence of powerful cultural continuities in that era of radical economic change. In general, it is suggested that throughout the entire period (1815–1920) the changing composition of the American working class caused the recurrence of 'premodern' patterns of collective behaviour usually only associated with the early phases of industrialization.

## I

The work habits and the aspirations and expectations of men and women new to factory life and labour are examined first. Common work habits rooted in diverse premodern cultures (different in many ways but nevertheless all ill fitted to the regular routines demanded by machine-centred factory processes) existed among distinctive first-generation factory workers all through American history. We focus on two quite different time periods: the years before 1843 when the factory and machine were still new to America, and the years between 1893 and 1917 when the country had become the world's industrial colossus. In both periods workers new to factory production brought strange and seemingly useless work habits to the factory gate. The irregular and undisciplined work patterns of factory hands before 1843 frustrated cost-conscious manufacturers and caused

5. J. F. C. Harrison, *Learning and Living* (London, 1961), 268; E. P. Thompson, 'Time, Work-Discipline, and Industrial Capitalism', *Past and Present*, 38, 1967, 56–97, p. 57.

frequent complaint among them. Textile factory work rules often were designed to tame such rude customs. A New Hampshire cotton factory that hired mostly women and children forbade 'spirituous liquor, smoking, nor any kind of amusement . . . in the workshops, yards, or factories' and promised the 'immediate and disgraceful dismissal' of employees found gambling, drinking, or committing 'any other debaucheries'. A Massachusetts firm nearby insisted that young workers unwilling to attend church stay 'within doors and improve their time in reading, writing, and in other valuable and harmless employment'. Tardy and absent Philadelphia workers paid fines and could not 'carry into the factory nuts, fruits, etc.; books or paper'. A Connecticut textile mill owner justified the twelve-hour day and the six-day week because it kept 'workmen and children' from 'vicious amusements'. He forbade 'gaming . . . in any private house'. Manufacturers elsewhere worried about the example 'idle' men set for women and children. Massachusetts family heads who rented 'a piece of land on shares' to grow corn and potatoes while their wives and children laboured in factories worried one manufacturer. 'I would prefer giving constant employment at some sacrifice,' he said, 'to having a man of the village seen in the streets on a rainy day at leisure.' Men who worked in Massachusetts woollen mills upset expected work routines in other ways. 'The wool business requires more man labour,' said a manufacturer, 'and this we study to avoid. Women are much more ready to follow good regulations, are not captious, and do not clan as the men do against the overseers.' Male factory workers posed other difficulties, too. In 1817 a shipbuilder in Medford, Massachusetts, refused his men grog privileges. They quit work, but he managed to finish a ship without using further spirits, 'a remarkable achievement.' An English visitor in 1832 heard an American complain that British workers in the Paterson cotton and machine shops drank excessively and figured as 'the most beastly people I have ever seen'. Four years later a New Jersey manufacturer of hats and caps boasted in a public card that he finally had '4 and 20 good, permanent workmen', not one infected with 'the brutal leprosy of blue Monday habits and the moral gangrene of "trades union" principles'. Other manufacturers had less good fortune. Absenteeism occurred frequently among the Pennsylvania iron workers at the rural Hopewell Village forge: hunting, harvesting, wedding parties, frequent 'frolicking' that sometimes lasted for days, and uproarious Election and Independence Day celebrations plagued the mill operators. In the early nineteenth century, a New Jersey iron manufacturer filled his diary with notations about irregular work habits: 'all hands drunk'; 'Jacob Ventling hunting'; 'molders all agree to quit work and went to the beach'; 'Peter Cox very drunk and gone to bed. Mr Evans made a solemn resolution any person or persons bringing liquor to the work enough to make drunk shall be liable to a fine'; 'Edward Rutter off a-drinking. It was reported he got drunk on cheese.'[6]

6. *Mechanic's Free Press* (Philadelphia), Jan. 17, 1829; Edith Abbott, *Women in Industry* (New York, 1910), 374–5; Silesia Factory Rules, Germantown *Telegraph*, Nov. 6, 1833, reprinted in William Sullivan, *Industrial Worker in Pennsylvania* (Harrisburg, 1955), 34; letters of Smith Wilkinson and Jedidiah Tracy to George White, n.d., printed in George White, *Memoir of Samuel Slater* (Philadelphia, 1836), 125–32; Carroll D. Wright, *Industrial Evolution of the United States* (New York, 1901), 296; Rowland T. Berthoff, *British Immigrants in Industrial America* (Cambridge, 1953), 146; Card of H. B. Day, 1836, printed in Paterson *Guardian* (N.J.), Aug. 6, 1886; J. E. Walker, *Hopewell Village* (Philadelphia, 1966), 115–16, 256, 265–8, 282–3, 331, 380–4; 'The Martha Furnace Diary', in A. D. Pierce, *Iron in the Pines* (New Brunswick, 1957), 96–105; Sidney Pollard, 'Factory Discipline in the Industrial Revolution', *Economic History Review*, 16 (1963): 254–71.

Employers responded differently to such behaviour by first-generation factory hands. 'Moral reform' as well as what Sidney Pollard calls carrot-and-stick policies meant to tame or to transform such work habits. Fining was common. Hopewell Furnace managers deducted one dollar from Samuel York's wages 'for getting intoxesitated [*sic*] with liquer [*sic*] and neglecting hauling 4 loads wash Dird at Joneses'. Special material rewards encouraged steady work. A Hopewell Village blacksmith contracted for nineteen dollars a month, and 'if he does his work well we are to give him a pair of coarse boots.' In these and later years manufacturers in Fall River and Paterson institutionalized traditional customs and arranged for festivals and parades to celebrate with their workers a new mill, a retiring superintendent, or a finished locomotive. Some rewarded disciplined workers in special ways. When Paterson locomotive workers pressed for higher wages, their employer instructed an underling: 'Book keeper, make up a roll of the men . . . making *fulltime;* if they can't support their families on the wages they are now getting, they must have more. But the other men, who are drunk every Monday morning, I don't want them around the shop under any circumstances.' Where factory work could be learned easily, new hands replaced irregular old ones. A factory worker in New England remembered that years before the Civil War her employer had hired 'all American girls' but later shifted to immigrant labourers because 'not coming from country homes, but living as the Irish do, in the town, they take no vacations, and can be relied on at the mill all year round'. Not all such devices worked to the satisfaction of workers or their employers. Sometime in the late 1830s merchant capitalists sent a skilled British silk weaver to manage a new mill in Nantucket that would employ the wives and children of local whalers and fishermen. Machinery was installed, and in the first days women and children besieged the mill for work. After a month had passed, they started dropping off in small groups. Soon nearly all had returned 'to their shore gazing and to their seats by the sea'. The Nantucket mill shut down, its hollow frame an empty monument to the unwillingness of resident women and children to conform to the regularities demanded by rising manufacturers.[7]

First-generation factory workers were not unique to premodern America. And the work habits common to such workers plagued American manufacturers in later generations when manufacturers and most native urban whites scarcely remembered that native Americans had once been hesitant first-generation factory workers.[8] To shift forward in time to east and south European immigrants new to steam, machinery, and electricity and new to the United States itself is to find much that seems the same. American society, of course, had changed greatly, but in some ways it is as if a film – run at a much faster speed – is being viewed for the second time: primitive work rules for unskilled labour, fines, gang labour, and subcontracting were commonplace. In 1910 two-thirds of the workers in twenty-one major manufacturing and mining industries came from eastern and southern

7. Walker, *Hopewell Village, passim*; Walker, 'Labor–Management Relations at Hopewell Village', *Labor History*, 14 (1973): 3–18; *Voice of Industry* (Lowell), Jan. 8, 1847; New York *Tribune*, June 29, July 4, Aug. 20, 1853; Paterson *Guardian*, Sept. 13, 1886; Massachusetts Bureau of Labor Statistics, *First Annual Report, 1869–1870* (Boston, 1870), 119; Paterson *Evening News*, Nov. 21, 1900.

8. Fining as means of labour discipline, of course, remained common between 1843 and 1893. See, for examples, *Illinois Bureau of Labor Statistics, Fourth Annual Report, 1886* (Springfield, 1887), 501–26; Pennsylvania Bureau of Labor Statistics, *Fourteenth Annual Report, 1886* (Harrisburg, 1887), 13–14.

Europe or were native American blacks, and studies of these 'new immigrants' record much evidence of preindustrial work habits among the men and women new to American industry. According to Moses Rischin, skilled immigrant Jews carried to New York City town and village employment patterns, such as the *landsmannschaft* economy and a preference for small shops as opposed to larger factories, that sparked frequent disorders but hindered stable trade unions until 1910. Specialization spurred anxiety: in Chicago Jewish glovemakers resisted the subdivision of labour even though it promised better wages. 'You shrink from doing either kind of work itself, nine hours a day,' said two observers of these immigrant women. 'You cling to the variety . . . , the mental luxury of first, finger-sides, and then, five separate leather pieces, for relaxation, to play with! *Here* is a luxury worth fighting for!' American work rules also conflicted with religious imperatives. On the eighth day after the birth of a son, Orthodox Jews in eastern Europe held a festival, 'an occasion of much rejoicing'. But the American work week had a different logic, and if the day fell during the week the celebration occurred the following Sunday. 'The host. . . and his guests,' David Blaustein remarked, 'know it is not the right day,' and 'they fall to mourning over the conditions that will not permit them to observe the old custom.' The occasion became 'one for secret sadness rather than rejoicing'. Radical Yiddish poets, like Morris Rosenfeld, the presser of men's clothing, measured in verse the psychic and social costs exacted by American industrial work rules:

> The Clock in the workshop,– it rests not a moment;
> It points on, and ticks on: eternity – time;
> Once someone told me the clock has a meaning, –
> In pointing and ticking had reason and rhyme. . . .
> At times, when I listen, I hear the clock plainly; –
> The reason of old – the old meaning – is gone!
> The maddening pendulum urges me forward
> To labor and still labor on.
> The tick of the clock is the boss in his anger.
> The face of the clock has the eyes of the foe.
> The clock – I shudder – Dost hear how it draws me?
> It calls me 'Machine' and it cries [to] me 'Sew'![9]

Slavic and Italian immigrants carried with them to industrial America subcultures quite different from that of village Jews, but their work habits were just as alien to the modern factory. Rudolph Vecoli has reconstructed Chicago's south Italian community to show that adult male seasonal construction gangs as contrasted to factory labour were one of many traditional customs adapted to the new environment, and in her study of South Italian peasant immigrants Phyllis H. Williams found among them men who never adjusted to factory labour. After 'years' of 'excellent' factory work, some 'began . . . to have minor accidents' and others 'suddenly give up and are found in their homes complaining of a vague indisposition with no apparent physical basis.' Such labour worried early twentieth-

9. Moses Rischin, *Promised City: New York's Jews, 1870–1914* (Cambridge, 1962), 19–33, 144–99 but especially 181–2; New York *Tribune*, Aug. 16, 1903; William Herd and Rheta C. Dorr, 'The Women's Invasion,' *Everybody's Magazine*, Mar. 1909, pp. 375–6; Melech Epstein, *Jewish Labor in the United States* (New York, 1950), 280–5, 290–1.

century efficiency experts, and so did Slavic festivals, church holidays, and 'prolonged merriment'. 'Man,' Adam Smith wisely observed, 'is, of all sorts of luggage, the most difficult to be transported.' That was just as true for these Slavic immigrants as for the early nineteenth-century native American factory workers. A Polish wedding in a Pennsylvania mining or mill town lasted between three and five days. Greek and Roman Catholics shared the same jobs but had different holy days, 'an annoyance to many employers'. The Greek Church had 'more than eighty festivals in the year', and 'the Slav religiously observes the days on which the saints are commemorated and invariably takes a holiday.' A celebration of the American Day of Independence in Mahanoy City, Pennsylvania, caught the eye of a hostile observer. Men parading the streets drew a handcart with a barrel of lager in it. Over the barrel 'stood a comrade, goblet in hand and crowned with a garland of laurel, singing some jargon'. Another sat and played an accordion. At intervals, the men stopped to 'drink the good beverage they celebrated in song'. The witness called the entertainment 'an imitation of the honor paid Bacchus which was one of the most joyous festivals of ancient Rome' and felt it proof of 'a lower type of civilization'. Great Lakes dock workers 'believed that a vessel could not be unloaded unless they had from four to five kegs of beer'. (And in the early irregular strikes among male Jewish garment workers, employers negotiated with them out of doors and after each settlement 'would roll out a keg of beer for their entertainment of the workers'. Contemporary betters could not comprehend such behaviour. Worried over a three-day Slavic wedding frolic, a woman concluded: 'You don't think they have souls, do you? No, they are beasts, and in their lust they'll perish.' Another disturbed observer called drink 'un-American, . . . a curse worse than the white plague'. About that time, a young Italian boy lay ill in a hospital. The only English words he knew,were 'boots' and 'hurry up'.[10]

Men who expect to spend only a few years as factory workers have little incentive to join unions. That was true of the immigrant male common labourers in the steel mills of the late nineteenth and early twentieth centuries (when multi-plant oligopoly characterized the nation's most important manufacturing industry). In those years, the steel companies successfully divorced wages from productivity to allow the market to shape them. Between 1890 and 1910, efficiencies in plant organization cut labour costs by about a third. The great Carnegie Pittsburgh plants employed 14,359 common labourers, 11,694 of them south and east Europeans. Most, peasant in origin, earned less than $12.50 a week (a family needed $15 for subsistence). A staggering accident rate damaged these and other men: nearly 25 per cent of the recent immigrants employed at the Carnegie South Works were injured or killed each year between 1907 and 1910, 3723 in all. But these men rarely protested in collective ways, and for good reason. They did not plan to stay in the steel mills long. Most had come to the United States as single men (or married men who had left their families behind) to work briefly in the mills, save some money, return home, and purchase farm land.

10. William M. Leiserson, *Adjusting Immigrant and Industry* (New York, 1924), ch. 1; R. J. Vecoli, 'Contadini in Chicago: A Critique of "The Uprooted" ', *Journal of American History*, 51 (1964): 404–27; Phyllis H. Williams, *South Italian Folkways in Europe and America* (New Haven, 1938), 30–2; A. Rosenberg, *Memoirs of a Cloak Maker* (New York, 1920), 42, quoted in Louis Levine, *Women's Garment Workers* (New York, 1924), 42; Peter Roberts, *New Immigration* (New York, 1912), 79–97, 118–19; Roberts, *Anthracite Communities* (New York, 1904), 49–56, 219, 236, 291, 294–5.

Their private letters to European relatives indicated a realistic awareness of their working life: 'if I don't earn $1.50 a day, it would not be worth thinking about America'; 'a golden land so long as there is work'; 'here in America one must work for three horses'; 'let him not risk coming, for he is too young'; 'too weak for America'. Men who wrote such letters and avoided injury often saved small amounts of money, and a significant number fulfilled their expectations and quit the factory and even the country. Forty-four south and east Europeans left the United States for every one hundred that arrived between 1908 and 1910.[11]

Immigrant expectations coincided for a time with the fiscal needs of industrial manufacturers. The Pittsburgh steel magnates had as much good fortune as the Boston Associates. But the stability and passivity they counted on among their unskilled workers depended upon steady work and the opportunity to escape the mills. When frequent recessions caused recurrent unemployment, immigrant expectations and behaviour changed. What Brody calls peasant 'group consciousness' and 'communal loyalty' sustained bitter wildcat strikes after employment picked up. The tenacity of these immigrant strikes for higher wages amazed contemporaries, and brutal suppression often accompanied them (Cleveland, 1899; East Chicago, 1905; McKees Rock, 1909; Bethlehem, 1910; and Youngstown in 1915 where, after a policeman shot into a peaceful parade, a riot caused an estimated $1 million in damages). The First World War and its aftermath blocked the traditional route of overseas outward mobility, and the consciousness of immigrant steel workers changed. They sparked the 1919 steel strike. The steel mill had become a way of life for them and was no longer the means by which to reaffirm and even strengthen older peasant and village life-styles.[12]

## II

Let us sharply shift the time perspective from the years before 1843 and those between 1893 and 1919 to the decades between 1843 and 1893 and also shift our attention to the artisans and skilled workers who differed so greatly in the culture and work-styles they brought to the factory from men and women bred in rural and village cultures. The focus, however, remains the same – the relationship between settled work habits and culture. This half century saw the United States (not small pockets within it) industrialize as steam and machinery radically transformed the premodern American economic structure.

In the year of Abraham Lincoln's election as president, the United States ranked behind England, France, and Germany in the value of its manufactured product. In 1894 the United States led the field: its manufactured product nearly equalled in value that of Great Britain, France, and Germany together. But such profound economic changes did not entirely shatter the older American social structure and the settled cultures of premodern native and immigrant American artisans. 'There is no such thing as economic growth which is not, at the same time, growth or change of a culture,' E. P. Thompson has written. Yet he also

11. David Brody, *Steelworkers in America: The Non-Union Era* (Cambridge, 1960), 26–8, 36, 96–111, 125–46, 180–6, *passim*; Brody, *Labor in Crisis* (Philadelphia, 1965),15–45;

12. Brody, *Steelworkers in America, passim*; Brody, *Labor in Crisis*, 15–45.

warns that 'we should not assume any automatic, or overdirect, correspondence between the dynamic of economic growth and the dynamic of social or cultural life.' That significant stricture applies as much to the United States as to England during its Industrial Revolution and especially to native and immigrant artisans between 1843 and 1893.[13]

It is not surprising to find tenacious artisan work habits before the Civil War, what Thompson calls 'alternate bouts of intense labour and of idleness wherever men were in control of their working lives'. An English cabinetmaker shared a New York City workplace with seven others (two native Americans, two Germans, and one man each from Ireland, England, and France), and the readers of *Knight's Penny Magazine* learned from him that 'frequently . . . after several weeks of real hard work . . . a simultaneous cessation from work took place.' 'As if . . . by tacit agreement, every hand' contributed 'loose change', and an apprentice left the place and 'speedily returned laden with wine, brandy, biscuits, and cheese'. Songs came forth 'from those who felt musical', and the same near-ritual repeated itself two more times that day. Less well-ordered in their daily pleasures, the shoemakers in Lynn, Massachusetts, nevertheless surrounded their way of work with a way of life. The former cobbler David Johnson recorded in minute detail in *Sketches of Old Lynn* how fishermen and farmers retained settled ways first as part-time shoemakers in small shops behind their homes. The language of the sea was adapted to the new craft:

> There were a good many sea phrases, or 'salt notes' as they were called, used in the shops. In the morning one would hear, 'Come Jake, hoist the sails,' which simply was a call to roll up the curtains. . . . If debate ran high upon some exciting topic, some veteran would quietly remark, 'Squally, squally, today. Come better *luff* and bear away.'

At times a shoemaker read from a newspaper to other men at work. Festivals, fairs, games ('trolling the tog'), and excursions were common rituals among the Lynn cobblers. So was heavy drinking, with the bill often incurred by 'the one who made the most or the fewest shoes, the best or the poorest'. That man 'paid "the scot" '. 'These were the days,' Johnson reminded later and more repressed New England readers, 'when temperance organizations were hardly known.'[14]

Despite the profound economic changes that followed the American Civil War, Gilded Age artisans did not easily shed stubborn and time-honoured work habits. Such work habits and the life-styles and subcultures related to them retained a vitality long into these industrializing decades.

13. Stuart Bruchey, *Roots of American Economic Growth* (New York, 1965), 139; George Rogers Taylor, *Transportation Revolution, 1815–1860* (New York, 1951), 249; E. P. Thompson, *The Making of the English Working Class*, (London, Victor Gollancz, 1964), 97, 192.

14. Thompson, 'Time, Work-Discipline, and Industrial Capitalism', 73; 'A Workingman's Recollections of America', *Knight's Penny Magazine*, 1 (1846): 97–112; David Johnson, *Sketches of Old Lynn* (Lynn, 1880), 30–1, 36–49. The relationship between drink, work, and other artisanal communal activities was described inadvertently in unusual detail for dozens of British crafts and trades on nearly every page of John Dunlop's *The Philosophy of Artificial and Compulsory Drinking Usage in Great Britain and Ireland* (6th ed.; London, 1839), a 331-page temperance tract. There is good reason to believe that the craft customs described in this volume were known to American artisans and workers, too.

Conflicts over life- and work-styles occurred frequently and often involved control over the work process and over time. The immigrant Staffordshire potters in Trenton, New Jersey, worked in 'bursts of great activity' and then quit for 'several days at a time'. 'Monday,' said a manufacturer, 'was given up to debauchery.' After the potters lost a bitter lockout in 1877 that included torchlight parades and effigy burnings, the *Crockery and Glass Journal* mockingly advised:

> Run your factories to please the crowd. . . . Don't expect work to begin before 9 a.m. or to continue after 3 p.m. Every employee should be served hot coffee and a boquet at 7 a.m. and allowed the two hours to take a free perfumed bath. . . . During the summer, ice cream and fruit should be served at 12 p.m. to the accompaniment of witching music.

Hand coopers (and potters and cigarmakers, among others) worked hard but in distinctly preindustrial styles. Machine-made barrels pitted modernizing technology and modern habits against traditional ways. To the owners of competitive firms struggling to improve efficiency and cut labour costs, the Blue Monday proved the laziness and obstinacy of craftsmen as well as the tyranny of craft unions that upheld venerable traditions. To the skilled cooper, the long weekend symbolized a way of work and life filled with almost ritualistic meanings. Between 1843 and 1893, compromise between such conflicting interests was hardly possible.[15]

Settled premodern work habits existed among others than those employed in nonfactory crafts. Owners of already partially mechanized industries complained of them, too. 'Saturday night debauches and Sunday carousels though they be few and far between,' lamented the *Age of Steel* in 1882, 'are destructive of modest hoardings, and he who indulges in them will in time become a striker for higher wages.' Blue Monday, however, did not entirely disappear. Paterson artisans and factory hands held a May festival on a Monday each year ('Labor Monday') and that popular holiday soon became state law, the American Labor Day. It had its roots in earlier premodern work habits.[16] Continuity not consensus counted for much in explaining working-class and especially artisan behaviour in those decades that witnessed the coming of the factory and the radical transformation of American society. Persistent work habits were one example of that significant continuity. Working-class and immigration history regularly intersected, and that intermingling made for powerful continuities. In 1880, for example, sixty-three of every 100 Londoners were native to that city, ninety-four coming from England and Wales, and ninety-eight from Great Britain and Ireland. Foreign countries together contributed only 1.6 per cent to London's massive population. At that same moment, more than seventy of every 100 persons in San Francisco (78), St. Louis (78), Cleveland (80), New York (80), Detroit (84), Milwaukee (84),

15. *Crockery and Glass Journal*, n.d., reprinted in *Labor Standard* (N.Y.), Sept. 9, 1877; Frank Thistlethwaite, 'Atlantic Migration of the Pottery Industry', *Economic History Review*, 10 (1957–8): 264–73.

16. *Age of Steel*, Aug. 5, 1882 (courtesy of Lynn Mapes); Berthoff, *British Immigrants in Industrial America*, 54–5, 146; announcement of 'Great Festival' on 'Labor Monday,' Paterson *Labor Standard*, May 29, 1880.

and Chicago (87) were immigrants or the children of immigrants, and the percentage was just as high in many smaller American industrial towns and cities. 'Not every foreigner is a workingman,' noticed the clergyman Samuel Lane Loomis in 1887, 'but in the cities, at least, it may almost be said that every workingman is a foreigner.' And until the 1890s most immigrants came from northern and western Europe, French- and English-speaking Canada, and China. In 1890, only 3 per cent of the nation's foreign-born residents – 290,000 of 9,200,000 immigrants – had been born in eastern or southern Europe.[17]

Immiserization and poverty cut deeply into these ethnic working-class worlds. In reconstructing their everyday texture there is no reason to neglect or idealize such suffering, but it is time to discard the notion that the large-scale uprooting and exploitative processes that accompanied industrialization caused little more than cultural breakdown and social anomie. Family, class, and ethnic ties did not dissolve easily. 'Almost as a matter of definition,' the sociologist Neil Smelser has written, 'we associate the factory system with the decline of the family and the onset of anonymity.' Smelser criticized such a view of early industrializing England, and it has just as little validity for nineteenth-century industrializing America. Family roles changed in important ways, and strain was widespread, but the immigrant working-class family held together. Tough familial and kin ties made possible the transmission and adaptation of European working-class cultural patterns and beliefs to industrializing America. As late as 1888, residents in some Rhode Island mill villages still figured their wages in British currency. Common rituals and festivals bound together such communities. Paterson silk weavers had their Macclesfield wakes, and Fall River cotton-mill workers their Ashton wakes. British immigrants 'banded together to uphold the popular culture of the homeland' and celebrated saints' days: St George's Day, St Andrew's Day, and St David's Day.[18]

Much remains to be studied about these cross-class but predominantly working-class ethnic subcultures common to industrializing America. Relations within them between skilled and unskilled workers, for example, remain unclear. But the larger shape of these diverse immigrant communities can be sketched. More than mythic beliefs and common work habits sustained them. Such worlds had in them what Thompson has called 'working-class intellectual traditions, working-class community patterns, and a working-class structure of feeling,' and men with artisan skills powerfully affected the everyday texture of such communities. Life-styles and subcultures adapted and changed over time. In the Gilded Age piece rates in nearly all manufacturing industries helped reshape traditional work habits. 'Two generations ago,' said the Connecticut Bureau of Labor Statistics in 1885, 'time-work was the universal rule.' 'Piece-work' had all but replaced it, and

17. Paterson *Labour Standard*, May 29, 1880; Samuel Lane Loomis, *Modern Cities and Their Religious Problems* (New York, 1887), 68–73; Henry George quoted in Carl Wittke, *Irish in America* (Baton Rouge, 1956), 193.

18. Neil Smelser, *Social Change in the Industrial Revolution* (Chicago, 1959), 193; Lillie B. Chace Wyman, 'Studies in Factory Life', *Atlantic Monthly*, 62 (1888): 17–29, 215–21, 605–21 and 63 (1889): 68–79; Berthoff, *British Immigrants in Industrial America*, 147–81, *passim*; Paterson *Labor Standard*, Oct. 2, 1897. Except for the fact that nuclear households declined greatly at the expense of households containing lodgers (augmented households), examination of the household composition among immigrant Jews and Italians in Lower Manhattan in 1905 shows that powerful familial and kin ties bound together later immigrant communities, too.

the Connecticut Bureau called it 'a moral force which corresponds to machinery as a physical force'.[19]

Asa Briggs's insistence that 'to understand how people respond to industrial change it is important to examine what kind of people they were at the beginning of the process' and 'to take account of continuities as well as new ways of thinking' poses in different words the subtle interplay between culture and society that is an essential factor in explaining working-class behaviour. Although their frequency remains the subject for much further detailed study, examples of premodern working-class behaviour abound for the entire period from 1815 to 1919, and their presence suggests how much damage has been done to the past American working-class experiences by historians busy, as R. H. Tawney complained more than half a century ago, 'dragging into prominence forces which have triumphed and thrusting into the background those which have been swallowed up'.[20]

19. Thompson, *Making of the English Working Class*, 194; Connecticut Bureau of Labor Statistics, First Annual Report, 1885 (Hartford, 1885), 70–3.
20. Asa Briggs, review of Thompson, *Making of the English Working Class*, in *Labor History*, 6 (1965): 84–91; R. H. Tawney, *Agrarian Problem in the Sixteenth Century* (London, 1912), 177.

# 6

# From Work to Employment and Unemployment: the English Experience

KRISHAN KUMAR

Unemployment, as a concept and as a structural phenomenon, is a relatively new thing in Western society, even Western industrial society. It was first elaborated and analysed in the 1890s. In the succeeding decades, and especially as a result of the Great Depression of the 1930s, the debate gradually moved from a concern with a subordinate element in social policy to one which saw unemployment as a central feature of the industrial economy, and the linchpin of all future social policy. The old socialist claim of 1848, of 'the right to work', was transmuted to 'full employment' as the goal in principle of all industrial societies. This goal was substantially achieved, virtually irrespective of social policy, in the two decades of rapid economic growth that followed the end of the Second World War. However, in the 1970s unemployment returned once more to haunt Western industrial societies.

What light can a historical perspective throw on this predicament? How realistic or desirable is it, in the long-term perspective of the evolution of industrial societies, to erect full employment as the norm by which all policies and options are to be judged? What other possibilities and ideas lie buried in the historical deposit left by developing industrialism? Can we seriously, without irresponsibility, contemplate a 'world without work' – work considered as employment?

The justification of a historical approach is not simply the perspective it allows us on an all-too-pressing matter of current concern. There are also, I suggest, lessons of a more concrete kind to be learned from the past: about the organization

This essay was first published in *Sociological Review*, 22(2), May 1984. An earlier version was given at an EEC–FAST seminar on attitudes to work, Marseilles, 23–6 November 1981. I should like to thank the participants for their comments. Thanks are also due, for help on particular points, to my colleagues at the University of Kent: Richard Disney, John Oxborrow, Ray Pahl.

of work, of the relation of work to other spheres of 'leisure', family, and community life, and of the primacy of values in governing the relations between these. Nothing of the past can be relived or restored in a literal sense. Nor is there any intention here to indulge in antiquarian nostalgia. But there are times – critical points, perhaps, in the evolution of societies – when the experience and attitudes of past epochs seem peculiarly relevant to considering present problems. 'History does not repeat itself; but historical situations recur.'

## 'UNEMPLOYMENT' AND THE LABOURING POOR UNDER THE OLD POOR LAW, 1601–1834

For over three centuries – from the Elizabethan Poor Laws of 1597 and 1601 to Lloyd George's unemployment insurance legislation of 1911[1] – the history of the attitude to the unemployed in England is essentially the history of the Poor Laws. H. L. Beales once said that 'like the House of Commons, the Poor Law provides an institutional microcosm of the English people . . . it is the history of the country's social conscience.'[2] For the greater part of England's modern history, the Poor Law established the framework of a unique system of public provision for all forms of poverty and destitution. Whether from sickness or old age, widowhood or desertion, low wages or unemployment, poverty was relieved, as a right and not simply as a call on charity, in a wide variety of ways by the parish endowed with a statutory duty and authority.

The Poor Law covered all forms of distress due to poverty, however caused. Any member of 'the labouring poor' might be caught by its safety net. The term 'the labouring poor', or simply 'the poor' as commonly used right to the end of the eighteenth century, designated an exceedingly comprehensive category. Besides those in need of relief, for the time being, because of hardship, it included many artisans and small farmers, as well as all wage-labourers in town and country.[3] The comprehensiveness of the phrase reflected fairly accurately the comprehensiveness of experience. The line between the independent artisan or wage-earner and the pauper on parish relief was always an extremely tenuous one. For shorter or longer periods, through sickness, low wages, high prices, bouts of unemployment, or simply an inconveniently large family, the independent labourer might frequently find himself thrown upon the parish for relief under the Poor Law.

1. The Poor Laws themselves were not repealed until 1948 (in the National Assistance Act), although the Local Government Act of 1929 transferred the functions of Poor Law Unions and Guardians to the county and county borough councils.
2. H. L. Beales, 'The New Poor Law', *History*, vol. XV (1931), reprinted in E.M. Carus-Wilson (ed.), *Essays in Economic History*, vol. III (London: Edward Arnold,1962), pp. 179–80.
3. All students of the period agree on this. See especially Edgar S. Furniss, *The Position of the Laborer in a System of Nationalism*(Boston: Houghton Mifflin Company, 1920), pp. 25n, 93n. Dorothy Marshall notes the large proportion of the population – anyone who did not inhabit a tenement worth £10 or more a year – over whom parish overseers had rights of removal under a clause of the 1662 Act of Settlement: 'This clause in theory affected not only the old, the infirm, the helpless, and the infants, but also all those agricultural labourers who worked for, and were dependent on, their wages; it affected most of the smaller manufacturers, such as the spinners, the weavers, the dyers, and the shearers; it affected, too, the large class of small craftsmen, the blacksmiths, the carpenters, or the tailors. In short, as the Poor Laws had power not only over those who were actually chargeable, but over those likely to become so, their operation included the greater part of the lower working class under the designation of "the poor" '; Marshall, *The English Poor in the Eighteenth Century* (London: George Routledge & Sons, 1926), p. 2.

Hence the labouring poor, those who actually or potentially fell within the scope of the Poor Law, constituted an enormous group, by far and away the most numerous group in English society. It has been estimated that in the sixteenth, seventeenth, and for the most of the eighteenth century the labouring poor made up at least between 50 and 60 per cent of the total population, and , at various times and places, the proportion could rise to three-quarters. The really poor, those more or less permanently on relief and so below the status of wage-earner, constituted at any one time between a quarter and a third of the population. But it has to be emphasized that in practice the distinction between the independent labourer and the dependent pauper was never firm. Gregory King in 1696 classed almost half the population of the kingdom as 'decreasing' rather than 'increasing' the national wealth, that is, their annual family expenditure was greater than their income and hence they were at least partly dependent on Poor Law relief. D. C. Coleman confirms this with an estimate that 'in Stuart England between a quarter and a half of the entire population were chronically below what contemporaries regarded as the official poverty line.' Jacob Viner, too, on the basis of an estimate that the labouring poor formed well over half of the population of England in the eighteenth century, says: 'The really poor portion of the "poor" I take to have comprised, with their dependants, at a minimum somewhere between 50 per cent at the beginning and 40 per cent at the end of the century.'[4]

This promiscuous classification of the poor, necessary in face of the realities of the situation, was however highly distasteful to the authorities. We can indeed

4. Jacob Viner, 'Man's economic status', in James L. Clifford (ed.), *Man versus Society in Eighteenth Century England* (Cambridge: Cambridge University Press, 1968), p. 27. R. W. Malcolmson, using hearth tax returns, suggests that 'at least 75 per cent of England's roughly 5.5 million people in the later 17th century were labouring people. My own judgement is that around 80 per cent of the population were labouring men and women. . . .'; *Life and Labour in England 1700–1780* (London: Hutchinson, 1981), p. 19. And see D. C. Coleman, 'Labour in the English economy of the seventeenth century', *Economic History Review*, vol. 8, no. 3 (1956), reprinted in E. M. Carus-Wilson (ed.), *Essays in Economic History*, vol. II, (London: Edward Arnold, 1962), p. 295. Macpherson also estimates that the labouring poor (wage earners, cottagers and paupers) constituted over two-thirds of the adult male population of seventeenth-century England, and that 'alms-takers' – those dependent on the parish for relief – made up between a quarter and a third; C. B. Macpherson, *The Political Theory of Possessive Individualism: Hobbes to Locke* (Oxford University Press, paperback ed. 1964), pp. 61, 301 (note T) and, especially, the appendix, 'Social classes and franchise classes in England *c.*1648', pp. 279–92. See also his 'Servants and labourers in seventeenth century England', in *Democratic Theory: Essays in Retrieval* (Oxford: Oxford University Press 1973). Macfarlane notes that in the township of Killingham, in Kirkby Lonsdale, in 1695 approximately one-third of the population were listed as being in receipt of poor relief, and that this figure seems to have been typical for the area; Alan Macfarlane, *The Origins of English Individualism* (Oxford: Basil Blackwell, 1978), p. 77. For the estimate of the poor in the sixteenth century, see John Pound, *Poverty and Vagrancy in Tudor England* (London: Longman, 1971), pp. 25, 79.

In her splendid study of the French poor in the eighteenth century, Olwen Hufton also observes that 'the poor'included 'the perpetual poor' – the old, sick, orphaned etc. – along with labourers and small peasant farmers. She estimates that 'both *pauvre and indigent* [i.e. the truly destitute] . . . together in 1789 formed something above a third (and, speculatively, perhaps as much as a half) of the total population'; and she continues: '. . . where one merged into the other was, to say the least, obscure. The closer one looks at the conditions of existence of this large proportion of the French population the more difficult it becomes to isolate *pauvre* from *indigent*; for a process of continual recruitment took place from the higher to the lower category: the difference between the two was one of degree; Olwen Hufton, *The Poor of Eighteenth-Century France 1750–1789* (Oxford: Clarendon Press, 1974), p. 24. Cf. Mathias on the eighteenth-century English poor: 'in practice a narrow and fluctuating margin separated the condition of destitution, where people became a charge upon the public purse, and poverty, where they remained poor but viable, making their own way in the world'; Peter Mathias, *The Transformation of England: Essays in the Economic and Social History of England in the Eighteenth Century* (London: Methuen, 1979) p. 158.

almost say that, from the authorities' point of view, the entire history of the Poor Laws was an attempt to impose a classification upon the undifferentiated poor, and to back up this classification to the utmost by parliamentary statute and rigorous parish administrations. One basic distinction that was usually made explicit in every Poor Law amendment and regulation was that between the 'able-bodied poor' and the sick, old, and infirm. Another, generally implicit but more or less corresponding to the first, was that between the 'deserving' and the 'undeserving' poor. It is the attempt to make and hold this distinction that runs like a red thread through three centuries of Poor Law policy. And it is the almost total failure to hold the line that constitutes the actual history of the interaction between the labouring poor and the Poor Law authorities on the ground, in the counties and parishes.

Thus, from the very start, the 1601 Act distinguished between those of the poor able to work – the able bodied – and those who could not – the physically and mentally ill, the old, abandoned or neglected children, and one-parent families (whether headed by widows, deserted wives, or unmarried mothers). About this second category there was no problem, at least in theory. These were the traditional recipients of private philanthropic and charitable gifts and endowments, administered in the past usually by the Church, the official guardian of the poor and distributor of alms. With the Reformation and the dissolution of the religious houses, the state partly took over this function through its Poor Law institutions, supplementing the still very extensive private charities. By means of pensions (regular cash payments), payments of rent, occasional distributions of fuel, food and clothing, the provision of infirmary and other medical care, and apprenticeships for the young, an elaborate system of 'outdoor relief' catered to the needs of the aged, infirm, and other dependent poor.

'Indoor relief' was provided in workhouses. The workhouse as an institution was implicit in the 1601 Act, with its provision for setting the poor to work. But for a long time parishes seem to have been reluctant to follow up this suggestion in the form of workhouses, and the workhouse system remained largely unrealized until the later seventeenth century. In 1696 Parliament gave recognition to the Bristol workhouse experiment, and so gave impetus to the workhouse movement, which was widespread by the mid eighteenth century. Contrary to its ostensible purpose, however, the workhouse rarely provided remunerative work. Workhouses became 'homes for the most needy of the deserving poor: the children, the sick, the insane, and the elderly, those with no homes of their own and no relatives to nurse and care for them. . . . In spite of the name, most workhouses were more like hospitals, boarding schools and old people's homes than factories.'[5] In particular, for the whole period up to 1834 able-bodied males rarely found their way into the workhouse.

5. Geoffrey W. Oxley, *Poor Relief in England and Wales 1601–1834* (Newton Abbot: David & Charles, 1974), p. 92. Oxley's book is the most comprehensive recent study of the old Poor Law. It corrects at various points, in the light of later research, Dorothy Marshall's older study (note 3, above), which however remains invaluable for its detail and breadth of coverage. Oxley notes that the character of the workhouse rather accurately reflected its 'stop-gap' provenance, and that of the Poor Law in general, filling the space between the alms-houses of the endowed charities on the one hand, and the houses of correction of the vagrancy laws on the other: hence its own hybrid nature (p. 80). Garraty remarks that 'the typical English workhouse became a combination of Bedlam and Bridewell, a place where idiots and lunatics, thieves and worn-out prostitutes, dotards and abandoned waifs existed side by side amid filth and chaos, and the effect was to drive all "idle poor" (read, *unemployed*) out, to make of them vagabonds and furtive beggars'; John A. Garraty, *Unemployment in History: Economic Thought and Public Policy* (New York: Harper Colophon Books, 1979) p. 48.

Parish vestries might grumble about the increasing cost of the poor rates; particular overseers might be unscrupulous and tyrannical; workhouses might attract criticism variously for being too like prisons or too like palaces. But in general, for the category of the traditional 'deserving' poor, the system seems to have worked remarkably well, and with fair measure of humanity. There was a widespread acceptance of the need for a Poor Law, and of the community's obligation to provide for the dependent or impotent poor. But about the able-bodied poor, whom virtually all thinkers regarded as the crux of the problem, there was no such unanimity, and a considerable confusion of both policy and practice. At the centre of the confusion we can discern, in fact if not in name, a dispute about the nature of unemployment, its causes and its remedies.[6]

In the earlier sixteenth century – as shown, for instance, in the Act of 1531 – the authorities followed traditional practice in allowing the 'impotent poor' to beg for alms; but severe penalties and sanctions against begging were laid down for 'sturdy rogues and vagabonds', all of whom were assumed to be capable of finding employment were they not culpably idle and workshy. As John Pound says, the 1531 Act 'distinguished between the able-bodied vagrant, who was to be whipped, and the impotent beggar who was to be relieved, but it made no provision whatsoever for the man who desperately desired to be employed but had no job to go to.'[7] An Act of 1572 acknowledged that there were certain groups of workers – such as returning sailors and soldiers, harvest workers, and servants who had been turned away – who were genuinely unemployed through no fault of their own. It exempted them from the penalties for vagrancy but made no provision for their relief.

What brought about a change of feeling was a series of four catastrophic harvests between 1593 and 1597. Food prices soared, there were widespread food riots, and a large increase in vagrancy. This was the immediate background to the Poor Law legislation of 1597–1601. The government was forced to accept that there were many thousands of men in both the rural and the urban areas who were out of work for reasons beyond their control. It also accepted that there would have to be provision for their relief. But there was to be no blurring of the old line between the able-bodied and the incapacitated. The government wished to discourage begging, seeing it as a threat to public order. The incapacitated poor were therefore to be given relief, in their own homes if that were possible, in

6. Cf. Dorothy Marshall: 'To both 17th and 18th century writers the crux of the problem was the position of the able Poor. . . . The question was, in fact, one of unemployment rather than of poor relief. It was thought on all sides that [in Locke's words] "could all the able hands in England be brought to work, the greatest part of the burden that now lies upon the industrious for maintaining the Poor, would immediately cease, for, upon a very moderate computation, it may be concluded, that above one-half of those who receive relief from the parish, are able to get their living" '; *The English Poor in the Eighteenth Century*, p. 26. And cf. also Oxley: 'The main achievement of the old poor law was . . . the establishment of an effective, comprehensive and flexible system for the relief of the deserving poor (the aged, sick, etc.). . . . Yet this task was only peripheral to what, in 1601, was thought to be its main purpose: to solve the problem of unemployment and its consequential evils by setting the able-bodied poor to work. To be effective this policy required curbs to be placed on begging, which necessitated provision for those who deservedly obtained their sustenance in this way. Two centuries or so later the failure of the old poor law to deal adequately with the able-bodied poor of the industrial revolution led to its being substantially amended. Thus the able-bodied poor may have been peripheral to the main activities of the old poor law, but they played a very significant part in the evolution of its legislative framework'; *Poor Relief in England and Wales 1601–1834*, p. 102.

7. Pound, *Poverty and Vagrancy in Tudor England*, p. 44.

almshouses if not. The able-bodied were to be removed to their parish of origin and there set to work. Provision was made for the raising, out of parish rates, of stocks of materials - flax, hemp, wool - on which the poor might be set to work in their own homes.

The 1601 Act set the pattern of thinking about the able-bodied poor for a very long time to come. The goal was the speedy resumption of independence by the head of the family, the able-bodied adult male. It was assumed that, unless incorrigibly lazy and so deserving punishment, most of the able-bodied would be able to find work relatively quickly. Aid would be needed only for short periods, in times of exceptional hardship, to tide over the worker and his family until the return of normal times. In the conditions of a pre-industrial economy for a good deal of the time this was indeed often the case, as we shall see. But there were far too many causes of hardship in the lives of the labouring poor for this ideal seriously to have much chance of attainment in practice. A string of recurrent bad harvests, falling demand for a particular craft skill, chronic underemployment, low wages, or simply the accident of a large family to support: all these could be the cause of persistent and severe hardship for individual families. At a different level there was the kind of distress caused by mass local unemployment due to the closure of a mill during a slump. Although the severity of the distress would clearly vary enormously from region to region, the fact that these were not haphazard but endemic features of the pre-industrial economy meant that the Poor Law authorities were constantly faced with the challenge of what to do with the able-bodied poor. As a problem they simply would not go away.

Setting the able-bodied poor to work at home on stocks of materials, the main hope of the 1601 Act, had turned out to be such a failure that well before the beginning of the eighteenth century the scheme had largely been abandoned.[8] The eighteenth century policy-makers pinned their hopes on employment in workhouses. In the full flush of the workhouse movement, an Act of 1722 laid down the imposition of a 'workhouse test' whereby relief, including employment, was only to be given in the workhouse. But most workhouses were quite unsuited to providing anything but the lowest level of textile work - spinnng, clothes-making and repairing - together with some pig grazing and allotment cultivation: work, in other words, reasonably suited to the women, children, and old people who largely made up the workhouse population. Since most workhouses were small,[9] they were in any case incapable of taking in large numbers of unemployed during a depression.

Certain visionaries, such as Josiah Child, John Bellers, and Lawrence Braddon, and later Bishop Berkeley and Jeremy Bentham, projected grandiose schemes for the large-scale exploitation of the labour of the able-bodied unemployed. Organized in 'colleges of industry', or set to work by private contractors in 'corporations of the poor', they would not only become self-supporting, but make sufficient profit to support the rest of the dependent poor, and so solve the problem of the poor once and for all. These schemes mostly remained where they

8. Dorothy Marshall, *The English Poor in the Eighteenth Century*, p. 125. Oxley suggests that the main reason for the failure of the scheme was the difficulty the parish faced in raising the capital sum needed to purchase the materials; *Poor Relief in England and Wales 1601–1834*, pp. 103–4.

9. The 1722 Act gave parishes permission to form unions for the construction of workhouses in common, so that they could be of reasonable size; but few parishes seem to have availed themselves of this provision; Marshall, *The English Poor in the Eighteenth Century*, pp. 128–30.

rightly belonged, on paper.[10] Had they been tried, they would almost certainly have encountered the main stumbling block that stood in the way of all attempts by the Poor Law authorities to create meaningful work for the unemployed: that, whether in the agricultural or the industrial sector, it simply was not possible to provide profitable work for workers whose skills were the very ones not required – for the time being at least – by commercial employers. All that could be offered were short-term palliatives, of which road-mending increasingly became the most popular towards the end of the eighteenth century.[11]

From the parish's point of view one fact in any case was a dominating consideration throughout: since employment in the workhouse was never self-supporting, it was always cheaper to make cash payments to able-bodied paupers than to bring them into the workhouse.[12] Most parish authorities therefore ignored the 'workhouse test' of the 1722 Act, just as they had largely ignored the injunction of the 1601 Act concerning the provision of work for the poor. Dorothy Marshall has wisely advised that 'to understand the old Poor Law it is necessary to concentrate on administration rather than legislation.[13] Nowhere is this truer than in the treatment of the able-bodied poor. Despite all the intentions of the national policy-makers, the authorities at the local level responded to the real conditions on the ground and went in for outdoor relief to the able-bodied on a massive scale. Outdoor relief, largely in the form of cash pensions, had become the well-nigh universal remedy by the end of the eighteenth century,[14] helped on

10. For these schemes see Furniss, *The Position of the Laborer in a System of Nationalism*, pp. 88–95; Marshall, *The English Poor in the Eighteenth Century*, pp. 42–7; Viner, 'Man's economic status', pp. 45–6; Karl Polanyi, *The Great Transformation: The Political and Economic Origins of Our Time* (1944; Boston: Beacon Press, 1957), pp. 105–9; John A. Garraty, *Unemployment in History*, pp. 48–50. Garraty's book contains a good general account of the workhouse movement as a whole in Europe since the seventeenth century; see pp. 44ff.

11. Oxley, *Poor Relief in England and Wales*, p. 117. Ashton notes that 'in the years of depression that followed the wars with the French, thousands of men, women, and children were employed . . . in breaking up rock with hammers, to provide material for use by the turnpike trusts'; T. S. Ashton, *An Economic History of England: The 18th Century* (London: Methuen, 1955), p. 113.

12. That is, where a workhouse existed at all in the parish. The 1722 Act was permissive, not mandatory, and many parishes did not take up the sometimes expensive option of constructing workhouses, or modifying other premises to that end. For many parishes cash payments remained the only, and clearly in their minds the cheaper, option.

13. Dorothy Marshall, 'The Old Poor Law, 1662–1795', *Economic History Review* , vol. 8, no. 1 (1937), reprinted in E. M. Carus-Wilson (ed.), *Essays in Economic History*, vol. 1 (London: Edward Arnold, 1954), p. 295.

14. Oxley, *Poor Relief in England and Wales*, pp. 105–6. Cf. Marshall: 'It is interesting to see that giving allowance in relief of wages was no new expedient adopted to meet the emergency of the French Wars, or to deal with the distress at the end of the eighteenth century. By that time the practice was at least a century old. . . . It is difficult, indeed, to know why it arose, for it was not contained in the provision of any statute. The overseer was ordered to relieve "the poor and impotent", not able-bodied labourers, however low their wages. Yet it seems to have been a responsibility which the parishes assumed at an early date'; *The English Poor in the Eighteenth Century*, p. 104. A parliamentary inquiry of 1776 showed clearly that a large amount of relief consisted of 'allowances-in-aid of wages', even in those parishes which had workhouses: ibid., pp. 154–5. See also Garraty, *Unemployment in History*, pp. 52–3.

Furniss notes that the dominant mercantilist theory of the time itself provided a justification for allowance-in-aid of wages. By keeping wages low, knowing that they would be supplemented out of the parish rates, manufacturers would be able to offer their products at lower prices and so compete more effectively in foreign markets. 'Under these circumstances the allowance in aid of wages was a form of bounty given to the export industries, the burden of that bounty being borne by the contributors to the rates'; *The Position of the Laborer in a System of Nationalism*, p. 196. See also Mathias, *The Transformation of England*, p. 157.

by a movement of thought that adopted a distinctly more 'benevolent' attitude to the labourer, and a greater understanding of his problems of work and employment.[15] Gilbert's Act of 1782 gave official recognition of this practice, by sanctioning the granting of aid-in-wages, that is, the supplementing of low wages by payments from the parish rates. This should make it clear that the widespread adoption of the 'Speenhamland system' after 1795 introduced nothing new in principle in the working of the system of the price of bread and the number of family members to support, the Berkshire magistrates were merely following the practice of most eighteenth century authorities.[16]

Thus by the end of the eighteenth century it was clear that the attempt to hold the line between the able-bodied poor and the rest, between the 'deserving' and 'undeserving' poor, had resulted in almost total failure. Those lacking work through unemployment, or on low wages through underemployment, were treated in a more or less uniform system of outdoor relief along with most other categories of the poor. Only those too young, too old, or too sick, to care for themselves, and with no one to look after them, were relieved in workhouses. Most others received cash pensions in lieu of or in addition to wages. Depending on the spirit in which these payments were given and received, they could be demoralizing and degrading, or they could be accepted as a right and an entitlement. There seems good reason to believe that, until the end of the eighteenth century, the second attitude was at least as common as the first. Most workers accepted that there would be temporary periods of unemployment in their trades, and that in particular agricultural work depended on a wide series of factors – such as the weather and the seasons – seemingly quite independent of human control. Hence there could be nothing especially degrading about accepting support from the local community to which one belonged, in those periods of distress that were a natural and apparently permanent part of the life of all pre-industrial communities. Certainly employers, who made up the main body of the ratepayers, could not be happy about paying out rates to support the poor. But they could see that there was a reciprocal interest involved in maintaining

15. See especially for this change of attitude, A. W. Coats, 'Changing attitudes to labour in the mid-eighteenth century', *Economic History Review*, vol. 11, (1958), reprinted in M. W. Flinn and T. C. Smout (eds), *Essays in Social History* (Oxford: Clarendon Press, 1974), pp. 78–99, and A. W. Coats, 'Economic thought and Poor Law policy in the eighteenth century', *Economic History Review*, vol. 13, no. 1 (1960), pp. 39–51. The contrast with the earlier 'mercantilist' conceptions of labour can well be seen from Furniss, *The Position of the Laborer in a System of Nationalism*; see also Eli F. Heckscher, *Mercantilism*, 2 vols (London: Allen & Unwin, 1955), vol. 2, pp. 112–68; Coleman, 'Labour in the English economy of the seventeenth century'.

16. 'It is clear . . . that the magistrates of Berkshire, in issuing their notorious bread scale, were acting in accordance with tradition and precedent. They followed the tradition that relief should generally be given in cash to bring insufficient wages up to subsistence level in periods of temporary crisis, and the precedents of other counties in ordering such assistance, both in other crises and in the one with which they themselves were now confronted'; Oxley, *Poor Relief in England and Wales*, pp. 111–12. This is a needed corrective to the influential view of Polanyi that 'allegedly Speenhamland meant that the Poor Law was to be administered liberally – actually, it was turned into the opposite of its original intent. Under Elizabethan Law the poor were forced to work at whatever wages they could get and only those who could get no work were entitled to relief; relief in *aid of wages* was neither intended nor given'; *The Great Transformation*, p. 79. Polanyi is right about the intent of the Poor Law legislation, wrong about the practice. In fact Gilbert's Act acknowledged that the practice of aid-in-wages had existed on a wide scale for a long time. As with practically all Poor Law legislation from the sixteenth century to 1834, Parliamentary acts merely consolidated or confirmed what had been going on in various localities, sometimes for decades.

their unemployed workers, many of whom would be familiar, long-standing members of the community, and whom they would hope to employ again when better times returned. As the eighteenth century progressed, this became an especially strong consideration for the farmers, anxious to stem the flow of labour to the towns. Hence, too, their continued support for the increasingly onerous burden of Speenhamland.[17]

## WORK, EMPLOYMENT AND UNEMPLOYMENT IN THE PRE-INDUSTRIAL ECONOMY

The support of the unemployed worker by the parish becomes even more intelligible when we consider that the links and associations between work, employment, and unemployment were very different from what they were to become with the developing industrial economy of the nineteenth and twentieth centuries. Certainly, there is no question that wage labour was the predominant form of labour in seventeenth and eighteenth century England. This is clear from the researches of Hill, Macpherson, Macfarlane, Coleman, and others.[18] Most workers, moreover, were dependent on wages for the essential part of their subsistence. Adam Smith may, for the sake of argument, have exaggerated somewhat when he said that 'many workers could not subsist a week, few could subsist a month, and scarce any a year without employment.'[19] But we do nothing to aid the understanding of unemployment today by resurrecting the old sociological myth of a pre-industrial subsistence economy of self-employed peasants and craftsmen – least of all for England.

But having said that, it is important to realize that while workers might be dependent on wages, this did not by any means necessarily assimilate their condition to that of modern wage workers in factories and offices. The organization and setting of work for most eighteenth-century workers, wage-earners as much as others, expressed an experience and an ethos of labour a world away from the time-governed discipline of the modern factory. The term and status of 'wage-labourer' was itself ambiguous, carrying diverse connotations. Building workers, for instance, were paid wages on a daily rate; but it turns out that part of these wages were in payment for the cost of training and maintaining the apprentices who worked alongside the building workers, thus suggesting a craft occupation of a kind very different from that of the standard day-labourer.[20] Ashton describes

17. See on this Polanyi, *The Great Transformation*, pp. 93–4, 297–9. On the attitude of the poor to cash payments, cf. Furniss: 'By the middle of the eighteenth century, two hundred years of official relief had filled the lower orders with the feeling that the overseers' dole was their right and due, was justice not charity, and could therefore be accepted without shame and without gratitude'; *The Position of the Laborer in a System of Nationalism*, p. 231. On the corresponding acceptance by the state and local elites of their obligations to the poor (and the control of disorder thereby), see J. Walter and K. Wrightson, 'Dearth and the social order in early modern England', *Past and Present*, no. 71, May 1976, pp. 22–42.

18. See, for instance, Christopher Hill, *Reformation to Industrial Revolution* (Harmondsworth: Penguin Books, 1969); D. C. Coleman, *The Economy of England 1450–1750* (Oxford: Oxford University Press, 1977); Macfarlane, *The Origins of English Individualism*; Macpherson, *The Political Theory of Possessive Individualism*; B. A. Holderness, *Pre-Industrial England: Economy and Society from 1500 to 1750* (London: Dent & Sons, 1976).

19. Adam Smith, *Wealth of Nations*, 2 vols (Everyman edition, London: Dent 1910), vol. 1, p. 59.

20. Donald Woodward, 'Wage rates and living standards in pre-industrial England', *Past and Present*, no. 91, May 1981, pp. 28–46, *passim*.

ironworkers – nailmakers and the like – in the west midlands who were wage-earners paid by the piece, and who did their work in little sheds attached to their cottages. At the same time there were other ironworkers in the same area who bought their materials from the ironmasters and sold their product back to them, often the same master in each case; these thought of themselves as independent producers, not as wage earners. Hosiery workers of the east midlands who superficially followed the work pattern of these ironworkers were however wage-earners. They collected materials and orders from the large merchant hosiers, for which they were paid wages by the piece.[21] Agricultural labourers often lived-in with the families whose farms they worked, or were provided with a cottage and a small plot of land. Money wages, often paid only at the end of the year, in most cases represented only a very subsidiary part of their subsistence.[22]

The varied pattern of eighteenth-century work allowed for a different 'mix', and a different relation, of 'work' and 'leisure', and of wage labour and subsistence activities, than was possible later. From this followed a now familiar set of characteristics of work and workers before the coming of the factory system: work was regulated by the task, rather than by time; bouts of intense labour alternated with long periods of idleness; the irregularity of the workday pattern imposed by the task was heightened by the irregularity of the working week and the working year; 'Saint Monday' and often 'Saint Tuesday' were piously honoured; and the summer season of the year, often for as long as from June to October, was given over to agricultural and farming activities as against the manufacturing work carried on during the rest of the year. The keynote throughout is irregularity: of time, of effort, of the payment of wages by employers, who often delayed for two or three months before paying for completed pieces of work. John Rule rightly says 'it was not the length of the factory day, but its regularity which contrasted with the cottage labour system.'[23]

Irregularity was also a central characteristic of employment. Uncertainty in the demand for labour marked practically every trade and occupation, although the problem seems to have been mainly one not so much of actual redundancy as of underemployment or 'concealed unemployment'. This was a function of the general structure of agriculture and industry, with the seasonal and cyclical fluctuations common to both. But the effects of this lack or loss of regular employment were significantly lessened by two crucial features of the eighteenth century labourer's position.

In the first place, the eighteenth century labourer was a 'pluralist' as far as occupation was concerned. Where one occupation went cold and slack on him, he could often resort to another. Rule has pointed out that one important

21. Ashton, *The 18th Century*, pp. 101–2.

22. Ibid., p. 206.

23. John Rule, *The Experience of Labour in Eighteenth Century Industry* (London: Croom Helm, 1981), p. 60. Most writers on labour in eighteenth-century England stress these general characteristics. Especially good are: T. S. Ashton, *The 18th Century*, pp. 201–35; Sidney Pollard, *The Genesis of Modern Management: A Study of the Industrial Revolution in Great Britain* (Cambridge, Mass.: Harvard University Press, 1965), pp. 160–208; E. P. Thompson, 'Time, work-discipline, and industrial capitalism', *Past and Present*, no. 38 (1967), pp. 56–97; Douglas A. Reid, 'The decline of Saint Monday 1766–1876', *Past and Present*, no. 71, May 1976, pp. 76–101; Rule, *The Experience of Labour*, pp. 49–69. For general characteristics of pre-industrial labour, see Keith Thomas, 'Work and leisure in pre-industrial society', *Past and Present*, no. 29 (1964), pp. 50–66; K. Kumar, 'The social culture of work', *New Universities Quarterly*, vol. 34, no. 1 (Winter 1979), pp. 5–28.

consequence of the domestic or 'putting-out' system was to disperse manufacturing to the countryside, while at the same time many rural craftsmen such as blacksmiths, wheelwrights, and thatchers were really part of the agriculture 'industry', and probably spent more time mending than making. Not only does this make it very difficult for us to distinguish occupational categories by economic sector, as 'industrial', 'manufacturing', or 'agricultural. It also meant that for workers of the time various occupational 'mixes' were possible, varying both as to region and as to the extent of the mix. Thus there was 'a continuum from the fully mixed in which a man might be equally dependent upon two occupations, through the seasonally mixed in which he might be employed in one or other of two occupations, depending on the time of the year, to the tending of a garden which added usefully but in a strictly collateral way to the family's comfort.'[24] Manufacturing and mining activities were often inextricably mixed with agricultural ones, so much so that, according to R. W. Malcolmson, 'some historians have spoken of the existence of an economy of dual-occupations: a household economy in which there was such an integral relationship between farming . . . and some kind of cottage industry that it may be misleading to speak of "by-employments" at all, for it is often the case that one means of livelihood cannot be clearly identified as predominant and the other as subsidiary.'[25] Prominent examples during the eighteenth century were the weavers, who regularly mixed weaving with husbandry; many communities of coal miners; the small self-employed clothiers of the West Riding of Yorkshire; and the tin-miners of Cornwall.[26] Defoe went so far as to describe those regions where the only source of livelihood was agriculture as 'unemployed counties'.[27]

24. Rule, *The Experience of Labour*, p. 12.

25. Malcolmson, *Life and Labour in England* , p. 38. Malcolmson gives this example: 'In the area of Frampton Cotterell, Gloucestershire, north-east of Bristol, a district that was full of rural industry, many men who were identified in contemporary documents as tailors, masons, weavers and other clothworkers, tanners, cordwainers, feltmakers and coal-miners can be shown from the probate inventories to have retained a substantial involvement in agriculture, in many cases equal in extent to that of yeomen and husbandmen . . . in some cases so much so that, were it not for the indisputable written attribution of their primarily non-agrarian occupation, one would have assumed they were either yeomen or husbandmen.' And he concludes: 'Occupational designations . . . can be seriously misleading, for in their apparent straightforwardness they often conceal much of the complexity of the household economies from which people supported themselves. A man was not always simply a farmer, or a weaver or a metalworker, or – the most difficult of all to interpret – a labourer, any more than most married women today could be usefully represented as "simply" housewives. We want to learn about the actual activities in which people were involved'; ibid., p. 40. For the integration of manufacturing and rural pursuits, see also Joan Thirsk,' 'Industries in the countryside', in F. J. Fisher (ed.), *Essays in the Economic and Social History of Tudor and Stuart England* (Cambridge: Cambridge University Press, 1961), pp. 70–88.

26. Rule, *The Experience of Labour* , pp. 13–15. Woodward shows the extensive involvement in agriculture of a wide range of craftsmen – carpenters, masons, thatchers – in the sixteenth and seventeenth centuries. For example, in Lincolnshire agricultural possessions accounted for over 50 per cent of the personal estates of seventy-nine craftsmen of these kinds, in Lancashire and Cheshire over 40 per cent; Woodward, 'Wage rates and living standards in pre-industrial England', pp. 40–1.

27. Quoted Coleman, 'Labour in the English economy of the seventeenth century', p. 302. Coleman, considering the question how far domestic industry might have been able to compensate for underemployment in agriculture, observes that 'the very ease with which an under-employed rural labour force . . . could at once form the basis of a domestic cloth industry and at the same time contribute to increasing national agricultural output suggests that some measure of success must have been achieved' (ibid.). For a remarkably similar mix of agricultural and industrial activities in seventeenth- and eighteenth-century Japan, see Thomas C. Smith, 'Farm family by-employments in preindustrial Japan', *Journal of Economic History* , vol. 29, no. 4 (1969), pp. 687–715.

This 'economy of dual-occupations' already points to the second important feature of the eighteenth-century labourer's position: that his work was organized around the home. This in itself reduced the degree of dependence on employment for wages. The household economy could and indeed had to draw on the labour of all its members. Few families could subsist for very long on the earnings of the head of the household alone. The household acted as an integrated subsistence unit, depending variously on contributions in the form of wages, food grown on allotments, and cattle grazed on the commons. As Malcolmson says, rather than speak of occupations in this period 'it is better to speak of the work itself – farm labour, weaving, housewifery – and to try and understand how such work contributed to a family's living.'[28] In the weaver's family, for instance, both husband and wife would be involved in 'manufacturing' – he weaving, she spinning – as well as 'agriculture' in the relevant seasons, while the wife would also do the domestic chores and probably also feed the livestock. The children would be employed as helpers in both weaving and spinning and would also do sundry domestic tasks. While it is probably true that for most labouring families the income from wages was the single most important means of support, in most cases it was rarely relied upon as the indispensable contribution to family subsistence. 'As long as domestic industry was supplemented by the facilities and amenities of a garden plot, a scrap of land, or grazing rights, the dependence of the labourer on money earnings was not absolute; the potato plot or "stubbing geese", a cow or even an ass in the commons made all the difference; and family earnings acted as a kind of unemployment insurance.'[29]

It should be clear from all this that 'unemployment', while not exactly welcomed, cannot have been the threat to livelihood that it later came to pose. And this in turn goes a long way to explaining the apparently lax attitude of the

28. Malcolmson, *Life and Labour in England*, p. 23.

29. Polanyi, *The Great Transformation*, p. 92. Furniss echoes Hammond's view that 'in the open field village the entirely landless labourer was scarcely to be found', and comments: 'Whether the cultivation of his own acres was an incidental or the chief part of his economic activity, the fact that the labourer controlled a portion of the earth's surface introduced a factor of vital importance into his struggle to win subsistence for himself and his family. As a source of income independent of the labour market the land would, it is apparent, become of supreme importance at times when prices were high and wages low. Access to the commons and wastes made possible the ownership of a cow which the produce of the labourer's scrap of land would have been unable to support; sometimes a pig or a few geese could be added to his little stock; fuel, which later became of so large importance in the family budget, could be obtained at odd times by cutting the turf or gathering the dead wood from the wastes. These together with the garden would furnish the foundation for his economic support, the capital which the labourer brought to the assistance of his muscular energy in his struggle for existence. Moreover, here as elsewhere in modern society the family must be taken as the economic unit, and from this point of view the garden patch and common rights acquire additional importance. For they made possible the exploitation of the economic opportunities of every member of the family over the age of infancy; each could contribute his share to the family income, the wife by her work in the garden, the children by their care of the stock on the commons. A single pair of hands need not attempt to carry the burden of the entire family, nor need the burden grow progressively greater as the family increased in size.' Furniss, *The Position of the Laborer in a System of Nationalism*, pp. 213–14. On the quantity and variety of common rights at this time, see Malcolmson, *Life and Labour in England*, pp. 23–35; on the perquisites of particular jobs, see Rule, *The Experience of Labour*, pp. 125–9. On the elimination and 'criminalization' of these rights and perquisites, see Peter Linebaugh in 'Conference Report', *Bulletin of the Society for the Study of Labour History*, no. 25 (Autumn 1972), p. 13; Jason Ditton, 'Perks, pilferage, and the fiddle: the historical structure of invisible wages', *Theory and Society*, vol. 4 (1977), pp. 39–71. For a parallel account of the French poor's 'economy of makeshifts' – including beggary, theft, and smuggling – see Hufton, *The Poor of Eighteenth Century France*, *passim*.

Poor Law authorities towards outdoor relief for the able-bodied poor. The loss of employment by the adult male head of the household produced hardship, and needed to be compensated in some way. But apart from the fact that unemployment was usually for intermittent short periods, and so a predictable part of family life, the wages lost made up only one part of the total family economy. The Poor Law overseers and Justices of the Peace were not faced, normally at any rate, with a situation of utter destitution and poverty as a result of unemployment. Hence it made sense, both out of humane consideration, and as a hard-headed financial calculation, to bring families up to a level of subsistence by supplementing their incomings of cash and kind, from whatever sources. By taking into account the total pattern of subsistence of labouring families, including their rights on the commons, the level of subvention would not normally have been very high. It was certainly cheaper for the parish to act in this way than to attempt to bring the labourer and his whole family into the workhouse, even had that been practicable. Aided by modest cash payments, together with what other income the wife and children might be able to bring in, the family was likely to emerge relatively unscathed from spells of unemployment.

There is one further point that should be mentioned in this account of the eighteenth century labourer's relation to wages and employment. The eighteenth century labourer did not *desire* income beyond a certain level. The idea of a continuously growing stream of income over the life span was alien to him. Eighteenth century commentators are unanimous in the view that workers preferred leisure to increased income. When wages were high, or prices low, they cut down the number of hours of work, as they were able to achieve the expected level of subsistence and comfort with less labour. It was one reason why many eighteenth century writers argued against high wages, if production were to be increased. In a famous expression of what later economists were gracefully to theorize as 'the backward-sloping supply curve of labour', Arthur Young declared that 'everyone but an idiot knows that the lower classes must be kept poor or they will never be industrious.'[30]

Once more, therefore, the importance of wages was qualified by a set of values and expectations that limited the needs and requirements of eighteenth century families. The truly fateful change came with the creation of a new set and structure of needs. As early as 1755 Bishop Berkeley threw out the suggestion 'whether the creation of wants be not the likeliest way to produce industry in a people?' Adam Smith was soon to argue that high wages, far from depressing industry, acted as an incentive to increased output, as it brought new standards of 'ease and plenty' within the range of the worker's perceptions, and encouraged him to 'exert his strength to the utmost' in striving to attain them.[31] The importance of money wages was to increase at the very time that the other supports of the family economy were being knocked away, as more and more of

30. The remark occurs in Arthur Young's *Eastern Tour*, 1771. An earlier tour had already produced a general law to cover this observation: 'Great earnings have a strong effect on all who remain in the least inclined to idleness or other ill courses, by causing them to work but four or five days to maintain themselves the seven; this is a fact so well known in every manufacturing town that it would be idle to think of proving it by argument'; *Northern Tour*, 1770.

31. Ashton, *The 18th Century*, pp. 213–14. See also, for the change of attitude, the articles by Coats cited in note 15 above.

the commons were enclosed and the factory system invaded the household economy. From being one among several components of the family economy, wages from employment threatened to be the sole precarious base.

## THE WORKING CLASS AND THE NEW POOR LAW IN THE NINETEENTH CENTURY

But not for some considerable time to come – not, in fact, until late in the nineteenth century. This fact is still not sufficiently appreciated. Because of a tendency to antedate the full impact of the industrial revolution in England,[32] the pattern of work and employment characteristic of twentieth century industrial man is read back into the earlier years of the nineteenth century. From this it is inferred, in particular, that unemployment must have had much the same consequences in the last century as in this – and without the support of the social services available today.

It is this, I think, that lies behind the traditional view that the Poor Law Amendment Act of 1834 constitutes a watershed in the treatment of the able-bodied poor – the category that, as we have seen, for most of Poor Law history covered (and concealed) the unemployed. The new Poor Law is seen as making a radical break with the past by abolishing outdoor relief and forcing all the able-bodied poor into the workhouse, on pain of abandonment to destitution outside. It is, on this view, not simply the product of a new toughness towards the poor, in keeping with the generally disciplinarian ideology of an expanding industrial economy, but the response of a society harbouring a different ethic of work, and a different attitude towards poverty and unemployment. It is thus truly the child of Bentham and Senior, Malthus and Ricardo.[33]

The view that the new Poor Law, 'the principles of 1834', marked a sharp break with the past is however a mistaken one. Even at the level of theory alone, without considering practices, it is not difficult to show that the Act of 1834 represented a continuation and indeed a culmination of the central philosophy of the 1601 Act. The 'new' Poor Law can in fact be seen as the last and grandest effort of the old order to establish and hold the line between the 'deserving' and the 'undeserving' poor, between the truly destitute – the sick, the old, widows and orphans – and the able-bodied poor, who could find their own means of support if they were not demoralized and pauperized by public subsidies. The 1834 Act wished to make this distinction as hard and thoroughgoing as possible. The 'less eligibility' feature of the Act – the principle that the pauper in the workhouse 'must cease to be really or apparently so eligible as the situation of the independent labourer of the lowest class' – merely reaffirmed, in a more rigorous form, the 'workhouse test' of the 1722 Act, designed to discourage the able-bodied from applying for relief unless

32. See on this K. Kumar, *Prophecy and Progress: The Sociology of Industrial and Post-Industrial Society* (Harmondsworth: Penguin Books, 1978), pp. 131–49.

33. For such a view, see e.g. Polanyi: 'The New Poor Law abolished the general category of *the poor*, the "honest poor", or "labouring poor".... The former *poor* were now divided into physically helpless paupers whose place was in the workhouse, and independent workers who earned their living by labouring for wages. This created an entirely new category of the poor, the unemployed, who made their appearance on the social scene. While the pauper, for the sake of humanity, should be relieved, the unemployed, for the sake of industry, should *not* be relieved'; *The Great Transformation* , p. 224.

utterly destitute. The ideal remained the same as that of the Elizabethan Poor Law, the same as it had been throughout the last two hundred years: the rapid resumption of independence by the labourer, who for whatever reason might be tempted or forced to fall back on the rates. Nassau Senior, the chief architect of the 1834 Act, in a review of Poor Law history in 1841 reserved his harshest condemnation for the 'over-generous' Speenhamland system, whose policy of wage subsidies had driven the labourer into a servile and dependent position not very different from that of the American slaves. 'Before the Poor Law Amendment Act, nothing but the power of arbitrary punishment was wanting in the pauperized parishes to a complete system of praedial slavery.'[34] The 1834 Act therefore pinned its highest hopes on the abolition of outdoor relief to the able-bodied, and the re-establishment of the 'workhouse test' with a vengeance. The 'deterrent' element, always latent and often practised under the old Poor Law, was here given its fullest expression in the hope that this would at last realize the long-cherished goal of removing the able-bodied from the sphere of the Poor Law.[35]

Mark Blaug is therefore quite right when he says that 'the Poor Law Amendment Act of 1834 marked a revolution in British social administration, but it left the structure of relief policy substantially unchanged.'[36] The parallels and continuities persist when we move from policy to practice. The 1834 Act had already compromised to some extent on the absolute prohibition of outdoor relief by allowing it to continue in the case of those of the old and the sick who could be

34. [Nassau Senior], 'Poor Law reform', *Edinburgh Review* , vol. 74, 1841, pp. 1–44, at page 3, reprinted in A. W. Coats (ed.), *Poverty in the Victorian Age*, 4 vols (Westmead: Gregg International Publishers, 1973), vol. II, 'English Poor Laws 1834–1870'. Senior's views on Speenhamland, accepted by generations of historians, were sharply and, it appears, successfully challenged in two important articles by Mark Blaug: 'The myth of the Old Poor Law and the making of the New', *Journal of Economic History* , vol. 23 (1963), pp. 151–84, reprinted in Flinn and Smout, *Essays in Social History* , pp. 123–53; 'The Poor Law Report re-examined', *Journal of Economic History* , vol. 24, no. 2 (1964), pp. 229–45. In the second article he summarizes the findings of the first as follows: 'Despite what all the books say, the evidence that we have does not suggest that the English Poor Law as it operated before its amendment in 1834 reduced the efficiency of agricultural workers, promoted population growth, lowered wages, depressed rents, destroyed yeomanry, and compounded the burden on rate-payers. Beyond this purely negative argument, I tried to show that the Old Poor Law was essentially a device for dealing with the problems of structural unemployment and substandard wages in the lagging rural sector of a rapidly growing but still under-developed economy. It constituted, so to speak, "a welfare state in miniature", combining elements of wage . . . escalation, family allowance, unemployment compensation, and public works, all of which were administered and financed on a local level. Far from having an inhibitory effect, it probably contributed to economic expansion; ibid., p. 229. A critical review of recent interpretations of Speenhamland concludes largely in favour of Blaug: see J. D. Marshall, *The Old Poor Law 1795–1834* (London: Macmillan, 1968); and see also J. R. Poynter, *Society and Pauperism: English Ideas on Poor Relief, 1795–1834* (London, Routledge & Kegan Paul, 1969), *passim*, and esp. pp. 278ff.

35. Social policy and social thinking throughout the nineteenth century and beyond continued to elaborate on this basic theme. Philip Abrams's account of policy-orientated research in Victorian England shows that, in the eyes of the researchers, 'the problem was to design reforms that would so ameliorate social conditions that individuals would be enabled, or forced, to improve themselves.' This led to 'the distinction that quickly developed as a cardinal analytical principle of this mode of social science, between the steady, industrious, self-reliant, rational, and therefore deserving poor on the one hand, and the feckless, weak, drunken, loafing, and therefore actually or potentially criminal and undeserving poor on the other'; Abrams, *The Origins of British Sociology 1834–1914* (Chicago: University of Chicago Press, 1968), pp. 31, 41.

36. Blaug, 'The Poor Law Report re-examined', p. 229. The 'revolution' referred to was the new centralized administration of the Poor Law, with a national Poor Law Commission supervising Boards of Guardians in local unions of parishes.

relieved in their own homes (those who could not were to be taken into workhouse). This was meant to be a severely limited provision. But as with so much Poor Law legislation in the past, what the national policy-makers sought after was undermined by the practice of the authorities at the local level. The formidable powers of the new Commissioners proved ineffectual to prevent the erosion of the central aspect of Poor Law policies by a large number of Poor Law Guardians, responding to the realities of the situation in their own areas.

In the northern counties, resistance to the new Poor Law was immediate, long drawn out, and crowned with an impressive degree of success. All sections of the community recognized the inappropriateness, in that region, of a policy which restricted relief of the able-bodied poor to the workhouse. In the northern industrial areas, the commonest experience of unemployment was of the temporary mass kind, when a slump threw thousands of workers out of work. It was impossible to attempt to relieve numbers as large as this in the workhouse, quite apart from the fact that this would destroy the worker's chances of re-employment when better times returned. A powerful coalition of manufacturers, magistrates, local clerics, and local Chartists combined to make the new Poor Law in many northern areas a dead letter for decades, by which time new ideas about poor relief were beginning to emerge. Outdoor relief to the unemployed poor continued to be given on a substantial and regular basis, even frequently in the form most anathematized by the Poor Law Commissioners, that of allowances in aid of inadequate earnings.[37]

The north exhibited the most spectacular resistance to the new Poor Law, but other regions carried out quieter wars of attrition which moved them more or less in the same direction.[38] In 1844 Sir James Graham, the Home Secretary, was forced to admit in the Commons that 85 per cent of relief was still given outside, and not inside, the workhouses.[39] The difficulty of enforcing central policy, and

37. On the failure of new Poor Law policy in the north, see Nicholas C. Edsall, *The Anti-Poor Law Movement 1834–1844* (Manchester: Manchester University Press, 1971). For the continuation of the provision of outdoor relief to the able-bodied, especially allowances in aid of wages, see Michael E. Rose, 'The allowance system under the New Poor Law', *Economic History Review*, vol. 19, no. 3 (1966), pp. 607–20; David Ashforth, 'The urban Poor Law', in Derek Fraser (ed.), *The New Poor Law in the Nineteenth Century* (London: The Macmillan Press, 1976), pp. 128–48.

38. For the continuity of pre- and post-1834 poor relief policies in the southern agricultural counties, see Anne Digby, 'The labour market and the continuity of social policy after 1834: the case of the eastern counties', *Economic History Review*, vol. 28, no. 1 (1975), pp. 69–83; Digby, 'The rural Poor Law', in Fraser (ed.), *The New Poor Law in the Nineteenth Century*, pp. 149–70. See also Anthony Brundage, *The Making of the New Poor Law: The Politics of Inquiry, Enactment and Implementation 1832–1839* (London: Hutchinson, 1978). Both Digby and Brundage emphasize the extent to which policies of continued outdoor relief were in the economic and political interests of the gentry and tenant farmer groups who dominated the countryside.

39. The situation did not change much during the course of the century. In Norfolk as late as the 1870s, 87 per cent of the able-bodied poor were receiving outdoor relief; Digby, 'The rural Poor Law', p. 163. For the country as a whole, Brundage comments that 'the profile of relief policies and the lines of authority remained remarkably constant throughout the 19th century. In towns as well as rural districts, four-fifths of those supported wholly or partly out of the poor rates were on outdoor relief. The union workhouse was relegated to the status of a general asylum for the very old, the very young, the infirm. It was also useful as a residual deterrent against insubordination'; *The Making of the New Poor Law*, p. 184. For urban areas specifically, Ashforth shows that throughout the latter part of the nineteenth century, 'never less than 85 per cent of all able-bodied paupers were in receipt of outdoor relief'; 'The urban Poor Law', p. 131.

the widespread flouting of it is shown in the frequent but unsuccessful campaigns of the Poor Law Commission (and later the Poor Law Board and the Local Government Board) to force local Boards of Guardians to abandon their practice of outdoor relief to the able-bodied (the last major campaign seems to have been in the early 1870s). In practice local Boards of Guardians were able to operate with considerable freedom of the central authority, and they used this freedom to maintain many of the features of the old Poor Law system. As with old Poor Law overseers and vestries, considerations of humaneness were mixed with calculations of cost. In London, for instance, in 1862 it was calculated that a pauper in the workhouse cost the ratepayer 4s 8d a week as compared to 2s 3d for an outside pauper. Motives of both kinds, therefore, often pointed in the same direction, in the maintenance of a considerable level of outdoor relief in the form of cash payments. The result was that the workhouse population of the nineteenth century was remarkably similar to that of the eighteenth in composition: that is, it was made up largely of the sick and infirm, the aged, and orphaned or abandoned children. The able-bodied poor, men and women, shunned the workhouse like the plague, and in many cases the Poor Law Guardians were willing accessories.[40]

## THE ECONOMY OF THE POOR IN THE NINETEENTH CENTURY

Still there remains a large question. The outdoor relief, in the form of cash payments, given to the poor was hardly generous. It was indeed the very meagreness of the dole that, in the eyes of many guardians, made it so attractive an alternative to the provision of relief in the workhouse. What, if any, additional resources did the poor have to draw on? What in particular was the pattern of work and employment that enabled the able-bodied poor to manage in the Victorian era? Did they in fact manage?

One answer, as revealed in the official statistics of the central Poor Law

40. For the relative cheapness of outdoor as opposed to indoor relief, see Rose, 'The allowance system under the New Poor Law', pp. 613–14. The rarity of finding the able-bodied poor in the workhouse was frequently commented on in the course of the century. As Ashforth says, 'in most years, in most urban unions, somewhere between 6 and 15 per cent of all those who were receiving relief, were receiving it in the workhouse. As a rule, the only able-bodied applicants sent to the workhouse were those considered to be idle, troublesome, morally unsound or Irish. The general attitude was expressed by the chairman of the Burnley board, when he stated that "the house was not a workhouse, it was a poor house. It was for the old and infirm and the destitute poor. It was never intended for able-bodied, hard-working, honest men" '; 'The urban Poor Law', p. 135. As a consequence, workhouses became, for most practical purposes, little more than 'hospitals of sorts; and indeed from the 1880s were described as such in official terminology'; Fraser, 'Introduction', in Fraser (ed.), *The New Poor Law in the Nineteenth Century*, p. 5. By 1870, the Poor Law Board could casually record that 'workhouses, originally designed mainly as a test for the able-bodied, have, especially in the large towns, been of necessity transformed into infirmaries for the sick'; Ashforth, 'The urban Poor Law', p. 148. A similar thing was noted of rural workhouses. In 1892 Mr Lockwood, inspector for the Norfolk Union, commented that 'during the last 20 years the rural workhouse has become almost exclusively an asylum for the sick, the aged, and children'; Digby, 'The rural Poor Law', p. 163. In the light of this well-attested position it is curious how strongly the Dickensian workhouse has dominated our image of the Victorian poor. Much of this no doubt has to do with the powerful propaganda of the anti-Poor Law movement, including of course Dickens's own writing.

authorities, was that the problem of the poor was being solved by the disappearance of poverty itself. Official statistics showed a gratifying and progressive drop in the number of paupers on relief throughout the century: from 1.26 million (8.8 per cent of the population) in 1834, to 1 million (5.7 per cent) in 1850, to 808,000 (just over 3 per cent) in 1880. By 1900 only 2.5 per cent of the population was estimated to be in receipt of poor relief. It was thought by many professional commentators that the rising standard of living of the working classes, together with improved Poor Law administration, were reducing poverty to a problem of relatively minor proportions.[41]

Such complacency could not however stand up to the extent of poverty revealed by the painstaking investigations of Booth, Rowntree, Bowley and others towards the end of the century and in the early years of the new one. These showed, with a striking degree of agreement, that something like 30 per cent of the population were living in poverty. When this is compared with the 2–3 per cent officially on relief in the same period, it is clear, firstly, that the Poor Law statistics are of little use as a measure of poverty and, secondly, that a significant proportion of the population were living in poverty without having recourse to poor relief.

And yet the Booth–Rowntree–Bowley picture is itself far from unproblematic. For one thing it is not clear how far back into the nineteenth century we can project these turn-of-the-century estimates, although Henry Mayhew's more impressionistic (and more vivid) observations of working class life at the mid-century reveal something of the same dimensions of poverty. But the real problem is the nature and significance of poverty itself. Who were the poor in the nineteenth century? What part did poverty play in the total picture of working class life? What aspects of that life, especially of working life, may have begun to change by the time Booth and Rowntree started their investigations?

Booth himself found old age to be the most frequent cause of poverty in the East End of London. The old made up one-third of all paupers in his 1892 study of Poplar and Stepney; while over half of all paupers on outdoor relief under the Poor Laws were aged and infirm. As in the eighteenth century, widows with dependent children constituted a high proportion of Poor Law relief cases. So did the sick; the Royal Commission on the Poor Laws of 1905–9 revealed that 30 per cent of paupers were receiving medical treatment. Large families again, were another major cause of poverty.[42] So far, the picture is one that shows a striking similarity with the eighteenth century poor, and suggests that many aspects – including some of the grimmest – of the eighteenth century working class life had persisted well into the nineteenth century.

Is this also true with another major cause, for many *the* major cause, of poverty –

41. For these figures see Michael E. Rose, *The Relief of Poverty 1834–1914* (London: Macmillan, 1972) pp. 13–15. For a good example of professional social research of the time, and the agreement on the diminishing extent of poverty, see Robert Giffen, 'The progress of the working classes', *Journal of the Statistical Society* 1883, reprinted in Abrams, *The Origins of British Sociology*, pp. 157–76; see also J. T. Danson, 'The condition of the people of the UK 1839–1847', *Journal of the Royal Statistical Society*, vol. XI, 1848, pp. 101–40.

42. For these findings, and a valuable brief discussion of the 'discovery of poverty', see Rose, *The Relief of Poverty*, pp. 20–34. See also E. H. Hunt, *British Labour History 1815–1914* (London: Weidenfeld & Nicolson 1981), pp. 120–5.

inadequate or irregular earnings? We have seen that eighteenth century workers frequently lost wages through spells of unemployment, but that these were at least in part compensated for by other resources of the household and local economy. How far was this still true in the nineteenth century? The precise contribution of unemployment to poverty in the nineteenth century is impossible to estimate, since the figures for unemployment before the establishment of labour exchanges in 1910 are notoriously patchy. The Board of Trade figures, based on returns from benefit-paying unions of members in receipt of 'out-of-work' benefit, show that between 1870 and 1912 average unemployment for the trades covered ranged between 3 and 6 per cent, with a rise to between 7 and 10 per cent for the bad years of 1879, 1885–7, 1893–5, and 1908–9.[43] These do not seem excessive, certainly as compared with some later levels. But as against this we have to set, for example, the estimates of Hobsbawm and Foster for the first half of the century. Hobsbawm shows that in the worst slump years, such as those of 1826 and 1839–42, anything between 25 and 75 per cent of particular occupational groups, and in some places of the whole working population, might be unemployed; although he makes the point that at most other times in this period 'underemployment, rather than cessation of work' was the main problem for most trades.[44] In the case of the Lancashire textile workers, Foster calculates that up to 30 per cent of the workforce were unemployed in the worst years of the 1830s and 1840s.[45] And generally it seems that a high degree of casual and irregular employment, and so a marked degree of underemployment, was a feature of the English economy right up to the end of the century, although patterns of stability and security of employment were beginning to be established in several trades.[46]

But of course we have to go behind these figures of 'the unemployed' to know what they meant in the lives of the workers concerned. And here there is sufficient evidence to indicate that, until about the end of the century, conditions of work and subsistence persisted which mitigated the bare fact of unemployment and modified its significance in the lives of workers. It was not merely that, as now, to be out of employment was not necessarily to be without work. More important was the 'undeveloped' state of the industrial economy itself, leaving significant pockets of 'pre-industrial' work organization and attitudes which militated against the complete identification of work with formal employment in the market economy. The statistics of 'unemployment' in the nineteenth century,

43. See José Harris, *Unemployment and Politics: A study in English Social Policy 1886–1914* (Oxford: Clarendon Press, 1972), appendix B, 'Unemployment statistics before 1914', table 2, p. 374. See also Sir William H. Beveridge, *Causes and Cures of Unemployment* (1931; Westport, Conn.: Greenwood Press, 1976) p. 6.

44. E. J. Hobsbawm, 'The British standard of living, 1790–1850', in his *Labouring Men: Studies in the History of Labour* (London: Weidenfeld & Nicolson, 1964), pp. 72–82. Hobsbawm quotes Henry Mayhew's estimate at the mid-century as 'worth our attention': 'Estimating the working classes as being between four and five million in number, I think we may safely assert . . . that . . . there is barely sufficient work for the *regular* employment of half our labourers, so that only 1,500,000 are fully and constantly employed, while 1,500,000 more are employed only half their time, and the remaining 1,500,000 wholly unemployed, obtaining a day's work *occasionally* by the displacement of some of the others'; ibid., p. 82.

45. John Foster, *Class Struggle and the Industrial Revolution: Early Industrial Capitalism in Three English Towns* (London: Weidenfeld & Nicolson, 1974) pp. 81, 258–9.

46. Hobsbawm, 'The British standard of living', pp. 80–2.

such as they are, conceal a very considerable amount of remunerative work actually done, and distort the real situation of families in the emerging industrial economy.

Take first the family economy, the traditional arrangement whereby virtually all members of the family contributed to its subsistence. This defensive bulwark against the involuntary unemployment of particular family members persisted throughout the nineteenth century, in the factory districts as much as in domestic industry. Smelser's suggestion that family employment declined in the cotton industry in the 1830s and 1840s has been shown to be untrue by Anderson and Pollard. At the mid-century, 'family employment was still characteristic, and as a result the local labour force was able to show superior resilience and attachment to the industry in depressions, even though wages were not high.'[47] There is even the possibility that early industrialization increased the employment of women and children, at a time when employment opportunities were declining in agriculture and domestic industry. Since, in addition, women and children earned more in the factories than elsewhere, 'with the Industrial Revolution their earnings became central to the domestic economy. They made a significantly larger contribution and they made it to a significantly larger number of families.'[48] Where family members did not actually work for money, they could contribute to family income indirectly, as in the case of grandparents who co-resided with their married children, 'caring for the children and home while the mother worked in the factory'.[49]

Thus the coming of the factory system did not for some time destroy the unity of the family economy. Thompson's remark that 'the family was roughly torn apart each morning by the factory bell'[50]is misleading, with its suggestion of a decisive fragmentation of family life, a radical separation of the spheres of work and family. Families continued to work as well as to live as a unit, a fact acknowledged indirectly by Engels in his appalled middle-class observation on the effects of working wives: 'It is inevitable that if a married woman works in a factory, family life is inevitably destroyed. ... [However] very often the fact that a married woman is working does not lead to the complete disruption of the home but to a reversal of the normal division of labour within the family. The wife is the breadwinner while her husband stays at home to look after the children and to do the cleaning and cooking. This happens very frequently indeed. ... One may well

47. Sidney Pollard, 'Labour in Great Britain', *Cambridge Economic History of Europe*, vol. 7, part 1 (Cambridge: Cambridge University Press, 1978), p. 133. And see Neil Smelser, *Social Change in the Industrial Revolution* (London: Routledge & Kegan Paul, 1959); Michael Anderson, 'Sociological history and the working-class family: Smelser re-visited', *Social History*, vol. 1, no. 3, pp. 323–4.

48. Neil McKendrick, 'Home demand and economic growth: a new view of the role of women and children in the Industrial Revolution', in N. McKendrick (ed.), *Historical Perspectives: Studies in English Thought and Society* (London: Europa Publications, 1974), pp. 185–6; Elizabeth Pleck, 'Two worlds in one: work and the family', *Journal of Social History* , vol. 10, no. 2, (1977), p. 185.

49. Michael Anderson, 'Household structure and the industrial revolution: mid-nineteenth-century Preston in comparative perspective', in P. Laslett and R. Wall (eds), *Household and Family in Past Time* (Cambridge: Cambridge University Press, 1972), p. 230. For the general contribution, material and non-material, of the wider kinship network to family support in nineteenth-century factory towns, see Michael Anderson, *Family Structure in Nineteenth Century Lancashire* (Cambridge: Cambridge University Press, 1971), esp. ch. 10.

50. E. P. Thompson, *The Making of the English Working Class* (London: Victor Gollancz, 1964), p. 416.

imagine the righteous indignation of the workers at being virtually turned into eunuchs.'[51]

Factory employment was of course a fact of experience for only a minority of nineteenth century workers, and least of all for adult males.[52] The persistence of the family economy was naturally even more evident in the small-scale domestic and outwork industries which, far from being extinguished by industrialization, actually expanded enormously as a result.[53] In mid-nineteenth-century Stourbridge, for example, by then a medium-sized industrial town based on iron, 'a good half of the workforce was employed in or about the home', with a family-based, task-orientated work pattern traditionally associated with domestic industry. This meant not simply the customary observance of 'St Monday' and 'St Tuesday' – until well into the 1870s and beyond – but the equally conventional interruption of industrial work to go harvesting and hopping (joined by the miners of the area) in the summer months. Children and women worked as a matter of course in these domestic industries – such as nailmaking and brickmaking – and shared in the long hours and laborious but intermittent toil characteristic of them.[54]

It was the continuation of domestic and outwork industry on an extensive scale that was mainly responsible for concealing from contemporary census enumerators – and later historians – a good deal of the remunerative work actually done in Victorian England, especially by women. This was especially true in a town like London, where few trades were transformed by the factory system until the twentieth century. The commentators and social statisticians tended to concentrate on women workers in factories, and so largely ignored the host of washerwomen, needlewomen, charwomen, landladies, baby-minders, midwives,

51. F. Engels, *The Condition of the Working Class in England*, trans. and ed., W. O. Henderson and W. H. Chaloner (Oxford: Basil Blackwell, 1958), pp. 161–2.

52. Cf. Chambers: 'The representative Englishman, it has been said, was still a countryman in 1831, and the representative workman was still a handicraftsman in a traditional workshop, working with traditional tools. In 1851, the distribution of the population had changed in favour of the townsman, but the representative Englishman was still far from being a worker directly employed in machine industry. The victory of the factory over the older forms of industrial organization was slow and it was not until the last decade of the century that it became the dominant form of organization in a majority of the industries. In 1851, those employed in the principal non-mechanized categories comprised about five and a half million workers and outnumbered those in the mechanized industries (including coal) by three to one; and of the one and three quarter million in the mechanized groups, half a million were cotton workers. The most numerous group after agriculture were domestic servants. In 1851, their number had risen to over a million and was still twice as large as the cotton workers. At 1,039,000 they were drawing nearer to the agricultural group which now numbered 1,790,000 and together these two groups numbered more than double those engaged in manufacturing and mining. When Britain was the undisputed workshop of the world, the "great industry" on which it was based actually employed 1.7 million out of a total British population of 21 million'; J. D. Chambers, *The Workshop of the World* (London: Oxford University Press, 1961), pp. 21–2. See also John Burnett (ed.), *Useful Toil: Autobiographies of Working People from the 1820s to the 1920s* (Harmondsworth: Penguin Books, 1977), pp. 256–65.

53. R. Samuel, 'Workshop of the world: steam power and hand technology in mid-Victorian Britain', *History Workshop*, no. 3 (Spring 1977), pp. 6–72; Pollard, 'Labour in Great Britain', pp. 128–9; F. F. Mendels, 'Proto-industrialization: the first phase of the industrialization process', *Journal of Economic History*, vol. 32 (1972), pp. 246–7; Pleck, 'Two worlds in one', pp. 181–2.

54. Eric Hopkins, 'Working conditions in Victorian Stourbridge', *International Review of Social History*, vol. 19, no. 3 (1974), pp. 401–25.

and other female domestic workers, including those married women who worked with their husbands in his trade. Even less visible to the enumerators were the ill-defined categories of female market workers and street-traders, not to mention street-walkers. Speaking of the London working class, Sally Alexander says:

> Women (and children) of this class always had to contribute to the family income.... It was often the household and not the individual worker, or even separate families, that was the economic unit. A mixture of washing, cleaning, charring as well as various sorts of home- or slop-work, in addition to domestic labour, occupied most women throughout their working lives. The diversity and indeterminacy of this spasmodic, casual and irregular employment was not easily condensed and classified into a census occupation.[55]

There was nothing idyllic about the family economy, either in its full pre-industrial form or in its increasingly attenuated and straitened state in the nineteenth century. It was nearly always stretched to its limit, with the Poor Law as a largely feared and disdained safety-net. But it remained, at its most besieged, a welfare system in miniature, with children, wives, and occasionally grandparents covering as best they could when the man was unemployed or unable to work. That for a good part of time the system provided at least a bare subsistence for the family is suggested by the fact that throughout the nineteenth century the Poor Law figures consistently show that only a small percentage of able-bodied paupers were destitute through want of employment.[56] It is this system that also partly explains the otherwise extraordinary clinging of many families to handicraft trades where these were in direct competition with factory production. Pollard refers to the plight of the hand-loom weavers, 'whose numbers did not decrease as their wages were inexorably depressed even further below subsistence level', as 'one of the best known and most puzzling episodes of the Industrial Revolution'. 'It will be better understood,' he suggests, 'if it is remembered that many weavers were now women, often part-time; others combined weaving with farming; and still

55. Sally Alexander, 'Women's work in nineteenth century London: a study of the years 1820–1850', in Juliet Mitchell and Ann Oakley (eds), *The Rights and Wrongs of Women* (Harmondsworth: Penguin Books, 1976), p. 65. The concealment of the degree of female employment is of course not confined to non-factory areas like London. Anderson notes that 'well over a third of all working wives in Preston in 1851 were employed in non-factory occupations, but were not recorded'; *Family in Nineteenth Century Lancashire*, p. 71. See also Hunt, *British Labour History*, p. 345, n. 36. For a good account of the contribution of women's part-time work – among other 'non-quantifiable' items – to family income in another Lancashire area, see Elizabeth Roberts, 'Working-class standards of living in Barrow and Lancaster', *Economic History Review*, vol. 30, no. 2 (1977), pp. 306–21.

It is his excessive reliance on census returns that largely vitiates the argument by Richards that women's employment *declined* in the Victorian age. See Eric Richards, 'Women in the British economy since about 1700: an interpretation', *History*, vol. 59 (1974), pp. 337–57. There seems no real evidence to support the view of a *quantitative* decline in female employment – rather the reverse. What is more plausible however is the idea of a 'qualitative' decline, a loss of status for women workers as they moved from pre-industrial household production to the factories and slop-shops of the nineteenth century. For this view, see e.g. Thompson, *Making of the English Working-Class*, p. 416. In another sphere of women's work, there was also the decline in the status of 'domestic service' itself, as reflected in the changing meaning of the word 'menial'; Burnett, *Useful Toil*, p. 165; OED, 'menial'.

56. Harris, *Unemployment and Politics*, p. 371. Given the relatively high levels of unemployment at various times in the century, this suggests that the unemployed were supported in other ways than by the public system of poor relief.

others clung to their spurious independence with the help of other members of the family working in the mills.'[57]

A further perspective on the still 'unmodern' nature of the Victorian economy is provided by a consideration of the two areas of employment that dominated throughout the nineteenth century: agriculture and domestic service. Domestic service did not simply give rise to the second largest occupational group after agriculture; it was far and away the most important source of employment for women. It expanded rapidly in the second half of the century, accounting for over 40 per cent of all employed women up to 1901. The denunciation of the conditions of domestic service has become so common that it is easy to forget that the alternatives for most women, and for their families, were far worse. It is in fact no idealization of domestic service to say that 'service provided country girls with a surrogate home and family', or that 'employment in a good household was akin to membership of an extended family group.'[58] For women and children, life in one's own home and family was at least as likely to lead to exploitation as life in someone else's service. Domestic service was a way out, both for them and their families, a means of externalizing some of the economic pressures on poor families living in cramped quarters on low wages, especially in the country districts. For the girls of these families, moreover, it was a secure, well-paid, and regular occupation for which there was a steady and rising demand throughout the century. The wages of domestic servants rose faster than those of almost all other wage-earners. In addition, 'servants' food and accommodation were in most cases far better than what they could have expected in their parents' home, and there were few workers so likely to receive medical attention paid for by their employers, pay during sickness, and regular paid holidays.'[59]

Nor did the movement out of the family disrupt the basic unity of the family economy. Girls in domestic service, like many of their counterparts in factory work, continued to regard themselves as part of the family enterprise. They regularly sent back much of their wages to their families, and made frequent visits for longer or shorter stays. For both themselves and their families, their movement into domestic service in the towns was no more than an extension, or an expansion, of the traditional contribution of girls to the family economy.[60] Moreover, once married, women workers were similarly occupied in 'domestic' employment – as homeworkers in the textile and dressmaking trades – and continued in a different guise to play their traditional part in the overall domestic economy. It is clear, then, that for this large section of the Victorian workforce – women accounted for about 30 per cent of the total labour force throughout the century – 'unemployment' could be neither as threatening nor as consequential as

57. Pollard, 'Labour in Great Britain', p. 132.

58. Hunt, *British Labour History* , p. 106; Burnett, *Useful Toil*, p. 137.

59. For this account of domestic service see Burnett, *Useful Toil*, pp. 135–42; Hunt, *British Labour History*, pp. 19–22, 105–7. See also Teresa M. McBride, *The Domestic Revolution: The Modernisation of Household Service in England and France 1820–1920* (London: Croom Helm, 1976).

60. Joan W. Scott and Louise A. Tilly, 'Women's work and the family in nineteenth century Europe', *Comparative Studies in Society and History*, vol. 17, no. 1 (1975), pp. 36–64. See also the various autobiographies of domestic servants in Burnett, *Useful Toil* , pp. 175–245. On domestic service as an extension of traditional family (and marital) roles for females, see Leonore Davidoff, 'Mastered for life: servant and wife in Victorian and Edwardian England', *Journal of Social History* , vol. 7, no. 4 (1974), pp. 406–28.

it was to become when domestic employment declined after the First World War.

Traditionalism, in work practices and attitudes, seems also to have been the hallmark throughout much of the countryside during the nineteenth century. The importance of this for the assessment of the impact of 'unemployment' is obvious when we consider that agricultural workers made up the largest occupational group for practically the whole century. 'Somewhere near mid-century British agriculture employed more workers than at any time before or since.' Agricultural workers then made up almost a quarter of the entire occupied population.[61] British agriculture was certainly being revolutionized, and the proportion of landless wage-labourers, already high relative to other countries, continued to grow throughout the century. But, as with work practices in the factory,[62] so in the countryside there was for long little attempt to 'systematize' and 'regularize' the workforce. Samuel comments that 'occupational boundaries in the nineteenth century countryside were comparatively fluid. They had to be, where so much employment was by the job rather than by the regular working week.' He goes on to echo Alexander's warning about the limitation of census-based accounts, in presenting a realistic picture of employment in the countryside:

> There is a whole spectrum of occupations which historians (following the census enumerators) have overlooked, either because they were too local to show up prominently in national statistics, like coprolite digging in Cambridgeshire and Bedfordshire, or because they were too short-lived to rank as occupations at all. . . . Industrial occupations in the countryside, such as limeburning, brickmaking, or quarrying, are ignored. So too is the whole range of country navvying jobs which kept the out-of-work farm labourer employed – sand getting and gravel drawing, for instance, clay digging, wood-cutting and copse work, and such locally important occupations as river cutting and dyking in the Fens. . . . We know very little about the alternative sources of employment open to the labourer; the census enumerators largely ignore them. 'Field labour' covers all.[63]

Something of the variety of work carried on in the countryside as late as 1892 comes out in the finding of the Royal Commission on Labour of that year that three-quarters of the farm labourers of Monmouthshire were engaged in wood-cutting, quarrying, and mine work. In a surprisingly direct echo of many statements about eighteenth century workers, they comment: 'With respect to many of them, it is difficult to determine whether they may be styled wood-cutters and quarrymen, coming to the land for hoeing, harvesting, and sundry piece-work, or whether they are in the main agricultural labourers, going to the woods, quarries and mines in the winter months.'[64]

61. Hunt, *British Labour History*, pp. 26–9. See also Pollard, 'Labour in Great Britain', pp. 139–47.
62. See E. J. Hobsbawm, 'Custom, wages, and work load in nineteenth-century industry', in his *Labouring Men* (London: Weidenfeld & Nicolson, 1964), pp. 344–70.
63. R. Samuel, 'Village labour', in R. Samuel (ed.), *Village Life and Labour* (London: Routledge & Kegan Paul, 1975), pp. 3–5.
64. Quoted Samuel, 'Village labour', p. 4. For a detailed account of the many different ways and means of 'making out' in the countryside in the late nineteenth century, see also R. Samuel, ' "Quarry roughs": life and labour in Headington Quarry, 1860–1920', in Samuel (ed.), *Village Life and Labour*, pp. 139–263. Samuel's account, based on oral evidence as with Roberts's similar study of Barrow and Lancaster (see n. 55, above), indicates the importance of local studies of this kind in correcting many of our notions about the nature of work and employment in Victorian England.

The nineteenth century farm labourer was clearly no stranger to the 'dual-occupation' economy. In addition he had access, on a declining scale no doubt, to the remaining rights (acknowledged or not) on commons, pasture, and woodlands, together in most cases with a small plot of land or allotment.[65] In the grim conditions of the agricultural labourer's life, especially in the south, these features were of inestimable value in gaining a subsistence. They also enabled farm families, even more than urban families, to act in a common enterprise. Women and children played a noticeable part in the family economy, not simply at harvest time but throughout the year, in such activities as laundry work, the keeping of ducks and pigs, poaching, and gardening.[66] In such an economic environment, 'unemployment' was decidedly not a meaningless thing – the winter months were especially hard – but it might be difficult to know precisely what it meant, or to assess the true consequences.

We should note, finally, that 'dual occupations' were not restricted to rural workers, but in a general sense involved a large proportion of the Victorian workforce as a whole. Victorian working life still showed a noteworthy 'irregularity' and diversity that in many ways harked back more to the eighteenth century pattern than to the twentieth. Raphael Samuel has shown a cyclical pattern of employment for many urban workers. The cycle, however, was not that of the economy but of the seasons. As the spring approached, families, sometimes in groups, would leave the town to seek employment in the countryside. At the height of the summer season, whole towns would be deserted and certain industries forced to close down temporarily. With the autumn and winter, the drift back to the town set in, with yet another change of occupations. The next spring set families moving again. Samuel makes it clear that the pattern was not really broken until the end of the century, with the 'regularization' of employment in factories and on farms.[67] Certainly the descent of East End London families on the hop fields of Kent in the summer months was still going strong at the turn of the century (and indeed for many decades thereafter).[68]

It is important to stress that the work pattern of these 'wandering tribes' was not something marginal and exotic in the Victorian workforce as a whole. Hobsbawm's examination of the 'tramping' system shows that a period of wandering in search of work – or simply of variety of place – was a normal part of the working lives of respectable artisans. The system combined elements of 'unemployment relief' with primitive labour-exchanges and the creation of a mobile labour market. It was, from the point of view of the artisans, a normal way of dealing with the threat of unemployment, setting men in motion from areas of scarcity of work to those where, with the help of local union branches, they could

65. Samuel, 'Village labour', pp. 6–10; 'Quarry roughs', pp. 189–94; G. Mingay, *Rural Life in Victorian England* (London: Futura Publications, 1979), pp. 116–17. Urban dwellers in certain regions also continued to eke out family income with the free produce of the countryside; see Roberts, 'Working-class standards of living in Barrow and Lancaster', pp. 316–17.

66. See D. Morgan, 'The place of harvesters in nineteenth-century village life', and J. Kitteringham, 'Country work girls in nineteenth-century England', both in Samuel (ed.), *Village Life and Labour* .

67. Raphael Samuel, 'Comers and goers', in H. J. Dyos and Michael Wolff (eds), *The Victorian City: Images and Realities* , 2 vols (London: Routledge & Kegan Paul, 1973), vol. 1, pp. 123–60.

68. See Gareth Stedman Jones, *Outcast London: A Study of the Relationship Between Classes in Victorian Society* (Harmondsworth: Penguin Books, 1976), pp. 90–2.

more easily find it. As Hobsbawm says, 'what we may call the non-capitalist sector of the economy long remained large enough, and the capitalist sector localized and diversified enough, to make temporary migration appear a feasible escape from slumps.' In the earlier part of the century, when the system – apparently as much a new growth as a continuation of eighteenth century practice – was at its height, the General Union of Carpenters commented that of late 'our highroads have resembled a mechanical workshop, or a mighty mass of moving human beings.' Hobsbawm adds that 'some men, in that period of rapid industrial growth, were semi-nomadic, leaving a permanent home for varying periods, or shifting their families from time to time, especially among builders, specialist craftsmen and supervisory workers.'[69]

These are simply glimpses. Many aspects of Victorian working life remain hidden from us by the preconceptions of officials, historians, and sociologists. But perhaps enough has been said to back up the main point: which is that work, employment, and unemployment in nineteenth century England still bore many of the hall-marks of the pre-industrial economy and society. Poverty was caused and relieved in much the same way as the previous century. Work was not so specialized that workers could not turn their hand to a variety of occupations in town and country. Urbanization itself had not yet gone so far that most workers and their families could not have some access to the 'free' resources of the countryside. The contingencies of life, including unemployment and underemployment, pressed as hard as ever; but a mixture of outdoor relief, a diversified labour market, and mutual aid in traditionally-oriented families and communities softened their stark impact.

## 'THE UNEMPLOYED MAN' AND THE CHARTER OF 'FULL EMPLOYMENT'

All this had begun to change fundamentally by the time Booth, Rowntree, Beveridge, and the rest began their researches on the poor. Industrialization was at last delivering up its fruits, and England was becoming the first fully recognizable urban-industrial society. The irregularity that marked work and the workforce was being eliminated in a number of ways, by specialization, mechanization, work organization and a firmer imposition of work discipline. For those workers in the right trades and industries this promised greater security and status. For others, de-casualization was a threat to their livelihood in circumstances where alternative ways of making ends meet were disappearing. For all, the 'right to work' was coming to carry almost exclusively one meaning, 'the right to employment'. The employed status was the only one entitling the worker to a claim on the society's resources; even when out of work, claims for benefits and support turned preponderantly on earned rights through previous employment.[70] Those who could not get employment at all, or for too short periods to build up

69. E. J. Hobsbawm, 'The tramping artisan', in his *Labouring Men*, pp. 48, 42, 44.
70. For this development see David Macarov, *Work and Welfare: The Unholy Alliance* (Beverley Hills: Sage Publications, 1980).

legitimate claims for support, were faced with a hostile and increasingly unsupportive environment.

The resources of the family itself, for so long the refuge of the unemployed, were squeezed by the withdrawal of labour of some of its members. The Education Acts of 1870 and later did what many factory acts had failed to do, gradually eliminating child labour on any but most insignificant scale. The number of working wives also declined. By 1911 only 10 per cent of married women were employed, compared with a quarter in 1851 and probably twice as much as that at the beginning of the nineteenth century.[71]

It is not surprising, therefore, and far from a coincidence that this is the period, beginning in the 1880s, in which 'unemployment' as a concept first received formal recognition, and was widely investigated and subjected to theoretical scrutiny.[72] We have often had occasion up to now to refer to 'unemployment' and the 'unemployed' before this period, and of course it is quite proper to do so. But the whole point of the discussion so far has been to stress the different meaning and significance of 'unemployment' in that earlier period, both for the workers themselves and the public authorities which had to deal with their situation. The appearance of a new word or concept, in the social world at least, sometimes does not mark more than a belated recognition of what has for long been going on. But in many cases, as with 'unemployment', it is a good indication that something in the social environment has significantly changed. A new awareness, a first response to a novel challenge, arises in the society. Such a challenge was now, for the first time, seen to be posed by unemployment, as an endemic structural feature of industrial economies, and as a social problem of potentially overwhelming proportions. A new phase of industrial life was signalled by the minority report of the Royal Commission on the Depression of Trade and Industry (1886) when it declared that the great problem of the age was not the scarcity and dearness of commodities, but 'the struggle for an adequate share of that employment which affords to the great bulk of the population their only means of obtaining a title to a sufficiency of those necessaries and conveniences, however plentiful they may be'.

71. Hunt, *British Labour History*, p. 18. The change reflected both the decline of domestic outwork and working class imitation of middle-class family life. Rural areas were as much affected as urban: 'One of the features of Rowntree and Kendall's investigation of rural poverty shortly before the First World War was how little wives were able to contribute to family earnings'; ibid., p. 23.

72. See John A. Garraty, *Unemployment in History: Economic Thought and Public Policy* (New York: Harper Colophon Books, 1979), pp. 103ff. The word 'unemployed' did not appear in its modern meaning in the *Oxford English Dictionary* until the late 1880s, and 'unemployment' was not a separate heading in *Hansard* until after the Boer War.

# Part II

# Employers' Strategies and Workers' Strategies

# Editor's Introduction

We have seen in part I something of the taming process whereby the alternative work rhythms and practices of pre-industrial society were made subject to the disciplines of factory organization. These disciplines and constraints that were imposed on the workforce were not the necessary consequence of an inevitable process of technological innovation. Certainly an earlier generation of economic historians claimed that the first factories arose largely for technical reasons, but others stressed the 'obvious advantages', in Mantoux's phrase, of organization and supervision. David Landes explicitly stated 'the essence of the factory is discipline – the opportunity it affords for the direction of and coordination of labour.' This was not a new notion devised by late-twentieth-century radical historians: its roots go back to the early nineteenth century.[1] In *The Philosophy of Manufacturers*, published in London in 1835, Andrew Ure perceived Arkwright not primarily as an inventor or as a technological innovator but as someone who was able 'to devise and administer a successful code of factory discipline'. Inventions such as the spinning jenny could operate equally well in a cottage as in a factory. Seen in this light, factory organization was primarily concerned with solving problems of discipline and control. This form of organization then helped to determine the forms of technical change that occurred.

Workers were bound to the disciplines of wage labour by their expanding needs as consumers and by the lack of alternative ways of maintaining their families and dependants. However, it was one thing to ensure that workers came to the factory on time and were docile and obedient to the demands of management; it was quite another matter to make sure that they worked hard and conscientiously. Overseers could hardly go round cracking whips over the backs of those workers

1. See the classic study by Reinhard Bendix, *Work and Authority in Industry*, first published by John Wiley and Sons in 1956; the Harper Torchbook edition, with new material, was published in New York and Evanston in 1963. More recently see Stephen A. Marglin, 'What do the bosses do? The origins and functions of hierarchy in capitalist production', *Review of Radical Political Economies* 6(2), 1974; reprinted in an abridged form in *Classes, Power and Conflict*, edited by Anthony Giddens and David Held, Macmillan, 1982.

whom they considered to be idle, although some might come close to that. Nor could workers be permanently cowed by the fear of dismissal: it was obviously a very wasteful strategy to encourage a rapid turnover of workers through indiscriminate firing with the consequent burden of hiring and training. It was clearly far better to retain a willing and productive workforce. Thus, from the very early days of the factory system there were a *variety* of styles of management. Some believed more in a benevolent paternalism and provided relatively good working conditions and fringe benefits. Such employers, often characterized as 'enlightened', cared for the health and welfare of their employees through providing model housing and other benefits. Leisure facilities were provided and great attention was devoted to workers' 'moral welfare'. Quakers and other Nonconformists, who had large and flourishing family businesses, were more concerned to use carrots rather than sticks to ensure the commitment of their workforce. Examples of such benevolent paternalism can be found in all the industrial nations from the early nineteenth century onwards.

Other employers adopted a different managerial style. In order to increase production they argued that it was necessary to understand more precisely what tasks had to be done and then arrange payment systems that would directly reflect the achieving of such tasks. In order to justify the authority that they imposed, attempts were made to devise a system of 'scientific management' to provide the justification and the means for extending control over the labour process. This line of thought found its clearest expression in the ideas and research studies of F. W. Taylor, who published books and articles at the end of the nineteenth century and in the early years of the twentieth century. Taylor recognized that it was necessary for management to observe very carefully how tasks were done, since it was hard to control the activities of workers unless management shared the knowledge the workers already had. With this knowledge it was possible to define jobs very carefully in terms of output, and this could then be linked directly with pay. Taylor devised his own techniques of time and motion study in order to work out the best possible levels of work performance with a given level of technology. He then tried to devise incentive systems that would secure these performance levels.

Taylor was also concerned with the quality and adequacy of machines, tools and materials but the aspects of his work that focused on the detailed supervision of the labour process came to dominate managerial consciousness. Fundamental lines of conflict were drawn up between management – insisting on its 'right to manage' – and workers, resisting the attempts to squeeze the last possible ounce of labour power from their muscles and brains. This rather crude struggle between, as it were, capital and labour was not what Taylor had in mind when he published the result of his time and motion studies. He imagined that workers would be motivated to work more effectively to increase productivity and consequently their own wages. From this perspective, management was a benevolent and supportive system enabling workers to achieve greater rewards and benefits. Indeed, Taylor believed more in cooperation than coercion as a basis for expanding scientific management and he saw the need for managers to change their attitudes too.

The most sustained critique of any such latent or implicit benevolence on the part of management was provided by Harry Braverman's vigorous polemic *Labour and Monopoly Capital* published in 1974. He assumed that 'skill' was a zero-sum concept, in that if management gained such knowledge, based on their detailed analysis of workers' activities, workers would have 'lost' something that could not be recovered. However, it is obvious that *sharing* is not the same as *dispossessing*. Workers do not lose their skill; they simply lose their monopoly of it. Braverman linked Taylorism with deskilling and what he termed 'the degradation of work in the twentieth century'. Taylor believed that any resistance to his scientific management would be on an individualistic and not a collectivist basis. Whilst control was essential, this was a control based on the authority of 'science', to which managers were equally bound. Hence there is an important distinction between the technical aspects of time and motion study and job design and the *style* of managerial implementation.

In chapter 7 Wood and Kelly point out that 'Taylorist techniques have been implemented within a number of quite different strategic frameworks.' The situation in Japan in the early twentieth century can be contrasted with that of Britain. In the former case the Taylorist focus on 'managerial control of workers and of work processes harmonized well with the paternalistic structures of large industrial organizations and with their drive to modernize Japan and to attack the arbitrary role of owners'. In Britain, on the other hand, Wood and Kelly claim that the existence of strong unions limited the spread of Taylorism and, where piece rates were introduced as a result of time and motion study, as in the British car industry, they were more likely to be the subject of various forms of bargaining and regulation rather than imposed paternalistically or automatically with the authority of science.

The 'scientific' aspects of Taylorism resonated well in the Soviet Union after the 1918 revolution, with Taylorite supporters arguing for the introduction of piecework and method study and increased labour intensity. 'Taylorism also found favour in Fascist Italy,' Wood and Kelly note, 'where it was often introduced in a very authoritarian manner and, instead of raising wages and reducing working hours, was used to achieve precisely the reverse (by contrast with the Soviet Union, where wages did increase in some sectors under piecework).'

It is important to stress the danger of conflating scientific management with specific techniques since this, in effect, was the confusion that Braverman's book did much to disseminate. An insistence on the potential for a whole range of managerial strategies undermines the fallacy that there is only *one* basic capitalist managerialist strategy, namely Taylorism.

The issue still has substantial contemporary relevance in the discussion about the introduction of new technology. The notion that a given form of technology carries with it one and only one managerial style, which it is ultimately in the workers' own self-interest to accept, is in itself a managerial strategy, based on the fallacy that has been mentioned.

Many sociologists and others were commissioned by managers and those in authority in industry to find ways of maintaining managerial control over what was perceived to be a stubbornly recalcitrant workforce. Workers in various countries, who did not welcome enthusiastically the imputed benefits of Taylorist techniques, were branded as being inadequately socialized into the value system of industrial society, as being mulishly and archaically class-conscious or as being simply obtuse. It was hoped that by exploring in greater detail what workers thought and how they operated, the blocks to even greater levels of production could be removed. Typically, the problem was seen to lie more with the workers than with management, reflecting a dichotomous approach to industrial organization on the part of management that they deplored when expressed by the workers. Sociologists who undertook such research reported, inevitably, that the reality was more complex than it originally appeared. In the same way that comparative analysis of managerial strategies undermined Braverman's stereotype of a single 'capitalist' strategy, so the distinctions between mass production, batch production and continuous process production undermined Braverman's monolithic stereotype of manufacturing industry. Fluctuation in demand and other factors undermined simple systems of planned work flow.

As Wood and Kelly emphasize, it is wrong to assume that the existence of any given managerial strategy implies in itself that it will be successfully *implemented*. It is not enough to observe workers as so many pieces of human machinery. It is also necessary to understand the social relationships in which the labour process is embedded and the attitudes and orientations of the workers concerned. One of the earliest and most thorough attempts to do this was carried out by Donald Roy, in his classic study made during eleven months of participant observation as a radial-drill operator in the machine shop of a steel processing plant in Chicago in 1944 and 1945. Despite all the attempts by management to develop a piecework payment system that would increase output, the paradox demonstrated by Roy was that the work group of which he formed a part had a regular daily programme of restricting output.

Michael Burawoy worked in exactly the same firm thirty years after Roy. He describes in chapter 8 'how the organization of a piecework machine shop gives rise to making out and how this in turn becomes the basis of shop-floor culture'. He goes on to argue that the changes he documents between 1945 and 1975 'do not seem to support theories of intensification of the labour process or increase of managerial control through separation of conception and execution'.

Not only did Burawoy have the opportunity of observing how the piecework system of payment changed over time in the same firm in Chicago; he was also able to work in a socialist society with, it might be assumed, a distinctive style of management and orientation to the role and activities of ordinary workers. His account of working as a radial-drill operator in a Hungarian machine shop in 1984 provides a rare and valuable insight into shop-floor life in a different cultural context. Burawoy writes in a non-academic, almost journalistic style, which does much to bring alive the everyday realities of what he calls 'the hidden abode of socialist production'. In doing this he provides an introduction to chapters 13 and 14, also based on empirical research in Hungary, which explore distinctive managerial and worker strategies. Burawoy notes how the workers spend their time on Fridays thinking about work outside employment; this provides a link with chapter 24 in part IV. However, the main point of Burawoy's Hungarian ethnography is that, perhaps counter-intuitively, production is *more* efficient in socialist Hungary than in capitalist Chicago: the workers work hard, the work flow is smoother and workers 'exude a natural and genuine generosity so absent from the brittle, competitive atmosphere at Allied'. Taken together, Burawoy's chapters on piecework, showing differences over time and between political cultures, provide a unique insight into the nature of the labour process. Despite all the research and discussion about scientific management over the last century, much factory work is still noisy, dirty and dangerous. As Burawoy remarks, 'machines don't recognize that they are run by fragile and fallible humans; they continue relentless.' Marx himself recognized that the burdens of a machine-dominated labour were inevitable and unavoidable in some degree. Even in the future socialist society of his imagination, the best that could be achieved would be a reduction of the length of the working day. Workers could then spend more time in what he called 'the realm of freedom' and less in 'the realm of necessity'.

In chapter 10 Child returns to managerial strategies, focusing more sharply on the introduction of new technology and moving beyond the debates about Taylorism that were fuelled by Braverman's work. He notes that managers still appeal to 'the ideology of market-driven technological determinism', perhaps more enthusiastically when the power of organized labour is weak. He shows how central a goal is the achievement of *flexibility* in production through such strategies as the elimination of direct labour, subcontracting, 'polyvalence' (that is, maintaining core workers who are able to perform a range of tasks which cut across or extend traditional skill and job boundaries) and, finally, the degradation of jobs. The main features of this last strategy are very similar to Taylorism, involving the fragmentation of labour with narrowly constituted jobs, deskilling and a use of direct control methods - whether through close supervision or structuring by technology.

The notion of a flexible firm based on a core of polyvalent workers and a periphery of subcontractors, outworkers, part-time workers (mostly female) and other forms of temporary labour is becoming more widespread in advanced industrial societies, as the following four chapters distinctively illustrate. Child argues that when management adopts a full-blooded strategy of the flexible firm, the consequence is that the labour force is segmented into different skill and status categories and the pool of labour in the external labour market is increased. He notes that this weakens the capacity of workers to mount an organized resistance against management and its use of new technology. This point is well understood in a recent report on *Flexibility and Jobs* from the European Trade Union Institute, but even this body admits that

> It would be wrong to exaggerate the extent to which such 'macho' management styles have predominated, even in countries where they received much press attention and acclaim from sympathetic government. Much management in Europe is fundamentally concerned at the long-term damage being done to industrial relations and labour efficiency as a result of this process. Nevertheless a clear trend does exist.[2]

This seems certain to be a crucial issue for the final years of the twentieth century.

In chapter 11 Fergus Murray takes a particular aspect of the core–periphery distinction and elaborates the consequences of the decentralization of production in Italy for the traditional labour movements. The introduction of new technology has encouraged firms to restructure production in a very distinctive way, which has encouraged some American commentators to see this model as

2. European Trade Union Institute, *Flexibility and Jobs – Myths and Realities*, Brussels, 1985, p. 101.

the pattern for the future in most other industrial countries. Control that was once best achieved through the concentration of production is now seen as better achieved through deconcentration and dispersal. The putting-out system that existed in eighteenth-century England, but was later destroyed by the introduction of the factory system in the nineteenth century, is now being reintroduced at the end of the twentieth century.

The rather general and partially polemical overview provided by Murray is elaborated in detail by Solinas, who explores in chapter 12 the social context of decentralized production in a specific industry. He describes typical worker careers, showing how women in particular move into home working after an early career as factory workers to fit in with their family-building period. Again, there are echoes of the eighteenth century as Solinas shows the interconnections of agricultural work, domestic work and manufacturing work in Emilia. Whilst factory workers in the early nineteenth century gave up their work flexibility for the disciplined routines of the factory, women in the knitwear industry in Italy 'forgo the advantages of direct employment in the factory in favour of a greater freedom to decide how much, how long, and how to work'. Whilst there may indeed be an element of increasing freedom associated with greater flexibility for some workers, there is also a danger of increasing powerlessness and potential for exploitation. We return to consider these issues in more detail in part V.

The final two chapters in this part relate to the interweaving of workers' strategies and employers' strategies. Kertesi and Sziráczki in chapter 13 attempt to interpret 'the behaviour of groups of workers in different positions, enjoying different interests and opportunities as a result of firms' and workers' conflicting aspirations and mutual compromises'. The authors describe the different elements in a multisegmented and diversified labour market. In Hungary it is important to distinguish between two economic sectors. The first is state *directed*, with budgetary dependence on the state. The second economic sector, by contrast, may be *regulated* by the state but the units use their own means of production and can decide for themselves when and for how long they operate. The two economic sectors have differing rules of operation and there is a kind of competition between them. The state would like to maintain the second economic sector in a secondary role but it is not always able to achieve this, and both sectors attempt to evade the regulations that are intended to keep their activities distinct.

Kertesi and Sziráczki describe the adaptation mechanisms of firms (in the West these would be called managerial or employers' strategies). However, unlike the situation in the West, in Hungary the same amount of work yields more consumable income in the second economic sector than in the first. Thus workers can not only improve their situation by moving between firms but also calculate the best strategy both inside the firm and outside in the second economic sector, trading off the relative benefits of each economic context to their best advantage. The choice between different ways of earning income is made on the basis of trade-offs between reward and effort. The authors then develop their typology of workers' strategies designed to both increase their incomes and improve their wage/effort ratios. As the authors recognize, the results of these various bargainings and trade-offs perpetuate new patterns of inequality amongst workers.

In the final chapter in part II David Stark develops the discussion of the various strategies adopted by both management and workers to reduce uncertainty, by focusing on subcontracting *within* Hungarian firms to partnerships of the same firm's workers. These enterprise business work partnerships, or VGMs, help the firm to overcome bottlenecks, reduce dependence on outside firms and provide the enterprise with increased flexibility in meeting deadlines. In the West, the flexible firm is based on core workers and peripheral part-time or temporary workers with substantial subcontracting to other firms. In Hungary flexibility is achieved inside the firm, where some privileged workers get additional payments for their work in the VGMs and also increase their bargaining power with management. Stark claims that

> for both professional and blue-collar partnerships, the outcome of bargaining about whether a particular project will be undertaken in regular hours or in the VGM is often not determined by immediate profitability criteria. Rather, bargaining involves a complex assessment of debits and credits, calculations about new clients brought to the firm, perceptions about indispensability, compensation at a later time for crucial tasks performed in an earlier period of difficulty, and anticipation of future needs. And although bargaining centres on calculations of earnings and efforts, these calculations are far from simple as they involve comparisons with the earnings of managers (who are excluded from VGM participation), side payments to non-members who perform support tasks for the partners ('pocket-to-pocket' payments from the partnership's common fund in what one worker described as the 'third economy' inside the firm), and considerations of the timing of bargaining in relation to the firm's planning cycle.

This complex and subtle pattern of bargaining between management and the VGMs is a long way from Taylor's scientific management in its most authoritarian version. The various forms of internal and external subcontracting, the growth of segmented labour markets also inside and outside the firm and other forms of dualism, which are described for Italy and Hungary in chapters 11 to 14, appear to be the best guides to the way much manufacturing work will be organized in the years ahead. The most privileged workers are able to enhance their position, both economically and politically. Other workers may be able to get other benefits from work outside employment. Whatever the precise pattern of work in a given context the final result seems to be a continued fragmentation of the workforce: some workers receive a cumulation of privilege, and other workers suffer multiple exclusions.

In part II we have limited ourselves to various strategies focused on the place of employment. However, for both the Italian outworkers and certain categories of Hungarian workers, the best strategy involves combining their employment with work outside employment, either in and around their own homes and smallholdings or in the second economic sector. This implies a wider consideration of other forms of work, to which we turn in part IV. Before leaving part II, it is important to recognize that the simple model of a single breadwinner, exchanging his labour power for a wage sufficient to support him and his dependent family and dominated at work by 'scientific management', is no longer tenable. New managerial strategies have to develop to cope with market uncertainties, the introduction of new technology or, in socialist societies, uncertainties in the bureaucratic environment. New workers' strategies emerge both in response to alternatives inside and outside the firm and also from the way households deploy their collective labour. Multiple-earner households typically bring together core and periphery workers under the same roof – and, indeed, in the same bed when a male core worker is married to a female part-time peripheral worker. The manager who is married to someone who is a consultant or does subcontracting work for her firm or organization is likely to become a more common phenomenon.

New divisions of labour are emerging that help to break down traditional lines of conflict and replace them with new ones. The arguments and issues that dominated the era of mass production and the collective workers are being replaced by new arguments and issues concerned with flexibility, fragmentation, deregulation and the distinctive strategies of management and workers.

# 7

# Taylorism, Responsible Autonomy and Management Strategy

STEPHEN WOOD AND JOHN KELLY

A curious feature of much previous discussion of Braverman's *Labor and Monopoly Capitalism* (1974) has been a marked tendency to portray capitalist management as virtually omniscient. The implementation of management strategy is therefore taken to be unproblematic. By equating Taylorism with capitalist management in its essence, Braverman is able to depict post-Taylorist developments as either complementary or irrelevant; anti-Taylorist strategies are inconceivable.

By contrast, Friedman (1977a,b) and R. Edwards (1979) have attempted to argue for the existence and importance of such alternatives. Friedman in particular has argued that it is precisely because of resistance to direct control that in certain situations managements have adopted less restrictive systems, involving the concession of 'responsible autonomy'. While Edwards lays equal stress on the need for managements to adapt to worker resistance, his argument rests as much on the reasons for the extensive non-implementation of Taylorism as on the problems created by its utilization. It was resisted by workers but was also not popular with managers and was not adopted in any general fashion. Those managements who adopted it did so in a piecemeal way; in short it was a failed experiment.

Despite this, Edwards concludes that managements did learn from and adopt some of the underlying ideas of Taylorism, such as the need to wrest control of production knowledge from workers or to define jobs in terms of output and to link this with pay, and these features were taken up and have endured. Any conclusion about the implementation and efficacy of Taylorism depends in part on how broadly it is defined at the outset. The broader one's definition of Taylorism, the more one sees it as all pervasive, as Braverman appears to regard it, while a narrower definition suggests a lesser degree of influence (cf. Palmer,

This essay was first published as chapter 4 in Stephen Wood, ed., *The Degradation of Work?*, Hutchinson, 1982.

1975). But there is equally the danger that in reacting to Braverman's over-reliance on Taylorism we fall into the trap of minimizing its importance. In this chapter we shall attempt to show that one way in which these problems may be circumvented is through a recognition of the limits and constraints of Taylorism. This involves more than simply emphasizing worker or managerial resistance to Taylorism: it also requires a reconsideration of the nature of Taylorism in order to clarify its limitations. This chapter will thus fall into three sections. The first deals with Braverman's treatment of Taylorism; the second outlines certain important but neglected features of Taylorism; and the third concludes by discussing the question of alternatives to Taylorism.

## BRAVERMAN: TAYLORISM AS THE QUINTESSENCE OF CAPITALIST MANAGEMENT

According to Braverman, *all* labour processes require some degree of co-ordination, in so far as they are based on division of labour. In modes of production based on social classes there also arises the necessity for control, a need which is far more thorough and more comprehensive under capitalism because of its dynamic character, evidenced by the constant drive to accumulate. Capitalism is also distinguished, however, by formally free labour - workers may dispose of their own labour power as they wish - and this, according to Braverman, further imparts to capitalist production an unusually antagonistic character.

These features of capitalism resulted, in Braverman's view, in constant attempts throughout the nineteenth century to develop a specifically capitalist mode of management that would exercise control over the labour process. Braverman sees the domestic, sub-contracting and putting-out systems as imperfect approximations to Taylorism, 'the specifically capitalist mode of management'. Detailed control over the labour process at the turn of the century was exercised, in Taylor's (and Braverman's) view, not by management but by skilled workers, who could and did thereby obstruct capitalist innovation and rationalization.

Deskilling originated historically in the management drive against such skilled workers, but the tendency is found throughout all sectors of the economy and continues well beyond the alleged decline of traditional craft work. This is because deskilling allows increased capitalist control over production, since opposed centres of knowledge are destroyed and the labour process is fragmented. It also permits, on the Babbage (1971) principle, a considerable cheapening of labour and an increased rate of exploitation.

For Braverman, Taylorism and its assumptions 'reflect nothing more than the outlook of the capitalist with regard to the conditions of production' (1974, p. 86), because it articulates the need to control labour, provides means (in the form of time-and-motion study and other techniques) for dispossessing workers of their knowledge of production and thereby provides management with the basis on which to *control* the labour process. Braverman describes Taylorism in the more abstract terms of three principles: the rendering of the labour process independent of craft, tradition or workers' knowledge, and their replacement with experiments (or science); the separation of conception from execution; and the use of the managerial monopoly over knowledge to control the labour process in detail. Post-Taylorist developments in management are seen as complementary to Taylorism ('human relations'), dismissed as inconsequential (for example, job redesign) or ignored (for example, productivity bargaining). Since management under capitalism is taken to have reached its purest expression in Taylorism, no further development of an anti-Taylorism character is possible. Braverman regards the human relations movement simply as a means for adjusting workers to the deleterious consequences of Taylorism.

The key to Braverman's assessment of Taylorism and its significance lies in his structuralist conception of capitalism as a law-governed system whose laws inevitably work themselves out without contradiction (Elger and Schwarz, 1980; Burawoy, 1978). For neither the capitalist mode of production itself nor the practices derived (analytically) from it, are treated as potentially contradictory. There is no notion of capitalist development itself issuing in pre-socialist forms, such as rudimentary planning, the growing interdependence of enterprises and the increasing democratization of work. Braverman's concept of control is also far from adequate, even in his own terms. His inflation of the control or autonomy exercised by pre-Taylorian craftsmen has been commented upon elsewhere but there is another difficulty, which is that he works implicitly with a zero-sum concept of control and its bases, particularly knowledge. Thus if management investigates, and acquires, knowledge of a production process, the workers are supposed either to lose this knowledge or to be incapable of regaining it, however partially. In other words, Braverman conflates acquisition of knowledge with monopoly of knowledge and examines control historically in terms of a simple shift from worker to employer control (see also Burawoy, 1978). He cannot, then recognize different modes of managerial control, post-Taylor, and as we have said must treat Taylorism as the highest form of management under capitalism and as incapable of being transcended.

Against Braverman's conception of a working class dominated by the laws of capitalism and its consequences has been counterposed worker resistance and struggle. This has been seen by many writers as a methodological corrective, but has also been used (Friedman 1977a) as the ground from which to explain the limits of management control as well as major changes in the means and relations of production. Yet the 'class struggle' critique of Braverman also remains within the Taylorist problematic of control. It does so by assigning great theoretical and empirical significance to the potential for working-class organization and struggle to evade full capitalist control of the labour process and thereby to thwart capitalist objectives. This tendency to inflate control to the point at which it becomes the central problem of capitalist management is at variance with most analyses of capitalism, including that of Marx, which emphasize the pursuit of profit as the directing aim of capitalist management.

But this is not all, because even in Marxist terms surplus value has not only to be *produced* but also to be *realized*. Control of the labour process by capital, the maximum rate of extraction of surplus value (consistent with continued accumulation and labour supply) and the realization of surplus value were analysed by Marx as integral but separate moments in capitalist production. This means that it is possible for contradictions to arise between any of these moments. Labour exploitation may be relatively high but control weak, as may be the case with skilled craft workers; or realization of surplus value may be constrained by structural or other limits to its production, such as output regulation.

## THE DEVELOPMENT OF TAYLOR'S SCIENTIFIC MANAGEMENT

While Braverman is correct to emphasize the significance of the labour process (Elger, 1979), and of Taylorism within that process, it should also be recognized that management in general does not revolve simply around labour. Taylorism is very much more complex than Braverman suggests, and although it has always centred on labour productivity, there was a growing emphasis throughout Taylor's work on the technical preconditions for raising it, such as adequate materials flow and machine maintenance, and implicitly on the problems of implementing his proposals in the face of worker suspicion or hostility. The initial and central concern was 'task management' – that is, the determination of possible levels of performance (given improved methods and so on) and the search for ways of securing these levels as effectively as possible. Hence Taylor emphasized the importance of financial incentives and the pay-performance link and later came to stress the importance of assigned work quotas for individual workers.

As Braverman notes, Taylor's system arose from his observations of output regulation by workers, a practice that was adopted as a defence against rate cutting and a possible loss of jobs as a result of an increase in productivity. For its part, management was compelled to resort to rate cutting to increase its exploitation of labour, because it lacked the detailed knowledge of production required to raise productivity. It was this knowledge which Taylor set out to acquire through time-and-motion study, though he soon came to realize that if labour productivity was to be raised, then simultaneous improvements had to be effected in machine maintenance, materials and tools supply, work flow and detailed supervision (F. W. Taylor, 1919).[1]

Taylor's conception of control, however, occupies an ambivalent position within his work, a fact obscured by Braverman's abstract and monolithic account of a 'Taylorism' that was free of contradiction and that underwent no development.[2] In *A Piece-Rate System*, Taylor's second published work, there was very little emphasis on control. At that stage Taylor still worked within a classical economics conception of the employment relationship as an economic exchange. Time-and-motion study would be accepted because workers would realize that with increased productivity would come increased wages. His own experiences at Midvale and Bethlehem Steel eventually convinced him that economic interest was insufficient to promote change, and that it was necessary to use the knowledge gathered through the 'scientific' investigation of production to control

1. Taylor's technical contributions were not therefore simply by-products, as Braverman (1974, p. 110) suggests, but necessary preconditions for raising and maintaining labour productivity; see Kelly (1982).
2. Equally 'monolithic' accounts of Taylorism derive from the practice of privileging a particular text as the clearest expression of Taylorism as a whole; cf. P. S. Taylor (1979), Sohn-Rethel (1978), Bendix (1974) and Drucker (1976).

the labour process. Thus in 1906 Taylor could write of the slide rule used to codify and apply knowledge of machining:

> The gain from these slide rules is far greater than that of all the other improvements combined, because it accomplishes the original object, for which in 1880 the experiments were started; i.e. that of taking the control of the machine-shop out of the hands of the many workmen, and placing it completely in the hands of the management, thus superseding 'rule of thumb' by scientific control. (Taylor, 1906, p. 252)

This much quoted statement is also much misunderstood, by Braverman and others. In short, they argue that if management does in fact acquire such knowledge of production, then workers either lose it or are unable to regain it. Yet knowledge is not a commodity that can be 'lost' in this manner, and Braverman has conflated the acquisition of knowledge with its monopoly (Burawoy, 1978). Even after time-and-motion study craft wrokers continue to possess their knowledge; they 'simply' lose the advantage of management ignorance. On this basis craft workers have continued to resist deskilling and have retained important positions in many branches of production (see Brown, 1977).

It is possible that Taylor himself recognized this problem, even if only dimly, because by 1912, in his Testimony to the House Committee, he was stressing heavily the necessity for a 'mental revolution' among workers and managers. In view of the American Federation of Labour's campaign against Taylorism (which culminated in the House Committee hearing) and the strike in the previous year at the Watertown Arsenal against time-and-motion study (Aitken, 1960; Nadworny, 1955), it is tempting to dismiss the 'mental revolution' as a public relations exercise designed to allay public hostility and suspicion. A more plausible interpretation, in the light of Taylor's experiences and the hostility of both employers and unions, was that Taylor was beginning to articulate the preconditions for the implementation of his techniques.[3] It was the same issue which led his associates, Cooke and Valentine, to the very different conclusion that Taylorism could only be implemented with trade-union co-operation in a framework of 'industrial democracy' (Haber, 1964, ch. 3; Nadworny, 1955, ch. 5).

Implicit in these observations is a distinction between techniques – time-and-motion study, control of work flow, stores inventories – and the strategy required for their implementation. For Taylor the introduction of scientific management did not require union co-operation and would in time render unions superfluous. It was to be introduced by a paternalistic but autocratic management which was itself subject to Taylorist principles. Managers would therefore demonstrate that their decisions were subject to the same discipline as the workers, namely, the authority of science, but in practice Taylor protested in 1912 that 'nine-tenths' of the problems of introducing his system could be laid at management's door. A key component of the strategy was individualism. Workers were to be paid by their individual performance; grievances and suggestions were to be received only from

3. Problems of implementation are also discussed in R. Edwards (1979) and Palmer (1975), both of which are useful correctives to Braverman. Fridenson (1978) illustrates, through the use of Taylorism in France, how managements may adapt the system to meet their own particular needs.

individuals; and the labour process, as far as possible, was to be composed of individualized work roles (Kelly, 1982). As the embodiment of collectivism, unions occupied no place in Taylor's world.

The techniques/strategy distinction[4] is absent from Braverman because he assumes its implementation to be unproblematic. In fact, Taylorist techniques have been implemented within a number of quite different strategic frameworks. In the Japanese context Taylor's emphasis on managerial control of workers and of work processes harmonized well with the paternalistic structures of large industrial organizations and with their drive to modernize Japan and to attack the arbitrary role of owners (Nakase, 1979; Okuda, 1972). Taylor's works were quickly translated into Japanese and sold in enormous quantities, and the Japanese branch of the Taylor Society was one of the first to be formed. It was the larger Japanese organizations, including government bodies and foreign companies inside Japan, that pioneered Taylorism. This strategy coexisted throughout the 1920s both with welfare strategies which constituted the foundation of the lifelong employment security system and with collective bargaining and joint consultation with trade unions. Taylorism as such began to decline during the Depression, when workers started to resist it more strongly and it began to be located within nationalist discourse as a foreign ideology alien to Japanese culture.

In Britain, by contrast, the existence of strong union organization in the major branches of production limited the spread of time-and-motion study. Where piece rates were introduced on the basis of such study, as in the car industry, they were often the subject of bargaining and regulated by mutuality clauses (limiting unilateral management changes) rather than by 'science' (Friedman, 1977b; Brown, 1977).

There was also a very intense debate on the nature of Taylorism and its applicability to a socialist mode of production in the early Soviet Union. Lenin's 1914 moral critique of Taylorism's oppression and exploitation of the workers (Lenin, 1965a) and its contrast with the economic anarchy outside the enterprise was replaced with a quite different view in 1918. Writing during the Civil War, at a time of serious economic dislocation, Lenin stressed the importance of using the 'scientific' components of Taylorism, such as time-and-motion study and planned work flow, as opposed to its 'bourgeois' ideological elements, principally intensification of labour. Having said this, Lenin introduced a critical ambiguity into his view by asserting that the overall intensity of labour in Russia was low by international standards and would have to be raised (Lenin, 1965b).

The ensuing debate in the USSR centred on the question of labour intensification, with one group (the Council on Scientific Management) arguing it was unnecessary and counter-productive, while the eventually successful Gastev and his supporters argued for the introduction of piecework and method study and increased labour intensity (Bailes, 1977; Traub, 1978). Taylorism also found favour in Fascist Italy, where it was often introduced in a very authoritarian manner and, instead of raising wages and reducing working hours, was used to achieve precisely the reverse (by contrast with the Soviet Union, where wages did increase in some

4. A similar distinction is implicit in R. Edwards (1979) and Palmer (1975).

sectors under piecework) (Carr, 1966; Rollier, 1979). What perhaps unites these otherwise distinct applications of Taylorism is, as Maier (1970) suggests, a radical, technocratic opposition to liberal capitalism. Equally, the insistence in Taylorism on the non-zero–sum basis of conflict, of the possibility of raising wages and profits simultaneously, appealed to the national, anti-class views of Fascism and the unitarist ideology of some American employers in the 1920s.

For many writers evidence of the diffusion of Taylorism emerges from its equation with enhanced division of labour. Braverman, as well as Littler (1978), argues that 'Taylorism' entails a 'dynamic of deskilling' because of its insistence on the division between conception and execution and its implicit acceptance of the Babbage principle. In 1835 Babbage wrote: 'The manufacturer, by dividing the work to be executed into different processes, each requiring different degrees of skill and of force, can purchase exactly that precise quantity of both which is necessary for each process' (Babbage, 1971, pp. 175–6). While it is undoubtedly the case that Taylorist techniques were used to further the detail division of labour, it is also true that the phenomenon was not peculiar to Taylorism and pre-dated it by a considerable period. Division of labur was subordinated in Taylor's work to his overriding objectives: securing control over the labour process and raising the productivity of labour (Haber, 1964; Kelly, 1982).

## DISTINGUISHING MANAGEMENT STRATEGIES

Given the importance of the context in which Taylorism is implemented and of avoiding the conflation of scientific management with specific techniques, it is necessary to develop modes of discussing strategies which are not rooted in Taylorism. The most recent attempt at such discussion is that of Friedman (1977a, 1977b, 1978). His attempt to delineate different managerial strategies is an important corrective to Braverman's view that one can isolate an invariant and essentially capitalist managerial practice, namely, Taylorism. Equally, Friedman implicitly rejects the arguments of a number of French sociologists that contemporary efforts to 'humanize' or reorganize work through the devolution of autonomy and by other methods are merely new forms of Taylorism (see, for example, Montmollin, 1974).

Although as we shall see there is some ambiguity in Friedman's conceptualization, he seems to identify two types of strategy according to their mode of control: direct control and responsible autonomy. In the first (of which Taylorism is the clearest expression) management exercises its control directly, by means of the specification of work methods, close supervision and coercion. The second type entails the concession of elements of control, or 'responsible autonomy', to workers so that they can exercise discretion over the immediate process of production. In another formulation he argues that the direct control strategy seeks to control or suppress the variability inherent in labour power, whereas the responsible autonomy strategy seeks to exploit it and to harness it to capitalist objectives.

These two types of strategy relate to a series of specific determinants, namely, the phase of development of capitalism, the competitive conditions of the industry, the production position of groups of workers (whether central or peripheral) and the central or peripheral position of particular industries. Direct control is thought to be more effective with peripheral workers and peripheral industries and in less developed areas of capitalism.

Despite its intuitive appeal, there are a number of difficulties with this conception. First, the components of both strategies are not clearly identified. Responsible autonomy is variously described as consisting of worker discretion and commitment to capitalist objectives (a job-redesign type of practice); as counselling, improvements in social relations, the stimulation of intergroup competition, suggestion schemes and participation (a classical 'human relations' type of exercise); and as the concession of improved material benefits - high wages and incentives, job security, good fringe benefits and working conditions (Friedman, 1977a, p. 97; 1977b, pp. 48–52). These practices may coincide empirically, but there are many cases where they do not, and it is thus important to be clear about the components of the posited strategy and to avoid defining strategies, or even tactics, in terms of techniques.

Equally, direct control is variously described as Taylorism (separation of conception and execution, centralization of conception and close supervision and pay incentives), and as an effort to limit the variable effects of labour power. The critical ambiguity in both conceptions (since they are related by exclusion) centres on the role of pay and pay incentives, described by Friedman as attempts both to control and to harness labour power variability (1977a, pp. 79, 93, 97; 1977b, p. 49). Friedman's attempt to resolve this issue by distinguishing money piecework (where work methods remain unspecified and payment is by the piece) from time piecework (where methods are specified and payment is by time saved) seems unsatisfactory. For many contemporary pay systems fall between these two extremes, combining method specification and piece payment, and both systems reflect the attempt to control output through the pay system, rather than by the manipulation of other non-financial rewards (1977a, p. 219).

Secondly, on the narrower conception of responsible autonomy (as argued especially in 1977b) which resembles forms of job redesign, Friedman is empirically incorrect to trace their origins to worker resistance or struggle, unless one wants to extend these latter terms to cover labour turnover and absenteeism. Thirdly, Friedman tends to accept at face value the theories of 'responsible autonomy' as defined in the terms of their originators and disseminators rather than subjecting them to independent and critical analysis. Thus when management theorists describe concessions of autonomy to work groups and posit a dichotomy between their practices and Taylorism (or 'direct control') Friedman accepts their arguments. He therefore fails to consider the possibility that autonomy, or control, may not be a zero-sum concept, and that management control over production may increase simultaneously with worker control over its more immediate aspects (Brighton Labour Process Group, 1977; Pignon and Querzola, 1976).

More seriously, Friedman fails to analyse the connections between responsible autonomy and direct control and to consider that certain forms of the former actually function because of classic Taylorist mechanisms and may conform to Taylorist principles. There is also a strong tendency in Friedman, as in Braverman, to treat management under capitalism principally as a control function, in which the recalcitrance of labour - class struggle - is elevated to paramount status. Yet for Marx the two principal defining features of the capitalist mode of production were that labour existed as a commodity and that the major objective of social production was the production and realization of surplus value. Although formally acknowledging these features, Friedman draws the conventional (but crude) distinction between the co-ordinating (or technical) and the authoritative functions of management: the latter is specific to capitalism while the former is 'part of any complicated economic process' (1977a, p. 77). What is missing from either of these functions is the production of profit in its various modes, an activity that has been reduced to the ahistorical category of 'co-ordination'. Capitalism therefore ends up being characterized in effect specifically by control over labour and its various modes.

A further consequence of Friedman's argument is that managerial activity tends to be abstracted from tactical or strategic frameworks, incorporating finance, sales, marketing, and to be conceptualized at the level of task management, or control over directly productive activity. He assigns considerable significance to the 'product cycle' under capitalism, in which sales of a new product rise at first only slowly, accelerate and then fall off, and links this with changes in managerial strategy towards 'responsible autonomy'. Yet this useful link is not carried through into an analysis of differences *within* managements.

Finally, one can question the justification for writing of management strategy, rather than say, tactics or practices. The first concept has connotations of comprehensiveness, coherence, long-term perspectives and consciousness. Do we really want to attribute these characteristics uniformly to capitalist management, or would the latter concepts (tactics, practices) be more appropriate?

Taken overall, then, Friedman's work may provide a valuable starting-point, but his central dichotomy as formulated seems unable to support the weight that one could reasonably expect it to bear. A more elaborated conception of managerial practices must recognize shifts in principal managerial objectives. Equally, such a conception must recognize both the connections between practices and the different forms which a single practice - such as Taylorism - may assume under different conditions.

What is important here is Friedman's insistence on the theoretical significance of analysing management practices in relation to class struggle. He argues that worker-initiated schemes of shop-floor control are more likely to reflect workers' own interests than those originating with management, and while this may be true in some cases, for example Fiat as compared with Volvo, there is a further level of analysis which complicates the picture. In their transition from conception to implementation, managerial schemes are invariably modified (to differing degrees) by workers' own counter-initiatives, and it would be necessary to appreciate such modifications in any analysis of managerial practices and their consequences (Goodrich, 1975; Wood and Kelly, 1978). We must also take into account some of the contradictions generated by Taylorism and the detail division of labour under the changing circumstances of the post-war economic boom (cf. Burawoy, 1978; Elger, 1979).

## LIMITS AND DEVELOPMENTS OF TAYLORISM AND DETAIL DIVISION OF LABOUR

During the economic boom after the Second World War both Taylorism and detail division of labour encountered problems, stemming in part from worker resistance but much more from structural contradictions (see Pichierri, 1978). To appreciate these contradictions, we must abandon Braverman's implicit treatment of manufacturing industry as a homogeneous sector and distinguish, for example, along the lines of Woodward (1958) mass production, batch production and continuous process industry (see also Heckscher, 1980).

The Ford moving assembly line, pioneered in the Highland Park vehicle works in 1914, was used solely for the mass production of the Model T Ford. Likewise, its extension into other car industries and into the manufacture of consumer goods such as electrical appliances was based on long production runs of a small range of products. Throughout the 1950s manufacturers of domestic appliances and of other mass-produced items expanded their product ranges in line with growing domestic and world markets (Corley, 1966). This process, however, increasingly came into conflict with the structure and limits of the assembly line. Realization of surplus value dictated that an ever-growing range of commodities be produced to meet diverse consumer 'demands'. Production of surplus value dictated that product range should be kept small to ensure long production runs and thereby to minimize production time lost because of product, parts and tools change-over (for examples, see Gowler, 1970; Kelly, 1982).

The major strategy used to resolve this contradiction was product obsolescence: this allowed old lines to be deleted from the product range (see Baran and Sweezy, 1968, ch. 5; Mandel, 1978, ch. 7). Manufacturers also attempted to reorganize distribution, either by stipulating a minimum batch size for wholesalers' orders or by allocating small orders into a 'queue' until there were sufficient orders for a single product to justify a production run. Other manufacturers tried (though unsuccessfully) to reach agreements on production swapping, whereby each of two companies would produce only one type of appliance in a particular factory and obtain other appliances through barter (Corley, 1966).

But a small number of firms reorganized production rather than distribution, either by shortening assembly lines or by abolishing them altogether. Instead of changing a long flowline every day or two in response to market fluctuations, firms could specialize in each of a number of shorter lines or single work situations on the same product, and thus reduce the frequency of product change-over. This trend was represented within management theory as an 'enrichment' of jobs – which, of course, it was, although its origins had less to do with under-utilized and bored workers than with overstretched production systems.

This reversal of detail division of labour did not signify the abandonment of Taylorism. On the contrary, such transformations of assembly lines frequently led to an individualization of work roles, to the replacement of group by individual incentives and to greater management control arising out of increased worker visibility (Kelly, 1982; Coriat, 1980). These new work roles were invariably determined by Taylorist techniques – time-and-motion study – within a Taylorist strategy of individualization. At the same time, many of these instances involved simultaneous increases in both worker's control over immediate aspects of production and management control, through the greater ease of accountability of individualized work roles. If we operate with a zero-sum concept of control, as is implicit in Braverman, this feature of mass-production systems cannot be grasped.

The limits to Taylorism are revealed in a different industrial sector, that of continuous process production. Precise specification of individual work roles depends for its efficacy on a relatively predictable input of work. Where there is considerable and unpredictable variability in production, either because of variations in the raw materials (for example, in coal mining, textiles, certain chemicals) or because of variations in the production process itself (for example, in certain branches of metal manufacture and processing), the application of Taylorist techniques generates a series of 'problems' for capital. Workloads are likely to vary significantly between individuals, and with an interdependent production process some individuals or groups are likely to be under-utilized while others are kept very busy. Sudden upsurges of work are likely to strain the production system or will generate higher labour costs if a reserve pool of utility workers is employed for such emergencies (Kelly, 1977).

The significance of sociotechnical systems theory, in this context, is that it articulated this contradiction between detail division of labour and the means of production, that is, between control over the labour process and the production of surplus value, and recommended the creation of autonomous groups. Each group is assigned a series of tasks and is responsible for their distribution within the group. The results of such initiatives have been to iron out work-load inequalities through flexibility of labour and, therefore, to raise the average intensity of labour, under the influence of group pay incentive schemes. Clearly, there are instances where shortened assembly lines and 'autonomous' groups have been inaugurated in response to trade-union initiatives, as Friedman has noted. Though the examples of Fiat and Volvo involve an industrial sector which is generally highly organized throughout the world, the majority of examples of the reorganization of mass-production systems have occurred not in vehicle manufacture but in electrical engineering, a sector characterized (in the UK) by lower union density, weaker union organization and a higher proportion of women employees.

The extent to which reversals of Taylorism or of detail division of labour are responses to structural contradictions and/or class struggle is a purely empirical question and cannot be determined *a priori* on the basis of a desire to upgrade the elements of class struggle or of contradiction, so obviously neglected in Braverman.

## CONCLUSIONS

Our discussion of Braverman and Friedman and our analysis of Taylorism and its limitations and contradictions clearly raise a wide range of substantive issues in the analysis of management and organization. Yet a number of key conceptual and methodological distinctions can be identified as necessary components of any analysis that aims to transcend some of the oversimplified views we have discussed.

The first point is that one cannot infer the successful implementation of a management strategy merely from its existence. In other words, the determinants of successful strategy formation are unlikely to coincide exactly with the conditions required for implementation. Taylor himself recognized the problems of implementation, even if he was unable to theorize about them effectively and could produce only the concept of a 'mental revolution' whose social determinants were not articulated.

Several writers have observed carefully the ways in which the implementation of a strategy or practice become the object of class struggle, and the best example here is that of incentive or piecework payment systems. By the more or less systematic modification of work methods and the regulation of output, workers have often been able to thwart the objectives of managerial initiatives (Roy, 1952, 1954; Lupton, 1963; Friedman, 1977a), and it has also been observed that Taylorism was implemented in the 1920s only in a piecemeal fashion (Edwards, 1979; Palmer, 1975). Once implementation is seen as problematic and uncertain, we can avoid the kind of error made by Bosquet (1972) in his assessment of increased worker participation in management decision-making. Bosquet argued that the concession of a degree of autonomy to workers would engender a desire for even greater influence and thereby precipitate an unstable and (to management) threatening process that could even call into question management's control of production. The argument is based on the premise that managerial initiatives are successfully implemented in the forms discussed by management theorists, which overlooks the problems of implementation, not to mention the ideological character of some management theory.[5]

The second conclusion we can draw is that it is dangerous to privilege one particular area of management concern as the overriding problem in need of solution. Braverman's (1974) insistence that the problem of management can be reduced to the problem of control is true in the sense that control can never be complete and predictable. But the significance of control over labour and the labour process has to be understood in the context of management's having a series of objectives (and hence potential problems) linked with the full cycle of capitalist production. Labour supply, job performance and surplus value extraction, product sale and product markets all can and do present problems for managements. The heads of several large British corporations such as British Steel or BL are currently less concerned with control over the labour process and surplus value production than with declining markets because of the world recession (see also Mandel, 1978).

The significance of a 'labour problem' is also likely to vary over time and to be associated with the capital–labour ratio of the company or firm, and we noted that detail division of labour had thrown up different kinds of problems in mass-production, flowline industries as compared with continuous-process production (see also Heckscher, 1980; Woodward, 1958). We cannot therefore assign priority to a single factor in management strategy, whether it be labour, technology or markets, but must determine such problems empirically.

Third, the notion of 'management strategy' is itself open to question on two counts. Management, except in very small firms or at departmental level in larger firms, is unlikely to function as a homogeneous entity, united in the pursuit of a single objective. Specialization of function has also generated specialization or differentiation of interests (Crozier, 1964). Equally, the notion of strategy cannot be taken at face value, with its connotations of conscious and clearsighted

5. For a discussion of the implementation of a job-enrichment scheme that highlights the differential responses of work forces, see Roberts and Wood (1982).

formulation of means and ends. In other words, the degree to which management holds and operates a strategy has also to be determined empirically (Thurley and Wood, 1982).

Both the differentiation of management and the variations between firms suggest, as we argued before, that alternative strategies are certainly available. Taylorism, for instance, may have been appropriate under conditions of an abundant labour supply, expanding markets and weak union organization but may reach the limits of its effectiveness in different circumstances.

Overall, the thrust of this chapter has been to argue for a more careful and more detailed study of management strategy, coupled with a sensitivity to the complexities of employing organizations, which together will enable us to transcend simplistic formulations and generalizations (Wood, 1980).

## REFERENCES


Aitken, H. G. J. (1960), *Taylorism at Watertown Arsenal: Scientific Management in Action 1908–1915,* Cambridge, Mass.: Harvard University Press.

Babbage, C. (1971), *On the Economy of Machinery and Manufactures*, Fairfield, NJ: Kelley (first published 1835).

Bailes, K. E. (1977), 'Alexei Gastev and the Soviet controversy over Taylorism, 1918–24', *Soviet Studies*, vol. 29, no. 3, July, pp. 373–94.

Baran, P., and Sweezy, P. (1968), *Monopoly Capital*, Harmondsworth: Penguin.

Bendix, R., ed. (1974), *Work and Authority in Industry,* Berkeley: University of California Press.

Bosquet, M. (1972), 'The prison factory', *New Left Review,* no. 73, May–June, pp. 23–34.

Braverman, H. (1974), *Labor and Monopoly Capital*, New York: Monthly Review Press.

Brighton Labour Process Group (1977), 'The capitalist labour process', *Capital and Class*, no. 1, Spring, pp. 3–26.

Brown, G. (1977), *Sabotage: a Study in Industrial Conflict,* Nottingham: Spokesman Books.

Burawoy, M. (1978), 'Towards a Marxist theory of the labour process', *Politics and Society*, vol. 8, nos 3–4, pp. 247–312.

Carr. E. H. (1966), *The Bolshevik Revolution*, vol. 2, Harmondsworth: Penguin.

Coriat, B. (1980), 'The restructuring of the assembly line: a new economy of time and control', *Capital and Class*, no. 11, Summer, pp. 34–43.

Corley, T. A. (1966), *Domestic Electrical Appliances*, London: Jonathan Cape.

Crozier, M. (1964), *The Bureaucratic Phenomenon*, London: Tavistock.

Drucker, P. (1976), 'The coming rediscovery of scientific management', *Conference Board Record*, vol. 13, no. 6. pp. 23–7.

Edwards, R. (1979), *Contested Terrain*, London: Heinemann.

Elger, A. (1979), 'Valorisation and deskilling – a critique of Braverman', *Capital and Class*, no. 7, Spring, pp. 58–99.

Elger, A., and Schwarz, B. (1980), 'Monopoly capitalism and the impact of Taylorism: notes on Lenin, Gramsci, Braverman and Sohn-Rethel', in T. Nichols (ed.), *Capital and Labour: A Marxist Primer*, London: Fontana, pp. 358–69.

Fridenson, P. (1978), 'Corporate policy, rationalisation and the labour force: French experiences in international comparison; 1900 to 1929', paper given at Nuffield Deskilling Conference, Windsor.

Friedman, A. (1977a), *Industry and Labour*, London: Macmillan.

Friedman, A. (1977b), 'Responsible autonomy versus direct control over the labour process', *Capital and Class*, no. 1, Spring, pp. 43–57.

Friedman, A. (1978), 'Worker resistance and Marxian analysis of the capitalist labour process', paper given at Nuffield Deskilling Conference, Windsor.

Goodrich, C. L. (1975), *The Frontier of Control*, London: Pluto Press (first published 1920).

Gowler, D. (1970), 'Sociocultural influences on the operation of a wage-payment system: an exploratory case study', in D. Robinson (ed.), *Local Labour Markets and Wage Structures*, London: Gower, pp. 100–26.

Haber, S. (1964). *Efficiency and Uplift: Scientific Management in the Progressive Era*, Chicago: University of Chicago Press.

Heckscher, C. (1980), 'Worker participation and management control', *Journal of Social Reconstruction*, vol. 1, no. 1, pp. 77–102.

Kelly, J. E. (1977), 'Scientific management and work "humanisation" ', paper read at BSA Industrial Sociology Group Conference, London School of Economics and Political Science.

Kelly, J. E. (1982), *Scientific Management, Job Redesign and Work Performance*, New York: Academic Press.

Lenin, V. I. (1965a), 'Taylorism: man's enslavement to the machine' (first published 1914), in V. I. Lenin, *Collected Works*, vol. 20, London: Lawrence & Wishart, pp. 152–4.

Lenin, V. I. (1965b), 'The immediate tasks of the Soviet government: raising the productivity of labour' (first published 1918), in V. I. Lenin, *Collected Works*, vol. 27, London: Lawrence & Wishart, pp. 235–77.

Littler, C. R. (1978), 'Understanding Taylorism', *British Journal of Sociology*, vol. 29, no. 2, pp. 185–202.

Lupton, T. (1963), *On the Shop Floor*, Oxford: Pergamon Press.

Maier, C. S. (1970), 'Between Taylorism and technocracy: European ideologies and the vision of industrial productivity in the 1920s', *Journal of Contemporary History*, vol. 5, no. 2, pp. 27–61.

Mandel, E. (1978), *Late Capitalism*, London: New Left Books.

Montmollin, M. de (1974), 'Taylorisme et anti-Taylorisme', *Sociologie du Travail*, vol. 16, no. 4, pp. 374–82.

Nadworny, M. (1955), *Scientific Management and the Unions 1900–1932*, Cambridge, Mass: Harvard University Press.

Nakase, T. (1979), 'The introduction of scientific management in Japan and its characteristics', in K. Nakagawa (ed.) *Labor and Management*, Tokyo: University of Tokyo Press, pp. 171–202.

Okuda, K. (1972), 'Managerial evolution in Japan', *Management Japan*, vol. 6. no. 1, pp. 28–37.

Palmer, B. (1975), 'Class, conception and conflict: the thrust for efficiency, managerial views of labor, and the working class rebellion, 1903–1922', *Review of Radical Political Economics*, vol. 7, no. 2, pp. 31–49.

Pichierri, A. (1978), 'Diffusion and crisis of scientific management in European industry', in S. Giner and M. S. Archer (eds), *Contemporary Europe*, London: Routledge & Kegan Paul, pp. 55–73.

Pignon, D., and Querzola, J. (1976), 'Dictatorship and democracy in production', in A. Gorz (ed.), *The Division of Labour*, Brighton: Harvester Press, pp. 63–99.

Roberts, C., and Woods, S. J. (1982), 'Collective bargaining and job redesign' in J. Kelly and C. W. Clegg (eds.), *Autonomy and Control at the Workplace: Contexts for Job Design*, London: Croom Helm.

Rollier, M. (1979), 'Taylorism and the Italian Unions', in C. Cooper and E. Mumford (eds.), *The Quality of Working Life in Western and Eastern Europe*, London: Associated Press, pp. 214–25.

Roy, D. (1952), 'Quota restriction and goldbricking in a machine shop', *American Journal of Sociology*, vol. 57, no. 3, pp. 427–42.

Roy, D. (1954), 'Efficiency and the fix', *American Journal of Sociology*, vol. 60, no. 3, pp. 255–66.

Sohn-Rethel, A. (1978), *Intellectual and Manual Labour*, London: Macmillan.

Taylor, F. W. (1906), *On the Art of Cutting Metals*, New York: American Society of Mechanical Engineers.

Taylor, F. W. (1919), *A Piece-Rate System* (first published 1895), in F. W. Taylor, *Two Papers on Scientific Management: A Piece-Rate System; Notes on Belting*, London: Routledge & Sons, pp. 31–126.

Taylor, P. S. (1979), 'Labour time, work measurement and the commensuration of labour', *Capital and Class*, no. 9. Autumn, pp. 23–38.

Thurley, K., and Wood, S., eds (1982), *Managerial Strategy and Industrial Relations*, Cambridge: Cambridge University Press.

Traub, R. (1978), 'Lenin and Taylor: the fate of "scientific management" in the (early) Soviet Union', *Telos*, no. 37, pp. 82–92.

Wood, S. J. (1980), 'Corporate strategy and organizational studies', in D. Dunkerley and G. Salaman (eds), *Organizational Studies Yearbook 1980*, London: Routledge & Kegan Paul, pp. 52–71.

Wood, S. J. and Kelly, J. E. (1978), 'Towards a critical management science', *Journal of Management Studies*, vol. 15, no. 1, pp. 1–24.

Woodward, J. (1958), *Management and Technology*, London: HMSO.

# 8

# Thirty Years of Making Out

MICHAEL BURAWOY

The study of changes in the labour process is one of the more neglected areas of industrial sociology. There are global theories, which speak generally of tendencies toward rationalization, bureaucratization, the movement from coercive to normative compliance, and so forth. There are the prescriptive theories of human relations, of job enrichment, job enlargement, worker participation, and so on, which do express underlying changes but in a form that conceals them. There are attempts to examine the implications of technological change for worker attitudes and behaviour, but these do not examine the forces leading to technological change itself. There are also theories of organizational persistence, which stress the capacity of enterprises to resist change. The few attempts at concrete analysis of changes in the labour process have usually emerged from comparisons among different firms. Such causal analysis, based on cross-sectional data, is notoriously unsatisfactory under the best of conditions, but when samples are small and firms diverse, the conclusions drawn are at best suggestive. As far as I know, there have been no attempts to undertake a detailed study of the labour process of a single firm over an extended period of time. Thus, my revisit to Geer, thirty years after Roy, provides a unique opportunity to examine the forces leading to changes on the shop floor.

## TECHNOLOGY

Whenever technology changes its character, it has a transformative impact on the organization of work. However, the study of technological innovation and adoption is still in its primitive stages. Apart from the conventional models of neoclassical economics, which stress the cumulative role of science in the pursuit of ever greater efficiency, there have been few attempts to examine the political and social forces leading to technological change in advanced capitalism. A notable exception is the work by David Noble, which suggests that capitalists choose among available technologies not only to increase productivity but, in addition, to

This essay was first published as chapter 4 in Michael Burawoy, *Manufacturing Consent*, University of Chicago Press, 1979.

gain control over the labour process and push smaller capitalists out of business.[1] A recent study of the mechanization of harvesting shows that growers develop new technologies but that adoption is contingent on the level of class struggle.[2]

Undoubtedly the examination of the forces leading to technological change is important. However, if we are to understand the changes in the labour process that are brought about by social imperatives other than those introduced by new machines, we must keep technology constant, since it would be impossible to isolate its impact. Fortunately, machine-tool technology, in its principles at least, has remained relatively constant over the past century, with the exception of the recent development of computer-controlled machines. It therefore provides a useful basis for studying 'non-technical' sources of change in the organization of work. Thus, the machine shops described in the writings of Frederick Winslow Taylor bear a remarkable resemblance to those of Geer and Allied.[3] The agglomeration of speed drills, radial drills, vertical and horizontal mills, chuck and turret lathes, grinders, etc., could be found in essentially the same forms in machine shops at the end of the nineteenth century as they are today. Even in the layout of its machines, the Jack Shop, where Roy worked, closely resembled the small-parts department where I worked. The organization of work and the incentive schemes, as well as the various forms of output restriction and the informal worker alliances, all described by Roy, are to be found today and can be traced back to the turn of the century.

However, outside the small-parts department there have been major changes in technology, in the direction of increased automation. The most impressive change at Allied came in the machining of rough cylinder-block castings. First introduced at a Ford plant in 1935, these monstrous integrated machine tools are programmed to perform several operations simultaneously (milling, tapping, boring, drilling, grinding, etc.) at each work station before the cylinder block is automatically transported to the next work station. Despite, or perhaps because of, its sophistication, this elaborate technology was out of order much of the time. In some departments one or two computer-controlled machines had been installed, but they, too, seemed to experience considerable downtime. Generally, the wide variety and relatively small volume of engines produced at Allied made it uneconomic to transform the technology of the entire plant, and, when new automated equipment was introduced, it frequently created more problems than it solved. As I shall suggest toward the end of this chapter, piecemeal technological innovation can easily become the focus of struggles on the shop floor.

1. David Noble, 'Before the Fact: Social Choice in Machine Design', paper presented at the National Convention of the Organization of American Historians, April 1978. For a more general history of the role of science in the development of capitalism, see his *America by Design: Science, Technology, and the Rise of Corporate Capitalism* (New York: Alfred A. Knopf, 1977).

2. William Friedland, Amy Barton, and Robert Thomas, 'Manufacturing Green Gold: The Conditions and Social Consequences of Lettuce Harvest Mechanization' (unpublished ms., University of California, Santa Cruz, 1978), and William Friedland and Amy Barton, *Destalking the Wily Tomato* (Davis, Calif.: Department of Applied Behavioral Sciences, College of Agriculture and Environmental Sciences, University of California, 1975).

3. See, for example, Taylor's *Shop Management* (New York: American Society of Mechanical Engineers, 1903).

Even in the small-parts department, by no means the most technologically sophisticated of the departments of the engine division, machines are now more reliable, flexible, precise, and so forth than they were in 1945. A very noticeable change from Geer is the absence of the huge belt lines that used to power the machine tools. Now each machine has its own source of power. In the remaining sections of this chapter I shall indicate how these small changes in technology have become part of, have facilitated, and have sometimes stimulated changes in productive activities and production relations.

## THE PIECE-RATE SYSTEM

In a machine shop, operators are defined by the machine they 'run' and are remunerated according to an individual piece-rate incentive scheme. While machine operators comprise the majority of workers on the shop floor, there are also auxiliary workers, whose function it is to provide facilities and equipment as well as assistance for the 'production' workers (operators). For each production operation the methods department establishes a level of effort, expressed in so many pieces per hour, which represents the '100 per cent' benchmark. Below this benchmark, operators receive a base rate for the job, irrespective of the actual number of pieces they produce. Above this standard, workers receive not only the base rate for the job but, in addition, a bonus or incentive, corresponding to the number of pieces in excess of 100 per cent. Thus, output at a rate of 125 per cent is defined as the 'anticipated rate', which - according to the contract - is the amount 'a normal experienced operator working at incentive gait' is expected to produce and represents 25 per cent more pieces than the base rate. Producing at '125 per cent', an operator will earn himself or herself an incentive bonus that adds around 15 per cent to the amount earned when producing at 100 per cent or less. Earned income per hour is computed as follows:

  Base earnings (determined by job's labour grade)<br>
\+ Base earnings × (% rate − 100%) (if rate is greater than 100%)<br>
\+ Override (determined by job's labour grade)<br>
\+ Shift differential (25 cents for second and third shifts)<br>
\+ Cost-of-living allowance

In 1945 the computation of earnings was simpler. The system of remuneration was a straight piece-rate system with a guaranteed minimum. There were no extra benefits. Each operation had a *price* rather than a *rate*. Earnings were calculated by simply multiplying the number of pieces produced in an hour by the price. If the result was less than the guaranteed minimum, the operator received that guaranteed minimum, known as the day rate. If output was greater than that corresponding to the day rate, an increase of 25 per cent in the number of pieces led to a 25 per cent increase in earnings. How the day rate was determined was not always clear. It reflected not only the job but also the operator's skill. Thus Roy received a day rate of 85 cents per hour, but Al McCann, also working on a radial drill on second shift but a more experienced operator, received a day rate of $1.10. The day rate on first shift was 5 cents lower than on second shift, so that, to make

85 cents an hour, Joe Mucha, Roy's day man, had to work harder than Roy. The price for a given operation, however, was the same for all operators.

The two systems thus encourage different strategies for achieving increased earnings. In 1945 Geer operators might fight for higher day rates by bargaining individually with management, but this did not guarantee them increased earnings if they were regularly turning out more pieces than corresponded to the day rate. Furthermore, the very operators who might be eligible for higher day rates would also be the ones for whom a guaranteed minimum was not so important. So the way to drive up income was to increase prices, and this could be accomplished either by fighting for across-the-board-increases on all prices or by fighting with the time-study man for improved prices on particular jobs. Operators did in fact spend a great deal of time haggling with time-study men over prices. These ways of increasing earnings are now relatively insignificant compared to two alternative methods. The first is via increases in the base earnings for the job and the fringes that go along with each labour grade. These are all negotiated at three-year intervals between management and union. Under the present system, the methods department is not necessarily involved in changes in the *price* of an operation, since this varies with base earnings. Increases in fringes, such as override, are also independent of the piece-rate system. The second method is to transfer to another job with higher base earnings – that is, of higher labour grade – or with easier rates. Frequently, the higher the labour grade, the easier the rates; for to encourage workers to remain on the more skilled jobs of the higher labour grades, and thereby avoid the cost of training new workers, the rates on those jobs tend to be looser. In 1945, when earnings were closely tied to experience and less associated with particular types of jobs, transfer to another job was frequently used as a disciplinary measure, since it was likely to lead to reduced earnings.[4]

The implications are not hard to foresee. Whereas in 1945 bargaining between management and worker over the distribution of the rewards of labour took place on the shop floor, in 1975 such bargaining had been largely transferred out of the shop and into the conference room and worker–management conflict on the shop floor had found a safety valve in the organization of job transfers on a plant-wide basis. As a consequence of changes in the system of remuneration, management–worker conflict has abated and individualism has increased.

## MAKING OUT – A GAME WORKERS PLAY

In this section I propose to treat the activities on the shop floor as a series of games in which operators attempt to achieve levels of production that earn incentive pay, in other words, anything over 100 per cent. The precise target that each operator aims at is established on an individual basis, varying with job, machine, experience, and so on. Some are satisfied with 125 per cent, while others are in a foul mood unless they achieve 140 per cent – the ceiling imposed and recognized by all participants. This game of making out provides a framework for evaluating the productive activities and the social relations that arise out of the organization

4. Donald Roy, 'Restriction of Output in a Piecework Machine Shop', (PhD diss., University of Chicago, 1952), p. 76.

of work. We can look upon making out, therefore, as comprising a sequence of stages – of encounters between machine operators and the social or nonsocial objects that regulate the conditions of work. The rules of the game are experienced as a set of externally imposed relationships. The art of making out is to manipulate those relationships with the purpose of advancing as quickly as possible from one stage to the next.

At the beginning of the shift, operators assemble outside the time office on the shop floor to collect their production cards and punch in on the 'setup' of their first task. If it has already been set up on the previous shift, the operator simply punches in on production. Usually operators know from talking to their counterpart, before the beginning of the shift, which task they are likely to receive. Knowing what is available on the floor for their machine, an operator is sometimes in a position to bargain with the scheduling man, who is responsible for distributing the tasks.

In 1945 the scheduling man's duties appeared to end with the distribution of work, but in 1975 he also assumed some responsibility for ensuring that the department turned out the requisite parts on time. Therefore, he is often found stalking the floor, checking up on progress and urging workers to get a move on. Because he has no formal authority over the operators, the scheduling man's only recourse is to his bargaining strength, based on the discretion he can exert in distributing jobs and fixing up an operator's time. Operators who hold strategic jobs, requiring a particular skill for example, or who are frequently called upon to do 'hot jobs' are in a strong bargaining position *vis-à-vis* the scheduling man. He knows this and is careful not to upset them.

By contrast, Roy complained that the scheduling man was never to be found when he needed him and, when he was around, showed little interest in his work.[5] This caused great annoyance when the time clerks were not sure which job Roy had to punch in on next. Equally significant was the relative absence of hot jobs in 1945.[6] In sum, the department takes its responsibility to get jobs finished on time more seriously, but, so long as operators are making out, this responsibility falls on the shoulders of the scheduling man rather than on the foreman or superintendent.[7] The change is possibly a result of heightened departmental autonomy and responsibility, reflected in departmental profit-and-loss statements and in the penalties incurred by the company when engines are delivered late to the customer.[8]

After receiving their first task, operators have to find the blueprint and tooling for the operation. These are usually in the crib, although they may be already out on the floor. The crib attendant is therefore a strategic person whose cooperation an operator must secure. If the crib attendant chooses to be uncooperative in dispensing towels, blueprints, fixtures, etc., and particularly, in the grinding of tools, operators can be held up for considerable lengths of time. Occasionally, operators who have managed to gain the confidence of the crib attendant will enter the crib themselves and expedite the process. Since, unlike the scheduling man, the crib

5. Ibid., pp. 419–23.
6. Roy refers to hot jobs on two occasions (ibid., pp. 405, 504).
7. When a job was really 'hot' the scheduling man might appeal to the foreman or even to the superintendent for support if the operator appeared recalcitrant.
8. I have not been able to discover the nature or existence of equivalent penalties during the war.

attendant has no real interest in whether the operator makes out, his cooperation has to be elicited by other means. For the first five months of my employment my relations with the crib attendant on second shift were very poor, but at Christmas things changed dramatically. Every year the local union distributes a Christmas ham to all its members. I told Harry that I couldn't be bothered picking mine up from the union hall and that he could have it for himself. He was delighted, and after that I received good service in the crib.

Many of Roy's troubles also originated in the crib. As in 1975, so in 1945: there were not enough crib attendants. Roy dramatically shows how the attendant who tries to serve operators conscientiously becomes a nervous wreck and soon transfers off the job. Problems may have been more acute under Geer, in Roy's time, since tools and fixtures were then located in the crib according to size and type rather than assembled in pans according to job, as in 1975. On the other hand, there were always at least two crib attendants when Roy was working at Geer, whereas in 1975 there was never more than one on second shift.

While I was able to secure the cooperation of the crib attendant, I was not so fortunate with the truck drivers. When I was being broken in on the miscellaneous job, I was told repeatedly that the first thing I must do was to befriend the truck driver. He or she was responsible for bringing the stock from the aisles, where it was kept in tubs, to the machine. Particularly at the beginning of the shift, when everyone is seeking their assistance, truck drivers can hold you up for a considerable period. While some treated everyone alike, others discriminated among operators, frustrating those without power, assisting those who were powerful. Working on the miscellaneous job meant that I was continually requiring the truck driver's services, and, when Morris was in the seat, he used to delight in frustrating me by making me wait. There was nothing I could do about it unless I was on a hot job; then the foreman or scheduling man might intervene. To complain to the foreman on any other occasion would only have brought me more travail, since Morris could easily retaliate later on. It was better just to sit tight and wait. Like the crib attendants, truckers have no stake in the operator's making out, and they are, at the same time, acutely conscious of their power in the shop. All they want is for you to get off their backs so that they can rest, light up, chat with their friends, or have a cup of coffee – in other words, enjoy the marginal freedoms of the machine operator. As one of the graffiti in the men's toilet put it, 'Fuck the company, fuck the union, but most of all fuck the truckers because they fuck us all.' Operators who become impatient may, if they know how, hop into an idle truck and move their own stock. But this may have unfortunate consequences, for other operators may ask them to get their stock too.

While it is difficult to generalize, it does appear that under Geer the service of the truck drivers – or stock chasers as they were called – was more efficient. For one thing, there were two truckers in 1945 but only one in 1975 to serve roughly the same number of operators. For another, as the setup man told me from his own experience,

> In the old days everyone knew everyone else. It was a big family, and so truck drivers would always try and help, bringing up stock early and so on. In those days operators might not even have to tell the truck driver to get the next load. Now everyone moves around from job to job. People don't get to know each other so well, and so there's less cooperation.

As they wait for the stock to arrive, each operator sets up his machine, if it is not already set up. This can take anything from a few minutes to two shifts, but normally it takes less than an hour. Since every setup has a standard time for completion, operators try to make out here, too. When a setup is unusually rapid, an operator may even be able to make time so that, when he punches in on production, he has already turned out a few pieces. A setup man is available for assistance. Particularly for the inexperienced, his help is crucial, but, as with the other auxiliary personnel, his cooperation must be sought and possibly bargained for. He, too, has no obvious stake in your making out, though the quicker he is through with you, the freer he is. Once the machine is set up and the stock has arrived, the operator can begin the first piece, and the setup man is no longer required unless the setup turns out to be unsatisfactory.

The quality and concern of setup men vary enormously. For example, on day shift the setup man was not known for his cooperative spirit. When I asked Bill, my day man, who the setup man was on day shift, he replied, 'Oh, he died some years ago.' This was a reference to the fact that the present one was useless as far as he was concerned. On second shift, by contrast, the setup man went about his job with enthusiasm and friendliness. When he was in a position to help, he most certainly did his best, and everyone liked and respected him. Yet even he did not know all the jobs in the shop. Indeed, he knew hardly any of my machines and so was of little use to me. Roy experienced similar differences among setup men. Johnny, for example, was not a great deal of help, but when Al McCann came along, Roy's life on the shop floor was transformed.[9] Al McCann had been a radial-drill operator of long experience and showed Roy all the angles on making out.

In 1945 there were more setup men than in 1975; this was due in part to wartime manpower policies but also to a greater need for setup men. Fixtures and machines have improved and become more standardized over the past thirty years, and the skill required in setting up has therefore declined. Moreover, under Geer, there was greater diversity in the operations that any one machine could perform, and it therefore took operators much longer to master all the jobs that they would have to run. On the other hand, it appears that mobility between different machines is now greater and average experience therefore less than at the end of the war. Roy also reports that, according to his fellow workers, the setup function was itself relatively new; this suggests again how recent was the specialization of the functions that earlier were performed by a single person – the foreman.

The assigned task may be to drill a set of holes in a plate, pipe, casting, or whatever; to mill the surface of some elbow; to turn an internal diameter on a lathe; to shave the teeth on a gear; and so on. The first piece completed has to be checked by the inspector against the blueprint. Between inspector and operator there is an irrevocable conflict of interest because the former is concerned with quality while the operator is concerned with quantity. Time spent when an operation just won't come right – when piece after piece fails, according to the inspector, to meet the specifications of the blueprint – represents lost time to the operator. Yet the inspector wants to OK the piece as quickly as possible and doesn't want to be bothered with checking further pieces until the required tolerances are met.

9. Roy, 'Restriction of Output', p. 307.

When a piece is on the margin, some inspectors will let it go, but others will enforce the specifications of the blueprint to the *n*th degree. In any event, inspectors are in practice, if not in theory, held partly responsible if an operator runs scrap. Though formally accountable only for the first piece that is tagged as OK, an inspector will be bawled out if subsequent pieces fall outside the tolerance limits. Thus, inspectors are to some extent at the mercy of the operators, who, after successfully getting the first piece OK'd, may turn up the speed of their machine and turn out scrap. An operator who does this can always blame the inspector by shifting the tag from the first piece to one that is scrap. Of course, an inspector has ample opportunity to take revenge on an operator who tries to shaft him. Moreover, operators also bear the responsibility for quality. During my term of employment, charts were distributed and hung up on each machine, defining the frequency with which operators were expected to check their pieces for any given machine at any particular tolerance level. Moreover, in the period immediately prior to the investigation of the plant's quality-assurance organization by an outside certifying body, operators were expected to indicate on the back of the inspection card the number of times they checked their pieces.

The shift since the war is clear. Under Geer, as Roy describes it, the inspector was expected to check not only the first piece but also, from time to time, some of the subsequent pieces. When the operation was completed on all the pieces, operators had to get the inspector to sign them off the old job before they could punch in on a new one. The responsibility has now shifted toward the operators, who are expected to inspect their own pieces at regular intervals.[10] Furthermore, improved machining, tooling, fixtures, etc. permit greater worker control over quality. It is now also argued that problems with quality result, not from poor workmanship, but from poor design of the product. For all these reasons, we now find fewer inspectors, and the trend is toward decreasing their numbers even further.[11]

When an inspector holds up an operator who is working on an important job but is unable to satisfy the specifications on the blueprint, a foreman may intervene to persuade the inspector to OK the piece. When this conflict cannot be resolved at the lowest level, it is taken to the next rung in the management hierarchy, and the superintendent fights it out with the chief inspector. According to Roy's observations, production management generally defeated quality control in such bargaining.[12] I found the same pattern in 1975, which reflects an organizational structure in which quality control is directly subordinated to production. Not surprisingly, the function of quality control has become a sensitive issue and the focus of much conflict among the higher levels of Allied's engine division. Quality control is continually trying to fight itself clear of subordination to production management so as to monitor quality on the shop floor. This, of course, would have deleterious effects on levels of production, and so it is opposed by the production management. Particularly sensitive in this

10. The change is one of degree, since Roy was also expected to check his pieces from time to time (ibid., pp. 267, 338).

11. Indeed, the general manager expected managers of quality control to make consistent efforts to cut the numbers of inspectors.

12. Roy, 'Restriction of Output', p. 388.

regard is control of the engine test department, which in 1975 resided with production management. The production manager naturally claimed that he was capable of assessing quality impartially. Furthermore, he justified this arrangement by shifting the locus of quality problems from the shop floor to the design of the engine, which brought the engineers into the fray. Engineering management, not surprisingly, opposes the trend toward increasing their responsibility for quality. Therefore, the manager of engineering supported greater autonomy for quality control as a reflection of his interest in returning responsibility for quality to the shop floor. To what extent this situation has been preserved by the vesting of interests since Allied took over from Geer is not clear.[13]

After the first piece has been OK'd, the operator engages in a battle with the clock and the machine. Unless the task is a familiar one – in which case the answer is known, within limits – the question is: Can I make out? It may be necessary to figure some angles, some short cuts, to speed up the machine, make a special tool, etc. In these undertakings there is always an element of risk – for example, the possibility of turning out scrap or of breaking tools. If it becomes apparent that making out is impossible or quite unlikely, operators slacken off and take it easy. Since they are guaranteed their base earnings, there is little point in wearing themselves out unless they can make more than the base earnings – that is, more than 100 per cent. That is what Roy refers to as goldbricking. The other form of 'output restriction' to which he refers – quota restriction – entails putting a ceiling on how much an operation may turn in – that is, on how much he may record on the production card. In 1945 the ceiling was $10.00 a day or $1.25 an hour, though this did vary somewhat between machines. In 1975 the ceiling was defined as 140 per cent for all operations on all machines. It was presumed that turning in more than 140 per cent led to 'price cuts' (rate increases).

In 1975 quota restriction was not necessarily a form of restriction of *output*, because operators *regularly* turned *out* more than 140 per cent, but turned *in* only 140 per cent, keeping the remainder as a 'kitty' for those operations on which they could not make out. Indeed, operators would 'bust their ass' for entire shifts, when they had a gravy job, so as to build up a kitty for the following day(s). Experienced operators on the more sophisticated machines could easily build up a kitty of a week's work. There was always some discrepancy, therefore, between what was registered in the books as completed and what was actually completed on the shop floor. Shop management was more concerned with the latter and let the books take care of themselves. Both the 140 per cent ceiling and the practice of banking (keeping a kitty) were recognized and accepted by everyone on the shop floor, even if they didn't meet with the approval of higher management.

Management outside the shop also regarded the practice of 'chiselling' as illicit, while management within the shop either assisted or connived in it. Chiselling

13. From conversations with various management officials and reading between the lines of Roy's dissertation, I am left with the impression that Geer Company tended to be more concerned with shipping the goods out than with quality control, particularly in view of the demand. (Managers of Geer have, of course, tended to deny this.) The problem of quality control has been endemic in the engine division since Allied took over. As long as quality control is subordinated to production, it is impossible to find good quality-control managers, What conscientious quality-control manager could possibly countenance subjugation to the imperatives of shipping? It is not surprising, therefore, to learn that there is a considerable turnover of quality-control managers.

(Roy's expression, which did not have currency on the shop floor in 1975) involves redistributing time from one operation to another so that operators can maximize the period turned in as over 100 per cent. Either the time clerk cooperates by punching the cards in and out at the appropriate time or the operators are allowed to punch their own cards. In part, because of the diversity of jobs, some of them very short, I managed to avoid punching any of my cards. At the end of the shift I would sit down with an account of the pieces completed in each job and fiddle around with the eight hours available, so as to maximize my earnings. I would pencil in the calculated times of starting and finishing each operation. No one ever complained, but it is unlikely that such consistent juggling would have been allowed on first shift.[14]

How does the present situation compare with Geer? As Roy describes it, the transfer of time from one operation or job to another was possible only if they were consecutive or else were part of the same job though separated in time. Thus Roy could finish one job and begin another without punching out on the first. When he did punch out on the first and in on the second, he would already have made a start toward making out. Second, if Roy saved up some pieces from one shift, he could turn those pieces in during his next shift only if the job had not been finished by his day man. Accordingly, it was important, when Roy had accumulated some kitty on a particular job, that he inform Joe Mucha. If Mucha could, he would try to avoid finishing the job before Roy came to work. Shifting time between consecutive jobs on a single shift was frequently fixed up by the foreman, who would pencil in the appropriate changes. Nonetheless, stealing time from a gravy job was in fact formally illicit in 1945.

> Gus told me that Eddie, the young time study man, was just as bad, if not worse, than the old fellow who gave him the price of one cent the other day. He said that Eddie caught the day man holding back on punching off a time study job while he got ahead on a piecework job. He turned the day man in, and the day man and the time cage man were bawled out.
>
> 'That's none of his damn business. He shouldn't have turned in the day man,' exclaimed Gus angrily.
>
> Gus went on to say that a girl hand-mill operator had been fired a year ago when a time study man caught her running one job while being 'punched in' on another. The time study man came over to the girl's machine to time a job, to find the job completed and the girl running another.
>
> Stella has no use for time study men. She told me of the time Eddie caught Maggie running one job while being punched in on another. Maggie was fired.[15]

These examples do suggest that, while chiselling went on, it was regarded as illegitimate at some levels of management.

14. My day man, Bill, never pencilled in the time but always got his cards punched in on the clock at the time office. This restricted his room for manipulation; but since he was very experienced on the miscellaneous job, this did not reduce his earnings by very much. When I filled in for him on first shift, I did in fact pencil in the times, and no one complained. This may have been a reflection of my power, since, with Bill away, hardly anyone knew how to do the various jobs or where the fixtures were. By pencilling in the times, I reckoned I could earn the same amount of money as Bill but with less effort.
15. Roy, 'Restriction of Output', p. 240.

What can we say about overall changes in rates over the past thirty years? Old-timers were forever telling me how 'easy we've got it now', though that in itself would hardly constitute evidence of change. To be sure, machines, tooling, etc. have improved, and this makes production less subject to arbitrary holdups, but the rates could nonetheless be tighter. However, an interesting change in the shop vernacular does suggest easier rates. Roy describes two types of jobs, 'gravy' and 'stinkers', the former having particularly loose and the latter particularly tight rates. While I worked in the small-parts department, I frequently heard the word 'gravy' but never the word 'stinker'. Its dropping out of fashion probably reflects the declining number of jobs with very tight rates and the availability of kitties to compensate for low levels of output. How do Roy's own data on output compare with 1975 data? Recomputing Roy's output on piecework in terms of rates rather than dollars and cents, I find that during the initial period, from November to February, his average was 85 per cent and that during the second period, from March to August, it was 120 per cent.[16] During the first six months of 1975, the average for the entire plant was around 133.5 per cent. For the different departments this average varied from 142 per cent among the automatic screw machines and automatic lathes to 121 per cent in the small-parts department, where I worked. The small-parts department functions as a labour reservoir for the rest of the plant because turnover there is high, rates are notoriously tight, and it is the place where newcomers normally begin. Nonetheless, of all the departments, this one probably most closely resembles Roy's Jack Shop in terms of machines and type of work. Thus, overall rates are indeed easier to make now, but my experiences in my own department, where most of my observations were made, bore a close resemblance to Roy's experiences.[17]

What is the foreman's role in all these operations? He is seen by everyone but senior plant management as expediting and refereeing the game of making out. As long as operators are making out and auxiliary workers are not obstructing their progress, neither group is likely to invite authoritarian interventions from the foreman. For their part, foremen defend themselves from their own bosses' complaints that certain tasks have not been completed by pointing out that the operators concerned have been working hard and have successfully made out. We therefore find foremen actively assisting operators to make out by showing them tricks they had learned when they were operators, pointing out more efficient set-ups, helping them make special tools, persuading the inspector to OK a piece that did not exactly meet the requirements of the blueprint, and so on. Foremen, like everyone else on the shop floor, recognize the two forms of output restriction as integral parts of making out. When operators have made out for the night and de-

16. Ibid., table 4, p. 94.

17. During the week 17 November 1975 to 23 November 1975, there were sixteen radial-drill operators in the small-parts department. Their average 'measured performances' for the entire year (or for the period of the year since they had begun to operate a radial drill) were as follows (all figures are percentages): 92, 108, 109, 110, 110, 111, 112, 115, 116, 119, 125, 133, 137, 139, 141, 142. The average was 120 per cent, which turns out to be precisely Roy's average in his second period. Moreover, the average period spent on radial drill in the *first eleven months of 1975* among these sixteen operators was of the order of six months, though a number of these operators had probably been operating radial drills for years. The data do not suggest significant differences between the rates on radial drills in Geer's Jack Shop and on radial drills in Allied's small-parts department.

cide to take it easy for the last two or three hours, a foreman may urge more work by saying, 'Don't you want to build up a kitty?' However, foremen do not act in collusion with the methods department and use the information they have about the various jobs and their rates against the operators, because rate increases would excite animosity, encourage goldbricking, increase turnover, and generally make the foreman's job more difficult.

However, the operator's defence, 'What more do you want? I'm making out,' does have its problems, particularly when there is a hot job on the agenda. Under such circumstances, operators are expected to drop what they are doing and punch in on the new job, 'throwing everything they've got' into it and, above all, ignoring production ceilings – though of course they are not expected to turn *in* more than 140 per cent. On occasions like this, unless the foreman can bring some sancions to bear, he is at the mercy of the operator who may decide to take it easy. For this reason, foremen may try to establish an exchange relationship with each individual operator: 'You look after me, I'll look after you.' Operators may agree to cooperate with their foreman, but in return they may expect him to dispense favours, such as the granting of casual days, permission to attend union metings during working hours, permission to go home early on a special occasion, etc. One of the most important resources at the disposal of the foreman is the 'double red card', which covers time lost by operators through no fault of their own at a rate of 125 per cent. Red cards may be awarded for excessive time lost while waiting for materials because a machine is down or some other adventitious event occurs that prevents an operator from making out. Bargaining usually precedes the signing of a red card; the operator has to persuade the foreman that he has made an earnest attempt to make out and therefore deserves compensation. Finally, one may note, as Roy did, that rules promulgated by high levels of plant management are circumvented, ignored, or subverted on the shop floor, with the tacit and sometimes active support of the foreman, in the interests of making out.

In 1945 foremen and superintendent played a similar role in facilitating making out, although they seemed to view many of these activities as illicit. The ambivalence of Steve, Roy's superintendent on second shift, is revealed in the following conversation.

> I told Steve privately that I was made out for the evening with $10.00.
> 'That's all I'm allowed to make isn't it?' I asked.
> Steve hesitated at answering that one. 'You can make more,' he said, lowering his eyes.
> 'But I'd better not,' I insisted.
> 'Well, you don't want to spoil it for yourself,' he answered.[18]

Shop management frequently sided with operators in their hostility to the methods department when rates were tight and making out was impossible. Yet operators were always on the lookout and suspicious of foremen as potential collaborators with the methods department. The primary criterion by which foremen were evaluated was their relationship with time-study men.

18. Roy, 'Restriction of Output', p. 102.

> As already indicated, the second shift operators felt, in general, that the 'better' supervisors were on their shift. They cited the connivance of Brickers, Squeaky and Johnson [day-shift supervisors] with the enemy, the methods department, pointing out that they were 'company men', would do nothing for the workers, would not permit loafing when quotas were attained, and 'drove' the operators on piecework jobs that were regarded as 'stinkers'. On the other hand, the night shift supervisors were known to have 'fought for their men' against the 'big shots', sought to aid operators in getting better prices from time study, winked at quota restriction and its hours of loafing, did not collaborate with methods in the drive to lower 'gravy' prices, and exhibited a pleasing insouciance when operators puttered away on day work.[19]

Another possible change revolves around the attitude of the foreman to goldbricking. Certainly, in 1945, foremen were not well disposed toward operators' taking it easy when rates were impossible, whereas in 1975 they tended to accept this as a legitimate practice. In general, Allied operators appeared to be less hostile and suspicious of shop supervision and exhibited greater independence in the face of authoritative foremen. As suggested earlier, foremen are now also relieved of some of the responsibility for the completion of particular jobs on their shift, this function being assumed by the assertive presence of the scheduling man. In all these respects my account of changes are similar to those described by Reinhard Bendix, Frederick Taylor, Richard Edwards, and others, namely, the diminution of the authority of the foreman and the parcelling-out of his functions to more specialized personnel.[20]

## THE ORGANIZATION OF A SHOP-FLOOR CULTURE

So far we have considered the stages through which any operation must go for its completion and the roles of different employees in advancing the operation from stage to stage. In practice the stages themselves are subject to considerable manipulation, and there were occasions when I would complete an operation without ever having been given it by the scheduling man, without having a blueprint, or without having it checked by the inspector. It is not neceesary to discuss these manipulations further, since by now it must be apparent that relations emanating directly from the organization of work are understood and attain meaning primarily in terms of making out. Even social interaction not occasioned by the structure of work is dominated by and couched in the idiom of making out. When someone comes over to talk, his first question is, 'Are you making out?' followed by 'What's the rate?' If you are not making out, your conversation is likely to consist of explanations of why you are not: 'The rate's impossible,' 'I had to wait an hour for the inspector to check the first piece,' 'These mother-fucking drills keep on burning up.' When you are sweating it out on the machine, 'knocking the pieces out', a passerby may call out 'Gravy!' – suggesting that the job is not as diffi-

19. Ibid., p. 290.
20. Reinhard Bendix, *Work and Authority in Industry: Ideologies of Management in the Course of Industralization* (New York: John Wiley, 1956); Frederick Taylor, *Shop Management;* Richard Edwards, 'The Social Relations of Production in the Firm and Labor Market Structure', *Politics and Society* 5 (1975): 83–108.

cult as you are making it appear. Or, when you are 'goofing off' – visiting other workers or gossiping at the coffee machine – as likely as not someone will yell out, 'You've got it made, man!' When faced with an operation that is obviously impossible, some comedian may bawl out, 'Best job in the house!' Calling out to a passerby, 'You got nothing to do?' will frequently elicit a protest of the nature, 'I'm making out. What more do you want?' At lunchtime, operators of similar machines tend to sit together, and each undertakes a post mortem of the first half of the shift. Why they failed to make out, who 'screwed them up', what they expect to accomplish in the second half of the shift, can they make up lost time, advice for others who are having some difficulty, and so on – such topics tend to dominate lunchtime conversations. As regards the domination of shop-floor interaction by the culture of making out, I can detect no changes over the thirty years. Some of the details of making out may have changed, but the idiom, status, tempo, etc. of interaction at work continue to be governed by and to rise out of the relations in production that constitute the rules of making out.

In summary, we have seen how the shop-floor culture revolves around making out. Each worker sooner or later is sucked into this distinctive set of activities and language, which then proceed to take on a meaning of their own. Like Roy, when I first entered the shop I was somewhat contemptuous of this game of making out, which appeared to advance Allied's profit margins more than the operators' interests. But I experienced the same shift of opinion that Roy reported:

> attitudes changed from mere indifference to the piecework incentive to a determination not to be forced to respond, when failure to get a price increase on one of the lowest paying operations of his job repertoire convinced him that the company was unfair. Light scorn for the incentive scheme turned to bitterness. Several months later, however, after fellow operator McCann had instructed him in the 'angles on making out', the writer was finding values in the piecework system other than economic ones. He struggled to attain quota 'for the hell of it', because it was a 'little game' and 'keeps me from being bored'.[21]

Such a pattern of insertion and seduction is common. In my own case, it took me some time to understand the shop language, let alone the intricacies of making out. It was a matter of three or four months before I began to make out by using a number of angles and by transferring time from one operation to another. Once I knew I had a chance to make out, the rewards of participating in a game in which the outcomes were uncertain absorbed my attention, and I found myself spontaneously cooperating with management in the production of greater surplus value. Moreover, it was only in this way that I could establish relationships with others on the shop floor. Until I was able to strut around the floor like an experienced operator, as if I had all the time in the world and could still make out, few but the greenest would condescend to engage me in conversation. Thus, it was in terms of the culture of making out that individuals evaluated one another and themselves. It provided the basis of status hierarchies on the shop floor, and it was reinforced by the fact that the more sophisticated machines requiring greater

21. Donald Roy, 'Work Satisfaction and Social Reward in Quota Achievement', *American Journal of Sociology* 57 (1953): 509–10.

skill also had the easier rates. Auxiliary personnel developed characters in accordance with their willingness to cooperate in making out: Morris was a lousy guy because he'd always delay in bringing stock; Harry was basically a decent crib attendant (after he took my ham), tried to help the guys, but was overworked; Charley was an OK scheduling man because he'd try to give me the gravy jobs; Bill, my day man, was 'all right' because he'd show me the angles on making out, give me some kitty if I needed it, and sometimes cover up for me when I made a mess of things.

## THE DISPERSION OF CONFLICT

I have shown how the organization of a piecework machine shop gives rise to making out and how this in turn becomes the basis of shop-floor culture. Making out also shapes distinctive patterns of conflict. Workers are inserted into the labour process as individuals who directly dictate the speed, feed, depth, etc. of their machines. The piece wage, as Marx observed, 'tends to develop on the one hand that individuality, and with it the sense of liberty, independence, and self-control of the labourers, on the other, their competition one with another'.[22] At the same times, the labour process of a machine shop embodies an opposed principle, the operator's dependence on auxiliary workers – themselves operating with a certain individual autonomy. This tension between control over machinery and subordination to others, between productive activities and production relations, leads to particular forms of conflict on the shop floor.

I have already suggested that pressures to make out frequently result in conflict between production and auxiliary workers when the latter are unable to provide some service promptly. The reason for this is only rarely found in the deliberate obstructionism of the crib attendant, inspector, trucker, and so on. More often it is the consequence of a managerial allocation of resources. Thus, during the period I worked on the shop floor, the number of operators on second shift expanded to almost the number on first shift, yet there was only one truck driver instead of two; there were, for most of the time, only two inspectors instead of four; there were only two foremen instead of four; and there was only one crib attendant instead of two or three. This merely accentuated a lateral conflict that was endemic to the organization of work. The only way such lateral conflict could be reduced was to allow second-shift operators to provide their own services by jumping into an idle truck, by entering the crib to get their own fixtures, by filling out their own cards, by looking through the books for rates or to see whether an order had been finished, and so on. However, these activities were all regarded as illegitimate by management outside the shop.[23] When middle management clamped down on operators by enforcing rules, there was chaos.

22. Karl Marx, *Capital*, 1: 555.

23. I vividly recall being bawled out by a manager who came into the time office long after he should have gone home. He found me going through the books to see how many pieces had been handed in on a particular operation. Second-shift shop-floor management allowed and even encouraged operators to look these sorts of things up for themselves rather than bother the time clerks, but senior management regarded this as a criminal act.

In the eyes of senior management, auxiliary workers are regarded as overhead, and so there are continual attempts to reduce their numbers. Thus, as already recounted, the objective of the quality-control manager was to reduce the number of inspectors. Changes in the philosophy of quality control, he argued, place increasing responsibility on the worker, and problems of quality are more effectively combated by 'systems control', design, and careful check on suppliers, particularly suppliers of castings. But, so long as every operation had to have its first piece checked, the decline in the number of inspectors merely led to greater frustration on the shop floor.

A single example will illustrate the type of conflict that is common. Tom, an inspector, was suspended for three days for absenteeism. This meant that there was only one inspector for the entire department, and work was piling up outside the window of Larry (another inspector). I had to wait two hours before my piece was inspected and I could get on with the task. It was sufficiently annoying to find only one inspector around, but my fury was compounded by the ostentatious manner in which Larry himself was slowing down. When I mentioned this to him, jokingly, he burst forth with 'Why should I work my ass off? Tom's got his three days off, and the company thinks they are punishing him, but it's me who's got to break my back.' In this instance, conflict between Tom and the company was transmuted into a resentment between Tom and Larry, which in turn provoked a hostile exchange between Larry and me. 'Going slow', aimed at the company, redounds to the disadvantage of fellow workers. The redistribution of conflict in such ways was a constant feature of social relations on the shop floor. It was particularly pronounced on second shift because of the shortage of auxiliary workers and the fact the more inexperienced operators, and therefore the ones most needing assistance, were also on that shift.

Common sense might lead one to believe that conflict between workers and managers would lead to cohesiveness among workers, but such an inference misses the fact that all conflict is mediated on an ideological terrain, in this case the terrain of making out. Thus, management–worker conflict is turned into competitiveness and intragroup struggles as a result of the organization of work. The translation of hierarchical domination into lateral antagonisms is in fact a common phenomenon throughout industry, as was shown in a study conducted on a sample of 3604 blue-collar workers from 172 production departments in six plants scattered across the United States:

> work pressure in general is negatively correlated to social-supportive behavior, which we have called cohesive behavior, and positively related to competitive and intra-group conflict behavior. Cohesive behavior is generally untenable under high pressure conditions because the reward structure imposed by management directs employees to work as fast as they can individually.[24]

The dominant pattern of conflict dispersion in a piecework machine shop is undoubtedly the reconstitution of hierarchical conflict as lateral conflict and competition. However, it is by no means the only redistribution of conflict. A

24. Stuart Klein, *Workers under Stress: The Impact of Work Pressure on Group Cohesion* (Lexington, Ky.: University of Kentucky Press, 1971), p. 100.

reverse tendency is often found when new machinery is introduced that is badly coordinated with existing technology. Here lateral conflict may be transformed into an antagonism between workers and management or between different levels of management.

To illustrate this point, I will draw upon my own experience with a machine that is designed to balance pulleys so that they don't break any shafts when they are running in an engine. The balancing machine, introduced within the past five years, is very sensitive to any faults in the pulley – faults that other machining operations may inadvertently introduce or that may have been embedded in the original casting when it came from the foundry.

The pulley is seated on a fixture attached to a rotating circular steel plate. The balancing plate and pulley can be automatically spun, and this indicates two things: first, the place where excess stock should be removed to compensate for imperfections in the pulley and, second, the degree of imbalance in the pulley. When an area of excess weight is located, holes are drilled in the pulley to remove stock; the pulley is then spun again and more holes are drilled as needed. This process is repeated until the pulley balances to within one or two ounces, according to the specifications on the blueprint. The most difficult part of the job is getting the balance set up. Before any pulley can be balanced, it is necessary first to balance the fixture and plate by placing clay on the plate. This complicated procedure for setting up is designed to ensure that the pulley is indeed balanced when the dial registers it as being balanced – that is, when the pulley is turned through 180 degrees on the fixture, the recording is still within one or two ounces, or whatever the specification happens to be.

The small pulleys were easy. Often they didn't even need balancing. Just a touch from the drill to indicate they had been attended to was all that was necessary. That was gravy. But the big seventy-five pounders presented a very different picture. They were the most difficult to balance and naturally the most critical. It was tough enough hauling them up onto the balance and then taking them off, let alone balancing them to within an ounce. Both Bill and I tried to pretend they weren't there, although there were always a good number sitting by the balance, four or five layers of sixteen, piled on top of one another. We balanced them only when we had to, and then with extreme reluctance. They often posed insuperable problems, due to defects in the castings or in the taper, which meant that they would not fit properly on their fixture. On one or two occasions I came on second shift to discover the unusual sight of Bill cursing and sweating over the mess the pulleys were in and hearing him say how, after ten years on the miscellaneous job, he was getting too old to face it any more. 'It's all yours, Englishman. Perhaps they'll give you a little bonus to keep you on,' he laughed. It wasn't so much that the pulleys were not offering him enough money, since Bill would have his time covered with a double red card. It was more that he had been defeated; his job had taken over; he had lost control. No amount of energy or ingenuity seemed sufficient to get those pulleys to balance, yet they still had to be delivered to the line. 'They expect me to make pulleys on this machine. Well, I only balance pulleys, and if they won't balance, they won't balance. They don't understand that if they've got blowholes in them they just won't come down.'

I came in one day at 3 p.m. and Bill warned me that the big shots would be breathing down my neck for the seventy-five pounders. 'Those pulleys are hot, man!' Sure enough, no sooner had he left than I found myself encircled by the foreman, the night-shift superintendent, the foreman of inspectors, the scheduling man, the setup man, and, from time to time, a manager from some other department. Such royal attention had me flustered from the start. I couldn't even set up the balance properly. The superintendent became impatient and started ordering me to do this, that, and the other, all of which I knew to be wrong. It was futile to point that out. After all, who was I to contradict the superintendent? The most powerful thought to lodge in my head was to lift the pulley off the balance and hurl it at their feet. As the clay piled up on the plate, way beyond what was necessary to balance it, the superintendent began to panic. He obviously thought his neck was on the line, but he had little idea as to how the machine worked. He was an oldtimer, unaccustomed to this new-fangled equipment. And so he followed the directions on the chart hanging from machine – directions that Bill had instructed me to ignore because they were wrong. When the superintendent thought the plate was balanced, we started drilling holes in the pulley – more and more holes, until the surface was covered with them. Clearly something was wrong. I'd never seen such a mess of holes. But the superintendent was more concerned with getting the pulleys out of the department and onto the engines. He didn't dare ask me to turn the pulleys through 180 degrees to see if they were really balanced – the acid test. I knew they wouldn't balance out, and probably so did he. By the end of the shift I had managed to ruin twenty-three pulleys.

The saga continued the following day. When I arrived at the balance, the superintendent was already there, remonstrating with Bill, who was trying to explain how to balance the plate. He was surrounded by yellow-painted pulleys – the pulleys I had 'balanced' the night before – which had been pulled off the engines just before they were due to be shipped out. Amazingly, no one was after my neck. The superintendent was fussing around, trying to vindicate himself, saying that the chart was misleading. It wasn't his fault, he complained, and how much better it was in the old days before we had these fancy machines that didn't work properly. Bill was not upset at all, even though he'd been on the pulleys all day. It didn't take much imagination to see why, since he was now a hero, having retrieved the situation. Management had come round to him in the morning demanding to know what incompetent had balanced the pulleys. Since he alone knew how to work the balance, Bill sensed his newly won power and importance. The superintendent, however, was in hot water, and his prestige, already at a low ebb, had taken a further dive. No one was particularly surprised at my ineptitude, since I had never demonstrated any mechanical skill or understanding.

I have just described two types of conflict that can result from the introduction of a new piece of technology. In my first example, the new machine was out of tune with the surrounding technology and as a result turned what was potentially a lateral conflict into one between management and worker. In my second example, the new machine allowed an operator to monopolize some knowledge (and this is quite likely when the machine is unique to the shop); this enhanced his power and led to a severe conflict between shop management and middle management when the operator was not around.[25] There is no space here to

25. This enhanced power was one of the attractions of the miscellaneous job, which no one wanted because it was rough, dirty, and dangerous as well as low-paying. Since the other operators on second shift knew virtually nothing about the jobs I did, I was able to develop a certain bargaining power, although by no means as great as Bill's.

explore other patterns of conflict crystallization, dispersion, and displacement. All I wish to stress is the way in which the specific organization of work structures conflict and how direct confrontation between management and worker is by no means its most common form.

Indeed, over the past thirty years conflict between management and worker has diminished, while that among workers has increased. This was how Donald Roy reacted to my observations at Allied:

> Your point in regard to the big switch of hierarchical conflict to the side of inter-worker competition pleases me immensely. . . . But in retrospect I see that in my time the main line of cleavage was the worker–management one. With the exception of the mutual irritations between machine 'partners' of different shifts, operator relations were mainly cooperative, and most of the auxiliaries (stock chasers, tool crib men, etc.) were helpful. There were employees in the Jack Shop then who recalled the 'whistle and whip' days before the local union was organized.[26]

There are a number of suggestions in his dissertation as to why there should have been greater antagonism between management and worker and less competition and conflict among workers. First, because of wartime conditions, there were more auxiliary workers for the same number of operators. Second, there was generalized hostility to the company as being cheap, unconcerned about its labour force, penny-pinching, and so on,[27] whereas the attitudes of workers at the engine division of Allied were much more favourable to the company. This was exemplified by the large number of father–son pairs working in the plant. If your son had to work in a factory, many felt that Allied was not a bad place. Third, Allied treated its employees more fairly than Geer. Part of this may be attributed to the greater effectiveness of the union grievance machinery in 1975 than in 1945. Furthermore, as part of Allied, a large corporation, the engine division was less vulnerable to the kinds of market exigencies that had plagued Geer Company. It could therefore afford to treat its employees more fairly. Also, Allied did not appear to be out to cut rates with the militant enthusiasm that Roy had encountered. Fourth, as Roy himself notes above, the period of CIO organizing was still close at hand, and many Geer employees remembered the days of sweatshops and arbitrary discipline. Among the workers I talked to, only the older ones could recall the days of the 'whistle and whip', and, when they did, it was mainly in reference to the tribulations of their fathers.

## CONCLUSION

Between Geer Company of 1945 and Allied Corporation, thirty years later, the labour process underwent two sets of changes. The first is seen in the greater individualism promoted by the organization of work. Operators in 1975 had more autonomy as a result of the following: relaxed enforcement of certain managerial controls, such as inspection of pieces and rate-fixing; increased shop-floor bargaining between workers and foremen; and changes in the system of piece rates – changes that laid greater stress on individual performance, effort, and

26. Personal communication, July 1975.
27. Roy, 'Restriction of Output', ch. 11.

mobility and allowed more manipulations. The second type of change, related to the first, concerns the diminution of hierarchical conflict and its redistribution in a number of different directions. As regards the relaxation of conflict between worker and management, one notes the decline in the authority of the foreman and the reduction of tensions between those concerned with enforcement of quality in production and those primarily interested in quantity. The greater permissiveness toward chiselling, the improvement of tooling and machines, as well as easier rates, have all facilitated making out and in this way have reduced antagonism between worker and shop management.[28] The employment of fewer auxiliary workers, on the other hand, has exacerbated lateral conflict among different groups of workers.[29]

These changes do not seem to support theories of intensification of the labour process or increase of managerial control through separation of conception and execution. What we have observed is the expansion of the area of the 'self-organization' of workers as they pursue their daily activities. We have seen how operators, in order to make out at all, subvert rules promulgated from on high, create informal alliances with auxiliary workers, make their own tools, and so on. In order to produce surplus value, workers have had to organize their relations and activities in opposition to management, particularly middle and senior management.

28. A similar argument, made by Lupton, is worth citing in full:

> In Jay's, I would also say that the 'fiddle' [chiselling] was an effective form of worker control over the job environment. The strength and solidarity of the workers, and the flexibility of the management system of control, made a form of adjustment possible in which different values about fair day's work, and about 'proper' worker behaviour, could exist side by side. I have no doubt that, if management controls had been made less flexible, and management planning more effective, the 'fiddle' would have been made more difficult to operate and probably output could have been slightly increased. But this might have destroyed the balance of social adjustment between management and the workers, and the outcome might have been loss in work satisfaction. The shop would no longer have been a 'comfortable', maybe not even a 'happy', shop. And, in turn, this might have produced higher labour turnover, absenteeism and the like. One can only guess about these things, since there are so many other considerations involved: the existence of alternative employment, the ability of existing management–worker relationships to withstand the impact of radical change, for example, but it seems to be that when relationships are adjusted in a way similar to that I have described, which resembles the indulgency pattern noted by Gouldner, then any attempt to 'tighten up' might lead to resentment and resistance. In the circumstances, management might prefer to live with the 'fiddle' at the cost of what they believe to be some slight loss of output, and regard this as the price they pay for a good relationship. (Tom Lupton, *On the Shop Floor* (Oxford: Pergamon Press, 1963), pp. 182–3)

Though Lupton fails to see the organization of work as the consequence and object of struggles between workers and managers, among workers and among managers, his characterization of the *functions* of the 'fiddle' are illuminating.

29. In interpreting these changes we will repeatedly come up against a difficult problem, namely, the degree to which Roy's observations reflect the exigencies of wartime conditions. For example, during the war, government contracts encouraged the overmanning of industry, since profits were fixed as a percentage of costs. Boosting costs did not change the rate of profit. As a consequence, we should not be surprised to discover cutbacks in personnel after the war. Thus, Roy informs us that after V-J Day, just before he left Geer, there was a reorganization in which foremen were demoted and the setup function was eliminated (Roy, 'Restriction of Output', pp. 60, 219). Hostility of workers to the company must have been, at least in part, engendered by wartime restraints on union militancy and by the choking-off of the grievance machinery.

# 9

# Piece Rates, Hungarian Style

MICHAEL BURAWOY

There are three workers: an American, a West German and a Hungarian. The American eats five eggs and steak for breakfast and goes to work in his Buick. At work he is exploited. The West German has three eggs and ham for breakfast and goes to work in his Opel. He is also exploited at work. The Hungarian has one egg for breakfast and no meat. He goes to work on a bus but he is not exploited. At work he rules.

*Joke from the Hungarian shop floor*

## I

Hungary is the consumer paradise of Eastern Europe. The Hungarian economic reforms of 1968, which gave more autonomy to state enterprises and more scope for private enterprise, have been consolidated and extended. The shortages of basic consumer goods that continue to benight other socialist economies have been more or less eliminated. Queues are now a curiosity – outside pawn shops, or for Cuban bananas. Meat, fruit, vegetables, all the basic and many luxury foods are always available and in many varieties. Every third family has a car, and almost all have refrigerators. State housing is still in short supply and apartments are pitifully small, but all over the country people are building themselves one- and two-storey homes. Except among the Gypsy population, one is hard pressed to find the poverty and insecurity that afflict a quarter of the population of the United States. And the Hungarian welfare system offers basic guarantees in old age, child-rearing, and illness. Consumer paradises, however, like all earthly paradises, are

This essay was first published in *Socialist Review*, 15(1), 1985. I am grateful to János Lukács for all the discussions we had together and his crucial role in making the study possible. A grant from the National Science Foundation, while gratefully accepted, nevertheless made it difficult to appreciate what it is like to earn and exist on five thousand forints a month. What I do understand is largely due to the extraordinary openness with which Hungarian workers and managers greeted my appearance on the shop floor and their enthusiasm to take me into their lives. M.B.

built not out of fine words, economic formulas or political slogans, but out of hard work. For two months I entered the hidden abode of socialist production.

When I am on the morning shift, as I am today and all this week, I catch the number five bus at 5.32 a.m. It's summer and already light. The bus is jam packed. Two and three stops back, towards the outskirts of the town, it picked up workers from the housing estate where fifteen thousand people live in one-room, one-and-a-half-room, two-room and, for the exceptionally lucky, three-room apartments. Although some have managed to buy their apartments from the state, most pay a monthly rent of 400 to 1000 forints (two to five days' work; the current exchange rate is 46 forints to one US dollar). Can a family of four ever get used to such cramped quarters in anonymous concrete blocks? Is work, like the open-air swimming baths, a welcome escape? If it is, you wouldn't know it from the grim faces on the bus. Perhaps it's just too early to be jovial. Probably one never gets used to the coercive routine of coming to work. There's silence on the bus, and I avoid catching my foreman's eye. The bus winds its way through the town, and in twelve minutes we are outside the factory. It could be a factory anywhere in the world, except that hovering over it is a dull red star. Its name is inscribed in broken lettering on the front wall.

We pass through a new three-storey building, housing the porter's lodge, the security check and the employment office. But most of the building is taken up by the workers' dormitory, built for long-distance commuters. These are usually young single men with skills to offer, although a few couples live here too. There's room for about a hundred workers, and at present there are about eighty. The rooms would be tiny enough for one person, but they manage to fit three beds together with a small shower and bathroom. At weekends workers go back to their homes, often in distant villages. This is not the sort of life one puts up with for long. But while it lasts it is at least cheap – 160 forints (six hours' work) a month for a bed.

After leaving the building I join a straggling line of workers walking toward Department B, the older of the two main shops – older workers and older machines. The entrance to the shop marks the real barrier between the factory and the world outside. Once I cross the line I have to cease day-dreaming, wrench myself into the present and concentrate on the realities at hand. I greet my fellow workers, shaking hands with some and recognizing others verbally. The nuances of social address, complicated enough for Hungarians, are much more so for a foreigner in an ambiguous status like myself. I stumble through it, clock in, and make my way to the changing room. It's 5.48, and already night-shift workers are showering. I open my locker and take out my work boots, still dripping with oil from yesterday, and brown overalls. At least they were brown when I got them four days ago. Now they are more black than brown, covered with oil stains and impregnated with metallic dust. As sure a sign of a novice as any, but no one draws attention to it. Shoes and clothes are given out free, and every two weeks I change my overalls. Brown identifies me as a member of Department B, while the workers in the newer shop, Department A, are decked in a more attractive bright green.

I return to the shop. It could be any machine shop. The familiar smell of oil, the familiar sounds – screeching of automatic lathes, the hum of drills drowned out by the roar of automatic mills. It evokes the same mixed feelings of dread and awe as did the small-parts department of Allied, the engine division of a multinational corporation in South Chicago where I worked as a miscellaneous machine operator for ten months in 1974–1975. It's about the same size – two hundred feet square. There are over a hundred machines, in nine parallel lines separated by five aisles, with another central aisle cutting across the shop. Six of the lines are dominated by lathes and automatic lathes, while the others are composed largely of mills and drills. Most of the machines are Czech or Hungarian, although one or two of the modern numerical-control machines are West German. There's even a broach used for cutting irregularly shaped holes, such as keyways in steel pulleys. I shudder every time I look at it, remembering the times I nearly killed myself on a similar machine at Allied.

The centre of the Allied shop was dominated by the scheduling office where we would pick up our work orders, the foremen's office, the inspectors' benches, and the crib, where we got our tools. Here the offices and crib are pushed against the wall; one of the inspectors' benches is too, while two are centrally located. But the shop's most central point is marked by a huddle of people around the coffee maker – always kept going by the woman who runs the speed drills. For four and a half forints (ten minutes' work), Zsuzsa will pour you a small glass of strong Hungarian coffee. However, I wait for mine to be brewed by the Dobó Katica Socialist Work Brigade – the women mill operators who have adopted me as one of their own. The noise is temporarily reduced to a hum, as the night-shift workers have left and the day-shift workers are gathered around to exchange gossip, what they did the night before or will do this weekend. The buzzer goes and we slowly scatter to our machines. The roar begins again.

## II

I operate a radial drill. Unlike other drills, with a radial drill the piece rather than the machine is clamped into position and the operator moves the spindle from hole to hole. From the steel base rises a column about two feet thick and ten feet tall, with a boom that extends six feet out from the column and swings around it. The head moves along the length of the boom. From its underside drops the spindle, which holds the chuck, into which various tools – drills, reamers, spot-facers, chamfers – can be inserted. So the spindle can be moved in three directions: horizontally, by pushing or pulling on the boom; vertically, by raising or lowering the boom on the column or by raising or lowering the chuck in the head; and in a horizontal, radial direction by moving the head backwards or forwards along the boom. A hollow steel table, with grooves used for clamping fixtures, raises the work to waist height.

How did I get landed with such a monstrosity? When I first appeared before the shop superintendent seven weeks ago as a prospective employee, I told him I had operated simple machines before. With no hesitation he marched me over to the vacant radial drill at the end of the line. There seemed to be no doubt in his mind where I belonged. I looked at the giant albatross and panicked. I wouldn't have dared touch such a machine at Allied. I protested feebly that I was not very skilled. Well, try it, he said. This was going to be a nightmare, I was certain. I soon understood why I had been dumped on the radial drill: no one else wanted it. The job was poorly paid and the norms were difficult to make; the machine demanded concentration and strength, and offered few opportunities for private earnings outside work – *maszek*. The trial would begin after I was marched from office to office, collecting a dozen signatures from seemingly every department and organization in the factory, registering me as a genuine socialist worker.

My foreman, Kálmán, seemed pleasant enough – a young engineer, getting practical experience on the shop floor. He introduced me to János, who would or would not teach me the tricks of the trade. János is a slight, moustached Gypsy, a skilled operator with twelve years in the factory and six on the radial drill. That day he had seven tools carefully lined up on the bench to his left. I watched him pick up each in turn, slap it into the whirling chuck, changing the 'speed' (revolutions per minute) and 'feed' (downward pressure, measured in centimetres per minute) on the head. He then guided the tool to the specified holes by pushing, pulling and turning the head on the boom, simultaneously bringing down the spindle until the tool cut into the small steel part, shaped like a beer bottle and clamped into its fixture on the work table. When this operation was finished he raised the spindle and detached the tool from the still-whirling chuck, replacing it with the next in sequence and beginning the process again. Periodically, he unlocked the fixture and revolved it on its axis to begin a new series of holes. After about eight minutes the piece was finished, full of holes in different directions, and unbolted from the fixture. A new piece from the large tub to his right was clamped into the fixture, and János began all over again. The piece-time norm for this job is seventeen minutes; János does it in half. It's an impressive sight – the easy flowing command with which this little man guides his machine in three directions, flicking tools in and out of the chuck. Would I ever be able to remember the exact sequence of tools and the holes each is supposed to cut? Would I ever dare slap a drill in and out of a chuck spinning at 1000 revolutions per minute? Who said industrial work has lost its skill?

János was friendly enough. Realizing my trepidation, he tried to assure me that it was not as difficult as it looked, and in any case my jobs would be simpler to begin with. Soon he took me for a drink of 'cola' at the buffet. Then Gabi introduced himself – the set-up man on the mills. Laci soon arrived on the scene. Everyone was curious about their new American worker. And then I was introduced to Lajos, the charge hand, who, it turned out, would really be responsible for my training. He is a charming, rotund, moustached fellow with curly hair and ruddy cheeks. I felt I was in good hands. He soon grasped my level and adjusted accordingly. Certainly it was not like my old machine shop in South Chicago, where Bill, the day-shift operator who was supposed to train me, was curt and hostile, showing me the bare minimum. Bill, of course, had every reason to protect job secrets from competition. His power on the shop floor rested on the monopoly of knowledge acquired from ten years as a miscellaneous machine operator. For the first three months, I remember, it was a nightmare. Every day I came in nervous, wondering what I had screwed up the night before. Here I never worry much. Not only Lajos but the radial drill operators themselves, János and Péter, are always prepared to help me. They show me the real route to success: abandoning the instructions on the blueprint.

Of course, I am not a typical newcomer. I am no threat to János and Péter. I do not compete for their gravy work or show how loose their norms are. That was clear from the beginning. They could afford to be nice to me. I would be here for only two months. Even when they show me the shortcuts I don't make more than 85 per cent, compared to everyone else's 100-plus. And there are positive incentives to be friendly. I am Misi, the sociologist from America who has come to write a book about factory life in Hungary, a guest worker with a difference. I am a curiosity that will enliven their days. They exude a natural and genuine generosity so absent from the brittle, competitive atmosphere at Allied – although even there, when I became more experienced and Bill realized he was going to have to live with me, he became more friendly. We would joke around when our shifts overlapped and even sometimes share a 'kitty' – work completed but not handed in, to be used in emergency situations when we couldn't make the rate.

## III

Today is Friday and everyone is thinking about the weekend. Even if it will mean more work, at least they will be working on their own gardens or weekend houses. They will decide the pace and own the product. But before the weekend I still have to get through the housings I began yesterday. The job has a lousy rate, and so I am not surprised Pista has not stolen them from me. When I'm on easier rates he sometimes does four hours overtime on my work after I have left. The gravy quickly disappears. There's nothing I can do about it, despite all the moral support I get from János and the women of the Dobó Katica Brigade. They tell me Pista is a *kulák* and *csizmás parászt* (boot-legged peasant). The problem is that Pista's automatic mill across the aisle from me often runs out of work, and if he doesn't manage to find more work for himself the shop superintendent will, generally lousy work. My first real encounter with Pista was one day when he stormed over to my machine swearing like a trooper about how he'd worked for the company twenty-one years and he was still being pushed around from one machine to another. He protested, 'I'm a mill operator, not a rough grinder or a lathe operator. Who the hell does this reactionary management think they are?' That time he knuckled under, moved onto the lathe, worked like fury, stormed out three hours before the end of the shift and didn't come in the next day. On another occasion, not finding any work to his satisfaction, he marched off home soon after beginning the shift.

At Allied workers were never punted from machine to machine. When there was no work – it rarely happend – we were guaranteed pay at 125 per cent. Here too, at least in theory, we are guaranteed 'standstill time' pay at 100 per cent, but workers are not satisfied with it. Nor is management. They prefer to transfer workers to other machines. Without the elaborate, union-protected job rights we had at Allied, workers' resistance depends on the bargaining power each can accumulate by virtue of his or her importance in the work process. Management's flexible deployment of labour is enshrined in the special bonus that foremen can distribute, a maximum of 300 forints a month (about one and a half days' pay). One of the criteria foremen use is operators' willingness and ability to work on a variety of machines.

But this doesn't affect me at all. I have difficulty operating one machine. My radial drill is not only the last in the line; it's also the oldest. According to the stamp on its base, it came from Csepel Machine Factory in 1959. Over the years it has developed a slight but noticeable wobble. It can shudder on the boom and the speed is difficult to change. But it does okay for the rough work it gets. And I can blame all my broken tools – I must hold the record – on my machine.

It's 6.30 a.m., and there are 104 housings left in the tub. Each requires five holes, carefully spaced around the circumference. I use an eleven-millimetre twist drill and the same speed and feed for each hole. Each piece, about twenty centimetres in diameter, is locked into the fixture by tightening a bolt with a wrench. After I have drilled the holes and taken the piece out of the fixture, I must break the edges of each hole by hand, turning a chamfering tool in the hole. All this takes between two and three minutes, depending on my work mood. The norm time is four minutes. When I first did this job I thought it was gravy. Then János told me there was another operation with another fixture. I assumed he was joking, and so continued merrily at two minutes apiece – 200 per cent, or so I thought. At last I was making some money. When I finished the series and was feeling rather pleased with myself, Lajos came round and said I had to spot-face them – enlarge the hole to a shallow depth, making a seat for a bolt head or nut, using a special tool called a spot-facer. I looked at Lajos as though he were crazy. 'No!' I exclaimed. So he showed me the blueprint, and sure enough there it was, spot-face all five holes. I was furious but powerless. What a rip-off – one norm for two operations. From one moment to the next gravy turns to dust. The spot-facing takes another two minutes, so even though it is possible to do one piece in four minutes, it would be impossible to keep that rate up for eight hours. In any case, who works for eight hours?

So I never make 100 per cent on this work. At Allied this wouldn't be so bad. When confronted with a lousy piece rate we simply took it easy and collected the guaranteed minimum of 100 per cent. Here it is quite another story. If you produce at 50 per cent, you are paid at 50 per cent. This is a socialist piece-rate system – payment strictly according to production. There may be employment security, but it is truly undermined by wage insecurity. The pressure doesn't let up. At the end of the month the piece times recorded on the 'work papers' we hand in for each job are totalled and we are paid accordingly. At the end of my first month I received a grand total of 3600 forints, about seventy dollars. My average percentage was eighty-two, but that included pieces I had produced in the first week when I was paid an hourly rate based on my worker category. These pieces were added into the subsequent weeks' production, so that my actual production level, averaged over the entire month, was more like 70 per cent. János, on the other hand, produced at 107 per cent and received 8480 forints for the month, after doing a lot of overtime. He wouldn't stick around the radial drill if he didn't get that overtime. That is the way management keeps its radial drill operators.

So as to avoid norm cuts, János doesn't hand in more than 110 per cent. But there is also a management-imposed ceiling of 110 per cent, which may be lifted on the twentieth of the month if shop supervisors think it necessary. Management wants to avoid arhythmical work patterns associated with high percentage outputs in some parts of the month and no work available in other parts. It also tries to keep the overall factory percentage below 110 per cent so as not to attract big norm cuts from the enterprise's central office. In this respect workers and management within the firm are in collusion against the central direction of the enterprise.

But there are ways to get around this upper limit without attracting attention from outside. Today, for example, János is working on the 'beer bottles' again. He can produce two shifts' work in one. The night before last he came in at around 9.00. He showed me his time card. Kálmán had written in that he had arrived at 5.45. On other occasions operators punch in one another for overtime they don't actually work. This is not as devious as it sounds, since we are paid for the work we do, not the hours we put in. The effect of this manipulation is simply to reduce the official average percentage so that, say, workers producing at 140 per cent will appear to be producing at only 108 per cent. The company has also begun to pursue an alternative strategy by creating a VGMK, an enterprise worker collective. Workers organize themselves into a collective in order to undertake some particular task assigned by management and to which management assigns a particular price. From the point of view of both management and the workers there are many advantages to this system, but two are particularly important. Income from VGMK work is not counted against the wage bill, and so is not part of the centrally-regulated average enterprise wage. And the time spent on VGMK work is not officially recorded. Thus if workers are officially paid at 110 per cent, they can receive the value of the extra 30 per cent they produce as VGMK earnings. Shop-floor management collaborates with workers, particularly the most scarce and needed workers, to circumvent official limits on their earnings.

At Allied things were simpler. We restricted our percentages to 140 per cent, or at least didn't hand in more than 140 per cent, so as not to attract the attention of the industrial engineers who studied our outputs. For all their scientific paraphernalia they didn't know which were the tight and which the loose rates. But here the system of norm cutting, apparently more arbitrary, is actually more effective. Norm cuts are dictated by the enterprise's head office based on the firm's overall performance. This figure, about 2 or 3 per cent each year, is translated into specific norm changes through bargaining between workers and shop-floor management. Although industrial engineers don't actually know which are the loose norms, worker participation ensures that the looser ones tend to get cut, although the more vulnerable workers obviously suffer most. Surely this is the managerial dream – workers who cut their own rates!

But all this is quite irrelevant to me. I don't have to worry about rate busting or the 110 per cent ceiling. I can't even make 100 per cent on these damned housings. I can't help but wonder what this system would be like for a newcomer who depended on this wage. For the first week you are on a personal wage. During this time you are 'trained' by a fellow worker and perhaps the charge hand or foreman will show you a thing or two. Then you are on your own. I had all the assistance possible and still made only 3600 forints. That's hardly enough to support a single person, let alone a family. No wonder new operators don't last long on my machine.

## IV

Norms are the true dictator. They drive one to fury and panic. I soon realized that I would have to risk life and limb to make the rates. I came in once to find that

Pista had already begun spot-facing some of the same housings I am doing today. The fixture was simple – two steel bars, two centimeters thick, bolted to the table in a V shape. It was obvious what I was supposed to do: hold the piece against the bars with one hand and bring down the spot-facer into the holes with the other. Knowing precisely what this was all about from my Allied experience, I was nervous at the thought. The piece might start shuddering against the bar, perhaps even leap over it, if my left hand wasn't strong enough to keep it in place. This piece of cast iron, the size of an average plate and the shape of a bowler hat, could then rip off a finger and fly into my chest. Machines don't recognize that they are run by fragile and fallible humans; they continue relentless.

I hovered around the machine, went for a walk, not knowing what to do. Lajos would never have allowed me to do it this way; he would have found another method. But he wasn't here. There was only Toni, who wasn't too concerned about safety. He simply showed me how to get hold of the piece with my hand. When Anna saw what was happening she immediately told me to leave it alone and called János. Annoyed that anyone should expect me to do it that way, he knocked the iron bars out of the table, flung them onto the floor in disgust, and found an alternative fixture – the one stipulated in the blueprint, but one that clearly no one used. It required that you bolt the piece in place, and rather than moving the piece, swing the drill from hole to hole, taking twice as long. There was no way I could make the rate.

I am lucky, I don't have to make the rate. I can afford to preserve my body intact, since I still have a second job in Berkeley. And, as often happens in Hungary, my second job brings in more money than my first. The money I earn here is pocket money, *pálinká* money. So why do I care what my percentage is each day? Why do I calculate how many hours' work, 'real work' at 100 per cent, I complete by the end of the shift? Is it the challenge to accomplish eight hours' work in a shift? The challenge of making the rates? The machine and its rates are an assault on my self-respect. When my performance is particularly low I am depressed and don't bother to add up the hours. But is challenge the whole story? How much challenge is there for János? He's done those beer bottles so many times now, it can hardly be a challenge – what keeps him going? Yes, money is an underlying factor, but there is something else involved in getting through the work day. It turns out to be much more exhausting to work slowly or irregularly. When one achieves a rhythm, when one is guiding the machine from hole to hole, turning the drill into the hole, flicking the feed on and off, slapping the tools in and out of the whirling chuck with fluency – in short, when one is controlling the machine rather than being controlled by it – time flies by and one is less exhausted. Unfortunately I am usually four or five hours into the shift before I get into rhythm, often already too tired to get moving. Today I am tired at 11.00 and I've only done thirty pieces. There are over seventy pieces still to do. Can I do it? It is certainly possible. So with renewed strength and concentration I begin the final assault. The last hours pass unnoticed as I see the pile gradually diminish.

Here there is no pressure from the foreman to hurry, as sometimes there was at Allied. There are no hot jobs that have to be done an hour ago, that require that I break the set-up and start on some new work. There is just me, my machine, the pieces and the norms. The norms are the decisive power. They are veritable relations of production. They shape my private relationship with my machine.

But it is private – I can seal myself off from everything around me, even the coercive reality of my day-to-day existence. But I can't transport myself into another world without courting danger: the machine and the tools demand my concentration. The holes have to be the right size, in the right place. And I have to be in the 'mood for work'. How often I see János wandering around the shop waiting for the mood to strike. Today and yesterday it never really came. He had been out on a drinking spree and this upset his work equilibrium. Instead he made himself a stand for his fishing rod out of materials he picked up from a friend in the storeroom. Tomorrow he will lie in the sun on the banks of the Tisza. Fishing is his favorite pastime, an escape from the housing estate and the factory. A city dweller with contempt for peasants, he doesn't grow paprika, grapes, cherries, potatoes in some garden. For him that's just another work trap.

## V

For the particularly privileged, management superimposes a personal domination on top of the impersonal domination of the piece rates. Typically, it is women who suffer under this double burden. With increasing numbers of women employed, management has devised clever systems of exploiting gender domination. Take the women of the Dobó Katica Brigade, who work on the mills. They have the assistance of Gabi, who sets up their machines and attends to any mechanical problems. But to encourage Gabi to work hard, management pegs his earnings, like the earnings of the individual mill operators, to the average percentage of the group. He is in fact the boss, who tells the women what work to run on which machines and decides if and when they can take their holidays. He is the intermediary between the women and management, and he has every interest in goading them to increase their output. For the most part they put up with his prodding, but when he comes in somewhat tipsy, as he did last week, they ostentatiously begin to gossip with one another.

Why do they put up with this subordination? They explain to me that if they want to work here, they have no alternative. The division into women's jobs and men's jobs is always accompanied by some form of gender domination. If it isn't integral to the jobs, it is added. Thus Zsuzsa, who operates the gang drills, has her independence undercut by having the role of coffee-maker thrust upon her. How she makes her rates I never understand.

Do the Dobó Katica women see themselves, or are they seen, as secondary earners? Certainly not. Anna is forty-one. She has two children, a boy of twelve and a girl of nine. She lives in a small town about half an hour's bus ride away. Two years ago she had serious heart trouble. Her life is hard. Her husband is a lathe operator in the same department but in the other production cycle. At home he's drunk a lot of the time. One morning Anna came in complaining that he had gone through a week's wages in one night. Anna has to clean and cook at the house of her mother, who is eighty and ill, as well as for her own family at home. At forty-six, Klára hasn't Anna's vitality or toughness, but she's always ready to suppress the seamy side of her life. Today she said she was tired because of her 'night work' – her whole face beamed with laughter. Her husband is a printer and drinks a lot. She worries because he also drives a car. She lives in a neighbouring village and commutes to work by bus. She also has two children, but they are much older than Anna's. And then there's Ági, the quietest of the three. She is forty-six too, but though she looks wearier than the others, like them she can always break into laughter when the occasion arises. When her daughter, who works in the crib on the other shift, comes by to visit, Agi lights up with pleasure and delight. At work these women feed the mills, at home they feed the family. The two jobs are equally exhausting, although there's no doubt which they prefer. But as Anna told me, 'Life is hard but not hopeless.' She lives for her two children, and would do almost anything for them.

Anna, Klára and Agi arrived together five years ago, and they have worked on the same shift and the same machines ever since. With Gabi, they form one half of the Dobó Katica Brigade. The other half is made up of three women and their setter from the other shift. Like everyone else, they switch shifts every week. The department also has another woman who migrated from the shop floor to the office, where she is a clerical assistant to the scheduling man. She records all the brigade's activities in a neatly-kept diary, with photographs of the nine members and Kálmań, the managerial representative. The diary records the two Communist Saturdays worked – one day's labour donated for a children's hospital and one day for the National Theatre – and three hundred hours of communal work on the factory grounds and donated for the construction of a new cultural centre. Then there are records of excursions they've taken together, parties they've had, and political meetings they've attended, such as the big one on war and peace organized by the regional party offices. The Dobó Katica women seem proud of their brigade. Last year they came first in the brigade competition and won nine thousand forints. That probably about covered their unpaid work. The runners-up got five thousand forints.

What's behind the brigades? They are not obligatory; why does anyone join them? No one really likes the brigades, but pressures from outside the factory, from the enterprise headquarters and the party, demand their establishment. So orders are passed down from on high to the shop superintendent: 'Form socalist work brigades!' The superintendent then expects each foreman to establish at least one brigade in his section. Given the hostility, this can be quite a tall order, but his bonuses depend on it. He approaches a likely candidate for leader, holding out the possibility of winning all this money. Whether there are also promises of favourable treatment is not clear. But it is more than likely that the formation of brigades will appeal more to vulnerable workers, such as women, than to experienced and skilled workers, who will have no part of such 'nonsense'. Certainly based on my experience here and in the champagne factory that I worked in a year ago, women workers seem to dominate in the brigade competition. By committing themselves to brigade work the women might hope to establish themselves more firmly within the shop, putting themselves in a better bargaining position.

Thus, Anna was furious when she didn't receive any monthly premium, known as *mozgóbér* ('moving pay'), for several months running. It is as if she felt her membership in the best brigade, her diligence at work, her meticulous cleaning of her work area, entitled her to the bonus. In practice, however, the premium is awarded to the more skilled and experienced workers, whose cooperation is essential to the effective organization of the shop. Such workers have no interest in brigade membership, and unlike Anna, they cannot be easily replaced.

There's another side to the feminization of work – deskilling. At Allied everyone set up their own machines, although there was a setter who might sometimes help out. Setting up was the part of the job that required the greatest skill and expertise. I can't imagine Allied workers tolerating the expropriation of that skill, its concentration in the hands of a single setter, while they just feed the machines. Nor can I imagine János, Péter and the other radial drill operators succumbing to such a system. Deskilling can proceed smoothly only if the old operators find satisfactory jobs elsewhere while the new operators are part of a more vulnerable labour force, and so it goes hand in hand with feminization. It's probably no accident that it was Gabi, a dedicated party member, who oversaw this transition.

The fact that these women face double labour (at home and in the factory) and double subordination (gender and class) doesn't mean that the men don't work hard too. Although he is the boss, Gabi's hourly wage is not much higher than Anna, Klára and Ági's. He earns more than they do because he does so much overtime. He too commutes from a village, about an hour and a half away. When he is on overtime and on morning shift he gets up at four a.m. to arrive at work at six. He leaves at six p.m. and arrives home not much before eight. He has dinner and goes to bed at ten or eleven. On weekends he works in his garden and helps his friends with theirs. In the shop he may sit around some of the time, but he is always ready to throw himself into his work should anything go wrong with one of the machines. He can look pretty worn out at the end of a shift.

## VI

For the men, at least, drinking becomes the quick escape from work. One can get sozzled by oneself at home or in a *kocsma* (pub), or do it in collective style in a private cellar. My first Friday I did it in style. It was Laci's idea. He runs one of the numerically-controlled mills. Once he has set up and the machine is running according to plan, he seems to have quite a bit of time to loaf around. He entertained me during my first week. Like Gabi, Laci is an *ingazó* (commuter), but his village is nearer than Gabi's. Laci is in his early thirties and strikingly handsome. Last year his wife had a serious operation in Debracen to remove an ulcer. She's now recovering at home, but is still very weak. Laci seems to have one major obsession: sex. His cupboards are plastered with pin-ups. He's always making passes at the women on the shop floor, who generally greet his advances with bored contempt. He's also a heavy drinker. Together with Gabi he organized my welcoming party at Béla's cellar. Béla, who towers over most of us, works on the horizontal boring machine. After work that Friday, Laci, Gabi, Béla, his mate on the 'horizontal' and I all went off to the cellar.

It was an old place hidden away in a hill, a cave with about fifteen wine barrels lining the walls, and a long table in an adjoining room. Béla's parents had been very successful wine growers until they were dispossessed of their land, first in 1945 and again with the consolidation into cooperatives in 1959. Each time his family had to begin again. Béla and his family now work two thousand *négyszögöl*, about three quarters of a hectare, growing some fruit and vegetables, but mostly cultivating vineyards. He makes about fifty hectolitres of wine a year – two white wines and one red. Béla doesn't sell any – he consumes it all with friends and family. He must have a lot of friends. As a guest I had to drink all three wines, and so was soon *totál.*

I swayed back to the town with Laci and Gabi. On the way we stopped at an *expresso* for a coffee and rum, whereupon they began to pound me with questions about working-class politics in the United States. What does the average worker think about the nuclear arms race? As I was to find time and time again, Hungarian workers cannot understand the mentality that would lead people to vote for a warmonger like Reagan. They had been well disposed toward Kennedy and Carter, but now they have difficulty distinguishing the American bear from the Soviet bear. They want to think well of America, land of opportunity and wealth. I'm always asked how much I earn – an amount that's mind-bogglingly vast to a Hungarian worker. Even when cost of living is taken into account it's much more lucrative to be a machine operator in the United States than in Hungary. In terms of hours of work, a car costs at least four times as much in Hungary; trousers, shoes and dresses cost seven or eight times as much, and food is also often more expensive. Only transportation, rent, and some entertainment can be cheaper. On the other hand, equally incomprehensible are the levels of violence, poverty and unemployment in the United States. And when I try to talk about the deep-seated racism in the United States, they compare blacks to Gypsies, who they say are 'lazy' and 'criminal'. In short, the comparison is complicated. But they do know they are much better off now than they were in 1956. Kádár has brought a continually increasing standard of living, but at a cost – an even greater increase in the expenditure of labour. They are running up the down escalator.

## VII

Next week will be my last, and Laci is organizing another gathering at Béla's cellar, this time, he promises, with 'goulash and shapely Hungarian girls'. But Gabi isn't here today to finalize arrangements, and we aren't sure when he will return. He's taken two weeks of his five weeks' holiday to work on the harvest in his village cooperative. In two weeks he gets five thousand forints, almost as much as he would get here in a month if he had no overtime. Miklós, the setter from the other shift, is working four hours overtime to cover half of Gabi's shift. He's having a frustrating time with the large numerically-controlled machine next to mine. It has been breaking down regularly, and now is making a huge racket. As at Allied, some of the numerically-controlled machines are down a lot. When this happens to Laci's mill he loiters around, gossiping, or goes home. It isn't worth taking 'standstill' pay. When the mill next to me breaks down, whatever member of the Dobó Katica Brigade is operating it is simply transferred to another mill. There are always more mills than operators.

The maintenance department has every incentive to get on with the job since their bonuses depend on keeping the down time below 320 hours a month for the whole shop. Józsi, one of the maintenance men, told me that they usually get their bonuses, if only because their boss is adept at juggling the figures. Sometimes

József has a lot of work to do, other days he has none. He told me that he averages three or four hours' work a shift. On afternoon shift he works less, and he often comes round to my machine to chat. But this week he has swapped shifts; his wife is expecting a baby any day. He is pretty nervous about it because the local doctors do not have a good reputation. He will have to hand over quite a sizeable tip, two thousand forints (some ten days' work), if he wants to be sure of proper attention. Józsi, who met his wife while he was working in East Germany, is always comparing Hungary with East Germany, saying that apartments are easier to get and things are much cheaper there. Here they live in a one-room apartment, although it has a television and a hi-fi. He desperately wants to move into a bigger place but doesn't know how he can manage it. A lucky few are now buying apartments from the state – a two-room apartment for about 600,000 forints. One can get a loan from the state bank of 360,000 forints plus 40,000 for each child; with two children a family still has to find about 160,000 forints. The enterprise might help some but most must rely on some other source, either private work or help from their parents. Józsi just doesn't know where he can get the money, and he doesn't have the time or energy to start building his own house.

On payday Józsi came over and showed me his pay slip for the month – 5300 forints. 'That's nothing, Misi. You can't live on that.' He has no overtime, but as a maintenance worker he has a skill which can help him find work on the side. Józsi mends washing machines in his spare time, bringing in another 4000 forints a month. His wife worked in a radiation laboratory until her pregnancy was well advanced. She gets five months' maternity leave at full pay from the state, and then for two and a half years while she is looking after her child she will get 1000 forints a month. But her earnings are nowhere near what they need for a new apartment. Life must be easier in the West, he assumes, but he knows from his own experience in West Germany how difficult it is to get a job.

## VIII

So today it seems I have myself to myself without interruptions. Even the mill next to me has ceased its racket. I am concentrating on my housings when one of the seven inspectors comes over to me. He's a little old guy who hides his fussiness behind a veneer of friendship. He asks me what happened to the two 'connectors' that were missing from the series I completed yesterday. That series, surely the worst job I've ever had, has dogged my existence for over ten days now. The story began a week ago Wednesday. I had just given up a series of 'housings' after smashing all the available spot-facers because there was too much steel to remove around the hole; so I was already depressed when these unfamiliar 'connectors' arrived on the scene – skittle-like objects about six inches long with a round head that had been milled flat to make two parallel sides. The blueprint said you had to drill a hole perpendicular to the milled sides through the head, ream (smooth out) the hole, and chamfer the edges. But who takes any notice of the blueprint? With János's help I eventually found the right fixture and we decided it was best first to drill all the pieces and then ream them all. All this took time and experimentation, and by the end of the day I had only drilled twenty-six pieces.

The next day was sweltering. When I came in at two p.m. the factory was like an oven – the temperature must have been over 100 degrees. There's no effective cooling system; the roof is low and part glass. Lajos was away and not a single radial operator showed up until later. It was too hot to work. And then I saw that someone had done another hundred of the connectors but had ruined them by making the hole too small. I didn't know and still don't know who left me with the headache. Obviously, they realized what they had done. I finished drilling the remaining 170 pieces and then for half a shift hovered around my machine, frustrated, not knowing what to do with the faulty connectors – the holes were too small to be reamed. I was very depressed: Lajos wasn't around to help, and János had no suggestions. I told Kálmán I'd had it. I wasn't coming in tomorrow. I'd wasted almost two shifts, and that was enough. I didn't need to waste another one. He tried to strike a deal with me: I could have tomorrow off if I did two lots of four hours' overtime next week. Some deal. Fuck that. There's no point in coming in if there's no work. I'm paid by the piece, not the hour. So I didn't go in on Friday, and I had already arranged to take Monday off as one of my two paid holidays. By Tuesday I expected someone else would have finished the connectors. But there they were, waiting for me, just where I had left them. At least Lajos was back. He started fooling around with the fixture, but it wasn't long before he realized that it wouldn't be possible to ream the defective pieces on my machine. The shop superintendent thought otherwise, so Lajos told him to have a go. To my delight, on the very first piece, with the reamer wobbling, he unhinged it from its sleeve. So we left the connectors and I started a new series of housings. What a relief!

That was Tuesday. Yesterday, Thursday, Lajos said I really had to finish up the connectors. But how? Well, he found another little fixture in which I could hold the connector by hand while I reamed. But it could only be done on a speed drill. Zsuzsa, who operates the speed drills, helped us set up. But I could see there was going to be trouble. Some of the holes in the connectors were so undersized that when the necessary pressure was brought to bear on the reamer my hand could not hold the piece steady. Sure enough, on Lajos' first attempt he couldn't hold the piece. It swung against the fixture and the reamer bent. We knocked it back into shape and after successfully reaming two pieces he handed it over to me. Zsuzsa told me to go very slow, but I guess I wasn't slow enough. On one particularly tight hole which required more pressure on the reamer the piece slapped against the fixture. I let go with the drill still whirling and the reamer smashed. I was furious. Why the hell was I having to pay for someone else's screw-up! I marched to the office and thrust the smashed reamer under Kálmán's nose. He shook his head and told me that would cost me a lot of money and signed for a new one. I got it replaced, but now I was nervous and agitated. After two more pieces it smashed again. Shit. I'd had it. I was ready to quit.

At this point János and Lajos turned up. They didn't give up as easily as I, but then they didn't have to run the job. Well, they figured out a way of holding the connector more steadily in the fixture by resting it against a steel bar. This worked. Slowly I got through the hundred pieces with undersized holes without further mishap. Two of the pieces, however, had not been completed in an earlier operation, so I tossed them into the next series and they were not registered as scrap. It is these two pieces that the old man has just come round to query. He says I can't just put them in the next series. That's officious baloney. So he forces me to sign for one more defective connector. It turns out that he wants to talk me into exchanging some dollars. He hasn't a chance.

In the middle of the fiasco around the speed drill yesterday Lajos couldn't understand why the holes were so tight. I explained that someone else had done them with a drill that hadn't been ground properly. Zsuzsa on the speed drills and Anna and Ági on the mills all backed me up, telling Lajos it was his fault because he had been on holiday. They continued to beleaguer him about management's ineptness and how I had been led round the bush, wasting so much time. What had been a total disaster and humiliation found its compensation in the solidarity the women exuded.

## IX

At Allied, while there may have been feelings of class consciousness, there were no such moments of solidarity. For all the trade union's importance, its effect was to atomize the workforce on the shop floor, reserving collective struggles for the triennial contract negotiations. The grievance machinery channelled struggles into the defence of individual rights and obligations, while the internal labour market encouraged workers to move to another job rather than fight out the issues in the present one. Here too struggles are individualized, not because of the presence but because of the absence of an effective union. There's no point in going to the union with a grievance, as I discovered when I wasn't paid for three hours overtime I had worked. I talked to Anna about it, and she laughed at the idea of going to the union representative. We decided to do it as a joke. The two representatives we consulted, both women, thought it was a joke too. I really had to go to the foreman, they said. So I went to Kálmán, who remembered he had given me the three hours and said he would file a grievance. I don't know if he did, but I never did get paid for that overtime.

So no one thinks of going to the union with any serious problem. Last year, when Anna was put on almost continuous weekend overtime, she went to the shop superintendent to complain that she could not do this because she had a family to look after. He simply told her that if she didn't like it she could leave. She explained to me how the union, the party, and management sit together on the 'director's council' and decide everything. When I told Janos that I hadn't gotten my overtime pay, he told me to go straight to the superintendent, rather than the foreman.

'Kálmán has no power.'

'What about the union?' I asked innocently.

'What about it? They are useless. Nulla-nulla.'

'But they at least provide cheap holidays,' I protested.

'Yes, but only for those who don't do any work, the bosses. The real workers don't get a chance to go to the holiday homes. I'm not a union member, a party member or a brigade member.'

'If they are all so useless why should anyone want to be a member?' I asked.

'When you want to get an apartment or a place in a nursery, these factors might be important.'

In fact party, union and brigade membership are becoming less and less important as the enterprise has less control over life outside work. Now flats are distributed largely on a point system linked to earnings, family size, and other factors independent of political activity inside the enterprise.

What is the party's role inside the factory? This is a difficult question. About 15 per cent of the workers are party members; these appear to be the more senior, experienced workers. The party secretary in Department B is one of the two scheduling men, a very popular young man. The party members meet every two weeks or so and are told of managerial problems. They are expected to help in the achievement of production targets and keep an eye open for trouble. But the significant power of the party is a potential one. In theory it can block any decision, from the employment of a given person to the introduction of norm cuts to the approval of the annual plan, since it is a signatory to every important document. In practice it interferes very little. It is this potential power that probably makes workers cautious in their attitudes toward the party. When expressing his bitterness and resentment Józsi would lower his voice and tell me there are 'red ears' all around. While I can joke about the party, no one else does. When a huddle of spectators gathered around my machine one night while I was trying to make out, I cried: 'What the hell is this – a party meeting?' They liked that, laughed, and even told the story to others. But I never heard anyone else joke about the party. In this respect the past casts a shadow over the present.

The party and union are essentially channels for communicating managerial decisions, and the absence of institutional means for expressing workers' collective interests fosters the individuation of struggles. But there is a basis for solidarity rooted in the organization of work. The one abiding characteristic of socialist economies is the generation of shortages, whether of workers, materials, machines, or investment resources. To be efficient in a socialist factory is to adopt a flexible work organization that can improvise effectively and rapidly. Labour is flexibly deployed by, for example, shunting experienced workers like Pista from machine to machine. At Allied job rights protected by the union and enshrined in the operation of the internal labour market prevented such arbitrary placement. Here flexibility is facilitated by the ample but by no means excessive supply of auxiliary workers – inspectors, set-up men, crib attendants, truck drivers and supervisors. At Allied these were cut to the bone in the name of capitalist efficiency, which created lines outside the inspector's window and the crib. The truck driver was turned into a king. This effectively turned piece worker against auxiliary workers, compounded by the ridiculous rules that came down from the bosses, further restricting the possibility of cooperation on the shop floor. Here there are also rules about checking the first piece and who should ride the lift truck, but no one takes much notice. Instead of being locked into opposition camps, nurtured by bureaucratic rules, the shop floor is a self-organizing autonomous unit. Every ten days it receives its production quotas and itself breaks them down into daily targets. Completed work and scrap move through the department with amazing speed. Here I have never seen the piles of defective pieces and unfinished engines that lined the aisles at Allied. As we approached the completion date for the half-year plan I waited for the mythical rush work to begin. Perhaps there was more overtime, perhaps the pace did become a little more hectic, but there was nothing like the rush work at Allied which recurred daily in the form of hot jobs and broken set-ups.

## X

In order to respond to the constraints of a shortage economy, the socialist firm engenders a limited form of workers' control. So long as piece rates are not screwed down so tight that we are turned against one another in the struggle to make out, so long as there are no arbitrary managerial interventions from on high, conception and execution can be effectively united on the shop floor. But this has consequences for attitudes toward management. Gabi, for example, refers to those who work and those who do nothing. Although a committed party member, he gets very resentful toward the *bürokrácia* in the 'glass house' where the bosses twiddle their thumbs. 'They don't know anything,' he said, shaking a blueprint under my nose. The potential for shop-floor solidarity against the glass house is always there. Only on my first day in the factory did I see a hint of its reality.

Management wanted to boost output without showing it on the books as an increase in percentage performance. They proposed a 2 per cent cut in norms in exchange for an immediate 2 per cent increase in basic wages and a promise of no more norm cuts next year. Obviously in some sort of trouble with the central enterprise, management took the extraordinary measure of calling a hasty meeting with the workers. The leader of the economic planning department, essentially the personnel manager, addressed the workers in Department A, while the chief engineer addressed Department B. I attended the meeting in Department A. It was introduced by the union secretary for the department. The personnel manager then explained the deal, suggesting that this was a way of keeping up with wage increases in other parts of the enterprise. But workers were suspicious at this unprecedented move. Why was management calling this meeting, consulting us? How would management guarantee that there would be no norm cuts next year? Would they put it in writing? Why were they cutting norms across the board, rather than selecting loose ones as they usually do? One party member said he would have to vote against the proposal because under it he would not be able to make the 106 per cent that the party expects from him! Among those attending, thirty-four voted against and seven in favour. Those in favour were all party members, union officials and supervisors.

In Department B, on the other hand, the proposal was unanimously endorsed. This is the oldest department, with older workers. Relations between management and workers are more harmonious, and the rates are said to be looser. In Department A they make parts under a Western licence. The rates are therefore tighter, the machinery more sophisticated, the workers younger and more skilled. So operators in Department A have more reason to resist norm cuts, and greater power to do so because they are more central to the firm's production and have skills that are badly needed by other enterprises. Nevertheless, they didn't believe that their opinion would have any effect on the outcome. Sure enough, the results were referred to the central trade union committee, which rapidly endorsed management's proposal. So why did management even hold the meetings? Perhaps they still remember the one-day strike that took place ten years ago when the new wage system was introduced. At that time the older workers lost their relative advantage *vis-á-vis* the younger workers and struck. Subsequently many of them left the plant.

## XI

Such collective struggle couldn't be further from my day-to-day life on the shop floor. It is 12.45, and the Dobó Katica women are already cleaning their machines and workplaces. On Friday their machines get an extra good clean. They are proud of their meticulous housekeeping. But I still have fifteen housings to drill. Determined to finish them off, I am flowing well with my old machine, and the possibility of coming to an end spurs me on to greater efforts. Pista comes round to inspect, to see if there will be any housings left for him to do in overtime. Even he is impressed by my pace, although not too happy. By 1.20 I finish the last one, and now I have to clean my machine and sweep up in the work area. I even take a rag to the old albatross itself, revealing a real green beneath the oily grime. I lock up my tools, scrub my hands and arms as best I can with the special soap, and I'm ready for lunch.

Although not entirely within the rules, I leave at 1.45 to go to the dining room. Lunch consists of a soup, a vegetable or pasta, and meat, and perhaps some fruit for dessert – all for eleven forints, twenty cents, or half an hour's work. Today it's cauliflower soup, liver fried in breadcrumbs with potatoes, and cherries to finish off. Tomás, the inspector whose desk is nearest to my machine, comes in with his factory companion, a woman who runs one of the lathes. They sit down next to me. I complain to him about the fussiness of his colleague who gave me a scrap notice for the connectors. He holds up his hands defensively, protesting that it has nothing to do with him. Indeed, Tomás seeks to maintain very friendly relations with the operators. Once when I had been drilling the thick oil-pumps, some hadn't fitted into the fixture properly. After they were clamped in place they would still move around when I was drilling, and the holes were skewed. About six were not good and sent back from the lathe, and another six defectives arrived from a previous series. Jokingly, Tomás asked me what he should do about them, how he should write them up. I told him, 'Put them down to bad castings.' He was suspicious but amused at my audacity. 'I can't do that,' he said, but he did. There was a similar problem of castings with the thin oil-pumps. Sometimes the grooves were not smooth enough to fit snugly onto the fixture, so the pumps couldn't be firmly clamped in place. I remember the problem of poor castings at Allied only too well. Some of the pulleys we had to balance came in with hugh blowholes in them. It was virtually impossible to drill out the right amount of steel in the right place so that the pressure on the axle would be evenly distributed. Somehow we had to balance them, blowholes or no blowholes. We didn't get much sympathy from management.

I make my way back to the shop, where a number of people are already gathered around Zsuzsa's coffee percolator. They are discussing what they will be doing this weekend. Kálmán beckons me to come over. He tells me Lajos will be mixing concrete for his new house and suggests I help him. 'His new house?' I repeat with some astonishment. Yes, Lajos is building himself a weekend house. Pista, it turns out, will be mixing concrete for his own new house. Tomás, the inspector, will be hard at work with his mates drilling a well in his 2000-square-metre garden. Indeed, many will be tending their gardens, plots of land rented from the city council for a nominal sum of sixty forints a year. It's usually the worst hilly land which, to get into shape, takes several years of sustained effort and much money. But then they can grow their grapes, cherries and peaches, cabbages and potatoes. They don't sell their produce but consume it at home. Others will be hiring out their skills, like Józsi repairing his washing machines. Laci will be running his mill all weekend. For the women the tasks of unpaid work are endless – washing, cooking, cleaning and nurturing. And János, I know, will be reclining on the bank of the Tisza, patiently waiting for the big catch.

The buzzer will be going in five minutes, and already the women are lining up. There's a note of urgency about their escape from this noisy, oily, heartless, metallic factory. I traipse off to the changing rooms to strip off my oily overalls, shirt and boots. Today I'm rather pleased with myself – I've scaled new heights in the realm of 'housings'. A line of bodies, rippling with fat around the midriff, files into the shower room. Now in the shower cubicle I can feel isolated once more as the hot water floods down from above – refreshing and peaceful. I have to get dried and dressed to catch the bus at 2.23, but that gives me another five minutes of bliss.

I leave, passing through the shop again to punch out. I wave goodbye to Péter, still working away on his radial drill, as diligent as ever. He'll be there for another three and a half hours – his cigarette to comfort him and perhaps a dash of *pálinká*.

# 10

# Managerial Strategies, New Technology and the Labour Process

J. CHILD

Any consideration of managerial policies towards the labour process must today take account of the new technologies based on microelectronics. The level of investment in new technology is substantial and is forecast to grow rapidly. It is already proving to be a vehicle for significant changes in the organization of work, and therefore in the position of workers within the productive process. Four managerially initiated developments, facilitated by new technology, are directed towards (i) the virtual elimination of direct labour, (ii) the spread of contracting, (iii) the dissolution of traditional job or skill demarcations, and (iv) the degradation of jobs through deskilling. These initiatives affect the ability of workers to control the conduct of their work through an exercise of discretion and skill, and each one has implications for the position of the workers concerned in the labour market.

New technology can play an important role in these changes to the organization and control of the labour process. The rationales applied to investment in new technology are not necessarily focused primarily on the labour process, but the technology does carry with it a potential for change in that process. The introduction of new technology in ways that change the labour process is therefore looked upon as the unfolding of a managerial strategy. This concept is, however, controversial, and its use here must be clarified before proceeding to the main argument.

This essay was first published as chapter 6 in David Knight et al. eds, *Job Redesign*, Gower, 1985. I am grateful to Edward Heery, Stephen Wood, colleagues in the Work Organisation Research Centre, and participants at the conference on the organization and control of the labour process held at Owens Park, Manchester in March 1983 for commenting on an earlier draft of this chapter. It draws in part on research funded by the Economic and Social Research Council.

## MANAGERIAL STRATEGY

Management normally exerts a major, if not the dominant, influence on the organization of the labour process in enterprises funded by private capital, excluding those of a professional and/or co-operative character. Contrary examples such as the national newspaper industry in Fleet Street are sufficiently exceptional as to prove the rule (Martin 1981). Nevertheless, doubts are raised about the concept of managerial strategy which expresses this influence and the intentions behind it. Three of these doubts concern (i) the concept's implication of rationality, (ii) the extent to which the labour process is the main point of reference for managerial policy, and (iii) the relation between policy intentions and implementation.

The concept of strategy implies a rational consideration of alternatives and the articulation of coherent rationales for decisions. In practice, some studies of senior managerial decision-making have identified as inherent characteristics: vacillation, the pursuit of factional interests, and even randomness (e.g. March and Olsen, 1976; Mintzberg, Raisinghani and Theoret 1976). Rationality often appears to be bounded and focused on the next step rather than on the long term. This critique, valid though it may be, is, however, only significant for an analysis of changes to the labour process if the persistence of disagreement within management (perhaps deriving from specialist values and interests) leads to attempts to dilute or sabotage the implementation of decisions once reached. Otherwise, the more significant factor is the substance of the policy that emerges, whatever quality of thinking underpins it, and the claims of rationality and hence necessity which managers may make for that policy.

In some of the labour process literature it is assumed that managerial strategies are formulated with labour's role in the productive process primarily in mind (e.g. Braverman 1974; Edwards 1979). In practice, consideration of that role could be quite secondary, with the actions taken on employment and job content being merely consequential upon other decisions. Management's priorities for the creation of surplus value may well be directed towards improving the conditions of market exchange or of financing. Investment in new technology which is subsequently applied towards securing changes in the labour process could therefore owe its origin to an intention of strengthening a company's position in its product market, perhaps by permitting the manufacture of new or improved products, when circumstances allow finance to be acquired on acceptable terms. The force of this qualification is to indicate a need to examine carefully the intentions behind managerial policies and not to assume that they are necessarily formulated with a conception of the desired labour process prominently, or even clearly, in mind. This does not mean, however, that managerial policies directed primarily by other objectives will be inconsequential for the labour process.

The possibility of attenuation between managerial policy and its implementation has been identified as a third problem with the notion of managerial strategy towards the labour process. As Wood and Kelly (1982) point out, one cannot infer the successful implementation of a managerial strategy simply from its statement as a policy. Nor can the existence of a strategic intention necessarily be inferred merely from conditions at the point of production or of service provision. These might result from interventions by junior managers or from informal practices introduced by the workers themselves. Supervisors have, for example, been found to make frequent *ad hoc* changes to workers' deployment and duties, particularly when the task system is variable by dint of inconsistent materials, product changes, or equipment breakdowns. The discretion and skills exercised by supervisors themselves can depend upon informal accommodations reached with middle managers (Child and Partridge 1982). Thompson (1983) also recalls that an important manifestation of the defence of craft identity has been the persistent practice of 'clawing back' concessions to management on questions of control and skill within the workplace; this will further attenuate actual practice from managerial policy. In short, attenuation can result from control loss within organizational hierarchies.

However, accommodations and informal practices lower down in the hierarchy can be conducive to efficient working (Gross 1953), in which case they might persist for a long time without the intervention or even the awareness of senior management. They would, in effect, be filling gaps in the systems laid down by management or correcting their dysfunctional effects. It is when such practices result in low efficiency that this is likely to register among senior managers as a problem and 'corrective' action will ensue. There are bound to be limits to the deviation of implementation from policy, though these require further empirical investigation. The substitution of technology for manual intervention in the conduct of tasks, and the technological improvement of control data, will tend to reduce such deviation. Thus not only does investment in new technology embody managerial intentions, but its introduction into the workplace may facilitate the implementation of these intentions.

One response to these qualifications would be to insist on a 'stringent' definition of managerial strategy in labour process analysis. This would restrict use of the concept to cases where (i) it can be demonstrated that managers hold a coherent set of policy rationales, which (ii) are directed specifically at key labour process dimensions such as control, discretion and skill, and where (iii) there is an effective follow through from policy to implementation. Rose and Jones (1985) also appear to follow this stringent definition when they question whether the concept of managerial strategy can be usefully applied to the situations uncovered by their case studies.

Rose and Jones note that managements in all the firms they studied were promoting greater flexibility in manning, though the industrial relations processes whereby this was progressed varied considerably. The firms they studied were located in different manufacturing sectors, and it is suggested later that there are likely to be considerable differences between sectors and between organizations in the character of managerial strategies and in their effectiveness. Thus while one sector of British industry such as shipbuilding, with its long tradition of demarcated craft control and a generally strong workplace organization, may exhibit relatively imprecise managerial strategies which have had limited influence on the labour process, another sector such as banking exhibits a centralized and specific managerial planning of the labour process which is implemented very effectively through managerially controlled pilot schemes and the imposition of precise work measurement, with little organized workplace opposition. Rather than rejecting the notion of managerial strategy because it is not always specific or effective, an alternative view would be to conclude that a model is required which allows for the possibility of variation in the nature of strategies and their implementation, and which draws attention to contextual factors pertinent to explaining such variation. In other words, the problem with the 'stringent' definition of managerial strategy lies in its failure to allow for the possibility that managerial strategies which are unspecific towards the labour process may nonetheless have relevance for it. The influence of managerial strategy on the labour process may be more complex, more variable and less direct than a stringent perspective allows. The alternative view is considered to provide a constructive basis for analysing the introduction of new technology, and is now outlined.

The point of departure is the observation that in capitalist economies corporate managerial strategies will necessarily reflect a consciousness of certain general objectives which are the normal conditions for organizational survival. These objectives are oriented to accumulation and are often expressed by senior managers in terms of 'profitable growth' (Child 1974). A portfolio of corporate strategies, amounting to what Spender (1980) has called a 'recipe', will typically be developed and will reflect the views of senior managers as to how the objectives can be realized in the specific context of the organization. These strategies are not necessarily formulated with the management of labour and structuring of jobs explicitly in mind.

It is noted later, for example, that investment in new technology is reportedly undertaken to meet targets such as improving the consistency of product quality, reducing inventory, or increasing the flexibility of plant. The appreciation of the production process held by the managers who approve the investment may not even include a clear conception of how the labour process is organized and controlled. Senior managers, particularly in larger organizations, often exhibit good understanding only of the work of a relatively small group of colleagues and subordinates, such that a 'psychological boundary' exists between them and the labour process (Fidler 1981). At this elevated hierarchical level managers tend to deal in terms of statistical abstractions such as throughput volume, wastage rates, stock levels, delivery performance, unit costs, budget variance, and employment costs. Managerial policies on new technology need not therefore articulate explicit statements about the organization of the labour process. Nonetheless, they effectively amount to strategies towards the labour process if the choice of a particular technology imposes certain constraints on its operation and manning, and if the strategic expectations attached to the new technology also impose constraints on labour process design. Moreover, management will influence the route by which these strategic intentions are operationalized, by selecting those specialists and subordinates who are to act as work organization designers. Each of these, be they production engineers, industrial engineers, systems analysts, craft-trained line managers, or social scientists, will have their own relatively specific orientation towards the organization and control of the labour process.

Managerial strategies therefore establish corporate parameters for the labour process which are unlikely to be inconsequential even when there is attenuation between policy and implementation. Purcell (1983) makes a comparable point in arguing that, within the modern large enterprise, managements have established corporate systems of centralized planning and financial control which have significant implications for the location of and control over bargaining about incomes and employment. The process whereby managerial intentions feed through to the workplace is therefore regarded as one in which managerial strategies play the role of 'steering devices' that have 'knock-on effects', to use terms suggested by Grieco (1983). This still allows for the fact that in different industrial sectors the extent to which strategies are formulated centrally or locally, unilaterally or bilaterally, can vary considerably. This perspective is also compatible with a recognition that the strategies may sometimes be unspecific and poorly understood, that they may be subject to reinterpretation and opposition by functional and junior managers, and that they may encounter worker resistance both informally in the workplace and through trade union action. Even in the absence of such opposition, the translation of policies and strategic decisions to the organization of the labour process will require detailed working out by lower levels of management, by specialists (who might include external consultants) and possibly by shopfloor and office workers themselves.

The tightness of coupling between senior managerial intentions and their actual implementation in the organization of the labour process is therefore regarded as a variable factor, which raises the question of the processes that may intervene in the transition from strategy to implementation. The flexible nature of new technology hardware and particularly its software may in fact permit a range of alternative working arrangements. The perspectives and values of middle managers, work organization designers and workers who have the potential to influence the implementation process therefore need to be taken into account, including factors determining their relative influence.

The role of managerial strategy developed here in connection with the introduction of new technology is represented in figure 10.1. Fundamental capitalistic objectives are seen to provide management's basic strategic motives. Strategies are developed as corporate steering devices, which are likely to inform decisions to invest in new technology. While it cannot be assumed that corporate strategies express an explicit view about the organization of the labour process, they will at the least establish certain parameters within which implementation and actual changes to jobs, and employment relations, take place. The transition to implementation is subject to intervening processes and actions. In short, actors, processes and contextual conditions all have to be taken into account.

## NEW TECHNOLOGY

The term 'new technology' is applied to a wide range of equipment utilizing microcircuitry and associated software. In some applications, microelectronic data handling capacity is combined with modern communications facilities to provide what has become known as 'information technology'. While there is as yet little agreement on the definition of these terms, it is possible to give examples of where new technology is being applied to work processes in manufacturing and services; these are listed in table 10.1.

The newness of new technology lies not so much in the application of electronics to data processing, which has been commercially available since the 1950s, but rather in the radically changed nature of the equipment now produced. This has enormously increased the range of its practical applications.

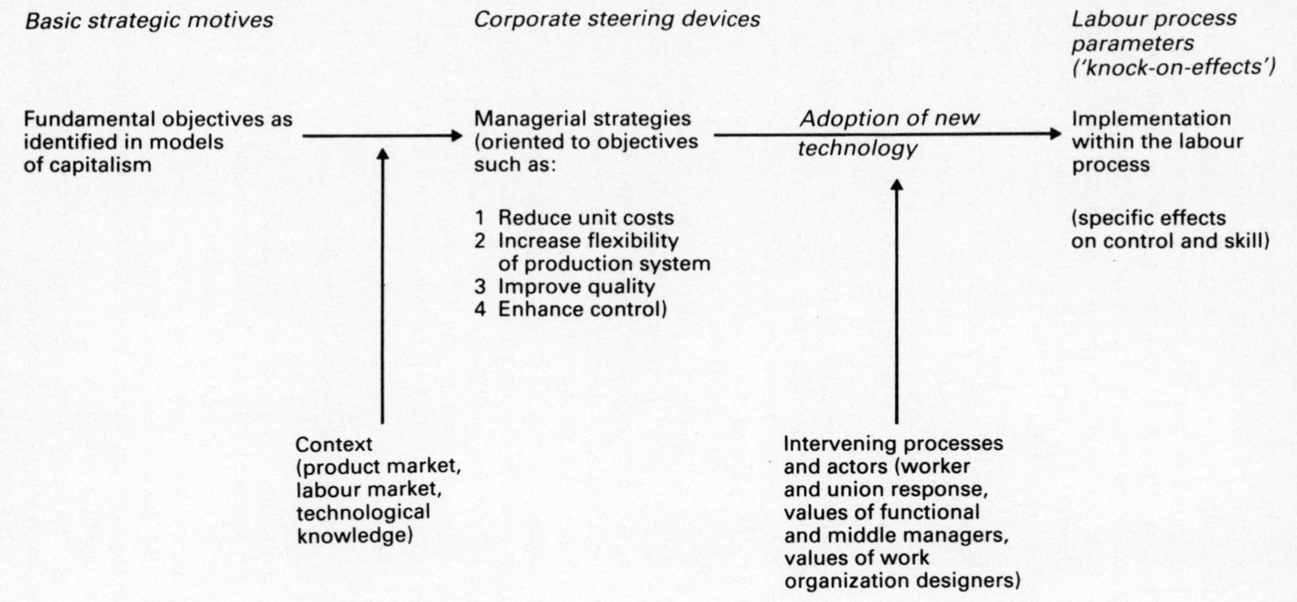


FIGURE 10.1 Representation of the role of managerial strategy

TABLE 10.1 Examples of new technology applied to processes in manufacturing and services

*Manufacturing*

1 **Computer-controlled manufacture:** CNC machines, robots, flexible manufacturing systems, process plant monitoring and control.
2 **Computer-aided design (CAD).**
3 **Computerized stock control and warehousing:** motor vehicle parts for manufacture and sale of spares. Also examples in service sector: retail store stocks, hospital pharmacies.

*Services*

4 **Financial:** automatic cash dispensers/tellers; customer records via VDUs, electronic funds transfer.
5 **Medical:** computer diagnosis, automated laboratory testing, intensive care monitoring.
6 **Retailing and distribution:** automated warehousing, stock control, electronic-point-of-sale (EPOS).
7 **Libraries:** computerized information systems, lending records based on use of bar-coding.
8 **Information services:** videotex (interactive and one-way systems via modified TV sets and telephone lines).

*Office and managerial work*

9 **Word processing and electronic filing.**
10 **Communications:** electronic mail and facsimile transmission, teleconferencing, networking (local area networks and to homeworkers via microcomputers and telephone lines).

Microelectronic technology is distinguished by its (i) compactness, (ii) cheapness, (iii) speed of operation, (iv) reliability, (v) accuracy, and (vi) low energy consumption. When combined with suitable data inputting and communication facilities, the new technology permits information to be collected, collated, stored and accessed with a speed not previously possible.

The real cost of new technology equipment is falling, and its programming is becoming easier (though software costs are not falling in proportion). It is also becoming more versatile. It is not surprising therefore that investment in new technology is already proceeding on an impressive scale, and that this is shortening the innovation cycle in both products and processes. Forecasts vary and obviously have to be treated with particular caution in such a new and changing field.

Investment is central to the process of capitalist development, and new technology has today become a significant component of that investment. Few studies of the labour process, however, have yet had an opportunity to take account of this technology, though there has been plenty of speculation about its generation of unemployment and deskilling. Braverman's analysis (1974) is already dated. The 'automation' he describes is more accurately termed 'Detroit automation', an advanced form of mechanization including automatic transfer which has been applied primarily to motor vehicle mass production lines. It is not representative of present-day new technology based on microelectronics. Edwards (1979: 122–5) briefly discusses the potential of new technology for extending 'technical control'. He comments that the feedback systems involved 'constitute qualitative advance over Henry Ford's moving line' (p. 125), the older form of technical control which provides the main technological point of reference for Braverman. However, Edwards has little to suggest by way of consequences for the labour process except to say that the new 'technology of production' now becomes the workers' 'immediate oppressor' rather than the supervisor.

Thomson (1983) provides a carefully considered assessment of the application of new technology based partly on his own research in telecommunications. New technology in his view 'does add to the power of capital to restructure the labour process' (p. 115). Thompson concludes that there is a tendency to use the technology in furtherance of a general trend towards deskilling. He sees this as an expression of management's motive for change, namely the desire to increase control over the labour process. New technology is also extending deskilling into the area of office work. Nevertheless, Thompson argues that there is no *technological* inevitability about deskilling. In so far as deskilling is under way, it results primarily from competitive market pressures and in many cases predates the introduction of new technology. Examples may also be found of alternative policies, such as 'responsible autonomy' identified by Friedman (1977), while certain new skills are being created as well.

Thompson's analysis is reinforced by the conclusions which Jones (1982a) and Wilkinson (1983) derive from case studies of numerical control technology. Both are critical of 'deterministic and universalistic conceptions of the direction and nature of skill changes' which accompany the introduction of new production technology (Jones 1982a: 181). Jones, for instance, found that firms differed in the forms of skill deployment accompanying the use of numerical control machines. He attributes this variation to differences in product and labour markets, organizational structures and trade union positions. Although cautious about according too much influence to managerial intentions, Jones suggests that one clue as to why he found a variety of skill deployments may lie in evidence that the criteria applied to investment in numerical control equipment did not necessarily include the reduction of labour costs as a determining objective.

Several significant points are suggested by the available research and statistics on new technology. First, it is a major area of investment and one that has important potential for the labour process. New technology therefore links managerial strategy to the labour process, as figure 10.1 suggests. Second, changes in the labour process accompanying the introduction of new technology can follow a number of possible routes. Third, this choice of possibilities is facilitated by the considerable flexibility offered by new technology, particularly by its software.

This degree of flexibility virtually transforms the application of electronic technology, driven by software, into an aspect of organizational design. Changes to the labour process must for this reason be attributed primarily to non-technological factors, such as managerial strategies formulated in the light of market decisions; established ideological definitions of appropriate structures and working practices can also be expected to play a role. The increasing flexibility of technology renders it far less of a constraint upon, and more of a facilitator of, working practices which emerge from the political processes of management's relations with labour.

Jones presumably had in mind the ability of workers to defend existing working practices when he commented that 'management cannot construct, *de novo*, the conditions under which labour is to function' (1982a: 199). The significance of the introduction of new technology at the present time when the power of organized labour has reached a low ebb is, however, precisely that this gives management considerably more scope than hitherto to use the technology to impose changes upon the labour process. Managers can, and do, justify these changes by reference to competitive pressures and in terms of a need to utilize the technology effectively – in other words, an appeal to the ideology of market-driven technological determinism. In present circumstances, when managerial strategies associated with new technology have teeth, it is particularly important to examine what these strategies are.

## MANAGERIAL STRATEGIES AND NEW TECHNOLOGY

Evidence from case studies (e.g. Buchanan and Boddy 1983) and surveys (e.g. Northcott, Rogers and Zeilinger 1982) suggests that the following objectives usually feature prominently in managerial intentions when introducing new technology: (i) reducing operating costs and improving efficiency; (ii) increasing flexibility; (iii) raising the quality and consistency of production; (iv) improving control over operations. There is clearly some interdependence between each of these strategic intentions. They are all directed towards enhancing opportunities to create surplus value, and enhancing the organization's ability to absorb the risks of competition.

Improvements in *costs and efficiency* may be secured in several ways relevant to the labour process. New technology may permit reductions in manpower via a substitution for direct labour (as in the automatic spot welding of Austin Metro bodies-in-white: see Francis et al. 1982); or via partial substitution for labour as in word processing (IDS 1980) and in laboratory automation (Harvey and Child 1983); or via the more economical allocation of manpower on the basis of superior workflow information such as that provided by electronic-point-of-sale (EPOS) systems in retailing (Cosyns, Loveridge and Child 1983). New technologies can also reduce costs by permitting improved stock control, the reduction of waste due to operator error, and better plant utilization via computerized scheduling. Advanced manufacturing systems offer a combination of these advantages on the basis of integrating the different elements of design, production, handling, storage and stock control (Lamming and Bessant 1983). They also offer greatly improved flexibility.

In an industry like engineering, many firms now have to compete on the basis of offering custom-built products produced in smaller batches and often involving complex machining. Achieving *flexibility* in production has therefore become an increasingly important goal. One of the most attractive features offered by new computer controlled technology is the ability to run a range of production items through a single facility with the minimum of cost and delay when changing from one specification to another. A somewhat comparable advantage in flexibility is now being sought in banking with experiments in computerizing customer files and linking these to VDUs used by bank staff. By providing individualized customer profiles, this facility would enable staff to adjust rapidly to the financial circumstances and history of each customer, and on that basis to make decisions rapidly on whether to grant loans or to offer other services. Increased operating flexibility based on new technology is likely to be accompanied by managerial demands for a complementary flexibility in manning and the breaking down of traditional task boundaries, or by attempts to avoid reliance on direct labour altogether.

Improvements in *quality* can be gained from the introduction of highly accurate automated equipment conducting repeatable operations, or from the use of microelectronics for more precise process control. These examples substitute for human intervention. Quality can also be enhanced when electronic assessment complements human judgement, an example being some forms of testing in manufacturing.

The new technology is one of information processing which depends upon the quality of its data inputs. If accurate measurement can be obtained, the ability to communicate information swiftly across distances, and the capacity to apply computational or synthesizing routines when required, clearly enhance the potential for managerial *control*. Senior managers may now no longer have to rely upon operators and middle managers for control data or for their interpretation, if these data can be captured directly at the point of operations. For example, EPOS systems in retailing can, via capturing data through the scanning of bar-coded or magnetically ticketed items, transmit control data on itemized sales, on throughput at each point of sale, and on stocks, directly to store managers and to central buying departments in a company's head office.

New technology is therefore being introduced to advance managerial strategic objectives, and it can be used as a means of facilitating the four types of change in the labour process which were listed at the beginning of the chapter. In keeping with the representation in figure 10.1, these changes are regarded as being in the nature of managerial strategies towards the labour process in so far as they are initiatives which stem originally from corporate objectives and decisions, whether directly and explicitly or not.

It will be evident that each of these managerial strategies effects a reduction in costs through the intensification of labour, whether directly through extending the labour power exerted or indirectly through improving the intrinsic performance of equipment. Moreover, by their very nature as interventions, they each constitute an extension of managerial control. However, the strategies provide different routes towards the increase of efficiency, and the perceived appropriateness of each is presumed to depend on specific circumstances of the kind outlined at the close of this chapter. The way in which labour cost reduction is balanced with other objectives also appears to vary with each strategy. Another variable factor is the extent to which proponents have so far come forward publicly, or have been uncovered by researchers, to articulate specific statements of intent towards the labour process in connection with each strategy. Further evidence on managerial intentions is required. Finally, the provisional character of the present fourfold classification needs to be recognized. If found to be useful, it will certainly require considerable elaboration.

### *Elimination of Direct Labour*

Abolition of labour has been the dream of both engineers and social visionaries, though from quite different perspectives. The concept of factories without workers has already reached the experimental stage. It is predicted that the wholly automated factory with virtually no direct workers will have become a reality in most advanced industrial countries within five years.

There are two main technological routes to the elimination of direct labour, which, though starting from different points in different industries, are becoming more similar. The process industries achieved an integrated flow of production many years ago and have operated with minimal direct labour forces. With increasing market pressures, employers such as chemical producers are turning increasingly to speciality products produced in batches. The ability of manufacturers to make several products and versions of the same product on a batch basis using the same basic plant is becoming particularly important. Computer controls linked to microelectronic sensors and intelligent data gathering instruments are essential to achieving the flexibility and they enable process producers to avoid dependence on human intervention outside the central control room (cf. Williams 1983).

A second main route to eliminating direct labour in manufacturing is via flexible manufacturing systems (FMS). These are computer programmed and controlled integrated production systems which bring to discrete item (i.e. non-process) production many of the continuous flow characteristics of process plants. The prospect of achieving greater flexibility in regard to batch changes on the same plant is often cited as a major attraction of FMS. Current interest in FMS is high, as witnessed by attendances at the three-day FMS conferences in Brighton (October 1982: 500 manufacturing managers and senior engineers listening to fifty papers) and London (October 1983: 400 delegates and seventy papers). The first prototype fully automated FMS factory in Britain, which opened in Colchester at the end of November 1982, attracted considerable press comment (e.g. *Guardian*, 1.12.82, p. 7; *Financial Times*, 8.12.82, p. 31; *Sunday Times*, 12.12.82, p. 50). Three-quarters of the factory managers polled by MORI in December 1982 said they were considering the introduction of FMS (*Sunday Times*, 12.12.82). While no doubt overstated, this is a clear expression of interest.

Discussions of FMS tend to emphasize the achievement of higher surplus value via the strategic advantage of being able to respond quickly to changes in market demand in both models and quantities ordered, and via the inventory/work-in-progress saving that results from dramatic reductions in manufacturing lead times. Saving labour has not been given much emphasis in public statements, perhaps for obvious reasons at a time of high unemployment. In fact, the incidence of labour saving can be very significant with even less than full automation. In the early examples of full FMS systems it is dramatic. The Colchester engineering factory, which produces a variety of shafts, gears and disks, is reported to run with three operatives rather than thirty (*Sunday Times*, 12.12.82). A manning of one person instead of 200 is reported on the night shift of the Fanuc FMS plant outside Tokyo (ibid.), while there are now many examples of the labour savings achievable through the installation of robotics which is an integral part of FMS (e.g. Cane 1982; Francis et al. 1982).

There is evidence of a conscious intention among some managers and engineers to use FMS and process control as a means of extending managerial control over the labour process. For example, Peter Dempsey of Ingersoll Engineers, which by 1982 had planned over 100 manufacturing installations in fifteen countries, stated in 'a keynote paper' on the first day of the 1983 FMS conference that 'ultimately [FMS] will mean wrestling manufacture away from human interference in much the same way as has happened in the oil refinery, sugar factory or cement plant'. Dempsey clearly viewed this as a managerial strategy rather than just a consequence of technology: 'FMS is a way of thinking. It is not about technology' (Charlish 1983). A line manager, who had led a project team to commission a new highly automated chocolate processing plant controlled by microprocessors, told the writer that 'we had through the commissioning period to decide how much flexibility [discretion] we can give the operator. Our objective was to reduce that to nil if possible.' This plant runs with a total complement of four people concerned with the process *per se*, only one of whom is an operator/controller who replaces the twenty-three operators previously required.

The managerial vision into which the elimination of labour through automation fits was developed in an interview with the recently retired technical director of a major international food processing company. (Although this company is itself a long way from full automation, it is nevertheless significant that largely under this man's influence a long-term plan was initiated in the late 1970s which has almost halved the labour force, partly on the basis of introducing rationalizing and labour-saving new technology.) His initial premise was that the technical relations of production were simple but that difficulties begin with the social relations – people mess things up. The object is therefore to eliminate labour, and in his view this should include labour at all grades. 'If you get rid of everybody, you've got an ideal factory, and most of your problems will disappear.' He saw automation as the key. It enables production levels to be maintained with less labour and with fewer plants. This permits an economy of space, even whole factories, which can be sold or put to other use. The rationalization of factories reduces the managerial and service overheads, while the remaining units are smaller and less complex. They are therefore simpler to manage and are likely to enjoy a 'better' climate of employee relations.

The labour-elimination strategy can also be found in some parts of the service sector, where it simply manifests the logical conclusion of a widespread trend to shift the labour costs of service provision onto the customer (for instance, self-service in retailing). One example, which is conceptually developed and is already operational in some locations abroad, is 'lobby' banking. This could substitute for branch banks an array of automatic cash transaction machines which have already been developed to perform services such as cash dispensing, cash depositing, crediting of other accounts, balance notification and ordering of statements. Such satellite branches would eliminate the present job of tellers, back office staff and branch managers.

The theoretical implications for labour process analysis of situations where the production process or service provision employs little or no labour are intriguing. Labour is obviously embodied in the plant and processed materials used, but what if it is absent from the workplace as such? This case, as yet largely hypothetical but prospectively significant, indicates that it is the productive process which is analytically significant as the main source of surplus value, and that labour is not necessarily involved *directly* in that process. The more that this situation comes into being, the more attention will need to be directed to the social relations of exchange, distribution and redistribution under capitalism rather than simply to the social relations of production in a narrow sense.

Automation has proceeded historically in the train of task simplification and routinization. The archetype of this earlier stage was the degradation of work through deskilling of the kind associated with Taylorism. As the employment of skilled craftsmen in direct production tasks became substituted by the employment of semi-skilled workers, and as the number of alternative employments in the labour market reduced through this process of change, so the market position of the production worker changed. In terms of the classification first developed by Mok (1975) and extended by Loveridge (1983), these jobs had changed from a location in the 'primary external market' to one in the 'secondary internal market'. In the primary external market, the craft jobs provided long-term stable earnings and permitted high levels of discretion – an advantageous 'primary' position founded upon special skills widely marketable in the general labour market 'external' to any one employing organization. In the secondary internal market, the new semi-skilled jobs enjoyed a relatively lower earning capacity with less long-term security (a less advantageous 'secondary' position). These jobs no longer utilized skills derived from specialized craft training but were instead now defined increasingly on the basis of specifications and training prescribed 'internally' by the particular employer. The benefit for the worker of generally sought-after skills commanding high value in the external labour market had gone.

The now emergent stage of direct labour elimination through the means of advanced automation gives rise to a further shift in labour market position for the workers concerned. In so far as they are displaced from regular employment altogether, their location will have shifted to the secondary external segment. They will have been forced onto the general labour market 'external' to the particular employing firm. Their position remains 'secondary' in that the absence of generally marketable skills eliminates the availability of long-term earning security as well as any opportunity to exercise discretion in the performance of tasks if work is secured. The labour market position of production managers displaced by the elimination of direct labour may shift even more dramatically from a relatively privileged primary internal position to one in the external market which will be of secondary standing unless their abilities and experience can still command a premium in the marketplace.

### *Contracting*

Contracting refers to an arrangement whereby the employer pays for an agreed delimited amount of production or period of labour time, but leaves the organization, manning and sometimes the equipping of the task to the worker or group of workers concerned. It has a long history. An early form of labour management in Britain was the putting-out system in which production was let out to physically dispersed domestic workers by a central employer-merchant.

Subcontracting to groups of workers on a central production site became widespread in the nineteenth century (Gospel 1983). Some putting out persists to the present day in the form of homeworking (Cragg and Dawson 1981) while subcontracting is still a common arrangement in the building industry.

These historical forms of contracting involved manual workers who were engaged on productive activities which could be performed as discrete tasks or stages. In such cases, the expense of maintaining continuity of employment and a superstructure of control could be avoided, and with it an economic risk when faced with market uncertainties and competitive pressures. There are distinct possibilities that where manufacturing can be carried out in discrete stages, a comparable development could re-emerge with the aid of new information technology. Here a standardization of language for specifying fabrication needs, combined with computer programming which can turn the specifications into production, may eliminate the need to incorporate the separate stages of manufacture within a single location serviced by a unified labour force.

It is noteworthy not only that employers today are displaying increasing interest in contracting arrangements, but that these are now being extended to office and managerial workers located at the core of bureaucracies. Arrangements for working from home while remaining part of a network connected electronically to a central office are clearly motivated by economic considerations, but their achievement relies heavily on new technology (Mandeville 1983).

Although the problem of controlling the growth of administrative and managerial overheads has been recognized for some time now (cf. Child 1978), it has not yet been resolved. A recent survey by the Institute of Administrative Management found that among 180 UK companies administrative costs had risen by 4 per cent in real terms during the five years to 1981 (Kransdorff 1983). Managements have in the past few years become acutely aware of overhead costs including those of wage and salary earners who had until recently come to expect long-term employment. Wage and salary earners incur many extra costs for the employer: heat, space, food, car parking, office and secretarial support, insurance costs and various requirements imposed by legislation. Additional investment in supervisory control is required to transform labour power into actual labour within the expensively serviced place of work. There is therefore a growing interest in the possibility of paying workers to work on their own premises on a contract basis. It has been predicted that fee paying short-term contracts will increasingly come to be substituted for long-term employment within organizations (e.g. Handy 1982).

Williamson (1975) analysed the development of hierarchical working relationships within large bureaucracies in terms of the lower transaction costs, including greater certainty and predictability, which often attended organizational as opposed to market relationships. New information technology, whether for transmission of data, facsimile documents or audio-visual exchange, is beginning to facilitate communication over distances and the precise logging (i.e measurement) of the transmission. Long-range communication can take place with increasing ease and reducing real cost, and less reliance has therefore to be placed on the close proximity of working that justifies the 'office'. Taking into account as well the burden of wage and salary costs, the balance of transaction cost advantage is thus moving back towards the market relationship in which smaller units and even people working at home are linked electronically and through market contracts to form a whole system of work.

According to a recently reported survey of 255 among the largest 1000 UK companies, almost two-thirds believe that by 1988 they will be employing executives working from home (Cane 1983). Already, over 20 per cent of companies with a turnover of more than £500m a year have some executives working from home using personal computers. It is not stated how many of these computers are linked to the corporate office. Rank Xerox has initated 'networking' arrangements with some of its specialists whereby they now work from their own homes on individualized contracts, and often have Xerox 820 microcomputers linked to the company's head office. The saving to the company is reported to be substantial since it estimates that a manager's or specialist's employment cost approaches three times his or her salary once overheads, secretarial and office services, and administrative back-up are taken into account. Under the 'networking' system, payment is only for a contracted number of days and/or services rendered and not for the non-productive time contained in full-time employment. Under such arrangements, the use of new technology increases the ability to record the networker's output, which further adds to managerial control.

Staff working at home under this kind of arrangement become self-employed contractors, and in fact Xerox encourages them to start up their own businesses or private practices to operate during the time not contracted to the company. In the case of high level specialists able to secure work on their own account, contracting therefore shifts them from the internal to the external labour market while retaining a primary standing. This standing would shift downwards towards a secondary status were the homeworkers not able to attract a market demand for their skills as consultants or private entrepreneurs. They, rather than their erstwhile full-time employer, now bear the risk of providing a secure income flow. They enjoy a greater control over how their work is actually carried out and over their pattern of working time, but the employer enjoys greater control over the conditions for extracting surplus value in that he can now specify the relation between work done and labour cost much more precisely – in addition to enjoying a much reduced overall labour cost.

Another strategic development in this category is already well established. This consists of contracting out whole areas of work, such as maintenance and services like cleaning and canteens which are regarded as peripheral to the core productive activity, in order again to save bearing the cost of a standing overhead for an activity which can be bought in more cheaply instead. New technology has some relevance to this strategy, particularly with respect to the external contracting of maintenance. Some new equipment has become so sophisticated and complex that its maintenance internally would require the employment of costly highly trained staff. On the other hand, with self-diagnostic systems and greatly improved reliability, the unanticipated need for major attention tends to reduce, and this may make it possible to use an outside contractor on a planned basis. Minor rectifications may now be adequately catered for by adding on the monitoring of plant condition and the replacement of standard parts and modules to the existing tasks of operatives, a form of 'polyvalence' discussed shortly. There is then less need to rely on specialized maintenance staff employed by the organization staff who, as Crozier (1964) indicated, occupy a strategic position *vis-à-vis* the labour process. In so far as external contracting of this kind substitutes for internal employment, the labour market consequences are to move former employees from either primary internal (maintenance) or secondary internal (most other services) segments onto the external labour market, though after relocation they may become members of the internal labour markets of contracting firms.

### *Polyvalence*

The third managerial strategy is frequently adopted in connection with new technology but does not depend on it. This is a strategy of 'polyvalence', in the French sense of the term, denoting a situation in which workers perform, or at least are available to perform, a range of tasks which cut across or extend traditional skill and job boundaries.

Polyvalence may be reached along several different routes. One involves the removal of skill demarcations and is horizontal in nature. In some cases the requirement for specific job skills which once commanded a premium in the external market has disappeared, because of technological change. The jobs concerned are extended to take in other tasks as a result. Lithographic workers in some provincial newspapers provide an example. In other cases, the route will be through the drive by employers to remove demarcation between skills which are still required. The intention here is to reduce employment costs and to increase the flexibility of manpower deployment. The fusion of electronic and mechanical features in the design of new technology is often cited by managers as a rationale for seeking polyvalence of this type among maintenance workers. In the service sector, a similar argument has been pursued in terms of integrating the application of specialist skills to meet the total needs of the customer, once new technology can provide the appropriate information system support. An example is provided shortly from banking, while Heery (1983) describes a development of this kind in local authority 'neighbourhood offices'.

A second main route to polyvalence is through enlarging the task competences of the worker in a job requiring relatively limited skills – usually an operative or routine office job. The dimension of this enlargement – how many additional tasks and how much additional responsibility or control – can vary and so correspondingly will the training required. A 'vertical' element of upskilling may be involved in job enlargement, but in other cases tasks requiring little skill are simply added together, and this may even be done in the hope of salving some worker job satisfaction in the wake of deskilling.

The job definition and routes of possible advancement for the polyvalent worker will in the main be highly specific to the employing organization, thus locating him or her firmly in the internal labour market. The standing of the polyvalent worker in the internal labour market will depend on the level of the skills which are now combined and on the discretionary content of the job. Whether or not polyvalence represents advance or regression, upskilling or degradation, will be a question of the route by which the worker has travelled to it.

The polyvalence strategy is often combined with the development of a 'responsible autonomy' type of control (Friedman 1977). 'Job enrichment' is a case in point, combining an extension of tasks with an increment of autonomy with regard to matters such as checking the quality of completed work. This will often form part of an employment policy which reinforces the internal labour market, through (i) the provision of opportunities to acquire new skills and tasks which are defined in the local organization's own terms, (ii) opportunities to advance at least some way up a grading ladder defined in terms of an organizational scheme of job evaluation, and (iii) emphasis upon long-term employment opportunities, involvement in communications and participation arrangements, corporate ceremonies and events, and other elements designed to build commitment to the corporate objectives defined by management. We are not, of course, very far from the so-called 'Japanese philosophy of management' here, though it is one which has characterized certain Western companies for some time (cf. Ouchi 1981). It approximates to the more sophisticated form of 'bureaucratic control' identified by Edwards (1979).

As well as offering the employer potential cost advantages by way of flexibility and reduced levels of manning, the polyvalence strategy is also an approach to control over the labour process which may be more effective than blatant and direct controls (as in close supervision) because it emphasizes the consensual and 'positive' side of the employment relationship. This strategy endeavours to tie the worker into the internal labour market of the organization and to render his or her skills specific to that organization. In so far as it succeeds in increasing the dependence of workers on employment in the particular organization and reduces their marketability elsewhere, then the polyvalent strategy enhances management's power in the employment relationship and hence its potential for control. Thus while, in the British situation at least, the initial stages of polyvalence may sometimes be forced through by confrontation with trade unions (though it is more often to be found in non-union situations), the strategy once it has reached a mature stage will tend to develop a more advantageous ground for managerial initiative. It may indeed generate a degree of acquiescence if policies of fostering normative commitment meet with success. It also has to be recalled that the 'responsible autonomy' which tends to complement polyvalence is a control strategy with its focus typically on output measurement. For instance, the allocation of responsibility to a worker or work group for a more 'complete' set of tasks – what is sometimes called a 'whole task' such as complete assembly of a TV set – can make it easier for management to identify accountability for substandard performance. The application of new microelectronic monitoring devices and information transmission systems facilitates performance measurement, and may thereby make a transition from direct personal supervision of the labour process to a responsible autonomy format that much more acceptable to management. In effect, new technology can substitute supervision at a distance for supervision in the workplace.

Polyvalence as a strategy is not necessarily pursued in connection with new technology – it may, for instance, take the form of a general managerial drive against craft or custom-and-practice demarcation and against multi-unionism. However, it can be associated with new technology in several ways: (i) as a policy to maintain the use of workers' capabilities when these would otherwise be underutilized because new technology takes over from the use of skills; (ii) in circumstances where new technology is introduced to enhance the organization's capability of competing – either on the basis of quick response and small job quantities, where flexibility in manning is therefore at a premium, or on the basis of introducing new technology to enhance the quality of service provided by staff whose range of tasks is thereby extended; and (iii) in cases where the new information processing capabilities accompanying plant investment permit polyvalence to a greater degree than before.

Wilkinson (1983) provides an example of the polyvalence strategy in a situation in which new technology might otherwise have resulted in deskilling. This was a firm manufacturing lenses and spectacles in which job rotation was introduced as a means of preserving the intrinsic content and interest of jobs concerned with lens preparation where the introduction of new computer-programmed machinery had reduced the skill and judgemental component of individual tasks. This policy of job rotation was supported by the careful selection of new recruits to ensure a certain level of competence and considerable attention was given to training. These measures in turn provided possibilities for future promotion to supervisory jobs. A craft-oriented management in this firm had adapted its policies on job design to the introduction of new technology so as in some degree to offset the reduction of skills, but also in a manner which tied the definition of those skills and opportunities for personal advancement more closely to the firm's internal labour market.

Banking provides an example of the second way in which polyvalence is associated with new technology. In one of the largest clearing banks, new technology is currently being considered as a means of enhancing the capacity of staff located behind desks in the lobbies of branches to offer a superior level of advisory service to customers. The idea would be to equip each desk with a VDU unit linked to a file containing customer details. It is argued that immediate file access of this kind would not only facilitate updating, but more significantly it would permit the member of staff to take on a marketing function by suggesting in the light of the customer information how the bank could be of service in terms of arranging insurance, providing a loan and so forth. It would also provide the staff member with data relevant to a judgement *not* to offer certain services – such as a further loan. The bank is already developing the concept of 'personal bankers' to deal with all non-cash transaction services to customers coming into bank branches: this new job is located at a grade above that of counter tellers, and it is claimed that the exercise of additional skills (including interpersonal ones) that it requires will provide a basis for further future promotion into posts such as back-office supervisor. If new technology is introduced in the manner described, then this is likely to enhance the polyvalence of the 'personal banker' role. The definition of this new job and the skills it requires is specific to the bank in question, though in the banking industry barriers already exist to the ready movement of workers from one bank to another through the external labour market. What should be noted with this example is that the new technology involved could just as readily be used to *reduce* the skill and control of the bank worker in dealings with the customer, by means of incorporating programmed decision hierarchies of a standardized form which serve as instructions to the worker over responses to the customer, given the latter's computerized profile. In the case of banks, such decisions are indisputably the direct product of managerial strategy: they are taken centrally, in detail, and with very little employee or union participation (Child et al. 1984).

A food company provides an example of the third type of connection between pursuit of the polyvalence strategy and the introduction of new technology. Having reduced its workforce considerably, the management of this company is now attempting to use the possibilities offered by microelectronics for integrating the monitoring of production workflow and the condition of equipment into a central control room (plus features such as the self-diagnosis of faults and ready replacement of faulty circuits) in order to introduce a new shopfloor role which combines operative and routine maintenance tasks. The new role offers some opportunity for upgrading once appropriate training has been successfully completed. Members of this particular management display a remarkable degree of consistency and unanimity in describing their labour strategy in connection with new technology: they see its purpose as enhancing flexibility and economy of manning by (i) workers taking on additional responsibilities, and (ii) a concomitant opening up of the job grading structure. These two thrusts are bringing management into direct confrontation with unions in a multi-union situation. The situation clearly illustrates the conflict between internal labour market managerial perspectives and those of occupational interest organization representatives holding to external labour market definitions of their members' jobs.

## *Degradation of Jobs*

A central argument in Braverman's book (1974) is that the conflict of classes around economic interest promotes a continual search by the capitalist for ways to control and cheapen the production process. While it may be his dream to eliminate the dependence on labour altogether, his desire for control and cost reduction are seen in the meantime to motivate a long-term trend towards the degradation of existing jobs.

The main features of this strategy are the fragmentation of labour into narrowly constituted jobs, with deskilling and a use of direct control methods either through close supervision or structuring by technology. Of all the developments discussed in this chapter, the degradation of jobs can be the most confidently identified as a managerial strategy – it has a long history, has been widely discussed and practised, and for many years found a place in managerial, engineering and even personnel literature (though never without its critics). It was pupil to F. W. Taylor's main theme: that skill, knowledge and hence control should be separated from the worker. Work study techniques were developed to operationalize this maxim, while the moving conveyor technology closely associated with Henry Ford added a 'technical control' over the pace of work and the physical location of the worker (Edwards 1979).

Managers are able today to use new technology in an attempt to avoid reliance on the skills and judgement of workers, and to regulate their performance more precisely. While this may be perceived by managers and engineers as a stage towards automation, a degradation strategy often has more effect on the intrinsic quality of jobs than on their quantity. It permits cost reduction through a substitution of less qualified workers, a minimization of training and a closer managerial definition of performance standards. These changes reduce worker control over the labour process and facilitate an intensification of work, but degradation will nevertheless probably involve fewer reductions in absolute manpower than polyvalence and certainly fewer than full automation.

Many examples of the pursuit of job degradation alongside the introduction of new technology are now recorded in the literature. Those concerning the use of numerical control have borne out Noble's (1979) contention that some managements have made a conscious choice to employ new technological possibilities for the purpose of job degradation even when there was an availability of alternative technologies or alternative modes of work structuring which could be used effectively with the technology (e.g. Jones 1982b; Wilkinson 1983). Another relevant example is newspaper production where new technology has been introduced in ways that have degraded and in some cases eliminated traditional skills. This has generated defensive measures by alarmed craft unions which appear to have poor prospects of long-term success (Cockburn 1983; Gennard and Dunn 1983). Degradation has also accompanied the introduction of new technology into areas of routine office work, such as local government treasurer's departments (Crompton and Reid 1982). However, a trend towards job degradation was already under way in office work well before the introduction of electronic technology, with the use of an advanced division of labour and close supervision within large open-plan offices (e.g. de Kadt 1979).

Policies of job degradation are even evident in areas of service provision where in the past the quality of the service has been associated with staff discretion concerning the appropriate response to individual customers' needs and covering, if necessary, a wide range of transactions (advice, purchases, services). Two instances, in retailing and banking respectively, may be illustrated from studies undertaken by the writer and his colleagues.

The major introduction of new technology within retailing consists of electronic-point-of-sale (EPOS) systems, which are fronted by electronic cash registers incorporating devices to scan bar-coded individual sales items. The cash registers are linked to a retail company's computer which will (in an advanced application) contain the prices to be applied to each item of sale – 'automatic price look-up'. With the exception of relatively few accounting and systems staff (who may be located at a head office rather than in local stores), the way EPOS has generally been applied so far is to reinforce a work degradation strategy. In the case of supermarkets, for instance, the system now permits management to impose much greater control over check-out 'girls'. Indeed, one of the claims made by those who supply EPOS systems is that they eliminate various forms of check-out fiddling. (This also applies to the loss of goods from stock.) Also because EPOS systems make readily available much more precise information on customer flows, they enable management to direct the deployment of staff more closely with regard to hours of working and job allocation within the store. There is a consequent intensification of the check-out operator's work. An interesting feature of EPOS is that it is also being used in a way that degrades jobs of higher standing within the organization. The information it provides on sales profiles and stock levels permits routine programming (such as automatic re-order routines) to be applied to some buying decisions for which management had previously to depend upon the judgement of buyers. In a similar way, the new information now reduces the dependency of store general managers upon the assessment of conditions and trends by departmental or section managers. The latter's role then tends to be reduced to that of a supervisor and in supermarkets there may be very few section staff left to supervise now that EPOS can eliminate the need to price-label individual items or to inspect the stock level of shelves visually. (Elimination of item price-labelling, of course, reduces the *level* of staffing as well.)

In the new or refurbished branches of one of Britain's largest banks, the traditional job of teller has been divided into routine and less routine components. While a relatively small number of staff now concentrate on dealing with non-routine customer requirements in a role that has actually been upgraded through taking on additional 'marketing' functions, the larger number of lobby staff now occupy jobs which have been degraded. They are required to specialize only on the handling of small cash transactions (and not even those involving large amounts of coin) and on customer balance enquiries. This policy has been developed by the bank's central management in order to speed up routine transactions for the customer and at the same time to intensify the work of the counter teller. It has been assisted by the introduction of new technology in the form of keyboard operated automatic electronic cash dispensers, in conjunction with a very old technology of pneumatic tubes to transmit cash deposited rapidly to a secure area.

The implications of job degradation for the labour market position of the workers concerned were summarized when discussing the elimination of direct labour through automation, for which degradation can be the forerunner. The application of techniques such as work study and clerical work measurement to the narrowing and deskilling of jobs is typically formalized in job descriptions and gradings which are particular to the employing organization. They serve to locate the worker more firmly within the organization's internal labour market, and along a historical path towards an increasingly secondary position. The worker's power to negotiate favourable terms and conditions as an individual is vitiated both by deskilling itself (the decline towards secondary status) and by the particularization of his or her skills away from substantive definitions or norms of experience which are recognized and command general value on the open external labour market. It is not surprising that workers who experience degradation often come to regard collective action as the only means of defending their position and securing a tolerable livelihood.

## DISCUSSION

Four managerial strategies have been identified to which the introduction of new technology can be allied. Each reflects objectives relating to the pursuit of capital accumulation under conditions of market competition, and represents in different forms an intensification of labour. All have definable implications for the labour process and for the labour market position of the workers concerned. When pursued severally by the management of a particular organization, these strategies increase the segmentation of its labour force into different skill and status categories as well as increasing the pool of labour in the external labour market. Both these results weaken the capacity of workers to mount an organized resistance against management and its use of new technology, or even to formulate common policies on the subject. The internal and external labour market consequences of managerial strategies towards the labour process will therefore tend to reinforce management's ability to pursue those strategies, unless wider contextual factors change significantly.

In so far as these managerial strategies are effectively implemented, they will generate variation in the labour process. The factors that influence the choice of strategy, and that determine whether workers seek or are able to resist its implementation, are therefore salient to an explanation of the specific form taken by the organization of the labour process. There are some pointers in the literature to these operative factors and, following the lead they provide, it is possible to outline the conditions which are likely to encourage each managerial strategy.

An extremely complex framework would be required for a full analysis of variations in the managerial strategies pursued towards the labour process and in the success with which they are implemented or resisted. It is possible only to suggest a bare outline here, which is approached along two planes or dimensions. First, as the previous discussion began to indicate, there are several levels of relevant contextual analytical unit: the mega socio-economic system, the nation or society, the industry or sector, the enterprise or organization. Second, there are conceptually distinct influences, including government policy, institutional and cultural features, product and labour market conditions, organizational and task variables.

It is accepted that the capitalist labour process will embody capitalistic objectives expressed in modern enterprises through management as the agent of capital. This implies a contrast with labour processes and modes of organization in non-capitalist mega systems: in principle with socialism but in practice with what Thompson has labelled 'state collectivism' (1983: 223n). While there is a common reliance on hierarchical work organization and the managerial function in both mega systems, the formal status of the worker in the production system is different as are the official organs which express that formal position. Managerial policies connected with the use of new technology are *prima facie* expected to reflect this fundamental difference.

Within the capitalist system, a divergence is apparent between countries in features that influence managerial strategies and the organization of the labour process. Sorge et al. (1983) illustrate this clearly through comparing British and West German companies in the extent to which the organization of computer numerical control usage is designed to build upon workers' existing skills rather than to substitute for these. Though other factors such as size of company are also found to be relevant, Sorge and his colleagues conclude that the tradition of craft reflected in the scale and quality of present-day German vocational training helps to account for the greater tendency in the German firms to rely on workers on the spot to control and edit machine programs as opposed to confining this to specialist programmers – in other words a polyvalent rather than a degradation policy. This tradition of craft and practical industrial knowledge is strongly represented in most German line management, and is likely to encourage a polyvalent strategy. Research adopting a cross-national perspective, and which is sensitive to the mode of industrial and social development in each country, points to a variety in capitalist labour processes and in the employer strategies which importantly shaped these. Littler's analysis (1983) of the managerial strategies adopted in Britain, Japan, the United States and Germany is particularly suggestive of the components of this variety.

The analysis of variety in managerial strategies has to be refined further, to more specific locations within a nation's system of productive relations. Littler (1983) cites Britain as the country most removed from what he calls the monopoly capitalism model of employment and labour relations incorporating a marked development of internal labour markets. At the same time, as he admits, within that one country, internal labour markets developed unevenly between different sectors. British banks and large chemical companies had, for example, developed internal labour markets at an early period, while these remained absent for a long time in other sectors such as textiles. Spender's research on strategic recipes (1980) has also indicated their industry-specific nature. Individual large firms will today typically straddle several industries and be internally divided into quasi-autonomous divisions or business units. A variety of managerial strategies towards employment is therefore not unexpected within the same company. Moreover, if managements are sensitive to the labour market position, skills and expectations of specific groups of workers, it is to be expected that they will adopt different strategies towards each group. Differentiated employment policies will therefore be evident even at the level of a single plant, such that particularly valued groups may be upgraded and encouraged to acquire new skills (polyvalence) while others are possibly degraded, eliminated or placed on limited contracts. In short, similarities and differences in managerial strategies need to be analysed at various system levels.

The second analytical dimension relevant to managerial strategies brings in the substantive factors which are likely to promote variety in labour process organization. The major factors to emerge from available research and discussion are government policy, institutions, culture, product and labour market conditions, organization and task.

The first three of these factors are predominantly national in scope. The importance of *government policy* is illustrated by the conclusion that legislation provides the most significant single stimulus to industrial democracy in the European countries (IDE 1981). Governmental encouragement has also been a major factor behind the West German vocational training programme previously mentioned. The role of government as promoter of certain applications of new technology is substantial and takes it effectively into the role of sponsoring certain managerial strategies. Thus the Colchester prototype FMS factory was largely funded by a £3m British government grant, and £60m has been set aside to meet FMS development and capital costs. Through the medium of policies for education and training, for recognition of professional privileges, and for industrial relations, governments play a substantial role in the development of the *institutional framework* which a number of studies have shown to impinge significantly on the organization and manning of the labour process (e.g. Maurice, Sorge and Warner 1980; Child et al. 1983). *Culture* is the third factor which is primarily identifiable at the national level. While its ontology and role is subject to considerable debate, the thesis has been strongly argued that cultural values such as those concerning the equality of individual worth within society and interpersonal trust will influence the strategies adopted by management: thus a low evaluation of workers' individual worth and trustfulness will encourage job degradation (cf. Hofstede 1980).

*Market conditions* can be both general and specific. Ramsey (1977) and others have pointed to the way that managerial strategies are adjusted to general business cycle conditions. In periods of recession and weakened labour power, it is suggested that strategies of labour elimination and degradation are likely to predominate, and that management's ability to enforce any chosen strategy will be greater. Conversely, the ability of workers to resist managerial strategies and to impose their chosen occupational definition of the labour process will be greater in periods of market buoyancy and labour shortage. Friedman (1977) examined the more specific labour and product market conditions of three British industries to reach the conclusion that these in large measure distinguished between the adoption of 'direct control' and 'responsible autonomy' strategies. The former tends to incorporate job degradation while the latter may incorporate polyvalence of the job enrichment type where a higher level of discretion is added. Labour supply conditions may also differ, of course, for particular groups of workers within a single firm. Even today, certain categories of skilled and specialist workers are claimed to be in short supply: the scarcity value of such workers is likely to be reflected not only in levels of pay but also in their ability to secure greater control over working practices.

Organizational and task factors are specific to the particular unit of production. Among *organizational factors*, company traditions can exert an important influence. They frequently have their origins in the ideology of an entrepreneurial founder who set out both a strategic perspective on the task of the organization and a philosophy on the form of the labour process to accomplish it. 'Fordism' as a labour process to accomplish the strategy of opening up the latent mass motor car market is simply the best known example out of very many. In this way, some companies have developed a mass production culture which encourages a trend towards job degradation, while others have maintained a bespoke tradition to which retention of craft skills and even polyvalence is more naturally related. Size of organization tends to be associated with this particular strategic choice, with mass producers usually being larger. A close relationship between larger size and greater specialization has been found in many studies conducted in a wide range of countries and organizational types (cf. Child 1973; Hickson et al. 1979). This means that larger size will encourage job degradation, over and above any mass production 'effect', through two processes. First, larger workforces will tend to become more internally specialized thus encouraging a narrowing of skills. Second, larger organizations will tend to employ more 'staff' specialists including industrial engineers and machine tool programmers who will work to control the labour process by narrowing the discretion of, and tasks performed by, workers.

There is some consensus among organizational theorists that the most significant *task dimensions* for an understanding of how work is organized are those relating to uncertainty and complexity (cf. Perrow 1970; Van de Ven and Ferry 1980). The number of exceptions encountered in performing the task and its general variability, a lack of clarity about what is required and about cause–effect relationships are all factors contributing to uncertainty. Complexity is increased by factors such as the amount of relevant information to be absorbed in carrying out the task, the number of steps involved, and the number of contributions required from different sources. A third relevant dimension is the cost of making an error, whether this falls primarily on property or on the person.

An analysis of the introduction of new technology into medicine, banking and retailing conducted by the writer and colleagues (Child et al. 1984) concluded that task uncertainty and the cost of error were particularly significant for enabling service providers to preserve the integrity of their jobs. New technologies will normally have a superiority in receiving, storing and providing rapid access to complex data, so long as these are in a structured form. Moreover, tasks involving uncertainty and risk require the exercise of judgement: the best way of carrying them out is not transparent. This 'indeterminancy' has considerable ideological potential for the defence of the worker's control over the labour process, as professional workers in particular have demonstrated (Jamous and Peloille 1970). In short, the greater the uncertainty and risk in tasks to be performed, the less likely are strategies of labour elimination or job degradation to be adopted. Since an organization will normally contain a range of tasks with different degrees of uncertainty and risk, this is another factor encouraging a diversity of management strategies towards the labour process within the firm.

Each of the four managerial strategies is likely to be pursued under different circumstances and in relation to different categories of workers. Within the purely British context, relevant product market, labour market, task and organizational influences may tentatively be identified, drawing from the framework just set out.

The *elimination of direct labour* through automation entails considerable investment in new equipment. Leaving aside process production where the properties of the materials are a major consideration, this strategy is most appealing to a management whose firm competes on the basis of embodying complex machining in products manufactured in small batches and subject to variability in specification. Investment of this order is also more likely in a recessionary period but when market opportunities are apparent and an upturn in demand is expected. In so far as FMS developments have so far involved new facilities, the relevance of labour market characteristics has not been clear. However, labour elimination strategies are more likely to be pursued and to succeed in existing establishments when the negotiating position of workers is weakened by unemployment, especially if severance terms are generous or alternative employment is offered elsewhere within the company or locality. Labour elimination would appear to suit tasks of which the performance dimensions are well understood, but which are complex and where precision is required. It is, finally, the strategy most likely to find favour in an organization with a strong professional engineering (as opposed to a craft) culture.

*Contracting* is a means of reducing the risk incurred in serving product markets which display unstable or seasonal patterns of demand. It commits the employer to maintaining a portion of his employment costs for a limited period only. The spread of contracting is likely to be facilitated by slack labour markets, in which a sufficient number of people come forward who are prepared to work on limited contracts and themselves bear the risk of providing a long-term income flow. Contracting is also more practical where there is a technical possibility of segmenting distinct tasks or stages in production, which can constitute a specific contracted obligation. Finally, the organization with high overheads and whose management has a strong (probably traditional) sense of a 'core' organizational competence, is the more likely to favour contracting.

It may be recalled that *polyvalence* takes the two forms of (i) removal of demarcations and (ii) job enlargement. Product market conditions in which quality of product or service is a significant competitive factor are likely to encourage both forms. An important impetus to removing demarcations may come from competitive pressures bearing on production costs, while job enlargement policies have been more common in buoyant product market conditions. The labour market factor is also relevant here. The removal of demarcation is likely to be seen as a threat to job control and will therefore be more readily introduced when organized worker opposition is weak. In contrast, job enlargement has typically been introduced in tight labour markets as an attempt to reduce high levels of absenteeism and labour turnover. The type of task conducive to a polyvalent strategy is one in which the use of worker discretion and judgement is believed to be functional, and one which permits flexibility of physical movement, of time budgeting and possibly of sequencing. The type of organization more likely to contain polyvalent strategies will have small work units (plants, departments or offices), a craft or professional tradition, and an emphasis on the training and development of workers. It may well have inherited a paternalistic tradition.

A *job degradation* strategy is likely to be stimulated by competitive pressures in product markets, but where the basis of that competition is keenly priced standardized production. Slack labour markets, with a pool of readily available compliant cheap labour from the 'secondary external' sector, are also conducive to the adoption and successful imposition of this strategy. Favourable task characteristics include repeated standard routine operations, for which methods can be readily defined and performance assessed without undue difficulty. The type of organization in which this strategy will tend to be found is large and without a strong craft or professional tradition. It may well have a history of autocratic management which maintained a considerable social distance from the workforce, and did not encourage opportunities for workers to gain advancement within the company.

These propositions suggest that the use of new technology to advance particular managerial strategies can usefully be understood in terms of contextual factors of a market, task and organizational nature within a particular country. Governmental, institutional and cultural factors come into account when broader cross-national comparisons are attempted. The analysis presented here implies that a study of job redesign within the labour process needs to be sensitive to specific historical and contemporary features which shape the patterns of its variation around the course of capitalist development.

## REFERENCES

Braverman, H. (1974), *Labor and Monopoly Capital: The Degradation of Work in the Twentieth Century*, New York: Monthly Review Press.

Buchanan, D.A. and Boddy, D. (1983), *Organizations in the Computer Age*, Aldershot: Gower.

Cane, A. (1982), 'The factory with no workers', *Financial Times* , 14 July.

Cane, A. (1983), 'More expected to work from home', *Financial Times*, 1 September,

Charlish, G. (1983), 'FMS – A way of thinking', *Financial Times*, 3 November.

Child, J. (1973), 'Predicting and understanding organization structure', *Administrative Science Quarterly*, **18**, 168–185.

Child, J. (1974), 'Managerial and organizational factors associated with company performance', *Journal of Management Studies*, 11, 175–189.

Child, J. (1978), 'The "non-productive" component within the productive sector; a problem of management control', in M. Fores and I. Glover (eds), *Manufacturing and Management*, London: HMSO.

Child, J. and Partridge, B. (1982), *Lost Managers: Supervisors in Industry and Society*, Cambridge: Cambridge University Press.

Child, J., Fores, M., Glover, I. and Lawrence, P. (1983), 'A price to pay? professionalism and work organization in Britain and West Germany', *Sociology*, **17**, 63–78.

Child, J., Loveridge, R., Harvey, J. and Spencer, A. (1984), 'Microelectronics and the quality of employment in services', in P. Marstrand (ed.), *New Technology and the Future of Work*, published for the British Association by Frances Pinter.

Cockburn, C. (1983), *Brothers: Male Dominance and Technical Change*, London: Pluto Press.

Cosyns, J., Loveridge, R. and Child, J. (1983), *New Technology in Retail Distribution – The Implications at Enterprise Level*, Report to the EEC, University of Aston Management Centre.

Cragg, A. and Dawson, T. (1981), 'Qualitative research among homeworkers', London: Department of Employment Research Paper, No. 21, May.

Crompton, R. and Reid, S. (1982), 'The deskilling of clerical work', in S. Wood (ed.), *The Degradation of Work?*, London: Hutchinson.

Crozier, M. (1964), *The Bureaucratic Phenomenon*, London: Tavistock.

de Kadt, M. (1979), 'Insurance: a clerical work factory', in A. Zimbalist (ed.), *Case Studies on the Labor Process*, New York: Monthly Review Press.

Edwards, R. (1979), *Contested Terrain*, London: Heinemann.

Fidler, J. (1981), *The British Business Elite*, London: Routledge and Kegan Paul.

Francis, A., Snell, M., Willman, P. and Winch, G. (1982), 'Management, industrial relations and new technology for the BL Metro', Imperial College, Department of Social and Economic Studies, November.

Friedman, A. L., (1977), *Industry and Labour*, London: Macmillan.

Gennard, J. and Dunn, S. (1983), 'The impact of new technology on the structure and organization of craft unions in the printing industry', *British Journal of Industrial Relations*, **XXI**, 17–32.

Gospel, H. F. (1983), 'Managerial structures and strategies: an introduction', in H. F. Gospel and C. F. Littler (eds), *Managerial Strategies and Industrial Relations*, London: Heinemann.

Grieco, M. (1983), Contribution to discussion, Conference on Organization and Control of the Labour Process, Owens Park, Manchester, March.

Gross, E. (1953), 'Some functional consequences of primary controls in formal work organizations', *American Sociological Review*, **18**, 368–373.

Handy, C. (1982), 'Where management is leading', *Management Today*, December, 50–3, 114.

Harvey, J. and Child, J. (1983), 'Green Hospital, Woodall, Biochemistry Laboratory: a case study', University of Aston.

Heery, E. (1983), 'Polyvalence and new technology', unpublished working paper, Department of Sociology, North East London Polytechnic.

Hickson, D. J., McMillan, C. J., Azumi, K. and Horvath, D. (1979), 'Grounds for comparative organization theory: quicksands or hard core?', in C. J. Lammers and D. J. Hickson (eds), *Organizations Alike and Unlike*, London: Routledge and Kegan Paul.

Hofstede, G. (1980), *Culture's Consequences: National Differences In Thinking and Organizing*, Beverly Hills, Calif.: Sage.

IDE International Research Group (1981), *Industrial Democracy in Europe*, Oxford: Oxford University Press.

Incomes Data Services (IDS) (1980), *Changing Technology*, Study No. 22, London.

Jamous, H. and Peloille, B. (1970), 'Changes in the French university-hospital system', in J. A. Jackson (ed.), *Professions and Professionalism*, Cambridge: Cambridge University Press.

Jones, B. (1982a), 'Destruction or redistribution of engineering skills? the case of numerical control', in Stephen Wood (ed.), *The Degradation of Work?*, London: Hutchinson.

Jones, B. (1982b), 'Technical, organizational, and political constraints on system redesign for machinist programming of NC machine tools', paper for IFIP Conference on 'System Design for the Users', Italy, September.

Kransdorff, A. A. (1983), 'Now for the white-collar shake-out', *Financial Times*, 18 April, 10.

Lamming, R. and Bessant, J. (1983), 'Some management implications of advanced manufacturing technology', unpublished paper, Department of Business Studies, Brighton Polytechnic.

Littler, C. R. (1983), 'A comparative analysis of managerial structures and strategies', in H. F. Gospel and C. R. Littler (eds), *Managerial Strategies and Industrial Relations*, London: Heinemann.

Loveridge, R. (1983), 'Labour market segmentation and the firm', in J. Edwards et al., Manpower Strategy and Techniques in an Organizational Context, Chichester: Wiley.

Mandeville, T. (1983), 'The spatial effects of information technology', *Futures*, February, 65–72.

March, J. G. and Olsen, J. P. (1976), *Ambiguity and Choice in Organizations*, Bergen: Universitetsforlaget.

Martin, R. (1981), *New Technology and Industrial Relations in Fleet Street*, Oxford: Clarendon Press.

Maurice, M., Sorge, A. and Warner, M. (1980), 'Societal differences in organizing manufacturing units: a comparison of France, West Germany and Great Britain', *Organizational Studies*, **1**, 59–86.

Mintzberg, H., Raisinghani, D. and Theoret, A. (1976), 'The structure of "unstructured" decision processes', *Administrative Science Quarterly*, 21, 246–275.

Mok, A. L. (1975), 'Is er een Dubbele Arbeidsmarkt in Nederland?', in *Werkloosheid, Aard, Omvang, Structurele Oorzakenen Beleidsatternatieven*, The Hague: Martinus Nijhoff.

Noble, D. F. (1979), 'Social choice in machine design: the case of automatically controlled machine tools', in A. Zimbalist (ed.), *Case Studies on the Labor Process*, New York: Monthly Review Press.

Northcott, J., Rogers, P. with Zeilinger, A. (1982), *Microelectronics in Industry: Survey Statistics*, London: Policy Studies Institute.

Ouchi, W. (1981), *Theory Z: How American Business Can Meet the Japanese Challenge*, Reading, Mass.: Addison-Wesley.

Perrow, C. (1970), *Organizational Analysis: A Sociological View*, London: Tavistock.

Purcell, J. (1983), 'The management of industrial relations in the modern corporation: agenda for research', *British Journal of Industrial Relations*, XXI, 1–16.

Ramsey, H. (1977), 'Cycles of control: workers participation in sociological and historical perspective', *Sociology*, **11**, 481–506.

Rose, M. and Jones, B. (1985). 'Managerial strategy and trade union responses in work re-organization schemes at establishment level', in D. Knight et al. (eds), *Job Redesign*, Gower, 1985, ch. 5, pp. 81–106.

Sorge, A., Hartmann, G., Warner, M. and Nicholas, I. (1983), *Microelectronics and Manpower in Manufacturing*, Aldershot: Gower.

Spender, J-C. (1980), 'Strategy-making in business', unpublished Ph.D. thesis, University of Manchester.

Thompson, P. (1983), *The Nature of Work*, London: Macmillan.

Van de Ven, A.H. and Ferry, D.L. (1980), *Measuring and Assessing Organizations*, New York: Wiley.

Wilkinson, B. (1983), *The Shopfloor Politics of New Technology*, London: Heinemann.

Williams, E. (1983), 'Process control boom near', *Financial Times*, 16 May.

Williamson, O.E. (1975), *Markets and Hierarchies*, New York: Free Press.

Wood, S. and Kelly, J. (1982), 'Taylorism, responsible autonomy and management strategy', in Stephen Wood (ed.), *The Degradation of Work?*, London: Hutchinson.

# 11

# The Decentralization of Production – the Decline of the Mass-Collective Worker?

FERGUS MURRAY

In this chapter I want to examine one of the changes that have been taking place in the organization of production and the labour process since the early 1970s, that is, the decentralization of production. While the geographical dispersal of production is a long established feature of capitalism, in the last ten years decentralization has undergone a quantitative increase and qualitative change. For example, in Italy large firms have reduced plant size, split up the production cycle between plants, and increased the putting-out of work to a vast and growing network of small firms, artisan workshops, and domestic outworkers.[1] In Japan large firms using advanced production techniques have insisted that their small supplier firms raise productivity through technological innovation, while moves are under way to link the small firms by computer to the large ones, thereby greatly increasing the control of the large corporations over production. In America and Britain increasingly mobile international capital in high technology small units has been moving into areas of high unemployment, for example in the southern 'sun belt' states of the US and in South Wales and Scotland in Britain, where careful labour recruitment exploits and exacerbates the segmentation of the labour market and divisions in the working class. And recently a statement in the Soviet press drew attention to decentralization when it criticized the way in which Russian industrialization continues to be based on huge factories and

This essay was first published in *Capital and Class*, no. 19, Spring 1983. I gratefully acknowledge the financial support of the SSRC for this research. And many thanks to Ash Amin, Bob Mannings, Donald MacKenzie, Mario Pezzini, Harvie Ramsay and everyone else who read and commented on earlier drafts of this essay.

1. For other articles on decentralization in Italy in English see Amin (1983), Brusco (1982), Goddard (1981) and Mattera (1980).

proposed a policy for the reduction of plant size and the development of small, flexible, highly specialized and technologically advanced production units. The article cited the example of General Electric which continues to reduce plant size despite the fact that all its 400,000 employees already work in factories of fewer than 1500 workers.[2]

There is then a growing body of evidence which challenges the idea that the progressive centralization and concentration of capital necessarily leads to a physical concentration of production – that the small production unit is the remnant of a disappearing traditional, backward sector of production. For generations Marxists have assumed that the tendency of capitalism was to the greater and greater concentration of production and massification of the proletariat. Indeed there were excellent historical reasons for making this assumption, as the development of both the basic commodity industries of the first industrial revolution and the mass production industries of the post-war boom led to a high concentration of workers in large integrated plants in large industrial towns.[3] Nevertheless the above evidence suggests that the size and location of production cannot be drawn from theoretical premises but rather that they are historically determined, depending on the particular circumstances capitalist production faces in different periods.

This chapter draws on empirical material from Italy to show how the use of decentralization has been intensified and has changed through the introduction of new technology as Italy's dominant firms have sought to restructure production in their struggle against declining profitability. In Italy the combination of automation and decentralization has been specifically aimed at destroying the power and autonomy of the most militant and cohesive section of the Italian proletariat, and this strategy has met with considerable success. This suggests that the political hopes pinned on the mass-collective worker in the seventies need to be carefully reconsidered in the light of decentralization and the recomposition of the proletariat this implies.

The chapter is organized as follows. The first section examines the determinants of the dominant organizational form of post-war industry, the large factory, and suggests that this form is historically specific, being contingent on the balance of class forces and the technologies available to capital. Using empirical material, the second section attempts to define the different forms of decentralization in order to bring out the wide variety of different workplaces and workers which decentralization creates through its physical fragmentation of the labour process. The third section analyses the way in which the application of information technology in production management not only gives capital a greater potential control over labour in the large factory, but also gives it the possibility of coordinating production and labour exploitation that is increasingly dispersed in small production units, artisan workshops and 'home-factories'.

The last part of the chapter suggests that decentralization has created new divisions in the industrial working class by increasing the number of workers

2. ' "Small is lovely" says Soviet economist', *Financial Times* 9 December 1982.

3 Blair (1972) says (p. 113): 'Beginning with the new technologies of the Industrial Revolution, the veneration of size has come to take on the character of a mystique, and, like most mystiques, it has come to enjoy an independent life of its own.'

living and working in conditions that greatly differ from those of the mass-collective worker. The transformation of the large factory and the rise of small production units has made collective action considerably more difficult. The chapter ends by asking how both old and new divisions can be effectively challenged by the labour movement and the left, with a strategy and organizations that give voice to the different needs and desires of different parts of the proletariat, while also giving them a unity that can overcome divisions rather than exacerbating them.

## THE LARGE FACTORY: IS IT INEVITABLE?

The term 'decentralization of production' has been used in Italy to describe a number of distinct features of the organisation of production. In general, decentralization refers to the geographical dispersal and division of production, and particularly to the diffusion and fragmentation of labour. However, this can take place in a number of ways:

1 The expulsion of work formerly carried out in large factories to a network of small firms, artisans or domestic outworkers.
2 The division of large integrated plants into small, specialized production units.
3 The development of a dense small firm economy in certain regions such as the Veneto and Emilia Romagna in Italy.

In Italy 'decentralization' has been used to cover all the above developments. In this chapter 'decentralization' is used to refer to the expulsion of production and labour from large factories, either in the form of in-house decentralization (splitting-up) or inter-firm decentralization (putting-out) within the domestic economy. This is because the chapter focuses on the way large and medium firms in Italy have used decentralization to reduce costs and increase labour exploitation, rather than on the development of districts of independent small firms that are not directly subordinate to larger firms. The analysis of this latter process has been an important part of the Italian debate on decentralization (e.g. Brusco, 1982; Paci, 1975 and 1980; Bagnasco et al., 1978).

An assumption has prevailed that large corporations operating in such sectors as engineering and electronics will organize production in large factories, in that they will amass large amounts of fixed capital and workers in particular, on any given site. However factory size is not given, and least of all does not necessarily correspond with the size of a firm or corporation's turnover, or their market and financial strength. Rather it is determined by the specific configuration of the conditions for profitable production prevailing in any given period. For example, the integrated car plant developed in rapidly expanding markets, with the balance of class forces initially in capital's favour, which made possible and profitable a particular combination of technology (mechanized flow line production) and labour domination (Taylorism). It was the coincidence of all these factors that made the integrated plant the most profitable form of production organization in the post-war consumer durables industries. When labour rebelled and markets began to stagnate, the 'efficiency' of this form of production was undermined and both capitalists and bourgeois economists discovered 'diseconomies of scale'. The ending of the long wave of expansion, the development of new technologies, and new management techniques have all contributed to change the form of the division of labour and the labour process within the large corporation. Five of the more important factors that influence factory size are the type of product being made, the technologies available, product control, industrial relations and state legislation. I shall consider the role of these factors in turn.

### *Product Type*

Product type is important in determining the degree to which the production cycle for a given product can be divided between separate factories. Industries where there is a high divisibility of the production cycle include aeronautics, machinery, electronics, clothes, shoes, and furniture. In contrast the steel and chemical industries tend to require a large unified production site, although the optimum plant size is not always as large as some people, for example BSC management, think (Manwaring, 1981: 72).

One particularly important development that has been taking place in the structure of some products is a process known as modularization. Although there has been a diversification in the number of models in many ranges of consumer goods, this has been underlain by a standardization of the major sub-assembled parts of the product. These sub-assembled parts are the basic modules of the product and can be made in different factories and put together at a later date. For example, as argued in Del Monte (1982: 154–6) at one time televisions were assembled in a linear manner on a long assembly line. The frame of the television would be put on the line, and individual parts then added to it. In modular production each module is assembled separately, and a much shorter process of final assembly is required. At present modular production is mainly limited to commodities from the electronics sector, but advances in product redesign facilitated by the introduction of microelectronic components suggest that it will be used elsewhere. (See the example of Fiat later.) If we recall how the bringing together of large numbers of workers on assembly lines in the sixties fuelled workers' spontaneous struggles, modular production, plus the increasing automation of the assembly areas themselves, can serve as important weapons for capital in reducing worker militancy through decentralization.

### *Technology*

Brusco (see FLM Bergamo, 1975) argues that Marx's explanation for the concentration of production in large factories was partly based on the necessity of running machines from a central energy source – the steam engine. As steam was replaced by electricity as the principal energy source for industry this particular centralizing tendency was weakened. Initially the expense of electric engines meant that one central engine and a system of transmission shafts and belts were used to drive the different machines. But as electrical technology developed and the price of engines fell, each machine was fitted with its own motor.[4] Other tech-

4. See Brusco in FLM Bergamo (1975: 45–7), Prais (1976: 52–3), Blair (1972: chs 5 and 6) and Marx (1976: 603–4).

nological changes that affect the product and the organization of production include shifts in materials, for instance, from steel to plastics, but the most important change that has been taking place in the last decade is the introduction of the microchip into the production of many commodities. While the microchip tends to a lessening of worker control over machines, it is also changing the nature of those machines. Generally there is a trend towards a replacement of electromechanical parts with microelectronic components, and from worker control of the machine to the installation of the unit of control in the machine which leads to changes in the production of the product and its associated labour process. Olivetti has been transformed from an engineering multinational to an electrical one over twenty years, and in many engineering firms electrical control systems are now taking over from mechanical ones. This implies a reduction of machine shop work in production. It is also interesting to note that electrical work, such as wiring and the assembly of circuit boards, has in some cases proved suitable for putting-out to tiny firms employing semi-skilled women workers – so suitable, according to Wood (1980), that in Japan there are an estimated 180,000 domestic outworkers in the electrical components industry alone. Similarly, a firm in Bologna making control units for machine tools did some quite radical experimenting with decentralization as it shifted from electromechanical to electronic control systems. According to the Bologna metalworkers' union (FLM Bologna, 1977: 78), with the appearance of microelectronics in the seventies the firm began to run down its machine shops and progressively intensified putting out which eventually accounted for 60 per cent of production costs. At this time the firm employed about 500 workers directly and over 900 indirectly as outworkers. A couple of years later with the introduction of automation the firm recentralized production and an estimated 600 outworkers lost their jobs.

There are then technological changes taking place that allow decentralization and falling factory sizes but it needs to be stressed that these changes don't automatically lead to decentralization. It is the particular capitalist's use of technology and the conditions of profitability that will determine how the organization of production changes.

### *Product Control*

The making of many commodities requires huge amounts of co-ordination and control of production, and the pressure to reduce dead time, stocks, and all types of idle capital has increased markedly since 1974. In a big plant, production is difficult to supervise at every level and the sheer size of the factory and the bureaucracy needed to run it can hide huge amounts of waste. This would suggest that for the capitalist the division of production and management into smaller and more easily controlled units would be a cost effective strategy.[5] The introduction of computer assisted management allows production to be split up by making the co-ordination of production in different plants considerably easier. General Motors's new 'S' car, for example, was being built in GM's European production network which employs 120,000 workers split up in thirty-nine plants in seventeen countries (*Financial Times*, 28 September 1982).

5. 'US auto makers reshape for world competition', in *Business Week* 21 June 1982. See also Griffiths (1982).

### *Industrial Relations*

The reduction of factory size and relocation of production are contingent upon the extent to which 'unfavourable' industrial relations are an important reason for restructuring in different industries in different countries. Prais (1982) suggests that factories in the UK with over 2000 workers are fifty times more vulnerable to strikes than those with less than 100 workers, and he goes on to say, in his academically refined union bashing tone, that big plants in UK car assembly, steel production, and shipbuilding develop endemic strikes 'which impedes the pursuit of efficiency, and leads ultimately to self-destruction' (p. 103).

In the late 1960s labour militancy in many Italian industries reached levels that directly threatened firm profitability and management undertook a series of strategies designed initially to reduce the disruptiveness of militant workers. One of these strategies, decentralization, was in part underlain by a management view, typified by the director of a Bologna engineering firm to whom I spoke, which saw a direct correlation between factory size and industrial relations in Italy in the 1970s. This director argued that a significant improvement in industrial relations could be achieved in a factory employing 100 rather than 1000 workers.

This is not to say there is an automatic relationship between industrial relations, labour militancy and factory size. Rather large plants in the post-war boom appear to have created conditions favourable to an intense and often 'unofficial' shop floor struggle that has been very disruptive for capital. It would be wrong therefore to equate the rise of smaller production units with the end of labour militancy on the shop floor. It seems that capitalists expect substantial 'improvements' in industrial relations from smaller scale production units. Clearly this will impose new and real difficulties for the autonomous organization of workers and the forms it should take in small plants. However, the struggles at Plessey Bathgate and Lee Jeans have shown that these are not unsurmountable.

### *State Legislation*

Central and local state legislation will be important in determining factory size and location in a number of ways. Incentives, grants subsidies, and factories themselves may all be used to persuade firms to set up additional sites, as can be seen by the uncoordinated efforts of the various regional development agencies in the UK.

Employment legislation, and its implementation, may also be very influential. In Italy important parts of the Worker's Statute do not apply in firms employing fewer than fifteen workers. And the smaller the plant the more possibility there is of using illegal employment practices, such as the use of child labour, and the evasion of tax and national insurance payments.[6]

## DIFFERENT FORMS OF DECENTRALIZATION

Using empirical material from the Bologna engineering industry, this section examines the two forms of decentralization that have been used most extensively

6. See Marx (1976: 604–5) for a discussion of the Factory Acts and the effect they had on domestic industry.

in Italy by large and medium sized firms. The intention here is to examine the way decentralization changes the nature of work and workers and the relationships that exist between firms. An analysis of the relationships between firms is important for the left, especially in view of assessing the accuracy and implications of two trends that are supposedly taking place; one is the vertical disintegration of many corporations, and the other is the growing wave of support (in Britain especially) for small business from the state and even the banks. On the basis of Macrae's analysis (1982), one would think that the power of monopoly capital was withering away to open a new golden age for the entrepreneur. However, while it may be true that some corporations are withdrawing from direct control of some production this in no way implies a weakening of their power. Rather, through decentralization these corporations may maintain a strict control over production while letting the small firm pay the costs and face the risks of production, thereby using decentralization as a means for reducing and shifting the corporation's risks and losses. In this way corporations maintain their ability to cover fluctuating markets while concentrating on the most profitable areas of production. This of course, does not mean that *all* small firms are subordinate to a particular corporation and many may even find a degree of independence.[7]

## *Putting-out*

Putting-out involves the transfer of work formerly done within a firm to another firm, an artisan workshop or to domestic outworkers. After the initial transfer, putting-out can be used to describe a semi-permanent relationship between firms.

Within the Italian economy putting-out appears to have contributed significantly to the rise of small firms and to the surprising shift that has taken place in industrial employment in the last ten years. In 1971 22 per cent of the total industrial workforce were employed in 'mini-firms' of fewer than nineteen employees. By 1978 this figure had risen to 29.4 per cent, an expansion of employment in the 'mini-firms' of 345,000. Furthermore the number of men employed in these firms rose by only 8.3 per cent in this period, whereas the number of women grew by 33.8 per cent. While it is difficult to generalize from such disaggregated data, they do indicate a steady growth of employment in very small production units for which the putting-out and the geographical fragmentation of production have been partly responsible. The period from 1974–8 is particularly interesting as a fall of employment of 52,000 occurred in firms of over 500 employees, whereas employment rose by 160,000 in the 'mini-firms' (see Celata, 1980: 85).

In the Bologna engineering industry, in the period 1968–80, the number of artisan firms employing 1–15 employees rose from 6602 to 9436, an increase of 42.9 per cent, and nearly a third of the Bologna engineering labour force of 88,000 was working in these workshops in 1980 (see FLM Emilia Romagna, 1981: 18–9).

The existence of this dense network of artisans, workshops and small firms, and

7. For a typology of small firms see Brusco and Sabel (1981). They suggest that a lot of small firms in Emilia are relatively independent whereas Del Monte (1982) is less optimistic about the position of small firms in the south of Italy (p. 125). And many small firms in Japan are 'wholly dependent on a single buyer' (Patrick and Rosovsky 1976: 509–13).

its expansion due to an initial restructuring of the Bologna engineering industry in the 1950s, have been among the vital preconditions for the development of putting-out and the increasing division of labour between small firms. As the example that follows suggests, decentralization has passed through two phases: a first phase between 1968 and 1974 when putting-out was used less out of choice than out of necessity owing to intense shop-floor struggles in the large and medium factories; and a second phase, since 1975, of more systematic use of decentralization, with the introduction of information technology into production planning and the appearance of numerically controlled machine tools in increasingly specialized artisan shops, accompanied by a gradual reversal of some of labour's gains on the shop floor. In this second phase it is possible to see an implicit shift from the direct control of labour on the shop-floor in the large Taylorized factory to a more articulated and flexible system of the organization of production where the labour process extends beyond the factory into the artisan workshop. In the artisan workshop the unmediated forces of the market that threaten the artisan's very existence ensure a high degree of 'self-exploitation' often reinforced by the paternalistic despotism of the small entrepreneur.

In the Bologna engineering industry there appear to be three motives for putting-out: to reduce fixed costs to a minimum; to benefit from wage differentials between firms; and to maximize the flexibility of the production cycle and of labour exploitation. The nature of putting-out is examined below through its use in a Bologna precision engineering firm.

The strategy of this firm, according to the management, has been to invest in labour and machinery just below the level of minimum expected demand. Any increase of production above this level has been met by putting-out, rather than risking an expansion of the factory or the workforce. However, contrary to management's claims, it is not true that the size of the labour force has always depended upon the level of demand. Until 1969, that is until when the first big strikes occurred, the size of the workforce grew steadily. However, after 1969, although production output rose rapidly for a number of years, the level of employment of production workers and productivity in the firm actually fell. It therefore appears that a decision was taken to limit employment in the firm as militancy on the shop-floor increased and to cover rising demand by massively raising putting-out. In 1972 of production work 46 per cent was put out of the firm, employing indirectly the equivalent of 570 full-time workers in small firms and workshops, whereas in 1969 only 10 per cent had been put out. In 1974–5 production fell rapidly, and work put out dropped to almost nothing, resulting in the loss of approximately 550 jobs. That is, while the level of employment in the firms working for the company went through a massive fluctuation, employment in the company itself was relatively stable. The company putting the work out did not then pay a penny of redundancy money and nor was there any disruptive and socially embarrassing struggle over job losses. This illustrates clearly the flexibility putting-out can provide. In this instance the reason for putting-out was not so much the exploitation of wage differentials as the minimization of costs and conflict over job losses with the union.

However, the same firm does also put out work for savings on wages, where the outworkers are paid up to 50 per cent less than their counterparts in the factory. The work put out here is not mechanical work, but wiring and circuit board assembly and involves women working in small firms and sweatshops where they have no legal or union protection.

With the introduction of computer assisted management and with the changes taking place in modular design, the firm has recently overhauled its putting-out system. Formerly, work of a once only basis was put out to artisan shops on the basis of very short lived and verbal agreements. The firm now encourages these artisans, who often employ fewer than five people, to group themselves together in order to amass the machinery and skills necessary for the production and sub-assembly of modules on a more regular basis. Meanwhile, management has won back some of its former power on the shop-floor with the help of computer aided production and an increase in internal labour mobility. The introduction of the computer has given management an increasingly refined control over the co-ordination of production both within and outside the factory, and putting-out is now used more routinely, while special and rush jobs are done in the factory due to the increased mobility of labour, achieved after six years of almost total rigidity.

Putting-out here has gone from a contingency solution of special problems to a more structured system. Initially flexibility was found in putting-out to artisan workshops to get around rigidity in the factory. Now it is the whole system, factory production and putting-out, that works to give flexibility.

Putting-out in Bologna engineering varies from skilled well-paid work using advanced technology to dirty, dangerous and deskilled work. Within this there is a clear division of putting-out based on sexual and racial divisions in the labour market. The skilled workers and artisans are almost exclusively middle aged men, while women, the young, and migrants from the south of Italy and North Africa are concentrated in the dirtiest, most precarious and worst paid work.

The other extensive form of putting-out is to domestic outworkers in industries like clothing, electrical components, and toys. This form of putting-out has received a good deal more attention than putting-out to small firms (e.g. Young, 1981; Rubery and Wilkinson, 1981; Goddard, 1981) and will therefore not be dealt with here.

Another increasingly important type of putting-out is that which takes place across notional frontiers where either parts of the production cycle are contracted out or the firm contracts out the production of the finished commodity it already makes, using its own specifications and technology for production in the subcontracting firm and its marketing network for the sale of the commodity. An example of the former type of international putting-out is cited in Frobel et al. (1980: 108) and refers to the extensive use the West German textile industry makes of textile firms in Yugoslavia, where firms send out semi-finished products from Germany to be worked up into the final product. And an example of the latter can be found in Del Monte's study (1982) of the electronics industry in southern Italy, where again West German firms making televisions contract out the production of complete sets to medium sized firms around Naples. The firms doing the work use the German firm's know-how and marketing services, not being big enough themselves to break into the world market. They, in turn, put out work to smaller firms in the area (pp. 150–1).

Putting-out then cannot be equated with an archaic and disappearing system of production. Rather it seems to have been reinforced as specific sectors of industry have faced altered conditions in the harsh economic and political climate of the seventies as the long wave of expansion ground to a halt. Therefore it would be mistaken to continue to segment firms in terms of the dualist opposition between large firms using high technology and small firms using outdated technology and traditional production techniques.[8]

## *Splitting Up Production*

The second form of decentralization is the splitting-up of production between factories of the same firm. Clearly firms will relocate factories, and change the organization of production between them for many and interlinked reasons. Here, I want to look specifically at splitting-up where it has been strongly motivated by management's desire to make the workers' organization as hard as possible, and where management has realized the potential dangers involved in concentrating large numbers of workers in large factories located in the large industrial town. While with the internationalization of production the fate of the domestic industrial working class is increasingly linked to the fate of the international working class, it is important to understand how the location and structure of the domestic proletariat is changing in a period of restructuring in the national and international economy.[9] Here I will examine some of the ways localized splitting has been used in the Italian economy.

In one of the Bologna engineering firms referred to previously, the upsurge of union militancy in the early seventies was met not only by an increase in putting-out but also by a partial splitting-up of production. While employment was allowed to fall in one factory in the firm, another small factory employing eighty workers was established an hour's drive away in a depressed agricultural region. Although the shop stewards were not slow to make contact with the workers in the new factory it has been difficult to take unified action. The workers at the small plant came from rural areas, do semi-skilled work, and are willing to work 'flexibly', that is they are prepared to change shifts and work overtime so that they can also work their plots of land. In contrast, the workers in the main factory are more skilled, they come from an urban background and are endowed with a militant trade union tradition.

Once the small factory was set up management then tried to put out work from it into the surrounding area, but found that there were not enough small firms in the area to allow this. However, the tendency to set up 'detached workshops' has been widespread where production permits this. One of the few studies of Fiat's decentralization of production into central Italy (Leoni, 1978) has shown how in its lorry division a mixture of splitting-up and putting-out has been used to maximize the dispersion of the directly and indirectly employed workforce in many very green 'greenfield' sites in a rundown agricultural area.

Another type of splitting-up is when the firm loses a central factory to become

8. In Japan there has been a 'rather rapid filtering down' in the form of numerically controlled machine tools from big to small firms (*Financial Times* Survey 1981). Macrae (1982) cites the example of the small Japanese firm where a leased, second hand robot system hammers out components in a 'backshed' workshop.

9. For work on Britain in this area see Massey and Meegan (1982), Fothergill and Gudgin (1982) and Lane (1982).

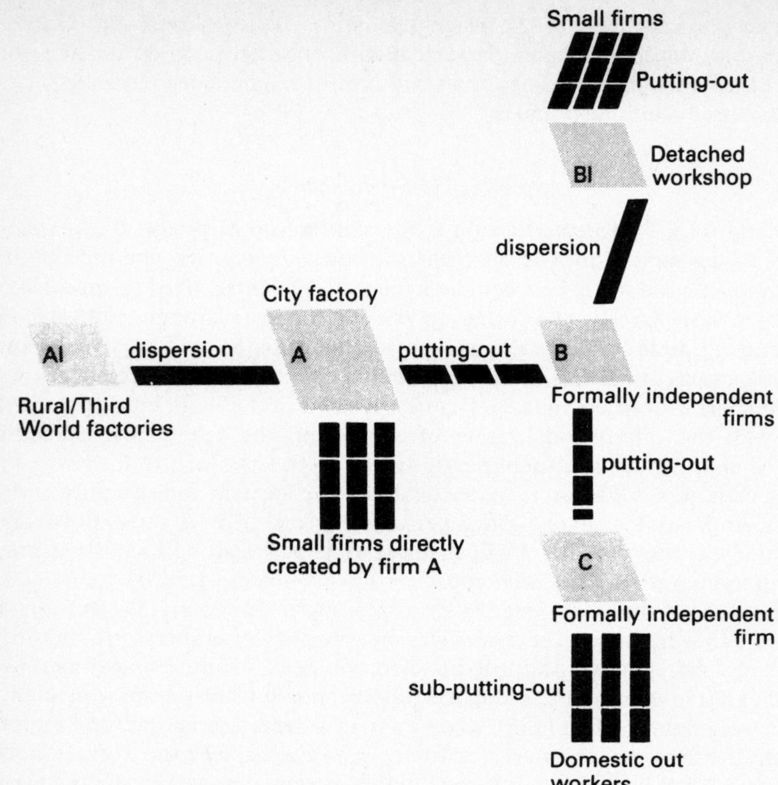


FIGURE 11.1 Schematic representation of the decentralization of production

an agglomeration of 'detached workshops'. Although this strategy is less common, one example from Bologna is striking. In this firm there are three 'major' production sites, three 'minor' ones, a stores site, a research site, and an administrative site spread out in the periphery of Bologna. In all, the firm employs 300 people dispersed in the different sites. Along with this fragmentation of production the firm also practises a high level of putting-out, and is progressively running down its machine shops to concentrate only on assembly, design and marketing activities.

A final example of splitting-up is provided by the electric domestic appliance company belonging to Vittorio Merloni, who is the head of the Italian employers' federation, the Confindustria. The firm employs 2000 workers who work in nine different sites and no factory has substantially more than 200 workers. The basis of managerial strategy is to take work to the workforce in the depressed agricultural regions of central Italy, where higher transport costs are easily offset by the 'industrial tranquillity' of the environment. One of the Merlonis specifically acknowledges that it is 'an advantage to have reduced concentrations of workers and, where possible, to know each worker'. And he goes on to explain that the firm has tried to create 'a group spirit in and outside the plants' to encourage workers to identify with the firm without losing their roots in the rural community. The idea behind this is to soften and control the traumatizing and often radicalizing transition from peasant production to work in a capitalist factory. Meanwhile, to keep things even more 'tranquil' the Merlonis concentrate their efforts on doing pressed steel, assembly and finishing work while the rest of production is put out to small firms and artisan shops often directly created by the Merlonis, who have paternalistically handed ex-workers the chance to 'go it alone' (see *Lotta Continua*, 22 May 1980 and 23 May 1980).

By way of completing this section on decentralization, figure 11.1 shows how different types of decentralization could be used by one firm to create a diffused production network or, as some Italians say, a 'diffused factory'.

## THE COMPUTER IN THE FACTORY

Within any mode of production the collection, analysis and circulation of information is vital. Within capitalism a particular form of factory production has arisen where one of the functions of the factory is the provision of a structure where information can be collected, co-ordinated and controlled. As communication technology has developed, the emergence of multi-plant and multinational enterprises has been made possible. Although telephones, telex, teletransmitters and the like are in no way determinants of the organization of production, they have allowed the centralization of control over capital to increase with the internationalization and geographical dispersion of production. However, the large factory has remained the basic unit of capitalist production.

The structure of the factory has developed, among other things, to ensure the free flow of information from the bottom of a pyramidal hierarchy to its top, and the free flow of control from the top downwards. Information, and access to it, are the keys to formulating and understanding a firm's strategy. For this reason a firm uses a lot of people to collect and transmit information in the factory and this information is carefully guarded. The people who have the greatest amount of information are in a superior position to judge and make decisions, and they will argue that they are 'objectively' correct because of their access to recorded 'knowledge'. In short, access to and the control of information is an instrument of class and sexual power.

In an engineering firm making complex automatic machines there may be as many as 20,000 separate pieces circulating in the factory. For management, this represents big problems and costs. As orders come in and are changed, the production of each piece must be planned and co-ordinated so that the final product is ready on time. Fixed capital and workers must not be allowed to stand idle; detailed plans of machine loadings, stocks and work schedules have to be made; and a change in orders, a delay by a supplier, a strike, an overtime ban or a breakdown can all upset these plans. At present many firms incur high management costs to ensure the co-ordination and monitoring of production within the factory. Traditionally this monitoring has been carried out by people writing things on bits of paper, passing them up the hierarchy, amassing them, analysing them and issuing orders based on them. Yet an increasingly flexible production organization is needed to get round worker-imposed rigidity, to ensure the full use of increasingly large amounts of fixed capital and to cut costs 'down to the bone', in the face of the burgeoning contradictions of the system.

The introduction of computer assisted management is a potentially valuable weapon for capital because it can increase management's control over all aspects of production, firstly through the further expropriation of worker's knowledge (mental labour), and secondly through an 'objectification' of control over labour that ensures the maximum saturation and co-ordination of labour time.

In one Bologna engineering firm there is a computer terminal for every thirteen employees. The terminals are used both to issue orders and to collect, feed back, memorize and co-ordinate information. The course of each part is monitored and information about individual machines and workers, such as work times and 'performance', are constantly recorded. Information from the four basic divisions of the factory – production, marketing, stock control, and planning – arrives at the central computer and data base and is recorded and analysed on a day-to-day basis. Information arriving from one department will automatically lead to co-ordination with other departments through the computer's central program. This gives the management the possibility of foreseeing where and when bottlenecks will occur, and allows management to experiment with 'dry' production runs on the computer to examine the ways in which potential blockages in production, including strikes, can be overcome through changing production plans in the factory and by increasing or changing plans for putting-out.

I'll now briefly point to three other areas where management benefits from the computer in production. Firstly, idle capital can be reduced to a minimum, whether through a greater control of labour or of stocks, as is achieved by the Japanese *kanban* (just in time) system of stock control. This system uses computers to co-ordinate in-house production and to link its surrounding ring of external suppliers so that stock requirements are calculated on an hourly and not a daily or weekly basis. Production is maintained by 'suppliers feeding a wide array of components, in the right order, through the right gate in the assembly complex to reach the line at the right time'. Secondly, automatic machines and robots can be linked together and run by a central computer, as is beginning to happen in the fully automated flexible manufacturing system. For example, General Electric has recently announced a new computerized system of information control and co-ordination which will enable robots 'to communicate with each other' and link all machines with electrical control into an integrated system, the remote parts of which can be connected by satellite links (*Financial Times* 30 March 1982). Thirdly, computerized information allows the decentralization of day-to-day management decisions while centralizing strategic control in the hands of a slimmed-down board of directors.[10]

For supervisory staff the introduction of information technology makes their information gathering role potentially obsolete, as the factory hierarchy changes from a function of production command to a more subtle one of political mediation. Fiat has taken this process further and, in workshops and offices where

10. See Manacorda (1976). See also the excellent pamphlet produced by the Joint Forum of Combine Committees (1982).

now there are no shop stewards, 'Fiat takes care of the problem of mediation with its sociologists, its new 'vaseliners' who talk to the workers about their problems.'[11] For shop-floor and office workers, computers mean stricter control through an impersonal and distant centre, rather than through face-to-face confrontation with the factory hierarchy. Anything a worker does may be recorded by the computer and used against her/him at a later date, while informal breaks won through struggle tend to be formalized and handed out as and when management see fit. Moreover the versatile computer doesn't lose its temper, and (as at Volvo) can issue orders in Swedish, Finnish, Yugoslavian and Turkish (see Zollo, 1979; Dina, 1981; Ciborra, 1979).

However, a computer system is only as good as its program and the degree to which workers are willing to co-operate with management. That is, the potential gains from the introduction of information technology are contingent upon management's ability to erode worker resistance to the technology and prevent new forms of resistance from developing. In one Bologna firm the introduction of terminals on the shop-floor was met by an 'information strike' where the workforce refused to co-operate in the collection of information.

One of the major benefits for capital is that computer assisted management can largely replace the function of the factory hierarchy as an information collecting network. And this in turn opens up the theoretical possibility of changing the organization of production radically through restructuring. Ferraris (1981) sums up the situation well.

> The new technology of the product (modularization), of production (automation), and information (distributed information and telecommunications) opens up new spaces to the process of decentralization of work and machines, which advances simultaneously with the concentration of management and control. This permits the overcoming of the historical tendency of the physical concentration of labour and fixed capital as a necessary condition for the centralization of command and profits. (p. 25)

So far, I have tried to show how the tendency towards decentralization of production and centralization of command is taking place. In order to reinforce the argument put forward, I shall cite some Italian examples where it is possible to see this process taking place.

## *Olivetti*

Olivetti's gradual transformation from an engineering group to an electrical one has been speeded up rapidly in the last few years, with the appearance of the dynamic management techniques of C. De Benedetti. Four particular processes can be seen at work:

1 At the financial level, Benedetti has arranged a bewildering series of deals with other international electronics producers which include Hitachi (marketing), St Gobain (funds and access to the French market), Data

11. Quote from a union militant in Turin, in *Il Manifesto*, special supplement on Cassa Integrazione, 1982.

Terminal System (acquisition) and Hermes (take-over of a Swiss typewriter producer).

2 Within Olivetti's Italian plants there is a move towards automation, using robots and the introduction of computer controlled testing of standardized modules.
3 Most assembly work is still done manually, but the increasing flexibility needed due to the rapid development and obsolescence of models led management to introduce non-linear assembly in the form of work islands.
4 While most assembly work is done in the factory some operations like circuit board assembly and wiring are put out to domestic outworkers in the north of Italy. This process is discussed in Perna (1980).

### *Benetton*

Benetton is an Italian clothes producer with a turnover of £250 million a year and sells under the names of Jeans West, Mercerie, Sisley, Tomato, OI2, My Market and Benetton. Production and marketing strategies are aimed at achieving two things: the minimization of costs, and the maximization of flexibility and (naturally) profits. This is achieved in the following ways:

1 Since the fifties Benetton has increasingly decentralized production. It now directly employs only 1500 workers and puts work out to over 10,000 workers. The directly employed workers work in small plants of 50–60 employees, where the union is 'absent or impeded'.
2 In its marketing structure, Benetton has 2000 sales points, but owns none of them. It gives exclusive rights to them. This strategy effectively reduces not only the selling price of the product by cutting the wholesaler out of the operation, but it also externalizes risks ensuing from fluctuating demand.
3 Computers are used to keep track of production and sales and to swiftly analyse market trends. Stocks are kept to a minimum of undyed clothes that are dyed when required (see Ferrigolo, 1982).

### *Fiat*

At Fiat there are four particular things to note:

1 A massive expulsion of labour after the defeat of the 1980 strike.
2 A big move towards automation with the LAM engine assembly plant and the Robogate body plant, both of which are highly flexible robot systems operated by a centralized computer system.
3 The introduction of work islands in the LAM system.
4 Fiat's use of decentralization. This has taken three forms: firstly, the export of integrated production units to Eastern Europe, Turkey and Latin America in the early 1970s; secondly, the splitting-up of the integrated cycle and the creation of small specialized plants in the south of Italy, which also began in the early 1970s; and thirdly, the putting-out of work from the Turin plants to local firms, artisans and outworkers.

Following the Japanese model Fiat has recently declared that in addition to assembly work, it will only produce the suspension systems and technologically important parts of the car in-house. All the rest of the work is to be decentralized, although it is unclear what form this decentralization will take. There has recently been a devastating rationalization of outside suppliers, with Fiat cutting the number of its suppliers by two-thirds and 'encouraging' the survivors to raise productivity and begin to sub-assemble parts in their own firms. Already 40 per cent of the Ritmo model is sub-assembled outside of Fiat's factories. Vittorio Ghidella, managing director of the car division, says 'what we have done is to transfer employment from Fiat to outside companies'[12] in order to disintegrate vertically as the Japanese have done.

A worker from Fiat's Lingotto pressed steel plant said in 1978 that small is hardly beautiful when you're working in one of the seventy firms with 30–50 employees that make parts of Fiat's decentralized lorry bodywork, where you work Saturdays, and do 10–12 hours overtime each week. He maintained that 'the question of decentralization and the lack of unity between small and big factories has been the weakest link in the struggles of the past years' (*Il Manifesto*, 5 October 1978).

Fiat's policy then seems to be aimed at automating what can be automated and decentralizing as much as possible so that 'decentralization is the other, almost necessary, face of robotization and the LAM' (*Il Manifesto*, 4 April 1980).

## THE DECLINE OF THE MASS-COLLECTIVE WORKER?

In Italy the increased pace of decentralization, automation, internationalization and an eventual frontal attack on the working class were provoked by two principal developments – the emergence of a militant, well organized labour movement and the stagnation of world markets. The heightened shop-floor struggles in the large and medium factories threatened the very 'efficiency' of Fordist production techniques, based on the maximum flexibility and total subordination of labour to capital. The strength and combativity of the large and medium factory proletariat made impossible a restoration of managerial control through economic recession and increased factory repression, as had happened in 1963–4. Increased competition in world markets and the slump of 1974 made it difficult for firms to pass on the costs imposed on them by labour's gains, while labour rigidity reduced their ability to respond to fluctuations in increasingly unstable markets. As a consequence large firm profit rates fell.

Decentralization was then grasped, initially as a shcrt-term strategy aimed at evading the labour movement's advances, in that it attempted to compensate high labour costs and low flexibility in the large and medium factories by directly creating or putting work out to small production units, artisans and domestic outworkers, where the influence of the unions was minimal (the small firms in question often being hidden in the submerged economy). However, the longer term aim of decentralization, automation, and the over-arching control of

12. Cited in 'Fiat follows Japan's production road map', *Business Week* 4 October 1982. See also *Sunday Times Business News* 10 October 1982 and Amin (1983)

production by electronic information systems is the destruction of the spontaneous organization of the mass worker on a collective basis. The dramatic confrontation at Fiat in 1980 hides a strategy which implies much more than a temporary political defeat for the large factory proletariat. Whereas decentralization was initially a short-term response, its very efficacy has largely precluded a recentralization of production. Indeed it has been used in conjunction with automation to begin to dismember the large factory proletariat through increasing division and dispersion into small plants and into the sweatshop where accumulation is unrestrained by organized labour.[13]

This is not to imply that the mass-collective worker is now politically insignificant. Indeed the power of organized labour based largely on the mass-collective worker is such that 'any company, almost irrespective of its size, which wishes to survive is now forced to initiate a transnational reorganization of production' (Frobel et al. 1980: 15) in order to take advantage of the cheap, abundant and well disciplined labour of the underdeveloped countries. Undoubtedly an international reorganization of capital is taking place but, as Graziani argues (1982: 34), decentralization draws attention to the fact that an abundant, potentially cheap and well disciplined labour force is also available within some advanced capitalist countries. In addition, decentralization reveals how capital gains access to that labour, while at the same time attempting to 'run down' the large factory proletariat, in an effort to restore the competitiveness of mature technology commodities in European markets.

If the aim of decentralization is ultimately the destruction of the large factory proletariat, its consequence is the recomposition of the industrial working class along new lines and divisions. As we have seen, decentralization takes many forms and to each of these forms correspond different and often new types of worker. The splitting-up of the production cycle, which is often combined with a restructuring of the labour process, creates highly mobile small production units. As Amin (1983) shows, the firm undertaking splitting-up may then search out a particular labour force that embodies the socio-economic characteristics that it considers to be optimal for profitability, taking the fixed capital to the labour force rather than risking its 'contagion' through migration and education in the large industrial town.

Putting-out creates a whole myriad of workers who are seldom immediately visible. In the small firm the labour process and conditions of work vary enormously between firms in the same industry, while the composition of the labour force, its traditions, experience and aspirations largely remain a mystery. An 'apprentice' working in a tiny firm in Turin expresses some of the contradictions that are lived by a small firm worker:

> The tiny firm is an inferno, but it is also a hope, and something near to yourself. Yes, but I know . . . that here the work is also being deskilled, but the idea still exists that you can learn a skill here, that they'll teach you something. You're a worker, but at least you can hope to become a good one. It's not really like this deep down, and everyone knows it, but where do you go if not here? Do you think Fiat's better? The big factory, in a certain sense, scares everyone; these days you only go when you've

13. For a discussion of Taylorism, the mass-collective worker and the changing class composition in Italy see Ferraris (1981), Rieser (1981), Santi (1982) and Accornero (1979 and 1981).

> given up hope . . . . Here they exploit but you're in your part of town, your place. You're treated badly, slapped around, but in that place, you see yourself in the work you do. (*Il Manifesto*, 16 May 1980)

Paternalistic relations are common on the shop-floor, with absolute power resting in the hands of the entrepreneur, whereas familial and social ties often link worker and boss outside the factory. In the small firm the relation of labour to capital is often unmediated by unions and labour legislation. It is factory despotism without the large factory and implies the reproduction of the mass, but non-collective, worker at a higher stage of the real subordination of labour to capital where the labour process is fragmented between many small production units, or into the minute division of labour between outworkers and artisans who supervise their own exploitation.

Graziosi (1979) who has done some fine work on restructuring in Italy, makes an important point when he says: 'The kernel of the strategy of decentralization lies in the marginalization, the increasing precariousness of vast social strata starting with the young, women and the old' (p. 152). It needs to be stressed that the marginality of these social strata is not economic – since they play a vital role in capitalist accumulation – but rather it is political and social.[14] The Bologna engineering industry illustrates the complexity of the composition of just one part of the proletariat, and the divisions and potential for marginalization that exist in it are many. In it are found so-called 'unskilled' women workers doing assembly work in the submerged economy, North African men in small foundries, workers in artisan shops supervising numerically controlled machine tools, workers with strong economic and cultural ties with the land working in remote rural factories, plus the workers in the larger factories with their militant union tradition and relatively privileged position. It is conceivable that at one time all these workers might have been employed in the same factory and joined by the formal and informal networks and organizations that workers establish, from which their demands and grievances are voiced and from which a collective response is developed. With workers in a firm scattered territorially, socially and culturally, in different conditions of work and often invisible from one another, the problem of uniting a single workforce, let alone the class, is daunting. This raises the question as to whether the shop-floor organization of unions – in Italy, the factory council and its delegates – can be an effective unifying organization if it is confined to one factory when the production cycle is being fragmented between plants and firms and domestic outworkers.

The recomposition of the Italian industrial working class is then exacerbating and creating new divisions which are leading to the growth of new sections of the proletariat and to the future weakening of a declining and besieged large factory proletariat. A first conclusion that can be drawn from this is that any faith in a

14. This process of marginalization and division has been aided by left analysis where 'women are seen as marginal workers and hence as marginal trade unionists' (CSE *Sex and Class* Group 1982), while the labour process debate has limited its analysis to those labour processes that are found in big factories largely employing men. The fact that in Britain men have largely theorized this labour process, while women have been largely responsible for an analysis of domestic outwork, is indicative of the difficulties facing the labour movement and the left. It is vital that left theorists should avoid reproducing the very divisions they are studying.

recuperation of the union movement 'in the economic upturn' is fundamentally misplaced and it is sadly ironic, but indicative, that the Fiat workers were beaten when the Italian economy was experiencing a mini-boom. A 'clawback' is made unlikely because the mass-collective worker is being displaced and probably no longer has the strength and cohesion to lead the industrial working class in future struggles. This does not imply however that the decline of the large factory and the mass-collective worker can be equated with the end of the shop floor or class struggle. Rather the problem is finding the strategy and organizational forms that will allow new and changed members of the proletariat to express their needs and desires and unite with the older sections of the class to fight for common ends.

The Italian experience shows that this is a difficult task and many mistakes have been made. Unions forged out of the struggles of the mass-collective worker have too often tried to impose unsuited strategies and organizations on small firms and diffused workers, while obstructing the creation of organizational forms more suited to their particular circumstances and grievances. This can be seen especially in the failure to form horizontal organizations that link workers in different firms at the local level in Italy, particularly in areas where decentralization has led to the weakening of informal social and political networks that link workers and collectivize their experiences. In Britain it can be seen by the continuing lack of official support for combine committees (see Lane, 1982:8).

The Italian labour movement has been quick to recognize that 'diffused' workers exist but for many reasons it has been extremely slow to find out what these workers want from the unions. A consequence of this is that there is a great deal of misunderstanding between the labour movement, which sometimes sees the 'diffused' workers as docile, passive and of marginal significance, and the 'diffused' workers themselves, who see the labour movement as being deaf and blind to their grievances and vulnerability.

Britain is not Italy and the mass-collective worker has not dominated the British labour movement to the same extent as in Italy, but this chapter has suggested that decentralization, automation and information technology are particularly effective means for attacking organized labour's power and autonomy, through the expulsion and dispersion of labour from large factories, sites and industrial towns. In Britain, the US and Japanese firms in south Wales and Scotland are the result of but one type of decentralization, while the domestic outworkers recently reported to be earning less than £35 a week are another. The textile firm director who 'optimistically' told the *Financial Times* (4 August 1982) 'I have this vision that St Helens could become the Hong Kong of the north-west' is the voice of a growing submerged and dispersed economy.

The British industrial working class is itself being rapidly restructured but the labour movement still largely clings to craft organizations and traditions. Hall (1982) and Lane (1982) have both drawn attention to decentralization in Britain and raised serious doubts about the unions' attempts to 'take themselves by the scruff of the neck and shake themselves into the shape necessary to cope with what is effectively a new environment' (Lane, p. 13). This chapter suggests that the reshaping of industry and the working class may accelerate further and faster than has yet been generally realized by the labour movement and the left in Britain. Hopefully the issues are becoming clearer, even if the answers seem to be a long way off.

## REFERENCES


Accornero, A. (1979) 'La classe operaia nella società italiana' *Proposte* no. 81.

Accornero, A. (1981) 'Sindicato e rivoluzione sociale. Il caso Italiano degli anni' 70' *Laboratorio Politico* no. 4.

Amin, A. (1983) 'Restructuring in Fiat and the decentralisation of production into southern Italy', in Hudson, R. and Lewis, J., *Dependent Development in Southern Europe*, Methuen, London.

Bagnasco, A., Messori, M. and Trigilia, C. (1978) *Le Problematiche dello sviluppo Italiano*, Feltrinelli, Milan.

Blair, J. M. (1972) *Economic Concentration; Structure, Behavior and Public Policy*, Harcourt Brace Jovanovich, New York.

Brunetta, R., Celata, G., Dalla Chiesa, N. and Martinelli, A. (1980) *L'Impresa in Frantumi*, Editrice Sindacale Italiana, Rome.

Brusco, S. (1982) 'The Emilian model; productive decentralisation and social integration' *Cambridge Journal of Economics* no. 2, June.

Brusco, S. and Sabel, C. (1981) 'Artisan production and economic growth', in Wilkinson (1981).

Celata, G. (1980) 'L'operaio disperso', in Brunetta, R. et al.

Ciborra, C. (1979) 'L'automazione nell' industria dell'auto' *Sapere* no. 816.

CSE Sex and Class Group (1982) 'Sex and class' *Capital & Class* no. 16.

Del Monte, A. (1982) *Decentramento internazionale e decentramento produttivo: Il caso dell'industria elettronica*, Loescher, Turin.

Dina, A. (1981) 'Lotta operaia e il nuovo uso capitalistico delle macchine' *Unità Proletaria* 3/4.

Ferraris, P. (1981) 'Taylor in Italia: conflitto e risposta sulla organizzazione del lavoro' *Unità Proletaria* 3/4.

Ferrigolo, A. (1982) 'Sogno italiano per famiglia veneta' *Il Manifesto* 3 June 1982.

*Financial Times* Survey (1981) 'Japan: the information revolution' 6 July 1981.

FLM Bologna (1975) *Occupazione, Sviluppo Economico, Territorio*, SEUSI, Rome.

FLM Emilia Romagnia (1981) *Quaderni di Appunti*, Bologna.

FLM Bergamo (1975) *Sindacato e Piccola Impresa*, De Donato, Bari.

Fothergill, S. and Gudgin, G. (1982) *Unequal Growth*, Heinemann, London.

Frobel, F., Heinrichs, J. and Kreye, O. (1980) *The New International Division of Labour*, CUP Cambridge.

Goddard, V. (1981) 'The leather trade in Naples' *Institute of Development Studies Bulletin* 12, no. 3.

Graziani, A. (1982) 'La macchina dell'inflazione e la mano invisibile dei padroni' *Unità Proletaria* no. 1–2, September.

Graziosi, A. (1979) *La Ristrutturazione nelle Grandi Fabbriche 1973–6*, Feltrinelli, Milan.

Griffiths, J. (1982) 'Robots march into European factories' *Financial Times* survey of the motor industry 19 October 1982.

Hall, S. (1982) 'A Long Haul' *Marxism Today* November.

Joint Forum of Combine Committees (1982) *The Control of New Technology*.

Lane, T. (1982) 'The unions: caught on the ebb tide' *Marxism Today* September.

Leoni, G. (1978) 'Economia sommersa, ma non troppo' *I Consigli* 57/8.

Macrae, N. (1982) 'Intrapreneurial now' *Economist* 17 April 1982.

Manacorda, P. (1976) *Il Calcolatore del Capitale*, Feltrinelli, Milan.

Manwaring, T. (1981) 'Labour productivity and the crisis at BSC: behind the rhetoric' *Capital & Class* no. 14.

Marx, K. (1976) *Capital*, vol. I, Penguin, Harmondsworth.

Massey, D. and Meegan, R. (1982) *The Anatomy of Job Loss*, Methuen, London.

Mattera, P. (1980) 'Small is not beautiful: decentralized production and the underground economy' *Radical America* October/September.

Paci, M. (1975) 'Crisi, ristrutturazione e piccola impresa' *Inchiesta* October/December.

Paci, M. (1980) *Famiglia e Mercato del Lavoro in un'economia periferica*, Angeli, Milan.

Patrick, H. and Rosovsky, H. (eds) (1976) *Asia's New Giant*, Brookings Institute, Washington.

Perna, N. (1980) 'L'operaio, punto debole du una macchina altrimenti perfetta' *Quaderni di Fabbrica e Staton* 14.

Prais, S. J. (1976) *The Evolution of Giant Firms in Britain 1909–1970*, CUP, Cambridge.

Prais, S. J. (1982) 'Strike frequencies and plant size: a comment on Swedish and UK experiences' *British Journal of Industrial Relations* March, XX, I.

Rieser, V (1981) 'Sindacato e composizione di classe' *Laboratorio Politico* 4.

Rubery, J. and Wilkinson, F. (1981) 'Outwork and segmented labour markets', in Wilkinson (1981).

Santi, P. (1982) 'All'origine della crisi del sindicato' *Quaderni Piacentini*.

Wilkinson, F. (1981) *The Dynamics of Labour Market Segmentation*, Academic Press, London.

Wood, R. C. (1980) 'Japan's multitier wage system' *Forbes*, 18 August.

Young, K. (1981) 'Domestic outwork and the decentralisation of production', paper presented to ILO regional meeting on women and rural development, Mexico.

Zollo, G. (1979) 'Informatizzazione, automazione e forza operaia' *Unità Proletaria* 3/4.

# 12

# Labour Market Segmentation and Workers' Careers: the Case of the Italian Knitwear Industry

GIOVANNI SOLINAS

## INTRODUCTION

This chapter reports on empirical research into the labour market in the knitwear and ready-to-wear industry in the province of Modena (Emilia). In particular, it looks at the careers of three categories of workers: homeworkers, those employed on the production lines of larger firms, and artisans[1]

Italy, in common with many other industrialized capitalist countries, has witnessed a growing decentralization of production. This tendency has been differently interpreted but a consensus is emerging that such developments are

This essay was first published in *Cambridge Journal of Economics* 6, 1982, 331–52. It is a revised version of a paper presented at the third conference of the International Working Party on Labour Market Segmentation, September 1981. I wish to thank Sebastiano Brusco, Paola Villa, and the referees and editors of *Cambridge Journal of Economics* for their valuable suggestions and comments. My thanks also to Paola Pagliarini for collaborating with me on the early stage of the research.

1. The bulk of the data to which reference is made is the product of direct interviewing. Since the aim of the research was not to deal with the actual dimensions of the strata of different workers but rather to look at their characteristic features, and given the difficulties in defining a representative sample, we chose to interview 100 workers for each group (production line workers, homeworkers and artisans). For each group interviewed we analysed the workers by age. In particular artisans and homeworkers were divided up thus: 25–34 yrs, 35–44 yrs, over 44 yrs; factory workers were divided differently: up to 25 yrs, 25–34 yrs, over 34 yrs. The survey relates to the second half of 1978.

In a decentralized industrial system such as this one, there will be an abundance and variety of outworkers amongst whom it becomes difficult to distinguish artisans from homeworkers. For the sake of convenience, we classify workers on the basis of the way they consider their own work. Therefore we define as homeworkers those who: (1) make no use of dependent labour; (2) do not utilize machinery or, at least, use only 'traditional' kinds of machine. Conversely, we classify as artisans those workers who: (1) avail themselves of some kind of dependent labour; (2) even when making no use of dependent labour whatever, utilize sophisticated types of machinery (automatic power looms or bobbin winders, etc.). It is worth noting that in Italian law a firm is defined as artisanal if it employs no more than ten workers (owners included) and up to five apprentices.

not evidence of economic backwardness.[2] On the contrary, an industrial structure consisting of firms of different size but with a large number of small and even 'microscopic' enterprises is increasingly being recognized as one possible avenue of economic development. Taking this for granted, the aim of these notes is to investigate the structure of the labour market in a prosperous area typified by economic growth which has the small firm as its base element.

The first two sections describe the industrial structure and the manufacturing processes; the second two analyse the different strata of the labour market; and the third two examine factors determining earnings, and the allocation of the work-force to the various jobs. The final section gives my conclusions.

## KNITWEAR AND READY-MADE GARMENTS: THE INDUSTRIAL STRUCTURE

### *The Industrial District*

The knitwear and ready-made garment industry is concentrated in Carpi and its surrounding boroughs which also constitute the local market within which workers are willing to move and do move comparatively freely. In this area the large majority of firms produce knitwear and ready-made garments; in these industries the level of vertical integration is low and so firms tend to specialize in one particular stage of production. Carpi and its surrounding area is a prime example of what Becattini calls an industrial 'district', for 'the elements uniting those firms making up the district . . . are a complex weave of external economies and diseconomies, interrelated costs and historical and cultural links which influence both business and personal relationships' (Becattini, 1979, p. 20).[3] These factors give cost advantages to the firm by virtue of favourable location, and form the basis for the development and maintenance of skills and specialized knowledge essential for the industrial system. In turn the concentration of skill and 'know-how' provides the foundation from which small businesses spring up, and from which 'that certain extra productivity' from labour derives (Becattini, 1979; Paci, 1978).

Such 'monocultural' areas characterized by a fragmented industrial structure have proved to have a remarkable capacity for resistance during times of crisis. This is due in no small part to the speed with which the industrial framework adjusts to changes in demand. In the last ten years Carpi's knitwear industry has demonstrated a marked vitality, despite wide fluctuations in manufacturing activity. Gross product and investment in fixed assets have increased and the industry has maintained its position in both the home and international market despite rapidly growing competition from third world countries. This success has preserved full employment.

2. See Bagnasco (1977); Bagnasco and Messori (1975); Brusco (1975, 1982); Capecchi 1978; Frey 1975; Paci (1975); Piore (1977, 1980); Rubery and Wilkinson (1981); Sabel (1982); Saliez (1979); Vianello (1975).
3. All quotations from Italian have been translated by me.

### *Industrial Organization*

The firms can be divided into three major categories:

1 firms with a comparatively high degree of vertical integration which produce directly for the consumer, which undertake all the main stages of production and which are only dependent on outside labour to a small degree;
2 subcontracting firms which undertake a single, intermediate stage of manufacture;
3 firms which have access to the consumer market, which produce individual styles and control the quality of the finished product within the plant but which commission outside labour for the larger proportion, and often the whole, of manufacture.

By Woodward's classification (1965) firms in groups one and two produce in large batches and small batches respectively whilst firms in group three produce 'prototypes' used to solicit orders which are then 'made-up'. The greater majority of the firms in group 1 are large (over 100 employees) whilst those in groups 2 and 3 are medium-sized or small.[4]

### *Market Organization*

The larger firms make standardized, generally good quality articles and operate as much in international as national markets. The small firms can be divided into two groups. The first group – firms which produce samples for the trade, receive orders and commission the manufacture externally, and also a fair number of subcontracting firms – have three notable characteristics. Firstly, by continuously redesigning products and diversifying production they show a marked capability of creating their own demand. These firms 'invent new needs and satisfy them at the same time. . . . The secret of this trick lies in the particulars of the firm's internal organization, its close relations with its clients and its collaboration with other firms in the sector' (Brusco and Sabel, 1981, p. 106). Secondly, they use advanced techniques which are comparable to those of the most successful large firms and are often equipped with the best machines available (ERVET, 1979). Moreover in industries such as knitwear and garment making where the manufacturing process may be fragmented without resorting to inferior techniques, small production units may benefit from the economies of scale. Becattini, quoting Marshall, argues

> the advantages of production on a large scale can in general be as well attained by the aggregation of a large number of small masters into one district as by the erection of a few large works. . . . In fact with regard to many classes of commodities it is possible to divide the process of production into several stages, each one of which can be performed with the maximum of economy in a small establishment. (Becattini, 1979, p. 19)

4. It is useful to point out that of the firms with fewer than twenty employees about 40 per cent produce for the consumer market.

The threshold level of operating efficiency at single stages of production is low enough in the knitwear and ready-to-wear industry to admit very small workshops (see Brusco, Giovannetti and Malagoli, 1979). For example, many knitting, stitching and finishing workshops employ from four to six workers. Finally, small firms are not necessarily or usually subordinate either in the market for their supplies or in their product markets. As Brusco observes:

> If subordination is to be judged by the 'capacity of one firm to limit the profits – and indirectly, in certain circumstances the wages of another', then the study of the firms functioning by filling orders, and the examination of their relations with the commissioning companies suggests that this really is not a widespread phenomenon. The subcontracting firms do not in fact usually operate in a monopsonistic market, where the power of the commissioning buyer is very strong, but rather in a market which, though by no means perfect, is basically a competitive one. (Brusco, 1975, p. 36)

This argument is also valid for the consumer market. Since, for the most part, the smaller production units have no direct channels to the market, their products bear the brandnames or trademarks of the wholesalers. Even here the opportunities are small for the commercial middleman to dominate the producers. The large numbers of wholesalers mean that they have little control over the market, and cannot 'make the price'.

The second group of small firms – small in number and much less representative – produce for the home market (in certain cases only for the local market) and manufacture lower quality articles. A not inconsiderable number of subcontracting firms also turn out lower quality components. These use a much lower level of technology and are in some instances merely 'offshoots' of other businesses. Frequently these firms operate on a margin of the market, springing up and vanishing with product market fluctuations.

## *Industrial Relations*

Industrial relations and working conditions vary widely with the size of firms and are determined by the degree of union organization and by aspects of Italy's labour legislation. In firms employing thirty employees and more union membership is high, the union is very strong, and has factory-level organization (Capecchi and Pugliese, 1978; FLM, 1977). From this well-organized position the unions can ensure compliance with social welfare provisions (sickness, pensions, etc.), enforce the *Statuto dei Lavoratori,* and obtain noticeable improvements upon the levels of pay and conditions agreed nationally. Moreover in medium-to-large factories workers have achieved significant control over the labour process and employment. Thus 'the presence of the union, and its involvement at every turn, make it extremely difficult for the management to dismiss workers. In fact, each time there is any difficulty it tends to become a political issue, the conditions for a strike are created, depositions are made to the Department of Employment, there is intervention by government agencies, etc.' (Capecchi, 1980, p. 30). In the smaller enterprises the picture is totally different: most have no shop-floor union organization, the legislation against unfair dismissals offers no protection in firms engaging fewer than fifteen persons, and workers are laid off at the first signs of a crisis. In many instances agreements between individual workers and the employer take precedence over collective contract, welfare norms are evaded, and variations in the workload and in working hours occur more frequently than in larger firms. The homeworking sector is even less well protected.

### *Relations with Other Areas*

Well-established Carpi firms frequently build new factories outside the region and direct a flow of orders to subcontractors in other areas, even at a distance from Carpi. In fact decentralization extends into the provinces of Mantua, Verona, Ferrara, Rovigo, Ancona, etc. Brusco (1982) has stressed that a 'core–periphery' relationship develops between areas where firms are long established, and those of recent establishment. The vast majority of firms, especially the smaller ones, have no access to the consumer market, are not usually equipped with sophisticated machinery, and carry out those stages of production with low value added. For the most part they make use of cheap labour: for example, 10 per cent of the employees of artisans in Modena are apprentices, whereas in other areas this proportion rises to 50 per cent (Malagoli and Mengoli, 1979). Similarly, the homeworkers are engaged in jobs calling for a lesser degree of qualification and (even where the job content is the same) are paid much less than their counterparts in Carpi. The periphery therefore provides core firms with the means of increasing profits, and gives the industrial structure an added degree of flexibility. In the event of a falling product market artisan subcontractors and homeworkers in Ferrara or Rovigo see a decline in the volume of orders well before outworks in Carpi. This shifting of risk to the periphery protects the core firms and allows greater security of employment and stability in labour relations even in small and 'mini' enterprises, and more continuity in the flow of orders to artisan businesses and home workers.

## THE MANUFACTURING PROCESS AND THE ACQUISITION OF SKILLS

Once the prototype has been developed and the patterns made the manufacturing process can be separated into knitting, shaping the knitted panels, making-up, finishing and pressing, quality control and packing. Not all the stages are indispensable and the number of single operations combining into a single production stage may vary according to the type and quality of the product. For example, in so-called 'diminishing-stitch' knitwear the cutting/shaping stage is eliminated; the making-up of 'fully-fashioned' garments invariably requires a greater number of single operations; and not every kind of product requires buttonholing and the attachment of buttons. The product's physical properties, its seasonal demand and the varying kinds of manufacturing techniques necessary for adapting to changes in fashion and to differing qualities of materials, are such that even the larger firms, with their longer production runs, are obliged to adopt remarkably flexible work organization. A change of product may require the rearrangement of what is usually termed the 'plant balance' and therefore involves worker mobility between machines within the same department and between departments.[5] Consequently it is not possible to define precise divisions between the different professional spheres. The scale of mechanization varies between the different stages of production. Only in the making-up operations and certain of the finishing operations are the machines engaged in different operations arranged in sequence so that production methods approximate to those of assembly lines. Most of the other processes use similar machines but not assembly line methods. Mechanization has gone furthest in knitting, certain kinds of finishing (embroidery) and, in some cases, cutting. Three types of automatic loom, the straight, the circular and the cotton loom, are used for knitting. Since cotton looms can be used effectively only for large batch production they are generally to be found in larger factories. Artisans and small enterprises mostly make use of circular machines and, above all, of straight looms.[6] All production line work uses more traditional fixed-cycle and single function power machines. This stage of the manufacturing process has not lent itself to automation, because of the special characteristics of material and of semi-finished products, and because of the physical properties of the final product, the profusion of styles and patterns and low levels of investment.[7] Two features of the operation of industrial sewing machines have an important bearing on the job content. About 70 per cent of the total work time is 'dead' time as the operator positions the work piece. On the other hand, when run at maximum speed the sewing machines produce six to eight thousand stitches per minute, so the 'real' work time is extremely intense. The successful operation of sewing machines therefore requires considerable manual dexterity and the demands of the machine limit the application of production line techniques and hence the degree of deskilling of the labour force. However, the relationship between mechanization and job qualification is by no means rigid (see table 12.1). The case of knitting is typical: even programmed machines will not run themselves. They require close attention and a great deal of intervention on the part of the operator and hence considerable knowledge of how the machine operates. Thus 'the intelligence of production has neither been built entirely into the machinery nor taken off the shop floor. It remains in the possession of the work force' (Noble, 1979, p. 42).

But the question of skill is not confined to the relationship between the operator and the machine. In an industry where the organization of production is so flexible, both inside and outside the factory, the question of professional skill centres not on manual ability and experience in the use of one particular machine but, rather, on the capability to operate a variety of machines and produce a range of qualities of weave. With this in mind, manual labour in the knitwear industry can be divided into three grades:

1 Craft workers: workers with complete knowledge of the manufacturing process, who may be utilized in any department, and who are capable of filling any position on the production line and performing any kind of

5. 'One may define the "balance" as being a process which aims at "optimizing" – in terms of time and cost – a set of individual jobs whose sequence is submitted . . . to specific constraints of precedence, and/or current contingencies' (Coriat, 1979, p. 121).
6. Looking at the relationship between technology and the structure of industry, the ascendancy of the straight loom over the 'cotton' would seem to be the most significant consequence of production decentralization and fragmentation.
7. For similar reasons it has been difficult to automate the making-up of footwear (Bright, 1958).

TABLE 12.1 Stage of production, degree of automation and worker qualification

| *Production* | *Automation* | *Worker qualification* |
|---|---|---|
| Sample | No | Craft |
| Knitting | Yes | Craft<br>Skilled operatives |
| Cutting/shaping | Yes/no | Craft<br>Skilled operatives |
| Making-up | No | Craft<br>Skilled operatives<br>Semi-skilled operatives |
| Finishing | Yes/no | Craft<br>Skilled operatives<br>Semi-skilled operatives |
| Pressing | No | Skilled operatives |
| Control/packaging | No | Semi-skilled operatives |

stitching, and workers who style, design and check products and who therefore have high skill and heavy responsibility.

2 Skilled machine operators: these include skilled production line workers and such non-production line workers as loom operators and pressers.
3 Semi-skilled machine operators: production line workers carrying out simple finishing and operating only one power machine, plus workers engaged in quality control and packing of the finished product.

Such skills cannot be regarded as firm-specific since the same product can be manufactured either by a large firm or by a group of co-ordinated small firms. Nevertheless, the features distinguishing types of firms are of central importance in determining the skill and knowledge of the workers. The large firms employ a heterogeneous work-force, with semi-skilled and skilled operators and craft workers within the same establishment. On the other hand the smaller firms' work-forces are more homogeneous, and the degree of skill and experience is dependent upon both the quality of the product and the kind of production techniques adopted. Subcontractors which carry out quality knitting or making-up employ skilled operatives and craft workers, whilst workers employed in firms where the finished products are inspected and packaged, or those carrying out special types of finishing (pleating, embroidering, etc.), are generally semi-skilled. It should also be noted that production line workers in the smaller firms have greater manual ability and superior knowledge of the manufacturing process than do their counterparts in the larger firms. Small firms have less rigid demarcation practices, require a greater degree of individual responsibility and process a wider variety of materials than large firms. However, in both large and small firms skills are acquired by a long period of 'on-the-job training', although the learning process is more rapid in small firms where production runs are shorter and hence experience is more varied. Finally, firms which put out the mass production of their prototype samples employ highly skilled workers. These firms have no production line and the workers collaborate closely in the designing of new models; moreover, the smaller the firm, the greater the individual contribution made by each worker. Each worker, if not actually designing products, knows every aspect of the job in the creation and adaptation of new models with the consequence that dividing lines between manual labour and intellectual effort tends to disappear (Brusco and Sabel, 1981).

Although the principal means by which professional abilities are acquired is by working in a factory, it is not, however, the only way. In such a 'mono-cultural' area, skills can be learned from the worker's mother, friend or relative who may be a home or factory worker. By this kind of apprenticeship sufficient skill will be acquired for a limited number of single tasks, but not an extensive expert knowledge of the manufacturing process.

Finally, the skills required in the knitwear and ready-to-wear clothing industry tend to be industry-specific. The tools and machines used in factory production differ markedly from those in the made-to-measure clothing trade and there is no continuity between the skills in the latter and those of factory workers. Even more tenuous is the link between household and industrial production, or with experience acquired in other industrial sectors and that needed in the knitwear and ready-to-wear clothing industry.

## HOMEWORKERS, PRODUCTION LINE WORKERS AND ARTISANS

There are considerable differences in the age and sex composition of the three categories. Production line workers and homeworkers are generally women whilst a large proportion of artisans are men. Futhermore, only a small fraction of the artisans and homeworkers are less than twenty-five years of age although the greater majority of factory workers are in this category. Lastly, women of forty to forty-five years of age more often than not work at home rather than in the factory.

Homeworkers, production line workers and artisans are mainly local labour or long-established immigrants and with the exception of certain young artisans are low both in scholastic achievement and social means. Recruitment into the industry can be divided into two main periods. In the 1950s and the first half of the 1960s the source of labour was the exodus from the rural areas, resulting from the combined effects of the crisis in the sharecropping farming system, and the increasing industrialization of the region. From the second half of the 1960s the main source of labour was from within the industry and the inflow of labour from other sectors slowed down markedly. The shape of industry during the first period differs in many ways from that existing today.[8] The 1950s and early 1960s

8. The industrial structure in the 1950s and early 1960s, in comparison with that of the present day, is essentially characterized as follows: in terms of job density, large firms outweighing the small; the more general diffusion of homeworking; and the existence of true 'intermediaries', that is 'links' between firms and out-workers. Against a background of growing international competition for standardized products, and a strengthening of trade union organization within the factories, many firms have tended to push out the middle stages of the manufacturing process. The imposition of VAT in 1971 and the passing of legislation concerning homeworkers in 1973 have meant that the route to 'undeclared' home labour (i.e. unprotected in terms of welfare) has become much more tortuous. The combined effects of these factors have brought about intense modifications in the structure of the industry. On the one hand, it has enlarged the proportion of firms developing prototypes and on the other – equally important – it has changed the general structure of out-work: intermediaries have more or less disappeared; homeworkers have reduced considerably; a large number of small subcontracting firms has sprung up (Malagoli and Mengoli, 1979; Solinas, 1981).

was an era of high unemployment and underemployment. In this period there was limited mobility between the different segments of the labour market, particularly between different sized firms, and most job changes resulted from dismissal. From the mid 1960s the industry increasingly adopted the 'contours' which it has retained. An important difference between the periods before and after the mid 1960s is the growing evidence from the latter period of the willingness of workers to move around within and between the different submarkets: from large to small firms, and from the firms into self-employment. It is on this second period that the analysis will be particularly centred.

In terms of pay, conditions of work, job characteristic and career patterns there is considerable overlap between homeworkers, factory workers and artisans. Features such as 'cash-in-hand' arrangements, underpayment, absence of union protection and collective sickness and insurance benefits are not exclusive to the sphere of homeworkers. More than 50 per cent of production line workers, and a comparable proportion of the artisans, have completed at least two years in a factory without any form of legal contract. Similarly, the termination of apprenticeship by dismissal, or the extension of apprenticeship beyond the normally accepted duration, was widespread even quite recently. Voluntary quitting is a common occurrence and the search for employment is not made through official channels (employment bureaux and the like) or union organizations: knowledge of the market and the nature of job opportunities is widespread and employment is sought amongst friends, relatives and through other social networks (Rees, 1966). Employers, especially small operators, make full use of similar channels when recruiting labour, by utilizing the grapevine existing between their own employees and acquaintances or by other informal methods (Mackay et al., 1971). It is also not uncommon for firms to employ workers who apply directly (Reynolds, 1971). Furthermore, the tightness of the labour market means that the periods of unemployment are very short especially when the worker quits voluntarily.

A consideration of the work histories of production line workers, homeworkers and artisans shows considerable mobility between home-based work and employment in small firms and large firms. Of those surveyed, one homeworker in four had been employed in large or medium-to-large firms (more than forty-nine employees) and one production line worker in three had worked at home; small and very small firms (fewer than twenty employees) recruited 30 per cent of workers from either production-line employment or home-based work; and amongst the artisans 20 per cent had been employed in large firms and 23 per cent in small firms, and 27 per cent had worked at home. Of the female artisans more than 50 per cent had previously been homeworkers.

There is no regular progression from homework and small firms to large firms. A study of the last ten years shows no evidence of any 'one-way' mobility carrying workers away from labour submarkets unprotected by unions into submarkets offering such protection. It is by no means rare for workers to quit large firms for employment in small firms. Such moves have been made by factory workers, homeworkers and particularly artisans. From interviews with the latter it emerges that no less than one in five artisans moved from large to small firms. In addition, 'homework' – which for most workers was the last stage in their career – also served as a stop-gap between factory jobs. It is also not uncommon to find spells of homework separated by stints of factory employment.

The routes by which skill is acquired are no more clearly defined than are the mobility chains. Progress from semi-skilled to the craft level may be achieved by advance within a large firm, or between small firms, or by a sequence of changes between firms of different size. Nevertheless, a comparison of the careers of production-line workers compared with those of the homeworkers and artisans allows three broad conclusions.

1 It is unusual for a movement between jobs to involve a loss of skill, mobility is generally along skill bands or not infrequently to higher skill levels.
2 'Ports of entry' into production work can be through large firms, or small subcontracting firms. The latter will, however, only hire inexperienced workers if very young. The specialized sample-producing firms normally take on only skilled and craft workers.[9]
3 Only large firms provide vertical mobility between each grade. But even in a large firm progress to the higher grades will be gained by only a small proportion of employees. The semi-skilled areas of large firms are 'transit zones' from which workers will be moved on after a relatively short time.

Thus there are two barriers to vertical mobility. The first, the most important, operates between small production units, and denies access to workers who are either unqualified, or no longer young, seeking entry into firms carrying out sophisticated and complex manufacturing procedures. The second operates within large firms, and constitutes a discriminatory barrier between the bulk of skilled operatives and workers who hold key positions in the factory (for example, sample producers and foremen).

There are, then, two transitional steps from the lowest to the highest professional level: one which takes the semi-skilled worker from the small to large firm; the other which leads the skilled worker from the large firm towards the smaller and, particularly, towards firms producing samples. Both steps require higher skill levels and consequently represent a promotion in the job ladder.

Since labour recruitment among the small firms is not subject to any kind of union-imposed constraints, the firms are free to base their recruitment policy on the match between experience or skill and the company's manufacturing characteristics. Consequently the relatively unskilled or the less able gravitate towards those firms carrying out functions in which the actual labour content is lower (embroidery, quality control and packaging, pleating, stitching of low quality materials, etc.). For such workers, the best opportunity to acquire professional knowledge and skills will be employment in a large firm. Indeed in large firms union control means that management is less selective in its hiring policy and ensures that most employees will manage some professional progress. Progress from packaging, the 'transit zone' for recently-engaged unskilled workers, depends on workers' and union control over the labour process rather

9. The fact that subcontracting firms carrying out knitting or making-up will take on unskilled labour, but only very young (preferably under eighteen years of age), would seem to be due to the lower cost, and the higher 'potential' productivity of that labour supply. Not only, in fact, will they be taken on as apprentices and therefore paid less; but they will also be easily 'pressured', and likely to succumb to the paternalistic kind of climate that is inherent in those small manufacturing units (Vianello, 1975). These advantages, however, cannot compensate for lack of skill in a firm of the kind which produces samples.

than, as is the case of the allocation of workers between small firms, skill and experience. Once on the production line, workers acquire skill by movement between jobs within and between departments. Only a small proportion of workers are promoted to key positions in the manufacturing process, and to the sample production department; moreover such transfers are managerial prerogatives with unions exercising little, if any, control. Thus the achievement of the highest skill level within large firms does not depend on a formal promotion system or on specific manning. Therefore access to the higher rungs of the job ladder for the large majority of production line workers is gained by winning entry into the 'upper stratum' of small firms. Mobility towards the smaller enterprises furnishes the worker with the ability to circumvent those obstacles to promotion resulting from managerial control of the top jobs in large firms.

The worker's career therefore evolves out of a succession of changes from one firm to another of differing size, as shown in figure 12.1. This results not only from the particular industrial structure and the specialist nature of the smaller firm, but also from the 'industrial relations system' governing the working relationship within small and large factories, and from policies of restraint pursued by larger firms in the sphere of craft labour.

Periods of working at home, while prolonging the time taken to rise to higher skill levels, do not usually break the factory career. It is rare to find examples where the move from home to factory work involves a downgrading of jobs. Generally the homeworking and factory jobs are on a similar skill level.

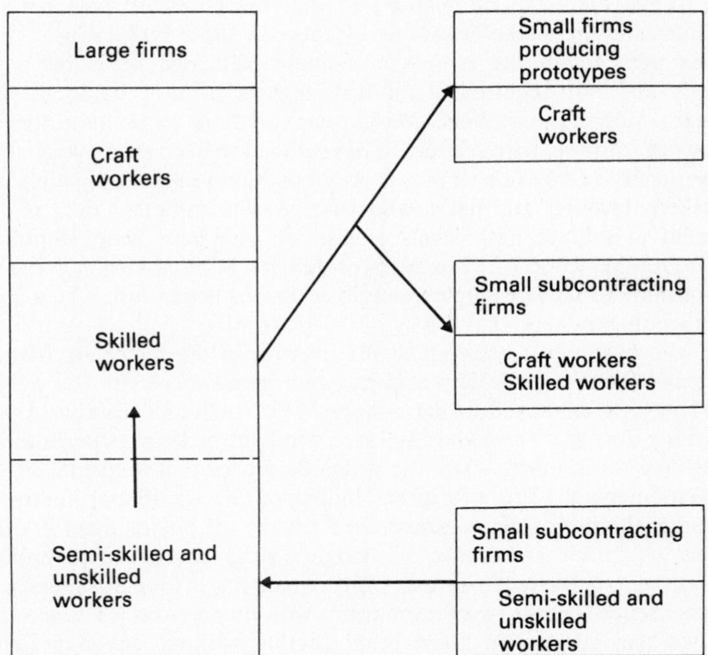


FIGURE 12.1 Directions of labour mobility and the acquisition of skill

## THE INTERNAL COMPOSITION OF THE CATEGORIES

### *Classification of Homeworkers*

Homeworkers can be classified into two groups on the basis of their 'career line', on the length of time spent working in the factory, and the kind of firm by which they were employed.

Thirty-four per cent of homeworkers surveyed were ex-factory production-line workers with a long history of skilled labour. Nearly all became homeworkers between the ages of twenty-five and thirty. In the course of eight or more years of factory employment they became highly skilled in at least one operation and usually mastered a range of operations calling for a medium to high degree of skill. Almost all of them are familiar with many aspects of the manufacturing process: they have operated many different kinds of machine, worked either with knitwear or with fabric, and performed various tasks on the production line. Their main attributes are ability and versatility, enabling them to adjust readily to changes in demand. They have little difficulty in switching to different kinds of work when new products and styles are in demand and when articles require special types of manufacture. Their ability to diversify also allows them to change buyers easily, and they are not necessarily formally hired by a firm. But this does not imply a lack of bargaining power. In fact, female workers who enjoy the security of a working husband often have no interest whatever in 'formalizing' their labour relations. There are also many cases where there is mutual agreement to avoid formal employment relations so that the employer pays no welfare contributions and the worker avoids tax (Capecchi, 1980; Fuà, 1976).

Sixty-six per cent of the sample of homeworkers had never been factory workers or had not acquired significant degrees of skill whilst in factory employment. Most of the workers aged 40 years and more are in this group, which can be divided into two main sections. Those who have been employed in the factory are generally ex-stitchers employed on production lines for only short periods or ex-packers, labellers and fixers who have spent insufficient time in factory employment to acquire high levels of skill or who have been employed on relatively unskilled work. The low levels of skill can be explained by frequent job changes or more usually be employment in a subcontracting firm where low-skill processes are undertaken.

Those who have never been employed in firms in the sector are mainly ex-labourers and farm-hands. Many of these were homeworkers in the 1950s and 1960s, whilst still employed in agriculture. This traditional Emilian worker – homeworking during winter, and then rice and fruit picking, labouring or odd-jobbing during the summer – was the principal source of low-cost labour in the early development of Carpi's knitwear industry. The traditional homeworkers often perform the sort of jobs commissioned 'out' by the buying firms in the early period but which, either because of changes in the product or in production techniques, are gradually dying out. The remainder of homeworkers without factory experience is made up of immigrants with no previous job experience, or manual workers coming in from other sectors without any experience of knitwear.

Homeworkers in the second category are normally engaged in jobs demanding a low degree of skill. Only the small minority move from simple to more complex operations. Furthermore, because of limited skill and experience, the relatively unskilled homeworkers are unable to adjust rapidly to changes in demand. The disadvantages of low skill levels and lack of adaptability place the second category of homeworkers at the mercy of the buyer. They are not hired by the commissioning firm because of their lack of bargaining power. Their employment is also susceptible to variation in demand, both seasonal and cyclical, and therefore in every sense they are marginal workers.

### *Classification of Production-Line Workers*

Production-line workers employed in the larger firms can be broadly classified into three groups by the length of time spent at work in the knitwear and ready-made section, and by age.

Workers who have completed no more than five years in the sector accounted for 29 per cent of the sample. Of these the highest proportion are under twenty-five years old. These are young girls working in their first job or who have been apprentices in the 'lower strata' of the small subcontracting firms. Few have ever worked at home. There is little difference between youngsters from small firms and those with no previous work experience except that the former who can stitch are put straight onto the production line, whilst the latter work on the control and packaging stations, or act as assistants for other workers. These girls carry out simple operations which require little skill but where great speed is essential (attachment of hooks, buttons and labels, etc.). Similar tasks are assigned to young women who are unskilled or have come into the industry from another sector.

Women of between twenty-five and forty years of age who have not less than six to eight years experience in the industry made up 62 per cent of the sample. These include long service workers in large firms, workers from small subcontracting firms and workers who have experienced both factory and home working. The different types of experience have no substantial effect on the workers' role in the factory. Those with continuous employment with large firms do the same jobs as those from small firms and as ex-homeworkers. However, nearly all have changed jobs and have worked in different departments. These are the most mobile element, production-line workers capable of carrying out a wide range of operations which, on occasion, call for a high degree of manual dexterity. In firms specializing in making-up ready-to-wear articles the organization hinges upon this section of the work force.

The rest of the sample – around 9 per cent – are forty years old or more and have usually worked for twenty or more years in industry. They may be ex-homeworkers or workers from small firms, or have been continuously employed in larger firms, and they have a thorough knowledge of the manufacturing process. However, they no longer possess the speed required for flow production and the majority have been transferred to other departments (especially pressing) while those who remain on making-up are given special jobs. In fact, most skilled and specialist workers in this age group either instruct apprentices, or do those jobs requiring a great deal of craft but where speed is less essential, for example 'making good' and finishing off, especially fine garments (attachment of trimmings, picking up threads, etc.).

### *Classification of Artisans*

Artisans can be divided into two groups by the length of time since setting up in business.

Twenty per cent of the artisans set up in business during the 1950s and the early 1960s. In this group, men outnumber women by two to one. The typical case history here would be of a salesman, travelling in knitwear, ready-to-wear or similar types of garments. This 'trader-entrepreneur' became independent by commissioning orders from the homeworkers – usually from his wife – before taking on his own first employees. Also typical of this era were tailors who were proprietors of small 'workshops' with one or two employed helpers but who made the transition from the rapidly declining 'bespoke' tailoring. Examples can also be found of workers without knowledge of either the market or the manufacturing process who nevertheless established small firms.

The early artisans were amongst the founders of the area's knitwear and ready-made garment businesses. Their particular traits were the ability to create a market for their own product, to develop new articles, and to organize a 'circle' of homeworkers. Moreover the oldest of artisan firms in this group were established in the same years as some of the bigger firms and both types of entrepreneurs have similar professional backgrounds. These 'artisanal' firms normally employ six to eight workers, and control a considerable volume of out-work. They turn out high quality goods, mainly for the consumer market, and have a turnover which is estimated to vary between £430,000 and £738,000 (at 1978 prices) and realize a margin over costs of not less than 30–35 per cent.

A 'second generation' of artisans set up shop from the second half of the 1960s onwards and provided 80 per cent of the sample. Unlike the first group, these are a product of the development of the sector and consist of men and women in equal proportion. For analytical purposes, it will be useful to distinguish between those who are ex-homeworkers and those who are ex-factory employees.

In more than half of the cases canvassed, the ex-homeworkers had factory experience but had become intermediaries between one, or more, firms and a 'circle' of homeworkers. Partly on their own initiative, and partly under pressure from the commissioning firms – particularly in the case of firms registered since the passing of legislation regarding homeworking, and the imposition of VAT – the parasitical 'middleman' or 'ringleader' without legal status has been transformed into a small entrepreneur. Many of these firms continue to maintain a structure reminiscent of the homeworker 'circle', employing few internal employees and a 'tight-knit network' of homeworkers to produce for other firms.

The most representative of the new generation of artisans who quit the factory to become self-employed are the specialist workers or the foremen. These may come from small or large firms or may have 'stepped up' the ladder by moving from a big to a small factory. One typical example is the woman who first of all worked at home for ten years, then was employed for six years on the production lines of two large knitwear factories, before 'up-grading' her skill level by moving to a small subcontracting firm. Finally she became foreman with an even smaller fashion business before setting up on her own. A second representative example is the artisan who went from skilled worker in a large concern to being head of department in a much smaller business; from there her career advanced in two stages to the head of department in successively larger firms.

Other typical male artisans were originally employed in the mechanical engineering industry and associated textile machinery sector. These were skilled in the production and maintenance of knitwear manufacturing machinery and established small production units supplying knitted cloth to the trade, a progression which has its own rationale. The supervision of the production of one or more powerlooms requires more in the way of the ability to keep the machine running efficiently than skill and dexterity in its operation.

Only a very small minority of the self-employed are not former skilled workers, or are not knowledgeable about the manufacturing process. In these cases it is usual for the artisan to have either entered into partnership in an existing business, or been employed in the knitwear industry (as for example a driver, or more often a warehouseman). In a firm engaged in making-up, these are the people in direct contact with the out-work. Not infrequently this grade of worker was delegated overseer of a 'circle' of homeworkers and from there progressed to self-employment.

Amongst the younger self-employed are those who have stepped from white-collar jobs to artisan positions. They come mostly from the smaller firms and are familiar with technical and administrative organization and have a central role in maintaining contact with suppliers, and clients, as well as co-ordinating the out-work.

Finally, a sizeable proportion of the 'second generation' of male artisans owe their status to being the sons or husbands of ex-'ringleaders', of ex-homeworkers, or of ex-factory workers. Some are 'heirs' who, before taking over the business, will train by securing employment with another firm, usually as a white-collar worker. The husbands who became artisans were usually workers in various industries who continued to be employed until their wives' businesses were sufficiently well established to guarantee sufficient income to allow the husband to give up his employment to take over managerial responsibility. In a sector where the work force is predominantly female and where skills are traditionally 'female property' the woman has a leading role in production whilst the husband has mainly administrative responsibility.

Between second-generation artisanal firms prosperity varies widely. Some enterprises produce for the consumer market, others for the trade market. Within this overall picture, a fairly typical stitching subcontractor with a staff of about six will have a turnover of something between £184,000 and £307,000, yielding a margin over cost of not less than 20–30 per cent, and an average of three to five commissioning buyers in any one year. However many firms have levels of turnover comparable with long-established firms, while others are very small indeed.

## FACTORS DETERMINING THE ALLOCATION OF LABOUR ACROSS THE MARKET

This section considers the factors determining differences in career pattern, variation in experiences within the skill strata and the allocation of workers to the various segments of the labour market. An important first question is what influences the choice between home and factory work.

Up to twenty years ago there was an extensive industrial reserve army in the Emilia region of Italy, made up of labourers, poor smallholders, peasants, farmhands and others. Then, the factors determining the allocation to factory or homework were different. The demand for labour in the firms was directed predominantly towards women who had acquired some degree of skill through having worked at home. Thus for the great majority of older women, as indeed for many of the younger workers, homeworking constituted the only possibility for employment. The firms – in those years especially the larger firms – 'creamed off' the more productive and professionally skilled element in the female workforce whilst the 'weaker' element gravitated towards the homeworking sector. Furthermore, many women who had a principally 'rural' background worked at home on a strictly part-time basis and regarded this activity as complementary to their rural waged labour. These women had a relationship with the industry which gave them no incentive to acquire professional skills and, in many cases, they did not seek factory employment (Sabel, 1979). However, the development of the knitwear and ready-to-wear industry has created an 'indigenous' labour force.

An examination of the careers and the family households of homeworkers, factory workers and artisans suggests that in half the cases spells of homeworking coincide with two sets of circumstances. Homework was usual where the woman had one or more children of pre-school age or the family included an aged relative or someone requiring constant attention and where there was no other woman within the family who could take over these domestic responsibilities. Conversely, those interviewed had worked in the factory when they were still living with their original family and when, although married, either had no children or children who were sufficiently grown up to be left alone. Where there were small children the tendency was for mothers to work in a factory only when an extended family household included another woman – mother, or mother-in-law – who either did not work or was herself a homeworker.

Women working in the factory then are, for the most part, those without heavy domestic responsibilities or from households where there were sufficient women to allow factory work and home duties to coexist 'peacefully'. As C. Saraceno observes: 'The inclusion of mother or mother-in-law within the family unit provides the domestic labour (including care of children) which would otherwise become precarious or impossible as a result of the wife's going out to work. By contrast, where such an inclusion is not possible . . . the economic necessity may draw the woman into working at home' (Saraceno, 1976, p. 105). It is worth noting that inter-generational family ties in the sense of 'mutual assistance' and economic relations which do not necessarily depend on cohabitation are of considerable importance. For example, there are many women who, although belonging to a simple family unit with small children, can continue in factory employment by delegating household duties to 'grannies' who live elsewhere.[10]

10. It is the writer's conviction that the presence of extended family households in the region and, what is more, the continuance of strong ties between families of differing generations is the main factor on the labour supply side allowing a high rate of female activity (as far as direct employment in the factories is concerned). In such circumstances, it is clear that the hardest-hit women will be the immigrants, those who have no means of turning to their families of origin for 'support'. It is in this area that one should look for answers as to why women from outlying provinces and central and southern Italy are obliged to work at home, rather than in discriminatory practices on the part of employers.

The research thus leads to the conclusion that the main factor regulating the allocation of women workers between homework and factory work is differentiation of family labour supply determined by the characteristics of its individual members, the family structure, and those inter-family relationships.[11]

The family position of women is an important determinant of their careers. Although many women do not interrupt their working career and many others return to the factory once the domestic situation permits, the job trajectory of most women is characteristically progression from the factory towards homeworking.

> Thus the women's career line seems to be an inversion of the men's which typically sees a progression at least until 45–50 years of age, to jobs of higher skill and status. In contrast women reach the highest level in their career whilst young . . .; then with the marriage and the arrival of the children . . . they move away from the central sector of the labour market . . . to return at length . . . into the marginal areas. (May, 1977, p. 62)

The age of workers is the second factor determining the allocation of labour to homework. Large and, even more, smaller firms operating a production line are very reluctant to take on workers of over forty years of age. Their efficiency, measured in terms of speed, is lower than average and after a certain age opportunities for factory employment dwindle.

The allocation of women to homeworking is therefore a product both of 'selection' within the market of the weaker strata of the labour force and of out-market factors determined by family responsibility. In this respect there is a close connection between the employment policy of the firms and the organization of working-class families. The firm discriminates against the older woman on the grounds of productivity and the family assigns to them domestic responsibilities. The younger women have secondary roles within the family and, being more in demand in the labour market, pursue full-time employment.

There is however a third reason which prompts certain women to abandon factory employment for homework which is independent of their relative efficiency and household responsibilities. Some women choose to work at home because of the greater degree of autonomy they enjoy in being able to organize their work. The homeworker is obliged to follow the required methods and to meet deadlines. Nonetheless, homeworking allows her to escape – in no small way – the control exercised by the 'bosses' in small firms, and by the 'hierarchy' in larger firms. These women forgo the advantages of direct employment in the factory in favour of a greater freedom to decide how much, how long, and how to work.

The principal factor which differentiates artisans from both homeworkers and factory workers is their degree of professional ability. The analysis of the previous section shows that workers who leave the factory in order to set up in business on their own generally have a thorough knowledge of the manufacturing process and, moreover, are capable of organizing and managing production. Whether owners of a firm producing for the consumer market or of one producing

11. Other surveys carried out in Italy in recent years come to somewhat similar conclusions (Ascoli, 1977; Balbo, 1973, 1978; Comba and Pizzini, 1975; Del Boca and Turvani, 1979; Saraceno, 1980).

intermediate goods, the artisans are the most skilled among their own employees, and they have organizing and other reponsibilities comparable with those of heads of department or production managers in the larger firms. They undertake the more complex manufacturing operations, organize the production line and manage the labour force. There are other bases for developing small businesses including administrative experience and the knowledge of the operation of the out-work system of the warehousemen. On the other hand access to skill, a knowledge of the manufacturing process, the internal structure of the firm and entry to the out-work system have been, and still are, generally the necessary conditions for establishing a small firm. Given these requirements, in a sector where technological barriers to entry are very low and demand in the product market is high, the decision to open a small business production unit is essentially a matter of willingness to do so. In these circumstances 'what is striking is not how many become artisans, but how many of those who are able do not' (Brusco, 1982, p. 175).

Finally it will be clear that the kind of tight personal and social relationships, the concentration of firms producing similar commodities, and the tradition of a ready movement from worker to artisan status must be taken very seriously into account when considering the differentiation of the supply of labour.

Professional skill not only provides a yardstick for determining the borderline between artisans and the other two categories of workers, but also provides a method of classifying homeworkers and production-line workers. However, the conditions for acquiring that skill also play a major role in allocating workers between labour market segments. Skill acquisition depends upon the chances of employment with one of the small innovating firms, the type of work carried out there and, in larger firms, the relative bargaining power of workers. Since skill and know-how are products of on-the-job experience and the worker's position within the factory, and since these depend largely upon the age of the worker and the skill acquired by that age, critical importance must be attached to the 'point of departure' of the career line. For example, a woman who comes into knitwear and ready-made from another industry will be employed on simple semi-skilled work; should she be forced to leave the factory for any reason with little experience she will become an extremely 'weak' homeworker, easily pressured by the buyer, and probably not formally employed by the commissioning firm – in every sense a marginal worker.

## FACTORS DETERMINING INCOME

The income of the artisan has two components: profit and wages (Sylos-Labini, 1974). Profit can be regarded as being determined by the degree of technology incorporated into the machinery, the product market, the type and quality of the product and the methods of production undertaken, and the level of wages. The possible variety in these variables means wide income differentials. At one extreme some artisans earn little more than a 'rich' homeworker, whereas other artisans earn as much as the owners of substantial firms.

The second component – wages – is a product of skill, effort and time. Skills being equal, even artisans belonging to the lowest group earn more than craft workers and foremen employed in the larger firms, although much of this difference may be accounted for by the longer hours worked by artisans. Even where the profit is at a minimum - in a family business with one or two dependants and a low level of investment in machinery - a high income can be obtained at the cost of hard, continuous work.

Homeworkers are paid by the piece. Their remuneration is determined by the type of work, their physical efficiency (determined at least partly by age) and the length of the working day. The highest-paid workers are those whose jobs demand the highest level of skill, for example cutting, sample production, making-up involving complicated operations; the worst-paid are those who do hand-finishing and other semi-skilled jobs. Relative earnings are therefore determined mainly by skills but the product market is an important influence on the level of pay. Changes in demand are rapidly reflected both in type and quality of articles, in the kind of out-work commissioned and consequently in the homeworkers' earnings. In these circumstances the ability to switch from one kind of work to another is an important determinant of earnings. The more versatile homeworkers receive hourly pay 25–30 per cent higher than the less experienced. The third important determinant of homeworker earnings is age. Individual tasks being equal, the hourly rate of earning decreases with age. Moreover, limited chances of employment in the firms for older workers and weaker competition among firms for less productive homeworkers will be translated into lower earnings. Homeworkers over forty years of age earn roughly a third less than their younger counterparts. The combination of differences in age and skill gives rise to wide wage differentials and an older worker carrying out a simple task may draw a wage as much as seven times less than a young skilled worker. The latter will at times receive higher hourly earnings than a similarly skilled worker employed in a large firm. Normally homeworkers work around the same number of hours as factory workers but the opportunities exist for longer working hours and hence higher pay than is taken home from the factory. Lastly, there is no evidence of any significant wage differentiation between workers directly employed by the commissioning firm and homeworkers who are not directly employed.

Earnings of workers employed in small firms are determined by the same variables as homeworker earnings. Those who are experienced, versatile, fast and willing to put in long hours have higher, and at times very much higher, levels of wages than comparable workers in the larger firms, whilst the reverse is true in the case of older, or less able workers.

Production-line workers' wages are determined by national agreements. The wage differentials (for example those relating to skills) are the products of a continuing bargaining process and have been eroded by the egalitarian policies pursued by unions during the 1970s. The presence of the unions within the large factory ensures that the national labour contract is applied, and also that the 'work-place margin' from production bonuses and other local additions will be at least partly controlled by the workers' organizations. Similarly, working hours are subject to union control at both national and company level. As a result, pay differentials within the large firms are narrower than outside and those factors which result in such wide earnings disparities between homeworkers and the employees of small firms, whilst present, are much less important in large firms. There wage differentials between the top and bottom grade of between 10 and 15 per cent are not unusual. Moreover the classification into the various pay grades does not depend only on skill. The production-line workers interviewed were divided into three pay groups and only in certain cases did inclusion in the highest group depend exclusively on skills. More usually grading of workers was determined by the company contract, the terms of which varied according to the strength of union organization amongst workers in the different firms. In the large firms then, age, skill, and the willingness to work long hours do not substantially affect the level and the structure of pay.

The brief analysis allows us to arrive at three important conclusions:

1 Whether employed in well unionized or weakly unionized firms, or whether working in a factory or at home, it is possible to get a relatively high wage.
2 In the large firm, high wages are gained through the strength of workers' organization; in the 'unprotected' sector they are tied to a worker's productivity and individual bargaining power which depends on scarcity.
3 Thus, for skilled workers with wide experience and at the height of their power, allocation among the various submarkets – especially the movement from large firms to small, and from thence to homeworking – does not necessarily reduce earnings and may well increase them; on the other hand relatively high earnings of older workers and those with lower levels of skill and little experience depend very much on employment in large firms.

## SUMMARY AND CONCLUSIONS

The main features of the labour market in Carpi are outlined in table 12.2. The first distinction that can be made is between large and small firms. The main feature of the large firm sector is the high degree to which workers are safeguarded both by legislation, which is effectively implemented, and trade union organization. In the small firm sector some parts of the labour legislation do not apply and, moreover, evasion is more common, the majority of workers are not effectively unionized and employment is less secure than in larger firms.

In the large factories there are wide skill differences, but unionization and union policy prevent wide wage differentials. However in the small firm sector wage differences depend on the one hand on the characteristics of the firm (technology, product and product market condition) and on the other on worker characteristics (skill, age and social and family position). Workers employed in firms which produce prototypes and subcontract production and in the 'non-subordinate' subcontracting firms turning out high quality pieces and using advanced technology have a thorough knowledge of manufacturing methods and receive high pay, often more than skilled workers employed in the large firms. In the smaller 'subordinate' and/or less technologically well-equipped firms, earnings for less well-qualified workers are substantially lower than those for comparable workers in large firms. The outworker labour force is similarly segmented, job insecurity, exploitation and low pay coexisting with high levels of professional capability, job security and pay (Capecchi, 1980).

TABLE 12.2 Characteristics[a] in different types of firms

| | *Large factories* | *Small firms producing prototypes or small non-'subordinate' subcontracting firms with 'good technology'* | *Small 'subordinate' subcontracting firms or firms with poor technology* | *Artisans* | *Homeworkers: upper stratum* | *Homeworkers: lower stratum* |
|---|---|---|---|---|---|---|
| Union protection | + | − | − | [b] | − | − |
| Job security | + | ± | − | + | ± | − |
| Degree of skill | ± | + | − | + | + | − |
| Career prospects | ± | + | − | + | ± | − |
| Level of income | + | + | − | + | + | − |

[a] The plus and minus signs indicate the relative job quality and the job characteristic. Where both plus and minus signs appear it means that the quality of the job characteristic varies both within and between firms.
[b] Artisans are not usually union members but belong to their own associations.

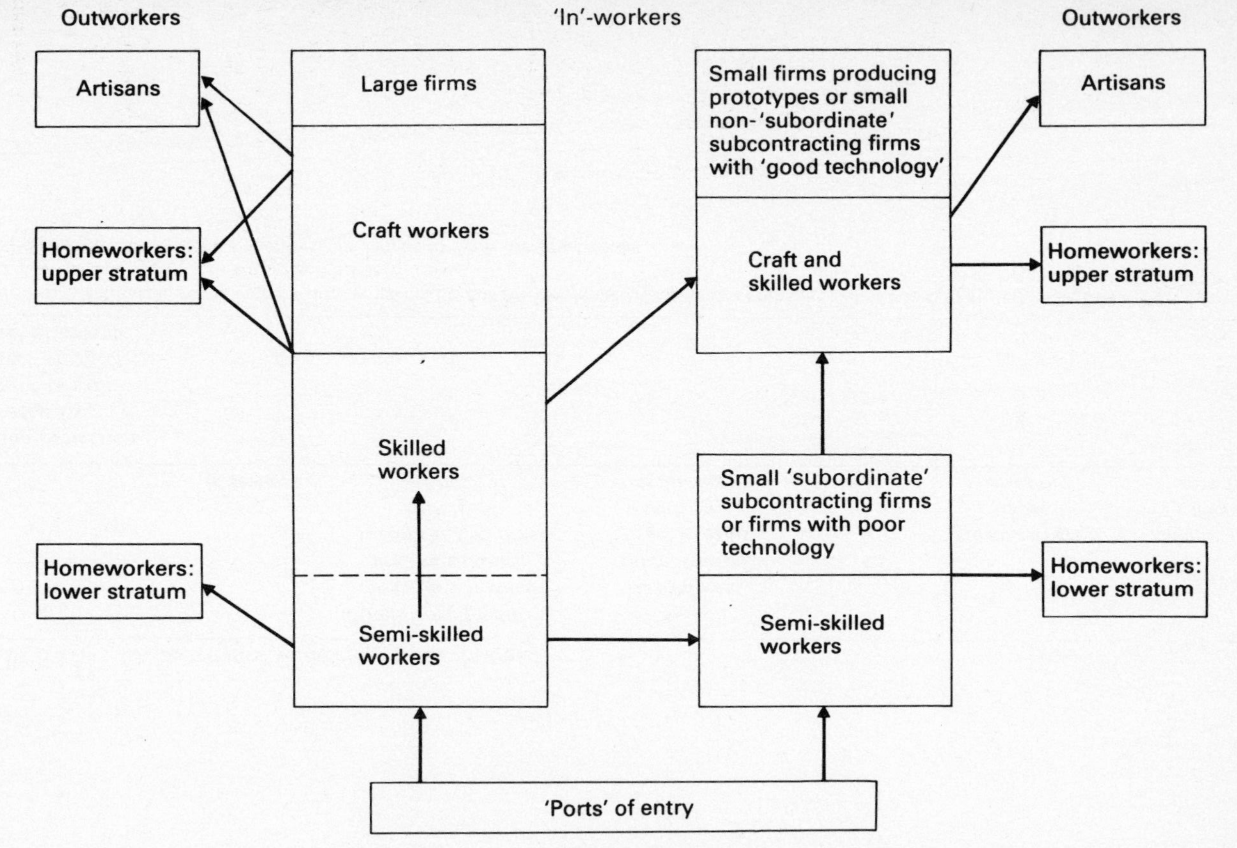


FIGURE 12.2 Job mobility and patterns of promotion

Significant differences also exist in the career patterns of the worker in the large and small firm sector (figure 11.2). In small firms, access to the higher rungs on the professional ladder is achieved by voluntary worker mobility towards firms offering good terms and conditions of employment. In larger firms career advancement is dependent upon control over the labour process exercised by unions and management.

The workers who are free of family commitments, young, able to work full-time and highly mobile between submarkets, progress toward higher paid and prestigious jobs and often travel from employment in a large firm to employment in a small firm and between different types of small firms. Moreover the only objective barrier to 'setting up in business' is lack of knowledge of the manufacturing process. Conversely older women and those with family responsibilities tend to be trapped into homework and are therefore excluded from the mobility chains to the better jobs.

It is clear that the structure of the labour market is determined by factors influencing the demand for, and the supply of, labour. The employment and wage conditions in large firms are guarded by secure product conditions. In the small firm sector, the quest for cheap labour, the flexibility in the organization of manufacture and the characteristics of firms operating within differing market segments (for example type and quality of product, degree of vertical integration, existence or not of dependence on other firms and methods of controlling and organizing the production process) are factors of prime importance in structuring the labour market. However, these demand-side factors only provide a partial explanation of the system of pay determination or of how labour is allocated between firms. The varying degrees of union bargaining power within the different submarkets, age and sex, the structure of the family, opportunities to acquire skill and experience and the network of personal and family ties all influence the strength or weakness of particular workers in the labour market. The structure of the labour market can only be fully understood if account is taken of how these demand and supply factors interact and in turn are modified. These results, then, would seem to confirm that 'segmentation requires multi-causal explanations and that the various explanatory hypotheses – based on the structure of technology, product markets, control over the labour process and labour supply – are complementary rather than competitive' (Rubery and Wilkinson, 1981, pp. 115–16). The striking feature of the Carpi knitwear labour market is that a large proportion of the work-force are able to assure themselves of 'good jobs' even within highly competitive small firms where union protection is minimal and government legislation more frequently avoided. It depends upon three closely interrelated kinds of influence:

1 the characteristics of the industrial 'district';
2 the subordination of both subcontracting firms and individual out-workers located outside Carpi's industrial 'enclave' to Carpi-based firms;
3 full employment, which stems from success in both national and international product markets.

The high concentration of firms within the area ensures that the market for intermediate produce from subcontracting firms is competitive. This protects the artisan from the monopsonistic power of the producers of the final products. More importantly the industrial 'districts form "compost" from which develop small innovative firms which are able to solve the clients' individual problems, (Brusco and Sabel, 1981). As Marshall pointed out:

> When the total number of men interested in the matter is very large there are to be found among them many who, by their intellect and temper, are fitted to originate new ideas. Each new idea is canvassed and improved upon by many minds; each new accidental experience and each deliberate experiment will afford food for reflection and for new suggestions, not to a few persons but to many. (Whitaker, 1975, vol. II, p. 198, as quoted in Becattini, 1979, p. 19)

However the survival and growth of innovative firms are conditioned by the utilization of sophisticated machinery (as emphasized by Brusco and Sabel) and also by the availability of highly-skilled, professional labour. Competition for these workers ensures that they are well paid.

The above circumstances are likely to be found in the provinces to which production is decentralized from Carpi. In most cases they have no access to the final consumer market, and in addition to their using somewhat inefficient production techniques, they are subject to the monopsonistic power of the commissioner-buyer. It is amongst these small subcontracting firms and home-worker circles that the most disadvantaged elements in the labour supply are concentrated. This distribution of low 'value-added' production stages and jobs with lower skill content along the decentralization route away from Carpi (to Mantova, Rovigo, Ferrara, etc.) increases the proportion of good jobs in Carpi. Consequently the low incomes of the home workers and artisans operating in the 'peripheral areas' enhance the income profits of Carpi entrepreneurs and workers.

Lastly high levels of demand for Carpi knitted products means a high level of employment of both worker ability and working time. Furthermore, the more the labour market is stretched, the more wages tend to rise, particularly for those with scarce skills and with knowledge of the manufacturing process. With growing experiences of high employment, 'risk factors' connected with job uncertainty lose much of their potency, and mobility increases within and between the various submarkets, between large and small firms and to self-employment. In this important sense the supply of skilled labour is demand determined. The growing number of good jobs provide the opportunities for acquiring both additional skills and experience; the experience of job security encourages workers to move in search of higher wages, better conditions and, particularly, more skills and experience.

## REFERENCES

Ascoli, U. 1977. Rigidità dei ruoli familiari e offerta di lavoro femminile, *Inchiesta*, no. 28.
Bagnasco, A. 1977. *Tre Italie: la problematica territoriale dello sviluppo*, Bologna, Il Mulino.
Bagnasco, A. and Messori, M. 1975. *Tendenze dell'economia periferica*, Torino, Valentino.
Balbo, L. 1973. Le condizioni strutturali della vita familiare, *Inchiesta*, no. 9.
Balbo, L. 1978. La doppia presenza, *Inchiesta*, no. 32.

Becattini, G. 1979. Dal 'settore' industriale al 'distretto' industriale: alcune considerazioni sull'unità di indagine dell'economia industriale, *Rivista di economia e politica industriale*, no. 1.

Bright, J. R. 1958. *Automation and Management* Boston, Harvard University.

Brusco, S. 1975. Organizzazione del lavoro e decentramento produttivo nel settore metalmeccanico, *Sindacato e piccola impressa* (a cura della FLM di Bergamo), Bari, De Donato.

Brusco, S. 1982. The Emilian model: productive decentralisation and social integration, *Cambridge Journal of Economics*, no. 2.

Brusco, S., Giovannetti, E. and Malagoli, W. 1979. *La relazione tra dimensione e saggio di sviluppo nelle imprese industriali: una ricerca empirica*, Modena, Studi e ricerche dell' Instituto Economico.

Brusco, S. and Sabel, C. F. 1981. Artisan production and economic growth, in Wilkinson, F. (ed.), *The Dynamics of Labour Market Segmentation*, London, Academic Press.

Capecchi, V. 1978. Sviluppo economico emiliano, ruolo dell'industria metalmeccanica, problema del mezzogiorno, in Capecchi, V. (ed.), *La piccola impresa nell'economia italiana*, Bari, De Donato.

Capecchi, V. 1980. Lavoro e condizione giovanile, *Problemi della transizione*, no. 4.

Capecchi, V. and Pugliese, E. 1978. Bologna e Napoli: due città a confronto, *Inchiesta*, nos 34–6.

Comba, L. and Pizzini, P. 1975. La donna che lavora e la famiglia, *Inchiesta*, no. 18.

Coriat, B. 1979. *La fabbrica e il cronometro* (Italian edition of *L'atelier et le chronomètre*), Milano, Feltrinelli.

Del Boca, D. and Turvani, M. 1979. *Famiglia e mercato del lavoro*, Bologna, Il Mulino.

ERVET 1979. *Indagine sullo stato e le prospettive della tecnologia del settore maglieria nel comprensorio Carpi-Correggio*, Bologna, Ente Regionale per la Valorizzazione Economica del Territorio.

FLM (Federazione provinciale di Bologna) 1977. *Occupazione, sviluppo economico, territorio*, Roma, Edizioni SEUSI.

Frey, L. (ed.) 1975. *Lavoro a domicilio e decentramento dell'attività produttiva nei settori tessile e dell'abbigliamento in Italia*, Milano, Angeli.

Fuà, G. 1976. *Occupazione e capacità produttiva: la realtà italiana*, Bologna, Il Mulino.

Mackay, D. I., Boddy, D., Brack, J., Diack, J. A. and Jones, N. 1971. *Labour Markets under Different Employment Conditions*, London, Allen and Unwin.

Malagoli, W. and Mengoli, P. 1979. Lavoro a domicilio e artigianato net comparto della maglieria, *Città e regione*, no. 5.

May, M. P. 1977. Il mercato del lavoro femminile in Italia, *Inchiesta*, no. 25.

Noble, D. F. 1979. Social choice in machine design: the case of automatically controlled machine tools, in Zimbalist, A. (ed.), *Case Studies on the Labour Process*, New York, Monthly Review Press.

Paci, M. 1975. Crisi, ristrutturazione e piccola impresa, *Inchiesta*, no. 20.

Paci, M. 1978. Le condizioni sociali dello sviluppo della piccola industria, in Capecchi, V. (ed.), *La piccola impresa nell'economia italiana*, Bari, De Donato.

Piore, M. J. 1977. Alcune note sul dualismo nel mercato del lavoro, *Rivista di economia e politica industriale*, no. 2.

Piore, M. J. 1980. The technological foundations of dualism and discontinuity, in Berger, S. and Piore, M. J., *Dualism and Discontinuity in Industrial Societies*, Cambridge, Cambridge University Press.

Rees, A. 1966. Information networks in labour markets, *American Economic Review*, no. 2.

Reynolds, L. G. 1971. *The Structure of Labor Markets* (1st edn 1951), Westport, Greenwood Press.

Rubery, J. and Wilkinson, F. 1981. Outwork and segmented labour markets, in Wilkinson, F. (ed.), *The Dynamics of Labour Market Segmentation*, London, Academic Press.

Sabel, C. F. 1979. Marginal workers in industrial society, *Challenge*, March–April.

Sabel, C. F. 1982. *Work and Politics: the Division of Labour in Industry*, Cambridge, Cambridge University Press.

Sallez, A. 1979. Subforniture, produttività del sistema industirale e sviluppo economico regionale, in Varaldo, R. (ed.), *Ristrutturazioni industriali e rapporti tra le imprese*, Milano, Angeli.

Saraceno, C. 1976. *Anatomia della Famiglia*, Bari, De Donato.

Saraceno, C. (ed.) 1980. *Il lavoro mal diviso*, Bari, De Donato.

Solinas, G. 1981. Il mercato del lavoro nell'industria della maglieria e delle confezioni in serie nella provincia di Modena, *Quaderni di rassegna sindacale*, no. 88.

Sylos-Labini, P. 1974. *Saggio sulle classi sociali*, Bari, Laterza.

Vianello, F. 1975. I meccanismi di recupero del profitto: l'esperienza italiana 1963–73, in Graziani, A. (ed.), *Crisi e ristrutturazione dell'economia italiana*, Torino, Einaudi.

Whitaker, J. K. (ed.) 1975. *The Early Economic Writings of Alfred Marshall: 1867–1890*, vol. II, London, Macmillan.

Woodward, J. 1965. *Industrial Organisation: Theory and Practice*, London, Oxford University Press.

# 13
# Worker Behaviour in the Labour Market

GÁBOR KERTESI AND GYÖRGY SZIRÁCZKI

## INTRODUCTION

Analysing the Hungarian labour market, we have witnessed, from the early 1970s, both the formation of stable structures of labour demand (sub-markets) on the one hand, and the spread of new types of worker behaviour on the other. In this chapter we attempt an interpretation of the behaviour of groups of workers in different positions, enjoying different interests and opportunities as a result of firms' and workers' conflicting aspirations and mutual compromises. The analysis of worker behaviour contributes to a better understanding of the mechanisms of the labour market and, at the same time, sheds light on the background and reasons for the reproduction of economic inequalities in the labour market between certain groups and strata. According to this approach, the survey of worker behaviour also sheds light on labour market segmentation. The conception and conceptual apparatus of this essay has much in common with modern Western labour market theories but there are a number of important differences as well. As to the differences, we should like to point out that the Hungarian labour market cannot be described using the categories of the dual (primary and secondary) labour market. Based on previous research in this area, we have to assume the existence of a multisegmented, diversified labour market.

In the first part of the chapter we divide the labour market into sub-markets (structures of labour demand) on the basis of firm behaviour and the job structure offered by these firms. However, the sub-markets are not automatically labour market segments, since in the given sub-markets there are groups of workers which are in a different position and follow totally different strategies concerning the utilization of their labour. They can be called segments only if in the given sub-markets there are mechanisms of reproduction, which, on the basis of conflicting interests of firms and workers and their mutual compromises, create stable patterns of labour market behaviour and strategies.

## FIRM ADAPTATION, SUB-MARKETS AND WORKERS' ASPIRATIONS

### *Possibilities for Firms: Market Adaptation, Bargaining for State Subsidies, Internal Labour Market*

Competition among firms and the resulting economic control lead to the adoption of three typical adaptation mechanisms. Economic units that are less dependent on hierarchical power relations and are able to adapt themselves to market demands (mostly small-scale enterprises, co-operatives and the auxiliary industrial enterprises of agricultural co-operatives) make attempts to raise their workers' wages by more than the average figure by improving profit and thus increasing their ability to attract and keep labour. This form of adaptation is characteristic of only a relatively narrow group of economic units and, as the new economic mechanism lost ground and the independence of economic units was limited and their number decreased, it has become less important. More commonly firms attempt to improve their labour market position by emphasizing their national economic importance, or by referring to central requirements and interests in the hope of obtaining special treatment, state subsidies and preferences (e.g. more advantageous forms of wage regulation, wage preferences, tax cuts etc.).

There has been, however, a third type of adaptation from the early 1970s. Here, firms transform their inner job structures, widen wage differentials, and thus create more possibilities for intra-firm labour allocation. These firms usually follow a particular wage policy, and allocate workers among jobs and tasks among workers in such a way that the jobs which are important to the firms – those that require skills and a good deal of firm-specific experience – are drawn out of inter-firm competition for labour and are isolated from jobs that are filled with newcomers.

This end is achieved by particular means. Jobs requiring different levels of skills or firm-specific experience are organized in a formal (reflected in job grades) or informal (established by intra-firm customs) hierarchy. Wages are determined according to this hierarchy. The demand for labour from the external market is narrowed down to jobs at the bottom of the hierarchy or to jobs outside the hierarchy in terms of both technology and labour organization. Only these jobs serve as points of entry to the firm; thus a newcomer starts at the bottom of the hierarchy. The firm opens up promotion paths for stable and loyal workers, offering higher wages and prestige and protecting them against competition from newcomers. The vacancies within the hierarchy are filled with workers from inside the firm, and the increase in individual wages is tied to seniority and promotion. This strategy has many advantages for the firm, since it does not exhaust its wage fund in wage competition among firms in order to meet the demand of new workers whose behaviour is unpredictable, and it makes it possible to keep the workers who are valuable to the firm.

In a firm that follows the above strategy, both entry to higher posts in the hierarchy and exit from them is limited.[1] This means that such jobs are rather closed and the significant labour processes (mechanisms for determining wages and labour mobility within the enterprise) are based on principles different from those of the external (inter-enterprise) labour market. These jobs are parts of a specific sub-market that we call the intra-firm or internal labour market.[2] Firms applied these means even before the 1970s, but as a coherent labour policy it was adopted probably only after 1968. The labour market, regenerated by the economic reform and less controlled labour management at firm level, made the formation of internal labour markets possible; because of the more and more severe labour shortage and its consequences, a growing number of firms had no alternative but to follow this form of adjustment. Since the internal labour market binds to the firm the group of workers that is most important to the management, it gives a certain security and protection, not only against the competition of other firms, but also against unpredictable changes in central regulations.

Most firms tried to profit from their bargaining position with central authorities, and, at the same time, to establish their internal labour markets; at the same time, in certain fields they had to face the competition of other firms in the labour market. This competition primarily concerned jobs where the management was not able to form or was not interested in forming job structures independent of the external labour market.

### *Elements of the Firm's Demand Structure: Internal Labour Market, Occupational Sub-Markets, Marginal Sub-Markets*

Basically, the technology and work organization adopted in a firm determines the hierarchical job structure formation. The more the technology is constituted of sequential elementary phases of work and the more the adopted technology and work organization are adjusted to the particularities of the products of a given firm, the more opportunity there will be for acquiring firm-specific skills in jobs determined by technological process and work organization. However, this is not enough: for the formation of an internal labour market it is also necessary that the firm, by a more or less deliberate wage policy and labour allocation, should build up or, by the continued application of rules, stabilize the internal hierarchy of jobs. There are, however, a great number of jobs within a firm where the functioning of the organization and the character of tasks are such that it is possible neither to bind workers to the firm by forming internal labour markets nor to attract them by promotion opportunities. The reason for this is that in such jobs firm-specific skills have no significant role in the performance of work, either because they are relatively isolated from the firms's hierarchy, or because the firm's production processess are disrupted into quite independent phases, which

1. There are various obstacles which block the mobility within and among firms: (1) administrative barriers; (2) formal qualification requirements (criteria for entry); (3) certain groups' attempts to monopolize positions; and (4) economic considerations (considerations of potential advantages and losses). In our analysis, when talking of barriers, we refer to any of the last three.

2. The most complex theory of internal labour markets was elaborated by Doeringer and Piore (1971).

can hardly lead to a homogeneous work organization. There are two types of such jobs. The first requires skills acquired through formal qualifications, or general practical experience accumulated during the years in the given occupation, or both. In the second neither formal qualifications nor skills acquired in the process of work have a role essential to work performance.

Jobs of the first type belong to an occupational sub-market, those of the second type to the unqualified – or, to use a term well known in the international literature which better indicates the workers' social status – marginal labour market. In both cases the sub-markets comprise a number of firms, and are built up from horizontally organized job structures. There is no vertical mobility, or, to put it differently, both the promotion and the role of further training of workers is negligible. As against the internal labour market there are fewer or no barriers to changing employer; thus labour mobility is higher than average.

However, there are significant differences between occupational and marginal sub-markets. In the occupational sub-markets labour mobility between economic units is intensive while changes of occupation are rare, that is, workers who change employer stay in the same occupation. When qualifications are a prerequisite for an occupation we call the sub-market an occupational one. In an occupational sub-market competition among firms leads to a wage mechanism regulated by supply–demand relations which distribute workers in the given occupation among the jobs. Apart from market mechanisms, individual wages are a function of the number of years spent in the given occupation. Wages and pay are thus differentiated according to the general occupational, practical knowledge acquired in the given occupation throughout the worker's career. The fact that in certain occupations in the building industry (carpenter, scaffolder, bricklayer, ferroconcrete fitter, concreter, joiner, electrician, house painter, central heating fitter etc.), in transport (lorry driver, car driver etc.) and in the engineering industry (engine fitter, locksmith etc.) the ratio of those who remain in the same occupation when changing employer is significantly higher than in other manual occupations also indicates the existence of such occupational sub-markets.

In marginal jobs neither formal qualifications nor practical skills have an important role. It is mainly physical strength that is needed. There is a high labour turnover also in the marginal sub-markets, but, unlike the occupational sub-markets, workers do not remain in the same occupation. When changing employer they usually change occupation. Male and female unskilled, storing and material handling jobs belong to this category (unskilled worker, boiler man, road builder, material handler, transport and dock worker, stock keeper, cleaner, unskilled agricultural worker etc.). In this sub-market labour allocation is regulated by a wage mechanism based on supply and demand to a great extent, while individual wage levels are much influenced by the worker's performance, especially under poor working conditions and when great physical effort is required.

The firm's job structure is a combination of the above-mentioned three demand structures – internal labour market, occupational sub-market, marginal sub-market – and it fundamentally determines the firm's labour demand. Every firm determines the quantity of its labour demand and in it the ratio of different occupations, qualifications and jobs with regard to its own work organization. The effect of labour shortages and labour market competition on the firm therefore depends basically on the firm's internal job structure; firms that have different structural characteristics try to and are able to solve these problems in different ways. Finally, job structures shape the forms of competition among firms and the mechanisms of bargaining between workers and management.

## *Dimensions of the Workers' Aspirations: Wage Maximization and Relative Net Advantage*

A firm offers jobs that are different in terms of skills and productivity, working conditions, wages etc. In addition, the labour supply itself is structured by sex, age, occupation, qualification etc. Not only does the firm attempt to attract and keep the labour force by various means, but also the workers have different opportunities to increase their incomes. The latter are basically determined by the place of the workers in the organization. In the effort to increase their incomes they can emphasize their dominant position in the organization (and the bargaining position stemming from it), the skills and qualifications they have and their work performance, but also they can make the most of their opportunities for earning additional income in the second economy, and profit from the firms' need to compete for labour.

The intensity of the workers' aspirations to increase their incomes also differs: it is a function of sex, age, life-cycle, size of family, and way of life. At times the main end is income maximization, and workers subordinate all other preferences to it. More often, however, the choice between the different ways of earning income is made on the basis of trade-offs between reward and effort. To put it differently: workers rationally economize their efforts (Gábor and Galasi 1981). This may hold true between parallel activities (e.g. between the work performed in one's 'main' job and the activities in the household plot or in the second economy) or within a single form of activity, between the wage level and the reward for effort. The resolution of these strategies has a great impact on the workers' employment and occupational stability, the extent to which they are attached to the state-organized labour market, and also on their income opportunities in the second economy.

We can say that in general, from a purely economic aspect, workers have two objectives within a given economic organization: to maximize their wage level and to improve or at least stabilize the reward/effort ratio (relative net advantage). These two objectives are present in workers' aspirations at the same time, although not to the same extent. There is a specific trade-off between the two objectives which leads to significant differences in the behaviour of different groups of workers, and in firms' attitude to these groups. There are workers who are able to increase both their wage level and their relative net advantage; there are others who achieve a wage increase only at the expense of their relative net advantage; still others aim at increasing their relative net advantage and, temporarily or permanently, accept a smaller increase in the wage level.

The rational behaviour of workers does not mean the uniformity of their aspirations. There are different spheres of rational behaviour. In this essay we focus our attention on how these aspirations, within a given frame (labour demand structures), add up to workers' strategies,[3] how the firm and the different groups of workers adapt, and how these adaptation mechanisms contribute to the reproduction of economic inequality between the various groups. From the conflicts and compromises between the firms' and the workers' aspirations, dominant behaviour patterns are crystallized in the sub-markets we have already described. In this conflictual process one can trace the typical worker behaviour patterns of the 1970s. Here we attempt to present and explain some of them.

## WORKER BEHAVIOUR: FIRMS' INTERESTS AND WORKERS' ASPIRATIONS - A MUTUAL ADAPTATION

Let us now outline the scope for firms to adapt to competition among firms for attracting and keeping labour, and let us see how much freedom of movement is left for the different groups of workers. In other words, are workers able to profit from the competition among firms, and from the conflicts between firms and the central economic management; and if so, how? This approach makes it possible to analyse specific labour market structures and behaviour patterns in the context of the firms' objectives and the workers' strategies.

### *Elite Workers: Key Position in the Internal Labour Market, Stability and Promotion*

From among the workers in the job structures of the internal labour markets we first deal with those who occupy the so-called *key positions*, i.e. the jobs on the top and in the middle of the hierarchy that require qualifications and skills.

For a better understanding of the character of these key positions one has to consider the work organization of a factory - which is most unlike a precision instrument! During the work process there are always hindrances, defects or other problems that the workers, in the interest of continuous production, have to solve on the spot. Under the conditions of the resource-constrained socialist economy, the shortages, associated conflicts and forced adaptations are much more frequent than in the demand-constrained market economies. From time to time there are shortages in raw materials, semi-finished goods, spare parts, labour etc. Firms working under such conditions frequently have to find *ad hoc* solutions. Within the various jobs, however, these problems arise with differing frequency. The jobs where, in the interest of continuous production, workers relatively often use different forms of improvization, we call key positions.

Workers who fill these key positions have special firm-specific skills, practical experience and informal connections in the firm, and this enables them to react flexibly to the various hindrances in order to keep up the continuity of production. It often means that they undertake some of the foreman's or shop

3. We use the terms 'workers' strategies' and 'firms' strategies' in the narrow sense of the word if both parties adjust to each other's expected behaviour, i.e. their aspirations are shaped according to the expected reaction of the other party (Schelling 1963, 21-2).

manager's organizational tasks. (Sometimes they get the missing spare parts from other workshops in the firm through personal connections; they often have special tools that they themselves have made with which work is easier and quicker; they are skilled in all the jobs in the workshops; and so on.)[4] These types of jobs and workers can be found - although to different extents - in every economic organization. Such is the universal skilled worker in the workshop turning out unique products for export in a machine industrial enterprise, the driver of trailer lorries in international transportation, or the foreman who controls the work process and corrects the technology in a chemical industrial plant. Workers in key positions, having firm-specific skills and experience, we call *elite workers*.

Special skills and experience are acquired, and informal connections within the firm are established, during long years with the same firm. The firm has specific means for picking out and keeping these workers. The formal career within the work organization or the informal advancement path, the wage increase tied up with promotion and seniority, all serve this purpose.

Most firms are growth oriented and thus strive to increase their labour force. Under the conditions of labour shortage and the pressure of labour market competition, new workers are hard to recruit. Therefore firms are unable to select newcomers according to their own requirements. For the firms, however, it does make a difference whether the jobs of decisive importance are occupied by suitable workers or not. This is why firms establishing an internal labour market narrow down their labour demand to jobs at the bottom of the hierarchy. Vacancies higher in this hierarchy are filled with workers from within. The process of internal selection of the labour force can be most closely controlled and influenced by the firm through promotion. The promotion ladder has an important role in improving the firms' ability to keep their labour force. Since advancement and its advantages attract a lot more people than those who actually attain it, the prospect alone has a labour stabilizing effect.

Sometimes firms arrange multistage vocational training at crucial career stages. Some kind of test is necessary for stepping up the promotion ladder. This training binds the worker to the firm since it has value only within the given firm and is acknowledged and recompensed only by that firm. More often, however, advancement paths within a firm are organized in an informal way and are embodied in the distribution of well or badly paying tasks, overtime work, and extra work for special bonuses within the work group or among work groups; sometimes they are tied up with the frequency of interference with the critical stages of the work process.

Wages increase gradually along seniority and promotion lines, and the gap between the basic wages determined by job grades and the actual earnings widens. The more firm-specific skills an individual has, or the more he knows the ropes, the more he is able to get well-paying extra work within the firm. Similarly, it is in the firm's interest that the occasional improvisations during production should

4. István Kemény was the first to call attention to the fact - in a case study of a firm in the machine industry - that even in the case of a seemingly coercive technology (assembly line) workers are able to transform the work process and work organization to a great extent because of the shortage economy (Kemény 1978).

function smoothly; therefore the necessary occasional special tasks are – by way of various extra bonuses – highly rewarded.[5]

In this way the firm manages to keep its elite workers. Should they leave the firm, most of their firm-specific skills and experience would be of little value elsewhere and they would lose their privileged positions and high wages. The losses associated with leaving bind them to the firm. However, the number of key positions and the advantageous opportunities for extra pay within the firm that go with these key positions are limited. Therefore the elite workers are interested in defending their own positions by making it difficult for other workers to achieve a similar status; if possible, by excluding them altogther.[6] The elements of such an exclusion strategy include attempts to monopolize 'quality' extra work and well-paying overtime work, and the claim that the distribution of jobs and tasks among workers should reflect seniority, with the hierarchy of earnings also following this allocation pattern.

This means that the elite workers' behaviour norms serve as a selection criterion for the whole firm.[7] As we have seen earlier, firms who attempt to establish internal labour markets do precisely that. As a result of the firm's labour and wage policy concerning the elite workers and the elite workers' behaviour towards other groups of workers, this labour market segment is fairly closed and protected.

The relatively small group of workers in this segment consists of middle-aged or older males who have spent a long time with the firm and who often have formal qualifications. An even more important differentiating trait is their firm-specific skills and extended system of informal connections. The great power

5. Firms can increase elite workers' wages by manipulating the job rating system. Workers in key positions are often put in the grade of 'hard working conditions' so that they can be paid higher basic wages. According to a representative survey covering 600,000 workers by the Ministry of Labour, the distribution of workers according to working conditions is as follows (1973–6, per cent):

| *Grades of working conditions* | | *1973* | *1976* |
|---|---|---|---|
| Good | 1 | 48.01 | 38.55 |
| | 2 | 32.43 | 38.07 |
| | 3 | 17.08 | 20.25 |
| Bad | 4 | 2.48 | 3.13 |
| Total | | 100.00 | 100.00 |

Since there was no real worsening in working conditions, the 10 per cent drop in the first grade of good working conditions indicates that many firms look for suitable grades for the wages they want to pay (Fülöp and Bokányi 1980, 18).

6. The closure of social groups is a very important element in understanding the nature of demarcation lines within the social structure and the social mechanisms that produce them. Since social groups become closed when, because of the scarcity of certain (physical or social) 'goods' or positions, there is keen competition for these 'things'. Weber called attention to this first, and stressed its consequences on the labour market (Weber 1976 (1921), 23 and 201–3). For a long time there was no reaction to it. Parkin (1974) was the first to deal with the problem in detail. Since then mostly German researchers use this conceptual framework for describing labour market processes (Kreckel 1980; Sengenberger 1981).

7. For example, in the Hungarian Wagon and Machine Factory: 'Although the old workers, having power and influence but without skills and experience, have some influence on wages in the plant producing tools, the distribution, following seniority lines, usually did not mean that the principle of work performance was ignored. On the contrary, it is made obvious to every young newcomer that, if he develops certain skills and experience and establishes his background within the plant, he will be able to step up the promotion ladder within the plant' (Fazekas 1982, 358–9).

(good bargaining position) they have to forward their interests springs from their role in the organization's functioning. Workers are exposed to the defects of the production process and, to the same extent, the firm is dependent on those workers, who are capable of removing these occasional obstacles. This situation puts the workers in a strong bargaining position with the firm. Given the right prerequisites, effort bargaining can be an important means in the workers' strategy, together with promotion (given for loyalty to – long service with – the firm). Bargaining aims at wage increases as well as an improved or, at least, a steady reward for effort ratio.

### *Double Status: Alternative Sources of Income and Restraining Work Performance*

In the internal labour market only a few workers actually obtain key positions. The majority are unable to accumulate special skills and get stuck in positions in the middle or bottom of the promotion ladder. Since the firm cannot bind these workers by the advantages that bind the elite workers, they have to follow different strategies: they can leave the firm, and thus increase their wages by taking advantage of the wage competition among firms; they can stay and increase their wages by increasing work intensity; or they can attempt to find alternative income sources outside the firm. Here we deal with the last solution.

The firm is able to keep workers who carry on income-earning activities outside the firm only if it offers them jobs that are suited to this double strategy. This is in fact true of a large number of jobs – those less important to the firm's functioning – where firm-specific skills and experiences are not required, and which are suited to workers holding back their efforts. Such a job has good working conditions, not too much physical effort, short monthly working hours (rare overtime hours) and shifts that are suited to permanent income-earning activities outside the firm.

The firm offers these types of jobs not only to workers stuck in the process of promotion but – as we will see – at every stage of its structure where labour market competition among firms, workers' aspirations for higher incomes and the second economy press the firm to do so. It can be both the labour supply of a given region, or the higher proportion of families active in the second economy, that make it imperative for the firm to create a large number of such jobs and to put up with such worker behaviour. However, when the advancement prospects are narrow or the workers' aspirations to go ahead are weaker, the possibility and attraction of long-term wage increases lessen. In this case, the firm and the workers make a compromise. The firm needs them and not only offers them jobs suited to their additional income-earning activities, but also puts up with the self-sparing behaviour that stems from the double employment status. The workers, in turn, rest content with wages below average, or smaller wage increases compared with other groups of workers.

In following this strategy, the firm's relative autonomy in establishing the wage differentials also plays a part. The firm, as regards internal wage differentials, economizes with the wage fund, or, more precisely, its yearly increment. From the annual fund for wage increases, the firm first of all pays the elite workers bonuses, overtime pay, fringe benefits, and also the increase in the basic wages, and – as we shall see – the 'workhorses'. This kind of wage policy is most easily accepted by workers who have alternative sources of income outside the firm. They might as well accept it since their total income approximates, and occasionally exceeds, the elite workers' earnings.[8]

In this way the firm has an opportunity to bind these workers as well. Although workers can increase their wages in the state sector by making the best of the wage competition among firms through frequent changes of employer, this involves uncertainties which would hinder their activities in the second economy. It is not always so easy to find a new job which gives the opportunity to work after the regular working hours outside the firm. Even if there is a good chance of obtaining such a job, it takes time. So turnover may lead to wage increases but it can happen that the total income from the two sources – the firm and the second economy – temporarily decreases. In the case of double-status workers it is also the potential losses that account for the relative employment stability.

Double-status workers differ from elite workers in the internal labour market not only in the characteristics of the jobs occupied by them (in the lack of firm-specific skills and lower wages), but also in their strategy of labour utilization. In their behaviour within the firm they aim to stabilize their wage/effort ratios even at the expense of moderate wage increases. They aim at attaining a stable wage level with moderate effort, instead of making efforts to increase their wages, since the latter would interfere with their earning activities outside the firm. The reason for this behaviour is that the same amount of work yields higher incomes in the second economy than in the state sector (Gábor and Galasi 1981).

The workers' preference for a stable wage/effort ratio as against earning maximization in the firm depends on the size, stability and frequency of income from the second economy. Beside the level of total income from various sources, two other questions have to be taken into consideration. One has to know the proportion of permanent income (stable in the relatively long run) to temporary income (uncertain, different amounts, unreliable) in the workers' or households' normal (customary for a relatively long time) real income. The ratio between permanent and temporary incomes from the second economy indicates the stability or instability of positions in the second economy. The proportion of permanent elements in the total income indicates the extent of the worker's attachment to the second economy. These connections have a definite impact on the behaviour of the various groups of double-status workers.

Because of their instability in the second economy, a relatively small number of workers can afford to regard the income from the first economy as a buffer. For the majority of workers the second economy is an important sphere of additional incomes but it is the stability and amount of the income from the firm which is dominant. There are naturally groups that can stabilize their positions and

8. The mutual separation of elite workers from double-status workers can be described best by the notion of demarcation, since neither group aspires after the other's position. A case study on a transport company shows that the shaping of an internal labour market leads to the separation of two major groups of workers. Elite workers move upward on the job hierarchy achieving higher wages and prestige in the function of the length of service. Double-status workers, however, are stuck at the bottom of the job hierarchy and the lower wages are offset by incomes from the household plot (Sziráczki 1983). A more extreme form of such a demarcation occurs when not only the jobs in a given occupation are split but also the different plants within one and the same firm (Köllõ 1982).

incomes in the second economy, but they are in number and percentage quite small.[9] Between these two extreme poles there are numerous mixed types.

However, behind the differences in opportunity for drawing income from the second economy, there lie more complex considerations that shed light on the importance of employment in the state sector; more precisely, the intra-firm social positions, connections and information of a large group of workers who carry on some activity in the second economy. However, there are certain spheres of the second economy (first of all in services) where workers of double status are in a strong position since the supply of materials and spare parts as well as the flow of information and market connections are guaranteed and, if they are not, the customers can be charged with these expenses. But most individuals who carry on activities in the second economy find a diffuse, unorganized market where even a basic infrastructure is lacking (the circle of customers is unknown, the producers are often invisible etc.) and there is not enough capital to bridge over the seasonal or business fluctuation of demand and supply. Indeed even if the necessary capital is given, the means of production (motor-car, van, small machines, special tools etc.) are not easily available. The flow of information and the system of market connections are not given to any newcomer; every individual has to organize and establish his own chain of market connections. It helps if the individual has a position and connections in the firm that enable him to obtain the necessary information and means. In any other case his position in the second economy may be uncertain and shaky, so that his income from it will be temporary and fluctuating – a characteristic of most double-status workers.

Household plots and small private farms around the house are exceptions. In the last decade, economic policy has allowed the development of channels for buying and selling and the connecting of these to the framework of state and co-operative sectors. However, this does not weaken but on the contrary reinforces our argument since, in the case of household plots, the connection beween the activity in the second economy and the position in the state sector is institutionalized. Here, instead of the destabilizing effects of the unorganized market and the fluctuations of demand and supply in other spheres, there are changes in the priorities of economic policy. An example of this is the 'vegetable crisis' in the mid 1970s which was caused by the sudden drop in the production of small farms as a result of unfavourable changes in economic policy.

Another important factor is that some of the activities in the second economy are on the border of illegality; sometimes they are tolerated, sometimes prohibited. But even legal activities are subject to extreme changes of economic control (higher or lower taxes, help or hindrance of the channels of buying and selling, the allowing of free prices and the official control of prices etc.). This is one reason for the uncertainty and unpredictability of the second economy, and why for most individuals it is only utilized as a means of supplementary income.

As a result of the limits on pay increases within firms and the higher incomes

9. They create a very special combination of behaviours within the two economies. They need, namely, the job in the first economy not because of the stability of their incomes, but because of legal protection. These workers want to maintain their positions of (quasi) wage-earners in spite of the fact that they are (really) small entrepreneurs in the second economy. That is the easiest way to evade taxes. So, although this group may be small in number, it has a great significance.

per unit of work in the second economy on the one hand, and the stability of earnings in the firm and the instability of additional sources of income on the other, the rational worker combines the advantage of security (stable employment and earnings) within the firm with additional income from the second economy. This strategy, by reason of the limiting factors discussed above, rarely results in outstandingly high incomes. Most workers can earn enough to keep up an average standard of living only by extending the legally compulsory working hours.

### *Workers at the Bottom of the Internal Hierarchy*

There is a third group in the internal labour market that is isolated from both the elite workers and the double-status workers. Workers in this group have neither firm-specific skills nor alternative income sources outside the firm. As to their social status, however, they are a heterogeneous group. There are young, urban skilled and semi-skilled workers who, because of their age, have not yet organized their income-earning activities in the second economy. There are young rural workers who are detached from their traditional rural surroundings (they do not have household plots) but are not yet accustomed to industrial or urban conditions. There are semi-skilled workers who do not have skills to be made use of in the second economy, for instance workers on assembly-line production (among them a lot of women). Most of them are young workers, just starting their career, in jobs at the bottom of the hierarchy of the firms' internal labour markets (points of entry), and are also beginners in their occupations.

In their case the lack of firm-specific skills, and the strategy of workers in key positions to monopolize the good sources of additional income, limit the possibilities for improving their positions. On the other hand, they have no alternative sources of income in the second economy, so they have less chance for an advantageous compromise with the firm by restraining work performance in a manner tolerated by the employer.

In order to understand the firm's attitude towards these workers, together with their behaviour, we have to consider some further peculiarities of their market position: the jobs that are filled by them belong to both the internal labour market and the inter-firm labour market (especially in certain occupations). Such mixed demand structures – they belong to occupational sub-markets, but the jobs in the given occupation form a hierarchy within the firm – are characteristic of firms in the machine and building industry and in transportation.

### *Workers in Occupational Sub-Markets: Labour Turnover as a Means of Accumulating Skills and Manoeuvring in the Labour Market*

In certain work organizations – where the given occupation is closely related to the firm's basic line of production – jobs in occupational sub-markets are also connected to the internal labour market hierarchy within the firm. However, most of the jobs constituting occupational sub-markets are technologically and organizationally independent of the firm's basic line of production and there are only a few such jobs within a firm. Therefore the firm is unable and unwilling to bind these workers by promotion and the advantages deriving from it. Since the number of such occupations is small, the firm is usually not interested in connecting these jobs – if that is possible at all – to its hierarchical organizational structures.

The fact that the occupational sub-markets constitute occupations that exist in many firms – i.e. the labour demand is relatively evenly spread among the firms – significantly increases the workers' chances for horizontal mobility. The workers' general skills, being useful in a number of firms, minimize the losses that spring from the devaluation of their firm-specific skills. The structure of labour demand and the lack of barriers to mobility within the occupation account for the fact that earnings and, with that, labour turnover closely follow the developments of demand and supply. No wonder that under the circumstances of labour shortage, labour turnover can be a means of forcing up wages. A relatively wide occupational sub-market offers chances for wage increase through frequent changes of employer; the workers make the best of the wage competition among firms while they stay in the same occupation.

However, there are other important reasons for the high rates of turnover. In the occupational sub-markets – especially in artisan-like repair and maintenance occupational sub-markets – the frequent changes of employer, a little like the case of the journeyman in the Middle Ages, contribute to the accumulation of practical skills and many-sided experience. Therefore, moving work place is an important means of acquiring various skills, experience and on-the-job training.

The above strategy of changing employer has its limits. The major limiting factors are firstly the need for stability in smaller settlements where employment opportunities are scarce, and where there are strong ties to the home, or a resistance to commuting (especially among middle-aged or older workers), and secondly the extent of opportunities to participate in the second economy. But the firm itself is able to keep the workers by offering certain possibilities for earning extra money. In the firm some working hours can be paid as overtime hours and the restraining of work performance is tolerated; or after working hours the firm's machines and lorries are lent to workers who use them in industrial, construction or repair and maintenance activities outside the firm. Agricultural plants provide their workers' small farms with fodder, seed-grain, insecticides and weed killers as well as offering security of purchase.

### *'Workhorses': Wage Increase at the Expense of the Wage/Effort Ratio*

Let us return to jobs that belong to an internal labour market (usually at the bottom of the job hierarchy at points of entry) and to an occupational sub-market that comprises a large number of firms. Workers in these jobs, usually having neither firm-specific skills nor established sources of income outside the firm, have two ways of increasing their wages. Within the firm they can increase their wages through acquiring firm-specific skills and gradually stepping up the promotion ladder. Alternatively, they can make frequent changes of employer, if they belong to an occupational sub-market, accumulating skills useful in a number of firms and making the best of the competition for labour among firms.

Under the conditions of labour shortage there is sharpening wage competition for labour among firms and workers can significantly increase their wages in a relatively short time through frequent changes of employer. Stable workers' wages increase to a much lesser extent since at the bottom of the hierarchy wages increase step by step along seniority and promotion lines. The forcing up of wages in the occupational sub-markets does not, in the short run, necessarily have an impact on the internal labour markets that are isolated from inter-firm demand and supply relations. However, the situation is different in the long run. One has to count on the spread of the wage-increasing effect of turnover on the whole economy, and the approximately equal rise in wages of all groups of workers. Nevertheless, workers in key positions and in positions where extra pay is available in the internal labour market usually have a strong bargaining position with the management since they have an important role in the firm's functioning. Consequently they may attain much higher wages than mobile workers in the occupational sub-market. Higher wages can therefore be attained through changing employers in the short run and through promotion in the long run.

At the intersection of the two labour market structures, jobs are occupied by young workers in the phase of their life-cycle when the accumulation need is the greatest in a family (founding of a family, obtaining a flat, etc.); the intensity of their income-increasing efforts is higher than that of other age groups. The behaviour of this group of workers is therefore motivated basically by their short-term need; consequently they prefer mobility to stability and promotion within the firm.

If the firm wants to keep these workers as well, then a higher wage level has to be guaranteed than the one they would attain through mobility in the occupational sub-market. In turn, these workers have to put up with a less favourable wage/effort ratio than is the generally accepted norm in the occupational sub-market where the wage level is lower.

It is important to understand that in Hungary, bodies representing workers' interests have only a small part in controlling the parity between effort and wages. That is why there are significant differences between the work intensity and wage levels of workers with the same occupation and qualifications in different branches of industry, firms and geographical regions. It is the practically free bargaining between firms and workers that is decisive in fixing the parity between effort and wages. This free – i.e. not institutionalized – bargaining mechanism is favourable for workers who have special skills in the firm and occupy key positions (elite workers) or who have a permanent source of additional income outside the firm (double-status workers). These groups of elite and double-status workers are able to advance their interests, often collectively, by way of mutual compromises with the firm: they have a strong bargaining position. While this holds true for the small group of elite workers, it applies to double-status workers (who have no decisive function in the firm) only if they represent a large group within a given firm and owing to their number are able to impose their interests upon the management. On the other hand, workers who are not in key positions in the economic organization, who have no income sources outside the firm and who strive at short-term income maximization – sometimes at any price – can be compelled to keep up a stiff pace of work for lack of a good bargaining position. The income maximization drive creates sharp competition within this group which further weakens their position since they cannot take a common stand in wage bargaining. Because of this situation, workers who do not aim at short-term income maximization, but aspire to promotion within the firm, are often compelled to take part in the competition. Consequently, competition sharpens and the pace of work stiffens.

The firm's incentive wages (piece rates) have the best results among the 'workhorses'. The usual outcome is that with the higher wage level output increases to an even greater extent, i.e. an improved wage/effort ratio from the firm's and a reduced one from the workers' viewpoint.[10]

Workers can keep up this stiff pace of work only for a certain time, even if the firm's pressure is not too hard. After this period the worker decides if he will remain with the firm permanently, or choose a strategy of changing employers. With time, workers attempt to get in key positions or find income sources outside the firm and get jobs suitable for work restraining behaviour. If neither of these is successful and the family's accumulation need is not too pressing any more, they usually leave the firm and look for a new employer. Although their earnings may decrease temporarily, it is compensated by the sudden improvement of wage/effort ratio.

## *Marginal Workers*

Jobs in the marginal sub-market require either the workers' natural physical strength or the performance of simple tasks that can be easily learnt in a short time. They never lead to the accumulation of firm-specific skills or experience, or general skills that are valuable in the occupational sub-markets comprising many

10. The extremely stiff pace of work often leads to the disorganization of the internal labour market structure. Fazekas describes a case very much different from the one in note 7. In the engine plant after the introduction of piece rates the higher productivity 'was a result almost totally of a non-official, silent extension of individual tasks. Some of the workers performed different tasks during the working hours (e.g. operated more machines at the same time), and produced much more than was officially prescribed during the same amount of time. . . . Since the prerequisite for achieving high productivity in the plant was only the increased work intensity, the old, highly qualified skilled workers in the engine factory were unable to keep up their positions in the wage hierarchy following the introduction of individual piece wages. The pace of work was set by the "workhorses" who aimed at short-term wage maximization. The old skilled workers left the factory one after the other' (Fazekas 1982, 265–73). However, the forced work intensity, the system of single workers operating more than one machine and the stiffening pace of work led to a spectacular worsening of quality. Wage increases based on the increase of work intensity are totally different from the elite workers' opportunities for wage increases or additional pay within the firm. Wage increases are tied to 'quality' work, to solving the problems of technological processes, undertaking production organization and overtime 'quality' work. For example in the Hungarian Ship and Crane Factory, 'actually, twenty welders control the whole plant in Angyalföld. Well, the welding is examined by X-ray and ultrasonics, so welding is 100 per cent perfect. We have a hundred welders and twenty of them produce at the highest quality. . . . If they turn nasty, no ship gets finished. . . . A key part of all portal-cranes and floating cranes is a great big cog-wheel. . . . If this machine or the workers on it turn nasty, we have to go to Vienna, to an Austrian firm to obtain the cog. Is it worth arguing with this chap about 20 fillers? Let's say we manage to talk him round, but next month there will be two cog-wheels missing. And there will be a drop in exports' (Polgár 1982, 62–4). Another example from a bus factory: 'Workers do not follow the line or its pace strictly. They run about for missing materials, reset the drill, they follow the bus to other workshops in order to finish previous phases of work, the foreman gives them other tasks according to the number of workers, they help one another within the work group, they correct defects in production' (Havas and Kardos 1975).

firms. The vocational skills needed to perform these tasks is minimal, so the training is very short, if there is any at all. Marginal jobs are, from the aspect of both qualification and the firm's job hierarchy, dead-end jobs; they rarely lead to an occupation or to jobs where one can accumulate skills and firm-specific experience. Marginal jobs, therefore, are isolated from the above-discussed labour market structures, the internal labour market and the occupational submarket.

In Hungary, marginal jobs were created in great numbers from the early 1950s until the mid 1960s, at the time of forced industrialization. During this extensive industrialization, many jobs were created to suit the unqualified, untrained (former poor) peasants' and itinerant workers' life-style of seasonal work, uncertain employment, and low wages (Kemény 1982). Furthermore, because urban housing construction lagged far behind the pace of industrialization it reproduced a distinctive life-style, namely, itinerant workers who found employment in the city but no permanent place to live. This is in turn led to family instability (Konrád and Szelényi 1971). In the new industrial enterprises there was a great number of jobs at the bottom of the hierarchy in which only physical strength or simple semi-skilled work was needed; the technology was based on primitive hand-tools, the work process was non-standardized, the quality requirements ignorable. Quantitative norms of production were changing, and from the aspect of technology and work organization they were not connected to jobs requiring quality and qualified work. The new industrial workers of poor peasant origin first occupied these jobs and many of them were never able to get into more qualified jobs and live a more regular life.

From the late 1960s the economic policy of extensive growth which was based on the abundance of unqualified workers came to a crisis. The agricultural labour reserve was practically exhausted and industrialization came up against a less rapidly growing and then stagnating labour supply. As the agricultural co-operatives' and household farms' position strengthened, there were extended work and income possibilities for rural workers which lessened the labour migration to cities. The decentralized industrialization (rural industrialization) further lessened migration on the one hand, and , on the other, shortened the distance of commuting; this, together with the spread of private house-building in the villages, contributed to the stabilization of family life-style. The extended educational system limited the reproduction of uneducated and unqualified workers in both rural and urban areas, and the expansion or preservation of obsolete structures characterized by jobs requiring uneducated labour came up against the narrowing supply of unqualified workers.

The sudden drop in labour supply from the late 1960s caused the most serious labour shortage in the labour market of unskilled workers. There were two reasons for this on the demand side. In the 1970s a great many firms still assumed the abundance of unskilled labour and invested in workplaces of low technological level. At this time firms in urban areas struggling with labour shortages created branches in rural settlements. On the other hand, if there was an opportunity for technological modernization firms often allotted their scarce means to the modernization of main technological processes, the backbone of their special line of production, or to new construction. At the same time the mechanization of unskilled work such as material handling, packing etc. was neglected.[11] Industrial reconstruction resulted also in the persistence of a great demand for unskilled labour within the structure of industrial plants, and these jobs were excluded from technological modernization. The establishment of internal labour markets further widened the gap between jobs requiring marginal and jobs requiring qualified workers.

*Marginal labour market and stable social position: provisional status in the state-organized labour market* The great demand for unskilled labour and the changed living conditions of these workers resulted in a number of particular labour market behaviour patterns and adaptation mechanisms. Many of the rural workers in marginal jobs (workers in canning and sugar factories, agricultural seasonal work, or unskilled work in construction etc.) practise small-scale agricultural production in the household plot or private small farm. They adjust to the seasonal character of employment and gradually organize small-scale production in the private small farm which is based on family work and yielded income. These workers react to the seasonal changes of employment and income possibilities in the state labour market by withdrawing to the household for some time (they regularly discontinue employment). This mainly female labour is unstable 'not necessarily because they frequently change employer but, which is more important from the aspect of the employable labour force at a given time, because they regularly leave the state-organized sector of production and appear in the private sector' (Galasi 1978, 8).

Many workers who frequently discontinue their employment often return to the same firm they left previously. With stable incomes from the private small farm they become so much used to alternating employment between the state sector and the private plot that they would not aim at continuous employment even if the firm were to abolish the seasonal fluctuation of its production. These workers have a provisional status between the state-organized labour market and the household; their loose ties to the state-organized labour market are not temporary but permanent.

*Marginal labour market and unstable social position: turnover as a compulsion* Unskilled workers in cities or in the outskirts of cities who often did not finish the eighth grade of compulsory elementary school and have no private small farms are in a different position, since they have to make a living on incomes mainly from the state sector. The possibilities open to them depend on the following factors: the relatively even distribution of marginal jobs among enterprises (in every firm there are unskilled workers - material handlers, cleaners etc.); the great demand for such workers; the lack of barriers to entry to marginal jobs (the openness of these jobs); the lack of stable sources of income in the second economy; the strict isolation from workers in other labour market positions.

11. We have to add that in the mid 1970s there were about 800,000 workers in Hungary (around 26 per cent of all manual workers) whose job, to some extent, involved material handling without any mechanized help (Pogány 1982, 147–8). The number of marginal workers in such jobs is probably smaller. Still, the data show the tendency of technological progress from the late 1960s onwards, and also the jobs left out of it.

The strict isolation of marginal workers from workers in internal labour markets and occupational sub-markets means that both ways of long-term wage increase are closed to them: by promotion through accumulating firm-specific skills and experience and by acquiring skills during the years in the same occupation. There nevertheless seems to be an opportunity for forcing up wages through frequent changes of employer; all the more so since there is a severe labour shortage in the urban labour market of unskilled workers for the above-discussed reasons. In order to retain these workers, firms may offer the alternative of either 'stiff pace of work and high wages' or 'restrained work performance and low wages'. However, both of these strategies are less effective among these workers than in the case of skilled young workers who keep up a stiff pace of work or the double-status workers who have a stable source of income in the second economy. Marginal workers are able to achieve high wages only in proportion to the number of working hours, or if performing tasks requiring great physical strength, under hard working conditions, where there is a direct relationship between effort and pay.[12] Since these jobs are dead-end jobs in the firm's job structure and do not lead to skills or promotion, there is no point in being a 'workhorse'. The unqualified worker's position is not much more favourable if he chooses to find work in the second economy (casual work for small shopkeepers and small producers, black work, casual unskilled work in construction) instead of becoming a 'workhorse'. These additional sources of income, however, rarely make up a regular system of activities suited to the firm's minimum requirements for the number of working hours and the way work is organized. The marginal worker is also in a marginal position in the second economy: he cannot organize his time, and his income opportunities are subject to great and sudden changes. He has to do without his low but guaranteed wage if he ceases employment, and if he frequently changes employer he must forgo the rights stemming from continuous employment - automatic wage increases, year-end bonuses if his monthly worktime is under twenty-one days etc. The marginal worker's behaviour is characterized by frequent changes of employers and occupations, and by income-increasing attempts. This behaviour is a response to a crisis. The available labour market strategies do not lead to a satisfactory, long-term maintenance of living standards or a solution to the double challenge of stability and security, either in the state-organized labour market or in the second economy, or even as a combination of the two. 'Such types of work do not allow, either individually or in their typical combinations, the establishment of a guaranteed, stable existence recognized by the majority and offering long-term perspectives'. The marginal workers' labour market instability (which is a decisive element of their unstable way of life) contributes to the disadvantages of this group and to the reproduction of social inequality.

12. 'An example: when the ship was finished, some of the iron sheets got rusty and it had to be removed so they could be painted. This is the most dirty, lousy job in the world, removing rust. It was done by a gipsy family. Four of them are employed here, but when work starts, the whole family comes, all thirty-six of them, and they do the job without overtime, on Saturday or Sunday, take the substantial sum of money and go away. They come again only when the next ship is finished. This is unbearable from the aspect of both labour discipline and legality since four of them are employed but thirty-six of them work so that the output of the four appears as 300 per cent. If this gipsy family ever becomes dissatisfied no one knows what the factory will do. Who will do this job? It could be mechanized, but then a machine would have to be bought. And equipment' (Polgár 1982, 63-4, excerpt from an interview).

## FINAL REMARKS

In our study we have attempted to demonstrate the typical patterns of workers' behaviour which evolved in the 1970s. These patterns can be regarded as specific strategies characteristic of the workers' behaviour, through which the groups of workers, differing in their goals, first of all increase their incomes and improve their wage/efforts ratios. These strategies, having evolved as a result of mutual adaptation processes of conflictual nature and thus being relatively stable (continually reproduced) through time, bear the marks of compromises between workers' endeavours and those policies which enterprises conduct towards the respective groups of workers.

With the existence of a significant variability in workers' positions and, as a consequence, in their chances to achieve their goals on the labour market, the operation of the labour market must contribute to the prevalence of social inequalities.

Throughout the study we have focused our attention on the most widespread patterns of worker behaviour. It is a task of future research to explore further strategies and sub-strategies to reach a fuller understanding of workers' behaviour in the Hungarian labour market.

## REFERENCES

Doeringer, P. B. and Piore, M. J. (1971): *Internal Labour Markets and Manpower Analysis*, Heath, Lexington.

Fazekas, K. (1982): 'Bér – teljesitmény alku a belsõ munkaerõpiacon' (Wage and performance bargaining on the internal labour market), in Galasi, P. (ed.) *A mukaerõpiac szerkezete és müködése Magyarországon* (*The Structure and the Functioning of the Labour Market in Hungary*), KJK, Budapest.

Fülöp, Gy. and Bokányi, I. (1980): 'A besorolási rendszer szerepe, funkciója' (The role and function of job grading), *Munkaügyi Szemle*, I–II.

Gábor, R. I. and Galasi, P. (1981): A második gazdaság (The Second Economy), KJK, Budapest.

Galasi, P. (1978): 'A fluktuáló munkaerõ néhány jellegzetessége' (Some characteristics of unstable manpower), *Munkaügyi Szemle*, no. 8.

Havas, G. and Kardos, L. (1975): 'Munkakultura és életforma, Esettanulmány az Ikarus Gyárban' (Work culture and life style, case study in Ikarus Bus Factory), unpublished manuscript.

Kemény, I. (1982): 'The unregistered economy in Hungary', *Soviet Studies*, no. 3.

Konrád, Gy. and Szelényi I. (1971): 'A késleltetett városfejlõdés társadalmi konfliktusai' (Social conflicts of delayed urbanization), *Valóság*, no. 12.

Köllõ, J. (1982): 'A külsõ és a belsõ munkaerõpiac kapcsolata egy pamutszövödében' (Connections between external and internal labour markets in a weaving factory), in Galasi, P. (ed.) *A munkaerõpiac szerkezete és müködése Magyarországon* (*The Structure and the Functioning of the Labour Market in Hungary*), KJK, Budapest.

Kreckel, R. (1980): 'Unequal opportunity structure and labour market segmentation', *Sociology*, no. 4.

Parkin, F. (1974): 'Strategies of social closure in class formation', in F. Parkin (ed.) *The Social Analysis of Class Structure*, London. Tavistock.

Pogány, Gy. (1982): *Munkaerõgazdálkodás és munkaerõpolitika* (*Labour Management and Labour Policy*), Kossuth, Budapest.

Polgár, M. (1982): 'A munkaerõ és bérviszonyok egyes kérdései a Magyar Hajó és Darugyárban' (Some questions of manpower and wage relations in the Hungarian Ship and Crane Factory), Pénzügykutatási Intézet, unpublished manuscript.

Schelling, T. C. (1963): *The Strategy of Conflict*, New York.

Sengenberger, W. (1981): 'Labour market segmentation and business cycle', in Wilkinson F. (ed.), *The Dynamics of Labour Market Segmentation*, Academic Press, London.

Sziráczki, Gy. (1983): 'The development and functioning of an enterprise labour market in Hungary', *Economies et Sociétés*, no. 3–4.

Weber, M. (1976): *Wirtschaft und Gesellschaft*, (1921), 5th edn, Tübingen.

# 14

# Rethinking Internal Labour Markets: New Insights from a Comparative Perspective

DAVID STARK

From the putting-out system of the early nineteenth century, to internal subcontracting at the turn of the century, to Frederick Taylor's system of 'scientific management', market economies have seen various organizational solutions to the problem of the allocation and reward of labour by the enterprise. Within the past decade, 'internal labour markets' have been identified by sociologists and economists as the prevalent institutional arrangement governing the allocation and reward of labour by the large capitalist firm in the contemporary period (Althauser and Kalleberg, 1981; Baron, 1984; Pfeffer and Cohen, 1984; Doeringer and Piore, 1971; Osterman, 1984; Williamson et al., 1975). Internal labour markets have been studied in comparative perspective in a number of advanced capitalist societies (e.g. Koike, 1983; Streeck, 1984); but the subject has not been explored in the context of a state socialist economy. This chapter undertakes such a comparison.

The purpose of this comparison is to contrast the mode of operation of internal labour markets in the capitalist firm with a quite different set of mechanisms in the socialist firm. To engage in comparison requires that we focus on the broadly similar functions performed by 'internal labour markets' in both systems. To understand the *specificity* of the institutional arrangements that perform comparable functions in both the capitalist and the socialist firm requires that we suspend

This essay was first published in *American Sociological Review*, 51, August 1986, pp. 492–504. Research was supported by a grant from the American Council of Learned Societies and by a grant from the Duke University Research Council. I would like to thank Robert Althauser, William Bridges, László Bruszt, Monique Djokić, István Gábor, Alan Kerckhoff, János Lukács, Teréz Laky, Csaba Makó, Angela O'Rand, and two anonymous referees for helpful criticisms and suggestions. An earlier version of this paper was presented at the 1985 Annual Meetings of the American Sociological Association in Washington, DC.

our initial assumption that internal labour markets have some invariant form (e.g. routinized promotions along ladders of bureaucratically defined job classifications).

The following analysis opens with a schematized model – a heuristic device to highlight the similarities and differences in the allocative and reward mechanisms within firms in the two economic systems. To anticipate the major lines of the argument developed below: in capitalist economies and in socialist economies, workers and firms face a number of uncertainties regarding labour that arise from the firm's coexistence, competition, and dependence upon other economic units in the organizational field. If the activities of other economic units cannot be controlled, then, at least, greater predictability can be attained within the (albeit permeable) boundaries of the enterprise itself. The mechanisms for accomplishing this goal are internal labour markets (generically defined) in both systems; but the specific institutional arrangements and the logics according to which they operate differ.

In both the capitalist and the socialist firm, internal labour markets perform broadly similar functions in tying workers to the firm, facilitating greater predictability of earnings and employment, ensuring cooperation in production, and thus reducing the effects of systemic uncertainties. The source and the nature of these systemic constraints and uncertainties, however, are not identical for the capitalist and the socialist firm. As a consequence, 'internal labour markets' take different forms in the two types of firms. Analysis of systemic uncertainties and the organizational responses of workers and managers yields a comparative model of mirrored opposition: in economies in which the firm operates in a *market environment*, systemic uncertainties regarding labour are reduced through internal *bureaucratic rules*. In the socialist economy, by contrast, where systemic uncertainties are produced by a *bureaucratic environment*, the firm responds through internal *market transactions*.

The use of internal market transactions to reduce the effects of systemic uncertainties in the socialist firm is brought into sharper relief in a recent organizational innovation in Hungary – the formation of semi-autonomous subcontracting units inside the enterprise. Discussion of these new market forms will (1) outline the ways in which the recent internal subcontracting arrangements promote organizational flexibility for the firm, and (2) analyse in greater detail the forms of bargaining that characterize the relations between subcontracting units and enterprises. These subcontractual links represent a formalized but non-bureaucratized development of the informal market transactions characteristic of internal labour markets in the socialist firm.

The aim of this comparative project is not to produce a more rigorous definition of internal labour markets, based on experiences inside the capitalist firm, which can then be used to ascertain the extent to which the allocation and reward of labour in the large socialist firm conforms to or departs from this definition. Instead, the goal is to develop a comparative strategy in which the specificity of the organizational problems and institutional 'solutions' in each system is revealed through their mutual contrast. The model of mirrored opposition allows us to grasp this dual specificity simultaneously as the institutional configuration of each system serves as a prism refracting the distinctive dimensions of the other.

## INTERNAL LABOUR MARKETS IN COMPARATIVE PERSPECTIVE

### *Reducing Uncertainties from a Market Environment*

For the purposes of this discussion, the central idea of the internal labour market approach[1] is that both managers and workers in the large capitalist firm (at the same time that they try to maximize opportunities for profits and wages, respectively) attempt to reduce uncertainties arising from the market environment. From the managers' perspective, a major cause of concern is the uncertainty of whether employees will stay with the firm. This uncertainty poses a problem for the enterprise because, although workers come to the firm with educational credentials and some skills, they often receive considerable training on the job. To ensure that the enterprise (and not some other firm) gets the returns on that investment, the enterprise takes certain steps to reduce the likelihood that its workers will take those skills out onto the external labour market. The results are regular, incremental wage and salary increases and promotions along internal job ladders, regulated by principles of formal bureaucratic rules. These routinized procedures, moreover, not only attach skilled employees to the firm but also facilitate the transmission of skills among workers themselves and provide long-term incentives to encourage performance by workers in the production process.

From the workers' perspective, the major uncertainty is that unfavourable labour market conditions (e.g. high unemployment) will drive down the costs of their dismissal and replacement by new workers. Thus workers, too, have an interest in institutionalizing those administrative rules that govern internal job ladders and the wage and salary increments correlated with promotion. And, especially through their trade unions, they attempt to enforce principles such as seniority as the salient criteria for determining the order of promotions or temporary layoffs. To the extent that they are successful, uncertainty of employment is differentially distributed across the working class and the actual or potential beneficiaries are more likely to cooperate in the production process (Edwards, 1979). The result of these efforts by both workers and managers to reduce the threat of uncertainties from the labour market is the increasing bureaucratization of the mechanisms of staffing and reward internal to the firm. In the US auto and steel industries we find, for example, a system of industrial relations characterized by narrow job classifications organized on well-defined ladders regulated by formal governance procedures.

Thus, in the contemporary period of the development of the capitalist economy, efforts within the enterprise to reduce uncertainties generated by a market environment take the form of bureaucratic rules. Although these arrangements are labelled 'internal labour *markets*', their character as bureaucratic rules is their distinctive trait (Osterman, 1984: 2–6).

The particular character of these rules, moreover, is not simply that they are

1. Various approaches are brought here under one rubric. For an excellent summary of competing and complementary theories of internal labour markets see Baron (1984). In terms of Althauser and Kalleberg's (1981) important conceptual reformulation of types of internal labour markets, the focus in these paragraphs is on the firm internal labour market (FILM) in the capitalist economy.

impersonal, but that they selectively bring into salience certain abstract attributes of persons. Not unique and singular properties, but categorical features are the only officially recognized criteria. The principle governing eligibility, selection, and reward is not membership in an interacting group, but membership in a category of persons. Internal labour markets in the West operate according to a classificatory logic.[2] For example, in the steel industry, individuals with certain credentials (a formal category) are eligible for promotions; only those at skill grade ten and with at least five years seniority can apply for jobs in the new rolling mill; and workers who fall into the category of those who entered the firm before 1971 will not be dismissed in the current layoffs. In the internal labour markets of the capitalist firm, individuals are differentially rewarded and/or protected in so far as they belong to a category in the official classifications. These categories are themselves the products of bargaining (that is, they are not naturally given but produced through negotiations concerning which criteria will be relevant in which circumstances). In this sense, negotiations about the 'terms of the contract' are not simply about numerical calculations (wage rates, productivity increases, cost of living, etc.) but in large measure about the terms in the officially recognized system of classification.[3] It is through this classification (categories of persons and categories of jobs) that an internal labour market is constructed.

### *The Socialist Firm in the Face of Uncertainties*

We turn now to the case of the state socialist economies of Eastern Europe; that is, we shift to the socialist firm operating in a bureaucratic environment. In the myth of planning there are, of course, no uncertainties in the system. Under conditions of administrative allocation of various factor inputs, the director of an enterprise is given a plan target, told from which firms supplies will arrive, and to which firms products will be sent; prices and wages are fixed, there is no credit market, and under Stalinist conditions even labour is directly, centrally, and administratively allocated. Under conditions of central planning it might seem that all sources of uncertainty have been eliminated.

The director of our socialist firm, however, would be quite surprised to learn that there are no uncertainties in the system. And he or she would locate the major source of uncertainties in the planning process, that is, the bureaucratic environment, itself. In the first place, plan targets are not fixed but can change in the middle of the period to which the plan applies (Berliner, 1956; Nove, 1980: 104–7). Moreover, although the supplying firm is specified, there is no guarantee that parts, materials, and other supplies will be delivered on time or will meet the requisite specifications. With few options to seek alternative suppliers, the manager must cope with these supply bottlenecks (Kornai, 1980; Berliner, 1976:

2. For insights on the classificatory politics through which social and organizational categories are constructed, defended, dissimulated, and challenged, see Bourdieu and Boltanski (1981) and Bourdieu (1984), especially pp. 466–84).

3. Systems of classification are thus both a resource and an object of contention. The terrain on which such classificatory politics occurs is not only at the bargaining table of contract negotiations but also in the courts and government agencies. A recent example of this classificatory politics can be seen in the current efforts to reclassify jobs around the issue of 'comparable worth' to counteract occupational sex segregation.

62–92). In Hungary (and, to a lesser extent in the other East European economies), plan targets are being replaced by 'indicators' and other more indirect regulating mechanisms. But even in those cases where the firm has more autonomy in choosing suppliers, nonetheless, supply bottlenecks arising from the 'shortage economy' continue to plague enterprise managers, and 'rush work' or 'storming' still characterize the work place at the end of monthly, quarterly, or yearly planning periods (Laki, 1980). The shift from plan targets to the more indirect indicators (which are subject to sudden and dramatic changes no less, and perhaps even more, than the notorious physical output measures of the plan targets) still means that the manager must navigate the firm through a process in which investment funds and, in many cases, wage funds, are allocated through central budgetary mechanisms (Kornai, 1983; Vági, 1982).

The nature of the bureaucratic environment bears directly on the allocation and reward of labour inside the firm. To cope with the uncertainties of supplies and shifts in either plan targets or indirect regulators, a substantial labour reserve is the surest protection. Firms that have hoarded labour have hidden labour reserves that can be mobilized when supplies finally arrive or when signals change. Because labour hoarding is not isolated but general, the systemic result is a situation of chronic labour shortage. This chronic labour shortage forms the basis of workers' bargaining power with management (Sabel and Stark, 1982).

From the perspective of *shop* management, the allocation of labour is also shaped by some fundamental features of the economics of shortage. Shop management faces repeated instances of forced substitution; i.e. when supplies or spare parts of a certain quality or specification cannot be obtained, they must make do with what is available. The consequence is that production runs must be interrupted, machines rapidly retooled, modifications made, normal sequences reversed, etc. To accomplish this, workers must be shifted (not simply within a month but often within a single day) from one machine to another across work groups and even across shops (Ladó and Tóth, 1985a). Not as a virtue but as a necessity in response to often occurring 'crises', the production process in state socialist economies requires a flexible allocation of labour on the shop floor. Moreover, the consequences of storming periods (intense bouts of work in which machinery is sometimes run without stopping for regular maintenance) combined with the fact that physical equipment is continued in operation past the point of normal technological obsolescence, are that foremen and superintendents face the imminent danger of breakdowns. To keep equipment running (either by speedy repair or by measures to prevent breakdowns under conditions when physical equipment is periodically over-utilized), shop management must rely on regular production workers to engage in certain maintenance and repair functions (Makó. 1985; Héthy and Makó, 1978). In short many of the material and organizational prerequisites of strictly Taylorist work methods and payment systems are absent on the socialist shop floor.[4]

Thus, to mitigate the effects of uncertainties from the bureaucratic environment, managers in the socialist firm depend on workers' cooperation at crucial

4. The attempt to bring an entire national economy under rationalized control through the instruments of central planning at the macro level poses insurmountable obstacles to 'scientific management' at the micro level.

moments and in key aspects of the production process. But they do not depend on all workers equally. Reduction of uncertainty therefore requires *differential* allocation of rewards targeted to those workers with firm-specific skills and less routinized tasks. The question is whether this goal is accomplished through bureaucratically regulated job classifications. At first glance, it might seem that this is the case: within the socialist firm, formal classifications according to educational credentials, skill, physically demanding or hazardous working conditions, and the like, abound (Nove, 1980: 206–7; McAuley 1979: 184–206). But these bureaucratic classifications are not the result of bargaining between managers and workers in a firm or industry, but are imposed on the firm by the central authorities. Central wage scales and job classification are, above all, an attempt to limit inter-enterprise wage differentials and restrict overall wage outlays. And because they are centrally established (and not the consequence of bargaining that reflects the specific conditions of the firm, locale, or industry), these formalized categories represent a further instance of constraints originating from the bureaucratic environment. Not by applying, but by circumventing these categories can a manager in the socialist firm achieve the flexibility in the allocation and reward of labour so necessary to meet production targets.

### *Selective Bargaining in the Socialist Firm*

If not through more bureaucratic rules at the level of the enterprise, through what mechanisms can shop management ensure the cooperation of key workers in a never-ending series of *ad hoc* arrangements? The hierarchically organized trade unions of Eastern Europe provide few channels for securing cooperation at the point of production. Instead, shop management engages in market-like transactions of selective bargaining. In this shadow bargaining, the 'bargaining units' are informal groups, membership in which is determined by position in the social networks of the shop floor.[5] These informal groups are constituted and reproduced by acts of exchange among workers themselves, e.g. special tools, spare parts, and information (Héthy and Makó, 1972a, 1978; Kemény, 1978; Fazekas, 1984). In their negotiations, both shop management and workers depend on the informal groups to construct equivalences and enforce the *quid pro quo* in the hidden bargaining, as, for example, when workers agree to perform special tasks during difficult times and are compensated (perhaps weeks later) by receiving easy overtime or payment for fictive work in a period when management has resources to distribute (Lukács, 1984; Kövári and Sziráczki, 1985; Ladó and Tóth, 1985b). This shop floor bargaining is, above all, transactive, and the conditions of exchange are often so incommensurate, particularistic, and complicated that this non-routinized exchange is not and cannot be governed by bureaucratic rules.

If managers in the socialist firm have an interest in the socialist 'internal labour market', many workers do as well, and for reasons directly related to the

5. Informal bargaining, of course, also takes place on the shop floor of the large capitalist firm. The point here is that whereas informal agreements are a subordinate mechanism within the capitalist firm, selective bargaining is the primary mechanism constituting the internal labour market of the socialist firm.

uncertainties specific to the socialist economy. Unlike workers in the West, workers in state socialist economies face few, if any, uncertainties about employment *per se*. The employment policies of the regimes and the structurally reproduced conditions of labour shortage ensure virtually no unemployment. Similarly, before the recent appearance of inflation in Eastern Europe, workers could be relatively certain of stable prices and a steady (but slow) increase in the standard of living. But they do face another set of uncertainties. The fact that the majority of manual workers in the socialist economy work on piece rates, and that only a small percentage are not on some kind of performance-based incentive system (International Labour Office, 1984: 144–5; Kirsch, 1972: 25–43), means that many workers are threatened by the same production problems that give headaches to management: in situations where the basic wage is a relatively small proportion of total earnings, breakdowns and supply bottlenecks disrupt production and can make it difficult to meet the norms.[6] This threat heightens the significance of the informal work group for two reasons: a strong informal group (1) provides resources for internal crisis management (the exchange of services among workers themselves to cope with these events) and (2) provides the channels for negotiations to even out earnings across good times and bad by calling in debts (incurred by shop management) when the occasion or need arises. Moreover, central wage regulations and job classifications lead to the uncertainty among workers that additional skills (especially those which are firm-specific) or additional effort will yield additional rewards. Workers who belong to the stronger informal groups on the shop floor are able to valorize their skills as the shadow bargaining provides an avenue of manoeuvre to achieve somewhat greater calculability in the ratio between effort (or skill) and reward (Héthy and Makó, 1972a; Kertesi and Sziráczki, 1985).

The ability to exploit uncertainties facing managers gives workers the opportunity to engage in transactive bargaining; the need to reduce the uncertainties they face themselves gives workers a real stake in these market-like transactions. But the shop floor is not a homogeneous field in which bargaining resources are equally distributed. Some workers are favourably located at critical production bottlenecks; others lack technical skills. Still others lack the 'political' skills to capitalize their assets (Makó, 1985). Not least important, workers differ in their possession of social capital (Bourdieu, 1980) – the contacts and connections that make up the informal groups, the affiliative ties on the networks of the shop floor that are so necessary for translating opportunities into advantageous bargaining. Workers' informal groups, the primary agency for transactive bargaining, vary in their density, extensiveness, and in the control they are able to exercise; or, in the language of the Hungarian shop floor, they are of different 'weight' (Fazekas, 1984; see also Farkas, 1983). In practice this means that not all workers participate (directly or indirectly) in the informal bargaining with management.

Within the selective bargaining of the socialist internal labour market, whether a given worker is included in the 'bargaining unit' and 'covered by its agreements' (to use conventional industrial relations terminology to highlight the contrast

6. For evidence of wide fluctuations in monthly earnings for Hungarian workers in a number of industries see Farkas (1983), Ladó and Tóth (1985b), Héthy and Makó (1972b) and Lukács (forthcoming).

with Western trade unions) is not determined by bureaucratic criteria. And although age, seniority, and technical skill are structural factors that influence the likelihood of being in an informal group with greater bargaining power, none of these attributes makes the individual automatically 'eligible for benefits'. In other words, it is personal membership in a group and not impersonal membership in a formal category that makes the individual a potential beneficiary of the informal bargaining. Similarly, although the gradient of workers' earnings is correlated with age (Kolosi, 1984) this outcome is not the result of promotion through well-defined job ladders (which, in any case, are unlikely due to the organizational features of the production process described above) but arises from the individual's movement from informal groups that have less opportunities for transactive bargaining to those that have more.[7] Thus, just as some workers in the capitalist economy are less advantaged on the internal job ladders (or are excluded from them altogether), so workers in the socialist economy differ considerably in the extent to which they benefit (or are excluded) from the transactive relations of informal markets inside the firm. Cast in the language of dual labour market theory, whereas in the capitalist economy occupants on the internal job ladders of the 'primary' sector differ from their counterparts in the 'secondary' sector in the degree to which they are *protected from the market,* dualism in the socialist economy is structured around differential opportunities for *participation in the market.*

## FROM INFORMAL BARGAINING TO INTERNAL SUBCONTRACTING

That market relations are cultivated inside the socialist firm as a means to reduce or surmount uncertainties from its environment becomes most transparent in the case of a new system of internal subcontracting inside Hungarian enterprises. Through legislative statutes enacted January 1, 1982, Hungarian workers received the right to establish subcontracting units, known as 'enterprise business work partnerships' (*vállalati gazdasági munkaközösségek,* or VGMs) inside their enterprises. These partnerships (of up to thirty members) have legal status, as semi-autonomous economic units, to negotiate contracts to produce goods or services on their 'off' hours using the firm's equipment.[8] Thus, a worker who belongs to a partnership is involved in two organizational forms: first, as an employee of the firm, working during the regular hours for wages and other benefits, and second, in the off hours, as a member of a partnership in which the organization of work, the election of representatives, and the internal distribution of earnings are decided at the discretion of the membership.

7. These moves are not 'promotions' but are often lateral shifts from one machine (or part of the production process) where rates are difficult or the opportunities for informal bargaining are limited to another with more favourable circumstances (access to 'easy overtime', special bonuses, etc.). See Lukács (forthcoming), and Kővári and Sziráczki (1985).

8. As forms of internal subcontracting, the VGMs bear some resemblance to the inside subcontracting system at the turn of the century in the United States. In contrast to the old 'sweating system', however, the relations among the members in the partnership are nonhierarchical and the internal division of labour is much more fluid. For a more detailed comparison and contrast see Stark (1985b).

The analysis of this new subcontracting innovation is based primarily on field research conducted by the author in eight Hungarian firms (in a range of industries - engineering and design, heavy and light industry) in the summer of 1984 with intensive follow-up studies in three of these firms in the winter-spring of 1985. Eighteen subcontracting units (of different skill composition - engineers, technicians, skilled workers, and semi-skilled workers) were included in the study. The research involved participation in meetings involving managers and workers, examination of company documents, and above all, many hours of open-ended interviews with thirteen managers and fifty-one workers in their factories and in their homes. Many of the interviews were recorded and transcribed, after familiarity was established with a subcontracting team and often at the suggestion of the workers themselves.[9] These studies at the level of firms were supplemented by aggregate statistics on the composition of the partnerships, newspaper articles, transcriptions of radio and television broadcasts, and personal interviews conducted with trade union officials at the national level, and with key figures in the decision to establish the new subcontracting form, including the former Deputy Prime Minister of the Hungarian government and a current member of the Central Committee.

## *Partners in Reducing Uncertainty*

As a further development and institutionalization of the socialist internal labour market, the new subcontracting form has its origins in the organizational features of the socialist firm. Its particular emergence in Hungary is also tied to a set of political and macroeconomic factors in that society at the beginning of the 1980s (Stark, 1985a). In brief, the particular timing of the decision to introduce the new form (a high-level, closed debate began in the summer of 1980) involved the conjuncture of a serious economic crisis, the cumulative effects of the expansion of the 'second economy' in the last half of the 1970s,[10] and the emergence of Solidarity in Poland. In the initial discussions, the Hungarian economic leadership hoped that the VGMs would improve the export performance of the large firms and also fill shortages for certain consumer goods and services. Enterprise management saw the VGMs as a way of resolving problems posed by the expansion of the second economy - namely, that workers were increasingly withholding their labour within the regular hours for moonlighting jobs in the off hours.[11] If workers were taking on extra work, better that they do so in the

9. Although the author's comprehension of Hungarian is good, to ensure accuracy of translation interviews were assisted by either János Lukács or László Bruszt (researchers at the Institute of Sociology of the Hungarian Academy of Sciences) who also arranged access to the firms.

10. The term 'second economy' refers to all income-generating activities which are outside the planned economy including, for example, legal private craftsmen and shopkeepers, private and household agricultural plots, unregistered moonlighting, etc. See Gábor (1979) and, for an estimate of the size of the second economy, Gábor (1985).

11. In terms of the model of mirrored opposition, the second economy in state socialist societies is, to a significant degree, structurally comparable to some parts of the welfare state in the West. For a similar argument see Szelenyi (1978). That is, whereas workers in capitalist societies receive some protection from the *uncertainty of employment* through unemployment compensation and sickness benefits from the *state* sector, workers in state socialist societies attempt to mitigate the *uncertainty of earnings* by taking their skills into an auxiliary *market* sector. The consequence, of course, is to increase the uncertainty for managers that workers will adequately perform their jobs in the regular hours.

partnerships where their energies could be reabsorbed to the benefit of the firm. For the political leadership, the VGMs were viewed as a means to augment the incomes of the politically and economically strategic group of skilled workers at the core of urban industry, many of whom could not take their specialized skills into the second economy. In a period of stagnating real wages in Hungary and worker insurgency in Poland, it was hoped that the new form would pre-empt political tensions among key groups of workers and tie their interests to the new wave of economic reforms.

With these macro-political motivations providing the possibility of the partnership arrangement, workers and managers inside Hungarian firms quickly realized that a system of internal subcontracting could be utilized to reduce many of the uncertainties described in the preceding section. After an initial period of hesitation in the early months of 1982, the partnerships have grown rapidly and continuously to the present. By mid-1985, more than 18,500 partnerships were in operation involving over 213,000 members. The partnerships are disproportionately located in heavy industry, and predominantly among skilled workers, i.e. the segment of workers of strategic concern both to the political leadership and to enterprise management. In some industrial branches, the proportion of manual workers in VGMs (administrative and clerical staff are rarely involved) exceeds 10 per cent, and in some large firms more than 20 per cent of manual workers are in the partnerships (Hungarian Central Statistical Office, 1986).

Typically, upper management in a given firm indicates that it would like to see a partnership formed in a particular field of activity. From that point on, selection is left to the social networks of the shop floor, with the result that VGM membership in the off hours is predicted by membership in a strong informal group in the regular hours. The additional earnings which these members receive from their work partnerships are much more than pocket change: hourly earnings in the work partnerships are usually 2 to 2.5 times higher than earnings during the regular hours. In the units studied, it was not uncommon to find VGM members whose hourly earnings from their partnerships were four times the average hourly wage in industry. For most of the work partners, the income from their VGM participation represents one-third to one-half of the yearly income from their regular job;[12] but for some members, VGM incomes equal, and even exceed, their regular earnings.

For the VGM member, then, participation in a work partnership provides access to an important set of benefits – an opportunity to marketize human capital (technical skills) and to gain new returns on investments in social capital (contacts and connections). For enterprise and shop-level management, as well, the partnerships provide a new avenue of manoeuvre to mitigate chronic problems facing the socialist firm.

12. This estimate extrapolates from published data: in 1984, average monthly VGM income per member was 4738 forints (Hungarian Central Statistical Office 1986:20–22) and the average monthly earnings for all workers in the main job in industry was 5615 forints (Hungarian Central Statistical Office 1985:45). The data on VGM incomes are based on reporting by enterprises to the Finance Ministry and are reliable. The estimate includes information on the dispersion of VGM earnings and assumes that VGM members earn higher than average incomes in the regular hours. More precise published statistics that express VGM incomes as a proportion of members' earnings from the regular job are not available. Detailed company records from a large firm show that partnership earnings increase members' income by more than 60 per cent.

Enterprise managers frequently approve the formation of partnerships in those areas in which the firm confronts troublesome bottlenecks, either in direct production or in special repairs and auxiliary services. In the latter case, partnerships are utilized to reduce dependence on outside firms. VGMs included in the study consistently underbid outside contractors in performing support functions such as installing new equipment, non-routine maintenance, or special design work that exceeds the firm's capacity. Over and above this immediate cost saving, inside subcontractors have the additional advantage of providing the enterprise increased flexibility in meeting production deadlines. Contracts with the work partnerships relieve managers of the inevitable delays encountered when such jobs are submitted for bids by other enterprises: VGM subcontractors are available on the spot and often have a thorough understanding of the particular needs of the firm, thus saving time in contract preparation or in the provision of additional information as the project unfolds.

The partnerships not only improve performance and flexibility in auxiliary services and maintenance, but also provide a novel form of economizing on scarce resources in the area of direct production. In deciding whether to subcontract to a VGM, the manager compares the partnership's fee with the labour costs of other ways of performing a production task in regular or overtime hours. Calculated as an 'hourly labour cost' to the firm, the hourly rate of enterprise expenditures to the VGMs is considerably higher than labour costs (hourly wage plus pensions and other benefits) for work performed in regular or overtime hours (for a detailed accounting from company records see Stark, 1985b). Nonetheless, the seemingly more 'expensive' subcontracting solution can be a preferred choice. Because the work partnership is a legally separate economic entity, the 'entrepreneurial fees' paid to the VGMs are not drawn from the enterprise wage fund (a fund that is both limited and highly regulated, with wage increases steeply taxed), but are charged against the firm's costs or 'other expenditures' account, just as they would be for a purchase or other transaction with any other economic unit in the economy. Thus, payments to the partnership members allow the enterprise to circumvent various aspects of the central wage regulations. In so doing, management can differentially reward strategic workers and tie their interests to those of the firm.

## *New Solutions and New Problems*

Hungarian managers are alert to the ways in which the partnership form, as a new system of selective rewards, offers new opportunities for reducing bottlenecks and all but eliminating turnover among workers in critical aspects of the production process. In the interviews and in their statements to the Hungarian business press, enterprise managers also tend to interpret the partnerships as providing a new structure of incentives, and they point to the faster pace of work, higher productivity, and better quality control in the VGMs as evidence of the improved performance that would be possible if central wage regulations were lifted altogether. Workers, for their part, are not dismissive of the partnerships as a new system of incentives. But they interpret the meaning of the partnership form in different terms by focusing on the collective nature of the new incentive, within a context in which workers have discretion to organize the work themselves. As one VGM member explained:

How can the VGM do the job more cheaply?

Our tool preparation [set-up] is better; everyone gets the tools he needs and then work begins. Yes, we use regular hours to do a lot of our set-up for the VGM. But we also use our heads to get the tools we need. Once we were told that we would have to wait two weeks to get some special tool that was needed for a job. But we just can't wait that long. So, I went to the small shop that makes the tool, I found that it was available, and it was purchased in a day. It would have taken forever if we had to wait to have it done through the regular purchasing channels. When we have a job to do that will make us some money, we make sure that we have everything to do it even if it takes a little bit of running around. Sometimes we will borrow tools from a partnership in another factory. We might have to pay a little for it; but often it all gets worked out informally since they might need to borrow something from us sometime.

Does that kind of thing ever happen for regular enterprise jobs?

In regular hours we're not required to use our heads. We wait for others to do that. Here [in the VGM] we use our heads. Several months ago there was an International Fair [trade exhibition] here in Budapest. Our VGM has a common fund that has various uses. From our common pool we sent everyone in the VGM to the exhibit to go to look out for tools or methods and pick up printed materials and ideas. We were able to find some good ideas. We found some fittings and tools that we were able to make ourselves and they have cut down on the time in the VGM. The enterprise never would have given us time off to go to the exhibit. They just wouldn't have thought about it. And if we weren't in a VGM there wouldn't have been any reason for us to waste our time going.

The astute manager can take advantage of the new division of labour and the higher morale within these self-managed micro units to improve the overall performance of his enterprise. One manager explained:

Here's an example. There used to be a bottleneck in producing a special shock absorber used in trucks. These shock absorbers were exported. We gave the task to a VGM. Earlier we had lots of quality control problems with this unit. The reject rate had gotten way out of hand at 23 per cent. After the job was undertaken by the VGM on their off hour, the reject rate fell to 9 per cent *on the regular hours*. What is learned in off hours can't be forgotten for the next day's morning shift.

Similarly, another manager observed that the VGMs are an important source of technical innovation:

The VGM brings the brain reserve out of people either in the organization of work or in technical things. Earlier we had a system where 'suggestions' could be made to the firm. There was some premium paid for them, but it was so small. Now, however, it's worthwhile for workers to make these small-scale innovations and these solutions can be used for regular hours. Ideas that were once left in drawers are now on the machines.

But since this micro-self-management is contained within the partnerships and does not extend to the rest of the organization, contradictions can develop between the incentives of the partnerships and the incentives of the firm.[13] Members of the VGMs have a dual set of interests and a dual morale. Self-management within one work unit leads to new problems: workers grumble that support activities (energy, tool rooms, parts, etc.) on which they depend during their off hours are not well organized. Managers complain that workers are holding back on performance on enterprise time and that members of the VGMs are hiding spare parts, raw materials, and machine fittings that are in short supply for use during their work for the partnerships. Thus, if ideas that were once left in drawers are now on the machines, it is also true that in some cases machine fittings that were once in the tool room are now hidden under a VGM member's work bench.

## INSTITUTIONALIZED BUT NON-BUREAUCRATIZED BARGAINING

Most importantly for the stability and reproduction of the socialist internal labour market, the partnerships provide a more formal mechanism in which the *quid pro quo* relations of the shop-floor bargaining can be institutionalized over a longer term. As a formalization of the selective bargaining that occurs during the regular hours, the new internal subcontracting system represents a transformation in which many of the original elements of the informal bargaining are conserved at the same time that a process of institutionalization has occurred. Institutionalization does not imply bureaucratization, however. As a form of the socialist internal labour markets, the work partnerships are not governed by impersonal rules. Official classifications, such as the credential or years of experience in the firm, are not criteria for membership in a partnership; furthermore, as we shall see, the content of their bargaining with the enterprise is not directed at establishing a set of eligibility requirements, rules for promotion, layoff schedules, wage increments, or associated benefits.

The customary practice in the price-setting between enterprise and VGM is that each partnership has an elected representative (*közös képviselö)* who negotiates for the collective membership. Within these negotiations, workers frequently use their tacit knowledge of the economic difficulties of enterprises to bargain for better rates for their partnerships. One particularly instructive case involved a team of semi-skilled assemblers. A mid-level manager approached the assemblers' representative with a job for their partnership. The firm, he said, had received a rush order that had to be filled by the end of the following week. The representative of the partnership feigned disinterest: the workers were tired, the partnership had more than enough work, the price was too low . . . and besides, he and the other partners knew that the components to be assembled for the supposed 'rush order' were sitting in railroad cars in the factory yard. Within a few days the firm would be required to pay a steep fine for every day that the cars were

13. The internal labour markets of the capitalist firm are also not without their contradictions. Bureaucratized job classifications that reduce uncertainties can also produce new rigidities. The recent increase of *outside* subcontracting by US firms is, in part, a means to circumvent the rigidities of narrow job classifications (Piore and Sabel 1984).

tied up. In the end a deal was struck: the price for the job was one-third higher than the initial offer, but still lower than the fine that the enterprise would have been forced to pay if the work partnership had not agreed to do the job promptly.

A similar case involves a VGM that produces sophisticated machine tools at a firm we shall call Minotaur, one of the largest in Hungary. This VGM consists of eighteen of the most highly skilled workers in a shop of 120 workers that produces machine tools for the enterprise and for the domestic market. Just prior to the establishment of the VGMs, management decided to increase its convertible currency earnings by producing some machine tools for Western export. But the work was poorly organized, deadlines were missed, and the first tools exported only narrowly met the technical standards of the foreign customer. Later, however, the export orders were given to the VGM in the shop, at that time in its second year of operation. The three expensive machine tools that it produced were delivered prior to the contract deadlines and surpassed the most rigorous performance standards.

At the end of 1984. Minotaur received several more such orders and intense negotiations began between the VGM and the enterprise about the terms of the subcontractual agreement. By February 1985 the bargaining reached an impasse; management's 'final offer' was only two-thirds of the price the VGM had proposed. The resulting situation resembled in part a strike, in part a lockout, in part a disagreement between two firms. The VGM refused to accept the lower offer and temporarily broke off negotiations. Management countered by refusing to give the VGM any other orders. The deadlock lasted four months, during which interviews were conducted with both sides in the negotiations. For the work partners it was a matter of how long they could continue to forgo the extra VGM earnings; for management, a case of how long they could bear to hear the ever loudening tick of the clock on the contract deadline with the foreign customer.

During the dispute, all the formal and informal resources of the VGM were brought into play. In the first place, their proposed subcontract price rested on exact knowledge of the final price of the negotiated sale to the West German purchaser and the hard currency profits that would accrue to the firm. One channel of information about the economic situation of the firm came from the 'Management VGM' that did the bookkeeping for the work partnership. Because of its divided loyalties it found itself pulled this way and that. As mid-level managers, on career lines within the enterprise hierarchy, they faced increasing pressure from plant management to disclose information about the personal financial difficulties of the VGM members. Yet as 'entrepreneurs' they were tied to the VGM machinists. Because their bookkeeping fees were based on a percentage of the proceeds of their VGM clients, they had a direct and immediate interest in seeing that the VGM got a lucrative contract and, thus, were not immune to requests for information that would help the work partners assess management's positions at the 'bargaining table'. Secondly, the VGM's resources were grounded in their strategic location within the production process. Each of the members spoke with pride of the fact that their VGM had no managerial personnel in its ranks. Their strength in the negotiations was based on their conviction that they alone were capable of fulfilling the export order. Moreover, they argued, it was not simply a case that they *would not* do the export work on the regular hours (since as employees of the firm they were bound to accept work tasks from their foremen), but that they *could not* do the job properly on the regular hours. Only in the VGM, isolated from the general disorganization of the shop during the regular hours and protected from the intrusions of foremen and engineers, could they achieve the complex internal coordination that was required to do the work smoothly and efficiently.

After four months of deadlock, management was forced to resume bargaining. The result was that the VGM was awarded contracts for three of the four machine tools for export at a price slightly lower than the work partnership's final offer. Unwilling to capitulate entirely, management forced one concession: the fourth tool was to be made during the regular hours. But this face-saving tactic did not have cost-saving effects. The time spent making this fourth machine tool in the regular shop was more than twice as long as the number of hours the partnership negotiators had specified, in their offer, would be required to construct the same tool in the VGM.

## *The Limits of Internal Competition*

Faced with partnerships that can play the problems of the enterprise to their advantage, managers are beginning to make a countermove in hopes of playing the partnerships against each other. In this strategy, managers encourage the formation of as many VGMs as possible, and then let them compete. Such a practice was adopted for some jobs in a large utility firm that was studied. As one VGM member in that firm describes the system:

> In many cases the VGMs bid for jobs. It's capitalism in a small place. The procedure is that management determines that a particular job needs to be done, say, repairing a pumping station. It then draws up an announcement for the job – such and such a place, of such a size, to these specifications. The job is posted and the various VGMs that are qualified to do that type of work are able to bid on the job. It goes to the VGM with the lowest bid. Sometimes there's very hard competition among the VGMs. Management definitely doesn't post a price for the job – because some VGM might submit a bid that is lower, cheaper, than management's estimate.

That such a system promotes competitiveness among the VGMs can be seen in this same worker's comments on communication across VGMs:

> Most people don't talk about their VGM. This is business. A typical conversation between two workers who are not in the same partnership would go something like: A: 'How are things going in your VGM?' B: 'So so. Could be better, could be worse.' Why is it so general and not specific? Because to reveal problems, especially when both are in VGMs that are in the same field, might make trouble in competitive bidding. So, everyone plays the game with their cards close to their chest. [Then, in English.] Business is business.

Unchecked competition among the affiliated VGMs, however, can sometimes rebound to the disadvantage of the firm. For example, the elevator division of one large enterprise established a number of VGMs in its elevator maintenance activity. Within a few months a fierce 'price war' developed among the VGMs.

One of the groups wanted to corner the market for elevator inspection in several of the western provinces of the country. In an attempt to drive the other VGMs out of business they reduced the price for routine elevator maintenance from 1000 to 900 forints. When a second VGM reduced its price to 800, the first countered with a bid of 700. The price in question was for a subcontract to the parent firm; the final price which the customer paid to the elevator division was higher and therefore the firm promised to benefit from the aggressive internal competition. Management's response, however, was to divide up the market, assign each VGM to a specific territory, and restore the price to its initial level of 1000 forints. Why? In the first place, managers were afraid that the 700 forints price was so low that the work would not be performed carefully. Since the parent firm is liable for faulty work, the firm had to take into account the threat of possible lawsuits. Such considerations were heightened by the fact that one of the groups in the price war was allegedly sabotaging the work of the others in an attempt to show that their competitors did 'sloppy work'. Secondly, the main purpose of establishing VGMs in this field was to hold on to the firm's employees. In fact, several maintenance teams had threatened to leave the enterprise to establish GMKs (another of the small-entrepreneurial forms) completely independent of the firm, or to join cooperatives that were competing with the firm. Because the firm's contacts in the provinces ran through its teams (who were in close touch with the managers of the housing estates where the inspections were done) such an eventuality would spell disaster for the elevator division. Inspection and maintenance were among its more profitable activities and, if the teams left the firm, they would take some of the clients with them. In effect, the firm could not afford the consequences of the low subcontract price that resulted from the price war, and therefore took steps to halt the unfettered competition.

Market competition among VGMs inside an enterprise, however, provides an exceptional means for setting prices and hours for the work partnerships. More typically, the VGM representative bargains with departmental or plant management to establish the terms of a contract, exploiting the group's network of contacts for information, as did the VGM machinists in their head-to-head battle with Minotaur. Other partnerships (especially in design and engineering) utilize their contacts with the firm's clients to bargain for more favourable terms, in some cases even competing with the firm by offering lower bids for design projects. Management tolerates such practices because the firm can often benefit from the partner's more aggressive efforts to seek new clients. Not parasitism but symbiosis characterizes the relationship between the partnership and the parent firm.

Thus, for both professional and blue-collar partnerships, the outcome of bargaining about whether a particular project will be undertaken in the regular hours or in the VGM is often not determined by immediate profitability criteria. Rather, bargaining involves a complex assessment of debits and credits, calculations about new clients brought to the firm, perceptions about indispensability, compensation at a later time for crucial tasks performed in an earlier period of difficulty, and anticipation of future needs. And although bargaining centres on calculations of earnings and efforts, these calculations are far from simple as they involve comparisons with the earnings of managers (who are excluded from VGM participation), side payments to nonmembers who perform support tasks for the partners ('pocket-to-pocket' payments from the partnership's common fund in what one worker described as the 'third economy' inside the firm), and considerations of the timing of bargaining in relation to the firm's planning cycle. As in any functioning market, the calculations in these partnership/enterprise transactions are not based solely on a single point in time but are retrospective and prospective, involving evaluations of past performance and of future possibilities on both sides. Moreover, this bargaining is also influenced by perceptions of the political atmosphere inside the firm, in the district or region, and at the national level. Since 1983, the political fortunes of the whole concept of the VGMs have been subject to cross-pressures from various quarters. Thus, both the manager and the VGM representative must look not only at the bottom line but also at competing political lines, and must be able to interpret political signals as well as read market conditions.

We have seen that the relations between the VGM and the firm create new forms of institutionalization in the bargaining among workers and management. But, if these processes represent a formalization of bargaining arrangements, it should also be clear that there is no simple formula that governs these relations. To reach agreement, the VGM representatives and their managerial counterparts balance not a simple *quid* for a singular *quo* but must construct equivalences between a plurality of *quids* and a number of disparate *quos*. This accountancy calculates in forints and fillers, but also dollars and cents. (Did the VGM project bring the firm convertible currency?) It counts clients and contracts, but also gauges the political winds. (Should a favour from management count differently when the tone of the district Party resolution is hostile to VGMs?) It sizes up the external labour market and looks to prevailing rates among private firms, but it also scans the social climate inside the firm. (How sharp is the envy among non-VGM members, how deep are the tensions, and will the local trade union protest the 'abuses of socialist principles?')

By establishing a system of institutionalized subcontracts inside the enterprise, the partnership form makes explicit the transactive relations of selective bargaining in the socialist internal labour market. But this innovation also introduces some new elements into the politics of the shop floor. The fact that the work partners participate on a daily basis in two competing and coexisting organizational forms – in the socialist enterprise in the regular hours and in the self-managed partnerships in the off hours – promotes an organizational reflexivity. An entirely unintended consequence of the new subcontracting form is that the members have concrete experiences with alternative forms of self-organizing work, an alternative model of representation, and alternative systems of payment inside the partnerships adjudicated by workers, themselves, and leading to new forms of calculation about the value of their work. Managerial prerogatives as of the 'natural order of things' are brought into question by the proximity (in space and time) of a functioning alternative.

If the partnerships produce new perceptions of the socialist enterprise on the part of the members, they also lead to new perceptions by non-members. Because the work partnerships have a more objectified institutional existence than the informal group (that is, they have officially recognized identities and clearly demarcated membership boundaries), their operations within the firm heighten the visibility of the internal labour market. The presence of the partnerships brings selective bargaining out of obscurity and into the bright light of debate and discussion at the level of the shop floor, the enterprise, and the nation. Especially for the non-members, it is now much more obvious that some workers are in, while others are excluded from, the socialist labour market.

## CONCLUSION

Internal labour markets have been analysed in this chapter as institutional attempts to mitigate systemic uncertainties facing actors in work organizations in modern industrial economies. The particular characteristics of these attempts, moreover, are a consequence of the social organization of the larger economic system in which the firm operates. But the specific institutional mechanisms in the micro sphere, that is, the organizational solutions produced by the contention and cooperation of workers and managers in both the capitalist and the socialist firm, are not simply derivative or reflective of the principles of the macro economy. In each case, the particular form of an internal labour market operates according to principles that are not homologous with, but are counteractive to, the principles regulating the larger economic system.

Thus, in large firms in market economies, systemic uncertainties regarding labour are mitigated by a set of bureaucratic rules governing promotion, layoffs, and wage increments. These rules operate according to a classificatory logic in which workers are differentially rewarded and/or protected in so far as they belong to a category of persons in an officially recognized system of classification.

Internal labour markets in the socialist firm, by contrast, operate according to a transactive logic based on affiliative ties. To mitigate the effects of supply bottlenecks or to circumvent the obstacles of centrally imposed wage regulations, neither workers nor managers have an interest in the routinization of internal systems of classification. On the contrary, the strategy of an internal labour market, in this case, is to create some space relatively insulated from the bureaucratic principles that govern the planned economy. To protect themselves from uncertainties in the production process and from rigidities in the central regulations, workers use resources at hand, starting with their knowledge of the peculiarities of the particular machines on which they work and including their contacts and connections for obtaining parts, materials, and information. They use the threat of exit as a means to be shifted to another position, perhaps one with no immediate promise of a pay increase but with more opportunity to build credit among other workers and with shop management, yielding higher rewards in the longer term. Managers, for their part, enter into the informal networks of the shop floor because only through cooperation with worker groups can production goals be realized. Above all these groups are not classes of persons – aggregations of individuals who fall into the same category based on shared abstract features; they are interacting groups, whose members share tools, information, and particular experiences, and are connected to each other (including shop management) through debts and credits, obligations and expectations. Most visible in the case of the Hungarian subcontracting system (whose members are formally affiliated to each other and to the firm), it is the *transactive* character of the socialist internal labour market that ties workers to the firm, reduces uncertainties, and produces inequalities in both the level and the predictability of earnings among different segments of the working class. Not collective bargaining but selective bargaining, not the union contract but the partnership subcontract, not human capital but social capital, not the credential but credit, not seniority on the employee's workbook but the connections that can be acquired over the years – these are the keys to mobility within the socialist internal labour market.

The purpose of the heuristic model of mirrored opposition presented here has been to grasp, in a single framework, the distinctive features of the capitalist and socialist internal labour market. The intention of this analysis has not been to argue that we can read back from the functions performed by internal labour markets to explain causes, that is, their historical emergence in the two systems. Such an account would require a shift in analytic strategy. To understand the *dynamics* of these institutional arrangements in particular countries (e.g. their evolution, and their eventual dissolution) requires careful attention to differences in state structures, unions, and parties across countries within each broad case, as well as to conflicts and coalitions in the distinctive micropolitics of the firm in each system. The argument presented here suggests that further analysis of internal labour markets in the capitalist firm should examine the *politics of classification*, the processes in which groups are formed and contend in the struggle over the salience of classificatory categories. The analysis of the *politics of markets* in state socialist societies is just beginning. The presentation of a comparative model of industrial organizations that includes the socialist firm was a necessary step in such a project.

## REFERENCES


Althauser, Robert P. and Arne L. Kalleberg. 1981. 'Firms, Occupations, and the Structure of Labor Markets: A Conceptual Analysis', pp. 119–49 in *Sociological Perspectives on Labor Markets*, edited by Ivar Berg. New York: Academic.

Baron, James N. 1984. 'Organizational Perspectives on Stratification.' *Annual Review of Sociology* 10:37–69.

Berliner, Joseph. 1956. 'A Problem in Soviet Business Administration.' *Administrative Science Quarterly* 1:83–101.

——. 1976. *The Innovation Decision in Soviet Industry*. Cambridge: MIT Press.

Bourdieu, Pierre. 1980. 'Le Capital Social: Notes Provisoires.' *Actes de la Recherche en Sciences Sociales*, no. 31:2–3.

——. 1984. *Distinction: A Social Critique of the Judgment of Taste*. Cambridge: Harvard University Press.

Bourdieu, Pierre and Luc Boltanski. 1981. 'The Educational System and the Economy: Titles and Jobs', pp. 141–51 in *French Sociology: Rupture and Renewal Since 1968*, edited by Charles C. Lemert. New York: Columbia University Press.

Doeringer, Peter and Michael J. Piore. 1971. *Internal Labor Markets and Manpower Analysis*. Lexington, MA: D. C. Heath.

Edwards, Richard. 1979. *Contested Terrain: The Transformation of the Workplace in the Twentieth Century*. New York: Basic Books.

Farkas, Zoltán. 1983. 'Munkások Érdek-és Érdekeltségi Viszonyai.' (Relations and levels of interest among workers). *Szociológia* 1–2:27–52.

Fazekas, Károly. 1984. 'Wage and Performance Bargaining on the Internal Labour Market.' *Wage Bargaining in Hungarian Firms*. Studies of the Institute of Economics, Hungarian Academy of Sciences 23:29–88.

Gábor, István R. 1979. 'The Second (Secondary) Economy.' *Acta Oeconomica* 22:291–311.

———. 1985. 'The Major Domains of the Second Economy', pp. 133–78 in *Labour Market and Second Economy in Hungary*, edited by Péter Galasi and György Sziráczki. Frankfurt: Campus.

Héthy, Lajos and Csaba Makó. 1972a. 'Work Performance, Interests, Powers and Environment: The Case of Cyclical Slowdowns in a Hungarian Factory', pp. 123–50 in *Hungarian Sociological Studies*, Sociological Review Series No. 17, edited by Paul Halmos. Keele, England: University of Keele.

———. 1972b. *A Munkásmagatartások és a Gazdasági Szervezet* (Workers' Behaviour and Economic Organization). Budapest: Akademiai.

———. 1978. *Munkások, Érdekek, Érdekegyeztetés* (Workers, interests, bargaining). Budapest: Gondolat.

Hungarian Central Statistical Office. 1985. *Magyar Statisztikai Zsebkönyv 1984* (Hungarian Statistical Pocketbook). Budapest: Statisztikai Kiado.

———. 1986. *A Kisszervezetek 1984 – ben és 1985. I. Feleveben* (The Small Organizations in 1984 and in the first half of 1985). Budapest: Statisztikai Kiado.

International Labour Office. 1984. *Payment By Results*. Geneva: ILO.

Kemény, István. 1978. 'La Cháine dans une usine Hongroise.' *Actes de la Recherche en Sciences Sociales*. November, no. 24:62–78.

Kertesi, Gábor and György Sziráckzi. 1985. 'Worker Behavior in the Labour Market', pp. 216–45 in *Labour Market and Second Economy in Hungary*, edited by Péter Galasi and György Sziráczki. Frankfurt: Campus.

Kirsch, Leonard. 1972. *Soviet Wages: Changes in Structure and Administration Since 1956*. Cambridge: MIT Press.

Koike, Kazuo. 1983. 'International Labor Markets: Workers in Large Firms', pp. 89–116 in *Contemporary Industrial Relations in Japan*, edited by Taishiro Shirai. Madison: University of Wisconsin Press.

Kolosi, Tamás. 1984. 'Status and Stratification', pp. 51–104 in *Stratification and Inequalities*, edited by Rudolf Andorka and Tamás Kolosi. Budapest: Institute for Social Sciences.

Kornai, Janos. 1980. *Economics of Shortage*. Amsterdam: North Holland.

———. 1983. 'Comments on the Present State and the Prospects of the Hungarian Economic Reforms.' *Journal of Comparative Economics* 7:225–52.

Kövári, György and György Sziráczki. 1985. 'Old and New Forms of Wage Bargaining on the Shop Floor', pp. 133–78 in *Labour Market and Second Economy in Hungary*, edited by Péter Galasi and György Sziráczki. Frankfurt: Campus.

Ladó, Mária and Ferenc Tóth. 1985a. 'A Hivatalos Szabalyok Arnyékában' (In the shadow of the official rules). *Mozgó Vilag* 6:3–10.

———. 1985b. 'A Munkaszervezet Centrumaban: A Centrális Helyzet Kialakulásának, Ujratermelödésének Feltételei és Következményei' (At the Core of the Work Organization: Conditions and Consequences of the Formation and Reproduction of Core Positions in the Work Process). Unpublished manuscript, Munkaugyi Kutatointezet, Budapest.

Laki, Mihaly. 1980. 'Year-end Rush Work in Hungarian Industry and Foreign Trade.' *Acta Oeconomica* 25:37–65.

Lukács, János. 1984. 'A Müvezetök Helye és Szerpe Munkaszervezeteinkben' (The Place and Role of Foremen in our Labour Organization). Unpublished manuscript, Institute of Sociology, Hungarian Academy of Sciences, Budapest.

———. (forthcoming). *Teljesitménybérezés és Munka Szerinti Elosztás* (Payment by Results: Ideology and Reality). Unpublished Ph.D. dissertation. Hungarian Academy of Sciences. Institute of Sociology.

Makó, Csaba. 1985. *A Társadalmi Viszonyok Erötere: A Munkafolyamat* (The Labour Process: An Arena of Social Struggle). Budapest: Közgadesági es Jogi.

McAuley, Alastair. 1979. *Economic Welfare in the Soviet Union:* Madison: University of Wisconsin Press.

Nove, Alec. 1980. *The Soviet Economic System* (2nd edition). London: Allen and Unwin.

Osterman, Paul (ed.). 1984. *Internal Labor Markets*. Cambridge: MIT Press.

Pfeffer, Jeffrey and Yinon Cohen. 1984. 'Determinants of Internal Labor Markets in Organizations.' *Administrative Science Quarterly*, 29:550–72.

Piore, Michael and Charles Sabel. 1984. *The Second Industrial Divide*. New York: Basic Books.

Sabel, Charles and David Stark. 1982. 'Planning, Politics, and Shop-Floor Power: Hidden Forms of Bargaining in Soviet-Imposed State Socialist Societies.' *Politics and Society* 11:439–75.

Stark, David. 1985a. 'The Micropolitics of the Firm and the Macropolitics of Reform: New Forms of Workplace Bargaining in Hungarian Enterprises', pp. 247–73 in *States versus Markets in the World-System*, edited by Peter Evans, Dietrich Reuschemeyer, and Evelyn Huber Stevens. Beverly Hills: Sage.

——. 1985b. 'Internal Subcontracting in the Socialist Firm: Recent Developments in Hungary.' Paper presented at the Fifth International Conference of Europeanists. Washington, D.C.

Streeck, Wolfgang. 1984. 'Co-determination: The Fourth Decade.' *International Yearbook of Organizational Democracy* 2:391–422.

Szelenyi, Ivan. 1978. 'Social Inequalities in State Socialist Redistributive Economies.' *International Journal of Comparative Sociology* 19:63–87.

Vági, Gábor. 1982. *Versengês a fejlesztési forrâsokért* (Competition for Investment Funds). Budapest: Kózgazdasági es Jogi.

Williamson. Oliver, Michael Wachter, and Jeffrey Harris. 1975. 'Understanding the Employment Relation: The Analysis of Idiosyncratic Exchange.' *Bell Journal of Economics* 6:250–80.

# Part III
# Most of the World's Work: Ideas, Concepts, Problems

# Editor's Introduction

In retrospect it is astonishing that until the early 1970s most sociologists neglected any serious consideration of those who did most of the world's work.[1] Early textbooks were overwhelmingly dominated by male employment: studies of miners, dockers, railroaders, lorry drivers, car workers, fishermen or steel workers were readily available to provide the typical ethnography of the world of work. Most general studies about management and 'the' workers were implicitly about male workers, as were many of the classic case studies of shop-floor or plant culture. Occasionally a female office worker might appear and there are, certainly, a few studies based on female employees, but the overall impression left on an uncritical student's mind must surely have been that work is for men and that, after marriage, family life is for women.

Evidently, such a view of work is ethnocentric and historically inaccurate. Few college textbooks in the United States have concerned themselves with historical issues and until very recently most have an implicit or explicit underlying assumption that the rest of the world is longing to get its work organized in the way that it is done in the United States. Peasants with other 'non-industrial' values present a problem that has to be overcome by the inculcation of a greater commitment to work and 'industrial values'. Since the world of work can be a

1. It is significant that it was not until 1980 that a United Nations report provided the following quotation now widely available printed as a postcard:

Women
constitute *half* the world's
population,
perform nearly *two-thirds*
of its work hours,
receive *one-tenth* of the world's income
and own less than *one-hundredth*
of the world's property.

This statement has shifted from being dramatically challenging to being conventionally acceptable in a very short time.

rough-and-tumble, aggressive and stressful environment, conventional attitudes held it to be important that an alternative set of values is available in the family and home to which work-wracked men can retreat for love, affection and regular hot meals. Happy is the woman who can support industrial America by providing the cosy little nest, whether for captains of industry or hard-pressed men on the assembly line. Even the First Lady should know how to arrange flowers.

Faced with this suffocating and patronizing complacency about women's work in industrial society it is understandable that feminists should have responded to the situation with considerable vigour, if not anger. During the 1970s the so-called 'domestic labour debate' flourished, and by 1979 more than fifty articles on housework had been published in the British and American socialist journals alone.[2] Different strands of feminist thinking became locked in debate as Marxists and less-than-totally committed Marxists argued over whether unpaid domestic labour was a source of surplus value. Do men exploit and oppress women through patriarchal attitudes and values? Does 'capitalism' exploit women by not rewarding them for the economic contribution they provide through their unwaged work? Or, finally, is there an unholy alliance between men and the capitalist system combining to oppress women? In political terms the answers to these questions were pretty important. There was little point in encouraging others to join in the class struggle if the 'main enemy' was in fact men; likewise, if men were the main enemy, the overthrow of capitalism would surely leave everything much as before. Whilst the subordination of women appeared to be linked to their role in the sphere of reproduction, freedom clearly could not be found through a refusal to reproduce.

There were, then, two forms of labour that were being expropriated from women: their labour power in reproducing this generation's labour by providing supportive domestic work for their husbands and, secondly, that involved in reproducing the next generation of healthy and docile labourers through bearing children. These ideas were all controversial. As Molyneux put it,

> it is not simply a question of the housewife's labour entailing a hidden benefit to the capitalist in lowering the value of the husband's labour power but rather that the maintenance of the domestic ensemble and of the individuals within it also entails a *hidden cost* which in this case is covered by the provision of a family wage to the husband.[3]

This statement helped to spark off a debate about the so-called family wage.[4] And so the spiral of the debate took another twist.

The discovery that a subordinated role for privatized domestic labour and various forms of the sexual division of labour predated capitalism swung the debate off to consider universalist patriarchal tendencies in most, if not all, societies, depending on how the varied ethnography was interpreted. The domestic labour debate lost its impetus by the end of the 1970s and the obsessive concern with housework and housewives gave way to a much broader analysis of

2. M. Molyneux 'Beyond the domestic labour debate' *New Left Review*, 116, 1979, pp. 3–27.
3. Ibid., p. 12.
4. H. Land, 'The family wage', *Feminist Review*, 1980, pp. 55–77; M. Barrett and M. Mackintosh, 'The "family wage": some problems for socialists and feminists', *Capital and Class*, 11, 1980, pp. 51–72.

the full range of women's economic and non-economic activities and the social relations in which they are embedded. Over the last decade interest has shifted away from the subordination of women in the home to the subordination of women in the (segmented) labour market.

At about the same time as the domestic labour debate became current in British sociology Ester Boserup published *Woman's Role in Economic Development* (1970) and another decade's debate ensued. The basic outline of her argument is set out in chapter 15 where Benería and Sen provide a sympathetic critique. Boserup was clearly correct in arguing that women's work included providing most of a household's food in many areas and that women's role in production had been grossly underestimated. She claimed that women's subsistence work was largely omitted in national statistics and that, overall, women's work is consistently underreported and underestimated. The latter point is uncontestable; in chapter 16 Benería elaborates it in some detail and explores the biases and limitations of official statistics and the definitions on which they are based. She also goes on to criticize those working within a Marxist framework for their neglect of subsistence production and the household economy. In the context of much of Latin America, Asia and Africa, such a neglect leads to the invisibility of most of the work done in those areas. Essentially Benería is arguing that a place must be found for non-commodity production in a relevant political economy, and she urges that we expand our concept of active labour so that economic activity may be related to human welfare more broadly conceived rather than to a given process of growth and accumulation.

In their criticism of Boserup, Benería and Sen fault her for being over-empiricist and for limiting her theoretical position to that of neo-classical economics. Boserup's apparently worthy goal of urging that women should receive more of the fruits of their labours in the process of modernization is not completely acceptable to her critics, since she assumes, too readily perhaps, that 'modernization' is a self-evident good. The introduction of commercial agriculture, for example, can be seen as a product of modernization but it is also associated with capital accumulation, which in turn produces new forms of class and gender domination:

> The single most powerful tendency of capitalist accumulation is to separate direct producers from the means of production and to make their conditions of survival more insecure and contingent. This tendency manifests itself in new forms of class stratification in rural areas – between rich peasants and capitalist farmers on the one hand, and poor peasants and landless labourers on the other. Capitalist accumulation can have a variety of effects on women's work depending on the specific form accumulation takes in a particular region. (Chapter 15)

Boserup is also castigated for ignoring the subordination of women in the sphere of reproduction and, indeed, many of the issues that were to emerge in the domestic labour debate in the ensuing years. Boserup writes as a progressive economist and not as a radical feminist. By focusing on non-domestic production as the main determinant of women's position in society, she neglects the household as a context for different styles of male domination. Indeed, it is hard to draw a firm line between household and non-household production.

These issues are explored by Mackintosh in chapter 17, who focuses on the role of domestic labour in a household-based economy. Drawing on her fieldwork in a village in Senegal, Mackintosh demonstrates the appalling burden of labour imposed on women by the rigidity of the sexual division of labour. Men may take over some of the agricultural tasks, leaving virtually all the non-agricultural tasks to be done by women. Her account of the 16-hour day of a 16-year-old girl is a graphic description of the extent of the burden of work such women carry. It would be cruel to minimize or to ignore in any way such work simply because it is not wage labour. In her very illuminating theoretical analysis of household and reproduction, she argues that the household is constituted on the basis of the relations under which women perform domestic labour for the feeding and care of all household members. The household 'is firmly rooted in certain kinds of economic activity: that is, the production and consumption of the products of domestic labour'. She then goes on to probe in more detail what precisely are the relations under which domestic labour is performed, and this leads directly to a consideration of the issue of reproduction. The arguments are complex and the issue is not helped, as she remarks, by the lack of clear definitions. Mackintosh provides an important analysis of the household's role in mediating between the social relations that produce the subordination of women in reproduction and those that govern social labour other than domestic labour:

> These two sets of social relations are mutually determining, and one set cannot continue to exist without the other. In a household-based system, the control by male elders of the whole system involves the maintenance of the subordination both of women to men and of younger men to male elders. To threaten the subordination of women would be to threaten the stability of the household and therefore of the system as a whole.

As Benería and Sen recognize, analysis of the spheres of both production and reproduction and the interaction between them is more than most economists can handle. The opening up of debate in this area has done much to stimulate a distinctive approach to women's work in Third World countries in recent years.

In chapter 18 Muntemba provides a valuable historical and comparative overview of women's work as food producers in Africa, with particular reference to Zambia. She shows how, over time, women's position has been consistently deteriorating. The marginalization of female productivity and food crop production consequent upon mechanization has had serious consequences. An emphasis on cash crops to produce food for urban populations has led to more land being used for commodity production and more labour (mostly male) working in that area. Women with small holdings of lower-quality land are left with the difficult task of maintaining their subsistence production with inadequate resources. It is understandable that many give up in despair. Government support, devised to increase cash crop production, went to men who attended courses at farm institutes, were granted loans and were taught improved production methods for food crops. Women were largely excluded from these benefits. Stereotypes about gender roles seriously inhibited women's capacity to support themselves on the land. They believed that the government systematically discriminated against them. Muntemba describes the work strategies that women adopted when faced with this situation.

It is in the context of these and other studies that Redclift attempts the ambitious task of drawing together (in chapter 19) the common themes surrounding gender, accumulation and the labour process. Her summary is compressed and it is distilled both from what has been termed the 'women in development' literature as well as from more conventional analyses of women's work. Clearly the debates of the 1970s have helped to produce a much more subtle and sophisticated analysis.

Much of the early work on domestic labour was weighed down with dogmatic theorizing, and it is refreshing to find Redclift reflecting the position of many scholars of the 1980s when she writes 'the articulation of capitalism with the sexual division of labour cannot be assumed to be uniform, but is a matter for concrete investigation.' This is admirable advice, and some detailed studies are presented in part V. (Perhaps Redclift does not always follow her own precept. She notes that 'in rural areas of developing countries where there are fewer commodities to "administer", the physical fabric of the dwelling, or the lack of it, allows for little fetishism.' The use of the word 'fetishism' in that context may reflect a radical feminist or Marxist ideology, but surely the point has to be empirically demonstrated rather than simply asserted.) The *meaning* of different forms of women's work in Third World countries has received much less attention than its articulation with the global processes of capital accumulation. Yet even this latter theme presents serious problems. As Redclift remarks: 'Bridging the conceptual gap between the international and the "domestic" economy is a difficult task.' That is certainly so, and Redclift takes us as far as the present literature allows. Her work is pivotal, surveying as it does a decade of research and looking forward to the problems and issues that are currently exercising the minds of scholars in this field. Students of the subject will find Redclift's survey particularly valuable in putting a large number of studies into an intellectual pattern. Read in the context of the previous chapter in this part, and also with the empirical case studies in part V, Redclift's essay helps to develop that deeper understanding of work in its wider context which is the theme of the book as a whole. Her undogmatic stance encourages her to be sceptical of all universalistic, enthnocentric or monocausal explanations, recognizing that similar symptoms do not necessarily result from only one disease and likewise that the same disease might have diverse symptoms. The historical and cross-cultural analysis of the process of capital accumulation and its impact on gender relations and women's work in general is far too complex a process to be encapsulated in one brief attempt at scholarly synthesis.

The final chapter in this part focuses on the female workforce of multinational companies and provides a close link with many of the chapters in part V. Like Redclift, Pearson demolishes stereotypes and shows something of the empirical variation by disaggregating the concept of women as 'cheap labour'. Different employers have differing needs and recruitment strategies, and 'women's potential labour power, as a commodity available for exploitation by capital, has to be negotiated for with forms of patriarchal control and with her childbearing and reproductive role.'

One strategy used by some employers is to recruit childless women to provide a more dispensable and flexible workforce. Women are also more likely to be employed on short-term or temporary contracts. However, the goal of increasing profitability has to be negotiated in relation to specific labour markets in specific contexts and to sets of cultural values which may or may not give way to employers' strategies. As Pearson argues, 'how their work process is organized will depend as much on the historically determined availability of female labour and the interaction of gender and class systems as on the demand for cheap labour from foreign capital.' 'Cheapness' on its own does not provide an adequate explanation.

Turning to consider the 'green female labour' employed in the electronics industry in both the First and Third Worlds, Pearson again introduces a note of caution to demonstrate that employers deploy a variety of strategies to ensure that they get a compliant workforce capable of high levels of output. A variety of different kinds of female worker can supply the same results. The sources and strategies may be different but the results are the same: women are confined to relatively lower-paid jobs which are classified as unskilled or semi-skilled. However, it is important not to make a universal consequence a universal cause. Women's cheap or 'green' labour is not a given fact of nature. Pearson shows that it has to be directly cultivated and she gives some indications on how this is done in both First and Third Worlds. Pearson's analysis points the way to important themes in the organization of work that are going to be of increasing salience in the years ahead, namely the interlocking relationships between North and South; the emphasis on historical and comparative analyses; the relationships between the reproductive or survival needs of the household and the demands for wage labour; and, finally, the crucial role of ideology in structuring and determining the complex interactions between production and reproduction.

The six chapters in this part are all, in their various ways, reconceptualizing the nature of work, focusing on the renegotiating of new divisions of labour and new modes and styles of work. It is significant that this conceptual and analytical work is being done by women on women. It is no accident that all of the contributors to parts III and V are women, as indeed are most of the contributors to this book. The reconsideration of all forms of work that is the focus of part IV would not have taken place without the stimulation of the reconceptualizations and fresh thinking of feminist scholars in the 1970s and 1980s. Some of the debates have been tortuous and inconclusive, to be sure, and some of the empirical studies have been unhealthily slender. This is partly due to the speed and excitement with which new ideas were formulated and disseminated: with so much pent-up research energy eager to apply itself to a rapidly developing and overwhelmingly relevant field, it is understandable that some material was published over-hastily. However, as the chapters in this part indicate severally and collectively, there is now a new caution and wariness about offering over-general statements about the work that women do. No longer is it convincing or acceptable to make a sharp distinction between studies focused on segmented labour markets on the one hand and studies limited to the domestic sphere of consumption, reproduction and survival on the other. These two spheres interact on each other, creating problems and contradictions that scholars are obliged to address. Similarly, a greater concern with food production and self-provisioning has directed attention away from the traditional concerns of agricultural economists to the sociology and political economy of the question of livelihood, broadly conceived. The wider conception of work that is being developed in this book has far-reaching implications for the study of development and of the nature and range of women's work. There can be no going back to the conventional stereotypes of the male-dominated textbooks of the sociology of work. That is a considerable advance.

# 15

# Accumulation, Reproduction and Women's Role in Economic Development: Boserup Revisited

LOURDES BENERÍA AND GITA SEN

Well over a decade has passed since Ester Boserup's book, *Woman's Role in Economic Development*, was published.[1] Probably no single work on the subject of women and development has been quoted as often. Given the importance of the subject and the appearance of a considerable amount of new material since 1970, it is now possible to evaluate the book from a fresh perspective; indeed such an evaluation is necessary. It is our purpose to summarize Boserup's main contributions, but also to present a critical analysis of her approach, particularly in view of recent scholarship on the subject.

When Boserup's work was published in 1970, it represented a comprehensive and pioneering effort to provide an overview of women's role in the development process. In the literature on development the specific role of women has been largely ignored, particularly the question of how development affects women's subordinate position in most societies. Boserup pointed out a variety of subjects that are systematically related to the role of women in the economy. Other authors, anthropologists in particular, had dealt with the role of women in changing societies; what distinguished Boserup's work was her perspective as an economist trained in the comparative study of developing countries and their problems. An analysis of her contributions is in order.

First, Boserup emphasized gender as a basic factor in the division of labour, prevalent across countries and regions: 'Even at the most primitive stages of family autarky there is some division of labour within the family, the main criteria

This essay was first published in *Signs* 7(2), 1981.

1. Ester Boserup, *Woman's Role in Economic Development* (London: George Allen & Unwin, 1970).

for the division being those of age and sex. . . . Both in primitive and in more developed communities, the traditional division of labour within the family is usually considered "natural" in the sense of being obviously and originally imposed by the sex difference itself.'[2] Despite the existence of stereotyped sex roles and the universality of women's concentration in domestic work, Boserup pointed out significant differences in women's work across countries and regions. She criticized the 'dubious generalization' that attributes the provision of food to men in most communities; women too have been food providers in many areas of the world. Her comparative analysis was particularly illuminating for Africa and Asia, where she emphasized the fundamental role women played in African agriculture in contrast to their lesser role in Asian countries and in Latin America as well. While there are many similarities in women's work in the industrialized urban sector, rural work exhibits diverse patterns associated with the particular characteristics of each area.

Second, Boserup provided some explanations for and analysed a variety of factors behind these differences. One of the most frequently quoted parts of her analysis is her comparison between the 'female' and 'male' systems of farming, which correspond to the African system of shifting agriculture and the Asian system of plough cultivation. In Africa, low population density, easy access to land, and less class differentiation than is found in Asian societies resulted in a division of labour where men cleared the land for cultivation and women actually cultivated the subsistence crops. In Asia – a region characterized by high population density – a ready supply of landless labourers available for hire and the 'technical nature of farming operations under plough cultivation' discouraged women's involvement in agricultural tasks and encouraged segregation of the sexes, including the seclusion of women in some areas.[3]

Boserup's analysis pointed to the correlations between women's work and factors such as population density and land holding. Although she was not always explicit about precise connections, she did suggest the existence of a relationship between these factors and different forms of women's subordination. For example, in her discussion of the economics of polygamy in traditional Africa, Boserup argued that polygamy made it possible for a man to control more land and labour, because each wife was assigned a plot of land to cultivate. Thus, her analysis pointed to an economic basis for polygamy and the bride price. Boserup's analysis did not explain polygamous arrangements in which wives seem to represent a cost rather than an economic resource for the husband, but it created a challenge for others to do so.

Third, Boserup's book began to delineate the negative effects that colonialism and the penetration of capitalism into subsistence economies have often had on women. She pointed out that European colonial rule, rather than being a 'liberalizing' factor for African women, contributed to their loss of status: 'Europeans showed little sympathy for the female farming systems which they found in many of their colonies.' Women often lost their right to land as a result of 'land reforms introduced by European administrators'.[4] These reforms, Boserup

2. Ibid., p. 15.
3. Ibid., p. 26.
4. Ibid., pp. 54, 60.

explained, were based on the European belief that cultivation was properly men's work. She argued that the introduction of modern technology and cash crops benefited men rather than women by creating a productivity gap between them; women were relegated to the subsistence sector of food production using traditional methods of cultivation.

Fourth, Boserup, among others, emphasized that 'subsistence activities usually omitted in the statistics of production and income are largely women's work.[5] Although there is a tendency for official statistics to underreport all subsistence activities, whether carried out by men or women, some of these activities tend to be specific to women, particularly domestic work and participation in agriculture as 'unpaid family labour'.[6] Despite some efforts to include subsistence work in statistics of production and labour force participation, women's work continues to be underreported and underestimated, particularly in the area of domestic production. In addition, the conventional theoretical concepts that underlie statistical categories are ideologically biased toward an undervaluation of women's work.[7] Boserup, therefore, raised an issue that is essential to a proper understanding of women's participation in economic life.

Finally, Boserup's comparative analysis projected the different sexual divisions of labour encountered in farming systems onto patterns of women's participation in nonagricultural activities. For example, she called attention to the influence of farming systems on migration patterns and on the participation of men and women in urban labour markets. African women's involvement in food cultivation generated a pattern of predominantly male migration, leaving women and children in the village. In contrast, Boserup argues, the Latin American pattern in which women participated less in farming involved a high degree of female migration, due also to the employment opportunities for young women in urban centres. Boserup's generalization, at times overstated, encouraged far more detailed analysis. Her scholarship inspired a great deal of the empirical and theoretical work that followed.

Despite Boserup's obvious contributions, critical analysis reveals three major weaknesses in her work. First, the book is essentially empirical and descriptive, and it lacks a clearly defined theoretical framework that empirical data can help elaborate. Although Boserup fails to identify an explicit framework, her underlying analytical concepts are often neoclassical. This seriously limits her analysis. Second, Boserup takes as given a unique model of development – the model that characterizes capitalist economies. Finally, despite her basic concern with the position of women in the development process, Boserup does not present a clear-cut feminist analysis of women's subordination. By concentrating on the sphere of production outside the household and ignoring the role of women in reproduction, her work fails to locate the basis of this subordination. In what follows we will elaborate each of these points in more detail.

5. Ibid., p. 163.
6. Adult men may also engage in unpaid family labour where extended families prevail.
7. Lourdes Benería, 'Accounting for Women's Work,' in *Women and Development: The Sexual Division of Labor in Rural Economies*, ed. Lourdes Benería (Geneva: International Labour Organization in press).

## THEORETICAL FRAMEWORK

One of the most common criticisms of Boserup's book is that it is repetitive. This problem becomes acute because the book fails to go beyond the data that it presents; Boserup rarely attempts to derive any overall theoretical or conceptual structure from her empirical data. These data are rich in insights about the patterns and variations in women's work across Africa and Asia, but most of her analysis is purely descriptive. *Ad hoc* introductions of values and ideology often take the place of explanations. In discussing the growing dominance of men over women in agriculture during Africa's colonial period, for example, Boserup contends that gender-based prejudice on the part of the colonialists caused them to teach advanced agricultural methods only to men.

When Boserup does use theoretical concepts, they tend to fall within the framework of neoclassical economics. In her discussion of the labour market and wage differentials between women and men, she suggests that the individual preference of employers and workers determines the nature of women's work, and hence their earnings. Boserup analyses demand in the labour market, stating that employers often prefer male labour over female labour; she analyses supply by stating that women prefer to work in home industries rather than in large enterprises.[8]

This emphasis on preferences constitutes a limited view of the forces that influence the labour market and the process of wage formation. There are many cases in which employers prefer women over men: examples include tea plantations, textile manufacturing firms, and labour-intensive industries operating in many areas of the Third World.[9]

Many of these are in fact large enterprises. Therefore the factors influencing preferences must be explained; preference is not the adequate explanatory variable. These influencing factors can range from the temporary character of employment among young, unmarried women – an important factor in hiring policies of multinational firms – to the tendency of women workers toward submissiveness, avoidance of tensions, and acceptance of low wages. In addition, women's own preferences need to be seen in dynamic perspective, and cannot be taken as given. They are the result of changing factors such as access to land, household work, family structure, family income, the availability of employment, and women's perception of their economic and social roles.

Boserup does go beyond a narrow focus on individual preference in her examination of hiring practices and wage formation in the export sector:

> It seems that the clue is to be found in considerations of costs in the plantation sector. . . . In Africa, the methods of food production are such that women can do nearly all the operations unaided by men. It is therefore possible to economize on labour costs in plantations (as well as in mines and industries) by employing only male workers, leaving the dependants . . . to be supported in the home village by the

8. Boserup, p. 113.

9. International Labour Organization (ILO), *Conditions of Work of Women and Young Workers in Plantations* (Geneva: ILO, 1970); Noeleen Heyzer, 'From Rural Subsistence to an Industrial Peripheral Workforce: Female Malaysian Migrants in Singapore,' in Benería, ed.; and Dorothy Elson and Ruth Pearson, 'Nimble Fingers Make Cheap Workers: An Analysis of Women's Employment in Third World Export Manufacturing,' *Feminist Review* (Spring 1981), pp. 87–107.

able-bodied women. The Asian pattern is in sharp contrast: there the predominant agricultural system requires the presence of men in the village. . . . Hence the plantation owner must face the fact that the whole family must get its livelihood from the plantation and this, of course, can be arranged most cheaply by having every able-bodied member of the family working on the plantation. Thus, in the Asian as well as the African case, the plantation (or the European farm) can avoid paying the male wages sufficient to support a whole family.[10]

The theoretical implication of such an argument is that the wage is not just a payment for productivity – the result of market forces of labour supply and demand. It is determined as well by the costs of maintaining and reproducing the labour force. This supports a Marxist theory of the wage rather than the neoclassical explanation, and is a concept that is compatible with a patriarchal vision of the male wage as the main source of family income. Women's wages, then, are viewed as complementary rather than primary, which explains women's willingness to work for a lower wage, and helps to explain why women's wages often remain barely above 50 per cent of male wages in cases where women's productivity is as high, if not higher, than men's.[11]

Boserup also hints at the existence of both wage differentials due to job segregation by sex, and labour market hierarchies related to race and nationality as well as gender.[12] Her empirical insights appear to support a theoretical model of fragmented labour markets rather than a model of a competitive labour market, which would suggest a neoclassical framework. Yet Boserup makes no attempt at reconciling her various and apparently contradictory descriptions of wage differentials and hiring practices. Her underlying neoclassical categories do not allow her to integrate her rich empirical observations within a coherent analytical framework. Similar limitations in her analysis result from her assumption of a unique development model.

## MODEL OF DEVELOPMENT: MODERNIZATION VERSUS ACCUMULATION[13]

Boserup's general argument is that women workers are marginalized in the process of economic development because their economic gains as wage workers,

10. Boserup, pp. 77–8.
11. ILO, passim.
12. Boserup, pp. 107, 147–51.
13. The modernization approach to economic development is based on a perception of social change as a linear movement from backwardness to modernity. Specifically, it calls for the adaptation of technology, institutions, and attitudes to those existing in the advanced capitalist countries of the West. The theory does not emphasize changes in class relations or the contradictory effects of the capitalist development process, nor does it acknowledge the possibility of alternative development models. In contrast, the capital-accumulation approach analyses the growth of interconnected processes of production – both quantitative and qualitative – motivated by profits, extension of the market, growing social division of labour and modes of production, and the proletarianization of the labour force. Private ownership of resources, and hence of the surplus generated in production (profits, rent, and interest), leads to class differentiation between owners and nonowners of the means of production. Private ownership also signals the private appropriation of productive wealth, and growing inequalities in the distribution of income and power.

farmers, and traders are slight compared to those of male workers. Hence, policy efforts should be directed to redress this problem, so that women share more fully in the fruits of modernization. Underlying this is the view that modernization is both beneficial and inevitable in the specific form it has taken in most Third World countries – a notion that has been extensively criticized by radical social scientists over the last two decades.[14] The modernization approach has two negative effects on Boserup's analysis. First, she tends to ignore processes of capital accumulation set in motion during the colonial period, and the effects of such processes on technical change and women's work. Second, she does not systematically analyse the different effects of capital accumulation on women of different classes.

Of the many variants of modernization theory, Boserup's work is one based on technological determinism that uses cultural values as filler for conceptual holes in the analysis. The technological determinism in her argument is clearest in her discussion of indigenous farming systems. For example, though Boserup argues that there is a negative correlation between the use of the plough and the extent of field work done by women, the basis of this correlation is never clarified. Nor does she discuss the possibility that there may be deeper causal reasons for the empirically observed correlation. Instead, one is left to presume that technical variation exercises some mysterious, if powerful, impact on the division of labour by sex. This sort of unexplained correlation is rife in modernization theory. The processes of modernization – in this case, the effect of plough cultivation on women's work – are rarely explained. Rather, the more modern is usually held up as the model against which the more backward is judged. To Boserup's credit, she does not make this last step. Instead she sees modernization operating concurrently with women's loss of economic independence.

However, this insight is not located in any coherent theory, but only in a sharp empirical intuition. Boserup holds cultural prejudices to blame for women's marginalization; overall the process of modernization is viewed as beneficial. Indeed, Boserup regards modernizing technical changes, such as the shift from hoe to plough cultivation, as the inevitable products of population growth.[15] But nowhere does she confront the causes of growing population density, particularly the Malthusian belief that population growth is somehow inherent in human nature.

Viewing the Third World from this perspective involves ignoring effects on population growth and density of the alienation of land and its private appropriation during the colonial period. The direct effects were felt most sharply in regions such as Southern Africa where most of the land (and, inevitably, the

14. Paul Baran, *The Political Economy of Growth* (New York: Monthly Review Press, 1959); André G. Frank, *Capitalism and Underdevelopment in Latin America: Historical Studies of Chile and Brazil* (New York: Monthly Review Press, 1967); Samir Amin, *Unequal Development* (New York: Monthly Review Press, 1976).

15. See Ester Boserup's earlier work, *The Conditions of Agricultural Growth* (London: George Allen & Unwin, 1965). In this book, exogenously given population growth provides the major impetus for technical change in agriculture. Her argument is intended to be anti-Malthusian – rising population density in a region is followed, not by the Malthusian checks of war or famine, but by technological adaptation (shorter fallow, higher cultivation intensity, the shift from hoe to plough) designed to facilitate greater food production.

best land) was taken over by settlers, squeezing the indigenous population into shrinking reserves, and leaving high person-to-land ratios.[16] The indirect effects have been felt in most regions where the privatization of land, labour, and subsistence have generated incentives for higher fertility among peasants.[17]

Such changes in the social organization of production and in the appropriation of the means of production also have powerful effects on the division of labour by sex and age. What appears to Boserup to be a technically determined correlation between plough cultivation and women's lower participation in field work has its roots in the social relations of production and reproduction. To be sure, Boserup does note that 'the plough is used in regions with private ownership of land and with a comparatively numerous class of landless families in the rural population.'[18] This, she says, creates the possibility of substituting hired workers, male and female, for the farm wife in field labour. But she does not explain why and through what processes this possibiliy is realized.

In fact, in her entire discussion of women's agricultural work, Boserup makes a rather artificial separation between women from landed peasant households and women from agricultural labour households. It is not clear why she focuses on the former when defining male and female farming systems, and discusses the latter in another section. Surely the landless women should also be part of the criterion by which a farming system is defined as male or female. This is especially true where women constitute a significant proportion of the agricultural wage-labour force in regions of plough cultivation.[19] In fact, the further along one reads in Boserup's book, the more it appears that the crucial distinguishing feature between African and Asian farming is not, as she suggests, the tools used - hoe versus plough - but the forms of appropriation of land, of surplus, and of women's reproductive capacity. The sexual division of labour is related to these factors.

Similiarly, while Boserup discusses the economic roots of polygamy, she fails to examine the process of change in this system as the possibilities of capital accumulation multiply. In some precolonial African communities, a large number of wives gave a man status and possibly a greater voice in the village councils. But women had at least partial control over the product of their labour. With the coming of long-distance trade and private appropriation of land, women's labour could be used to produce a surplus, which formed a basis for accumulation of land and wealth.[20] In turn, class differentiation began to intensify, women came to have less and less control over the product of their labour, and additional wives became, in fact, simply additional field workers who facilitated the accumulation of use-rights to more land. These changes probably indicated a major alteration in gender relations to the detriment of women. By failing to examine such matters, Boserup's argument remains divorced from any coherent analysis of the

16. Robert Palmer and Neil Parsons, eds, *The Roots of Rural Poverty in Central and Southern Africa* (Berkeley and Los Angeles: University of California Press, 1977).

17. Mahmood Mamdani, *The Myth of Population Control* (New York: Monthly Review Press, 1972).

18. Boserup, *Woman's Role*, p. 26.

19. In India, for example, plough cultivation coexists with a wage-labour force in agriculture that is one-third female. See Committee on the Status of Women in India, *Towards Equality* (New Delhi 1974).

20. Penelope Ciancanelli, 'Exchange, Reproduction, and Sex-Subordination among the Kikyu of East Africa,' *Review of Radical Political Economics* 12, no. 2 (1980): 25–36.

interconnections between the social process of accumulation, class formation, and changes in gender relations.

Another example of the work's weak conceptual basis is Boserup's discussion of women's declining status under colonial rule. The biases of modernization theory are evident in her presumption that the introduction of commercial agriculture was generally beneficial, except for the consequent decline in women's status. This presumption ignores entirely the long history of resistance to forced cultivation of crops such as cotton and coffee in Africa and other Third World regions.[21] Cultivation involving the increased use of land and labour in the production of commercial crops was a major mechanism for the transformation of land relations and class differentiation, and it opened possibilities for exploitation by commercial capital. The active intervention of the colonial state in such cultivation and in attempts to disseminate technological improvements is hardly surprising. The subsistence crops of the local people were not a source of surplus value. Subsistence farming drew the government's attention only under two circumstances: first, whenever the labour and land used for subsistence crops acted as a barrier to the expansion of commercial crops; and second, whenever subsistence production deteriorated to the point where there was excessive migration to the urban areas, or eruptions of political resistance.[22]

Teaching the women better techniques in subsistence cropping, as Boserup suggests, would have been like treating cancer with a bandaid. That such teaching did not take place could hardly be the cause of women's worsening situation under conditions of rapid land alienation and class differentiation. Nor is Boserup correct in implying that all men benefited from commercial production. The possibilities of accumulation inherent in commercial farming undoubtedly enabled some men to raise themselves up in the indigenous class hierarchy, but most men did not experience such mobility. The narrow truth of Boserup's thesis is that while some men could be integrated into the ruling class, almost no women could be, at least on their own. The concentration of women in subsistence farming undeniably caused this unevenness. That commercial cropping came to dominate over subsistence cropping was a product not of European patriarchal culture, but of the process of capital accumulation. Thus, women's loss of status results from the interweaving of class relations and gender relations.

Recent scholarship emphasizes the close connections between processes of accumulation and changes in women's work and in the forms of their subordination. The single most powerful tendency of capitalist accumulation is to separate direct producers from the means of production and to make their conditions of survival more insecure and contingent. This tendency manifests itself in new forms of class stratification in rural areas – between rich peasants and capitalist farmers on the one hand, and poor peasants and landless labourers on the other. Capitalist accumulation can have a variety of effects on women's work depending on the specific form accumulation takes in a particular region.

21. A. T. Nzula, I. I. Potekhin, and A. Z. Zusmanovich, *Forced Labour in Colonial Africa*, ed. Robin Cohen, trans. Hugh Jenkins (London: Zed Press, 1979).

22. Henry Bernstein, 'African Peasantries: A Theoretical Framework,' *Journal of Peasant Studies* 6, no. 4 (1979): 421–43; Judith Van Allen, 'Sitting on a Man: Colonialism and the Lost Political Institutions of Igbo Women,' *Canadian Journal of African Studies* 6, no. 2 (1972): 165–82.

In some areas, the sexual division of labour may change and women's workload may be intensified. For example, Jette Bukh shows how the concentration of men in commercial crops and male migration to urban areas in search of work have forced women in Ghana to take up additional tasks in subsistence agricultural production, lengthening and intensifying their work day.[23] The pressure on women in these largely female-headed households is aggravated by increased school attendance among their children, which has induced changes in the crops cultivated. For example, women have begun to substitute cassava production for labour-intensive yam production, though cassavas are less nutritious. They have also decreased vegetable production. Furthermore, as land becomes privately appropriated, common sources of water, fuel, and food are lost to poorer peasants and landless labourers, forcing women to spend more time and labour in finding, fetching, and foraging.[24]

In other areas, women may lose effective control over productive resources and over the labour process and its product. Kate Young describes the changes in the sexual division of labour that resulted from the penetration of merchant capital and its interaction with local capital in the Mexican region of Oaxaca in the 1920s.[25] Merchant capital was already taking away women cloth weavers' control of their terms of purchase and sale. The shift from traditional crops to market-oriented coffee production introduced new changes; women's work shifted from weaving to seasonal participation in coffee production. As a result, they lost control over economic resources and over the labour process, and became secondary and marginal workers in agricultural production.

A third possible effect of capital accumulation involves a new division of labour in which young women become migrant wage earners. The increasing internationalization of capital offers vivid examples of woman's place in the capitalist labour process. Noeleen Heyzer describes the participation of young migrant Malaysian women in the labour-intensive industries of Singapore.[26] Migrant workers make up 51 per cent of the total manufacturing work force in Singapore, and about 45 per cent of the workers in the sector are women working at the bottom levels of the wage structure. Heyzer's analysis illustrates the conditions under which women are becoming important participants in the industrialization process taking place in Third World countries. As Dorothy Elson and Ruth Pearson have pointed out, women's employment is a logical outcome of the increasing fragmentation of capitalist production, in which technology enables industrialists to shift the labour-intensive processes of production to the Third World. Female labour meets the needs of capitalists searching for a disciplined and low-cost labour supply.[27] Helen Safa illustrates this point in her discussion of runaway shops in Latin America and Asia, where about 80 per cent of the employees are women.[28] A common feature of this type of employment is that it is temporary, either because contracts are of limited duration or because there is a

23. Jette Bukh, *The Village Woman in Ghana* (Uppsala; Scandinavian Instit. of African Studies, 1979).
24. Gita Sen, 'Women Workers and the Green Revolution,' in Benería, ed.
25. Kate Young, 'Sex Specificity in Migration: A Case Study from Mexico,' in Benería, ed.
26. Heyze in Benería, ed.; Aline K. Wong, 'Planned development, social stratification, and the sexual division of labor in Singapore', *Signs*, winter 1981.
27. Elson and Pearson, see note 9.
28. Helen I. Safa, 'Runaway shops and female employment: the search for cheap labour', Signs, winter 1981.

high turnover of workers. In addition, working conditions are oppressive. Heyzer describes the prevalent 'atmosphere of compulsion' and the alienation of the workers. Safa describes the lack of public transportation, inadequate health care and other social services, and management resistance to unionization.

In some areas, capital accumulation may weaken traditional forms of patriarchal control over women and introduce new forms. Carmen Diana Deere shows how changes from servile to capitalist relations of production in mid-twentieth-century Cajamarca, Peru, loosened patriarchal controls over women's work.[29] Increasing male migration to the coastal plantations gave women greater autonomy, but access to land shrank, and a new structure emerged by which women became dependent on male wage earners. Similarly, in South-East Asia patriarchy within the family has been replaced by a capitalist control that takes very patriarchal forms; young women's lives and sexuality are circumscribed by the firm's labour control policies.

Finally, class differentiation accompanying the capitalist transformation of a region provides a new basis for differentiation between women. This is well illustrated by Ann Stoler in her study of Javanese women. In analysing the impact of agricultural change on labour force participation, Stoler states that 'for the poorer majority of village society, both men and women suffer as more and more land is concentrated in the hands of the wealthier households. However, the decline in female employment opportunities is more easily observable.'[30] While Boserup points to the ability of some women from landed households to withdraw from field work when landless labourers are available, she does not point out the implications of this situation for women who are landless labourers. Poor and landless women, for example, are often forced to seek agricultural work despite declining employment opportunities due to mechanization of agriculture.[31]

In brief, these studies show the specific ways in which women are affected by the hierarchical and exploitative structure of production associated with capitalism's penetration in the Third World. Modernization is not a neutral process, but one that obeys the dictates of capitalist accumulation and profit making. Contrary to Boserup's implications, the problem for women is not the lack of participation in this process as equal partners with men; it is a system that generates and intensifies inequalities, making use of existing gender hierarchies to place women in subordinate positions at each different level of interaction between class and gender. This is not to deny the possibility that capitalist development might break down certain social rigidities oppressive to women. But these liberating tendencies are accompanied by new forms of subordination.

## ANALYSIS OF SUBORDINATION: THE REPRODUCTIVE SPHERE

One of the most pervasive themes of the present feminist movement is the emphasis placed on the role of reproduction as a determinant of women's work,

29. Carmen Diana Deere, 'Changing Social Relations of Production and Peruvian Peasant Women's Work,' *Latin American Perspectives* 4, no. 1-2 (1977): 48-69.
30. Ann Stoler, 'Class Structure and Female Autonomy in Rural Java,' *Signs: Journal of Women in Culture and Society* 3, no. 1 (Autumn 1977): 74-89.
31. Sen.

the sexual division of labour, and the subordinate/dominant relationships between women and men.[32] It is precisely this emphasis that is lacking in Boserup's book. As a result, her analysis does not contain a feminist perspective that speaks directly to the problem of women's subordination. To be sure, the book is about different forms subordination can take, but it fails to elucidate the crucial role of the household as the focal point of reproduction. Nor does it explain the social relations among household members in the making of 'the woman problem' and in determining women's role in economic development.

Boserup's analysis of polygamy in Africa offers an illustration in this regard. Her analysis, as mentioned earlier, is grounded in economic factors, namely, the greater access to land and labour resources provided by each wife. Boserup's interesting insight, however, is not accompanied by an analysis of the significance of this type of household arrangement for the dynamics of male domination. Nor does it explain why polgamy can also be found in Middle Eastern countries where women are secluded and do not represent an addition to land and labour resources. In these cases, polygamy becomes a luxury that not all households can afford. A similar situation can even be found in parts of Africa where women are secluded, such as the Hausa region in northern Nigeria where polygamy has been on the increase during this century.[33] In the Middle East and in the Hausa region polygamy might be related to social reproduction, that is, to the access each wife provides to family networks and resources. Seclusion may be an effort to control female sexuality for the purpose of identifying paternity and transmitting resources from one generation to the next.

Thus Boserup's analysis falls within a traditional approach to women's issues (and it echoes traditional politics). This approach focuses on nondomestic production as a determinant of women's position in society. Consequently, the solution to women's oppression is seen in the sphere of economic and social relations outside the household. Recent feminist analysis points out the shortcomings of this approach, stressing that it is one-sided and does not address itself to the root of patriarchal relations. In the three areas discussed below - domestic work, spheres of production and reproduction and population and birth control issues - the emphasis on reproduction has contributed to an understanding of women's economic role, of the material base of their oppression, and of its implications for policy and action.

## *Domestic Work*

During the past decade, feminist attempts to understand the roots of women's oppression have resulted in a growing body of literature on domestic labour and household production, as well as on the patriarchal structure that controls them. Most of this literature is based on conditions prevalent in industrialized, urban

32. Reproduction here refers not only to biological reproduction and daily maintenance of the labour force, but also to social reproduction - the perpetuation of social systems. Related is the view that in order to control social reproduction (through inheritance systems, for example) most societies have developed different forms of control over female sexuality and reproductive activities. This control is the root of women's subordination.

33. Richard Longhurst, 'Resource Allocation and the Sexual Division of Labour: A Case Study of a Moslem Hausa Village in Northern Nigeria,' in Benería, ed.

societies where the nuclear family has been, until recently, the most basic form of household organization, and wage labour has been the most important source of family subsistence. Under these conditions, the great bulk of domestic work consists of the production of use values through the combination of commodities bought in the market and domestic labour time. The goods and services produced contribute to the reproduction of the labour force and to its daily maintenance. Thus, domestic work performs a crucial role for the functioning of the economic system. It is linked with the market both by way of what it purchases and by what it provides – the commodity labour power that is exchange for a wage.[34] In the average household, this work is done by women and is unpaid. Women's unique responsibility for this work, and their resulting weakness in the labour market and dependency on the male wage, both underlie and are products of asymmetric gender relations.

The form, extent, and significance of domestic work, however, vary according to a society's stage of economic transformation. In a subsistence economy, the materials used for domestic production are not bought in the market; they are transformed in such a way that household and nonhousehold production are closely linked – to the extent that it is hard to draw a line between them. Domestic work extends itself into activities such as gathering wood for the domestic fire, picking vegetables for daily meals, and baking bread in village public ovens for family consumption. Domestic work also becomes part of the agricultural labour process when, for example, the meals for agricultural workers are cooked in the home and transported to the fields. Similarly, the agricultural labour process extends itself into household production, as when cereals are dried and agricultural goods are processed for family consumption.

In agricultural societies, then, the degree of production for the household's own consumption is higher than in societies where a good proportion of home production has become commoditized. In farming areas domestic and agricultural work contribute most to subsistence needs. The African female farming system places the burden of subsistence largely on women. In most cases, despite a clearly defined sexual division of labour, men's and women's work is integrated in time and space. The separation between productive and reproductive activities is often artificial, symbolized, perhaps, by a woman carrying a baby on her back while working in the fields. By contrast, under the wage-labour systems of industrialized, urban societies, the burden of subsistence falls upon the wage; domestic work transforms the wage into use values consumed in the houshold. A clear separation between domestic and commodity production exists, and unpaid housework becomes more and more isolated and differentiated from nonhousehold production.

Despite these differences, the extent to which domestic work is performed by women across countries is overwhelming. Women perform the great bulk of

34. For an elaboration of these points, see Veronica Beechey, 'Some Notes on Female Wage Labor in Capitalist Production,' *Capital and Class* 3 (Autumn 1977): 45–66; Terry Fee, 'Domestic Labour: An Analysis of Housework and Its Relation to the Production Process,' *Review of Radical Political Economics* 8, no. 1 (1976): 1–8; Susan Himmelweit and Simon Mohun, 'Domestic Labour and Capital,' *Cambridge Journal of Economics* 1, no. 1 (1977): 15–31; Maureen Mackintosh, 'Domestic Labour and the Household,' in *Fit Work for Women*, ed. Sheila Burman (London: Croom Helm, 1979).

reproductive tasks. To the extent that they are also engaged in productive activities outside of the household, they are often burdened with the problems of a 'double day'. As mentioned earlier, Boserup includes an interesting discussion about the tendency of conventional statistics to underestimate subsistence activities, including domestic labour, which represent a high proportion of women's work. Yet nowhere does she indicate how central women's primary involvement in household activities is to an understanding of their subordination and of their role in the economy.

## *Reproduction and Production*

The emphasis on reproduction and on analysis of the household sphere indicates that the traditional focus placed upon commodity production is insufficient to understand women's work and its roots in patriarchal relations. In order to understand fully the nature of sex discrimination, women's wages, women's participation in the development process, and implications for political action, analysts must examine the two areas of production and reproduction as well as the interaction between them. An example from the field of economics – the internal labour market model of sex differentials in the work force – illustrates this approach.

This model represents a step forward from neoclassical explanations of women's secondary status in the labour market. It focuses on the internal organization of the capitalist firm to explain sex segregation and wage differentials, rather than on factors of supply and demand developed by other models.[35] The dynamics of this internal organization tend to foster the formation of job ladders and clusters that create hierarchies among workers. Sex is one factor by which workers can be separated. In this model, occupational segregation, wage differentials, and other types of discrimination by sex are viewed as resulting from the hierarchical and self-regulatory structure of production.

Two policy implications can be drawn from this model. Radical policy would involve elimination of the hierarchical structure of production, perhaps by some form of workers' control and equalization of wages. To the extent that this would eliminate or reduce differences among workers, it would tend to eliminate or reduce differences by sex. A less radical policy would involve equal opportunity/affirmative action plans that take the structure of production and the labour hierarchy as given, but would make each job equally accessible to men and women. Both of these policies have a major flaw; they focus only on the structure of production and do not take into consideration women's role in the area of reproduction. If women face a double day and if child-care facilities are not available to them, neither of the two policies is likely to solve fully the problem of women's secondary status in the labour market, given that their participation in paid production is conditioned by their work in and around the household. All of this points out how necessary it is to eliminate discrimination within the reproductive sphere. Domestic work must be shared between women and men,

35. Francine Blau and Carol Jusenius, 'Economists' Approaches to Sex Segregation in the Labor Market,' in *Women and the Workplace*, ed. Martha Blaxall and Barbara Reagan (Chicago: University of Chicago Press, 1976).

child-care services must become available, and both patriarchal relations and gender stereotyping in the socialization process must be eliminated.

Within the Marxist tradition, it is interesting to note that the Engels thesis does contain an analysis of the interaction between reproduction and production.[36] His view of the origins of women's subordination links the productive sphere – the introduction of private property in the means of production and the need to pass it on from one generation to the next – with reproduction, that is, with the need to identify paternity of heirs through the institution of the family and the control of women's sexuality and reproductive activities. The Engels thesis can be projected to situations, such as those prevalent in industrialized societies, where large segments of the population do not own the means of production, but where there still is a hierarchy and class differences within the propertyless classes. It can be argued that to the extent reproduction implies the private transmission of access to resources – education, for example – the need to identify the individual beneficiaries of this transmission remains.[37]

Engels himself did not extend the analysis in that direction. For him, as for Marx, the production of means of subsistence and the reproduction of human beings are the two fundamental levels of human activity. However, both assumed that the elimination of private property and women's participation in commodity production, made possible by industrialization, would set the preconditions for their emancipation. Thus the initial connection between production and reproduction found in Engels became blurred with the assumption that transformation of productive structures would automatically erase women's oppression. Traditional Marxist thinking and traditional leftist and liberal politics have followed a similar pattern. The new emphasis on reproduction is the result of the questions posed by feminists; it can be viewed as an elaboration of the simplifications inherent in Engels's initial formulation.

A variety of recent studies on women in Third World countries have focused on the interaction between production and reproduction to analyse women's work. Maria Mies's study of Indian women lace makers in Narsapur, Andhra Pradesh, for example, shows how the seclusion of women has conditioned their participation in nonhousehold production.[38] Although lace making is a producing industry geared toward the international market, it is highly compatible with seclusion and domestic work. Women are engaged in lace making as much as six to eight hours a day, in addition to their household chores. Their average daily earnings amount to less than a third of the official minimum wage for female agricultural labourers. This situation persists even though the industry has grown considerably since 1970 and represents a very high proportion of the foreign exchange earnings from handicrafts in the region. Many of the women are the actual breadwinners in their families. Mies argues that this highly exploitative

36. Friedrich Engels, *The Origins of the Family, Private Property and the State,* reprint edn (New York: International Publishers, 1975).

37. See Lourdes Benería, 'Reproduction, Production and the Sexual Division of Labor,' *Cambridge Journal of Economics* 3, no. 3 (1979): 203–25, for an elaboration of the point. This notion can explain, for example, why sexual mores are less strict among the poor than among middle- and upper-class people in many urban as well as rural areas.

38. Maria Mies, 'The Dynamics of the Sexual Division of Labor and the Integration of Women Into the World Market,' in Benería, ed.

system has in fact led to greater class differentiation within local communities as well as greater polarization between the sexes. The system is made possible by the ideology of seclusion that rigidly confines women to the home, eliminates their opportunities for outside work, and makes them willing to accept extremely low wages. A strict focus on the productive aspects of lace making – this is Boserup's approach – to the exclusion of reproductive aspects, such as seclusion, presents only a partial picture of the nature of women's exploitation.

### *Population Control and Birth Control*

The 1970s were particularly fruitful in highlighting the issues of reproductive freedom in the advanced capitalist countries; movements for abortion rights, safe contraception, and adequate day care, and struggles against sterilization abuse abounded. For women in the Third World, however, the question of reproductive freedom has been complicated by the issue of overpopulation and by opposition to imperialist-dominated programmes of population control. This is, of course, also true for poor women from ethnic and racial minority groups who face the threat of sterilization abuse within the advanced capitalist countries. Much of the literature on Third World countries has focused on the question of population control without directly addressing the problem of reproductive freedom for women or the possible contradictions between class and gender.[39] A feminist perspective can modify the analysis of population growth and control in the Third World.

The concept of reproductive freedom includes the right to bear or not to bear children and, by implication, the right to space childbearing. To the extent that children are potential labourers, or inheritors for the propertied classes, decisions about childbearing affect not only the woman but her entire household. For example, in very poor peasant households that possess little land and are squeezed by usury and rent payments, the labour of children both on and off the peasant farm may be crucial to the ongoing ability of the household to subsist and maintain land. Pronatalist tendencies in rural areas may have a clear economic basis. Even neoclassical economists are becoming increasingly aware of the effect of class-related factors – level of schooling, size of land holdings, and access to technology – on fertility rates.[40] Marxist writers have shown the conflict between the economic rationality of the individual household and social programmes of family planning and population control.[41] This conflict may be expressed in subtle ways, such as ignoring available contraception, or in more overt resistance to programmes of forced sterilization. While leftists have correctly opposed forced sterilization and have pointed to the social causes of unemployment – the real population problem – there has been a tendency to ignore a critical aspect of childbearing: it is performed by women.

39. Martha Gimenez, 'Population and Capitalism,' *Latin American Perspectives* 4, no. 4 (1977): 5–40; Mamdani; Bonnie Mass, 'Puerto Rico: A Case Study of Population Control,' *Latin American Perspectives* 4, no. 4 (1977): 66–81.

40. Mark Rosenzweig, 'The Demand for Children in Farm Households,' *Journal of Political Economy* 85, no. 1 (1977): 123–46.

41. Mamdani.

It is true that decisions about childbearing may affect the survival of the entire household over time; still, the most immediate burden of multiple pregnancies falls on the mother. In conditions of severe poverty and malnutrition where women are also overworked, this can and does take a heavy toll on the mother's health and well-being. The poor peasant household may survive off the continuous pregnancy and ill-health of the mother, which are exacerbated by high infant mortality. The mother's class interests and her responsibilities as a woman come into severe conflict.[42]

The result of this conflict is that a poor woman's attitude toward birth control, contraception, and even sterilization are likely to be different from those of her husband or mother-in-law. Research on these problems in the Third World should address questions such as: (1) Who makes decisions about childbearing and birth control within rural households, families, and communities, and on what basis are the decisions made? (2) What indigenous forms of family limitation are available to poor women, and how are they used? (3) Are there differences of opinion and interest between the childbearers and other family members? (4) How does childbearing affect women's participation in other activities?

Answers to these questions require careful empirical research of a sort that is barely beginning in the Third World. The insights gained from empirical research must affect one's assessment of birth control programmes, especially the more enlightened programmes that focus on the health and education of the mother. The reduction in infant mortality, improvement in health and sanitation, and better midwife and paramedic facilities can give poor, rural women more options than having to resolve class contradictions through their own bodies. Such programmes, however, clearly cannot be a panacea for the basic problems of extreme poverty and inequality in land holding; the contradictions of class and capital accumulation in the countryside can be resolved only through systemic social change.

## CONCLUSION

In our analysis we have assessed the positive contributions of Boserup's work to a decade of feminist research on women in the Third World. We have also tried to show the limitations of her analysis, which arise from a flawed and inadequate conceptual basis.[43] There has been a great deal of fruitful research in the past decade that is thoroughly grounded in theory, particularly in class-based and feminist perspectives, which provides a richly textured understanding of the position of women in the Third World.

It is very important to delineate the policy implications that emerge from this analysis. Boserup's own conclusions on policy emphasized women's education as

42. Nancy Folbre, 'Patriarchy and Capitalism in New England, 1650–1900' (Ph.D. diss., University of Massachusetts, 1979), and 'Patriarchy in Colonial New England,' *Review of Radical Political Economics* 12, no. 2 (1980): 4–13.

43. For an earlier critique of Boserup's discussion of farming systems, see Suellen Huntington, 'Issues in Woman's Role in Economic Development: Critique and Alternatives,' *Journal of Marriage and the Family 37*, no. 4 (1975): 1001–12.

the major mechanism by which modernization would begin to work to women's advantage. Through education, women can compete more successfully in urban labour markets and gain access to improved agricultural techniques in the rural areas. This conclusion ignores two crucial features that an analysis based on the concepts of accumulation and women's role in reproduction would highlight. On one hand, it ignores the high incidence of unemployment among educated people in the Third World. Unless the systemic causes of unemployment are removed, women's education by itself is purely an individualist solution; it attempts to alter the characteristics of individual women rather than those of the system of capital accumulation. On the other hand, even if there were dramatic systemic changes, education by itself would not alter women's position, in that education cannot address issues of child care and domestic work. The high incidence of the double day in countries like the Soviet Union and China supplies ample evidence of this policy's limited success.

Short-term programmes involving the basic-needs strategy have definite motivational limits, but they cannot be ignored entirely.[44] Since the principal outcome of tensions between gender and class are that women are overworked and in ill health, systems of water provision, electrification, and sanitation and health are immediately beneficial. One must remain aware, however, of how such programmes are implemented and whom they benefit. Strategies that involve the self-organization of poor women for control over such programmes are crucial.

The long-term goal, however, remains, and that is the elimination of class and sex hierarchies through a radical transformation of society, a struggle that requires not only an analysis of class and of accumulation, but a recognition of the importance of reproduction at all levels. We can no longer ignore the questions of what goes on within households, nor the interweaving of gender relations and class relations. The feminist analysis of the Third World in the past decade has lent support and clarity to this vision.

44. For a clarification of the basic-needs strategy, see ILO, *Employment, Growth and Basic Needs: A One-World Problem* (New York: Praeger Publishers, 1976).

# 16

# Conceptualizing the Labour Force: the Underestimation of Women's Economic Activities

LOURDES BENERÍA

## INTRODUCTION

The growing amount of literature on women's issues that has appeared during the last ten years has been instrumental in deepening our understanding of the nature and extent of women's participation in economic activities. It has also increased our awareness of the conceptual and empirical problems that exist regarding this subject. One such problem is the definition and measurement of women's work. As studies on women's labour force participation have proliferated the inadequacies of available statistics in capturing the degree of their participation in economic life has become progressively more obvious.

Survey work, detailed studies of women's activities, and even mere observation of everyday life has led to a general agreement about the obscurity and low value generally attached to women's work in most societies. There are in fact two issues that are interrelated along these lines. One is ideological and is associated with the tendency to regard women's work as secondary and subordinate to men's. An aspect of this tendency relates to the fact that an important proportion of women's work is unpaid. Both the ideological and monetary aspects are clearly symbolized by an expression such as 'my mother doesn't work' even though she might be working longer hours than any other household member. 'Work' in this case

This essay was first published in *Journal of Development Studies*, 17, 1981, pp. 10–28. The original research was carried out while the author was working as coordinator of the Programme on Rural Women of the International Labour Office. The views expressed here are the author's and do not necessarily reflect those of the ILO. A different version is included in *Women and Development: The Sexual Division of Labour in Rural Societies*, published by the ILO and edited by the author. Many thanks are due to the ILO colleagues who read the manuscript and helped at different stages of the project, in particular to Z. Ahmad, D. Ghai, F. Lisk, M. Loutfi and G. Standing, and to N. Nelson and G. Sen.

means participation in paid production, an income-earning activity. The ideological aspect is reinforced by the pervasive lack of a clear conceptualization of the role played by women at different levels of economic life. For example, while an effort has been made to evaluate the contribution of subsistence agricultural production to, for example, national output, similar efforts to evaluate subsistence work carried out by women in the household have been the exception rather than the rule.

This ideological bias, as will be seen below, is deeply embedded in most of the concepts widely used in the social sciences; dealing with it requires an effort to analyse the very roots of this bias and to reconstruct these concepts in such a way that the role of women in society can be placed in its proper perspective. In the light of the arguments presented in this chapter, it is ludicrous to include women among the 'passive' or 'inactive' groups in society such as pensioners, housewives and the handicapped (Blanchard, 1979). (Note that Blanchard was speaking as Secretary General of the ILO, an institution highly concerned with refining labour force concepts and improving statistical information on the labour force).

The second issue is a consequence of the first and is of a less fundamental but more practical nature. It refers to the actual statistical evaluation and accounting of women's work either as participants in the labour force or in terms of GNP estimations. It is by now well known that most labour force and national accounting statistics reflect a gross underestimation of women's participation in economic activity. Concern over this problem has been growing during the past decade. Boserup, in her analysis of women's role in the development process, put it clearly when she wrote that 'the subsistence activities usually omitted in the statistics of production and incomes are largely women's work' (1970:163). This concern has been expressed repeatedly by other authors as well (Gulati, 1975; Standing, 1978). Yet subsistence production, as will be seen below, is not the only area of underestimation of women's work.

Although we do not want to fall into the trap of making a fetish of statistics, it is important to point out shortcomings of available data for the purposes of evaluating women's work. Those data are commonly used for planning purposes and can be the source of numerous biases. The purpose of this chapter is to show how those shortcomings are rooted in the conceptual categories used. The focal point of the essay is the analysis of statistical biases and of the concepts that feed statistical categories. The second section analyses the conventional definitions of active labour used, how they affect data collection and, more specifically, how they bias the evaluation of women as economic agents. The third deals with the more theoretical aspects of the problem, linking these definitions to a given conceptual framework of what constitutes economic activity. A redefinition of economic activity is suggested and its implications for statistical purposes are discussed in the fourth section.

## BIASES OF AVAILABLE STATISTICS

Until the Second World War, statistics on the 'economically active population' depended primarily on population censuses. The emphasis on problems of unemployment derived from the 1929 crisis and generated an increased interest in the collection of reliable statistics on the subject. In 1938 the Committee of Statistical Experts of the League of Nations recommended a definition of the concepts of 'gainfully occupied' and 'unemployed' population and drew up proposals to standardize census data with the purpose of facilitating international comparisons. As a consequence, many countries expanded the collection of statistics on what, from then on, would be called the 'labour force' (ILO, 1976; League of Nations, 1938).

The 1938 definition of gainful occupation was that 'for which the person engaged therein is remunerated, directly or indirectly, in cash or in kind'. The labour force was defined as comprising the gainfully occupied and the unemployed, the objective being to measure not only the employed population but the total labour supply. Updated labour force definitions adopted by the Statistical Commission of the United Nations in 1966 defined the economically active population as comprising 'all persons of either sex who furnish the supply of labour for the production of economic goods and services' (ILO, 1976:32). The basic difference between the 1938 and 1966 definitions was that while the former responded to the objective of including the unemployed as forming part of the labour supply, the latter reflected an increasing concern not only with unemployment but also with underemployment. The objective was to reach an estimate of the potential labour supply in order to best estimate the underutilization of labour resources; the potential labour supply was to include not only individuals contributing 'to the incomes of their families and to the national product' (p. 36), but also the unemployed and underemployed.

We can see from this definition that there are two focal points in the conventional measurements of the labour force. One reflects the concern over unemployment, the potential labour supply, and the full utilization of labour resources. The other reflects the link between the concepts of labour force and the national product – active labour being defined as that which contributes to the national product plus involuntary inactive or unemployed labour. Both lead to questionable measurements of the labour force – symbolized by the fact that a domestic activity such as cooking will be classified as performed by active labour when the cooked food is marketed and as inactive when it is not. And family members might be classified as underemployed when working in agriculture but not when engaged in household production.

This is because the underlying definition of the national product includes essentially only goods and services exchanged in the market. The problem of underestimation of the labour force is therefore more acute in areas where the market has not penetrated many spheres of human activity. While in industrialized societies the only major exception is domestic production – to the extent that it has not been commoditized[1] – nonmarket production is more prevalent in the Third World.

In order to deal with this problem, continuous efforts have been made, on the part of national and international bodies in charge of labour force statistics, to include nonmarket subsistence production in GNP estimations and subsistence

1. Throughout this chapter the concept of commodity is used in its usual meaning of an output produced for the purpose of being exchanged in the market and sold for a price.

workers as active labour.[2] Hence the introduction of the concepts of 'potential labour supply' and of 'marketable goods' in order to measure the contribution of some sectors not yet penetrated by the market. But despite the increasing sophistication in data collection and labour force estimations, important problems remain and the tendency to underestimate the active population – especially among women – is still a major flaw in available data. Let us examine more specifically the significance of these definitions from the point of view of measuring the female labour force.

The League of Nations 1938 definition specified that '*housework done by members of a family in their own homes is not included in that description* of the gainfully occupied, *but work done by members of a family in helping the head of a family in his occupation is so included*, even though only indirectly remunerated, (ILO, 1976:28–9; emphasis added). Under this definition, when members of a household are assumed to help the head of the family (presumably a male), as for example agricultural workers, they are classified as 'unpaid family workers'; on the other hand, when the same individuals perform domestic work, such as food processing or water carrying, they are not defined as workers, the rationale being that the former are assumed to be engaged in income-earning activities while the latter are not.

Despite the considerable effort made since 1938 to improve labour force statistics, these concepts have remained essentially untouched to the present time; subsequent work has mainly concentrated on techniques of data collection. For example, the concern for estimating the potential labour supply reflected in the 1976 definitions had implications for female labour: 'Particular attention should be given to groups which may be especially difficult to classify, such as female unpaid family workers in agriculture' (ILO, 1976:32). However, the problem of underestimation of women's participation in the labour force has not disappeared, as a glance at the relevant ILO literature on the subject indicates (Standing, 1978; Standing and Sheehan, 1978). Given the above definitions of the labour force, this underestimation is due to several factors.

First there is the problem of defining who is an unpaid family worker. In 1954, an ILO resolution recommended that, in order to be defined as such, an unpaid family worker must work in nondomestic activities for at least one third of the normal hours.[3] The problem of defining what are normal hours and for how long a family member has worked affects both male and female workers. A typical approach in many countries is that, in order to be classified as an active worker, an individual must have worked a minimum of 15 hours during the two weeks before a census takes place. However, given that involvement in home production does not merit inclusion in the 'labour force', and to the extent that women's unpaid family work is highly integrated with domestic activities, the line between what is conventionally classified as unpaid family worker and domestic worker becomes very thin and difficult to draw. The result is a logical underestimation of women's nondomestic work.

2. The ILO, for example, has maintained a continuous interest in devising new approaches to deal with the problem. In addition to the sources already mentioned, see Richter (1978), Frank (1977), Bienefeld and Godfrey (1975).

3. Resolution adopted at the Eighth International Conference of Labour Statisticians, Geneva, Nov.–Dec. 1954. See Standing (1978:30) for a discussion on the subject.

Second, when censuses classify workers according to their 'main occupation', the tendency to underreport women as workers in agriculture or any other type of nondomestic production is very prevalent. In India, for examply, the 1971 Census excluded women whose main occupation was classified as housewife but who were also engaged in other work outside of the household; it has been estimated that, in this case, the exclusion of 'secondary' work implied a fall in the participation rate from almost 23 per cent to just over 13 per cent (Gulati, 1975). The problem of underreporting has been observed across regions, even though certain Moslem countries are often mentioned as extreme cases: 'With few exceptions, where censuses or surveys have been conducted in these countries . . . the female unpaid family workers were, to a large extent, not recorded' (ILO, 1977, VI:11). In Algeria, the number of women reported as unpaid family workers in the 1956 census was 96,000; after a post-census re-evaluation of data, it was estimated that 1,200,000 women working as unpaid family members had not been reported (ibid).

There are several reasons for this underreporting: they range from the relative irregularity of women's work outside the household – that is, the greater incidence among women of seasonal and marginal work – to the deeply ingrained view that women's place is in the household. If census and survey workers do not ask about primary and secondary occupations, they are likely to classify a good proportion of women as working only in the household when this is not actually the case. In many countries it is considered prestigious to keep women from participating in nonhousehold production;[4] when asked whether women do so both men and women tend to reply negatively even if this is not the case. In addition, underreporting might be due to any economic incentive derived from 'hiding' women's income-earning activities – such as the loss of paid security benefits and family subsidies tied to the full time dedication of the housewife to domestic activities (Benería, 1977).

Thirdly, some activities are performed by women at home even though they are clearly tied to the market. This is the case when they sell food and drinks in or near their own home. Cloth-making for nonfamily members and selling of handicrafts and other products inside the family compound are other examples. The proximity and integration of these activities with domestic work makes them highly invisible too; they are likely to go unreported as market activities unless census and survey researchers are conscious of the problem.

Consequently, conventional labour force statistics must be approached with a high degree of scepticism when evaluating women's participation in production. Women working as wage labourers will tend to be automatically classified in the labour force, but women working in agriculture or in any other activity not clearly connected with the market might not be – depending upon each country's definition of labour force and upon methods followed to estimate it.

Table 16.1 provides an illustration of available figures on regional and country activity rates. Compiled by the ILO, they are drawn from country surveys and censuses, and widely used for international comparisons of labour statistics. The

4. An extreme case is the observance of *purdah*, or the seclusion of women, which is often seen as a 'luxury' poor women cannot afford. This attitude is found in parts of South Asia, the Middle East, North Africa and West Africa (Abdullah and Zeidenstein, 1978).

table shows that activity or labour force participation rates (the proportion of the population classified as gainfully occupied and as unemployed) are much higher for men than for women across regions. It also shows that variations in activity rates are higher among women; while the lowest average regional rate corresponds to Latin America, the highest rates, for the three years given, are registered for the more industrialized countries of Europe and North America. Given the very high degree of involvement of women in agricultural production and trade in many African countries, the relatively low rates shown for Africa might immediately be questioned. However, the degree of variation is greater among countries, especially when differences between age groups are taken into consideration. For example, activity rates for the 25–44 age group in 1970 ranged from 4.2 per cent in Saudi Arabia to 67 per cent in Zaire and 93 per cent in the USSR (Standing, 1978).

TABLE 16.1 Actual and projected activity rates, by region (per cent)

| | *Males* | | | *Females* | | |
|---|---|---|---|---|---|---|
| | *1975* | *1985* | *2000* | *1975* | *1985* | *2000* |
| Asia | 53.8 | 53.1 | 54.0 | 29.1 | 28.4 | 28.2 |
| Africa | 51.6 | 49.3 | 47.8 | 24.4 | 22.9 | 22.0 |
| Europe | 58.2 | 58.5 | 56.9 | 31.4 | 33.0 | 34.3 |
| Latin America | 48.9 | 48.0 | 48.5 | 14.0 | 15.4 | 18.3 |
| Northern America | 56.3 | 57.4 | 57.4 | 32.2 | 34.3 | 37.2 |
| World | 53.8 | 53.0 | 53.0 | 29.1 | 28.2 | 28.2 |

*Source:* ILO, *Labour Force Projections*, 1977

These figures should only be read as rough estimates of women's labour force participation rates. For example, the very low activity rates reported for the Arab countries should not be taken at face value. A census taken in Sudan in 1956, which included questions about both primary and secondary occupations, resulted in a labour force participation rate of women of almost 40 per cent (Standing, 1978:29), in contrast with other official statistics that report rates barely above the 10 per cent level.

In a survey taken by Deere in the Andean region, it was found that the proportion of women participating in agricultural work was 21 per cent instead of the 3 per cent officially reported (Deere, 1977). This type of underestimation is common across countries, and especially in agricultural areas (Anker and Knowles, 1978; ILO, 1978). To the extent that the amount of agricultural work that women perform is greater for the poorer strata of the peasantry (Deere, 1976; Stoler, 1976), it implies that this underestimation differs according to class background and affects women from the poorer strata to a greater degree.

Two conclusions can be drawn from this. One is that studies on women based on conventional labour force statistics must use a great degree of caution in their analyses and inferences about women's work. The danger of tautological conclusions is obvious: if active labour is primarily defined in relation to the market and if production and labour not clearly exchanged in the market tends to be grossly underestimated, the positive relationship often found between women's activity rates and some index of economic development is clearly erroneous. This is especially the case when comparing predominantly agricultural with predominantly industrial countries and geographical areas. Yet numerous studies on women's labour force participation continue to ignore the problem.[5]

In addition, the implication often derived from this positive relationship, namely that economic development and industrialization have positive effects on women's emancipation, is far from being obvious. This is not just because women's participation in production and control over resources in less economically developed agricultural societies might be greater than statistics lead us to believe (Boserup, 1970; Bukh, 1979; Rubbo, 1975). It is also because, although participation in the industrial/urban labour force might provide women with a source of earnings, participation *per se* does not guarantee freedom either from subordination to patriarchal structures or from other forms of exploitation (*IDS Bulletin*, vol. 10, no. 3, 1979).

The second conclusion is that the great disparity in women's participation in the labour force across countries is likely to be exaggerated and international comparisons are likely to be misleading as long as a comparable statistical base is not adopted. Although country and regional differences do exist, comparisions based on figures such as official female labour force participation rates must be qualified with a scrutiny of data collection in each country. In addition, it is necessary that the concepts that have nourished statistical definitions be clarified. It is to this subject that I turn now.

## THE CONCEPT OF ACTIVE LABOUR

The problem of underestimation of women's work becomes even more acute if we question the conventional definitions of active labour. It is at this level that the ideological dimension in the evaluation of women's work comes in. The basic question arises from the need to define who is engaged in the production of goods and services during a given time-reference period. (See the definition by the Statistical Commission of the UN given above.) In the last resort, it amounts to defining what constitutes an 'economic activity' and understanding the conceptual and functional boundaries between it and other types of activity.

For orthodox economics, the focal point for the analysis of economic activity is the process of capitalist growth and accumulation, with emphasis given to quantitative relations in commodity production. The basic mechanism through which these relations are expressed is the market which becomes the formal expression of economic activity. Through the process of exchange, the price of commodities is an indicator of their relative worth. Market exchange is tied to the division of labour which, as Adam Smith typically emphasized, is viewed as the basis for productivity increases and as the source of the wealth of nations. The production of exchange values is viewed as economic activity whereas use value production is normally not viewed as such. Exchange values take their concrete

5. See Tienda (1977), Cordell and McHale (1975), Boulding (1977), Denti (1968), Safiotti (1977). Tienda, for example, elaborates the proposition that 'the proportion of female active labour varies according to indices for economic development' (p. 307) and finds that this is the case for Mexico. Yet her conclusion is based on conventional labour force statistics.

form through the market, and, in that sense, the market becomes the basic source of information for a quantitative evaluation of society's output.

This explains why orthodox economics focuses its attention on the market; although the economic system is regarded, as Robbins has put it, 'as a series of independent but conceptually discrete relationships between men [*sic*] and economic goods' (1932:69) these relationships are viewed essentially from a quantitative perspective. In fact the almost exclusive attention paid to quantitative relations in neoclassical economics has often led to identifying these relations with the essence of economic analysis.

It follows from this that activities falling outside the market mainstream are considered peripheral to the economic system and not defined as 'economic'. The history of national income accounting and of labour force statistics, as explained in the previous section, has followed this basic theoretical framework. Efforts to incorporate 'marketable goods' in national income accounts represent an attempt to apply this framework to nonmarket activities. In the same way, when home-based activities produce goods for exchange, they become 'income-earning activities' and the labour engaged in them becomes active labour. That is, *when work becomes commoditized*, in the sense that it produces goods and services for exchange, *it is regarded as an economic activity; participation in the labour force is then measured in terms of labour's links with market activity.*

Within the nonorthodox tradition, these concepts have often been used in a similar way despite basic differences with the orthodox tradition. Marxists, for example, have argued that economics cannot be confined to the sphere of quantitative relations between people and economic goods, and that social relations underlying commodity exchange need to be considered as part of the economic realm; as Sweezy (1942) has pointed out, 'the quantitative relation between things, which we call exchange value, is in reality only an outward form of the *social* relation between the commodity owners' (p. 27). However, despite the fact that Marx talked about all labour producing use values as productive labour,[6] the most prevalent position within the Marxist tradition has been in accordance with his contention that 'use value as such lies outside the sphere of political economy' (Marx, 1911:19). Sweezy explains this exclusion of use value production from the field of investigation of political economy on the grounds that Marx 'enforces a strict requirement that the categories of economics must be social categories, i.e. categories which represent relations between people' (p. 26).

The reason for this exclusion must be sought in Marx's concentration on the analysis of the capitalist mode of production and the dynamics of accumulation. Thus, despite the broader definition of economic categories within the Marxist framework, a relative neglect of noncommoditized sectors – such as subsistence production and the household economy – has been a common feature until recently.

During the past few years there has been an increasing realization of the importance of understanding the nature and significance of noncommodity production and its role within the economic system. What is argued in this section

6. 'If we examine the whole process from the point of view of its results, the product, it is plain that both the instruments and the subject of labour are means of production, and that the labour itself is productive labour' (Marx, 1967:181).

can be summarized in two points: (1) use value production *does* embody a social relation and should therefore not be excluded from the field of political economy; (2) exclusion of use value production renders the analysis of economic activity incomplete, leads to distortions in the measurement of the labour force, and can reinforce ideological biases related to the undervaluation of women's work. The central argument of this chapter is that any conceptualization of economic activity should include the production of both use and exchange values, and that active labour should be defined in relation to its contribution to the production of goods and services for the satisfaction of human needs. Whether this production is channelled through the market and whether it contributes directly to the accumulation process are questions that can be taken up at a different level of analysis and should not affect our understanding of what constitutes economic activity. The argument is far from implying that there is no difference between commodity and noncommodity production, but rather that the latter type of production is also part of the realm of economics and must be valued accordingly.

The basis for this argument is provided by the literature on domestic work, reproduction and subsistence production which has been developed during recent years. In what follows, I present a brief summary of the contributions that are relevant for the purpose of this argument.

## *Domestic Work and Subsistence Production : the End of Invisibility*

The analysis of the household has gradually increased in sophistication over recent years. Within the field of economics,[7] neoclassical analysis pioneered this effort with theoretical and empirical work on the factors affecting women's participation in paid production. Further work along these lines was concentrated on subjects such as the quantification of domestic production through time - allocation studies, the estimation of the market value of home production, fertility analysis, and the economic factors affecting marriage and divorce. This work has centred around the application of utility maximization and cost-benefit analysis to the domestic economy. That is, it has applied conventional micro-economics to the analysis of the household, with an emphasis on quantitative relations.

In contrast, feminist and Marxist literature has centred on the significance of unpaid household production for an understanding of the economic role of women within both the household and the larger economy, and of its implications for an understanding of the reasons behind women's subordination. It has emphasized the role of women in the reproduction and daily maintenance of the labour force - a fundamental point made being that household production cheapens the costs of maintenance and reproduction. This is so in comparison with the costs that would be incurred if the goods and services produced domestically with unpaid labour were bought in the market. Household production therefore reduces labour costs in commodity production and, in this

7. The analysis of domestic work has taken place within the orthodox as well as the Marxist traditions. Typical examples of the first are compiled in Lloyd's book (*1975*), while a summary of the Marxist literature on the subject is provided by Himmelweit and Mohun *(1977)*. Subsistence production and its links with commodity production is analysed in Benholdt-Thomsen (1978), Deere (1977) and Wolpe (1975). On the subject of reproduction see Edholm et al. (1977) and Benería (1979).

sense, can be regarded as having, if not a *direct* link with it, an *indirect* effect on the accumulation process (Beechey, 1977; Deere, 1976; Fee, 1976).

Two basic differences between the two approaches can be pointed out. One is that while orthodox economics, in applying the concepts used in market-oriented micro-economics to the domestic economy, tends to blur the distinction between use values and exchange values, feminist and Marxist analyses have stressed this distinction. The other concerns the political significance of the analysis; while conventional analysis takes the economic system *uncritically* and tends to *describe* changes taking place within it, the second approach asks political questions more directly and emphasizes the link between women's roles and the economic system. These questions are formulated both from the point of view of examining women's subordination to men – a problem that can apply to any given economic and political system – and from the point of view of seeking to understand how this subordination is integrated with exploitation in class society.

Yet both approaches share a common result: domestic labour and its connections with the nondomestic economy are no longer invisible. The incorporation of domestic work in the mainstream of analysis reflects the progressive realization of its importance for a full understanding of women's work and of the sexual division of labour in and outside of the household.

Similarly, the analysis of the subsistence sector and of the role that it plays within the larger economy has recently received new attention. This analysis has raised further important questions. Many authors have pointed out the permanence of this sector in many countries of the Third World, not only in agricultural areas, but also in urban areas under the form of a marginalized population which is either not absorbed by the capitalist sector or repelled by it as unemployed labour. Yet subsistence production is *indirectly* related to market production. As Wolpe (1975) has argued in relation to South Africa, the existence of the subsistence sector allows the capitalist sector to pay a wage which covers only the subsistence needs of the wage labourer – normally a male migrant – instead of family subsistence. The role of women in providing unpaid work within the sector, in domestic and agricultural production, and in cheapening the wage has also been pointed out by other authors (Bukh, 1979; Deere, 1976; Mueller, 1976). The subsistence sector constitutes therefore a source of cheap labour from which wage labour can be drawn as capital accumulation proceeds. Far from being two separate sectors, as the dual economy analysis argues, the subsistence and the capitalist sectors are highly interconnected to the extent that the latter feeds upon the former.

Use value production outside of market exchange takes place both in the household and in the subsistence sector. Efforts have been made to include it in GNP calculations[8] even though its market value is difficult to estimate. In particular, agricultural production not exchanged in the market is viewed as 'marketable output' and labour engaged in it as being part of the labour force – as the concept of 'family worker' indicates. Problems of underestimation in this case are due to practical difficulties in data collection, not to conceptual biases.

8. This is so even in the much less frequent case of estimation of domestic production. Illustrations can be found in Walker (1969), Scott (1972), Vanek (1974).

In contrast, the few attempts made at estimating domestic production have for the most part not generated a clear definition of household production as an economic activity and especially of domestic workers as being part of the labour force unless they be wage workers. In the last resort, housework is linked with consumption rather than with production by most authors. Galbraith, who included a chapter on 'Consumption and the Concept of the Household' in his *Economics and the Public Purpose*, regards housework as 'the labor of women to facilitate consumption' (1973:33). Yet, part of the recent literature on domestic labour contains a clear conceptualization of domestic work as an integral part of the economic system. Within the Marxist tradition, several authors have discussed the need to view the concept of mode of production as including 'the relations and forces involved in the production of use values but also those involved in the reproduction of the species [reproduction of people]' (Himmelweit and Mohun, 1977). However, in the last resort housework is linked with consumption rather than with production since it concerns 'production of use values for immediate consumption outside of any direct relation to capital' (p. 28). While this point is important for the purpose of differentiating use value from exchange value production and of delineating what activities contribute directly to the process of capital accumulation, it does not justify the asymmetry in the conceptual treatment given to the two types of use value production. Although it is important to differentiate between activities directly related to capital and activities that are not, and between labour that participates in the commodity sector or not, this does not justify the exclusion of any type of non-commodity production from our definitions of economic activity and active labour.

In the conventional definitions of national product and labour force, the rationale for this asymmetry seems to be the assumption that subsistence agricultural production consists of goods normally sold in the market while household production does not. Yet this assumption becomes even more arbitrary when household production is looked at from an historical perspective. The extent and nature of household-related work – overwhelmingly women's work across countries – varies according to the stage of economic transformation of a given society. The gradual penetration of the market into economic life generates a shift of production from the domestic to the market sphere of production. In industrialized societies, where subsistence depends predominantly on the wage, the function of domestic work is to 'transform' family income into consumable goods and services, only a small part of which is produced within the household. The burden of subsistence therefore falls on the wage, parts of production get gradually removed from the household, and domestic labour tends to concentrate on the transformation of market goods for household consumption.

By contrast, domestic labour in predominantly agricultural societies contains a higher degree of production – as symbolized by the fact that all stages of food transformation are often carried out in the household. In addition to strictly domestic activities, women's work around the household consists of a great variety of subsistence activities – such as water carrying, wood gathering, and food transportation – which often require long hours of work. The burden of subsistence in this case falls on these types of activities together with agricultural work in which women's participation is also high. In this case, agricultural and household-related tasks are highly integrated in time and space, and productive and reproductive activities highly intertwined. The introduction of the notion of 'marketable goods' in such cases for the purpose of evaluating subsistence production and measuring the labour force constitutes a projection of a concept specific to commodity production for the purpose of differentiating two types of output – marketable and nonmarketable. These in fact serve similar functions and can hardly be separated out. The gradual penetration of the market into rural economies introduces different degrees of direct contact with commodity production and capital. Yet it does not change the productive and reproductive *nature* of these activities; what changes is the degree of their integration into commodity production and into the economic system.

## *Social Relations and Use Value Production*

Now that domestic and subsistence production are becoming analytically more visible, and their proper role within the economic system is being re-evaluated, it is increasingly difficult to argue that the production of use values does not embody a social relation. The penetration of analysis into the household and subsistence production has been instrumental in bringing into the open the complexity of 'social relations' in use value production. We can talk, for example, about differences in access and control over the household means of production and about the unequal distribution of resources among different household members. A closer analysis of differences in household organization also documents the complexity of relations in regard to household hierarchies by sex and age and of the division of labour even among members of the same sex (Benería, 1979) Similarly, under a wage labour system in which subsistence depends on the male wage, we can identify, as Seccombe (1974) has done, two levels of exchange – between employer and wage labourer and between wage labourer and domestic worker – existing in the interaction between the household economy and commodity production. Thus, it is logical to view the two levels of exchange as generating a set of social relations. In the same way, social relations are generated in the interaction between domestic and agricultural production in a subsistence setting to the extent that these activities can be viewed as part of the agricultural production process, when women cook and carry meals to the men working in the fields.

Two different conclusions spring from these observations. One is that the assumption of the household as the most basic unit of analysis – which is often made in the social sciences – is not appropriate. The household cannot, for example, be assumed to be a harmonious unit of consumption and production/reproduction; it is precisely the conflicting nature of the relations generated by these functions that is being disentangled by feminist analysis. And this implies that it is important to distinguish between the household as a collective unit and the individual members that are part of it. This is especially so if our interest focuses on the analysis of mechanisms and forms of subordination/domination.

The other implication is that the household cannot be viewed as being isolated in the 'private' sphere and distinct from the 'public' sphere. Both spheres are highly interconnected and have an influence upon each other. Once the role of use value production and its importance within the larger economy is understood, the separation between the two spheres becomes artificial. It is in fact this separation which is at the root of the asymmetric treatment given to different types of use value production.

A full understanding of these implications leads to the conclusion that whether we are dealing with agricultural production or domestic work within either a polygamous household or the nuclear family, use value production generates 'social relations between people' and forms part of 'the categories of economics'. Once this is understood it is still possible to differentiate between activities that are *directly* related to capital accumulation and those that are not, or between that part of the labour force that produces exchange values and the part that is engaged in use value production.

## MEASURING WOMEN'S WORK

The purpose of the previous section was to discuss the concepts that underlie economic categories and to present a framework that can move us beyond conventional concepts of the labour force. Practical implications for data collection and statistical evaluation of women's work can follow from new concepts. But first we might ask about the usefulness and significance of such an exercise. The two main questions here are *why* do we want to expand our concept of active labour to include use value production and, especially, *what difference* can it make for women. Obviously it is possible that censuses and survey work might be addressed to evaluate all economic activities, as defined above, and yet be totally irrelevant for dealing with women's subordination.

Having recognized this possibility, I want to argue that such an exercise responds to three main objectives. One is to counteract the ideological undervaluation of women's work and to give recognition to the long hours of labour in which women are engaged. We are in fact only arguing that domestic labour should receive the same treatment as other types of labour engaged in use value production. But, in addition, we are also underlining the crucial function played by women within the larger economy and pointing out the interaction between use value and commodity production.

The argument presented here should not be taken as a tacit acceptance of the traditional sexual division of labour by which women remain predominantly in unpaid work. What is intended is to focus on the economic significance of this work and to point out, for example, that women clearly engage in a 'double day' load when they are responsible for household duties in addition to a similar load to men's outside of domestic production. This implies that it is essential to understand that it is not enough to emphasize the need to increase women's participation in paid production as a basis for their economic self-reliance; any development scheme, be it a limited employment policy or an ambitious radical change, must deal with the question of how to organize production so that women are not burdened with a double load.

A second objective is related to the simple need to have as much information as possible about women's activities and their role in economic life. Planning development programmes, employment policies, training and educational programmes, introduction of technological change at all levels (including the household), etc., must be based on accurate information on women's work if they are to be fully relevant to about 50 per cent of the world's population.

A typical example of the need for more information is the problem of unemployment and underemployment among women. The lack of accurate estimations of these variables in most countries is a natural consequence of the problems described so far; if women are either not classified or underestimated as workers, it is logical that they will also be underestimated among the unemployed since, in order to be counted as such, they must first be defined as part of active labour. Some hints at the high underemployment and unemployment of women in the Third World exist,[9] but for the most part systematic information on the subject is not available. In the industrialized countries, unemployment rates among women are higher than among men practically across the board. Yet this type of information should be a starting point of any development strategy and employment policy. This information cannot be obtained accurately without an estimation of the proportion of women that are 'taking refuge' in domestic and subsistence production because there is no employment elsewhere available to them.

Finally, a third objective in expanding our concept of active labour is to define economic activity in such a way as to relate it to human welfare rather than to a given process of growth and accumulation. As pointed out earlier, it is important to focus on commodity production if we are interested, for example, to understand the process of production and growth in a capitalist economy; a different question is to move beyond commodity production and focus on all activities contributing to the satisfaction of material needs - as required, for instance, by a basic needs development strategy. By differentiating between the broader level of economic activity and the narrower level specific to a given process of growth and accumulation, we are differentiating between all activities contributing to human welfare and those linked to a particular economic system. In this way, we transcend the conceptual framework that evolved out of the specific categories linked to capitalist production, of labour put to use for accumulation and profit.

We must now examine the pragmatic implications of the arguments made in this chapter for statistical work, lest we be charged with being impractical. It should be pointed out that some of the discussion carried out by the ILO on the issue of labour force statistics and by neoclassical economists working on household time-use data comes close to asking some of the questions posed in this chapter. The issues raised include the difficulty of drawing a dividing line between economic and noneconomic activity, and the distinction between

9. In India, for example, it is clear that among the proportion of the population that have lost access to land, women are less likely than men to find wage employment (Mies, 1978). As a result, unemployment figures for women are high; the Committee on the Status of Women in India estimated that, in 1971, women represented 60 per cent of rural unemployment and 56 per cent of urban unemployment (p. 160). Yet it is highly likely that these figures underrepresent female unemployment because women can always take refuge in the household and move out of the conventionally defined labour force. A second example comes from Latin America where it has been estimated that in the rural areas underemployment is more than twice as high as the national unemployment rate, and that most of the unemployed are young people and married women (ILO/PREALC, 1976).

economic activity and housework.[10] Some authors have talked about *economic activities* that are 'marginal' (such as hunting, handicrafts and raising vegetables) and 'auxiliary' (repairing tools for one's work and marketing home-produced goods) which are not likely to be included in labour force statistics unless they are clearly performed for the market (Mueller, 1978).

In one ILO recommendation on household survey statistics of the labour force, it is suggested that data collection should concentrate on 'how people earn their living' (Turvey, 1978). The difficulty, however, appears where we want to be more specific about what earning a living means. While some authors have insisted on concentrating on income-earning activities, i.e. on following a market-oriented bias, others suggest that the number of hours of work can be used for an indication of work for a living – which implies that work might not produce an income but is implicitly a part of 'economic activity'. The exact meaning of economic activity is never defined, but what is made clear is that there are problems with the conventional definitions and that an understanding exists of the fact that many tasks performed in and around the household are related to 'earning a living'.

If we use the expression 'make' instead of 'earn' a living, it is even clearer that very little difference exists between the various types of subsistence and domestic activities with regard to their contribution to making a living. A similar argument can be made for activities such as food processing, cooking, washing, repairing the house, and taking care of the aged. If in addition we add reproductive tasks as an integral part of the overall process of production/reproduction, we are adding activities such as the care of children to the above list. Taken together, they include all use value production – of tangible goods as well as services. On the other hand, the list would not include nonwork activities such as recreation and leisure.

For statistical purposes, an evaluation of use value production and of the labour force participating in it requires a detailed investigation of the tasks and the work involved. Survey research carried out at the household level and the subsistence sector has pioneered the type of research that is necessary. However, what is also needed is a systematic data collection by country that can provide a continuous source of information and that is moderately standardized. One of the problems that immediately comes to mind is how to measure work and labour participation. Use of number of hours of work might be misleading since, given the flexibility of scheduling in subsistence and domestic tasks, work can be carried out with different degrees of intensity, interspersing it with leisure time, with breaks of different duration, etc. This makes it difficult to measure not only labour force participation but also underemployment and labour utilization.

10. There is a problem of specifying what is meant by 'work' thus drawing a dividing line between economic and noneconomic activity. The problem is an important one with respect to such activities as growing vegetables, repairing a dwelling, collecting firewood, processing food or scaring away birds (Turvey, 1978:8). A similar concern is expressed by Mueller: 'the distinction between economic activities and housework is basic to the *traditional measurement of employment*. Yet for the self-employed, and specially for people engaged in subsistence agriculture, the distinction is rather artificial. Activities that may occupy much of their time are on the borderline between economic work and housework, with the result that difficult classification and measurement problems arise (Mueller, 1978:2 emphasis mine).

One possible way to deal with these questions is the estimation of the *average* number of hours that household members spend in use value production – the average based on survey work and depending upon the specific characteristics, such as the level of technology, and the extent of use value production in each country. For those who might be sceptical about estimating an average, it should be pointed out that evidence exists to show that the amount of time spent on domestic work has not changed considerably through time and has been found to be very similar in countries with very different socio-economic characteristics;[11] the variations among countries and through time are related to the *composition* of housework and the *duration* of specific tasks. Thus, while shopping is more time-consuming in some countries, less time is spent on other activities such as taking care of children or cleaning. Averages can take into consideration other differences such as those between rural and urban households and variations by class.

However, the use of averages should be accompanied by detailed information about the composition and duration of specific tasks. In particular, classification of work and activities can respond to a range of questions:

1 Overall, we want to know the involvement of household members in use value production. In particular, the objective is to evaluate women's participation in all tasks contributing to production and reproduction.
2 The distinction between commodity and use value production can be made clear by distinguishing between income-generating tasks and production for the household's own consumption. To the extent that conventional estimations have included subsistence agricultural production in labour force and GNP calculations, they do not totally coincide with the category of commodity production which is directly tied to the market and to capital. These estimations often blur rather than clarify the distinction between commodity and use value production. The distinction can be made clearer if statistical data are gathered with this purpose in mind.
3 This distinction is also important for the purpose of measuring unemployment; questions can be drawn up in such a way as to determine whether a worker, male or female, is 'taking refuge' in the subsistence or domestic sector due to a lack of employment opportunities in the commodity sector, and this requires a clear distinction between these sectors.
4 Further breakdown of activities in different categories can provide information for a variety of purposes. Thus, tasks related to reproduction will provide information about demographic factors, child care and schooling needs, time spent in shopping and food transformation, the effect of household technology on domestic work, the need for community services, etc.

11. Although research on the subject has taken place mostly for the industrialized and more developed countries, they include a variety of countries at different levels of development and economic and political organization. Szalai's studies (1972), for example, refer to twelve countries, including Peru, Eastern European and Western countries. An analysis of the constancy in time spent on housework in the United States can be found in Hartmann (1974). However given that these are the countries that have experienced the greatest amount of change, it is reasonable to expect that a similar situation will be found in other countries.

This list is meant not to be exhaustive but to illustrate at the general level the type of data collection that can be taken for a full account of women's work (as well as of other household members, such as children and the aged, whose activities are also underestimated). This account *per se* tells little about the mechanisms of subordination that this work might entail, but it can provide basic information to pursue the analysis of women's position in society.

## CONCLUDING COMMENTS

I have argued in this chapter that, within conventional definitions of the labour force, women's participation in economic activities tends to be grossly underestimated, particularly in areas with a relatively low degree of market penetration in economic life. This is due mostly to conceptual and ideological biases concerning the nature of women's work and to difficulties in collecting accurate statistics of their labour force participation. As a result, available information on women's work must be used with caution and international comparisons in particular can be very misleading if the statistical concepts and data collection methods used by different countries are not taken into account.

The main thrust of the chapter, however, is to point out the shortcomings of conventional labour force concepts. These concepts are geared to measuring labour participation in commodity production, that is, in production for exchange instead, for example, for the satisfaction of basic human needs. The reason for this bias is to be found in the view that economic analysis and economic categories have been defined in relation to the process of growth and accumulation; only workers engaged in activities *directly* related to that process are conventionally defined as being in the labour force. The main argument of this chapter is that active labour should include all workers engaged in use value as well as exchange value production which includes activities such as household production and all types of subsistence production. At a more concrete level, narrower categories of labour can be distinguished – such as labour engaged in commodity production and that which is not. Within a capitalist economy, this implies that the concept of active labour goes beyond labour engaged *directly* in capitalist production for the market.

From the point of view of women's work, the purpose of this conceptualization was underlined in the previous section and can be summarized under two main objectives. One is *ideological* and it has to do with the proper evaluation of women's work and the eradication of sexist concepts. A full understanding of the economic significance of household production, for example, implies that women's work is economically productive and essential for the functioning of the economic system. Society as well as women themselves must recognize this function in order to avoid succumbing to the view that it is of secondary importance, a basic source of women's subordination. This can remove the paradox, so commonly found in the Third World, in which a local economy survives thanks to women's involvement in subsistence production while men are unemployed; yet official statistics show low labour force participation for women and high participation for men respectively.[12] The other objective is of a *practical* nature and concerns the dynamics of change: a more general definition of labour force implies that development strategies and programmes of action must be concerned with the whole spectrum of active workers. Thus the introduction of more productive technology in household production will free household workers from time-consuming tasks while widening the range of possibilities of choice between domestic and nondomestic work. Similarly, employment programmes must take into consideration the degree of unemployment and underemployment 'hidden' in use value production. Under conventional statistics unemployed women who concentrate on household activities due to lack of opportunities to work outside the household are not included in the category of 'discouraged workers', or as 'unemployed'. The implications of this chapter indicate that they are part of the labour force and should be a matter of concern for any employment programme.

## REFERENCES

Abdullah. A., and Zeidenstein. S., 1978, 'Village Women of Bangladesh. Prospects for Change', unpublished ILO study, Jan.

Anker, R., and Knowles, J., 1978, 'A Micro Analysis of Female Labor Force Participation in Africa', in Standing and Sheehan (1978).

Beechey, V., 1977, 'Some Notes on Female Wage Labour in Capitalist Production', *Capital and Class*, Autumn, 45–66.

Benería, L., 1977, *Mujer, Economia y Patriarcado Durante el Periodo Franquista*, Barcelona: Anagrama.

Benería, L., 1979, 'Reproduction, Production and the Sexual Division of Labor', *Cambridge Journal of Economics*, Sept.

Benholdt-Thomsen, V., 1978, 'Subsistence Reproduction and General Reproduction', paper presented at the Conference on the Subordination of Women and the Development Process, IDS, Sept.

Bienefeld, M., and Godfrey, M., 1975, 'Measuring Unemployment and the Informal Sector. Some Conceptual and Statistical Problems', *IDS Bulletin*, vol. 7, no. 3, 4–10.

Blanchard, F., 1979, 'Demographic Pincer Closing on Industrialized World', *ILO Information*, vol. 15 no. 2.

Boserup, E., 1970, *Woman's Role in Economic Development* , London: George Allen and Unwin.

Boulding, E., 1977, *Women in the Twentieth Century World*, Sage Publications, New York: John Wiley and Sons.

Bukh, J., 1979, *The Village Woman in Ghana*, Uppsala: Scandinavian Institute of African Studies.

Committee on the Status of Women in India, 1974, *Towards Equality*, New Delhi.

12. I have called this type of situation 'the paradox of Chaouen' to describe the conditions in this northern Moroccan town where most men are idle due to the unemployment created by the replacement of traditional crafts by modern imported products; women, on the other hand, can be seen busily moving around town and in the countryside carrying on the main burden of subsistence and family production. Yet, according to 1975 statistics for Morocco, only 15 per cent of the labour force were women (ILO, 1977).

Cordell, M., and McHale, J., 1975, *Women in World Trends*, Center for Integrative Studies, State University of New York at Binghamton.

Deere, C. D. , 1977, 'The Agricultural Division of Labor by Sex: Myths, Facts and Contradictions in the Northern Peruvian Sierra', paper presented at the Joint National Meeting of the Latin American Studies Association, Houston, Texas.

Deere, C. D., 1976, 'Rural Women Subsistence Production in the Capitalist Periphery', *Review of Radical Political Economics*, vol. 8, no. 1.

Denti, E., 1968, 'Sex-Age Patterns of Labor Force Participation by Urban and Rural Populations', *International Labor Review*, vol. 98, no. 6, 525–50.

Edholm, F., Harris, O., and Young, K., 1977, 'Conceptualizing women', *Critique of Anthropology*, vol. 9/10, 101–30.

Fee, T., 1976, 'Domestic Labor: An Analysis of Housework and its Relation to the Production Process', *Review of Radical Political Economics*, vol. 8, no. 1, 1–17.

Frank, W., 1977, 'The Necessity and Possibility of Comprehensive Information Systems for Agriculture', International Association of Agricultural Economists, *Members Bulletin*, no. 1, Oxford: Agricultural Economists Institute, July.

Galbraith, J. K., 1973, *Economics and the Public Purpose*, Boston: Houghton Miflin Co.

Gulati, Leela, 1975, 'Occupational Distribution of Working Women. An Inter-State Comparison', *Economic and Political Weekly*, 25, Oct, 1692–1704.

Hartmann, H., 1974, 'Capitalism and Women's Work in the Home, 1900–1930', Ph. D. dissertation, Yale University.

Himmelweit, S., and Mohun, S., 1977, 'Domestic Labour and Capital', *Cambridge Journal of Economics*, vol. 1, Mar.

ILO/PREALC, 1976, *The Employment Problem of Latin America, Facts, Outlooks and Policies*, Santiago.

ILO, 1976, *International Recommendations on Labor Statistics*, Geneva.

ILO, 1977, *Labor Force Projections*, Geneva.

ILO, 1978, 'Condiciones de Trabjo, Formacion Profesional y Empleo de la Mujer', report prepared for the 11th Conference of American States Members of the ILO.

League of Nations, 1938, *Statistics of the Gainfully Occupied Population, Definitions and Classifications Recommended by the Committee of Statistical Experts*, Studies and reports on Statistical Methods, no. 1. Geneva

Lloyd, C. (ed.), 1975, *Sex, Discrimination and the Division of Labour*, New York: Columbia University Press.

Marx, K., 1911, *A Contribution to the Critique of Political Economy*, Chicago: Charles Kerr & Co.

Marx. K., 1967, *Capital*, vol. 1, New York: International Publishers.

Mies, M., 1978, 'Consequences of Capitalist Penetration for Women's Subsistence Reproduction', paper read at the Seminar on Underdevelopment and Subsistence Production in South East Africa, April 1978.

Mueller, E., 1978, 'Time Use Data', Population Studies Center, University of Michigan.

Mueller, M., 'Women and Men, Power and Powerlessness in Lesotho', included in *Women and National Development.*

Reiter, R. (ed.), 1975, *Towards an Anthropology of Women*, New York: Monthly Review Press.

Richter, L., 1978, *Labour Force Information in Developing Countries*, Geneva: ILO.

Robbins, L., 1932, *The Nature and Significance of Economic Science*, London: Macmillan.

Rubbo, A., 1975, 'The Spread of Capitalism in Rural Columbia' in Reiter (1975).

Saffiotti, H., 1977, 'Women, Mode of Production, and Social Formations', *Latin American Perspectives*, vol. IV, nos 1 & 2, 27–37.

Scott, Ann Crittenden, 1972, 'The Value of Housework: For Love or Money?', *Ms* Magazine, July.

Seccombe, W., 1974, 'The Housewife and her Labour under Capitalism', *New Left Review*, no. 83.

Smith, A., 1975, *The Wealth of Nations*, Harmondsworth: Penguin Books.

Standing, G., 1978, *Labor Force Participation and Development*, Geneva: ILO.

Standing, G., and Sheehan, G. (eds), 1978, *Labor Force Participation in Low Income Countries*, Geneva: ILO.

Stoler, A., 1976, 'Class Structure and Female Anatomy in Rural Java', in Wellesley Editorial Committee (1976), 74–88.

Sweezy, P., 1942, *The Theory of Capitalist Development*, New York: Monthly Review Press.

Szalai. A., et al. 1972, *The Use of Time*, The Hague: Mouton Press.

Tienda, M., 1977, 'Diferenciacion Regional y Transformacion Sectoral de la Mano de Obra Femenina en Mexico, 1970', *Demografia y Economia*, XI, 3, 307–25.

Turvey, R., 1978, 'Household Labor Statistics of the Labor Force in Developing Countries', Geneva: ILO internal circulation.

Vanek, J., 1974, 'Time Spent in Housework', *Scientific American*, Nov, 116–20.

Walker, K., 1969, 'Homemaking Still Takes Time', *Journal of Home Economics*, vol. 61, no. 8.

Wellesley Editorial Committee (ed.), 1976, *Women and National Development: The Complexities of Change*, Chicago University Press.

Wolpe, H., 1975, 'The Theory of Internal Colonialism: The South Africa Case,' in Oxaal, I., et al. (eds), *Beyond the Sociology of Development*, London: Routledge.

# 17
# Domestic Labour and the Household

MAUREEN M. MACKINTOSH

A central theoretical concern of the women's movement in Britain and elsewhere in the capitalist West has always been the analysis of the relation of the family to capitalism, or, more precisely, the relation of women's struggles within and concerning the family to her struggles in the sphere of wage work and other aspects of more public life. The debate over the theoretical analysis of domestic labour[1] was just one of many attempts to address this concern. Starting from the Marxist analysis of the capitalist mode of production, the contributors to the debate set out to analyse the nature of housework and its relation to work done under conditions of wage labour.

This debate, it is widely agreed, argued itself into a cul-de-sac from which it was very difficult for it to get any further in its own terms. I shall argue in this chapter that one reason for the creation of this impasse was the lack of a wider perspective, historical or cross-cultural, on the question of the content, the use value nature, of the work involved. In order to present this case, I shall examine the performance of tasks typical of domestic labour within capitalism – child care, cooking, cleaning – in a society which is as yet incompletely dominated by the law of value and

This essay was first published as chapter 8 in Sandra Burman (ed.), *Fit Work for Women*, Croom Helm, 1979.

1. See especially J. Gardiner, 'Women's Domestic Labour', *New Left Review*, no. 89, 1975; J. Gardiner, 'The Political Economy of Domestic Labour in Capitalist Society', in D. L. Barker and S. Allen (eds), *Dependence and Exploitation in Work and Marriage* (London, Longman, 1976); J. Gardiner, S. Himmelweit and M. Mackintosh, 'Women's Domestic Labour', *Bulletin of the Conference of Socialist Economists*, vol. 4, no. 2, 1975; S. Himmelweit and S. Mohun, 'Domestic Labour and Capital', *Cambridge Journal of Economics*, no. 1, 1977; J. Harrison, 'Political Economy of Housework', *Bulletin of the Conference of Socialist Economists*, vol. 4, no. 1, 1973; W. Seccombe, 'The Housewife and Her Labour under Capitalism', *New Left Review*, no. 83, 1974; W. Seccombe, 'Domestic Labour – Reply to Critics', *New Left Review*, no. 94, 1975; M. Coulson, B. Magas and W. Wainwright, 'The Housewife and her Labour under Capitalism – A Critique', *New Left Review*, no. 89, 1975.

where therefore a great deal of other production – agriculture, fishing, craft work – is still household-based. The society in question is part of the rural economy in Senegal in West Africa, where I lived from May 1975 to August 1976.

I shall then use the results of this examination to reflect upon the domestic labour debate in Britain, and to suggest one possible direction of future work. I should be clear from the beginning as to what I see as the purpose of this kind of 'comparative' analysis. I am not in any sense suggesting that the situation which I describe in Senegal is identical to the situation in pre-capitalist Britain. Only historical research can analyse the evolution of the household in Britain. Instead, I am using international comparison between Britain and a society subject to imperialism but incompletely penetrated by the law of value, to illuminate the nature of the assumptions on the basis of which we – those of us with a training in economics in particular – have analysed capitalist society.

## DOMESTIC LABOUR AND CAPITALIST PRODUCTION

The central theoretical issue on which the domestic labour debate turned was the value analysis of domestic labour within capitalism: is domestic labour value-creating, and if not, what is its relation to the creation of value? Another way of posing precisely the same question would be: how does the production of goods and services within the home relate to the accumulation of capital? This debate was of course not resolved to everyone's satisfaction, and among those still interested there are conflicting views. I do not propose to summarize these positions, since the subject of this chapter is the limits rather than the details of the debate. I begin, however, by describing briefly the position which I find the most satisfactory, since this position informs a great deal of what is to follow.

Housework in the capitalist West, as I and others have argued in more detail elsewhere,[2] is production within the home of use values (goods and services such as cooked meals and washing) for immediate consumption. The products of housework do not pass through the market. Housework is therefore not value production, the goods and services produced are not produced for exchange, and the conditions of their production are not directly subject to the law of value. Domestic labour is private labour, not socialized labour. Since it is labour which is not brought into relation, through the buying and selling of commodities, to labour performed in the production of commodities, it does not enter into the formation of abstract labour, which is the basis of value. It is therefore not subject to the same pressures for increased productivity as is labour subject to the wage relation. Labour within the household cannot be directly compared to wage labour, for theoretical purposes, because it is not commensurate with it through the market.

This does not mean however that domestic labour within capitalism is unaffected by the operation of the law of value. On the contrary, pressures from the sphere of wage labour have had an impact on the content of housework in

2. Especially Gardiner, Himmelweit and Mackintosh, 'Women's Domesitc Labour'. Himmelweit and Mohun, 'Domestic Labour and Capital', is a survey of the debate written from the same theoretical point of view.

ways that a number of writers have documented.[3] Some goods and services which used to be produced within the home are now bought and sold as commodities, certain kinds of household equipment have reduced the time necessary to produce an adequate standard of cooked meals and cleanliness. But it does mean that domestic labour is performed under relations of production which are not those of value production and wage labour.

It is here that we reach one of the limits of the domestic labour debate as it has so far been conducted. None of the writers on the subject, myself included, has been able to specify in a satisfactory way the social relations under which domestic production is conducted. Discussions of the subject have been descriptive rather than analytical: the description of ideal-typical relations between men and women within the home. The sexual division of labour within the home – that is, the fact that it is women who perform most of the domestic labour – had within the terms of the debate to be taken for granted. Once it was taken for granted that it is women who do the housework, then the analysis of domestic labour could be used to examine the question of how women's work within the home is related to her subordination both within the home and outside it.[4] But the original begging of the enormous question of the nature of the sexual division of labour within the home has meant that the nature of the social relations of domestic production has remained unspecifiable, and therefore the potential contribution of the theoretical work on domestic labour to our understanding of the family under capitalism has been extremely limited. Hence the marked loss of interest within the women's movement in the domestic labour debate.

Why was the domestic labour debate set up in terms which led it into this cul-de-sac? One answer to this question is that our perspective, limited to the experience of housework within the capitalist West, and lacking a historical or international perspective on the phenomenon we were analysing, led us to equate or conflate certain phenomena which are in fact distinct. One example of this is that we held our concept 'domestic' to be unproblematic, whereas in fact we were using the word in two analytically distinct senses: domestic work as work done within the home, and domestic work as a particular kind of work, such as child care, cooking and cleaning, servicing the members of a household. In our society, work which is domestic in the first sense is also generally domestic in the second sense, but this fact is specific to our society (that is, not universal) and it requires explanation.

Once the debate was set up in these terms it was inevitable that the question of the sexual division of labour within the home should be begged. We took domestic labour as an unproblematic unity, the relation of which to value production was the subject of analysis: the result was that we could analyse neither the use value nature of the work nor the nature of the home in which the work was done. There has been, of course, a good deal of description of the content of domestic work, and a frequent reiteration that the work was in some sense reproductive work, work to do with the reproduction of labour. But this perception could not be integrated into an analysis which did not question the relation between the nature of the domestic work and the form taken by the household.

3. Through transferring some use values to the commodity sphere, and the use of domestic equipment.

4. Thus there has been a discussion of the way in which women's work in the home constrains her participation in the wage labour force.

We need therefore to deconstruct the concept of domestic work and examine its components. The next section seeks to do this through the examination of the sexual division of labour, and the distinction between types of work, in a society where many kinds of work (including agricultural production) are household-based.

## DOMESTIC LABOUR IN THE HOUSEHOLD-BASED ECONOMY: THE THEORETICAL PROBLEM

If Marxist economists studying domestic labour under capitalism have tended to take the work done within the household as an unproblematic whole, Marxist anthropologists have tended to do the same thing when studying societies where a wide range of production is household-based and not produced for the purpose of exchange. A number of economic anthropologists have variously tried to define a mode of production whose defining characteristic is that production is carried out within the household. Universally, these attempts, while admitting the existence of a sexual division of labour in production within the household, do not integrate this division of labour into the analysis of the mode of production as a whole, but merely comment upon it in a descriptive way. This is true of anthropologists working with a wide range of ideological perspectives.

Thus Sahlins's 'domestic mode of production'[5] refers to 'economies organised by domestic groups and kinship relations', where the 'household is as such charged with production, with the deployment and use of labour power, with the determination of the economic objective'. 'Domestic' in Sahlins is used to mean internal to the household; non-domestic work would involve co-operation between households. Sahlins's discussion of relations between members of the household in production is purely on the descriptive level. Thus: 'Division of labour by sex is not the only economic specialisation known to primitive societies. But it is the dominant form, transcending all other specialisation in this sense: that the normal activities of any adult man, taken in conjunction with the normal activities of an adult woman, practically exhaust the customary works of society.' There is no further discussion of the content of, or the explanation for, this division of labour.

Besides the lack of reference to the concrete nature of the work of men and women within the household, there is also in Sahlins an assumption that there is no important division of labour either among men or among women. In the work on domestic labour under capitalism also, the lack of a division of labour in the domestic sphere is another aspect of domestic labour which is taken for granted, since it cannot be explained independently of an explanation of the structure of the household. This assumption is, however, much less factually plausible for the household-based economy.

In the work of Meillassoux[6] one can trace the same absence of investigation of the division of work within the household. This is even more striking because

5. M. Sahlins, *Stone Age Economics* (London, Tavistock, 1974).
6. Especially C. Meillassoux, *Femmes, Greniers et Capitaux* (Paris, Maspero, 1975).

Meillassoux's work is much more carefully theorized than that of Sahlins, and because his concern to explain the reproduction of the 'domestic community' leads him to examine in some detail the relations between the sexes. Production, for Meillassoux, is agricultural production, and the relations of production are the relations of production in agriculture. The relations of reproduction on the other hand are purely relations of marriage and kinship, the relations of men to their progeny. The work of caring for children, washing, cooking, cleaning - the work which feminists see as fundamental to an understanding of the whole sexual division of labour in capitalist society - has vanished. Extraordinarily, this work, in the rare references to it in Meillassoux's most recent work, is casually referred to as 'domestic work' in spite of the fact that the whole household community is called the 'domestic community'. The confusion of definition is apparently unrecognized, presumably because the importance of the work is totally discounted. The dependence of men upon women for food, because of the sheer incapacity of men to produce cooked food, is recognized at one point, but no conclusions are drawn beyond the need (which is a *non sequitur* except on specified assumptions) of a man for a wife.

One could multiply examples of the absence of analysis of the sexual division of labour in production from contributors to this literature. Two such examples would be the work of Terray[7] and that of Hindess and Hirst[8] on primitive communism. These writers tend simply to omit the typically female tasks of cooking, cleaning and child care from their catalogue of production: they fall down the divide between agricultural work on the one hand, and the relations of kinship and filiation on the other, between production and 'reproduction'.

To some extent, Marxists who ignore the importance of cooking, cleaning and so on are simply reflecting the prejudices of orthodox development economists. Typically, at least until very recently, these economists have transferred the prejudices of their own society against the classifying of cooking or child care as work at all directly to the household-based village economy. Thus one writer of Marxist politics but orthodox economics could list for India, under the heading of 'non-work and leisure' in the village economy, the following 'domestic duties': cooking, collecting firewood and water, mending the roof, and child-bearing.[9] However even within this tradition, evidence is gradually accumulating concerning the hours of work involved in these tasks, and the importance of their performance to the standard of living of the household in the village economy. Those of us attempting to examine these economies from a Marxist-feminist perspective have to take this evidence into account, not simply in order to add it into the total quantity of work which has to be done to maintain the household, but in order to develop an understanding of the way in which this work differs from other types of work in society, even when the society is one where agriculture too is in a different sense also a domestic task.

7. E. Terray, *Le Marxisme devant les Sociétés 'Primitives'* (Paris, Maspero, 1972). For a critique of Terray, see especially M. Molyneux, 'Androcentrism in Marxist Anthropology', *Critique of Anthropology*, vol. 3, nos 9 and 10, 1977.

8. B. Hindess and P. Q. Hirst, *Precapitalist Modes of Production* (London, Routledge and Kegan Paul, 1975).

9. B. Dasgupta, 'New Technology and Agricultural Labourers in India', in S. Hirashima (ed.), *Hired Labour in Rural Asia* (Tokyo, Institute of Developing Economies, 1977). 'Child-bearing' may (?) be a misprint for 'child-rearing'.

## DOMESTIC LABOUR IN A SENEGALESE VILLAGE ECONOMY

The Senegalese village which I shall now discuss is one where, until the very recent arrival on part of its land of a foreign-owned plantation, all the production done within the village boundaries was household-based. That is to say, for the agricultural production which produced both the main subsistence (non-marketed) crop and the cash crops which were the main source of money income in the village, the household was the unit of decision-making and of effective land appropriation. A large majority of the agricultural labour time spent on the fields of a household was drawn from within that household. Besides agriculture and tasks of cooking, cleaning and child care, the only activities productive of goods and services within the village were cattle herding, charcoal-making, one or two artisan activities such as the making of clothes, and retail selling of some goods from outside the village such as fresh fish and rice. Since 1973, the plantation had been providing the first ever local source of large-scale agricultural wage work.

Leaving aside the cattle herding, artisan work and retail selling, I shall examine the agricultural and non-agricultural work for similarities and differences in its organization. The non-agricultural activities then include the following: food preparation, cleaning, washing, care of children, wood and other gathering activities, care of the sick, physical maintenance of the house and its fencing.

Men and women engage in both agricultural and non-agricultural activities in this village. Men do the bulk of the agricultural labour but some women have fields of their own and there are some agricultural tasks on the men's fields which are typically done by women. In the non-agricultural sphere, men do the repair, building and maintenance of the house; women do all the other tasks.

The division of labour between the sexes is, however, much more rigid in the non-agricultural sphere. There are tasks where men and women work side by side in agriculture; there are none in the non-agricultural sphere. Technical change in agriculture – the introduction of donkey- or horse-drawn equipment – has eroded the women's role in agricultural production since the women do not use the equipment. Men have taken over tasks that used to be done by both men and women, and even sometimes tasks that were generally done by women alone. An example of the latter is the winnowing of the peanuts, previously done by women pouring from a bowl, now sometimes done by men with newly-introduced forks. Furthermore, in agriculture, young male labour is quite frequently used to replace female labour, winnowing again being an example or the dehusking of peanuts, without there being a stigma attached to a young man who does this. The rigidity of the sexual division of labour in agriculture is most marked in the subsistence crop (millet) and it is least marked in the newest cash crop (wet season vegetables) where there is considerable fluidity of definition of the sexual division of tasks.

No such fluidity exists in the non-agricultural sphere. Men construct and maintain the physical buildings and walls. All other tasks of caring for and maintenance of the people in the household are done by the women of that household. There are no tasks done by both men and women. Men provide the subsistence food, millet, either by growing it or occasionally buying it for cash when the crop is finished. Once provided, it is under the control of a woman in the household. Otherwise, the provision of food is the sphere of the women. They may gather or cultivate plants to eat with the millet; if additions to the millet – oil or tomato, for example – are bought, the women will do the buying, even if the men have sometimes provided the cash. Food preparation is done by the women exclusively, and all members of a household eat from a common pot. The physical caring for other human beings is entirely a women's task, including washing clothes and caring for the sick. This division of labour according to gender is not undergoing any process of change. Whereas children, girls and boys, may both be taken to work in the fields on tasks which, while generally divided on lines of gender, are not rigidly so, in the non-agricultural sphere there is strong hostility from both men and women towards the use of boys to assist in women's tasks.[10]

The non-agricultural tasks are extremely time-consuming. The following is a description of a day's work for a young woman who does all the tasks for the household in which she lives. She gets up at around (we decided) 5 a.m.: that is, well before it is light. She pounds millet for perhaps one hour. Then she goes to the well for water (which may mean a long wait) and prepares breakfast, which consists of millet couscous largely prepared the day before. The next stage is preparing the ingredients for lunch, which may be millet porridge or rice, and may involve gathering or going to the village shop. They eat at midday or 1 p.m. The couscous for supper and the next day's breakfast is prepared during the afternoon, to be eaten about 7.30 p.m. If her mother-in-law is working at the plantation she takes food to her. In the evening she pounds millet again. She goes to bed at around 9 p.m. During the day, usually in the morning, she does the washing as necessary for six adults and a child, and she has a one-year-old child constantly with her. She herself is sixteen years old.

There is one time-consuming activity which is not in this list: the gathering of wood. The women do this intensively at certain periods of the year, of which this (the description was taken in March) was not one. The heaviest work is the pounding of the millet and the fetching of water, especially for washing clothes.

A young woman doing all the non-agricultural labour for a household therefore spends her whole working day upon it. She does not have a field of her own, and does little agricultural work, though in the rainy season she takes food to the people in the fields. Later, as she becomes older and has daughters to help her with the cooking and washing and child care, she may take on more agricultural labour.

The rigidity of the sexual division of non-agricultural work has become even more evident since the arrival of the plantation, offering wage work during six months of the year to both men and women. The participation rate of the women as well as the men in the plantation labour force is extremely high, there being no feeling among the men that the women should not do this work. The working day on the plantation is normally from 7.30 in the morning to mid to late afternoon, though packers often work more irregular hours in shifts. For the men, this plantation work is an alternative to other activites during the plantation season, which is the dry season in Senegal when they do not work on their own crops. From this village some younger men used to go away to work for the dry season;

10. One manifestation of this hostility is the attribution of male homosexuality to the performance as a young boy of women's household tasks (an explanation I heard several times, but in the city, not the village).

older men stayed in the village, doing various tasks of maintenance of fields and houses and tending a longer-duration cash crop which has now largely been abandoned. The men who remained did not work long hours in this season, so the plantation has not meant an intolerably long working day. The women on the other hand, inevitably, have simply added their plantation work to their non-agricultural tasks which they undertake all the year round, thereby stretching their physical endurance almost to breaking point.

This, for example, is a working day of a woman, doing the non-agricultural work for a household all on her own, and also working at the plantation. She gets up at least an hour earlier than the young woman just described, to pound her millet, fetch water and make breakfast for the household. She prepares and leaves something for lunch, perhaps couscous to be heated, for the children, which has been partly prepared the night before. She leaves the children with an old woman in the compound and goes to work at about 7 a.m. She returns from work around 4 or 5 p.m., and goes to the well or the plantation tap for water on her way home. Once home, she prepares the couscous for supper and for the next day, and pounds the millet again. When there is washing to be done she does it at night. She always goes to bed later than when she is not working at the plantation, and when she is washing perhaps as late as 11 p.m. or midnight. She is up again the next day at 4 a.m.

With the women under this kind of pressure, there has nevertheless been no breaking down at all of the division of labour by sex in non-agricultural tasks. Not only do men never do any of this work, but young boys also do none, despite the fact that they are in the household, and do not begin to work on the plantation at as young an age as the girls. As the woman just described explained, 'I have only sons, so there is no one to help me.'

There are a number of ways in which women try to cushion the appalling strain of this double day. One is by simply not working as regularly as the men. As one woman said: 'I work until I see that all my clothes are dirty, then I take a day off, do all my washing, and start all over again.' To the extent that it is possible, women shift the way in which their work is spread over the year – for example, they all make sure that they have collected their firewood before the start of the plantation season – but the very nature of their work, daily maintenance of a household, means that there is very little they can do in this respect. Therefore they inevitably need days off when their household work piles up or a child is ill. The result of this constraint on women's work outside the household is the start of a process with which we are also extremely familiar in Europe. Employers take advantage of these constraints on women to treat their female employees differently from the men they employ. The men's jobs tend to be stabilized, to last all season, and they are paid at least the minimum wage. The women's jobs tend to pay less, the women are treated as an interchangeable mass of workers, frequently hired at the gate each day, and the management make far less effort to stabilize the work force. Within a year of the plantation's establishment, a familiar pattern of sex-based hierarchy of pay and conditions in the labour force had been set up. The women, trapped by their home obligations, can do nothing about this inequality of conditions. Thus the rigidity of the sexual division of labour in domestic tasks is visibly the source of women's greater oppression within the sphere of wage work.

The other way in which women cushion the strain of doing two days' work in one is through the use of an already existing division of labour among women in the household. Not all women do non-agricultural household labour. There are only a few exceptions to the generalization that women only do this work if their status in the household is that of wife or daughter. Nor do all wives do this work. This village is virilocal, wives moving soon after marriage to join their husband's household; it is also polygamous. Furthermore, in general as a man gets older, he will retain a married son in his household. The result of this is that 60 per cent of households in this village contain more than one married woman.

A girl starts to help her mother with her household work when she is quite young; by ten she is doing quite a lot of cooking and fetching water, but is not yet strong enough, for example, to get the washing clean. By thirteen, two years before she is likely to marry, a girl may be doing virtually all her mother's work in the home. Once she marries and leaves her parental home, a young woman works for her mother no more. Instead, if she is the first wife of a young man, she is likely to take on all her husband's mother's household work. This is the main way in which an older women is finally relieved of the burden of housework. In principle the mother-in-law does no more work, and she will say that she does none. In practice she may help, but it will be her own decision to do so. This means that an older, active woman with a daughter-in-law at home can go to work on the plantation without exhausting herself in the way that the younger women do. The young woman whose working day was described earlier agreed that the division of labour was always organized in this way and that her mother-in-law 'would never agree to stay in the house while I went out to work'.

If a woman is the second wife of her husband, the situation is different. In this case the first wife will already be doing the work in the household, and the second wife will share the work, turn about, so many days (the number varies) each. The only break in this will be if a woman has just had a child, when she will have a break from the work.

There are also in households a number of women who are neither wives nor daughters of the household head (the household head being almost always male in this village). The most common case is the divorced sister of the head of the household, and in general this sister will do no work in the household, except as an irregular favour to one of the other women. Adult female kin of the household head do not do the work in the household: the rules that determine who does the housework depend on the marriage relation and kin ties between men. Thus, by extension, a woman marrying a younger brother of the head of the household had replaced in the housework the oldest wife of that older brother of her husband. Furthermore, a woman whose bride-price was not fully paid, though she was living in her husband's household, was doing no housework.

All that has been said above about the division of non-agricultural household work between women refers chiefly to cooking and does not extend to child care. Child care is the individual mother's responsibility, and any sharing of this by other women is done as a favour. Only older daughters can be relied upon to look after younger children when necessary. Child care therefore obeys somewhat different rules from other non-agricultural tasks, and, as in our society, very young children are the strongest constraint preventing women from going out to work for a wage. A woman, if she is prepared to work very long hours indeed, can reorganize cooking, cook in the morning for lunch time and do her washing at night; but if she has no one to look after a young child she is tied. Sometimes sisters married into different households help each other with child care in these circumstances, something which never seems to happen for other household tasks. The extent to which co-wives help each other with child care seems to vary greatly from household to household, and to depend a lot on individual personalities.

Thus there exists a division of labour among women in the performance of non-agricultural household tasks. I return below to the rules by which this work is allocated and their implications. Before this I want to discuss one more piece of evidence concerning the strength of the social boundary cutting off these household tasks from the rest of the productive work of this society. This evidence concerns what happens to this non-agricultural work when the economy becomes much more monetized than the village economy I was describing above. This evidence comes from the village in which I actually lived in Senegal, which is closer to Dakar, the capital city, than the above village, and as a result much more penetrated by monetary exchange relations.

In this situation there comes to exist what is almost a separate sphere of exchange in the village: that of petty selling between women. This selling is either of vegetables and fish bought in small-quantity lots and broken down for retail resale, or partially prepared food (couscous only needing final steaming), or small cooked foods (fried doughnuts for example, or grilled peanuts). There is an enormous amount of this petty selling, which I only slowly became aware of through living in a household, and it is very important to the way in which women succeed in providing for their families. Its proceeds supply the small sums of money of which women are in constant need, in order to buy small quantities of relish to add to the staple foods, or to take a child to the dispensary. Women may even sell some of their crops from their fields in this small-scale way, though if they have many crops they will sell them wholesale.

Men never go in for this small-scale petty selling. They sell their crops wholesale, they buy millet when they have to do so (and in the village now in question they frequently have to, millet growing having declined) in as large lots as possible and leave it to the women to break it down. If they pay money for minor ingredients to the meals they give the cash to the women to shop, but they would never have a woman buy a sack of grain for them.

It is the sexual division of the non-agricultural tasks in the household which creates these two separate types of exchange and the sex-typing of petty selling. Women also grow crops, but men do not cook food or care for children, and so they also do not become involved in this petty exchange economy.

I have established therefore that in this Senegalese village economy, where there is agricultural as well as non-agricultural labour which is non-value-producing, and where the production unit for the cash crop is also the household, one can nevertheless make distinctions between the women's non-agricultural labour (which I shall henceforth refer to as 'domestic labour' for the purpose of theoretical discussion) and the other household-based labour, largely in agriculture. In particular, the sexual division of labour, the allocation of certain tasks exclusively to women, is much more rigid in domestic labour than in agricultural labour (or, though I have not discussed this in detail, in other tasks). One can justifiably refer to a sphere of domestic labour which requires separate analysis in this society, as in societies where the domestic labour, also done largely by women, is the only non-value-producing labour.

What kind of separate analysis, then, is required? The final section of this chapter can only begin to attempt an answer to this question. I examine the relation of the sphere of domestic labour to the constitution of the household and to various concepts of reproduction, first for the Senegalese case, and then for our own society.

## THE HOUSEHOLD AND REPRODUCTION

'The household' is a very different kind of concept from such concepts as 'kinship' or 'the family'. It is a much more concrete category than these, and it is firmly rooted in certain kinds of economic activity: that is, the production and consumption of the products of domestic labour.

In the Senegalese case, the forms of co-operation of women in domestic work were firmly enclosed by the household walls; there was no cross-household co-operation except of an extremely sporadic and exceptional sort. By 'co-operation' I do not mean the harmonious sharing of tasks, but rather the creation of the complex unit within which division of labour for these domestic tasks occurs. This unit consists of the women in one household, household membership being determined by birth, or possibly co-optation and assimilation (nieces brought in to help), for unmarried girls, and by marriage for women, except that divorced or widowed women may temporarily or permanently join male kin. But the latter, as we have seen, are not part of the domestic labour unit. It is as daughters or wives that women work in the household, and they aid and replace each other within the household as a single unit. There is only one cooking pot on the fire for any household at any moment.

In fact, for there to be more than one cooking pot at any moment would be contradictory, because the household in this village is virtually defined in terms of the sharing of a common pot. However this does not mean that the household is a redundant concept, another word for the domestic unit of work. No doubt it is true that a concept of the household and its boundaries has sometimes been imposed by researchers on a reality in fact far more complex; nevertheless, in the village I am describing the unit which I am calling the household is a category that the villagers use to organize their descriptions of their society. It has a physical existence – boundary walls within the larger compound – and the implications of membership of the household go beyond the fact of the common cooking pot which it contains. To say that the household contains those who eat from a common pot, that is those who consume the product of a single unit of domestic labour, is not a tautological statement at all.

There is an institution in this village society which reinforces this conception of the household, which I am suggesting is one based in the economic relations of domestic labour, and that is the formation of joint households at the time of the heaviest village agricultural labour. At this time, brothers who have separated to form households of their own will regroup into a single household, the women forming a single unit of domestic labour and taking it in turns to cook. This larger unit is referred to by the same word as the smaller units from which it is constituted: it is a household in the full sense of the word. It is easy to suppose that this serves to capture any available economies in the performance of domestic work at a period when women, more in the past than at present, were also performing agricultural labour. In pursuit of this hypothesis, it would be interesting to compare the organization of domestic labour, and its technical conditions, in similar villages where this joint household system is nevertheless lacking. This is, however, impossible from existing data, since research into the organization of domestic labour in Senegal - indeed in Africa - is virtually non-existent.[11]

I am suggesting, therefore, that the social institution of the household should be seen not as defined in terms of the unit of domestic labour, but as derived from it. The relations which constitute the domestic labour unit also constitute the household, though the household has, in this society, many facets other than simply that of the production of the products of domestic labour. I am proposing this derivation of the household as one which has greater generality. The household, defined as the smallest co-residential unit in a society, is constituted on the basis of the relations under which women perform domestic labour for the feeding and care of all household members, including men and children. Its size and organization will be partly determined by the technical conditions under which the domestic labour is performed in the society in question. Membership of his household may also be the basis for the performance of a great deal of other labour in the society, or it may not. The former is true in the Senegalese village; the latter is true in most social classes in Britain.

I should add a comment on the technical conditions of domestic production. Although the content of the work that I am calling domestic labour is the same in the Senegalese example and in Britain (cooking, cleaning, child care), the technical production processes involved are of course very different. The time taken for each task, and the heaviness of the labour involved, are much greater in the Senegalese village, and the products of this labour cannot be replaced by products bought on the market. The result is that a household without a woman in good health and strength cannot survive. There are a number of ways in which a man unable to take on the full burden of the agricultural labour for the support of his household can be assisted in this society, but assistance with domestic work for a woman who is chronically ill or weak is much more problematic, unless she has in the same household co-wives or daughters or a daughter-in-law. A really viable household in this village society requires more than one woman able to take on the full burden of the domestic tasks. This is not so in Britain today. I find it curious how much of the debate about the changing nature of the household has centred on the direct demands of work outside the home[12] and how little on the mediating effects of the changing technical demands of the domestic labour within the home.

11. Thus an elaborate discussion of the organization of agricultural production of a village whose population is drawn from the same ethnic group as the village I am describing, in J. M. Gastellu, B. Delpech, M. Diouf and Y. Diouf, *Maintenance Sociale et Changement Economique au Sénégal, II Pratique du Travail et Reéquilibres Sociaux en Milieu Serer* (Paris, Travaux et Documents de l'ORSOM, 1974) contains no detailed discussion of domestic labour.

12. In particular, the need of capital for a mobile population.

What then are the relations under which domestic labour is performed, the relations which constitute the unit of domestic production? This is the question which raises the issue of reproduction, in the various senses in which that word is used in the literature, since the feature of domestic labour from which we began and to which we have returned is that it is all, or almost all, done by women, and it consists of the production of essentially identical types of use values in two very different societies. The interest of feminists in the concept of reproduction has always – all confusions of definition apart – been because of our desire to understand the link between the inferior position of women in society and the fact that it is women who bear and rear children. This is still clearly the question that we should be asking.

The confusions of definition have, however, been dreadful, in the feminist as in the non-feminist Marxist writing. I shall consider the theories of the household-based economy first. In an earlier commentary on Meillassoux's work I argued[13] that Meillassoux, in common with other writers who have tried to formulate modes of production for this type of society, detached the relations governing the production of people and their distribution through the society – the relations of kinship, marriage and filiation – from all basis in social production and thereby emptied them of content. The effects of this show up at their worst in Hindess and Hirst,[14] where no content for kin relations is specified at all: 'All that is required for the economic level is some system of social relations where children are reared by adults.' Meillassoux admits the subordination of women as part of the content of the kin relations that he describes, but he sees the maintenance of this subordination as unproblematic. I went on to argue that we need to distinguish the social relations of human reproduction from the ways in which the reproduction of the mode of production as a whole is ensured or enforced. I now think, looking back on this formulation, that it offers no way out of the problem just stated. No amount of reformulation of definitions will help, in the absence of a theory of how women's subordination is reproduced through her participation (or absence of participation) in social production.

It is this theory which an analysis of domestic labour should help us to work towards. The institution of the household is a mediating link in societies. It mediates two sets of social relations, both of which have economic content in the sense that they are based in production activities, and is itself an economic institution. The first set of relations is those which reproduce the subordination of women and the alienation from her of the control of her body, her progeny and the products of her domestic work. The second set of relations is those governing the performance of social labour other than domestic labour, relations which may be more or less oppressive or exploitative.

In the household-based economy, the household is the institution which contains within itself both of these sets of relations. But, and this is the force of the analysis of the Senegalese case above, even in this case one can see that there are two mutually imbricated sets of social relations present, the division between them coming to the surface in the differences between domestic labour and other

13. M. Mackintosh, 'Reproduction and Patriarchy: A Critique of Claude Meillassoux, *Femmes, Greniers et Capitaux*', *Capital and Class*, no. 2, 1977.
14. Hindess and Hirst, *Precapitalist Modes of Production*.

labour. On the one hand one has the set of relations which involves the marriage, filiation and residence rules, the performance and control of domestic labour, and the resultant exclusion of women from certain roles in the rest of social production. These relations are those that constitute the household and control its membership. On the other hand, one has the relations involved in the performance and control of agricultural labour. This second set of relations is the one that has been the subject of the debate concerning the lineage mode of production,[15] and the debate has centred on the control by the older men of the younger. These two sets of social relations are mutually determining, and one set cannot continue to exist without the other. In a household-based system, the control by male elders of the whole system involves the maintenance of the subordination both of women to men and of younger men to male elders. To threaten the subordination of women would be to threaten the stability of the household and therefore of the system as a whole. The specific way in which in a household-based society these two sets of power relations are mutually dependent for their reproduction has yet to be the subject of detailed research. There will be forms of these mutual determinations which are specific to the household-based economy. But the existence of the two sets of relations and the existence of some forms of mutual dependence between them is something one should look for in all societies.

Which brings us back to domestic labour in capitalist society. The domestic labour debate established one point quite clearly: that domestic labour is production, it produces goods and services which contribute to the standard of living in our society. It embodied one particular confusion which concerns us here: the tendency to see the nature of these goods and services, for the purpose of our analysis, as use values like any others, which happened to be produced within the home.[16] This confusion was precisely that also perpetuated by the theorists discussed above, who, in their analyses of household-based economies, failed to distinguish domestic from other labour.

The interpretation of domestic labour within capitalism which I am now proposing does not, in a sense, contain anything which we did not already know about domestic labour. What I am trying to do is to reassemble what we know, the results of the domestic labour debate, and all that has been said in the women's movement about the way in which women's work in the home constrains and constructs her position in the rest of society, in such a way that it makes sense as theory and in particular in such a way that we can begin to answer the question: what are the social relations of domestic production?

First I am arguing that we must stop sliding between 'the household' and 'the family' in our discussions of domestic labour in capitalist society. The household is an institution which we must examine for itself, without taking it for granted that we know what we mean by the term. I am proposing that the household, in capitalist society as in other societies, is an economic institution, because it is

15. C. Meillassoux, *Anthropologie Economique des Gouro de Côté d'Ivoire* (Paris, Mouton, 1964); C. Meillassoux, 'From Reproduction to Production', *Economy and Society*, vol. 1, no. 1, 1972; Terray, *Le Marxisme*; P.-P. Rey, *Les Alliances de Classes* (Paris, Maspero, 1973).

16. In case this seems very unfair to the contributors to the debate, I should repeat what I said earlier: I mean by this that the description of these use values was not integrated into the economic analysis.

rooted in the production of the products of domestic labour: use values such as cooking or child care, and especially child care. The theoretical issue which then has to be examined is how the marriage relation operates to constitute the household in our society. Clearly most households in this society are still constituted on the basis of marriage, and the performance of domestic labour is still closely linked to the status of being a wife. Equally clearly, however, the marriage relation does not have the same force as in a society where household is the basis for all social production, nor does the control of progeny have the same importance as in a society where filiation is the basis for the control and allocation of labour. Yet the marriage bond is still a subordinating one for women, and domestic labour is the economic content of that subordination. A woman is not in control of her work within the home – the upbringing of children for example – since she does that work within an institution in which she is subordinated. And the fact that she does that work operates to maintain that subordination by excluding her from certain other forms of participation in social production.

For the set of social relations that constitutes the household, and which creates and maintains women's subordination, is mutually interwoven – and therefore to some extent mutually determining – with the set of social relations that governs other social production, in this case the relations of capitalist value production and wage labour. The household, the location of women's domestic labour, is the mediating institution for these two sets of relations: women's position and work within the household traps her and forces her into a subordinate position also within the wider society.

If one sorts out two sets of social relations in this way, then one can to some extent sort out the confusion of meanings of 'reproduction' in both the societies I am discussing. Since I have not been attempting to construct a complete theory of either society (a construction which would obviously have involved many issues outside the scope of this chapter) I can only sketch this. However, if one refers to the first set of social relations, those through which women are subordinated and the household constituted, as 'relations of reproduction', then one is doing so in recognition of the fact that oppressive societies seek to subordinate women in order to control the process and results of human reproduction. That is one meaning of the word. The other sense in which one might wish to use 'reproduction' is quite different: one wishes to investigate, for any society, how the two kinds of oppressive or exploitative social relations manage to be maintained against the opposition of the oppressed or exploited.

# 18

# Women as Food Producers and Suppliers in the Twentieth Century: the Case of Zambia

SHIMWAAYI MUNTEMBA

In this chapter we argue that women's ability to produce and supply food has been deteriorating over time. This may have started in pre-colonial times, particularly with the advent of merchant capital. But twentieth-century economic and political developments have accelerated the process. While this situation applies to peasant production as a whole,[1] our discussion here is limited to food production and supply. This is because today the food crisis is one of the major problems facing many African countries.[2] Despite capitalist expansion and state policies favouring large-scale state-controlled production, peasants continue to play an important role in national food strategies. Moreover, we believe that questions dealing with food production will, of necessity, address female producers in their capacity as part of, and not in isolation from, the peasantry. The last ten years have witnessed an upsurge in peasant studies in Africa.[3] Most works conceive of the peasant as a male and use the male gender. They also largely deal with issues affecting male peasants: cash crops, marketing,

This essay was first published in *Development Dialogue*, 1(2), 1982, pp. 29–50.

1. See, for example, Muntemba, M. S., 'Rural Underdevelopment in Zambia: Kabwe Rural District, 1850–1970', Ph.D. dissertation, University of California at Los Angeles, USA University Microfilms; Phimister, I., 'Peasant Production and Underdevelopment in Southern Rhodesia, 1890–1914, with Particular Reference to the Victoria District', and Vellut, Jean-Luc, 'Rural Poverty in Western Shaba, 1890–1930', in Palmer, R. and Parsons, N., (eds), *Roots of Rural Poverty in Central and Southern Africa*, London, 1977, pp. 225–6 and pp. 294–316 respectively.
2. See FAO, Food Outlook, no. 7, July 1982, pp. 7–8.
3. The two volumes *The Roots of Rural Poverty*, op. cit., and Klein, Martin, A., (ed.), *Peasants in Africa*, Beverly Hills, 1980, have pulled many studies together. Tanzanian scholars have put out several studies on Tanzanian peasants and many theses and dissertations can be found on these subjects, particularly at the universities of Dar es Salaam and Zambia.

agricultural education, mechanization. Even such important questions as land dislocations, migration and social stratification, which affect women most poignantly, are analysed in relation to male peasants.

It is only in a few selected regions of eastern and southern Africa that some work is being done, mainly by female researchers, which addresses the female question.[4]

Focus on food production must of necessity deal with female producers because they have, in the main, carried the burden of food production. This is deducible from researches into African peasantries. The intensification of cash crop production, dominated by men, has led to male shifts away from food production. In addition, as a result of higher male migration to other rural or urban areas, women now form the larger percentage of peasant producers. (As examples, in Zambia in 1969 there were eighty males to 100 females in some rural districts, while 30–50 per cent of the households were headed by women in others; in Lesotho 40–60 per cent of able-bodied males are away working in South Africa at any one time.[5]) Food problems cannot, therefore, be analysed or remedies suggested without addressing this single major producing group.

This chapter will attempt to understand and discuss the position of women as food producers and suppliers within the framework of the social relations of production, distribution and surplus appropriation. We believe that by so doing, we shall be getting to the fundamental cause of the problem. Control over, and access to, the physical means of production – land or fertile soils, communications, transport; and the productive forces – human labour, implements and inputs, coupled with more efficient methods, ensure labour's productivity. But that is not enough. To ensure non-appropriation and fair distribution there has to be control over one's own labour and the product of that labour. At every reconstructible period in history there has been a struggle over these factors at household, village, national and international levels. How women fared in this struggle influenced their ability to produce and supply food.

Evidence suggests that although this struggle may have existed in pre-colonial times, it was not until the penetration of capitalism and the money economy that the position of women was most markedly and devastatingly challenged. Then, the struggle heightened at every level. First, the relation to land was altered. In theory, chiefs remained the custodians of land. In actual fact, absolute control rested with colonial powers. In the process of alienating land to companies for mineral and agricultural production, or to settlers for capitalist farming, some African producers were dispossessed of cultivable land altogether, while others moved to less fertile areas. In countries where white settlement did not occur, alliances and other processes associated with the colonial state resulted in land shortages and incipient landlessness for poorer peasants. The majority of peasants are not any better off under the independent states. Some land shortages and land-

4. See Mascarenhas, O. and, Mbilinyi, M. *Women and Development in Tanzania: An Annotated Bibliography for Tanzania*. Pala in Kenya, Muntemba in Zambia and Olivia Muchena in Zimbabwe have written and published on the topic.

5. *Census of Population and Housing 1969, Final Report, Total Zambia*, Republic of Zambia Government, and Gordon, Elizabeth, 'An Analysis of the Impact of Labour Migration on the Lives of Women in Lesotho', *The Journal of Development Studies*, vol. 17, no. 3, April 1981.

lessness have occurred during this period. The commercialization of agriculture put constraints on the amount of land available for the production of food crops.

Labour posed a major problem. Capitalist enterprises demanded male workers. As a result, there was a high rate of migration by able-bodied males. As rural areas became more impoverished, even women, particularly the young, migrated. There arose, in the rural areas, a shortage of productive workers, particularly males, and this, in turn, altered the sexual division of labour. Women undertook jobs formerly performed by men; the old those of the young. Struggle over labour occurred in another way. The introduction of the money economy, as well as the demand for cash crops, resulted in competition for labour within households. More labour went into cash crop than food crop production. Emphasis on exportable crops also led to a shift from women to men as the main agricultural producers. In promoting agricultural production, states did not include women in their efforts to increase peasant productivity. Thus what little technology and financial assistance filtered through to the peasants went to selected men in selected regions. Begun in colonial times, this practice has persisted in many African countries despite political rhetoric or intentions. Consequently, women's productivity, particularly of food crops, has stagnated and in some cases actually diminished.

In situations where food crops, such as maize, are the major marketable ones, more of the crop was marketed, less stored for consumption. It has been the case historically that the need for cash sometimes leads producers to sell their food. In times of stress, for example drought or war, peasants may choose to concentrate on food production to feed themselves. Whenever this happened, pressure was exerted on them to sell. To date national food shortages or political crises have resulted in greater hardships for peasants who are pressured to sell or whose food is requisitioned by the armed forces.

Reinforced by general capitalist biases against female producers, patriarchal modes of control over land (in patrilineal and virilocal societies), control over women's labour and the product of that labour, have lingered on. The man who controls the cash crop field as well as the women's labour and who possesses modern knowledge and implements, exercises absolute control over agricultural income. This has made it difficult for women to independently purchase inputs for their fields and, occasionally, supplementary food. The man decides whether or not implements may be used in the woman's food crop field. If he decides in favour of using them, cultivation often takes place at the tail end of the rainy season resulting in poor yields. In this way men control food production and supply, sometimes to the detriment of food availability for the household.

Within the stated framework of our enquiry, three themes emerge as central to an examination of food production and supply. These are: land, labour and the sexual division of labour. Because of space constraints we shall speak generally about these themes in relation to Africa south of the Sahara. We shall then briefly illustrate the case in historical perspective by drawing on the Zambian experience.

Contrary to the generally held view that land is plentiful in Africa and therefore cannot act as a constraint, there is evidence that the land issue has been critical in food production. There are cases of poor quality land, of land shortages and of outright landlessness. Registration and privatization of land has particularly affected women peasants, and consequently food production, quite adversely.

In pre-colonial times land was generally under the control of the community with the chief having custodial rights and headmen administrative responsibilities. In patrilineal societies, men had usufructuary rights. Women had these rights in relation to plots allotted to their male relatives. In matrilineal communities all lineage adult members had usufructuary rights. In virilocal societies women cultivated their husbands' plots or they got usufructuary rights to fields of their own through the husbands' membership of the village community. In Nigeria, however, there is evidence that some wealthy individuals had started to control land privately. But this is an area which requires further research to see the extent and mechanisms of such controls. Cultivable land and the availability of water influenced the settlement patterns of agricultural people.

When capitalism reached its industrial and financial height in the metropolitan countries, colonialism was introduced over most of Africa. Two approaches were adopted in terms of the appropriation of agricultural raw products from African countries: white settlement or production through local peasants. In West Africa and Uganda, peasants were delegated the production task, whereas in southern and eastern Africa (Tanzania to a lesser extent) countries experienced white settlement.

Despite the fact that production was in the hands of peasants in West Africa, the land problem recurred there too. The metropolitan countries introduced or encouraged three main cash crops: cocoa, coffee and nuts. They sought alliances for their desired production among local chiefs and elders. In almost all cases the latter ended up with large plots of land for themselves.

Later, the few African state functionaries joined their ranks. Mechanisms of such acquisition varied from country to country. In the Ivory Coast peasants were subjected to forced labour,[6] while notables were exempted. They were thus able to devote more time to their own production. In addition, the colonial state aided them with labour. As a result, they accumulated capital with which they bought larger land holdings. Others managed medium-sized plantations. However, from the late 1920s the metropolitan economy needed more cash crops. Consequently, forced labour was discontinued. The former conscripts went into small-scale plantation agriculture. By 1974 some peasants, particularly those who had cultivated small-sized plantations, could not expand because there was not enough new land.

A similar process occurred in the peanuts basin of the SeneGambia.[7] Chiefs and elders bought land to the detriment of small farmers. In Niger[8] intensified cash crop production, which started in the 1930s but accelerated after the war, coincided with land shortage. Over the century the state had been aiding some peasants in increasing their production. Later, they were given access to credit facilities and were thus able to buy up land. Although landlessness as a whole is

6. My discussion on the Ivory Coast draws on Chauveau, Jean-Pierre, 'The Baule Region of Toumodi Kokumno in Historical Perspective', in Klein, Martin, A., *Peasants in Africa*, op. cit., pp. 143–74.

7. For the SeneGambia I have relied on Copans, Jean, 'The Evolution of Peasants', in *Peasants in Africa*, pp. 77–103.

8. I have drawn on DeJean, Elaine de Latour, 'Shadows Nourished by the Sun: Rural Social Differentiation Among the Mawri of Niger', in *Peasants in Africa*, pp. 105–74.

rare in the rest of Niger, there are now indices of it in the south. Nigeria[9] has reached the most advanced stage of land privatization in response to intensified cocoa growing. The many land disputes, which have become common since the sixties, bear witness to the struggle over land.

None of the works which we drew upon for this description discussed the effects of the land development on female producers. But we can deduce that women formed the majority of the disadvantaged peasants. They had no direct access to land in these mainly patrilineal societies, they had not been political office holders, and they did not own any cash crop fields.

Since the introduction of cash crop production in West Africa, land has gradually been taken away from food crops, partly to enlarge acreages for cash crop production and partly to utilize the available family labour to the maximum. This process has been observed in the Ivory Coast and Cameroun,[10] and in Niger where 'when land began to run out, people planted peanuts in their own millet fields.'[11] But the most telling example comes from Nigeria where, in 1974, it was estimated that most households were putting 70 per cent of their holdings under cocoa production. Holdings averaged three acres for migrants and ten for locals.

Peasants in southern and eastern Africa experienced land dislocation according to the scale of white settlement. In South Africa,[12] Boers started expanding their frontiers in the nineteenth century. The growth and development of mining resulted in large land sales. In addition, land was also taken up for mineral production, for towns, and by speculators. This, plus the need for labour, resulted in the 1913 Land Act allocating to Africans 13 per cent of the land. The 13 per cent included Lesotho and comprised the most unfertile land. The Bantustan development has crowned and enshrined the dispossession. From this land women, who stayed behind while their men went to the mines and towns, eked out a living for themselves and their children. They also supplemented their husbands' wages by providing them with food whenever they visited home. The deterioration of the already poor quality soils, together with population growth, gradually placed greater hardships on women. An example of women's difficulties in connection with production and labour problems in such lands comes from Lesotho. In recent research involving 524 wives of migrant men, 55 per cent of the respondents mentioned problems connected with their fields; 28 per cent referred to this as their greatest problem; 71–72 per cent worried about their ability to feed themselves and their children, while 6 per cent actually lacked food.[13]

9. See Clarke, Julian, 'Peasantization and Landholding: A Nigerian Case Study', in *Peasants in Africa*, pp. 177–219.
10. I have drawn on Levin, Michael D., 'Export Crops and Peasantization: The Bakosi of Cameroun', in Klein, Martin, A., *Peasants in Africa*, op. cit., pp. 221–41.
11. DeJean, Elaine de Latour, 'Shadows', op. cit., p. 122.
12. My main sources are Bundy, Colin, 'The Transkei Peasantry, *c.*1890–1914: Passing Through a Period of Stress', *Roots of Rural Poverty*, op. cit., pp. 201–20; Wilson, Monica and Thompson, Leonard, (eds), *The Oxford History of South Africa* vol. II, Chapters I–V; Bundy, Colin and Beinart, William, 'State Intervention and Rural Resistance: The Transkei, 1900–1965', *Peasants in Africa*, op. cit., pp. 271–315.
13. Gordon, Elizabeth, 'An Analysis of the Impact of Labour Migration on the Lives of Women in Lesotho', *The Journal of Development Studies*, op. cit., p. 65.

From the 1890s land in Zimbabwe[14] started to pass into settler hands. Settlers then began to squeeze peasants out of production. As in South Africa, land in Zimbabwe was divided between whites and Africans. Native reserves (for Africans) were mainly located in rocky and less productive areas. Much of the area was infested by tse-tse fly and baboon. Peasants could not keep cattle (essential for more productive plough cultivation) while baboons damaged their crops. The reserves were also set farther away from the urban markets. This had a double effect of curtailing peasant participation in the market and inflating prices in the reserves.

Under the 1930 Land Apportionment Act, 49.1 million out of about 90 million acres were under white control. African land included Native Purchase Areas (actually deducted from reserve land), where Africans could buy land. By 1970 the division was thus: 44.9 million acres for whites against 43.6 million for Africans, or 1000 acres per head to Europeans and twenty-nine per head to Africans. As in South Africa, women were supposed to reproduce labour in the reserves under dire production conditions. Formerly, women did not have direct access to land in these patrilineal societies. But now their access was curtailed even further because of the constraints placed on their men. Poor quality land led to lower crop yields. Land privatization, which started after 1951 in the reserves, has continued after independence. Settlement schemes have not taken women into consideration except as labour providers on their husbands' plots.

Large white settlement in the highlands of Kenya[15] resulted in dislocation for Kikuyu peasants. As in southern Africa, reserves were created for Africans. As in West Africa, but to a far smaller extent, collaborating Africans bought land. After 1953 the colonial government encouraged land privatization. This process gained momentum after independence when, with British aid, the new state initiated settlement schemes to cater for landless peasants and to ease pressure in the reserves. The situation is that peasants in settlements take title to land. And, of course, they are all men. The question, then, is: what happens to female producers? In these patrilineal societies, women had usufructuary rights to their husbands' or sons' lands. Can they be sure of this right under these developments, for if the son sells his land he will for ever forfeit his right to it? The old system allowed for temporary land loans negotiated directly. Will the new system have room for this? Are development strategies calling for land privatization the best ones, seen in the perspective of the main food producers – the women?

The questionable effects of settlement schemes have also been noted in other countries. The attempts at socialized production through Ujamaa villages in Tanzania seem not to have addressed the question of control of both land and labour by women. Wives do not have access to land. As a result women must leave

14. I have relied mainly on Palmer, Robin, *Land and Racial Domination in Rhodesia*, London, 1977, and 'The Agricultural History of Rhodesia', and Phimister, I., 'Peasant Production and Underdevelopment in Southern Rhodesia, 1890–1914, with Particular Reference to the Victoria District', *The Roots of Rural Poverty*, op. cit., pp. 221–54 and pp. 225–67 respectively; and Olivia Muchena who has written various discussion papers on the position of rural women producers.

15. See, in particular, Leys, Colin, *Underdevelopment in Kenya: the political economy of neocolonialism 1964–71*, London 1975. Also, Dr Achola Pala has been carrying out research on rural women producers and has written several discussion papers on which this chapter has drawn.

the villages when their husbands die. Those who may have had access to land through their matrilineal rights now face losing this altogether.[16] However, there are indications that the experiment at socialized production through communal villages in Mozambique might benefit women producers. There, women have the same rights to land as men.[17] But the experiment is still too new for effective analysis.

As in West Africa, so here too, those peasants involved in cash crop growing allotted more land to these than to food crops. From Tanzania come examples of men who put under cash crop production even the land that belonged to their wives through their matrilineages.[18]

But land dislocation and privatization had another effect on food supply. Previously, women supplemented their food supplies, particularly fruit and vegetable, through gathering. In times of shortage, this became a strategy for survival. But this strategy failed as people moved to new areas whose ecosystems they did not know; or where gathering could not be undertaken. Privatization has limited their operational areas. Viewed from the 1980s and different socio-economic cultures, we might find this mode irrelevant to analyses of the food problem and to strategy formulation. But for people faced with malnutrition and famine these additional food sources are of great significance.

The question of land is, however, meaningless without consideration of labour: without the latter, land is nothing. Throughout the century, male labour has been extracted from local into capitalist production. Although less marked in West Africa some regions in the savanna experienced migration. With no cash crops, men sold their labour in order to meet cash needs. From Niger comes the case of conscripted labour which continued until the later 1920s. But the process has been more marked in eastern and southern Africa. From the early days of capitalist penetration, male labour was deployed into the mines and settler farms – initially through forced labour, then through the tax mechanism and later through the people's desire for cash. In all cases, as the impoverishment of rural areas deepened, migration accelerated. It started to include young women. Rural–urban migration has become a thorn in the flesh of many independent countries.

The branches of production in the pre-colonial economies sometimes observed a sex division. There was also a sex division within agricultural production. The absence of men meant that women had to perform those tasks formerly undertaken by men. There were cases where they could not do this and overcropping and lower yields were the result. Servicing activities such as smithing were discontinued and this resulted in shortages of the tools of production of the right quality and shape. Women in the labour reservoirs of southern Africa: Botswana, Lesotho, Swaziland, Malawi, Mozambique and some parts of Zambia, suffered enormous hardship as their burdens of responsibility and the shortage of labour

16. Brain, J. L., 'The Position of Women in Rural Settlement Schemes in Tanzania', *Ufuhamu*, VI (I). Cited in Mascarenhas and Mbilinyi, op. cit.
17. Isaacman, B. and Stephen, J., *Mozambique Women, the Law and Agrarian Reform*, United Nations Economic Commission for Africa, Addis Ababa, 1980, Chapter V.
18. Hamdani, Salha, 'Peasantry and the Peasant Woman in Tanzania', mimeo. Cited in Mascarenhas and Mbilinyi, *Bibliography*, op. cit.

increased. Elderly women in particular have continued to experience hardship, lower yields and malnutrition.

From the 1930s, but especially after the 1939–45 war, governments all over Africa attempted to increase peasant productivity. In some cases more land was released; credit facilities were made available; inputs were distributed; training in more efficient methods of production was introduced; and markets were organized. But in all cases governments adopted the 'reinforcement of success' approach. In the SeneGambia the Porteres plan of 1950 advocated this.

After independence the government, with the help of the French Société d'Aide Technique et de Cooperation, implemented the policy of extending 'services to those producers with the capacity and will to mobilize enough land and labour'. In Zimbabwe the government introduced the Master Farmer programme, even in the face of land problems – thus causing many of the 'master farmers' to migrate to Zambia. In all the countries, poorer peasants were not reached and in all cases women were excluded from the programmes. The independent governments have perpetuated the approach so that women, who are the poorest and yet the major food producers, do not have these means of increasing their yields. Poor cropping methods have been reported in many parts of Africa. Where we have evidence of this, it largely affects women in relation to production of food crops.[19]

Our analysis of the food problem cannot ignore natural disasters such as drought. Notwithstanding this, it is important to note that international and local state control over the products of labour has interfered with what strategies of survival women might have adopted. Both the colonial and neo-colonial states have emphasized the production of cash crops. Peasants responded in some of the ways noted above, to the detriment of food production. However, there is evidence that, in times of stress caused by climatic conditions, or in war situations or when there are national shortages for the non-producing groups, governments squeezed out even the little food peasants would have grown. This happened during the drought years of the early 1930s in West Africa. Then, peasants gave up cash crop production in favour of millet. State power was used to extract the millet. During the 1939–45 war peasants in eastern and southern Africa had to 'sell' food crops to the war effort. District Commissioners were given the task of ensuring this. When white settlers turned away from maize production during the UDI days in Zimbabwe, peasants made up the food crop deficit. Government propaganda, regimentation and sometimes brutal appropriation (for example by soldiers) have been used to extract food from the peasants.

We have already referred to the sexual division of labour in terms of job performance. But our concept goes beyond this to encompass control over labour and labour's product. Whether patrilineal or matrilineal, husbands have always controlled the labour of women. Because of this control, men have dictated that their wives spend less time in food production. The official preference for male producers resulted in men's control of the more efficient tools and methods of production. This affected women's food production in two ways. In the first place,

19. See, for example, Jiggins, J., 'Female-headed Households: Mpika Sample, Northern Province', *Occasional Seminar 3*, RDSB, University of Zambia mimeograph.

men used the implements to cultivate cash crops, or they hired them out for cash. A recent village study of ninety households in Tanzania revealed that 90 per cent of the women surveyed used the hoe while, from the same households, ox-drawn ploughs were used for cash crop production.[20] Secondly, as we shall see in the following, men's control over produce heightened.

In pre-colonial times women had control over food produce and could distribute it as they saw fit, often as gifts to needy relatives. But in the rare cases of exchange for non-subsistence items they had to confer with their husbands (the exception to this comes from Nigeria, where men controlled yams). With increasing cash needs male control has sharpened. In this context it would be unfair to underplay factors which compel male household heads to sell food to meet immediate cash needs. The women's position is that they themselves should decide whether to sell food or not. If they have to, then they must have control over the income. They believe that, given the opportunity to choose between raising cash or food for their household, they would go for the latter. Indeed there are indications that female household heads tend to borrow money for immediate needs rather than sell food. On the other hand, there is evidence that women heads have sold food crops to their own disadvantage in order to invest in, for example, the health or education of a child.

In summary, then, land and labour issues have affected women's food production capabilities adversely, and their ability to supply food has been deteriorating. In those countries where their husbands go into wage labour, women have both fed themselves and their children and have supplemented their husbands' wages through food gifts and by maintaining them during their stay at home before the cycle starts again. Although they could not adequately do so, men were obligated to start partially maintaining their families 'back home' through cash remittances. But cash came at irregular intervals, or it was insufficient, mainly because of the meagre wages. Some women have sought to increase their food supply capacities by going into seasonal wage labour. Often the wages are too low and the prices of food too high for this strategy to work. The time spent in wage labour could be better spent in their own production, provided the factors of production are favourable to them. The intensification of cash crop production has drawn land and labour away from food crops resulting in local food shortages. This process was realized earlier in West Africa when, instead of encouraging peasants or allowing them to cultivate enough food crops, the colonial government started to import rice from China. Gradually this became an acceptable food crop. But attempts to grow it in sufficient quantities have benefited only men. With the growing urban population rice became a viable marketable crop, to the disadvantage of sufficient food supplies for the producers themselves. Elsewhere, marketable food crops have been sold to the disadvantage of household requirements. Peasants have had to supplement their needs through imported foods.

20. Ngalula,T. K. F., 'Women as a Productive Force in Tanzanian Rural Society: A Case Study of Buhongwa Village in Mwanza District', unpublished M.A. dissertation, University of Dar es Salaam. Cited in Mascarenhas and Mbilinyi, op. cit.

## THE ZAMBIAN CASE

### HISTORICAL PERSPECTIVES: THE PRE-COLONIAL SITUATION

Pre-colonial Zambia was largely populated by matrilineal peoples.[21] But there were pockets of patrilineal societies in the eastern and northern parts of the country. Matrilineal societies in the northern and north-central areas were also uxorilocal so that access to land was through the woman's lineage. Others were virilocal. Broadly speaking, people followed three main agricultural practices. In the northern and north-central areas cultivators practised the *chitemenë* and *chiteme* systems involving lopping and felling of trees. Elsewhere, trees were cut when new fields were opened. They cut brambles for fertilization. Along the flood plains of the western region and in the north-west, cultivators also built mounds. Both men and women performed specific agricultural tasks within the agricultural cycle. Men lopped or felled trees, built mounds and turned fresh soils. Together with the women, they scared birds, harvested and built granaries. Women turned the soils, planted, weeded, scared birds, harvested and carried the produce to the villages for storage. They also cultivated additional crops such as pumpkins, sweet potatoes, cassava and nuts. Clearly, women performed more tasks than the men. But while this was the case in the agricultural sector, men were more active in hunting, fishing, smelting and interregional trade.

In all situations, in uxorilocal societies as well, theoretically it was the men who controlled the agricultural produce. Women distributed the produce for household consumption and sometimes to needy relatives. But beyond this, they consulted their husbands. In matrilineal, virilocal societies women who wanted the freedom to consume and distribute without interference got extra land whose produce they controlled absolutely. They got this land in two ways: from the husband's lineage through him or from their own lineage if they were close to their natal villages. We do not have evidence of this practice in patrilineal societies. Patriarchal modes of control also applied to single women. Before marriage, they were controlled by their fathers or uncles and could not cultivate fields independently, and, if divorced or widowed, control by fathers, brothers or sons persisted in patrilineal societies. While women in matrilineal societies had access to land independently, brothers or uncles could control the labour of their children.

Because of the low level of technology, fields were limited in size. The possible shortage of staple grains was compensated by a variety of other foods: nuts, pumpkins, sweet potatoes and cassava. When these did not see them through the year or when the climate was unfavourable, women gathered. Throughout the year, they gathered especially for relishes.

But even in pre-colonial times food production and supply did not always work smoothly and was often disturbed by the political institutions. Chiefs demanded tribute through labour services, thus deploying labour from individual households, and they wanted tribute in the form of gifts of produce. When producers

21. Much of the discussion is based on the research on women in agriculture that the author carried out in 1980–81. The research was funded by the Ford Foundation, whom the author thanks.

did not give, the chiefs carried out raids. Powerful chiefs like those of the Lozi in the west and the Bemba in the north raided farther afield. Their raids were for people, cattle and grain; tribute to them included grain, iron tools, skins, and ivory. The dominating role of chiefs, then, deprived households of labour, tools and produce. We do not know the effects deployment of labour had on household production, although we can surmise what they could have been. But its results on food supplies have been documented.[22] Chiefly raids left some households without food. Women resorted to gathering as the sole mode of survival until the next crop was ready.

## HISTORICAL PERSPECTIVES: THE COLONIAL SITUATION 1900–1945

A review of women as food producers during this period can be divided into two broad categories: women from areas with a lower rate of male out-migration and closer to the main lines of communication and urban centres; and women from areas which experienced high male labour migration. The first area included today's south-central parts of the country and portions of the east. Most white farmers who came to Northern Rhodesia (as Zambia was called before political independence in 1964) settled here and therefore struggle over land, agricultural labour, the productive forces and the market was sharpest in this area.

The Administration of Northern Rhodesia did not have a clear land policy until after 1924. However, by 1910 much of the land along the railway line had been alienated either to mining and railway companies or to white settlers. More land was alienated after the 1914–1918 war to resettle British ex-soldiers. In today's Eastern Province the North Charterland Exploration Company controlled 10,000 square miles in addition to settler farms. The number of settlers in Northern Rhodesia was negligible compared to Southern Rhodesia (Zimbabwe). By 1911 there were 159 settlers in the country. In 1919 the number had risen to 250 for the railway region alone. These numbers notwithstanding, the settlers controlled large amounts of land on either leasehold or freehold tenure. Settler lands almost always coincided with the previously more densely populated areas because of the soil's higher productivity.

Initially, most settlers did not have much capital or technical knowledge. They relied on labour-intensive methods and African knowledge and produce. Thus they retained Africans, who had previously occupied these lands, as tenants. Because they were tenants, Africans could only cultivate land as allowed by their landlords. In the early period, they could cultivate as much as they would, although this was limited by technological and labour constraints.

Tenants were legally required to work for their landlords for two months in a year. In practice, however, they worked for longer periods. Moreover, settlers had difficulties in recruiting and retaining labour. They often signed their tenants on as wage labourers after the tenants had fulfilled their tenancy obligations. The burden of agricultural work started to shift more heavily onto women. But, at peak

22. See, for example, Muntemba, M. S., 'The Evolution of Political Systems in South-Central Zambia, 1890–1953', unpublished M. A. thesis, University of Zambia.

periods, settlers also utilized the labour of women to work in the house and in the fields. Women thus had less time to devote to production to meet their own requirements. Another way settlers collected their rental dues was through produce, while some demanded that tenants sell at least one bag of maize to them.[23] Thus many tenants ran out of food before the end of the agricultural season. Women supplemented these shortfalls by gathering. Those tenants who found the situation unbearable, moved. Sometimes they went to alienated but unoccupied lands; at other times to unalienated lands within the same ecosystem.

Not regarded as a permanent labour resource, women were evicted at the death of a husband. The story of the old woman Lweembe, in Kabwe Rural District, illustrates the situation most poignantly. Lweembe's husband had been a tenant. Although she sometimes worked for the farmer at peak periods and helped around his house, she mainly worked in the small household plot. Her household produced enough to meet the rental and food requirements, and she sold one bag every so often to the landlord. These obligations were met because her husband used to hire an ox-drawn plough from the landlord. When her husband died, she was left with four dependent children. She wished to continue cultivating her plot and meet rental obligations because 'that land was all I had and I had grown up there.' This was not to be. She was evicted. She moved to the next farm to live with a brother. She could stay but could not cultivate independently. She moved to another settler farm to live with an uncle. She could not stay because he was a tenant. In the next ten years, she moved from relative to relative until she heard of a chief 'who had a good heart'. She went and begged for a piece of land. This was granted, and she and her children settled there.[24]

As settlers' capital formations improved, coupled with increasing knowledge, they found the tenancy system unproductive. Some started to evict their tenants under the Agreement of Surrender of 1912.[25] Those Africans who attempted resistance met with state force. By 1930, most of the tenants had moved.

The Colonial Office took over direct administration of the country from the British South Africa Company in 1924. One of the first tasks the new government undertook was to enact a land policy. In 1928–9, land in Northern Rhodesia was divided into Native Reserves (for Africans) and Crown Lands (for towns, mineral development and for actual or anticipated white settlement). Africans were required to move into the reserves demarcated for them. Those who did not wish to move were overpowered. Many moved to less productive lands. Consequently, they had to stop growing some of their foods.[26] In some cases they crowded together in the few fertile places. Before removal some of them had started selling surpluses to settlers and the urban centres to meet their tax and other cash requirements. After the depression the mining industry's labour force grew, and with it the urban market. Along with its need for cash, was the state's desire for food for the urban workers. White settlers could not fulfil this task and there was pressure on peasants to sell food. Land over-use developed, a situation which started to worry some government officials because of its implications for food

23. National Archives of Zambia (N.A.Z.), BS 3/399, Enclosure no. 3, Tenancy Agreement.
24. Luwale Lweembe, interview, 24 June 1981.
25. N.A.Z., BS 3/399, Enclosure no.1, Memorandum of Agreement of Surrender.
26. Senior Chief Chipepo, interview, HD/08/File 1/37.

supplies for mine workers. Nevertheless, the government did not do much to improve the situation until after the war.

There were also problems connected with water supplies for human beings and for stock. Previously, African peasants settled mainly along rivers, particularly perennial ones. Here, women cultivated vegetables and other supplementary foods throughout the year. In their new homes, they could not do so. Males who previously sought strategies to avoid wage labour, were now forced to sell their labour because of the foreclosing economic opportunities in the reserves. To other problems of production in the reserves began to be added those of labour shortages. Some males were recruited as fighters and porters for the war effort. Yet, throughout the war, peasants were also required to produce food. In addition to maize, they were to send millet. District Commissioners were commended according to the amount of grain they 'bought' from the peasants. The burden of meeting these requirements fell on women. 'Those were hard days', said one woman interviewee. They did not have enough even for their own households.

While land dispossession played an important role in altering the position of women as food producers in the agricultural regions, labour was mainly responsible in the rest of the country. From the outset, international capital was more interested in mineral extraction. But until the late 1920s, mineral production was negligible and required little labour. However, as part of the larger southern African economic region, stretching from South Africa to the Congo (Zaire), African labour from Northern Rhodesia circulated among these countries. Men from the northern, north-western, western and parts of eastern areas migrated in great numbers. Yet in these areas their contribution to agriculture, i.e. to lop or fell trees for the *chitemenë* system, to build mounds in the valleys and to help scare birds because sorghum and millet remained the main staples in some places, was more important. In these parts, the soils were generally of low productivity. The land rotation system,[27] whereby fields had to be continuously extended, was essential. By the 1930s, some villagers could not practise this owing to the absence of young men.[28] Women, who had started to perform most tasks, could not fell or lop trees. Less fertilization of soil occurred. Because women could not easily extend their gardens, overcropping, a curse of later years, started to take place. The men's contribution to scaring birds and harvesting was important because, although these tasks could be, and were undertaken by women, both were undertaken in the morning and evening. At the latter time, women's labour was also required for food preparation. During the dry months, relishes were not plentiful and women had to cover huge distances to fetch them. The heavier burden which started to fall on them sometimes resulted in their getting too tired by the end of the day to prepare the major and, in some cases, only meal of the day. As agricultural production became too onerous, women started to rely more heavily on gathering. Paradoxically, on account of the increasing burden, some found it difficult to supplement their agricultural shortfalls through gathering. In an already precarious agricultural system, villagers experienced

27. Allan, W., *The African Husbandman*, London 1965, p. 6.
28. Richards, Audrey I. and Widdowson, B. M., 'A Dietary Study in North-Eastern Rhodesia', *Africa*, vol. 9, no. 2, pp. 179–81; and von Horn, Laurel, 'The Agricultural History of Barotseland', in Palmer, R., *Zambian land and labour studies*, vol II, pp. 14–16.

actual hunger during the three dry months, the 'hunger months'. Some women sent their children to relatives in urban centres even though the situation there was not better. Another development, which became accentuated later with urbanization, was that as their agricultural burden grew, in some instances they started to shift to less onerous but also less nutritious foods such as cassava.[29] This development sharpened according to the rate of out-migration and urbanization.

## HISTORICAL PERSPECTIVES: THE COLONIAL SITUATION 1946–1964

This period witnessed the intensification of commodity production. The shift to production of marketable crops became pronounced. At the same time, mines adopted a policy of labour stabilization, while the influx of young men to urban centres in search of wage employment accelerated. The demand for food increased accordingly. Furthermore, in its efforts to revamp its weak economy following the 1939–1945 war, the British Government wished to extract as much raw materials, including agricultural products, from its colonies as possible. Cotton, tobacco and groundnut were the main crops required from Northern Rhodesia. Maize production was essential to feed the copper producers. But the Northern Rhodesia Government was operating within certain economic constraints. Besides, it was essential to retain some areas as labour reservoirs. Therefore, the government limited its financial, technical and marketing assistance to the south-central and eastern parts of the country. These were the major maize, tobacco, cotton and groundnut growing areas. But even here it was confined to few producers, none of them women. Since the aim was to boost production of cash crops, only men formed the target group.

The first step the government took in realizing higher production by Africans was to release more land. Native Trust Lands were created in 1947. The government also initiated the Peasant and Improved Farmers Schemes, aimed at introducing peasants to modern technology. It established bonus schemes to reward those producers who followed modern methods of production, thus encouraging others to adopt them. The government gave financial assistance through loans, and it advanced implements. None of these benefits was extended to women. In spite of discrimination against poor peasants and women, the government required from them maize to feed urban workers. Depots were set up in areas not covered by agricultural assistants. In these areas, many men had left for wage labour. Women were the major target. They sold two, three or four bags of maize and were left small quantities to supplement their sorghum which they could not grow in large quantities because of labour problems. By 1964 many had stopped growing sorghum altogether and had turned to maize as the staple grain.

Between 1946 and 1964 the money economy had thoroughly penetrated most of south-central and eastern Zambia. Money was required to buy agricultural implements and inputs and essentials such as clothing and blankets, to purchase certain items of food and to pay school fees. This, plus government assistance and

29. Richards, Audrey I., *Land, Labour and Diet in Northern Rhodesia: An Economic Study of the Bemba Tribe*, London, 1969, pp. 104–5.

propaganda, resulted in greater efforts by peasants to grow marketable crops.

There were several implications of these developments for food production in these areas. First, pressure on land mounted. In one of the chieftancies which I researched, pressure on land mounted because of the large number of ex-soldiers who settled there in the 1950s. These went into tobacco production and ranching. The government settled them in Native Trust Lands, thus defeating the purpose of the scheme, which was to relieve pressure on land in the reserves. Africans were pushed into less fertile 'rock and rubble' areas where cultivable land was most limited and scattered. Here, they joined those who had moved there before 1945. Land clearing was most arduous, so that by the time older women finished clearing a quarter of an acre, men would have taken up much of the cultivable land. The social fabric had been so broken that even headmen could not protect them. In the words of their chief, 'how can you expect elderly women to clear all those stones? How can you expect a man to clear enough land for his wives and children and mother and aunt?' This problem was compounded by the fact that younger men fled the reserves, leaving mothers to fend for themselves.

In another part of this region peasants were moved to make room for the Kariba dam. The amount of land they were allocated was based on the number of male household heads. Yet in this matrilineal society, women had always had usufructuary rights to land through their lineages. Located away from the urban markets, along the routes used by men who recruited labour for the Southern Rhodesian mines, the area had seen a high rate of male migration. Women had maintained themselves and their dependants by cultivating the rich alluvial soils along the Zambezi river. This was disturbed by the new developments. In the new less fertile and rocky lands, even male kin did not have sufficient land to allocate to female kin members, or, if they did, they did not have the time or energy to help with the clearing. As in similar situations, younger males joined the throng of wage labourers. Single women, those who might later be divorced or widowed, were placed in a very precarious position indeed.[30]

Elsewhere, peasants started to move to those parts of the reserves with more fertile land and/or closer to the main lines of communication and markets. Men had an advantage over women in this respect. Women could not migrate as easily, both for social reasons and because headmen tended to allocate land to males unless the woman was also a relative. When overcrowding developed, women were the first to get squeezed out so that their acreages got smaller and smaller. Though land in the reserves was not saleable legally, in fact a few peasants in the agricultural region started to sell some. A substantial number of them were elderly single women who 'sold' land to meet an immediate cash need. In fact because the concept of selling land did not exist in their communities, women thought that they were merely loaning the land, hence the paltry prices. When the lands they were cultivating became exhausted because of inefficient farming methods, they tried to regain those which they had 'sold'. Often they could not. Appeals to the local courts did not succeed.[31]

In matrilineal societies a husband could allot a piece of land to his wife where she could grow crops over which she had absolute control, as already stated. A few

30. Colson, E. *The Social Consequences of Resettlement*, Kariba Studies, IV.
31. Court Cases, Chief Mungule's court.

women in south-central Zambia grew enough from these plots in pre-colonial times to sell and thus built up herds of cattle. Most importantly, in the twentieth century, women resorted to produce from these fields to feed members of their households. We said earlier that maize was the major cash crop. By this period it had completely ousted sorghum and millet as the staple grain. To fully utilize the available labour, households did not cultivate separate fields for domestic consumption. Instead, they reserved some bags of maize out of the total production. Men, although not food processors, made the decision and often underestimated the household requirements. There were instances when cash was needed most desperately at harvest time. Thus they ran out of maize before the next season's crop was ready. Women turned 'their' produce into household produce. It was not until after 1964 that most women lost these independent lands, but the process started during this period. Men wanted to bring as much land as possible under cash crop cultivation; they also wished to utilize women's labour to the maximum. They started to deny their wives these independent lands or to give them less acreage. Maximum utilization of their labour did not leave them sufficient time or energy to travel to their matrikin villages to exploit their land.

The struggle for household labour manifested itself in another way. As stated earlier, households have always supplemented their staple food with other foodstuffs such as pumpkins, cassava, sweet potatoes and yam, while groundnuts and vegetables served as relishes. With the commercialization of agriculture, women did not have sufficient time to gather food. Domestically produced supplements, especially relishes, became crucial. However, in order to increase cash crop production they now put less time into the production of these 'minor' crops (in official parlance – the term minor itself reveals a lot about government attitudes to food production for household consumption). Women's labour was most desired during the rainy season when most of these crops were also planted. To increase the yields, they had to use more efficient methods, modern technology and inputs. Men who controlled household implements or the cash to purchase seed and fertilizers preferred to use them for cash crop production; others hired out their implements in order to raise cash. They only allowed them to be used in the wives' fields when they did not need them, often at the tail end of the rainy season. Consequently, yields did not increase. In some cases, they actually diminished.

We mentioned that government programmes aimed at increasing peasant productivity were directed towards men only. In order to increase household production some men imparted knowledge to their wives so that female productivity did actually rise. However, control over knowledge and household implements, strengthening the patriarchal attitudes, gave men leverage to control agricultural income. They gave their wives a disproportionate share, even taking into account joint household expenses.[32] Some women informed me that direct or indirect pressure was brought on them to sell women's crops such as groundnuts and vegetables. This was particularly the case if implements were used in the fields. This practice deprived household members of some important foodstuffs.

32. Muntemba, M. S., 'Women in Agricultural Change in the Railway Region of Zambia: Dispossession and Counter-Strategies, 1930–1970', in Bay, E. (ed.), *Woman and Work in Africa*, Colorado 1982, pp. 83–103.

Single women faced even worse constraints on food production. We have already referred to some of the problems they encountered in relation to land. They were not given any training. Because they did not have husbands who wanted to increase their productivity through modern techniques, many continued to use the old methods. Moreover, use of more efficient implements was important because of the need both to increase production and to replace the labour of the now absent younger people. In the 1950s many women depended on male relatives to plough for them and apply fertilizers. By the 1960s, many of the latter could not afford the time away from their own fields to perform these tasks. The women's productivity, therefore, did not increase. Sometimes they were forced to sell three out of the five bags they had harvested. Thus, some found themselves short of food before the year was out. Younger ones resorted to beer brewing through which they bought grain. For older ones, this was too taxing.

Efforts to increase peasant production were restricted to the 'agricultural' region, as stated earlier. From 1960 the government attempted to sublimate nationalist aspirations by extending 'rural development' projects to 'non-agricultural' areas. Efforts were half-hearted and did not make any impact. Furthermore, the government wished to keep the 'non-producing' region as a labour reservoir. For these reasons, male outward migration grew, while visits by migrant workers to their homes became few and far between. Many more were becoming urbanized. The mining companies' policies of labour stabilization encouraged urbanization. Some men took their 'village' wives to towns; many set up 'temporary' marriages with women from the neighbouring reserves. Thus, although land remained 'abundant', problems connected with labour accelerated. Women continued to use old implements such as the hoe; they continued to overcrop. Production of less nutritious food increased. With the penetration of the cash economy even to these areas, women started to sell crops such as cassava and groundnuts.[33] However, they did not produce these in large quantities because of labour shortages, and by selling some they were left without enough for domestic consumption. In the 1950s some producers from maize-producing areas in south-central Zambia profited by travelling to 'non-producing' areas where they sold maize at double the price offered by the Maize Control and Grain Marketing Boards. But, of course, many poor women could not afford the prices.

## THE NEO-COLONIAL SITUATION 1964–1981

Initially, the independent government was committed to 'rural development' through the money economy. It also wished to increase agriculture's contribution to the GNP. From the early 1970s copper prices started to slide down on the world market. Copper contributed more than 90 per cent to the GNP. Agriculture was seen as a way of earning foreign exchange. For these reasons peasants were exhorted to increase their cash crop production, particularly of cotton, sunflower and tobacco. They were also urged to grow maize and other food crops

33. Spring, A. and Hansen, A., 'Women's Agricultural Work in Rural Zambia from Valuation to Subordination: Agricultural Changes in Zambia since the late 1930s', African Studies Association Meeting, Los Angeles, mimeograph.

to feed the nation (i.e. the urban workers), and to increase their groundnut production for oil extraction. The formerly 'non-producing' labour reservoirs were also encouraged to produce maize, not as a domestic food but as a saleable crop. To aid them in increasing productivity, the state heightened its support and improved the agricultural prices of cash crops but not those of maize. More and more peasants were given training in efficient methods of production. Some were settled on unoccupied settler farms. In 1975, the President announced measures to alleviate problems connected with land. Henceforth all land in Zambia was under state guardianship, although chiefs could administer it in the reserves. In all cases land was to cease being a saleable commodity.[34]

Peasants reacted to these initiatives and their overall production of cash crops increased. The country became almost sufficient in cotton, for example (although in 1981, vegetable oil extracts, sunflower seeds and groundnuts were not being produced in sufficient quantities to meet national oil requirements). But this increase was at the expense of maize and other food crops. Thus the country found itself short of maize to feed the urban population. Some producers also experienced shortfalls themselves and looked to stores for their maize meal supplies. State officials chided rural producers for laziness, suggesting that the peasants were unable to feed themselves. But, as one rural District Governor was quick to remind the government in 1979, people in his area were not lazy. They were merely responding to party and government calls for increased cash crop production. The deteriorating food situation in rural areas, resulting in malnutrition in some households, started to worry some state officials and from the 1970s rural people were urged to produce food for domestic consumption. The National Food and Nutrition Commission came to the forefront. These efforts notwithstanding, the problem of food for both urban and rural populations reached a critical stage in the later part of the 1970s. Problems connected with land and labour and the sexual division of labour continued to undermine production.

Pressure on land mounted as state lands (formerly Crown lands) remained closed to peasants who did not have the necessary securities. The few local bourgeoisie who had the securities started buying up this land. Government resettlement schemes affected few peasants. In the words of one chief, 'how can taking one *man* out of a village of 200–300 people relieve pressure on land?' The 1975 declaration does not seem to have released much land for the peasants. Mounting pressure on land hit women worse than it did men. Seventy per cent of the plaintiffs in some land cases in south-central Zambia were mainly elderly divorced or widowed women. Their holdings averaged three acres of poorer quality land. Many women in this region had turned to vegetable growing. Seventy-five per cent of them singled out land as the major constraint. As noted above, state concerns for food and nutrition took place against strong propaganda for the production of cash crops and food for urban populations. Emphasis on commodity production perpetuated and accelerated the struggle over land and labour within households. More land was given to cash crop production than previously. More labour was directed into these and other saleable food items.

34. Address by His Excellency the President Dr K. D. Kaunda to the National Council of the United National Independence Party, Mulungushi Hall, June 30–July 3, 1975, mimeograph.

While in theory women could receive government support, in practice they remained relatively insufficiently supported. Married women could not easily get loans because they were not household heads. Most single women did not have the necessary securities. Courses at farm institutes were still largely male-oriented; women's programmes continued to emphasize home economics. 'We were taught how to make scones. How could that help us with our farming? Flour was too expensive to get anyway. Later, you could not even get it', said one woman in an interview in 1976. Another in 1981: 'It is all very well to learn about good nutrition and hygiene. Where is the food to give nutrition?' From the later 1970s there were few courses for women in the production of food crops, such as groundnuts. Much of the crop ended up in the urban markets.While as many as 90 per cent of the women in the Southern Province could handle the ox-drawn plough, only 20 per cent could manage any other implement (minus the tractor where I recorded zero female knowledge). As the implements were owned by husbands, married women continued to face difficulties of access to them for production in 'their' fields. Male control over their wives' labour and household income marched alongside the intensification of saleable crops.

In what were formerly labour reservoirs men became the target of government support, despite the fact that there were more women living there. Improved production methods of food crops were not taught to female producers, although state agencies organized the collection of these items for urban markets. At the same time, the general state of deterioration led to increased migration of both men and women from the more productive age group. This exacerbated the problem of labour supply. Studies carried out in the Northern Province revealed accentuated overcropping. They reported malnutrition. There was a higher incidence of both in female-headed households.[35] In the North-Western Province stagnating or diminishing yields of crops such as cassava and groundnuts have been documented.[36] Struggle over household labour also developed because of the introduction of maize as a cash crop. Increasing male control of agricultural income forced women to sell more of the little cassava and groundnuts they grew than had been the case previously.[37] The tendency for women to sell food crops in order to raise cash continued to bedevil nutrition efforts. But the cash raised this way was in turn used to buy food at prices peasants often could not afford.

## WOMEN'S REACTION AND STRATEGIES

Women analysed their position within the context of the role of the state and, to a lesser extent, that of their male relatives, particularly husbands – 'the government has forgotten us'; 'As long as you people in towns eat, what does it matter that we cannot?' They blamed government precisely because of its role as the major agent for increased productivity. The state controlled overall distribution. In their view the state systematically operated against them. We have seen in this chapter that their perception is not wrong. Both colonial and neo-colonial state policies

35. Jiggins, J., op. cit.
36. Spring and Hansen, op. cit.
37. Ibid.

contributed most decisively to the deteriorating position of women in production. Women reacted in many ways. Some lowered their production efforts so that the state could not appropriate surpluses for the urban people. As some women conceded to me, this was the wrong strategy. In times of national needs food was extracted from them anyway. Furthermore, this strategy had the overall effect of lowering production so that even their own consumption was not always assured. Because men owned the implements, the man's relatives inherited them even though they may have been bought out of agricultural income. Older women, who would have already put their children through school, were particularly bitter. Said two polygamously married women, 'Our household production has been deteriorating over the last five years. How can it not when we, the women, have decided to work as little as possible?'

In the 'agricultural' region many women turned to vegetable growing. They saw in this a way to produce crops which they could control. They could also work in the vegetable gardens for short periods after working in the major fields. Household relishes were assured. We have already mentioned problems connected with land and labour, despite the husband's acknowledgement of the importance of vegetables for household food supply. Because of water supply problems, this activity should largely be undertaken during and soon after the rains. But women's labour was most needed during the wet season.

The inability to grow enough to feed themselves and through which they could also raise cash, led some women, particularly younger and single ones, to turn to other activities, such as beer brewing. While this activity was lucrative in the 'agricultural' region where there was a cash circulation and also surplus grain to buy, it was not quite as rewarding in poorer areas. Some women stated that they could only make 30n (40 US cents) per brew. Often they gave the beer away for lack of customers to buy.

Finally, some women migrated to urban centres where they hoped for better social and economic opportunities. This, of course, added greater labour-related burdens to those who remained in the rural areas, while urban centres have not held much hope for those with little or no academic qualifications.

## CONCLUSION - AND WHAT THEN?

In this chapter we postulated that women are central to a discussion of the food situation. We argued that their capacity to produce and supply food has been deteriorating, and posited three major areas of enquiry in analysing this situation. While these areas have been dealt with in relation to women producers, land and labour are central to an enquiry into peasant production generally. We traced the process of deteriorating fortunes within the framework of the three themes by drawing on the Zambian case. It is our contention that despite country or regional particularities, these themes can be applied in an analysis of the situation in other parts of Africa. Our brief and general description in the first part seems to substantiate our claims. Through the Zambian case, we have concluded that the situation of women producers and of food production worsened at a pace responding to the nature of capitalist appropriation of land and labour and the intensification of cash crop production. Thus the phenomenon became more marked after 1945 when everywhere colonial states intensified cash crop production. The situation has persisted after formal independence. State attitudes and practices reinforced and sometimes deliberately promoted patriarchal systems of control placing further constraints on food crop production. We conceded the role that natural disasters play but showed that, even in such situations, food supply in peasant households is further undermined by state appropriation. It was indicated that mechanization has contributed to the marginalization of both female productivity and food crop production. We briefly surveyed women's options and noted the negative undertones in most of them.

The question, therefore, is: What then? Women's food production has deteriorated and with it food supply for their households and for nations still dependent on peasant production. We identified three problem areas – land, labour and, connected with the latter, the sexual division of labour. Women themselves identified two major responsible factors – the state and men, whether husbands, headmen, or male kin members. In the search for alternative development strategies – food and surplus food being key to poor peasants – Another Development must start by tackling these fundamental problems. Control by women of land, of the productive forces, of their labour and the product of that labour must be viewed as the most urgent priority. Thus land reforms and schemes resulting in privatization as the means of bolstering small-scale production must be challenged: they do not take women into consideration. It is imperative to consider women not because they are women but because, as we hope we have shown, they are central to food strategies. Instead, socialized forms of land systems in which *all* producers have usufructuary rights must be fostered. But this is not enough. Peasant women have to participate in the political machinery to assure equitable distribution of the productive forces and non-appropriation of food from them. Women must be conscientized to challenge the sexual division of labour which subjects their labour to men. They must translate 'the thought of this [male control of implements and labour and the inheritance laws] upsets me too much to want to go to the fields' into something more positive. But the forces at national and international levels are so strong that, alone, women cannot succeed and through this success move toward alleviating some of the food problems bedevilling many African countries.

# 19

# Gender, Accumulation and the Labour Process

NANNEKE REDCLIFT

Discussion of gender and work has so far been pursued in three separate and to some extent self-contained debates. First, there has been the lengthy exploration of the significance of domestic labour as a special form of work, in which the focus has been on the productive or non-productive character of household work and the extent of its autonomy from the capitalist mode of production (Delphy 1977; Gardiner 1975; Harrison 1973; Himmelweit and Mohun 1977; Molyneux 1979; Seccombe 1974).

A separate area of discussion has been the sexual segregation of the labour market, the particular characteristics of women as wage labourers and the role of a reserve army (Amsden 1980; Anthias 1980; Beechey 1977, 1978; Bruegel 1979; West 1982). Occupational stereotyping, low pay, dual labour markets and deskilling have been central issues here, and there has been considerable historical investigation of the role of gender in the development of specific aspects of the labour process. Both these themes have been examined in the context of advanced industrial societies.

Meanwhile, a third body of literature has considered the changing nature of the economic roles of the sexes in developing and non-Western societies, the consequences of capital penetration for the sexual division of labour and the survival or destruction of subsistence economies. The so-called 'women in development' literature has revealed a variety of forms of incorporation of the household and the differential impact of economic change on the work of women and men[1]

This essay was first published as a chapter in Enzo Mingione and Nanneke Redclift (eds), *Beyond Employment*, Basil Blackwell, 1985. It was presented at the World Congress of Sociology, Mexico City 1982. I would like to thank members of the Women's Studies MA at the University of Kent for their stimulation and encouragement. I am also grateful to Peter Fitzpatrick, to Bryan Roberts for excellent editorial advice, and to Michael Redclift for helpful comments on the final draft.

1. The term 'development' is sometimes misleadingly used as if it referred to 'development projects' (i.e. the impact of planned change, which has often been directed at men to the detriment of women), rather than the wider processes of economic change.

(Ahmed 1980; Benería 1979; Benería and Sen 1981; Benholdt-Thomsen 1981; Boserup 1970; Deere 1976; Deere and Léon de Leal 1982; Harris and Young 1981; ILO 1980; Loutfi 1980; Mies 1980; Nelson 1980; Pala 1977; Palmer 1977, 1979; Papanek 1977; Remy 1975; Tinker 1976; Young 1978).

As Molyneux has pointed out (1979), feminist analysis of women's work under advanced capitalism has tended to treat household and wage-work as separate topics for investigation, thus precluding a discussion of the full range and interrelationship of women's economic and non-economic activities, and the development of a 'comprehensive theory of the political economy of women'. A comprehensive theory may still elude us; it is nevertheless important to examine some of the contradictory hypotheses that have emerged from the discussion of women's work. To do this not only housework and wage-work but also the diverse accounts generated in advanced industrial and in developing economies need to be brought to bear more closely on each other.[2]

The issue of value has been central in these debates, whether or not in explicitly Marxist form. As Bradby asks, 'How could one maintain a labour theory of value in face of the recognition that the labour of half the world did not take the form of value? . . . the use value of labour power, the capacity to work is itself the appropriation of unpaid female labour' (Bradby 1982: 1–25). The undervalorization of women's work relative to men's is one feature to be identified with apparent consistency. They are paid less for comparable tasks or concentrated in low-pay activities, or hired on a different contractual basis, such as piecework, which works to depress the wage in relation to male earnings. More importantly, a large proportion of their daily activities are unpaid. This includes both work that is strictly for the maintenance and reproduction of the domestic unit and production that ultimately enters the market in which unpaid family labour makes a significant contribution, either as part of peasant production or as an element of a wage-labour relation in which it is the male who is formally contracted.

Notable among the attempts to provide a general explanation of this phenomenon is Beechey's explanation of the characteristics of women's employment, which argues that it is the relationship between the family and the

2. As Norma Chincilla noted in her study of Guatemalan industrialization:

> It gives an incomplete understanding to study occupational structures or industrial growth independently of an international context of investment, production and control. . . . The fate of women, the way they carry out their daily tasks and the view of the world they derive from these experiences depends . . . not so much on the policies of their governments, or the enlightenment of the men around them, as on the function that the economy of which they are a part serves in the world system. (1977: 39)

The implication here is that the experience of women is merely a dependent variable, derivative of the macro-economic system, and the writer gives greater priority to the impact of monopoly capitalism than to the interaction between capitalism and forms of patriarchy. Despite the functionalism of this approach it nevertheless underlines the necessity of developing a conceptual framework which encompasses the national and international economic context within which women's productive activities are located (Ifeka-Moller 1975; Pala 1977; Remy 1975) and it is this issue which will be taken up here. The question of the autonomy of patriarchy versus the historical and cultural specificity of gender subordination remains a central theme for feminists (Beechey 1979). Less attention has, however, been given to the North–South dimension of forms of capitalist oppression, the problem which has polarized the international feminist movement.

productive system that accounts for the conditions of female participation (Beechey 1977). Her paper is part of the wider body of feminist literature which has sought an explanation for gender role ideology in terms of the historical changes in the economic function of the household within capitalist production. Beechey locates the explanation for women's low wages outside the labour process itself, within the economic exchanges of the household. Thus her basis for an analysis of the position of women under capitalism is the separation of the family from the means of production in the course of capitalist accumulation. She maintains, however, that this disjunction is largely illusory, in that the family appears separated but is 'actually only divorced from the labour process'. The central task, as she sees it, is therefore to analyse the relationship between the family and organization of production as capitalist accumulation develops.

This useful point is somewhat undermined by a rather mechanistic connection between the household and the productive process. Drawing a direct analogy between 'married women workers' and the semi-proletarianized migrant labourers on the periphery, she argues that both can be paid below the value of labour power because of the secondary nature of their wage and the availability of subsidies external to their own wage relationship.

Beechey thus bases her analysis on a specific form of the family, in which the household consists of a woman married to a man who is earning the primary wage. Men are bread-winners and women are dependants.[3] It is evident from her account that she sees this not merely as an ideal model of family roles but as a statement of fact. Only at one point does she use the words 'on the assumption that'; the precise form of words chosen in the rest of her paper suggest that she believes that it is because all women workers *are* members of households with male bread-winners that women can be paid below the value of labour power.[4] Her explanation therefore rests on empirical reality, not on the existence of ideological mystification.

At one point in her paper she counters the obvious criticism that her theory deals inadequately with single women. Here she argues that they are dependent in exactly the same way as married women on their families of origin. In other words, that daughters are dependent on fathers. Again this is presented as a statement of fact and exceptions (women without husbands or families of origin to subsidize their costs, living in households that are not formed around kinship or marriage) are seen only to prove the rule, in that they are unable to cover the costs of their own reproduction adequately and, as she puts it, 'are depressed into poverty' – a generalization that implies that poverty is somehow an aberration from the normal workings of the capitalist system.

3. For example, Beechey writes of women workers:

> It is their dependence on male wages within the family for part of the cost of the production and reproduction of labour power which accounts for the possibility of individual capitalists paying wages which are below the value of labour power. The married woman does not therefore have to pay for the entire cost of reproducing her labour power or for that of her children who will become the next generation of wage labourers and domestic labourers.

4. In a later article (1983) Beechey substantially modifies her argument, emphasizing the importance of the construction of gender divisions within the production process itself. Unfortunately this was not available at the time of writing this chapter.

There are thus several problems with this kind of approach. First, if the terms 'female labour' and 'married women's labour' are conflated and confused, it becomes difficult to apply the model to an analysis of specific categories of women. Beechey writes as if she assumes that female wage earners actually are married to male bread-winners. Those who are not are merely an exception to the underlying logic of her argument. The labour process is not only gender specific but is also often marital-status specific, a fact that Beechey's hypothesis cannot explain.

Second, whether married or single, the model assumes women's dependency on a male wage. Several recent articles have questioned the validity of this as a generalization based on statistical evidence of household income sources. While it appears that in terms of national averages, for example, women in the UK contribute a smaller proportion of total household income than men do,[5] one could equally well argue that this was the result rather than the cause of women's low pay. More significantly for Beechey's argument, however, is the fact that it is clear that even if women do not cover the entire costs of their reproduction nor do many low-income earning men. In the Third World, the wage has never been a 'family wage' and the abundant supply of labour has always undercut the value of labour power. What exactly does 'dependent' mean in terms of percentages? The man who is dependent on a wife to provide one-third of total household costs is rather less dependent than the wife who is dependent on the husband's contribution of two-thirds of those costs, but her income may nonetheless be crucial. Quantitive measures are not at issue, however. The point is that it is tautological to argue that women are economically advantageous to capitalism because they are economically dependent, while at the same time they are economically dependent because they are low paid. Low pay for men has not been analysed in this way. The 'presumed' dependence of women and their ideological construction as 'housewives' (Mies 1980) may be extremely significant but this is a different issue.

Third, Beechey makes the important point that 'the existence of the family must be presupposed if Marx's implicit arguments about the advantages of female wage labour are to constitute a satisfactory explanation'. However, she then goes on to presuppose not only the *form* of the family, which she treats unproblematically as a constant, but also the nature of the distribution of income within it.[6] The end result of her own account is an analysis in which changing forms of the family, the experience of other ethnic groups, and the changing relationship between households and the productive process cannot be explained.

A somewhat different approach is offered in Barrett and McIntosh's discussion of the family wage (1980). They are concerned with 'a description of the means by which the reproduction of the working class has in fact been accomplished'. Unlike Beechey, they emphasize that the notion of the male chief bread-winner is ideological. It has been an expectation or a moral prescription emanating from the social construction of women's subordinate role and reproductive obligations

5. In 1980 this was at least 25 per cent, or for the USA a decade earlier, 36.8 per cent, if a woman worked full time all year, according to Rowntree and Rowntree (1970).

6. This is somewhat surprising, since Beechey explicitly states that it is important to transcend an approach such as that offered by Engels, in which the family form is presumed to change as a mechanical result of changes in the organization of production.

rather than a reality, since many working class households have always covered the costs of their reproduction from multiple sources. They see the *idea* of the family wage as the *outcome* of a historical process in which male predominance in the labour process is a distinctive feature of the development of British capitalism, and they link this with the need for better conditions of reproduction for the working class. They stress that this was both an aspect of working class struggle and congruent with the needs of capitalism. On this point, their conclusions about the *source* of the idea of the family wage are somewhat contradictory. Was it the result of the logic of capitalist development or the outcome of working class struggles? If both, what was the precise relationship between them?[7] The strength of Barrett and McIntosh's article is their discussion of the evolution of the notion of the male bread-winner as an aspect of labour history, and their account of the complex play of interests involved in the emergence of the family wage as ideology. Ultimately, however, such explanations are teleological, since the basic supposition is that 'Women's wage-labour can be explained through its economic advantages (to capitalism) and it is these economic advantages that structure the forms of that labour' (Anthias 1980: 51). By treating capital as a homogeneous category, one must logically suppose that the costs of the male wage are met within the same system; therefore no real reduction of costs to collective capital can be made. Beechey's direct analogy with migrant labour is not a valid one, since implicit in that argument is the existence of a pre-capitalist or non-capitalist mode of production. Since she had explicitly stated that the separation of the family from the production process is more apparent then real, she cannot argue for a domestic mode of production that is analytically separable from the capitalist system.

In summary, Beechey argues that women are paid low wages because they are enmeshed in a family structure in which they are dependants. Therefore, the value of their labour power actually *is* less, because the costs of their reproduction *are* less, being partially met through male wages. The wages of all women are assumed to be covered by this general formulation, since all women are regarded as economically dependent on a male, whether husband or father. Barrett and McIntosh, however, emphasize that there may be no necessary congruence between the 'expectation' of women's economic dependence as ideology and the reality of income distribution. They nevertheless remain ambiguous as to the sources of this ideology. Thus, a somewhat inconsistent account of women's waged work emerges from these two papers. On the one hand, the 'needs' of capitalism are served by cheap female labour, on the other they are served by paying men enough to keep women at home. To say that capitalism will attempt to pursue the most profitable labour strategy is a *post hoc* argument that cannot explain why certain categories of worker should be more exploitable than others at

7. Barrett and McIntosh (1980: 56) conclude:

> Certainly it was a demand that found support mainly among bourgeois reformers and the upper strata of male workers. On the other hand, the bitter opposition of many employers to the factory legislation and even more to its implementation suggests that individual capitalist did not favour the exclusion of women from the factories. Yet it seems clear that the collective interests of capital as a whole, as eventually articulated in state policy, lay in establishing the principle if not the practice of the male bread-winner.

particular times or why particular combinations of domestic and/or factory production should be optimal at any given moment. Ideological forces and the requirements of political control are also important in this contradictory process in which the family both shapes and is shaped by the process of accumulation (Stolcke 1981).

## FORMS OF INCORPORATION AND THE VALUE OF LABOUR POWER

Capitalism is not only interested in labour power as an abstract commodity. It is interested in cheap labour. However, there are various ways in which production may be related to reproduction to obtain this. In some contexts, male migrant labour that retains a foothold in some rural area may be drawn on; in others, whole families labour under a male contract; in others, female, part-time or homeworking labour will be incorporated. As yet, we know little about the determinants of these patterns.

Thus, the concrete manifestations of capitalism and patriarchy give rise to diverse outcomes which are the results of a series of interactions between economic forms and between ideological representations and productive systems. While many of the characteristics of female labour, such as labour intensity, low productivity, 'ghettoization' in specific sectors of production and differential wage rates, appear to be widespread, the explanations of these patterns developed in a European context do not necessarily hold good for peripheral capitalist economies where the capitalist transition and the nature of women's economic participation takes different forms.

As we have seen, functionalist explanations relating the nature of women's labour to the needs of capitalism have been prevalent in these debates. They provide conflicting accounts which are difficult to reconcile with cultural or historical variations in women's economic roles. There has been a tendency to draw generalizations about the relationship of gender to capitalism on the basis of an experience which should be seen as historically specific. The articulation of capitalism with the sexual division of labour cannot be assumed to be uniform, but is a matter for concrete investigation. As Deere has pointed out:

> To the extent that capitalist expansion engenders a process of underdevelopment in the periphery, the economic participation of women in the Third World differs significantly from women's economic participation within the centre of the world capitalist system.
>
> On the one hand, capitalist development in centre economies has required greater labour force participation, while, on the other, capitalist expansion in the periphery has often intensified women's economic participation in non-capitalist modes of production, particularly in rural areas where women's work is geared to subsistence agricultural production and petty commodity production and circulation. (1976: 9)

It is precisely because the concepts of housework and waged-work have often been treated as universals and applied uncritically across time and space that the 'problem' for women in the non-Western world was initially defined as one of *lack* of integration in development. Because women commonly work as unpaid family labour, the economic significance of their role in food-crop production was often ignored, rendering women and their activities invisible (Boserup 1970).

Several writers have subsequently criticized the 'integrationist' position, documenting the wide range of economic activities, both remunerated and unremunerated, performed by women, whether as unpaid family-subsistence producers, agricultural wage labourers, independent artisan producers, subcontracted homeworkers, petty-commodity producers, or small traders in the informal sector. They have noted the inadequacy of a simple dichotomy between wage-labourers and the self-employed in peripheral economies (MacEwan Scott 1979). These studies have made clear that women are already fully integrated into the economy, whether as domestic or extradomestic labour, and have emphasized that the problem lies rather in the exploitative nature of their integration (Roberts 1979).

Clearly, considerable variation exists in the forms of women's participation, even among countries at a similar level of economic development, and there are substantial differences in the response of the female labour force to this process (Youssef 1974). The class-based nature of this response has been noted in several ethnographies (Stoler 1977; Young 1978). Benería and Sen (1981) have also drawn attention to the inaccuracy apparent in Boserup's original characterization of Africa and India as female and male farming systems respectively, pointing to the crucial significance of landless women wage labourers in Indian agriculture and stressing the relevance of major underlying differences between the two continents historically in terms of social stratification, access to land and relations of production.

While giving full recognition to this diversity, three points can nevertheless be stressed in the comparison between the Western European experience and that of currently developing countries.

First, the wage sector absorbs fewer people and pays them less for comparable tasks in peripheral as opposed to core economies. Thus, full employment and a family wage have never been options for more than a minority of the labour force and women's contribution, through both waged and unwaged work, has always been crucial for the reproduction of the family.

Second, because of the smaller proportion that formal wage employment represents in the overall economy, we cannot assume that the relationship of the family to the means of production is necessarily the same as that which obtained during the expansion of capitalism in Europe, since the continuance of subsistence production and the production of use values assumes greater importance. Countries like Bangladesh, for example, remain largely subsistence economies, in which 73 per cent of the consumption of rural people is made up of food and 14 per cent is taken up by housing (Abdullah and Zeidenstein 1981).[8] Post-harvest food processing, the boundary beyond which statistical measurement virtually ceases, is an area of crucial economic importance and a central aspect of women's activity. Merely to render some foodstuffs edible can take as much as four times as long as the time expended in their cultivation (Abdullah and Zeidenstein 1981). Given the division into male semi-proletarians and female subsistence producers that has been identified for some regions (Deere 1976), it may not be helpful to

8. The sharp rise in landless labourers has nevertheless meant that increasing numbers of rural peasants cannot produce their own subsistence and are forced to buy in food.

consider the family as a unit in its relationship to the means of production. Differentiation by gender within it may be of greater importance.

We must also consider family structure itself. Female-headed households are now estimated to represent between one-quarter and one-third of all households world-wide, and in Latin America and the Caribbean the trend is particularly marked. It is statistically very difficult to document the difference between 'stable' and 'unstable' consensual unions. What has merged from recent microstudies, however, is the importance of the pattern in which the stable unit is the matrifocal household of women and children, in which male partners come and go (Phizaclea 1981). The explanation offered for this is precisely the reverse of that suggested by the British case, since it is argued that this is an economic strategy that is adaptive to highly unstable employment opportunities for men and women, when labour market conditions as a whole preclude the existence of male bread-winners. Under such circumstances, it has been argued that women can sometimes 'make out' better on scarce resources on their own (Stack 1974).

Third, within the overall population redistribution that is a crucial feature of many developing economies, sex-specific migration is of continuing importance. In some areas males are selected, leaving women responsible for the provision of daily subsistence, as they have always been in many parts of Africa for instance, but also leaving them with cash-crop responsibilities and the need to generate income for other necessities (Hanger and Moris 1973). In other areas, such as Latin America, female migration remains significant. Young (1978) documents this clearly for the Mexican state of Oaxaca, where migration was also highly age specific, and where sex and age-specific outmigration had wide local ramifications in terms of the reduction of unpaid family and domestic labour:

> Girls were the principal victims of population redistribution: in the 1940s, 50s and 60s never less than 40 per cent of female migrants between ten and twenty-nine were under twenty years of age, the majority were under fifteen and had neither completed their schooling nor gained any specific skills . . . only 28 per cent of male migrants between ten and twenty-nine were under twenty years of age. (p. 142)

This pattern is reflected also in the age structure of the female work-force. In most Latin American countries, for example, peak activity in the non-agricultural labour force occurs between twenty and twenty-five years old, and as Youssef (1974) has pointed out: 'The propelling factor in the growth of the female labour force came in the form of an influx of single women into the labour market.'

We should note, too, that the limited development of the internal market in most developing economies and the corresponding lack of commoditization means that the woman's role as consumption agent is much less significant than in the central economies.[9] In rural areas of developing countries where there are

9. This role has been described thus by Galbraith:

> Without women to administer it, the possibility of increasing consumption would be sharply circumscribed. With women assuming the tasks of administration, consumption can be more or less indefinitely increased. In very high income households, this administration becomes an onerous task. But even here expansion is still possible: at those income levels women tend to be better educated and better administrators. And the greater availability of divorce allows a measure of trial and error to obtain the best [*sic*]. Thus it is women in their crypto-servant role of administrators who make an indefinitely increasing consumption possible. As matters now stand . . . it is their supreme contribution to the modern economy. (1974: 34)

fewer commodities to 'administer', the physical fabric of the dwelling, or the lack of it, allows for little fetishism. The domestication of women around commodity management is less pronounced, even though it may permeate as ideology or status marker. Housework in this sense of the term occupies less time; however, the production and transformation of primary subsistence and the acquisition of basic resources (water, fuel, etc.) remains paramount and occupies considerable amounts of time (as much as sixteen hours daily in some cases). The generation of additional cash to buy in food that is no longer produced locally is also increasingly important in many areas.

Lastly, the process of proletarianization takes different forms for men and for women, and one of the outcomes frequently commented on for women has been increasing conflict between their productive and reproductive roles. Young's account of the changing sexual division of labour in Oaxaca, for example, describes a process in which the introduction of coffee as a cash crop, a consequent narrowing of other economic opportunities and the resulting out-migration, lead to a decline in inter-family labour exchange and in increased emphasis on the fertility of the individual family, reflected in higher birth rates. Young stresses that women from each stratum of local society were differently circumscribed by the customary division of labour and that the impact of capitalism on them is cross-cut by their class position. However, she sees a basic contradiction between their insertion in the labour force and the cultural norms that constitute their subordination. Since each married couple is now more dependent on producing the labour it needs, women's reproductive role is reinforced, thus creating a basic contradiction between the women's need to produce labour and to sell labour. Poor households are dependent for their survival on women's labour, which means, she argues, that they are less dependent on their husbands economically. However, as she points out: 'the cultural prescription that a woman's place is in the home ensures that those who have to work outside it derive no social benefit from it' (p. 151). Thus, in this account, women's low pay derives not from economic dependence, since they are vital both to the reproduction and maintenance of labour, but from their 'specialization in reproduction' or the expectations surrounding it. She concludes: 'Their labour can thus be devalued both because of their "real" role, and because this role itself places constraints on the type of work they can undertake' (p. 153).

It is interesting to compare this account with Stolcke's (1981) discussion of coffee cultivation in Brazil in which changing labour needs lead to an increasing emphasis on a matrifocal household unit. Although in some cases urban industrialization may have tended to reinforce the nuclear-family pattern, in others it has encouraged the proliferation of a wider range of kin ties. The spread of capitalism into the periphery has also led to the break-up of the traditional family as the location for reproduction. Mies (1981) states: 'Often the men find it difficult to make enough money to send to their wives in the village. Therefore, the women, often without any means of production, turn to begging, to prostitution, or to employment for less than the minimum wage. In any case, they become the main bread-winners of the broken family' (p. 10).

As Chen and Guznavi (1979) found in their account of 'Food for work' programmes in Bangladesh, rural, male unemployment, out-migration and increasing landlessness have reduced many female-headed households, particularly those of widows, to destitution. Many women are forced by economic necessity to forgo social acceptability and contravene cultural norms of female seclusion entirely in order to survive.

Thus, class and sexual polarization intersect, and a contradictory pattern may emerge in which the upper strata of rural women may become domesticated and removed from agricultural production altogether. At the same time many small peasant households become increasingly indebted, lose their land and are forced to seek wage employment which may often take them out of the rural economy entirely. Women from the poorest strata may thus be forced to seek gang work on construction projects and public-works schemes and, far from becoming domesticated, become literally 'defeminized', in the sense that in order to exist they must often abandon the norms around which their sexuality was constructed. Whatever the nature of these norms may be, relinquishing them under circumstances in which they remain the dominant model merely reinforces their exclusion.

It is evident, then, that the differing paths of transition to capitalism give rise to varying forms of relationship between the family and the productive system, and that these themselves are influenced by the precise configuration of the local labour market and its insertion in the national and international economy.[10]

## PATTERNS OF ACCUMULATION AND THE SEXUAL DIVISION OF LABOUR

The relationship between the international and sexual division of labour has so far been approached through the interesting but limited case of the so-called world market factories, the multinational assembly operations established within free trade zones in several newly industrializing countries, such as Mexico and Malaysia, which draw heavily on cheap female labour (Cardosa-Khoo and Khoo 1978; Fernandez-Kelly 1978; Heyzer 1981; Lim 1978; Pearson and Elson 1981). This case has attracted attention as a 'new' type of wage employment for women,

10. This micro-level data can be statistically supported, for some areas. In India, for instance, a drop has been noted in the female participation rate in all categories of employment except transport (Mitra 1977). Between 1911 and 1971 the ratio of women to men in the work force declined from 525 per 1000 males to 210 per 1000 males. Between 1951 and 1971 the number of women workers in agriculture declined from 31 to 25 million. The total number of female workers suffered a decline of 12 per cent, while male workers increased by 27 per cent (Indian Council of Social Science Research):

> Whereas the number of female cultivators dropped by 52 per cent, the number of male cultivators increased by 6 per cent. This is a clear indication of the fact that women are losing control over land as a means of production, i.e. they are gradually becoming pauperized. Similarly, the female agricultural workers increased by 43 per cent, whereas the male agricultural workers increased by more than double that rate to 88 per cent; women are also not becoming proletarianized at the same rate as men. (Mies 1980: 4)

In Latin America, on the other hand, the trend is different, and rates of labour-force participation are increasing more rapidly for women than for men. Although statistical measures of women's work are among the most unreliable data yet collected (Benería 1979), they do indicate broad regional differences in the incorporation of the female labour force, and in the balance between unpaid, unenumerated family labour and some form of wage-labour.

in which the connections between the internationalization of capital and the employment of a gender-specific labour force are particularly clear. Pearson and Elson (1981) point out that although the capitalist labour process is not gender ascriptive, it is the bearer of gender, and women enter with a predefined status as inferior bearers of labour. Thus, while employment may offer them certain advantages, it does not necessarily provide a challenge to traditional patterns of authority and can 'intensify', 'decompose' and 'recompose' existing forms of subordination.

The focus of their valuable study is on the 'need to evaluate world market factories from the point of view of the new possibilities and new problems which they raise for the women who work in them'. In doing this they provide an important counterbalance to earlier accounts which had concentrated on the structural determinants of production (Fröbel et al. 1980). In emphasizing the experiential aspects, however, it is important not to lose sight of the fact that this new process is new chiefly for its visibility, for the fact that it is characterized by the mobility of capital rather than labour, and for the physical relocation of parts of the production process, made possible by the combined effects of communications technology, deskilling and fragmentation (Braverman 1974). However, the significance of cheap female labour for international patterns of accumulation is not new, as Safa (1981) has shown in her historical account of labour intensive industries in the USA. Nor is it confined to the wage-labour relationship alone. It is merely the latest stage in a constant search for cheap labour, each of which has drawn on a different type of female labour; in the case Safa describes this has been rural, migrant and non-Western in turn.

Bridging the conceptual gap between the international and the 'domestic' economy is a difficult task. However, some recent steps have been taken towards this (Deere and de Janvry 1978; Meillassoux 1981; Portes 1978). Portes, for instance, has argued in the context of the informal economy debate that the apparently micro-level relationships which characterize it are fundamental to the understanding of the operations of capitalism as a world system, and provide the 'missing element' in current models of the relationship between core and peripheral economies. He too suggests that the informal economy is more than 'an exercise in self-preservation' but is a basic element in maintaining the disparities between core and peripheral wages, stemming the falling rate of profit and preventing downturns in core economies, through its ability to provide cheap goods to a low-paid work-force.

As we have seen, 'informal economy' is a gender-neutral term which covers the work of both sexes but which conceals an internal sexual division of labour (Moser 1980). Women's subsistence and petty commodity production form important elements of these activities and, as Moser points out, men and women occupy different economic 'spaces' in which their work is interdependent. Similar arguments have been put forward about the continuing role of 'subsistence agriculture', also used in a gender-neutral sense. It is clear that fully proletarianized wage labour is not the only link that can be established between women's work and the evolution of the international economy; various aspects of self-provisioning and domestic labour, i.e. subsistence reproduction, can also be seen in this light.

There is now a large literature, both empirical and theoretical, on the penetration of capital in developing economies. This has given rise to two different accounts, which identify different roles and outcomes for women. The first, which might be called the 'subsidy thesis', stresses the role of subsistence reproduction in the general process of accumulation. It argues the necessity for the continued re-creation of pre-capitalist modes of production, following Rosa Luxemburg's interpretation of the need for ongoing primitive accumulation for the extraction of surplus labour and surplus product:

> In the central economy the freeing of labour serves a double purpose: it lowers the cost of labour by giving to the employer flexibility in hiring and firing, and simultaneously it increases the size of the market. It implies the destruction of the subsistence economies, and complete proletarianization of the workers. In the periphery the cost of labour is also reduced through its freeing, but there is no rationality of market expansion though proletarianization. Hence, wherever possible, as in agriculture, the subsistence economies will be maintained. This will permit further lowering of labour costs since it allows for the indirect exploitation of family labour occupied in the production of use values and petty commodities that cover part of the subsistence of the workers. (de Janvry and Garramon 1977: 210)

In many accounts 'family', 'household' and 'domestic' are synonyms for female and child labour. As de Janvry writes: 'Surplus value is increased . . . by collapsing the price of agricultural labour by an amount equal to the production of use values by the worker's family in the subsistence plot. In this way subsistence agriculture supplies cheap labour to commercial agriculture which in turn supplies cheap food to the urban sector where it sustains low wages.' The subsidy hypothesis has been influential both in the debate about the nature of capitalist transition itself and, as we have seen, in explanations of women's work in advanced and in peripheral capitalism. The concept of domestic economy has often been used as a generalizable category applicable to both. Yet the economic content of women's roles is very different, and the production of subsistence or the transformation of commodities implies a different relationship with the capitalist system.

The precise nature of the linkages that are thought to exist between households, domestic economies, pre-capitalist forms and capitalism proper is therefore far from clear. These forms predate capitalism, implying that they have a certain autonomy, yet they cannot be seen as entirely distinct modes of production. To the extent that capitalism penetrates a particular region, they become 'subsumed', yet they are not 'directly' integrated in that the relations that obtain within them are different from capitalist labour relations.

The terms of these relationships are themselves influenced by the coexistence of capitalist relations and the exchanges that are established between them. These exchanges are themselves seen as unequal, with capitalist relations comprising the 'structure in dominance' to which other relationships are subservient. However, the form of this articulation and the exchanges involved have recently been the subject of much debate (Banaji 1977; de Janvry and Garramon 1977; Vergopoulos 1978). While it is argued that capitalist enterprises in the periphery shift replacement and welfare costs of their work-force onto the subsistence sector, it has also been suggested that remittances from migrant workers are crucial in the continuance of some subsistence economies (Arizpe 1982;

Bustamante 1979). To take the case of Mexico, for example, migrants to the US are said to provide remittances of between three and four billion dollars annually, and it has been estimated that as many as 21 per cent of Mexican households, particularly in rural areas, may be partially supported by migrant incomes. A simple one-way model of subsidies from one to the other thus seems hardly adequate to describe the complexities of the transfers that occur.

While proponents of the subsidy thesis have provided a theoretical model to explain the persistence of subsistence production and the role of the domestic economy, other writers have provided empirical accounts of local conditions of change which stress the *decline* in women's economic roles, their loss of control of productive activities and/or the decline in the economic importance of those activities (Boserup 1970). Several studies have documented the way in which the development of export-oriented crops undermines domestic production, stimulates the cultivation of a limited product mix dominated by male labour and restructures local economies, creating increased differentiation along both class and sex lines (Benería 1979; Hanger and Moris 1973; Loutfi 1980; Mies 1980; Palmer 1977; Rogers 1980). The principal outcome of this process is seen as the decline in overall importance of women's handicraft and subsistence production, and increasing reliance on income from wage labour. The precise mechanics of this 'simple reproduction squeeze', as Bernstein (1979) has called it, are complex, but common elements reported for a number of cases can be identified. These include:

1 increasing commitment of labour *time* to cash crops, especially in traditionally female work such as weeding (this is particularly acute in the case of high yielding 'green revolution' varieties which allow multiple cropping and thus greatly increase women's already heavy work burden, allowing less time for subsistence production);
2 expansion of cash crops into land formerly used for food crops;
3 relegation of food crop land to less fertile areas;
4 increasing distance of food crop land from dwelling;
5 absolute loss of household plot due to indebtedness, expropriation or resettlement;
6 control by men of new technologies and agricultural inputs (through their greater access to credit and information, and the assumption by extension agencies that household heads are males, and that males are the principal cultivators);
7 control by men of new sources of income;
8 alienation of women from their customary land rights, through land registration or land reform policies which recognize males only as family heads;
9 increasing need for cash to buy food no longer produced domestically, competing needs for available income and possible decline in family nutritional standards and women's control over resources.

In this model the squeeze occurs both in women's available labour time and in their resource base, and it is argued that cash incomes remain inadequate to counterbalance this tendency. Moreover, not only do women lose food-production capacity but they often lose previous income sources of their own. Examples of this have been noted in the technological impact on women's food processing. Case studies have shown that rice huskers, tortilla machines, mechanized looms, sago processors and grinding mills of various kinds have often been introduced and taken over by men to the detriment of women. Women's loss of control over distributional systems has also been documented, e.g. where increased scale ousts the smaller traders (Dixon 1978; Mies 1980), where capitalist marketing penetrates indigenous market systems (Mies 1980; Young 1978); or where new organizational forms, such as co-operatives, are introduced as intermediaries.

It is important to stress that though many writers have talked about the increasing limitations on economic access for women, in the sense that the subsistence economy becomes increasingly marginalized or even disintegrates, it does not follow that women then become economically inactive, as is sometimes implied. As we have seen, a sharp distinction between the subsistence and wage-earning sectors is largely inaccurate and women may be pushed into an intermediate position in which their subsistence base is reduced but their ability to earn income is fragmentary and intermittent. Often they are seasonal and part-time workers, sometimes contracted through male household members as auxiliaries, and they frequently build up meagre incomes from multiple sources that remain unrecorded.

Can we reconcile the contradictions of these two positions, both of which have been put forward as generalizable processes or universal theoretical models of the relationship between capitalist development and the sexual division of labour? The available empirical evidence suggests that both patterns occur under different circumstances. If this is the case, however, the theoretical logic of necessity in the subsidy model is severely weakened.

Proponents of the 'necessity' view in discussions of the family wage similarly argued that the 'requirement of reproduction of the working class' made a family wage essential. It has not proved essential in the Third World, and the continuing 'super-exploitation' of women and children has been central to the development process (Leacock 1981). As we have seen, supporters of the exclusion thesis would argue that the ability to produce subsistence is under threat in many areas. As Sen (1981) has shown in his study of the Bangladesh, Sahel and Ethiopian famines, natural resource crises played a much smaller part in mass starvation than failures of purchasing power to buy in high-priced foodstuffs that could not be produced by landless labourers. Sometimes this is a problem of landlessness *per se* but frequently it is gender related, in that men become semi-proletarianized while women's subsistence base is eroded.

Clearly, these variations reflect specific regional patterns. Deere (1976), for example, drawing on Columbian material, argues that male semi-proletarianization at low wages is facilitated by the *continuance of* the female subsistence base. Hanger and Moris (1973), however, in their account of the Mwea rice scheme in Kenya, have argued that the introduction of rice as a cash crop, coupled with the resettlement of a peasant population, reduced the land available for subsistence and introduced time constraints that made it impossible for women to produce enough food for family consumption. Males were increasingly pulled into wage labour elsewhere but cash incomes were too low to buy in enough staple foodstuffs or fuel. Nutritional levels reportedly declined dramatically and family poverty increased. Thus the conditions which in nineteenth century England gave rise to a family wage ideology and the domestication of women are being repeated in the periphery, but given the different nature of the capitalist transition, a frequent outcome is inequality of distribution between classes and genders and increasing pauperization. It is clear that contradictory patterns are found between regions, suggesting once again the dangers of regarding 'the penetration of capitalism' as a homogeneous process or assuming that the response to it will be everywhere the same.

## REPRODUCTION AND DOMESTIC PRACTICES

The concept of the costs of reproduction has been central to the attempt to explain sexual inequality in the economy. Many Marxists and Marxist feminists have used the concept in its broadest sense in order to develop a theoretical account of the relationship between the family/household and the wider society, which does not necessarily prejudice the notion of the family as a locus of contradiction and which is based on process rather than on bounded units of analysis. Yet reproduction has also proved to be an elusive and confusing notion.

Harris and Young (1981) suggest that reproduction is a concept which allows for the discussion of the complex variety of relationships between the genders. They go on to indicate three separate levels of analysis at which the concept operates, usefully breaking down its unitary nature and showing that it encompasses several processes, which may even be in conflict. As in their previous articles, they are justly critical of the use of the term 'women' as a universal category. They reject a simplistic association of reproduction with women, and emphasize the significance of their productive roles. Nonetheless, at each level of their analysis they see reproduction 'as the field within which women's positioning is defined', suggesting that they should, in fact, be equated. They are also concerned throughout to specify the relationship between women and various aspects of reproduction in which they 'occupy clearly defined and significant positions'. For social reproduction, for example, they ask how crucial certain forms of control over women's reproductive powers are for the creation of the conditions of existence for production and the reproduction of the system. For the reproduction of labour, they are concerned to demonstrate the connections between women and various aspects of the process, such as allocation to specific class positions, ideology, early socialization and material reproduction (daily care and maintenance). For human, or biological, reproduction they are interested in how different patterns of fertility give males greater or lesser power over women. Thus, on the one hand, they oppose unitary notions of reproduction and support substantivist positions, arguing throughout for the specificity of pre-capitalist modes of production. On the other, despite initial disavowal, their paper is devoted to showing aspects of the connection between women and reproduction. They conclude by suggesting that the need to control women's generative powers is a universal feature that overrides differences, not because the needs of reproduction are unchanging but 'precisely because of differences over time in the requirements of human groups *vis-á-vis* biological reproduction'.

The link between the control of women's reproductive capacities, including their capacity to reproduce labour (which is sociologically rather than biologically given), and their subordination by means of marriage exchange, regulation of sexuality, limitation of access to resources, etc., has been debated in a variety of forms. However, of itself 'control' tells us very little about the gender relations that result. Harris and Young, in contrast to Engels for example, phrase the problem in terms of the 'requirements of human groups' rather than the requirements of individual property-owning males. The difference is surely important, for the perennial question is, of course, why women are not controlling their own reproductive powers, exchanging men in marriage, regulating male sexuality, etc. As some anthropological accounts of women's alternative power have suggested, in some contexts perhaps they are. As far as the eventual outcomes for women are concerned it is the *forms* of control which are crucial. In a society such as the Trobriands, so compellingly described by Annette Weiner, where women's reproductive powers are fundamental to positive evaluations of their selfhood and to the regeneration of society as a whole, we get a very different reading of the consequences of group requirements, one which is far removed from suggestions of passivity and oppression (Weiner 1979). On this point, Deere and Léon de Leal (1982) are surely correct to argue that women's role in reproduction cannot fully explain the sexual division of labour since the former is relatively constant, while the latter is very varied.

Harris and Young leave till last the question of the relationship between production and reproduction and the degree of autonomy of the latter. They note that various feminists have posited a separate set of structures for the social relations of human reproduction and they find this separation of production and reproduction appealing. They regard as too simplistic the orthodox Marxist approach that sees them as a single system with the mode of production determinant in the last instance (Gimenez 1977). Certainly it is possible to find similar modes of production in which gender relations are significantly different. Though how we assess 'difference' and 'similarity' is not always very clear, and there are obvious difficulties in establishing criteria by which the gender relations of societies could be ranked on some sort of a sliding scale. Young's own work, cited earlier, does however suggest that even if there is no absolute functional fit or strong line of determinancy, the sexual division of labour, domestic practices and reproductive strategies do indeed vary significantly with changing relations of production.

A final problem lies in the conceptualization of change and the definition of what is necessary for a system to continue to exist in a defined form. Various authors have criticized the concept of reproduction for implying that a given mode of production exists to reproduce itself and can, of itself, assure the conditions of its own existence. They have argued that the conditions of existence for social formations, such as that described by Meillassoux for instance, lie beyond their own boundaries, a fact that must be central to any theory of imperialism. Reproduction is commonly held to entail the 'adequate' provision of the material means of survival, but how is adequacy to be defined? It is not only a question of culturally specific requirements, as defined by Marx. Inequalities in adequacy are fundamental to stratified societies, and any model of reproduction must be able to capture the dynamics of unequal entitlements in which some groups are perpetually reproduced less adequately than others. The central issue in the analysis of the penetration of capitalism and its effects on social groups must be the differential levels of reproduction that are created in the process. Levels and styles of reproduction are the markers of class, and to blanket them all by the assumption of some absolute standard of need is to confuse the issue.

In general, then, it seems hard to escape a return to dualism in these models. The difficulties of empirically separating production from reproduction are evident; they must be rooted in their material base, yet to see either one as determinate seems problematic. Rather they form a unity in which the possibilities for contradiction and some degree of autonomy for the relations of reproduction must be included. Nor can we automatically correlate them with gender differences, although the reproduction of labour on a daily basis and over time is characteristically women's work in a wide variety of contexts. We have widespread evidence of the descriptive fact that women are particularly associated with a set of processes that we label 'reproductive', over-represented in the informal sector, yet not exclusive to it, and exhibit certain characteristics in relation to the valorization of their labour. However, regularities are not the same as explanations and it can be argued that the difficulties outlined above suggest that we are posing the question in the wrong way. It may be more fruitful to see a totality in which each is enmeshed in the other, to see determination as lying in the process of interaction itself and to examine the relationship between the way systems are reproduced and the gender relations which constitute them.

Production and reproduction are a unity, but of an often contradictory rather than a functional kind. They are neither independent, determined nor determinate in any simple mechanical way. Nor is an explanation of one necessarily to be found in the other; rather their intersection shapes the form of the whole at any given time. Dualism and the concept of 'articulation' serves to reinforce the notion of separate spheres. The conditions for the reproduction of the household lie partly outside itself, and the reproduction of capitalism is premised upon unpaid domestic labour. Each is embedded in the other. Just as the reproduction of labour has seldom been guaranteed by the wage alone, so capitalist relations are 'engendered' (Harris and Young 1981) in that they are based on covert but crucial assumptions about gender and reproduction. Relations of appropriation are concealed by ideas about what is natural, biological or institutional, concealed behind the idea of a timeless domestic relationship. However, as Weiner (1979) points out: 'The system of reproduction is never in equilibrium, it is always in flux, in movement, containing points of limitation and points of possible expansion which demand continual attention.'

## CONCLUSION

Several strands of argument have been considered in this chapter. One has to do with structural changes in advanced industrial capitalism which lead to the reduction of employment and the increasing importance of forms of work based on other activities, usually considered 'non-economic'. The problems in defining these 'other' activities as 'non-capitalist' have been mentioned, but some way of handling their distinctiveness must still be preserved, while emphasizing their interdependence with capitalist relations proper. The terms 'household', 'domestic' and 'informal' present problems both because they tend to bound too firmly units which are themselves changing in response to the process of restructuring, and because they conceal internal sexual divisions and gender inequalities. As in wage relations, women tend to be clustered in the activities of lowest returns to labour and to predominate in labour-intensive areas of work. At a very general level, women's greater responsibility for the reproduction of basic subsistence can be identified as a common element. However, what it means to subsist in different socio-economic environments produces very different outcomes for women. Thinking about these economic processes in terms of types of activity is also misleading since the same task can have very different meanings when done by different sexes, and whether it is valorized or non-valorized, visible or invisible, esteemed or not esteemed, will depend as much on the sex of the performer as on the job itself and the relationship within which it is done. Thus the sexual and domestic divisions of labour do show an element of cross-cultural consistency but they also show important historical and cultural variations which need to be taken into account in the development of general theoretical explanations.

It proved difficult to apply explanations of these characteristics based on women's actual economic dependency to many non-Western settings, though the *ideology* of dependency and the secondary nature of women's 'non-reproductive' work remain a powerful influence. Functionalist accounts based on the needs of capitalism also left many things unexplained. Why should it be in the interests of capital to domesticate some women at some times or to proletarianize them at others, to pay some groups of workers a family wage or to rely at other times on the self-provisioning of women and children to make up deficiencies? The political power of groups of workers, the size of the relative surplus population, the nature of the subsistence base in terms of products and landholding, the type and extent of capitalist and/or multinational penetration, all have an important bearing on the patterns of reproductive and productive relations that develop.

At an international level the search for profitability can also have diverse outcomes. As Aranda and Arizpe (1981) put it, the 'comparative advantage' of women's 'disadvantage' is a powerful incentive: in many areas of developing countries, a deteriorating rural economic situation, increasing needs for income and high rates of male unemployment make available a young, cheap, female pool of labour which may be incorporated in various ways; or it may be excluded; or, yet again, included in invisible ways as when women are compelled to invest more time in specific tasks in cash-crop production, such as weeding, yet remain categorized as unpaid family labour.

The variety of these patterns make it hard to see the subsidy function as an adequate general explanation of the persistence or expansion of subsistence production. It cannot capture the complexities of the transfers taking place at different levels of the system, nor can it encompass the chronic erosion of the subsistence base that is occurring in many regions. As Mies argues, the process of accumulation appears to create an expanding mass of relative surplus population, which will never be absorbed into the formal wage-labour pool, who will remain structurally non-wage labourers and who are forced to produce their own survival in various forms.

## REFERENCES


Abdullah T. and Zeidenstein S. (1981) *Village Women of Bangladesh: Prospects for Change.* Pergamon Press, Oxford.

Ahmed Z. (1980) The plight of rural women: alternatives for action. *International Labour Review*, July–August.

Amsden A. (1980) *The Economics of Women and Work.* Penguin, Harmondsworth.

Anthias F. (1980) Women and the reserve army of labour: a critique of Veronica Beechey. *Capital and Class* 10, 50–63.

Aranda J. and Arizpe L. (1981) The 'comparative advantages' of women's disadvantages: women workers in the strawberry export agribusiness in Mexico. *Signs* 7(2), winter, 453–73.

Arizpe L. (1982) Relay migration in the survival of the peasant household. In Safa H. (ed.) *Towards a Political Economy of Urbanization in Third World Countries.* Oxford University Press, Delhi.

Banaji J. (1977) Modes of production in a materialist conception of history. *Capital and Class*, 3.

Barrett M. and McIntosh M. (1980) The 'family wage': some problems for socialists and feminists. *Capital and Class*, 11, 51–72.

Beechey V. (1977) Some notes on female wage labour in capitalist production. *Capital and Class* 3, 45–66.

Beechey V. (1978) Women and production: a critical analysis of some sociological theories of women's work. In Kuhn A. and Wolpe A. M. (eds) *Feminism and Materialism*, pp. 155–97, Routledge and Kegan Paul, London.

Beechey V. (1979) On patriarchy. *Feminist Review* 3, 66–82.

Beechey V. (1983) What's so special about women's employment? A review of some recent studies of women's paid work. *Feminist Review* 15, 23–45.

Benería L. (1979) Reproduction, production and the sexual division of labour. *Cambridge Journal of Economics*, 3, 203–25.

Benería L. and Sen G. (1981) Accumulation, reproduction and women's role in economic development. *Signs*, 7(2), 279–98.

Benholdt-Thomsen V. (1981) Subsistence production and extended reproduction. In Young, K., Wolkowitz, C. and McCullagh, R. (eds) *Of Marriage and the Market.* CSE, London.

Bernstein H. (1979) African peasantries: a theoretical framework. *Journal of Peasant Studies*, 6(4) 421–43.

Boserup E. (1970) *Woman's Role in Economic Development.* Allen and Unwin, London.

Bradby B. (1982) The remystification of value. *Capital and Class*, 17, summer, 114–33.

Braverman H. (1974) *Labor and Monopoly Capital.* Monthly Review Press, New York.

Bruegel I. (1979) Women as a reserve army of labour: a note on recent British experience. *Feminist Review*, 3, 12–23.

Bustamante J. (1979) Emigracion e inmovilidad. *Uno Mas Uno*, 14 May 1979.

Cardosa-Khoo J. and Khoo K. J. (1978) *Work and Consciousness: The Case of Electronics 'Runaways' in Malaysia.* Paper presented to the Conference on the Continuing Subordination of Women in the Development Process. IDS, University of Sussex, Brighton.

Chen, M. and Guznavi R., (1979) *Women in food-for-work: the Bangladesh experience.* World Food Programme, Rome.

Chincilla N.S. (1977) Industrialisation, monopoly capitalism and women's work in Guatemala. In Wellesley Editorial Committee (eds) *Women and National Development: The Complexities of Change.* University of Chicago Press, Chicago.

Deere C. D. (1976) Rural women's subsistence production in the capitalist periphery. *Review of Radical Political Economics*, 8(1), 9–17.

Deere C. D. and de Janvry A. (1978) A Theoretical Framework for the Empirical Analysis of Peasants. Working Paper no. 60, Giannini Foundation, University of California, Berkeley.

Deere C. D. and Léon de Leal M. (1982) Peasant production, proletarianization and the sexual division of labour in the Andes. In Benería L. (ed.) *Women and Development, the sexual division of labour in rural societies*. Praeger, New York.

de Janvry A. and Garramon C. (1977) The dynamics of rural poverty in Latin America. *Journal of Peasant Studies*, 4(3), 206–15.

Delphy C. (1977) *The Main Enemy*. Women's Research and Resources Centre, London.

Dixon R. (1978) *Rural Women at Work: Strategies for Development in South Asia*. Johns Hopkins University Press, Baltimore.

Fernandez-Kelly M. P. (1978) Mexican Border Industrialisation, Female Labour Force Participation and Development. Unpublished paper.

Fröbel F., Heinrichs J. and Kreye O. (1980) *The New International Division of Labour*, Cambridge University Press, Cambridge.

Galbraith J. K. (1974) *Economics and the public purpose*. Deutsch, London.

Gardiner J. (1975) Women's domestic labour. *New Left Review*, 89.

Gimenez M. (1977) Population and capitalism. *Latin America Perspectives*, iv, 4.

Hanger J. and Moris J. (1973) Women and the household economy. In Chambers R. and Moris J. (eds) *Mwea: an Irrigated Rice Settlement in Kenya*. Weltforum Verlag, Munich.

Harris O. and Young K. (1981) Engendered structures: some problems in the analysis of reproduction. In Kahn J. S. and Llobera J. (eds) *The Anthropology of Pre-capitalist Societies*, Macmillan, London.

Harrison J. (1973) The political economy of housework. *Bulletin of the Conference of Socialist Economists*.

Heyzer N. (1981) Towards a framework of analysis: women and the informal sector. *IDS Bulletin*, 12(3), 3–7.

Himmelweit S. and Mohun S. (1977) Domestic labour and capital. *Cambridge Journal of Economics*, 1, 15–31.

Ifeka-Moller C. (1975) Female militancy and colonial revolt: the women's war of 1929, Eastern Nigeria. In S. Ardener (ed.) *Perceiving women*, pp. 127–57, J. M. Dent, London.

International Labour Office (1980) *Women in Rural Development: Critical Issues*. ILO, Geneva.

Leacock E. (1981) History, development and the division of labour by sex: implications for organization. *Signs*, 7(2), winter, 474–491.

Lim L. (1978) *Women Workers and Multi-national Companies in Developing Countries: The Case of the Electronics Industry in Malaysia and Singapore*. Occasional Paper no. 9, University of Michigan.

Loutfi M. (1980) *Rural Women: Unequal Partners in Development*. International Labour Office, Geneva.

MacEwan Scott A. (1979) Who are the self-employed? In Bromley R. and Gerry C. (eds) *Casual Work and Poverty in Third World Cities*, pp. 105–29, John Wiley and Sons, Chichester.

Meillassoux C. (1981) *Maidens, Meal and Money*. Cambridge University Press, Cambridge.

Mies M. (1980) Capitalist development and subsistence reproduction: rural women in India. *Bulletin of Concerned Asian Scholars*, 12(2), 3–14.

Mies M. (1981) Lace, Class and Capital Accumulation. Unpublished paper, Institute of Social Studies, The Hague.

Mitra A. (1977) The status of women. *Frontiers*, 18 June.

Molyneux M. (1979) Beyond the domestic labour debate. *New Left Review*, 116 (3–27).

Moser C. (1980) Women's work in a peripheral economy: the case of poor urban women in Guayaquil, Ecuador. Paper presented to Institute of Development Studies Workshop on Women, the Working Poor and the Informal Sector. Brighton, Sussex.

Nelson N. (1980) *Why Has Development Neglected Urban Women?* Pergamon Press, Oxford.

Pala A. O. (1977) Definitions of women and development: an African perspective. *Signs*, 3(1), autumn, 9–13.

Palmer I. (1977) Rural women and the basic needs approach to development. *International Labour Review*, 115(1), 97–107.

Palmer I. (1979) New official ideas on women and development. *Institute of Development Studies Bulletin*, 10(3).

Papanek H. (1977) Development planning for women. *Signs* 3(1), 14–21.

Pearson R. and Elson D. (1981) Nimble fingers make cheap workers: an analysis of women's employment in Third World export manufacturing. *Feminist Review*, 7, 87–107.

Phizaclea A. (1981) Migrant women and wage labour: the case of West Indian women in Britain. In West J. (ed.) *Work, Women and the Labour Market*, Routledge and Kegan Paul, London.

Portes A. (1978) The informal sector and the world economy: notes on the structure of subsidised labour. *Institute of Development Studies Bulletin*, 9(4), June, 35–40.

Remy D. (1975) Underdevelopment and the experience of women. In Reiter R. (ed.) *Towards an Anthropology of Women*, Monthly Review Press, New York.

Roberts P. (1979) The integration of women into the development process: some conceptual problems. *Institute of Development Studies Bulletin*, 10(3).

Rogers B. (1980) *The Domestication of Women: Discrimination in Developing Societies*. Tavistock, London.

Rowntree M. and Rowntree J. (1970) More on the political economy of women's liberation. *Monthly Review*, 21(8), 26–32.

Safa H. (1981) Runaway shops and female employment: the search for cheap labour. *Signs*, 7(2), winter.

Seccombe W. (1974) The housewife and her labour under capitalism. *New Left Review*, 83.

Sen A. (1981) *Poverty and Famine*. Oxford University Press, Oxford.

Stack C. (1974) Sex roles and survival strategies in an urban black community. In Rosaldo M. and Lamphere L. (eds) *Women, Culture and Society*, Stanford University Press, Stanford, California.

Stolcke V. (1981) The unholy family: labour systems and family structure – the case of Sao Paulo coffee plantations. Paper presented to La Conferencia sobre Aspectos Teóricos del Parentesco en A. Latina, Ixtapan de la Sal, Mexico, 1981.

Stoler A. (1977) Class structure and female autonomy in rural Java. In Wellesley Editorial Committee (eds), *Women and National Development*, University of Chicago Press, Chicago and London.

Tinker I. (1976) The adverse impact of development on women. In Tinker I. and Bramsen M. B. (eds) *Women and World Development*, Praeger, New York.

Vergopoulos K. (1978) Capitalism and peasant productivity. *Journal of Peasant Studies*, 5(4), 446–65.

Weiner A. (1979) Trobriand kinship from another view: the reproductive power of women and men. *Man*, 14(NS), 328–48.

West J. (1982) *Work, Women and the Labour Market*. Routledge and Kegan Paul, London.

Young K. (1978) Modes of appropriation and the sexual division of labour: a case study from Oaxaca, Mexico. In Kuhn A. and Wolpe A. M. (eds) *Feminism and Materialism*, pp. 124–54, Routledge and Kegan Paul, London.

Youssef N. (1974) *Women and Work in Developing Societies*. Population Monograph Series, University of California, Berkeley.

# 20

# Female Workers in the First and Third Worlds: the Greening of Women's Labour

RUTH PEARSON

## WOMEN WORKERS AND THE NEW INTERNATIONAL DIVISION OF LABOUR

Nimble-fingered young women working in serried ranks in a South East Asian electronics factory is by now a widespread image. More than that, it is *the* image of women industrial workers in the Third World. Virtually all of the analysis of women's work in the industrial sector in the Third World is based on the experience of export platform factories. From a number of often first-hand research and other reports about women working in a variety of sectors, regions and countries in the Third World an ideal and universal picture has emerged which has tended to coalesce the Third World into a single undifferentiated country where women factory workers are young, industrious, naive and passive. And it seems likely that the same kind of generalizations are being translated to the analysis of women working in the new technology industries of the industrialized world.

This simplistic analysis captures some aspects of the emergence of a specific demand for female labour for assembly operations in factories mainly owned by foreign capital and producing for the world market as part of what has been termed the new international division of labour. However, this framework of analysis, which refers to the trend during the 1960s and 1970s for foreign companies to relocate production to low-wage countries, belies the complexity of

This essay was first published as chapter 5 in K. Purcell et al. (eds), *The Changing Experience of Employment*, Macmillan and the British Sociological Association, 1986.

the wider process of capitalist restructuring at a global level.[1] The analysis assumes the existence of an ubiquitous pool of 'suitable' female labour – a kind of global reserve army activated directly, and without contradictions, by international capital seeking low-paid workers with high productivity.

Partly responsible for this undifferentiated image of Third World women workers is the way in which the analysis of the new international division of labour has ignored the complexities and contradictions of producing the desired social relations of production involved in creating a new sector of waged labour. The analysis focuses primarily on the international mobility of capital which facilitates rational location decisions on the basis of comparative costs (Frobel et al., 1980). Labour is cheap in Mexico but cheaper still in Sri Lanka and even cheaper in Malawi (USTC, 1970). Which location was chosen depended, of course, on a number of other considerations, including the scope of incentives provided by Third World governments eager to attact foreign investment in the industrial sector, for such investment offers foreign exchange earnings and industrial employment opportunities and at least the promise of escape from the Third World's traditional place in the international division of labour. Indeed the competition to attract international investment of this kind is so intense that many Third World countries have established special locations – free trade zones (FTZs) or export processing zones (EPZs) which provide international capital with relevant industrial infrastructure and services and effectively cede large areas of sovereignty over foreign companies operating within these areas in terms of trade and employment regulations. By 1984 there were some eighty such zones with another forty planned or in the process of establishment (UNTC, 1983, p. 25).

It is clear, therefore, that location decisions are not just a matter of seeking the lowest cost environment; in addition the state, in the guise of the host government, has to intervene to deliver such environments to international capital in a variety of ways.[2] They have to guarantee political and economic security, which could be provided by a strong military regime or could be delivered by enacting legislation about the control or absence of labour unions (Lauridsen, 1984, p. 6; Edgren, 1982), as well as provide the industrial inputs necessary to make the environment feasible for an internationally controlled and organized operation. This means providing telecommunications, air freight services, power and water supplies and basic infrastructural and internal transportation investments (UNIDO 1979). The governments representing the multinational companies' home State have also been required to intervene to provide a feasible environment for this mode of international accumulation. The United States, for example, made special provision in its tariff schedule to allow US components assembled abroad to be allowed back into the United States free of import tax on the value of those components (USTC, 1970).

1. For a critical analysis of the new international division of labour, see Jenkins, 1984. For conventional economic analyses of exports of manufactures from the Third World, see Helleiner, 1973; Lall, 1978; Nayar, 1978.

2. I am indebted to Diane Elson who presented a paper entitled 'The Interrelation of Capital, Gender and State in the World Market for "Nimble Fingers" ' jointly with an earlier draft of this paper at the 1984 BSA Conference, and contributed many of the ideas about the role of the State in liberating women's labour to capital.

What has not been addressed is the availability or construction of cheap labour. It has not been acknowledged that either capital or the State might need to intervene to deliver the suitable labour required; it has been assumed that this was axiomatic on the existence of high levels of unemployment or underemployment in the Third World locations. Given that it has been female labour which was targeted to provide labour power for Third World export factories it was assumed that the absence of industrial employment for women in the immediate economic history of the country meant that there would be no problem in making this labour available in the quantities and qualities required.

## THE IDEAL WOMAN FACTORY WORKER IN THE THIRD WORLD

The analysis of women's employment by multinationals involved in manufacturing for export in the Third World has established that women constitute an overwhelming proportion of the 'operator' (i.e. unskilled and manual worker) level of employment and that such employment constitutes up to 90 per cent of total employment generated by such investments (Edgren, 1982; Pineda-Ofreneo, 1984; Konig, 1975). It is also clear that women are employed in both traditional and 'new technology industries' in spite of the unequivocal existence of unemployed male labour in the Third World. The reason why women's labour is the preferred 'cheap' labour in a situation of surplus labour of both sexes is complex. Firstly women's wages are generally lower than those paid to male workers in comparable occupations, though this is not always the case (Cardosa and Khoo, 1978). But also it has been demonstrated that women's productivity under the production conditions determined by specific production processes are higher than men working under the same conditions (Elson and Pearson, 1980).

From this analysis of how and why women are the preferred labour force, a stereotypical picture of the average or ideal Third World woman factory worker has emerged, comprising four essential components:

1 that she is young – recruited from an age cohort ranging from fifteen to twenty-five, concentrated in the 18–21 age group;
2 that she is single and childless;
3 that she is 'unskilled' in the sense of having no recognized qualifications or training;
4 that she has no previous experience of formal wage employment in the industrial sector – 'virgins in terms of industrial employment that need not be retrained or untrained' (Konig, 1975), to quote one not untypical researcher writing about women's employment in the Mexican border industries.

## BEYOND THE STEREOTYPE

In fact, when we come to examine in detail different case studies of women factory workers in different areas and regions of the Third World it becomes clear that there exists considerable variation in the characteristics of the workers recruited. For what the management of multinational companies consciously, if not explicitly, operated was indeed a strategy of providing for themselves a labour force which would incur minimum costs in terms of wages, fringe benefits, management control, discipline and militancy. And these are not necessarily supplied by recruiting a single age cohort from the vicinity of these factories and setting them to work in a standard context.

The mostly deeply held aspect of the stereotype of women workers in Third World factories is that they are young women; the age range varies in different accounts, but it is generally within the range of 15–25, bunching in the 18–21 age group. However, research has indicated that there is in fact a considerable variation in the age range. In some countries women as young as twelve are employed; in other countries (e.g. Barbados) the labour force in the electronics factories are considerably older, starting in the late twenties and going throughout the thirties age group (CEREP, 1981).

This last example is interesting because it relates to another aspect of the stereotype, that women factory workers in the Third World are *single*. It is clear why this should form part of the employers' construction of their ideal labour force; single women, with few alternative industrial job opportunities, can deliver the highest level of compliance and loyalty to the firm. They are deemed not to have domestic and economic responsibilities to their own conjugal households and children – a kind of international teenager ready to exchange their hours of industrial activity for the monetary rewards and concomitant independence this brings. However, what single really means in the context of this analysis is *childless*, and in different social contexts the two characteristics do not necessarily go together.

In Barbados, where the age of first childbirth is earlier, and age at marriage later (which is the English speaking Caribbean pattern; see Standing, 1981), and the provision of maternity leave and payments more historically integrated into the island's labour practice, older women are recruited who have passed through their intensive phase of childbearing.

In locations where there is a large supply of women applicants for jobs in export processing factories, the criterion of childlessness can be used as part of a complex recruitment mechanism for selecting 'ideal' applicants. In Mexico where there is an excessive supply of female labour and a range of export factories in different sectors, and where for social, economic and cultural reasons there is a high rate of illegitimate births, electronics factories include pregnancy tests as well as declarations of childlessness as a routine measure (INET, 1975). In Malaysia where recruitment takes place within a less homogeneous and different social and cultural context, different strategies have been adopted. Amongst the social classes from whom electronics workers are recruited, there is a strong prejudice against married women working in factories, and a much more cohesive family structure, so recruitment of single high-school graduates will provide motivated childless women (Cardosa and Khoo, 1978). But where the prejudice against factory work extends to daughters because of its implications in undermining forms of control of fathers and brothers over young women, capital may have to alter its strategy in order to 'release' the required labour power. One multinational company operating in Malaysia pursues a policy of reinforcing traditional forms of patriarchal power. Instead of undermining the father's authority over the daughter by encouraging modern, Western independent behaviour, it pursues a policy of reinforcement: 'the company has installed prayer rooms in the factory itself, does not have modern uniforms and lets the girls wear their traditional attire, and enforces a strict and rigid discipline in the workplace' (Lim, 1978, p. 37). In another case the firm has allowed traditional leaders onto the production line to talk to the women and check the modesty of the company uniform (ibid., p. 36). Young women recruited from rural areas may be provided with supervised hostel accommodation and in some cases the wage is paid to the male kin rather than directly to the women workers.

What these variations in the composition of the labour force and in the employment conditions demonstrate is that women's potential labour power, as a commodity available for exploitation by capital, has to be negotiated for with forms of patriarchal control and with her childbearing and reproductive role; and at the same time these can be used to control the composition and characteristics of those employed. In addition, it must be recognized that different production processes and industrial branches require different kinds of labour power which may be supplied by different sub-sectors of the female labour force. For example, Fernandez-Kelly (1983) has documented wide variations in the characteristics between women recruited into the electronics and garments sectors on the Mexican border – demonstrating that workers in the garments plants are less educated, older (median age 26 years compared to 20 years in electronics plant), more likely to have held waged employment before (70 per cent compared to 40 per cent) and have a greater number of children. This is related to the 'enfeebled position of "older" women in the labour market and the inability of the garment sector to attract workers who are seen to be ideal (i.e. young single childless women) because of the higher instability and temporality of employment as well as the extremely inadequate working conditions' (Fernandez-Kelly, 1983, p. 51). In addition to this it can be argued that workers employed making garments whose design, size, material, etc. change frequently are required to bring a specific kind of experience and skill to the job, suggesting that older women with previous experience are a preferable work force in this sector (Pearson, 1978).

> The reduction of workers to the notion of 'cheap labour' may fail to identify variations which have theoretical and practical significance. Variations derive from the different competitive and technological conditions of different manufacturing branches which will determine the nature of labour recruitment strategies and the form that control over workers takes in each industry. (Fernandez-Kelly, 1983, p. 85)

Moreover the firms do not face an undifferentiated supply of homogeneous cheap female labour and can utilize differences within the potential female labour force to structure their recruitment strategy according to their own perceived requirements.

## HOW WOMEN WORKERS BECOME CHEAP LABOUR

One such strategy is the practice of recruiting childless women for certain sectors of export manufacturing. This provides capital with a mechanism which serves a number of purposes in its attempt to release the ideal female labour power. Recruiting women with children, or who are liable to bear children during the course of their employment, potentially involves additional costs to the firm, such as maternity benefits, maternity leave, sick leave, absence from work, contributions to State health services for dependants. But it is not just the potential cost of employing women actively involved in these stages of reproduction which leads management to avoid them, for in many instances legal requirements for maternity payments are waived for this particular form of industrial production (Yoon, 1979). It also provides a mechanism for ensuring whatever turnover rates are appropriate; for if the argument is that Third World women factory workers perform unskilled tasks, then several years of experience will not enhance a woman's productivity compared with a newly recruited worker. But the dispensability of the labour force in terms of the ease with which it can be retrenched in response to fluctuations in demand, or made redundant if a decision is taken to cease production or relocate in another country, is a further advantage of this carefully selected labour force. Avoiding recruitment of pregnant women and those with children and terminating the employment of those who become pregnant is one of the many mechanisms which is used to maintain an ideal structure of the labour force.

Other features of management practice and employment conditions provide further evidence of ways in which the composition of the labour force can be controlled. One example is the widely reported practice of contracting women on short-term and/or temporary contracts (Lim, 1978; Green, 1980; Pearson, 1978). This ensures that women have no long-term employment rights and can be dismissed as variations in production levels demand, at no cost to the firm.

## WORKING CONDITIONS

A further mechanism which increases the turnover of a given factory's labour force is the working conditions themselves. Occupation-related health hazards in the different sectors, ranging from myopia caused by close microscope work, nausea and cancer from contact with chemicals and solvents, bronchial and respiratory disorders from working with textiles, etc. are extensively detailed in the literature (NACLA, 1975; Grossman, 1979; Cardosa and Khoo, 1978; Blake and Moonstan, 1981). In such situations health problems, for which the firm takes no formal responsibility, can be used to maintain and increase productivity in the plant; workers whose physical condition prevents them maintaining the required level of productivity will withdraw themselves from employment, without needing to be dismissed by management.

Another feature of working conditions in many multinational Third World operations is the absence of any effective structure for promotion, increased earnings and technical advancement for the women operators (Blake and Moonstan, 1981; Ong, 1984). While there may be minimal possibilities for advancement, e.g. to group heads (i.e. head of sections) in the electronics assembly plant, this only offers minimal improvements in hourly wage rates and has the disincentive of separating the woman from the companionship of her fellow workers, which is highly rated as being one of the main sources of job satisfaction for the women concerned.

The lack of promotional structure must be seen in the context of the rigidly enforced sexual hierarchy within the plants (Pearson, 1978; Wong, 1983). This is a feature common to all manufacturing industry regardless of location and ownership, but one which is significantly intensified in Third World export processing plants in the electronics sector. Estimates vary between countries but the sexual stratification is so marked in Third World electronics that women workers often account for over 95 per cent of all unskilled jobs, themselves 80–90 per cent of total employment. The few supervisory, management and technical jobs are generally occupied by men (INET, 1975).

A further aspect of working conditions refers to one of the characteristics of the multinational company's target female labour force frequently cited by commentators, that of docility. Many commentators, often quoting management and industrial promotion agencies in the Third World, have pointed to the docility of women operators in the face of boring, tedious and repetitive work (Elson and Pearson, 1981; Lim, 1978; Joekes, 1982). The explanations for why women should be so accepting of these conditions varies from the fact that women are naturally submissive, that domestic work suffers from the same disadvantages, to cultural factors concerning the pattern of behaviour of women in a given society. The rigid sexual hierarchy of production in the factories contributes to the promotion of such a response from the women workers as all authority and responsibility is firmly in the hands of male technical, managerial and supervisory personnel. So too are the elaborate management strategies aimed at emphasizing the 'femininity' and accepted feminine characteristics of women workers (Cardosa and Khoo, 1978). Management sensibly does not rely entirely on nature to ensure an unresistant labour force, though it does take advantage of the various historical reasons why women are less likely to respond to unionization, where legally permitted (Pearson, 1980; Grossman, 1979; Heyzer, 1987).

One final point about the variations in conditions of employment in the Third World must be made. Much of the literature assumes a single type of production situation and relations of production; that is, of young women recruited from the school leaver cohorts with no industrial experience, working in manufacturing plants organized along conventional factory lines. In reality, as we have seen, there is a range of production relations which vary according to the historically determined situation of women in any given situation. While the majority of Third World women industrial workers are employed as 'free' wage labour , this is not always the case. In Turkey, women weaving carpets for export in village-based workshops do not receive any payment from the subcontractor, who instead pays according to a piece-rate scale to the male head of the household (OU, 1983). In Haiti women employed in American-owned firms making toys and soft goods frequently take work off the plant to their homes to complete (Viezzer, 1980); in Puerto Rico a large proportion of the production of garments for the export market takes place in illegal 'underground' domestic workshops whose output is then marketed by the multinational retail groups in the United States (Riviera Quintero and Gonzales, 1980).

What this analysis demonstrates is that the female labour recruited for Third World market factories is not available in a pre-packaged form. While it is clear that women workers offer capital labour power which can be low paid and highly productive, both the State and capital need to intervene to release this labour power in the particular form required by concrete production conditions. Nor can it be assumed that this labour is available in unlimited quantities from a given age cohort anywhere in the world; the characteristics of the female labour force – in terms of age, education, marital status, class and ethnic origin – and how their work process is organized will depend as much on the historically determined availability of female labour and the interaction of gender and class systems as on the demand for cheap labour from foreign capital.

## MULTINATIONAL COMPANIES AND WOMEN WORKERS IN THE FIRST WORLD

We have argued that much of the analysis of women industrial workers in the Third World rests on the assumption that changes in the international division of labour are responsible for recruiting women for the first time into waged industrial work. It is, therefore, curious to find that the literature discussing the composition of the labour force recruited by multinational companies to work, particularly in the new technology sectors located within the industrial countries such as Britain, uses a parallel set of stereotypes to explain the location decisions of international firms and to describe (or dismiss) the composition of the female labour force. For it is clear that women workers in advanced industrial countries have also been targeted by management to provide, for given production tasks, a category of labour power which can be differentiated from the male labour force and utilized under specific conditions to provide a highly efficient and cost effective labour force.

Compared to the extensive literature on Third World multinationals, much less attention has been given to the recruitment of women workers by multinationals in advanced countries, in spite of the fact that the developed market economies continue to receive by far the greatest proportion of all flows of foreign direct investment, over 75 per cent of the total in 1980 (UNTC, 1983).

Most of the literature on foreign investment in Britain is concerned with the location of production investments by foreign companies in the peripheral regions of the British Isles – Wales, Scotland and Ireland, particularly in what are described as the 'high technology sunrise industries', electronics goods and components, computers, etc. Why these sectors are dominated by foreign companies is irrelevant to this analysis, except for the fact that the multinationality of these firms is deemed to operate to allow them to make rational location choices as they do in the Third World.[3] However, the emphasis in this literature is different from that concerned with Third World market factories. Much stress is placed on the investment and tax incentives offered by the different regional development authorities (Hood and Young, 1983). It is not that the labour force is not considered, but it is assumed in an uncontradictory way that areas experiencing industrial decline and high unemployment will automatically provide a suitable labour force in much the same way as it was considered that such labour was available in any Third World location.

3. For an analysis of foreign investment in Britain, and other industrialized countries, see Stopford, 1979; Hood and Young, 1983; Stever et al., 1973; Hymer, 1976.

## THE BRITISH EXPERIENCE

As far as British experience is concerned, there is no doubt that firms starting up new production sites expected to recruit women workers for the labour intensive, unskilled or semi-skilled operations involved in the assembly of electronics-based consumer goods and electronic components. Hood and Young (1983) report that 51 per cent of all workers employed by foreign firms in the electrical engineering sector in the United Kingdom are women. Soete and Dosi's study (1983) shows that the average female share of employment in the electronics sector was 34 per cent in 1981, while specific sub-sectors showed a range from 52 per cent for electronic consumer goods to 26 per cent for electronic computers. There is also evidence which suggests that the electrical engineering sector as a whole has a much lower capital/labour ratio (Hood and Young, 1983) reflecting the intensive use of manual workers within the sector.

It should be noted that these figures reflect a much lower level of female intensity than those reported for Third World electronics factories where 80–90 per cent of the labour force were women. Is this to be explained by the fact that such a rigid sexual division of labour is not maintained by employers in the UK and that men are being recruited into what elsewhere is exclusively women's work? Or that there is no available supply of women workers with the qualities and characteristics apparently so easily produced in situations of urban poverty in the Third World?

## CHANGES IN PRODUCTION TECHNOLOGY AND THE SEXUAL DIVISION OF LABOUR

Part of the reason for the lower female intensity in the electronics sector in the UK, compared to that in a range of Third World countries, is that the industrial structure includes the more capital intensive research and development activities, as well as production and assembly processes (Massey, 1983, p. 78). Recent research on the electronics industry would suggest that the trend of investment in the production end of the electronics sector is towards more automated technology and a relative integration of production processes than that common in Third World factories. The bulk of foreign investment in these sectors has been located in the peripheral local economies of Wales and Scotland, much of which in the 1970s included assembly operations for standard mass produced products, similar to those carried out in South East Asia and elsewhere. But recent years have seen a decline both in overall employment in the electronics sector, and a sharp decline in female employment. Some 31,700 women lost their jobs between 1975 and 1981, while there was an increase in male employment of 3500 and women's employment fell by 30 per cent between 1971 and 1981. The female intensity of the industry, measured by women's share in total employment, fell from 42 per cent to 34 per cent between 1971 and 1981, and current prognostications indicate that this trend will continue (Soete and Dosi, 1983).

The changing sexual composition of the labour force, following the changes in the production process, reflects a tendency for a change in the skills composition of the labour force, where new techniques of production and investment in integrated production units have increased the demand for inputs of (male) skilled labour. As Morgan and Sayer (1984, p. 110) have pointed out, 'notwithstanding the post-Braverman preoccupation with deskilling, the proportion of skilled workers in the British electrical engineering industry is increasing both relatively and absolutely', indicating a process of polarization of skills which is reflected in the bifurcation between female and male employees as well as between unskilled workers and technically qualified and skilled employees.

But unskilled women operators still constitute the largest single category of employment in the industry. As we argue below, the changing technical and managerial policies within the industry are tending to utilize female unskilled workers in a different way from their use in assembly plants or conventional technology. However, in spite of the changing technical and sexual composition of the labour force, the undifferentiated notion of women's labour as being suitable and available for employment is still part of the accepted analysis of why firms locate production in depressed peripheral regions and why they recruit women's labour. This notion is described as 'green' labour and differs little in terms of the stereotypical assumptions and characteristics it carries from the notion of 'cheap labour' used in the analysis of the female labour force in world market factories in the Third World.

Several accounts of restructuring in Wales, of which investment by foreign firms in the 'sunrise' industries forms an important part, refer to the pool of 'green female labour' which it is claimed was a strong pull factor in the locational decisions of electronics firms coming into the region in the post-1960 period (Massey, 1980). Morgan and Sayer (1983) claim that the operators for electronics plants were specifically recruited from those with 'little previous experience, and hence little to unlearn' – a description reminiscent of the notion of the 'industrial virgin' cited above with reference to Mexican electronics workers. Winkler (1987) claims that the availability of 'large reserves of female labour' was the most important factor in the dispersal of civil service departments to peripheral areas in Britain as the result of the introduction of new technology, which requires an 'unskilled, cheap and docile labour force'. Hence, dispersal to areas where there are large reserves of female labour, lacking work and trade union experience.

Historically there is indeed evidence of a low female participation rate in Wales (Massey, 1983). The economic and political history of the area, dominated by the coal and later the steel industries, both exclusively male employers, together with the political hegemony exercised over this relatively homogeneous labour force, explain to a large extent the exclusion of women from the industrial labour force and thus their lack of union experience. To imply that women are by nature unpolitical and unlikely to organize in the workplace is inaccurate; indeed with reference to the service sector it is significant that the highest growth of union recruitment in Britain has been from female clerical workers by NUPE, NALGO and others, and militant action by women workers within and against official union structures has been extensively documented (cf. the Plessey occupation – Findlay, 1984; the Lee Jeans occupation – Elson, 1983; Grunwicks – Rogaly, 1977; Ford workers in 1968 and 1984). But as Massey argues (1983) the organization of women workers being drawn into the labour force in the current phase of industrial restructuring must be understood in the context of the fragmentation of previous patterns of industrial hegemony in terms of large scale heavy industrial employment.

Indeed, both unions and management have recognized the potential for industrial militancy amongst women workers in South Wales, which has resulted in the signing of 'sweetheart' agreements breaking with traditional craft-based union structure within the manufacturing sector and organized on the basis of a closed company shop.

## THE ELECTRONICS INDUSTRY CREATES ITS 'GREEN' LABOUR FORCE

Management has had to intervene in several ways to ensure other aspects of the 'natural docility' of the female industrial workers in electronics plants, despite the fact that empirically it could be demonstrated that they have had no previous industrial experience. Morgan and Sayer (1984) report that recruitment, management and organizational strategies of foreign companies in the electronics sector in South Wales have had to be rethought in the light of recent experience of the involvement of women in industrial disputes in the region as well as the changing nature of the production process. Post-1977 investors, in which Japanese companies are highly represented, are reconsidering their whole labour strategy. Having for long regarded labour as a 'cheap commodity' which can be disposed of according to market fluctuations, they were now hiring in accordance with long term corporate strategy, recruiting workers with relevant 'skills' which include behavioural attitudes as well as technical skills (ibid.).

This is not to say that there is any uniformity in the way different firms seek to acquire suitable labour, though it would seem that in the post-recession situation of intense competition, management is more conscious of the need to construct its labour force carefully. Interviews with managers report planned interviews, dexterity tests, elimination of specific categories of applicants, such as single parents and those with school-aged children and other family responsibilities. In a letter to all employees at their South Wales factory at Hirwaun in December 1984, the Japanese firm of Hitachi invited all workers aged thirty-five or over to take voluntary retirement, arguing that older workers are more prone to sickness, are slower, have poorer eyesight and are more resistant to change. Although they did not single out women assembly and testing workers, they justified their action with reference to the effect of redundancies earlier in the year which were carried out on a last-in-first-out basis, which meant 'we lost most of our younger people, *particularly in production areas*' (*Financial Times*, p. 1, 11 December 1984; emphasis added), adding enigmatically that they needed to achieve a balance of the workers over thirty-five despite their physical and mental shortcomings, the young despite their being more difficult to control and less mature, 'and those in between despite their increasing domestic problems' (ibid.) It would appear that Hitachi are trying to re-create an ideal labour force which might be less easy in the South Wales environment, with its history of unionization, than it would be in South East Asia. They complained that the average age at the Hirwaun plant of forty compared unfavourably with other plants and offered an inducement allowance of £1800 to any employee taking up their offer, together with an opportunity to nominate a sixteen-year-old 1984 school leaver to fill the resulting vacancy.

Clearly the accepted view that location in a local labour market, which offers few alternative job opportunities, gives workers 'little option but to accept the ideologies, situational definitions and rules of the game imposed by local employers' (Norris, 1978, p. 475; cited by Maguire, 1984) must be challenged. Maguire's account of the specific recruitment and management strategies employed in a Northern Ireland electronics factory reinforces the evidence from South Wales that the required social relations within the workplace, that of compliancy and flexibility, cannot be and are not taken for granted.

Scotland's Silicon Glen provides a further example of heavy recruitment of women workers to the largely foreign-owned electronics sector. Some 50 per cent of those employed are 'women semi-skilled operators and testers' (SDA unpublished figures, cited in Goldstein, 1984), but projections made against trends in changing technology and new investment in automated wafer fabrication plants would suggest that this proportion will fall by 1986 to 'less than 30–40 per cent'.

Detailed information about the composition of Scotland's women electronics workers presents a much more complex picture than the notion of 'green' female labour would suggest, reflecting how 'the previous social characteristics of the areas impart a reflection of the previous use of . . . [the] . . . area by capital' which creates the preconditions for the new roles that segments of the labour force, such as women, are coming to play (Massey, 1983, p. 50). The recruitment patterns of different firms suggests a considerable variation in the composition of the labour force. Goldstein (1984) reports that in one semi-conductor plant, 50 per cent of the women were married to skilled shipyard workers, while in another there was a preponderance of 'upper working class wives and wives of white collar professionals'. Wong (1983) found that in one company the average age of production workers was seventeen, indicating school-leaver recruitment, while in another there was a high proportion of women with older children and school-aged children. One manager is quoted as stating: 'we seek people who have had previous machining or light assembly experience' (Wong, ibid.) reflecting the high levels of wage employment for women in the Scottish economy throughout the twentieth century (Breitenbach, 1982). Some firms in fact deliberately exploited the different characteristics of women of different ages and industrial experience, placing young school leavers alongside older women 'to limit the potential disruption of "giggly girls" and effectively to discipline older women, reminding them of their dispensability' (Goldstein, 1984, p. 11).

Far from seeking a homogeneous workforce which spontaneously delivers the desired qualities of docility and high productivity, management is actively using the differences between different women – age, class, cultural attributes – to aid its objective of developing the internally applied discipline it requires in order to achieve a highly productive and flexible workforce. This strategy not only includes scientific management techniques such as quality control, but also direct and paternalistic forms of management–employee relationships. An example of this from Scotland is the granting of fringe benefits, such as company loans to ease financial problems, a useful strategy in a country where non-payment allows the creditor to possess the debtor's assets for resale. One manager utilizing this strategy clearly recognized its implications: 'if we are nice to people, we win their loyalty for ever' (Goldstein, 1984, p. 11).

Technical change in the electronics industry in both product and process technology is also forcing a reformulation of the role of female labour. Some firms with conventional assembly plants still require women as a flexible, efficient, docile and dispensable manual labour force. New automated silicon wafer fabrication plants require different skills and attributes from their female labour force. Rather than required manual dexterity for microscope assembly tasks, women are to become 'machine minders, monitoring the movement of wafer batches through highly complex equipment, reading the computerized performance data output and sounding the alarm if something goes wrong'. Workers will be required to work within a 'clean room environment' where meticulous adherence to antistatic procedures is required (Goldstein, 1984, p. 7).

While such jobs continue to be described as unskilled or semi-skilled[4] they are also crucial to the successful operation of these plants, and it is clear that women are recruited to do them because they can be *relied* on to adhere to the 'clean room' procedures, to remain within the environment for long stretches of time, and to learn how to monitor the computerized data for problems in the production line. The companies are, therefore, anxious to maintain a stable female workforce, seeing characteristics previously regarded as negative ones, such as docility, willingness to carry out monotonous tasks, as positive attributes of reliability and conscientiousness.[5] Far from being dispensable, in a situation where there is a local shortage of skilled and trained technicians, management is concerned that the women workers who carry out their required jobs satisfactorily, should remain at the same plant because of their crucial role in the production process which cannot be instantly fulfilled by 'green' labour recruited from the reserve army of female school leavers and the unemployed.

Japanese electronics firms in South Wales are also developing a concept of 'core workers', which includes the technically semi-skilled operators. Morgan and Sayer (1984) report that management are actively trying to insulate these 'core workers' from the vagaries of the external labour market by a dual strategy of offering them supplemental payments and at the same time increasing subcontracting to act as a buffer between the 'permanent' core workers and those recruited temporarily to meet changes in demand.

In California's Silicon Valley the electronics industry exhibits a similar polarization between skilled and unskilled workers and between men and women, where the labour force is divided between technical research and development workers and unskilled blue collar workers (Keller, 1984; Snow, 1980). However, an additional factor in the US is the high utilization of immigrant non-English-speaking workers in assembly operations, which makes it easier for firms to keep unions out, to keep wages low and to dismiss workers according to the demands of the market (Howard, 1981). Subcontracting is also taking place in the California electronics industry. Katz and Kemnitzer (1984) report the significant

4. Production-line workers are described as unskilled in the Third World and semi-skilled here. For a discussion of the concept of skill in respect of women workers, see Phillips and Taylor, 1980.

5. See Humphrey, 1984 for a discussion on the differential evaluation of women's and men's abilities and characteristics in production processes.

development of putting-out systems for some elements of the production process which are carried out in the homes of women workers, generally former factory employees, under a variety of formal and other contractual relations. This has the advantage for the companies of not having to pay the capital costs, and not being responsible for environmental and safety factors; as a result many industrial accidents have taken place in domestic premises for which the women workers have no protection or compensation.[6] Whether or not this will lead to the development of a similar core–periphery polarization amongst female factory workers has yet to be established.

## CONCLUSION: THE GREENING OF WOMEN'S LABOUR

This chapter has argued that women employed by multinational companies producing consumer goods for the world market do not necessarily have identical characteristics, nor are one group of workers infinitely and instantly substitutable for another. But it also demonstrates that in both the First World and the Third World women are confined to relatively low paid jobs which are classified as unskilled or semi-skilled. This confinement is implemented through a number of complex mechanisms provided by capital through the recruitment preferences and production practices of management, the legislative and political actions (or inactions) of the State, and the ideology of gender roles which provides sex stereotyping of male and female jobs which are enforced by the community in general, the organized male skilled working class, and by women's own perceptions of what constitutes appropriate work for women.

The resultant rigid sexual hierarchy within the production process which is widely reported in many studies of industrial work in both the Third and the First World[7] presents women with a limited range of job opportunities. Within this range their participation is prescribed in certain defined ways in order to release their labour power in a manner most appropriate to the form of capital accumulation represented by a given production process in a given competitive and technological, geographical and social environment. Therefore, the nature of the tasks women are required to perform, the specific characteristics of the labour power that is required from them (be it dexterity, reliability, unskilled manual work, or meticulous computer monitoring) and the demographic and social composition of the female labour force, will vary among individual industrial (sub)sectors and between and within regions and countries. It is also true that multinational companies which decided to locate production in whichever part of the industrialized or Third World bring with them management policies, practices and prejudices which reflect both their perception and their experience

6. The issue of environmental and factory safety is one that is not given much prominence in discussions of location decisions of international capital, though the larger scale accidents in Bhopal and Mexico City in 1984 bear witness to the scale of the problem. Harris (1984) found the women employed in foreign-owned plants in County Mayo were well aware of the health hazards but knew that the continuation of their jobs depended on them not publicly discussing the risks.

7. For recent studies on women's industrial employment in Britain, see Cavendish, 1982; Coyle, 1982; Cockburn, 1983; Pollert, 1981; Westwood, 1984. For further studies on women industrial workers in the Third World see Michel, 1983; Hancock, 1977; Elson 1981.

of whether and which women are likely to constitute the most appropriate labour force. But these policies have to interact with the existing supply of (potential) female labour which bears the characteristics produced by the outcome of different sets of interactions between patriarchal, class, racial, ethnic and spatial relations (Anthias and Yuval Davies, 1983; Massey, 1983).

We are, therefore, arguing two different but related propositions. Firstly, that women are sought out by capital for specific roles in new and emerging forms of production, as well as old and declining forms. And that in both old and new production processes, women continue to occupy the bottom layers of the occupational structure, reflecting the way in which women workers, doing women's work, are socially constructed as a subordinate group differentiated from the dominant labour force.[8] But secondly, we have argued that the recruitment of women workers in new industrial situations – either new sectors and processes or parts of the world new to given kinds of industrial processes – does not of itself provide capital with suitable labour power. This labour has to be constituted, taking into account the pre-existing sexual division of labour. It is constructed directly by the recruitment, selection, management and personnel policies of individual companies and indirectly by the intervention of the State, and negotiation within local and traditional modes of gender control. Women's labour, in an appropriate form, that is 'cheap' labour, or 'green' labour, does not exist in nature; it has to be directly cultivated, a process we have called the greening of women's labour.

## REFERENCES


Anthias, F. and Yuval-Davies N. (1983) 'Contextualising feminism – gender, ethnic and class divisions', *Feminist Review*, no. 15.

Blake, M. L. and Moonstan, C. (1981) 'Women and transnational corporations: the electronics industry in Thailand', East West Centre, Honolulu.

Breitenbach, E. (1982) *Women Workers in Scotland*, Pressgand, Glasgow.

Cardosa, J. and Khoo, K. J. (1978) 'Workers in electronics runaways: the case of Malaysia', IDS, University of Sussex, (see Young, forthcoming).

Cavendish, R. (1982) *On the Line*, Routledge and Kegan Paul.

CEREP (1981) Report of Joint Study Seminar organized by the Centro di Estudio de la Realidad Puertoriquero and IDS, University of Sussex, on women and social production in the Caribbean, San Juan, June–July 1980.

Cockburn, C. (1983) *Brothers*, Pluto Press.

Coyle, A. (1982) 'Sex and skill in the organisation of the clothing industry', in West (ed.), *Work, Women and the Labour Market*, Routledge and Kegan Paul.

Edgren, G. W. (1982) 'Spearheads of industrialisation or sweatshops in the sun?', ARTEP–ILO, PO Box 2-146, Bangkok.

Elson, D. (1983) 'Jeans and the international division of labour', *Links*, vol. 17.


8. The use of the terms dominant and subordinate to refer to men and women workers relates to the literature on segmented labour markets, and to an attempt to avoid the undynamic and historical constraints of the analysis of primary and secondary labour markets. The benefits of salvaging something useful from this body of literature for the analysis of women industrial workers is amply discussed in Green (1980).

Elson, D. (1981) 'Women workers in export oriented industrialisation in South East Asia', a selected annotated bibliography, IDS, University of Sussex.

Elson, D. and Pearson, R. (1980) 'The latest phase of the internationalisation of capital and its implications for women in the Third World', IDS discussion paper no. 150, University of Sussex.

Elson D., and Pearson, R. (1981) 'Nimble fingers make cheap workers: an analysis of women's employment in Third World export manufacturing', *Feminist Review*, no. 7.

Fernandez-Kelly, M. P. (1983) 'For we are sold, I and my people: women and industry in Mexico's frontier', SUNY.

Findlay, P. (1984) 'Fighting plant closure: a case study of the Plessey occupation', Department of Industrial Relations, University of Strathclyde, paper presented at workshop of women and multinationals, University of East Anglia.

Frobel, F. , Heinrichs, J. and Krey, O. (1980) *The New International Division of Labour*, Cambridge University Press.

Goldstein, N. (1984) 'The women left behind: technical change and restructuring in the electronics industry in Scotland', paper presented at workshop on women and multinationals, University of East Anglia.

Green, S. (1980) 'Silicon Valley's women workers: a theoretical analysis of sex segregation in the electronics industry labour market', East West Centre, Honolulu.

Grossman, R. (1979) 'Women's place in the integrated circuit', *South East Asia Chronicle* (joint issue with *Pacific Research*), vol. 9, no. 5.

Hancock, M. A. (1977) 'Women and TNCs: a bibliography', East West Centre, Honolulu.

Harris, L. (1984) 'Women and foreign firms in the west of Ireland: consciousness and organisation', paper presented at workshop on women and multinationals, University of East Anglia.

Helleiner, G. K. (1973) 'Multinational exports from less developed countries and multinational firms', *Economic Journal*, vol. 83.

Heyzer, N. (1987) 'The relocation of international production and low-pay female employment; the case of Singapore', in Young (forthcoming).

Hood, N. and Young, S. (1983) 'Multinational investment strategies in the British Isles: a study of MNEs in the UK assisted areas and Republic of Ireland', HMSO, London.

Howard, K. (1981) 'Second class in Silicon Valley: if engineers are the artisans of high-tech society, production operatives are its migrant workers', working papers no. 8, *New Society*, Sept./Oct.

Humphrey, J. (1984) 'Gender, pay and skill: manual workers in Brazilian industry', Sociology Dept, University of Liverpool.

Hymer, S. (1976) 'International operations of national firms: a study of direct foreign investment', MIT.

Jenkins, R.O. (1984) 'Divisions over the international division of labour', *Capital and Class*, no. 22.

Katz, N. and Kemnitzer, D. (1984) 'Fast forward: the internationalisation of Silicon Valley', in Nash and Fernandez-Kelly (1984).

Keller, J. F. (1984) 'The division of labour in electronics', in Nash and Fernandez-Kelly (1984).

Konig, W. (1975) 'Towards an evaluation of international subcontracting activities in developing countries', report on Maquiladoras in Mexico, UNECLA, Mexico City .

INET (Instituto Nacional de Estudios Sobre el Trabajo) (1975) 'Incorporacion de la mano de obra feminina a la industria maquiladora de exportacion'.

Joekes, S. P. (1982) 'Female led industrialisation: women's jobs in Third World export manufacturing, the case of the Moroccan clothing industry', IDS research report no. 15.

Lall, S. (1978) 'Recent trends in exports of manufactures by newly industrialising countries', paper prepared for the National Economic Development Office (NEDO), London, December.

Lauridsen, L. (1984) 'Export oriented industrialization and the working class: the case of Taiwan', in Norlund et al. (1984).

Lim, L. (1978) 'Women workers in multinational corporations in developing countries. The case of the electronics industry in Malaysia and Singapore', Women's Studies Program occasional paper no. 9, University of Michigan.

Maguire, M. (1984) 'Location and recruitment as a means of control: the case of a Northern Ireland electronics factory', paper presented to BSA Conference.

Massey, D. (1980) 'Industrial restructuring as class restructuring: some examples of the implications of industrial change for class structure', CES working note 604.

Massey, D. (1983) 'Industrial restructuring as class restructuring', *Regional Studies*, 17.

Michel, A. (1983) 'Multinationals et inegalites de classe et de sexe', *Current Sociology*, vol. 31, no. 1.

Morgan, K., and Sayer, A. (1983) 'The international electronics industry and regional development in Britain', Urban and Regional Studies working paper 34, University of Sussex.

Morgan, K. and Sayer, A. (1984) 'A "modern" industry in a "mature" region: the remaking of management and labour relations', University of Sussex, School of Social Sciences.

NACLA Latin American and Empire Report (1975) 'US runaway shops on the Mexican border', vol. IX, no. 7, July.

Nash, J. and Fernandez-Kelly, M. P. (1984) 'Women, men and the international division of labour', SUNY, Albany.

Nayar, D. (1978) 'Transnational corporations and manufactured exports from poor countries', *Economic Journal*, vol. 88, March.

Norlund, I., Wad, P. and Brun, V. (1984) *Industrialisation and the Labour Process in Southeast Asia*, Papers from the 1983 Copenhagen Conference, repro serie no. 6, Institute of Cultural Sociology, University of Copenhagen.

Norris, G. (1978) 'Industrial paternalist capitalism and local labour markets', *Sociology*, 12, no. 3.

Ong, A. (1984) 'Global industries and Malay peasants in peninsular Malaysia', in Nash and Fernandez-Kelly (1984).

Open University (OU) (1983) 'Migrants from Sakultuten', video, Third World studies course, U204.

Pearson, R. (1978) 'Women workers in Mexico's border industry', IDS, University of Sussex (see Young, forthcoming).

Pearson, R. (1980) 'Women's response to the current phase of internationalisation of capital', paper presented at the women's symposium, International Union of Anthropological and Ethnological Sciences Intercongress, Amsterdam, April.

Phillips, A. and Taylor, B. (1980) 'Sex and skill: notes towards a feminist economics', *Feminist Review*, no. 6.

Pineda-Ofreneo, R. (1984) 'Subcontracting in export-oriented industries: impact on Filipino working women', in Norlund et al. (1984).

Pollert, A. (1981) *Girls, Wives, Factory Lives*, Macmillan.

Riviera Quintero, M. and Gonzales, L. (1980) 'La industria de la Aguja: puento invisible en la historia del trabajo feminino en Puerto Rico', CEREP.

Rogali, J. (1977), *Grunwick*, Harmondsworth: Penguin.

Snow, R. (1980) 'The new international division of labour and the US workforce', East West Centre, Honolulu.

Soete, L. and Dosi, G. (1983) 'Technology and employment in the electrical and electronics industries', TEMPO Project, Science Policy Research Unit, University of Sussex.

Standing, G. (1981) *Unemployment and Female Labour: a study of labour supply in Kingston, Jamaica*, Macmillan.

Stever, M. D. et al. (1973) 'The impact of foreign direct investment on the UK', Department of Trade and Industry.

Stopford, J. (1979) 'Employment effects of multinational enterprises in the UK', ILO, Geneva.

UNIDO (1979) 'World industry since 1960', *Progress and Prospects*, New York.

United Nations Commission on Transnational Corporations (UNTC) (1983) *Transnational Corporations in World Development: An Update.*

United States Tariff Commission (USTC) (1970) 'Economic factors affecting the use of items 807.00 and 806.30 of the tariff schedule of the US', Washington DC.

Viezzer, M. (1980) 'Women's employment in foreign manufacturing plants in Haiti', IDS-CEREP study seminar on women in social production in the Caribbean.

Westwood, S. (1984) *All Day, Every Day.*

Winkler, V. (1987) 'Tertiarisation and feminisation at the periphery: the case of Wales', Department of Town Planning, UWIST, Cardiff. In Newby et al. (eds), *Restructuring Capital: recession and reorganisation in industrial society*, Macmillan.

Wong, Y. (1983) 'Oriental female "nimble fingered lassie" women with patience: ghettoisation of women workers in the electronics industry', M. Phil. dissertation, IDS, University of Sussex.

Yoon, S. Y. (1979) 'The halfway house – MNCs, industries and Asian factory girls', UNAPDI, Bangkok.

Young, K. (ed.) (forthcoming) *Serving Two Masters*, Cambridge University Press.

# Part IV
# Forms of Work and Sources of Labour

# Editor's Introduction

In this part the focus shifts to the divisions of labour within and between households and to the various forms of communal and informal work that are not conventionally considered in the contemporary sociological analysis of work. The contemporary interest in other forms of work apart from waged labour has been prompted partly by the intellectual debates discussed in part III, and partly by other new issues that have emerged in the last twenty years. Forms of work that were part of the necessary work of 'getting by' or surviving in pre-industrial times (see Malcolmson, chapter 2) have been rediscovered and put forward as putative solutions to contemporary problems.

In order to understand the significance of the recent developments in thinking about work, it is necessary to have in mind the conventional stereotype of the divisions of work between 'the family', the workplace and the state. In this stereotype, the chief earner is a male who earns a 'family wage' to support his wife and dependent children. When he retires he expects to be supported by his state pension, by the services of his wife and possibly, although not necessarily, by his children. In return for the taxes on his wages he and his family expect to get considerable welfare benefits to enable them all to keep healthy, to be educated and trained and to be cared for if they suffer disability or misfortune, whether of biological, social, psychological or economic origin. Instead of the household being, as it were, a relatively self-supporting 'getting-by unit', the model based on the male breadwinner assumed that many of the burdens and responsibilities which in the past fell to the immediate family, the wider kinship network or to neighbours in the locality should be, as it were, shared out to become burdens and responsibilities of the society as a whole.

In order for such a model to work in practice there must, of course, be a strong collective desire to achieve it, since it must depend on people paying more in individual taxation in order to gain more in collective benefits. Most people see the benefits of municipal parks but not all see collective provision for the care of the elderly, say, as being universally desirable. Similarly, employers readily see the advantages of state-provided roads but may be less enthusiastic about state-controlled factory health and safety measures or employment protection legislation.

However, leaving aside such ambivalence in values, there are other elements in the late-twentieth-century context that have led to a change in the stereotypical model. The dramatic increase in married women's activity rates since 1950 has made it more likely for households to have two or more earners. Fewer children enable women to return to work after only a very short break. It is now increasingly the pattern for women to return to employment whilst still having dependent children in the household and, indeed, a quarter of married women in Britain whose youngest child is under five return to work, albeit probably on a part-time basis.

At the same time that the relationships between the household and the economy were changing, with the collapse of the breadwinner model of a single earner, the relationships between the state and the family were also changing. The provision of the so-called welfare state became problematical for a number of reasons: as people required better and more specialized education, lived longer and so on, so (it was claimed) their expectations of state provision grew unrealistically high in relation to the resources available. Faced with such demands, social democratic governments responded by arguing that they could not afford to maintain welfare services and benefits at the levels now expected, given their commitments to other expensive areas, such as defence, and given also the high cost of renewing and maintaining a declining or deteriorating infrastructural base. This so-called 'crisis of the welfare state' has been analysed by commentators from a wide variety of political, ideological and theoretical perspectives but all agree that, for whatever reasons, the old conventional stereotypes of the structure and sexual divisions of employment, the divisions of domestic labour and the divisions between the public and private provision of welfare have permanently disappeared. Whether or not the crisis is real, if believed to be true it will be true in its consequences.

As a result of these and other changes in structures and perceptions, old divisions are changing or being renegotiated and new divisions are emerging. The chapters in this part of the book are concerned mainly with work outside employment and how this is divided within and between households. Forms of work that in an earlier period might have been dismissed as archaic, as belonging more to a less satisfactory past before 'the golden age of full employment' and a beneficient state, are now being rediscovered. Self-provisioning work in and around the household by household members or the reciprocal exchange of labour between one household and another are forms of communal work not untypical of the eighteenth century but not conventionally considered in texts in the sociology of work. It is important to remember that the actual form of work may not be new: the novelty lies in the interrelationships between different forms of work or the particular significance of a given form of work in the contemporary context.

Thus, the growth of married women's employment outside the home prompts a concern with the balancing and sharing of the work outside employment in and around the home. The decline of employment in manufacturing prompts a concern with the mix between the collective and the individual or the public and the private provision of services. Allied with that last point, there has been a growth in the development of technological innovations which allows the manufacture of new goods enabling people to provide more or better services for themselves. People have to spend more time, perhaps, driving and maintaining their cars but the greater freedom and control over personal lifestyles makes such efforts seem worth while. There are other potential renegotiations, switches or substitutions that may be seen, depending on one's point of view, as new problems or new solutions. Some see the growth of unemployment as providing the potential freedom of wage earners, who can throw off their chains as they flock to the riches of the informal economy. Others, with empirical evidence on their side, point to the serious disadvantages faced by unemployed people who, whilst they may have 'free' time, lack the money to buy tools or materials, to pay for a telephone or private transport and to enable them to join in the social contexts in which most paid work outside employment is found.[1] Typically, those who get extra money that is not declared for taxation purposes are already in employment and have the social contacts to find the work and the money and skills to carry it out. 'Money finds money' is the general rule, although there are certainly exceptions – whether of places or of social categories.

These new tensions and lines of cleavage, based on the way different forms of work are accomplished within and between households, have not received the same attention as that given to the issues that were discussed in part II. Nevertheless, there is some very interesting work emerging on these topics in various countries. The problems are seen to be similar in many different contexts and it would not be possible to do justice to this topic without adopting a comparative perspective.

Chapter 21 provides a snapshot of the divisions of domestic labour in Canada in 1971 based on the time budgets of a sample of wives and husbands in the Greater Vancouver area. Work on time-budget analysis has become much more sophisticated in the last fifteen years (see, for example, Gershuny's work in chapter 26) but the Vancouver study provides a useful benchmark and, since research in this area is expensive and time consuming, the number of replicatory studies is always likely to be limited. The authors show unequivocally how the workload of the women increases disproportionately where they have the 'double burden' of paid employment and domestic work outside employment. As the authors laconically conclude, 'women's job time is sensitive to demands at home while men's is not.' On the face of it the research reported in this chapter suggests that men are doing very modest amounts of renegotiating of the divisions of domestic labour in response to their spouses' increasing involvement in the labour market. However, values do change and it is sociologically implausible to expect an established 'traditional' pattern to change quickly (even though such a traditional pattern may itself have a shorter history than may be thought by those whose knowledge and experience is limited to the middle class in Western industrial society).

Part of the singular importance of Gershuny's research is that it covers a

1. For an accessible and well-researched introduction to the informal economy, see Philip Mattera, *Off The Books*, Pluto Press, London and Sydney, 1985. The constraints on unemployed people preventing them from doing extra work are discussed in Claire Wallace and Ray Pahl, 'Polarisation, unemployment, and all forms of work', in *The Experience of Unemployment*, edited by Sheila Allen et al., Macmillan, 1986.

considerable time span – a period of nearly half a century. Thus he is able to make his data compatible with similar studies of time budgets in a number of other countries over the same period; his sample size is large enough for him to make meaningful comparisons between social classes in Britian over the full period; and, finally, he is able to situate his work in a broader model of socio-economic change. Thus, chapter 26 is central to our overall theme of understanding the changing structure, context and meaning of work at the end of the twentieth century. Gershuny shows how the growth of what I would call self-provisioning – or what Gershuny would more precisely term that set of processes in which unpaid labour is combined with materials and capital equipment installed in private houses to produce final services – is related to wider changes in technology and the organization of production inside and outside the home. Gershuny is, in effect, providing us with a new model, based on the use of time, that enables us both to measure the relative salience or importance of different forms of work and to show how their interrelations change over time. In very simple terms, it can be readily understood that the same task – washing clothes – can be done outside the home at the communal well or pump; inside the home at the sink with hands, wringer and posser; at the laundry; or in the home again by a washing machine. It may be done by women or men, by the mistress or the servant. These and other changes are well recognized, but their collective significance has not been fully grasped. The interesting and important issue that Gershuny explores, both in chapter 26 and in his work elsewhere, is how to relate such different ways of getting a task done to broader changes in the balance between formal and informal work and between manufacturing and services industries. He shows how there have been shifts in 'modes of provision' and 'chains of provision' that have fundamental impacts on the way work is done, who does the work, and what kind of work it is. Domestic work is a different kind of activity in 1984 from what it was in 1937.

The arguments in chapter 26 are complex and demanding but they enable us to look with clearer eyes at some of the changes in the way work is done in contemporary society. The provision of certain kinds of domestic services involves more paid manufacturing employment for some – not necessarily in the same country – and more highly mechanized unpaid work for household members. By devising a complex system of accounts, based on units of time rather than units of money, Gershuny demonstrates how the development of new demands in service provision can create new employment, both in manufacturing and in services. Tele-shopping, for example, would be a new activity, based on a new technology, which would create jobs in the manufacturing of the new equipment involved and would also release time which, with more money provided by increased productivity, would increase the demand for new services. Gershuny concludes with a rhetorical question: 'If our needs are met by a combination of formal and informal production, and technical change alters the relationship between these, can we be satisfied with an economics which concentrates just on the formal economy?' We might add here: can we similarly rely on a sociology that limits itself to the analysis of only one form of work, namely employment?

There have been other studies of time budgets, particularly in the Soviet Union, where scholars pioneered the use of this research tool early in this century. A particularly valuable study, based on four Russian cities, was carried out by L. Gordon and E. Klopov between 1965 and 1968. Methodologically sophisticated and analytically sensitive, this study was published in English in 1975 with the curiously inappropriate title of *Man after Work* (Progress Publishers, Moscow). For some reason this book was overlooked by scholars in the West. Whilst this is understandable in the case of American sociologists, who are notoriously isolationist, it is odd that German, French and Italian researchers interested in work outside employment should also have neglected it. Gordon and Klopov, when examining the renegotiation of the divisions of domestic labour, observe that men with higher levels of education do more work in and around the home, leading to 'a certain equalization of the work load of men and women in the daily routine' (p. 237). However, the evidence suggests that it is not the men with the highest grades who do most but rather those in the middle levels. Presumably the most highly educated men have the most demanding employment and higher satisfactions in their careers. Clearly more studies linking different forms of work are needed.

The study by Glatzer and Berger (chapter 23) is important for providing a detailed account of household production - or self-provisioning - based on a representative survey of the adult West German population carried out in 1980. Overwhelmingly the jobs in and around the household are done by members of the households themselves and there is little of the reciprocal exchange of labour described by Sik for Hungary in chapter 24. In Germany the authors show that 'even for household repairs and housing renovations requiring handicraft skills, market firms are not used on a large scale. Two-thirds of households usually do such work themselves. Only one-fourth call on a craftsman, and the remaining households ask people in their social network.' The authors consider several factors that may be related to variations in the various forms of self-provisioning. The unequivocal conclusion emerged that it was *household composition*, rather than income, class or any other variable, that was of the greatest significance in explaining variations. As in other studies, household composition (associated, of course, with stage in the life cycle) is of crucial importance in understanding the complex mixes of forms of work and sources of labour outside employment. Glatzer and Berger also explore the provision of welfare and social services and demonstrate various shifts between collective institutions, private households, the market and the informal economy based on paid work.

Two other chapters explore in more detail the work that members of households do for each other (chapter 24) and the 'caring' work that household members do for each other (chapter 22). Whilst, as might be expected, Parker shows in chapter 22 that most studies report that women bear the main burden of informal care, there was a strong feeling that they should not have to cope alone and that the state had an undiminished if not increasing role in providing professional support. Parker concludes from her review of a number of relevant studies in Britain that there is no evidence of a 'wholesale abrogation of responsibility by families'. The euphemism 'care in the community' means care in the family, which, in turn, means care by women. Once women have, individually, taken on particular burdens it is unlikely that they will receive much practical support from other relatives. In the case of mentally handicapped children most work, both domestic and child care, fell to the mother; whilst fathers made a contribution, it never approached half the workload. Parker's summary of a number of empirical studies gives a clear view of the source of labour for a broad range of burdensome work outside employment.

Sik's account of the reciprocal exchange of labour in Hungary is part of a much larger study, and the material presented in chapter 24 is more illustrative than conclusive. The implications are that a pattern of collective and communal work amongst peasants, typical of pre-industrial Hungary as well as many other parts of Europe, has continued, though in a modified form - particularly in the way people combine together to build houses for themselves. He points out that historically it was the middle-level peasants who were most likely to cooperate together. This has been shown - in considerable detail - to have been the case in England too.[2] The extraordinary point emerging from Sik's work is his claim that 85 per cent of Hungarian households used the reciprocal exchange of labour in some kind of social or welfare work. This is presumably a reflection of the low level of development of the statutory services, but he also mentions the high cost of informal sources of labour, and the size of the Hungarian household, which is too small to handle all the various demands for labour made upon it. Because Hungary industrialized relatively late, many of the peasant traditions still linger on, so that the pattern he describes has probably been lost in other contexts. However the reciprocal exchange of labour could well emerge or re-emerge in unfamiliar contexts such as the inner cities of Britain.

There is considerable interest in neighbourhood support networks in Britain elsewhere.[3] Nevertheless, one of the most distinguished sociologists who has worked in this area has criticized the notion that informal care could be a low-cost alternative to formal government statutory provision:

> Governments have been pushing what they call the informal system of care, and they have got it all wrong. They will need to spend money to provide back-up services. If we want to go into neighbourhood care in a big way in urban areas, the evidence we have points to the conclusion that caring must be turned into a proper job with paid wages, and we cannot rely on volunteer housewives who simply don't have the time or sufficient numbers to do the work.[4]

Finally, in chapter 25 Mingione situates various forms of informal work into the specific socio-economic context of southern Italy. This is a crucial and necessary corrective to any tendency to generalize notions about the 'informal sector' of the economy to many different contexts. In southern Italy the informal sector is composed partly of irregular temporary and mainly young male wage labourers and partly of female workers, who combine a range of domestic, self-provisioning and wage-labour activities. By locating this form of informal labour in its economic, social and geographical contexts, Mingione provides an important conceptual link between part IV and part V. Taking one form of work out of context can be very misleading, and Mingione's concern to relate different forms of work to regulation, deregulation and the sources and types of 'surplus

2. R. M. Smith , 'Kin and neighbours in a thirteenth-century Suffolk community', *Journal of Family History*, 4(3), 1979, pp. 219–56. See also the discussion of this and other studies in R. E. Pahl, *Divisions of Labour*, Basil Blackwell, Oxford, 1984.

3. For example, Martin Bulmer, *Neighbours: the work of Philip Abrams*, Cambridge University Press, 1986.

4. Philip Abrams, quoted in *The Guardian*, 18 October 1981; given in Bulmer, *Neighbours* .

population' is part of a more general attempt to theorize work outside formal, regulated employment elsewhere as diverse field studies and empirical data are put into broader frameworks.[5] Sociologists interested in work have at last left the offices and factories of the formal economy to explore the changing pattern of all forms of work. My own attempt to come to terms with these problems by focusing on a very detailed study of the Isle of Sheppey in the Thames estuary is simply one building block in cumulative and comparative analysis.[6] As more and better studies appear in the 1990s, it is likely that towards 2000 students will have the ethnography and the improved conceptual apparatus to come to terms with all forms of work outside employment.

5. It is curious that the diversity and strength of many European studies is not so far matched by similar work in the United States. Indeed, in one recent publication very small businesses were simply taken as a proxy for the informal sector. This very limited and partial approach to a complex problem is sure to be soon superseded as more scholars come to grips with the complexities of the comparative evidence. However, it is good that this debate has at least started. See Alejandro Portes and Saskia Sassen-Koob, 'Making it underground: comparative material on the informal sector in Western market economies', *American Journal of Sociology* 93(1), 1987, 30–61.
6. See my monograph *Division of Labour* (Basil Blackwill, 1984) and the very comparable Italian study by Roberto Serpieri and Antonella Spanò, 'Scelte informali nell'agire di consumo', *Inchiesta*, no. 74, 1986, 32–51. That complete issue of *Inchiesta* is devoted to the problems discussed by Mingione in chapter 25.

# 21

# No Exit for Wives: Sexual Division of Labour and the Cumulation of Household Demands in Canada

MARTIN MEISSNER, ELIZABETH W. HUMPHREYS, SCOTT M. MEIS AND WILLIAM J. SCHEU

This chapter is concerned with the sexual division of domestic labour and provides hitherto unavailable descriptive data of the distribution of daily activities of married couples. The analysis of these data is designed to choose between two accounts of the relationship of wives and husbands to the production of household services. It will examine differences between the hours which husbands and wives contribute to housework and their total workload, when demands on the household accumulate due to two paying jobs and young children. The response of husbands to their wives' workload is a contentious question, and complete time budgets of the workday and weekend activities of married couples have so far not been available. For these reasons, this essay will be concerned with the provision of detailed descriptive data and with the consistency of results in the analysis of several components of the problem. These components include (1) the conditions of participation in paid work; (2) the length of the work week and its impact on the distribution of work between the couple; (3) the composition of housework activities and the proportionate contributions of each spouse; (4) the reflection of cumulating demands in the overall time budgets of wives and husbands; and (5) their relative share of the increasing costs in total and domestic labour time.

## CONTRADICTIONS

Work in the relationship of married women and men is facing growing contradictions. More women work for pay away from home, a fact which holds the promise of greater economic independence from their husbands' income. At the

This essay was first published in *Canadian Review of Sociology and Anthropology*, 12(4), part 1, 1975.

same time, the conventional division of functions continues to allocate domestic obligations to women, a fact that could prevent women's achievement of independence through work for money. This first contradiction is reflected in a second: women take on a mounting share of the collective labour while being denied the characterization of their efforts as work.

This chapter is intended to describe the consequences of the contradiction between change and stability in the allocation of work in public and private production. In order to account for these consequences, two theories can be formulated. We will first sketch a 'theory of adaptive partnership' and the empirical findings which have consistently supported it in the sociology of the family. We will then identify the cumulation of demands on a household in a 'dependent labour theory' and present findings which can be related to it. The analysis of data which follows should permit an assessment of the correspondence of one or the other of these two accounts with the consistent structure of the results.

## ADAPTIVE PARTNERSHIP

The sociology of work in the household has until recently been confined to research in family relationships. According to its account of the division of labour in the household, 'the work of the woman is a resource which gives her more weight in the balance of power and in the division of domestic tasks in the couple: the resource "work" permits her . . . to take a greater part in family decisions and to obtain from the husband more help in domestic tasks' (Michel, 1970:290). A subsidiary account explains the shift to more 'help' from husbands by the relative availability of time of either wife or husband. When the wife goes out to work for pay, 'the husband feels obliged to help out more at home and takes over an appreciably larger share of the housework' (Blood and Wolfe, 1960:63). 'Or the wife may be so heavily burdened with childcare responsibilities that she just plain runs out of time. Then the only way of getting the work done is to tap the husband's time' (p. 57). 'Correspondingly, the husband will contribute more to housework when his job requires fewer hours' (p. 63).

According to this argument, the 'family' (i.e. marriage and household) is a self-balancing system which adapts to structural changes and internal requirements. As more women work for pay, their employment increases their relative power in domestic decisions, and decreases their available time and, accordingly, their relative share of housework. Husbands respond to the greater demands of their wives' job and of children through increasing contributions to domestic obligations. In short, marriages are becoming more equal relationships, and the contradiction between the job participation of women and the conventional division of household labour becomes resolved in 'the symmetrical family'.

The empirical findings of this field of research have confirmed its theoretical expectations. Comparable research projects in America (Blood and Wolfe, 1960:62), in Sweden (Gendell, 1963:121, 128–9), in France (Michel, 1970:285), and in Britain (Young and Willmott, 1973:115) found approaching equality in the household division of labour and more equality when wives held paying jobs. It was also shown in some reports that more husbands helped in housework when their wives worked longer hours away from home and when there were younger children. In the interviews, either women were simply asked if their husbands helped in housework or they were given a list of eight or nine selected domestic activities in order to indicate whether they were always done by the husband or the wife, more by one than the other, or equally. A summed score indicated the degree of equality. One such list included making out tax declarations, correspondence, home repairs, shopping for appliances, for clothes and for groceries, cleaning up for visitors, washing dishes, and cleaning floors (Michel, 1970:291).

## DEPENDENT LABOUR AND THE CUMULATION OF DEMANDS

The 'adaptive partnership theory' is confined to the internal balance of the resource of paid work and time in the personal relationship of wife and husband and was not addressed to the actual use of time. An alternative account would consider the structure of control of resources in the social environment of the household and recognize the conditions which create demands on actual time use. Women and men have a different relationship to work organizations, to the class structure, and to the means of controlling the value of different kinds of labour. Their circumstances are constrained by this difference, and their personal conduct, in domestic decisions for example, can ameliorate the constraint but cannot undo it.

This alternative argument, then, takes into account men's and women's relationship to productive and social resources and its consequences for demands on their work and the time it requires. The principal condition of men's life chances is the structure of work organization to which they are tied by careers and other inducement devices. Men's relationship to the organization of work defines their class position. Work organizations in turn are controlled by men who consistently occupy positions of greater authority, skill, and income, while subservient, monotonous, and unrewarding jobs are allocated to women.

In law and in practice, marriage is a contract for the domestic services of a woman who is kept by her husband in return. Its meaning becomes apparent when it is threatened. A husband can sue the source of damages to his wife's sexual and other services; his choice of residence (usually related to his work place) takes precedence over his wife's; and the wife's economic security is endangered by the potential of desertion (Zuker and Callwood, 1971). The economic function of the household formed on marriage is the servicing of men (and the preparation of children) as resources for the corporate organization of production. While men's class position is a function of their work, women's position is a function of their husband's or father's, that is, of their kin relationship as constituted through their dependent labour in the household. When women take paid jobs, their income can enhance the display of their husbands' social rank but not their own, and the jobs which are available to them in the corporate organization of work confirm their dependent labour status.[1]

1. We are aware that this argument contradicts Eichler's (1973), according to which women's occupational position affects their social rank independently from their status of personal dependant. In our view the subservient character of much of women's employment in all ranks confirms their personal dependency as does the effects of their daily domestic labour. This is what our analysis will demonstrate.

Stable expectations follow from, and are maintained by, this relation of dominance and dependence. They provide a belief structure which consistently re-creates the conception of the primacy of paid and organized work in the life of men, according to which it is right that women's principal obligation is to household services and their paid work is secondary both to the household and to their husbands' jobs. Correspondingly, the prevailing meaning of 'work' is in the privileged interest of men who control its organization. As reflected in the language of social science, domestic labour is not work, and even the status of women's employment as work is tenuous. Husbands treat their wives' employment either as temporary 'help' in earning supplementary income or as a form of personal entertainment. In symmetry with that conception, both housewives and social scientists define husbands' contributions to domestic obligations as 'helping' their wives.

What form does this structure and meaning of work take in the sexual division of domestic labour? Govaerts has introduced the concept of the cumulation of roles in order to account for differences in the free time available to women (1969:105–6). However, the relevant 'roles' have quite different implications for women and men, and it is more appropriate to speak of the cumulation of 'demands' on the shared household enterprise. Seen from the perspective of women, these demands accumulate through (1) a husband, (2) the establishment of a household, (3) two paid jobs, and (4) children. Subsidiary additions to demands consist of full-time versus part-time work for pay; younger versus older or no children; a greater number of children; and the urgency for a second job, depending on the amount of money brought in by the first.

Men meet their obligations through 'their' work, and the conception of housework as nonwork facilitates their neglect of domestic obligations. Whether they work for pay in addition to housework or not, married women's continued dependence assures that household services are being maintained. Instead of the internal balance of resources in the 'adaptive partnership,' the cumulation of demands on the household becomes the cumulation of women's 'dependent labour'. In short, the contradiction between the changing structure of the labour force and the conventional division of domestic work is widened by the disparate effects of women's employment and young children on the allocation of men's and women's time.

According to this argument, one would expect the following results in the analysis of the data:

1 The principal inducement for women to be in the labour force is an insufficient income of their husbands, and having young children will reduce their labour-force participation; neither condition has an effect on the proportion of men in paid work.
2 Increases in the paid working hours of husband or wife will increase the wife's workload and will require adjustments in the balance between her paid and domestic work time , while men's workload will be unaffected by their wives' working time.
3 The proportion of men performing each of the centrally necessary and regular domestic work activities will be consistently small, and their involvement in irregular and more discretionary domestic work will be

larger than women's only in the most conventionally masculine activities.

4 Throughout the entire structure of daily activities, the time allocation of women will be drastically affected by the cumulation of demands from their paid work and a young child, while the composition of men's days remains in large part unchanged.

5 As demands increase, the combined overall workload of the couple increases; but the husband's workload remains stable and his share in the workload, as well as in the increase, declines.

6 The demands resulting from his wife's paid work will have little effect on the husband's total workload or his contribution to housework, and the questionable legitimacy of the wife's employment will be expressed in the tendency of the husband's domestic work hours to increase somewhat in response to the demands from a young child, that is, demands which fit his conventional conceptions.

The opposite of what has been expected and found through the theory of adaptive partnership, these predictions are in consistent agreement with the argument of the relationship of women's dependent labour and the cumulation of demands. This argument tends to find empirical support in the results of time-budget studies. The time budgets of some 30,000 people in twelve countries show that married women with paying jobs are overworked in comparison to employed men and to housewives (Szalai, 1972:128, 583–93). A study of American married women (Walker, 1970) has demonstrated that women's overall workload and housework hours are dramatically affected by their paid work and the number and ages of children, while their husbands' hours remain unchanged except in the extreme case when their wives worked for pay *and* they had either five or more children or the youngest was under two.

We will now indicate the characteristics of the data and the way in which they are more complete than previous time-budget studies. The consistency of results of the analysis of these data will permit an assessment of the plausibility of the two theories.

## THE DATA

The 24-hour time-budget studies, such as the multinational projects, have always relied on data from separate individuals, making it possible to compare aggregated information on independently sampled women and men, but not on actual couples, and without reference to the spouse's corresponding data. Other studies, like Walker's pioneering work, have relied on married women's reports on their husbands and themselves and accounted only for parts of the day, excluding nonwork activities. In both cases time-use data were obtained from an individual only for a workday or a weekend day, but not both, and weekend compensations for workday experiences could only be assessed by inference from data of groups of different individuals.

The data for this analysis describe married couples interviewed separately by

TABLE 21.1 Job status on time-budget workday and child under ten (number of couples)

| *Paid job status on time-budget workday* | | | *Child* < 10 | |
|---|---|---|---|---|
| Women | Men | Total | No | Yes |
| No paid job | Worked in paid job | 237 | 131 | 106 |
| Worked in paid job | Worked in paid job | 103 | 85 | 18 |
| Subtotal (1-job and 2-job couples) | | 340 | 216 | 124 |
| Off job | Worked in paid job | 11 | | |
| Worked in paid job | No job or off job | 10 | | |
| Off job or no job | Off job | 11 | | |
| Subtotal (off-the-job couples) | | 32 | 21 | 11 |
| Total with usable time budgets | | 372 | 237 | 135 |
| Cases omitted: | | | | |
| 1 Husband woked on time-budget workday, but not in last seven days (likely inconsistency between wife's and husband's time budgets) | | 17 | | |
| 2 No time budget, or incomplete | | 22 | | |
| Total number of couples interviewed | | 411 | | |

two interviewers in 1971.[2] They contain time budgets of wives and husbands for a full workday and one full day off (usually a weekend day). Sampling involved the selection of eight areas of Greater Vancouver which were characterized by different combinations of socioeconomic status and stage in the family life cycle. Households in each area were selected randomly with the provision that their members must include both husband and wife and that at least one of the two hold a paid job. Table 21.1 shows the distribution of cases according to the main characteristics. Most of the analysis is limited to the 340 couples in the first two categories in which the husband, or both wife and husband, were working away from home on the workday for which the time-budget record was taken.

## JOB PARTICIPATION AND THE COLLECTIVE WORKLOAD

The length of the working week as well as the labour-force participation of men has tended to decline. The labour-force participation of women is increasing. According to several comparisons of earlier and more recent time-budget studies, the average hours of women's housework have either increased overall or, at best,

2. The source of data for this chapter was a comprehensive study of the social, temporal, and spatial ecology of urban dwellers. It was designed and executed by George Gray, Scott Meis, Jack Scheu, and Kathie Storrie. This is the occasion for the two authors of this essay not included in that group to thank the members of the group, and for the other two to thank the members of the group not among the authors, for access to and encouragement in the unrestricted use of the data from the project.

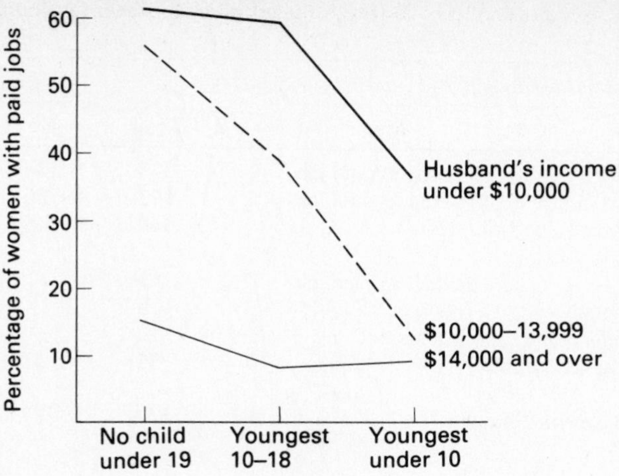


FIGURE 21.1 Women's labour force participation by children's age and husbands' income

remained the same despite changes in household technology (Walker, 1969; Robinson, 1971; Vanek, 1974; Michel, 1974). Average hours of work, multiplied by the proportion of persons performing it, make for the amount of collective effort. These observations suggest that the collective burden of women has increased at home and on the job, a change of conditions to which men appear to respond through a collective reduction in their contributions to work.

According to Canadian national data, the factors which crucially affect women's labour-force participation in addition to those of age and education derive from the demands of the household. The proportion of women with paying jobs is reduced through marriage, the number of children, and young children, and it increases where husbands' income is smaller. These conditions have little or no effect on men's labour-force participation (Kalbach and McVey, 1971:222–31).

As shown in figure 21.1, the married women in our study respond similarly to the necessities. They make up for their husbands' inadequate incomes through working for pay in greater proportions and they are more likely to stay at home for younger children.

## THE PAID WORK WEEK

When the hours in paid work of one or both spouses increase, the demands on the overall workload shared by wives and husbands becomes greater. If 'adaptive partnership' prevailed, one would expect increases in the job hours of one spouse to be mitigated through accommodation in the hours of paid and domestic work of the other. Under conditions of 'dependent labour,' it would be women who make up for the difference.

In two-job couples, the proportion of *both* wives and husbands with full-time or

TABLE 21.2 Effects of wives' and husbands' job hours on each other's work

| (a) | | *Husband's paid work week* | | |
|---|---|---|---|---|
| | | *Part time* | *Full time* | *Overtime* |
| Percentage of employed women who worked full time or more (103 two-job couples) | | 47 | 59 | 79 |
| (b) | | *Wife's paid work week* | | |
| | | *Part time* | *Full time* | *Overtime* |
| Percentage of employed men who worked full time or more (103 two-job couples) | | 74 | 79 | 95 |
| (c) | | *Husband's paid work week* | | |
| | | *Part time* | *Full time* | *Overtime* |
| Percentage of women employed (340 one-job or two-job couples) | | 40 | 31 | 24 |
| (d) | *Husband's paid work week* | | | |
| | *None* | *Part time* | *Full time* | *Overtime* |
| Housewives' regular housework hours (all 372 couples) | 24.5 | 30.3 | 32.9 | 33.3 |
| (e) | *Wife's and Husband's paid work week* | | | |
| | *Both none* | *Both part time* | *Both full time* | *Both overtime* |
| Total workload hours in estimated weekly time budget: | | | | |
| Wives | 42.7 | 51.9 | 61.8 | 72.5 |
| Husbands | 47.1 | 56.5 | 53.6 | 55.4 |
| (couples with same job hours) | (11) | (11) | (16) | (7) |

overtime job weeks increases as the hours of their spouses increase (table 21.2a and b), that is, there is no mutual accommodation. However, women accommodate men's longer job hours when the proportion of women with paid work declines (table 21.2c), and the hours of regular housework increase for the women who stay at home (table 21.2d). Table 21.2e shows the estimated weekly workload of job time, necessary travel, and all domestic work for the cases where both husband and wife have comparable hours of paid work. Between the condition in which both did not work for pay and the condition where both worked overtime, the wives' workload increases by 30 hours and the husbands' by 8 hours. Excluding the cases where both did not work for pay, the husbands' overall workload decreases slightly, as the work week extended from part time to overtime, and their wives' goes up by 20 hours.

Having found in the small number of couples with relatively equal job hours that the husband's contribution tends to be insensitive to increasing shared demands, we can now consider all cases and assess the effect of the wives' weekly job hours on the conduct of both husbands and wives. Figure 21.2 shows graphically that as the wives' job hours increase: (1) their hours of regular housework decline without being made up for because their husbands' housework remains virtually at the same low level of some four to five hours a week; and

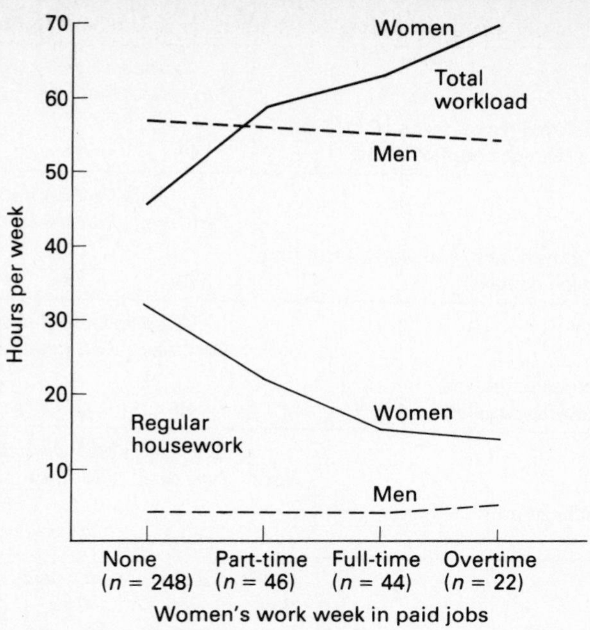


FIGURE 21.2 Wives' hours of paid work, and husbands' and wives' total workload and regular housework

(2) despite the successively more compressed hours of housework, the wives' total workload increases a great deal while their husbands' declines slightly. When men's workload and regular housework are plotted against their own job hours (not shown in the graph) and compared with the data for women, men always work less than women in each of the strictly comparable conditions.

## THE DOMESTIC WORK WEEK

At the core of the problems of the sexual division of labour addressed in this chapter lies a complex set of activities - housework. It has been denied recognition as work and has often been reduced to the simple question of whether husbands 'help' their wives. Some of the influential studies in family sociology have argued that time is an important resource in the husband–wife relationship, but have not considered how much time is required by the activities contained in their selective lists and how much by those which were omitted.

The contradiction between the importance of housework in the sexual division of labour and its obscured and neglectful treatment in social research demands an examination of its internal structure of component activities and of the question of what proportions of wives and husbands contribute to them and how much. Table 21.3 shows the percentage of wives and husbands who reported having engaged in each category of domestic work on a workday and a day off on the weekend, and for either of these two days combined, as well as estimates of the average hours they likely spent in a week.

The distinction between regular and irregular domestic work implies a discretionary dimension. Regular housework includes those activities which are, in most households, a daily to weekly necessity and leave less choice of the time at which they have to be done. Greater regularity is also indicated through the proportion of households for which the activities were reported. In the order shown in table 21.3, the proportions of women reporting each of the regular housework activities, for either workday or weekend day, range from 93 per cent in cooking to 43 per cent in child care, while the proportions for irregular items range from 42 per cent to 1 per cent.

The two largest items, in proportion as well as average time, are daily cooking and house cleaning. They take up about half of the time of women's regular and irregular housework and over one-fifth of men's. The contributions of husbands to these essentials and other regular requirements are always but a fraction of their wives'. The 26 per cent of husbands cleaning house on either workday or

TABLE 21.3 Percentage of time and hours in housework activities

| | Workday | | Day off | | Either day | | Estimated Weekly hours | |
|---|---|---|---|---|---|---|---|---|
| *Activities* | *Wife* | *Husband* | *Wife* | *Husband* | *Wife* | *Husband* | *Wife* | *Husband* |
| | % | % | % | % | % | % | *hours* | *hours* |
| *Regular housework* | | | | | | | | |
| Daily cooking | 86 | 13 | 77 | 18 | 93 | 27 | 8.0 | 0.7 |
| House cleaning | 74 | 8 | 61 | 20 | 86 | 26 | 7.8 | 1.1 |
| Kitchen wash-up | 47 | 4 | 41 | 8 | 64 | 11 | 2.1 | 0.2 |
| Regular shopping | 54 | 15 | 14 | 11 | 61 | 24 | 3.9 | 1.2 |
| Laundry | 36 | 1 | 21 | 1 | 48 | 2 | 2.9 | 0.0 |
| Child care | 36 | 7 | 33 | 18 | 43 | 21 | 3.3 | 0.9 |
| All reg. housework | 97 | 39 | 95 | 51 | 99 | 69 | 28.0 | 4.1 |
| *Irregular housework* | | | | | | | | |
| Irr. food/clothes | 25 | 0 | 23 | 1 | 38 | 2 | 3.3 | 0.0 |
| Irr. purchases | 8 | 4 | 7 | 8 | 14 | 11 | 0.7 | 0.2 |
| Sundry services | 31 | 22 | 21 | 28 | 42 | 43 | 1.4 | 1.1 |
| Repair, maint. | 5 | 11 | 6 | 22 | 10 | 28 | 0.2 | 2.2 |
| Building | 0 | 3 | 1 | 5 | 1 | 6 | 0.0 | 0.4 |
| All irr. housework | 54 | 36 | 46 | 52 | 70 | 65 | 5.6 | 3.9 |

(a) Estimated weekly hours are the sum of five times the average workday hours and two times the average weekend-day hours.

(b) $N = 340$ couples, excluding those with wife or husband off the job on the time-budget workday.

(c) Shopping and work involving food and clothes have been divided into regular and irregular categories. Irregular work on food and clothes includes canning, baking, sewing, mending, and fruit and vegetable picking. Irregular purchases include shopping for clothes, household equipment, car, leisure goods, house or apartment, and commercial services. The corresponding regular housework items are cooking the daily meals, laundry and ironing, and shopping for groceries and toilet articles. Sundry services include pick-up and delivery of persons and things, the rare case of getting a cleaning person or gardener, household accounting, animal care, and work entailed by leisure activities. Repairs and maintenance apply to appliances, car, bicycles, boats and other leisure equipment, the yard and garden (but not gardening proper). Building includes major construction and remodelling.

weekend day spent an estimated 4.25 hours per week while 86 per cent of the wives cleaned up for 9 hours. In cooking, 27 per cent of the husbands contributed an average 2.5 hours a week and 93 per cent of the wives 8.5 hours.

Only 39 per cent of the husbands contributed to any regular housework on a workday and 51 per cent on a weekend day in comparison to 97 per cent and 95 per cent of their wives. Only seven of the 340 husbands reported doing laundry in comparison to nearly half of their wives: men's inclination for machine technology does not extend to the washing machine. The largest proportions of men can be found in two of the irregular items of domestic work whose characteristics often approximate a state of leisure and where discretion is greater: repair and maintenance, and sundry services such as animal care, small errands, and work related to leisure activities. Surprisingly, even the typically masculine household chores, such as fixing things around the house (i.e. repair and maintenance), were reported by only 28 per cent of the husbands on a workday or weekend day. However, together with major construction work, it was the only kind of domestic work in which the proportion of men was greater than that of women. The average 2.5 hours of these manly efforts are at best equivalent to the time which wives have to devote to dishwashing in a week, an activity in which men are supposed to be so glad to 'help' (one out of ten men spending less than two hours a week). In total, men devoted about half of their domestic effort to the more discretionary, irregular kinds of work. Their total time was less than one-fourth of that of their wives and nearly one-third of them did not even make a token contribution to the regular necessities.

These data indicate that most married women do the regular, necessary, and most time-consuming work in the household every day. In view of the small and selective contribution of their husbands, they can anticipate doing it for the rest of their lives. The condition of their dependency finds daily expression in the structure of the domestic working day. The following examination will show in the temporal context of entire time budgets whether husbands respond to the cumulation of demands from young children and their wives' employment, however limited their response may be.

## TIME BUDGETS AND THE CUMULATION OF HOUSEHOLD DEMANDS

Because our data describe only married couples in established households, the lowest demand level from which we can begin consists of the two obligations created by having a spouse and living in a household. We will assess (1) the effect of an additional paid job, that is, the difference made by both wife and husband working for pay in comparison with couples in which only the husband is gainfully employed; and (2) the effect of the obligations created by having children in the household, determined here by the presence of at least one child under ten years of age.

The effect of each of the two conditions will be considered simultaneously so that we can tell the relative difference made by each. They will be ordered on the single dimension of increasing demands: (1) one paid job, no child under ten; (2) one paid job and a child under ten; (3) two paid jobs, no child under ten; and

(4) two paid jobs and a child under ten. In this ordering, a second paid job is given greater weight, even though the condition of 'one job, child under ten' would seem equivalent to 'two jobs, no child under ten'. The time required for a job and its related travel is generally greater than the time required for children. Work on the job cannot be combined with housework, but the additional work generated by children is part of domestic work and often combined with other household tasks.

Tables 21.4 and 21.5 display entire time budgets for a workday and a weekend day, each divided into eight combinations of sex, wife's employment, and the presence of a child under ten. Their examination makes it possible to assess the responses of wives and husbands to the problems of sharing the exigencies of cumulative demands and to understand the internal composition of their main blocks of time in work, self-maintenance, and leisure.

The time which women with paid work devote to their jobs is less than their husbands' because a larger proportion of women than of men work part time and a smaller proportion work overtime. Congruent with other findings, women's job time is sensitive to demands at home while men's is not. Women with a child under ten work for pay nearly one hour less than women without. In comparison, men in all categories work for pay about eight hours on a workday, and the small variations in their job time are unrelated to having a wife with a job or a younger child.

Even more pronounced differences can be seen in the composition of times spent in housework activities. Most obviously, women's time in child care goes up sharply when there is a child under ten, but the child-care time of women with paid work is half that of women without, on both workday and day off. Only a small proportion of husbands with a child under ten contribute to child care and, significantly, their contribution on weekends tends to be less, in average time and percentage of men, when their wives have a paying job than when they do not. In all the regular housework activities, a paid job tends to reduce drastically the average time spent by women on a workday. In an item-by-item comparison, the weekend record suggests that women with paid work revert to the full level of housework of jobless housewives. In house cleaning, particularly, they make up for time lost and spend virtually as much time as unpaid housewives do during the week. There is no noticeable change in husbands' regular housework items on workdays, in response to the necessary reduction in their employed wives' housework times, although the sum of their small efforts doubles to an average of 50 minutes in the extreme case of a child under ten *and* a job-holding wife. Husbands do a little more housework on weekends than on workdays, primarily in shopping and child care, but remain indifferent to the burdens of their wives' paid work.[3]

Repair and maintenance is the only category of domestic work in which husbands respond to greater household demands, both on a workday and a weekend day. While many of these typically masculine activities are undoubtedly

3. The question may be asked whether younger husbands would not be inclined to contribute more to housework than older ones and to respond more noticeably to cumulating demands. A similar question concerns education. According to our data, the husbands' housework hours remain essentially the same for older or younger, and more or less educated husbands, whether or not their wives work for pay or have a child under ten.

TABLE 21.4 Workday time budget hours by sex, wife's job and child under ten

| | *Women* | | | | *Men* | | | |
|---|---|---|---|---|---|---|---|---|
| | *1-job couple* | | *2-job couple* | | *1-job couple* | | *2-job couple* | |
| | *No ch.* | *Child* | *No ch.* | *Child* | *No ch.* | *Child* | *No ch.* | *Child* |
| Job | 0.0 | 0.0 | 6.5 | 5.8 | 7.7 | 8.1 | 7.6 | 7.2 |
| Job-related | 0.0 | 0.0 | 0.4 | 0.3 | 0.2 | 0.3 | 0.3 | 0.4 |
| Moonlighting | 0.0 | 0.0 | 0.0 | 0.0 | 0.0 | 0.0 | 0.1 | 0.2 |
| Total job work | 0.0 | 0.0 | 6.9 | 6.0 | 8.0 | 8.4 | 8.0 | 7.9 |
| Necessary travel | 1.0 | 1.0 | 1.3 | 1.1 | 1.4 | 1.4 | 1.4 | 1.3 |
| Daily cooking | 1.3 | 1.5 | 0.7 | 1.0 | 0.1 | 0.1 | 0.1 | 0.2 |
| House cleaning | 1.5 | 1.4 | 0.5 | 0.9 | 0.1 | 0.1 | 0.1 | 0.1 |
| Kitchen wash-up | 0.3 | 0.3 | 0.1 | 0.1 | 0.1 | 0.0 | 0.0 | 0.0 |
| Regular shopping | 0.9 | 0.8 | 0.4 | 0.6 | 0.1 | 0.1 | 0.2 | 0.2 |
| Laundry | 0.6 | 0.7 | 0.1 | 0.3 | 0.0 | 0.0 | 0.0 | 0.0 |
| Child care | 0.1 | 1.3 | 0.0 | 0.6 | 0.0 | 0.1 | 0.0 | 0.2 |
| Total reg. housework | 4.8 | 6.1 | 1.8 | 3.5 | 0.4 | 0.5 | 0.3 | 0.8 |
| Irr. food, clothes | 0.8 | 0.4 | 0.2 | 0.2 | 0.0 | 0.0 | 0.0 | 0.0 |
| Irr. purchases | 0.0 | 0.1 | 0.0 | 0.0 | 0.0 | 0.0 | 0.0 | 0.0 |
| Sundry services | 0.4 | 0.2 | 0.1 | 0.1 | 0.1 | 0.1 | 0.1 | 0.0 |
| Repair, maint. | 0.1 | 0.0 | 0.0 | 0.0 | 0.1 | 0.1 | 0.2 | 0.4 |
| Building | 0.0 | 0.0 | 0.0 | 0.0 | 0.0 | 0.0 | 0.1 | 0.0 |
| Total irr. housework | 1.3 | 0.8 | 0.4 | 0.3 | 0.3 | 0.3 | 0.5 | 0.4 |
| Sum workload | 7.1 | 7.8 | 10.4 | 11.0 | 10.0 | 10.5 | 10.2 | 10.4 |
| Sleep | 8.7 | 8.4 | 8.2 | 8.2 | 7.9 | 8.0 | 8.2 | 8.1 |
| Personal care | 0.7 | 0.7 | 0.7 | 0.8 | 0.6 | 0.5 | 0.6 | 0.6 |
| Eating | 2.2 | 2.1 | 1.8 | 1.9 | 1.9 | 1.8 | 1.9 | 1.8 |
| Sum self-maint. | 11.6 | 11.2 | 10.7 | 10.9 | 10.3 | 10.3 | 10.7 | 10.6 |
| Associations | 0.3 | 0.2 | 0.0 | 0.1 | 0.1 | 0.2 | 0.1 | 0.0 |
| Church | 0.0 | 0.0 | 0.0 | 0.0 | 0.0 | 0.0 | 0.0 | 0.0 |
| Active sports | 0.2 | 0.1 | 0.1 | 0.0 | 0.2 | 0.2 | 0.2 | 0.1 |
| Hobbies | 0.1 | 0.1 | 0.1 | 0.0 | 0.1 | 0.1 | 0.1 | 0.2 |
| Gardening | 0.5 | 0.4 | 0.0 | 0.0 | 0.2 | 0.1 | 0.2 | 0.1 |
| Total active leisure | 1.0 | 0.9 | 0.3 | 0.1 | 0.6 | 0.6 | 0.6 | 0.3 |
| Visiting | 0.7 | 0.8 | 0.6 | 0.4 | 0.5 | 0.4 | 0.5 | 0.4 |
| Talk or write | 0.5 | 0.5 | 0.4 | 0.2 | 0.2 | 0.2 | 0.2 | 0.3 |
| Drink, parties | 0.4 | 0.3 | 0.2 | 0.1 | 0.4 | 0.5 | 0.3 | 0.1 |
| Outings | 0.0 | 0.0 | 0.0 | 0.0 | 0.0 | 0.0 | 0.0 | 0.0 |
| Total sociability | 1.6 | 1.7 | 1.2 | 0.6 | 1.1 | 1.1 | 1.0 | 0.8 |
| Drive or walk | 0.1 | 0.1 | 0.1 | 0.1 | 0.1 | 0.0 | 0.0 | 0.2 |
| Publ. entertainmt | 0.1 | 0.1 | 0.1 | 0.0 | 0.1 | 0.1 | 0.1 | 0.1 |
| TV, radio | 1.1 | 1.1 | 0.9 | 0.7 | 1.0 | 1.0 | 1.4 | 1.7 |
| Reading | 0.7 | 0.5 | 0.4 | 0.0 | 0.5 | 0.4 | 0.5 | 0.3 |
| Relaxing | 0.4 | 0.2 | 0.2 | 0.1 | 0.2 | 0.2 | 0.2 | 0.1 |
| Total entertainment | 2.4 | 2.0 | 1.6 | 1.0 | 1.9 | 1.7 | 2.2 | 2.4 |
| Sum leisure | 5.0 | 4.6 | 3.1 | 1.8 | 3.6 | 3.3 | 3.9 | 3.4 |
| Unclassified | 0.3 | 0.4 | 0.1 | 0.3 | 0.4 | 0.3 | 0.2 | 0.3 |
| Total time budget | 24.0 | 24.0 | 24.4 | 24.0 | 24.3 | 24.5 | 25.0 | 24.6 |
| (*N*) | (131) | (106) | (85) | (18) | (131) | (106) | (85) | (18) |

Table excludes couples with wife and/or husband off the job on workday

TABLE 21.5 Day-off time budget hours by sex, wife's job and child under ten

| | *Women* | | | | *Men* | | | |
|---|---|---|---|---|---|---|---|---|
| | *1-job couple* | | *2-job couple* | | *1-job couple* | | *2-job couple* | |
| | *No ch.* | *Child* | *No ch.* | *Child* | *No ch.* | *Child* | *No ch.* | *Child* |
| Job | 0.0 | 0.0 | 0.5 | 0.1 | 0.1 | 0.6 | 0.4 | 0.4 |
| Job-related | 0.0 | 0.0 | 0.0 | 0.0 | 0.0 | 0.0 | 0.0 | 0.0 |
| Moonlighting | 0.0 | 0.0 | 0.0 | 0.0 | 0.0 | 0.0 | 0.0 | 0.0 |
| Total job work | 0.0 | 0.0 | 0.5 | 0.1 | 0.2 | 0.6 | 0.4 | 0.4 |
| Necessary travel | 0.7 | 0.7 | 1.1 | 0.7 | 0.9 | 1.1 | 1.1 | 0.7 |
| Daily cooking | 1.0 | 1.1 | 0.9 | 1.1 | 0.1 | 0.2 | 0.2 | 0.1 |
| House cleaning | 0.8 | 0.8 | 1.3 | 1.2 | 0.3 | 0.3 | 0.4 | 0.1 |
| Kitchen wash-up | 0.2 | 0.3 | 0.2 | 0.4 | 0.0 | 0.1 | 0.1 | 0.2 |
| Regular shopping | 0.2 | 0.2 | 0.3 | 0.0 | 0.1 | 0.1 | 0.2 | 0.3 |
| Laundry | 0.2 | 0.2 | 0.4 | 0.2 | 0.0 | 0.0 | 0.0 | 0.0 |
| Child care | 0.1 | 1.1 | 0.1 | 0.6 | 0.1 | 0.5 | 0.0 | 0.3 |
| Total reg. housework | 2.5 | 3.6 | 3.2 | 3.6 | 0.6 | 1.2 | 0.9 | 1.0 |
| Irr. food, clothes | 0.5 | 0.2 | 0.3 | 0.5 | 0.0 | 0.1 | 0.1 | 0.1 |
| Irr. purchases | 0.0 | 0.1 | 0.1 | 0.0 | 0.0 | 0.1 | 0.1 | 0.0 |
| Sundry services | 0.3 | 0.2 | 0.1 | 0.1 | 0.3 | 0.3 | 0.2 | 0.3 |
| Repair, maint. | 0.1 | 0.1 | 0.0 | 0.4 | 0.5 | 0.7 | 0.6 | 1.3 |
| Building | 0.0 | 0.0 | 0.0 | 0.0 | 0.1 | 0.2 | 0.3 | 0.0 |
| Total irr. housework | 1.0 | 0.6 | 0.6 | 1.0 | 1.0 | 1.4 | 1.3 | 1.6 |
| Sum workload | 4.2 | 5.0 | 5.4 | 5.5 | 2.7 | 4.3 | 3.7 | 3.8 |
| Sleep | 8.4 | 8.5 | 7.9 | 8.4 | 8.2 | 8.0 | 8.0 | 7.9 |
| Personal care | 0.5 | 0.5 | 0.9 | 1.0 | 0.6 | 0.6 | 0.6 | 0.4 |
| Eating | 2.4 | 2.2 | 2.0 | 2.2 | 2.0 | 1.9 | 1.8 | 1.7 |
| Sum self-maint. | 11.3 | 11.2 | 10.8 | 11.6 | 10.8 | 10.4 | 10.3 | 10.0 |
| Associations | 0.1 | 0.0 | 0.0 | 0.0 | 0.1 | 0.1 | 0.1 | 0.0 |
| Church | 0.1 | 0.2 | 0.1 | 0.1 | 0.1 | 0.2 | 0.0 | 0.3 |
| Active sports | 0.2 | 0.2 | 0.1 | 0.1 | 1.1 | 0.6 | 0.5 | 0.4 |
| Hobbies | 0.2 | 0.1 | 0.0 | 0.0 | 0.1 | 0.3 | 0.5 | 0.2 |
| Gardening | 0.5 | 0.3 | 0.4 | 0.0 | 0.8 | 0.7 | 0.9 | 0.3 |
| Total active leisure | 1.1 | 0.8 | 0.6 | 0.2 | 2.3 | 1.9 | 1.9 | 1.2 |
| Visiting | 1.2 | 1.3 | 1.3 | 0.2 | 0.9 | 1.1 | 1.2 | 0.4 |
| Talk or write | 0.4 | 0.4 | 0.5 | 0.6 | 0.4 | 0.2 | 0.3 | 0.6 |
| Drink, parties | 0.6 | 0.2 | 0.2 | 0.3 | 0.6 | 0.3 | 0.5 | 0.3 |
| Outings | 0.1 | 0.0 | 0.2 | 0.0 | 0.1 | 0.0 | 0.1 | 0.1 |
| Total sociability | 2.3 | 1.9 | 2.2 | 1.2 | 1.9 | 1.6 | 2.1 | 1.3 |
| Drive or walk | 0.5 | 0.3 | 0.3 | 0.8 | 0.8 | 0.5 | 0.6 | 0.8 |
| Publ. entertainment | 0.1 | 0.2 | 0.2 | 0.1 | 0.3 | 0.3 | 0.2 | 0.2 |
| TV, radio | 1.7 | 1.4 | 1.3 | 1.4 | 1.9 | 1.6 | 1.9 | 2.7 |
| Reading | 0.6 | 0.6 | 0.6 | 0.4 | 0.7 | 0.7 | 0.5 | 0.2 |
| Relaxing | 0.4 | 0.6 | 0.6 | 0.8 | 0.8 | 0.7 | 0.3 | 1.2 |
| Total entertainment | 3.3 | 3.0 | 3.1 | 3.4 | 4.5 | 3.8 | 3.5 | 5.1 |
| Sum leisure | 6.6 | 5.7 | 5.8 | 4.9 | 8.7 | 7.3 | 7.5 | 7.5 |
| Unclassified | 0.4 | 0.6 | 0.4 | 0.3 | 0.5 | 0.4 | 0.8 | 0.7 |
| Total time budget | 22.5 | 22.5 | 22.5 | 22.3 | 22.7 | 22.4 | 22.4 | 22.1 |
| (*N*) | (131) | (106) | (85) | (18) | (131) | (106) | (85) | (18) |

Table excludes couples with wife and/or husband off the job on workday

necessary, there is no rationale for an increase in time devoted to fixing and washing the car or cleaning up the back yard when the household is under greater pressure to maintain the essentials. These time-budget records confirm the token conception of husbands' willingness to 'help' wives: they like 'to change lightbulbs and move the furniture' (Meinardi, 1972:124).

The same consistent structure of reactions can be observed in the principal self-maintenance and leisure activities. Over the range of four categories of rising demands, women have less and less time for sleep and meals, while men's times remain the same throughout. Each of the three main classes of leisure contains one most prominent activity in terms of average hours spent as well as the proportion of people engaged: gardening, visiting, and watching television. The time which women have for each is consistently reduced under the pressure of mounting obligations, particularly on a workday. The leisure experience of men in these three most popular activities is oblivious to rising household requirements. On both workday and weekend, their time in front of the television set tends to *increase* while visiting and gardening show no consistent change. For a gross summary, let us take the sum of the five most important nonwork activities, estimated for an entire week, and compare the extreme demands levels (i.e. 'one job – no child' versus 'two jobs – child under ten'). In this comparison women lose 14 hours a week and men make a net gain of 1.4 hours a week in sleep, meals, gardening, visiting, and television watching – activities which take up about half of the total hours of a week.

A growing number of couples are confronted by the demands which the wives' paid work makes on their household, and these demands accumulate with those created by young children. According to the adaptive partnership theory one would expect the potential contradiction between women's involvement in public production and the demands of the household to be resolved, or at least mitigated, in a sharing of changed burdens and benefits. However, the detailed time budgets tell a story of the dependent labour of married women whose entire days are affected, activity by activity, while their husbands keep the day of 'their' work and their leisure intact in its overall composition and its component activities.

## THE SHARE OF THE INCREASING WORKLOAD

We have described the proportions of husbands and wives who contribute to the activities of domestic work and then have shown how the distribution of time for the activities of their entire day responded to the cumulation of demands. We should now address the question of the wives' and husbands' relative share in the overall workload and its regular housework component as demands accumulate.

A measure of the burdens shared by the couple is the sum of husband's and wife's total weekly workload, estimated from the hours of the workday and weekend time budget they both devote to work for pay, necessary travel, regular housework, and irregular domestic work. The left half of figure 21.3 shows that this combined workload rises consistently with each step of accumulating demands, in the four categories of wife's employment and a child under ten, from a weekly total of 99.3 hours in one-job couples without a young child to 125.6 hours in two-job couples with a child under ten. The lower line in the graph

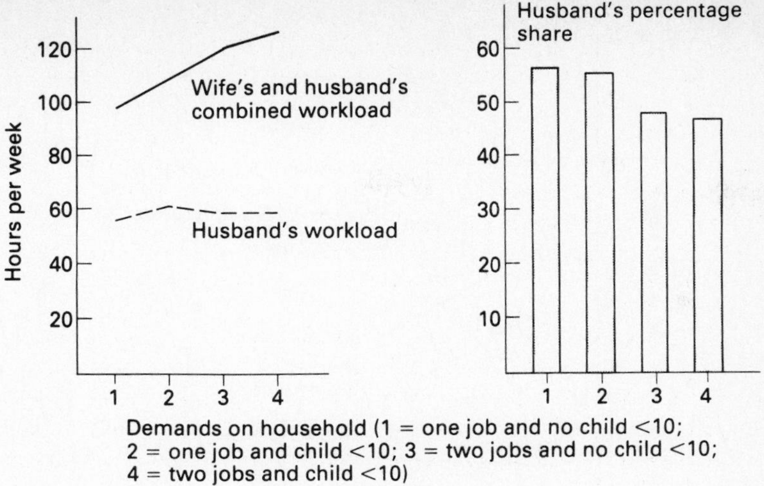


FIGURE 21.3 Household demands and husband's share in combined total workload

describes the husbands' component in that combined total, and it shows little variation relative to increasing demands. The bar graph on the right of figure 21.3 sets the combined workload to 100 per cent and describes the percentage share of husbands. It declines step by step with additional demands.

The crucial problem, when a married woman holds a paying job, is the housework. The domestic work week of housewives without outside employment is a full equivalent (give or take three hours, depending on whether they have a young child) to their husbands' 40-hour week on the job.[4] Is the obstacle of a double burden overcome through a redistribution of housework in an adaptive partnership of husband and wife, or does the dependent-labour status of married women come to a point because they have to come to their own terms with an excessive workload? Our data make clear that women must find their own 'solutions': (1) through more part-time and less overtime work, they keep their job hours on a workday to an average of over one hour less than their husbands'; (2) they reduce their domestic work hours on a workday to half the amount of housewives without employment; (3) they make up for some of the weekday reduction on the weekend but manage to compress the necessities of the regular housework of the entire week by more than 13 hours. Despite these modifications, their total weekly workload increases by 18 hours. If husbands do not share the problem, do they at least 'help' in mitigating it? In couples without a child under ten and a wife without employment, husbands do an estimated 3.2 hours of regular housework a week, increasing it by an insignificant 6 minutes

4. This equivalence is confirmed in the multinational time-budget studies, where the domestic work hours of housewives, as a percentage of the job hours of men, range from a low of 99 per cent in Belgium and 100 per cent in the USA to 133 per cent in the Soviet Union (Szalai, 1972:583–93).

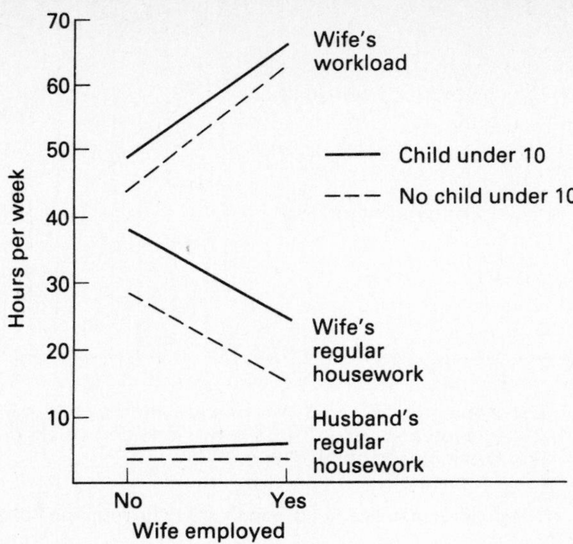


FIGURE 21.4 Change and stability in wives' work week and husbands' housework

when their wives go out to work. In couples with a young child, things are only slightly better. The husbands' 5 hours of regular housework increase by one hour a week when their wives work for pay. As shown in figure 21.4, despite the radical difference which a paid job makes in the working week of married women, their husbands' contribution to the regular necessities of the household remains small and virtually unchanged.

We have argued that husbands have an interest in maintaining conventions according to which their life is devoted to work and their wives' to the family. Do husbands perhaps contribute differently to increased demands due to a young child than they do due to their wives' employment? When controlling for the effects of a child under ten, the wife's job makes for a reduction of 12.7 hours in the regular housework of husband and wife combined. The husbands' small increase makes up for 5 per cent of that reduction. A child under ten requires an increase of 11.2 hours in the couple's regular housework and the husband contributes 20 per cent to that increase.

Turning now to the couple's overall workload, the combined increase from the wife's employment is 18.7 hours (when controlling for the effect of a child under ten), that is, 2.5 times as much as the average increase of 7.6 hours due to a young child (with the effect of wife's employment controlled). Husbands shared 4 per cent of the large increase required by their wives' paid work but 45 per cent of the smaller increase necessitated by a young child. The husbands' conduct corresponds with their conventional interest: a modest demand of more time for children is legitimate but the exigencies of their wives' paid work count for next to nothing.

## ADAPTIVE PARTNERSHIP OR DEPENDENT LABOUR?

This chapter has provided an analysis of the workday and weekend time budgets of married couples. The analysis was designed to choose between two theories of the sexual division of household labour. Both theories were formulated to account for the consequences in the household of the contradiction between economic change resulting in a greater demand for women's work, on the one hand, and the stability of sexist conventions in the allocation of work, on the other. The analysis extended over the conditions of participation in paid work; the length of the paid work week; the composition of housework activities; the structure of entire time budgets relative to cumulate demands of wife's employment and young children; and the share of wives and husbands in their combined workload. If the results in these components had been inconsistent, both or neither of the two theories could have potential plausibility.

The 'adaptive partnership theory' was derived from family sociology, according to which the moral force of equity would have done its work in a greater sharing of domestic obligations as a result of a change in the internal balance of wives' and husbands' resources of paid work and time. Derived from the recognition of the different relationship of women and men to the organization of production, an alternative theory predicted that the cumulation of demands on men's and women's shared household would become the cumulation of the 'dependent labour' of women. Throughout the range of data, the results were consistent. These results deprive the 'adaptive partnership' conception of plausibility and put the methods of research associated with it into question. The consistency of results makes it more difficult to reject the 'dependent labour' argument.

Not designed to improve the status of women but to assure a pool of cheap and compliant labour, the rising demand for the employment of married women contains its own contradiction. Paid work offers to married women the potential of at least some financial independence from their husbands but, at the same time, confirms their domestic dependency in the menial and subordinate character of much of their paid work. The larger contradiction, according to which employment demand and domestic requirements accumulate in their dependent labour, leaves no exit for wives.

## APPENDIX: WHAT HUSBANDS HAVE TO SAY

After a preliminary analysis of the time budgets, ten of the couples of the original study were reinterviewed in order to explore with them in more qualitative depth their feelings and conceptions of their division of paid and domestic work. We are compiling here a small selection of recorded comments in which eight husbands express their sense of obligations of housework, women's jobs, and their rewards. They represent a full range of class differences and of wives' work status. These comments speak loud and clear for themselves and need no further interpretation. (A full report of these ten case studies is contained in Humphreys, 1974.)

A machine operator in his mid-thirties, whose wife works nearly full time as a keypunch operator (three children, aged 3 to 11), on the subject of the 'heavy work' which he takes as his share of the housework: 'I think – why the hell do I have to scrub these bloody walls and she couldn't get up on a step ladder and do the same bloody thing. My dad never did it. Why the hell do I have to do them?'

A forklift driver in his mid-fifties, whose wife works two days a week as a switchboard operator (three children, aged 13 to 22), on the conditions for sharing housework: 'If a woman *has* to work, then the husband and wife should share the housework, but if it isn't necessary for her to work then she should consider looking after the house first. It isn't necessary for her to work in the first place. She's doing this for herself and to satisfy herself, where the man has to work to keep the house going.'

The same man, on the question of the possibility of changing the share of housework: 'If my wife wanted change I'd have to think about it, but there's no point in thinking about something that may or may not happen.'

A skilled repairman in his early forties whose wife had been upgrading her education and is contemplating further training, on the question of his wife taking a job (four children, aged 5 to 16): 'I'd want her home when the kids come home from school or at least when I get home from work. I'm sure as hell not cooking my own supper. I didn't get married for that.'

The same man, on women's jobs in his shop: 'There are a lot of jobs in the repair shop that are so damn monotonous that the men don't want them, so the girls do it. Women are better at these sorts of jobs. They have more patience and are more conscientious.'

A policeman in his early forties whose wife works a few hours a week as a salesperson in a store (two children, aged 9 and 13), on his wife's income: 'It doesn't mean anything because it's so little. I told her to put it away into a little account, do whatever you want with it.'

His wife's view of her income: 'It's not that you make a lot of money, but as you see your money grow and that it can do something for the family, well I think it's rather nice.'

The same man, reacting to two weeks recently when his wife's job was full time: 'To stand back and say there's no way she's going to work steady if this is what it's going to do. It wasn't the money, it was just getting a break from housework to cut the boredom down a little bit and having fun at it and no stress or strain or nothing. Once a job starts to develop the stresses and strains it's not worth it any more. You've lost your sense of direction.'

A sales representative in his mid-forties said he is happy about his wife's full-time bank job and does the 'outside chores' at home. About the 'inside' housework, he feels: 'I wouldn't want it. It doesn't interest me and women are more capable of doing it. It's her responsibility because it's just accepted that she looks after that area. It's just the same as finances. I don't want to be bothered with it and I think it's good for her to do it.'

The same man, on women's paid work: 'I'm against seeing women on the end of a jackhammer. I don't think they're capable of producing the same as what a man is. They can do it, but they can't produce as much as a man could so they should get paid accordingly.'

A manager in his mid-thirties whose wife is a full-time housewife (3 children, aged 7 to 14), on the hypothetical question of his wife taking a job: 'I wouldn't stand in her way, if that's what she wanted to do, but fortunately for me she doesn't want to do that. My wife's first priority should be the family and the home as long as I'm able to provide for the family.'

An executive in his mid-fifties, whose wife is a codirector in their own company and works there almost full time (two children at home, aged 14 and 17), on women's and men's jobs and the division of housework: 'I don't say a woman's place is in the home. I just don't see why a woman should blacktop roads, for instance . . . not when there are able-bodied men that can do it. Women should complement rather than compete with men. If I'm capable of doing it and it falls into the male sphere then why the hell should she have to do it? She should acknowledge the fact that he does it better and let him do it and vice versa. If you have a dirty job to do, it should be the male that goes out and does it. When he comes home from that dirty job there's a clean bed, a nice meal and a nice chair to sit in. What the hell – you can't have that if your wife's out doing the same thing as you.'

A lawyer in his late forties whose wife has just quit a part-time professional job because the double burden was too much (three children, aged 15 to 19), about the sharing of housework: 'If the guy comes home completely beat because he's got a job of much more pressure and his wife has a job because she's bored with the housework, this gives her a lift and she's more up to doing the housework.'

## REFERENCES

Blood, Robert, and Donald Wolfe (1960) *Husbands and Wives: The Dynamics of Married Living*. New York: Free Press.

Eichler, Margrit (1973) 'Women as personal dependants,' pp. 38–55 in M. Stephenson (ed.), *Women in Canada*. Toronto: New Press.

Gendell, Murray (1963) *Swedish Working Wives*. Totowa: Bediminster.

Govaerts, France (1969) *Loisirs des femmes et temps libre*. Bruxelles: Editions de l'institut de sociologie, Université Libre de Bruxelles.

Humphreys, Elizabeth W. (1974) 'Role bargaining: a means of adaptation to strain within dual work families.' MA thesis. Vancouver: University of British Columbia.

Kalbach, Warren, and Wayne McVey (1971) *The Demographic Bases of Canadian Society*. Toronto: McGraw-Hill.

Meinardi, Pat (1972) 'La politique du travail ménager,' pp. 123–130 in *Le livre de l'oppression des femmes*. Paris: Belfond.

Michel, Andrée (1970) 'Statut professionnel féminin et interaction dans le couple en France et aux Etats-Unis,' pp. 281–91 in A. Michel (ed.), *La sociologie de la famille: recueil de textes présentés et commentés*. Paris: Mouton.

Michel, Andrée (1974) 'Emploi féminin, techniques ménagères et budgets-temps.' *Society and Leisure* 6:185–90.

Robinson, John (1971) 'Historical changes in how people spend their time,' pp. 143–53 in A. Michel (ed.), *Family Issues of Employed Women in Europe and America*. Leiden: Brill.

Szalai, Alexander (ed.) (1972) *The Use of Time: Daily Activities of Urban and Suburban Populations in Twelve Countries*. The Hague: Mouton.

Vanek, Joann (1974) 'Time spent in housework.' *Scientific American* (November): 116–20.

Walker, Kathryn (1969) 'Homemaking still takes time.' *Journal of Home Economics* 61:621–4.

Walker, Kathryn (1970) 'Time used by husbands for household work.' *Family Economics Review* (June): 8–10.

Young, Michael, and Peter Willmott (1973) *The Symmetrical Family: A Study of Work and Leisure in the London Region*. London: Routledge.

Zuker, Marvin, and June Callwood (1971) *Canadian Women and the Law*. Toronto: Copp Clark.

# 22

# Who Cares? A Review of Empirical Evidence from Britain

GILLIAN PARKER

## INTRODUCTION

One of the most persistent misconceptions about 'modern society' is that the family no longer cares for its dependants, especially the elderly. Yet, as Brody (1981) has pointed out:

> Research during the past several decades has systematically disproved the notion that contemporary families are alienated from the aged and do not take care of them as used to be the case in the 'good old days'. The accumulated evidence documents the strength of intergenerational behaviour, the frequency of contacts between generations, the predominance of families rather than professionals in the provision of health and social services, the strenuous family efforts to avoid institutional placement of the old, and the central role played by families in caring for the noninstitutionalized impaired elderly.

Unfortunately, as Brody continues, though science has signed the death certificate of 'family alienation from older people' the popular misunderstanding has eluded burial. So successful has this elusion been that another commentator (Shanas 1979) has likened the misconception to 'a hydra-headed monster'.

The aim of this chapter is to identify clearly where care is usually based, who does the caring, why caring is mostly a female task and who 'ought' to care. Information about the extent of residential or institutional care for elderly people and for children and adults with disabilities is reviewed; the extent to which families and others are involved in the day-to-day care of dependent people is documented; and those within the family who bear the major responsibility for care are

This essay was first published as chapter 2 in Gillian Parker, *With Due Care and Attention*, Family Policy Studies Centre occasional paper no. 2, January 1985. 

identified. Some evidence on the role of women as carers and on who 'should' care for dependent people is also included.

## THE LOCUS OF CARE

Expectations and assumptions about where care for dependants should take place and who should undertake it vary with the type of dependant. Family responsibility for care of the elderly is, in most cases, assumed by offspring after they have led a 'normal life' (Moroney 1976). For families with a disabled child the position is radically different: 'Families, especially parents, are not faced with the prospect of providing care for a matter of years after a 'normal life' but for decades. For these families the idea of a normal life has to be redefined' (p. 64). While there is, in theory, an element of choice over whether or not an adult child assumes responsibility for an ageing parent, society rarely sanctions the same degree of choice for a parent in regard to his or her young children. Moreover, many elderly people have no family who might take on responsibility for their care; this is true of only a very small proportion of children with disabilities. For adults with disabilities the issues are different again. Adults who acquire disabilities after a normal life might expect, and be expected by others, to continue to live where and with whom they were living while in full health. By contrast, young people with congenital disabilities or disabilities acquired in childhood, especially where these are physical and not mental impairments, might hope to leave home and establish an independent life in much the same way as their contemporaries. (Although it must be acknowledged that the reality of the situation is very different from this ideal; Hirst 1984.)

Expectations for adults with mental handicaps are less clear cut. In the past, certainly, there has been an implicit expectation that they could not live independent lives and, consequently, that where not in institutional care they should remain with their families. Indeed the 1971 White Paper *Better Services for the Mentally Handicapped* (Cmnd 4683) assumed that each handicapped person should live with his own family as long as this did not impose an undue burden on the family or on the handicapped person. The report of the Jay Committee (1979) (Cmnd 7468) challenged this assumption, however, proposing that 'the family should *not* be regarded as the central agent in the care and support [of a mentally-handicapped person] until the parents are old and infirm.' It was suggested instead that 'a range of accommodation should be available which would allow the handicapped person to choose with his family whether to move out and establish a life independent of the parental home' (Wertheimer 1981, pp. 168–9). Moves towards 'normalization' of the lives of people with mental handicaps have also prompted questions about where they should live: 'if we say that mentally-handicapped people have the same rights as other people in British society, does that not include the right to leave home at eighteen?' (p. 169)

That 'society' holds these differing expectations about the locus of care for different dependency groups is given some empirical confirmation by recent research carried out in Aberdeen (West et al. 1983 and 1984). In three separate locations in Scotland, 727 adults were asked to study vignettes of people of different ages and different types of disability. They were then asked to indicate which of several possible care arrangements should be adopted for each 'vignette'. In all cases the options ranged 'from family and informal care only (including the possibility of transfer to close kin) through domiciliary professional support, community based professional care [e.g. a day centre] to residential care of a partial or total kind'. Table 22.1 summarizes the results of this study.

The authors conclude that there is a consensus for care arrangements which can be 'termed community based professional care – day care centres, day hospitals, and notably in respect of elderly physical disability, sheltered housing', i.e. community rather than institutional care. However, it is also pointed out that:

> The public are discriminating. Their advocated preferences are strongly associated with the nature of the medical problem and the implications entailed for the (vignette) carers and dependants. This varies from relatively strong support for family and informal care in the psychiatric case, the only occasion this option is relatively preferred, to overwhelming support for residential care in respect of the confused elderly. There is evidence in the young and more particularly elderly dependency groups that mental impairment is more strongly associated with advocacy of professional involvement than physical impairment.

Although West et al. found little difference between the three samples in their expressed preferences, or between age groups or socio-economic groups, they did find that preferences differed slightly between men and women: 'In respect of sex . . . there [was] a statistically significant difference between males and females in regard to both young mental and physical handicap and elderly physical disability. In these cases, women less often advocate family and informal care alone and more often prefer community based professional care options'. This finding is, of course, important because it is women who shoulder the major burden of informal care. The effect was not, however, consistent over dependency groups and it seems more than likely that marital status, age and sex of the respondents would be interactive. For example, one could speculate that elderly married women would differ in their preferences for different dependency groups from, say, young adult single men. Unfortunately, the Aberdeen study could not explore these issues.

TABLE 22.1 Advocated care preference for the physically and mentally impaired of different ages (percentages)

| | *Young (school leaver)* | | *Adult* | | *Elderly* | |
|---|---|---|---|---|---|---|
| *Advocated care preference* | *physical* | *mental* | *physical* | *mental* | *physical* | *mental* |
| Family and informal care *only* | 20.2 | 16.0 | 29.3 | 44.8 | 14.8 | 9.2 |
| Domiciliary professional help | 17.7 | 9.0 | 28.7 | 16.4 | 17.7 | 7.4 |
| Community based professional care | 29.2 | 43.0 | 38.8 | 24.8 | 58.1 | 17.3 |
| Residential care | 33.0 | 32.0 | 2.2 | 14.0 | 9.5 | 66.0 |
| Total (100%) | 713 | 721 | 711 | 721 | 718 | 715 |

NB Both the adult and elderly 'mental impairment' vignettes related to psychiatric conditions rather than mental retardation.
*Source*: West et al. 1983, 1984.

Another Scottish study (Weeks n.d.) which questioned middle-aged people about preferences for their own care in old age, revealed that only a minority expected their families to look after them when they became old. A substantial majority 'had favourable attitudes towards being looked after in nursing homes or residential homes'.

Recent work in America has shown how age, or more correctly life-cycle status, is related to differing attitudes about, and preferences for, the locus of care for the elderly. A study of elderly women, their middle-aged daughters and young adult grand-daughters documented quite substantial differences between the groups (Brody 1981; Davis 1981). Grand-daughters 'felt more strongly than the middle generation and much more strongly than the grandmothers about . . . "grandfilial responsibility", that is, that older people should expect help from their grandchildren' (Brody). While grandmothers strongly endorsed family care of the elderly they 'were more likely (75%) than the daughters (61%) and grand-daughters (59%) to favour paying someone for . . . care rather than obliging a working daughter to leave her job' to take on responsibility. In addition, 'grandmothers were least likely to think that adult children with their own families should do household tasks for their parents.'

When the researchers asked questions which focused less on what people in general should do and more on what the individual women would like for themselves, they found that 'middle-generation women were less likely than either the grandmothers [or] grand-daughters to prefer an adult child as provider of housework and personal care services.' The authors suggested that these preferences reflected the pressure of multiple responsibilities that the middle-generation women were feeling themselves or observing in their contemporaries.

While the majority of people in these studies saw the family and other informal settings as the right locus of care for dependants very few felt that families should be left to cope alone and most saw an active role for the state in the provision of professional support and care. At the same time it was clear from the Aberdeen study that different mixes of care were felt appropriate for different types of dependency. Another important point, although not discussed by the authors, is that while there was a degree of consensus about the locus of care it was not complete. Individual differences are important; just as those cared for will have different preferences for where and by whom they should be cared for, so those doing the caring will have differing preferences.

## RESIDENTIAL VERSUS NON-RESIDENTIAL CARE

### *The Elderly*

Misconceptions about the abrogation of family responsibilities are, perhaps, strongest in relation to the elderly. Yet, while it is certainly true that the absolute number of elderly people in residential care has grown over the past 20 years, the proportion of the elderly who are so cared for has not; only a tiny minority are in residential care and, moreover, the proportion in such care has not risen significantly since the turn of the century.

In 1981, the number of residents in local authority and private or voluntary homes for those aged sixty-five or over (England and Wales) was 170,300 (*Social Trends 1983* , table 7.30). This represents only 1.55 per cent of the population aged sixty-five or over. Even if all these residents were seventy-five or over they would still represent only 5 per cent of the population of similar age. By comparison, in 1900, 2.8 per cent of the population of seventy and over, and in 1920, 1.6 per cent of those aged sixty-five and over, were in public care (Halsey 1972, table 12.4).

A related misconception about the elderly who do not live in residential care is that they are neglected by their families to a greater degree than in the past. This misconception arises in part, perhaps, from the increasing number and proportions of elderly people who live alone. In 1961, 7.0 per cent of all households were elderly people living alone; by 1971 this proportion had risen to 12 per cent, and in 1981 was 15 per cent of all households (*Social Trends* 1983, table 2.2). At least part of this increase is accounted for by the increase in childless marriages and fall in the birth rate generally.

However, living alone does not necessarily mean that an elderly person is without support from his or her family, where one exists. As early as 1948, Sheldon's study of elderly people in Wolverhampton showed that widowed people often decided to live alone rather than move in with family members because relatives, usually children, lived close at hand (Sheldon 1948, p. 154). A large representative study of elderly people in the community (not in residential care) in the 1970s (Hunt 1978) discovered just under a third living alone, although this proportion increased with age. However, when people did live alone support was often available from relatives. For example, shopping for bedfast or housebound elderly people was done by relatives in almost half the cases reported. Even among elderly people suffering from dementia, whom one might expect to be receiving hospital or institutional care, family care appears to be more important than formal care (Kay et al. 1970; Bergmann et al. 1978; Isaacs et al. 1972).

While it is difficult to draw any conclusions about changes in the pattern of family care for the elderly from the studies reviewed here – they are based on dissimilar samples from dissimilar communities – there is no apparent evidence of wholesale abrogation of responsibility by families. The provision of statutory services to the elderly has certainly increased since 1948 but this has largely been to support the elderly without families close by rather than replace or supplement family care (Bergmann et al. 1978; Moroney 1976). Indeed, it can be argued that care of the elderly by their families may be more common now than in the past. Johnson and Johnson (cited in Greengross 1982) have suggested that today's 'modified extended families' care more extensively and for longer than ever before. As more elderly people live to a very old age it is inevitable, then, that a greater proportion of the next generation will become responsible for their care.

### *Children with Disabilities*

It has been estimated (Court Report 1976, Cmnd 6684, vol. 1 p. 220) that in an average health district (pre-1982) only around 840 children under the age of sixteen will suffer from handicaps severe enough to warrant some form of special education although the numbers warranting special health care will be around 5500. Of the 840 children approximately 240 would be severely mentally retarded. However, there is very little up to date information about the *proportions* of children with severe handicaps who are cared for in residential or institutional settings. The DHSS paper 'Better services for the mentally handicapped' (1972, Cmnd 4683) estimated that slightly over 70 per cent of children with severe mental handicaps were living with their families.

However, it seems that the number of young children who become long stay residents is declining. Children who *are* admitted to hospital care now tend to remain for short periods only (Moroney 1976, p. 78); 'Long term or permanent institutionalization among [mentally handicapped] children is not the norm.' The number of children resident in NHS hospitals in England, Scotland and Wales in 1976 was 4879 (Jay Report), a population some 4405 lower than in 1970. In addition, in 1977, 1721 children with disabilities were living in local authority homes but this represented an increase of only 300 or so since 1970. There had also been an increase of around 1500 in the number of places funded by local authorities in voluntary and private homes but it is not possible to estimate how many of these places were for children.

There is no clear or recent indication of the number or proportions of children with severe physical disabilities only who are in long-term residential care. The Court Report (p. 248) cites figures from a 1969 DHSS survey which indicate that, at that time, around a fifth of children in long stay hospitals were not mentally handicapped. What we know of children with physical disabilities only, however, suggests that only a very small proportion ever become long-stay residents in institutions after having been cared for at home (e.g. Hirst 1982). Some children with physical disabilities may attend boarding schools but again reliable information on the numbers and proportions involved is not available.

In summary, the information we are able to glean all points to a relatively small, and declining, proportion of children with severe disabilities being cared for in residential or institutional care. That the majority of children with severe disabilities are cared for by their families 'in the community' does not, however, mean that the community at large is involved in their care. The question of who is actually involved in providing care is discussed later in this chapter.

### *Adults with Disabilities: Mental Handicaps*

Of the groups so far considered, adults with mental handicaps seem to be most likely to be in some form of institutional or residential care. Bayley's (1973) study of all the people with mental handicaps registered with the Sheffield Mental Health Service in 1968 showed quite clear differences in age structure between those still at home and those who had been admitted to institutional or residential care. Although around two-thirds of all those with severe mental handicaps were living at home this proportion dropped with age.

Government estimates (HMSO 1971, Cmnd 4683) suggest that over a half of severely mentally handicapped adults do not live with their own families. While there has been a trend towards the reduction of numbers of long-stay residents in mental handicap hospitals it seems likely that the increase in places in local authority, private and voluntary homes has more than made up this reduction ( *Social Trends* 1983). Consequently, it seems unlikely that there will have been any major increase in the proportion of adults with mental handicaps living in non-residential care.

The indications are, indeed, that people with mental handicaps may be admitted to residential care at a later stage than before, rather than not being admitted at all (Moroney 1976, table 4.9). However, as Tyne (1982) has pointed out, we do not know for certain that this is the case.

### *Adults with Physical Disabilities and Chronic Illnesses*

It is extremely difficult to estimate the proportion of non-elderly people with physical disabilities who are living in institutional or residential care, although, as indicated earlier in this section, one would probably expect both the proportion and the numbers to be small. We do know that in 1981 there were some 13,200 adults under retirement age living in local authority, voluntary and private residential accommodation (*Social Trends* 1980, table 13.23) but there is no indication of how many people with physical disabilities only might also be living in long-stay hospitals. Moreover, we can make no estimate of what proportion of the total population of people with similar disabilities this number represents.

There are some hints in the literature about the high incidence of family care for people with physical disabilities and chronic illnesses. For example, a recent study of young adults (Hirst 1982) has shown how few are able to move away from home and establish independent lives in the same way as their contemporaries.

In a study by Cartwright et al. (1973) only 9 per cent of a sample of 785 people (including some elderly people) who had recently died, had been in a hospital or institution for the twelve months before their death. A similar proportion (8 per cent) of Sainsbury's (1970) original sample of adults on local authority disability registers were living in residential establishments or hospitals. None of Blaxter's (1976) sample of non-elderly adults with a disability condition went to live in residential care when discharged from hospital and, it appears, all were still in their own homes a year later.

Despite the paucity of information about the extent of residential or long-term hospital care for adults with physical disabilities, it appears that such care plays little part in the lives of the vast majority. We do know from Harris's survey (1971) that less than a tenth of the most severely impaired non-elderly adults (this includes some people with mental impairments) live alone. All but 2 per cent of the remainder live with relatives. It is clear, then, that the major part of caring for non-elderly dependent adults takes place in informal settings and it almost always involves relatives.

## WHO CARES WITHIN THE FAMILY?

We have seen that the majority of children and adults within the dependency groups considered in the review live 'in the community', rather than in any form of residential care. Although the proportions of each dependency group who live with relatives varies, the family is still the most important locus of care for all of them. However, to talk about 'care by the community' or even 'family' care is to disguise the reality. In fact, as is shown in the following sections, 'care by the community' almost always means care by family members with little support from others in 'the community'. Further, care by family members almost always means care by female members with little support from other relatives.

It appears that 'shared care' between family members is uncommon; once one person has been identified as the main carer other relatives withdraw. However, the extent to which particular relatives or others are involved in the care of dependent people varies both between dependency groups and also within – influenced, as one might predict, by where the dependent person lives.

### *The Elderly*

Surveys of elderly people have shown that, where care is provided by family members, daughters are usually the main carers. Both Sheldon's (1948) and Townsend's (1957) studies of elderly people found that not only did daughters carry the major burden of caring for dependent parents but also that elderly people were more likely to live with a married daughter than with a married son. When elderly men became ill their wives cared for them; when elderly women became ill they were cared for by their daughters. Although daughters were less likely to be looking after their fathers, they thus often became involved indirectly by supporting their mothers in the care of their father.

Daughters and daughters-in-law were more likely to be helping elderly people with household and other tasks than were sons and sons-in-law in Hunt's (1978) study of old people at home. Only in the matter of visiting the elderly did male children help to anywhere near the same extent as female children.

More recently, Nissel and Bonnerjea (1982) (in their exploration of the ways in which caring for elderly relatives constrains 'women's participation in the community') have underlined the heavy burden borne by women caring for elderly relatives. Husbands rarely gave direct help to their wives with the care of the dependent relative living with them, even where the wife was employed outside the home. The majority 'gave the impression of being quite distant from the situation. Many of them denied there were any serious problems' (p. 35). Among the elderly mentally ill also, where the stresses of care are greater, women bear the brunt of responsibility (Isaacs et al. 1972; Sandford 1975; Levin et al. 1983).

Gilhooly (1982), in a recent study of the carers of people suffering from senile dementia, found that the expectations among family members influenced who cared: 'when there were both sons and daughters who could potentially give assistance sons were rarely expected to give as much help as daughters.'

Daughters and daughters-in-law become the main carers for elderly people not because they are the only people available to take on the task. Many researchers have identified that often 'one person in the family [is] singled out to carry more than a fair share of the burden of care' (Townsend 1957).

Nissel and Bonnerjea (1982) noted that 'once the relative was settled with one of his/her children, the other "children" contributed very little. This caused growing resentment as the relative needed more and more attention, and as the carer had less and less time for her previous work and other activities' (p. 32). Similar patterns are evident from Gilhooly's work: 'It seemed that once one person had formally taken on the responsibility of care, the rest stopped helping at all' (Gilhooly 1982, p. 70). '"Family" care means care by *one* member of the family. It was exceedingly rare to find cases of real "shared" caregiving. In those few cases of genuine shared caregiving it was a son and his wife, never the dependant's daughter and her husband' (Gilhooly n.d.). This unequal sharing of the burden of care pertained even though other relatives might live in the district and visit or telephone the elderly person. The reasons for this low level of shared caregiving were various. Sometimes spouses who were carers kept their difficulties hidden from relatives; sometimes relatives who were not the main caregivers could not appreciate the full extent of the burden carried; 'finally, there were quite a few families in which only the primary caregivers believed that home care was the most appropriate form of care. In other words, there were family members who simply did not want to give the amount of care that would enable the dependant to remain at home.'

The evidence, then, is unequivocal. While the family, where it exists, still cares for its elderly members within the family, it is wives, daughters, daughters-in-law and other female relatives who shoulder the main burden of responsibility. Moreover, when the carer has taken on the burden she is likely to receive little practical support from other relatives.

### *Children with Disabilities*

As in the great majority of families with children, the bulk of caring for a disabled child is done by his or her mother with little help from other family members.

Wilkin (1979) found that large proportions of mothers caring for mentally handicapped children received no help with child care. Neither was any help with basic domestic tasks given. The 'majority of mothers carried a very heavy burden with very little support' (p. 118). The father's role in most families 'varied little from the dominant cultural pattern' yet 'most could have and should have done more to ease the burden on their wives' (pp. 129, 133). Wilkin also concluded that his study 'cast considerable doubt on the importance which should be attached to networks [of kin, friends and neighbours] as sources of support with the daily routine of child care and housework' (p. 195).

Glendinning (1983) in her in-depth study of seventeen families with a severely disabled child, while acknowledging that fathers did not take as much responsibility for the day-to-day child care as did mothers, felt that objective measures or assessments of the fathers' participation were probably less important in mediating mothers' stress than their *perceived* willingness to help. Older children were often, but not invariably, 'an important source of practical support' to the families in Glendinning's study. None of the families had substantial regular or frequent practical help from other family members outside the household. 'Relatives' own family commitments or grandparents' advancing age meant that some parents just did not expect any help' (p. 99), while others recognized family members' reluctance to offer help because of 'their apprehension about medical, nursing or behaviour problems' which might arise. Practical help from neighbours was similarly limited.

In Glendinning's more recent study (Glendinning, n.d.) fathers' involvement with child care was found to be greater than might have been expected but was concentrated on the more pleasurable and less taxing activities such as playing with or amusing the child. Around 44 per cent of the families who had relatives living nearby received practical help from them on a regular basis and just under two-thirds received some emotional or moral support. Less than a third of families had regular practical help from friends and neighbours, and under a half received any moral support.

Carey's (1982) study of the carers of mentally handicapped children in North Wales revealed, like the other research reviewed here, that most work, both domestic and child-care related, fell to the mother. Although fathers made a contribution this never approached half the total workload and, where help was offered, it was with child minding rather than child care, and with child care rather than household chores. Shared tasks were most likely to be those involving lifting and carrying children and child minding in the late evening. The tasks most likely to be undertaken by the mother alone were cleaning and tidying the house, dressing children and childminding during holidays. Help from siblings was at a lower level than that identified in Glendinning's study and help from the extended family, friends and neighbours was limited. As did Wilkin, Carey concluded that fathers' contributions to household duties and child care were insufficient to 'support the conclusion that role relationships in handicapped families are approaching symmetry'.

Results from the Child Health and Education Study (Cooke 1982) reinforce scepticism about sharing of child care and housework in families with a disabled child. While 88 per cent of fathers spent some time during the week keeping children amused at home only 42 per cent ever took the children out without their mother at least once or twice a week. Help with domestic tasks was at an even lower level overall. Under a half helped with shopping at least once or twice a week and around a third helped to clean the house or with the cooking. The only 'substantial' contribution was made with washing up; just under two thirds of husbands helped with this at least once or twice a week. The lowest level of help was given with washing (12 per cent) and ironing (6 per cent). Help with household tasks did not appear to increase with severity of the child's disability: 'The tendency was for greater severity of handicap to be associated with slightly greater participation in child care and slightly less participation in housework. However, in general it was mothers who bore the main burden of responsibility' (p. 71).

A study of the family life of children with cystic fibrosis in Northern Ireland (Burton 1975) has produced a picture of family care and support somewhat at variance with those painted by the other studies reported here. While the mothers were most closely involved in giving therapy to the children (mothers devoted an average of 5 hours a week to this on top of their normal domestic duties compared to fathers' 45 minutes a week) it seemed that they had considerable support from both family and community. Mothers who managed to work outside the home 'often substituted the care of relatives and domestics for their own care'. Additional domestic help was available to most mothers, usually coming from their immediate family. 'From the spontaneous comments of most mothers, it was obvious that family members were a great source of strength and practical assistance offering whatever services were required' (p. 122). Only 9 per cent of the mothers had no such support available; all of these were recent immigrants to

Northern Ireland. In addition, 50 per cent of all mothers accepted occasional help from friends or neighbours.

It is not entirely clear why the mothers in Burton's study should have been apparently better supported than mothers in the other studies. However it seems that cultural factors may have been important. Certainly, as already indicated, recent arrivals in Northern Ireland did not have the same support network available to them as did mothers who were native to the province.

In summary then, the major share of caring for children with disabilities or chronic illnesses falls to mothers with relatively little help from fathers, siblings, relatives, neighbours or friends. A major problem revealed by review of these studies is, however, the inadequate way in which 'help' is measured. Wilkin (1979) identified this problem when he contrasted his finding, that the mothers of mentally handicapped children received little support from families and neighbours, with earlier studies (Bayley 1973; Carr 1976; Burton 1975) which apparently demonstrated the availability of considerable support. This he felt was due to none of the other studies having 'systematically collected information about what individuals actually did with respect to a wide range of domestic tasks' (p. 145).

### *Adults with Disabilities*

One of the difficulties with the major sources of information about the care of non-elderly dependent adults is that they are not exclusive in their scope. Harris (1971) included both physically and mentally impaired people and elderly and non-elderly in her survey. Similarly, the subjects in Cartwright et al.'s (1973) research about the 12 months prior to death included both the elderly and non-elderly. Studies which are limited to specific types of disability and/or to non-elderly adults only tend to be small and consequently more limited in their applicability. These limitations should be borne in mind in the rest of this section.

*Adults with mental handicaps* Perhaps because so many adults with mental handicaps have, in the past, been cared for in institutional accommodation of one form or another their care in the community does not appear to have attracted as much attention from researchers as has the care of children.

In-depth interviews with families caring for mentally handicapped adults in Sheffield revealed a very low level of support for the mothers of these people (Bayley, 1973). Only fourteen out of the thirty-six fathers interviewed in the study helped 'much' with the care of their mentally handicapped son or daughter. Siblings still at home helped even less but this was often as a result of deliberate policy on the parent's part. In sixteen out of fifty cases other relatives were said to give 'much' help and support to the mother but it was more common for one relative, almost always a woman, to be of particular help than it was for there to be a wide spread of family helping. Neither was support from neighbours extensive although some families preferred this. Some families desperately needed help but were unable or found it difficult to accept it.

Most families managed to develop some coping structure but this weakened as the mentally handicapped person and his parents aged. When other children left

TABLE 22.2 Main and secondary carers of mentally handicapped adults living at home (percentages)

| | *Main carer* | *Secondary carer* |
|---|---|---|
| Mother | 80 | 3 |
| Father | 9 | 49 |
| Sibling | 6 | 4 |
| Spouse | 1 | — |
| Other relative | 4 | 8 |
| No carer | — | 36 |
| Total (100%) | 352 | 352 |

One male subject was not included in these figures as he was himself caring for his elderly, infirm mother.
*Source:* City of Bradford MDC Social Services Department 1983.

the parental home a source of help departed with them. When they had children of their own the amount of help they might be able to offer diminished still further. In general, however, the 'coping structure' depended on one person, nearly always a mother. Consequently the most likely reason for breakdown of care was the death or illness of that person.

A recent study in which the carers of 352 mentally handicapped adults in West Yorkshire were interviewed (City of Bradford MDC Social Services Department 1983) identified both main and secondary carers. The findings are reproduced in table 22.2. The average age of main carers in this study was fifty-seven (although the range was wide, from 20 to 86 years); 41 per cent of them were aged sixty or over. The secondary carers were of a similar average age and range. Even though the researchers did not explore the inter-relationships between main and secondary carers and household composition (indeed, no information on household composition is included in the report), it can be seen that just over a third of the main carers had no support from household members or others. Even if one assumed that there was no secondary support for any of the main carers, *except* mothers, this would still leave nearly 20 per cent of the mothers without secondary support.

Another recent study of mentally handicapped people (including some children) living in rural and remote areas of Scotland discovered that in households with only one parent the presence of, particularly, grandmothers appeared to be important in keeping the mentally handicapped family member at home (Seed 1980). Support from relatives outside the household was noted in two-thirds of the social networks studied but there were 'more instances of contacts with relatives in the case of mentally handicapped children than adults' (p. 47). Families with little or no contact with relatives did not appear to compensate for this by other social contacts.

*Adults with physical disabilities and illnesses* The majority of adults with physical disabilities, who are not in residential care, appear to live with family members. Harris's (1971) survey (which as we have already noted contained some people with mental handicaps) showed that only 9.4 per cent of adults aged 16–64 who were handicapped or impaired lived by themselves. The majority lived with their spouse and/or children, others with parents or siblings and a few with unrelated people. Most, then, lived in households where, in theory, others were available to help care for them.

Sainsbury (1970) found that 16 per cent of those under pension age in a group of registered disabled adults lived alone while 20 per cent still lived with their parents. Striking differences were evident in the patterns of help and support received by the disabled person, depending on the composition of their households. Thus only 26 per cent of those living alone received help from relatives while 84 per cent and 92 per cent, respectively, of those in two person and three or more person households did. However, very little of this help came from relatives *outside* the household. Indeed 'in spite of other relatives in the neighbourhood, where a disabled person required considerable help during the day, the burden of care was usually undertaken by one relative within the household' (p. 130).

In one-person households where relatives were providing support the helper was most often a single relative, usually a daughter. Only where care was not available within the family did statutory services step into the breach. Help from relatives outside the household was obviously a 'thorny' topic for some of the households Sainsbury studied:

> Most of the persons interviewed were defensive about the scope of help provided by relatives living beyond the household. People tended to emphasize their distance from relatives who were not living in the neighbourhood, and the family commitments of those who lived nearby. In both cases, they were at pains to justify the lack of help, or their reliance on help outside the family. (p. 135)

Only 16 per cent of all the households received help from neighbours although this type of help was more important to those living alone than to others.

Similar variation in source of help with household composition was evident in Cartwright et al.'s (1973) study of the 12 months preceding the deaths of a sample of elderly and non-elderly adults. Those who had been living only with their spouses before death (33 per cent of those under 65 years) had most often been helped by the spouse while people living with relatives of a younger generation had been helped most often by their children or children-in-law.

There was usually (in 83 per cent of cases) one person who 'bore the brunt' of care even though others might be involved. Wives and husbands generally bore the brunt of caring for the married, daughters for the widowed, sisters and other relatives for the single. The 'brunt bearer' was 'almost always a family member (nine-tenths), and generally a woman (three-quarters)' (p. 155). It was found that neighbours 'rarely undertook nursing care' although relatives often did so, indicating perhaps that there were certain personal tasks which it may be impossible to expect the 'community' rather than the family to undertake (cf. Wright 1983).

In one study (Blaxter, 1976) non-elderly men discharged from hospital with a disability were most likely to have non-employed spouses at home to care for them. Fewer problems of personal care and daily living thus arose for them than for discharged women patients. Difficulties with personal care were mostly 'solved' by the care of 'daughters, or to a lesser extent sisters, mothers, other kinsfolk and neighbours' (p. 57). Neighbours 'were essential only if there were no female relatives available' (p. 57).

Family support in the city Blaxter studied seemed rather stronger than that reported in other studies. Some of this appeared to be due to expectations of the cared for or of professionals rather than of the carers. 'It appeared to be taken for granted by all that if female relatives were available, no problem could exist' (p. 58). In some cases patients refused to contemplate alternative forms of outside help, expecting their (usually female) relatives to cope. Although the caring relatives appeared to take this duty for granted, for some it caused considerable hardship. Indeed this unquestioned assumption that mainly female family members would provide care led to 'some of the most obvious failures in ensuring necessary care' when professionals colluded with it. The needs of young wives and mothers with disabilities tended to be overlooked by professionals. Thus, not only were women more likely to take on, and be expected to take on, the duties of caring for a disabled relative, when the disabled person was a young woman she was, in some way, expected to have fewer problems in caring for herself!

## SUMMARY AND CONCLUSIONS

The evidence reviewed here shows unequivocably that families do already care for their dependent relatives but that the major part of the burden of care falls on women - whether wives, mothers, spouses, siblings or friends and neighbours. There is little evidence of any real shift in the 'social division of community care' (Walker 1982). These broad factors which define carers and are common between them should not, however, blind us to the *differences* which exist between them, or to the questions that these differences raise.

For example, it seems that cultural factors, identified in studies in Northern Ireland and Aberdeen, may influence both carers' expectations about who *should* care for dependent relatives and the support that they can expect from other relatives and neighbours. However, we know very little about how these expectations arise or how they translate into action. Do the people who believe that the family should always care for its dependants actually do so when the opportunity arises? If not, what factors prevent them from doing so or, conversely, what factors help those who wish to care for their dependants continue to do so?

Most research finds that one family member tends to become the main carer even when others are available to help (although some, for example Cantley and Smith 1983, have questioned the concept of a 'main carer'). Would practical help and support from other relatives help the main carer or would it make effective care of the dependent person more difficult? We currently have little idea of the views and wishes of carers in this respect.

Indeed we have little idea of carers' wishes for support in general. Research into preferences for care patterns indicates that informal care with professional support would be the preferred option for most people and most dependency groups but we do not know whether this is what would meet *carers'* present needs. Nor do we know how carers' needs vary between dependency groups.

Another topic about which there is little information is the inter-generational nature of care. There are hints in the literature about women bearing the burden of care for two and sometimes three generations. However, because research tends to focus on the cared-for person rather than the carer, there is no adequate measure of the real amount of informal caring that goes on.

Another, and related, gap in the research so far reviewed concerns the measurement of care provided. Wilkin has already drawn attention to the inadequacy of many accounts of the amount of help provided by relatives, friends and neighbours to those who are main carers. These subjective measurements of help given, whether assessed by interviewer, or interviewed, allow neither within nor between group comparisons of the impact of caring. Measurement of the effect of supportive intervention is, in consequence, almost impossible. Recent attempts at the use of time budgets warrant further attention and development (Nissel and Bonnerjea 1982).

Finally, there are considerable and growing discrepancies in our knowledge about the locus and nature of care for different dependency groups. Many surveys have been and are being carried out concerning the nature of informal care for elderly people. However, there is much less information about, for example, children and non-elderly adults with physical disabilities. This dearth of information reflects, in part, both the relatively smaller number of children and non-elderly adults with disabilities, and their consequent 'low visibility' for policy makers. This low visibility is compounded by the lower likelihood of people in these dependency groups entering residential care with all the costs to the state that involves.

The apparent assumption, in policy, that parental family care is all that is needed for non-elderly adults should, perhaps, be challenged, especially as more children with disabilities survive into adulthood.

## REFERENCES

Bayley M. (1973) *Mental Handicap and Community Care* Routledge and Kegan Paul, London.

Bergmann K., Foster E. M., Justice A. W. and Matthews V. (1978) 'Management of the demented elderly patient in the community' *British Journal of Psychiatry* 132:441–9.

Blaxter M. (1976) *The Meaning of Disability* Heinemann, London.

Brody, Elaine M. (1981) ' "Women in the middle" and family help to older people' *The Gerontologist* 21, 5:471–480.

Burton L. (1975) *The Family Life of Sick Children* Routledge and Kegan Paul, London.

Cantley C. and Smith G. (1983) Paper presented to the Social Administration Association Conference, University of Kent at Canterbury, July 1983.

Carey, Gwyneth, E. (1982) 'Community care – care by whom? Mentally handicapped children living at home' *Public Health* 96:269–278.

Carr J. (1976) 'Effect on the family of a child with Down's Syndrome' *Physiotherapy* 62, 1:20–23.

Cartwright A, Hockey L. and Anderson J. L. (1973) *Life before Death* Routledge and Kegan Paul, London.

City of Bradford Metropolitan District Council Social Services Department (1983) 'The future accommodation needs of mentally handicapped people presently living in the community.' Clearing house for social services research, University of Birmingham, no. 2.

Cooke K. (1982) '1970 birth cohort – 10 year follow-up study: interim report' University of

York, Department of Social Policy and Social Work, Social Policy Research Unit, Working Paper, DHSS 108.6/82 KC.

Davies, Linda J. (1981) 'Service provision and the elderly: attitudes of three generations of urban women' *The Occupational Therapy Journal of Research* 1, 1:32–52.

Gilhooly, Mary (1982) 'Social aspects of senile dementia' in *Current Trends In Gerontology: proceedings of the 1980 conference of the British Society of Gerontology* Rex Taylor and Anne Gilmore (eds) Gower, Aldershot.

Gilhooly, Mary (n.d.) 'Family care of the dementing elderly' *Practiciens et 3 Age.*

Glendinning C. (1983) *Unshared Care* Routledge and Kegan Paul, London.

Glendinning C. (n.d.) *The Resource Worker Project* George Allen and Unwin, London.

Greengross, Sally (1982) 'Caring for the carers' in *Care in the Community: recent research and current projects* Glendenning F. (ed.) Beth Johnson Foundation, Stoke.

Halsey A. H. (ed.) (1972)*Trends in British Society Since 1900* Macmillan, London.

Harris A. (1971) *Handicapped and Impaired in Great Britain* HMSO, London.

Herbert Y., Willison J. and Zaborski A. (1983) 'Strength in sadness' *Social Work Today* 15, 7:14–15.

Hirst M. (1982) 'Young adults with disabilities and their families' University of York, Department of Social Policy and Social Work, Social Policy Research Unit, Working Paper DHSS 112.7/82 MH.

Hirst M. (1984) 'Moving on: transfer from child to adult services for young people with disabilities.' Unpublished paper.

Hunt A. (1978) *The Elderly at Home* OPCS Social Survey Division, HMSO, London.

Isaacs B., Livingstone M. and Neville Y. (1972) *Survival of the Unfittest: a Study of Geriatric Patients in Glasgow* Routledge and Kegan Paul, London.

Kay D. W. K., Bergmann K., Foster E. M., McKechnie A. and Roth M. (1970) 'Mental illness and hospital usage in the elderly: a random sample followed up' *Comparative Psychiatry* 2:26–35.

Levin E., Sinclair I. and Gorbach P. (1983) *The Supporters of Confused Elderly People at Home: Extract from the Main Report* National Institute for Social Work Research Unit, London.

Moroney R. M. (1976) *The Family and the State: Considerations for Social Policy* Longman, London.

Nissel M. and Bonnerjea L. (1982) *Family Care of the Handicapped Elderly: Who Pays?* Policy Studies Institute, London.

Sainsbury, Sally (1970) 'Registered as disabled' *Occasional Papers on Social Administration* no. 35, London.

Sandford J. R. A. (1975) 'Tolerance of debility in elderly dependants by supporters at home: its significance for hospital practice' *British Medical Journal* 3, 471–3.

Seed P. (1980) *Mental Handicap: Who Helps in Rural and Remote Communities?* Costello Educational, Tunbridge Wells.

Shanas E. (1979) 'Social myth as hypothesis: the case of the family relations of old people' *The Gerontologist* 19:3–9.

Sheldon J. H. (1948) *The Social Medicine of Old Age* The Nuffield Foundation/OUP.

Townsend P. (1957) *The Family Life of Old People* Routledge and Kegan Paul, London.

Tyne A. (1982) 'Community care and mentally handicapped people' in Walker A. (ed.) *Community Care: The Family, the State and Social Policy* Basil Blackwell, Oxford.

Walker A. (1982) 'The meaning and social division of community care' in Walker A. (ed.) *Community Care: the Family, the State and Social Policy* Basil Blackwell, Oxford.

Weeks David, J. (n.d.) 'Ageism and being alone – a suitable case for prevention?' (preliminary report) Jardine Clinic, University of Edinburgh.

Wertheimer A. (1981) 'People with mental handicaps' in Walker A. and Townsend P. (eds) *Disability in Britain: A Manifesto of Rights* Basil Blackwell, Oxford.

West P., Dalley G., Thompson C., Brown S., Hewitt A., Illsley R. and Kelman H. (1983) 'Social responsibility for the care of dependency groups' *International Journal of Rehabilitation Medicine.*

West P., Illsley R. and Kelman H. (1984) 'Public preferences for the care of dependency groups' *Social Science and Medicine.*

Wilkin D. (1979) *Caring for the Mentally Handicapped Child* Croom Helm, London.

Wright F. (1983) 'Single carers: employment, housework and caring' in Finch J. and Groves D. (eds) *A Labour of Love: Women, Work and Caring* Routledge and Kegan Paul, London.

# 23

# Household Composition, Social Networks and Household Production in Germany

WOLFGANG GLATZER AND REGINA BERGER

## HOUSEHOLD PRODUCTION AND WELFARE PRODUCTION

Welfare is a general goal in modernized societies; it is here defined as the combination of people's objective living conditions and their subjective well-being. People's welfare is influenced by many actors and events, but four institutions are of essential significance in the process of welfare production: the market system, the welfare state, associations and private households (Zapf 1981). In this process private households have a key position because they decide which outputs they demand and where they try to get them. In principle they can choose to get goods and services from the market system, the welfare state, collective organizations of organized self-help and charitable institutions, and also from the illegal underground economy, the informal social network, and their own household production. These institutions specialize in certain goods and services, e.g. the welfare state in public goods, the market system in private goods; sometimes there is a relationship of competition, sometimes of complementarity. Each of these institutions has its specific capacities and limits of performance. In recent years the limits of the market system and the overloading of the welfare state have become more apparent. The consequences in political discussions were twofold: on the one hand a political debate began about how to obtain better use of household capacities and to relieve the welfare state; on the other a political campaign was initiated to direct demand from the underground economy to the market economy. Because it is difficult to draw a sharp line between household production and underground economy, these are somewhat conflicting goals.

This essay was first published in Wolf Gaertner and Alois Wenig, *The Economics of the Shadow Economy*, Springer Verlag, 1985.

The aim of our study is to describe some productive performances of private households in West Germany (FRG), and to analyse their determinants. Our data base is the Welfare Survey 1980, a representative survey of the adult West German population.[1] Theoretically we start from the assumption that the capacities and limits of the institutions of welfare production are closely related to the number and the size of the respective units, the firms in the market, the central, regional and local authorities in the state area, and the groups and organizations in the collective field. The same seems to be applicable to the household economy; the composition of the household with respect to the number and the relationship of its members is an important determinant of the household's production. A one-person household has different needs and different ways of satisfying those needs compared with an extended family. An incomplete family differs from a complete family in respect of who contributes and who receives how much. So we can argue that the changes in the distribution of the household types will have consequences for the level of household production and its role in the process of welfare production.

To give a description of the distribution of household forms in West Germany we differentiate first between family and non-family households; about half of the households belong to each category (see table 23.1). The non-family households are households without children, and they mainly consist of people living alone, of couples living alone and to a lesser extent of non-married adults living together. The family households mainly consist of households with one child and two children. In addition, there is a small number of couples with three children, families with many children, extended families and incomplete families. A very small number of households falls outside this classification.

In addition to household composition we take into account that further factors influence the amount of household production. The most important is household income, which determines the ability to acquire goods and services.[2] If goods can be bought then there are fewer incentives to produce them by one's own work. As the income level is positively correlated with the number of employed household members it can be assumed that in households with higher income there is less time for household production activities. For both reasons income should influence household production. Household production also requires special attitudes towards activities and special skills. These aspects differ between social classes

1. In the Welfare Survey 1980 we interviewed 2396 adult inhabitants of the FRG in respect to four themes. One-fourth of the questions are as in the Welfare Survey 1978, which focused on the evaluation of living conditions. Another fourth concerns standard demography and the measurement of well-being. The remaining parts are related to household production and occupational placement. The survey was carried through by Wolfgang Zapf, Wolfgang Glatzer, Heinz-Herbet Noll, Wolfgang Brachtl, Roland Habich, Sabine Lang, Maria Müller-Andritzky and Christian Siara.

2. The income level is the total monthly net income of the household weighted by the size of the household. The weighting takes into consideration that different household sizes need different incomes. The weighting procedure which we have used assumes that a two-person household needs 1.7 times as much as a one-person household. The income of three-person households is weighted by 2.3. With every additional household member the weight increases by 0.5. In the statistical analysis three income levels are distinguished: the lowest quintile, the second to the fourth quintile summed, and the highest quintile.

TABLE 23.1 Families and non-family households in West Germany 1978 and 1980

| | *Households* | | | | *Respondents* | |
|---|---|---|---|---|---|---|
| | *1978* % | *1980* % | *1978* N | *1980* N | *1978* % | *1980* % |
| *Households without children* | 48.6 | 48.3 | 916 | 1048 | 41.5 | 42.6 |
| Living alone | 22.2 | 20.5 | 418 | 445 | 14.5 | 12.9 |
| Couples living alone | 23.0 | 23.3 | 433 | 505 | 23.8 | 24.7 |
| Unmarried adults | 3.4 | 4.5 | 65 | 98 | 3.2 | 5.0 |
| *Households with children* | 49.8 | 51.8 | 965 | 1122 | 58.4 | 57.4 |
| Couples with one child | 19.1 | 19.0 | 360 | 411 | 21.0 | 19.9 |
| Couples with two children | 15.5 | 16.6 | 292 | 360 | 16.9 | 17.8 |
| Couples with three children | 5.1 | 5.2 | 96 | 112 | 6.2 | 5.9 |
| Couples with many children[a] | 2.6 | 2.0 | 49 | 44 | 3.1 | 2.7 |
| Extended families[b] | 3.5 | 3.1 | 66 | 66 | 5.7 | 5.2 |
| Incomplete families[c] | 4.0 | 4.5 | 76 | 98 | 3.6 | 3.5 |
| Special cases[d] | 1.4 | 1.4 | 26 | 31 | 1.9 | 2.4 |
| Total | 99.8 | 100.1 | 1881 | 2170 | 99.9 | 100.0 |

[a] Couples with many children: couples with four or more children.
[b] Extended families: couples or a parent with children and further relatives in the household.
[c] Incomplete families: one adult with one or more children.
[d] Special cases: households, to which belong not related persons, with or without children.
*Sources:* Welfare Survey 1978 ($N = 2012$); Welfare Survey 1980 ($N = 2396$)

and, therefore, we assume that household production varies between social classes.[3]

It is also hypothesized that household production depends on the age of the household members. On the one hand greater age is often combined with a restricted ability for activities, and on the other new needs emerge, such as those resulting from ill health. More generally it is assumed that the life-cycle stage of a household is responsible for many household production activities. We try to measure some of these influences by using the age of the head of the household as a variable.[4]

In the following study we show how selected aspects of household production are related to these factors. Their connection with the household forms is

3. Social class is not measured by objective criteria, for example by occupation, education or income. It represents a subjective rating of the respondents. The possible answers are 'lower class', 'middle class', 'upper middle class', 'upper class', 'none of these classes' (don't know, rating refused). In the presented analyses the upper middle class and the upper class are summed. Between this subjective rating and the objective criteria of social class there are strong correlations.
4. The head of the household is determined by the respondent of each household. The statistical analyses are done with three age groups: 18 to 30 years, 31 to 59 years, 60 and more years.

presented section by section; a final table shows how they depend on income level, class position and age of the head of the household (table 23.8). In addition to the bivariate analyses we did multiple classification analyses[5] to obtain the combined effect of the four factors, and the predictive power of each factor if the other factors are controlled.[6]

## ANALYSIS OF HOUSEHOLD ACTIVITIES

### *Producing, Using and Maintaining Goods*

In a widely held view the development of private households is characterized by an increasing loss of economic functions. In contrast it has been postulated in recent years that economic tasks are returning to private households. Instead of demanding services on the market, private households purchase 'producer goods' and add their own work in order to achieve the desired outcomes. According to this view, private households show a high amount of productive activities which nowadays are carried out using a high level of technical equipment.

Our empirical results make clear that private households in the FRG are predominantly self-supporters in doing everyday housework; market alternatives like the employment of a household help or the use of outside firms are seldom used. For example, only 3 per cent of households give their bedlinen to a laundry and only 4 per cent have the windows cleaned by a paid household help. Such household tasks are rarely assigned to relatives, friends and neighbours. Even for household repairs and housing renovations requiring handicraft skills, market firms are not used on a large scale. Two-thirds of households usually do such work themselves. Only one-fourth call on a craftsman, and the remaining households ask people in their social network. On average, households perform 5.9 of the seven household tasks listed in table 23.2 by themselves. Fifty-four per cent of households usually do all of the seven tasks with their own hands, and only 8 per cent assign four or more tasks to others.

Gardening is an example of an activity which, in contrast to everyday housework, has at least partly the characteristics of leisure. In spite of advanced urbanization in the FRG it is nevertheless a standard activity which is done in slightly more than 50 per cent of the households.

The most expensive commodities enabling self-supply by private households are cars and houses. As 70 per cent of all households, and 80 per cent of

5. Multiple classification analysis is a procedure comparable with multiple regression. It examines the effects of several independent variables on one dependent variable. The differences between multiple classification analysis and regression analysis consist in the lower requirements of multiple classification analysis. Interval measurement is only required for the dependent variable; the independent variables may be nominal scales. No assumptions are made about the form of the relationships between the variables, but, like regression analysis, the effects of the independent variables must be additive. The $\eta$ coefficients indicate the bivariate correlations; the $\beta$ coefficient is a measure for the effect of an independent variable on the dependent variable, controlling for all other independent variables.

6. We also took into account that rural–urban differences are correlated with household production activities, but we did not find that this variable had an influence comparable with that of household type, age of the head of the household, income level and class position.

TABLE 23.2 Household tasks and by whom they are performed, West Germany, 1980 (per cent)

| | | *The household task is usually done by*[a] | | | | | | |
|---|---|---|---|---|---|---|---|---|
| | | Social network | | | Market system | | | |
| *Household tasks* | Household members | relatives | friends | neighbours | house worker | firm | Does not occur | Total |
| Shopping | 98.6 | 1.0 | 0.4 | 0.4 | 0.3 | 0.1 | 0.2 | 101.0 |
| Preparing meals | 98.2 | 1.4 | 0.3 | 0.1 | 0.3 | 0.5 | 0.2 | 101.0 |
| Keeping the dwelling clean | 97.1 | 1.2 | 0.5 | 0.1 | 2.6 | 0.1 | 0.7 | 102.3 |
| Cleaning the windows | 92.5 | 2.4 | 0.7 | 0.2 | 4.0 | 0.9 | 0.2 | 100.9 |
| Washing the bedlinen | 92.2 | 2.8 | 0.7 | 0.2 | 1.3 | 3.4 | 0.2 | 100.8 |
| Repairing the water tap | 67.7 | 4.5 | 3.2 | 1.0 | 0.2 | 25.4 | 0.8 | 102.8 |
| Wallpapering the dwelling | 65.2 | 7.0 | 5.5 | 0.2 | 0.2 | 26.0 | 1.1 | 105.2 |

[a] Two answers are possible.
*Source:* Welfare Survey 1980 ($N$ = 2396 households)

households with several members, possess a car, and 15 per cent of all households run a second car, the saturation point of car supply has almost been reached. The widespread wish for one's own dwelling is realized in only 42 per cent of German households despite a continuous increase since the 1950s.

In respect of private households' demand for market goods one can argue that the purchase and maintenance of these goods represent a new source of market demand. But this is only partially true because private households perform such tasks by themselves too. So 8 per cent of households do all car repair and maintenance work by themselves, and 70 per cent do maintenance work always or sometimes by themselves. Only 28 per cent assign all car repair and maintenance work to service stations.

Houses are constructed to a considerable extent using self-help. Thirty per cent of households that own their house built the shell of the house themselves, and 37 per cent performed most of the interior design work. Self-help in house construction is often the only way that less wealthy households can acquire a house of their own; in addition, technical and handicraft skills are required which are not available in all households.

The production, use and maintenance of goods vary to a high degree with the composition of households (see table 23.3). The lowest degree of self-support can be found in one-person households. Incomplete families are in general below the average level. By contrast, complete families and especially extended families show a high amount of self-support. The differences remain significant if income level, social class and age of the head of the household are controlled. By multiple classification analyses we get the result that income level, social class and age of the head of the household have some influence on household production, but not

TABLE 23.3 Production, use and maintenance of selected goods by household composition, West Germany, 1980

| *Household composition* | *Housework* no.[c] | *Gardening* % | *Possession of a car* % | *Possession of a second car* % | *Car repair*[a] % | *Dwelling owner* % | *Self-help*[b] % |
|---|---|---|---|---|---|---|---|
| Living alone | 4.9 | 25.5 | 27.2 | 1.4 | 33.9 | 23.0 | 16.1 |
| Couples living alone | 5.8 | 53.3 | 65.8 | 9.1 | 35.5 | 43.1 | 36.8 |
| Unmarried adults | 6.2 | 34.7 | 74.7 | 15.5 | 51.6 | 24.3 | 16.9 |
| Couples with one child | 6.3 | 59.8 | 88.5 | 21.0 | 51.9 | 44.9 | 49.7 |
| Couples with two children | 6.5 | 65.1 | 91.6 | 24.3 | 50.9 | 51.0 | 32.6 |
| Couples with three children | 6.3 | 75.3 | 96.2 | 24.0 | 59.1 | 55.4 | 38.5 |
| Couples with many children | 6.6 | 71.8 | 93.2 | 29.6 | 43.1 | 58.9 | 16.9 |
| Extended families | 6.2 | 90.4 | 97.7 | 38.4 | 51.6 | 87.3 | 47.1 |
| Incomplete families | 5.4 | 34.0 | 66.7 | 6.7 | 17.5 | 30.8 | 30.7 |
| All households | 5.9 | 52.2 | 70.2 | 14.8 | 45.2 | 42.1 | 36.3 |
| Correlation $\eta$ | 0.30 | 0.35 | 0.53 | 0.28 | 0.20 | 0.29 | 0.23 |

[a] Car repair is performed by household members always or sometimes (only households which possess a car).
[b] Interior design work during house construction was performed as 'self-help'.
[c] Average of seven household tasks as in table 23.2.
*Source:* Welfare Survey 1980 ($N$ = 2170 households)

in each area, and generally not as strongly as has household composition (see table 23.4). The income level of households is only a good predictor for the possession of a car. We had expected household income to show a stronger influence, and we conclude that economic pressures and incentives are not the most important determinants of household production activities. Social class influences the amount of housework and repairs of cars. This is supposed to depend on class-specific attitudes and skills. In the working class we find the highest amount of car repairs; in the upper class we find the lowest degree of self-performed housework. The age of the head of the household is also a good predictor for different household production activities. This means that housework and car repairs are less self-performed in retirement than before. The possession of one's own house and car is also less in the highest age groups. This is not true for gardening: it is relatively high in retirement, and the garden is an area where old people can still be active.

TABLE 23.4 Determinants of selected dimensions of household production, West Germany, 1980 (multiple classification analyses)

| *Domain of performance* | *Household composition* $\eta$ | $\beta$ | *Social class* $\eta$ | $\beta$ | *Income level* $\eta$ | $\beta$ | *Age of the head of the household* $\eta$ | $\beta$ | *Explained variance* $R^2$ |
|---|---|---|---|---|---|---|---|---|---|
| Dwelling owner | 0.27 | 0.24 | 0.03 | (0.03) | 0.04 | (0.03) | 0.25 | 0.11 | 0.12 |
| Possession of a car | 0.52 | 0.46 | 0.16 | (0.08) | 0.18 | 0.18 | 0.47 | 0.32 | 0.42 |
| Possession of a second car | 0.25 | 0.31 | 0.15 | (0.06) | 0.22 | 0.26 | 0.14 | (0.02) | 0.14 |
| Car repair | 0.19 | 0.19 | 0.20 | 0.17 | 0.13 | (0.05) | 0.22 | 0.23 | 0.12 |
| Housework | 0.43 | 0.38 | 0.11 | 0.12 | 0.7 | (0.03) | 0.31 | 0.22 | 0.24 |
| Gardening | 0.34 | 0.33 | 0.06 | (0.04) | 0.02 | (0.04) | 0.22 | 0.15 | 0.14 |

Parentheses indicate no significant influence (level of significance: $\alpha \leqq 0.001$).
*Source:* Welfare Survey 1980 ($N$ = 2170 households)

## *Performing Personal and Social Services*

One characteristic feature of household production activities is their broad variety. Therefore our study of the performance of personal services has to focus on some selected aspects. An important part of personal services is termed 'social services', and in so far as households and families carry out such activities they accomplish the task of social services (Moroney 1976). Social services differ from the other personal services in that they constitute social support for people who cannot help themselves, for example handicapped people, sick people, people needing care, and also children. The responsibility for taking care of such people is mainly attributed to the family and kin, but also to the welfare state with its collective institutions. Public bodies that assist private households in the fulfilment of their tasks are not well developed.

The division of labour between private households and collective institutions in respect of social services is roughly shown by the figures in table 23.5. In 7.6 per cent of households there are people with health impairments, and nearly as many households (namely 5.6 per cent) have close relatives in some kind of collective institution. People with health impairments in private households are mostly handicapped (5.6 per cent), some are in need of care (1.9 per cent) and some are sick at home (2.6 per cent). These household members are mainly nursed by other members of the household. The households are supported to a small extent by relatives outside the household, while neighbours, friends, parish nurses and social workers are very seldom mentioned as helpers. A high percentage (49 per cent) of households with handicapped people say that members handicapped, in need of care or sick do not receive any special care by other people. Household types do not differ in having close relatives in collective institutions, but they differ remarkably in having health-impaired people at home. As expected, a high proportion of the extended families have members with health impairments. Contrary to the assumption that there is no capacity in small households to

TABLE 23.5 Persons cared for in private households by household composition, West Germany, 1980

| *Household composition* | *Handicapped persons in household* % | *Handicapped, sick persons, and persons needing care in household* % | *Handicapped, sick persons, persons needing care, children under 10 in household* % | *Near relatives outside the household in institutions* % |
|---|---|---|---|---|
| Living alone | 4.3 | 5.2 | 5.2 | 7.5 |
| Couples living alone | 8.7 | 11.2 | 11.2 | 5.0 |
| Unmarried adults | 4.3 | 6.9 | 6.9 | 4.4 |
| Couple with one child | 4.6 | 6.7 | 39.9 | 5.0 |
| Couples with two children | 3.9 | 5.3 | 49.3 | 6.0 |
| Couples with three children | 4.4 | 5.7 | 61.3 | 5.5 |
| Couples with many children | 0.0 | 4.3 | 59.6 | 2.7 |
| Extended families | 8.1 | 13.1 | 41.8 | 3.4 |
| Incomplete families | 6.4 | 7.6 | 33.7 | 4.4 |
| All households | 5.6 | 7.6 | 27.3 | 5.6 |
| $\eta$ | 0.10 | 0.11 | 0.44 | 0.05 |

*Source:* Welfare Survey 1980 ($N$ = 2170 households)

perform social services, people with health impairments are also often found in households of couples living alone. Obviously one spouse often takes care of the other, especially in higher age groups.

If we examine how the presence of health-impaired people at home is related to income level, social class and age of the head of the household, we find that apart from household form only age has a significant influence. But the variables mentioned together explain only a very small part of the variance. The same is the case when we try to explain statistically why a household has close relatives in an institution. Only income significantly influences this percentage; the highest income group of households has fewer people in institutions. This might be explained by a causal influence in both directions: households can obtain higher income if nobody is health-impaired; and households which have higher income can more easily employ nursing help at home for their sick members.

The percentage of households which have to care for children is much higher than the percentage which takes care of health-impaired people (see table 23.5). The bulk of social support for people who usually need social services is performed in family households. As for child care, one-third of the respondents with small children say that their children are also looked after by people and institutions outside their own household. This support in child care has to be paid for by the families demanding it. The average costs amount to 97 DM per month.

The same applies to the care of school children. Thirty-six per cent of the respondents with school children help them with doing homework. The supervision of homework by public institutions is not very common, whereas paid private lessons are of somewhat greater importance. Five per cent of the respondents having school children pay for private lessons, at an average amount of 55 DM per month. This is an example of shifts between collective institutions, private households, the market and the shadow economy. The services for which schools are primarily responsible are partially left to private households. If they want to relieve themselves from this burden they transfer it to the market or the shadow economy and spend part of their income on this relief.

## SOCIAL NETWORKS AND SOCIAL SUPPORT

Social networks consist of contacts between individuals, groups and organizations by which individuals and households can mobilize material and personal support in everyday life and in emergencies. Relatives, neighbours and friends form informal social networks. According to the predominant view, modern forms of formal social networks, from self-help groups to welfare state institutions, have reduced the significance of informal networks. But nevertheless there is a high amount of given and received social support in modern society.

The frequency of social support given to relatives, friends and neighbours varies with the kind of service. In the informal networks, psychological support seems to be widespread; the most common support given to relatives as well as to friends and neighbours is help in personal problems.

To add illustration to the figures we mention two examples. Supervision of small children was undertaken in the past two to three years by 16 per cent of the respondents for relatives, 9 per cent for friends and 4 per cent for neighbours. Housing renovations were done by 17 per cent for relatives, 11 per cent for friends and 3 per cent for neighbours. These are examples of fairly widespread services, and they show that the frequency of support is highest for relatives, less for friends and less still for neighbours, with high differences between the categories.

Our data also show that informal social networks rarely support everyday housework and the care of handicapped people. These activities are permanent and have to be undertaken continuously, whereas the special capabilities of informal social networks consist in giving support in emergency situations. A housekeeping emergency may arise if the person doing the bulk of the housework falls ill. In such a case many households try to get along with the support of members of their own household, but some ask for help from relatives outside their own household. This is an indicator of the limited support potential inside smaller households in particular. After relatives, it is to friends and acquaintances that people turn for help. Among the informal reference groups, neighbours are the least asked for help. Compared with relatives and friends, paid houseworkers as well as state and religious institutions play a minor part too.

We sought households' opinions of the support received. The vast majority of household members consider the support received from other households as 'just right'. Between 5 and 7 per cent , however, think the support received from informal social networks is rather too little. In particular, people living alone take this view. A small number of households are of the opinion that network support is too much. So there is no widespread desire for more network support. Obviously support is not always viewed positively. Two important reasons may be mentioned for this. First, such support may interfere with the wish for privacy and may involve unwelcome social control. Secondly, the support may be considered to create an obligation to help in return, which may be unwanted or unrealizable. Support seems to follow to some extent the principle of reciprocity. Most households expect to give as much help as they take (see table 23.6). But there are important exceptions to this rule. More households believe that they give more support than they get than vice versa. People living alone, unmarried people living together, and incomplete families are household forms which comparatively often receive more support than they give. This indicates that social support is also regulated by need.

Social networks enable a majority of the households to enlarge their capacities temporarily. But 27 per cent of the households report that they have no support relations at all. From the aspect of social support this is the problem group; apparently it cannot mobilize appropriate relief in emergency cases. The household forms which most frequently have no support relations are people living alone and incomplete families. In addition, under less favourable living conditions there are fewer support relations. The low-income groups and the lower social classes more often have no support relations if the composition of the household and the age of the head of the household are held constant. The influence of income level and social class is, however, weak. The household composition and the age of the head of the household have stronger effects on the

TABLE 23.6 The subjective balance of received and given support between private households by household composition, West Germany, 1980 (per cent)

*Question*: Does your household receive more, less or just as much support from other households than your household gives?

| *Household composition* | *Just as much* | *Receives more* | *Receives less* | *No support relations* | *Total* |
|---|---|---|---|---|---|
| Living alone | 44.6 | 12.4 | 12.4 | 30.6 | 100 |
| Couples living alone | 48.7 | 3.9 | 14.4 | 33.1 | 100 |
| Unmarried adults | 58.7 | 7.9 | 14.7 | 18.7 | 100 |
| Couples with one child | 57.2 | 4.1 | 15.7 | 23.0 | 100 |
| Couples with two children | 66.2 | 2.2 | 11.5 | 20.0 | 100 |
| Couples with three children | 60.2 | 0.6 | 11.3 | 27.9 | 100 |
| Couples with many children | 42.9 | 4.0 | 11.9 | 41.2 | 100 |
| Extended families | 69.7 | 0.0 | 13.9 | 14.4 | 100 |
| Incomplete families | 58.6 | 5.5 | 7.5 | 29.0 | 100 |
| All households | 54.6 | 4.8 | 13.1 | 27.4 | 100 |

*Source:* Welfare Survey 1980 (*N* = 2170 households)

frequency of support relations. In particular, with increasing age support relations become more rare.

Overall, the results point to the fact that support relations within social networks are primarily characterized by a balance of giving and receiving. As it seems there are, however, important exceptions, one can argue that within limits the deficiencies of certain household forms can be compensated by the social support of the informal networks.

## NON-MATERIAL OUTCOMES OF HOUSEHOLD PRODUCTION

The influence of household production on the subjective well-being of individuals may happen in various ways. The household members can judge favourably the goods and services which are produced and used in their household, and for that reason may be satisfied. The mere availability of social support, for example confidence that nursing will be available during illness, may positively influence satisfaction. Moreover, subjective well-being will result not only from goods and services, but also from the intrinsic value of activities. Household activities have positive and negative benefits which affect subjective well-being (Juster, Courant and Dow 1981).

The non-material welfare benefits of household production are partly by-products of the activities and the availability of goods and services, but a broad concept of household production also includes direct contributions to subjective well-being. Belonging to a household community may protect from social isolation and loneliness; needs for social relations, love and affection may be satisfied. Such contributions are often considered to be the essential function of the modern nuclear family. However, in each household or family temporary or permanent deficiencies can exist and diminish well-being. In particular, when several individuals live together there is always the chance of conflict and of a reduction in well-being through quarrels and disagreements. Overall, one has to take into account the positive and negative influences of households and families on subjective well-being.

The significance of household production for subjective well-being is empirically indicated by its influence on the satisfaction with housekeeping. With an increasing number of household tasks performed by the members themselves, satisfaction with housekeeping rises. The satisfaction with housekeeping also depends on the evaluation of the social network support. In particular, if the received support is considered as not sufficient, the satisfaction with housekeeping is low. These results explain the differences in satisfaction with housekeeping between household types (see table 23.7).

Satisfaction with housekeeping is below average in households of people living alone and of incomplete families; both have a low amount of household production activities and informal network support. Satisfaction with housekeeping is above average especially in extended families and families with three children, which both show a high amount of household production activities and informal network support.

As housework is mainly done by women, we can assume that sex differences are related to satisfaction. Indeed, men are much more satisfied with housekeeping than women, who do most of the work. Women are also less satisfied than men with the division of labour in households. The satisfaction with the division of

TABLE 23.7 Satisfaction with the household and deficiencies of satisfaction by household composition, West Germany, 1980

| *Household composition* | *Satisfaction*[a] *with house-keeping* | *Satisfaction*[a] *with division of labour* | *Deficiency*[b] *of family* % | *Deficiency*[b] *of love* % |
|---|---|---|---|---|
| Living alone | 7.9 | — | 19.4 | 18.4 |
| Couples living alone | 8.8 | 8.6 | 8.8 | 8.5 |
| Unmarried adults | 8.2 | 7.5 | 11.2 | 11.8 |
| Couples with one child | 8.5 | 7.8 | 7.2 | 5.8 |
| Couples with two children | 8.4 | 7.5 | 8.3 | 8.7 |
| Couples with three children | 8.8 | 7.6 | 5.2 | 5.5 |
| Couples with many children | 8.5 | 6.9 | 21.1 | 15.4 |
| Extended families | 8.9 | 8.0 | 2.6 | 2.1 |
| Incomplete families | 7.8 | 7.1 | 17.9 | 22.8 |
| All households | 8.5 | 7.9 | 9.9 | 9.6 |
| Correlation $\eta$ | 0.20 | 0.24 | 0.16 | 0.17 |

[a] Satisfaction is rated on a numerical scale from 0 (fully dissatisfied) to 10 (fully satisfied).
[b] Deficiencies in satisfaction are rated on a verbal scale 'very much/much/somewhat/nothing at all'; the percentages in the table are the answers 'very much and much' summed.
*Source:* Welfare Survey 1980 ($N = 2195$)

labour is also a question of household form. The highest satisfaction with the division of labour in the household is found among those couples living alone, whereas the lowest satisfaction is found in families with many children.

More general welfare benefits which result from the living together of the household members are roughly indicated by a comparison of subjective well-being in one-person households and in households with several persons. People living alone think relatively often that they have deficiencies in their satisfaction with family and love. Deficiencies of well-being above the average are noticed not only for people living alone, but also for members of incomplete families, couples with many children and households composed of unmarried adults. The subjective deficiencies in these domains have negative consequences for general well-being, for feelings of loneliness, for life satisfaction and for happiness. In complete families the subjective well-being is more often reduced by quarrels and disagreements than in other household forms. But these negative influences do not have the weight of the positive influences. In general it seems to be easier to develop a high level of subjective well-being in complete families and in the households of couples living alone than in households of different composition.

## SUMMARY

Our investigation concerns the amount of household production and its determinants in selected dimensions. The main data base is a representative survey of 2400 interviews which were carried out in the FRG in 1980. The

TABLE 23.8 Selected indicators for activities and evaluations in private households, West Germany, 1980

| | | Income level | | | | Social class | | | | Age groups (years) | | | | |
|---|---|---|---|---|---|---|---|---|---|---|---|---|---|---|
| | | lowest quintile | 2nd to 4th quintile | highest quintile | $\eta$ | working class | middle class | upper class | $\eta$ | 18–30 | 31–59 | 60–99 | $\eta$ | All respondents |
| Housework | no. | 4.8 | 4.7 | 4.6 | 0.06 | 4.7 | 4.7 | 4.4 | 0.11 | 4.7 | 4.7 | 4.5 | 0.08 | 4.6 |
| Household repairs | no. | – | – | – | – | 1.4 | 1.3 | 1.1 | 0.11 | 1.5 | 1.5 | 0.7 | 0.40 | 1.3 |
| Possession of a car | % | 56.6 | 74.4 | 83.1 | 0.19 | 62.3 | 74.7 | 84.1 | 0.16 | 84.9 | 82.5 | 32.4 | 0.48 | 71.1 |
| Car repair | % | 51.8 | 51.0 | 36.1 | 0.13 | 59.2 | 42.1 | 34.9 | 0.17 | 55.6 | 45.7 | 20.4 | 0.20 | 45.9 |
| Dwelling owner | % | – | – | – | – | – | – | – | – | 28.6 | 48.9 | 41.1 | 0.17 | 41.9 |
| Gardening | % | – | – | – | – | – | – | – | – | 40.2 | 58.9 | 47.8 | 0.16 | 51.5 |
| Health-impaired people at home | % | – | – | – | – | – | – | – | – | 1.7 | 6.1 | 9.5 | 0.12 | 5.8 |
| No help is received | % | 37.6 | 30.5 | 30.3 | 0.06 | 38.4 | 32.7 | 26.4 | 0.08 | 17.6 | 37.1 | 46.0 | 0.22 | 34.2 |
| No support relations | % | 28.5 | 22.9 | 19.7 | 0.07 | 28.9 | 24.2 | 19.2 | 0.07 | 13.2 | 25.7 | 34.8 | 0.18 | 24.7 |
| Satisfaction with division of labour[a] | | 7.6 | 7.9 | 7.9 | 0.06 | – | – | – | – | 7.6 | 7.7 | 8.4 | 0.14 | 7.9 |
| Satisfaction with housekeeping[a] | | 8.3 | 8.5 | 8.5 | 0.06 | – | – | – | – | 8.1 | 8.5 | 8.7 | 0.14 | 8.5 |

[a] Personal weighting; elsewhere household weighting.
Only values with significant difference (level of significance: $\alpha \geqq 0.001$).
*Source*: Welfare Survey 1980 ($N$ = 2396 households)

descriptive results show that the households are fulfilling many economic tasks in the handling of goods and the care of people. Neither the market system nor the collective institutions of the welfare state could take over these tasks. Nowadays it is often proposed to transfer tasks from the welfare state back into the households; but the limits of the households' capacities have to be taken into account. The political answer to these problems should not be to substitute one institution by another but to find the appropriate mix of welfare production.

The role of the informal social networks enjoyed by most of the households is to broaden their capacities beyond the limits set by the composition of the household. But support from social networks is seldom continuously received; its function is rather to overcome emergencies. Our analyses hint at the notion that support relations are primarily regulated by a principle of reciprocity. But the received social support also depends on need, and within limits the social network compensates the deficiencies of those households with low self-support capacities.

Household production is connected with subjective well-being in several ways. For example, satisfaction with housekeeping depends on the amount of self-support of household members and on the evaluation of the network support. But more important for subjective well-being are the direct contributions resulting from living together, for example feelings of belonging and love on the positive side, and quarrels on the negative side. Both vary to a high degree with household composition.

The composition of households is a determinant of all the dimensions of household production which were investigated. Alternative hypotheses which postulate the influence of income level, class position and the age of the head of the household are valid, but the influences of these variables are weaker (table 23.8). In general, household composition is the best predictor of household production. In particular, those household forms which today are increasing in number have self-support below the average. This is most striking for the one-person households. If the development of the household structure continues as now, this will be one reason for a decrease in overall household production. But there are more factors to be taken into account which change the overall amount of household production. The influence of the growing labour force participation of women is also in the direction of a decrease. A factor which pushes in the opposite direction is the technical equipment of households, which increases the labour productivity in the household. The reduction in working time and the high unemployment rates are also forces which seem to contribute to increases in household production.

## REFERENCES

Juster, F. Thomas, Paul N. Courant and Greg K. Dow (1981): The theory and measurement of well-being: a suggested framework for accounting and analysis. In Juster, F. Thomas and Kenneth C. Land (eds), *Social Accounting Systems*. Academic Press, New York/London.

Moroney, Robert M. (1976): *The Family and the State: considerations for social policy*. Longman, London/New York.

Zapf, Wolfgang (1981): Wohlfahrtsstaat und Wohlfahrtsproduktion. In Albertin, L. and W. Link (eds), *Politische Parteien*. Droste, Düsseldorf.

# 24

# Reciprocal Exchange of Labour in Hungary

ENDRE SIK

The reciprocal exchange of labour (REL) is a widespread institution of labour allocation in contemporary Hungary. Households use this institution either as a means of coping with predictable crises and unexpected emergencies or as a means of increasing efficiency and eliminating shortages in labour-intensive self-service, self-production and 'self-welfare' processes.

In this chapter I introduce and illustrate the concept of reciprocal exchange of labour, analyse its role in rural housebuilding, present its advantages and disadvantages, and finally discuss its incidence by strata.

## THE CONCEPT OF RECIPROCAL EXCHANGE OF LABOUR

The terms 'reciprocal exchange of labour'[1] denotes those transactions in the course of which households exchange their labour for other households' labour on a 'non-market' basis. The *household* is the unit of analysis because it is the household which defines economic goals, makes the decisions necessary to achieve them, and has the power (to some extent) to organize the labour of its members.[2]

1. For a more detailed description of REL see Sik (1985).
2. There may be several transitional forms between the household and the enterprise. The majority of households do carry out venture-type activities, and as long as they are not distinct from the basic function of the household (namely the meeting of household needs) but merely assist it, the term 'household' can still be used. A second case is when the products of agricultural small-scale producers are sold, an economic calculation is made both on the production and the sale, investment and profit accounts are kept separately from other activities of the household, but the profit is used only to meet the needs of the household (and to replace tools and equipment used in production). Here the term 'venture household' can be used. This is particularly appropriate if the activity is occasional and if the proportion of the household's consumer goods purchased from this income is small. But if the profit from production is kept separate from the household budget every year and only a constant amount is transferred to the household, the remainder serving rather to increase production rapidly, and if the production – separated from the household – produces fixed assets, the term 'venture' (mini-enterprise) would be appropriate.

This chapter will focus upon the reciprocal exchange of *labour*. Wallmann (1979) and Pahl (1984) have given illustrative examples to demonstrate the variation in the content of labour between cultures and even within one culture as well as the difficulties faced by researchers involved in comparative research. In the light of these examples, a minimum working definition of labour will be employed here which has been borrowed from Max Weber. This definition would not be sufficiently precise if this study was seeking a comprehensive treatment of labour *per se*. Weber's definition of labour is as follows : 'Economically speaking, human activities may be either directive or executive. The latter type is called labour while the former is called disposal over goods or labour' (Weber, 1979, pp. 15–16).

Obviously the notion of the reciprocal exchange of labour assumes an exchange. An important condition for the realization of this exchange is the *independence* of the two partners who make decisions regarding the method of using their own labour capacity as well as organizing 'outside (non-domestic) labour'. It follows from this that the labour carried out by members of the household *cannot* be considered as reciprocal exchange of labour.

Finally, following this definition, any transaction will be regarded as a reciprocal exchange of labour if the exchange is made on a *non-market* basis. This *negative* definition means simply that striving after profit is not supposed to be determinant in the exchange.

It is difficult to come to a precise, operational definition of the reciprocal exchange of labour without some discussion. The organization of exchanges is regarded as subordinate to a series of principles along a continuum between two poles – maximum altruism and maximum self-interest. No single definition is sufficient to separate them. Reciprocal exchange transactions are in equilibrium in the long run, near to the midpoint of Sahlins's reciprocity continuum, which he calls 'balanced reciprocity':

> 'Balanced reciprocity' refers to direct exchange. In precise balance, the reciprocation is the customary equivalent of the thing received and takes place without delay. Perfectly balanced reciprocity, the simultaneous exchange of the same types of goods in equivalent amounts, is not only conceivable but ethnographically supported in certain marital transactions, friendship compacts, and peace agreements. 'Balanced reciprocity' may be more loosely applied to transactions which stipulate returns of commensurate utility within a finite and narrow period. Balanced reciprocity is less 'personal' than generalized reciprocity: we would see it as 'more economic'. The parties confront each other as distinct economic and social interests. The material side of the transaction is at least as critical as the social: there is more or less precise reckoning, as what is given must be responded to within a limited period. So the pragmatic test of balanced reciprocity becomes an inability to tolerate one-way flows; the relations between people are disrupted by a failure to reciprocate within limited time and equivalence tolerances. It is a feature of the main run of generalized reciprocities that the material flow is sustained by prevailing social relations; whereas, for the main run of balanced exchange, social relations hinge on the material flow. (Sahlins, 1965, pp. 194–5)

Perhaps the following case study of rural housebuilding may help towards a better understanding of why I have defined the reciprocal exchange of labour only in a very loose, 'non-taxonomic' way. It will be seen that there are important differences among the transactions of the following case study in the time frame, in the mode of bargaining and so on, unless *all* these transactions are reciprocal ones.[3]

In June we began laying the foundations. The lion's share of the work was done under my guidance by my wife and my mother-in-law. At that time we got considerable help from two other families of relatives – the granddaughters of my godmother, and their husbands. In the past they had visited us a maximum of once a year, and they sometimes helped us if there was anything to do. I, in turn, did or made this or that for them, but they had never before come to help us on a major task. When they visited us last Easter they saw the materials in the yard. They immediately offered their help and told us to let them know when to come, adding that they would also want to build a cottage and garage.

So one day we gave them a ring, they came by car, and we began laying the foundation on a free Saturday. They brought along their wives, too, who did the cooking and the easier work. Even my old and sick foster mother kept herself busy, though she could hardly walk.

Making the foundation was a hard job. We worked from 6 a.m.to 6 p.m., and ate five chickens and six pounds of meat, washing it down with two crates of beer. Even so we could only keep up a good pace because I could borrow a mixer. It belonged to a young fellow in the village who was also busy building something. I tried out the machine and went along to ask him if he would let me have it. He lent it to me without even asking for any money, and said he would let me know when he needed it. You see, in villages people are ready to lend small machines, trestles, and left-over building materials.

Then we had to put up the walls. It took us two weekends and two afternoons, with me and the family always doing this or that before and after work. The helpers were the relatives from a nearby village, the two neighbours, and some new chaps, two of my colleagues. One of the them is a mason whom I helped with some masonry work for a couple of days two or three years ago. He and his grown-up sons would have been able to manage on their own but for the imminent price rise that spurred them on to finish most of the work before it hit them. So he accepted my offer, and promised to help me when I needed him. The other one, Uncle Lajos, is an unskilled worker, for whom I had worked a lot for a very reasonable pay.

We had agreed that whenever we had less official work to do, and the weather permitted, I should go and do the skilled work for him. Sometimes I even took a day off to get a good run at it. We kept a regular check of the hours I worked. Now he came along to help, for I had helped him to build his cottage well, quickly, and at a more than reasonable price. He knew then that he would have to pay me something because – not being a skilled worker – he would never have been able to return my work with work of the same quality. He was glad to have had a good skilled worker at that low price.

Another neighbour of mine, Uncle Dániel, also came to help us with this work. I had a financial transaction with him earlier, when I rebuilt and tiled his kitchen. I made him pay only the price of the materials, adding that he should come along and help when I was in the thick of building my cottage. And sure enough, he always

3. The case study was carried out in 1980 in a village in central Hungary (Sik, 1981). To build a house using domestic labour and money and add to these resources via REL and a state mortgage (using the latter mostly to buy materials and hence do less work) is quite typical in Hungary (Sik, 1986). Readers who are interested in the microprocesses of REL should read Fél and Hoffer's (1969) description of the society of Atány, a village near Tiszaigar where the following case study was made.

kept an eye on how we were getting along, and came whenever there was something for him to do. He popped over when a cartload of material arrived, and he helped unload it. He also fetched adobes from nearby, driving a small gardening tractor. Such things can amount to considerable savings, because, without help, bad weather can spoil a great many materials.

Uncle Mihály, my neighbour, also helped to erect the roof, for I had helped him with the building of his cottage and a stable. He had asked me to go and help because he was afraid of a change for the worse in the weather. He said he paid a man, who had begun building the cottage, 150 forints (a little over £2) a day, and he offered me the same amount. I took four or five days off my work, and put my nose to it. I would not have asked him for any money, since he had also done me good turns when, for instance, I needed some tools or help with this or that, but he insisted, because that was the surest way of making me stay on the spot all the time.

Well, you can imagine the crowd of people erecting the roof. No wonder that later none of them turned up to help. Of course the members of the family went on toiling, and others came as well. For instance, my foster mother's godson came to help us when we were making adobes. I had never helped him, he simply came around and saw me working. He said, 'My dear Pista, can I help you, or shall I beat it?' I said it would come in handy if he could help. And so he came, then later he let on that he would also need some help and some gravel. He wanted to install a water-meter. I worked for him about three hours, but he had spent the same amount of time working for me.

A former workmate of mine, a house painter and decorator, also helped me with making adobes. He is a strong young man. We knew he would also need help since he was a newly-wed. I spared him the painting of the rooms. Everybody should help with what they are most skilled at. So the painting cost less than we would have paid to a stranger, though the most important thing was that there was somebody to do the work, because, in summer, house painters are in great demand and they are hard to get.

Putting in the doors and windows, I had only the role of an unskilled worker, for the skilled part of it was done by Uncle Mihály, an old friend of Sárika's [his wife's] people. Once when he came to see us he saw we were planning to build a house. When he left he said he would help us with the doors and windows if we wrote to him when the time came. And that's what happened. He stayed here for three days, working out of frienship, no money asked for or given. Who knows, some day he will ask us for a favour, and then we shall help him as much as he helped us, but so far no mention has been made of it at all.

Now I think I owe work to about a score of people, though I, Sárika, and my mother-in-law were almost always at it, working our fingers off during these two years. But we could not even have started building if we had had to pay each and every skilled and unskilled worker. On the one hand, a cottage built with such help is much cheaper than one when everything has to be paid for; on the other hand, the person who builds in this way cannot go to bed without the burden of feeling that he owes this and that to a lot of other persons, and how much he, in turn, will have to work for others when so requested.

It may also happen that help cannot be returned because the helper moves away, or simply he never wants to build, and so you feel you are a bad debtor. And it is not good to be a debtor, since it makes meeting people unpleasant. That is what I mean when I say that this kind of building is advantageous financially but disadvantageous morally.

It seldom happens that people refuse to return help. There are people who keep a log-book of help rendered by them, with entries like: 'I helped Uncle Józsi five days then, and three days this and that time'. Yet it is not like a contract, some people do not even commit it to paper. I did not write it down myself either, though to tell the truth I did not help so much. At the same time I made a point of not forgetting about it. I never wanted anybody to help me for love, I am going to return it when I am expected to. We agreed upon it at the time of the work. And when they tell me, maybe in three or five years' time, 'Well, come then, we need your help, we have begun building', then you cannot say 'No.' It can even be taken amiss if you say you are willing only to help that much because you were given such and such amount of work. You are to work, only to work.

## THE ROLE OF RECIPROCAL EXCHANGE OF LABOUR IN OVERCOMING THE CONSTRAINTS OF RURAL HOUSEBUILDING

Almost the only way rural households are able to get a house is by building one for themselves. In rural areas the state and cooperatives build practically no flats or houses.

The need for housing is increased by the custom for the younger generation to move away from the parental home (Zsigmond, 1978). As a result the parents are faced with the choice of either building more than one house during their lifetime or building their own house large enough to allow the younger generation to live as a separate household.

Most rural households do not have enough money to complete work on building their houses before they move in. It is true that the use of mortgages has become more and more widespread since the 1960s (Kenéz, 1978) and incomes from the second economy have increased (Gábor, 1983). Nevertheless in most cases households can only afford to pay for the building materials and for those basic construction works which are required by the mortgage. Hence in order to be able to afford to build their own house households generally have to borrow additional money from other households, reduce their consumption spending and do extra work (Sik, 1984; Róbert, 1986; Dávid, 1980).

The rising cost of land and building materials imposes a large and increasingly severe burden on households' financial resources. It has three sources. The first is the permanent shortage of land and building materials which leads to a 'black market' operated by local monopolies.[4] The second is the frequent official price increases.[5] The third is the important fact that to obtain and transport scarce

4. 'The centres of the black economy are the building materials' depots and the brick factories. Have you heard about the brick dealers? They are the people who buy bricks at the state's depot and resell them for a couple of hundred forints more to the real users. The carriers buy a thousand bricks for 900 forints and sell them for 1400-1500 forints including delivery. They make a big profit and they do almost no work for it' (Szekulity, 1974).

5. 'The real per capita income of the population has been increasing since 1974 (with some fluctuations). The average annual increase is 3.5%. The average annual increase of the consumer price index between 1971 and 1975 was 5.1% and between 1976 and 1980 8.1%. But the average increase in prices of building materials between 1971 and 1980 was 8.8% per year. Prices of building materials have thus increased more rapidly than consumer prices, and 2.5 times faster than real incomes. On the basis of the average price increase alone we can see that from 1971 to 1980 the cost of houses has increased at least 50 per cent. This estimate does not even include increases in land and utility prices' (Hoffmann, 1983).

building materials in rural areas is already very expensive and is becoming even more so because of the lack of transportation facilities.[6]

Building skills acquired by experience are widely found among people living in rural areas and are adequate for the construction techniques in use. There are two reasons for this, which reinforce one another. On the one hand housebuilding has always been more or less a household duty and hence a certain pool of 'local skills' has been created - skills which are possessed by almost all rural inhabitants. On the other hand it is the rural population which provides the majority of state and cooperative construction workers (Galasi, 1976); in this way they are able to acquire the building skills possessed by skilled workers. The inertial power of their 'inherited' knowledge is considerable and makes the acquisition of new building skills a slow process. However, since housebuilding technology does not change rapidly, housebuilding skills also change slowly.

Despite the building skills possessed by the rural population, there is a constant shortage of skilled workers for rural housebuilding. This is partly because there are phases in the work which cannot be carried out without real training because they need special skills or an ability to use special tools. It is also because the council insists on the involvement of a properly trained skilled worker. The building industry draws away rural labour power into the cities. This happens in two ways: through the 'official' eight hours of people's 'first' jobs, and through the higher wage opportunities in the second economy.[7]

The labour market in the second economy in self-initiated housebuilding is organized by state construction workers.[8] Brigades of rural workers take the jobs together and this way they join the second economy of the cities, where they are passed from hand to hand for an income much higher than they could earn in the rural area (Kenedi, 1981).

Rural housebuilding relies largely on local small artisans but there are too few of them to meet the demand.[9] An artisan has described his situation as follows:

> I build approximately two houses a year. One can be known for this job. If someone likes it, he comes and asks me if I'm ready to take on the job. I'm able to help to get

6. 'It's very hard to get building materials. We have to look hard to find them. We travel a lot and by the time we arrive at the building materials' depot they're sold out. On Monday I was in Egyed village, with my brother-in-law. They had got building materials at the depot; they had been sorted out and they had even got some extra supplies as well, but the sales assistant told us that he would not let us, strangers, have any of them. He would only sell to those living in the same village. Besides, Egyed belongs to another county, called Hajdú-Bihar, not ours [Szolnok]. If you show them your building permit and it says that you belong to Szolnok county, depot salesmen in other counties [like Hajdú-Bihar or Heves] will not sell you anything' (Varga, 1983).

7. The first economy refers to full-time jobs in the state sector (together with a small minority of full-time private sector jobs). The second economy refers to all income-producing activities outside these situations. It is normal for people to take part in the second economy after finishing work in their full-time job.

8. Those who require 'second economy' building work done therefore make contact with state construction workers, who because of their social networks can readily provide a team with the appropriate skills.

9. The participation of artisans in self-initiated housebuilding has decreased because of the tax system. Only the 'big fish' dare to build more than three or four houses a year. The others stop work for a while or - as stated in the interview quoted - just supervise (Havasi, 1982; Hegedüs, 1982). According to the data of the Hungarian *Yearbook of Housing Statistics* (1982), only 30 per cent of self-initiated housebuilding was done by artisans in 1982!

> the plans drawn up and give advice about how to start the construction. If I can see that he is serious about it I'm ready to do all I can. Sometimes I get the plans made for him; he only has to send them to the council. I've got good connections with the planners, too. When I take on the job I insist that the unskilled workers should be organized by him. I don't like having to find them. Besides I'm afraid of being cheated by any unskilled worker who does not work well. By the 1960s or early 1970s the wage of an unskilled worker employed on such a building job was 150 forints per day, working from 6 a.m. till 6 p.m. with one hour lunch break. It is now 300 forints. But it is very hard to get hold of them. People, if they are able, prefer not to work but to tend to their gardens and vineyards, so it's usually relatives whom you can find taking part in self-initiated construction. Houses are almost always built with this kind of help. Often they need an artisan only because the law requires someone to direct the work and give advice. He advises on what kind of concrete should be mixed, and how it should be used, how the walls and roof should be built. I don't really work, just direct, give advice and check the work. I'm paid hourly for this kind of advisory work. It's not a good business, because if I do the work myself, I sleep better and I know that I have done a good job. Besides I have to be there from morning till evening, and get paid 200–300 forints a day for this kind of supervision. It's not so much money. But if I work as a skilled worker I get paid 400–500 forints per day. (Sik, 1980)

This part of the interview shows that even the supply of unskilled labour is limited in rural areas. This is partly because unskilled workers are drawn away to work in the cities, and partly because their unskilled labour can probably be better used as small-scale producers in agriculture (Szekulity, 1974; Tóth, 1976).

As a result of all these processes the wages of rural artisans and day labourers are increasing rapidly. In the monopoly situation created by the labour shortage it is not surprising that rural housebuilders lacking both skill and knowledge of the law are at the mercy of artisans, many of whom have good connections.[10]

10. 'László Cs., a railway worker, who had a flat which had only one room and a kitchen and which was so wet that all his furniture became rotten, could not think for a long time whom to get to do the job of housebuilding. He had to find a builder quickly, because it was a condition of his mortgage (granted by the state bank) that he had to complete the building of his new house by 31 December 1967. He could not even think about employing a state building company since the local one (the cooperative) considered the amount of the mortgage – 129,000 forints – given to him too small to cover the cost. The building branch of the agricultural cooperative could not take on the job because they were too busy with other work. László Cs. could not do anything but turn to the only artisan in the village, Janos M., who agreed to do the work. According to the contract the artisan should have provided the materials. When the bricks were transported László Cs. noticed that many of them were faded and broken. When he remarked on this he was told that the bricks had to be bought in advance and the fading had happened while they were being stored. László Cs. wanted the master builder to direct the work personally, but since he was working on many houses at the same time, he obviously could not be everywhere. László Cs. had paid 121,000 forints to the artisan by instalments, when he realized that the work would cost more than the agreed figure. The remaining 8000 forints of his mortgage would not cover it. He told the entrepreneur that he would pay the last 8000 only when the house was completed. The master builder immediately stopped work. He refused to paint the outside or inside walls of the house, the doors or the windows, and he did not build an access to the attic. The floor boards were already cracked because the wood had not been seasoned, the ceiling was full of cracks, and the plaster was coming down. László Cs. complained to the village council, and despite all these problems he was given permission to occupy the house. He also complained to the OTP [National Savings Bank] but he was informed that his house counted as a private one, despite the state mortgage, so the authorities were not able to interfere. Hence he has to turn to the courts (Berkovits, 1971).

Despite the increase in prices of building materials and the high wages available it is impossible to economize on the use of materials and labour in building. On the one hand it is impossible to reduce the amenities of the house, because they are imposed both by the building permission and urbanization standards, and by prestige considerations.[11] The location, size and height of a house have always been important attributes, expressing status and prestige, since they are striking and enduring indications of the social position of the household.

> Today it is the house now, which has taken the place of land, in the centre of the values of [the village of ] Varsány. . . .
>
> The almost symbolic importance of the house can be seen by the way people judge it by the number of features it possesses. There are constant innovations (windows with shutters for example), which are soon considered obligatory by everyone. For example, one such innovation in Varsány was the pitched roof, which is purely decorative. The building of this kind of roof was later forbidden by the council, and made subject to a fine of 5000 forints. But even after this rule was introduced, twenty more such roofs were built by people willing to pay the fine.
>
> The height of the house is also very important in people's eyes. On one occasion, somebody rebuilt the roof of his house just to be a couple of centimetres higher than his neighbour's
>
> There is a newer fashion: parquet flooring. It's not very practical as it is very often muddy outside the house, but people lay parquet floors at least in the inner room, which is very rarely used.
>
> The number of rooms is very important too. Two kitchens is the norm, for example: one inside the house, and the other one, the so called 'summer-kitchen', in the yard. It's remarkable that 'most young couples find it more important to build a second kitchen than a bathroom.' (Jávor, 1978)

Previously, acceptance in local society depended on making one's house as similar to other houses as possible. More recently prestige has come to depend on the individuality, luxury and height of the house. The role of the house as a measure of prestige has increased because the other traditional measures (land, horses, animals) have lost their function. The incentive to build houses which are bigger and have more comforts is the fact that houses preserve the value of money accumulated in periods of rural prosperity. This money is almost impossible to invest in means of production or land. The accumulation of consumer goods is an investment aim only among those who have been 'left behind' in the prestige race. The role of consumer goods in expressing prestige is therefore limited.

A variation of this is when a house is built through reciprocity with an eye to the future increase in its market value, as in the following example:

> In Buzsák [village] there was a custom that if somebody married, the whole family went to build the house. . . .
>
> Our family is big. My mother has got six brothers and sisters, my father has got

11. This extract from an interview gives a good example (Szekulity, 1974): 'People always clutch at something. They see a house and say, "Hell, if he can build a house like that, so can I." This feeling can push everybody to build a house. If my neighbour had not built one I probably would not have built one either. My neighbour's brother had bought half a plot of land and said to me, why don't you buy the other half? However, although my neighbour's brother was often ill he still started building the house. Why don't I do the same? Am I afraid?'

> another three. Their families came to help, too. They are my cousins. Then my father and mother came too. They worked there from early in the morning till late at night. They started on 1 May and we were able to move in in September. . . . I was pregnant at that time. I didn't even go there very often. The women used to carry the bricks, mix the concrete. There were four bricklayers in the family. They directed the work. In September we moved into the new house. My daughter was born soon afterwards, I could bring her home to the new house. We have got a kitchen and one room, a cellar, a boiler room, electricity, running water, a bathroom with gas cylinders. We lived there five years, four kilometres from the town centre. I didn't like living there, there was no kindergarten, but we had to stay for five years. But we were sure from the beginning that we were not going to stay in that house. But without that one we couldn't buy another one. This way we could sell it five years later for 350,000 forints and then we could buy a cooperative flat in the town centre, which is where we live today. (Dobos, 1983)

A typical rural household is not able to carry out the work needed to build a house on its own. This is because on average the household consists at most of two men of 'full value' (an adult man and an older son) and one or two people of 'part value' (woman, younger child, elderly people). This is just too few for many phases of housebuilding. Moreover, the labour power of the male members of the household is already occupied on weekdays for 8–10 hours on average. But it is also the duty of men to organize housebuilding, to obtain the materials, and to obtain the necessary permissions. This takes a lot of time during the construction and crucially affects the cost (Kenedi, 1981; Kunszabó, 1983).

Because of the high cost of new building materials the household has to use its own labour to obtain substitutes. This is possible by pulling down old buildings (Kunszabó, 1980a) and by self-producing building materials (Kenéz, 1978):

> Households with lower incomes and less wealth may cover part of the building costs by using their own labour, by producing building materials for the house themselves, making adobes, digging the foundations, making breeze blocks or – where possible – quarrying stone. To make adobes is not a gipsy privilege. In the late 1950s and early 1960s, when housebuilding started in the villages, it was still usual for people to self-produce building materials. Those who were able to produce their own walling materials only had to pay for the woodwork and roof material. That is why the use of these self-produced wall materials such as adobes, earth walls or breeze blocks was so widespread.

Another possibility is for the household to pay for the costs of building materials in labour or by exchanging other goods:

> Secondhand building materials are sold cheaply, but they may even be given free on the understanding that 'you will give me something in exchange when I need it.' But sometimes people don't even have to say anything, because it is taken for granted, so that it appears that they pay no attention to the value of what is given. 'It is left over, I cannot return it to the building materials depot anyway.' 'It is all right then, I will show you my gratitude.' In fact, when the opportunity for reciprocation comes, the person returning the good or service calculates its value very precisely, and tries to provide something of equal value as far as possible. This might be occasional transport, manual help or even surplus fruit at the end of the summer. Reciprocation may be delayed until the next building season. No urgency, only honour: those who are unreliable, greedy or forgetful soon drop out of the system. (Kunszabó, 1983)

There are two other facts which make it difficult for households to carry out the bulk of the construction tasks themselves: the labour-intensive nature of the construction technology, and the time constraints on finishing the work.

Building technology has not changed for a long time. It is obvious that the ugliness of rural houses, so criticized by architects, and the inefficiency of the construction method are not due to people's 'bad taste' and backwardness. They are much more a defensive response to a situation where there is little choice.[12] This is well summarized by Ferenc Kunszabó (1980b):

> The newest, so-called box form of the houses had become very popular by the end of the 1950s and was almost the only design in use in the 1960s. . . . It is simple to build: it minimizes the length of outside walls and uses the smallest and simplest type of roof: the pitched roof. The result is that this is the cheapest construction method. Through the use of concrete cornices, walls of equal length in any direction can be joined, and generally those building materials (stone, bricks, lime, cement, ballast, sand, concrete, ferro-concrete, timber frames and slate) which are readily available allow the work to be carried out in the best, simplest and most robust way. In other words those hundres of thousands of families who have self-built their houses in the last twenty-five years, and have 'sweated' maybe half of their lives, and the hundreds of thousands who will build them in the future are doing so not to irritate the experts but because present-day techniques and technologies make this method the most economical and efficient way of building.

The use of traditional technology to build houses means not only that much manual labour is required, but also that especially in certain phases of the construction the collective work of many people at the same time is needed, and this involves a high degree of organization. However, the number of people needed for certain tasks can be fairly well planned and these groups of people can be brought together for single weekends or during their holidays to help build the house. The people who are recruited into such groups are often employed in different workplaces and live in different settlements, and this collective reciprocal work is carried out in their leisure time instead of working in their second jobs or on their own household tasks. The construction work has to be very well organized in order not to waste the time of the helpers, as this would threaten the

12. 'The poor man who has no money now cannot be convinced about advantages which will show up in the future since it seems such a long time off. This happens in the case of the people's choices of building materials, too. Most of the artisans, master builders, insisted on the traditional small sized bricks. They did not take on any job using other kinds of bricks. Houses made of small sized bricks are simpler to build. People have become accustomed to using them over hundreds of years, and because of the growing number of family houses built with small sized bricks by reciprocal collective work using the help of neighbours and friends. At first sight the use of modern building materials looks more expensive since small bricks cost less individually. It is only after a detailed calculation of the cost of using bigger sized bricks, taking into account their volume and better insulation qualities, that it becomes clear that they are actually cheaper'(Bossányi, 1983).

'There has been almost no change in the use of bricks. New types of brick for dividing walls, and porous wall bricks, are available but there is no demand for them. The brick producers try to convince the spare-time housebuilders that modern walling materials are better and will last longer but the buyers cannot afford them because they are more expensive to buy. Besides, the unskilled but capable handy workmate or relative are used to building the main walls from B–30 blocks and the dividing walls from small sized solid bricks. They would not be able to build a house using modern bricks; to do this would require special skills rather than experience gained over years' (Keller, 1985).

existence of the whole network and the prestige of the household who is initiating the building as well as the efficiency of the work.

According to statistical evidence housebuilding can be completed within one or two building seasons by this kind of technology.[13] The judgement that the house is considered by the household 'completed' depends very much on their finances, tolerance of chaos, ambitions and capacity to do extra work after carrying out their first jobs. Once the household has moved in to the new house it is up to them what kind of luxury fittings they will add and at what pace.

The urgency of construction has many causes. Housebuilding disrupts the whole life of household members. All their leisure time – the weekends, evenings and holidays – is devoted to planning and carrying out the building of the house. The whole household drives itself to do the work; all other household activities are subordinated to housebuilding. The situation can be even worse because the household has to live in cramped living conditions, and may even move several times during the construction. It can create a special 'construction way of life', which produces the risk and danger of pauperization if it lasts too long.

The need to build quickly is also due to the fact that the income-generating agricultural activities of the household cannot be suspended for too long. The lack of these extra earnings cannot last too long either, because this can disrupt the household budget so much that it can affect the pace of housebuilding itself, perhaps further reducing the consumption of the household, a situation which cannot be tolerated for long without incidental social effects.

The pressure to finish building is also due to the constantly rising cost of building materials and the need to minimize the time spent on searching for them, obtaining them and storing them. Construction is also influenced by the weather. On the one hand it is better to move into the new house before the winter arrives; on the other hand housebuilding has to be stopped during the winter.

Given all these facts it can easily be seen that the ordinary rural household is unable to build a house using household members' own labour alone or using only labour bought on the labour market.

We can summarize our argument about the constraints on rural housebuilding by saying that households are tossed between the Scylla of self-exploitation and the Charybdis of financial impossibility. They are able to survive the construction of their house only through the use of reciprocal labour. The main reason for the widespread occurrence of this reciprocal labour is not its cheapness, pleasantness or efficiency, but the fact that there is no alternative to it.

## ADVANTAGES AND DISADVANTAGES OF THE RECIPROCAL EXCHANGE OF LABOUR IN CONTEMPORARY HUNGARY

The reciprocal exchange of labour (REL) is used by households in many different situations, and for a variety of purposes. By studying these cases it can be shown that they conform to certain patterns: these can be categorized as follows.

In a first type of case REL is used for primarily non-economic purposes, such as

13. Of the self-initiated houses and flats built in 1982, 33 per cent had been completed in one year, 64 per cent in eighteen months, and 77 per cent after two years. The average length of time to build a house was 19 months (Hungarian *Statistics about Houses and Flats,* 1983).

sociability, or to create personal relationships. In such cases economic reasons may be secondary, for example when the aim is to increase the efficiency of collective tasks such as housebuilding (this decreases the monotony of the work as a short-term effect and educates people into work roles as a long-term effect).

In a second type of case increased work efficiency is the primary reason for the use of REL. The households might have been able to perform the work on their own, but by using REL they can complete the work more efficiently as they share out the work and/or combine their labour power. Those households who use their resources rationally adopt REL instead of suffering individually. The advantages that the sharing of work tasks brings to the household parallel those which accrue to countries through specialization in the production of certain crops or goods – referred to as the law of comparative advantage. Households possess several kinds of skill but they are free from any investment or maintenance costs (education). By drawing on collective labour power, the quality of the work becomes more professional without any extra effort, the work can be done faster and more effectively, and the number of workers can be reduced.

There are two cases in which the reason for the use of REL is the lack of domestic labour power. In the first the balance in the labour power economy of the household is disturbed because of some kind of difficulty or crisis (e.g. a celebration, the absence of a household member, an illness, bad weather etc.). The main common features of these situations are that they occur unexpectedly and are temporary. As long as the household is not in difficulty it does not use REL. But the fact that the trouble appears unexpectedly and is temporary does not mean that households do not plan in anticipation of it. However, they do not know when they will find themselves in a situation of need, what kind of need it will be, or how long it will last. But such situations are virtually certain to occur for all households, and they plan for this eventuality. Ideally such planning should allow recourse to REL on an immediate basis, i.e. without the actual date, duration or type of need for labour being predictable. The best type of REL contact for this purpose is one which is long lasting and secure, which is strengthened by altruistic elements, but which is not often used, i.e. it remains available despite not being activated.

The second case of labour power shortage is when the task is predictable and household labour needs calculable. Here REL is used as a 'defence', because household members are unable to carry out all the tasks themselves. This is often due to external constraints. In cases in this category households are able to plan in advance and can even decide to draw on REL when they need a job of work done. Such uses of REL do not involve an unexpected and temporary lack of labour power; rather there is no solution for the household other than reliance on REL.

Categorizing the reasons for the use of REL in this way does some violence to reality but is justifiable for analytical purposes. For example REL which increases efficiency necessarily increases the household's ability to defend itself, just as the defensive type of REL increases the household's efficiency. REL which is undertaken without an economic aim can be understood as a network-creating action which will assist in establishing other types of REL; this helps the household in providing for needs occurring in the future as well as in ensuring that the needs are met promptly when they occur.

The characteristics of the types of REL are set out in table 24.1. REL which

TABLE 24.1 Characteristics of the types of REL

| | *Types of REL* | | | |
|---|---|---|---|---|
| | *Organized for non-economic purposes* | *Efficiency increasing* | *Constrained by the lack of labour power* | |
| | | | *Crisis avoidance* | *Defensive* |
| Dominant types of exchange | Altruistic exchange of work or REL | REL | Altruistic exchange of work or REL | REL |
| Typical types of work | Household work, service | Agricultural | Social service, agricultural | Housebuilding, service |
| Characteristic organization of work | In groups, at the same time | In pairs or in groups at the same time | In pairs at different times | In groups, at different times |
| Its frequency of use for long-term purposes in contemporary Hungary | Rare | Rare | In general use | In general use |
| Alternative institutions to REL for allocation of labour power | None | Labour market | Altruism, labour market, domestic work | Domestic work (self-exploitation), labour market |

*lacks an economic purpose* is naturally the least 'economic oriented'. It can be regarded as creating or reinforcing the structure of the primary group, at the same time as the 'labour' is taking place. Its main purpose is the creation of the network itself. The use of REL to *increase efficiency* occurs when the household finds it more advantageous than the use of other sources of labour. This presupposes the permanent use of REL and rational, but not market-based, planned behaviour. (For example characteristically this kind of REL is used in agriculture, for seasonal tasks which require a sudden peak of labour supply. This is met by two partners or groups of people using REL, and has helped REL to survive to the present.) *Crisis avoidance* REL is able – unlike the previous type – to cope with difficulties which occur unexpectedly. As the actual need for it cannot be predicted in advance, but because when it appears it must be dealt with immediately, the best way of organizing this type of REL is a permanent connection between two partners, who have an altruistic type of reciprocal exchange of labour. The *defensive* type of REL is similar to the efficiency-related type in that the household can plan for it in advance, because on the basis of its own and the other households' experiences it can be expected to happen. But it is similar to the crisis avoidance type of REL in that the need for it arises from a lack of labour power, due to some cause external to the household.

So far I have described REL as a useful institution which households choose in most cases in preference to the market or to altruistic action (i.e. unreciprocated help). As we have seen, REL is used to meet domestic labour needs at home and work, to increase the efficiency of collective work, to help in 'defence', and to cope with crises. The reader might therefore gain the impression that REL is a panacea, a cure-all, without any side effects. In fact, the use of REL can cause difficulties and strained relationships for households. It has many characteristics which can give rise to conflicts among households, for example the lack of precise records of the work done by one household for another, the difficulty of valuing tasks which are utterly different, the need to spend time organizing groups of people and the social costs of maintaining the network.

Let us examine in turn the positive and negative effects for households of three types of REL: increased efficiency; crisis avoidance; and defensive.

The positive effects of REL used to *increase the efficiency* of work are the increased output of work done at home, the reduction of costs, and the increased efficiency of work; there can even be an increase in the quality of the work. REL can also strengthen the social structure, e.g. as the network expands, conflicts disappear; and it can increase the standard of living of those involved.

However, as long as it increases only the traditional forms of living labour, REL has the unintended negative effect of retarding the introduction of new machinery and equipment. Since REL uses more living labour it helps traditional skills to survive and postpones the purchase of equipment. In the short term this can seem to be an advantage: use of REL involves little investment compared with the use of modern techniques; it maintains traditional skills; and it brings benefits to those who participate through the maintenance of the network. But in the long term these can lead to disadvantages.

In fact it is not REL itself which reduces the incentive for innovation. As new machines appear in the community, REL may be involved in their use. The lack of machines is due to the lack of capital and skills, and definitely not the use of

REL: REL is an effect rather than a cause. For example, the 'backwardness' of the technology used in collective housebuilding is not the result of the use of REL. However, REL helps the old technologies to survive; it provides a 'soft' alternative to the use of new technologies because it needs more living labour.

*Crisis avoidance* REL cannot be substituted in the short term: this, together with altruistic action, is the most important external labour power source for households in need. The negative effect of this type of REL in the long term is that it signals that household members are not able to provide for themselves in times of crisis or that they are in constant difficulty. As a result the household loses its independence and becomes a 'subordinated-independent' client of another household. The use of crisis avoidance REL increases altruistic reciprocity, as it becomes clear for both parties that reciprocation by work is impossible. This negative effect does not occur automatically if the difficulties are occasional or are caused by factors which are obviously beyond the control of both parties participating in REL, for example if a disaster is involved which involves all the people using REL. The effects of *defensive* REL differ fundamentally from those of the previous two types. While the negative effects of the previous two types of REL only apply in the long term and under specific conditions, since the effects are subordinated to other factors, the negative effects of defensive REL can occur even over the short term. We should not undervalue the strength of these negative effects, since they occur together with the positive ones (figure 24.1). The use of REL changes the economy of labour power of the households in four ways:

1 external labour power enters into the household's possession; it
2 has to be returned
3 in a later period,
4 and this presumes active participation in the network.

These four dimensions are shown in the upper part of figure 24.1.

The extension of the network has three effects. On the one hand the costs to the household of maintaining the network increase, as do the possibilities of strain in the structure of the primary groups; on the other hand the network is able to work more effectively, the more extended it is. (The range of skills contained in the network will be greater; the time spent searching for the appropriate person and the costs of organizing the work will decrease; etc.) Households feel that the greatest danger of REL is the increase in costs of maintaining the structure of the social relationships and the possibilities of strain. This can be seen from our next example, which refers to the pattern of working which developed in the immediate postwar period because of the shortage of draught animals:

> The lack of horses brought people together. A pair of horses usually had two owners. They had to agree which day and for whom to work the horses. For example, at the times when the demand for labour in the fields is highest everybody would prefer to spend all the time on their own field, and one can imagine how difficult it would be to agree. It needed a lot of self-control and patience. (Duba, 1974)

Whether the increased efficiency of the network outweighs the increased strains within the structure of the primary groups depends on the success of REL. The

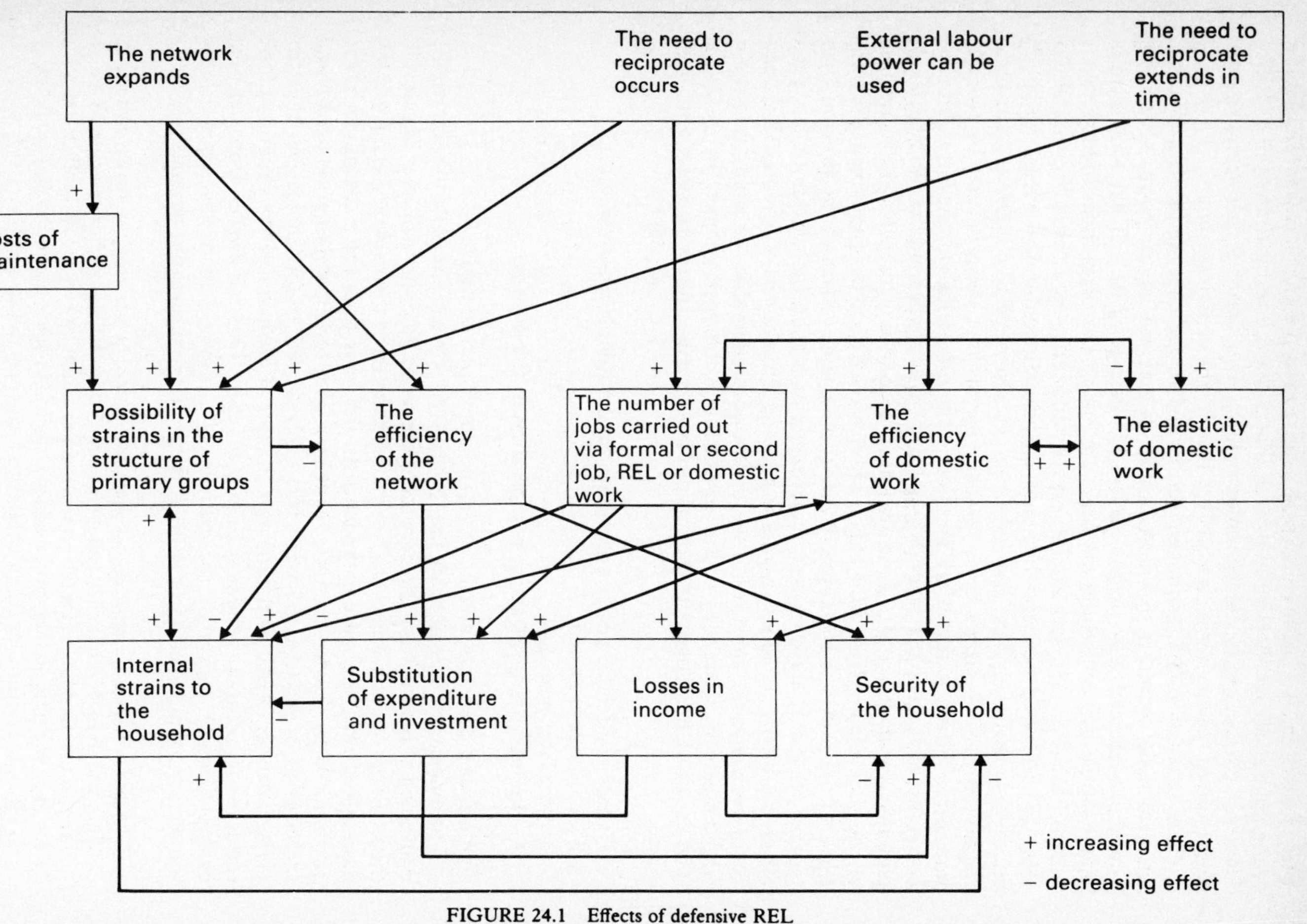


FIGURE 24.1 Effects of defensive REL

cohesion of the household (its 'internal stock of strains') may thus depend upon the success of REL.

The strongest negative effect of defensive REL arises through the obligation to return help. The special nature of REL means that returning help is complicated, and has to be done with the proper ceremony and with care about the timing and form of help. REL always carries the possibility of some misunderstanding, miscalculation, or forgetfulness by one or other partner, or a change of view regarding the value of the service, any of which might lead to increased strains within the structure of primary groups. The obligation to return the help increases the amount of extra work done by the household; it disturbs the domestic routine, and can even cause losses in a household's income, as instead of working in their second jobs household members have to return the help they have received.

The main positive feature of defensive REL is that it enables the household to obtain external labour power. This helps make good the lack of money available to the household, or substitutes for purchases in the labour market, and increases the efficiency of the work (by drawing on diverse skills, and combining labour). This results in a decrease in the household's needs for money and investment as well as increasing the efficiency of the network.

By allowing work to be spread out over a longer time, defensive REL has many advantages too. However, as the length of time involved increases, so too does the likelihood of strains on the household and negative impacts on the household's domestic work. The timing of REL can be a particular source of conflicts. The following is an example in agriculture:

> I have sixteen acres of land. Most of it is forest, meadow and marshes. I could not sow wheat because I had to help the others. In reciprocity. We joined together with the neighbours. We reap and plough together and share our tools. I have a plough, and a harrow. We even rent a tractor together from the local agriculture cooperative. (Berkovits, 1980)

In housebuilding, too, timing can lead to conflict:

> I started to collect the materials for my house when I was a bachelor. I calculated, made a note of how many rafters I collected and told myself 'here grows my house'. I had collected twenty-three rafters when I married. After the wedding we moved into my parents summer-kitchen: we started to build our house immediately. All my brothers and sisters, six of us. . . . We found a disused stone quarry nearby. We quarried the stone from there. All our holiday was spent on this, we were digging the stone for two weeks from morning till evening. If the family had not worked together on this, my wife and I would have spent two months breaking the stones.
>
> By the third year of our marriage we had used up the rafters, our house was completed, we even managed to plaster the inside walls and paint them. But then we had to start it again: my sister got married. She needed stone and adobes, too. She needed the help of the family, too.
>
> In the fourth year of our marriage we managed to render the outside walls of our house and in the fifth to paint them. . . . That year my second sister married. So we started it all again.
>
> In the following year my brother married. We went to the stone quarry, made adobes, dug the foundations, built walls again.

> Two years later my second brother married. Stone quarry, adobes, foundations, walling . . . you must know the whole process by heart already. (Berkovits, 1980)

To cope with these kinds of strain people choose appropriate technologies and methods of work organization, and plan to spread their commitments over time. Two more examples follow, one from agriculture and one from housebuilding:

> People who rent larger plots and grow certain crops can experience peaks of labour demand: for example, those who grow grapes, onions, garlic, lettuce, vegetables or who have peach, sour cherry or apple orchards. In the Szabolcs, Szatmár and Kiskunság regions, on the outskirts of the three cities one can even observe some areas of plots where people have chosen to grow fruits of particular types and times of ripening in order to minimize peaks of labour demand. They harvest the earlier ripening varieties on the plot belonging to the first family, with the help and labour power of the relatives, and then go on to the second family's plot, etc. (Szabó, 1981)

> We were going to start building our house, but my aunt and my neighbour were going to build houses too, so we decided to delay starting. We didn't want to have all three houses being built at the same time. I delayed starting for a year. But this way it was good for them and for me, too. I was able to go and help them, and now they come and return the help to me. (Varga, 1983)

As can be seen, without REL many households would have been unable to realize their aims, their standard of living would have decreased, and the level of economic activity would have suffered from the constant disruptions or would have decreased because of the shortage of labour power.

However, REL increases households' social costs and their internal conflicts and strains. It can disrupt the labour power economy of the household for a longer period, and this can affect households' incomes and cause difficulties in domestic work or life which reduce the security of the household.

## THE INCIDENCE OF RECIPROCAL EXCHANGE OF LABOUR BY STRATA IN CONTEMPORARY HUNGARY

Finally, I examine which strata use the reciprocal exchange of labour more and less frequently. I assume that the use of REL cannot lie outside lower and upper limits. There are various reasons for this assumption. In every stratum there is at least a minority of households who are not obliged or who are unable to enter into the REL network. In the lowest strata those whose domestic work capacity is large enough to fulfil all their needs can survive without using REL, while isolated and poor households, especially the sick and elderly, are unable to participate in reciprocal relations since they lack any resource to return. In the highest strata the minority who are financially secure have no reason to use REL, though they may participate in the REL network for social reasons, e.g. to express sociability, to gain popularity.

I will now set out the arguments for two theoretically possible models to describe the distribution across classes of REL in contemporary Hungary. In the first model the frequency of usage of REL is uniform across strata. The validity of this model in contemporary Hungary can be supported by three arguments: empirical, socio-economic and cultural. They suggest that only a minority of Hungarians do not use this institution. In Hungary during a five-year period 85 per cent of households used REL for social purposes (e.g. care of the sick, the elderly), 34 per cent for service, 22 per cent in small-scale agriculture, 6 per cent in chores and 5 per cent in housebuilding (but almost 80 per cent of those who build their own houses use REL!) (Sik, 1985).

The socio-economic factors which make households use REL are equally valid for all social strata. They are:

1 The shortage and poor quality of services and social welfare facilities which affect almost everybody (with the exception of the most powerful or wealthiest households).
2 The extremely high price of labour in the second economy, which hampers most housebuilding and prevents farming households from buying labour on the market.
3 The working capacity of an average Hungarian household, which is too small to fulfil all the domestic, self-servicing tasks etc.

As for cultural background, on the one hand because of their rural origins the vast majority of Hungarian households have the skills to take part in REL. They may even have an inherited network of exchange partners. On the other hand, in the provision of care there are also fundamental norms which exist in every stratum, e.g. generalized reciprocity in the provision of care among kin, and the norm of reciprocity (Gouldner, 1960).

A second model hypothesizes that REL is restricted to middle strata – that the highest and lowest income groups are not involved. This model has aiso been described by Hungarian ethnologists. For example Kós (1949) writes as follows:

> Wealthy peasant farmers did not participate in reciprocal lending because . . . their family labour force was too small relative to the large size of their estates. Neither did the least wealthy take part in it since they were the sharecroppers or day labourers of farmers, so they had to spend their time on the latter's land. Reciprocity was typical of the middle peasant strata whose family economies and labour forces were roughly equal and so could perform various urgent and lengthy jobs together, faster and better. They were similar in being engaged in traditional agricultural activities and, in most cases, were each other's relatives.

In my view, this second model is appropriate because, especially in the rural economy, compared with the lower strata the middle strata are considered to have stronger social organization, more skills and manual labour abilities, and higher aspirations as well as a greater – but not limitless – quantity of capital goods for their satisfaction.

## CONCLUSION

In this short essay my intention has been to introduce the reader to a distinctive form of labour allocation. The main characteristics of REL are caused by the facts that households lack sufficient resources to purchase goods and services on the market, and that they do not possess sufficient labour power to rely on self-production. The vitality of social networks and tradition in contemporary Hungarian society also helps the survival of this institution. This is partly why REL is more widespread in the rural context. Of course there can be very different combinations of constraint and tradition in particular subcultures, work processes and localities, and this affects the use of REL.

It would be of great interest to learn the mechanisms of constraint and tradition which create REL and how REL reacts upon them. This would be a step towards an understanding of households' work strategies as well as the labour allocation process of the economy as a whole.

## REFERENCES

Berkovits, Gy. (1971) Befejezetlen házak. In Berkovits, Gy. (1980).

Berkovits, Gy. (1980) *Terepszemle*. Szépirodalmi, Budapest.

Bossányi, K. (1983) Központositott téglahiány. *Heti Világgazdaság*, Nov. 19.

Dávid, J. (1980) A magánlakásepités formái és feltételei. *Valóság*, 10, 56–70.

Dobos, I. (1983) Népszokások a városban. *Valóság*, 10.

Duba, Gy. (1974) *Vajudó parasztság*. Madách, Bratislava.

Fél, E. and Hoffer, T. (1969) *Proper Peasants*. Viking Fund Press, NY.

Gábor, R.I. (1983) A második gazdaság és 'környéke' Magyarországon: Az 1960-as évektöl napjainkig. *Bulletin sz. MSZMP KB Társ. Tud. Int.*, 6, 66–166.

Galasi, P. (1976) A községben élö ipari-épitöipari munkások mint a munkaerö sajátos csoportja. *Közgazdasági Szemle*, 3.

Gouldner, A. (1960) The norm of reciprocity. In A. Gouldner (ed.) (1973), *For Sociology*, Penguin, London.

Havasi, D. (1982) A helyi tanácsok feladata a magánerös lakásépitésben és lakásgazdálkodásban. *Állam és Igazgatás*, 131–42.

Hegedüs, M. (1982) A magánerös lakásépités továbbfejlesztésének lahetöségei Bp. XVI. kerületében. *Állam és Igazgatás*, 243–50.

Hoffmann, I. (1983) A folyamatos árszinvenalemelkedés hatása a lakásépitésre. *Közgazdasági Szemle*, 5, 608–21.

Jávor, K. (1978) Kontinuitás és változás a társadalmi és tudati viszonyokban. In Sárkány (1978).

Keller, S. (1985) Az épitöanyagpiacról. *Heti Világgazdaság*.

Kenedi, J. (1981) *Do it Yourself: Hungary's self-help economy*. Pluto, London.

Kenéz, Gy. (1978) A falusi, illetve a családi házas épitkezés összefüggése a háztartások fogyasztói adott-ságaival. *Szöuetkezeti kutatóintézeti Közlemények*, 134, 135.

Kós, K. (1949) Kalákák és egyéb munkaformák a régi Bondonkuton. *Népélet és Néphagyomábny*, Bucharest.

Kunszabó, F. (1980a) Kaláka. In *Makacs maradandóság*, Magvetö, Budapest.

Kunszabó, F. (1980b) *Jászföld*. Szépirodalmi, Budapest.

Kunszabó, F. (1983) *Gyarapodásunk története*. Magvetö, Budapest.

Pahl, R. E. (1984) *Divisions of Labour*, Basil Blackwell, Oxford.

Róbert, P. (1986) *Származás és mobilitás*. MSZMP KB Társadalomtudományi Intézet, Budapest.

Sahlins, M. B. (1965) On the sociology of primitive exchange. In M. Banton (ed.), *The Relevance of Models for Social Anthropology* (ASA monograph, no. 1) Tavistock, London.

Sárkány, M. (ed.) (1978) *Varsány*. Akadémiai, Budapest.

Sik, E. (1980) Onkizsákmányolás és munkacsere. Budapest, unpublished paper.

Sik, E. (1981) A munkacsere Tiszaigaron. *Szociologia*, 1, 49–72.

Sik, E. (1984) Munkacsere és társadalmi struktúra. In *Gazdaság és rétegzödés*, Társadalomtudományi Intézet, Budapest.

Sik, E. (1985) Kaláka vidéken. Budapest, unpublished paper.

Sik, E. (1986) The welfare system and its future in Hungary: towards the 'self-welfare' society? Paper for XIth World Congress of Sociology, New Delhi.

Szabó, L. (1981) A paraszti munkaszervezet mai formái. Muzeumi levelek, Szolnok.

Szekulity, P. (1974) *Határjárás*. Kossuth, Budapest.

Tóth, Z. (1976) A szekszárdi kockaházak társadalma. *Valóság*, 4, 74–84.

Varga, M. (1983) Kaláka. Filmscript, Szeged.

Wallman, S. (1979) Introduction. In S. Wallman (ed.), *Social Anthropology of Work* (ASA monograph no. 19), Academic Press, London.

Weber, M. (1979) *Gazdaságtörténet*. KJK, Budapest.

Zsigmond, G. (1978) Az 1960-70-es évek fordulójának családtipusa. In Sárkány (1978).

# 25

# Work and Informal Activities in Urban Southern Italy

ENZO MINGIONE

## INTRODUCTION

One of the important 'discoveries' by social scientists in their analysis of contemporary society is that the world of work is becoming increasingly heterogeneous. A complex division of labour is in fact nothing new; on the contrary, from the classic analysis by Durkheim to the most recent studies on labour market segmentation a certain diversity in working activities, subject to constant change and growth, has always been assumed. These interpretations, however, were framed around the predominance and increasing importance of one particular kind of labour. Although it found expression in different forms, it was considered to be the most important if not the only paradigm of the relation between working activities and the social system. The kind of labour in question is lifelong employment for a family wage in large or medium firms in industry or services, that is, permanent blue- or white-collar jobs. The existence of housework, casual labour, temporary or seasonal employment, self-provisioning and various kinds of self-employed activities could not be denied. However, it was assumed that they would decline and, above all, that they were of very little relevance for interpreting industrial societies and their prospects. The heterogeneous picture of work has, therefore, always existed (see Pahl, 1984) and its recent 'discovery' – to which, among other things, the ample literature on the so-called informal sector has contributed – has been more concerned with one particular aspect. This is the fact that working activities previously excluded from interpretations of society, because they were considered to be on the decline or insignificant, must now be reintegrated into any interpretation of the social division of labour since they are taking on an increasing importance, at times merely explanatory and theoretical, but more often also in terms of numbers. In this sense, the change is more of a scientific than a radical social revolution. We will come back to this point in our concluding remarks.

The aim of this study is to analyse the heterogeneous situation regarding work in one region, southern Italy, where the working activities 'typical' of industrial societies have never been prevalent. As a conclusion, we wish to put forward some suggestions for reformulating in comparative terms the theory of the relationship between working activities and society.

It may well be the case that southern Italy is still the most densely populated underdeveloped region of some size to be found in an industrialized country. In saying this, however, the intention is not to deny that a series of profound social changes have taken place in the area since the end of the Second World War. In the immediate post-war period, the term 'underdeveloped' was applied especially to the high incidence of very low-income agricultural activites (accounting for 50 per cent of the working population compared with about 30 per cent in central and northern Italy) and to the parallel absence or sporadic nature of modern industries in the area. But by 1981 the rate of agricultural employment in southern Italy (also called the Mezzogiorno)[1] had decreased to 17.3 per cent;[2] the greater part of the population now live in urban centres, one-third in cities with over 100,000 inhabitants.

The thirty years from 1950 to 1980 were characterized by large-scale emigration from the region; the almost total depopulation of the poorer agricultural areas; a very profound change in agricultural systems; at least two much debated phases of industrialization;[3] and the drastic effects of the social and economic policies adopted by governments with a Christian Democrat majority. These governments promoted employment through patronage in the public tertiary sector and transfers of money to families in the form of pensions and allowances (Boccella, 1982; Mingione, 1986a), which led to the modernization and unification of consumption patterns at the expense of an ever-increasing dependence by the south on resources produced outside the area.

Today, 'underdevelopment' means above all weak fluctuating industrialization relying on investment from outside, the parallel concentration within the region of unemployment and underemployment in all economic sectors (as can be seen

1. Southern Italy is usually understood to include the following regions: Abruzzi, Molise, Campania, Apulia, Basilicata, Calabria, Sicily and Sardinia. Bagnasco (1977) also includes the region of Latium. In our opinion, the best definition includes Latium but excludes the province of Rome. Most of the data given here, elaborated by Marina La Rocca and myself, comply with Bagnasco's definition, while the data taken from other authors exclude Latium.

2. The figure for the employment rate in agriculture in the south is swollen, at least in the last two censuses, by a large number of bogus agricultural day labourers or family workers who work for a very limited number of days per year.

3. In approximate terms, it can be said that there have been two phases of industrial decentralization to the benefit of southern Italy. The first began weakly in the 1950s and, after a peak of intensity at the beginning of the 1960s, declined throughout the following decade with a few upsurges before the oil crisis in 1973. The leading protagonists in this phase were predominantly state-owned firms in heavy industry, iron and steel and petrochemicals. The second phase got under way at the start of the 1960s and, through a series of ups and downs, is still is progress (the automated Fiat factory at Termoli in Molise was inaugurated in 1984). In this phase the leading role has been played by light industry, above all metallurgical, engineering and electromechanical firms; they are mainly in the private sector and are experiencing a period of radical restructuring. Both phases have led, on the whole, to the creation of fewer jobs than the number lost in the same period in traditional local industries (Graziani and Pugliese, 1979).

*TABLE 25.1 The employment structure in southern Italy at the 1971 and 1981 censuses (including Latium)*

| | 1971 | | 1981 | | Change |
|---|---|---|---|---|---|
| | no. (000) | %[a] | no. (000) | %[a] | 1971–81 % |
| Resident population | 23,564 | 43.5 | 24,801 | 44.3 | + 5.2 |
| Active population | 7,843 | 39.6 | 8,975 | 40.3 | + 14.4 |
| First job seekers | 594 | 60.9 | 1,547 | 67.7 | +160.3 |
| Unemployed | | | 624 | 62.0 | |
| Employed plus unemployed | 7,249 | 38.5 | 7,428 | 37.2 | + 2.5 |
| Employed: agriculture | 1,850 | 57.05 | 1,289 | 57.6 | − 30.3 |
| industry | 2,495 | 29.9 | 2,237 | 28.1 | − 10.3 |
| services | 2,905 | 40.2 | 3,902 | 39.8 | + 34.3 |
| Precariously employed workers in industry | 1,173 | 63.8 | 667 | 81.6 | − 43.1 |
| Precariously employed workers in services | 84 | 68.7 | 288 | 63.2 | +244.8 |
| Workers in small firms (fewer than ten employees) | 158 | 20.7 | 209 | 21.6 | + 32.4 |
| Self-employed and family workers in agriculture | 831 | 44.1 | 445 | 41.0 | − 46.4 |
| Agricultural workers and (mainly) day labourers | 999 | 76.1 | 818 | 75.8 | − 18.2 |
| 'Central'[b] workers in medium and large firms (more than ten 'regular'employees) | 590 | 16.4 | 830 | 21.8 | + 40.7 |

[a] Percentage of the national data.
[b] The term *centrale* is used to refer to workers in big and medium industry who have job security and regular contracts, and in most cases belong to a trade union.
*Source:* The figures are elaborated from the data contained in the ISTAT censuses (industry and commerce 1971, 1981; population 1971; provisional and final results of population 1981) by Dr Marina La Rocca in her doctoral thesis 'Changes in the Italian social structure in the 1970s', Faculty of Political Science, University of Messina, June 1984.

in table 25.1), and a relative lack of or inefficiency in public welfare services. The latter have been greatly penalized in this region by the priority given to monetary transfers to families over the modernization of such services.[4]

The approximate picture that can be drawn from the socio-occupational data and from certain important items of structural information is of use in estimating the presence and extent of informal activities in the area. Almost a quarter of the active population – 36.2 per cent according to the official estimate – is made up of people seeking employment, and a further 20 per cent is accounted for by

4. Innumerable data exist on the scarcity of public services in southern Italy: from overcrowding of hospitals to pupils attending schools in two shifts; from average train speeds of 30–40 per cent less than in central and northern Italy to the almost total absence of day nurseries, homes for the aged and specialist centres for the handicapped; from the sporadic and insufficient nature of state-financed housing to the fact that twice the normal time is needed to carry out public works.

precariously employed workers[5] in industry and the tertiary sector and farm labourers hired on a daily basis. The remaining 56 per cent of the working population includes a very substantial number of self-employed workers and workers without job security employed by small or very small firms in all three sectors of the economy. For these workers income from work is usually low and irregular. To sum up, only just over one-third of the active population in southern Italy enjoys a stable average or above-average income. In this area there is a conspicuous number of civil servants and employees in the modern private tertiary sector (banking and insurance), while the workers in large and medium industrial firms form less than 10 per cent of the active population. The numbers of the latter increased considerably in the 1970s, however, as a result of an appreciable decentralization of factories belonging to big private industrial groups in the north of Italy and abroad.

What is said below may be clearer if we explain at the outset some of the ways in which the picture of the urban Mezzogiorno based on the assumed presence of informal work fails to correspond with the types of such work described in the vast literature on the subject. In particular, there are four areas in which we shall define precisely the general non-correspondence of the present informal sector in the cities of southern Italy to the established models: the 'traditional' type of 'street-corner' economy; the type of informal sector characteristic of the large metropolitan areas in the Third World; the informalization found in widespread suburban industrialization, namely the type based on small and medium specialized manufacturing firms; and, lastly, the innovative/creative and alternative informal type in both the German/Californian version of young people's alternative lifestyles and the 'technological/self-service' version identified by Gershuny (1978, 1983; Gershuny and Miles, 1983).

The first type is important because it was formulated as a direct result of the kind of phenomena witnessed twenty years ago in the large cities of southern Italy and, above all, in Naples (Allum, 1975). The 'street-corner' economy was a poor community system of economic organization at the very margins of legality and with a strongly hierarchical set-up. The inhabitants of an alley combined their resources and submitted to a set of regulations, alternative to those of the market and the state, in order to organize their survival. The principal 'ingredients' in this informal community organization were hawking, traditional handicrafts and services, contraband, prostitution, petty theft and receiving; but reciprocal relations based on a group-specific code also played a considerable role. In general, we agree with those who maintain that present informal activity in the urban Mezzogiorno is not an offshoot of the 'street-corner' economy (Pinnarò and Pugliese, 1985; Pugliese, 1983). In the course of the last twenty years this economy has, for the most part, been swept away by intensified modernization of the social structure and of consumption and behaviour patterns. Even those activities in the 'street-corner' economy which have survived in present-day

5. In a well-known article Sylos-Labini (1964) has suggested that the level of precariously employed people (that is, underpaid clandestine workers without job security) be measured by taking the difference between the employment figure in the population census and that in the census of industry. The latter is always lower than the former, a difference which is attributed 'to the fact that in the census of industry employers fail to declare a large number of casual workers, who state that they are in work in the population census' (Braghin, Mingione and Trivellato, 1978, p. 270, note 9).

informal occupations – for example, hawking and illicit activities – are now organized on very different bases and the 'street-corner' community is dying out.

The problem of comparing informal activities in the Mezzogiorno with those in the cities of the Third World is a complex one and can only be definitively resolved by specific analysis. However, it is important to make a few observations in advance, since superficial comparisons between southern Italy and the Third World are made all too frequently; this is also the case regarding other aspects. The specific features of the informal sector in Third World cities and, above all, the processes of social transformation underlying this sector are in reality very different from those that characterize the Mezzogiorno. Illicit street markets and trading, handicrafts in the home, informal urban transport (rickshaws and jepneys), independent and semi-independent occupations linked to multinationals, the rearing of domestic animals in overcrowded huts, and the thousand different ways of squeezing a little money out of an increasing number of tourists do not play a very important part in the economy of southern Italy. In this respect, it is worth emphasizing that in the towns of southern Italy the informal sector is principally made up of clandestine labour and precarious wage work, while in the cities of the Third World informal self-employment with very low earnings is almost always predominant. But, above all, there is one important basic fact that makes the informal sector in southern Italy, as a process of social transformation, different from that in underdeveloped countries. In the former, the recent consolidation of the informal sector took place for the most part after urbanization, which is already slowing down and accompanied by persistent economic stagnation rather than by economic growth as happens in the Third World, though based on dependency and indebtedness.

The informal sector in the Mezzogiorno does not have much in common either with the knock-on effect of widespread industrialization, such as in the centre and north-east of Italy and in other similar experiences. Here small and medium firms and specialized workshops make use of outwork, the 'flexible' utilization of all members of the family and the complementary relationship between a relatively rich part-time agriculture and the modernization of those specialized handicraft and manufacturing activities which have not been swept away by the international integration of markets during the last few decades. In southern Italy, these informal systems of small manufacturing enterprises, revitalized by the industrial decentralization and restructuring of the last fifteen years, are only found sporadically and are not particularly significant. The traditional specialization of leatherware production (gloves, shoes and clothing) in small workshops in the city of Naples may be considered to be in a phase of decline. The decentralization of small and medium industry from the 'Third Italy' (central and north-eastern Italy) to the Adriatic side of the Mezzogiorno assumes local importance only in the region of Abruzzi; in Apulia it is already failing to deal with the persistent employment crisis and absorb a significant number of young people. Finally, the ever-pressing and chronic restraints of 'a life with no options', a relatively poor local market demand increasingly dependent on income transfers from outside, and a social fabric which is segmented yet homogeneous in its expectations (the desperate search for secure employment, preferably in public administration) end by suffocating the type of potential source of alternative creativity which is said to exist in the new informal activities as practised by young people in California or Germany or in the technological innovation of the personal computer and the informatics revolution.

In the case of southern Italy, the informal sector is characterized by two main areas which, even though they do not account for the whole, certainly go a long way towards explaining part of it. Firstly, there is the question of informal wage employment, mainly of male workers, which in the past was more simply and accurately called 'black' labour (that is, clandestine labour). Then there is the area of predominantly female labour consisting in housework and other family-based self-provisioning activities. Here we must include both the persistently high number of full-time housewives and the pressures from recent social transformation in the south. Manifested in the destruction of traditional forms of community and family solidarity, in the need for modern services and bureaucratic regulation and in the parallel inefficiency of public services, they have led to the opening up of an ever-widening gap, one which is difficult to bridge, between demands and needs on the one hand and the resources to satisfy them on the other. In this part of the country, both in the true domestic sphere and in the services sector, a process of informalization is making headway since it is the only possible short-term answer in the absence of other solutions. However, it is a situation full of difficulties and problems caused by social tensions and discrimination.

## THE FEATURES OF INFORMAL LABOUR IN DIFFERENT SECTORS

### *The Building Industry*

In the last few decades, events in the building industry have constituted a very important and too often underrated factor in terms of the social structure underlying the question of the Mezzogiorno. In the immediate post-war period the massive financial resources of landowners, freed by sales and expropriations, were to a great extent poured into this sector. In parallel, the economic policy of the moderate governments in the 1950s was directed towards large-scale public works in the country's infrastructure and, in addition, the demand for houses increased progressively – this on the part of the urban upper and middle classes, strengthened economically by public intervention, bureaucratic expansion, the abandoning of rural areas and the corresponding growth of the urban bureaucratic centres. The building industry took on a controversial and speculative aspect in the sense that high profits were made in this sector and the interweaving of public affairs and private business was permeated by corruption and misappropriation of public money. The result was that the large criminal organizations in the south were soon able to corner a major part of these activities. However, what we are really interested in are the characteristic ways labour is employed in this industry. The presence of a large and growing overpopulation prepared to accept precarious underpaid jobs without a contract led to the excessive spread of the practice of using clandestine labour.

This speculative building, based on clandestine labour on the 'big' construction sites, reached its peak in the 1960s. In this period, the precariously employed

TABLE 25.2 The employment structure in the building industry in southern Italy at the 1971 and 1981 censuses (including Latium)

| | *1971* | | *1981* | | *Change* |
|---|---|---|---|---|---|
| | *no. (000)* | *%* | *no. (000)* | *%* | *1971–81 %* |
| Total employees | 1002 | | 872 | | − 13.0 |
| % of employees in industry | | 40.2 | | 39.0 | |
| Male employees aged 14–24 | 242 | | 183 | | − 24.4 |
| % of employees in building | | 24.15 | | 21.0 | |
| Total employees | 884 | | 726 | | − 17.8 |
| % of total employees | | 88.2 | | 83.3 | |
| Precariously employed workers | 726 | 82.2 | 481 | 66.2 | − 33.7 |
| Workers in small firms | 39 | 4.4 | 90 | 12.3 | +127.5 |
| 'Central' workers | 119 | 13.4 | 156 | 21.5 | + 31.2 |
| Precariously employed workers in building as % of: | | | | | |
| Employees in building | | 72.45 | | 55.2 | |
| Employees in industry | | 29.1 | | 21.5 | |
| Precariously employed workers in industry | | 61.9 | | 72.1 | |
| All precariously employed workers (except agriculture) | | 57.8 | | 50.4 | |

*Source:* Our elaborations of ISTAT data in the 1971 and 1981 censuses of population and industry and commerce

labourers in the building industry alone represented almost 40 per cent of all the employees and 45 per cent of all the workers employed in industry in the south. Then, in the following decades, this type of building activity declined – as can be seen in table 25.2 – owing mainly to the saturation of the market.[6]

None the less, even in the 1980s, the precariously employed labourers in the building industry constitute the greater part of all non-agricultural workers and more than one-fifth of all industrial employees in the Mezzogiorno. Besides, as we will see below, it can be assumed that there has been a tendency in the last ten years for this estimate no longer to include an entire group of even more precariously employed labourers who work intermittently on 'small building jobs'. It must be emphasized that even that part of the small army of clandestine building labourers which has been accounted for is equivalent to almost 60 per cent of the number of workers employed in large and medium firms, that is, those workers who are considered to form the backbone of the working-class and the trade union movement. In other words, for every ten 'central' workers (see

6. The saturation in the building of dwellings by large firms began to emerge in the 1960s and led to a severe crisis in the formal sector in the 1970s. It was indicated by the steep rise in new flats remaining vacant (Ginatempo, 1976: Ginatempo and Fera, 1985).

table 25.1) in industry potentially belonging to a trade union, two of whom are permanently employed in the building industry itself, there are six precariously employed workers in the building sector.

It is interesting to re-examine the last fifteen years for possible changes in the condition of these precariously employed workers following the radical transformation that has taken place in the residential building industry in this same period. In the 1970s the big construction sites suffered a drastic decline, and the 'official' residential building industry appeared to have almost entirely vanished. It is with some surprise, therefore, that we learn of the enormous volume of residential building that took place in the 1970s, as recorded by the census data for 1981. Of this volume, 70–80 per cent is covered by unauthorized building of three main kinds: self-help (do-it-yourself) building; holiday homes; and renovation and extension work (see Ginatempo and Fera, 1985).

The number of precariously employed workers in the building industry has decreased considerably, even though the decline is less accentuated than the reduction in the number of such workers in all of industry (see tables 25.1 and 25.2). In the case of the building industry, this decrease is the combined result of trends that at first sight are difficult to understand. The census of industry and commerce shows that a substantial increase in employment has in fact occurred in this sector, especially as regards small firms (with fewer than ten employees). At the same time, according to the population census the overall number of employees has gone down. Consequently, the hypothesis may be put forward that in the ten years which witnessed a revolution in unauthorized building, the activity of a vast array of small firms was consolidated and formalized.

This apparent paradox can easily be explained by taking into consideration the type of activity that was becoming widespread (relatively small-scale renovation, finishing-off work and commissioned construction of family houses and villas) and the parallel modifications in fiscal and economic legislation which, in some cases, made it worth while to put one's activity on a legal footing. As a consequence, a certain number of workers in the building industry were taken out of precarious employment. However, one wonders if there has really been such a large drop in precarious employment in building. There is good reason to believe that a not inconsiderable number of young men apparently seeking their first job are, in reality, precariously employed in the building industry.[7] However, whereas ten or twenty years previously their fathers and elder brothers declared themselves to be workers because employed clandestinely, but at fairly regular intervals, on big construction sites, the younger generation 'rightly' describe themselves as looking for a job since the casual labouring work they do in building is much more clandestine and precarious. Although their number is still high, precariously employed building labourers can be said to be on the decline. Despite this, it cannot be taken for granted that informal building activity is also

7. This possibility is confirmed by the substantial drop in youth employment in the building industry in southern Italy: the number of workers under 24 years of age has gone down from one-quarter of the total in 1971 to little more than a fifth in 1981. In central and northern Italy, on the other hand, where unauthorized building plays a reduced role, the percentage of young workers is greater. The assumption that the number of young workers who are very precariously employed in building is high and on the increase is borne out by qualitative research.

effectively diminishing. On the contrary, it is a well-known fact that small and medium enterprises in the field of renovation, self-help building and the building and repairing of unauthorized dwellings operate outside the law. New small-scale building still remains one of the main areas of tax evasion and non-compliance with legal regulations.

Using quantitative data and information of a qualitative kind, it is possible to build up a picture of the precariously employed workers in the building industry. They are almost exclusively males and either illiterate or with a very low level of education. A large number of them begin working when minors and as a result figure among the young age groups over a long period. During the twenty years of large-scale emigration, one of the possible first stages of mobility was precarious employment in the building trade. Today, however, it increasingly represents a dead end without long-term prospects or opportunities for social mobility. It is therefore a strong factor in the creation of poverty, which is also transmitted from one generation to the next.

### *Agricultural Labour and Self-Provisioning by Town Dwellers*

Our qualitative research on the low-income strata in the towns of Messina, Reggio Calabria, Milazzo and Barcellona Pozzo di Gotto identified very few cases of cultivation for personal consumption and few families who regularly receive non-marketed agricultural products from relations or friends who are farmers (see Mingione, 1985). A previous investigation of the workers in the chemical centre of Siracusa/Augusta and those in the steel centre of Taranto showed that this kind of resource represented a minimal factor, even in families of peasant origin with near relations still engaged in agriculture (see Mingione, 1977). Neither is this contradicted by the more recent research on consumption patterns in Naples (see Serpieri and Spanò, 1986). Agricultural resources for personal consumption appear to be of little relevance for either workers or the poorer and more marginal strata in southern Italian towns. An exception must be made in the case of some families which include agricultural pensioners and in that of suburban areas where there is still an appreciable amount of cultivation on 'small plots' for personal consumption (see Randazzo, 1986). It may be estimated, therefore, that agricultural production for personal consumption involves directly or indirectly, but with some degree of commitment and continuity, less than 5 per cent of the low-income urban population in the south.

It is very difficult to estimate if and how many members of low-income families living in towns work intermittently as farm labourers by the day, especially at harvest times. In 1982, more than 650,000 agricultural day labourers were recorded in southern Italy; of these a good 80 per cent worked fewer than 100 days in the year (Pugliese, 1985). Moreover, this army of part-time agricultural day labourers is concentrated in several agricultural regions, and so an obvious supposition is that it includes a number of part-timers who live in the towns. Given the fact that it is in the interest of both labourers and employers to formalize and register this agricultural work, it is plausible to assume that such seasonal farm labourers also engage in unregistered informal activities in the towns where they live. It is interesting to note that this category may comprise an appreciable number of young women (aged 14–24). In fact, the rate of female youth employment in agriculture in the Mezzogiorno is extremely variable and reaches its peaks in the same areas where the army of seasonal day labourers is to be found most. In 1981, the rate was still over 60 per cent in the provinces of Reggio Calabria and Brindisi, while it was about 50 per cent in the provinces of Taranto, Catanzaro, Messina and Benevento, and over 40 per cent in those of Cosenza, Salerno and Potenza.

### *The Growth of Precarious Employment in the Service Sector*

Table 25.1 shows that workers precariously employed in the tertiary sector represent the category which increased most in the 1970s, even more than the category of young people looking for their first job. In general terms, this fact confirms the hypothesis that the growth of the tertiary sector in a relatively poor economic environment is accompanied by a considerable expansion in clandestine employment and in the informalization of working conditions (Mingione, 1986b). In this case, however, we need to remark on and adjust the estimated figure. The fact that precariously employed workers are still 7.4 per cent of all those working in this sector must be put in perspective for two important reasons: first, clandestine workers in the tertiary sector are concentrated in only some branches, whereas they are almost completely absent in others (public administration, credit and insurance companies, provision of advanced services to firms, transport); and secondly, a large part of the clandestine labour known to exist in these branches is excluded from the estimated figure.

In commerce, especially in the retail trade, in services to the public (bars, restaurants, garages) and in services to families (domestic help and services rendered in the home), the incidence of clandestine labour is not only growing rapidly but is also quite high compared with the number of people in regular employment (more than a third). In particular, the estimate in table 25.1 excludes a number of cases that are found in this area to a relevant extent: clandestine workers who gain by declaring that they do not work, for example, a large number of maids who are paid by the hour; undeclared family helpers; young apprentices looking for their first job; minors; foreign workers from Third World countries; the unemployed; and housewives working very occasionally outside the home. So what we are dealing with is a vast and growing area of informal labour, but one which also covers very disparate kinds of work. It includes occasional activities – the small jobs done by young people during long periods of unemployment – and others which are continuous, though never regularized, true informal occupations, such as undeclared waiters and unauthorized hawkers. Much of the work is of a self-employed or semi-independent kind (for example, the immigrants who sell goods at street corners in Naples often operate under the control of a local entrepreneur); and there are several types of outwork in rapid expansion (for example, commissioned typewriting). However, there also exists a large number of clandestine wage workers.

We find a similarly heterogeneous picture when we look at the informal worker. All categories of workers are in supply, especially the weaker ones: minors and young people looking for their first job, women who wish to re-enter the labour market, elderly people (pensioners and non-pensioners), and immigrants from the Third World. However, where the labour market is in an extremely weak position, it is plausible to assume the presence of a substantial number of males in the central age groups who have heavy family responsibilities, no educational or professional qualifications and are condemned to erratic employment by particularly difficult lives, by no means unusual in the towns of southern Italy. They give up compulsory school education in order to earn a bit of money and help their families. For four or five years they work for very low wages as helpers in bars or as shop boys. Later, they do undeclared work as unloaders or manual labourers in the wholesale trade or in engineering plants. They spend the whole of their lives like this, changing jobs and working in many different fields.

The service sector, then, is permeated by kinds of informalization which do not conform to official job categories and are typical of the economic poverty of the region, the failure to set up a modern system of welfare and the pervasiveness in the south of patronage and corruption in public office. What we are dealing with, first of all, is the extension of housework to cover all those assistance and service activities (concerned with the care of children, old people, the sick etc.) that are not covered either by the social services or by a 'modern' branch of low-cost private services. Secondly, there are forms of community and family solidarity which act as supplementary resources to the shortcomings of the state and the market. These resources, however, may be used in very debatable ways and distributed unfairly because they have to a large extent gone into disuse as a result of the 'modernization' and geographic mobility of the population. Lastly, a whole area of informal activity must be considered which originates from personal dependency and patronage in the public welfare system. By this is meant not only corruption and the exchange of political favours but also all those services supplied against cash payments by public employees in and outside their normal working hours, such as nurses and doctors who offer their services privately without declaring the fact (see Jedlowki, 1986).

### *Clandestine Labour in Manufacturing Industry*

It can be seen from the data in table 25.1 that in 1971 the number of precariously employed workers in manufacturing industry in the south was almost 450,000 and that this had fallen to 186,000 in 1981: a drastic reduction of nearly 60 per cent. During the same period employment in small and very small firms remained stable, unlike in the north where it increased substantially. This second figure is the result of aggregating decreases and increases in different branches. An appreciable fall occurred in the numbers of independent craftsmen and small family firms in the regions hardest hit by the crisis of the 1970s. Against this, employment went up as a result of industrial decentralization in some branches in which Italian industry typically specializes (electromechanics, clothing and knitwear), in particular in the regions of Abruzzi, Latium and the northern part of Apulia. The decrease in precariously employed labour is in part due to a manipulation of the statistics, since a large group of such workers in engineering workshops were transferred from the secondary to the tertiary sector during the decade in question (1971–1981). This fact also puts the exceptional expansion of the tertiary sector into perspective.

Nevertheless, the drop is for the most part real and reflects the persistent crisis in traditional local industry. Furthermore, this has not been compensated for by a substantial extension to southern Italy of the model of widespread industrialization based on small and medium firms which is characteristic of the centre and the north-east. From this we can assume that the types of informal manufacturing labour connected with such a model - work done in the home, undeclared overtime, subcontracting, long hours of family labour - are not particularly present in the south. It is not surprising, therefore, that our research on the towns of Sicily and Calabria revealed few cases of this kind.

The situation of clandestine labour in manufacturing in the city of Naples needs to be looked at separately. Here there has always existed a widespread industrial and handicraft production in small workshops, often located in the home, which specialized in leather working, but also comprises other branches of the clothing industry. This is, for the most part, a highly fragmented industry which makes abundant use of clandestine and overwork by family members, often greatly exploited by those who buy and market such products. Always in great difficulty in terms of economic survival and already in decline owing to competition from more large-scale enterprises and from producers in developing countries, it was particularly hard hit by the 1981 earthquake in Irpinia and the way in which reconstruction was carried out: there was no longer any space for the small home workshops (IRES CGIL, 1981; Giannola, 1983).

The results from a recent examination of the records relative to the settlement of disputes on termination of clandestine work (Fortunato, Ligouri and Veneziano, 1986) show that the footwear and clothing industry is especially characterized by the presence of clandestine workers. While this branch of industry accounts for just over 20 per cent of manufacturing employment in Naples, clandestine labour disputes make up 55.9 per cent of the total. The authors of this research maintain that 'footwear is apparently the branch which employs clandestine labour most "integrally", in all the various kinds of enterprises and productive units. In both branches there is a high concentration of women workers. As a matter of fact, nearly all the workers are women' (p. 85).

## *Multiple Job-Holding*

It is worth referring briefly to the question of multiple job-holding or 'moonlighting' since the results and interpretations are now available of at least three investigations in areas that include important towns in southern Italy: Caserta (Ragone, 1983); Catania (Reyneri, 1984); and Bari (Chiarello, 1985). They were part of a project to ascertain the rate of incidence and draw up a detailed qualitative picture of 'moonlighting' by workers with guaranteed jobs.[8]

By definition, the three surveys did not take into account multiple job-holding by individuals having a first occupation with no job security. This means they are unable to supply data for the figure of the 'clandestine multiple job-holder', quite common among low-income groups in the Mezzogiorno.[9] The surveys report a

8. 'In the three surveys of southern Italy, the area of guaranteed work included the employees in the normal and extended public sector (central and local state administration, state-funded public services, local authorities, state-controlled enterprises, schools and universities, state-owned banks, municipalized firms), in partially state-controlled industry and in private non-agricultural firms with more than 100 employees' (Chiarello, 1985, p. 33).

9. Many investigations into social marginality in southern towns have shown that there exists a type of precariously employed worker, known as a *saltafossi* in Sicily, who engages in many working activities, all of a casual kind (see Cammarota, 1977).

fairly high number of multiple job-holders: 15.7 per cent for the district of Caserta; 21.7 per cent for the conurbation of Catania; and 22.8 per cent in the sample taken in Bari. The second jobs are mainly self-employed activities which are continuous, of long duration and clearly informal in the sense that they evade tax regulations and are not officially registered. In the Catania and Caserta surveys, half of the cases concern non-manual workers with relatively above-average incomes. In the case of Bari, the figure for this kind of 'moonlighter' is much lower (21 per cent of the total).

Multiple job-holding in medium- to low-income groups - semi-skilled manual workers or those with basic qualifications - accounts for 54 per cent of the cases in Bari, 38 per cent in Catania and 34 per cent in Caserta. These workers are part of a traditional family structure in which the wife/mother is a housewife, the children have great difficulty in finding work, and the husband/father manages to make ends meet by also taking up a second and, if need be, a third activity. In these circumstances, economic motives play a more important role in starting another activity than in other cases. This situation fully reflects the highly rigid and segmented state of the labour market, since those already working are able to find a second job whereas it is almost impossible for women or young people to find a first job. The surveys show that in the majority of cases the first job constitutes an important social resource making a second activity possible both for direct reasons of social connections, professional qualifications etc.[10], and for indirect reasons - such workers can face the economic uncertainty of the second occupation because they have a first job to fall back on. As Reyneri rightly points out (1984, pp. 253–73), the combination of a high incidence of multiple job-holding with parallel high levels of unemployment and 'non-employment' (that is, the condition of not seeking employment as in the case of students, housewives and pensioners) is a feature of southern Italy that is extremely difficult to eliminate. The reason for this is that in the majority of cases second jobs are not jobs taken away from the unemployed but rather activities invented within the interstices of the economic and institutional system.

## *Self-provisioning Activities*

We are unable to make any remarks about the historical development of this kind of work, because no research material is available which documents to what extent and in what way activities like production in the home of preserved foodstuffs, clothing or furniture have changed in the last few decades. The self-provisioning activity which appears to be most widespread and which expanded greatly in the 1970s is self-help (do-it-yourself) building. This category comprises not only renovation, extension work, finishing or maintenance but also the complete construction of dwellings by urban families with the aid of informal la-

10. In southern Italy, those with a second job are mostly public employees and workers in the modern private tertiary sector. They often use their professional credentials and the power conferred by the first job to obtain a second one. Take, for example the bank clerk employee who also works as a financial consultant (professional credentials); it sometimes happens that in his second capacity he prepares the documents relating to the request for a loan which it is his job to examine in his first capacity (power credentials).

bour offered for a similar favour in return or for payment in cash (Ginatempo and Fera, 1985). The presence of this kind of activity is not surprising if we put together three elements typical of the specific situation in the Mezzogiorno: the high incidence of experienced workers specialized in the building of dwellings; the crisis of large building sites specializing in houses for above-average income groups, a crisis which has left a substantial number of potential labourers 'unemployed'; the chronic underproduction of dwellings for low-income and lower-middle-income groups by state-financed bodies, cooperatives or private builders. Nor is it surprising that the self-help builders are predominantly lower-middle-income families. Unlike the case of England (Pahl, 1984), in southern Italy it is easier and more convenient for families with above-average incomes to use informal workers for this kind of work. However, it is the case in this region also that very low-income groups do not engage in self-help building because they do not have the necessary resources (above all, money for materials, given that the land itself is often occupied illegally).

What has been said above also applies to other types of self-provisioning, such as those identified by a recent investigation into consumption patterns in Naples (Serpieri and Spanò, 1986). The numerous group of lower-middle-income earners are very active in self-provisioning, especially in those activities carried out by women but also in typically male activities. Although largely inspired by local culture (for example, traditional use of home-made tomato sauce and pasta), it can readily be assumed that such activities are now mostly carried out using modern do-it-yourself equipment, which means that the traditional skills of a region are not reproduced as a matter of course. In middle-income families the housewife has more time available, both because she does not have to face problems of real poverty and because she is often helped by relatives, as well as more monetary resources for investing in self-provisioning activities. This is reflected in the fact that the production of foodstuffs in the home is very widespread (bottling of tomato sauce and making jam, other kinds of preserves, home-made pasta, wines and liqueurs etc.), as is also dress-making. These families almost always possess a sewing machine and often a small knitting machine as well.

Apart from self-help building, the question of male self-provisioning activities (carpentry, electrical repairs and plumbing, furniture-making, decorating, constructing door and window frames, agricultural cultivation for own use, repairing vehicles) is a debatable one. As Serpieri and Spanò (1986) rightly point out when analysing the results from the research on consumption patterns in Naples, this type of work is widespread and is correlated mainly with need and ability. Unlike those in poverty, the large majority of families enjoy a social status which brings with it many additional needs. Normally they have sufficient monetary resources to be able to have recourse to the market, preferably the informal market. This occurs where their own technical skills are insufficient to do the job by themselves or if they possess no particular skill which they can exchange for the help of neighbours and friends. This is the case, above all, with electrical repairs, plumbing and carpentry, which are less common than self-help building repairs and painting jobs. However, more than a third of families are self-sufficient for all repairs in the home, a further 10 per cent resolve all their problems except for one particular repair job, and only a small minority turn to the market in all cases. The number of families who do their own repairs to motor vehicles is relatively low – about 30 per cent.

Before attempting to draw some general conclusions on the estimates for informal working activities, it is worth mentioning two areas that have not been considered so far: crime and housework. It is a well-known fact that criminal activities, especially those organized by the Mafia and the Camorra, deal with considerable sums of money; they pervade people's daily lives (think of the protection racket against shopkeepers), involve a not insignificant part of the population in the large towns of southern Italy, and range from drug trafficking to protection rackets, receiving stolen goods, theft, contraband and prostitution. It is very difficult, if not impossible, to carry out specific research in this field and so we are reluctant to put forward general estimates on the amount of money and the number of people involved. It does seem, however, that the recent judicial investigations in Naples and Palermo have revealed a very extensive and complex network in which a small number of bosses at the head of a military-style hierarchy extend their control over the illegal activities of several thousand people, more or less aware of their involvement in a criminal organization. A survey carried out on young deviants in Messina (Tomasello, 1986) shows that the patterns of deviant behaviour are closely intertwined and lead these young people into the hands of those who control drug trafficking, even where they are at first far from involvement in such activity – such as petty thieves who, paid in heroin by receivers, then become drug addicts and pushers. It is obvious that a youth unemployment rate of about 50 per cent, with ever-lengthening periods in search of work, constitutes a very useful 'reserve army' of labour for organized crime.

With regard to housework in the urban south, it must be said that few married women go out to work and most of them are full-time housewives: in 1981 36.6 per cent of the total number of women were full-time housewives and the official rate of female employment was low, namely 22 per cent. If the towns only are considered, the percentage of housewives is higher and the rate of female employment lower; in the countryside the latter is especially high in agriculture. If we then take only the urban strata with relatively low incomes, the percentage of housewives is still higher and the rate of employment drops to very low figures. Our own research also shows that those in or seeking employment are almost exclusively made up of young women and a few older unmarried women. We leave aside ideological prejudices of the type 'A woman's role is to stay at home and look after the family, and a man's is to look for work' – these are still deeply rooted, though they are basically kept alive and find their justification in labour market conditions – and the real difficulties and weaknesses of the labour market. The qualitative research shows that housework is an unavoidable necessity for the less prosperous families in the towns of southern Italy, involving long hours of work for at least one woman per family (Randazzo, 1986). In these towns, because of the failure on the part of both the public and the private sector to develop them, there are no modern services to offset the social imbalance brought about by modernization and the weakening of traditional forms of community and family solidarity, the old ways to satisfy the need for services. This dual process has had the effect of extending the tasks involved in housework so that it covers any gaps which open up and any new emerging needs.

In conclusion, it can be said that the extended form of housework is to be found in almost all low-income families, and that the housewife who also engages in self-provisioning and service activities is the most common type of informal worker in the urban south.

Next we find a large number of informal workers – informal in the sense that they are precariously employed and clandestine. Most of them are males, the most substantial and homogeneous group – though in decline – being concentrated in the building industry; however, similar types of worker are also found in manufacturing industry and increasingly in the service sector. Apart from these, there is a large area of fragmented informal work (small jobs) of two kinds: first multiple job-holding, and secondly very precarious and/or intermittent informal activities carried out from time to time by the 'non-employed' (students, housewives, pensioners) and by young people and women in search of work, and on a more regular basis but for very low pay by minors.

If we limit our calculations to the part of the population with low and lower-middle incomes, it can be estimated that just under 10 per cent of urban families are involved in multiple job-holding (in middle to high-income families the figure is also just under 10 per cent). But it is very difficult to estimate the extent of the second category: fragmented informal labour. All we can do is state our conviction that it is almost impossible to find low- or middle-income families in southern Italian towns where at least one member of the family has not engaged, at least once in his or her life, in informal labour in this sense. We have also seen that self-provisioning is very widespread. In particular, self-help building increased dramatically in the 1970s in both small and medium towns and in the surburban peripheries of large cities. Except for the building industry, it has proved difficult to put forward a hypothesis about current trends in self-provisioning. We can do no more than make the observation that this kind of activity will probably increase considerably as the surplus population rises on the one hand, and the use of cheaper do-it-yourself equipment (for example, durum-wheat pasta machines, microwave ovens, electronic home knitting machines) becomes more widespread on the other.

## AN INTERPRETATION IN COMPARATIVE TERMS OF THE CASE OF THE MEZZOGIORNO

The analysis carried out so far leaves many questions unanswered. It is evident that an interpretative paradigm based on the specific features of industrial societies and on a narrow understanding of work as lifelong employment for a family wage cannot explain the nature of society in southern Italy today, just as it failed to explain the same society twenty or thirty years ago. It is true that a few decades ago the main trends pointed towards an explanation of this kind – from the abandonment of the countryside to emigration, increasing employment in the bureaucracies of the public and, to a much lesser extent, the private tertiary sector, and the decentralizing of industries. However, it is becoming more and more difficult to argue that these trends still exist. Nor is it easy to say on the basis of our analysis whether or not informal activities are spreading in the present-day

Mezzogiorno. Up to the end of the 1960s quite high numbers of precariously employed (above all in the building and traditional local industries) and underemployed (mainly in agriculture) workers were recorded, who may have been involved in geographical and work-based mobility. The dramatic change in the last twenty years concerns not so much the number of workers in precarious or informal employment but rather the question of mobility, the role of informal work during a person's lifetime and in the organization of the family, and the type of work and its environment. As in many other cases, it is more the decline of the 'industrializing trend' in the Mezzogiorno that makes it difficult to interpret the social situation than the greater or lesser - never completed[11] - extension of the paradigmatic features of an industrial society: lifelong blue- and white-collar employment with the family income provided by the husband/father, the domestic role of the wife/mother, the trend towards the nuclear family, the commodification and standardization of consumption and the decline in community and 'mechanical'[12] forms of solidarity, and so on. It is important to underline this observation since it could serve as a starting-point in a comparative interpretation. It may in fact be possible to provide a unifying explanation for the different definitions and interpretations of the informal sector (see Mingione, 1987) by assuming that we are dealing with the various local effects of a global change in trends affecting all contemporary societies.

This potential common origin might also explain why the international debate on the informal sector and informal activities, though expressing very different situations and interpretations, has in general remained on common ground and why the interpretation of these phenomena is still so problematical even after many years of research and discussion. Although it could not explain the whole of social reality, the idea of an industrializing trend has been very effective in making the problem less complex, when and wherever it has been applicable. In

11. Pahl (1984) correctly notes that casual labour and numerous types of occasional and temporary clandestine jobs or of self-help activities have always been a characteristic feature of the division of labour. Like a high working mobility and instability, they have been particularly widespread in those countries which went through a long phase of competitive industrialization in the last century. Moreover, the employment of young people has always been characterized by some degree of instability, 'irregularity' and mobility. These factors are not decisive enough, however, to nullify the interpretative scope of the concept of industrializing trend; on the contrary they could even be put forward to support it. Casual forms of labour decrease or vanish when industrial societies develop or when young people become adults and set out on a career as blue-collar, white-collar or professional workers. These kinds of employment form the real paradigm for understanding the work–society relationship. What is more important, in our opinion, is the case of certain countries with retarded development and that of underdeveloped countries. Here the tendency to 'confirm' the process of industrial modernization does not function at all, throwing into a crisis all the different models of development on which the social sciences, at least in their classic versions, are more or less based.

12. What is meant is that the industrializing trend is formed in a different way by combining many of these features. The basic assumption is more or less the same, even though evaluations and methods may differ greatly. Take, for example, the central role in Durkheim's thought of the decline in 'mechanical solidarity' rooted in the interests of the extended family, clan or community, that is, in interests determined by traditional similarities and not modern differences. Marx,Weber, Tonnies and many others are said to have agreed fully with the idea that industrial societies are characterized by a decline of this type; however, the ways in which they incorporated this process in their theories and methods are very different.

other words, it has acted as means of both selecting those phenomena which are considered important and specifying why and in what way they are important.[13] For example, the hypothesis that forms of employing labour based on wages or salaries are no longer central to understanding and explaining present-day societies necessarily calls into question all accepted sociological (or economic or even psychological) thinking founded on the assumption that the forms of employing labour which guarantee job security are central to society. The pitfalls and uncertainties regarding methodology and theory in this type of approach are obvious and should lead the researcher to adopt great caution and be more clearly aware of his own limits.

Our specific theme is the significance to be attached to the existence and possible spread of various informal activities (in the areas of work and consumption) in society. In this regard, three main and complementary questions of theory have emerged which are undergoing a radical redefinition: a devastating criticism of the paradigms based solely on an explanation in terms of formal and officially recognized work;[14] attempts at theorizing the different ways in which material social reproduction takes place (the reasons for and social consequences

13. The idea of the industrializing trend as a device for simplifying interpretation is clearly present in several theoretical schools in the social sciences, from the classical economists to the positivist tradition, to structural functionalism (see Parsons's theory of the family) and Keynesian and neo-Keynesian economics (see the role in Keynes's thinking of labour policies - official ones, naturally, and aimed at potential or current heads of families - as a means of stabilizing the economic cycle). It is also clearly found in the different Marxist currents (for example, the theory of capital accumulation), giving rise - among other things - to Polanyi's criticism, also aimed at Marx, and to the more recent criticism from feminists. It may be the case, however, that Marx could be read outside his historicist perspective or reformulated on the basis of some of his interesting 'openings', like the one regarding the different methods of surviving and the principle that given a certain context, typical features occur in different modes of production which cannot be totally reduced to one another within each specific social formation.

Weberian sociology appears to be the least influenced by the idea of the industrializing trend. However, one should not leave out of consideration what is supposed to be an important theme in Weber's method: the spread of rational behaviour and economic calculation as a potential form of scientific knowledge. In other words, although Weber never assumes that the different areas of rational behaviour extend in a linear process compared with behaviour dictated by non-rational motives, what is there left of an already highly relativistic scientific system if one explicitly accepts the determining importance of centrifugal tendencies that are uncontrollable in comparison with rational behaviour?

We believe that these are very serious questions, and they introduce the problem of whether a social science, a limited form of science or a non-scientific and variable method of understanding is possible. For those who believe a scientific approach is possible (even one limited by specific conditions), it is nowadays indispensable to put forward schemes for 'translating' the patrimony of classical science. An operation of this kind is extremely difficult because of the interference from the debate on interpreting the scope of each different current of thinking and from that on the dissimilarity or opposition between them (the current debate on social classes gives an idea of the complexities involved).

14. Criticism of the interpretive paradigm which attributes exclusive or predominant importance to some forms of employing labour as compared with others represents a necessary step 'backwards'. The exclusive or dominant paradigm implies, explicitly or implicitly, a reductive attitude to everything that is different from the dominant paradigm itself; its criticism compels reconstruction of what different forms of labour mean relative to one another and of their entire possible range relative to the overall social organization. A slightly stereotyped example will illustrate better what we mean: if the idea that unpaid housework (the dependent or residual factor) 'serves' only or chiefly to reduce the cost of wage labour (the independent or dominant factor) is rejected, it will be necessary to redefine the links between wage labour and housework and between both and the organization of society.

of different lifestyles or family survival strategies);[15] and efforts at redefining a theory of surplus population so that it explains why and how it arises and what are the social relations by which it is characterized over a long period. In this concluding section we shall dwell on the last question, beginning with several phenomena described as belonging to informal activities in the Mezzogiorno and found among the numerous types analysed in contemporary literature on the subject. As can be assumed from what has just been said, our theoretical experiment is also necessarily of a preliminary and limited kind.

It is fairly obvious that the existence of a widespread informal sector calls for some concept or other of surplus population. By this is meant an excess population which either willingly or unwillingly and for different reasons works and survives, wholly or in part, outside formal labour channels, which are subjected to regulation in a wide sense by various legal, political and market mechanisms.[16] Closer inspection, however, shows that any concept of surplus population is very likely to suffer from theoretical inconsistency. Such a concept arises as a negative response to the hegemonic claims of political institutions and of explanatory models based on a regulated and organized market, despite which the existence of surplus population, especially of the long-term kind, is explained with no reference at all to these same models. In this sense, the only theory of surplus population that is not too superficial, that of Marx, insists on its relative and transitory nature. According to Marx, the growth and spread of capitalist relations of production continues to produce surplus population which is relative to the capacity to absorb labour at the moment it is formed and acts as a reserve army of labour for the subsequent waves of capitalist expansion. Neither Marx nor later Marxist writers are particularly interested in explaining the 'mystery' of why surplus population persists. This is because its theoretical role is limited in the Marxian theory of capital to its 'function' as a reserve army of labour and to its historically 'relative' nature.[17]

15. Elsewhere (Mingione, 1985), we have dealt mainly with this second aspect, which we consider very important. Naturally, in this case too there are all the same difficulties arising from the gaps in explanation owing to the crisis of the 'industrializing trend'. We intend to examine in the near future to what extent it is possible to combine explanations based on a new theory of the variety in modes of social reproduction with those resulting from a similar treatment of surplus population.

16. Bagnasco (1985) starts from the idea that there are 'four main mechanisms for regulating economic activity' (p. 10): reciprocity, the market (the invisible hand), organization and political exchange. Socio-economic systems can be interpreted according to the particular mix of these four elements, taking into account the fact that over a long period industrial development has witnessed the growing importance of the last two as against the first two. In this perspective, what we have termed 'decline of the industrializing trend' could be seen as equivalent to an inversion of the tendency during the last few decades. In his proposed method Bagnasco insists on the non-linearity of social development, on the local diversity in combining the four mechanisms and on the specific discontinuities in the trade-off between the different mechanisms in various historical phases and in differing contexts. Given the present state of highly accentuated heterogeneity and discontinuity of social change, Bagnasco holds that partial or medium-range theories must be worked out, starting from local conditions and defining theoretically comparative perspectives.

17. This is not the place to refer to the Marxian theory of relative surplus population. None the less, it is worth underlining that the need to provide a theory arose in Marx as a polemical thrust against those who maintained that industrial growth would have soon absorbed all available labour and thereby caused high and irresistible wage increases in the long run. Marx's reasoning with regard to the creation of surplus population by industrial development evinces great intelligence and deep analysis (far more

Nowadays, the Marxian theory of relative surplus population is for the most part inadequate since the emphasis has necessarily been shifted on to the 'absolute' nature of the phenomenon (Paci, 1982; Ginatempo, 1983), its existence over a long period and, therefore, the ways in which it continues to exist; the latter are difficult to locate in the social-economic processes that may explain its origins. At the same time, however, it would at present be difficult to deny the fact that the growth and spread of industrial capitalism (not necessarily understood in the Marxist sense) and the formation of surplus population are historically connected, when one cannot fail to note the effects of labour-saving innovations, the increasingly rapid internationalization of capitalist competition, the penetration of modern market relationships into the outermost reaches of the Third World, and so on. Perhaps of more use would be to deepen further the analysis of the relationship between specific modes of industrial development and the creation of different forms of surplus population. In our view, it is possible to argue that chronically low labour productivity, the relative waste of resources and the scarcity of products on official markets, together with the expansion of the 'second economy' in the countries of real socialism, represent another way of expressing the link between growth and surplus population. Correspondingly, the high increase in working married women might also reflect a tendency for a growing number of housewives to become part of the excess population.[18] If this is the case, future research will have to pay greater attention to the complex processes of economic-social development and, in particular, to those aspects connected with the formation of different types of surplus population.[19]

Before passing on to the informal sector and the very different types of activities

convincing, in our view, than that of Malthus who on this specific question comes to the same conclusion). However, he started off a theoretical controversy in which he was not interested for the very reason that, in his eyes, surplus population is an instrumental or 'functional' concept. How and why it persists; what are the possible consequences of a strong growth in surplus population on social stability and instability and of a concrete geographical-social separation between areas where surplus population is formed and areas where it is absorbed: these are questions which are not worth going into, at least outside the theory of the final crisis of capitalism and of the relative, but overall, impoverishment of the working class. Marx implicitly assumes, therefore, that clear dividing lines (geographical, political, cultural and social) between the working class and the surplus population are never formed. Whereas most of his theory of surplus population has stood the test of industrial history during the last century, the assumption of a definitive absence of dividing lines (which is translated into the 'functional role' of surplus population relative to wage levels and the standard of living of workers in employment) is questionable to say the least, and not only with regard to present times.

18. Put in these terms the question is undoubtedly of an economistic kind. However, in its original terms at least, the whole problem of surplus population cannot be viewed otherwise in as much as it is founded on comparing current with possible higher levels of labour productivity, taking into account the real potential in each specific working activity. Moreover, it is clear that the question of cultural factors and choices of alternative behaviour must be looked at further; this applies not only to the supply of married women's labour but to all the other factors.

19. We wish to underline that almost all the approaches in the field of social and economic policy assume an 'already formed surplus population' and do not consider as a cost the creation or avoidance of a very high surplus population. In this case also, we are faced with the inherited assumption of the industrializing trend according to which the formation of surplus population was first inevitable and secondly advantageous, that is, an essential feature of industrial development. In this regard, it would be possible to work out a paradoxical 'Keynesian' principle: 'It is a good thing to create high surplus population, it is a bad thing not to absorb it as quickly as possible.'

it now encompasses, there is at least one other extremely complex phenomenon that must be examined: that of the specific ways in which labour resources are 'formally' utilized when conditioned by the regulation of socio-occupational structures, a process all too often undervalued or seen in mythical terms. It cannot be denied that there has been a tendency over a long period, at least in the industrialized countries (and in very different ways in the socialist countries), to subject the socio-occupational structure to an increasing number of regulations which vary from country to country. Such a tendency clearly creates obstacles to inclusion in the socio-occupational structure and thereby prevents additional layers of surplus population from being absorbed under 'formal' conditions.[20] The most obvious examples of such regulations are those against child labour; those which exclude from certain professions people who have the ability but not the required educational or professional qualifications; and those which stifle the economic initiative of anyone who, at least when starting up, does not have sufficient resources to register at the chamber of commerce, pay taxes or purchase a licence. This tendency has been too hastily labelled by several political parties as the consequence of a trade-union/socialist conspiracy against the free market or that of an authoritarian state capitalism against the workers. On the other hand, it is clear to us that the interests which have worked and are still working in favour of regulation are many and diverse: the economic interest of those who want protection against unfair competition (or even against the dynamism of newcomers ready for any sacrifice); the interest of workers in increasing guarantees of better working conditions, welfare services and an acceptable income; and the interest of state apparatuses in controlling greater resources so as to be in a position to manage an increasingly complex and differentiated society. By taking into account this complex plurality of interests behind the tendency towards regulation, the relative meaning and specific conditions of 'over-regulation' (with respect to which interest groups?) or 'deregulation' (against and in favour of whom?) can be more fully understood. But, above all, it will be possible to understand better an entire aspect of the heterogeneous nature of the informal sector.

We will now continue our analysis on the basis of a model (figure 25.1). Starting from the processes by which surplus population is produced and labour resources are absorbed, it attempts to explain all the possible heterogeneous aspects of the informal sector and to avoid the functionalist short cuts typical of classic theories of surplus population. The model is based on the formation of a gap which persists over time and on the plausible hypothesis that it is tending to increase at present. We have already briefly mentioned the arguments in favour of this hypothesis in terms of the creation of surplus population. Detailed research into the specific and local forms of economic growth could clarify what are today the main ways in which surplus population arises in various economic and social contexts. Here, however, we must be satisfied with the general observation that

20. In the countries of real socialism the formal conditions which exclude the absorption of surplus population are hypothetically very different and arise, paradoxically, from the need to avoid unemployment. In order to achieve the latter, any tendency for labour productivity to rise in the socialist system of production is stifled by institutional means. The result is both the chronically insufficient supply of official commodities and the growth of the 'second economy.'

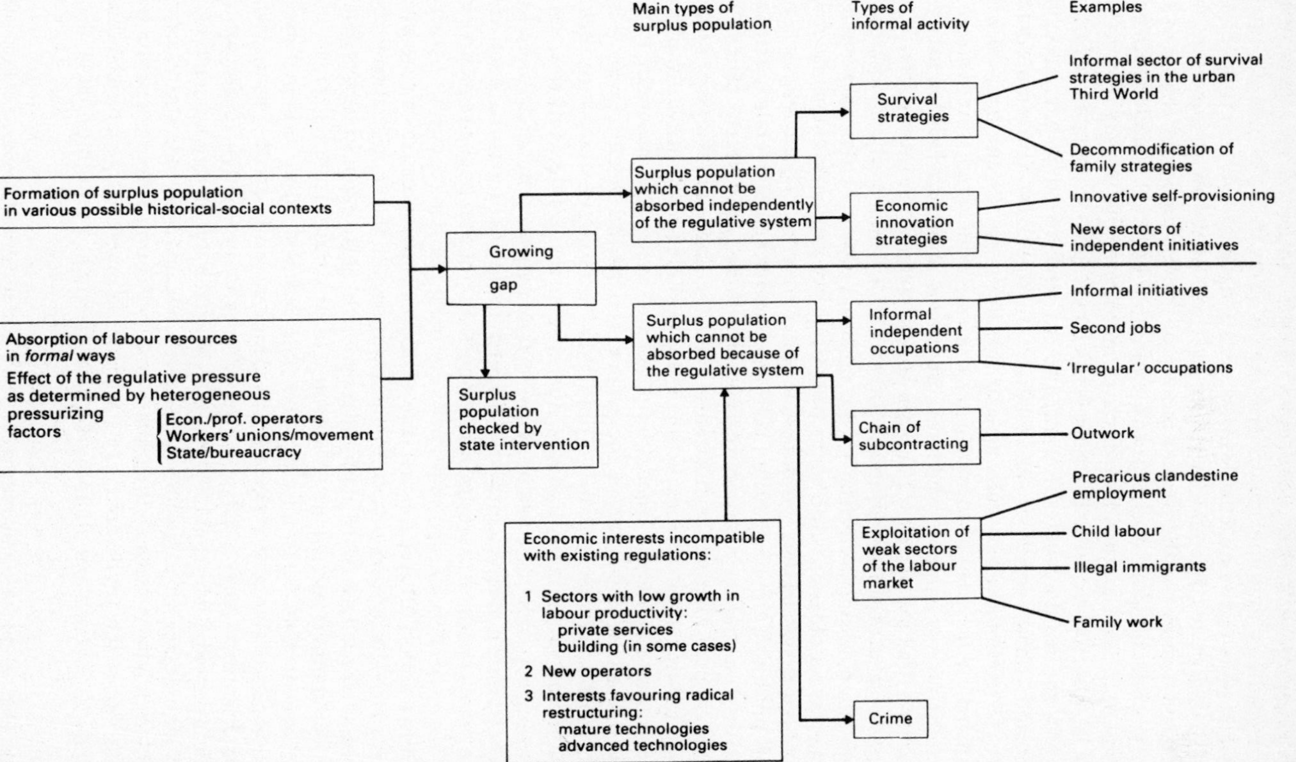

Main types of surplus population
Types of informal activity
Examples
Formation of surplus population in various possible historical-social contexts
Absorption of labour resources in *formal* ways
Effect of the regulative pressure as determined by heterogeneous pressurizing factors
Econ./prof. operators
Workers' unions/movement
State/bureaucracy
Growing
gap
Surplus population checked by state intervention
Surplus population which cannot be absorbed independently of the regulative system
Surplus population which cannot be absorbed because of the regulative system
Economic interests incompatible with existing regulations:
1 Sectors with low growth in labour productivity:
private services
building (in some cases)
2 New operators
3 Interests favouring radical restructuring:
mature technologies
advanced technologies
Survival strategies
Economic innovation strategies
Informal independent occupations
Chain of subcontracting
Exploitation of weak sectors of the labour market
Crime
Informal sector of survival strategies in the urban Third World
Decommodification of family strategies
Innovative self-provisioning
New sectors of independent initiatives
Informal initiatives
Second jobs
'Irregular' occupations
Outwork
Precaricus clandestine employment
Child labour
Illegal immigrants
Family work


FIGURE 25.1

despite the many different forms it assumes throughout the world, present social-economic development is still producing a high percentage of surplus population.

The hypothesis that the gap is tending to grow rests, above all, on an observation which is connected with what we have called 'inversion of the industrializing trend'. It could be argued that one of the most important and characteristic features of the present process of irreversible social change is the potential – and in some areas already existing – decline in lifelong salaried employment in large and medium firms in industry or the tertiary sector. This type of labour receives a family wage (sufficient, that is, to support a nuclear family and not just the worker himself) and is characterized by internal labour markets and a high degree of job stability.[21] In this case, too, more detailed research is required which goes beyond the limits set to our analysis here. Nevertheless, it is essential to underline one important point: the distinction between the varying extent to which this process has at present asserted itself and its even more radical potential consequences if taken to be irreversible. When Gorz (1982) talks of a 'farewell to the proletariat' or when we speak of absolute overpopulation, we are referring to the potential extent of the phenomenon. Lifelong jobs for blue- or white-collar workers do not vanish from one day to the next, and it may well be that a considerable part of the surplus population will find work of this kind in the near future. The likelihood of such a tendency still has important consequences today in all contexts, though in different terms. The question is in part different for those areas – like the English midlands or some of the early industrialized regions in the USA – where this process is still very conspicuous and intense at a local level. What is especially important for our analysis is the potential scope of the process and all the specific forms it may assume; these do not exclude the possibility that in some situations such lifelong jobs will increase in number or that in others the increase will merely slow down.

A growing gap engenders two principal types of surplus population: one which cannot be absorbed independently of the system for regulating working activities, and one which cannot be absorbed under the conditions set by the regulative system. This distinction is important for interpreting the heterogeneous nature of the informal sector, because the first type of surplus population will be more likely to adopt survival strategies that are neutral with regard to the regulative system. The second type, on the other hand, will be more likely to adopt strategies that, in one way or another, run counter to this system.

This line of argument must also be regarded with due caution, since a methodological leap has been made which cannot be justified with certainty when we pass from ascertaining the existence of surplus population to the survival strategies adopted. Some examples may clarify what is meant by a methodological leap. A high degree of persistent youth unemployment is an indicator of surplus population. It tells us that a considerable number of young people fail to find work in the formal sector, yet do not die of starvation, despite having no official source of income. A part of them do not undertake any kind of paid informal work and

21. In the literature on the segmentation of the labour market (Edwards, Gordon and Reich, 1976; 1982) this particular type of labour tends to correspond with the main segment. It is no accident that in their most recent work (1982) these same theorists view the crisis in this segment as the characteristic aspect of the present phase of development.

are maintained by their families while they seek employment. Some of these may engage in self-provisioning activities so as to help their families to maximize their resources. For example, it is not unusual for young unemployed girls to help with domestic chores or temporarily in a family's economic activity where their contribution is not essential but useful as unpaid help (such as shopkeepers' children who make home deliveries, earning tips for themselves and new customers for the shop). Others, on the other hand, carry out various types of temporary informal activities which may or may not conflict with the regulative system. Still others end up in criminal circles.[22]

It still remains true, none the less, that if we compare the results of research into the strategies of the young surplus population in southern Italian towns (an overpopulation conditional upon the regulative system) with the strategies of young people in the shanty towns of Rio de Janeiro (a surplus population in part unconditioned by the regulative system), we find in the latter a greater incidence of informal activities independent of the regulative system, that is, work which is not illicit. Another example from among the many available could serve equally well to illustrate the way in which the distinction between the two types of surplus population is hazy from the perspective of the strategies that can be adopted. The state of surplus population may also be partial; that is, there are workers in employment who for family or individual reasons or from personal interest or choice are ready to spend additional time in working activities to produce income or resources. This partial condition of surplus population may be resolved by self-provisioning strategies. Such an answer lies outside the regulation of working activities, but it presupposes possession of the necessary material and labour resources (it is possible, for example, to make furniture for the home using the latest do-it-yourself equipment) or a second job; the latter case may involve evasion of the regulative system (as is almost always true in the cases identified by Italian research).[23]

22. It would be worth examining in more detail the relationship which is formed between a high surplus population of young people and the spread of various juvenile criminal activities (individual, in gangs, at the service of organized crime) (see Tomasello, 1986). Compared with other informal strategies, criminal activities clearly have the 'advantage' of being more profitable and the 'disadvantage' of greater risk (see Valladares, 1986).

23. In this regard it is helpful to think of one possible progression from self-provisioning to informal work and then, subsequently, to the formal sector. Our hypothetical worker has an average income and adult children. In his spare time he likes to make furniture, using all the latest do-it-yourself equipment (self-provisioning). His friends and neighbours admire his inventiveness and ask him to make items for them; these are paid for in cash (informal). He realizes that his network of connections could become very profitable if he gave up his main job (early retirement) and opened a craft workshop, possibly employing one of his sons who is out of work. After a period of clandestine activity, business picks up and this neo-artisan decides to formalize his activity (pay taxes and register at the chamber of commerce) so that he can count on having more customers and the protection offered to officially registered operators.

The transition from the informal to the formal sector is not an occasional phenomenon. Many activities which at the take-off stage need to rely on being clandestine are compelled later on to assume a formal status, since the regulative system offers a better safeguard for their interests. An example of this is the increased incorporation into the formal sector of small and medium firms in the 'Third Italy' during the 1970s. In the preceding decade these same firms had become active participants in rapid industrial growth by exploiting very flexible conditions, also the result of their informal status (Bagnasco, 1977).

It is worth making a digression in this regard on the importance of the individual and social characteristics (family, environment, local culture etc.) of surplus population both at the moment the latter is formed and for evaluating possible informal activity options or strategies. The formation of surplus population must be analysed in its quantitative and qualitative complexity. It is evident that if a growing supply of well-educated labour demanding continuous work for a family wage receives increasing offers of occasional (seasonal and temporary) and poorly paid unskilled jobs, a substantial layer of surplus population will also be formed. It is all right for a 17-year-old to work in a fast-food restaurant or pick fruit for low pay during the summer holidays. But he cannot be expected to do this kind of work after he has obtained his degree or diploma and is married with a family to support. The main reason for such an attitude is not the unwillingness of new generations to accept heavy or dirty work, or work with insufficient guarantees or professional content relative to 'too sophisticated' expectations – on the contrary, one finds more and more young people who in desperation accept for the time being very poor working conditions – but lies precisely in the fact that such work does not provide for their survival in the specific social-historical terms established beforehand in different social contexts. To peddle wares on the streets of Naples means something different to a young Egyptian with a diploma who is saving up a sum of money with which to return to his native country, raise a family and open a shop in Cairo than it does to a Neapolitan of the same age. If he were to do the same, he would have no opportunity to take part in as many public examinations as possible in search of a permanent job; as a result he saves nothing and develops no life strategy.

Before attempting a brief final look at the model as applied to the situation in southern Italy and to other different situations, it is worth stating clearly several considerations regarding the area we have labelled 'economic interests incompatible with regulation'. Such interests are incompatible with the regulative system in specific ways and, consequently, vary widely in different places and historical phases; some general observations are however possible, which can then be incorporated into the interpretation of differing forms of informal activity. It may be readily supposed that the regulative system is shaped by the pressure from those interests which are strongest and best represented within a given political-institutional order. There exists the possibility, therefore, that weaker or newly formed interests are penalized by the regulative system. From this a whole series of possible 'convergences' may arise between the surplus population whose absorption is prevented by the regulative system and economic interests which are incompatible with this system. The most interesting and widespread example, at least in countries with a market economy, is given by those economic sectors with a high labour intensity and a low margin for increasing labour productivity. They include many branches of the service sector and, in numerous countries, residential building. In such cases the cost of 'regulated' labour is decisive and puts a growing number of economic operators into difficulty. The partial or total alternative to the disappearance or radical transformation of the economic activity in question – for example, the spread of self-service as proposed by Gershuny (1983) or do-it-yourself building – or to very high price increases, impracticable in some fields, is often a growing informalization of work in violation of legal regulations (illicit jobs, child labour, illegal immigrants) or, in some cases, also by exploiting family and/or ethnic resources.[24] It is therefore important to analyse the specific nature of the possible convergences between economic demands incompatible with the regulative system and types of surplus population strategies, because this will allow us to explain, in general, the presence or absence of certain areas of informal activity.

From the very beginning, post-war southern Italy has provided an example of an area in which the gap between the formation of surplus population and the local absorption of labour resources is a wide one. There is extensive surplus population in the towns, and it was even more extensive in the countryside in the first years. For a certain time surplus population remains to a large extent a transitory phenomenon. As waves of young labourers precariously employed in building and clandestine workers in industry emigrate to find permanent jobs, they are replaced by new generations and the same cycle is repeated. However, a growing number remain within the surplus population. In the last fifteen years the reduction in formal outlets has led to a very considerable qualitative change, even though the widening of the gap has been contained by a massive injection of public spending in the form of direct money transfers to the family and expansion of the state bureaucracy.[25] The specific types of informal activities that have been developed can be explained, at least as a first approximation, by tracing the interconnections between the surplus population's characteristics and local economic interests incompatible with existing regulations. During the first twenty years after the War most of them were to be found in building and traditional industries, while today informal outlets are increasing in the private service sector.

Innovative strategies, both of the type which is neutral with respect to the regulative framework and that which violates it, have been irrelevant owing to the chronic weakness of the economic fabric, mummified by the growing intervention of the welfare state. A submerged world has come into being, difficult to grasp in its entirety, in which the domestic strategies of families are less influenced by the market; in other words, isolated nuclear families have had to get by without modern services and strong family and community networks. This process has undoubtedly overloaded the role of the full-time housewife.

24. The case of the retail trade and restaurants is especially interesting. It is no accident that in many industrialized countries the food trade, for example, has come under the almost exclusive control of family businesses run by recent ethnic immigrants (Koreans in New York and Los Angeles, Afro-Indians in England). What is worth emphasizing in the catering sector is the polarization between, on the one hand, ever more sophisticated and expensive luxury restaurants and, on the other, the proliferation of small family restaurants (often run by ethnic minorities, and nearly always based on the long hours worked by family members and some clandestine helpers), self-service and fast-food businesses. The latter rely on the simultaneous use of customers' free labour and on fairly unskilled labour which tends to be casual, clandestine and always extremely low paid.

25. This is another subject which needs to be examined in more detail in an appropriate context. As a first approach, we would say that there are three ways in which social policy helps to partially or completely halt the formation of surplus population: (a) creation of public sector jobs, besides those resulting from the growth of bureaucracy and the expansion of social services; (b) payment of substantial unemployment benefit on condition that it is not supplemented by an income-earning activity; (c) payment of other kinds of welfare benefits, likewise on condition that they are not supplemented by an income-earning activity (for example, in southern Italy one could point to the notorious disability pensions paid to healthy persons provided they are registered as officially unemployable).

Nowadays, the surplus population is increasingly made up of young people, with that percentage of young women on the increase, and there is a tendency for it to persist over time; consequently, this frustrating situation is handed down to a large part of the next generation.

The informal sector in the Mezzogiorno is more and more taking on the appearance of an ever-expanding and fragmented kaleidoscope of working activities, which rests on its much discussed complementary function relative to family and state resources. This function is managed, however, in such a way that it produces immediate ineffectual solutions but no prospects of reducing the social unease caused by the present jobs crisis. In addition, it must be said that the qualitative features of the current surplus population in southern Italy, mainly composed of young people with a moderate or high level of education and with particular job expectations, render the picture of the local informal sector even more complicated. A series of jobs can no longer be filled by a considerable number of potential local workers - like, for example, domestic services, fishing, some seasonal male employment in agriculture, or several casual jobs in commerce and services to the public - precisely because of the above-mentioned tendency to create increasingly informal working conditions. In this respect, the role of the waves of immigrants, especially from the Arab countries of North Africa, is also relevant in southern Italy.

The application of the model to the case of the Mezzogiorno might lead one to make the serious mistake of thinking that the three concepts of surplus population (and informal work strategies), unemployment and poverty overlapped one another. However, the model should in fact help to keep them clearly separate. Although there is some overlapping between the three phenomena in this region, it must not be overestimated even in specific cases, and so the existing informal activities cannot be interpreted as survival strategies of the poor or unemployed.

We will look first at the question of the unemployed. In theory, they should all be counted as part of the surplus population and their survival should be explained by the supposition that they engage in informal activities while waiting for formal employment. But we know from the real experience of almost all industrialized countries that, at least for a certain period and for certain categories of the unemployed, the possibility of receiving unemployment benefit - at times higher than the income which can be earned from informal activities - is dependent on receiving no other form of income (sometimes even the benefit received is wholly or partially reduced by deducting an amount equivalent to the incomes of members of the unemployed person's family). The other important thing to note is that in order to carry out informal activities, it is often necessary to have and to develop special connections and resources; this is unlikely in the case of the unemployed who receive benefit and are in search of formal employment. Taking both considerations together, one begins to understand why all the specific investigations into informal work in the industrialized countries have shown that the unemployed and their families are only involved in it to a small degree. With this in mind, we thought it was worth extending the model to include a section for that part of the surplus population which is prevented, to a greater or lesser extent, from engaging in informal activities by the policies of the welfare state.

In the Mezzogiorno the figure of the unemployed and that of the informal worker coincide in two special cases, building labourers and young people; here there exists a real compatibility. With regard to the former – at least in the Italian situation – there is a presupposition that in every case the job is for a limited time, which almost always compels them to alternate rare and short periods of formal employment with long periods of unemployment on very low benefit (in Italy only those workers who are laid off but still officially on a firm's books – the so-called *cassintegrati* – receive 'unemployment benefit'); during these periods it is essential to engage in a good deal of informal activity or clandestine work in building. Young people and women seeking their first job, on the other hand, either are not generally entitled to unemployment benefit or they receive paltry sums. Consequently, if their families are not able to support them, they undertake informal work whenever and wherever possible.

However, both the model and the analysis of the situation in southern Italy clearly assume that the state of surplus population and the practice of informal work go far beyond a technical concept of unemployment and involve the full or partial working potential of persons who for various reasons are not seeking formal employment (they have no desire to; they are already working; they know they would not find the job they want; they are unable to look for work; and so on). In this area the model is fully compatible with the interpretation by Gershuny (1983) of social innovation and the spread of the self-service sector, or with the observation of Pahl (1984) that middle-income families in England have a propensity towards self-provisioning, although such types are not very widespread in the Mezzogiorno. The ways in which economic growth occurs places an increasing number of potential workers in families among the surplus population, while at the same time supplying some families with the resources to utilize this potential in informal activities. To what extent the latter are engaged in depends, naturally, on specific local conditions. The members of middle-income family in Kent may have the opportunity and resources with which to renovate their house by themselves and let out some rooms to holiday-makers; likewise a Fiat mechanic in a new suburb of Turin could with the help of his children begin by repairing his neighbours' cars with the aim of opening up a small garage in the future. But it is much more unlikely that such possibilities arise in Messina or Calcutta.

For similar reasons, the informal strategies of those making up the surplus population cannot necessarily be viewed as a response to poverty. Although there is in the Mezzogiorno an important link between informal work and poverty, it does not account for the whole of the story. In this region it is a question of young males who were entrapped, in the 1960s, in the world of precarious employment in the building industry. Often their wives worked as hourly paid domestics before the birth of their first child. Later these women became full-time housewives, sometimes able to earn some extra income through work done at home (sewing and mending, laundering etc.). Their children have probably left school as soon as permitted by law (at present the proportion of young people in the south without a compulsory school certificate is still above 10 per cent) to become child workers: the females to go into service or work as farm labourers, or to help their mothers with household chores; the males to work in building or as low-paid helpers in workshops, cafés and restaurants. In this way the cycle of precarious work, semi-illiteracy and poverty is often handed down from one generation to the next.

We have seen, however, that informal activities in southern Italy extend well beyond this slice of social reality. There are also those who have two jobs; the practice of self-provisioning by a very wide range of families; the informal microfirms for specialized building, self-help building and renovation; the activities of young people with a higher level of education from middle- or lower-middle-income families; and possibly, though rarely, also innovative activities which in an informal phase invent new or strengthen old economic undertakings and, later on, may be formalized. Although the specific realities are different, the same methodology could be applied to the survival strategies within the informal sector in Third World cities. Despite the fact that urban poverty and the informal sector here appear to be two faces of the same reality, not all informal strategies start, stay or end up in poverty (Valladares, 1986).

If the world-wide growth of a highly heterogeneous informal sector is a continuing trend and reflects the increase in layers of surplus population in different environments, we must learn to understand the complex reasons behind such a trend. This means going beyond the two more simplistic opposing interpretations that hold a spell over the academic: withdrawal from a capitalism in crisis, or regeneration (restructuring the capacity to accumulate) in new terms, with an ever-widening gap between super-exploitation and poverty on the one side and privilege, wealth and waste on the other. In the market-based economies, if not elsewhere, the concept of the informal sector has taken on all the theoretical ambiguity inherent in the idea of surplus population. Its origins can be explained but it is difficult to attribute a general meaning to its existence. In reality, what is to be learnt from the informal sector, and even more on a global level from the great and growing diversity of the connections between labour processes and social forms, is the need to know how to redefine the basic simplifications established by the social sciences in over a century of problematical accumulation of scientific knowledge (an accumulation which took for granted at least the persistence of several general trends, though their meaning has been interpreted in different ways). Whether or not it is possible to carry out such a redefinition we do not know. But if it is, it can only be done on the basis of small-scale experiments with no pretensions to offer global or definitive answers. In our view, it is an important step forward to begin to understand that the industrializing trend is no longer at work (and in some cases never really has been), that surplus population remains even when it does not 'serve' to lower the cost of labour to the benefit of capitalistic growth, and that informal strategies cannot be reduced to a potential withdrawal from capitalism or to its potential regeneration. This is the case, even though such strategies are mainly negative steps of little significance for defining the near future of a specific social organization, and of even less significance with regard to the more distant future or destiny of human societies on a global level.

## REFERENCES

Allum, P. (1975): *Potere e società a Napoli nel dopoguerra*. Torino: Einaudi.

Bagnasco, A. (1977): *Tre Italie: la problematica territoriale dello sviluppo italiano*. Bologna: Il Mulino.

Bagnasco, A. (1985): 'La costruzione sociale del mercato: strategie di impresa e esperimenti di scala in Italia'. *Stato e Mercato*, no. 13, 9–45.

Boccella, N. (1982): *Il Mezzogiorno sussidiato*. Milano: Angeli.

Braghin, P., Mingione, E. and Trivellato, P. (1978): 'Per un'analisi della struttura di classe dell'Italia contemporanea'. In M. Paci (ed.), *Capitalismo e classi sociali in Italia*, Bologna: Il Mulino, 257–304.

Cammarota, A. (1977): *Proletariato marginale e classe operaia*. Roma: Savelli.

Chiarello, F. (ed.) (1985): *Sistema economico, bisogni sociali e occupazione: Il doppio lavoro nell'area barese*. Bologna: Il Mulino.

Fortunato, R., Liguori, M. and Veneziano, S. (1986): 'Il lavoro irregolare dal sommerso alle istituzioni: le vertenze di lavoro nell'area napoletana'. *Quaderni IRES CGIL – Campania*, no. 2, 57–92.

Edwards, R., Gordon, D. and Reich, M. (eds) (1976): *Labour Market Segmentation*. Massachusetts: Lexington Books.

Edwards, R., Gordon, D. and Reich, M. (1982): *Segmented Work, Divided Workers*. Cambridge: Cambridge University Press.

Gershuny, J. I. (1978): *After Industrial Society*. London: Macmillan.

Gershuny, J. I. (1983): *Social Innovation and the Division of Labour*. Oxford: University Press.

Gershuny, J. I. and Miles, I. (1983): *The New Service Economy*. London: Frances Pinter.

Giannola, A. (1983): 'Delocalizzazione e deindustrializzazione nella città di Napoli'. *Quaderni IRES CGIL - Campania*, no. 1.

Ginatempo, N. (1976): *La città del Sud*. Milano: Mazzotta.

Ginatempo, N. (1983): *Marginalità e riproduzione sociale*. Milano: Giuffré.

Ginatempo, N. and Fera, G. (1985): *L'autocostruzione spontanea nel Mezzogiorno*. Milano: Angeli.

Graziani, A. and Pugliese, E. (eds) (1979): *Investimenti e disoccupazione nel Mezzogiorno*. Bologna: Il Mulino.

IRES CGIL (1981): *L'evoluzione delle strutture economiche e sociali dell'organizzazione del territorio a Napoli*. Edited by DAEST, Napoli.

Jedlowski, P. (1986): 'Il servizio informale: servizi socio-sanitari, processi di informalizzazione e sistemi di relazioni in una comunità montana del cosentino'. *Atti del Convegno: strategie famigliari, stili di vita e attività informali*, Università di Messina, 30–31 maggio 1986.

Mingione, E. (ed.) (1977): *Relazione Finale della Ricerca sui Poli di Sviluppo Industriale nel Meridione*. Roma: Formez.

Mingione, E. (1985): 'Social reproduction of the surplus labour force: the case of Southern Italy'. In N. Redclift and E. Mingione (eds), *Beyond Employment*, Oxford: Basil Blackwell, 14–54.

Mingione, E. (1986a): 'Ristrutturazione del Welfare e politiche sociali nel Mezzogiorno'. *Politica ed Economia*, no. 6, 65–9.

Mingione, E. (1986b): 'Ciclo dei servizi e complessità sociale'. *Economia e Lavoro*, XX(1), 111–22.

Mingione, E. (1987): 'Urban survival strategies, family structure and informal practices'. In Smith M. and Feagin J. R. (eds), *The Capitalist City – Global Restructuring and Community Politics*, Oxford: Basil Blackwell.

Paci, M. (1982): *La struttura sociale italiana*. Bologna: Il Mulino.

Pahl, R. E. (1984): *Divisions of Labour*. Oxford: Basil Blackwell.

Pinnarò, G. and Pugliese, E. (1985): 'Informalization and social resistance: the case of Naples'. In N. Redclift and E. Mingione (eds), *Beyond Employment*, Oxford: Basil Blackwell, 228–47.

Pugliese, E. (1983): 'Aspetti dell'economia informale a Napoli'. *Inchiesta, Numero Speciale sull'economia informale*, XIII(59–60), Gennaio-Giugno, 89–97.

Pugliese, E. (1985): 'Stratificazione sociale e part-time'. *La Questione Agraria*, no. 18, 27–45.

Ragone, G. (ed.) (1983): *Economia in trasformazione e doppio lavoro: il doppio lavoro nell'area casertana*. Bologna: Il Mulino.

Randazzo, R. (1986): 'Strategie familiari, ruolo e identità femminile in trasformazione nell'Italia meridionale'. *Atti del Convegno: strategie famigliari, stili di vita e attività informali*, Università di Messina, 30–31 maggio 1986.

Reyneri, E. (ed.) (1984): *Doppio lavoro e città meridionale: il doppio lavoro nell'area catanese*. Bologna: Il Mulino.

Serpieri, R. and Spanò, A. (1986): 'Scelte informali nell'agire di consumo'. *Atti del Convegno: strategie famigliari, stili di vita e attività informali*, Università di Messina, 30–31 maggio 1986.

Sylos-Labini, P. (1964): 'Precarious employment in Sicily'. *International Labour Review*, March.

Tomasello, S. (1986): 'Devianza giovanile: strategie e tipologie famigliari a Messina'. *Atti del Convegno: strategie famigliari, stili di vita e attività informali*, Università di Messina, 30–31 maggio 1986.

Valladares, L. (1986): 'Growing up in the favela'. Paper presented at the XIth World Congress of Sociology, New Delhi, India.

# 26

# Time, Technology and the Informal Economy

JONATHAN GERSHUNY

Conventional economics is concerned to an overwhelming extent with the formal economy – those human activities which are mediated through monetary exchanges. The 'blue books' (to use an old-fashioned colloquialism for the yearly national accounts) describe economic behaviour through such money-valued abstracts as value added through employment, capital investment, final expenditure, government transfer payments, imports, exports and so on. These sorts of blue book concepts, and the changing relationships between them, constitute the reality to which economists normally address their theories. The significance of the informal economy perspective lies in its assertion that 'economic' processes, of great importance to the development of the society, take place *outside the blue book economy*.

This chapter has four sections. The first reviews the concept of the informal economy. The second and third discuss briefly the historical changes in the organization of production that have resulted in the shift of work between the formal and informal sectors of the economy. The fourth attempts to integrate the discussion of informal production into a broader view, which considers all the different sorts of work, paid and unpaid, that go to satisfy particular categories of need. Most needs are satisfied by a *combination* of formal and informal production activities; the fourth section uses time-budget material to investigate the historical change in the mix of different sorts of production and consumption activities that go together to satisfy particular needs.

## FORMAL AND INFORMAL ECONOMIES

The formal economy can be conceptualized as consisting of flows of money and commodities between households and the formal production system (figure

Parts of this chapter are drawn from the author's 'Technology, social innovation and the informal economy', *Annals of the American Academy of Political and Social Sciences*, August 1987, and from *Social Innovation and the Division of Labour*, Oxford University Press, 1983.

26.1a). Households put labour into the formal production system, and receive in exchange money wages. They buy goods and services from the formal production system in exchange for money payment. These exchanges are *specific*: each commodity flow, be it labour, good or service, in one direction is balanced by a money flow in the opposite direction.

The sum total of the money flow in one direction – either total wages or total payments for goods and services – may serve as an indicator of the extent of formal economic activity. Each of these flows is accounted for by some arm of government or by some official survey. In the UK, for example, the tax and national insurance authorities, together with the annual family expenditure survey, census of production and the census of employment, can in principle enumerate all of these flows – and this enumeration forms the basis of the national accounts.

It has always been recognized that there is some economic activity *outside* these flows. Subsistence agriculture in developing economies, for example, would certainly not appear in this sort of accounting framework. And in developed economies, there is ready recognition of the statistical anomalies that result from such events as the marriage of a householder to his or her erstwhile housekeeper.

Nevertheless, the nature of these sorts of unaccounted economic activities is rather different from the accounted ones. We can symbolize this by a slight revision of our previous picture of the working of the formal economy (see figure 26.1b). The household buys goods and services from the formal economy, it *consumes* the purchased services, and it *uses* the purchased goods *as capital*, in combination with household labour, in the production of more services for final consumption. Each of the flows between the formal production system and the household is carried out on the basis of a specific and explicit exchange. The

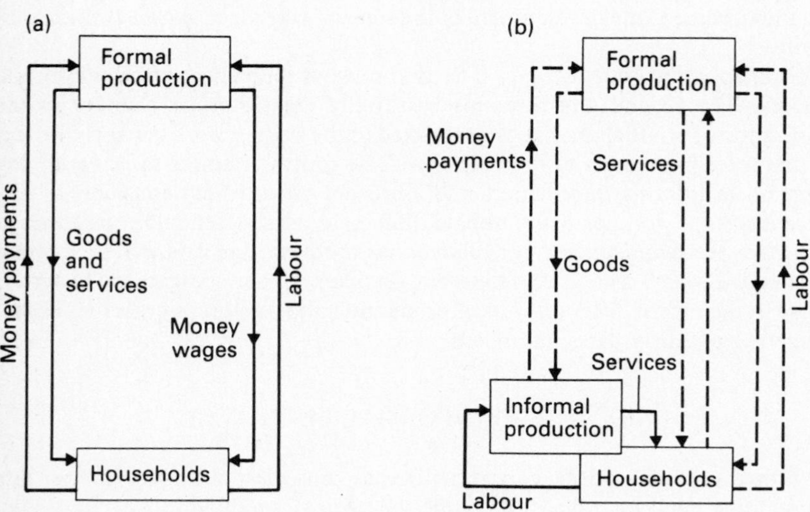


FIGURE 26.1 (a) The formal economy and (b) the informal economy: household production

flows between the two are *conditional;* they consist of short-term contracts to exchange a definite quantity of some commodity for a given amount of money. The flows within the household are not in general based on any specific and explicit exchange of definite quantities of commodities.

Social theorists such as Homans may be correct in asserting that in the longer term there may be exchange relationships implicit within family structures,[1] but these are rarely specific to particular historical instances; a wife can rarely be said to have carried out some particular household operation on some particular day in exchange for some other particular household operation carried out by her husband. And these exchanges are typically between non-quantifiable or incommensurable values – e.g. the exchange between cooking and social status effected by some spouses (almost invariably wives).

So we could distinguish (1) exchanges between the formal production system and households, which are specific, i.e. explicit, quantified and relatively short term; and (2) exchanges within the household, which are generalized i.e. implicit, non-quantified and often very long term – indeed, often never consummated.[2]

Closely associated with the household production system, and encouraged by the same social and technical developments, is what might be called the 'communal' production system. Included in this are 'voluntary' or religious organizations, baby-sitting circles, transport cooperatives and housing improvement cooperatives. At one extreme are those organizations on the verge of the formal production system – the baby-sitting circles or car pools – which operate on the basis of a quasi-money exchange, tokens or credits, and which break down if equal values are not exchanged within a relatively short period. But more generally there is only a rudimentary system of specific exchange, and a major reason for the involvement of those who carry the burdens are the intangible, symbolic, unquantified returns for their activities.

What distinguishes this category of production is that real money is not used as an indicator of exchange of value for value. Where money is paid it is explicitly not in exchange for value received. Thus officers of communal organizations are paid honoraria, in *recognition* of rather than *exchange* for services; and expenses, even though they may be fiddled, are rarely used as complete compensation. And in extreme cases – such as making meals for sick neighbours – the form of exchange can hardly be differentiated from that within the household.

As I have argued previously, growth in the household economy (and in the closely associated communal sector) is promoted by the rising cost of purchased services relative to the declining cost of 'domestic capital goods'.[3] Jobs are exported from the formal economy into these sectors of the informal economy; and as it becomes economically rational for individuals to provide services informally, it becomes correspondingly difficult to persuade people to purchase formally provided services, or to pay higher taxes in order to receive more public services. Thus, cheap and effective washing machines mean less purchase of

1. See G. C. Homans, *Social Behaviour: its elementary forms* Routledge and Kegan Paul, London, 1962.
2. For an extensive discussion of theories of social exchange, see A. Heath, *Rational Choice and Social Exchange*, Cambridge University Press, 1976.
3. J. I. Gershuny, *After Industrial Society*, Macmillan, London, 1978; Humanities Press, Atlantic Highlands, New Jersey, 1978.

laundry services, private cars replace buses, TV replaces cinema, and so on. The growth of household sector production implies an increasing proportion of total demand devoted to products of the high-productivity-growth, formal, manufacturing sector, and a declining demand for low-productivity-growth, formal, service sector products – and, hence, rising unemployment.

In a 'free' labour market, this situation would be self-correcting. Wage levels would fall, particularly in some relatively low-skilled service occupations, as a result of the entry into the market of labour displaced from manufacturing industry, with the dual effects of lowering the price of services, and thus increasing the demand for them, and at the same time (because of the lower price of labour relative to capital) increasing the labour input per unit of service output. By this argument, wages would fall until all those looking for jobs were employed.

But in most developed economies, labour markets are not free to behave in this manner. There are inflexibilities in the formal economy's demand for labour resulting from employment protection legislation, employers' social security contributions, and labour union restrictive practices. And the supply of unskilled labour is restricted by the high marginal tax rates which result from the high rate of loss of social security benefits with low earnings. These market imperfections mean that full employment in the formal economy cannot be achieved by lowering wage rates.

There is, however, another sector of the informal economy where these imperfections are not present: the underground, hidden or black economy.[4] This third category of informal production activity is very close to the formal system. In fact it exists in the interstices of the formal economy, consisting largely of economic activities also undertaken in the formal economy, often by the same people. It is distinct from the formal production system, in principle, because those involved in it wish it to be so; it consists of economic activities which are hidden from the state authorities because of their illegality – either through avoidance of tax or other regulations, or because they involve thefts. Activities in this sector also bear some similarity to those in the other two informal sectors (the household and the communal) since, though the main mode of exchange between sectors in the underground economy is specific and money based, there is still a strong subsidiary element of generalized exchange. So, for example, Mars and Henry find a wide range of symbolic and unquantified values in people's explanations of why they are involved in occupational theft – 'helping out a friend' or 'because it's exciting'.[5] Even though these explanations may be coloured by a need to justify illegality, they do presumably reflect some reality.

The underground economy, which is by definition free of external restrictions, may to some extent counteract the inflexibility of the formal labour market; wages are not free to fall in the formal economy, but a low-wage informal sector develops instead. There are also reasons other than rising unemployment for the growth of this sort of economic activity. The falling cost of capital makes it easier for individuals to own their own tools – which makes 'own account' working more

4. S. Smith, *Britain's Shadow Economy*, Clarendon Press, Oxford, 1986 provides a useful review of the literature on this phenomenon.

5. S. Henry and G. Mars, 'Crime at work: the social construction of amateur property theft', *Sociology*, 12(2), September 1978.

convenient and less easy to detect. And the high costs of working within the formal sector, both high marginal rates of taxation and the administrative costs of dealing with the official state, make it attractive for those active within the formal economy to transfer all, or more usually part, of their activities into the underground economy.

We should however be clear that the underground economy is no substitute for conventional employment. 'Hidden' work depends critically on access to suitable markets. Recent studies have shown that only a small proportion of those formally unemployed have any substantial involvement in the underground economy.[6] On the contrary, it appears that the majority of all hidden work is done 'on the side' by those who already have jobs. Underground production is also rather small scale when compared with the unpaid household sector: economists' estimates put the value of household production in a modern economy as being of the same order as that of the whole of the formal economy.[7] The black economy, by contrast, might amount to no more than one-twentieth of the total of formal production.

## THE DEVELOPMENT OF A DEVELOPED SOCIETY

Economic development is normally viewed as a one-way progress: a march through the sectors, from reliance on primary production through manufacturing production to a society whose major efforts are devoted to the production of services; a transition from a traditional society in which economic relationships are based on custom, in which such processes of exchange that exist are generalized, to a modern society in which an increasing proportion of social relationships are monetized, converted from generalized to specific exchange. I argue here that this view is wholly misleading.

Instead, it may be proposed that technical innovations, changes in capital endowments, and modifications in legal institutions and in patterns of social organization, combine to produce a rather less tidy pattern of development. Instead of the steady one-way flow of economic activity from the household or communal basis to the industrial production system – Polanyi's 'great transformation' – we have to consider a whole series of little transformations of production, perhaps taking place simultaneously, between the formal economy, the household or communal sector, and the underground sector, whose directions are determined by the particular social and technical conditions pertaining to the production of particular commodities at particular times.

We can list some of the circumstances which bring about these transformations. Consider the six possible transitions of production among the formal economy, the household or communal sector, and the underground sector (figure 26.2).

Transformation 1, from household or communal to formal production, is the conventional development process, relying on the economic principles identified by Adam Smith – economies of scale, division of labour, advantages of specialization, and efficient use of factors of production. The processes he

6. See for example R. E. Pahl, *Divisions of Labour*, Basil Blackwell, Oxford 1984.

7. A helpful review of this literature is found in Ann Chadeau, 'Measuring Household Activities: Some International Comparisons', *Review of Income and Wealth,* 31, 3, September 1985.

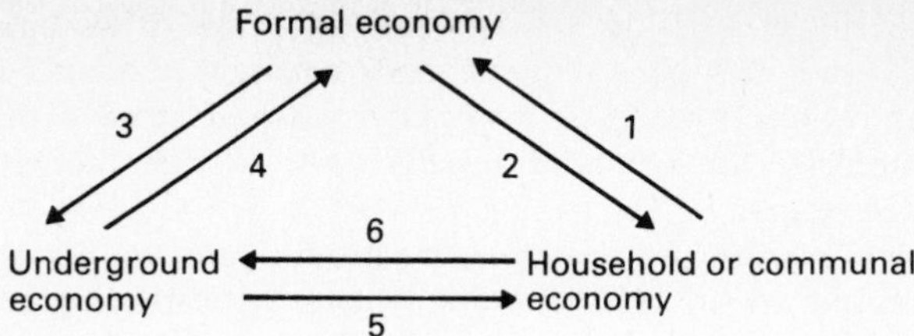


FIGURE 26.2 The six transformations

described are of course still valid. And, indeed, in the production of a wide range of commodities these processes are still the predominant determinants of the pattern of development but not for all commodities. Social and technical conditions have changed.

I have previously argued that the changes in the relative prices of domestic capital goods and service labour have led in the past to a transfer of production of some services from the formal economy into the household, and that this process is likely to extend to other services in the future: thus, transformation 2. The exact conditions under which these transformations occur are rather complex, and are discussed at length in my *Social Innovation and the Division of Labour*. However, to simplify somewhat, we might say that this sort of transformation is likely where the capital goods used in the production of a particular commodity become so cheap that they need not be used intensively (and where the necessary skills may be expected within households).

Three conditions for transformation 3 have already been mentioned: unemployment combined with an inflexible formal labour market, declining real price of capital, and high costs in formal production. It may be useful to add a fourth, the criminalization of particular sorts of formal production; for example, government restrictions on the use of labour-saving capital equipment in the formal economy might simply drive such production underground. Transformation 4, from underground to formal production, has the converse conditions. Full employment might tempt workers from insecure underground employment to better-protected formal jobs. Lower tax rates would reduce the attraction of the underground sector. And more extensive or effective policing would certainly raise the costs of involvement in underground production.

Examples of transformation 5, from underground to household production, are rather difficult to find at present. We might perhaps speculate as to the effects of selectively decriminalizing the unlicensed distillation of whisky for domestic consumption. Or, more generally, we might imagine the effects of the introduction of construction materials which demand less skilled labour (for example, plastic hot-water pipes, currently uncommon in the UK) in reducing 'underground' construction activities in favour of do-it-yourself household construction. There are close analogies here with transformation 2.

Finally, transformation 6, from household to underground production, has converse conditions to transformation 5. Here we can identify an example of criminalization of a household activity dating before the industrial revolution;

certain forest rights possessed by the community before enclosures were revoked by Enclosure Acts, so that those who continued to trap small game were subsequently classed as poachers. Of more present-day relevance, the existence of high unemployment may encourage the growth of low-paid 'hidden' domestic employment – a transfer of production from the household to the underground economy.

The six sorts of transformation described here are of course not exhaustive; they result from my particular threefold classification of formal and informal economic activity. My argument is simply that, at any time, the particular circumstances – of technology, labour supply, and public regulation and organization – which pertain to the production of any commodity, may lead to one of a wide range of different sorts of transformation. Certainly, in the two centuries since Adam Smith's birth, the *aggregate* effect of all these little transformations has been the great transformation from household or communal production to formal industrial production. But over the last few decades the transformation of some sectors of production from a formal economic basis to a household basis has been of critical importance to the development of the economy as a whole. And it may well be that, in the future, the aggregate effects of transformations 2 and 3 may outweigh the effect of transformation 1 with respect to the level of formal employment.

One conclusion from this line of argument is that if we are to understand the processes of structural change in the 'economy', we need to consider evidence about behaviour outside it. We need to know more about the detail of daily life. To understand the operations and historical dynamics of the household economy, we need evidence of how people spend their time, and what they do with the goods and services that they buy. Economic statistics, unsurprisingly, describe 'the economy'. But there is a technique for collecting quantitative statistical evidence about the household economy: the *time-budget survey*.[8] The final section of this chapter outlines one way that time-budget data can be used to extend our understanding of the relationship between the formal and informal economies. It suggests a new way of organizing socio-economic accounts, using time rather than money as a *numéraire*. And it very briefly summarizes the intermediate results of a study which yields some clues about how current new technologies may be expected to affect the informal economy over the coming decades.

## HISTORICAL CHANGE IN CHAINS OF PROVISION

It may be helpful at this point in the exposition to lay out, in a preliminary way, some of the sorts of changes in chains of provision that we may expect to find over a historical period. We might divide these changes into three classes, of which the third is of particular importance to the evolution of the informal economy.

First, there are changes in the organization of production in the formal economy. There is occupational specialization; the Adam Smith processes

8. J. P. Robinson, *How Americans Use Time*, Praeger Scientific, New York, 1977 provides a concise description of time-budget techniques and their application.

continue whereby jobs are subdivided, and demand for the more skilled classes of labour increases. And there is also industrial specialization; industries become more willing to subcontract elements of their production processes to other specialist firms, so that the extent of vertical integration in the economy is reduced.

Secondly, there are changes in the distribution of time between the various categories of human purposes (or, as we might alternatively term them, needs). As the level of satisfaction of particular purposes rises, so individuals and societies will wish to transfer their resources – their production and consumption time – to the satisfaction of other purposes. Part of the explanation of change in economic structure comes from this sort of development.

But how does the level of satisfaction come to rise? Central to the arguments about the non-money informal economy is the third class of change: radical innovation in chains of provision, that is changes in the mode of provision for particular needs or purposes.

Consider, for instance, the provision of domestic services in the 1930s. We can see what are in fact two quite distinct ways of satisfying requirements for the maintenance of the domestic environment. One involved a good deal of paid work time – the work of domestic servants. Middle-class households might have to contribute a certain amount of unpaid work in the form of supervision, and perhaps household marketing, but (as we shall see in a moment) the greater part of the domestic services in such households was purchased from the formal economy. The result of the purchase of this skilled service labour was a high level of domestic comfort for the household members (if not necessarily for the servants). This high-income mode of provision of domestic services very adequately satisfied this particular purpose – for a minority of the population.

By contrast, the other mode of provision involved much less paid work. The majority of households could not afford to employ servants, but acquired domestic services largely through their own unpaid labour. Some paid work was still involved – such households would still have to acquire materials from the money economy – but this would be on balance quite a different sort of paid labour (primary or manufacturing rather than service), and on a much smaller scale, than the use of paid labour in the high-income chain of provision. And, accordingly, the low-income mode of provision involved very much more unpaid work – heavy, largely unmechanized drudgery which produced, at the end of the day, less satisfactory domestic services than the alternative. Spending more time in unpaid work, such households would have less time available for domestic consumption, and enjoyed much lower standards of food and shelter: colder, damper and dirtier housing, and less, worse prepared, colder and less nutritious food. A minority were well provided with domestic services; the majority were substantially underprovided. How would it be possible to increase the extent of satisfaction of the society's needs for domestic services? It certainly would be possible, in the 1930s, to increase the capital equipment used in the high-income mode, making servants somewhat more efficient at their work. This might have the effect of marginally improving the welfare of the high-income households, or of slightly reducing the amount of paid domestic labour necessary to provide the same level of welfare. The introduction of new domestic equipment in the context of the high-income mode of provision, might be described as merely

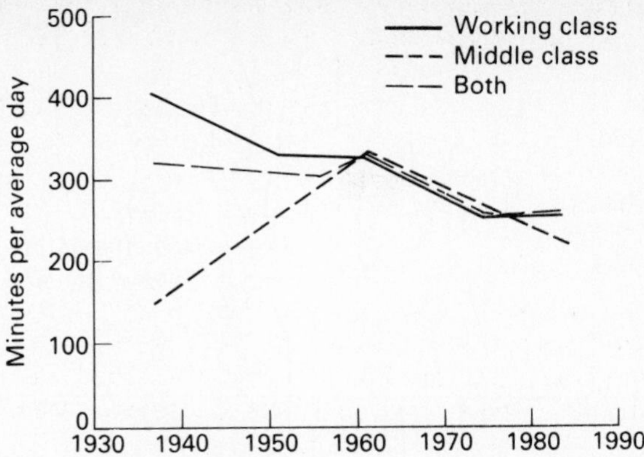


FIGURE 26.3 Routine domestic work: British 'housewives', 1937–84

incremental innovation. Marginal additions of capital equipment to be used by servants could hardly make a very substantial impact on the major problem, which was that the majority could never expect to employ servants. If some want servants, others must *be* servants; it might be possible to increase the output from the high-income mode of provision marginally, but not in such a way as to make a substantial impact on the overall welfare of the society.

Of course, what actually happened was a very much more radical innovation. More capital equipment was introduced – but in conjunction with unpaid labour. Economic development during the 1950s and 1960s was dominated by a particular sort of consumer expenditure, which we might helpfully think of as capital investment in the informal economy – investment in vacuum cleaners, washing machines, electric or gas cookers, refrigerators – which served to increase the efficiency of unpaid domestic production. In effect a new mode of provision of domestic services emerged, involving different sorts of paid work (manufacturing rather than service employment) and new sorts of housework (less physical drudgery).

Figure 26.3 shows the results of an attempt to reconstruct the evolution of domestic work time for women (unemployed, or employed very little) in the UK.[9] It may be interpreted as showing (1) the very substantial disparity between middle- and working-class 'housewives' in the 1930s, reflecting the differential effects of the high-income and low-income modes of domestic service provision on unpaid work time; (2) the increase in middle-class women's domestic work time through the 1950s as the high-income mode became progressively more inaccessible to all except a minority of the rich; and (3) the convergence, and continuing decline through the 1960s and 1970s, of the domestic work of both

9. The data for this table is drawn from surveys carried out by Mass Observation during the 1930s and 1950s, the BBC during the 1960s and 1970s (see BBC, *The People's Activities and the Use of Time*, BBC Publications, London, 1978) and the UK Economic and Social Research Council (J. I. Gershuny, I. D. Miles, S. Jones, C. Mullings, G. S. Thomas and S. Wyatt, 'Time budgets: preliminary analyses of a national survey', *Quarterly Journal of Social Affairs*, 2(1), 1986, pp. 13–39).

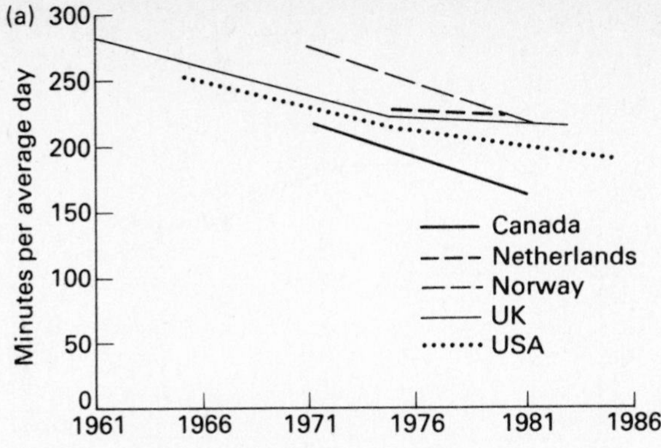


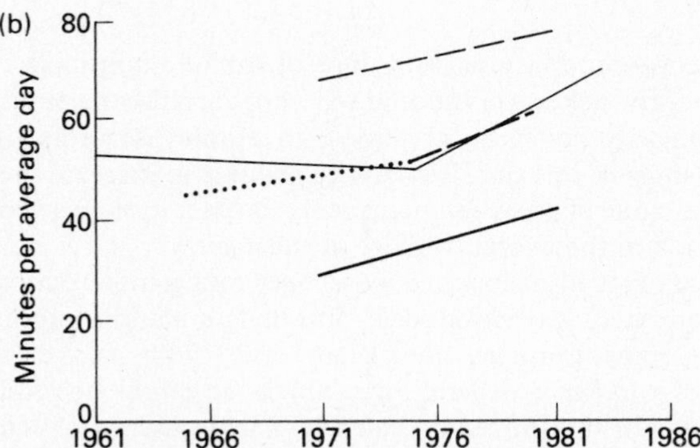


FIGURE 26.4 Routine domestic work, in five countries: (a) women (b) men; controlling for change in employment and family structure

classes. The same evolution of women's domestic work through the 1960s and 1970s is found in the USA, Canada, Holland, Denmark and Norway.[10] We might parenthetically note that men's domestic work, though remaining at a much lower level than women's, seems to have been increasing in these countries over the same period (figure 26.4a and b).

We have here an example of radical innovation in a chain of provision for a particular need. There are different ways that a given purpose can be satisfied – alternative modes of provision – which have different mixes of costs and advantages. Different groups in the society will have differential access to the alternative modes at any time, and accordingly receive different levels of benefit. In the example of domestic service in the 1930s, the rich minority had access to a

10. The multinational comparative data set used here is not yet properly documented in a published form, but a brief description will be found in J. I. Gershuny, 'Time use, technology and the future of work', *Journal of the Market Research Society*, 28(4), October 1986.

mode of provision which gave them very substantial benefits, whereas the majority enjoyed much less satisfactory domestic conditions and at a considerable cost of unpaid work time. Over time the relative costs and advantages of competing modes of provision change, altering the distribution of advantages across the society. Through the 1950s and 1960s the money costs of the high-income mode rose, so that it very nearly disappeared from this chain of provision. At the same time the costs of the innovative, domestic-capital-intensive mode of provision fell, and its performance improved, so as to replace the high-income mode. Hence, over time, the acquisition of domestic services, which used to demand paid service labour, came instead to require very much more manufacturing employment. And though the better-off minority of the population, who in the 1930s had very little unpaid domestic work, now have more, the consequence for the majority has been a substantial reduction in unpaid work input to this chain of provision.[11]

So this is the conceptual scheme. A society's time may be divided into 'chains of provision' for particular purposes or needs. These chains consist of the amounts of time spent in paid or unpaid work, or in leisure and consumption, which are devoted to the satisfaction of each class of human purpose. All of the time spent by members of the society can be attributed to one or other category of production or consumption, in one or other of the chains. Over a historical period, the allocation of time among these categories changes in three distinct ways:

1 There is change in the organization of the money economy, such that different kinds, or different quantities, of paid labour time are required for the production of different commodities (e.g. less paid manual labour time, more paid 'information work').
2 The society redistributes its time between various of the purposes (less time devoted to the acquisition of domestic services, more to out-of-home leisure activities).
3 There is a change in the mix of activities involved in the satisfaction of particular purposes (domestic services involving more paid manufacturing employment, and more highly mechanized unpaid work).

## A SYSTEM OF ACCOUNTS

The notion of 'chains of provision' provides a straightforward basis for a system of socio-economic accounts which includes both the formal and the informal economy. We can relate time use outside paid employment to final expenditure on (or state provision of) goods and services, and hence to employment. And, since both paid employment and extra-economic activities may be measured in terms of time, we arrive at a time-based account of changes in lifestyle and economic structure.

The first step relies on the observation that each sort of activity is associated

11. This process of transformation in the mode of provision of services is described in more detail in J. I. Gershuny, *Social Innovation and the Division of Labour*, Oxford University Press, 1983.

with the use of particular final goods and services. Time spent at the cinema requires the purchase of entry; travel time requires a passenger ticket; time at school requires either state expenditure on a final service or, more occasionally, some household expenditure on private education. Washing clothes may require laundry services, or household expenditure on soap, on water rates, on electricity, and on a washing machine and a service contract for it. Each time-use category is associated with a distinct bundle of goods and services (though of course each category of good or service may be associated with more than one category of activity; the same kitchen table may be used for food preparation and eating and for school homework).

In principle, these associations between activity categories and the commodities used while engaged in them could be determined empirically. We could, for example, ask within the time-budget diary, not only 'What were you doing? Where? With whom?' but also 'Using what?' In practice, of course, such a research instrument would be quite unmanageable - but the same end could be achieved by other, observational, techniques. For the moment, however, as a first pass through the sequence of analysis, I have allocated commodities to their appropriate activities purely on the basis of *a priori* reasoning; table 26.1 summarizes this set of assumptions.

These associations between activities and commodities are crucial in forming the link between the time-budget-based 'lifestyle' indicators, and conventional economic statistics. The time expenditure categories in table 26.1 include the full range of activities other than paid work; the money expenditure categories cover all the sorts of final goods and services consumed in the economy. The table thus enables us to translate time use into final demand - and, using the conventional economic statistical sources (input/output and industry/occupation matrices), we can in turn translate final demand into industrial output, industrial employment, and thence into occupational employment patterns. (This process of translation is a non-trivial task, requiring an intricate sequence of calculations which I shall not attempt to outline here; the general principle is nevertheless quite straightforward. and the set of associations in table 26.1 is really the only unconventional aspect of it.)

Employment is itself a time use category; furthermore, it is the one category missing from table 26.1. So, in the time use column of table 26.1 we have all the activities other than paid work; and the money expenditure columns may be translated into time spent at work in different occupations. We can, in short, replace table 26.1 by an alternative formulation, which represents all the society's activities, inside and outside 'the economy', in terms of a single indicator: time.

Table 26.2 provides a very simplified version of such a system of accounts, which divides paid work summarily into just two categories: manual and non-manual. For each of the two years, the time use columns sum to the total 1440 minutes of the 'average' day of the population (aged 14+). In 1961, for example, this average day was made up of 236 minutes paid work, 989 minutes of leisure or consumption time (if we were to look at more detailed activity data, we would find that it includes 560 minutes of sleep and 98 minutes of eating) and 215 minutes of instrumental activity (cooking, cleaning, shopping etc.), which I summarily classify as unpaid work. The table is organized around six groups of activities or 'purposes', of which two (shelter, household maintenance; shopping, travel) involve just instrumental activities, two involve only consumption activities (out-of-home leisure; medicine and education), and two (home leisure, child care; food, sleep) include a mixture of unpaid work and non-work activities. Most of the paid employment in the economy can be explained in terms of the final demand for commodities associated with these six classes of activities.

Most, but not all: we have to take into account, in addition, employment associated with foreign demand for UK products – which generates in all 38 minutes of the total of 236 minutes of paid work in the average UK day, but is not related to any unpaid work or consumption time in the UK. (Of course, these exports are related to consumption time in foreign countries – and, similarly, some UK consumption time is related to expenditure on imports, which serve to explain some foreign employment. The column headed 'foreign work' estimates this effect; the 40 minutes of foreign work related to UK activities – which I have estimated crudely by assuming that the productivity levels in countries exporting to the UK are on average the same as those in the UK – approximately balance the 38 minutes of UK work associated with foreign consumption activities.)

Another category of UK production which cannot be matched with particular consumption or domestic work activities is the provision of 'background' or 'environmental' services – law and order, defence, public administration – whose effects are diffused through all of our experiences. (An alternative way of handling these might be to treat them as an intermediate product whose costs are distributed evenly across all branches of production.) For the purposes of table 26.2 I have grouped these in a single category together with employment associated with the provision of analogous private background services such as life insurance, pensions and personal savings.

Consider the change, over the period 1961 to 1984, in the 'shelter, household maintenance' chain. Unpaid work in this category has fallen, for the adult population as a whole, by about 15 minutes per average day. This is the phenomenon we discussed in the previous section – 'social innovation' in the production of domestic services. Now we can see the connection of the change in domestic work to change in paid employment. The reduction in unpaid work was enabled by increases in households' purchases of capital equipment and materials in the formal economy. Though less time was spent in the unpaid 'instrumental' non-market tasks – indeed precisely *because* less time was spent in them – unpaid work time became more intensive in its demand for purchased commodities. The reduced housework time is in effect purchased by an increase in domestic equipment.

So in spite of very high rates of productivity growth (an approximately threefold increase) in the manufacturing sector over the period, paid work time related to this category of purpose did not fall very fast (compared, for example, with paid work related to food, where the increase in agricultural and manufacturing productivity was not balanced by increasing consumption intensity). Indeed, when we consider that the normal hours of work per employee actually fell by about 10 per cent over the period, we find that the number of jobs only declined by about 0.5 million from the 1961 total of 6.1 million, and white-collar and other service work associated with the provision of shelter has risen over the period we are considering. Thus associated with this purpose, and as a result of the process of social innovation I have described, less time was spent in unpaid

TABLE 26.1 Activities, time use and related expenditures

| | *Time use activities (mean min per average day) (time budget survey)* | *Goods (family expenditure survey)* | *Marketed services (family expenditure survey)* | *Non-market services (national accounts)* |
|---|---|---|---|---|
| Shelter/clothing | Housework | Housing (rent, rates, other charges), power and fuel, clothing, furniture (inc. cutlery, china, and oddments) cleaning materials, matches etc. | Repairs, maintenance, decoration, household etc. insurance, laundry and cleaning, domestic help, other repairs not allocated elsewhere | Sewerage, refuse disposal, fire, local welfare, and other welfare services |
| Food: cooking | Cooking, washing-up | | | Agriculture, fishing and food |
| meals | Eating meals, snacks | All food and non-alcoholic drinks | | |
| Child care | Child care | | | Child care |
| Shopping | Shopping | | | |
| Travel and communications: | | | | |
| Domestic | Domestic travel | Postage, telephones, telegrams; purchase of car, bicycle etc. | Maintenance and running costs of motor vehicles, bus, train fares etc. | Roads, lighting, transport and communications |
| Other | Leisure travel and excursions | | | |
| Personal care | Dressing, toilet, sleep | Toilet requisites, cosmetics | Hairdressing | |
| Restaurants | Restaurants | | Meals bought away from home | |
| Pubs | Pubs and social clubs | Alcoholic drink | | |
| Cinema, theatre | Cinema, theatre, dances, parties etc; at church; civic duties; watching sports | | Cinemas, theatres and other events | Libraries, museums etc. |
| Playing sports | Playing sports | | | |
| Walking | Walks | | | |
| Visiting/entertaining | Entertaining or visiting friends | | | |

| | | | | |
|---|---|---|---|---|
| TV, radio | TV, radio, music | Radio and television, and musical instruments (including repairs) | Radio and television licences and rental payments | |
| Reading, study | Reading books or papers, or studying | Books, magazines and periodicals | | |
| Talking, relaxing | Conversation, relaxing | Cigarettes, tobacco, pipes etc. | | |
| Odd jobs, gardening | Odd jobs, gardening | Seeds, plants, flowers and pets | | |
| Games, hobbies | Hobbies and pastimes, knitting, sewing | | | |
| Holidays | | | Hotel and holiday expenses, and miscellaneous other services | |
| Medical services | Personal services | Medicines and surgical goods | Medical, dental, and nursing fees | National health service |
| Education | | | Educational and training expenses | Education |
| Admin./defence | | | Pocket money and other expenditure assigned elsewhere; life assurance, pension contributions; sickness and accident insurance; savings of all kinds, including contributions to Christmas and holiday clubs | Defence, external relations, employment services, research and other industry, police, prisons, Parliament, finance, records and other services |

TABLE 26.2 A time-based system of accounts

| | *Time outside employment* | | *Time in employment* | | *All paid work in UK* | *Foreign work from imports* | *All employment (000)* | *Distribution of employment* |
|---|---|---|---|---|---|---|---|---|
| | *Non-work* | *Work* | *white-collar work* | *Manual work* | | | | |
| | *(min per average day)* | | *(min per average day)* | | *(min per average day)* | | | |
| *1961* | | | | | | | | |
| Shelter, household maintenance | 0 | 93 | 25 | 36 | 61 | 14 | 6278 | 0.26 |
| Food, sleep etc. | 659 | 68 | 16 | 24 | 40 | 10 | 4123 | 0.17 |
| Home leisure, child care | 268 | 12 | 7 | 10 | 16 | 4 | 1672 | 0.07 |
| Shopping, travel | 0 | 41 | 6 | 7 | 13 | 1 | 1344 | 0.06 |
| Out-of-home leisure | 45 | 0 | 8 | 3 | 11 | 2 | 1169 | 0.05 |
| Medicine, education | 16 | 0 | 20 | 7 | 27 | 2 | 2814 | 0.12 |
| Background services | 0 | 0 | 15 | 14 | 29 | 1 | 3018 | 0.12 |
| Exports | 0 | 0 | 13 | 25 | 38 | 6 | 3919 | 0.16 |
| All time use | 989 | 215 | 110 | 126 | 236 | 40 | 24337 | 1.00 |
| *1983* | | | | | | | | |
| Shelter, household maintenance | 0 | 73 | 25 | 21 | 46 | 16 | 5591 | 0.24 |
| Food, sleep etc. | 647 | 63 | 8 | 8 | 16 | 6 | 1934 | 0.08 |
| Home leisure, child care | 284 | 17 | 7 | 5 | 12 | 3 | 1411 | 0.06 |
| Shopping, travel | 0 | 70 | 5 | 4 | 9 | 2 | 1119 | 0.05 |
| Out-of-home leisure | 70 | 0 | 9 | 2 | 11 | 2 | 1386 | 0.06 |
| Medicine, education | 22 | 0 | 30 | 5 | 36 | 3 | 4347 | 0.18 |
| Background services | 0 | 0 | 17 | 7 | 24 | 1 | 2951 | 0.13 |
| Exports | 0 | 0 | 19 | 21 | 39 | 10 | 4824 | 0.20 |
| All time use | 1023 | 224 | 120 | 73 | 193 | 43 | 23564 | 1.00 |
| *Change 1961–83* | | | | | | | | |
| Shelter, household maintenance | 0 | −21 | 0 | −15 | −15 | 2 | −687 | −0.02 |
| Food, sleep etc. | −12 | −5 | −7 | −17 | −24 | −4 | −2189 | −0.09 |
| Home leisure, child care | 15 | 5 | 0 | −5 | −5 | 0 | −261 | −0.01 |
| Shopping, travel | 0 | 29 | −1 | −3 | −4 | 0 | −225 | −0.01 |
| Out-of-home leisure | 24 | 0 | 1 | −1 | 0 | 0 | 217 | 0.01 |
| Medicine, education | 6 | 0 | 10 | −2 | 8 | 1 | 1533 | 0.07 |
| Background services | 0 | 0 | 2 | −7 | −5 | 0 | −66 | 0.00 |
| Exports | 0 | 0 | 6 | −5 | 1 | 4 | 905 | 0.04 |
| All time use | 34 | 9 | 10 | −53 | −43 | 3 | −773 | 0.00 |

production, but providing overall very nearly as many paid jobs in 1984 as in 1961.

Of course, the time freed from unpaid domestic work, and from the reduction in employed people's paid work time, must be spent somehow. One use to which this extra time is put is in the consumption of out-of-home recreational, educational and medical services. This sort of change does not involve increasing consumption intensity (i.e. increased expenditure and hence paid employment per moment of consumption time), but rather the increase of the total of time devoted to activities in which consumption intensity remains constant. A sit-down meal at a restaurant, for example, involves just about as much labour time now as it did thirty years ago; but more people eat out in the 1980s than in 1961, which means more consumption time and hence more paid labour time (though the argument is complicated by the emergence of the fast-food industry over this period). In the chain of provision of shelter, a reduction of the total of unpaid work time was balanced by an increase in the consumption intensity of that time, so that levels of paid employment hardly fell in spite of very substantial increases in labour productivity. In the 'out-of-home leisure' category – pubs, restaurants and sports – an increase in time devoted to time-extensive service consumption leads to an increase in jobs. And a similar process may serve to explain the growth in employment in the chain of provision connected with medical and educational services.

Consider, finally, 'the shopping and related travel' category. Time spent by consumers in this activity has increased from about 45 minutes per average adult in 1961 to about 70 minutes in 1984. And as we see from figure 26.5, this increase is part of a longer-term trend in the UK, and (figure 26.6) corresponds to similar increases in a number of other European countries. The North American data in figure 26.6 is at a higher overall level, but does not show the same upward trend; the explanation of the increase seems to be innovation in the retail industry, leading to larger self-service shops in which the shopper spends more time selecting and paying for goods, and shops which are geographically removed from town centres, which means more travel time. The lower prices of goods bought

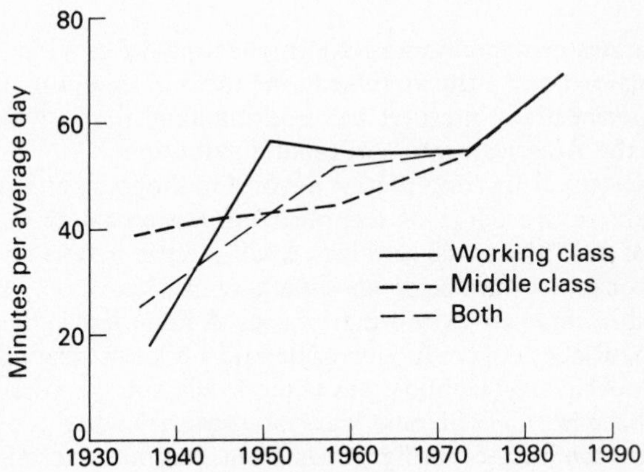


FIGURE 26.5 Shopping: British 'housewives', 1937–84

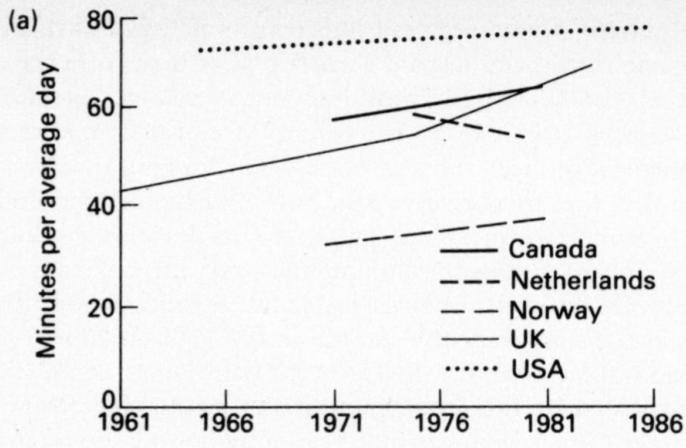


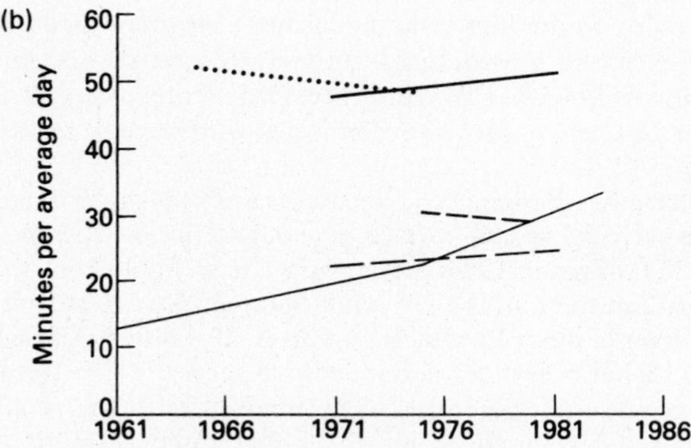


FIGURE 26.6 Shopping and associated travel, five countries: (a) women only (b) men only; controlling for change in family and employment structure

from supermarkets or hypermarkets are in effect paid for by the increased non-money 'transaction costs' – the increased time spent in shopping. We might, from a European perspective, interpret the multinational comparative evidence in figure 26.6 as the Americanization of retail distribution.

The very substantial amounts of time devoted to shopping and related activities suggest a likely future effect of technical innovation on time use. The new technologies of the 1930s, such as valves, small electric motors and plastics, were embodied in consumer durable goods – washing machines, vacuum cleaners and the like – used in innovative 'informal' modes of provision of domestic services, which led to new jobs and a reduction of unpaid work time from the 1940s to the 1970s. Might not the new technologies of the 1980s, such as microprocessors and fibre optics, be embodied in new ways of organizing the provision of retail services? Tele-shopping, ordering goods from computer terminals in homes, making use of a range of associated services – consumer advice, funds transfers and home delivery, for example – could substantially reduce the amount of time currently devoted to marketing, and increase the paid employment associated with the distribution chain. And just as, in the past, time freed from domestic work went in part to enable the consumption of time-extensive leisure services, so in the future might time freed from the burden of shopping.

## CONCLUSION

This very brief presentation hardly scrapes the surface of the potential applications of an analysis of the interrelationships between technical innovation, production in the money economy, informal production and consumption. The model outlined in this paper shows how lifestyle - in the quite concrete sense of the allocation of time between alternative activities - relates to demand for products from the formal economy, and how technical innovations affect the relationship between activity patterns and final demand. If our needs are met by a combination of formal and informal production, and technical change continuously alters the relationship between these, can we be satisfied with an economics which concentrates just on the formal economy?

# Part V

# Disaggregated Capitalism: New World Factories, New Technologies, New Strategies and New Contradictions

# Editor's Introduction

It has been repeatedly asserted in this book, in both the editorial introductions and the contributed chapters, that the world's work is changing as a result of the re-negotiation of different divisions of labour. Historically minded readers might well wish to ask: 'But was it not ever thus?' Certainly, as we saw in part I, there were changes in the way work was done in the eighteenth and early nineteenth centuries in Britain that were every bit as dramatic as anything that is happening in the world today. The unprecedented fact is that contemporary changes are now taking place on a world scale. Early industrialization and the development of the factory system was a very geographically localized phenomenon. Even within societies the 'industrial part' remained relatively separate from large areas in which agricultural production continued in traditional ways. Thus, for example, in Russia industrial development before the Crimean War was quite different from that typical of Western Europe, and those in government hoped to maintain a system of patriarchal manufacture based on the traditions of Russian handicrafts. Specialized peasant craftsmen organized themselves into quasi-cooperatives called *artels* and different groups of villages became widely famous for their knives, locks, nails, shoes, icons and so on. During the first half of the nineteenth century these peasant industries flourished owing to their cheapness, their flexibility and their close touch with their market. Machine-made factory goods did not force them to reorganize with the use of machinery until late in the nineteenth century.

The process of industrial development was relatively slow in many areas and it took decades to achieve what some countries can now do in a very few years. A recent study of the dozen or so European countries that were peripheral to the main industrial nations of Britain, France and Germany concluded:

> Successes and failures, partial successes and half-hearted tries give us the variegated picture of the European periphery's development during the age of the industrial revolution. While at the beginning of 'the long nineteenth century' these countries appeared as a unit in virtue of their backward and traditional economic structure

> when compared to the core – the great differences in their geographic position, historical development, social structure and international position notwithstanding – by the end of the period the similarities among them had largely ceased to exist.[1]

That is a considered but still a very extraordinary statement. Industrialization led to greater divergence and dissimilarity as these nations were more or less effective in 'catching up' with the core.

Now, in the last years of the twentieth century, with the growth of multinational or transnational companies deploying world factories to supply the needs of world markets, the changing nature of work is a truly global phenomenon. Similar processes are taking place in Latin America, Africa and Asia. The new international divisions of labour appear to ride relatively easily over political and cultural differences. The Fiat cars made under licence in Poland or Spain, the Volkswagens made in Brazil and similar examples elsewhere are produced with exactly the same technology and work routines – whether in socialist or capitalist societies and whether in the First or Third Worlds.

Cash crops take the place of subsistence production, men migrate to find employment, women carry excessive burdens of household production and survival, the multinational companies seek out and create green labour (as Pearson showed in chapter 20), and new technology affects manufacturing production from Silicon Valley to Taiwan and from Liverpool to Mexico City. There is a global domino effect that is not checked by national boundaries.

In this part of the book it becomes even more difficult to decide which studies reflect most tellingly these new ways and styles of getting the world's work done. Examples are taken from Britain, Mexico, Israel and the United States but there are many other contexts that could have provided similar empirical studies. Catherine Hakim's chapter on homeworking in Britain requires more introduction than do the other chapters in this part. Most previous studies of homeworking have been local, limited studies, often of women working as outworkers in the garment manufacturing industry. The image held in Britain, even by informed commentators, would be of immigrant women in Bradford or East London stitching, sewing and pressing for pitiably low wages on which, being maybe husbandless, they have to support many small children. The image might also include assumptions about such women suffering eye strain or other manifestations of physical or psychological ill-health. Receiving low wages and with no fringe benefits and neglected by the unions, such women may be supposed to have an inarticulate resentment that radicals might wish to organize and to focus.

Certainly there is some substance in such a stereotype and I raise some of these issues in my discussion of chapter 29 below. However, Hakim's work should make us cautious about extending such a stereotype to the complete universe of homeworkers. Her analysis is based on a special national survey carried out in the autumn of 1981. Hence we are provided with a much more comprehensive overview than has hitherto been available.

Hakim begins by emphasizing that homeworking is part of the so-called 'flexible' workforce that has grown so substantially in Britain in the early 1980s, so

1. I. T. Berend and Gy Ranki, *The European Periphery and Industrialization 1780–1914*, Budapest and Cambridge, 1982, pp. 159–60.

that by mid-decade the labour force divided neatly into two-thirds 'permanent' and one-third 'flexible'. Half of all women in employment and a quarter of the men are in this 'flexible' sector. A significant and, perhaps, surprising finding is that 'homework jobs are very diverse, being spread across all ten industry groups and most of the fifteen main occupation groups.' Hakim's evidence is quite counter to current myth and stereotype both in this and also in a second and, what Hakim admits was a 'completely unanticipated' respect. As many as four-fifths of all homeworkers are owner-occupiers and are relatively well educated. Only a quarter of the sample reported that their home-based job was also their main or usual job. The main disadvantage appeared to be that the women in particular are not able to utilize to the full their skills and capacities.

Overall, homeworkers appeared to be in good health, suffered few accidents and only 5 per cent expressed dissatisfaction with their work.

Leaving aside the men whose work is based on their homes and two-thirds of whom work full-time, we may focus on the two-thirds of the homeworking women (excluding the child-minders) who work very short part-time hours of less than 16 hours a week. Why should they not feel resentful at their low wages, lack of fringe benefits and lack of rights as employees? The answer must surely be that, for the majority of women, their wages are added to the wages of a 'core' or 'permanent' worker, namely their husband or partner. Young couples with a mortgage and a young family find it very hard to get by on the wages of a single chief earner. Some extra income is essential and, given the distribution of workplaces in relation to the location of residential areas, the only way in which women with young children with no alternative child-minding support can engage in the labour force is by working from home. Even though the rewards from part-time work may be small in absolute terms, their marginal utility is high. Hence the lack of any substantial expression of resentment. Any putative conflict between 'permanent' and 'flexible' workers is largely defused by the fact that so many of them meet each other as partners in bed each night.

The growth of homeworking, then, must be seen in the context of the need for increased *household income* at certain critical stages of the life course. The dramatic growth of 'flexible' workers and homeworking that is documented by Hakim must be understood, therefore, as the result of a tacit alliance between employers' strategies, seeking to maintain maximum flexibility in an uncertain economic environment, and households' strategies, concerned to maximize household income through additional earners.

The *component wages* provided by the female partner may be based on more than one part-time job and, similarly, the chief earner may be moonlighting with a second, weekend or evening job. One of the most significant developments in the distribution of work in the 1980s is that money-generating jobs are being clustered in work-rich households leading to a privileged 'middle mass' with a relatively comfortable standard of living. Such households with multiple contacts in the labour market and the sphere of employment are better placed to find further employment for their offspring as they leave school and, for a time, seek to add their wages to their natal family income.

These work-rich households with multiple sources of income, owning their own homes and engaging also in self-provisioning and other forms of work, draw apart from those work-starved households who, when they lose their chief earner's wage through unemployment or redundancy, find it very hard, in Britain certainly, to find any other source of income other than that provided by the social security system. This process of polarization is one of the consequences of a more disaggregated capitalism.[2] Hakim's article needs to be seen in the context of these wider developments and, as such, it provides the first solid documentation of a significant new trend. As we shall see, women's component wages may serve different purposes and functions in different contexts but there are strong parallels between the growth of homeworking in Britain and the insurance companies' strategies in the United States to decentralize employment in the way described by Barbara Baran in chapter 31.

Arizpe and Aranda show in chapter 28 that a woman's loss in one country may be another woman's gain elsewhere. They pose the extremely interesting and relevant question as to whether the fluidity of the international labour market has become more a zero-sum game for women than for men. The authors studied young Mexican peasant women who had recently entered salaried employment in strawberry packing plants to see how this might affect their consciousness, their living conditions and their situation within their families. Most of the women concerned had not previously been in employment and all were still living with their family or kin. Eighty-five per cent of the women were single, and during the time that they were laid off from the plants they remained at home, helping out with domestic work. Most young girls gave nearly all their earnings directly to their parents.

However tiring and burdensome such work may be, the young women prefer it to being shut in their homes: 'Almost all the younger workers consider their job in the agroindustry as a stage in their life that allows them to get out of the daily routine of the village.' This echoes very directly the pattern in Europe at the end of the nineteenth century. Peter Stearns, in his detailed study of industrial work from 1890 to 1914, concluded that daughters who worked for a few years before marriage contributed directly to the family economy: 'In England they paid board and room to their parents, keeping some earnings back for spending money. On the continent they turned their wages over directly.[3]

In Mexico in the late twentieth century, as in Europe in the late nineteenth century, companies can take advantage of the 'traditional idea that any income earned by a daughter, wife, or mother is an "extra" over and above the main income of the father, husband, or son'. Women are paid *component wages* that can be added to the earnings of other household members to provide a more substantial composite household income. For this reason, the factories prefer young, unmarried workers and, indeed, about half the workers in the strawberry packing plants would be completely out of employment if the plants did not exist. Almost without exception the women cease waged labour on marriage:

2. I have discussed this process of polarization in a number of publications. It is introduced in my *Divisions of Labour*, Basil Blackwell, Oxford and New York, 1984, and developed in subsequent publications. See, for example, my articles, 'The Politics of Work', *The Political Quarterly* 56(4) 1985, pp. 331–45; 'Polarizzazione sociale e crisi economica', *Inchiesta*, 74, 1986, pp. 4–11; 'The Distributional Consequences of Informal Work', in R.G. Heinze and Claus Offe (eds) *Organisierte Eigenarbeit: Eine neue Wohfahrtsquelle?* (provisional title – forthcoming).

3. Peter N. Stearns, *Lives of Labour: work in a maturing industrial society*, Croom Helm, London, 1975, p. 269.

> This impermanence allows a company considerable savings in wage increases due to seniority as well as in payments for maternity, disease, or disablement and in old-age pensions. It also prevents the workers from accumulating information and experience that would lead them to organize and to demand improvements in hiring and working conditions. Meanwhile the traditional culture itself assures continuous instability by making marriage the only aspiration for women.

The authors emphasize that the employers have reinforced certain of the social and cultural patterns of the region, so that the female workers gain only modest economic benefits for themselves, although their families may be marginally better off. The young women see their hope for the future as being more closely related to their prospects in marriage than to their advancement in employment. The authors come to the pessimistic conclusion that when, as seems inevitable, the strawberry agribusiness collapses, little will have changed in any substantive way for the women. The organization of employment serves to reinforce patriarchal and authoritarian structures. Inevitably, it seems, the industry will leave for other countries with even lower production costs: jobs that have shifted from the US to Mexico will move on to benefit Haitian or Honduran women. As they remark, 'all women lose along this chain', and it is essential to understand the overall process in an international perspective.

Bernstein's contribution (chapter 29) on the subcontracting of cleaning work in Israel echoes many of the points made in the previous chapter. The low level of education, the lack of occupational options and the patriarchal control of Arab women has led to their mass entrance into the labour force as subcontracted workers. There is, again, a congruence between traditional social arrangements and the needs of the employers. The strong control of Arab women by men leads to a preference for a workplace where a young unmarried woman is not on her own: 'Preferably she should be working with a larger group of women from her own settlement, under the direct supervision of a man well known to her family, and best of all a member of her own extended family, and with as little contact as possible during the workday with other people, especially strange men.' Subcontracted work fits these requirements very well.

Like the previous authors in this part, who see the pattern of work they describe as being likely to increase in the future, Bernstein also suggests that forms of subcontracting and outwork are likely to increase and that the case of cleaning that she describes may be indicative of an important trend. Certainly, recent evidence suggests that cleaning is now big business in Britain. It has been claimed that in 1980–1 the average return on capital invested in the cleaning business was 27.5 per cent, compared with an average 10 per cent for British industry as a whole. By 1986 it was calculated that the industry had a turnover of £400 million. The trade journal of the Contract Cleaning and Maintenance Association – *Reflections* – argued that contract cleaning would be seen as one of the great business success stories in the period 1968–90: 'By 1990 the contract cleaning industry could well have grown to such a size that it will justify a separate investment category in the share register of the *Financial Times*. . . . How can anyone deny that we are winning the struggle to become a large mature industry like the insurance, retail and other such service industries?'[4]

4. Quoted in Angela Coyle, *Dirty Business*, West Midlands Low Pay Unit, 1986, p. 6.

Angela Coyle suggests that 'employers' strategies for reducing their wage bill have developed to an art form. The secret is to employ a lot of people for a short time, rather than to employ a few for longer. Short hours remove the necessity either to pay employers' National Insurance contributions, or to provide tea and lunch breaks.'[5] Women are recruited locally to join the team for any given contract. Each cleaner works for between 10 and 15 hours a week but she may have one or two more similar jobs in order to make up the overall component wage. The supervisors of the predominantly female cleaners are also more likely to be women, whose job is to control the workers and placate the customers under severe budgetary constraints. If the British government's commitment to privatization continues it is likely that the industry will continue to expand to have an annual income of perhaps £1000 million by 1990. Women who work for contract cleaning companies in Britain are more likely to be aged between thirty-five and fifty-nine with family responsibilities and a history of a range of low-paid women's employment. Many of such women are black. This peripheral part of the workforce grew at an unprecedented rate in the mid 1980s.[6]

In chapter 30 an attempt is made to show the employment consequences for the US workforce of transferring manufacturing operations in the electronics industry to low-wage developing countries. Taking the example of the manufacture of television sets, the authors show that from 1971 to 1981 output nearly doubled - from 5.4 to 10.5 million sets - whereas jobs for production workers dropped by a half over the same period. Productivity on a unit output basis grew dramatically over the decade. During the same period American consumer firms moved many of their manufacturing operations to low-wage developing countries, and the US Department of Labor estimated that more jobs were created in these new plants overseas making TV sets than were employed in domestic television manufacture. Quite evidently, whether this process is called deindustrialization or whether it is seen as the restructuring of manufacturing industry will depend on the point of view of the observer.

At the same time that employment in the US consumer electronic industry was declining, owing to productivity gains and the shifting of operations overseas, import penetration grew dramatically. The authors argue that import competition 'must be counted as the primary cause of job losses in the US consumer electronics industry'. However, they do not present convincing arguments for this assertion and one has the suspicion that they are reflecting 'official' views. The information they provide suggests that American companies that seek cheap labour overseas were indeed directly responsible for job losses. The authors seem anxious to absolve US companies from any blame in adopting such a policy, and rather lamely they assert that 'movement abroad was a defensive reaction, not a strategy aimed at expanding markets and improving productivity.'

In the case of microelectronics the trends are even more striking. The authors calculate that 'in recent years, US merchant manufacturers have carried out perhaps 90 per cent of all assembly work overseas.' In this case the authors say clearly that this shift directly displaces American workers. As a result of this new international division of labour, 'some workers, companies, industries, and

5. Ibid., p. 12.
6. *Financial Times*, 5 February 1987. See also chapter 27.

regions will lose out. Unskilled and semi-skilled manufacturing workers are in the greatest jeopardy.' The authors conclude by pointing up the need to rethink public and private programmes of training, retraining and education and also to rethink the meaning of work. This chapter illustrates very neatly some of the contradictions in the global process of capital accumulation and indicates something of the logic that could encourage the US to move to a much greater degree of protectionism. If the US did move in that direction, international political alliances would be affected. Increased intervention into the market, which such protectionism implies, should involve an ideological shift about the involvement of the state in the economy. There is a clear clash of interests here between the state's concern to provide employment for its citizens and private capital's concern to buy products from the cheapest source and to employ labour at the cheapest rates. Such are the contradictions of disaggregated capitalism.

Finally, in chapter 31 Barbara Baran considers the impact of office automation on women's employment in the insurance industry. Her review begins by linking in to the debates generated by Harry Braverman's *Labour and Monopoly Capital* that were also raised in part II. She argues that whilst the first wave of office automation was in line with the Braverman deskilling thesis, the second wave of innovation will have different consequences. The emergence of computer-linked multiactivity jobs will combine tasks previously carried out by data entry clerks, other clerical workers and professionals. As a result of these changes unskilled clerical work has been largely eliminated. The organization of work has also changed so that new multiactivity teams operate in new open plan offices in which status differentiation is much reduced. As Baran remarks: 'In order for information flows to be managed in a conscious and explicit way as the new technologies require, the old power bases have to be destroyed.' She goes on to claim that much of the labour force is professional and more highly trained than in the past. Geographically the work is being disaggregated and decentralized; Baran mentions one firm which has one-sixth of its claims adjustors working at home. These are all women – educated, married and mostly white – who are paid on a piece-rate basis. 'Productivity is extremely high; overhead and labour costs are low. Although both the information and physical production remain centralized, the labour process itself has been decentralized, decollectivized, and rendered asynchronous.'

Baran's work is important as being one of the few empirical studies in a rapidly changing field. As she significantly remarks, 'whereas the factory socialized production, the new technologies are paving the way for an organization of work that is extraordinarily isolating.' She concludes that, overall, skill levels will rise as total employment in the industry declines. It does not follow that the quality of work life will necessarily improve: 'The new jobs in the insurance industry may be not only dead-end, but also boring, stressful, and deeply unsatisfying. Even fairly skilled work that is driven by the logic of computer algorithms seems to subject workers to unusually high levels of stress.' Baran believes that cheaper female labour is being substituted for more expensive male labour throughout the occupational hierarchy. Women are also said to be more 'flexible' than men. There are huge pools of cheap, docile, educated, white women in suburbia ready to 'trade higher wages for flexible or shorter hours, and benefits may be less important to them if they and their children are covered by their husbands' plans.'

Insurance companies are tending to decentralize and to relocate to tap this cheap, high-quality clerical workforce. The converse of these trends is that employment opportunities for minority and less well-educated white women may decline: 'For women at the bottom of the clerical hierarchy, jobs are simply disappearing.'

The new divisions of labour and spatial redistributions are producing new tensions and forms of social polarization. The incorporation and exploitation of female labour at various levels and in various ways is one of the main themes of this part. The problems for male workers were discussed in part II. The interaction between individuals', households' and employers' strategies has emerged as one of the fundamental themes that is sure to be an increasing focus of attention in the next decade.

# 27

# Homeworking in Britain

CATHERINE HAKIM

The typical British homeworker is usually regarded as a woman tied down by the needs of her family, exploited by her employer and working for low wages on tedious, repetitive tasks. A 1981 special survey of home-based workers in Britain carried out by the Department of Employment has done much to dispel this image, and in this chapter key findings from the survey are examined and set in the context of new patterns of employment. (See Hakim, 1980, 1982, 1984a, 1984b, 1985; Cragg and Dawson, 1981; Hakim and Dennis, 1982; Leighton, 1982, 1983a, 1983b; Huws, 1984; Kay, 1984.)

## CHANGING PATTERNS OF WORK

It is widely believed that one of the effects of the recent recession has been to produce new patterns of work and an increase in labour market flexibility. For example Atkinson argues, on the basis of case-study research in the main, that firms are reducing their 'core' workforce of full-time permanent employees who offer functional flexibility in favour of expanding use of 'peripheral' (or non-core) workers who offer numerical flexibility: self-employed freelances, temporary workers obtained from agencies, people on short-term contracts, homeworkers, public subsidy trainees and part-time workers (Atkinson, 1984a, 1984b; Atkinson and Meager, 1986; Institute of Manpower Studies, 1984, 1986). The thesis has gained some credence, although it is not conclusively proven by case studies, and the evidence from the *1984 Workplace Industrial Relations Survey* is equivocal.[1]

This essay was first published in *Employment Gazette*, February 1987. 

1. Although Millward and Stevens were clearly aware of Atkinson's thesis about the increasing size of the 'non-core' workforce, they carefully avoided offering any clear conclusions on trends over the period 1980–84 from their analysis of the results of the *1984 Workplace Industrial Relations Survey* (WIRS). For example, their analysis of employment practices notes a small but significant increase in the use of part-time workers, a substantial decline in the use of outworkers and homeworkers, a significant decline in the use of freelancers and no change at all in the use of people on short-term contracts, although they hold back from noting that their survey results also show a decline in the use of agency temps. Overall, their report on the 1984 WIRS, and comparisons with Hakim's analysis of the 1980 WIRS, suggest a general *decline* in the size of the non-core workforce in the period 1980–84 (Hakim, 1985; Millward and Stevens, 1986, pp. 203–12), at least in relation to establishments with 25 or more employees.

The results of the spring *Labour Force Survey* show an enormous growth in temporary work, a substantial growth in self-employment, and a significant growth in part-time work since 1981. The growth in part-time jobs is the smallest: no more than 300,000 over the period 1981–85. The number of part-time jobs rose from 4.184 million in spring 1981 to 4.475 million in spring 1985, that is, from 19.7 per cent to 21.7 per cent of all employees in employment. More attention has been focused on the unprecedented growth in self-employment, most of which is due to an increase in single-person businesses, that is individual workers who are self-employed without any employees. Between 1981 and 1984, the numbers of people who were self-employed in their main job grew by 442,000 to 2.6 million or from 9.2 per cent to 11.2 per cent of total employment (Creigh et al. 1986). But the most dramatic increase has been in temporary work. The numbers of temporary workers rose from 621,000 in 1981 (*including* some people on government schemes) to 1,314,000 in 1985 (*excluding* people on government schemes) – an increase of almost 700,000 jobs, with relatively large increases in the numbers of men doing temporary work. A continuing upward trend in the numbers of temporary workers is confirmed also by the Institute of Manpower Studies, based on a postal survey of 175 employers in a broad cross-section of industries, and case studies of twenty firms using temporary workers of one sort or another (IMS 1984, 1986).

Looking at each of these groups separately can give a misleading impression of growth, as some of the groups overlap, at least in part, and all of them can contain home-based workers as well. So the figures quoted above involve some double-counting.

To date, no estimates have been attempted on the relative sizes of the different sections of the labour force, or on the magnitude of changes in recent years. However, by using a simple but robust distinction between full-time permanent employees and all other workers, the spring *Labour Force Survey* can be used to measure trends since 1981. For convenience the two groups will be called the 'permanent' workforce and the 'flexible' workforce, although these short-hand labels rather oversimplify the distinctions. Table 27.1 shows a small but steady decline in the relative size of the 'permanent' workforce among both men and women, from 70 per cent of all in employment in 1981 to 66 per cent in 1985. So steady and consistent is the decline that one can already foresee a figure of 64 per cent for spring 1987. By the mid-1980s the labour force divided neatly into two-thirds 'permanent' and one-third 'flexible'. On this measure, one-quarter of all men in work and half of all women in work are now in the sector offering numerical flexibility. The proportions are slightly reduced if the figures are related to the economically active population (everyone in work or seeking work) instead of the population in employment (whether as employees or self-employed). The importance of the 'flexible' sector has clearly been underestimated; it is hardly a narrow and insignificant fringe on the edges of the labour market. In spring 1981 the 'flexible' workforce consisted of almost seven million workers in Great Britain (table 27.1). The autumn 1981 survey of home-based workers yields a national estimate of 1.68 million for England and Wales, which can be grossed up *pro rata* to an estimate of 1.88 million in Great Britain. So home-based workers are clearly not a large proportion of this sector of the labour force – just over one-quarter (27 per cent). And the very fact of being home-based, or off-site, workers distinguishes

TABLE 27.1 Changing patterns of work 1981–5 (thousand and per cent)

| | *Males* | *Females* | *All* |
|---|---|---|---|
| *1981* | | | |
| Economically active | 15,653 | 10,435 | 26,089 |
| In employment | 14,093 | 9,512 | 23,606 |
| Unemployed | 1,560 | 923 | 2,483 |
| Full-time regular employees | 11,581 | 5,058 | 16,639 |
| As % of economically active | 74 | 49 | 64 |
| As % of in employment | 82 | 53 | 70 |
| All other workers | 2,512 | 4,454 | 6,967 |
| As % of economically active | 16 | 43 | 27 |
| As % of in employment | 18 | 47 | 30 |
| *1983* | | | |
| Economically active | 15,379 | 10,418 | 25,797 |
| In employment | 13,565 | 9,379 | 22,943 |
| Unemployed | 1,815 | 1,039 | 2,853 |
| Full-time permanent employees | 10,896 | 4,759 | 15,655 |
| As % of economically active | 71 | 46 | 61 |
| As % of in employment | 80 | 51 | 68 |
| All other workers | 2,668 | 4,620 | 7,288 |
| As % of economically active | 17 | 44 | 28 |
| As % of in employment | 20 | 49 | 32 |
| *1985* | | | |
| Economically active | 15,569 | 10,984 | 26,553 |
| In employment | 13,853 | 9,886 | 23,739 |
| Unemployed | 1,715 | 1 098 | 2,814 |
| Full-time permanent employees | 10,805 | 4,814 | 15,619 |
| As % of economically active | 69 | 44 | 59 |
| As % of in employment | 78 | 49 | 66 |
| All other workers | 3,049 | 5,072 | 8,121 |
| As % of economically active | 20 | 46 | 31 |
| As % of in employment | 22 | 51 | 34 |

*Source*: *Labour Force Survey*, figures for Great Britain based on results for spring 1981, 1983 and 1985

them sufficiently to suggest that they are not representative of the whole sector. On the other hand, they exhibit *all* the characteristics of the 'flexible' workforce, and may be regarded as more broadly illustrative, and of more general interest, than any other single group taken in isolation. As the 1981 special survey demonstrates, the home-based workforce encompasses large numbers of nominally self-employed people as well as tiny one-man businesses, part-time workers, people with temporary and casual jobs, and some short-term contract jobs. And most of the issues that have been debated in relation to homework also arise in relation to other groups of non-core workers.

## 1981 NATIONAL HOMEWORKING SURVEY

In order to allow the survey results to be grossed up to national estimates, the spring 1981 *Labour Force Survey* (LFS) was used as the sift survey and sampling frame for a specially designed interview survey of home-based workers which was carried out by the Office of Population Censuses and Surveys in autumn 1981. Purely for reasons of costs, the survey was limited to England and Wales, but the pattern of results is thought to be representative of Great Britain as a whole, even though national estimates have to be up-rated *pro rata* to obtain figures for Great Britain.

The *National Homeworking Survey* is often confused and conflated with the 1981 LFS, by researchers as well as research users. So it must be emphasized that the autumn 1981 special survey of home-based workers is completely separate from the spring 1981 LFS, that data from the 1981 LFS is not incorporated into the special survey, and that the information collected in the specially-designed survey could not have been collected in the LFS. The separateness of the two surveys needs to be underlined because the 1981 LFS sift questions did not work as well as hoped, and may be misunderstood by some researchers as being equivalent to the special survey data. It follows that the data collected in the 1981 LFS bears no clear relationship to the information obtained in the autumn 1981 survey, and cannot be used as a substitute for it.

Homework is notoriously difficult to define, while even small adjustments to the definition adopted can dramatically affect any national estimates produced (Hakim, 1984a; Bisset and Huws, 1984, p. 4; TUC, 1985, p. 4). The special survey was thus designed to encompass a large number of quite distinct sub-groups, as shown in figure 27.1.

The primary focus of the 1981 survey was on the 229,800 people working at home (excluding childminders), and more especially the 100,000 homeworkers with a single employer: the most detailed information was collected from this group,[2] which is shown in tinted boxes in figure 27.1. For a number of reasons less detailed information was also collected from people who worked from home as a base, who are estimated to number some 400,000 – or about 700,000 if construction and road haulage workers, and family workers, are included. Firstly, the distinction between working mainly at home or from home as a base is not sufficiently clear-cut for a precise cut-off point to be applied with assurance. In the event the detailed information collected in interviews led to some reclassification of the sample between the two categories. The second, more important reason is that people working from home as a base provide a controlled comparison group: like homeworkers they are unusual in not working at the employer's workplace, but unlike homeworkers they are not tied to working at home. For those topics and issues which are specific to home-based work – such as employment status or the frequency of delivery/collection of the work – it is useful to have equivalent information for people working from home as a base for

2. Homeworkers with a single employer constitute the key group around which proposals for new legislation and for other forms of intervention by trade unions and employers have focused. For example, a Private Member's Bill, the Homeworkers (Protection) Bill, introduced unsuccessfully by Frank White MP in November 1979 and again in January 1981, proposed that its scope should effectively be limited to homeworkers with a single employer. However, the TUC's revised *Statement* on homeworking stops short of endorsing this approach – possibly because results from the 1981 survey, published in 1984, showed that the size of the group, at around 100,000, was much smaller than anyone had thought.

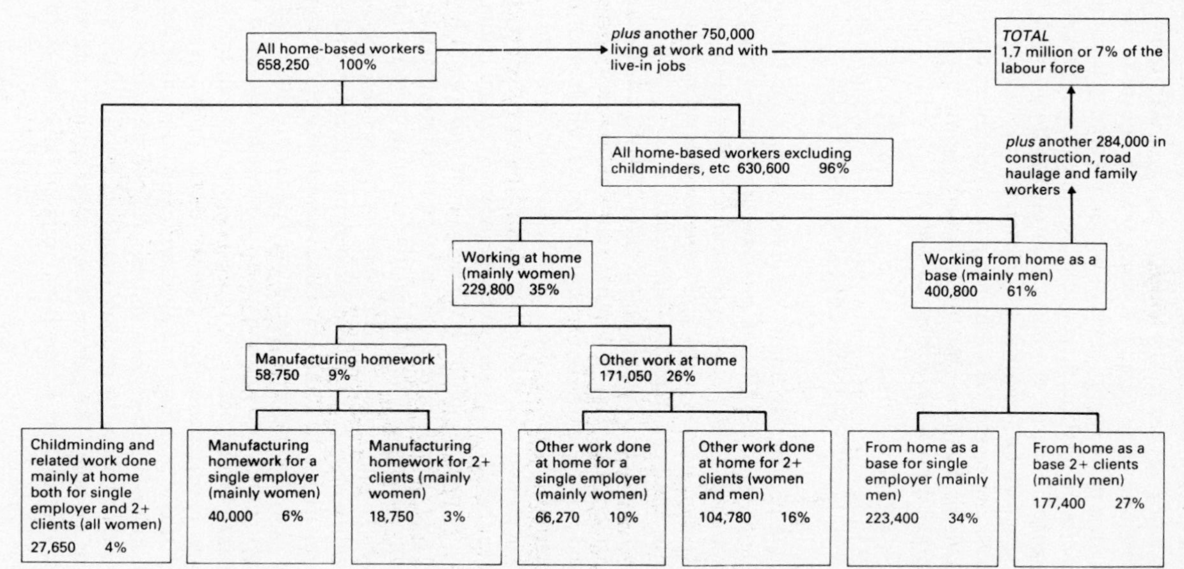


FIGURE 27.1 Composition of the home-based workforce, England and Wales, 1981

comparison with the information collected from homeworkers.[3] One might readily expect that employers would treat homeworkers differently from their on-site workforce. So the key issue is whether they treat *all* home-based workers in a consistent manner, or whether there is evidence of homeworkers in particular being discriminated against in the sense of being offered terms and conditions inferior to those offered to people working from home as a base. So the survey design allows for a fairly rigorous test of whether working at home *per se* is a significant factor. Extending the survey coverage in this way means that it can also be used as a general source of information on the home-based workforce as a whole, a group on which there has so far been no information at all.

Thus the 1981 survey provides information on homeworkers narrowly defined, that is *people who work at home*, and on the broader home-based workforce, that is *people who work at home or from home as a base.*

## PERSONAL CHARACTERISTICS

The majority (71 per cent) of homeworkers are women, and the majority (71 per cent) of people working from home as a base are men. So comparisons between homeworkers and others are often confounded with sex comparisons. However, differences between homeworkers and others, between women and men, were generally less pronounced than the similarities.

Comparisons between the results of the 1981 homeworking survey and nationally representative data from other sources show that home-based workers generally – and homeworkers in particular – do not differ at all from the labour force as a whole in terms of their health, household incomes, their spouse's workforce participation and experience of unemployment. They differ to a small degree in being slightly less likely to be members of ethnic minority groups, and more likely to be married and to have dependent children at home. Women in particular are more likely to have one or more children under 16 years at home. However, homeworkers are most distinctive in their pattern of housing tenure, with an extremely high proportion of owner-occupiers and relatively few council tenants: four-fifths of all homeworkers are owner-occupiers and over half have a mortgage, compared to half and one-third respectively of all private households. Only among those doing manufacturing homework does the proportion of council tenants come close to the national average of one-third. Overall, homeworkers appear to be distinctive, to some extent at least, in that a relatively high proportion are experiencing the dual financial pressures of relatively new mortgages for house purchase and a young family to provide for.

In general, home-based workers and especially homeworkers are also distinctive in being well-educated by national standards and far better qualified than the labour force as a whole. The pattern is consistent among both women and men. For example, one in four home-based workers (and one-third of the home-

3. People doing childminding and related work (caring for people or animals) were treated as a separate group throughout the analysis, although some of them work mainly at home and some work from home as a base. The national estimate of 14,000 quoted for this group in the earlier *Employment Gazette* article (Hakim, 1984a) was in fact an error; the correct figure is about 28,000, as shown in figure 27.1.

workers) have degree-level or other higher education qualifications compared to only one in seven of the working population as a whole. As a result, many home-based workers are over-qualified for the jobs they do, or under-employed in relation to their qualifications. (This was far less likely among people doing manufacturing homework, however.) They are unable to capitalize on their skills and work experience due to the limited range of home-based jobs: only one-quarter reported that their home-based job was also their main or usual job. This finding was completely unanticipated, and has strong implications for attitudes towards home-based work and the earnings achieved from it. For instance, few homeworkers think that their homework skills and experience will be helpful in obtaining an on-site job, when they return to working outside the home in due course, and those doing manufacturing homework are quite clear about wanting to get work *different* from their homework job.

## HOMEWORK JOBS

As was foreshadowed in the report on the survey of employers (Hakim, 1985, pp. 36, 52–57), homework jobs are very diverse, being spread across all ten industry groups and most of the fifteen main occupation groups; the same is even more true of jobs done from home as a base (table 27.2). Manufacturing homework jobs[4] are in the minority, even among homeworkers. The more numerous white-collar homework jobs exhibit rather more diversity, and include jobs in management and administration, professional jobs, design and artistic work, clerical and secretarial jobs and small numbers of jobs in selling, hairdressing and catering. Overall, homework jobs are found in all fifteen occupation groups except for two: security (order 8) and transport operating (order 9) seem to be the only types of work in which working at home is completely ruled out.

As expected, people working from home as a base exhibit even greater variety, with jobs spread across the full spectrum of occupation groups and no concentration in particular kinds of work. The sole exception to this pattern is selling. There are roughly 160,000 jobs in selling in England and Wales that are home-based, or one-third of all jobs done from home as a base. Sales work accounts for half of the jobs done by people with a single employer and one-fifth of those working for two or more bodies.

## HOURS WORKED

There are sharp differences between men and women in the number of hours per week devoted to their home-based job: two-thirds of the men work full-time (31

4. The definition of manufacturing homework jobs applied in the main report on the 1981 survey is different from that applied in previous reports (Hakim 1984a, 1985, pp. 23, 55, 56) and yields a slightly lower national estimate of no more than 60,000 instead of 72,000 as reported previously. The key feature of the revised definition is that it excludes some professional, artistic and other white-collar jobs which were originally classified as manufacturing homework jobs by interviewers. So the slightly lower revised figure refers to a more homogeneous group of purely manual jobs.

TABLE 27.2 National estimates: occupational distribution of home-based workers

| *KOS orders* | *Occupational groups* | *All working at home* | *Manufacturing homework* | *Other work at home* | *Working from home as a base* | *Childminding and related* | *All home-based work* |
|---|---|---|---|---|---|---|---|
| 1 | Professional and related (management and administration) | 21,040 | — | 21,040 | 19,320 | — | 40,360 |
| 2 | Professional and related (education, health, welfare) | 33,670 | 310 | 33,350 | 46,860 | 6,270 | 86,790 |
| 3 | Literary, artistic and sport | 33,370 | — | 33,370 | 20,270 | — | 53,640 |
| 4 | Professional and related (science, engineering, technology) | 9,780 | — | 9,780 | 14,690 | — | 24,470 |
| 5 | Managerial | 15,770 | — | 15,770 | 26,100 | 370 | 42,240 |
| 6 | Clerical and related | 39,720 | — | 39,720 | 36,040 | — | 75,770 |
| 7 | Selling | 13,920 | — | 13,920 | 157,730 | — | 171,650 |
| 8 | Security | — | — | — | 1,180 | — | 1,180 |
| 9 | Catering, cleaning, hairdressing and other personal services | 2,630 | — | 2,630 | 23,220 | 21,020 | 46,870 |
| 10 | Farming, fishing and related | 380 | — | 380 | 11,150 | — | 11,530 |
| 11 | Processing, making, repairing (excluding metal and electrical) | 42,680 | 42,680 | — | 5,230 | — | 47,910 |
| 12 | Processing, making, repairing (metal and electrical) | 3,440 | 3,090 | 350 | 21,090 | — | 24,530 |
| 13 | Painting, assembling, product inspecting, packaging and related | 8,960 | 8,960 | — | 3,910 | — | 12,860 |
| 14 | Construction, mining NEC | 3,060 | 3,060 | — | 380 | — | 3,440 |
| 15 | Transport operating, etc. | — | — | — | 13,290 | — | 13,290 |
| | Inadequately described | 1,380 | 650 | 720 | 360 | — | 1,740 |
| Total | | 229,790 | 58,750 | 171,050 | 400,810 | 27,650 | 658,250 |

hours or more a week) while two-thirds of the women (excluding childminders) work very short part-time hours of less than 16 hours a week. Short hours are not attributable to the fact that many homework jobs are second or subsidiary jobs. For the great majority of both men and women, their home-based job is their only job, and it is a subsidiary job for only one in ten. So the large differences between men and women in hours worked must be accounted for rather by the extent and nature of their domestic and childcare commitments. These differences between men and women are mirrored within the various groups of home-based workers. The great majority of homeworkers work part-time hours whereas most people working from home as a base are doing their job full-time.

## JOB TENURE

The home-based workforce is not fundamentally different from the labour force as a whole in terms of job tenure. Excluding those working for two or more employers/clients, the majority of home-based workers work continuously for the same employer, so there is a large degree of overlap between the total duration of all home-based jobs and the duration of their current job. About one-third have been doing their current job for less than two years; about one-third have been doing their job for 2–5 years; and another third have been doing the job for six years or longer, extending in a minority of cases to 21 years or longer. Both for homeworkers and others, this generally represents their total experience of home-based work.

There are substantial differences between men and women. Women generally have shorter histories of home-based work, with less than six years being typical. Men generally have longer histories of home-based work, six years or longer being typical, and almost half had six years or longer in their current home-based job.

## EMPLOYMENT PROTECTION LEGISLATION RIGHTS

All the rights under the employment protection legislation depend on the worker being an employee. And most depend also on them having worked a specific qualifying period of continuous employment, varying according to the right. For most of the rights, an employee must have worked at least 16 hours a week. For the major rights (redundancy pay, unfair dismissal and maternity rights) employees must meet certain minimum conditions defining their job tenure with the employer: those who work 16 hours or more per week must have at least two years or more in the job, and people working at least eight but less than 16 hours per week must have at least five years or more in the job. People who do not yet qualify because their length of service, or job tenure, falls below the required minimum of two or five years may, of course, eventually qualify for these rights.

The analysis presented in table 27.3 ignores the issue of home-based workers' employment status to focus on the job tenure and weekly hours conditions. Although a large proportion of home-based workers are able to fulfil the requirements regarding length of time in the job, substantial proportions fail to meet the requirements regarding weekly hours worked. One-third of the homeworkers, but

TABLE 27.3 Employment protection legislation conditions (per cent)

| *Hours of work and length of service in current home-based job* | *All working at home* | *Manufacturing homework* | *Other at home* | *From home base* | *Childminders* | *Total with childminders* |
|---|---|---|---|---|---|---|
| Working 16+ hours per week, two years or more in the job | 34 | 41 | 32 | 56 | 55 | 48 |
| Working eight but less than 16 hours per week, five or more years in the job | 9 | 10 | 8 | 3 | 1 | 5 |
| Working 16+ hours per week, less than two years in the job | 10 | 19 | 6 | 19 | 23 | 15 |
| Working eight but less than 16 hours per week, less than five years in the job | 18 | 19 | 17 | 9 | 8 | 12 |
| Working less than eight hours per week | 30 | 10 | 37 | 14 | 12 | 20 |
| **Base = 100%: all home-based workers, excluding those not providing the information** | 606 | 165 | 441 | 986 | 73 | 1,665 |

only one in seven of those working from home as a base, will never be able to qualify for most employment protection rights due to working less than eight hours a week. Two-fifths of the homeworkers and three-fifths of the others already meet the conditions of eligibility, and about one-quarter of each group has not yet had a sufficiently long period of service to qualify (although they may do so at a future date).

However, these results take no account of the issue of home-based workers' employment status, or of the question of whether continuity of employment has been maintained over the whole period of work (that is, despite any breaks), and the evidence suggests that most home-based workers might fall at one or another of these additional hurdles.

The national survey confirms the findings of all small-scale studies – that home-based workers almost invariably have experience of full-time jobs outside the home, with between six and 20 years' experience being typical. There is therefore no substance in the explanation sometimes offered for the low earnings of homeworkers: that these women have no experience of on-site jobs and so have very low productivity.

Equally there is evidence that what may have started as a short-term option can readily become a permanent career rather than a temporary work arrangement. About 10 per cent of all home-based workers have been doing this type of work for over 20 years, not necessarily in the same job. And it is notable that the tiny group of people who had never held an on-site job, whose work experience consisted solely of home-based work, was dominated by men rather than women. Sales work seems to be the most important source of permanent careers in home-based work, but there are also others.

An earlier, in-depth study showed that many female homeworkers did not really regard themselves as having 'jobs': they were working in a somewhat amateur way and therefore their earnings could not fairly be compared with earnings from on-site work (Cragg and Dawson, 1981, p. 21). The national survey throws further light on this ambivalent attitude to homework jobs. Homeworkers are almost three times more likely to describe their job as 'casual' than are people working from home, irrespective of whether it is their only job or not. Almost all the manufacturing homeworkers had only the one job, yet they are also the group most likely to describe their home-based job as 'casual': half of them did so compared to only one-quarter of people doing white-collar homework jobs and just over one in ten of those working from home. Yet half of those doing manufacturing homework already meet the length of service and hours conditions of eligibility for employment protection rights (table 27.3), and on that criterion are regular workers. Thus 'casual' and 'regular' jobs exist side by side within the home-based workforce, with large differences in the hours worked and job tenure despite small differences in the nature of the work done, and no doubt with significant implications for work orientations and work attachment. The 'casualness' of homework seems to have been exaggerated – since it is often presented as the dominant mode rather than a minority perspective – but it cannot be overlooked either. For example, it probably accounts for non-reporting of homework to a much larger extent than has so far been recognized, and is possibly more significant than 'fear of repercussions', which is usually offered as the sole explanation.

## PAY AND EARNINGS

The weekly earnings of homeworkers are widely dispersed, but are typically low: in 1981 one-third earned less than £10 a week and three-quarters earned no more than £40 a week. In large part this is attributable to the fact that most homeworkers work only very short part-time hours, as noted above. Some homeworkers intentionally restrict their hours and earnings so as to keep them below the level at which income tax and National Insurance contributions become due. In addition, payment systems and rates of pay vary enormously, even for the same type of work. And the majority of homeworkers report that earnings fluctuate a good deal over a year.

Overall, homeworkers (and home-based workers more generally) have hourly earnings concentrated disproportionately at the upper and lower ends of the national earnings distribution. From this, two apparently contradictory conclusions can be drawn: homeworkers are among the highest paid workers in Britain (one-fifth have hourly earnings in the top 10 per cent bracket) but they are also very poorly paid (over one-third have hourly earnings in the lowest 10 per cent bracket). The lowest-paid jobs are in manufacturing homework and child-minding – jobs typically done by women. So the great majority of people with very low hourly earnings are women, while the majority of high earners are men. Nonetheless, three-quarters of all homeworkers said they were satisfied with their pay, women being slightly more satisfied than men overall. The lowest levels of satisfaction with pay were found among homeworkers who were aware that they could earn more money in a job outside the home – which as noted earlier would often be different from their homework job.

## COLLECTION/DELIVERY OF WORK

Home-based work is distinctive in that the work has to be delivered to and collected from the workers, instead of them travelling daily to the employer's workplace. The survey confirms that it is almost invariably the employer who organizes – and bears the costs – of delivery and collection of work. However, most homeworkers and the great majority of people working from home also collected/delivered work. The frequency of collection/delivery was relatively high in all groups, typically at least once a week and often daily.

## WORKSPACE

The need to provide workspace and storage space in the home is clearly an inconvenience for many homeworkers, but it is not the most important disadvantage. Only a minority of homeworkers are able to confine all their work and storage within a separate workroom. About half of all homeworkers reported that both the work itself, and storage of equipment or finished products, had to be accommodated in parts of the home used by the family. This sometimes presented problems, in terms of the dirt created and the space taken up, particularly among manufacturing homeworkers. But when asked about this disadvantage in relation to all the others, problems such as the social isolation of working at home loomed much larger than this one.

## ASSISTANTS

By and large, homeworkers do not use any assistants at all, whether paid workers or unpaid family helpers. In the minority of cases where assistants are used, both women and men typically draw on other members of their family or household for help with the work, non-relatives being much rarer, with a single occasional helper being the norm. On this evidence, there is no basis for regarding homeworkers as independent subcontractors, especially as they are all doing the job themselves for the most part.

Another, weaker, definition of a subcontractor was also applied to the survey results: someone who regularly employs two or more paid assistants. On this criterion, only 1 per cent of the homeworkers could be classified as independent subcontractors, most of them being men and doing white-collar homework rather than manufacturing homework.

## CONTINUITY AND BREAKS

As noted earlier, to establish eligibility to employment protection rights, homeworkers must demonstrate not only that they have the requisite length of service with the employer but also that they have been employed continuously for that time. Definitions of continuity of employment can be fairly complex, especially in relation to home-based workers and others working away from the employer's workplace, given the need to demonstrate some continuing availability for work even when not attending daily for work. The recent case of *Nethermere (St Neots) Ltd* v. *Taverna and Gardiner* made legal history by resulting in a decision that the two women homeworkers were employees despite working part-time hours with periodic breaks in the work, because they had sufficient continuity to establish 'mutuality of obligation'. The detailed weighing-up of the evidence on each individual case that is characteristic of the courts cannot be attempted in a large-scale structured survey. But the survey was used to provide some relevant information on the number of, and reasons for, breaks in the supply of work to home-based workers who worked for one particular employer. The results suggest that many homeworkers would be unable to establish continuity of employment, whereas the great majority of people working from home as a base would have no difficulty in establishing continuity. Interruptions in the supply of work from the employer, and breaks chosen by the homeworker, are the norm rather than the exception, especially among those doing manufacturing homework. For example, as many as one-quarter of the homeworkers experienced breaks (for whatever reason) totalling more than three months in the previous year, compared to only 6 per cent of people working away from home. Homeworkers are less likely than people working away from home to voluntarily *choose* to have breaks from work, but this is largely due to the fact that they experience a very much larger number of *involuntary* breaks, when no work is available from the employer. In effect the choice is made for them, most of the time. This can fuel resentment that the flexibility of homework is weighted rather more in the employer's favour than the worker's. But more significantly, a large number of extended breaks in the supply of work constitute a serious impediment to establishing continuity, and hence eligibility for employment protection rights.

## EMPLOYER'S CONTROL

The traditional test applied in common law to distinguish the employee in a master–servant relationship from the self-employed entrepreneur is the degree of *control* exercised by the employer over the nature of the work, when and how it is done, and so forth (Leighton, 1983b, p. 198). Unfortunately there is no standard set of tests of control that can readily be applied to all jobs and all work situations. For example, the frequency of collection/delivery of work constitutes a measure of control over the volume and pace of the work in most – but not all – jobs. The seven specific tests of control included in the survey were thought to apply reasonably well to all jobs done by people working at home for a single employer, the group of special interest throughout the survey.

When asked whether they would lose the job if they did not do a certain minimum amount of work, only half the homeworkers said they would – that a minimum volume of work was required by the employer.

When asked whether they could stop taking on work for a time if they wanted to, without losing the job, two-thirds of the homeworkers said they could. Clearly, continuity of employment is not a feature of the employment contract (whether written or implied) for most homeworkers.

Homeworkers were asked about deadlines set by the employer and the likely response to these not being met. Almost half the homeworkers said deadlines were effectively not set by the employer, in that nothing would happen even if a deadline for delivery had been set. The other half said that they never failed to meet any deadlines set for completing the work or that specific action would follow if they did. The nature of the employer's reaction to work not being ready on time ranged from losing the job, warnings of dismissal and deductions from pay on the one hand, to reprimands, demands for an explanation and other reactions too vague for classification on the other hand, with the two types fairly evenly balanced.

Another test of the employer's control is whether specific instructions are given on how the work should be done. Half the homeworkers said the employer left it all to the worker. The other half received specific instructions; typically these were detailed enough to cover the whole job. On this test, manufacturing homeworkers emerge as subject to the highest levels of control, with half being given very detailed instructions.

Another aspect of control is monitoring the quality of completed work. However, quality control seems to be a universal feature of home-based jobs (and perhaps all work!). The vast majority of homeworkers said their work had never been below the quality wanted; or that if it was, the employer would react by deducting money from their pay, returning the work for improvements, and so on.

Another indicator of the employer's control is the degree of choice allowed in the work taken on, more specifically whether the homeworker could refuse any particular kind of work offered by their employer. Almost two-thirds said they could, the proportion being only marginally lower among manufacturing homeworkers.

Homeworkers were also asked whether they had ever been asked to take on a rush job for their employer. Two-thirds said they had, with rush jobs being an almost universal characteristic of manufacturing homework jobs.

On the basis of these particular indicators of employer control, no more than half of all homeworkers working for a single employer appear to be employees – in that they are subject to the kind of control typical of direct employment. On some measures, the proportion is higher: two-thirds are asked to take on rush jobs, for example. But, on the other hand, two-thirds can refuse particular jobs, and even stop taking any work at all for a while. So on balance only about half appear to be consistently subject to the sort of control characteristic of an employer–employee relationship. Although there are some small differences between those doing manufacturing homework and those doing white-collar homework jobs, the conclusion applies to both groups equally.

In recent years the courts and tribunals have moved away from the 'control' test in deciding employment status and now frequently adopt the more complex 'multiple' test, in which numerous aspects of the employment relationship are weighed up to determine whether a worker is an employee or self-employed. A multiple test containing thirteen separate items was devised for this study and applied to home-based workers with a single employer. On this (somewhat stringent) test, virtually none of them were employees: only 4 per cent satisfied *all* thirteen conditions for employees status. However, as noted earlier, virtually none of the home-based workers could be classified as independent subcontractors in terms of regularly employing assistants. Given these somewhat contradictory classifications, it is not surprising that many home-based workers are not sure whether they are employees or self-employed.

## EMPLOYMENT STATUS

One-third of homeworkers (and of home-based workers more generally) are confused or uncertain about their employment status. Doubts about employment status are not explained by homeworkers being uninformed or unable to grasp the legal issues in question; they seem to arise rather from the characteristics of the job.

In many cases the uncertainty would be due to the fact that the homeworkers in question earned too little over the year, worked too few hours or had too many breaks in continuity of employment, for there to be any practical need to decide what the employment status was. For example, there is little incentive to sort out the employment status of someone who works less than eight hours a week as they cannot be eligible for employment protection benefits in any event. If earnings remain below the limit where income tax and National Insurance contributions become payable, neither worker nor employer are forced to decide which of them would be responsible for making such payments.

As noted earlier, large proportions of homeworkers have low earnings, irregular earnings, breaks in the continuity of employment, and relatively short hours of work. However, people who work from home as a base tend to work full-time hours, with fewer breaks in continuity and higher earnings - yet here too one-third have doubts about their correct employment status. So it is the objective conditions of home-based work that produce such high levels of doubts about employment status - as noted earlier in relation to the various tests of employer control.

## LABOUR TURNOVER

Supplementary interviews for the 1981 survey were carried out in the autumn (mainly October), roughly five to six months after the *1981 Labour Force Survey* interviews (which were concentrated in May), by which time a few people were no longer doing home-based work because their previous job had ended for one reason or another and they had failed to obtain (or had not sought) another home-based job. As a result, a very small proportion of people in the 1981 survey gave information about the home-based job they had been doing in spring 1981 (at the time of the LFS interview) rather than about home-based work being done in autumn 1981. The proportion of people whose home-based job had ended between spring and autumn 1981 provides an indicator of labour turnover in the home-based labour force over a six-month period, which can be doubled to give an estimated annual labour turnover rate. Overall about one in seven (14 per cent) home-based workers' jobs had ended for one reason or another within the previous six months, giving an annual turnover rate of about one-quarter (28 per cent) for all home-based workers. The turnover rate was the same for those working at home and those working from home as a base, but it was much higher for women than for men: 40 per cent compared to 17 per cent. As a rough basis for comparison, labour turnover in 1981 was 31 per cent of all employees in employment in that year, so labour turnover in the home-based workforce as a whole is, if anything, below rather than above the national average. (Inevitably, it is above or below average in particular occupations.)

## HEALTH AND ACCIDENTS

Throughout the debates on homeworking the health and safety risks of homework have been emphasized, leading to demands for new legislation and regulations, most recently by the Low Pay Unit (Bisset and Huws, 1984, pp. 31-2) and the TUC (1985, pp. 12-14). Yet concrete evidence of health and safety problems in homework has been hard to come by (Cragg and Dawson, 1981, p. 25; Bisset and Huws, 1984, pp. 31-2). Another reason for paying special attention to health problems in the national homeworking survey is the popular view that homeworkers include disproportionate numbers of people with chronic illnesses or disabilities which prevent them going out to work - and also prevent them achieving average earnings for their occupation. In the event both propositions were shown to be unfounded.

If anything, the health of home-based workers is somewhat better than the health of the working population as a whole in Britain. More particularly, people working at home do not differ at all from the working population as a whole, or from all working women, in terms of the incidence of chronic illness or of limiting chronic illness; and they are somewhat more likely to assess their health as 'good'. So homeworkers' reports of health problems resulting from the work done at home would not be confounded with, or exacerbated by, a previous history of health problems to any greater extent than would be the case in the population generally.

In fact, the occurrence of accidents and of health problems resulting from the work being done at home is very low indeed: only 2 per cent of all homeworkers reported that an accident connected with the work done at home had ever occurred, either to themselves or to another person; and only 3 per cent reported that health problems resulting from the work done at home had ever arisen, either for themselves or for any other person (table 27.4).

People doing manufacturing homework and those doing childminding and related work at home report accidents and health problems connected with the work done at home two to three times more often than white-collar homeworkers; but even in these groups only 3 to 5 per cent report such problems, a maximum of one person in twenty. Since the information relates to accidents and health problems that had *ever* arisen in connection with the homework job, either to the homeworker or to anyone else, the conclusion must be that their incidence on an *annual* basis must be very rare indeed.

Apart from being extremely rare, accidents are typically of a trivial nature. Among the handful of accidents reported by homeworkers, these consisted of cuts, falls, bruises, sprained wrists and similar problems of a short term character, the most serious being a woman who got a sewing machine needle through her finger. In the majority of cases the accident happened to the homeworker, and only rarely to someone else.

Health problems suffered as a result of the work done at home divided into two broad groups of equal importance: those that had a clear physiological element (such as backache, the effects of fumes, headaches, aggravation of poor eyesight

TABLE 27.4 Accidents and health problems resulting from homework (per cent)

| | *Proportion in each group reporting that homeworker or another person:* | |
|---|---|---|
| *Homeworkers* | *had an accident connected with homework* | *health suffered as a result of homework* |
| All working at home | 2 | 3 |
| Manufacturing homework | 3 | 5 |
| Other work at home | 1 | 2 |
| Childminding | 4 | 5 |
| Women | 2 | 3 |
| Men | 1 | 3 |
| Single employer | 1 | 4 |
| 2+ clients | 3 | 2 |

or asthma attacks) and those that were primarily psychological in nature (such as feelings of depression, anxiety and phobia), presumably resulting from the social isolation of working at home rather than from the nature of the work itself. It is notable that men only reported problems of the second type; possibly men feel more acutely the isolation of working at home, which may be seen as their wife's (or a woman's) domain. Women reported problems of a physiological and psychological character in roughly equal proportions, irrespective of the type of homework they did. However, none of the childminders reported problems of a psychological nature, presumably because their work is not socially isolating as it involves interacting with children and, to some extent, their parents. This also helps explain why both men and women working for a single employer are somewhat more likely to report health problems than those working for two or more clients (table 27.4). The degree of social isolation is increased among those working for a single employer, and is reflected in a higher incidence of psychological as compared with physiological problems.

Overall then, accidents connected with homework are both rare and typically of a trivial nature. Health problems resulting from homework are also rare, and they arise from the social isolation of working at home as often as from the work itself. As might be expected, manufacturing homework has the highest rates of accidents and health problems, but even in this group no more than one in twenty reported an accident or a health problem having ever arisen, either to themselves or to anyone else. A very similar picture was obtained in a recent Low Pay Unit study, which found headaches, eyestrain, stress and depression to be the most common problems mentioned by homeworkers (Bisset and Huws, 1984, pp. 31–2).

## TRADE UNION MEMBERSHIP

Historically, the trade union movement has been opposed to homeworking and sought to abolish it. As Bisset and Huws note: 'For the greater part of this century it was the majority opinion in the trade union movement that homeworking was a social evil which should be abolished; that homeworking undermined workplace union organisation and perpetuated conditions of poverty and squalor in the home' (Bisset and Huws, 1984, p. 13). Within the last decade a new perspective has emerged which seeks rather to incorporate homeworkers into the trade union movement, as reflected in the 1978 TUC *Statement* on homeworking, updated in 1985 (TUC 1978, 1985). How receptive are homeworkers to these new opportunities? And do they perceive trade unions as having anything to offer homeworkers? The evidence so far points to very low levels of trade union membership, and a high degree of ambivalence about the usefulness of trade unions for homeworkers (Cragg and Dawson, 1981, pp. 25–6; Hakim, 1985, pp. 40–2, 89–93; Bisset and Huws, 1984, pp. 32–3).

The special survey confirms that levels of unionization are extremely low among home-based workers: only 14 per cent (10 per cent of homeworkers) are currently trade union members compared to 45 per cent of the working population and 33 per cent of those aged 18–64 years (tables 27.5 and 27.6). Nationally, a substantial proportion of people who are not currently union

TABLE 27.5 Trade union membership by sex (per cent)

| | *Home-based workers* | | *Working* | | |
|---|---|---|---|---|---|
| *Trade union membership* | *men* | *women* | *at home* | *from home* | *Total* |
| TU member connected with home-based work, all | 18 | 8 | 7 | 17 | 13 |
| previously | 3 | 1 | 1 | 2 | 2 |
| currently | 15 | 7 | 6 | 15 | 11 |
| TU member connected with other job, all | 34 | 38 | 38 | 34 | 36 |
| previously | 29 | 36 | 34 | 31 | 32 |
| currently | 5 | 2 | 4 | 3 | 3 |
| Never TU member | 45 | 52 | 52 | 46 | 49 |
| Previous members, all | 32 | 36 | 35 | 34 | 34 |
| Current members, all | 19 | 9 | 10 | 17 | 14 |
| No information on TU membership | 3 | 2 | 3 | 3 | 3 |
| **Base = 100 per cent** | 899 | 785 | 671 | 1013 | 1684 |

TABLE 27.6 Trade union membership by employment status and sex, Great Britain 1983–4

| | *Trade union membership (per cent)* | | | |
|---|---|---|---|---|
| *Employment status* | *Currently* | *Previously* | *Never* | *Base* |
| **All aged 18–64** | 33 | 28 | 39 | 2,626 |
| All in paid work 10+ hours/week | 45 | 23 | 32 | 1,702 |
| Employee | | | | |
| full-time (30+) | 53 | 21 | 26 | 1,273 |
| part-time (10–29 hours) | 28 | 27 | 45 | 251 |
| Self-employed | 10 | 34 | 56 | 176 |
| Unemployed | 14 | 50 | 36 | 220 |
| Economically inactive or working < 10 hours | 9 | 34 | 58 | 704 |
| All not in paid work | 10 | 38 | 52 | 924 |
| **Men aged 18–64** | 43 | 29 | 28 | 1,273 |
| **Women aged 18–64** | 23 | 28 | 49 | 1,353 |

*Source: 1983–84 Social Attitudes Survey*: figures for Great Britain derived from unpublished tables supplied by Social and Community Planning Research, excluding a small number of people not providing information on TU membership

members have been members of a union in the past and this is also the case for all groups of home-based workers. But half of all home-based workers, both men and women, have never been members of a trade union (or staff association) - well above the national average of about one-third.[5]

The low level of unionization is not attributable to the fact that two-thirds of all homeworkers, and half of those working from home, report themselves as self-employed in their home-based job. Nationally, only 10 per cent of the self-employed are trade union members, and about half have never been union members, a pattern very similar to that for people of working age who are *not* in paid work (table 27.6). However, within the home-based workforce there are virtually no differences in the pattern of trade union membership between homeworkers and those working from home, between employees and the self-employed, between people working for a single employer or for two or more. Clearly, the pattern of unionization is specific to home-based work, within which employment status is an insignificant additional factor. The general pattern across all groups is of trade union membership in the past connected with another job, and a very low level of current trade union membership connected with home-based work, the level being twice as high among men as among women: 15 per cent compared to 7 per cent (table 27.5).

Further information on attitudes to the trade unions generally, awareness of trade unions relevant to homeworkers and views on trade union access to lists of homeworkers' names and addresses was collected only from homeworkers. Only 2 per cent of the non-union homeworkers said they had ever been approached about joining a trade union in connection with the work they did at home. Only 14 per cent were aware of any trade union representing people doing the type of work they did at home, but some of them believed homeworkers were not eligible to join it. Overall, only one in ten non-union homeworkers knew of a relevant trade union that would accept homeworkers as members. The vast majority of both male and female homeworkers did not know of any suitable union they might join. On the other hand two-thirds did not see union membership as being important for homeworkers; only one-third thought unionization was very, or fairly, important for homeworkers. In line with these attitudes, only one-third of homeworkers were prepared to allow trade unions the right to obtain lists of homeworkers' names and addresses from employers; two-thirds were against the idea. Responses were solidly consistent; but they were also divided into two camps; the majority of homeworkers see no advantages in unionization, but a sizeable minority of one-third are in favour.

## ATTITUDES TO HOME-BASED WORK

There is every reason to expect that the attitudes of homeworkers to their jobs are determined not only by the jobs in question but also by a host of other, quite separate factors, in particular the marked differences between men and women in

5. The best source of comparative national data on patterns of trade union membership was found to be the *British Social Attitudes Survey*, which was initiated in 1983 as an independent multifunded regular survey. See reports by Jowell and Airey (1984). Jowell and Witherspoon (1985) and Jowell, Witherspoon and Brook (1986).

their breadwinner role, in their work expectations and aspirations. For example, the *General Household Survey* consistently finds higher levels of job satisfaction among women than among men, partly due to lower expectations or needs, and partly due to the fact that it is often the more satisfied women who remain in the labour force - given that more women than men actually have a choice (OPCS, 1982, pp. 85–7). Similarly, the homeworking survey found marked sex differences in work orientations.

Neither of the two standard but competing views of homework are supported. One view presents homeworkers as women with young children who are trapped at home by their domestic responsibilities. But only one-third of women working at home (and only one-quarter of all homeworkers) say that they have to work at home. The other view presents homework as an especially attractive option for women, preferable in many ways to going out to work at an on-site job. But only one-third of women working at home say it is a clear preference (rather than a forced choice). In contrast a two-thirds majority of men working at home are doing so out of preference. Overall fewer than half of all homeworkers express a positive preference for this work arrangement; and one-third of all homeworkers seem to be doing so fortuitously, in that they either have no preferences as between working at home or elsewhere, or else they prefer to go out to work. Descriptions of the stress experienced by women in combining paid work with their domestic and child care activities, especially when all these activities are confined to the home, provide an explanation for the survey finding that more women than men actually prefer to go out to work (Cragg and Dawson, 1981; Martin and Roberts, 1984, pp. 64–7; Allen and Wolkowitz, 1986). On the other hand, when asked why they are doing home-based work, the majority of men and women list all the advantages, emphasizing in particular the sense of freedom and flexibility it offers.

One factor which reinforces homeworkers' appreciation of the advantages of working at home is a clear awareness that homework is scarce, particularly manufacturing homework, with supply and demand weighted strongly in the employers' favour. The great majority are aware that their employer can easily replace the homeworker, whereas they would have difficulty finding an alternative homework job. People doing manufacturing homework for a single employer are especially vulnerable.

Overall, the vast majority of homeworkers declare themselves satisfied with their homework job; only a tiny minority of 5 per cent feel dissatisfied. The proportion who are dissatisfied rises to a maximum of only 11 per cent among manufacturing homeworkers, notwithstanding the relatively low levels of hourly pay for this type of homework.

## VIEWS ON THE NEED FOR LEGISLATION

Although awareness of relevant employment legislation is generally high among homeworkers, opinion is very divided as to whether it covers people working at home: one-third thought that none of the existing legislation (such as employment protection legislation, health and safety regulations, and Wages Council regulations on minimum pay) had any application to homeworkers, one-third were unsure, and one-third thought that at least some of the existing legislation already covers homeworkers. So the vast majority of homeworkers do not think with any degree of certainty that existing legislation applies to them.

When asked whether the conditions of people working at home needed to be improved at all, opinion was again divided: one-quarter of homeworkers thought conditions were all right as they stood, one-quarter were not sure, and half wanted improvements. Details of the particular improvements sought by homeworkers were not collected, but two-fifths of all homeworkers endorsed the idea of special laws, action by the government and by employers. Action by trade unions was endorsed by a minority of homeworkers, but almost as many rejected the idea that trade unions could help to achieve improvements, so that, on balance, only a tiny proportion favoured this approach. As noted earlier, most homeworkers do not support unionization as a solution to their problems, looking rather to action by the government and by employers.

## CONCLUSIONS

Overall the 1981 survey shows that the picture of homeworking that is usually presented - of work typically done by women, who are working at home largely due to family responsibilities, with few or no skills, doing low-paid manufacturing work, exploited, and suffering health problems because they lack the protection of health and safety legislation - is highly misleading. Only a small proportion of women doing manufacturing homework approximate to this picture - at least in part. But they are not representative of all homeworkers, who number some 250,000 in England and Wales.

To complete the picture it has to be noted that homeworkers are more highly qualified than most, in better health than most, and more likely to own their own homes, and their usual occupations may be more skilled than is reflected in their homework job. Many of the women are making conscious trade-offs between the flexibility of homework and the relatively low-paid jobs available - just as the *1980 Women and Employment Survey* showed more generally that women who work part-time are trading off convenience against pay (Ballard, 1984, p. 416). This process explains why the majority of homeworkers express themselves as satisfied with their job and pay.

One of the key features of the research design was to allow comparisons between homeworkers and people working from home as a base, in order to assess whether home-based workers generally are treated consistently by employers, or whether working at home *per se* is a significant factor in the terms and conditions offered by employers. The results are instructive. Although in many areas there are no differences at all between those working at, or from, home, the overall picture is of significant differences between the two groups. Further tests show that the distinctive treatment of homeworkers is not due to direct sex discrimination but rather to the differential treatment of part-time workers and full-time workers.

However, it should not be assumed that these results can be projected into the the future unaltered. An expansion of home-based work could be expected to increase the range and variety of jobs available on this basis - especially if more home-based jobs are created by developments in new technology. At the minimum, this would begin to reduce the astonishingly high proportion of home-based workers who are *not* doing their usual job and are often underemployed, with lower-than-usual earnings. Manufacturing homework would diminish - both in absolute terms and as a proportion of the total - since it is rarely a positive choice and preference. At the maximum, entirely new types of business might eventually develop, offering services highly tailored to local markets and needs, and allowing a flexibility in work patterns that has so far remained a luxury in ordinary on-site jobs.

## REFERENCES

Allen, S. and Wolkowitz, C. (1986) 'Homeworking and the control of women's work', pp. 238-264 in *Waged Work: A Reader*, edited by *Feminist Review*, London: Virago Press.

Atkinson. J. (1984a) *Manning for Uncertainty: Some Emerging UK Work Patterns*, Brighton: University of Sussex Institute of Manpower Studies.

Atkinson, J. (1984b) 'Manpower strategies for flexible organisations', *Personnel Management*, August 1984, pp. 28-31.

Ballard, B. (1984) 'Women part-time workers: evidence from the 1980 Women and Employment Survey', *Employment Gazette*, vol. 92, no. 9, pp. 409-16.

Bisset, L. and Huws, U. (1984) *Sweated Labour: Homeworking in Britain Today*, London: Low Pay Unit.

Cragg, A. and Dawson, T. (1981) *Qualitative Research Among Homeworkers*, Research Paper no. 21, London: Department of Employment.

Creigh, S. et al. (1986) 'Self-employment in Britain: results from the Labour Force Surveys 1981-1984', *Employment Gazette*, vol. 94, no. 6, pp. 183-94.

Hakim, C. (1980) 'Homeworking: some new evidence', *Employment Gazette*, vol. 88, no. 10, pp. 1105-10.

Hakim, C. (1982) 'Homeworking in the London clothing industry', *Employment Gazette*, vol. 90, no. 9. pp. 369-76.

Hakim, C. (1984a) 'Homework and outwork: national estimates from two surveys', *Employment Gazette*, vol. 92, no. 1, pp. 7-12.

Hakim, C. (1984b) 'Employers' use of homework, outwork and freelances', *Employment Gazette*, vol. 92, no. 4, pp. 144-50.

Hakim, C. (1985) *Employers Use of Outwork:* A study using the 1980 Workplace Industrial Relations Survey and the 1981 National Survey of Homeworking, Research Paper no. 44, London: Department of Employment.

Hakim, C. and Dennis, R. (1982) *Homeworking in Wages Council Industries:* A study based on Wages Inspectorate records of pay and earnings, Research Paper no. 37, London: Department of Employment.

Huws, U. (1984) 'New technology homeworkers', *Employment Gazette*, vol. 92, no. 1, pp. 13-17.

Institute of Manpower Studies (1984) *Flexibility, Uncertainty and Manpower Management*, Report CN 526, Brighton: University of Sussex Institute of Manpower Studies .

Institute of Manpower Studies (1986) *Changing Working Patterns:* How companies achieve flexibility to meet new needs, London: National Economic Development Office.

Jowell, R. and Airey, C. (1984) *British Social Attitudes - the 1984 Report*, Aldershot, Hants: Gower.

Jowell, R. and Witherspoon, S. (1985) *British Social Attitudes - the 1985 Report*, Aldershot, Hants: Gower.

Jowell, R., Witherspoon, S. and Brook, L. (1986) *British Social Attitudes – the 1986 Report*, Aldershot, Hants: Gower.

Kay, H. (1984) 'Is childminding real work?', *Employment Gazette*, vol. 92, no. 11, pp. 483–6.

Leighton, P. (1982) 'Employment contracts: a choice of relationships', *Employment Gazette*, vol. 90, no. 10, pp. 433–9.

Leighton, P. E. (1983a) *Contractual Arrangements in Selected Industries:* A study of employment relationships in industries with outwork, Research Paper no. 39, London: Department of Employment.

Leighton, P. (1983b) 'Employment and self-employment: some problems of law and practice', *Employment Gazette*, vol. 91, no. 5, pp. 197–203.

Martin, J. and Roberts, C. (1984) *Women and Employment: A Lifetime Perspective*, London: HMSO.

Millward, N. and Stevens, M. (1986) *British Workplace Industrial Relations 1980–1984: The DE/ESRC/PSI/ACAS Surveys*, Aldershot, Hants: Gower.

Office of Population Censuses and Surveys (OPCS) (1982) *General Household Survey 1980*, London: HMSO.

Trades Union Congress (1978) *Homeworking: A TUC Statement*, London: TUC.

Trades Union Congress (1985) *Homeworking: A TUC Statement*, London: TUC.

# 28

# The Comparative Advantages of Women's Disadvantages: Women Workers in the Strawberry Export Agribusiness in Mexico

LOURDES ARIZPE AND JOSEFINA ARANDA

In recent years, the women's movement the world over has stressed the need to provide women with increased access to salaried employment in order to improve their living conditions. In some industrialized countries, however, the recession and long-term economic trends are making it more difficult for women to get adequate employment, because, among other reasons, many of the jobs traditionally held by women in industries - particularly in textiles, garment manufacturing, and electronics - are being relocated in developing countries.[1] For several decades, many of the labour-intensive agricultural activities in which women worked as wage labourers have also been shifting to developing regions. In these regions, where male and female unemployment has been perennial, most governments welcome capital investments that will create employment and bring in foreign currency through exports. For example, many jobs formerly held by women in the northern cities and in the southern rural areas of the United States have moved south to Mexico and to other Latin American and Caribbean countries.

Behind this movement lie both the market pressures that force companies into a constant search for lower production costs, and the rationale of 'comparative advantages', according to which different economies are advised to specialize in

This essay was first published in *Signs*, 7(2), 1981.

1. Helen I. Safa, 'Runaway Shops and Female Employment: The Search for Cheap Labor', Signs 7(2), 1981; United Nations Industrial Development Office (UNIDO), 'Women in the Redeployment of Manufacturing Industry to Developing Countries' (UNIDO Working Paper no. 3, United Nations, 1980).

those products that they can sell profitably in the international market. But it so happens that such 'advantages' are closely linked to the cheap labour costs that come from women's social and economic 'disadvantages'; a woman's loss in one country may be some woman's gain in another country. Thus, it could be said that women in developing countries are gaining the jobs that have been redeployed from industrial countries. In fact, companies are using women's liberation slogans in deprived areas to justify giving jobs to eager young women rather than to older women or men who also desperately need jobs.[2]

The main issue raised by these events - whether the fluidity of the international labour market has become more of a zero-sum game for women than for men - cannot be fully discussed in this chapter, but some light can be shed on it by examining the extent to which such a 'gain' for women in a developing country actually improves their status and living conditions. A survey through interviews of young Mexican peasant women who have recently entered salaried employment in the strawberry-export packing plants of Zamora in the state of Michoacán helps us to understand the changes created by salaried work in their consciousness, their living conditions, and their situation within family and community.

## AGROINDUSTRY AND RURAL EMPLOYMENT IN DEVELOPING COUNTRIES

Worldwide, the optimism generated in the 1950s by the projects for rural community development and after that by the increase in agricultural production due to the Green Revolution came to an end in the 1970s. Meanwhile, in the last three decades rural unemployment, movement of peasants toward the cities, demographic growth, and the marginalization of rural women from the technological and economic benefits of development have increased rapidly in many countries of Latin America, Africa, and Asia.

Import-substitution policies as a strategy for development in such countries led to rising foreign debts due to the high costs of technology and of capital goods imported from the industrialized countries.[3] The governments of developing countries, in order to acquire foreign exchange to improve their balance of payments, have encouraged export-oriented agriculture, which in many African, Latin American and Asian rural areas has led to food scarcity.[4] Attempts to compensate for this scarcity by purchasing food from abroad have only perpetuated the vicious circle of dependency and poverty.[5]

The use of technological improvements from the Green Revolution increased yields and efficiency in rural production, but also led to higher concentration of agricultural resources in the hands of capitalist entrepreneurs.[6] In many countries

2. Linda Lim, *Women Workers in Multinational Corporations: The Case of the Electronics Industry in Malaysia and Singapore*, Michigan Occasional Papers no. 9 (Ann Arbor: University of Michigan, 1978).
3. Michael Todaro, *Economics for a Developing World* (London: Longman, 1977).
4. Francis Moore Lappe et al., *Food First: Beyond the Myth of Scarcity* (Boston: Houghton Mifflin, 1977).
5. Susan George, *How the Other Half Dies* (Montclair, NJ: Allanheld, Osmun, 1977).
6. Ingrid Palmer, 'Rural Poverty in Indonesia,' in *Poverty and Landlessness in Rural Asia* (Geneva: International Labour Office, 1977); Cynthia Hewitt de Alcantara, *La modernizacion de la agricultura Mexicana* (Mexico: Siglo XXI Editores, SA, 1978).

this concentration has displaced small family producers who have become agricultural labourers or migrants surviving precariously in the outskirts of overpopulated cities.[7] The expansion of this surplus population in rural and urban areas is being attacked through massive family planning campaigns, even though it is clear that population growth is closely linked to the conditions of extreme poverty and insecurity that prevail on the land. Another solution now being proposed to stop the rural exodus lies in the creation of rural employment through agroindustries, a policy sponsored both by national governments and by multinationals who have found a fertile field for investment.

Following this trend, in Latin America the per capita production of subsistence crops decreased by 10 per cent between 1964 and 1974, while that of agricultural products for export increased by 27 per cent.[8] During this same period US capital investments in agriculture for export in this region increased considerably, since investments in the food industry provide a 16.7 per cent profit abroad, compared to an 11.5 per cent return within the United States.[9] Since World War II, food processing companies have invested more in Mexico than in any other country of the Third World. An example of this type of investment is the strawberry industry in Zamora, which since 1970 has provided employment for approximately 10,000 young peasant women in its packing plants. Significantly, as in the textile and electronics industries that are also redeploying their production units abroad, the employment of women rather than men is clearly preferred in these agroindustries.[10] Why are young women preferred? Is it sufficient to say, as do the managers of such plants, that it is because they are 'more dextrous' and 'less restless'?

## PEASANT WOMEN AND RURAL DEVELOPMENT IN LATIN AMERICA

According to recent census statistics in Latin America, women's agricultural work shows a relative decrease in all countries and an absolute decrease in many.[11] This may be due, partly, to inadequate census registration of rural women's activities, but it also reflects increased female migration from rural areas, as well as the shift to other self-employment (especially petty trade) and intermittent domestic service – occupations that fall between the borders of organised economic activities and unpaid female domestic and community work.[12] Another important shift in rural women's activities has been reported among small family producers, where the agricultural labour of household women is intensified in order to

7. Lourdes Arizpe, *Migracion, etnicismo y cambio economico* (Mexico: Colegio de México, 1978).
8. R. Burbach and P. Flynn, 'Agribusiness Targets Latin America,' *NACLA Report on the Americas* 12 (January–February 1978): 5.
9. Ernst Feder, *El imperialismo fresa* (Mexico: Ed. Campesina, 1977).
10. Lim; and George.
11. International Labour Office (ILO), *Women in the Economic Activities of the World: A Statistical Analysis* (Geneva: ILO, 1980).
12. United Nations Development Program (UNDP), 'Rural Women's Participation in Development,' UNDP Evaluation Study no.3 (Geneva: United Nations, 1980); and Jocelyn Massiah, 'Family Structure and the Status of Women in the Caribbean, with Particular Reference to Women Who Head Households,' UNESCO, SS-80/Conf. 627/COL. 34 (paper delivered at the Conference on Women, Development and Population Trends, Paris, 1980).

increase or maintain productivity in deteriorating market conditions.[13] Finally, a fourth trend in which poor, rural women enter wage labour in agricultural and livestock production or in agroindustrial activities is also becoming widespread.[14]

These four trends appear separately or in combination in different countries and regions. But all of them stem from the same process:the economic crisis of small peasant family production in rural areas in Latin America. Discussion of the causes of this crisis go beyond the scope of this chapter, but the major trends in the status and employment of poor rural women in Latin America must be understood in the context of strategies these households use to survive in an increasingly difficult environment. There are also, of course, large numbers of women who have broken completely with their parents' or their husbands' households and who live and make decisions on their own. We find them, for example, along the Mexico-US border or in the shantytowns of all the major Latin American and Caribbean cities.[15] Their choice of economic activity and lifestyle constitutes an individual decision-making process that should be analysed as such within the narrow limits set by widespread unemployment and underemployment, cramped housing, and strict social pressures.

But in agrarian societies, there is little room for individualistic response. Especially in the case of young peasant women, the decision to work or to migrate is either made by the family patriarch or through permission granted by him. In any case, even more than sons, daughters are bound to their parents' households by the religious and social norms that prescribe absolute obedience, docility, and service toward others. In fact, this chapter will argue that it is precisely these qualities that make the young women so attractive as a work force. The data that follow should make this abundantly clear.

## STRAWBERRY PACKING AND FREEZING PLANTS IN ZAMORA

The strawberry agribusiness in Zamora began to expand in the mid-1960s, first through US capital and later through Mexican capital. Its competitiveness in the international market comes from the fact that Mexican strawberries are cultivated in the winter and that their transport and especially their labour costs are very low.[16] Production is completely dependent on US companies: the seedlings are imported from California; the export trade is handled entirely by six US

13. Carmen Diana Deere and Magdalena Léon de Leal, 'Peasant Production, Proletarianization, and the Sexual Division of Labor in the Andes', *Signs*, 7(2), 1981 and Cheywa Spindel, 'Capital Oligopólico e a producao rural de base familiar papel socio-economico da mulher' (unpublished research paper for the Rural Employment Policies Branch, ILO, Geneva, 1980).

14. Lucila Diaz Ronner and Maria Elena Munoz, 'La Mujer asalariada en el sector agricola,' *America indigena* 38 (April-June 1978): 327-34; Alicia E. Silva de Rojas and Consuelo Corredor de Prieto, 'La explotacion de la mano de obra femenina en la industria de las flores: Un estudio de caso en Colombia' (unpublished research paper for the Rural Employment Policies Branch, ILO, Geneva, 1980); Diana Medrano, 'El caso de las obreras de los cultivos de flores de los municipios de Chia, Cajica y Tabio en la sabana de Bogota, Colombia' (unpublished research paper for the Rural Employment Policies Branch, ILO, Geneva, 1980); and Marta Roldan, 'Trabajo asalariado y condicion de la mujer rural en un cultivo de exportacion: El caso de las trabajadoras del tomate en el estado de Sinaloa, Mexico' (unpublished research paper for the Rural Employment Policies Branch, ILO, Geneva, 1980).

15. María Patricia Fernández Kelly, 'Mexican Border Industrialization, Female Labour Force Participation and Migration,' *International Migration Review*.

16. Feder.

commercial brokers who have stopped attempts by Mexican plants to sell directly to the European market; and the strawberry prices are dictated by conditions in the US market, especially by the success of the California strawberry harvest.

Eighteen packing and freezing plants for strawberries functioned during the 1979–80 cycle in Zamora and in Jacona, a neighbouring village. Among them the hiring characteristics and working conditions for women, as well as male personnel, vary little: for example, some pay $14.70 (US¢66) per hour of work on the conveyor belts and others $14.00 (US¢63), but the lower wage is counterbalanced by payment of bus tickets and by better treatment for the workers. As Marta Rodriguez put it: 'X is the packing plant where women workers are treated the worst, and that is why they have many problems in hiring people. Even though they pay more there, the girls prefer better treatment, such as they get at Bonfil, where no overtime or commissions are paid. At X the bosses are almost Nazis.' It is interesting to note that firm X is the one that consistently shows the highest productivity and efficiency; it is the only one, for example, that has devices under the roofing to prevent swallows from nesting there. In most of the plants there is a minimum investment in installations: they are prefabricated metal structures that can be easily dismantled. Everything reflects short-term investment.

Fifty per cent of production for export in the 1978–9 cycle, which produced 88 million pounds of frozen strawberries (though the official figure given for exports was lower, 72.7 million pounds), was handled by the six companies we studied. Of these, three hire as many as 900 women workers at the height of the season, one hires 650, and two hire up to 350. One of the worst conditions of work women face in these plants is the acute annual fluctuation in labour demand according to changing conditions in cropping and in the price of sugar (sugar is added to the frozen strawberries). Figure 28.1 shows the typical annual fluctuation in Frutas

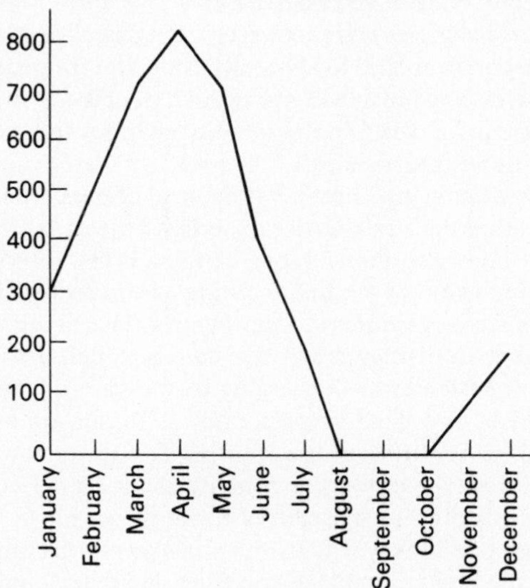


FIGURE 28.1 Annual fluctuation in number of female workers employed in the Frutas Refrigeradas plant

Refrigeradas, one of the companies surveyed. Except in special conditions, all plants are closed from four to six months each year and have a peak season for hiring from March to May. Later on we shall see how the hiring is organized and how the women workers adjust their working lives to such conditions.

## THE SITUATION OF WOMEN WORKERS IN THE STRAWBERRY PLANTS

Approximately 10 per cent of the personnel in the plants do administrative work; of these usually all managers and accountants are men, and the secretaries are young, single women from the town of Zamora. In production work, except for the young men who unload the strawberry crates from the trucks and those in charge of the refrigerators, the great majority of workers are young peasant women who live in outlying villages of the Zamora valley and the region.

The 300 women workers interviewed were selected at random from each of the six plants. On the average, between 5 and 10 per cent of the total female workers in each plant were interviewed, with the exception of El Duero, where 18.3 per cent of the women were surveyed. Interviewed in proportional numbers, they perform the different tasks described below:

*Stem removers* Women who remove the stems of the strawberries do piecework, that is, they are paid $5.00 (US¢23) per crate of strawberries, each weighing seven kilograms. A worker with magic hands is able to remove the stems of up to thirty-five crates of strawberries per day; one with slow hands can barely manage five crates per day. But the number of crates available to work on varies from week to week. For example, on February 4, 1980, the 400 workers at Frutas Refrigeradas were assigned only one crate of strawberries each, because it rained the previous week and very few strawberries were harvested. On days like this the expenses of the workers for transportation and food are the same, but they earn only according to the number of crates they finish. On average, 80 per cent of the women workers in the plants do this type of work; in the sample taken for the survey , they represent 75 per cent of those interviewed.

*Supervisors* These women are chosen by the head of personnel, or by the union leader, to check whether the strawberries tossed into the canals have had the stem properly removed. They represent 4 per cent of those interviewed, which is equivalent to the proportion of women working as supervisors in most plants.

*Selectors* Once the stem is removed, strawberries float along canals filled with water and disinfectant until they reach the conveyor belts, where the selectors pick out defective or rotten strawberries. As in the case of the supervisors, the selectors are chosen by the head of personnel or by the union leader, both of whom frequently show favouritism toward their friends or toward women from their own villages. This type of work is done by about 15 per cent of the women workers in the plants and by 18 per cent of those surveyed.

*Tray workers* From the conveyor belts the strawberries are put in tins or small boxes to be frozen, the best being placed on trays and frozen individually. This is also done by women who are selected in the manner described for those performing the two previous tasks. The women who performed the last three tasks mentioned were paid hourly, at the rate of $14.00 (US¢66) per hour during the 1979–80 cycle. Though a stem remover who works with amazing dexterity might earn a higher wage than women engaged in the other tasks, normally supervisors, selectors, and tray workers earn more. Those who work on an hourly wage enjoy greater prestige because they earn more and are closer to the higher-level employees. Many of the stem removers would prefer to work on the conveyor belts, especially those who, because of their age, are no longer able to work at high speed. But seniority normally is not taken into account for either promotion in tasks or other fringe benefits. The younger workers sometimes resent the favouritism, not so much for personal reasons, but rather because of loyalty to their villages: 'See here – why aren't there more from Tinguincharo on the conveyor belts?' But others say that it is a tiring job. For instance, Berta Olivares prefers working as a stem remover because, 'We can at least go and walk around a little when we go get a crate for strawberries to de-stem. . . but those on the conveyor belts are damned uncomfortable, they don't even let them move, they can hardly even sigh. We can even sing.'

Now that the scene of their work has been described, the first questions to be answered are: Who are these women? Did they work before? If so, what jobs did they hold?

### *Occupational Background of the Workers*

Of the women surveyed, 61 per cent stated that they had never worked before. It must be noted that these included those who, because they are very young, had not yet entered the work force. Those who had worked before going into the packing and freezing plants (41.3 per cent) performed the types of jobs indicated in tables 28.1 and 28.2. More than half worked in agriculture previously, and a third passed through paid domestic service. Their agricultural wage labour in the region has been replaced by immigrant labour, but this is not the case in paid domestic work, since housewives in Zamora repeatedly complained that 'you just can't find servants around here anymore.'

TABLE 28.1 Workers' previous employment by sector

| *Sector* | *Cases (N)* | % |
|---|---|---|
| Agriculture | 69 | 55.7 |
| Services | 38 | 30.7 |
| Industry | 7 | 5.8 |
| Trade | 7 | 5.8 |
| Agroindustry | 2 | 1.7 |
| Handicrafts | 1 | 0.3 |
| Total | 124 | 100.0 |

TABLE 28.2 Workers' previous occupations

| *Position* | *Cases (N)* | *%* |
|---|---|---|
| Agricultural labourer | 52 | 41.9 |
| Servant | 25 | 20.2 |
| Unpaid family worker in agriculture | 17 | 13.7 |
| Office or shop employee | 13 | 10.5 |
| Factory worker | 11 | 8.9 |
| Trader | 2 | 1.6 |
| Others | 4 | 3.2 |
| Total | 124 | 100.0 |

Table 28.2 shows that of the formerly wage-earning women whom the strawberry agroindustry has attracted most have been servants and agricultural labourers. We can now ask: why have they taken jobs in the strawberry plants? Most of the female employees prefer to work in these plants rather than as servants because, as Irma Cortes said, 'We are not subject to the will of *la patrona* [the employer] and we can live in our own homes in the village where we have friends.' Some of them like working in agriculture, but they find the work harsh. One of them said she preferred work in the fields 'because we are out in the air, and not under the discipline of the factory, even though it is much more tiring work; for example, pulling out the weeds growing in the fields is awful hard work, and one ends up with one's back real tired.'

Did they change jobs because of wage differentials? The income of 76.6 per cent of those interviewed increased with their employment in the plants, while that of 7.6 per cent remained the same. The high percentage of those who earned lower incomes (16.6 per cent) can be partly explained by the fact that many of these had only recently joined the plants and had not yet acquired the necessary skills, while others attended work irregularly. Of those who previously held jobs, 66.1 per cent worked in their own community, 28.2 per cent in the region, and only 0.7 per cent in another state, in Mexico City, or in the United States. Clearly, the strawberry companies have not brought back women working outside the region, nor have they attracted migrants from outlying regions, for the recruitment system precludes doing so. In fact, only 6.7 per cent of the female workers were born in another state, and more than half (60 per cent) were born in Zamora and Jacona, or in Ecuandureo, a neighbouring municipality. The rest come from other municipalities in the same region.

None of the women workers live by themselves or with friends. With one exception – a woman who was adopted by the family with whom she lives – they all live with family or kin. The fact that they still live with their families is due to a very deeply rooted social rule that forbids a young woman's leaving her father's home unless it be through marriage. But their choice of residence is also directly enforced by the acute housing scarcity in Zamora and Jacona and by the fact that the wages they earn are clearly insufficient to permit living in a boardinghouse, the only socially acceptable form of habitation for single women living away from home.

### Age, Marriage, and Schooling

Most of the workers, 68.7 per cent of the sample, are between fifteen and twenty-four years of age (table 28.3). Managers of the plants stated that they prefer to hire young women because of their higher productivity, and because they are 'very quick with their hands' and 'concentrate better than the men'. In fact, the younger women's manual dexterity is crucial in the task of removing the stems, but it is of only secondary importance in selecting and packing the strawberries; older women could do the latter tasks just as well. In only two of the plants, however, were older women predominantly chosen for these. Additional factors that influence the preference for hiring young women are analysed in the next sections.

Girls usually begin to work in the plants when they are twelve to fifteen years old, and they work until they marry, normally between the ages of seventeen and twenty-one. As one of them put it, 'The women marry before they are twenty because at that age the men say we have already missed the last boat'. Those who do not marry continue working, and a few young married women return to work in the plants.

Of the female workers interviewed, 85.3 per cent are single, 9.0 per cent are married, 3.0 per cent are divorced or abandoned, and 2.7 per cent are widows. Almost all workers over the age of thirty are widowed, divorced, or separated from their husbands. Most of them support their children and perhaps their parents or siblings. The few married women workers state that their husbands do not send back enough money from the United States where they are working.

One older woman told us that in the early times of the packing plants women stood in long lines outside the plants hoping to be hired: 'There were little girls, young girls and adults, even old women.' But, at present, the increase in the number of plants has led to a relative scarcity of women workers, particularly during the peak time of the season. At this busy time, plants hire women of all ages, including twelve-year-olds and older women. Then, as strawberries begin to come in at a slower rate, the management begins to eliminate workers: 'First the little girls, then the lazy ones, then others begin to drop out by themselves when they see that there is very little working time left,' one worker told us.

Sixteen per cent, mostly the older workers, have not been to school at all, while 31 per cent attended primary school up to the third grade. This low average in schooling can be explained by conditions in their communities, but it is

TABLE 28.3 Ages of female workers

| *Age* | *Cases (N)* | *%* |
|---|---|---|
| 12–14 | 30 | 10.0 |
| 15–19 | 141 | 47.1 |
| 20–24 | 65 | 21.6 |
| 25–29 | 16 | 5.3 |
| 30–50 | 39 | 13.0 |
| 51–80 | 9 | 3.0 |
| Total | 300 | 100.0 |

significant to note that 3.7 per cent have reached the high school or preparatory school level, since in theory their education should have given them access to jobs with higher incomes and prestige. But the fact is that very few such jobs are available in Zamora, and, besides, these women explained that they earn more money working at a fast pace in the plants than they would working in a shop or an office.

Although they seem to recognize this, the great majority of the women are convinced that their low degree of schooling prevents them from getting other jobs, and they complain bitterly that their parents, especially their fathers, did not allow them to go on studying:'Women are not allowed to finish [school] because our parents say it does not pay for itself because we then go and get married, and it has only been a waste.' 'If I were to study,' said another, 'I could be a secretary, and I would stop doing this very tiring job.' The mythical nature of this hope becomes clear if we realize that, as has happened in other developing countries, an increase in levels of education would lead to an increase in job entrance requirements, and consequently the same proportion of less qualified women – even if their educational level were higher in absolute terms – would continue filling the lower-level jobs.

This hypothesis is further strengthened if we compare the plant workers surveyed in Zamora with a group of female agricultural labourers, surveyed in the state of Aguascalientes north of Michoacán, who pick grapes seasonally.[17] The profile of marital status among the grape pickers resembles that of the workers in the strawberry plants: 80 per cent are single, 8 per cent are married, 3 per cent are divorced or separated, and 9 per cent are widowed.[18] In ages and schooling, the percentage distribution is also similar, but there are significant differences.

The similarities in both age structure and schooling indicate that roughly the same social group of women enter either of those jobs (tables 28.4 and 28.5). But more women with higher schooling between the ages of twelve and nineteen enter strawberry-factory work in Zamora. The foregoing suggests that many young, single girls enter agroindustry who otherwise would not work for wages and, second, that strawberry-plant work attracts women whose higher educational levels make it unlikely that they would accept work in agriculture. However, additional data not included in the surveys on the educational levels in the communities would be necessary to confirm the latter hypothesis.

### *Social Attitudes toward Women's Work in the Factories*

When the strawberry industry first began, it was very difficult for the plant managers to recruit enough women workers. They could get those who were already working in other jobs but were unable to attract young women whose families were not in dire need of additional income. The women's reluctance to enter paid employment was due to the very real fear, confirmed by women's experiences, that unaccompanied young women in public places would be 'stolen'. Carmen Garcia summarizes it neatly: 'Previously, it was really rotten for the girls, because they were frequently stolen when they were going to fetch water, or to wash clothes or to bring the *nixtamal* [maize dough]. . . . They were

17. Ronner, p. 331.
18. Ibid.

TABLE 28.4 Ages of female agricultural labourers in Aguascalientes and women workers in agroindustry in Zamora

| Age | *Women workers in Zamora (%)* | *Women labourers in Aguascalientes (%)* |
|---|---|---|
| 12–19 | 57.0 | 52 |
| 20–29 | 27.0 | 21 |
| 30–39 | 7.7 | 10 |
| 40 or over | 8.3 | 17 |
| Total | 100.0 | 100 |

*Sources:* For the Aguascalientes: Lucia Diaz Ronner and Maria Elena Munoz, 'La Mujer asalariada en el sector agricola,' *America indigena* 38 (April–June 1978): 327–34. Other statistics from authors' research

even stolen with the help of a gun or a machete. They were taken into the woods and then the men would come to ask their parents for the girl [in marriage]. Most of the girls did marry them, even if they did not want to, and here divorce is out of the question. If they don't get on together, the woman just puts up with it. Here it is customary for the husbands to beat the women when they are drunk, they say that blows make women love them more.' Yet, as it happens, the fact that the young girls are no longer 'stolen' as often in the peasant villages of the region as they were in the past is attributed mainly to their working in the strawberry plants, although no one ever explains exactly why this is so.

At first, the fathers flatly refused their daughters permission to work in the factories. One woman told us: 'The parents are not used to one's working and in the village people gossip a lot, they say that the women who go out to work go with many men.' Not long ago it was still forbidden for men and women in the villages

TABLE 28.5 Schooling of female agricultural workers in Aguascalientes and women workers in agroindustry in Zamora

| *Education* | *Women workers in Zamora (%)* | *Women labourers in Aguascalientes (%)* |
|---|---|---|
| None | 16.0 | 32.0 |
| 1st–3rd grade, primary | 31.0 | 28.0 |
| 4th–6th grade, primary | 49.3 | 40.0 |
| Secondary or preparatory | 3.7 | — |
| Total | 100.0 | 100.0 |

*Source:* See table 28.4

to address one another on the street. What the parents most feared, did occasionally happen. An experienced worker, Ines Gomez, explained: 'When it [work in the plants] began, it turned out that many of the girls got pregnant because they did not know how to look out for themselves, and as we move in an environment of "machismo" and paternalism, it happened frequently . . . but now the girls know how to handle themselves, now they even want to study and improve themselves.' The young women workers see their situation in a different way and complain bitterly: 'All they do is spread rumours about us. Many boys say they won't marry those who work in the plants, and all the girls from the village work there, but of course later they themselves are after us. They spread many untrue stories about us. Some of our nieces even went around saying that we were pregnant, and that we had left the children at the Social Security.'

The young women workers' situation is further complicated by the migration of most of the marriageable men: 'The girls don't go North [to the United States] because people talk badly about them. Even if we just go to Zamora they talk badly, we can never go anywhere. . . . The boys are allowed to go North and they come back real proud, some of them shack up with the American girls over there. They say they are very loose, that they even go after the boys. Others do return here to get married.'

Initially the local priests were opposed to the women's factory work too. One incident illustrates the situation very clearly. The strawberry plants in Jacona were unable to get female workers because every Sunday the local priest thundered that women would go to hell if they sinned by going out to work in the factories. It is said that the problem was solved when the owners of the plant spoke with the priest and offered to pay for the cost of a new altar for the parish church. Since that day, the local priest has exalted the dignity of work.

## *Wages and Expenditures*

As has been noted, the workers' wages are subject to the rate at which the plants buy strawberries during the year and to their own level of skill. The monthly average wage among workers surveyed is $1126 (US$51.18). Eleven per cent earn an average of $1750 (US$79.51), 26 per cent earn an average of $750 (US$34.09) per month , while 8 per cent earn an average of $350 (US$15.90). These wage levels are very far below the legal minimum wage, which amounted to $4260 (US$193.63) for that region in 1980. Since a single person, let alone a family with children cannot survive on this income, such low wages can only be considered as complementary to the main income of a family.

Worse still is the fact that the wages these women get vary enormously on a day-by-day and week-by-week basis. The season begins in November or December and lasts until July or August. However, during that period there are 'bad months', as the women call them – November, December, January, February, August, September – in which they earn an average of less than $500 (US$22.72) per month. During the good months they may earn as much as $2200 (US$90.90) per month. Most of the women are not hired at the plants for the whole year; 56 per cent work from seven to nine months; 5 per cent work from ten to twelve months; 16 per cent from four to six months; 11.6 per cent from one to three; and 11.3 per cent do not get to work even one month per year. Many of those in this latter group work only on the Saturdays during the peak season, or they are younger sisters of the workers who tag along a few days per week.

During the months when there is no work in the plants, 75.3 per cent remain at home helping with the domestic work; some do embroidering or knit pieces for sale. The surprisingly large number of women who follow this pattern indicates that these families do not urgently require a constant income from the women workers. In some cases – as, for example, one where the daughter supports herself and her mother – the income earned in the plant in the months of seasonal work is sufficient to keep them during the three months without work. Among the 24.3 per cent of the workers who do work during these months, 7 per cent work as servants, 11 per cent go harvesting in the fields as day labourers, 1.0 per cent work in offices, and 0.3 per cent migrate to the United States. The remainder work in the informal sector in a variety of ways.

To what extent do these predominantly peasant families depend on the women workers' income? The majority (61.6 per cent) answered that their work only partially supports their families, 20.7 per cent replied that they give no financial help to their families, and 17.7 per cent stated that they offer major support. It is usual for one of the younger girls to hand over the entire weekly wage to her father or mother, who then little by little lets her have whatever money she requires for her expenses. Table 28.6 shows that the correlation between the amount a worker gives her parents and the amount she earns is not significant.

How are their wages spent? What the workers keep for themselves, they spend on fashionable clothes, costume jewellery, romantic comics and stories, and beauty products. But the larger part of their wage, handled by their parents, goes into buying household consumer goods. This has been a boom for shops selling furniture and electric appliances. Some of the consumer goods purchased in the poorer households are basic items such as gas stoves, beds, wardrobes, and sewing machines; in other households the goods may be television, radios, blenders, and record players. Only a few households buy luxury items such as enormous consoles, fancy furniture, porcelain figurines, wine glasses, and so on. The survey indicates, however, that the parents buy these items not only for prestige but also because they can sell or pawn them when times get hard. It must be noted that the commercial boom in Zamora is due only in part to the women workers' income; it is mainly a result of the income in dollars sent back by the male migrants working in the United States. Even so, the pattern of consumption is the same in both cases.

TABLE 28.6 Workers' monthly wages by proportion given to parents (per cent)

| *Monthly wages (pesos)* | *All* | *Almost all* | *One-half* | *A little* | *Nothing* |
|---|---|---|---|---|---|
| 200–1000 | 36.9 | 15.7 | 23.8 | 10.5 | 13.1 |
| 1001–2000 | 30.1 | 25.3 | 27.4 | 12.4 | 4.8 |
| 2001–3000 | 38.2 | 27.4 | 25.4 | 7.2 | 1.8 |
| Over 3000 | 11.2 | 44.4 | 11.1 | 22.2 | 11.1 |
| All wage categories[a] | 31.0 | 24.0 | 25.7 | 11.0 | 5.7 |

[a] 2.6 per cent of workers surveyed did not answer this question.

### *Recruitment of Workers for the Plants*

Women workers are recruited each season through social networks in the communities. In the plants that have unions, the union secretary chooses women delegates in each village or hamlet; in plants that don't have a union, the head of personnel chooses these delegates. Once the word is sent to them that they should begin recruiting, these delegates go around the village letting everyone know that they are hiring. They list the names of those women who want to go to work, purportedly giving preference to experienced workers. But Antonieta Castro complained that previous experience matters little: 'Some of the new ones are given preference by the bosses, because they give them *gollete* [some present]. We don't get angry about this, we only feel hurt.' The 'loyalty' that a worker has shown toward the general secretary of the union or the company is also taken into account during compilation of the lists, as are personal preferences and group rivalries within the community. In hiring, the company follows the list made by the delegate, moving through it progressively as the season advances. The recruiter in the village, usually an older woman, is socially responsible for the young girls she recruits as workers. Parents sometimes allow their daughters to go only if they trust the recruiter. This responsibility also gives the latter the power to decide who will work in the plant.

### *Conditions of Work*

Hiring conditions and benefits in most plants are clearly below legal requirements stated in Mexican law. In the first place there are no contracts or permanent jobs for the workers. (According to the law the companies should pay the minimum wage, establish fixed working schedules, and hire the workers permanently during the entire year.) In the second place, fringe benefits are nonexistent: plant workers have no Social Security, nor do they have adequate medical services. More mothers could work if the plants had nurseries, and by law factories must provide one whenever there are more than thirty permanent women workers. When the women ask for a nursery, however, they are turned down. One manager said: 'We saw that the nursery was not really necessary because only two or three children come along with their mothers, and that is why we did not put one in.'

### *Women's Perception of their Work in the Plants*

Although these conditions persist, and in spite of the fact that many of the women employed in the plant consider the work to be tiring and oppressive, they prefer it because their only alternative would be to remain shut in their homes doing domestic work or to work in jobs that are even more underpaid. Of the workers surveyed, 65 per cent said that they prefer to work outside their home. As Amalia Vega put it: 'We like so much to go out and work in the packing plant that when we return to our village in the evening we skip along the road dancing and singing. We don't mind about being tired [after a working day of eight to eleven hours]; because we have earned our few pennies and have left the little ranch for a while, we are very happy. In the village you get bored by seeing the same faces all day long and listening to the same gossip. By working we entertain ourselves.'

This is, in fact, a very fair assessment of the situation. When asked what type of work they like best, 59 per cent answered that they prefer to work in a strawberry plant; only 4.5 per cent prefer to work on the land, and 36.5 per cent would prefer to be employed in an office.

Although four out of every five workers interviewed said they wanted improvements in their working conditions, particularly in wages and in the treatment they receive from their bosses, there are no real channels for protest. Only half of them belonged to a union, but this was due to the fact that only four of the six plants had a union. However, less than half of the workers (46.7 per cent) though that unionization could help them get better working conditions. This distrust reflects the fact that the existing unions closely collaborate with management. The pragmatic attitude of the union leaders, some of them women, is evident in the statement of one woman leader. Asked how she and other leaders got along with management, she said: 'Fortunately there has always been a good relationship. People get to understand each other by talking. Also, we are interested in the company not having a loss, otherwise, we don't get *utilidades* [a profit-sharing government scheme].' In actual fact, workers rarely receive *utilidades*, which are sometimes used to pay for the annual fiesta and Mass in the plant. As a result, workers hardly participate in union activities: 'We get bored going to the meetings,' one worker told us. 'We don't understand anything and we get nothing out of it. We just waste our time.'

Almost all the younger workers consider their job in the agroindustry as a stage in their life that allows them to get out of the daily routine of the village. More than half (58 per cent) answered that they do not plan to go on working once they get married. In so many words, they were saying: 'Why, that's what I'm getting married for, to stop working!' Of those who say they may continue to work, most believe they will marry a bum and will end up having to support their household.

## CONCLUSIONS

Why does the strawberry agroindustry predominantly employ women? It is true that the jobs of removing stems and selecting strawberries require a manual dexterity that men do not usually achieve, but this is not the main reason that the industry employs women. In the region of Zamora, agroindustry cannot compete with the wages paid in the United States in order to attract and retain migrant male labour. At the same time there is a large population of young women who have very few alternatives for work. The strawberry plants do not have to compete with urban wages for women workers, since the emigration of women from the region is not frequent; male emigration largely covers the deficit in the budget of most peasant families. Moreover, the great majority of young women in peasant families have access only to paid domestic work or to wage labour on the land, both of them unrewarding jobs.

Therefore, the main reason for employing women is that they can be paid much lower wages than those stipulated by law, and can be asked to accept conditions in which there is a constant fluctuation in schedules and days of work. Here it seems to us that the companies take advantage of the traditional idea that any income earned by a daughter, wife, or mother is an 'extra' over and above the main income of the father, husband, or son. If such wages were paid to male workers, the low income and the instability of the job would be untenable in the long run; workers would either move to other jobs or organize and strike to get higher wages.

Other results of the analysis support this view. That the percentage of women household-heads in the packing and refrigerating plants is very low - 5.7 per cent as compared to 12 per cent in the region as a whole - suggest that the wages paid by the plants cannot constitute the central income of a household. In a circular fashion, of course, it also reflects the factories' preference for young, unmarried workers.

Thus, the plants attract many young women - approximately one-half of the women workers - who normally would not enter wage-earning jobs if the plants did not exist. So it seems, at least, from a comparison made with a group of agricultural labourers from Aguascalientes and from the fact that 42.4 per cent of the workers surveyed gave only half or less than half of their wages to their households. Further support for this hypothesis is found in the large majority of women workers who do not seek alternative work during the months they are not employed in the plants. Another advantage for the plants is the constant turnover among women workers. This impermanence allows a company considerable savings in wage increases due to seniority as well as in payments for maternity, disease, or disablement and in old-age pensions.It also prevents the workers from accumulating information and experience that would lead them to organize and to demand improvements in hiring and working conditions. Meanwhile, the traditional culture itself assures continuous instability by making marriage the only aspiration for women.

Clearly, the strawberry agroindustry in Zamora can exist only thanks to particular conditions by which cheap female labour is readily available. This conclusion coincides with that reached by Ernst Feder, who points to the low cost of labour as one of the most important factors in making the Mexican strawberry industry competitive internationally.[19] Thus, the 'comparative advantages' of this industry in the international market are closely associated with the 'comparative disadvantages' of young, inexperienced, rural women who suffer social, legal, and economic discrimination. From a sociological point of view, what the agribusiness capitalists have done is to make use of certain social and cultural characteristics of the region, that is, the high demographic growth, the traditional cultural values that assign a subordinate role to women, the family structure of the communities, and the local patterns of consumption. The key question to be asked is whether this way of using resources will improve the living conditions of the women and of their communities.

Have conditions for women changed with their entry into salaried industrial work? This study shows that they have changed very little. The great majority of workers continue to live in their parents' homes; a very few go to live with other relatives in Zamora, but always under the same conditions of subordination and restriction they experienced in their own homes. About half of them hand over the greater part of their wages to their parents or use their earnings to support

19. Feder.

their own families. Thus they have only slightly increased their personal consumption. Their families, of course, have an improved standard of living, at least temporarily.

Although the women have more freedom when working outside their homes, they are harassed by the men in the streets and are not free to move around the town or the villages on their own. Even when travelling to and from the plants the young women are closely supervised by the recruiters and the union leaders. There have been some changes: the young girls are not 'stolen' as frequently as before, and apparently they have a more decisive voice as to whom they will marry. Also, some have become eager to study and to get ahead.

But work in this agroindustry, for the majority of women, is certainly no way to get ahead. There are no promotions; the workers get no encouragement or help to acquire skills or education; and the instability and low wages of the jobs, as mentioned previously, do not offer any prospects for improvement in the future. Predictably, under these conditions no significant cultural change is taking place. On the contrary, the lack of prospects for promotion in the agroindustry, the low wages, and the high level of unemployment only push the workers back into the traditional hope of marriage as the only road toward a better future. Only a few of the young women, mostly those who have not married, have acquired new aspirations about employment possibilities and lifestyles. For these too, however, it will be very difficult to find employment once the strawberry industry declines. The strawberry companies take advantage of the traditional values and conditions that subordinate women and end up reinforcing this traditional order. In fact, it is in their interest to oppose any initiatives to change the passive, submissive role of women in Zamora. In this sense, no 'modernization' of women's roles is evident in the region.

What has been the impact of the strawberry agroindustry on the communities of the region? In the short run the industry has provided a better standard of living for rural families. The majority use the women's incomes to improve their housing and, particularly, to purchase household goods – furniture and electric appliances – which also serve as a form of saving. The workers' wages, then, flow rapidly through the merchants of Zamora toward the urban industries that manufacture these consumer goods.

But while the market for consumer goods has expanded, the poorer groups in the region have not been brought into the market. Because of the hiring practices in the plants, work is not given to women heads of households, or to the poorer male and female labourers – those who most require an income. Rather, since the survey shows that the majority of the workers do not support themselves, it would seem that jobs are given mostly to young women of the middle-level peasant families, whose wages serve to improve their families' standard of living. Although such a gain is not to be underestimated, it benefits only minimally those households whose economic survival depends entirely or partially on women's wages. As a result, older women who are heads of households are pushed back into the strenuous, harsh, and even more poorly paid job of strawberry picking in the fields.

The strawberry agroindustry is not creating conditions for the future development of the region. It is not training workers, nor is it promoting or improving the social services. It does not serve to stem emigration of men to the United States.

The cultivation of strawberries, on the contrary, tends toward the concentration of land and capital while it displaces and undermines production in small landholdings.

Thus, it seems to us that the strawberry agroindustry has provided some short-term improvements, but in the long run - aside from the profits that flow mainly to US agribusiness concerns and to affluent local entrepreneurs - it will leave behind nothing but ashes when it collapses. The collapse is expected, according to two plant managers, in about three to five years. It is difficult to refrain from apocalyptic forecasts when we can see that the decline of this agroindustry will plunge the region back into underdevelopment: peasant household incomes will fall, massive unemployment will force countless women and families to migrate, and the hopes for a better life that have been raised among women will, once again, be destroyed. Basically, nothing will have changed for women. Since the strawberry industry requires female workers whose income is not essential for the household, it bypasses the needy and predominantly employs women from middle-income groups. Since it requires submissive and docile workers, it reinforces partriarchal and authoritarian structures. Since it benefits from a constant turnover of workers, it does not oppose the machismo that confines women to home and marriage.

The basic dilemma emerges very clearly under a feminist analysis. Much of the data - for instance, Amalia Vega's touching description of the joy she and other women feel at being allowed to leave the narrow horizons of their villages - shows that the plants improve the lives of women and therefore from a feminist point of view should be defended. At the same time, salaries and working conditions at these plants are dismally exploitative, comparing unfavourably both to the norms set down by Mexican law and to actual situations elsewhere in Mexican industry; for this reason they should be denounced and opposed.

An even more painful dilemma faced by women's movements in situations such as this is that women whose consciousness has been raised by a temporary prosperity will be left stranded when economic and social survival again becomes difficult if not impossible, while industries that were once a source of hope move to regions populated by another group of docile and disadvantaged women. Thus, by the time the strawberry agribusiness - or the US assembly plants along the Mexican border, for that matter - move to other countries that offer lower production costs, the jobs Mexican women had temporarily gained from the loss experienced by their US counterparts will also be lost to them. The jobs will then become a temporary gain for, perhaps, Haitian or Honduran women.

In this way, women's 'comparative disadvantages' in the labour market in any given country can, at some point in time, be translated into 'comparative advantages' for companies, capitals, and governments in the international markets. When disadvantaged women organize to get even minimal improvements in wages and working conditions, the 'comparative advantages' are lost, and investments go elsewhere. Clearly, all women lose along this chain. This being the case, one can only conclude that discrimination against women in employment, reflecting as it does the disadvantages women suffer from attitudes about gender, from social customs,. and from their lack of political power, cannot be fought effectively in one place or country unless an appropriate international perspective is developed.

29

# The Subcontracting of Cleaning Work in Israel: a Case in the Casualization of Labour

DEBORAH BERNSTEIN

## THE CHARACTERISTICS OF CASUAL LABOUR

Casual labour has been defined as labour lacking a moderate degree of security of income and employment. It is, in these respects, the reverse of organized labour, which has attempted to make security of employment and income one of its central goals. Casual labour is often equated with the secondary, or peripheral, labour market and, in the context of Third World countries, with the informal economic sector. This implies characteristics such as low pay, few rights, few skills, little training, little security, easy firing, few options for vertical mobility or for movement into the primary labour market, and large turnover. It has often been pointed out that the secondary labour market, or the peripheral economy, attracts and recruits the more vulnerable segments of the labour force: immigrants, both legal and illegal; racial, ethnic and national minorities; women; and vulnerable age groups, primarily the young and the elderly. A number of more recent studies have attempted to illuminate some of the specific forms of casual labour. Bromley and Gerry, in discussing casual labour in the Third World, distinguish between four categories:

1 Short term wage-work – paid and contracted by the day, week, month or season, or paid and contracted for fixed terms or tasks, with no assurance of continuity of employment.

This essay was first published in *Sociological Review*, 34(2), 1986. An earlier version was presented at the BSA conference at Bradford, 1984. I would like to thank the participants of the session for their comments and suggestions.

2 Disguised wage-work – [the case in which] a firm or group of firms regularly and directly appropriates part of the product of a person's work without that person being legally an employee of the firm or group of firms.
3 Dependent work – [the case in which] the worker is not in wage work but is dependent upon one or more large enterprises for credit, the rental of premises, a monopolistic, or oligopolistic supply of raw material [etc.].
4 True self-employment – a person [who] works independently, obtaining an income without engaging in wage-working, disguised wage-working or dependent working. (1979: 5–6)

Most students who discuss forms of labour organization within the secondary labour market have focused on wage labour. The forms of casual wage labour which have gained some attention have been: outwork (Rubery and Wilkinson 1981), especially subcontracting (e.g. Wong 1983) and homework (Hoy and Kennedy 1983; Allen 1983; Haug 1983); piece-work (e.g. Herzog 1980); part-time work (Dombois and Osterland 1982); and temporary work (Caire 1982).

The initial discussion of secondary labour characteristics stemmed from a dual economy perspective, which led to a clear demarcation between primary and secondary markets, primary and secondary industries and core and peripheral geographical locations. As studies became both more detailed and more concrete it became clear that different types of labour can and *do* exist within the same industry, at times in the same firms and even the same public office or institution. Rubery and Wilkinson have argued that:

> The persistence and even expansion in the use of a wide range of forms of casualized labour, from home-working to on-site labour-only subcontracting combined with evidence of the vertical disintegration of production in advanced, as well as declining sectors, demands a reinterpretation of the relative importance of different forms of labour organization. (1981: 116)

Detailed case studies in a variety of countries have pointed to the restructuring of the labour process within the primary sector and the incorporation of various types of secondary workers through a variety of means, such as integrating outwork as part of the process of production (Friedman 1978); decentralizing production (Murray 1983); and introducing temporary workers into the office. In many cases these changes entail physical separation between segments of workers involved in the production of the same commodity. In other cases, when the temporary worker or even some types of subcontracted workers are introduced into the same location of production or service, the separation is not physical but social.

Attention has also turned to the relations *between* the different segments of workers within the same industry, questioning the role of secondary casual workers not only in relation to capital but also to the core of organized, secure, and at least potentially mobile primary workers.

As noted above, one of the essential features of casual labour is the temporariness of its employment. Such temporariness can result from a variety of factors, among them seasonal fluctuations in the demand for the particular labour, the impact of technological innovations, the competitiveness of the industry and the effects of recession and budget cuts. The temporary duration of employment or even the realistic prospect of it being a temporary duration, inevitably affects the relation between worker and employer. The employer will be motivated to extract the maximum labour for the duration of employment, thus intensifying the labour process. At the same time he will be motivated to limit his remuneration to the immediate payment for labour actually given, rather than to forms of payment which affect the reproduction of labour in the long term, such as pension schemes, sick funds and even paid leave and sick leave. Thus the aspects inherent in capitalist relations, the extraction of labour for the maximization of profits in return for the reproduction of labour power, will be interpreted in the most immediate and narrow sense. A long term view of the workers and their needs will be lacking to a much greater extent than in the case of non-casual labour, even though all capitalist relations entail the same basic problem.

The temporariness of employment severely inhibits the ability of workers to organize effectively and to enforce their own understanding of their needs, which would include not only adequate pay, but also rest, recreation, physical well-being, old age security, etc. Furthermore, in those cases where such benefits have been secured by law, through the political power of an organized working class, casual workers will have severe difficulty in ensuring the implementation of the law. The employer, in turn, will have little incentive, in terms of his own interests, in taking on the costs of long term benefits as he does not expect a long term relation with his labour force. Thus casual labour is characterized by temporary employment and income, intensified extraction of labour, immediate forms of payment and weak organization among the workers themselves. This last feature both reinforces the former ones and in itself affects the workers' sense of powerlessness and vulnerability.

The distinction between casual and non-casual labour is not a stable or static one. In the beginning of the twentieth century it appeared as if causal work was a residue of the earlier periods of the industrial revolution and would soon completely disappear.[1] The latter part of the twentieth century seems to show that casual labour has remained an integral part of production and service. Furthermore, some changes in the process of production have increased the importance of casual labour and introduced it in industries and processes where work had previously been centralized and organized.

The process of casualization both reflects and shapes existing class relations. An erosion of the level of organization among segments of workers, a weakening of their control over the extraction of their labour, as well as over the returns they receive, are possible when the working class in general either loses ground in relation to capital and state, or is highly segmented within itself. Such segmentation distinguishes between organized and non-organized, strong and weak, secure and insecure elements, a distinction often overlapping other distinctions of gender, race, nationality and age. Such segments do not merely exist side by side but relate to one another. It is still an open debate as to whether the relationship is one in

1. A report of the Chief Inspectorate of Factories and Workshops for 1925, quoted by Hoy and Kennedy takes this position clearly: – 'There is a consensus of opinion that homework is on the decline' (1983: 229). Rubery and Wilkinson (1981: 118) point to a similar position in the literature dealing with subcontracting, mentioning, among others, Braverman (1974: 63–4).

which the casual workers reinforce the ability of the core workers to retain their privileged position or whether these are threatened by the former.

To conclude, we have been arguing so far that casual labour, typical of the secondary labour market, is not a distinct separate and marginal form of economic activity. Rather, it is embedded in all economic sectors and is an integral element in class relations, giving flexibility to capital and enabling some segments of the working class to enjoy a more secure and advantageous position. Nevertheless, an extended period of recession, which witnesses not only wide scale unemployment but also a restructuring of labour processes and organization, raises the question of how secure the latter segments are, and for how long.

This chapter deals with one form of casual labour, that of subcontracted cleaning work. Cleaning work is in many respects the epitome of secondary labour, and is a clear example of recruitment of already vulnerable groups; primarily women, often immigrant women or women of ethnic, racial or national minorities. We shall argue that subcontracted cleaning work manifests all the characteristics of casual labour discussed above. On the other hand, cleaning workers employed directly by the institutions in which they work, enjoy a more secure, organized and rewarded position. Thus the emergence of subcontracted cleaning work entails a process of casualization for existing and for potential cleaning workers. The chapter discusses the reasons for the transition from one form of labour to another, and the implications of this transition on workers' conditions of labour and their organization.

The study of subcontracted cleaning work was carried out in Israel during the year of 1984, in the area of Haifa. The study involved the interviewing of close to one hundred workers from ten different institutions: four hospitals, four institutions of education and two industrial enterprises. Workers were asked about their previous work experience, their conditions of pay and social benefits, extent of organization and relations with the subcontractor and/or his supervisors. The interviews were conducted in various locations: in the work place, in the workers' homes and at seminars of the Haifa Workers' Council. Difficult methodological problems arose, to a large extent, from the nature of casual labour. Most information given by the workers was not substantiated by documents such as pay slips. As the workers were not well informed in many cases, it was difficult to determine whether they were referring to their net or gross income. It was very difficult to have a satisfactory conversation during work hours as the workers were in fear of the subcontractors, who, in fact, on a number of occasions chased the interviewers away. Meeting at other locations was also difficult, as many of the workers were young Arab women who commuted daily from villages outside Haifa. Access to the women in their villages was also difficult.

Additional interviews were conducted with management personnel concerning the reasons for the transition to subcontracted cleaning; with trade union officials concerning the attempts at organizing subcontracted workers; and with a number of subcontractors concerning the workers they recruit and their conditions of work. The latter were extremely reluctant to meet us, and their information, as far as it could be substantiated by other sources, was far from accurate. A number of observations were carried out in two institutions but once again they were discontinued because of the objection of the subcontractor.

The cleaning work studied took various forms. One form was that of individual women cleaning offices, shops, banks, etc. after work hours. In such cases the pay was usually according to the area cleaned and there was no direct, on the spot, supervision or control. The other characteristic form was that of a number of workers, sometimes a very large number, cleaning an institution under direct control and supervision of the subcontractor or his inspectors. In some cases, such as hospitals, work went on all day, in two shifts. In other cases, such as the university, it was carried out after classes were finished or before they began. In such cases pay was usually calculated according to time rather than area. The exact tasks to be carried out were specified in detail. In all cases the work was primarily manual, washing floors, wiping surfaces and cleaning toilets. Machines were only introduced to a limited extent for the cleaning of linoleum or marble floors.

## CLEANING WORK

There are three main types of paid cleaning work: paid domestic work or domestic service; direct wage labour employed by institutions; and subcontracted labour employed by cleaning contractors. While cleaning workers employed directly by private and especially public institutions in Israel have increasingly acquired, over the last two or three decades, some important features of organized labour, the other two categories - domestic workers and subcontracted cleaners - demonstrate practically all the features of casual labour. In the following discussion we shall focus on one of these categories, that of subcontracted cleaning workers.

The contracting out of cleaning work has spread rapidly in Israel over the last decade, though it does not appear to be a totally new phenomenon. Scattered evidence exists of public institutions contracting out their cleaning work in the late 1950s and early 1960s. Those early instances of subcontracting appear to have aroused strong opposition among both the workers thus employed and trade union officers, especially those active among female service workers.[2]

The opposition to subcontracting combined, at the time, with a general trend within the General Federation of Labour - the Histadrut - aimed at incorporating temporary workers into the ranks of organized labour to a much greater extent than had existed before. The mass immigration of the 1950s led to large scale temporary employment in almost all spheres. Workers employed on a temporary basis were often members of the Histadrut, thus enjoying some of the services it provided, but were not considered part of the organized work force at the work place level, so were not represented by the workers' committee and did not benefit from collective bargaining. By the early 1960s unemployment caused by mass immigration had all but ceased, and the Histadrut turned its attention to strengthening its position among those workers who had for many years remained temporary workers, recurringly dismissed and re-employed. During these years, such workers improved their position markedly, often securing permanent employment and payment on a monthly, rather than daily, basis. This process included temporary cleaning workers who were employed by public and state

2. A discussion of a strike of subcontracted female cleaning workers in Tel Aviv appears in the journal of the Women Workers' Movement *Dvar Ha-Po'elet*, vol. 28, no. 6 (June) 1962, p. 180. In it the prevalence of subcontracting in public institutions is strongly condemned.

institutions. The opposition to subcontracting expressed by cleaning workers, in a milieu in which the labour movement was attempting fully to incorporate the weaker, secondary elements of the labour force, appears to have led to the reduction, and possibly total disappearance, of contracting out of cleaning work for approximately one decade, until the early 1970s.

Subcontracting of cleaning work reappeared in the early 1970s and has spread rapidly since then. It has appeared and spread in all industrial spheres – education, health, financial and marketing establishments, government administration, etc. – as well as in all sectors of the Israeli economy – the private sector, the state and public sectors, and the economic sectors owned by the Histadrut. By the mid-1980s it is difficult to claim that contracting out is more prevalent in any one sector, although in the 1970s the state seems to have played a leading role in directing its institutions, or those financed by it, to contract out their cleaning work instead of directly employing cleaning workers. Two major considerations affected this process. The first was a desire to cut costs caused by direct employment. These costs had increased markedly during the 1960s because of the stabilization in the status of directly employed cleaning workers as a result of their inclusion among the organized workers at the work place level. The second was a severe shortage of labour, which led employers to look for alternative sources of labour to those available to them so far.

### *Reduction of Costs*

The costs to be met by the employer in the case of direct wage employment can be seen at a number of levels. The first is immediate costs to be met on a monthly basis. These include the monthly wage paid to the workers and the various taxes paid by the employer to the state. In addition, there are a wide range of social benefits paid on a monthly or annual basis, such as national insurance, travelling expenses, employer's share in workers' pension and sick funds, work clothes, and annual paid leave and recreation expenses. In the case of cleaning workers whose work place belongs to a sector with a strong workers' organization, such benefits could add between 60 and 70 per cent to their basic wage. An additional direct cost is caused to employers by benefits which ensure shorter working hours on a daily and monthly basis to specific groups of workers. Thus, for example, cleaning workers employed by state hospitals worked seven rather than eight hours per day, and twenty-two rather than twenty-four days per month.

The second level, long term costs of wage employees, arose from the fact that almost all organized labour was employed on a permanent basis, i.e. until retirement.[3] This could be especially problematic for employees in the case of workers doing manual, unskilled work, whose labour did not improve with years of experience but, more probably, deteriorated with age.

The third level is costs of control and management, both in terms of controlling

3. Permanent employment was, and still is, a very central issue for organized labour in Israel. Even though according to collective agreements such a commitment can be broken under specific circumstances, these are few and strenuously resisted by unions. The relative ease of acquiring tenure and the difficulty of then dismissing workers have become a striking feature of labour relations in Israel, even though there are indications of a weakening of these features in the current recession.

the work process and inspecting it, and in terms of book-keeping and administration. Once again, bearing these costs is more worthwhile, from the point of view of the employer, in the case of a more complex labour process than that of unskilled manual labour.

### *Shortage of Labour*

Shortage of labour, or in other words the increasing difficulty of obtaining new workers either in place of those who retired or left, or as new workers for the expanding public and private services. was often mentioned as a major reason for the transition to subcontracting. This was repeatedly emphasized in interviews with medium level management, primarily those in charge of either maintenance or personnel. Such shortage is also documented by the Employment Bureau all through the 1970s.[4]

A number of factors can explain the shortage of labour for cleaning work felt at that time. New opportunities were opening for women as a result of the rapid growth of the Israeli economy from the early 1950s, halted only by a severe depression (1965–7). The rapid growth was influential for women's employment mainly from the early 1960s when the unemployment of the previous decade had all but disappeared. The new opportunities were mainly in clerical work and public services.

The expansion of opportunities was complemented by changes within the potential female labour force. The new generation of Jewish women were not willing to enter many of those occupations taken by their mothers, a phenomenon known from other contexts of immigration (Piore 1979: 87). Their level of education was more advanced than their mothers (CBS 1982, Tb. xxii/3), enabling them to take advantage of the new and expanding positions in the labour market. As a result of the dwindling of the main source of female cleaning workers, that of new immigrants in general and oriental ones in particular, new sources of labour had to be tapped. The main sources were rural Arab women from villages within the state of Israel, preferably those living in easy commuting distance from the main Jewish urban centres and women and, to a much lesser extent, men from the territories occupied by Israel since 1967. The new forms of labour organization and employment used to reach and recruit this labour had a marked advantage in the labour market.

As noted above, the state played an important role in pushing through the transition to subcontracted cleaning work. Nevertheless the state, as an employer and thus as an immediate partner in class relations, does not function in a vacuum. The Histadrut, in its capacity as the General Federation of Labour and the overall association of individual trade unions, did little to oppose this process or to counter the considerations discussed above. The absence of such opposition is especially notable in the light of two structural factors. First, the Histadrut itself serves in a dual capacity. On the one hand it is the workers' movement and thus their representative in issues of negotiation and struggle. On the other hand, the

4. E.g. *Be'Sherut Ha-Ta'asuka* (In the Employment Bureau) (July), 1976, p. 119; (January) 1978, p. 274; (October) 1977, p. 176.

Histadrut has its own economic sector and thus is the employer of workers who formally own the means of production. In practice the Histadrut serves in the dual capacity of employer and labour representative at one and the same time. This situation has in some instances led to the significant improvement of the conditions of Histadrut employees as compared to those employed by the private sector. Nevertheless, in the specific case of subcontracting, there does not appear to have been such an effect. The Histadrut as an employer did not function any differently than did state or private employers. Second, for an extended period, until 1977, the Labour Party was in control both in the government and in the Histadrut. This additional duality did not lead to any systematic intervention in opposition to the new system of labour organization and employment being introduced by state authorities.

## DIRECT WAGE LABOUR AND SUBCONTRACTED LABOUR

There is much in common between direct wage labour and subcontracted labour, especially in the specific form the latter takes in the case of cleaning work. In both instances there is a wage relation which is embedded in capitalist relations. In both situations there is a hierarchical work situation which entails differentials of wage, authority and prestige. In both cases there is a clear distinction between manual and non-manual labour. In both case the employment of labour is related to the making of profits. And yet there is a significant difference in the relation between maximization of profits and employment of labour in the two instances. In the case of direct employment, the reason for the employment is the task which has to be done. The relation to profit making will be more long term and indirect, especially in the case of state institutions such as hospitals, government offices and institutions of education, which are related to profit making through the state support of capitalist interests rather than by a direct and immediate striving for profits. On the other hand, labour employed by a contractor is hired for the sole purpose of being sold to a third party at an immediate gain to the contractor-mediator. The dual incentive of the contractor, to sell the labour subcontracted by him and to maximize his own profits at the same time, compels him to find workers who will enable him to cut expenses to the greatest possible extent and to extract the maximum labour in return for the wages paid by him. While this pressure is true for subcontracting in general, it is especially so in the case of cleaning work. The expenses faced by the contractor are relatively few and the major one by far is that of labour. Thus it is easy for new contractors or subcontractors to enter the scene, increasing its competitiveness and the insecurity of the competing contractors. As the main expense is that of labour, the push to lower labour expenses and intensify the use of labour employed becomes even stronger.

### *Intensification of Labour*

The intensified use of the labour of subcontracted cleaning workers takes on various forms, all of which have in common the extraction of more labour in a given period of time than would have been extracted under more relaxed circumstances. Observation in places of work point to a number of recurring patterns.

1 *Transfer of workers* The contracting out of cleaning work means that the workers are then employed by the contractor and *not* by the institution being cleaned at any specific time. Thus the contractor can transfer his workers from place to place, using the same labour force in a number of institutions during the same day or week. This will usually lower the expenses per capita on the part of the contractor, and create an extremely intense work day for the cleaning worker.

2 *Reduction of workers* The most prevalent form of intensification is the providing of fewer workers than required by the original agreement between the contractor and the institution. To quote only one example, a large state hospital had signed a contract requiring ninety-five cleaning workers daily, approximately two-thirds in the morning shift, and one-third in the afternoon shift. In practice the contractor supplied approximately thirty-five workers in the main shift and fifteen in the afternoon shift.

3 *Short-term employment* Subcontracted labour is characterized by rapid turnover. This reflects, on the one hand, the will of the worker to get out of a situation which she (or he) cannot change. On the other hand, it is also desirable to the subcontractor and often initiated by him. It enables him to avoid employing workers who have become less efficient over the years due to age and fatigue, and also to avoid the large severance payment required by law.

4 *Self-imposed intensification* As mentioned above there are many cases where payment is calculated according to the area cleaned. Under such circumstances workers will often speed their own work to finish as quickly as possible regardless of the long term effect of such speeding on their health and stamina.

## *Wages and Benefits*

The conditions under which subcontracted cleaning workers are employed demonstrate the emphasis inherent in casual labour on immediate forms of payment to the almost total exclusion of long term rewards and benefits. These payments are kept to a minimum because of the labour intensive, unskilled and competitive nature of the sector. As noted above it was extremely difficult to receive accurate information concerning pay. Nevertheless, the basic information given was consistent enough to enable a number of general conclusions.

1 Two main categories of subcontracted workers could be clearly distinguished: those workers who were paid according to the legal minimum income and those whose wages fell far below the required minimum.

2 The legal minimum income is in itself a highly problematic category. For reasons we shall not go into, the relation between the minimum income and the average income tends to deteriorate rapidly, from 40 per cent when the minimum income is adjusted to the average income rate to as low as 25 per cent after approximately half a year.

3 There is a significant number of subcontracted workers whose wage falls far below the minimum income, by as much as 50 per cent. The extent of

undercutting the minimum income appeared to be increasing during the year in which our study was conducted, though it is difficult to document such a trend with certainty.

4 There is a large gap between the wages of those cleaning workers who are still directly employed by institutions and those of subcontracted workers, though this gap varies markedly according both to the nature of the institution and the specific conditions of the subcontracted workers. Cleaning workers employed by hospitals enjoy better wages than those employed by schools, for example, so that the former earn approximately 50 per cent above the minimum income, while the latter earn only 20 per cent above it. The gap is, of course, much greater between directly employed workers and the subcontracted workers. Within the same institution a subcontracted worker doing the same work can earn as little as 30 per cent of what is earned by the directly employed cleaning worker.

The drive to keep wages as low as possible is implemented in a number of ways:

1 As noted above there is frequent undercutting of the minimum income which is both required by law and stated in the contract between Histadrut and the organization of cleaning enterprises and contractors.
2 Other legal requirements are also undercut or bypassed, such as extra pay for working on Saturday (the legal rest day), extra pay for working additional hours, or accurate compliance with the cost of living expenses.
3 Many subcontractors delay the payment of wages and otherwise manipulate the payslip so that they appear to be paying a higher wage than is actually being paid. In a number of cases subcontractors avoided giving payslips altogether, making it impossible for the worker to calculate whether the sum paid at the end of the month was in accordance with the work which had been done.

In addition to the gap in wages, there is a large gap in the social benefits enjoyed by directly employed as compared to subcontracted workers. The benefits range from work clothes and travelling expenses to sick pay, recreation, sick fund and pension schemes, from subsidized meals to a cut in required hours of work per day, and days per month for female state employees. In the case of hospital workers the various social benefits added as much as 60 to 70 per cent to their basic wage, and in the case of other sectors the social benefits added at least 40, at times 50 per cent. Some of the social benefits had an immediate effect on the workers' monthly income. Most benefits had a long term effect both on the worker's income and general well being. The employer's contribution to the workers' sick fund and pension scheme are clear examples of benefits with such a long term effect.

To conclude, the effect of the form of employment becomes evident when comparing the conditions of subcontracted workers to those directly employed doing similar work, in the same or similar institutions. It is also evident when observing the change in the conditions of workers who were directly employed by an institution which decided to contract out its cleaning work. In this latter case some of the workers usually continued doing the same work, but as employees of the subcontractor who took over the work. Despite the assurance that these workers received from their previous employers that they would continue working under precisely the same conditions, their situation in fact deteriorated rapidly. Social benefits were cut and wages increased at a rate which did not keep up with inflation. New workers employed by the subcontractor were taken on on the basis of lower wages and fewer benefits, serving to push down the conditions enjoyed by the more veteran workers.

And yet, the distinction between organized and casual workers is not so clear cut. Some of the social benefits mentioned above do apply to subcontracted workers as well. The Histadrut has signed a collective work agreement with the organization of cleaning enterprises and contractors. While this agreement does not include the whole range of benefits enjoyed by strong groups of workers, such as state employees, it does include significant benefits such as sick leave, sick fund and pension scheme. Nevertheless, almost all the workers we interviewed did not enjoy these benefits. Just as a legal minimum income exists which is not respected by most subcontractors, so a collective contract exists which is unfamiliar to most workers. Thus a closer look must be taken at prevailing forms of labour union organization and their inadequacy in the case of subcontracted workers in general and cleaning workers in particular.

## WORKER ORGANIZATION AND SUBCONTRACTED LABOUR

The basic pattern of worker organization within the Histadrut is based on collective bargaining by trade union functionaries and the implementation of the collective bargain at shop floor level by workers' committees. A collective agreement is negotiated bi-annually, at the national level, between the trade union of a given industry and the association of employers. The agreement is then ratified by the Minister of Labour, who, in some instances, extends specific items of the collective agreement to apply to unorganized workers and employers as well. At the local level trade union functionaries negotiate specific agreements with individual employers with the aim of improving on the collective agreement applying to the industry as a whole. The third level, that of the workers' committee at the work place, has the vital role of the watchdog. It must learn the national and local agreements through the the trade union and see that all items are carried out, and possibly even improved upon. On a day to day basis the worker's committee deals with individual problems of workers in accordance with the various agreements at hand. This pattern of organization developed in large sectors with a strong trade union apparatus and large concentration of workers. None of its links, neither the national, the local, nor the shop floor, are effectively applicable to subcontracted cleaning work.

Subcontracted cleaning workers who are members of the Histadrut[5] belong to the Service Workers' Union. This is one of the weakest trade unions belonging to the Histadrut, and its bargaining power is highly limited. Two issues can demonstrate the union's weakness. First and foremost, no effective opposition was

5. Many wage employees in Israel belong to the Histadrut primarily due to its very large Sick Fund, rather than out of trade union consciousness or affiliation.

put up by the union concerning the contracting out of cleaning work. Thus the union accepted the far reaching change in the structure of the work as a *fait accompli* without even acting to restrict it within institutions owned by the Histadrut itself.[6] Secondly, the union accepted the legal minimum income as the basis for the wage scale agreed between it and the employers' association, without insisting on improving upon it, thus leaving the workers at the lowest possible legal income. While the national secretariat of the Service Workers' Union is a weak and ineffective body, the local level is even more so. In most local workers' councils little attention is paid to subcontracted cleaning workers and little attempt is made to improve upon the existing agreement. The Haifa Workers' Council, the area where our study was carried out, is a significant exception. Over the last four years the local union functionary has put much effort into negotiating with subcontractors over the conditions of work, but the weakness of the contractors' organization on the one hand, and the absence of workers' committees on the other, have made these efforts quite fruitless.

The clearest expression of subcontracted cleaning work as casual labour is the inability to establish workers' committees at the work place level. From the point of view of the worker, the significant work place, in terms of organization, is not the institutions where she (or he) works, but the contractor *for whom* she (or he) works. Thus the labour force of a given work place is made up of all workers employed by the same contractor. But this labour force is not concentrated in any one location. It is scattered among a variety of institutions, offices, banks, supermarkets, etc., so that most workers have no knowledge or contact with each other. The only basis for organization is therefore those workers employed by a given contractor whose actual work is carried out on the same site. This is a very weak and highly temporary basis.

An additional complicating factor is the high proportion of workers who come from different villages and small towns outside the city where the work takes place. They are transported to work and back by the subcontractor or one of his supervisors. They have little chance to make contact with one another outside working hours, and even less chance to make contact with local workers' council and trade union functionaries. As a result the workers usually have no knowledge of the rights assured them according to the collective agreement which, theoretically, applies to them, and are usually ignorant even of the rights assured them by law.[7] No stable workers' committee can develop in these conditions and thus there is no channel through which the local union functionary can pass on information or receive complaints. Under these structural circumstances it is not surprising that expressions of resistance reported to us during our study were of a sporadic and spontaneous nature, aimed at dealing with *ad hoc* problems rather than expressions of sustained organization aimed at more long term changes. The

6. For example, hospitals belonging to the Histadrut Sick Fund and some of the Histadrut's office buildings.

7. To quote one example. A cleaning worker, presently employed by the Education Department in the Haifa Municipality, told me of her previous experience with a cleaning contractor. After giving birth she was told by him that she was not entitled to a three month paid maternity leave because he had not insured her in the National Insurance and thus 'could not pay for her from his own pocket'. Even at the time of recalling the incident she was not yet aware that he was legally obligated to insure her, and thus she was in the position to sue him for her maternity leave rather than accept his 'explanation'.

latter point, the migratory nature of much of the work force, highlights a further issue directly relevant to casual labour: the relation between the structure of employment and the composition of the labour force, or, in other words, the tendency of casual labour to predominate among weak segments of the population.

## SUBCONTRACTED LABOUR AND THE COMPOSITION OF THE LABOUR FORCE

### *The Mass Entrance of Arab Women*

Shortage of labour for cleaning work under conditions of direct employment was one of the important causes of the transition to subcontracting. Thus subcontracting as a system, and specific subcontractors individually, have to be able to tap new sources of labour unavailable for direct wage employment. The availability of such a source or sources and their specific features reinforces the process of casualization discussed above, and enables it to take on the extreme form which it has acquired over the last decade.

The main supply for subcontracted cleaning workers is Arab women. Some of the women live in the large Jewish cities or on their outskirts, but most of them come from the hinterland, from villages and small towns at a travelling distance of between half an hour to one hour. An additional, related source are Palestinian women (and to some extent men) from the territories occupied by Israel since 1967. The extent to which subcontractors recruit workers from the occupied territories depends primarily on the distance at given points. Thus Haifa, where our study took place, does not have many workers from the West Bank[8] while Jerusalem, Tel Aviv and Beer Sheba have a much larger number.

It has been impossible to obtain accurate figures or even sound estimates as to the proportion of rural Arab women among subcontracted workers. Estimates vary between 50 per cent, a figure quoted by a trade union officer, and 90 per cent claimed by a large subcontractor, who referred in this case both to Arab women living in Haifa and to those coming from the Arab settlements outside it. In either case the proportion of Arab women is very high, raising the question of why such women turn to cleaning work in general and to subcontracted cleaning work in particular. Three main factors are relevant: the lower level of education of Arab women as compared to Jewish women; the highly limited occupational options open to them, especially outside the urban centres; and the patriarchal control evident in many Arab families, especially in the rural settlements.

The level of education among Arab women is markedly lower than that among Jewish women. Even though there has been a striking increase in the education of Arab women over the last two decades, the gap is still very clear (CBS 1982: Tbs xxii/1, 2, 3). Thirty-five per cent of all 18 to 24 year olds has only five to eight years of schooling as compared to 8.3 per cent among the equivalent age group in

8. A large contractor in the Haifa area claimed that it was not profitable for him to transport workers from the occupied territories because of the distance. Observation in large places of work tends to confirm his claim, though not in all cases.

the Jewish population. Eight years of schooling is not enough to enter any vocational training for skilled occupations. At least as important is the scarcity of employment opportunities for young Arab women. Those with post high-school education turn primarily, like their Jewish peer group, to teaching, nursing and social work. But the second main avenue of employment for women, that of clerical work, is highly restricted. The large public and state administration offers few options to Arab women, and financial institutions are much fewer in Arab settlements, as are private enterprises and companies.[9] Thus many young women with high school education are faced with similar problems to those of women with less schooling. A large source of employment for Arab women in rural and semi-rural settlements is the clothing industry,[10] much of which is also organized on the basis of subcontracting. While such work, according to most of our informants, has a higher prestige than cleaning work, it also pays very low rates, is highly intensive and is sometimes viewed as more confining and oppressive (Margalit-Gintzburg 1984: 29–31).

Finally, the strong patriarchal control of men (whether fathers, older brothers or husbands) over women in the Arab, especially Moslem and Druse, society, further restricts women's employment options.[11] The preference in many households is for a workplace where the woman, especially the young unmarried woman, is not on her own. Preferably she should be working with a larger group of women from her own settlement, under the direct supervision of a man well known to her family, and best of all a member of her own extended family, and with as little contact as possible during the workday with other people, especially strange men.

Subcontracted work fits these requirements to a much greater extent than direct wage employment. The women have little contact with anyone in the institution or establishment where they work. They are recruited by a member of their own village or town who serves as the contact person for the subcontractor or subcontracting enterprise. The recruiter, in most cases, arranges the transportation to the workplace and back, and in many cases supervises the work during the day as well. This structure is most fully developed in the case of the cleaning of large institutions such as hospitals, where thirty or forty young women come into town and work a full eight hour shift. Women cleaning banks and offices tend to live in the town itself and to have more direct contact with the subcontractor or, more commonly, with one of his supervisors. The preference of many male guardians for controlled and supervised subcontracting supplies the subcontracting enterprise with a large, though not very stable, labour force. At the same time,

9. For the importance of these occupational options for young Jewish women, see Bernstein (1983).
10. Statistics concerning Arab workers are few and unreliable. A doctoral study concerning the Arabs living in the Galilee reported 48 per cent of the women workers being employed in the textile and clothing industry (presentation of Aziz Kheidar, Haifa University, 30 March 1984).
11. The position of women in the Israeli Palestinian community is in itself undergoing change, and is presented in the literature with varying emphases as to the extent of subordination and actual patriarchal control. Rosenfeld (1980) tends to emphasize the continuation of women's subordination and dependence, as compared to Ginat (1982) who emphasizes their indirect power. While Mar'i and Mar'i (1985) point to a variety of processes of change seeming to weaken women's subordination, they argue that the specific political position of the Palestinian minority in Israel tended, and probably still tends, to reinforce traditional aspects concerning the attitude toward women. This position is also taken, even more strongly, by Pedersen (1983).

the workers are highly dependent on their recruiter and supervisor, who is often their main (and at times sole) contact and mediator with their actual employer.

These three factors – the low level of education, few occupational options and patriarchial control – help explain the relation between subcontracted labour as *casual* labour and the composition of the labour force. Arab women, especially rural ones, have little ability or power to acquire basic information concerning the rights and benefits assured to them, or to organize to ensure the implementation of such rights when aware of them.

All the disabilities discussed are accentuated in the case of Palestinian women from the West Bank and Gaza Strip. Their opportunities are fewer and the control over them greater. In addition they lack any form of protection. The Histadrut is not authorized to organize workers from the occupied territories. A special state labour exchange is supposed to supervise conditions of payment and social benefits but many workers, among them subcontracted cleaning workers, obtain their work outside the labour exchange. They become, in effect, illegal workers totally dependent on their recruiter. As a result the dynamics of casual labour, the lowering of wages and intensification of labour can continue unimpeded.

### *Displacement of Workers*

The rapid spread of subcontracted cleaning work and the marked increase of female Arab workers raise the question of whether a process of displacement has been taking place, the displacement of direct wage labour by subcontracted labour and the displacement of Jewish by Arab workers. The issue of such displacement has been stated clearly by Bonachich: 'Displacement of high-priced with cheap labour can occur in a variety of ways. The basic principle, regardless of differences in detail, is that capital shifts from one labour source to another, in the process undermining gains high-priced labour has achieved' (1979: 23). The immediate answer to the question of displacement raised above appears to be negative. The difficulty of finding workers under the condition of direct wage labour was one of the central causes for the transition, as was the resistance of Jewish women, mainly the younger women, daughters of immigrants, to such work. Thus subcontracting can be seen as entering a vacuum created by the increase in demand for and drop in supply of cleaning workers. Nevertheless, a closer look does reveal both direct and indirect expressions of displacement.

First, the contracting out of cleaning work has been introduced over the last decade and a half not only in new or enlarged establishments but also in existing ones which had previously employed their own workers. In some cases the same workers continued doing the work and thus one *form* of employment displaced another. In other cases workers resigned and new ones were brought in by the subcontractor, in which case one group of workers displaced another.

Secondly, there are some indications that the introduction of subcontracting kept workers away, thus reinforcing the already existing shortage. This point is made in the Employment Bureau's Journal in reference to Haifa in the late 1970s: 'Cleaning services are given in this area by subcontractors, and as the working conditions under subcontractors are very poor, the women badly exploited, their wages minimal, many prefer to turn down such work and remain at home.'[12]

12. *Be'Sherut Ha-Ta'asuka* (In the Labour Employment Bureau) October 1980, p. 84.

Thirdly, the improvement in the working conditions of directly employed cleaning workers has come to a stop over the last few years , according to the secretary of the workers' committee in the largest state hospital in Haifa, which employs its own cleaning workers in one part of the hospital and contracts out the cleaning work in its large new extension. One can only speculate whether the availability of subcontracted workers has served to limit the ability of the directly employed to follow up on their earlier gains. And finally, the shortage discussed above was a real and concrete problem. Nevertheless, the availability of subcontracting, and thus the recruiting of a large supply of cheap and mobile labour, eliminated the necessity of finding other solutions which might have been far more beneficial for actual and potential workers. As Sassen-Koob noted regarding immigrant workers: 'The availability of immigrant workers and their willingness to take undesirable jobs facilitated the reproduction of these jobs which otherwise might have to be upgraded in order to meet the standards of native workers' (1980–1: 28).

## *Patterns of Differentiation*

Despite the direct and indirect effect of subcontracted cleaning work on direct wage labour, the differentiation between them is still marked. As noted above there is a clear discrepancy in both wage and work conditions between subcontracted workers and those directly employed. But this is not the only discrepancy. There are additional lines of differentiation which can be distinguished among subcontracted workers themselves. One of these is the distinction between male and female workers. While the majority of workers are women, there are also male workers. Usually these are young Arab men, either from the rural settlements close to the urban centres or from the occupied territories. In a minority of cases they include older Jewish men who have no other options for one reason or another. At times the men do the same work as the women, though more frequently there is a division of labour according to which specific tasks are allocated according to sex. For example, in large hospitals young men will be found doing the window cleaning and will usually be the ones to operate the machines used for the cleaning of marble, linoleum or carpeting. In all the cases we came across in our study, men's wages were higher than women's. This was explained by the male workers as due primarily to the difference in their specific tasks. A large contractor, on the other hand, insisted that such a discrepancy was only reasonable, even when the same work was carried out, due to the man's commitment to provide for his family, commitment from which women, so it seemed, by his definition, were exempt.

A further differentiation appeared between the wages of Arab and Jewish women. This was more difficult to determine as usually the workers in a given location were either all Jewish or all Arab rather than mixed. Nevertheless, it appeared that, on the whole, Jewish women were able to strike a better deal with the subcontractor than Arab women working for the same subcontractor on a different location. Finally, a third distinction appeared consistently between Israeli Palestinian women and those from the occupied territories. The higher transportation expenses from the occupied territories were deducted from the workers' wages. In addition, as noted above, their dependence on subcontractors and other middlemen, all of whom took their own share of the pie, was even greater. Thus the differentiation between groups of cleaning workers which emerged in our study was based not only on the difference in form of employment and related production factors, but also on other criteria of dominance central to the structure of Israeli society, those of gender, nationality and citizenship.

The organizational activity of the Histadrut served to exacerbate the distinctions among subcontracted workers rather than to moderate them. At the individual level, Jewish women found it much easier to approach the trade union officer at the Workers' Council. These workers lived near by and, at least relatively speaking, had greater knowledge of the help they could get and suffered fewer cultural and language barriers. At the work place level, the Arab rural women were also at a disadvantage. The union officer had greater difficulty making contact with them due to a variety of barriers, the most prominent among them being the far more stringent supervision to which they were subjected. Thus the few attempts made to establish workers' committees at the work place level, highly problematic attempts for the structural reasons discussed above, were carried out among Jewish women only.

Finally, at the trade union level, three-day seminars were organized for workers, aimed at enhancing their knowledge concerning the Histadrut and their commitment to it, as well as their knowledge of their own legal and contractual rights. Over the last few years cleaning workers have also attended such seminars.[13] The seminars were held in centres of recreation established by the Histadrut and provided a rare opportunity for rest from both wage and domestic labour. The women who took part in these seminars were baby minders, domestic cleaning workers and subcontracted workers. They were all women who lived in the city or on its immediate outskirts, and in over 90 per cent of the cases were Jewish women. The Arab women who attended the seminars were urban women, and in no case were they representatives of the large component of rural Arab women. Even so, the organization of such seminars, and the ensuring of the women's attendance, was extremely difficult. The women appeared to benefit greatly from the experience, as much from the rest and companionship, as from the information passed on to them. Nevertheless, despite the fact that those who attended the seminar were also members of a highly exploited group of workers, the mass of subcontracted workers were left untouched.

To conclude, the activity of the Histadrut varied from no action in most Workers' Councils to a variety of organizational attempts, which, at best, affected a narrow stratum of more easily accessible workers, leaving the main source of subcontracted workers - rural Arab women and workers from the occupied territories - totally unaffected.[14]

13. I personally attended three such seminars as part of this study.

14. The Histadrut is formally exempt from dealing with the conditions of work and wages of workers from the occupied territories. Special state run employment bureaux for workers from the occupied territories are supposed both to supply employment (or rather supply workers on demand) and supervise payment and social benefits. This is not very satisfactory even for those workers who do get their work via the employment bureau. A large proportion of the workers obtain their work through other channels over which there is no supervision (see *Ha'aretz*, 13.2.85; 14.2.85).

## CONCLUDING COMMENTS

Cleaning work is done primarily by women. It is usually done by women of subordinate or marginal groups. Often the cleaning is done 'after hours.' One leaves the office, classroom, supermarket, bank, etc. and finds it clean the following day. Physically, but far more important socially, it is easy for many people, including many workers and among them women workers, to treat cleaning work and thus cleaning workers as 'invisible'. This is possibly one of the reasons that the process of casualization of cleaning work has passed unremarked by labour functionaries and activists, let alone other workers. This in itself, is an important reason to turn attention to the process and its effects. But the 'invisible' process discussed in this chapter is part of a larger phenomenon, that of casual labour in the Israeli labour market in general. The existence of such a component has remained, if not invisible, at least outside any significant debate concerning the Israeli labour force and working class.

The high rate of membership in the Histadrut, and the impressive political and economic power of the Histadrut, created the impression of a wholly organized and cohesive labour force, all members of which enjoyed, to a lesser or greater extent, the benefits of primary labour. This was, no doubt, a misleading impression. While the level of organization was high, and the benefits to be gained from organization real, this was never the whole picture. Since the establishment of the state there have been significant components of casual labour. The large oriental immigration remained largely unskilled, low paid, and unsure of secure employment during the 1950s and at least to some extent during the first part of the 1960s as well (Bernstein and Swirsky 1982), and this in spite of membership in the Histadrut. Palestinian Arabs in israel have been in a far more marginal position. In 1959 they were accepted as members of the Histadrut, organized within a special Arab department, directed by Jews, but even in later years occupied many of the insecure and unstable positions in the labour market, whether as casual petty entrepreneurs or as casual wage labour (Rosenfeld 1978). The West Bank and Gaza Strip, occupied by Israel in 1967, added a further component of casual labour, by far the most vulnerable component, lacking labour union protection and in many cases without a legal working permit.[15] Finally, women have also been a constant source of casual labour in specific female occupations such as personal services, clerical work in small private offices and subcontracted homework.

The above mentioned cases point to the margins of the labour market, but there are at least initial indications that forms of casual labour are infiltrating into the more secure and central spheres of the labour market as well. Forms of subcontracting and outwork can be found in a wide variety of industries and services, supplemented by new forms of temporary employment. The economic crisis in Israel and the recession which is clearly evident at the time of writing will most likely lead to further restructuring along similar lines. Thus the case of cleaning work discussed in this article, rather than being a 'curiosity', may very well be

15. Estimates put the numbers of workers, legal and illegal, from the occupied territories at approximately 100,000 workers.

indicative, in an extreme form, of a far more central trend. It can only be hoped that once casualization begins to hit the stronger segments of the labour force it will become less 'invisible' and lead to new forms of labour organization and resistance.

## REFERENCES


Allen, Sh. (1983), 'Production and reproduction in the lives of women home-workers', *Sociological Review*, 31(4): 649-65.

Bernstein, D. (1983), 'Economic growth and female labour: the case of Israel', *Sociological Review*, 31(2): 263-93.

Bernstein, D. and Swirsky, S. (1982), 'The rapid economic development of Israel and the emergence of the ethnic division of labour', *The British Journal of Sociology*, 33(1): 64-85.

Bonachich, E. (1979), 'The past, present and future of split labor market theory', *Research in Race and Ethnic Relations*, vol. 1: 17-64.

Braverman, H. (1974), *Labour and Monopoly Capital*, New York, Monthly Review Press.

Bromley, R. and Gerry, C. (eds) (1979), *Casual Work and Poverty in Third World Cities*, Chichester, Wiley and Sons.

Caire, G. (1982), 'The increase in temporary work and the regulation of the labour market', *Sociologie du Travail*, 24(2): 135-58 (French).

CBS (1982), *Statistical Abstract of Israel – 1982*, Jerusalem.

Dombois, R. and Osterland, M. (1982), 'New patterns in the flexible utilization of labour: part time work and labour subcontracting', *Sozial Welt*, 33(3-4): 466-81 (in German).

Friedman, A. (1978), *Industry and Labour: Class Struggle at Work and Monopoly Capitalism*, London, Macmillan.

Ginat, J. (1982), *Women in Muslim Rural Society*, New Brunswick, Transaction Books.

Haug, M. (1983), 'Miami's garment industry and its workers', *Research in Sociology of Work*, vol. 2: 173-89.

Herzog, M. (1980), *From Hand to Mouth*, Middlesex, Penguin Books.

Hoy, J. and Kennedy, M. (1983), 'Women's paid labor in the home: the British experience', *Research in Sociology of Work*, vol. 2: 211-39.

Margalit-Gintzburg, Y. (1984), 'There are Arab women workers who earn too little', *Dvar Ha-Po'elet*, no. 72 (April): 29-32 (Hebrew).

Mar'i, M. and Mar'i, S. (1985), 'The role of women as change agents in Arab society in Israel', in *Women's Worlds*, eds Bernard, Mednik, Izraeli and Sufer, Praeger.

Murray, F. (1983), 'The decentralization of production – the decline of the mass-collective worker?' *Capital and Class*, no. 19: 74-97. See also chapter 11.

Pedersen, B. (1983), 'Oppressive and liberating elements in the situation of the Palestinian women', in *Women in Islamic Societies*, ed. Bo Utas, London, Curzon Press.

Piore, M. (1979), *Birds of Passage*, Cambridge, Cambridge University Press.

Rosenfeld, H. (1978), 'The situation of the Arab national minority in Israel', *Comparative Studies in Society and History*, 20(3): 374-407.

Rosenfeld, H. (1980), 'Men and women in Arab peasant to proletariat transformation', in *Theory and Practice*, ed. Diamond S. Mouton, The Hague.

Rubery, J. and Wilkinson, F. (1981), 'Outwork and segmented labour markets', in *The Dynamics of Labour Market Segmentation*, ed. F. Wilkinson, London, Academic Press.

Sassen-Koob, S. (1980-1), 'Immigrant and minority workers in the organization of the labour process', *The Journal of Ethnic Studies*, 8(1): 1-34.

Wong, M. (1983), 'Chinese sweatshops in the United States', *Research in Sociology of Work*, vol. 2: 357-79.

# 30

# Employment Lessons from the US Electronics Industry

JOHN A. ALIC AND MARTHA CALDWELL HARRIS

In the US electronics industry, competition – domestic as well as international – has led to increases in labour productivity through changes in product design and automation and to transfers of manufacturing operations to low-wage developing countries. For example, in the consumer electronics industry, annual output of colour television sets per production worker in the United States increased from 150 in 1971 to 560 in 1981. Total output nearly doubled, from 5.4 million sets to 10.5 million. At the same time, domestic employment in colour television manufacture dropped by half – a result of greater foreign value-added, redesigned televisions with fewer parts and less need for assembly labour, and automation. The example is not atypical, and the implications are clear: new technology can cut into job opportunities even though output rises substantially.

In two other sectors of the electronics industry – microelectronics (which includes semiconductors) and computers – employment has grown rapidly. (The 1985 layoffs will, as in earlier business slumps, prove temporary.) Microelectronics technology made redesigned colour television sets possible, and far more Americans now work for semiconductor manufacturers than were ever employed in consumer electronics. Skilled and professional jobs predominate in microelectronics, accounting for nearly 60 per cent of employment, compared with about 30 per cent in consumer electronics. Similar patterns exist elsewhere in high technology electronics: continuing advances in both products and processes leave relatively fewer openings for unskilled and semiskilled workers. Indeed, jobs for production workers in US computer firms declined slightly during 1984, although overall employment in the computer sector rose.

This essay was first published in *Monthly Labor Review*, 109(2), 1986. It is based in part on *International Competitiveness in Electronics* (Washington, DC, Office of Technology Assessment, US Congress, November 1983), chapter 9. An earlier version was presented at the 2nd International Conference on Human Factors in Manufacturing, Stuttgart, Federal Republic of Germany, June 11–13, 1985. The authors thank Philip A. Mundo for assistance with the statistical data.

American consumer electronics firms have faced stiff foreign competition since the latter part of the 1960s. But only in the last few years have US-based microelectronics and computer manufacturers found competitors from Japan able to match their product offerings. Given declining advantages in product technology, and Japan's proven capabilities in process technology, American manufacturing companies have been forced to change their priorities. Within any manufacturing organization, quality and productivity, and hence costs and competitiveness, depend on the integration of workers and machines into an efficient and effective production system. Highly automated plants will demand new ways of using skills, resolving conflicts, and making decisions. The emphasis on shared responsibility and decision-making in Japanese organizations appears to give them a head start in integrated production systems. Japan's manufacturers are more adept at utilizing the skills and capabilities of their work force, and are further along at integrating workers and machines - an important source of competitive advantage.

In a given industry, job opportunities change with demand for the industry's products with shifting patterns of international competition, and with increases in labour productivity. The latter stem not only from automation and work reorganization, but from products redesigned for easier, cheaper manufacture. Rising worldwide demand for the output of a given industry will create new jobs only if demand rises more rapidly than productivity. From the perspective of a national economy, net job creation also depends on trends in imports and exports and on foreign and domestic investments. Imports may displace domestic production; overseas investment by domestic companies may do the same.

In any economy, new jobs are continually being created, old jobs eliminated. At the level of the firms, jobs are created as companies are established or expand, and jobs disappear as companies atrophy and die or move production overseas. Over time, automation, work redesign, and organizational change help fewer workers produce more. If a firm cannot sell enough of the additional output, it may have to reduce its labour force. Even if it can increase sales, improvements in efficiency necessarily cut into future job opportunities. Aggregate economic growth provides the gross context for job creation and job destruction; the organization of work within the enterprise creates the fine structure.

This chapter discusses factors which affect employment in two components of the US electronics industry - consumer electronics (SIC 3651) and microelectronics (SIC 3674), touching briefly on computer manufacturing (SIC 3573).[1]

## EMPLOYMENT TRENDS IN ELECTRONICS

Employment in US manufacturing has been essentially static since the late 1960s, but declined relatively over the 1974-84 period from 26 to 21 per cent of the non-

1. These industries are categorized under the following Standard Industrial Classification (SIC) codes as published in the Office of Management and Budget's *Standard Industrial Classification Manual, 1972:* consumer electronics - SIC 3651, 'Radio and Television Receiving Sets, Except Communication Types', microelectronics - SIC 3674, 'Semiconductors and Related Devices', and computer manufacturing - SIC 3573, 'Electronic Computing Equipment'.

TABLE 30.1 Growth in employment in the electronics industry

| | 1974 | 1984 | 1985, first half |
|---|---|---|---|
| *Numbers of employees* | | | |
| Consumer electronics | 113,600 | 71,800 | 68,400 |
| Microelectronics | 148,300 | 273,000 | 283,300 |
| Computers and peripherals | 217,000 | 460,900 | 456,900 |
| *Percentage production workers* | | | |
| Consumer electronics | 74 | 68 | 66 |
| Microelectronics | 51 | 43 | 41 |
| Computers and peripherals | 39 | 37 | 35 |

agricultural workforce. However, in electronics, employment expanded rapidly over the period – although not in all parts of the industry. Employment has nearly doubled in microelectronics and has increased even faster in computers, while the consumer electronics category (which includes many types of products other than television sets) has shrunk. Table 30.1 shows the number of employees and the percentage of production workers in consumer electronics, microelectronics, and computer and peripherals industries, in 1974, 1984 and the first six months of 1985. By mid-1985, the 808,600 workers in consumer electronics, microelectronics, and computer firms accounted for more than 4 per cent of the US manufacturing labour force. Although these firms make up only a portion of the electronics industry, they employ more than twice as many workers as the steel industry.[2]

Figure 30.1 compares trends in labour productivity and production employment over the past decade for each of the three categories discussed in this chapter. (Productivity is plotted as value-added per production worker hour in inflation-adjusted terms.) Value-added productivity growth in consumer electronics – where employment declined – has roughly paralleled the all-manufacturing average. In contrast, computer manufacture shows a rapid rise in employment, with productivity rising almost as fast until the mid-1970s. Many jobs have also been created in microelectronics, where productivity gains were again substantially above the all-manufacturing average. With both computers and microelectronics suffering from business slowdowns during 1985, layoffs have been common and total employment has dropped.[3] No doubt these declines will prove temporary, with employment levels rebounding once the slump has passed, as occurred twice during the 1970s for both the microelectronics and computer sectors. Over the long term, however, employment prospects in the US computer industry appear far better than those in microelectronics.

2. Including communications equipment and components other than semiconductors would double the total, to more than 1.7 million workers, while employment in the American steel industry fell to about 330,000 during 1984.

3. Both sectors' troubles have been widely reported. See, for example, 'Those Vanishing High-Tech Jobs', *Business Week*, July 15, 1985, p. 30. Although the averages for 1984 and the first half of 1985 do not yet show the decline in microelectronics, employment fell each month during 1985 through June in both microelectronics and computers.

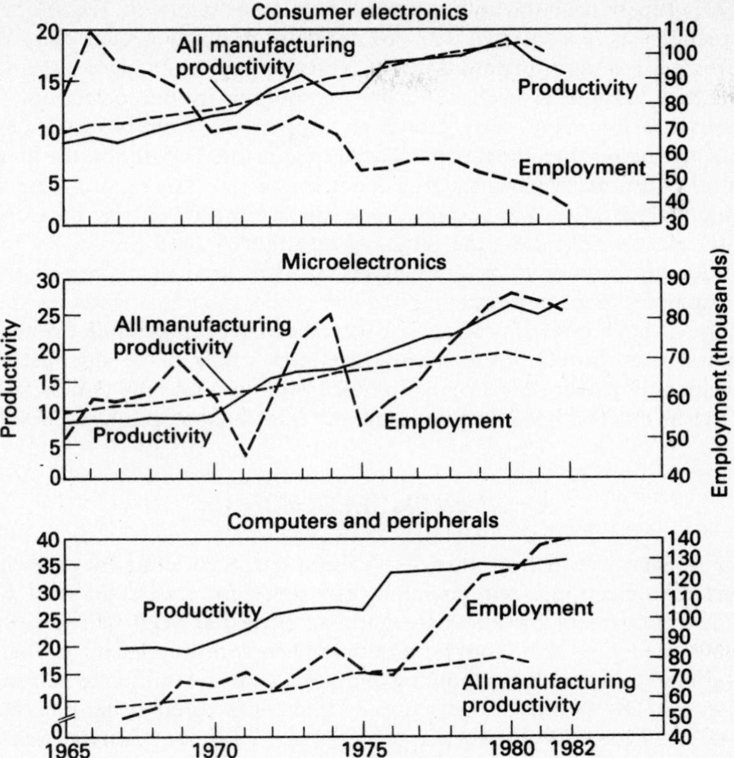


FIGURE 30.1 Trends in productivity and production worker employment in consumer electronics, microelectronics, and computers, 1965–82. Productivity is value-added productivity per production worker hour in 1972 dollars

*Source:* 1977 and 1982 census of manufactures

Productivity trends are seldom unambiguous. Their significance can be questioned when technological change is as rapid as it has been in computers and peripherals and in microelectronics. In these sectors, product performance has advanced rapidly; today's dollar buys far more capability than it did a few years ago.[4] In colour television manufacture, technical change has been much slower, with intense price competition depressing value-added productivity measures compared with other US industries over the 1965–82 period; the retail price index for colour television sets increased by less than 5 per cent, while that for all consumer durables more than doubled. Productivity on a unit output basis for colour television manufacture has, however, risen far more rapidly than on a value-added basis.

As figure 30.1 demonstrates, the portions of the electronics industry with the

4. See *International Competitiveness in Electronics*, p. 89.

highest rates of value-added productivity growth (microelectronics and computers) also experienced the highest rates of employment growth. Rapid increases in productivity were associated with the creation of jobs, not their elimination. The reasons are straightforward: spurred by technological changes opening vast new markets, export as well as domestic, output in microelectronics and computers has for many years grown at rates in the vicinity of 15 per cent annually, far higher than the rate for all manufacturing. In contrast, the domestic market for consumer electronics grew less than half as fast, exports were small, and import penetration was severe; the value-added productivity measures for consumer electronics reflect the plight of an industry hard pressed by foreign competition and striving to make relatively standard products more cheaply.

The examples of microelectronics and computers show that when technological change is rapid, rates of productivity increase may be high while employment nonetheless rises. Similar correlations sometimes follow at the aggregate level; rates of unemployment may drop nationwide while productivity climbs, particularly if coupled with high investment and the introduction of new technology.

## CONSUMER ELECTRONICS

In many respects, the manufacture of television sets, accounting for about half of US consumer electronics employment, can stand for the sector as a whole. Domestic employment in television manufacturing has been falling since the mid-1960s (see figure 30.2). Jobs for production workers dropped by half between 1971 and 1981, despite a near doubling of output, from 5.4 million to 10.5 million television sets. During this period, a dozen US manufacturers either merged with Japanese or European producers or left the business; General Electric's departure, announced late in 1985, will leave only two major US firms. The US industry now includes more than 10 foreign-owned companies. While contributing to the employment totals in the chart, US production by foreign-owned companies such as Sony or Gold Star tends to reflect higher fractions of foreign value-added than the output of American-owned firms such as Zenith or RCA.

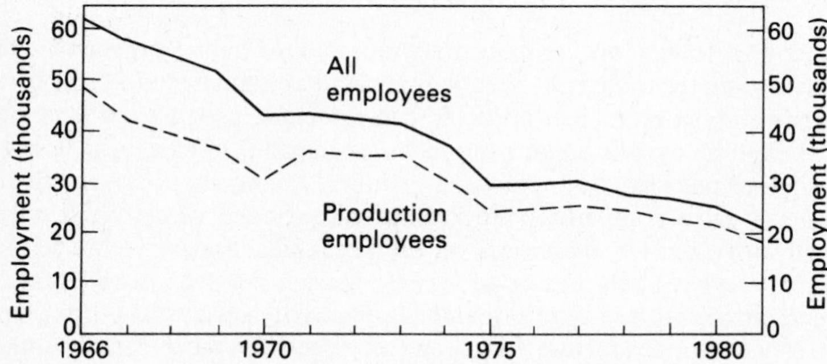


FIGURE 30.2 US employment in television manufacturing, 1966–81. Data for 1966–75 are for all television employment; data for 1976–81 are for colour television only
*Source:* Office of Technology Assessment, *International Competitiveness in Electronics*, Washington DC, November 1983, p. 354

As television sales grew, apparent productivity on a unit output basis (measured as annual output divided by the number of production workers) jumped from 150 sets per worker in 1971 to 560 in 1981. In terms of value-added per production worker, productivity was up by about 40 per cent – a trend similar to that for consumer electronics as a whole.[5] The productivity improvements came from multiple sources. As colour television sets replaced black-and-while receivers, manufacturers introduced more highly automated production processes. Somewhat later, reductions in the number of parts – resulting from solid-state chassis designs – meant reduced labour content. Only 6 per cent of the colour television sets made in the United States were solid-state models in 1970, but by 1976 essentially all had been redesigned around transistors. The number of parts dropped by half or more – for example, from 1023 components for a Panasonic colour model in 1972 to 488 in 1976.[6] Often, component insertion was mechanized at the same time. A good deal of the productivity growth during the 1970s resulted from these interrelated changes in chassis design and manufacturing methods. Clearly, the causes of the employment declines in television manufacturing extend well beyond import penetration or offshore assembly; the spread of solid-state chassis designs and automated manufacturing dramatically reduced labour requirements in this sector of the electronics industry. Import competition did have the effect of speeding the changes.

Over the same period, American consumer electronics firms relocated many of their manufacturing operations to low-wage developing countries. While there are no precise numbers on foreign workers employed in these plants, the US Department of Labor believes there may be more than 30,000 – a greater number than now employed in domestic television manufacture. As a result, the proportion of domestic value-added dropped during the 1970s; more parts and subassemblies were produced overseas for final assembly in the United States, whether by American- or foreign-owned companies. Given these trends, simply dividing the total output of television sets by the number of employees overstates productivity gains (although value-added productivity adjusts for this). By 1980, the United States imported more than $1 billion worth of circuit boards and picture tubes for colour television sets, about one-third of the total value of domestic output. Two basic causes, then, account for the employment decline in television manufacture: greater labour productivity, achieved through product redesigns as well as automation; and transfers of labour-intensive operations overseas. Intense competitive pressures, centred on manufacturing costs, drove both trends.

Improvements in productivity and manufacturing efficiency may eliminate jobs in the short term, but help to slow down job losses over the longer term. In 1974, for example, Matsushita, a Japanese company, bought Motorola's money-losing Quasar television operations. Matsushita invested heavily in automated manufacturing (some of it in Mexico); redesigned Quasar's product line; and reorganized shopfloor operations, with particular emphasis on quality control and

5. *1977 Census of Manufactures: Communication Equipment, Including Radio and TV, MC77-I-36D* (Department of Commerce, June 1980), p. 36D-5; *1982 U.S. Industrial Outlook* (Department of Commerce, January 1982), p. 343.

6. *International Competitiveness in Electronics*, p. 223.

employee participation programmes. Greater labour productivity and higher quality – stemming from new capital equipment and redesigned products as well as work reorganization – helped save the jobs of several thousand American workers. At the same time, the production process was more automated, cutting into job opportunities. Quasar's investments in Mexico also came at the expense of job opportunities for Americans. But without these steps, Quasar's US plants might have closed – at the cost of many more jobs.

In the Quasar example, impacts on manufacturing efficiency had many sources; it is impossible to isolate and account with any precision for each. As figure 30.2 and the Quasar example illustrate, rationalization of production may improve manufacturing efficiency and keep some people at work while making others redundant. Prospects for avoiding displacement are far better in US industries that are more technologically dynamic and are expanding more rapidly than consumer electronics. But nowhere can the tradeoffs between productivity and job opportunities be avoided. In general, productivity must rise to improve competitiveness. Unless output expands at least as fast, some jobs will vanish.

### *Import and Offshore Production: How Important?*

The US consumer electronics industry has faced strong external competition since the late 1960s, largely from producers in the Far East. Half the US consumer electronics market has been taken by imports; most products still assembled in the United States contain many imported components. Penetration of consumer electronics markets coincided with employment decline. For example, imports of black-and-white television sets rose from one-quarter to three-quarters of US sales over the 1967–77 period. Imports of colour television sets peaked in 1976 at a level nearly ten times greater than in 1967, then dropped because of quotas termed Orderly Marketing Agreements negotiated with Japan, South Korea, and Taiwan.[7] The quotas cut imports roughly in half.

To what extent have imports cost US jobs? First, we must determine the causes of import penetration. Imports may rise because demand exceeds domestic capacity or because consumer preference shifts to foreign-made goods (perhaps they are judged better values). In the first case – exemplified by video cassette recorders, where US capacity is zero – jobs may not be lost directly but the rate of increase in job opportunities may slow. In the second case, typified by imports of Japanese cars and to a lesser extent by sales of television sets, immediate decreases in employment are likely.

Nor are the consequences of offshore production straightforward. Today, the remaining American-owned television manufacturers all operate overseas production facilities. In addition to the attraction of low-wage labour, the US tariff schedules serve to encourage offshore assembly. (Items 806.30 and 807 permit re-imports with duties computed only on foreign value-added.) All wages and salaries paid overseas could be viewed as a loss to American labour and the US gross domestic product. But what if American firms can only lower their costs and maintain or expand their markets by moving abroad? In some cases, American firms may seek offshore production to take advantage of low-cost labour. In other

7. See *International Competitiveness in Electronics*, pp. 112–13 and 446–9.

cases (computer plants in Western Europe, for example), US manufacturers may wish to manufacture near their overseas customers.

It is oversimple to argue that the total number of foreign workers engaged in production for shipment to the United States - whether employed by US or foreign firms - represents domestic employment loss. In most cases, US consumer electronics firms had little choice concerning offshore production. Movement abroad was a defensive reaction, not a strategy aimed at expanding markets and improving profitability. To assume that jobs overseas substitute directly for US employment is tantamount to assuming a stable competitive environment - not at all the case. Rather, employment declines followed losses in competitiveness. American firms had higher costs than their rivals. They pursued the obvious route: increases in automation to raise productivity at home, combined with transfers of labour-intensive operations offshore. Only some companies survived; the others left the industry or were purchased by more successful manufacturers. In this complex chain of events, then, import competition must be counted as the primary cause of job losses in the US consumer electronics industry.

## MICROELECTRONICS

Since the mid-1950s, US employment in semiconductor manufacture has increased rapidly, from a few thousand when production of transistors was just beginning, to more than 280,000 by the first half of 1985 (see figure 30.3). In addition to merchant firms selling on the open market, the totals in the figure include captive production by vertically integrated manufacturers such as IBM and AT&T. During two periods, 1969–71 and 1974–5, employment dropped sharply as a result of recession. Since late 1984, total employment in semiconductors has again been dropping, with the number of production workers falling more sharply. These recent declines come when the economy is not in recession; given the new strength of Japanese competition, it appears that the microelectronics sector has entered a new phase in its evolution.

The proportion of production workers in the US microelectronics industry

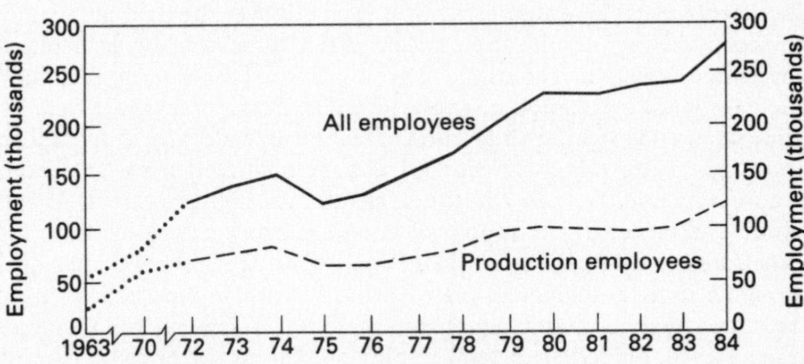


FIGURE 30.3 US employment in semiconductors and related devices, 1963–84
*Sources:* Office of Technology Assessment, *International Competitiveness in Electronics*, Washington DC, November 1983, p. 356; Bureau of Labor Statistics

dropped from 66 per cent of the total work force in 1963 to slightly more than 40 per cent in 1985. American semiconductor manufacturers, particularly the merchant firms, have been moving labour-intensive assembly operations offshore for years; technological advance has contributed to the shift toward skilled and professional jobs in the United States. Demand for technicians and other nonproduction workers has risen with each succeeding generation of more sophisticated (and expensive) fabrication equipment. With movement through large-scale and now very large-scale integration, design and development of new circuits has become far more complex and time consuming; the ranks of engineering and R&D personnel have grown much faster than those of unskilled and semiskilled production employees.

### *Imports and Offshore Manufacturing*

In comparing current layoffs, particularly for production workers, with those in previous downturns, one major difference is this: Japanese competition was not a factor during the 1970s. Today, Japanese firms account for substantial fractions of world market share for some types of devices, holding 85–90 per cent of the burgeoning worldwide merchant market for 256K RAM memory chips. (Note, however, that this percentage excludes devices produced by such companies as AT&T for internal use.) Furthermore, huge investments by Japanese semiconductor manufacturers over the last few years have created a great deal of overcapacity. This excess capacity, as much as 30 or 40 per cent for some types of chips, aggravated the price cutting that has been endemic in the industry. After informal complaints against the Japanese going back a number of years, US semiconductor manufacturers filed three major trade-related complaints with the Federal Government over a four-month period in 1985. Partly in consequence, Japanese firms have been cutting back on shipments to the United States, while also accelerating their investments here – paralleling their earlier investments in consumer electronics.

Imports are not new to this sector. In 1971, the United States exported twice as many semiconductors as it imported, but by 1982 imports exceeded exports. Do the trends now visible portend job losses? Will employment suffer here as in consumer electronics? The answer is no, at least not over the next decade. There are two reasons. First, despite the current sales slump, worldwide demand for microelectronic devices will continue to grow over the longer term. Although the Japanese have made substantial inroads, American firms retain more than half of worldwide sales, and are still in a position of technical leadership in some if not all varieties of integrated circuits. Second, US semiconductor firms have exported much more aggressively than consumer electronics manufacturers. Moreover, about three-quarters of all US imports of microelectronic devices consist of intracorporate transfers by American-owned firms – that is, re-imports after offshore processing. Offshore employment may continue to rise, and perhaps continue to increase faster than domestic employment, but US jobs in microelectronics should rise as well. Nonetheless, total employment in the sector could continue to grow while the number of production jobs declines.

American semiconductor firms transferred labour-intensive 'back-end' operations overseas – primarily assembly steps such as wire bonding and encapsulation

– at a rapid pace beginning in the 1960s. During that decade alone, US companies established more than 50 foreign manufacturing plants.[8] Wafers, fabricated domestically, were shipped to low-wage sites, mostly in Asia, for the final stages in processing, then returned to the United States or sent on to other markets. In recent years, US merchant manufacturers have carried out perhaps 90 per cent of all assembly work overseas.[9]

The reason is simple. Typical estimates for the 1970s indicated that production costs could be cut in half through offshore assembly.[10] Given these potential savings, cost/price competition became the primary motive for such investments; American semiconductor firms moved offshore to reduce costs and expand markets. Once the first US manufacturer invested in low-wage countries, others followed. With questionable prospects for automation during the 1960s and early 1970s, and a rate of technological advance that threatened to render investments in automated equipment obsolete, the choice was plain: move offshore or be undersold. In contrast to consumer electronics, the competitors in microelectronics were American firms almost exclusively; large-scale foreign investments by US manufacturers predated Japanese thrusts in microelectronics by more than a decade. If in the case of consumer electronics, offshore manufacturing was a reaction to import competition, in microelectronics the motives were offensive.

Because most offshore jobs are filled by assembly workers, overseas manufacturing has contributed to the declining fraction of production employees in the United States. US firms employ perhaps three-quarters as many people in their foreign operations as they do here; but, while only 40 per cent of the domestic jobs are in production, the figure is more than 80 per cent for offshore plants.[11] As a result, American companies employ many more production workers overseas than at home – roughly 150,000, compared with about 115,000. Although domestic jobs more than doubled during the 1970s, offshore employment grew even faster.

To what extent do foreign workers employed in the overseas operations of US firms, or the employees of foreign-owned companies which export to the United States, stand for job opportunities lost to Americans? In contrast to offshore facilities, most of which are in Asia, point-of-sale plants in industrialized countries have been established largely for strategic reasons: market access, customer liaison, and, sometimes, the avoidance of import barriers. While these point-of-sale plants have arguably small consequences for US employment, offshore investments driven by lower wages directly displace American workers, just as in consumer electronics. Periodically, speculation arises that advances in automated production equipment will mean that American firms can return back-end processing to the United States. With more automation, the labour cost advantages of offshore sites diminish, although they may not vanish. But even when costs remain lower overseas, strategic advantages – similar to those for

8. *A Report on the US Semiconductor Industry* (Department of Commerce, September 1979), p. 84.

9. J. R. Lineback, 'Automation May Erase Offshore Edge', *Electronics*, Apr. 21, 1982, p. 94.

10. W. F. Finan, 'The International Transfer of Semiconductor Technology Through US-based Firms', Working Paper no. 118 (National Bureau of Economic Research, December 1975), p. 60.

11. *Summary of Trade and Tariff Information: Semiconductors* (US International Trade Commission Publication 841, July 1982), p. 8.

point-of-sale plants in other industrialized countries - may mean that American companies will bring some of their production back home.[12] If they do (keeping in mind that it is automation that would make this possible), the result is not likely to be an increase in jobs for production workers. Employment is far more likely to increase for engineers, technicians, and supervisors.

### *The Production System*

The picture outlined above is not quite so simple as it might seem. Generalizations about the microelectronics industry conceal a good deal of diversity within. Low production costs are far more important for some firms than for others. Companies that depend on product leadership must develop manufacturing systems geared to device technologies pushing the state of the art. Those with broad product lines will place greater stress on costs and quality. Needless to say, no microelectronics manufacturer can neglect costs or quality; the question is one of priorities. Still, unique product designs - for example, a microprocessor with capabilities outstripping those of the rest of the industry - will generate competitive advantages almost irrespective of manufacturing costs.

Nonetheless, in microelectronics as in any industry, unique products remain the exception; generally, manufacturing capabilities are critical for competitive success. Microelectronics, first of all, is an industry where product and process knowhow interact more closely than in perhaps any other. As an example, in mid-1984, Trilogy Systems abandoned its attempts to achieve wafer-scale integration, which would have increased scale and complexity by factors of 100 or more - companies must be able not only to design but to build new types of devices. More than this, quality has become, since the end of the 1970s, central to competitive dynamics. As in many other industries, Japanese manufacturers made quality and reliability a major element in their export strategies. This helped Japanese semiconductor firms penetrate US markets. They concentrated on standard devices such as memory chips, meeting or undercutting the prices of American manufacturers while offering better quality and hence better value.

What does it take to achieve high quality in the production of integrated circuits? Certainly it takes good manufacturing equipment. Japanese semiconductor firms purchased most of their equipment from the same vendors that supplied the US industry; hence they had no advantage on the factory floor as far as equipment was concerned. Integrated circuits from different manufacturers do differ in design, even when functionally identical. Design details influence costs and quality; Japanese firms made design choices aimed at quality and reliability, sometimes at the expense of cost or performance. But more than this, Japan's factory system as a whole - plant layout, integration of people into the production process, task allocations, management style, and internal training and retraining programmes - leads to high quality as well as low costs. From a systems perspective, their production processes helped Japan's semiconductor manufacturers to penetrate world markets, competing successfully with American firms that had the lead - and still do - in many functional aspects of circuit design.

12. See, for example, S. P. Galante, 'US Semiconductor Makers Automate, Cut Chip Production in Southeast Asia', *The Wall Street Journal*, Aug. 21, 1985, p. 28.

## DO IMPORTS, TECHNOLOGY COST US JOBS?

Import competition, automation, and offshore investment take place in a context of global shifts in market structure, with long-term consequences for jobs and job opportunities in a national economy, as well as immediate impacts on workers, firms, and industries. In expanding markets, a firm that can respond quickly to new opportunities anywhere in the world may be able to increase exports and consolidate its position. During the 1970s, for example, American semiconductor manufacturers capitalized on the shift toward metal-oxide-semiconductor integrated circuits ahead of their foreign rivals. In doing so, they created many new job opportunities for Americans, unskilled as well as skilled.

In consumer electronics, particularly television manufacture, the dynamic has been far different. Much of the technology is conventional, accessible to firms in many parts of the world. Markets grow more slowly. In the United States, competition at the retail level has been fierce, with prices declining relative to other consumer durables. As productivity increased, employment declined. Overall, then, while employment in the US electronics industry has grown, the increases have been far from uniform. Few of the workers who once made vacuum tubes found work in microelectronics.

Of course, growth and technological change in electronics also exert influences far beyond this industry. Computer manufacturing, where US competitiveness remains high, has seen rapid employment increase with simultaneous productivity improvements. At the same time, advances in computer systems have created and destroyed vast numbers of jobs in other industries.

Figure 30.4 illustrates employment growth in computer manufacture, including peripherals. Even more than in microelectronics, the trend has been away from production employees and toward more skilled workers and professionals. Unlike either semiconductors or consumer electronics, neither imports nor offshore production has as yet affected employment greatly. American computer firms have invested heavily overseas, but foreign plants generally serve foreign

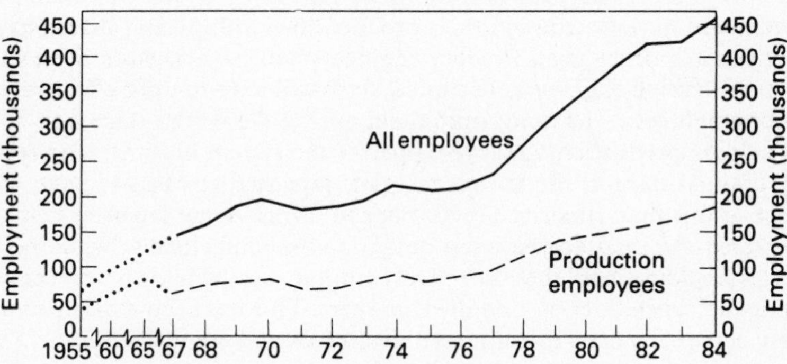


FIGURE 30.4 US employment in computer and peripheral equipment manufacturing, 1955–84

*Sources:* Office of Technology Assessment, *International Competitiveness in Electronics*, Washington DC, November 1983, p. 359; Bureau of Labor Statistics

markets. As in microelectronics, some foreign production may substitute for exports from the United States. But in industrialized (and some developing) countries, American firms often must invest in manufacturing facilities if they expect to sell in volume, limiting the extent to which point-of-sale plants can be viewed as displacing domestic workers. Imports of peripherals and components have been more important; many disc drives and terminals now come from overseas.

In computers, competitive threats lie well in the future.[13] But in consumer electronics, US competitiveness began to slip 20 years ago. Employment typically falls when industries lose ground in either domestic or international markets. Even if aggregate economic growth brings greater demand, only the more efficient companies can take full advantage; firms seldom have any choice but to adopt new technologies, process as well as product, if they wish to remain competitive. Those that move quickly (but not too quickly) may be able to gain an edge over their rivals through efficiency improvements or differentiated product designs. Companies may be forced to automate or pursue alternative routes to lower costs and greater productivity simply to survive. Such strategies have enabled Zenith and RCA, the two largest American colour television manufacturers, to maintain their approximate market shares, but to do so they had to cut their payrolls. If modernizing production facilities and moving offshore costs US jobs in the short term, such strategies may help maintain the total market for American-made products over the longer term.

Like all technical change, then, advances in electronics will continue to bring a mix of positive and negative outcomes. Firms manufacturing electronics products will, for some years, continue to create substantial numbers of new jobs. In US manufacturing as a whole, however, jobs – at least for production workers – may go down in absolute terms. A major source of decline in employment opportunities will be redesigned production systems utilizing computers and computer networks along with other tools for improving organizational efficiency.

For firms determined to maintain their competitiveness in world markets while retaining a production base in high-wage economies, computer-assisted automation will be necessary but not, by itself, sufficient. To be successful, these companies will have to redesign their product lines with greater manufacturing efficiency as a primary goal. Product engineers will have to work more closely with manufacturing engineers. Technical staffs will have to work effectively with shopfloor employees – learning from them during the design stage and, at later stages, helping production employees operate the system in something approximating optimal fashion. In the recent past, Japanese companies have done a better job at this than American (or European) firms. Some Japanese firms have nearly erased the interface between design and manufacturing, while building corporate organizations that effectively utilize available human resources, including the capabilities of 'unskilled' workers. This has been a major source of Japanese competitiveness in consumer electronics and microelectronics.[14] While

13. J. A. Alic and R. R. Miller, 'Export Strategies in the Computer Industry: Japan and the United States', in P. Edwards and R. Gordon, eds, *Strategic Computing: Defense Research and Computer Technology*.
14. *International Competitiveness in Electronics*, chapter 8.

we prefer to stress similarities rather than differences between Japanese and Western management styles, it seems clear that the Japanese are well ahead in introducing more highly integrated production systems. A major reason is decision-making processes that lend themselves to conflict resolution and the development of shared values, necessary attributes of integrated systems. Designing products for manufacturing efficiency will be one of the keys to competitive success for American firms over the next few decades. So will integration of workers – at all levels, but particularly on the shop floor – into the production process.

Only by using labour effectively and efficiently – which often means changes both in product design and in the production system – can firms in high wage economies maintain their international competitiveness. Not all firms will be successful. Some workers, companies, industries, and regions will lose out. Unskilled and semiskilled manufacturing workers are in the greatest jeopardy.

How can the negative impacts be minimized, while capitalizing on the potentials of new technology? The relationships between technical change, employment, and international competition may be complex, but from the standpoint of public policy, many of the negative effects are quite predictable. Adjustment problems cannot be avoided, but governments can prepare for them, both to ease the inevitable shifts and to help maintain the competitive ability of domestic industries. Because shifts in industrial structure bring new jobs with new skilled requirements, it may be time to rethink both public and private programmes of training, retraining, and education. With jobs and job opportunities for production workers declining, it may be time to rethink the meaning of work in advanced industrial societies.

# 31

# Office Automation and Women's Work: the Technological Transformation of the Insurance Industry

BARBARA BARAN

Not only is the majority of the US work force now engaged in various forms of white-collar activity, most of it in offices, office work is also largely women's work. Of the total female work force, 67 per cent is employed in white-collar occupations, compared to only 40 per cent of the male work force. More than one of every three working women is a clerical (US Department of Labor, 1981a). Today, the introduction of computer-based technologies into offices promises to affect dramatically the working lives of these women. Although the 'office revolution' has been much heralded but long awaited, this chapter will contend that in the last few years the combined forces of heightened competition and technological innovation have sped the process of diffusion. Automation of white-collar activities is proceeding much more slowly than its enthusiasts had hoped; nevertheless, in a number of industries information technologies are beginning to have a major impact on the size of the work force and the nature of work.

To date, however, there has been little empirical analysis of these changes. Most of the literature on the effects of technology on work design and manpower requirements has been, and remains, focused on manufacturing. In addition, in so far as a literature on office automation does exist, it is remarkable for the disagreement among researchers.

This essay was first published in M. Castells (ed.), *High Technology, Space and Society*, Sage, 1985. Research was done in conjunction with Suzanne Teegarden, Barbara Facher, and Jean Ross. In addition, I would like to thank Stephen Cohen, Ben Harrison, Ann Markusen, Michael Teitz, and, of course, Manuel Castells for their help along the way, and Eileen Appelbaum for sharing her own work on the insurance industry. Finally, I am especially indebted to three loyal critics and supporters: Amy Glasmeier, Margaret Baran, and, as always, Jim Shoch. A portion of this research was performed under contract with the United States Congress Office of Technology Assessment through the Berkeley Roundtable on the International Economy; however, the opinions expressed here are mine.

The intent of my research on the insurance industry, then, was to contribute to this nascent literature – with a particular emphasis on the probable impacts of office automation on the female work force. I selected the insurance industry for observation for several reasons. First, it is a prototypical white-collar industry in the sense that the production of its product, as well as the supporting administrative activity, involves the processing and generation of paper. Second, insurance is a major employer of office workers, especially clericals; of the more than 14 million 'administrative support personnel' employed in 1980, close to 1 million were working in this one industry alone (US Bureau of the Census, 1981). As a result, of course, approximately 60 per cent of the work force is female (US Department of Labor, various years: percentages computed by comparing tables B-3 and B-2). Finally, insurance is also one of the most highly automated of the white-collar industries; for example, it has been estimated that insurance companies account for a remarkable 16 per cent of IBM's entire installed base (interview with executive in the Life Office Management Association).

Because aggregate data are both woefully incomplete and, at best, fail to capture with any richness changes occurring in labour process, I chose a methodology that combined case work and elite interviewing. Initially, a case study was conducted of a major national property/casualty insurer that included twenty-six interviews with employees in various parts of the company's operations (home office, branch office, data processing centre, commercial group, and personal lines centre) and analysis of extensive personnel data that the company made available. The second stage of the study involved interviews with executives, personnel managers, and systems analysts in twenty-five other companies, loosely stratified by size, product type, growth rate, distribution system, and so on. Finally, members of the industry's trade associations, agents' associations, and vendor companies were also interviewed. This fieldwork has been supplemented with secondary source material from government agencies, trade publications, and documents and surveys kindly provided by the trade associations and consultants to the industry.

This chapter begins with a brief review of the existing literature as the context for my own observations. In the following two sections I then argue that, in the insurance industry at least, current and future applications of computer technologies are likely to differ significantly from earlier implementations of office automation equipment (with which most of the literature is concerned); this is because of important changes that are occurring in the competitive environment, in markets, products, and in the technology itself. Finally, I will explore the likely effects of the new implementations on manpower requirements, the occupational structure, and women's labour.

## THE DESKILLING DEBATE

Although the deskilling debate certainly preceded Braverman, his contribution was particularly provocative and therefore formed the starting point of this investigation. Braverman (1974) argues that despite the differences between the old and the new technologies, the dynamic of the transformation is a familiar one. Just as the industrial revolution robbed skilled artisans of their trade, automation of the office will deskill and degrade white-collar labour.

As in the factory, office work is being divided into hundreds of minute fragments parcelled out among thousands of 'detail' workers who thereby lose control over the product of their labour and any variety in their daily activity. The greatest portion of every day, or perhaps the entire day, is spent operating a machine. As middle-level jobs are deskilled, the work force is polarizing into a mass of unskilled workers on one hand and a tiny coterie of managers and professionals on the other.

In recent years the most important challenge to this perspective has come from a disparate group of writers whom I will label the 'postindustrialists'. I include within this category analysts of diametrically opposed ideological persuasion, such as Daniel Bell (1976) on one hand, and Fred Block and Larry Hirschhorn (1979) on the other, and futurists such as Alvin Toffler (1980).

The common core of the postindustrialists' argument is that the inherent logic of an information-based economy differs in fundamental respects from the first wave of mechanization. First, whereas the assembly line socialized and centralized production, the new technologies offer the possibility of radical decentralization. Second, whereas the industrial revolution intensified the division of labour, computer technologies promise less functional specialization. And, third, whereas partial mechanization produced degraded job configurations, fully automated labour processes expel unskilled labour; within the capital-intensive sectors, then, average skill levels will rise.

In the most optimistic and popular of these accounts, the end product of this transformation is a society of knowledge-workers. Hirschhorn and others, however, warn that so long as outmoded social relations confine the direction of development, we are instead likely to produce a society characterized by serious underutilization of workers' skills and widespread permanent structural unemployment.

Finally, the numerous feminist writers who have intervened in this debate (see, for example, Barker and Downing, 1980; Davies, 1975; Glenn and Feldberg, 1977, 1983; Hacker, 1979; Nussbaum and Gregory, 1980; Werneke, 1983; West, 1982) argue that, because of the pervasiveness of occupational sex segregation within the office work force, women will bear the brunt of the restructuring process. Whereas women's jobs are disproportionately disappearing and their opportunities for upward mobility declining, men may actually benefit both because they will dominate the more highly skilled technical and professional jobs being created and because automation may centralize control in the hands of (male) senior managers and systems analysts.

The limited number of case studies that have been published report conflicting findings. In regard to changes in the occupational structure, some researchers have found that job loss is concentrated among low-skilled clericals (Faunce et al., 1962; Shepherd, 1971), implying a general upgrading of labour; other studies indicate, on the contrary, the elimination of skilled clerical activities, resulting in a polarization of the occupational structure (Glenn and Feldberg, 1977; Hoos, 1961; *BLS Bulletin* no. 1468). Similarly, whereas some analysts have reported less task fragmentation as the technology becomes more sophisticated (Shepherd, 1971; Matteis, 1979; Sirbu, 1982; Adler, 1983; Appelbaum, 1984), others suggest that job content is narrowed and worker autonomy reduced (Murphree, 1982; Greenbaum, 1979; Cummings, 1977; Glenn and Feldberg, 1983, 1977). Finally, although in all cases women experienced the greatest job loss, in some reports it appeared that after automation women were relegated to lower-skilled activities (Glenn and Feldberg, 1977; Murphree, 1982), whereas in other accounts female clericals seemed to benefit from the new labour process (Matteis, 1979; Cummings, 1977).

This chapter will address a number of these questions based on my empirical observations in the insurance industry; briefly, however, my critiques of the dominant perspectives can be summarized as follows.

First, although the strength of the Bravermanist account lies in its insistence on an enduring capitalist logic that constrains the implementation of new technologies, in so far as this analysis elevates the factory – with its assembly line and detail workers – to an essential aspect of the capitalist organization of production, the Bravermanists miss much of what is radically new about the new technologies. The leading postindustrialists and futurists, on the other hand, make the reverse error. Bell (1976), for example, seems to have implicitly assumed that the US economy would escape the unpleasant consequences of serious competition, permitting a friendly accommodation between capital and labour. Toffler (1980) similarly ignores the implications of capital's current drive to reduce costs, particularly labour costs, and the extent to which control over the labour force looms large in managerial choice of appropriate technologies, job design, and so on.

In terms of specific analyses of the effects of office automation, the feminist work has, from my perspective, been the most interesting, although, unfortunately these investigations have relied almost exclusively on the Bravermanist framework. Nonetheless, the feminists have correctly insisted that in the face of the historic and extensive sex segregation of the office, analyses of the likely effects of automation on this work force can ill afford to be gender blind; indeed, these analyses must address the broader questions of changes that are occurring in gender relations and in the role of female labour in the economy.

Finally, however, I will argue that office automation cannot be analysed as a unitary phenomenon. Impacts vary on the basis of the specific kind of technology introduced, the nature of the work being automated (originating in the unique characteristics of the product, markets, organizational structure, and competitive dynamics of the industry), and perhaps also the characteristics of the available work force. Similarly, it is necessary to periodize the process of office automation. The first wave did, indeed, correspond to the expectations of the Bravermanists. Nevertheless, in the last few years it has been possible to discern the outlines of a fundamentally new dynamic that I will attempt to describe here.

## THE FIRST WAVE

The first applications of computer-based technology in the insurance industry involved simple mechanization of extremely structured, high-volume operations. The early mainframes were used primarily as number-crunching machines. The automated tasks were fairly discrete so that the shift from manual to computerized performance had little effect on the organization as a whole; task fragmentation, or Taylorization, had already isolated these routinized functions. Word processors, duplicating machines, private branch exchanges, and so on similarly were introduced to mechanize a particular task without regard for the nature of the overall office procedure.

Both the cost and technical requirements of the early machines and the tendency to automate in conformity with the rationalized structure of traditional administrative bureaucracies resulted in intensification of the long-term trend toward task fragmentation and functional centralization. Conceptually and in practice at this stage of development, Taylorization and mechanization were integrated processes.

Routine keyboarding was separated more sharply from other clerical functions and was often spatially isolated from the rest of the firm. Work in these processing centres (both data processing and word processing) was machine-linked, machine-paced, and often machine-supervised.

Task fragmentation was not limited to processing functions. Overall, in the last two decades the labour process in insurance companies was centralized by narrow function. For example, in a number of companies even the main professional occupation, underwriting, was rationalized. At the bottom end, low-level underwriting functions were transferred to a newly created clerical position; at the top end, more speciality underwriting categories were created. Workers were grouped into sections of underwriters, raters, typists; paper flowed from one section to another, mimicking the assembly line. This spatial segregation by occupation was tantamount to spatial segregation by gender. The professional and managerial categories were overwhelmingly male; the growing clerical work force solidly and increasingly female.

In line with the Bravermanist mode, then, the first stage of automation in the insurance industry tended to increase job fragmentation, centralize production by narrow function, heighten occupational sex segregation, and make many routine keyboarding functions spatially 'footloose'. More recently, however, the greater sophistication of the technologies and transformed market conditions are dictating a new organizational logic that promises to reverse many of these early trends.

## THE OFFICE OF THE FUTURE

### *Competition and Organizational Change in the Insurance Industry*

During the 1970s the implementation of advanced office systems proceeded much more slowly than observers and especially the vendors had expected. The barriers to rapid diffusion were both technological and organizational. First, at the level of the technology itself, the task of representing more complex white-collar activities in computer algorithms proved to be exceedingly difficult. To paraphrase systems analyst West Churchman, it was not so easy to get a machine to behave as competently as a clerk (Mintzberg, 1972). The attempt to impose a standardized logic on unstructured procedures generated too many exceptions to be cost-effective and in some cases even diminished the efficiency of the organization (Strassman, 1980). In addition, competition within the vendor community slowed the development of the effective communications networks that are critical to the implementation of sophisticated, integrated office systems.

Second, however, resistance to automation within the user community proved to be an equally serious barrier to diffusion of the new technologies. Professionals, managers, and even executive secretaries balked at the introduction of machinery that threatened to transform the character of their work and the relations of power in their workplaces. In the past few years it has taken a dramatic change in the competitive dynamics of the industry to begin to erode this resistance.

Falling interest rates and the slow but steady deregulation of the financial services sector has brought new competitors into the game and cut sharply into insurers' profit margins. Whereas formerly, as a regulated industry, insurance carriers were virtually assured a reasonable rate of return, today even some giants in the field are struggling for survival. Companies in which paternalism protected job security even through the great depression have recently been rocked to their foundation by layoffs of up to 1500 employees virtually overnight.

## *Technological Change in the Insurance Industry*

At the same time, three technical developments in particular have improved the cost-effectiveness of systems implementation and widened the possible range of applications. First, the increasing miniaturization of electronic circuits has produced quantum leaps in the computing power of ever smaller and cheaper machines. Second, significant improvements in telecommunications technology and the merging of communications and computer technologies have allowed insurers to link their data processing equipment to numerous other office machines (such as word processors, facsimile transmitters, microfilmers, and optical character recognition devices) both within buildings and across continents. Third, the simplification of computer language and greater sophistication of computer software has made possible a whole new range of applications.

In contrast to many office environments, systems development in the insurance industry has been propelled by data processing needs. In the last decade mainframes have become increasingly fast and storage capacity has grown geometrically; nevertheless, the most important development in data processing hardware has probably been the dramatic increase in the capabilities of minicomputers and now microcomputers.

Together with the improvements in communications technologies, these sophisticated small computers have allowed insurers to develop integrated, decentralized data processing systems. Such systems typically link a single host computer to a node, which might be a cathode ray terminal (CRT), intelligent terminal, mini or microcomputer, printer, teleprinting terminal, and so on; the network may be either local or long distance. Local area networks connect a number of components at the same site, often by means of a coaxial cable. Long distance networks perform the same function for remote sites; data transmission is usually through ordinary telephone circuits or leased lines, although some companies have begun to experiment with satellite transmission.

On the basis of these integrated systems insurers have been able to consolidate all policyholder data into central master records stored in the company's main computer installation; in the past, these records were duplicated in up to a dozen functional units. Now users in remote sites can access and manipulate the same data base. As a result, both data entry and data processing functions are often distributed and decentralized; and given the improvements in both mainframe mass storage capacity and communications networks, these decentralized systems are moving rapidly to increase the numbers of on-line, real-time applications.

The development of more sophisticated software is also allowing companies to automate complex, less structured functions; and the new 'user friendly' languages are encouraging professionals and managers to directly access and make use of the wealth of information that the integrated data bases make available for strategic planning, marketing, and so on. As a result, true management information or decision support systems are beginning to be possible and professional functions are being automated for the first time.

### *A New Approach to Automation*

Beginning in the late 1970s, then, as the range of possible computer implementations widened and systems analysts began winning their battle against middle-level knowledge workers, approaches to the problem of automation changed as dramatically as the machines. This evolution can be characterized as the movement from functional approaches to systems approaches; that is, from automating discrete tasks (e.g. typing, calculating) to rationalizing an entire procedure (e.g. new business issuance, claims processing) to restructuring and integrating all the procedures involved in a particular division, product line, or group of product lines.

The transition to a systems approach to automation began, as we might expect, with the simplest procedures - procedures that involved a very small number of discrete tasks, such as payroll, accounting, billing, and so on. Over the last decade more and more complex procedures have been automated and the attention of managers and systems analysts in the industry has turned to the problem of a rational reorganization of the entire firm, including its distribution system, on the basis of fully integrated computer systems. All the work involved in a particular product line is analysed; the labour process is restructured and, where possible, automated. But automation follows the new logic of the organization; older functions may simply be eliminated as artifacts of an outmoded production process. New business issuance is a good example.

The trend in new business processing has been toward on-line, single source entry. In a great many of these applications, rating, billing, and printing functions are performed entirely by the computer. The underwriting function is computer-assisted; that is, the computer provides actuarial guidelines, performs calculations, facilitates rapid access to policyholder files, and so on. Increasingly the policy moves electronically through the various steps in this process, producing daily reports on policy status at each work station. In the case of highly standardized policies, the computer may even perform the underwriting function.

Most of these systems are based on distributed processing networks that give remote site users access to the company's master records. Often they also reflect the trend toward consolidation, integrating functions such as rate quoting, billing, and calculation of commissions with the new business production.

On the basis of these integrated, on-line systems, insurance companies have recently begun a serious redesign of the labour process. Although Taylorist logic continues to inform their efforts, the emerging organization of work bears little resemblance to the assembly line.

## *The Redesign of Work*

The ideal operative on Ford's assembly line turned one bolt. The ideal production worker in the 'insurance company of the future', with the aid of a sophisticated computerized work station, rates, underwrites, and issues all new policies for some subset of the company's customers, handles the updates and renewals on those policies, and, as a by-product, enters the information necessary for the automatic generation of management reports, actuarial decisions, and so on.

In many companies studied, two closely related processes are occurring. The first is the emergence of highly computer-linked, multiactivity jobs that combine tasks formerly performed by data entry clerks, other clerical workers, and professionals. Typically, data entry, rating, routine underwriting, and sometimes policy preparation have been transferred to a skilled clerical worker; a similar configuration has developed in the claims handling process.

In these cases, unskilled clerical work has been largely eliminated; workers in the new clerical jobs, although closely circumscribed in their decision making, are a long way from the typing pool. Judgement calls do have to be made by these clerks. Often they are required to interact directly with the agents, a level of responsibility formerly reserved for professional underwriters. But, perhaps most important, because these workers are accepting risk and directly issuing policies, they are almost solely responsible for 'quality control'. Some kinds of quality checks are, of course, built into the computer systems, but at this stage at least such monitoring only functions to catch gross errors and inconsistencies. Basically, in increasing numbers of insurance lines, clerks are responsible for the soundness and accuracy of the millions of routine risks their companies write and claims they settle.

In these automated processes professionals are also having their work redefined as clerks take over their lower-level functions. First, they have become 'exceptions' handlers; that is, they are responsible only for the policies or claims that fail to fit into the 'pigeon-holes' of the computerized system (which, of course, includes large risks); therefore, their work has become more interesting and complex. Second, in the case of underwriters at least, there has been a reorientation of the job function away from churning out policies and toward planning and marketing. Increasingly, underwriters are being required to go into the field and work directly with agents to develop, evaluate, and encourage the sale of new products. In this way their job has been enlarged or reintegrated as it combines tasks formerly divided among managerial, professional, and sales personnel; 'mental' and 'manual' labour are also to some extent being combined as higher-level employees are required to enter the data directly into the machines, eliminating numerous clerical intermediaries.

The second major reintegrative process that is occurring is the elimination of single-activity units in favour of multiactivity teams. Whereas formerly typists, raters, and underwriters were divided into separate units, each with its own supervisor, now a small team consisting of one or two of each kind of worker will service some subset (often geographical) of the company's customers. In some cases, this form of organization probably simply presages and prepares the organization for the more complete electronic reintegration of work just described. In other cases, however, where the products are more specialized, complex, low volume, or changing rapidly, the team structure is likely to be a long-term arrangement.

Significantly, even the physical environment reflects this new approach. The walls of private offices have been torn down and managers, professionals, and clericals work side by side in shoulder-high cubicles. Open office plans not only reduce overhead costs and permit flexible response to changing technologies; they work to erode outmoded social relations.

Paul Strassman (1980), of the Xerox corporation, has argued that one of the most serious barriers to the improvement of white-collar productivity is 'the view [of managers and professionals] that information is a private good, a source of [their] power'. In order for information flows to be managed in a conscious and explicit way as the new technologies require, the old power bases have to be destroyed. The new office designs have the dual effect of permitting visual scrutiny of everyone's activities and of removing an important symbol of the old managerial role in which power was based on secret information and private loyalties. The pooling of secretaries has a similar impact.

Finally, however, as Sabel (1982) has suggested in the case of manufacturing, the trends just outlined are translating into different actual job configurations, depending on the nature of both the product and its market. The insurance industry, like many other US industries, has been moving in the direction of more sophisticated market segmentation. As one result, a bifurcation seems to be occurring in their product offerings between highly standardized products aimed at mass markets on the one hand, and a proliferation of specialized products, many directed at the upscale market of households with yearly incomes of $50,000 or more, on the other.

Both developments are being spurred by the new technologies, but the production process varies significantly in these two situations. High-volume insurance products – such as homeowners' packages, health, and auto – are being increasingly standardized so that their production and/or servicing can be almost fully automated. In numbers of these lines, low-level and high-level labour is being expelled, leaving primarily skilled clerks and a few managers. In others, the occupational structure is bifurcating; the computerized system is able to handle all but the most complex decisions so that only data entry clerks and exceptions underwriters are needed to process the policies. Again, the nature of the product seems to be critical in determining which of these two configurations emerges, although factors such as the importance of quality control and the prejudices of top management also play an important role.

At the other end of the spectrum, many of the new speciality and financial services products are too complex, unique, or flexible to lend themselves to this kind of automation. Much of the labour force is professional and is more highly skilled than in the past, as evidenced in some cases by new training and licensing requirements. Tailored products could not be sold profitably without the use of the computer, but here the machine augments rather than assumes the functions of professional labour. Routine clerical functions are also less automated, although they are decentralized in the manner described earlier to reduce redundancy, and the trend is toward elimination of as many manual tasks as possible.

### *Spatial Reorganization of Work*

Predictably, a transformation of the industry's spatial organization is accompanying this redesign of the labour process. The direction of change is not a simple one of more or less centralization; several driving principles are operative, producing a variety of configuratons. Perhaps the two most important motivations are the desire to eliminate expensive redundancies and, more generally, a push to reduce land, labour, and overhead costs (although companies are also shifting work to improve customer service, data quality, and the sales effort). Small powerful computers and expanding telecommunications capabilities have opened up numbers of new ways to meet these goals. Companies no longer have to locate whole procedures in the same site; the various component functions can be performed in spatially disparate locations and then reintegrated electronically.

For example, to eliminate redundancy and take full advantage of scale economies, high-volume, standardized processing is being centralized for an entire multilocational corporation. In the case of insurance fleets (that is, combinations of numbers of separate companies), one data centre sometimes services the entire fleet. Because the occupational composition of these centres is largely technical and clerical, they are usually located away from the expensive land and labour of the central cities, but in areas where telecommunications hookups are adequate.

At the other extreme, the drive toward greater efficiency has led insurers to decentralize numbers of functions; data entry and often certain kinds of printing and processing functions are being pushed down to the point of data generation, in this case often the agency or field office. Single-source entry and decentralized production eliminate innumerable redundant steps, improve the accuracy of the data, and dramatically speed turn-around time.

In some cases even more radical decentralization is occurring. Although still rare, insurance companies are beginning to experiment with telecommuting, or homework. The motivation is both cost reduction and the desire to attract or retain the preferred work force – educated, preferably married, and usually white women.

One company studied now has about one-sixth of their claims adjustors working at home. These women (and they are all women) operate as independent contractors and are paid on a piece-rate basis. Using interactive terminals linked to the company's mainframe, they can log onto the sytem at their convenience; the computer stacks the claims in a queue, automatically updates the master file, and creates the checks and explanations of benefits. Productivity is extremely high; overhead and labour costs are low. Although both the information and physical production remain centralized, the labour process itself has been decentralized, decollectivized, and rendered asynchronous.

Finally, however, whole procedures are also being relocated. For example, in order to automate an entire product line, many companies have consolidated work formerly scattered in numerous branch offices into two or three regional centres. Often there is no longer any reason that production has to occur in proximity to the customer base.

### *Summary*

In all of these ways the emerging labour process in the insurance industry is the antithesis of the traditional factory. Electronically reintegrated job categories are combining numerous narrow occupations; in a very real sense, the functioning of the assembly line is now internal to the machine. Similarly, whereas the factory socialized production, the new technologies are paving the way for an organization of work that is extraordinarily isolating.

In the new offices more and more categories of employees now sit alone in small cubicles riveted to their terminals. In many companies the ratio of terminals to employees is already 1 : 2. With the move to interactive on-line systems, these workers are increasingly engaged in 'conversations' with the machine rather than with coworkers.

In the most advanced systems there is also little immediate, physical interdependence among workers - either because the various steps in the production process can be separated in both time and space or because one clerk assumes all the functions of the production team. The current experiments with home work are the radical extreme - and perhaps the logical extension - of this process.

## REDUNDANCY, SKILL, AND THE NEW EXPERIENCE OF WORK

On the basis of these observations, then, information technologies are likely to have two major impacts on the manpower requirements and occupational structure of the insurance industry over the next decade. First, employment should fall, at least in relation to output and probably in absolute terms. Second, skill levels should rise as routine clerical work is eliminated and professional work becomes more complex. At the same time, however, opportunities for occupational mobility will probably decline, the quality of work life may deteriorate, and workers may have less discretion and independence in the conduct of their jobs.

### *The Elimination of Work*

Although true productivity figures are almost impossible to calculate for the insurance industry,[1] there is considerable evidence that automation is improving efficiency and reducing labour inputs. In the life segment, where automation of policy production has proceeded most rapidly in the last decade, purchases of life policies increased by 49.2 per cent between 1970 and 1980 while the labour force expanded by only 9.8 per cent. Between 1980 and 1982 sales grew by 20.8 per cent and employment remained essentially stable.[2]

1. The US Department of Labor, Bureau of Labor Statistics (BLS) has given up its attempt to develop productivity figures for the insurance industry, in large part because it is almost impossible to adequately measure the inputs from brokerage houses, real estate agencies, and so on.

2. This is a very rough estimate of labour productivity within insurance companies alone; labour inputs from independent agents, brokers, and so on have been excluded. Source: US Department of Labor (n.d., various years), *Economic Report of the President* (1983: table B-30), *Best's Aggregates and Averages* (1983), *Insurance Information Institute* (1983).

The situation in the property-casualty segment is more complicated for several reasons: fewer lines of business have been automated; greater reliance on an independent agency force makes it more difficult for insurers to develop fully integrated systems; and for the last decade companies have been scrambling to expand sales to reap the investment benefits of high interest rates.[3] As a result, between 1970 and 1980 employment kept pace with gains in output.

Recently, however, reckless expansion caught up with these companies; losses and layoffs have been widespread. Between 1980 and 1982 sales plunged by 6.5 per cent and employment by 3.8 per cent.[4] Since then labour-shedding has probably increased. With one exception, every property-casualty company visited had experienced serious layoffs in the last four years, ranging between 5 and 15 per cent of their work force. None of these companies foresees new hiring. Heightened competition has brought renewed concern with the bottom line; property-casualty insurers are moving rapidly to automate new product lines and develop an industrywide agency value-added network (with IBM) to improve the efficiency of their distribution system.

Although the layoffs in response to overcapacity were felt throughout the occupational hierarchy, the impacts of technological change have been more discriminate.[5] Routine clerical categories were the first to be eliminated and, for the next few years at least, will continue to be the hardest hit. Between 1970 and 1978 clerical employment as a percentage of total employment in the industry fell from 50 to 45 per cent; in effect, 73,000 clerical jobs were eliminated by the shift in the occupational structure. Keyboarding and filing occupations were particularly seriously affected; the number of keypunch operators dropped by 22 per cent, the number of file clerks by 20 per cent, and the number of typists by 12 per cent (see table 31.1).

Other categories of clerks also experienced absolute declines in employment. For example, between 1978 and 1981 the number of stenographers fell by 31 per cent and the number of manual bookkeepers by 15 per cent. Because of the newly automated claims and underwriting support systems, in the space of these three years the industry also employed fewer claims adjustors and raters (see table 31.2).

Since 1978 also, the impacts of automation on professional work are beginning to be visible in the aggregate data. Between 1978 and 1981 underwriters lost employment share and the number of accountants and auditors plunged

3. For various legal reasons, property-casualty companies were better able than life companies to move their capital into short-term, high-yield investment products.

4. See note 2.

5. Unfortunately, there is no good time-series data available on employment by occupation in the insurance industry. The 1980 Census of the Population has still not developed an occupation-by-industry table; in addition, occupational categories have been so significantly redefined as to make comparisons with the 1970 Census very problematic. Data are available from different sources for a limited number of years. Occupational data for 1960 are reported by the US Department of Labor (1969). These data are comparable to data for 1970 and 1978 reported by the US Department of Labor (1981b). More recent unpublished data is available from the BLS *Occupational Employment Survey of Insurance, 1978 and 1981* . Unfortunately, there are serious and irreconcilable differences between the OES and Industry-Occupation Matrix data. All I can do is report both data sets here. Fortunately, they basically agree on the direction of occupational change and support the expected trends. The OES data, because it is employer-based, may be the more reliable. In any case, it provides the first evidence concerning the crucial later time period when serious restructuring of work in the industry had begun.

TABLE 31.1 Percentage distribution of insurance employment by occupation: 1960, 1970, 1978

| *Occupation* | *Percentage employment* 1960 | 1970 | 1978 | *Percentage change* 1970–8 |
|---|---|---|---|---|
| Managers/officers | 13.3 | 11.8 | 12.1 | 21.4 |
| Prof./tech.workers | 3.2 | 5.8 | 6.0 | 24.0 |
| Clerical workers | 47.4 | 50.0 | 45.4 | 8.0 |
| computer operator | | 0.7 | 1.3 | 119.0 |
| keypunch operator | | 1.8 | 1.2 | −21.9 |
| statistical clerk | | 2.8 | 2.5 | 6.4 |
| bookkeeper | | 3.6 | 2.8 | −7.4 |
| adjustor/examiner | | 7.3 | 9.8 | 58.8 |
| file clerk | | 2.5 | 1.7 | −19.7 |
| mail handler | | 0.7 | 0.5 | −10.7 |
| secretary | | 13.2 | 12.0 | 8.2 |
| typist | | 6.9 | 5.1 | −11.7 |
| Sales | 33.6 | 30.0 | 34.5 | 37.2 |

*Sources:* US Department of Labor (1969 and 1981b)

TABLE 31.2 Percentage change in employment in insurance carriers by selected occupation: 1978–81

| *Occupation* | *Percentage change in employment* |
|---|---|
| Total employment | 5.6 |
| Managers and officers | 10.9 |
| Professional and technical | 9.5 |
| actuary | 21.7 |
| systems analyst | 42.5 |
| accountant/auditor | −51.1 |
| claims examiner, P/C | 10.8 |
| underwriter | 3.0 |
| computer programmer | 36.2 |
| Clerical | 3.5 |
| computer operator | 0.4 |
| bookkeeper, hand | −15.2 |
| claims adjustor | −7.7 |
| correspondence clerk | −1.5 |
| file clerk | −15.9 |
| general clerk | −5.9 |
| rater | −1.6 |
| secretary | 6.6 |
| stenographer | −31.4 |
| typist | −2.9 |
| Sales | 6.6 |

*Source:* US Department of Labor (1981/1979)

dramatically. Although the professional and technical category continued to grow faster than total employment, most of this expansion was directly attributable to the rapid addition of computer professionals (systems analysts and programmers); excluding these two categories, professional occupations grew at about half the rate of total employment (see table 31.2). Because computerization of professional underwriting and claims functions did not begin in earnest until the end of the last decade, we should expect these trends to accelerate.

### *Changes in Skill Requirements and the Occupational Structure*

In contrast to analysts, then, who argue that automation tends to eliminate higher- and middle-level clerical occupations, my own work suggests that most traditional clerical categories are declining - routine, semiskilled, and skilled - including fairly new, but now obsolete, computer-linked jobs such as keypunch. At the same time, however, because computers are best able to perform highly structured functions, narrow routine clerical jobs are disappearing the most rapidly. Whereas the first round of automation did, indeed, deskill and 'proletarianize' much clerical work, the second round is totally eliminating many of those degraded functions.

What is being deskilled, on the other hand, is professional work. Today both users and vendors of office automation equipment have largely shifted their attention away from the task of automating routine activities and are struggling with the problems of how to translate the functions performed by knowledge-workers into computer software. As they are successful these functions are turned over to cheaper labour.

Ironically, in net, the rolling process of deskilling and redundancy is probably raising average skill levels within the industry. Large numbers of low-skilled clerks who formerly made up the bulk of the work force are being expelled; skilled clericals are taking over low-level professional functions; and (a smaller) professional staff is having its work upgraded. In all categories, then, there are relatively fewer jobs, but the remaining work is, overall, more skilled. In this case, therefore, it is critical conceptually to separate the individual workers from their functions. Elements of the work process are being degraded, but the specific agents now performing those functions are either being upgraded or rendered redundant.

### *Occupational Mobility*

Despite rising skill levels in the industry, career paths may be structurally truncated. In the past the barrier to mobility between clerical and professional occupations was primarily sex discrimination. Women were raters; men were underwriters. Theoretically, a rater could be prepared by her job and on-the-job training for an underwriting position, although in practice this rarely happened because of the gender-identification of job categories.

The affirmative action victories of the last decade created new opportunities for women to move up. Perhaps a third of the female underwriters and managers interviewed in one company had entered the firm 10 to 12 years before in clerical positions. Now, however, as lower-level professional functions are automated, the 'bridge' jobs between clerical and professional occupations are being eliminated. In the words of one personnel manager, there will be a 'quantum jump' between the new machine-linked clerical or paraprofessional categories and the remaining, more highly skilled professional, managerial, or sales work.

Barriers to mobility, then, are not new. But if bridge jobs disappear, a new kind of structural barrier to upward mobility will be created just as the older sexual barrier is being eroded.

### *A New Experience of Work and the Question of Control*

The new jobs in the insurance industry may be not only dead-end, but also boring, stressful, and deeply unsatisfying. Even fairly skilled work that is driven by the logic of computer algorithms seems to subject workers to unusually high levels of stress (Adler, 1983; Zuboff, 1982; Gregory, 1982). Partially this is the product of what Zuboff called the 'curious combination of abstraction and routinization' that characterizes computer-mediated work. Daily activity is centred around the comprehension and manipulation of abstract symbols. Not only is this labour more socially isolating, it requires sustained concentration. Because the fruits of their labour 'disappear behind the screen,' workers complain that they lose the sense of accomplishing a task (Zuboff, 1982).

Similarly, although labour is being electronically reintegrated, the autonomy of the worker may be diminished. As numerous commentators have argued (see, for example, Noble, 1979; Braverman, 1974; Greenbaum, 1979), the question of control over the labour process brings into sharp relief the extent to which job design is socially determined. The implementation of the new technologies is posing an important set of choices.

On one hand, productive exploitation of the vast amounts of information made available by the integrated data bases would dictate a diffusion of that information throughout the organization. Zuboff (1983) and Hirschhorn (1981) have suggested that this is, indeed, occurring in continuous process manufacturing; and Sable (1982) makes a similar argument about the effect of CAD/CAM technologies. On the other hand, American managers have an old and deep distrust of their work force, as witnessed by the remarkable proportion of managers and supervisors in US industry.

Today this tension is evident in the insurance industry, both within and between companies. In some situations former data entry clerks are being given wider responsibilities for policy issuance and claims processing and professionals are taking on tasks of data analysis and strategic decision making formerly reserved for management. In other situations task variety has been diminished and the daily work process is closely monitored by machines. For example, in some companies supervisors can keep track of the number of cases handled by each customer service representative and standards have even been set for the number of times the telephone is allowed to ring before it is answered (Appelbaum, 1984).

Significantly, in either case, although the integrated systems may reduce the role of middle management, they provide senior managers with an important new source of control over the daily operations of the organization. And, as Zuboff (1982) has argued, because the integrative logic, decision rules, and operating procedures are designed into the computer programs by a small group of managers, systems analysts, and programmers, users have little comprehension of the system's overall function or the normative criteria on which it was based.

Finally, in this regard, it is interesting to speculate on how a largely female labour force is likely to affect job design in the insurance industry. Although historically one of the defining characteristics of female-typed occupations has been the absence of substantial power over the organisation (Oppenheimer, 1968), women have frequently been preferred for highly responsible jobs (such as nursing and secretarial labour) in which authority is extremely constrained. It is possible, then, that in the context of a female work force, lower-level decisions may be pushed down to cheaper labour without threatening top management's control.

## CHEAP BUT EDUCATED LABOUR

The critical questions when I began this study were not only how is automation likely to affect the lives of the almost 1 million women office workers currently employed by the insurance industry, but also what kind of role might female labour play in the process of economic restructuring. In this section, I would like to offer some admittedly tentative answers to both of these questions.

### *The Growing Importance of Female Labour*

First, despite the fact that female-dominated jobs are disappearing in great numbers, empirically the proportion of women in the insurance industry has grown dramatically in the last decade. By 1982 women comprised 61 per cent of the industry's entire work force, up from 54 per cent in 1970 (US Department of Labor, various years).

Between 1970 and 1980 women claimed approximately 307,000 of the 352,000 new jobs created; and over the next two years women gained 8900 jobs, whereas men lost 5500. In total during this period female employment rose by 46 per cent compared to a meagre 7 per cent rise in male employment. In contrast to the economy as a whole, where the ratio of women to men increased by 4.7 percentage points, in the insurance industry the ratio climbed by 7.2 percentage points (see table 31.3).

In this same period, however, as I discussed earlier, clerical workers declined as a percentage of the work force. In other words, the increase in female employment cannot be explained by the disproportionate growth of traditionally female-typed jobs. On the contrary, in fact, what seems to be occurring is a major movement of women into traditional male occupations – professional, managerial, technical, and even clerical.

Between 1970 and 1979 the number of female managers and officers grew from 11 to 24 per cent of the insurance work force; professionals from 17 to 38 per cent; and technicians from 38 to 65 per cent (see table 31.3). The percentage of women insurance examiners and investigators (formerly male clerical occupations) grew from 9 per cent in 1962 to 26 per cent in 1971 and 58 per cent in 1981 (Appelbaum, 1984).

Overall in the insurance industry, the ratio of women to men in professional and technical occupations rose by 19 and 27 percentage points respectively, as opposed to a 4.3 percentage point gain for women throughout the economy in professional and technical occupations combined. Although the disaggregated comparative statistics are not extremely reliable, women in the insurance industry during this period seem to have increased their share of professional employment more rapidly than in any other major sector of the economy (see table 31.3).

TABLE 31.3 Percentage point increase in the proportion of female employment by industry and occupation: 1970–80

| | Occupation | | | | Percentage total |
|---|---|---|---|---|---|
| *Industry* | *Prof.* | *Mgr* | *Sales* | *Cler.* | *employment* |
| Total labour force | 4.3 | 9.5 | 5.9 | 6.5 | 4.7 |
| Manuf. | 9.0 | 5.9 | 11.9 | 6.7 | 2.8 |
| Trans. and utilities | 7.7 | 9.9 | 22.8 | 3.1 | 3.7 |
| Wholesale | 8.8 | 5.9 | 4.0 | 8.9 | 3.4 |
| Retail | 13.4 | 11.3 | 5.4 | 6.3 | 5.5 |
| Services | 0.9 | 10.1 | 2.6 | 11.8 | 7.7 |
| Fire | 13.0 | 15.7 | 17.5 | 5.1 | 8.3 |
| Insurance[a] | 19.0 P<br>27.0 T | 13.0 | | | 7.2 |

[a] Data for the insurance industry is from the Insurance Information Institute and is based on EEOC statistics. Although it is not strictly comparable to the BLS data, because insurance carriers tend to be large, the EEOC data on the percentage of female employment is virtually identical to the BLS report. Here, P = professional, T = technical workers as the EEOC data is captured in this form.

*Source:* Computed from figures in US Department of Labor (1981b and 1980) and unpublished data from the Insurance Information Institute

There are a number of plausible explanations for this rapid transition from male to female labour. The first is simply affirmative action victories. Successful affirmative action suits have been waged against insurance companies, and, as a result, companies throughout the industry have developed more egalitarian hiring and promotion policies. For example, because of affirmative action litigation between 1977 and 1983 one company studied increased its percentage of female managers from 4 to 33 per cent; professionals from 27 to 46 per cent; and technicians from 29 to 67 per cent.

There is also, however, reason to believe that cheaper female labour is being substituted for more expensive male labour throughout the occupational hierarchy and that women are being used to smooth the process of job redesign and introduction of the new machinery. The professional staffs in the new highly automated personal lines centres of the company where I conducted my intensive case study are so overwhelmingly female that the chief administrator of one joked that they are under pressure to develop affirmative action goals for men. She explained that the reason they chose to hire women was that women are more 'flexible' than men in adjusting to the computer-mediated labour process.

In another company the introduction of computer-assisted underwriting has shifted the bulk of policy processing from a department that is over 60 per cent male to one that is entirely female. In still another the change to a computerized claims process not only brought protests from the older male adjustors, but was accompanied by an increase in the percentage of female employees from approximately 25 per cent of the claims force to over 60 per cent.

Similarly, in line with this hypothesis, the percentage of female professional and technical workers in the industry varies widely by product line. In the more highly automated life and medical/health segments, women's share of employment in these occupational categories is considerably higher. In 1979 40 per cent of all professionals in life carriers and 43 per cent of professionals in medical/health carriers were women, as opposed to 35 per cent in property/casualty companies. Similarly, 68 per cent of all life insurance technicians were female and 81 per cent of all medical/health technicians, whereas women held only 50 per cent of all technical jobs in the property/casualty segment (see table 31.4).

Significantly, also, although women are moving up in the occupational hierarchy, female wage rates in the industry remain extremely low. In this case study company, for example, female professionals earn only 16 per cent more than male clericals (whereas male professionals earn 50 per cent more); and the majority of white female managers (57 per cent) earn on the average $4 *less* per week than white male clericals. Between 1970 and 1979 in the finance, insurance, and real estate (FIRE) sector as a whole, wages for nonsupervisory personnel fell more dramatically than in any other sector of the economy; whereas total real wages increased by 2 per cent, in the FIRE sector real wages fell by 8 per cent.

In summary, then, drawing together these statistics with the earlier description of changes occurring in the labour process, automation in the insurance industry seems to be creating precisely the kinds of jobs for which women always have been preferred – semiskilled, low paid, and dead end. As a result, the deskilling of professional functions may be acting as a countertendency to the elimination of routine clerical jobs, maintaining employment opportunities for women.

At the same time, as women move into men's jobs the occupational hierarchy is becoming less gender-segregated than in the past. Perhaps, more precisely, as Burris and Wharton (1982) have recently suggested, the more middle-class jobs (managerial, professional, and some technical categories) are desegregating, whereas clerical occupations continue to be solidly and increasingly female. Although this change opens up new opportunities for college-educated women, it

TABLE 31.4 Percentage of female employment in the insurance industry by industry segment: 1978

| | *Percentage industry segment female employment* | | | |
|---|---|---|---|---|
| *Occupation* | *All carriers* | *Life* | *Med./health* | *Prop./casualty* |
| Total employment | 60.9 | 53.8 | 69.2 | 64.8 |
| Mgr/admin. | 23.8 | 20.5 | 31.4 | 24.1 |
| Prof. | 38.0 | 40.3 | 42.9 | 34.5 |
| Tech. | 65.3 | 68.2 | 81.4 | 50 |
| Cler. | 92.4 | 92.0 | 91.4 | 93.6 |

*Source:* Equal Employment Opportunity Commission (1979)

probably not only reflects affirmative action gains but also the fact that in the current restructuring process skill levels are remaining fairly high, whereas much of the actual work is routinized and unsatisfying; and in the face of growing competitive pressures, the substitution of women for men across a range of occupations serves to depress wage levels without sacrifices in the quality of labour. In this regard there is a danger, as one personnel manager suggested, that some formerly male occupations may be resegregating female and will be devalued as a result.

### *Female Labour as a Locational Determinant*

Although a literate but cheap female work force is of growing importance to the industry, feminism and affirmative action gains have made it increasingly difficult to attract educated women into dead-end, low-wage work. White suburban housewives offer companies a partial solution to this dilemma. Because of their household and childcare responsibilities, these women are less career-oriented and, therefore, more willing to accept jobs with limited occupational mobility; they may trade higher wages for flexible or shorter hours, and benefits may be less important to them if they and their children are covered by their husbands' plans. These women also, according to clerical organizers, are considerably less likely to be responsive to union initiatives than are minority women in the central cities, many of whom are the sole supporters of their households.[6]

Nelson's (1982) study of the locational determinants of automated office activities (including insurance) concluded that, holding land costs constant, companies have chosen to site these portions of their operations in areas with a disproportionately high percentage of white married suburban housewives. Similarly, in a fairly recent interview an executive of the Fantus Company, a subsidiary of Dun and Bradstreet that specializes in corporate location, argued that automation is raising skill requirements and forcing insurance companies to relocate in order to maintain a low-cost but high-quality work force:

> The increased sophistication of word processors and the growing use of computers to handle claims have forced insurance companies to hire more skilled workers than in the past. As demand for this kind of skilled labor grows, recruiting and training will become increasing problems. To be successful [in a market where demand is high], the company must have salaries and working conditions that make it one of the more attractive employers in the area. Because insurance companies tend to have modest pay scales relative to other employers . . . this will create pressure to locate in intermediate and smaller cities. (*Best's Review*, 1979: 62–3).

My own limited case work tends to corroborate these observations. Executives in one company explained in great detail the analysis of census data that preceded the siting of their new automated centres; the chosen workers for the first of these to open in a small town in the north-east were 'white housewives of Germanic descent'. Similarly, four companies studied had recently moved parts of their

6. Based on interviews with organizers for Service Employees International Union no. 925 and Office and Professional Employees International Union no. 3.

operations from major cities to adjacent suburban areas reportedly in search of a higher-quality clerical work force. The company described earlier that is experimenting with homework consciously saw this programme as a way to take advantage of the labour pool of educated women with small children. In so far as skilled labour is increasingly important to the profitability of the insurance industry, then, it is also becoming a central determinant in its location decisions.

### *Opportunities for Women Will Vary by Class and Race*

For all these reasons, however, although there will continue to be jobs for women in these automated insurance companies, employment opportunities for minority and less well-educated white women may decline sharply.

According to 1979 statistics from the Equal Employment Opportunity Commission, insurance carriers over the last decade have employed a relatively high percentage of minority clericals - 22 per cent of their clerical work force as compared to the industrywide average of 17 per cent. Undoubtedly this is because insurance has unusually large numbers of routine, back office jobs, the categories of clerical labour in which minority workers tend to be overrepresented. In 1980, for example, blacks constituted 11.2 per cent of the work force but 21.6 per cent of all file clerks, 17.5 per cent of office machine operators (including 22 per cent of all keypunch operators), and 15.5 per cent of all typists. In contrast, only 5 per cent of all secretaries and 7 per cent of all receptionists were black (US Department of Labor, 1981b).

As the data processing centres begin to close and routine clerical categories shrink, minority clericals are in real danger of losing their jobs. Hacker's (1979) study of technological change at AT&T concluded that the single best indicator of a job slated for elimination by automation was the disproportionate presence of minority women.

The threat to minority workers is especially great in so far as the new offices are sited outside the central cities in white suburbs and small towns. For example, the three new personal lines centres described earlier were set up in towns where minorities represented 3.1, 3.3 and 14.3 per cent of the population. Finally, also, as Nelson (1982) has argued, the move to teams that involve close working relations among higher and lower level employees may well favour the hiring of 'socially compatible'white women.

### *Summary*

Overall, then, although the new technologies may be freeing women from the pink-collar assembly lines and even raising skill levels of the female work force, there is, in the end, little cause for good cheer. For women at the bottom of the clerical hierarchy, jobs are simply disappearing. For skilled and particularly white clericals there will be jobs but not opportunities; in this sense, their situation may actually worsen in so far as the last decade had begun to open up possibilities for advancement. Similarly, numbers of college-educated women may make their way into professional and managerial ranks only to find their talents underutilized and undervalued.

At the same time, however, because of the significantly greater opportunities available to college-educated women, the female occupational structure is apt to bifurcate more sharply than in the past, diminishing even further the egalitarian thrust of feminist strategies such as affirmative action. In general, in fact, the new technologies should make it more difficult for women to organize on their own behalf as work is increasingly isolated and footloose.

## CONCLUSION

Finally, to conclude, I would like to return to the beginning and place all these observations within the context of the deskilling debate. On one hand, as the postindustrialists predict, a reintegration of the labour process does seem to be occurring in this industry, unskilled labour is being expelled and, as a result, average skill levels are rising. At the same time, however, labour is being degraded, the occupational structure is polarizing, and, although work has been electronically reintegrated, this is not necessarily translating into greater autonomy or task variety on the job; on the contrary, numerous categories of workers may be much more closely supervised.

One explanation for these contradictions perhaps lies in the critical distinction the postindustrialists make between simple mechanization and total automation. Whereas early forms of mechanization relegate the worker to the role of machine appendage, in the advanced stages of automation workers assume responsibility for 'controlling the controls' (Hirschhorn, 1981). In this account, ultimately, full use of the new productive force – information – depends on its (more democratic) diffusion throughout the organization.

Significantly, it seems unlikely within the next decade that many white-collar activities will lend themselves to the kind of total automation found in continuous process manufacturing plants, even in an intensive paper-processing industry such as insurance. Too many events in the office are unique, unstructured, or (most important) are dependent on interpersonal interaction to permit them to be easily computerized. Past attempts to freeze these activities in computer algorithms often have had negative repercussions on the effectiveness of an organization. As a result, the postindustrialists might argue, in offices we should expect to continue to see the proliferation of degrading job configurations deriving from partially automated work processes.

Although this is a plausible explanation, the contradictions may be more fundamental in nature. As numerous commentators have suggested, the critical question is not the logic of the new technologies but the element of social choice. Neither the assembly line nor the hierarchical division of labour between men and women were inevitable. In the face of heightened competition and little organized labour resistance, managers may well choose the immediate benefits to their bottom line that deskilling strategies promise. That is, despite the liberating potential of the computer revolution – and probably even ultimately at the expense of full exploitation of its productive capacity – the old and by now well-criticized tendency of US corporations to maximize short-term profits may well prevail.

## REFERENCES

Adler, P. (1983) Rethinking the Skill Requirements of New Technologies: Working Paper. Cambridge, MA: Harvard Business School.

Appelbaum, E. (1984) 'The impact of technology on skill requirements and occupational structure in the insurance industry, 1960–1990.' Temple University (unpublished).

Barker, J. and H. Downing (1980) 'Word processing and the transformation of the patriarchal relations of control in the office.' *Capital and Class* 10 (spring): 64–99.

Bell, D. (1976) The Coming of Postindustrial Society. New York: Basic Books.

*Best's Aggregates and Averages* (1983) 'Property-casualty edition.' Special issue.

*Best's Review* (1979) 'Insurance office locations in the 1980s' August: 62–3.

Block, F. and L. Hirschhorn (1979) 'New productive forces and the contradictions of contemporary capitalism' *Theory and Society* 7.

Braverman, H. (1974) Labor and Monopoly Capital. New York: Monthly Review Press.

Burris, V. and A. Wharton (1982) 'Sex segregation in the US labor force.' *Review of Radical Political Economics* 14(3): 43–55.

Cummings, L. (1977) 'The rationalization and automation of clerical work.' Master's thesis, Brooklyn College.

Davies, M. (1975) 'Women's place is at the typewriter: the feminization of the clerical labor force', pp. 279–296 in R. C. Edwards et al. (eds) Labor Market Segmentation. Lexington, MA: D. C. Heath.

Economic Report of the President (1983) Table B-3. Washington, DC: US Government Printing Office.

Equal Employment Opportunity Commission (1979) Minorities and Women in Private Industry. Washington, DC: author.

Faunce, W., E. Hardin and E. H. Jacobson (1962) 'Automation and the employee.' *Annals of the American Academy of Political and Social Science* 340.

Glenn, E. N. and R. L. Feldberg (1983) 'Technology and work degradation: effects of office automation on women clerical workers', in J. Rothschild (ed.) Machina Ex Dea. Elmsford, NY: Pergamon.

——(1977) 'Degraded and deskilled: the proletarianization of clerical work.' *Social Problems* 25 (October): 52–64.

Greenbaum, J. M. (1979) In the Name of Efficiency. Philadelphia: Temple University Press.

Gregory, J. (1982) 'The electronic office: a stress factory for women clericals.' Prepared for the Office Automation Conference, April.

Hacker, S. L. (1979) 'Sex stratification, technology, and organizational change: a longitudinal case study of AT & T.' *Social Problems*.

Hirschhorn, L. (1981) 'The post-industrial labor process.' *New Political Science* (fall).

Hoos, I. (1961) Automation in the Office. Washington, DC: Public Affairs Press.

Insurance Information Institute (1983) Life Insurance Fact Book. Washington, DC: author.

Matteis, R. J. (1979) 'The new back office focuses on customer service.' *Harvard Business Review* (March–April).

Mintzberg, H. (1972) 'The myth of MIS.' *California Management Review* (fall).

Murphree, M. (1982) 'Impact of office automation on secretaries and word processing operators.' Presented at the International Conference of Office Work and New Technology, Boston.

Nelson, K. (1982) 'Labor supply characteristics and trends in the location of routine offices in the San Francisco Bay area.' Presented at the 78th Annual Meeting of the Association of American Geographers, San Antonio.

Noble, D. F. (1979) 'Social choice in machine design: the case of automatically controlled machine tools', in Case Studies in the Labor Process. New York: Monthly Review Press.

Nussbaum, K. and J. Gregory (1980) Race Against Time: Automation of the Office. Cleveland: Working Women Education Fund.

Oppenhemer, V. (1968) 'The sex labeling of jobs.' *Industrial Relations* 7(3).

Sabel, C. F. (1982) Work and Politics: The Division of Labour in Industry. Cambridge: Cambridge University Press.

Shepherd, J. (1971) Automation and Alienation: A Study of Office and Factory Workers. Cambridge, MA: MIT Press.

Sirbu, M. A. (1982) 'Understanding the social and economic impacts of office automation ' MIT (unpublished).

Strassman, P. (1980) 'The office of the future: information management for the new age.' *Technology Review* (December–January).

Toffler, A. (1980) The Third Wave. New York: Bantam Books.

US Bureau of the Census (1981) US Census of Population, 1980. Washington, DC: author.

US Department of Labor, Bureau of Labor Statistics (BLS) (1981a) Employment and Unemployment: A Report on 1980; Special Labor Force Report 244. Washington, DC: author.

—— (1981b) The National Industry-Occupation Employment Matrix, 1970, 1978, and Projected 1990, vol. I. Bullletin 2086. Washington, DC: author.

—— (1981/1979) Occupational Employment Survey of Insurance (unpublished).

—— (1980) Handbook of Labor Statistics. Bulletin 2070. Washington, DC: author.

—— (1969) Tomorrow's Manpower Needs, vol. II. Bulletin 1606. Washington, DC: author.

—— (various years) *Employment and Earnings* (March issue) Washington, DC: author.

Werneke, D. (1983) Microelectronics and Office Jobs: The Impact of the Chip on Women's Employment. Geneva: International Labour Office.

West, J. (1982) 'New technology and women's office work', in J. West (ed.) Work, Women, and the Labour Market. London: Routledge and Kegan Paul.

Zuboff, S. (1983) Some Implications of Information Systems Power for the Role of the Middle Manager: Working Paper. Cambridge, MA: Harvard Business School.

—— (1982) 'Problems of symbolic toil.' *Dissent* (winter): 51–61.

# Part VI
# Why Work?

# 32

# Making Work: a Perspective from Social Science

WILLIAM RONCO AND LISA PEATTIE

Mack, the fifty-two-year-old small-boat captain, will tell you that for him fishing is 'just a living, only a living'. But he will also admit that he would never consider any other kind of work and has never had any other kind of job 'except the army', and that fishing appeals to him because 'I can be independent – no bosses.'

A day on Mack's boat is exhausting: sixteen hours of baiting hooks, laying and hauling lines, and cleaning and dressing hundreds, often thousands, of pounds of fish. Or perhaps having no fish at all if it has been an unlucky day. Parts of the workday are boring in the extreme: putting bait on hooks, hauling and coiling line, travelling slowly to the fishing grounds and back. Other parts of the work are not routine enough for comfort, for even in this day of meteorology, small storms can appear unpredictably and do significant damage. Even in the relatively small port from which Mack fishes, several fishermen die each year in storms and accidents at sea.

Mack appreciates the natural beauty in ocean and sky; he will stop to watch a whale. He is proud of having and exercising the skill that successful fishing demands. Recently developed electronic equipment no doubt helps him make a living, but it spoils the work a little for him. He says the equipment threatens to 'make anyone a fisherman'.

Dan, the principal of large high school in a wealthy suburban community, knew what he was up against when he took the job. His predecessor and his predecessor's predecessor both left a legacy of conflict and ill feeling from parents, teachers, and students alike. Thriving on the controversy, Dan immersed himself in the work. He weathered – and won – the inevitable power skirmishes and settled back to attempt to 'really make the organization sing'.

This essay was first published as chapter 1 in William Ronco and Lisa Peattie, *Making Work: self-created jobs in participatory organizations*, Plenum Press, 1983.

Dan's workday is meticulously planned well in advance. His schedule is always full, and he devotes considerable energy to filling it with tact, concern, and political acumen. He hates crises and surprises, and he uses the schedule as a weapon against management by default.

Dan likes to think of himself – and hopes others will think of him – as a scholarly manager. Savouring the smoothly running organization he has engineered, he takes on the larger issues of redefining the organization's mission. At this point, he is troubled less by surprises than by the inability of others to see and respond to his efforts.

Jeanne is a fine arts major, a sculptor and ceramic artist, but right now she is working as a production potter in her own studio. All by herself, all day long, in a low-ceilinged workroom full of grey, unfired pots, she makes mugs, one handle after another, exactly alike. Pushing herself one day, she made sixty; those were the best of all. 'It is in the hands and the more you do, the better they get. If you're going to do something like this for a living, you have to like the grungy things – like wedging clay, firing kilns. The things clay makes you do are things I like'.

Jeanne's marathon, lone potting contrasts sharply with the sociable work-world of Richard, who works in a collective studio, of which he was one of the founders. Richard started potting as a hobby while a student of architecture and planning, and only a couple of months later, he began thinking, 'How many cups would I have to sell to live from this?' He still makes a living from planning, and he pots for pleasure, even though he also gets pleasure from organizing the studio and trying to push the members into selling more seriously. 'I'm interested in making art more like other professions,' he says. 'Selling can be just as creative.'

Our interests reflect two themes that Rosabeth Kanter identified as characterizing the ambience of work in America in the late 1970s: work as a source of self-respect and meaning, and work as a political environment in which people demand various rights.[1]

The theme of work as a source of self-respect and meaning is a result of several major social trends: the increasing educational level of most workers, the growing proportion of younger workers, and more general attitude shifts among many workers of all ages. Younger, more educated workers, and more workers overall, expect more of work as an experience, not only as a source of economic sustenance.

The demand that work should be satisfying seems to be a modern one. Commenting on the autobiographical documents left by nineteenth-century British working people, John Burnett noted that 'For most, work was taken as given, like life itself, to be endured rather than enjoyed; most were probably glad enough to have it at all, and to expect to derive satisfaction or happiness from it was an irrelevant consideration.'[2]

There are evidently many Americans for whom work today is still the necessary toil that earns a living, the daily alienation that makes possible family life and

1. Rosabeth Kanter, 'Work in a New America', *Daedalus: Journal of the American Academy of Arts and Sciences* 107 (winter 1978): 47–78. See also Harold L. Sheppard and Neal Q. Herrick, *Where Have All the Robots Gone?* (New York: Macmillan, 1972).

2. John Burnett, ed., *Useful Toil: Autobiographies of Working People from the 1820s to the 1920s* (London: Allen Lane, 1974), p. 15.

leisure enjoyment. But younger, better educated, and more affluent workers (and there are proportionately more of all of these categories) are increasingly manifesting a 'concern for work as a source of self-respect and non-material reward - challenge, growth, personal fulfilment, interesting and meaningful work, the opportunity to advance and to accumulate and the chance to lead a safe, healthy life.'[3]

With such increasing demands placed on the quality of the work experience, it becomes crucial to understand fully the nature of work that provides the high levels of meaning and self-respect that workers want. Reviewing the literature on work and job satisfaction, we found that most existing writing and research are not concerned with the nature of highly satisfying work. Most of what we found fits within these categories:

1 statistical public opinion studies that document shifts in levels of job satisfaction, determinants of job satisfaction, and comparative analyses of subgroups with different levels of job satisfaction;
2 studies of alienation or job satisfaction in specific organizations and settings;
3 articles and books about various kinds of worker ownership schemes and job redesigns in large organizations;
4 journalistic profiles of the work experience in general.

None of these approaches seems to do justice to the topic of a high-quality work experience. The statistical studies quantify something called *job satisfaction*. The journalistic profiles make it clear that *satisfaction* is a woefully inadequate term for a variety of complicated ways of getting different kinds of pleasure out of work, but these profiles usually focus on only one kind of work. The studies of worker ownership and job redesigns identify some of the characteristics of satisfying work, but always within a planned and usually a large organizational setting, where the needs of the management limit what individuals can do about their work life.

We thought we could learn something about the nature of highly satisfying work if we could examine work in 'natural settings' that resemble the intentionally structured job-redesign experiments in larger corporate settings. We believed that the absence of a larger organizational environment might make it possible to observe basic principles of satisfying work uncluttered and unconstrained by bureaucratic crosscurrents and contingencies.

We chose as our research subjects people who told us that they like their work, and who work either on their own, with minimal supervision, or in small, participatory organizations. Such work situations are, of course, unusual, and not merely in being satisfying: they are unusual also in scale. Most Americans work in very large organizations.

Rosabeth Kanter provided some perspective on just how many Americans work in large organizations:

> Nearly 20 per cent of the total nonagricultural employed labour force works for local, state or federal government. Another 30 per cent are employed by business

3. Kanter, op. cit., p. 53.

> enterprise with more than 500 people on the payroll. And this half of the labour force in government and big business does not include a variety of other large organizations that cannot be called 'business' but are often increasingly run like them: private universities, private hospitals. Over 12 million Americans work in firms which employ over 10,000 people. In manufacturing, the dominance of large organizations in providing jobs is even more striking. Recently, 60 per cent of all persons employed in manufacturing were in firms with a least 1000 people, 42 per cent in companies with over 10,000 employees. Over 3 million people work in firms employing over 1,000,000 people.[4]

We don't know exactly how large organizations shape the work experience. It seemed to us, however, that their very size limited the possibilities for the sort of worker autonomy and control that the research identifies as essential to high levels of job satisfaction.

Thus, we chose to study small organizations. To further ensure that the organizations we chose provided at least the structural elements of worker autonomy and control, we focused on participatory organizations: co-ops and collectives whose members have a say in governing the organization and in designing its work and theirs.

In addition to their providing the structural characteristics of satisfying work, the organizations we chose have relevance for exploring a second trend in the workplace, also identified by Kanter: the demand for worker rights. While not concerned with the traditional worker rights issues of safety or equality of opportunity, the members of the organizations we studied are quite concerned with the more general issue of their rights in the workplace. Many of them came to their present work arrangement in explicit pursuit of 'rights' that had eluded them at former places of work. Nearly all are dedicated to the general worker rights issue of workplace democracy.

Besides their relevance to worker rights and their provision of structural elements of job satisfaction, the organizations we studied have an intrinsic interest as examples of 'hip' or 'cockroach capitalism'. In the United States (and it would appear elsewhere, judging by reports from France), 'the desire to create, to invent, to confront reality maintains itself or even develops outside the established institutions,'[5] and individuals or small groups are making their own work situations. There are young people selling leather work along the sidewalks of Berkeley; there are cooperative restaurants; there are law and medical collectives. It is hard to know how many there are of such alternative entrepreneurs and, if it may be called a movement,. how seriously to take it as such.

In any case, our interests in the politics of work have focused on the characteristics and the potential of self-employment and small participatory organizations. 'Cockroach capitalists', independent self-employed work arrangements, and democratically run small businesses seem to us to offer opportunities for personal and political expression as well as a work organization more amenable to democratic operating principles than the large corporations that dominate the US economy. From the outset, we have hoped that this research

4. Ibid., p. 66.
5. Jules Chancel and Pierre-Eric Tixier, 'Le désir d'entreprendre', in *Et si Chacun créait son emploi?* (Paris, autrement no. 20, Sept. 1979), p. 8.

would provide some insights into the problems and potentials of the'small' workplace.

Our interests in the nature of highly satisfying work and the 'small' workplace led us to a research design involving an almost anthropological study of a half-dozen workplaces: a fishing cooperative, a pottery studio, an architecture firm, a sheltered workshop, a food co-op warehouse, and several managerial jobs with a high degree of autonomy and control, for example, the principalship of a large, suburban high school. We interviewed, observed, and occasionally worked with our subjects, attempting to explore what their work is and how it is satisfying to them.

## JOB SATISFACTION

We chose the research subjects out of an interest in what is ordinarily called *job satisfaction*. We focused on people who told us they liked their work and on situations in which work seemed to have a strong potential for providing a satisfying experience.

Even more than the jobs that are redesigned to provide increased autonomy and control, the workplaces we were studying afforded workers the opportunity for much independence. Within such environments, it became apparent that the ways in which people *structure* their work life when they have the freedom to do so provide important clues to the nature of job satisfaction.

As we went on trying to understand the individuals we studied, we came to view 'job satisfaction' as a dynamic *process* more than as a stable set of attitudes. The 'job satisfaction' studies we read seemed to focus on the discomforts of working: monotony, boredom, safety. Herzberg[6] labelled such factors 'hygiene factors' several decades ago and insightfully identified them as 'dissatisfiers'.

We found ourselves exploring more of what Herzberg called the 'satisfiers' in the work experience: features of the work experience itself rather than features in the work environment. We quickly encountered a number of predictable features of highly rewarding work among our subjects: challenge, intellectual stimulation, variety, personalization of the work, a sense of meaning of the work, and of course autonomy and control of the work.

Beyond these, we also encountered several recurring characteristics of the work experience that we did not entirely anticipate:

1 An apparent need for occasional repetition and monotony. Given the fullest breadth of choice, many of the people we studied frequently opted to work on boring, repetitive tasks that they could easily take care of in other ways. The fisherman who baits his own hooks (hundreds of them) while his crew looks on was our most poignant example.
2 An occasional, but recurring, expansion of 'challenge' to out-and-out 'risk'. The school principal we studied – as much as the fishermen – describes his work in terms of chances taken. Such people seem to savour the risk almost as much as the ultimate outcome.

6. Frederick Herzberg, *Work and the Nature of Man* (New York: Thomas Y. Crowell, 1966).

3 An interest in the public statement made by the work. All of our subjects are deeply interested in how they and their work are perceived by peers and members of their community. They do not care much about status, but they all have an *image* they hope to project.
4 Emotional ups and downs. Perhaps resulting from their internalization and personalization of the work, our subjects experienced fairly wide swings in their emotions. At the frequent high points, they could be exhilarated by and deeply pleased with their work. At the low points, they could be completely drained.

Most generally, we were surprised at the extent to which our subjects had thought through their own understanding of their work. Perhaps because of the work's fostering of autonomy and control, each person we interviewed had a well-thought-out rationale, approach, and philosophy of his or her work. Much as Robert Lane[7] found in *Political Ideology*, we discovered in a small cross section of workers an extensive body of careful thinking coupled with an appreciation of the activities and skills that consumed their working hours.

## MAKING WORK

Growing out of, and somewhat beyond, any static characteristics of satisfying work we found, we were struck by the dynamic nature of job satisfaction, by the processes of making work. Our subjects' extensive autonomy in and control of their work and work organizations forces them to make work in two ways: drawing external boundaries that separate work from nonwork, and creating internal boundaries that separate and create order among all the possible ways of getting the job done.

In many instances, making work is an exercise in joy and commitment; in some cases, it is painful and difficult. The process seems to emphasize the balancing and containment of, the occasional immersion in, and the restructuring of all aspects of the work, ranging from the most abstract and intellectually enjoyable to the most uncomfortable, humiliating, and monotonous.

Much of what we see as making work has to do with drawing boundaries:

1 *Internal boundaries:* making work within work. Within the flexibility and autonomy of their work arrangements, our subjects must create internal boundaries to organize their days, projects, and tasks. They create schedules. They create categories of different kinds of tasks and segments of the work, personal priorities and preferences. They create mechanisms that allow them to change priorities. These internal boundaries must account for and balance changing economic realities, timing, and personal desires.
2 *External boundaries:* making work distinct from nonwork. Our subjects have to separate work from nonwork activities. Emotionally invested in their work, they must make sure to make the meaning they expect the work

7. Robert Lane, *Political Ideology* (New York: Free Press, 1967).

> to provide them. Surprisingly, distinguishing work from nonwork is not easy. For the fishermen, for example, what is work and what is sport? For the potters, what is hobby? The answers are not academic – to them.

For the workers we studied, there is an element of voluntarism in the activity that, by blurring the distinction between 'work' and 'hobby', calls into question the boundaries of the category *work* itself. The combination of these led us to examine more closely the social construction of work.

## THE SOCIAL CONSTRUCTION OF WORK

The fishermen, teachers, and potters don't typically engage in debates to resolve the question 'What is work?', but the issue is alive, to a degree, for all of them. In particular, they often have to answer the question when they feel that they are working too hard, when every part of their day has something to do with work. Their difficulties with the ambiguity of work as a social category signal for us a set of issues that comprise a backdrop for this research: the blurring of 'work' and 'hobby'.

It may seem odd that as basic a social category as work is not clear. 'Working' is contrasted with 'fooling around', 'being unemployed', 'hobby', 'being on welfare', 'being a housewife'. We need such distinctions and use them to place people socially, to determine what they are entitled to, and decide how seriously to assess what they are doing. All this assumes that we can identify work when we see it, and that the category of work is more-or-less self-evident.

Yet a number of trends question the self-evidence of work. The demand that work be a source of respect and fulfilment, for example, suggests that work might come to resemble art or hobby. The women's movement's inquiry into the nature of housework is calling into question the extent to which that cluster of activities can be ignored as 'work'. The economy of the 1980s, which features an expanding service sector, is giving rise to a number of jobs (e.g. social worker) whose component tasks may more closely resemble friendly conversation than any of the more traditional occupations.

The evolution of the job structure involves a continual creation of 'occupations, of "work", out of nonwork human activities'. If 'work' is activity that contributes to the production of goods and services for the market, it is plain 'that activities move into the official labor force as the statuses of workers or work change [sic] due to changes in legislation and changes in the administrative rules by which membership in the official labor force is determined and legitimized'.[8] What economists speak of as the expansion of the tertiary sector is in part the creation of new jobs to serve the requirements of evolving technology and institutions – computer programmers, airline attendants, customer service representatives – but also the transformation of nonmarket human activities into 'work'. Thus, we have day-care workers, masseurs, group leaders, community organizers – activities that have moved into the market economy and become official occupations. Thus, the

8. Eliot Friedson, 'The Official Construction of Occupations: An Essay on the Practical Epistemology of Work' (unpublished).

occupational categories are man-made and changing – work descriptions cannot be taken for granted.

Work can be seen as elicited from the individual by others, through payment, force, or persuasion; it can also be seen as a form of self-expression. In the first aspect, it is the cost of life; expelled from Eden, Adam was cursed by having to earn his living by the sweat of his brow. We pay for work; what we do by choice, unpaid, is our avocation. Societies build systems of incentives, both positive rewards and negative sanctions, so that work will get done. But in the second aspect, work has also been seen as man's 'calling', his craft, his means of self-expression, his way of joining with his fellows in some common purpose.

All the group activities we studied – and many others – could be pursued either as 'work' or as a 'hobby'. Some people fish for a living; some people fish for sport. The fishermen we studied felt superior to 'sport fishermen' – but they fished with a kind of macho zest that certainly had elements of sport in it. Potting for many is a hobby; some of the potters we studied actually earned a living in other ways than by their pots. Working with children can be pursued as a volunteer effort, but the teachers we studied were extremely serious about their occupation.

The distinction between 'work' and 'hobby' is thus not inherent in the activity; it lies in the social context in which the activity is carried out. The social arrangements that structure the activity also set for it a social meaning. The same activity may fall into the 'work' or the 'hobby' category, depending not on the activity itself, but on the surrounding social context.

What marks an activity as work? Being paid and monetary remuneration as a prime motive for engaging in the activity certainly mark 'work' off from 'hobby'. Being paid is, under the rules of sports, what distinguishes the amateur from the professional. But we may speak of 'voluntary work', meaning an activity that is like ordinary work in every respect but payment, and for some of the people whom we came to know in this study, payment or the possibility of payment takes a secondary place to commitment to the activity. Mixed motives are general. Even the care of children by women, while motivated by affection, is surely not independent of the customary support of women by their husbands.

Sometimes 'work' seems to be distinguished from 'hobby' by a greater degree of commitment, by sustained effort over time. But we find that amateur actors accuse professionals of 'egoistic' or 'nonartistic' (i.e. less engaged) acting, and that amateur basketball players complain that their professional counterparts 'don't play for the sport itself but play for the money'.[9] Thus, a high level of commitment may be associated with either voluntarism or professionalism.

Work may be distinguished from leisure or hobby as being an activity that appears to be a burdensome necessity. Thus, when Peter Willmott and Michael Young discussed work and leisure with ordinary Londoners, they found that 'women in overwhelming numbers regarded domestic cleaning, washing clothes and washing-up as work. These were jobs generally disliked. As for meals, routine ones were more of a drudgery than meals for guests or the great weekly ritual of Sunday dinner.'[10] On the other hand, it is clearly possible for work to be a source

9. Robert A. Stebbins, *Amateurs: On the Margin between Work and Leisure* (Beverly Hills: Sage, 1979), pp. 73–4, 213.

10. Peter Willmott and Michael Young, *The Symmetrical Family: A Study of Work and Leisure in the London Region* (London: Routledge and Kegan Paul, 1973), p. 209.

of gratification as well as a burden. Stevenson's *Home Book of Quotations*[11] has a long set of entries under 'Work: a curse', but it has an equally long set of entries under 'Work: a blessing'. The Lewisham postman who told Willmott and Young that 'I get more leisure at work than I do at home'[12] seems to have been atypical among their interviewees, chiefly in positively evaluating a working-class occupation; similar comments were not unusual among professionals. Indeed, middle-class people interviewed for the study characteristically saw in their work what the authors characterized as generally 'an alliance of duty and pleasure', described in terms of a 'sense of commitment'.[13] Certainly, a strong positive commitment to the work activity is characteristic of the groups involved in this study. 'Work' is also associated with notions of a useful product; on the other hand, a disillusioned bureaucrat who cooks, gardens, or does carpentry as a hobby may well feel that the latter are more useful than a kind of 'work' seen as 'processing papers'.

It has also been pointed out repeatedly[14] that 'work' is associated with the experience of being confined by the scheduling and disciplining of others, by loss of autonomy, and by a distribution of the product so that some persons (employers) benefit from the efforts of others (workers); this selling off or alienation of one's activity may have its experiential counterpart in the experience of alienation. At the same time, we recognize in the notion of self-employment that a person may be 'working for himself'. While at least one economist[15] sees the long hours characteristic of self-employed workers as representing pleasure in an independent working activity, the more conventional view is to treat the long hours as *self*-exploitation.

It seems that in human practice activities can become at a given moment more or less 'work' or 'hobby' in terms of the mental set of the persons engaging in them. On the one hand, persons in controlled and routinized paid working situations more often than not manage to find satisfactions in the exercise of craft and initiative within the constrained situation of 'the job'. Unusually gifted in this, perhaps, but not atypical in making the attempt, was the cushion builder at the Ford Motor Plant interviewed by Studs Terkel:

> I could look at a job and I would do it. My mind would just click. I could stand back, look at a job, and two minutes later I can go and do it. I enjoyed the work. I felt it was a man's job. You can do something with your hands. You can go home at night and feel you have accomplished something. (Did you find the assembly line boring?) No, uh-uh. Far from boring. There was a couple of us that were hired together. We'd come up with different games – like we'd take the numbers of the jeeps that went by. That guy loses, he buys coffee.[16]

But on the other hand, a person may dignify his hobby by treating it as a sort of

11. Burton Stevenson, *The Home Book of Quotations* (New York: Dodd Mead, 1967).
12. Willmott and Young , op. cit., p. 208.
13. Ibid., p. 209.
14. See for example the discussion in E. P. Thompson, 'Time, Work-discipline and Industrial Capitalism', *Past and Present* 38 (1967): 56–97.
15. Tibor Scitovsky, *The Joyless Economy: An Inquiry into Human Satisfaction and Consumer Dissatisfaction* (New York: Oxford University Press, 1976), pp. 89–101.
16. Studs Terkel, *Working: People Talk about What They Do All Day and How They Feel about What They Do* (New York: Pantheon, 1974), p. 250.

work, with its own place and time commitments. A recent study of a project for the elderly in San Francisco reports how a group of widows living in the infinite leisure of a retirement community structured part of their time as a sort of quasi-work. They met together at set hours in the common room to make craft items to sell for group projects. When one of their number proposed using for her family two of the items she had produced, the idea met with general resistance. She was taking as her private property what would otherwise be the group's, and in this way, she was breaking the frame that dignified what would otherwise be private 'hobbies' by making them 'work'.[17]

Furthermore, in contrasting a general class of freely chosen and expressive activities we call *hobbies* with the more necessity-compelled category we call *work*, we note that there is also ambiguity in the evaluation of the two. Marx looked forward to a future in which economic necessity would no longer be the driving force behind work, so that each individual could freely choose to 'do one thing today and another tomorrow, to hunt in the morning and fish in the afternoon, rear cattle in the evening, criticize after dinner, just as I have a mind',[18] but it does not seem to have occurred to Marx to rejoice in the prospect of citizens of the new society's rejecting work altogether, for he saw people as making sense of their lives only in being 'productively active'. In proposing a distinction between 'labour', which arises in the realm of necessity and serves to reproduce human life, and 'work', which creates a true product, Hannah Arendt drew on a long (and one might well argue class- and sex-biased) tradition of invidious comparison between the creative activity of the leisured classes and the servile work of the masses,[19] but this tradition has in Western thought its own antithesis: the Protestant ethic strain that sees useful work as central to ethical practice as a human being [20]

At the same time that alienation through wage labour debases work, respect is given to work as the serious business of life because in the monetized society, it acquires exchange value. Thus, at the same time that our work groups try to make work less like a job and more like a hobby, we also see them giving the activity more weight by making it more economically serious. For example, one of the members of the potters' collective says that if the group would organize to sell collectively and to sell more, they would work harder and better.

It thus turns out that the categories of 'work' and 'hobby' are fuzzy categories. They are not defined by the inherent nature of the task to be performed. They are not defined by a clear differentiation of the motives with which the activity is performed. Nor is there an evaluative standard that clearly differentiates the two.

This set of ambiguities is hardly captured by concept of *job satisfaction* on which most work studies are focused. The concept of *job satisfaction* seems to imply a taking-for-granted of the separation between 'work' and 'hobby' that we see as an underlying issue for all of the groups we have been examining. It is not simply the

17. Arlie Russell Hoschschild, *The Unexpected Community* (Englewood Cliffs, NJ: Prentice-Hall, 1973), p. 42.

18. Karl Marx and Friedrich Engels, 'The German Ideology', excerpted in Lewis S. Feuer, *Basic Writings on Politics and Philosophy: Karl Marx and Friedrich Engels* (Garden City, NY: Doubleday, 1959), p. 254.

19. Hannah Arendt, *The Human Condition* (Garden City: NY: Doubleday, 1959).

20. See Max Weber, *The Protestant Ethic and the Spirit of Capitalism* (New York: Scribner, 1930) and R. H. Tawney, *Religion and the Rise of Capitalism* (Magnolia, Mass.: Peter Smith, 1926).

relative balance of utilities and disutilities, and of compensation for disutility with reference to a clear category, but the categories themselves that are at issue.

Each of the work groups we have been studying has in one way or another been structured so as to make it possible for the members to maximize the 'hobby' aspects of the occupation in the sense of leaving the worker free to structure, to create, to play. But the organizations are also structured to make the activity – which, as we have said, could in other circumstances be a 'hobby' – function as work. The way in which members of these groups structure their work, as well as their own commitment to it, makes the activity sit right across the structural ambiguities of the boundary between 'work' and 'hobby'. Thus, our attention to these work groups turns out to be attention not only to work satisfaction and work commitment, but to the social construction of work itself.

## INHERENT DILEMMAS OF 'GOOD WORK'

It is no doubt a sort of triumph to construct for oneself a satisfying work situation. But it turns out that good work has some inherent dilemmas.

It is important for people – some of them, anyway, and the people we came to know are among them – to have work that they can feel positively committed to. Good work for these people is work they *want* to do, work they do for more than the money. But committed work is hard to limit. Because the workers are in it for more than the money, they find themselves at it outside working hours, and putting in more energy than they would have to hold the job. Though they may not at the time be able or willing to predict it, the result may be burnout.

For example, a number of the people who were most active in organizing a school we studied, where teachers managed and made policy, put in a year or two of furious energy and then left the school altogether for other, usually much less demanding, positions. The school, now running with people who work without the passion of the early days, has a tamer feeling to it.

A second dilemma has to do with the flip side of burnout: good work is flexible enough to allow people to withdraw as they feel the need. This flexibility is not only convenient and pleasant, it also enables workers to feel that engagement is voluntary. But to feel that an activity is serious (i.e. work rather than play), the worker needs to feel a sense of necessity. The fishermen we studied set their own days and hours for an activity that for other people out in the same bay in similar boats is 'sport'. The fishermen we studied make much of the difference between themselves and the sportfishermen: for them, fishing is a living, an economic necessity.

The potters we studied work intermittently and spend a good deal of their 'working day' in chatting with each other and watering the plants. Their commitment to the studio as an organization is important in part because it represents a serious commitment to potting as work.

A third dilemma is that good work allows for people to be creative and inventive. However, there can be some real satisfaction in repetition and boredom. The repetitive fishing work of baiting and winding and cleaning the fish gives a satisfying rhythm for dependable routine in an environment where uncertainty can often be an enemy. Good work involves variety and surprise – but also the repetition and limitation that make it possible for the worker to acquire and exercise specialized skill. A young potter, making mug after identical mug, twelve hours a day in her studio, and a gifted teacher who all day long allows herself no moment of undisciplined response, no span in inattention – these are two very different kinds of work and worker. But they are alike in their solitary pride in the exercise of disciplined skill.

Good work is work that can be made, shaped, formed by the workers themselves, that can be an extension of their will to create. But a fourth dilemma is that making work can be a burden; the worker has to make the decisions and provide continuing initiative. The fishermen like very much the fact that no one orders them to come to work – the decision each day is their own. But making that decision every day means forcing oneself up out of bed, usually in the dark, and entering the world of the noisy, lurching boat. The principal and the teacher in the worker-controlled school spend a good chunk of their Sundays planning their work for the coming week. This teacher is justly proud of the way in which she has organized her class so that all day every day, the children carry out learning activities in varying sizes of groups with appropriate materials. But to make that happen requires endless ongoing planning, and that seems to hedge against the sort of spontaneity that both she and the children might enjoy.

A fifth dilemma arises particularly in work with people – a growing category, as the increasing size of the service sector suggests. Close interactions with other people add a dimension of warmth and sociability and have the potential to enhance even otherwise boring jobs. But people work often leaves no clearly visible output and may leave workers wondering if they are performing well. Persons intensely committed to effectively carrying out people work (the school principal, for example) may not have an empirical, objective confirmation of their effectiveness. In the absence of such measures, they have to make them themselves – another dimension of making work.

A final dilemma has to do with a worker's ability in 'good' work to express her or his values and politics. The dilemma is that while good work offers this possibility, it may take some additional difficult steps to realize the potential. Political expression implies some interaction with others; individual self-employment efforts have limited ability to make a strong symbolic political statement. Working in a group, however, almost inevitably entails compromises, and compromises may comprise a worker's original political interests. Furthermore, making participation function requires another kind of effort that may be experienced as a burden, rather than as freedom.

These dilemmas are evident in varying degrees in our research. They are linked with our notion of *making work*. Each of the dilemmas is a balancing-act, 'good' aspect of work that needs to be constrained and moulded in order to be fully enjoyed. As far as we could see from our research subjects, 'job satisfaction' depends on resolving these dilemmas with grace and inventiveness.

The internal structuring of work – schedules, tasks, coordination, placing in space – is not independent of the external boundaries that set off work from non-work. There is always an implicit audience. The meaning of work, which we refer to usually by the term *job satisfaction*, is both personal and social. The potters arguing about whether they should present themselves on their card as a pottery collective or as a studio are arguing both about the social setting of their activity and about its meaning, and therefore its structuring, to themselves. The fishermen taking pride in their macho individualism do so against an implicit background of the regimented work of the factory or the white shirt and the bureaucratic order of the office. Thus, those who are free to structure their work in their own way are engaged in a complex process on both the societal and the individual level. They do not have the job as a shell into which they fit. They do not just go to work; they make their work. In so doing, they may suggest something of what the social construction of work involves for us all.

# 33

# The Need to Work: a Perspective from Philosophy

SEAN SAYERS

My theme is work. At a time when mass unemployment is a major social and political problem throughout the industrial world, it is a theme which needs little introduction. Nevertheless, I shall begin with some. For I must confess that work is a subject that did not much occupy my thoughts until recently. I have a steady and relatively congenial job teaching philosophy in a university. There is little danger of my losing it, and scant prospect of changing it. From my own immediate experience, therefore, I have little occasion to think about the issue of work.

This complacency was gradually disturbed, however, by the great British miners' strike of 1984–5. The strike was against pit closures – in defence of jobs and communities. The cause seemed doomed from the outset, for the miners were pitting themselves against economic forces beyond even the power of governments to control. Nevertheless, the months passed, and the miners stayed out on strike and even increased the intensity of their struggle – on their own, without significant support from the rest of the labour movement, and in the face of a concerted attempt to break the strike by the whole organized force of the state and the propaganda power of the media. As the extraordinary level of the miners' unity, determination and commitment to their cause gradually became evident, one began to wonder: why are they fighting so hard, what are they struggling for?

At one level the answer was clear enough. They were fighting for their jobs and their communities; they were fighting for the traditional socialist principle of the right to work. For socialism is based upon the view that social productive labour is, in Marx's words, man's essential activity (and woman's too) and, potentially at least, the main avenue to human self-development and fulfilment. Beyond that, working people have also struggled for a decent portion of leisure as equally a

This essay was first published in *Radical Philosophy*, 46, summer 1987, pp. 17–26.

human need. These are the ideas that I will be seeking to explain and defend in what follows.

They are not, of course, peculiar to socialism. In particular, the idea that people need work, and that unemployment is a human evil and one of the greatest of current social problems, is common ground amongst almost all shades of political opinion. Yet, at a more philosophical level, it is not always clear why this should be so. For work is very often conceived as unwanted and painful toil which people would avoid if they could.

This is how it is portrayed by an influential and pervasive social philosophy – the hedonist account of human nature, which underlies utilitarianism and classical economics. According to this theory, the pursuit of pleasure and the avoidance of pain are the sole motive forces of human life. Work involves painful exertion and the deferral of gratification; we undertake it only because we are forced to, as a means to satisfy our needs. If we are fortunate enough to be able to meet our needs without working – to consume without the toil of producing – we will readily do so. So the hedonist theory has it.

Thus Russell, for example, writes 'in praise of idleness'.[1] Ideally, he suggests, we would live a life of luxurious indolence. Hume, who shares this view, envisages this ideal life as follows:

> Let us suppose that nature has bestowed on the human race such a profuse *abundance* of all *external* conveniences, that, without any uncertainty in the event, without any care or industry on our part, every individual finds himself fully provided with whatever his most voracious appetites can want, or luxurious imagination wish or desire. . . . No laborious occupation required; no tillage, no navigation. Music, poetry, and contemplation form his sole business: conversation, mirth and friendship his sole amusement.[2]

Appealing and plausible as this vision may at first appear, there are good reasons to question it. Empirical studies reveal that people's attitudes to work are more complex and contradictory than it suggests. They show that the great majority want work and feel a need for work, even when they find it unsatisfying in all sorts of ways: dull, repetitive, meaningless. Moreover, there is much evidence to demonstrate the harmful and destructive effects of unemployment.

At the simplest level, a remarkably high percentage of people in work respond in positive terms if asked whether they find their work satisfying. In a British survey of this kind carried out in 1978, 75 per cent replied that they liked their work a lot. Figures were higher among managers (81 per cent) than among skilled workers (73 per cent); but even 66 per cent of the unskilled workers said that they liked work 'a lot'.[3] Of course, caution is needed in interpreting such crude findings. It is clear that answers are given in the light of available alternatives, which are usually unattractive, as Kahn explains:

> For most workers it is a choice between no work connection (usually with severe attendant economic penalties and a conspicuous lack of meaningful alternative

1. B. Russell, *In Praise of Idleness and Other Essays*, London, 1935.
2. D. Hume, *Enquiries*, Oxford, 1894, p. 183.
3. M. Jahoda, 'The impact of unemployment in the 1930s and the 1970s', *Bulletin of the British Psychological Society*, 32, 1979, p. 311.

activities) and a work connection which is burdened with negative qualities (routine, compulsory scheduling, dependency, etc.). In these circumstances, the individual has no difficulty with the choice; he chooses work, and pronounces himself moderately satisfied.[4]

Other studies, however, indicate that very few people would happily give up their work, even if the alternative meant no loss of income. They call into question the idea that what people want is a life of mere consumption and that they work only as a means to earn a livelihood. When a cross-section of Americans were asked if they would continue working even if they inherited enough to live comfortably without working, 80 per cent said they would keep working.[5] Moreover, the percentage of people who say that they would work in such circumstances rises as people approach retirement age. This is a striking fact, as Marie Jahoda observes, 'for at the age of sixty-five the alternative to a job – no work – must be a highly realistic comparison, while for younger people the question invites fantasy.'[6]

Studies of the unemployed and of the retired, furthermore, suggest that the effects of the absence of work extend far beyond the financial sphere. An investigation among the unemployed workers of Marienthal in Austria in the early 1930s, for example, showed that 'their sense of time disintegrated; having nothing to do meant that they became less able to be punctual for meals or other arrangements. Budgeting, so much more necessary than before, was progressively abandoned. . . . Family relations . . . deteriorated and family quarrels increased.'[7] Many subsequent studies have confirmed these findings. They have shown a lowering of self-esteem and morale, and increases in the suicide rate and the incidence of psychiatric treatment.[8] In short, there is strong evidence that 'work plays a crucial and perhaps unparalleled psychological role in the formation of self-esteem, identity, and a sense of order.'[9]

## ALIENATION

Yet people are sceptical of philosophies which tell them that they need to work or that they should find fulfilment in work; and not without some reason. For such philosophies seem grotesquely at odds with the reality of work as the majority experience it. Work is often routine, oppressive and stultifying. So far from offering possibilities of fulfilment and self-realization, more typically it is alienating and destructive of soul and body. In Marx's well-known words, industrial forms of

4. R. Kahn, quoted in Department of Health, Education and Welfare Report, *Work in America*, Cambridge, Mass., 1973, p. 15.
5. *Work in America*, p. 9. Results from Britain are similar; see Jahoda, 'The impact of unemployment', pp. 311–12.
6. Jahoda, 'The impact of unemployment', p. 312.
7. Ibid., p. 309.
8. Summaries of such evidence can be found in *Work in America*; M. Jahoda, *Employment and Unemployment*, Cambridge, 1982; and J. Hayes and P. Nutman, *Understanding the Unemployed*, London, 1981.
9. *Work in America*, p. 4.

work 'mutilate the labourer into a fragment of a man, degrade him to the level of an appendage of a machine, destroy every remnant of charm in his work and turn it into hated toil.'[10] These highly charged words, though written more than 100 years ago about Victorian factory conditions, still apply today – and not only to factory work, but equally to a growing range of office and service sector jobs, which are being subjected to the industrial division of labour.[11]

Evidence of the alienating and destructive effects of modern work has been extensively documented by social scientists in recent years. Much of this evidence is based upon personal accounts of the experience of work by workers.[12] This sort of evidence is sometimes regarded as unreliable, as 'subjective' and 'impressionistic'. The overwhelming weight of it, however, means that it cannot be dismissed, even by the most unsympathetic writers. The term 'alienation' is one of the few theoretical concepts of Marxism that has passed into everyday currency; and this is because the features of work that it describes are experienced on a very wide scale. Alienation is a common feature of work as we know it.

Apparently less 'subjective' indications of the extent of alienation can be gathered in the form of statistics for rates of absenteeism, unofficial strikes and other forms of indiscipline at work. Such evidence is more readily quantifiable; but not necessarily better for that reason. For, like all evidence, its significance requires interpretation. At the end of the 1960s and in the early 1970s such rates were increasing. At the time this was often cited as proof of the increasing alienation of workers and of the demise of the 'Protestant work ethic'.[13] We hear less of this theme these days. Such forms of indiscipline are now less prevalent; but it would be unwise to conclude from this that attitudes to work have changed fundamentally in recent years, or that alienation in work has significantly diminished. The threat of unemployment, as we all know, is a harsh task-master. 'Tranquility is found also in dungeons,' as Rousseau observes, but that does not make them desirable places in which to live.[14]

There is no doubt of the alienation and dissatisfaction involved in much modern work. Does this refute the idea that there is a need to work? Not at all. To insist that there is a need to work, and a need for fulfilment in work, is not to say that these needs are adequately met in present society. On the contrary, it is only by recognizing these needs that we can understand the phenomenon of alienation and appreciate the critical force of this concept. For the concept of alienation *presupposes* that there is a need for work and for fulfilment in work that modern conditions of work deny. This point is well known and needs little emphasis. It is clear in the description that Marx gives of alienated labour, which consists in the fact that in his work the worker

10. K. Marx, *Capital*, vol. I, Moscow, 1961, p. 645.
11. H. Braverman, *Labour and Monopoly Capital*, New York, 1974.
12. For example, S. Terkel, *Working*, New York, 1975; R. Fraser (ed.), *Work*, 2 vols, Harmondsworth, 1968; M. Haraszti, *Worker in a Worker's State*, Harmondsworth, 1977.
13. 'The old workhouse morality seems to have eroded. Wildcat strikes, riots, occupations, absenteeism and indiscipline broke out in a world plague in the late 1960s,' according to A. Skillen, *Ruling Illusions*, Brighton, 1977, p. 60. The same view is expressed more cautiously in *Work in America*: 'In some industries there apparently is a rise in absenteeism, sabotage and turnover rates' (p. 11).
14. J. J. Rousseau, *The Social Contract and Discourses*, London, 1973, p. 169.

> does not affirm himself but denies himself, does not feel content but unhappy, does not develop freely his physical and mental energy but mortifies his body and ruins his mind. . . . His labour is therefore not voluntary but coerced; it is *forced labour*. It is therefore not the satisfaction of a need; it is merely a *means* to satisfy needs external to it.[15]

Implicit in the concept of alienation is the view that we are not mere passive consumers but active and creative beings. Productive work is 'the first premise of all human existence'[16] – the most fundamental and essential human activity, and the basis upon which both human nature and society develop. And, although Marx never fails to stress that in present conditions most forms of work are alienating and humanly destructive, he entirely rejects the view that work is mere toil and that mankind has a natural and inherent aversion to it. Given the necessary conditions, labour can be 'a liberating activity', it can become 'attractive work, the individual's self-realisation'.[17]

These ideas are not confined to the socialist tradition. Similar views are at the basis of the work of Maslow and other humanistic psychologists. They also underlie the 'job enrichment' school of industrial psychology. In opposition to the hedonist account, Frederick Herzberg and others have argued that people are active and productive beings for whom work can and should be attractive and involving.[18]

This approach helps to explain and illuminate the need to work. In the first place, and at the most abstract and general level, work requires activity. It is clear that people, in the modern world at least, have a need to be active. They are not, in fact, satisfied by a life of mere passive idleness with 'no laborious occupation required'. One of the great psychological problems of unemployment is coping with the inactivity it brings. Moreover, work not only demands activity; in the form of a job, at least, it imposes a time structure on the waking day. The absence of such a time structure is also usually experienced as a problem by those who are unemployed.[19]

Secondly, work is *productive* activity. The exercise of our powers to shape and form the objective world and appropriate it to our needs is in itself a satisfaction and a need. In Marx's words, 'the object of work is . . . the objectification of man's species life' in which he can 'contemplate himself in a world that he has created'.[20] Summarizing numerous recent psychological studies, the authors of *Work in America* report that 'through the . . . awareness of one's efficacy and competence in dealing with the objects of work, a person acquires a sense of mastery over both himself and his environment.'[21]

Moreover, work is essentially the exercise of these powers towards *useful* ends.

15. K. Marx, *Economic and Philosophic Manuscripts of 1844*, New York, 1964, pp. 110–11.
16. K. Marx and F. Engels, *The German Ideology*, part I, New York, 1978, p. 48.
17. K. Marx, *Grundrisse* (Selections), ed. D. McLellan, St Albans, 1973, p. 146.
18. F. Herzberg, *Work and the Nature of Man*, Cleveland, 1966. See also Skillen, *Ruling Illusions*, pp. 68–9.
19. Jahoda, *Employment and Unemployment*, pp. 22ff; Hayes and Nutman, *Understanding the Unemployed*, pp. 40–1.
20. Marx, *Economic and Philosophic Manuscripts of 1844*, p. 114.
21. *Work in America*, p. 4.

The product is a use value: something that satisfies human needs. 'Whatever his or her occupation the worker feels needed,' write Hayes and Nutman:

> Work roles are not the only roles which offer the individual the opportunity of being useful and contributing to the community but, without doubt, for the majority they are the most central roles and consequently people deprived of the opportunity to work often feel useless and report that they lack a sense of purpose.[22]

In the third place, work (in most of its modern forms, at least) is a social activity, both in its organization and in its product. In most cases a job is a directly social activity. It takes people out of their homes and puts them into contact with others. In modern industry, indeed, the very process of work has become a cooperative one. As Marx says: 'The product ceases to be the direct product of the individual, and becomes a social product, produced in common by a collective labourer, i.e. by a combination of workmen.'[23] Moreover the product, when it is destined for the market, is intended to meet needs beyond those of the individual or the immediate household.

For many people, work is the main basis of their social life, and also of their sense of identity and status. Indeed, in the case of large enterprises like mines or factories, it may be the basis for a whole community. In a wide review of attitude studies, Herzberg and his associates found that the social aspect is the most frequently mentioned source of satisfaction from work.[24] Conversely, as Jahoda says, 'case studies of the unemployed. . . repeatedly draw attention to the demoralising effect of social isolation.'[25] This is also, of course, a recurrent theme in the literature about women whose work is confined to the home.

## WOMEN AND WORK

So far I have implicitly been equating work with a job, with employment, and contrasting it with unemployment. It has been possible to do so because employment has become the predominant form of work in contemporary society. Nevertheless, it is clear that there are many kinds of work which do not take this form. It is particularly important to recognize this fact when talking about the issue of women and work.

Traditionally, women's work has been confined to the domestic sphere, and this has been reflected in the view that women's 'place' is in the home. However, as has often been observed, work patterns are changing. Since the Second World War, at least until the present recession, women have increasingly been drawn into employment outside the home. As a consequence, attitudes are also changing. 'In a society in which money determines value,' writes Margaret Benson, 'women are a group who work outside the money economy. Their work [at home] is not worth money, is therefore valueless, is therefore not real work.'[26]

22. Hayes and Nutman, *Understanding the Unemployed*, p. 43.
23. Marx, *Capital*, vol. I, p. 505.
24. Hayes and Nutman, *Understanding the Unemployed*, p. 42.
25. Jahoda, 'The impact of unemployment', p. 313.
26. M. Benson, 'The political economy of women's liberation', in M. Evans (ed.), *The Woman Question*, London, 1982, p. 195.

The modern women's movement is a product of, and a response to, these changes; and it has reflected the ambivalent attitudes to work that I have been describing in a particularly clear and conscious way. Two distinct and opposed reactions are apparent within it. On the one hand, some women have resisted and rejected the pressures towards public employment. The world of work is a 'man's world' - an alienated world - where women can expect nothing but further oppression and exploitation. They have consequently sought to reverse the attitudes that Benson describes and 'revalue' the domestic, the female sphere.

The main tendency of the women's movement, however, has been to accept - indeed, to affirm - the need for women to work outside the home, and to demand the conditions necessary to make practical and tolerable the fulfilment of this need. These conditions are, in the workplace, equal pay and opportunities, and the provision of créches, nurseries, maternity leave etc.; and, in the home, an equal division of domestic labour. It is not here a question of opposing the domestic role to work outside the home, as though they were exclusive opposites. The strand of the women's movement that I am describing has characteristically affirmed the need for *both*, with the implication that it must be the same for men. As Margaret Stacey puts it: 'Many women no longer want to be presented with an "either-or" "choice" *between* work on the one hand and a family on the other.'[27]

No doubt the forces that have driven women out to work are mainly economic ones. Nevertheless, the women's movement is an expression and an indication of the fact that, quite apart from the economic motives, women feel a *need* - an inner need - for work: a need for a job as an end in itself, and not merely as a means to earn a livelihood.

Some of the psychological evidence for this conclusion is strikingly similar to the evidence about the psychological effects of unemployment in general which I have just described. Housewives increasingly feel constrained by the purely domestic role, and unable to use their talents and capacities to the full. Empirical studies show that the incidence of depression and psychiatric symptoms is higher among housewives than among women with jobs.[28]

What this suggests is that the purely domestic role - no matter how fulfilling and productive aspects of it may be - is not a sufficient one for women in modern industrial society. This is the message of the main strand of the women's movement. Long ago, in this context, Betty Friedan talked of 'the problem that has no name'.[29] But this problem does have a name, and that name is 'unemployment'. In the modern world, that is to say, women just like men have a need for jobs, for employment, for work.

## WORK AND LIBERATION

The criticisms that I have made of hedonism have been widely voiced in recent years; but the turn my argument has just been taking is likely to be less familiar and to provoke a more sceptical response. For many who would agree that we are

27. M. Stacey, quoted in E. Wilson, *Only Halfway to Paradise*, London, 1980.
28. A. Oakley, *Subject Women*, London, 1982, pp. 75-81, reporting the studies of G. W. Brown and T. Harris, *Social Origins of Depression*, London, 1978.
29. B. Friedan, *The Feminine Mystique*, New York, 1963, chapter 1.

essentially active and productive beings who in some sense need to work, would also maintain that work, in the form of a job, can never be fulfilling. A job is something we do only because we have to, in order to earn a living; satisfying productive activity can exist only outside the sphere of employment and jobs, in free time. Thus, it will be argued, a sharp distinction must be made between work in the world of employment and autonomous creative activity outside it. What people want and need is not employment, not jobs, but the very opposite. In Gorz's phrase they want the 'liberation from work' - a reduction of the working day to the inescapable minimum and an extension of leisure time.[30]

The socialist principle of the 'right to work' is a demand for jobs. According to libertarian writers like Gorz, this demand is both reactionary and outdated. Reactionary in that the work ethic it embodies is, and always has been, a ruling-class ideology which is preached to working people in the attempt to get them to accept their work and do it without complaint. Until now, the lifelong labour of the vast majority has been a social necessity. However, the introduction of automation and the new technology is rapidly creating the conditions that could free people from this need. We are on the brink of the 'post-industrial' age, in which the 'liberation' from work will be a real possibility, and in which the old ethic of work will be neither appropriate nor applicable.

Ideas and arguments like these are enormously influential at the moment, particularly on the left. Nevertheless, it is impossible to comprehend either our present attitudes to work or their history on the basis of them. They are unsatisfactory in almost every aspect. That is what I will now argue.

In the first place, the widespread view that the work ethic is necessarily reactionary must be challenged. The history of ideas about work clearly reveals that a belief in the human value of labour has by no means always been the outlook of the ruling class. On the contrary, those who have been exempted from the need to work by their social position have often tended to look down upon work - and particularly upon manual work - and denigrate it as the lowest and least worthy of human activities.[31]

Historically, the idea of the dignity of labour is associated particularly with Protestantism. Nowadays, especially on the left, it is customary - almost obligatory - to sneer at the 'Protestant work ethic' and reject it as a piece of reactionary and oppressive ideology. I shall come back to the question of its present significance in due course. First, however, it is important to see that in its own time, in the hands of the early Protestants at least, it had a progressive and radical aspect.

30. A. Gorz, *Farewell to the Working Class*, London, 1982; and *Paths to Paradise: On the Liberation from Work*, London, 1985.

31. This view is familiar in the philosophies of Plato and Aristotle, who both write from the point of view of slave owners in a society based upon slavery. However, these attitudes are echoed in more recent writing: see for example J. S. Mill, *Utilitarianism*; S. Sayers, 'Higher and lower pleasures', in B. Lang et al. (eds), *The Philosopher in the Community*, Lanham, MD, 1984 pp. 112–29; and also H. Avendt, *The Human Condition*, Chicago, 1958. An important strand of medieval social thought about work tended to portray it as an unwanted necessity - the curse to which mankind was subjected at the time of the fall. However, there are also other and more positive aspects to this tradition. It is perhaps too simple to suggest, like P. D. Anthony (*The ideology of work*, London, 1978), that 'the ideology of work' is a distinctively modern phenomenon which emerges only with Protestantism; but there are surely some grounds for the view that work is given a distinctive moral emphasis in the modern era.

It is well known that Protestant ideas about work helped to form the attitudes and to create the habits and discipline which were needed for the development of modern capitalism and modern industry.[32] However, the initial development of capitalist industry was not the work of the ruling class of the time, and these ideas did not express its interests. On the contrary, they expressed the outlook and needs of what Christopher Hill, using a seventeenth-century phrase, calls 'the industrious sort of people . . . yeomen, artisans and small and middling merchants'; in other words, 'economically independent men, householders, to the exclusion both of the propertyless and of the privileged classes'.[33]

So far from being a ruling-class ideology, the views of the early Protestants were often aimed quite specifically against the ruling class of the day – the aristocracy and landed gentry – as an idle and parasitic class; and they formed the basis of the revolutionary ideas of the Civil War period. As Christopher Hill says:

> A theory that dignifies labour is as double-edged as the labour theory of value which is its secularised counterpart, already to be found in the writings of Hobbes and Locke. . . . 'They are unworthy of bread that in their deeds have no care for the commonweal.' This was the lower-class heresy throughout the centuries. The propertied class had always been able to suppress it until the sixteenth century; but then it won its way to respectability, thanks in part at least to the growing social importance of the industrious sort of people.[34]

Subsequently, as capitalist relations of production were established, it was no longer so much a matter of persuading people of the virtue of the modern habit of work as of keeping them at it. As the nascent bourgeoisie won increasing economic power and political influence, the political implications of the Protestant work ethic were gradually transformed. In Hill's words: 'As the Nonconformists sloughed off their political ideals, so their emphasis on the duty of labour outweighed their emphasis on the rights of those who work.'[35]

And yet, at the same time, the 'lower-class heresy' to which Hill refers lived on, and ideas of the dignity of labour continued to be 'double-edged'. Indeed, as I have argued, they remain at the basis of much radical and socialist political thinking, and form the basis of its critique of modern conditions of work.

In this connection, it is important to see that such ideas also underlie the libertarian outlook of writers like Gorz. Although he calls for a 'liberation from work', his position should not be confused with the hedonist theory I criticized earlier. Gorz is not writing in praise of a life of mere consumption and idleness. Quite the contrary: he advocates that our free time should be filled with creative and productive activities. For he, too, believes that people are essentially active beings, who can find fulfilment only through the exercise of their creative powers. However, he also argues that such fulfilment is possible only outside the sphere of employment, which is unavoidably alienating.

32. Classic accounts are M. Weber, *The Protestant Ethic and the Spirit of Capitalism*, New York, 1958; and R. H. Tawney, *Religion and the Rise of Capitalism*, London, 1926. I have found particularly helpful C. Hill's brief discussion in *Society and Puritanism in Pre-Revolutionary England*, London, 1969, chapters 4, 15.
33. Hill, *Society and Puritanism*, p. 130.
34. Ibid., p. 135.
35. Ibid., p. 140.

powers. However, he also argues that such fulfilment is possible only outside the sphere of employment, which is unavoidably alienating.

The question of whether alienation can be overcome in some future society is outside my present scope; but it is beyond question that much present work has alienating and unsatisfying features, as I have already stressed. Moreover, it is surely the case that there are some jobs that are so menial and degrading that most people would rather remain without work than do them. Nevertheless, it is a mistake to regard all forms of employment in a purely negative light. For the evidence, I have been arguing, shows that for most people work is a more complex and ambivalent experience. It shows that most people gain genuine and important satisfactions from their work.

No doubt these satisfactions – the satisfactions of the active and social exercise of our creative powers – can be obtained in ways other than through a job. Some people indeed do find them outside the structure of employment, as the report on *Work in America* recognizes:

> Although *work* is central to the lives of most people, there is a small minority for whom a *job* is purely a means to a livelihood. To them a job is an activity that they would gladly forgo if a more acceptable option for putting bread on their table were available. What little evidence there is on this point indicates that for most such individuals the kind of jobs that they see open to them do little to provide the sense of self-esteem, identity or mastery that are the requisites for satisfying work. These individuals turn to other activities (music, hobbies, sport, crime) and other institutions (family, church, community) to find the psychological rewards that they do not find in their jobs.[36]

For most people, however, the experience of being without a job is a profoundly demoralizing and unfulfilling one. This is particularly so if joblessness takes the form of unemployment in its usual sense, but to a lesser extent it is also true of the experience of retired people and of women engaged solely in housework, as I have argued. Here it is worth noting Jahoda's striking finding that when they were made unemployed, the men she studies in Marienthal actually *decreased* their leisure activities, 'their attendance of clubs and voluntary organisations, their use of the free library, their reading.'[37]

No doubt it is possible to live a fulfilling life without a job. However, those who succeed in doing so constitute only a small minority, for the inner resources required are very great. Jahoda puts the point well: 'It is true that nobody prevents the unemployed from creating their own time structure and social contacts, from sharing goals and purposes with others or from exercising their skills as best they can. But the psychological input required to do so on a regular basis under one's own steam entirely, is colossal.'[38]

36. *Work in America*, p. 10.

37. Jahoda, 'The impact of unemployment', p. 309. See also M. Jahoda, P. Lazarsfeld and H. Zeisel, *Marienthal: the Sociography of an Unemployed Community*, London, 1972.

38. Jahoda, 'The impact of unemployment', p. 313. Elsewhere Jahoda also notes that 'even with all their material and educational advantages, some academics, freed for a year from their regular time structure, flounder and feel lost' (*Employment and Unemployment*, p. 23).

## A FALSE NEED?

This is what the bulk of the evidence indicates, and there is virtually none to the contrary. However, the writers I am criticizing are unlikely to be greatly upset by this. They do not seriously dispute the view that a majority, as a matter of fact, feel the need for a job. Rather, the crucial question for them is how this fact is to be interpreted. For they would argue that the supposed 'need to work' is ultimately a product of the training and moral conditioning to which we are subjected. It is a 'false' and 'artificial' need, not a natural one: it is a social and historical product.

My main purpose so far has been to argue that people gain real and important fulfilment from work; the need to work is genuine and real. But I do not mean to imply that this need is an inherent and universal feature of human nature. Protestantism, no doubt, involves such a view. It portrays work as the God-given duty and 'calling' of mankind. In more contemporary terms, moreover, it is often argued that human beings are endowed with a unique creativity, and that this is an essential feature of human nature which distinguishes us from the rest of animal creation. Man is *homo faber*, the productive species.[39]

The socialist view of work has some similarity to these ideas, it is true. In its Marxist form, however, it differs fundamentally from them in rejecting the idea of a universal and eternal human nature. Human nature, for Marx, develops and changes historically. Human powers and human needs are a human and social product. In particular, they are a product of the essential human activity of labour. 'By acting on the external world and changing it, [man] at the same time changes his own nature.'[40]

Through the activity of labour, people develop their powers and capacities and create new needs – including the need to work. I have been arguing that this is a real and fundamental need in present society. However, there are reasons to believe that it has not always been so, and that attitudes to work have changed greatly in the course of history.

A frequently heard complaint of Western employers in the Third World is that the 'natives' make poor workers: they are 'unreliable', they are 'lazy'. These complaints are not new. Marx quotes an amusing example:

> In *The Times* of November 1857 there appeared a delightful yell of rage from a West Indian planter. With great moral indignation this advocate, in support of his pleas for the re-establishment of Negro slavery, describes how the Quashees (the free Negroes of Jamaica) were content to produce what was strictly necessary for their own consumption, and looked upon laziness itself ('indulgence' and 'idleness') as the real luxury article alongside this 'use value'. They said that sugar, and all the fixed capital laid out in the plantations could go to hell; they smirked with ironical, malicious glee at the ruined planters. . . . They had ceased to be slaves, but were not yet wage-earning labourers but only self-sustaining peasants working for their own necessary consumption.[41]

39. See R. Norman, *The Moral Philosophers*, Oxford, 1984, chapters 8–9 for a brief and clear presentation of these ideas in a philosophical context.
40. Marx, *Capital*, vol. I, p. 177.
41. Marx, *Grundrisse*, p. 101.

The same complaints are heard still. Writing in 1961 the anthropologist Gusinde declares, more in resignation than in anger:

> The Yamana are not capable of continuous daily hard labour, much to the chagrin of European farmers and employers for whom they often work. Their work is more a matter of fits and starts. . . . Repeated irregularities of this kind make the European employer despair, but the Indian cannot help it. It is his natural disposition.[42]

It is absurd to talk of 'natural dispositions' in this way, and to regard these matters in purely moral terms. Nevertheless, this should not blind us to the real differences in attitudes to work that such judgements indicate.

These differences are strikingly confirmed by numerous anthropological studies. On the basis of a great deal of empirical evidence Sahlins, for example, convincingly refutes the common idea that primitive – hunter and gatherer – people have to work without cease in the constant battle to survive, and lack the leisure time needed to 'build culture':

> There is nothing . . . to the convention that hunters and gatherers can enjoy little leisure from tasks of sheer survival. . . . The traditional formulas might be truer if reversed: the amount of work (per capita) increases with the evolution of culture, and the amount of leisure decreases.[43]

For example, the Arnhem Land aborigines, according to Sahlins,

> do not work hard. the average length of time per person per day put into the appropriation and preparation of food was four or five hours. Moreover, they do not work continuously. The subsistence quest was highly intermittent. It would stop for the time being when the people had procured enough for the time being, which left them plenty of time to spare.[44]

Similar patterns are found among other hunter-gatherer groups. 'Reports . . . suggest a mean of three to five hours per adult worker per day in food production.'[45]

What do these peoples do with their free time? According to Sahlins, 'much of the time spared by the Arnhem Land hunters was literally spare time, consumed in rest and sleep.'[46] If such primitive societies fail to 'build culture', he concludes, it 'is not strictly from want of time. It is from idle hands.'[47] The choice to avoid embarking on the path of civilized development, he suggests, may even be a

42. Quoted by M. Sahlins, *Stone Age Economics*, London, 1974, p. 28. The Yamana are a group of South American hunters. Similar complaints were made about newly recruited Mexican mineworkers at the beginning of this century. 'His lack of initiative, inability to save, absences while celebrating too many holidays, willingness to work only three or four days a week if that paid for necessities, insatiable desire for alcohol – all were pointed out as proof of natural inferiority' (quoted in E. P. Thompson, 'Time, work-discipline, and industrial capitalism', *Past and Present*, no. 38, 1967, p. 91).
43. Sahlins, *Stone Age Economics*, p. 35.
44. Ibid., p. 17.
45. Ibid., p. 35.
46. Ibid., p. 19.
47. Ibid., p. 20.

conscious one: 'Why should we plant when there are so many mongomongo nuts in the world?' ask the Bushmen.[48]

## INDUSTRY AND HUMAN NATURE

Such attitudes are not confined to 'other cultures'. People of pre-industrial Europe shared them. At the outset of the industrial revolution, working people strongly resisted the new work discipline required in the factories; and the early factory owners complained of the unreliability of their workers in precisely the same terms as do today's employers in the Third World. In the textile mills, for example, 'on the first introduction of the business the people were found very ill-disposed to submit to the long confinement and regular industry required of them.'[49] Indeed, the first manufacturers faced not only technical and mechanical problems; they also had to find ways of 'training human beings to renounce their desultory habits of work and to identify themselves with the unvarying regularity of the complex automaton.'[50]

Moreover, initially at least, the inducements of higher wages and piece rates were ineffective. In the eighteenth century, the received wisdom had been that 'the hands work better the less they are paid.' Payment by results was an innovation of industrialism, introduced only gradually as attitudes to work and its rewards changed.[51] The pre-industrial worker, it seemed, lived with no care for the morrow: when he had earned sufficient he 'returned to his village . . . [or] went on a drunken spree.'[52] As with the Quashees described by Marx, 'ambitions to rise above his own idea of a "subsistence" income by dint of hard work were foreign to him. He had to be made ambitious and "respectable". . . . For unless the worker *wished* to become "respectable" . . . none of the other incentives would bite.'[53]

The inculcation of Protestant morality, with its emphasis on the virtues of work, regularity, orderliness, sobriety and thrift, no doubt played an important part in changing attitudes to work and its rewards. Likewise, schooling was a significant factor in training the young in the habits of the new industrial order. 'Once within the school gates,' as E. P. Thompson says, 'the child entered the new universe of disciplined time.'[54] However, the role of preaching and schooling should not be over-emphasized. While work remained on a domestic and small workshop scale, such influences had only limited effect. It was the introduction of large-scale machinery that made the new discipline imperative and enforced it upon the workers. This was clear enough to the manufacturers, as their 'philospher' Ure observes. In a workshop, he says, 'when a mantua maker chooses to rise from her seat and take the fresh air, her seam goes back a little, that is all;

48. Quoted, ibid., p. 27.

49. Quoted by S. Pollard, *The Genesis of Modern Management*, London, 1965, p. 161.

50. A. Ure, *The Philosophy of Manufactures*, London, 1835, p. 15.

51. Pollard, *The Genesis of Modern Management*, p. 191. See also E. P. Thompson, *The Making of the English Working Class*, Harmondsworth, revised edn, 1980, p. 393.

52. Thompson, *The Making of the English Working Class*, pp. 392–3.

53. Pollard, *The Genesis of Modern Management*, p. 195.

54. Thompson, 'Time, work-discipline and industrial capitalism', p. 84.

there are no other hands waiting on her.' In a cotton mill, by contrast, 'all the machinery is going on, which they must attend to.' And so, Ure stresses, it was 'machinery [which] ultimately forced the worker to accept the discipline of the factory.'[55]

The first factory workers bitterly resisted the new system; but the system eventually prevailed. The habits and attitudes it required were gradually accepted and internalized: human nature was transformed. 'How superior in vigour and intelligence are the factory mechanics in Lancashire . . . to the handicraft artisans of London,' exclaims Ure in a typically ecstatic passage;[56] but the same changes were noted by other and more sceptical observers, including Marx and Engels.

By the standards of industrial society, people from pre-capitalist societies are 'unreliable' and 'lazy', they lack 'discipline' and 'energy'. These are facts noted by writers of the most widely differing moral perspectives. It is not illuminating to see these matters in moral terms, however; for what these observations make clear is that attitudes and habits of work are ultimately a product and a reflection of the mode of production in which they occur. In particular, the modern need to work that I have been describing is a product of the historically developed conditions of modern industry. The 'habit of industriousness', as Hegel calls it, is a product of work itself. 'Practical education, acquired through working, consists first in the automatically recurrent need for something to do and the habit of simply being busy.'[57] Likewise Marx describes how capitalism in particular 'drives labour out beyond the limits of its natural needs':[58]

> The historical vocation of capital is fulfilled as soon as, on the one hand, demand has developed to the point where there is a general need for surplus labour beyond what is necessary, and surplus labour itself arises from individual needs; and on the other, general industriousness has developed (under the strict discipline of capital) and has been passed on to succeeding generations, until it has become the property of the new generation.[59]

Rousseau was one of the first modern writers to make these points. He recognized and described with great insight and originality the way in which our needs – and, in particular, the modern needs to be sociable, active and productive – have developed historically. Man 'in the state of nature' – primitive man – he argues, is a creature of few needs and no concerns beyond them. 'He desires only to live and be free from labour . . . . Civilised man, on the other hand, is always moving, sweating, toiling, and racking his brains to find still more laborious occupations.'[60]

Primitive man, says Rousseau, is 'indolent'. However, he repudiates the moral condemnation usually implied by that term. He does so by simply *reversing* the customary moral judgement. For he regards the 'laziness' of earlier people as the 'natural' condition of mankind; and the modern needs to be busy and productive

55. Quoted by Pollard, *The Genesis of Modern Management*, p. 184.
56. Ure, *The Philosophy of Manufactures*, p. 23.
57. G.W.F. Hegel, *Philosophy of Right*, Oxford, 1952, p. 129.
58. Marx, *Grundrisse*, p. 101.
59. Ibid., p. 100.
60. Rousseau, *Social Contract*, p. 104.

as 'artifical' and 'false' needs – harmful and corrupting developments of human nature.

Sahlins, in common with many other recent writers, is inclined to take the same view. Thus he warns against judging the work habits and attitudes of the hunters and gatherers he describes 'from the anxious vantage of European compulsions';[61] and he suggests that 'the more appropriate deduction from the cultural differences might have been that Europeans are overworked.'[62]

Such ideas provide the basis for much of the currently fashionable scepticism about the human value of work. Gorz's outlook is similar, as we have seen: for he, too, argues that the need to work is a false and artificial creation of modern industrial society. In other, non-industrial societies we see different – truer and more natural – attitudes to work; and it is these that provide the touchstone for his criticisms of the attitudes that I have been describing.

However, there is another view we can take of these matters. The developments that I have been describing provide no basis for the romantic idea of a 'natural' attitude to work. Rather, they indicate that, in this area at least, human nature is social and historical through and through. Attitudes to work, *all* attitudes to work – those of pre-industrial societies just as much as contemporary ones – are social and historical products. They are created by and reflect the mode of production in which they occur. Thus the modern need to work, although it is undoubtedly a historically developed need, should not be judged 'false' or 'artificial' simply for that reason. On the contrary, it is a real and ineliminable feature of contemporary psychology. For in the course of the historical developments that I have been outlining, new habits, new attitudes, new needs have been created and old ones relinquished. Human nature itself has been transformed.

## THE NEED FOR LEISURE

As well as needing work, it is clear that we also need time off work – leisure – both for rest and relaxation, and also for the pursuit of activities and needs not fulfilled in work. Gorz puts strong emphasis on this point. He even quotes some evidence for it: namely a large European survey of 1977 which found that a majority (55 per cent) of people in work, if granted the choice, would prefer a reduction in their working hours to an increase in wages.[63] Moreover, the reduction of working hours is something for which working people have long struggled, although it is important to stress that this has usually been in the context of the demand for full employment. As Jahoda says, the labour movement has traditionally taken the view that 'leisure hours are a complement to work hours, not a substitute for them.'[64]

Gorz, by contrast, sees leisure precisely as a desirable substitute for work. As we have seen, his view is that work is a coercive necessity and freedom consists in the 'liberation from work'. In a well-known passage, Marx contrasts the 'realm of

61. Sahlins, *Stone Age Economics*, p. 63.
62. Ibid., p. 51.
63. Gorz, *Farewell to the Working Class*, p. 140.
64. Jahoda, *Employment and Unemployment*, p. 24.

necessity' (the realm of 'labour . . . determined by necessity and mundane considerations') with the 'realm of freedom' which involves 'that development of human energy which is an end in itself.'[65] Gorz makes much of this passage. He talks of the autonomous, creative activities – arts and crafts, hobbies, sports and recreation – which the liberation from work will allow. However, his account of this 'realm of freedom' is just as questionable as his account of the psychology of work. Although he sees well enough that work is a socially conditioned need, he writes as if autonomous and creative leisure activities will flourish quite naturally when we are freed from the coercive need to work. He fails to see that the desires and needs for these activities are equally social and historical products.

No doubt I will be thought to be misrepresenting Gorz at this point. After all, he says quite explicitly that a reduction of work time is not in itself 'intrinsically liberatory', and that it will bring freedom only if there exists a network of 'collective facilities' – community centres and workshops – and of 'local, non-market, collective services', etc.[66] What this suggests, however, is precisely that the *need* for 'autonomous' activity is present naturally; all that is required for it to flourish are the *means* – free time and the appropriate facilities. It is this view that I am questioning.

Mere free time, even with a network of cooperatives and so on, is something quite different from the realm of freedom as Marx describes it. The need for the positive and active use of non-work time is, in fact, a modern phenomenon: it hardly exists in pre-industrial societies. Rousseau describes how his 'natural man', once he has satisfied his few basic needs, simply falls asleep under the nearest tree. The abundant free time of hunter-gatherers, as we have seen, involves little that can properly be put under the heading of the 'development of human energy as an end in itself'. The ceremonies and rituals which are often a well-developed feature of the life of such societies tend to be as coercively necessary for their members as mundane labour, and bear little relationship to Gorz's 'autonomous creative activity'. Moreover, as E. P. Thompson writes, popular culture before the industrial revolution in England was 'in many ways otiose, intellectually vacant, devoid of quickening'.[67] This conflicts, I know, with the picture of people in pre-industrial communities spending long hours in conversation, in singing and dancing, and in other convivial pursuits; but we must beware of romanticizing these societies. The truth rather appears to be that their autonomous non-work activities are desultory and limited, and not for lack of free time.

The extensive active, free and creative use of non-work time by working people is a development of modern industrial society.[68] The growth of public leisure activities begins in the eighteenth century and has continued steadily until it has become, today, the basis of huge and still expanding areas of industry. Of course, a great deal of modern leisure activity involves people only as consumers, in a

65. K. Marx, *Capital*, vol. III, Moscow, 1971, p. 820.
66. Gorz, *Paths to Paradise*, pp. 103–4.
67. Thompson, 'Time, work-discipline and industrial capitalism', p. 93.
68. See S. Sayers, 'Work, leisure and human needs', *Thesis Eleven*, no. 14, 1986, pp. 79–96; H. Cunningham, *Leisure in the Industrial Revolution*, London, 1980; and T. Burns, 'Leisure in industrial society', in S. Parker et al., *Leisure and Society in Britain*, London, 1973.

passive fashion. The developments I am describing are still in process: their general direction, however, is unmistakable.

What these observations indicate is that the 'realm of freedom' is not attained simply by having free time – although free time is, to be sure, a necessary precondition for it. Rather, the active and creative use of free time is a historical development. It is itself a *need*, the development of which is gradually transforming non-work hours from being a time of mere torpor and idleness into a sphere in which they will truly be a time of free human development of the sort envisaged by Marx. In short, the 'realm of freedom' is best seen as a *development* of the 'realm of necessity' – its complement and not its mere opposite.

## THE POLITICS OF WORK

I have been defending the view that work and leisure are real and fundamental, though historically developed, needs in the modern world. These ideas, as I have stressed, are central to the socialist outlook. However, they are widely dismissed as conservative attitudes which have ceased to have any application to contemporary politics. In conclusion, I will argue that there is no basis for these charges.

We are frequently told, for example, that the 'work ethic' is in decline, although it is seldom clear just what this means. However, it seems quite likely that work attitudes are changing. Young people in particular, it appears, are becoming more demanding in relation to work: they are less willing to submit quietly to arbitrary authority, and they want fulfilment from their work. The idea that work of whatever kind is a duty and a virtue is passing – if, indeed, it was ever widespread. However, if the arguments that I have been giving are at all correct, it would be wrong to imagine that this is because people are coming to deny the importance of work in their lives. On the contrary. The evidence, as I have shown, points in quite the opposite direction: it demonstrates that people are coming to regard work no longer as a *duty* but rather as a *need* which has become an essential part of human nature.

Libertarians like Gorz, by contrast, put a very different interpretation on these developments. They celebrate the 'demise of the Protestant work ethic' as proof that people are at last coming to appreciate that the need for work is a false and unnatural compulsion produced by modern society. This is often presented as though it was the most far-reaching and radical critique of industrial capitalist society.[69] It is nothing of the kind. Such scepticism tells people that their desire for work and for fulfilling work is a delusion, the artifical product of social conditioning, which they should discard. In effect, in present circumstances, this is to tell the unemployed to reconcile themselves to unemployment; it is to tell alienated and dissatisfied workers to renounce their desire for fulfilling work as illusory and put up with their lot; it is to tell women to keep to their domestic 'place'.

A similar message is expressed in entirely different terms and from an entirely different quarter: not by would-be radicals, but by politicians who like to think

69. As well as Gorz *passim*, see also P. Willis, *Learning to Labour*, Farnborough, 1977; and Anthony, *The Ideology of Work*.

that they are facing the current situation in the most hard-headed and realistic terms. The prospect now, in much of the Western world, is of long-term mass unemployment. Present government policies, in Britain at least, seem almost deliberately designed to this end. If the experience of the 1930s is any guide, the recommended alternative of a programme of public works (unless on a massive scale), while it might do some good, is unlikely to alter the situation fundamentally. It is a sobering thought that it was only the policies of fascism in Germany and the approach of world war in other countries that lifted the capitalist world out of the great depression.[70] In this context, we have heard talk (even from some trade union leaders) of 'training for leisure', where 'leisure' is a euphemism for unemployment. The idea is that unemployment is inevitable; people must be trained to accept the fact and adapt to it.[71]

It may seem that the view that I have been presenting gives some encouragement to the idea that people can be trained to accept unemployment. If the need for work is socially created, then surely it can be uncreated by social means – by education, by training? This does not follow. Indeed, what I am saying is directly opposed to such views. When I talk of the need to work in modern society as a *real* need, and when I stress that it is an outcome and a product of modern industry, I mean precisely to deny that it is a product simply of education, or that it is a purely ideological phenomenon. On the contrary, it is a need which arises out of the most basic *material* conditions of modern society, and which cannot therefore be altered by the methods of indoctrination alone.

## SOCIALISM AND WORK

The need for work, and the need for leisure too, I am arguing, is ultimately an aspect and an expression of the development of modern industry; it is a product of the productive forces. These have developed within the framework of capitalist relations of production. Increasingly, however, the development of industry is coming into collision and conflict with these relations of production. 'From forms of development of the productive forces these relations turn into their fetters.'[72]

These conflicts and contradictions have never been more clearly apparent. The gigantic forces of production developed by modern society lie underused and even idle: not only factories and machinery but, even more importantly, people – millions of men and women with their socially developed habits and skills. And not because the capitalist system is incapable of mobilizing and employing them. Even when they are employed, as Marx says,

> everything seems pregnant with its contrary. Machinery, gifted with the wonderful power of shortening and fructifying human labour, we behold starving and overworking it. The new fangled sources of wealth, by some weird spell, are turned into sources of want . . . . All our inventions and progress seem to result in endowing material forces with intellectual life, and in stultifying human life into a material

70. M. Stewart, *Keynes and After*, Harmondsworth, 2nd edn, 1972.
71. C. Jenkins and B. Sherman, *The Collapse of Work*, London, 1979.
72. K. Marx, 'Preface [1859]', in *Selected Works*, vol. I, Moscow, 1958, p. 329.

> force. This antagonism between modern industry and science on the one hand, modern misery and dissolution on the other hand; this antagonism between the productive powers and the social relations of our epoch is a fact, palpable, overwhelming, and not to be controverted.[73]

The productive potentiality of modern industry is immense, and so is its potentiality for human liberation. In a rationally and humanely organized society, it could be used not only to meet the real needs of the most basic kinds – the real poverty and want which still exist, even in the most economically advanced societies – but also to create more humane conditions of work, including a reduction of the working day. But such statements are likely to arouse scepticism in many quarters. For people are fearful and apprehensive of the productive power of modern industry, and inclined to reject such views as naively 'productivist' ones.[74]

To this charge socialism must plead guilty, for it is quite avowedly a 'productivist' philosophy – not in the sense that it recommends production simply for the sake of production, but in the sense that it regards production as 'man's essential activity' and as a primary human and social value. Its fundamental criticism of capitalism follows from this. Capitalism is no longer able effectively to employ the productive forces – the means of production and the labour power – which it itself has brought into being. It is not able to meet the needs – including the needs for fulfilling work and leisure – which it itself has created. What socialism demands, therefore, is not the liberation of people from work – capitalism is already doing that all too successfully by throwing millions on the dole – but rather the liberation of work, of the productive forces (including people), from the stultifying confines of the capitalist system.

As for what a possible future society may hold in store, we have learned to be cautious and sceptical of utopian visions. The problems of 'actually existing' socialist societies are a sufficient warning . Marx, too, was notably restrained when it came to 'dreaming up recipes for the cookshops of the future'. In one of his few attempts to envisage the character of a future communist society, he talks of labour becoming 'life's prime want'.[75] This has often been dismissed as one of his more utopian and fantastic ideas. But is it really so? The arguments that I have been presenting raise this question – and not only on the basis of what can be envisaged for an ideal future, but on the basis of what we can see in the present. According to Lenin:

> The feudal organisation of social labour rested on the discipline of the bludgeon, while the working people, robbed and tyrannised by a handful of landowners, were utterly ignorant and downtrodden. The capitalist organisation of social labour rested on the discipline of hunger. . . . The communist organisation of social labour . . . rests . . . on the free and conscious discipline of the working people themselves who have thrown off the yoke both of the landowners and the capitalist. This new

73. K. Marx, 'Speech at the anniversary of the *People's Paper*', in *Selected Works*, vol. I, Moscow, 1961, p. 39.
74. See for example Gorz, *Farewell to the Working Class*, p. 33.
75. K. Marx, *Critique of the Gotha Programme*, in *Selected Works*, vol. II, Moscow, 1961, p. 25.

> discipline does not drop from the skies, nor is it born from pious wishes, it grows out of the material conditions of large-scale capitalist production, and out of them alone.[76]

Lenin was writing in 1920, when Russia was still predominantly a peasant-based agricultural society. His words must have seemed as utopian and as distant from reality as Marx's.[77]

If today, in our society, they still seem so it is for different reasons. We live in a capitalist society, based upon large-scale industry. For most people in our society, work is in many respects an alienating and oppressive experience. The spur that drives them to it may no longer be the threat of hunger as such, but certainly the threat of serious material deprivation plays its part.[78] There is no question but that there are material incentives to work. And yet the evidence, I have been arguing, shows that work (at least of any but the most repulsive and degrading sort) is also now felt subjectively as a need. It may not yet be 'life's *prime* want', but it is a vital want, a need, nevertheless. So far from being a utopian dream, Marx's vision is increasingly becoming a fact of modern psychology. That is to say, the *subjective* conditions for a more satisfactory and rational organization of the work of society are developing here and now. What is lacking is the *objective* framework of economic and social relations, and the objective organization of work, which would allow this need to be satisfied.

73. K. Marx, 'Speech at the anniversary of the *People's Paper*', in *Selected Works*, vol. I, Moscow, 1961, p. 39.
74. See for example Gorz, *Farewell to the Working Class*, p. 33.
75. K. Marx, *Critique of the Gotha Programme*, in *Selected Works*, vol. II, Moscow, 1961, p. 25.
76. V. I. Lenin, 'A great beginning', *Selected Works in Three Volumes*, vol. III, Moscow, 1975, p. 171.
77. Lenin was well aware of this. 'It must be clear to everybody,' he wrote, 'that we, i.e. our society, our social system, are still a very long way from the application of *this* (i.e the communist) form of labour on a broad, really mass scale .... It will take many years, decades, to create a new labour discipline, new forms of social ties between people, and new forms and methods of drawing people into labour.' ('From the destruction of the old social system to the creation of the new', *Selected Works*, vol. III, p. 289).
78. The government is continually seeking ways of cutting social security payments, in order 'to force the unemployed to take any low paid job on offer' (*The Sunday Times*, 17 February 1985, p. 1).

# Epilogue:
# On Work

R. E. PAHL

The final two chapters in this book are about work in the widest sense and do not require an introduction. Most readers will want to explore within themselves the issues raised by Ronco and Peattie. Their question 'What marks an activity as work?' is not easily answered by common sense. Does reading this book out of interest become 'leisure', whilst reading it in order to prepare for an essay in a course on work become 'work'? What if someone who is paid to review the book for a journal were to read enough to write the piece in question but then carried on reading for fun? Was the first period of reading work, and did the gradual growth of interest lead to the work changing to leisure or pleasure? These issues have worried philosophers for centuries.

Ronco and Peattie argue that the 'mental set' of the person may be important in determining what is or is not work. We choose to do our hobbies but we may feel compelled to do our work: thus the notion that 'a realm of necessity' must be contrasted with 'a realm of freedom' is deeply embedded in our ideas about work. Yet even as we are about to say we avoid it if we can, we know that for many people it is work that provides the essential meaning to their lives. We understand what Sayers means when he argues that the need for work is 'ultimately an expression of the development of modern industry'. Yet it is unclear from Sayers's essay whether the forces of production have, indeed, created ideological fetters in the form of a false consciousness that binds people to the notion of a need to work. His stance smacks of over-determination. People may be bound in a given historical conjuncture to the dominant ideas of the time, but do they not have the hope – if not the capacity – to transcend their ideological fetters?

## THE SOCIAL RELATIONS OF WORK

Sayers is surely right to argue that the subjective need to work is socially constructed, but that itself is a real and objective fact which has clear social consequences. One way to link the arguments of chapters 32 and 33 is to consider work as an activity in terms of the social relations in which it is embedded. These social relations can be structured by the patterns of domination generated by the capitalist economic system, by the principles of both the market and of reciprocity and by the social hierarchies of age, gender, kinship, neighbourhood and informal group. An individual may apparently be engaged in a work task but simply observing that individual may provide little understanding of what kind of work it is or, indeed, whether it is work at all. Not all purposeful activity is work; but if it is non-work or play we again cannot be sure until we know more of the social relations in which the play activity is embedded. We see people at a drinks party: one person may be there sharing a convivial activity and engaging in a pure form of sociation or play. Another person may work for the British Council or the Embassy staff and is heavily and intensely involved in the employment for which she is paid. There *is* a distinction between work and play but it is not based on the intrinsic nature of the task or activity. In order to clarify this and to introduce further complexities a particular example may be explored in some detail.

Consider an image of a woman ironing. She is standing by an ironing board on which there is a garment – a blouse or a shirt. Is she at work or is she at play and, if the former, what kind of work is she engaged in? The answer will depend on the social relations in which her task is embedded. Let us explore some possibilities.

First, the woman could be a full-time wage worker producing garments as a domestic outworker. If she has been hired on a piecework basis she could have an incentive to iron as many garments as quickly as possible. Alternatively, she may have been hired on a fixed contract with no incentive to increase the number of garments she irons, although there may be some quality control so that the style or quality of her work is more important than her pace. Her approach to her task is likely to be related to the contractual arrangements that exist between her and her employer. She may be working part-time, she may be working shifts which include a period at home, or she may be doing casual work, covering for regular employees at a holiday time or taking on extra work at a particularly busy period. Whatever the precise details, she is, in all these cases, basically a wage labourer: she is selling her ironing skills to an employer who provides her with the materials and also, possibly, the tools. If she had an accident and lost her sight or injured her ironing arm her labour power would disappear or be reduced.

There is a further twist. We may learn that she is basically a wage labourer, determined by the social relations in which her task is embedded, but we cannot be sure that her employer is honest. It is possible that this female outworker is not recorded in the firm's official returns to the appropriate government department. This may be a strategy to avoid the obligation to pay certain taxes or insurance contributions and also to avoid granting certain rights and benefits to the employee, such as the number of days holiday with pay, rights to sickness benefit and maternity leave, and insurance in the event of, say, an accident with the iron. If the worker is being hired informally or illegally that will not affect the basic social relations of wage labour; it will, however, determine whether it is formally recorded which, in turn, will have fundamental implications for the individual concerned. If the work is done informally this does not, of course, put it in any separate informal economy but it should be described as shadow or hidden wage labour to distinguish it from the formally recognized and recorded form.

The woman could be preparing the garment for sale but she may own the material and the iron; she may have dyed the cloth, designed the style or decorated the garment in some distinctive way. She may have her own stall or boutique or she may be selling by contract to specific retail outlets. Whatever the details, she is a self-employed worker engaged in petty-commodity production. She is responsible for her own pace of work and the quality of what she produces; she may employ others, who may or may not be members of her family. If the latter she may be engaged in family capitalism with its own distinctive sets of social relations. Again, her activities may be more or less officially recognized and she may prefer to defraud the tax authorities, despite the risks involved. This may involve the simple underdeclaring of profits, or it may be coupled with paying other people in cash so that she has no contractual obligations towards them.

So far the woman at the ironing board has been viewed as an income-generating agent. We know nothing about her age, marital status, race or subjective preconceptions and attitudes. She could be married or single and in both cases she may or may not have a child. Let us assume that she is ironing the garment for another member of the household in which she lives. What kind of work would that be? Again we need to know more about the nature of the social relations in which the task is embedded. This time we are not concerned with social relations of capitalist production but with the familial or patriarchal relations, which may get very complex. There is a great range of possibilities. The woman may be ironing a shirt for her lover. Her mind is full of loving or erotic thoughts so that the task is highly charged emotionally and provides substantial pleasure as she, perhaps, fantasizes about the person as she irons the various parts of the garment. She may have offered to do the task as an act of love, knowing that her lover was willing and able to do the task himself and, indeed, in the past has done the same for her. The work is thus symbolic: it is work with a purpose, done for love, and is similar to the toil of monks or nuns who work literally for love as a means of self-expression. The distinction between this kind of work and play is that in the latter case the pleasure would be solely in the activity of ironing. It would not matter for whom the shirt was being ironed: the important activity would be the ironing itself and the pleasure would be similar to that experienced by those who play tennis or go fishing as a recreational activity.

However, the woman may have been married for many years to a man she barely tolerates. He insists on a clean, well-ironed shirt every day. He may hit her if she fails in what he claims is her duty. She resignedly goes about her task heavily dominated by patriarchal social relations. The task is a burden and brings no pleasure: she feels constrained, oppressed and resentful. She is but one example of the oppression of women and she may be brooding on the unfairness and injustice of her situation. Even if she is ironing her children's garments the resentment may be much the same if she feels constrained by her domestic role and the social relations established by the power of her spouse.

If the woman is ironing her own blouse then much will depend on the context in which she is to wear it. If on the following day she has to wear the garment at the office then she is, as it were, working to reproduce herself as a smart worker. She knows that the way she presents herself is part of the way she is able to demonstrate her effectiveness as a worker. She has internalized the expectations of employers and colleagues – whether male or female – and thus feels constrained to dress in a given way. She is thus working for her employer in her own time but, of course, she is also reproducing herself as a worker when she is cleaning her teeth or eating muesli. However, she would do these things even if she were not in employment. Hence, the task of ironing her blouse is more directly related to her employment and she would not do the task if she was on holiday. Some occupations require specific uniforms or work clothes that are provided and maintained by the employer. Other jobs make no demands on their incumbents and the workers may wear what they like. By exploring the task in this way we can see that some women do have extra employment-related work to carry out in their own time. Unmarried men may have the same burden: married men typically pass on the burden to their wives.

It may be that the woman is ironing her elderly mother-in-law's blouse. A combination of social pressures have put her in the position of being responsible for the care of someone who is unable to care for herself. She may be engaged in what is euphemistically termed 'community care'. She is an unpaid community worker and the obligation she is made to feel to care for her husband's mother may prevent her from engaging in paid employment. Such burdens of family and kin are highly gender-specific. Men would not be expected to care for the elderly in the same way and in the case of an unemployed single man with a dependent relative the social services would, in Britain, provide support that would not be available to a woman in the same position. The social relations of family obligation are sharply divided by gender.

Let us now turn away from the labour market and the ageist or sexist domination of the household and consider the situations where the woman is ironing for someone who is not a household member. She might be doing a little casual work as a domestic cleaner and getting extra cash for doing the ironing at home. She would be sharing in the social relations of the casualized lumpenproletariat, however sweetly her employer asked her to do the work. The more likely situation, however, is that she is doing the ironing for a non-household member without receiving payment. She may be a member of the local dramatic society and the producer has flattered her into pressing the costumes of the leading actors. She may have agreed to do the work calculating that her willingness will put her, as it were, into credit with the producer: she has entered into a relationship based on the norm of reciprocity. Her reasonable assumption is that by giving her time and effort in doing the ironing she will be repaid with a comparable favour in the future. She may be wanting a part in a play; she may hope that the producer will be stimulated by his appreciation of what she has done to notice other more personal qualities; she may want the esteem and support of other members of the dramatic society. Whatever the reward for which she hopes, she will perceive the task as an investment: she is banking reciprocity and she may expect to get her return in due course. If, on the other hand, the producer has looked round the room and simply cajoled or flattered the nearest woman to do a tedious chore, then she has suffered the effects of normative patriarchal oppression (assuming that the producer does not equally victimize men to stay behind to move scenery or to paint the theatre). The woman could, of course, volunteer to iron the garments solely and simply because she enjoys the chance to help the group. The task is a pleasing relaxation, perhaps, from a mentally exhausting job and she enjoys the chance to share in the collegial style of the amateur dramatic group. She may not care whether or not she is socially rewarded with thanks and gratitude. The activity is genuinely a pleasure and would not, therefore, be classed as work. However, it would cease to be play if, after offering to do the task a number of times, the group started to assume that it was her job and began to apply the pressures of collective domination to trap her into regular labour.

This is not meant to be an exhaustive survey of all the possible patterns of social relations in which the task of ironing could be embedded. It is simply a way of exploring the various structures of constraint that are created by social relations in which wage labour, domestic labour and communal labour are embedded. It would clearly be quite wrong to say that our busy ironing woman was not working when she was not engaging in wage labour. However, it is important to recognize that her orientation to the task substantially altered the form of work in which she was engaged. It matters a great deal whether she is a subordinate, physically and economically powerless person living with a domineering husband or someone living with a man in a spirit of partnership. In the former case it could be claimed that she is living in a situation of patriarchal domination whereas in the latter case the lifting of the domination structure of social relations changes the nature of the task. This point is important. It is not always necessary to change the nature of the task in order to reduce the burden of work but rather, more significantly, it may be more effective to change the nature of the social relations in which the task is embedded. Thus the dramatic society could turn the pleasurable task into work by taking the activity too readily for granted. Similarly, the woman who was producing her own garments for sale on her stall could make some to give to friends or to exchange for their craft products. In such a case principles of altruism and reciprocity would transform a product aimed at the exchange values of the market to something produced solely for its use value to a friend or relative. It is not the nature of the task that determines whether use values or exchange values are being produced: it is a combination of the social relations and the social orientations in which the task is embedded that defines the form of the work. The meanings that individuals bring with themselves as they face a given task are critical. Throughout our example we have been thinking about a woman doing the task. If the example had referred throughout to 'a person' many readers would still assume that it was a woman doing the work. The tyrannies of custom and convention may create work as much as the economic relations of production.

This specifically sociological approach to work has substantial practical importance. In much contemporary discussion there is an assumption that work is changing dramatically, simply because there are now proportionately fewer men employed in manufacturing industry. When discussion is based solely on paid employment and that is contrasted with all other activity, implicitly seen as leisure, then reducing the hours of paid employment is equated with reducing the amount of work that is done, or work-sharing is seen solely in terms of redistributing paid employment. By focusing on only one form of work new inequalities in the distribution of work could get overlooked and those doing other forms of work could become even more heavily burdened.

Perhaps the point can be made another way: assume a society with a vast source of some rare raw material that cannot be made synthetically. The world market for this product provides the society that owns it with enough money to provide every inhabitant with an average income index-linked to the average per caput income in Switzerland or whichever country is taken as the norm. Certainly, work would not then cease in that society. There would be a very great demand for services. Some people would want to spend their income in cafés and restaurants where part of the pleasure would be the smiling and efficient service. Since the attraction of wage labour might be dramatically reduced, what other rewards will be needed to produce the cooks and waiters? Critics will dismiss the notion as fanciful, claiming that there are still many poor people in economically advanced societies and that most people have many material wants still to satisfy. Certainly there can be no absolute limit to wealth, but if workers in early-nineteenth-century Britain had been offered the prospect of the present system of national social security they would have been likely to dismiss such a vision as utopian. There may, indeed, be more people now who do not feel impelled to engage in wage-labour work, although they will readily engage in other forms of work with quite oppressive forms of social domination. Alternatively others may prefer to mix different forms of work on a part-time basis.

A relatively rich society may find that it needs other forms of work more urgently than it needs wage labour. Work in the services in particular may have to combine different forms in order for the quality of the service to be adequate. Perhaps an example will make the point. The success of a wine bar depends very heavily on its atmosphere and style. The proprietor may engage someone to serve the wine for which he or she gets paid a wage. However if that person is getting an index-linked social wage it may be more amusing to drink the wine than to serve it. If, on the other hand, the proprietor is a convivial jazz pianist he may wish to have the wine bar largely to fulfil his own musical ambitions in an appreciative context. If the quality of the music is good enough he may have many people volunteering to take part. Serving the wine may be a way of taking part in a convivial activity; more introductions may be made, and one may get merit that is repaid through the principle of reciprocity on other sociable occasions in the future. Serving the wine is like the woman doing the ironing for the dramatic society in order to be part of the collegial context. Even if the work of serving the wine is not embedded in the social relations of wage labour, people still pay for their drinks, taxes are still levied and the state still gathers in resources which it can then redistribute. From that point of view it is paradoxically more important that people spend money than that they earn it.

This example is given in all seriousness. It may be very dangerous for rich societies to emphasize only one or two forms of work at the expense of all others. The value system that encourages competition or greed at the expense of collaboration and altruism may not ultimately succeed. In the same way that the woman, resentful of the patriarchal domination of her husband, may still willingly iron costumes if her lover is the producer of the local dramatic club, so may all forms of work be transformed.

This is not the place to draw up a utopian political programme. However, it is worth recognizing that discussions about the politics of work or the future of work will not get very far if they limit themselves to the current notions about what work actually is. In the same way that those concerned about the position of women in society found it necessary to analyse gender relations in a more conceptual or theoretical way before they could make sense of their contemporary situation, so, too, those concerned with work must come to terms with the social relations in which it is embedded.

In the eighteenth century households engaged in a variety of forms of work unselfconsciously simply as part of the means of getting by. Now, at the end of the twentieth century, we have to make a conscious effort to unlearn the model of work as a male-dominated wage-earning activity. The good society may depend less on how much money we can get from our work and more on how we rearrange the social relations in which that work is done. These issues concerned an earlier generation of sociologists, who saw that the way wage labour was organized and the way it was coming to dominate all other forms would have extremely serious consequences for society. Marx wrote of alienation and saw the reduction of hours in the working day as the necessary preliminary to a less oppressed socialist society. Durkheim was concerned with the forced division of labour in the uneasy transition between a society held together by mechanical solidarity, in which most people were much the same, to one held together by organic solidarity, where people perceived each other's differences and were held together by them.

People work for a whole range of rewards and incentives: there are almost as many combinations of carrots and sticks as there are workers. Some employers urge a greater concern with the individual needs and motivation of workers, others would find it simpler to have robots as workers and to deal solely with machines. However, rather than spending much time and effort finding out why employees do not work harder, are not 'happier' or whatever, it might be more useful to explore the social context of the other forms of work in which employees also engage. The indications are that households are working harder and longer than at any time in the past. As long as we realize that employment is only one form of work we are in a better position to get a true perspective on contemporary household work practices.

This book of readings, *On Work*, has been concerned with *all* forms of work and has adopted a broadly comparative and historical perspective. The casual reader might imagine that I have over-emphasized the role of women's work, simply because nearly half of all the essays I have included are specifically about that topic. If anything I should perhaps have devoted *more* space to the changing role of women's work and employment, but happily an increasing number of texts and readers focusing specifically on women's work are now being published, so the position is not as bad as it was a decade ago. There is no need to repeat arguments I have already outlined in the introductions to the previous five parts of the book. The linkages and contradictions between production and consumption, between production and reproduction and between the social relations of the domestic and the social relations of the formal economy have been referred to in different contexts and are threads that are interwoven in the fabric of the book as a whole.

## THE 'FUTURE-OF-WORK' INDUSTRY: A POLEMIC ON POLEMICS

There will be other readers who may be surprised that I do not pay more attention to what might be termed the 'future-of-work' industry. In the 1980s a number of books were published which suggested that the way work was arranged was changing so substantially and fundamentally that the world would never be the same again. André Gorz published *Adieux au Proletariat* in Paris in 1980 and it appeared two years later in Britain with the title *Farewell to the Working Class*. Barry Jones's book *Sleepers, Wake*! was also published in 1982 in both Britain and Australia, and these two books set the trend for the decade; other authors made the same points more polemically or more accessibly.[1]

This present reader could be seen as a sustained attack on the naivety and superficiality of some of the popular polemics of the decade. Many future-of-work books are embarrassingly ethnocentric and are obsessed with the imputed consequences of new technology. They are also frequently intentionally or unintentionally highly misleading. Thus, for example, Charles Handy writes very persuasively and thus reaches a wide audience but his material is unashamedly anecdotal and he rarely draws on scholarly research. His book has been accorded a degree of authority well beyond that which he himself would claim for it. When he writes about the growth of subcontracting (discussed in this book in part V) his style is deceptively authoritative. Organizations, he claims, 'are waking up to the possibilities of more subcontracting on a bigger scale. . . . Whether we like it or not (and there are many who don't) the contractual organization is with us, is growing and is likely to grow faster. We would be wise to wake up to that fact because the management of contractual organizations is different from, and in many ways more difficult than, the management of employment organizations'.[2] This flip style, urging us to 'wake up' to the inevitable, is dangerous; it implies there is no alternative. Since Handy's book seems aimed more at management than at workers, he does not feel it is necessary to explain to his readers why some people don't like subcontracting. Handy does not write about impoverishment, exploitation and the subordination of women that many research studies show are associated with subcontracting. His stance is of the worldly-wise 'inside dopester' who can provide us with tips on the horses to back in the race to the future. His style is to argue by anecdote and it will undoubtedly seem persuasive and convincing to the unwary. One such anecdote refers to the Rank Xerox company's scheme whereby redundant workers were rehired as independent 'consultants' working from home with communications equipment provided by the company. Handy claims that this creates 'a dispersed office, perhaps the office of the future'.[3] Certainly the company saved on overheads and the individuals concerned got substantial redundancy payments and a subsidized start to their new freelance life. Much is made of the Rank Xerox story and it is widely quoted and discussed in TV documentaries and quasi-academic articles. 'It is a reorganization of work from which, so far,' Handy asserts, 'everyone seems to have benefited.' Readers of chapter 31 in this book will be sceptical of such a suggestion. This widely quoted example of a new way of working was established in

1. Popular examples are Charles Handy, *The Future of Work*, Basil Blackwell, Oxford, 1984; and James Robertson, *Future Work*, Gower, Maurice Temple Smith, 1985. Also in this genre but with a greater concern with the ethics of work is *Will the Future Work*?, edited by Howard Davis and David Gosling, World Council of Churches, Geneva, 1985. Gorz's book was published in England by Pluto Press, and Jones's book was published by Wheatsheaf Books.
2. Handy, *The Future of Work*, pp. 29–82.
3. Ibid., p. 77.

1981. In 1987 there were only fifty-nine people operating as 'networkers' in the scheme.

It would be easy but very unfair to multiply such criticisms of Handy's book which, in general, is well intentioned and makes no pretensions to scholarly objectivity. Its purpose is to stimulate, to jolt and to encourage fresh thinking, and inevitably it is partial and idiosyncratic. It includes many sensible, practical suggestions for coping with a society with high levels of unemployment and with an unstable and volatile labour market for the middle-class salaried. Handy is urging people to consider new options and new possibilities. He is outlining a programme of survival strategies for the middle class and many people, particularly managers in industry, will find some of his practical suggestions helpful.

Handy's book, however well meaning, is potentially dangerous if it persuades many people of the inevitability and beneficence of changes that are neither inevitable nor benign. The world of work (as this book shows ) is becoming more polarized, more divided and more disaggregated. The future-of-work industry's products, such as those by Handy or Gorz, are not being adequately tested. The criticisms I have applied to Handy, and which I suspect he would largely accept, could be directed at Gorz, who bids farewell to the working class at a time when the exploitation of a global workforce has become more effective and, because it is so dispersed and disaggregated, so invisible. Handy does not acknowledge the new exploitations inherent in subcontracting, and Gorz does not acknowledge that the growth of unemployment to over 30 million in the OECD countries is more a burden than a liberation for those concerned. Certainly, many manual workers prefer to construct their social identities from the activities they engage in outside employment. But they are still totally and completely dependent on the money that comes from employment to enable them to engage in these more meaningful activities of leisure and consumption in the realm of freedom. Gorz uses the term ' "a non-class of non-workers" to designate a stratum that experiences its work as an externally imposed obligation. . . . Its goal is the abolition of workers and work rather than their appropriation.'[4] Clearly Gorz is referring to changes in consciousness and the implication of that for political action, but if the *structural* situation of the workers has not changed, Gorz may be turning his back on the fire to watch the flickering shadows on the wall.

Now whilst I am claiming that many of the polemical books produced by the future-of-work industry are highly misleading, they have certainly succeeded in stimulating interest quite impossible to achieve with a book such as this, which to many will appear much less accessible. I began with the idea of writing a short, relevant text that would open up to a wider readership some of the current scholarly debates on work. I decided that such a project was premature. A more urgent need was to make recent evidence and arguments available, so that readers would have the material with which they could construct new debates for themselves. That material is complex, wide-ranging and, in some cases, intellectually demanding. I agree completely with those in the future-of-work industry who urge us to look with fresh eyes at all forms of work. My fear is that too many will turn their eyes but not much will come into focus. Understanding the new strategies of employers and households and how they interact from the

4. Gorz, *Farewell to the Working Class*, p. 7.

local to the global level is obviously a demanding and wide-ranging project. The political economy of an expanding global capitalism has to be understood in parallel with intra-household dynamics and processes and the renegotiations of distinctive divisions of labour.

Yet, paradoxically, much of this book is arguing that change is less pervasive than it may seem. Women are still overwhelmingly responsible for their traditional work. They simply now do more of other kinds of work as well. Where the goal of most employers throughout the world is to get the work of one full-time male done by one part-time female at a fraction of the cost, talk of the new liberation from toil can sound offensive.

In order to come to terms with the new global, national and sexual divisions of labour there is no substitute for hard, critical thinking, and it is in that spirit that I have made the selections in this reader. The new politics of work of the 1990s will have to engage with the issues raised in this book. There are no easy solutions and there is much pain and hard work ahead before anyone can realistically bid 'farewell to the working class'.